I0754938

Engd by W.G. Jackman, N.Y.

Robert Southey.

W.E. Ashton, Printer.

NEW-YORK, HARPER & BROTHERS.

THE LIFE AND CORRESPONDENCE OF ROBERT SOUTHEY.

EDITED BY HIS SON,

THE REV. CHARLES CUTHBERT SOUTHEY, M.A.,

CURATE OF PLUMBLAND, CUMBERLAND.

NEW YORK:

HARPER & BROTHERS, PUBLISHERS,

82 CLIFF STREET.

MDCCCLI.

PREFACE.

For the delay which has taken place in bringing forth this work I am not responsible, as it has chiefly arisen from the circumstance that no literary executor was expressly named in my father's latest will, and, in consequence of the difficulties which thus arose, it was not until the spring of 1848 that the materials, as far as they had then been collected, were put into my hands. I have, since then, made what speed I might in the preparation of them for the press, amid the engagements of other business, and with my hand often palsied by causes over which I had no control.

It were useless to endeavor to refute the various objections often made to a son's undertaking such a task ; yet one remark may be permitted, that although a son may not be a fit person to pass judgment upon a father's character, he yet may faithfully chronicle his life, and is undoubtedly, by a natural right, the most proper person to have all private letters submitted to his eye, and all family affairs intrusted to his judgment.

With this feeling, and with the full conviction that I am acting in accordance with what would have been my father's own wish, I have not thought it right to shrink from an undertaking for which I can not claim to have in other respects any peculiar qualifications. Accordingly, my object has been, not to compose a regular biography, but rather to lay before the reader such a selection from my father's letters as will give, in his own words, the history of his life ; and I have only added such remarks as I judged necessary for connection or explanation ; indeed, the even tenor of his life, during its greater portion, affords but little matter for pure biography, and the course of his literary pursuits, his opinions on passing events, and the few incidents of his own career, will all be found narrated by himself in a much more natural manner than if his letters had been worked up into a regular narrative.

My father has long been before the public, and has obtained a large share of praise, as well as of censure and misrepresentation ; he has yet, however, to be *fully known ;* and this I have a good hope will be accomplished by the publication of these volumes ; that in them all his mind will appear—in its playfulness as well as its gravity, in its joys and its sorrows, and the gradual progress of its opinions be fairly traced, from the visionary views of his early youth, up to the fixed and settled convictions of his riper years ; and if I have inserted any letters or passages which relate principally to his domestic life, and the affairs of the family circle, it has been with the conviction that he himself would not have wished them to be excluded, and that, although without them the events of his life might have been recorded, these would have formed only the outlines of the picture, which would have wanted all those finer touches that give to human nature its chief interest and its highest beauty.

I must now make my acknowledgments generally to those friends and correspondents of my father who have most kindly placed their letters at my disposal, and in particular to Mrs. Henry Bedford for those addressed to Grosvenor Charles Bedford,

Esq., from which I have drawn my chief materials for this volume, and which I have used largely throughout the work; to William Rickman, Esq., for those addressed to his father, the late John Rickman, Esq.; to the Right Hon. Charles W. W. Wynn; to John May, Esq.; to J. G. Lockhart, Esq., for those addressed to Sir Walter Scott; to Joseph Cottle, Esq.; to Mrs. Neville White and the Rev. James White; to the family of the late Sharon Turner, Esq.; to Walter Savage Landor, Esq.; to the family of the late Dr. Gooch; to the family of the late Rev. Nicholas Lightfoot; to Mr. Ebenezer Elliott; to Mr. Ticknor, of Boston; to Miss Elizabeth Charter; to Mrs. Hodson; to John Kenyon, Esq.; to Mrs. H. N. Coleridge; to William Wordsworth, Esq., Poet Laureat; and to Henry Taylor, Esq.

Other communications have been promised to me which I shall take a future opportunity of acknowledging.

While, however, my materials from these sources have been most extensive, there must still be many individuals with whom I have not been able to communicate, who have corresponded with my father upon literary subjects; and, should this meet the eye of any of these gentlemen, they would confer a great obligation upon me by permitting me the use of any of his letters to them, which are likely sometimes to possess an interest different from those addressed to intimate friends and frequent correspondents.

I may say, in conclusion, that whatever defects these volumes may possess, I have the satisfaction of feeling that they will verify my father's own words—words not uttered boastingly, but simply as the answer of a conscience void of offense both toward God and man—"I have this conviction, that, die when I may, my memory is one of those which will smell sweet, and blossom in the dust."

CHARLES CUTHBERT SOUTHEY.

CONTENTS.

RECOLLECTIONS OF THE EARLY LIFE OF ROBERT SOUTHEY, ESQ., LL.D., WRITTEN BY HIMSELF.

LIFE AND CORRESPONDENCE.

The editor is requested to correct a misstatement in the Autobiography, p. 38. It is there said that "Mr. Dolignon, in some delirium, died by his own hand." This is an error; Mr. Dolignon having died of paralysis in the prime of life, "in the full enjoyment of domestic happiness and worldly prosperity."

THE

LIFE AND CORRESPONDENCE

OF

ROBERT SOUTHEY.

RECOLLECTIONS OF THE EARLY LIFE OF ROBERT SOUTHEY,

WRITTEN BY HIMSELF, IN A SERIES OF LETTERS TO HIS FRIEND, MR. JOHN MAY.

LETTER I.

HIS ANCESTORS—THE CANNON SOUTHEYS—HIS FATHER SENT TO LONDON—REMOVED TO BRISTOL.

Keswick, Wednesday evening, July 26th, 1820.

MY DEAR FRIEND JOHN MAY,

SOME old divine has said that hell is paved with good resolutions. If Beelzebub has a tesselated pavement of this kind in one of his state-rooms, I fear I shall be found to have contributed largely to its unsubstantial materials. But that I may save one good resolution at least from being trodden under hoof by him and his imps, here I begin the performance, hoping, rather than promising, even to myself, that I may find leisure and courage to pursue it to the end—courage, I mean, to live again in remembrance with the dead, so much as I must needs do in retracing the course of my life. There are certain savages among whom the name of a deceased person is never mentioned; some superstition may have attached to this custom, but that the feeling in which it originates is natural I know both by experience and observation. My children never speak of their brother Herbert, and I never utter his name except in my prayers, unless some special cause acts upon me like a moral obligation.

I begin in the cloudy evening of a showery, louring, ungenial day: no desirable omen for one who is about to record the recollections of six-and-forty years, but a most inappropriate one in my case, for I have lived in the sunshine, and am still looking forward with hope.

I can not trace my family further back by the Church registers than Oct. 25, 1696, on which day my grandfather Thomas, the son of Robert Southey, and Ann, his wife, was baptized at Wellington, in Somersetshire. The said Robert Southey had seven other children, none of whom left issue. In the subsequent entries of their birth (for Thomas was the eldest) he is designated sometimes as yeoman, sometimes as farmer. His wife's maiden name was Locke, and she was of the same family as the philosopher (so called) of that name, who is still held in more estimation than he deserves. She must have been his niece, or the daughter of his first cousin. The register at Wellington goes back only to the year 1683. But I have heard that Robert's grandfather, that is, my great, great, great grandfather (my children's *tritavus*), was a great clothier at Wellington, and had eleven sons, who peopled that part of the country with Southeys. In Robert's days there were no fewer than seven married men of the name in the same parish. Robert himself was the younger of two sons, and John, his elder brother, was the head of the family. They must have been of gentle blood (though so obscure that I have never by any accident met with the name in a book), for they bore arms in an age when armorial bearings were not assumed by those who had no right to them. The arms are a chevron argent, and three cross crosslets, argent, in a field sable. I should like to believe that one of my ancestors had served in the crusades, or made a pilgrimage to Jerusalem.

One of them has left the reputation of having been a great soldier; in the Great Rebellion I guess it must have been, but I neither know his name, nor on what side he fought. Another (and this must have been the Robert with whom my certain knowledge begins) was, as the phrase is, out in Monmouth's insurrection. If he had come before Judge Jeffries in consequence, Nash would never have painted the happy but too handsome likeness of your god-daughter, which I have risen from my work ten times this day to look at in its progress, nor would you have received the intended series of these biographical letters. The entail of my mortal existence was in no small risk of being cut off by the executioner. My father had the sword which was drawn (not bloodied, I hope) in this unlucky quarrel, but it was lost in the wreck of his affairs.

John, the elder brother of this bold reformer and successful runaway, settled as a lawyer in

Taunton, and held the office of registrar for the archdeaconry. He married the heiress of the Cannon family, and upon the death of her father fixed his residence at the manor-house of Fitzhead, in Somersetshire, which was her property. By this marriage he had one son and two daughters. John Cannon Southey, the son, practiced the law; one daughter married the last of the Periam family, and survived him; the other married one of the Lethbridges, and had only one child, a daughter. That daughter married Hugh Somerville, then a colonel in the army, and brother to James Lord Somerville; she died in childbed of John Southey Somerville, her only issue.

My grandfather settled at Holford Farm, an estate belonging to his uncle John, in the parish of Lydiard St. Laurence, about ten miles north of Taunton, under the Quantock Hills. This removal was made when John obtained possession of his wife's property; the first use he made of it, therefore, seems to have been to befriend his nephew. And I have discovered another good indication concerning him: his name appears among the subscribers to Walker's Sufferings of the Clergy, a presumption, at least, that he had some regard for books, and a right way of thinking. He was very much respected and beloved. My grandfather regarded him with the greatest reverence, as one from whose judgment there could be no appeal; what his uncle said or thought was always sufficient authority with him. Lydiard St. Laurence is a very retired hamlet, containing only three farm-houses, and having no other habitations within two miles of it. My grandfather brought his grandmother there, and there she died at the great age of 102. A maiden sister lived with him. She had a small estate held upon three lives; two of them fell, and the third, a worthless profligate, contrived from that time almost to support himself upon it. Knowing that my poor aunt Hannah was now dependent upon his life, he would never strike a stroke of work more. When his debts became troublesome, away went his wife to the poor old woman with a tale about writs, bailiffs, the jail, and jail fever; and in this manner was she continually fleeced and kept in continual fear, till the rascal died at last of close attention at the ale-house. This story is worthy of insertion in an account of English tenures.

The removal from Wellington to a lonely hamlet seems to have brought my grandfather within the pale of the Established Church, for he had been bred up as a Dissenter. (The old sword, therefore, was probably pursuing its old courses when it went into the field in rebellion.) Aunt Hannah, however, though an inoffensive, kindhearted woman in other respects, retained so much of the essential acid of Puritanism in her composition, that she frequently chastised her niece Mary for going into the fields with her playmates on a Sunday: she and her brothers and sisters, she said, had never been suffered to go out of the house on the Sabbath, except to meetings.

My grandfather did not marry till he was forty-five; probably he could not have maintained a family before he was settled upon his uncle's farm. His wife's name was Joan Mullens. They had three sons, John, Robert (who was my father), and Thomas, and two daughters, Hannah and Mary, all born at Halford. The boys received what in those days was thought a good education. The elder, being designed for the law (in which his name and family connections would assist him), learned a little Latin; he lived more with Cannon Southey than with his parents, both in his boyhood and youth, as his sister Mary did with Madam Periam or Madam Lethbridge (this was in the time when that title was in common use in the West of England), being always with one or the other as long as they lived. But Cannon Southey's house was a bad school for him. He was looked upon as the probable heir of the family after the birth of young Somerville, who was always a weakly child. The two younger brothers were qualified for trade. My father had preserved his ciphering-book, and I would have preserved it too, as carefully as any of my own manuscripts, if it had not been lost at the household wreck at his bankruptcy. If you will look in that little treatise of mine upon the "Origin, Nature, and Object of the New System of Education," you will find a passage at p. 85, 86, written in remembrance of this ciphering-book, and of the effects which it produced upon me in early boyhood.

When my uncle John was about to begin business as an attorney in Taunton, Cannon Southey, who was then the head of the family, lent him £100 to start with. "That hundred pounds," he used to say, with a sort of surly pride, "I repaid, with interest, in six months, and that is the only favor for which I was ever obliged to my relations." Cannon Southey, however, though not very liberal to his kin, had a just regard to their legal rights, and left his property in trust for his great nephew, John Southey Somerville, and his issue, with the intention that if he, who was then a child, should die without issue, the estates should descend to the Southeys; and, that the whole property might go together, he willed his leasehold estates (which would else have been divided among the next of kin) in remainder, upon the same contingency, to my uncle John and his two brothers, and to the sons of each in succession, as the former branch might fail.

Robert, my father, was passionately fond of the country and of country sports. The fields should have been his station instead of the shop. He was placed with a kinsman in London, who, I believe, was a grocer somewhere in the city —one of the eleven tribes that went out from Wellington. I have heard him say, that as he was one day standing at this person's door, a porter went by carrying a hare, and this brought his favorite sport so forcibly to mind that he could not help crying at the sight. This anecdote in Wordsworth's hands would be worth as much as the Reverie of poor Susan. Before my father had been twelve months in London, his master died; upon which he was removed to Bristol, and placed with William Britton, a linen-draper in Wine Street. The business at that time was a profitable one, and Britton's the best shop of its kind in the town, which is as much as saying that there was not a better in the West of England. This must have been about the end of George the Second's reign. Shop-windows were then as little used in this country as they are now in most of the continental towns. I remember Britton's shop still open to the weather long after all the neighbors had glazed theirs; and I remember him, from being the first tradesman in his line, fallen to decay in his old age, and sunk in sottishness, still keeping on a business which had dwindled almost to nothing. My father, I think, was not apprenticed to him, because, if he had served a regular apprenticeship, it would have entitled him to the freedom of the city, and I know that he was not a freeman: he lived with him, however, twelve or fourteen years. Among the acquaintance with whom he became intimate during that time was my half uncle, Edward Tyler, then employed in a Coventry warehouse, in Broad Street, belonging to the Troughtons. This introduced him to my grandmother's house.

LETTER II.

THE HILLS—THE BRADFORDS—WILLIAM TYLER—ANECDOTE OF HIM—HIS GRANDFATHER'S DEATH.

Tuesday, August 1st, 1820.

Mrs. Hill, my grandmother, was, at the time of which I am now writing, a widow; her maiden name was Bradford. I know nothing more of her father than that he was a Herefordshire man, and must have been of respectable property and connections, as appears by his having married into one of the best families in the county, and sending a son to college. His wife's name was Mrs. Margaret Croft. I have it written in gold letters, with the date 1704, in a copy of Nelson's Festivals and Fasts, which descended as a favorite devotional book to my mother. They had three children: Herbert, so named after the Croft family; another son (William, I think, by name), who was deaf and dumb, and just lived to grow up; and my grandmother Margaret.

My grandmother was very handsome: little Georgiana Hill, my uncle says, reminds him strongly of her; and I remember her enough to recognize a likeness in the shape of the face, and in the large, full, clear, bright brown eyes. Her first husband, Mr. Tyler, was of a good family in Herefordshire, nearly related I *know* he was, and nephew I *think*, to one of that name who was Bishop of Hereford. He lived at Pembridge. The seat of the family was at Dilwyn, where his elder brother lived, who either was not married or left no issue. I have hardly heard any thing of him, except that on his wedding day he sung a song after dinner, which could not be thought very complimentary to his bride; for, though it began by saying,

> "Ye gods, who gave to me a wife
> Out of your grace and favor,
> To be the comfort of my life,
> And I was glad to have her"

(thus much I remember of the rhymes), it ended with saying that, whenever they might think fit, he was ready to resign her. It happened, however, that the resignation was to be on the wife's part. He died in the prime of life, leaving four children, Elizabeth, John, William, and Edward; and his widow, after no very long interval, married Edward Hill, of Bedminster, in the county of Somersetshire, near Bristol, and was transplanted with her children to that place.

Edward Hill was the seventh in succession of that name. His fathers had lived and died respectably and contentedly upon their own lands in the beautiful vale of Ashton, the place of all others which I remember with most feeling. You see it from Clifton, on the other side of the River Avon; Warton has well characterized it in one of his odes as Ashton's *elmy* vale. The Hills are called gentlemen upon their tombstones in Ashton church-yard, where my father, two of my brothers, my three sisters, and my poor dear cousin Margaret, are deposited with them. Edward Hill, the seventh, was a lawyer and a widower; he had two children by his first marriage, a son, Edward, the eighth, and a daughter, old enough, I believe, at the time of his second marriage, for the daughter to be married, and the son very soon to hold a commission in the marines. He was a fine, handsome man, of considerable talents, and of a convivial temper. I have heard him spoken of with admiration by persons who were intimate with him in their youth. He could make verses, too, after the fashion of that age. I have somewhere a poem of his, in his own writing, which came to my mother after *her* mother's death, and, in like manner, descended into my possession: it is not, therefore, without a mournful feeling that I recall to mind the time when it was first shown to me, and the amusement which it then afforded me. It was a love poem, addressed to my grandmother during the days of courtship: it intimated some jealousy of a rival, who was called Strephon, and there was a note at the bottom of the page upon this name, explaining that it meant "the young justice."

William Tyler, the second brother, was a remarkable person. Owing to some defect in his faculties, so anomalous in its kind that I never heard of a similar case, he could never be taught to read; the letters he could tell separately, but was utterly incapable of combining them, and taking in their meaning by the eye. He could write, and copy in a fair hand any thing that was set before him, whether in writing or in print; but it was done letter by letter, without understanding a single word. As to self-government, he was entirely incompetent, so much so that I think he could hardly be considered responsible as a moral being for his actions; yet he had an excellent memory, an observing eye, and a sort of *half-saved* shrewdness, which would have qualified him, had he been born two centuries earlier, to have worn motley, and figured with a cap and bells and a bawble in some baron's hall. Never did I meet with any man so stored with old saws and anecdotes gathered up in the narrow sphere wherein he moved. I still remember many of them, though he has been dead more than thirty years. The motto to Kehama,* as the Greek reference, when the abbreviations are rightly understood, may show, is one of my uncle William's sayings. When it was found impossible to make any thing of him by education, he was left to himself, and passed more time in the kitchen than in the parlor, because he stood in fear of his step-father. There he learned to chew tobacco and to drink.

Strange creature as he was, I think of him very often, often speak of him, quote some of his odd, apt sayings, and have that sort of feeling for his memory that he is one of the persons whom I should wish to meet in the world to come.

The man of whom he learned the use, or, rather, the abuse of tobacco, was a sottish servant, as ignorant as a savage of every thing which he ought to have known—that is to say, of every thing which ought to have been taught him. My mother, when a very little girl, reproved him once for swearing. "For shame, Thomas," she said; "you should not say such naughty words! for shame! say your prayers, Thomas!" "No, missey!" said the poor wretch, "I sha'n't; I sha'n't say my prayers. I never said my prayers in all my life, missey; and I sha'n't begin now." My uncle William (the Squire he was called in the family) provoked him dangerously once. He was dozing beside the fire with his hat on, which, as is still the custom among the peasantry (here in Cumberland, at least), he always wore in the house. You, perhaps, are not enough acquainted with the mode of chewing tobacco to know that in vulgar life a quid commonly goes through two editions; and that, after it has been done with, it is taken out of the mouth, and reserved for a second regale. My uncle William, who had learned the whole process from Thomas, and always faithfully observed it, used to call it, in its intermediate state, an old soldier. A sailor deposits, or, if there be such a word (and if there is not, there ought to be), *re*-posits it in his tobacco-box. I have heard my brother Tom say that this practice occasioned a great dislike in the navy to the one and two pound notes; for when the men were paid in paper, the tobacco-box served them for purse or pocket-book in lack of any thing better, and notes were often rendered illegible by the deep stain of a wet quid. Thomas's place for an old soldier between two campaigns, while he was napping and enjoying the narcotic effects of the first mastication, was the brim of his hat, from whence the Squire on this occasion stole the veteran quid, and substituted in its place a dead mouse just taken from the trap. Presently the sleeper, half wakening without unclosing his eyes, and half stupefied, put up his hand, and taking the mouse with a finger and thumb, in which the discriminating sense of touch had been blunted by coarse work and unclean habits, opened his mouth to receive it, and, with a slow, sleepy tongue, endeavored to accommodate it to its usual station between the double teeth and the cheek. Happening to put it in headforemost, the hind legs and the tail hung out, and a minute or more was spent in vain endeavors to lick these appendages in, before he perceived, in the substance, consistence, and taste, something altogether unlike tobacco. Roused at the same time by a laugh which could no longer be suppressed, and discovering the trick which had been played, he started up in a furious rage, and, seizing the poker, would have demolished the Squire for this practical jest, if he had not provided a retreat by having the doors open, and taking shelter where Thomas could not, or dared not follow him.

Enough of uncle William for the present. Edward, the remaining brother of the Tyler side, was a youth who, if he had been properly brought up, and brought forward in a manner suitable to his birth and connections, might have made a figure in life, and have done honor to himself and his family. He had a fine person, a good understanding, and a sweet temper, which made him too easily contented with any situation and any company into which he was thrown. My grandfather has much to answer for on his account. Except sending him to a common day-school, kept by a very uncommon sort of man (of whom more hereafter), he left him to himself, and let him grow and run to seed in idleness.

My grandfather would have acquired considerable property if he had not been cut off by an acute disorder. He had undertaken to recover some disputed rights for the church of which he was a parishioner, at his own risk and expense, on condition of receiving the additional tithes which might be eventually recovered during a certain number of years, or of being remunerated out of them in proportion to the cost, and hazard, and trouble of the adventure. The points were obstinately contested; but he carried them all, and died almost immediately afterward, in the year 1765, aged sixty.

LETTER III.

RECOLLECTIONS OF THE HILLS—PARSON COLLINS.

Nov. 16th, 1820.

My grandmother's jointure from her first husband was £200 a year, which was probably equivalent to thrice that sum in these days. The Tylers had from their father £600 each. Miss Tyler lived with her uncle Bradford, of whom and of her I shall speak hereafter. I

* I have heard my father say that this proverb was rendered into Greek by Mr. Coleridge.—Ed.

must now speak of the Hills. My uncle (it is so habitual to me to speak and write of him, and of him only by that name, κατ' ἐξοχὴν, that I will not constrain myself to use any further designation)—my uncle, and his brother Joseph, and Edward Tyler, went by day to a school in the village kept by one of the strangest fellows that ever wore a cassock or took up the trade of tuition. His name was Collins. He was clever and profligate, and eked out his ways and means by authorship—scribbling for inclination, and publishing for gain. One of his works I recollect among my uncle's books in Miss Tyler's possession; its title is "Hell's Gates open;" but, not having looked into it since I was a mere boy, I only know that it is satirical, as the name may seem to import. I sent for another of his publications some years ago from a catalogue, not as any thing of value, but because he had been my uncle's first schoolmaster, and I knew who and what he was. It is to be wished that every person who knew me would think that a good reason for buying my works: I should be very much obliged to them. It is a little book in the unusual form of a foolscap quarto, and because it contains one fact which is really curious as matter of history, I give its title* at the bottom of the page. This publication is in no respect creditable to its author, and, on the score of decency, highly discreditable to him. But the fact, which is well worth the two shillings I gave for the book (though but a halfpenny fact), is, that, as late as the end of George the Second's reign, or the beginning of George the Third's, there were persons in Bristol who, from political scruples of conscience, refused to take King William's halfpence, and these persons were so numerous that the magistrates thought it necessary to interfere, because of the inconvenience which they occasioned in the common dealings of trade and of the markets. William's copper money was then in common currency, and, indeed, I myself remember it, having, between the years 1786 and 1790, laid by some half dozen of his halfpence with the single or double head, among the foreign pieces and others of rare occurrence which came within my reach.

Devoid as his Miscellanies are of any merit, Parson Collins, as he was called (not in honor of the cloth), had some humor. In repairing the public road, the laborers came so near his garden wall that they injured the foundations, and down it fell. He complained to the way-wardens, and demanded reparation, which they would have evaded if they could, telling him it was but an old wall, and in a state of decay. "Gentlemen," he replied, "old as the wall was, it served my purpose; but, however, I have not the smallest objection to your putting up a second-hand one in its place." This anecdote I heard full five-and-thirty years ago from one of my schoolmasters, who had been a rival of Collins, and was satirized by him in the Miscellanies. His school failed him, not because he was deficient in learning, of which he seems to have had a full share for his station, but because of his gross and scandalous misconduct. He afterward kept something so like an ale-house that he got into a scrape with his superiors.

One of his daughters kept a village shop at Chew Magna, in Somersetshire, and dealt with my father for such things as were in his way. She used to dine with us whenever she came to Bristol, and was always a welcome guest for her blunt, honest manners, and her comical oddity. Her face was broad and coarse, like a Tartar's, but with quick dark eyes and a fierce expression. She was one of those persons who could say *quidlibet cuilibet de quolibet.*

I perceive that I should make an excellent correspondent for Mr. Urban, and begin to suspect that I have mistaken my talent, and been writing histories and poems when I ought to have been following the rich veins of gossip and garrulity. All this, however, is not foreign to my purpose; for I wish not only to begin *ab ovo*, but to describe every thing relating to the nest; and he who paints a bird's nest ought not to represent it nakedly *per se*, but *in situ*, in its place, and with as many of its natural accompaniments as the canvas will admit. It is not manners and fashions alone that change and are perpetually changing with us. The very constitution of society is unstable; it *may*, and in all probability *will*, undergo as great alterations, in the course of the next two or three centuries, as it has undergone in the last. The transitions are likely to be more violent and far more rapid. At no very distant time, these letters, if they escape the earthquake and the volcano may derive no small part of their interest and value from the faithful sketches which they contain of a stage of society which has already passed away, and of a state of things which shall then have ceased to exist.

LETTER IV.

HIS MOTHER'S BIRTH AND CHILDHOOD—HER MARRIAGE—HIS OWN BIRTH.

My mother was born in 1752. She was a remarkably beautiful infant, till, when she was between one and two years old, an abominable nurse-maid carried her, of all places in the world, to Newgate (as was afterward discovered), and there she took the small-pox in its most malignant form. It seemed almost miraculous that she escaped with life and eyesight, so dreadfully severe was the disease; but her eyebrows were almost destroyed, and the whole face seamed with scars. While she was a mere child, she had a paralytic affection, which deadened one

* Miscellanies in Prose and Verse; consisting of Essays, Abstracts, Original Poems, Letters, Tales, Translations, Panegyrics, Epigrams, and Epitaphs.

"Sunt bona, sunt quædam mediocria, sunt mala plura;
Quæ legis hic aliter non fit, abite, liber."—Martial.

"Things good, things bad, things middling when you look,
You'll find to constitute, my friends, this book."

By Emanuel Collins, A.B., late of Wadham College, Oxford. Bristol: printed by E. Farley, in Small Street. 1762.

side from the hip downward, and crippled her for about twelve months. Some person advised that she should be placed out of doors in the sunshine as much as possible; and one day, when she had been carried out as usual into the fore-court, in her little arm-chair, and left there to see her brothers at play, she rose from her seat, to the astonishment of the family, and walked into the house. The recovery from that time was complete. The fact is worthy of notice, because some persons may derive hope from it in similar cases, and because it is by no means improbable that the sunshine really effected the cure. The manner by which I should explain this would lead to a theory somewhat akin to that of Bishop Berkeley upon the virtues of tar water.

There are two portraits of my mother, both taken by Robert Hancock in 1798. My brother Tom has the one; the other hangs opposite me, where I am now seated in my usual position at my desk. Neither of these would convey to a stranger a just idea of her countenance. That in my possession is very much the best: it represents her as she then was, with features care-worn and fallen away, and with an air of melancholy which was not natural to her; for never was any human being blessed with a sweeter temper or a happier disposition. She had an excellent understanding, and a readiness of apprehension which I have rarely known surpassed. In quickness of capacity, in the kindness of her nature, and in that kind of moral magnetism which wins the affections of all within its sphere, I never knew her equal. To strangers she must probably have appeared much disfigured by the small-pox. I, of course, could not be sensible of this. Her complexion was very good, and nothing could be more expressive than her fine, clear hazel eyes.

Female education was not much regarded in her childhood. The ladies who kept boarding-schools in those days did not consider it necessary to possess any other knowledge themselves than that of ornamental needle-work. Two sisters, who had been mistresses of the most fashionable school in Herefordshire fifty years ago, used to say, when they spoke of a former pupil, "*Her* went to school to *we*:" and the mistress of which, some ten years later, was thought the best school near Bristol (where Mrs. Siddons sent her daughter), spoke, to my perfect recollection, much such English as this. My mother, I believe, never went to any but a dancing-school, and her state was the more gracious. But her half sister, Miss Tyler, was placed at one in the neighborhood under a Mrs. ——, whom I mention because her history is characteristic of those times. Her husband carried on the agreeable business of a butcher in Bristol, while she managed a school for young ladies about a mile out of the town. His business would not necessarily have disqualified her for this occupation (though it would be no recommendation), Kirke White's mother, a truly admirable woman, being in this respect just under like circumstances. But Mrs. —— might, with more propriety, have been a blacksmith's wife, as, in that case, Vulcan might have served for a type of her husband in his fate, but not in the complacency with which he submitted to it, horns sitting as easily on his head as upon the beasts which he slaughtered. She was a handsome woman, and her children were, like the Harleian Miscellany, by different authors. This was notorious; yet her school flourished notwithstanding, and she retired from it at last with a competent fortune, and was visited as long as she lived by her former pupils. This may serve to show a great improvement in the morals of middle life.

Two things concerning my mother's childhood and youth may be worthy of mention. One is, that she had for a fellow-scholar at the dancing-school Mary Darby (I think her name was), then in her beauty and innocence, soon afterward notorious as the Prince of Wales's Perdita, and to be remembered hereafter, though a poor poetess, as having, perhaps, a finer feeling of meter, and more command of it, than any of her cotemporaries. The other is, that my mother, who had a good ear for music, was taught by her father to whistle; and he succeeded in making her such a proficient in this unusual accomplishment, that it was his delight to place her upon his knee, and make her entertain his visitors with a display. This art she never lost, and she could whistle a song tune as sweetly as a skillful player could have performed it upon the flute.

My grandmother continued to live in the house at Bedminster which her husband had built, and which, after his death, had been purchased by Edward Tyler. It was about an hour's walk, εὐζώνῳ ἀνδρὶ, from Bristol; and my father, having been introduced there, became, in progress of time, a regular Sabbath guest. How long he had been acquainted with the family before he thought of connecting himself with it, I do not know; but in the year 1772, being the 27th of his own age, and the 20th of my mother's, they were married at Bedminster Church. He had previously left Britton's service, and opened a shop for himself, in the same business and in the same street, three doors above. Cannon Southey had left him £100; my mother had a legacy of £50 from her uncle Bradford; my father formed a partnership with his younger brother Thomas, who had such another bequest as his from the same quarter; perhaps, also, he might have saved something during his years of service, and the business may have begun with a capital of £500; I should think not more. Shop signs were general in those days; but the custom of suspending them over the street, as is still done at inns in the country, was falling into disuse. My father, true to his boyish feelings, and his passion for field sports (which continued unabated, notwithstanding the uncongenial way of life in which his lot had fallen), took a hare for his device. It was painted on a pane in the window on each side of the door, and was engraved on his shop-bills. This became interesting when he told me of his shedding tears at the sight of the hare in the porter's hand in London; and I often think of having one cut upon a seal, in remembrance of him and of the old shop. Bryan the Prophet told me, in the days of Richard Brothers, that I was of the tribe of Judah—a sort of nobility which those prophets had the privilege of discovering without any assistance from the Herald's Office. Had he derived me from Esau instead of Jacob, my father's instincts might have induced me to lend a less incredulous ear.

The first child of this marriage was born August 1, 1773, and christened John Cannon. He lived only to be nine or ten months old. He was singularly beautiful; so much so, that, when I made my appearance on the 12th of August, 1774,* I was sadly disparaged by comparison with him. My mother, asking if it was a boy, was answered by her nurse in a tone as little favorable to me as the opinion was flattering. "Ay, a great ugly boy!" and she added when she told me this, "God forgive me! when I saw what a great red creature it was, covered with rolls of fat, I thought I should never be able to love him."

LETTER V.

FIRST GOING TO SCHOOL—BIRTH OF BROTHERS AND SISTERS—MISS TYLER.

March 20th, 1821.

The popular saint of the democratic cantons in Switzerland, St. Nicolas de Huë (to whom I paid my respects in his own church at Saxeln), remembered his own birth, knew his mother and the midwife as soon as he was born, and never forgot the way by which he was taken to be christened, nor the faces of the persons who were present at that ceremony. But he was an extraordinary child, who, though he neither danced, nor sung, nor preached before he was born (all which certain other saints are said to have done), had revelations in that state, and saw the light of heaven before he came into the light of day. It has pleased the metaphysico-critico-politico-patriotico-phoolo-philosopher Jeremy Bentham to designate me, in one of his opaque works, by the appellation of St. Southey, for which I humbly thank his Jeremy Benthamship, and have in part requited him. It would be very convenient if I had the same claim to this honor, on the score of miraculous memory, as the aforesaid Nicolas; but the twilight of my recollections does not begin till the third year of my age.† However, though I did not, like him, know the midwife at the time when she had most to do with me, I knew her afterward, for she brought all my brothers and sisters into the world. She was the wife of a superannuated Baptist preacher, who, as was formerly common for Baptist preachers to do, kept a shop, dealing in medicines and quackery among other things. Preachers of this grade have now nearly or entirely disappeared; and even the Methodists will not allow their ministers to engage in any kind of trade. I mention this family, therefore, as belonging to a class which is now extinct. They were stiff Oliverians in their politics. The husband was always at his studies, which probably lay in old Puritanical divinity; he was chiefly supported by his wife's professional labors, and I well remember hearing him spoken of as a miserable, morose tyrant. The only son of this poor woman lost his life by a singularly dismal accident, when he was grown up and doing well in the world. Hastening one day to see his mother, upon the alarm of a sudden and dangerous illness which had seized her, he came to the draw-bridge on St. Augustine's Back just as they were beginning to raise it for the passage of a vessel. In his eagerness he attempted to spring across, but, not calculating upon the rise, he fell in, and the vessel passed over him, inevitably, before any attempts to save him could be made. I used to cross the bridge almost every day for many years of my life; and the knowledge of his fate warned me from incurring the same danger, which otherwise, in all likelihood, active as I then was, and always impatient of loss of time, I should very often have done.

It was my lot to be consigned to a foster-mother, a girl, or, rather, a young woman, who had been from childhood employed by my grandmother, first in the garden, then in household affairs; a poor, thoughtless, simple creature, who, however, proved a most affectionate nurse to me. The first day that I was taken to school she was almost heart-broken at the scene between me and the schoolmistress—a scene which no doubt appeared to me of the most tragical kind. Having ushered me into the room and delivered me into custody, she made a hasty retreat, but stood without the door, looking through a curtained window which gave light into the passage, and listening to what ensued. It was a place where I was sent to be out of the way for a few hours morning and evening, for I was hardly older than Cuthbert is at this time, and, though quite capable of learning the alphabet, far too young to be put to it as a task, or made to comprehend the fitness of

* My birth-day was Friday, the 12th of August, 1774; the time of my birth, half past eight in the morning, according to the family Bible. According to my astrological friend Gilbert, it was a few minutes before the half hour, in consequence of which I am to have a pain in my bowels when I am about thirty, and Jupiter is my deadly antagonist; but I may thank the stars for "a gloomy capability of walking through desolation."—*Letter to Grosvenor C. Bedford, Esq., Sept.* 30, 1797.

† My feelings were very acute; they used to amuse themselves by making me cry at sad songs and dismal stories. I remember "Death and the Lady," "Billy Pringle's Pig," "The children sliding on the ice all on a summer's day," and Witherington fighting on his stumps at Chevy Chase. This was at two years old, when my recollection begins; prior identity I have none. They tell me I used to beg them not to proceed. I know not whether our feelings are blunted or rendered more acute by action; in either case, these pranks are wrong with children. I can not now hear a melancholy tale in silence, but I have learned to whistle.—*Letter to G. C. Bedford, Esq., Sept.* 30, 1797.

sitting still for so long a time together on pain of the rod. Upon this occasion, when, for the first time in my life, I saw nothing but strange faces about me, and no one to whom I could look for kindness or protection, I gave good proof of a sense of physiognomy which never misled me yet, of honesty in speaking my opinion, and of a temerity in doing it by which my after life has often been characterized. Ma'am Powell had as forbidding a face (I well remember it) as can easily be imagined; and it was remarkable for having no eyelashes, a peculiarity which I instantly perceived. When the old woman, therefore, led me to a seat on the form, I rebelled as manfully as a boy in his third year could do, crying out, "Take me to Pat! I don't like ye! you've got ugly eyes! take me to Pat, I say!" Poor Pat went home with the story, and cried as bitterly in relating it as I had done during the unequal contest, and at the utter discomfiture to which I was fain to submit, when might, as it appeared to me, overpowered right.*

My sister Eliza was born in 1776, and died of the measles in 1779. I remember her as my earliest playmate, by help of some local circumstances, and sometimes fancy that I can call to mind a faint resemblance of her face. My brother Thomas came into the world 1777; Louisa next, in 1779. This was a beautiful creature, the admiration of all who beheld her. My aunt Mary was one day walking with her down Union Street, when Wesley happened to be coming up, and the old man was so struck with the little girl's beauty that he stopped and exclaimed, "Oh! sweet creature!" took her by the hand, and gave her a blessing. That which in affliction we are prone to think a blessing, and which, perhaps, in sober reflection, may be justly thought so, befell her soon afterward—an early removal to a better world. She died of hydrocephalus, a disease to which the most promising children are the most liable. Happily neither her parents nor her grandmother ever suspected, what is exceedingly probable, that in her case the disease may have been induced by their dipping her every morning in a tub of the coldest well water. This was done from an old notion of strengthening her: the shock was dreadful; the poor child's horror of it, every morning, when taken out of bed, still more so. I can not remember having seen it without horror; nor do I believe that among all the preposterous practices which false theories have produced, there was ever a more cruel and perilous one than this. John, the next child, was born in 1782, and died in infancy.

My recollections of Eliza and Louisa are more imperfect than they might otherwise have been, because during those years I was very much from home, being sometimes at school, and sometimes with Miss Tyler, of whose situation and previous history I must now speak, because they had a material influence upon the course of my life.

Miss Tyler, who was born in the year 1739, passed the earlier part of her life with her maternal uncle at Shobdon, a little village in Herefordshire, where he resided upon a curacy. Mr. Bradford had been educated at Trinity College, Oxford, and was in much better circumstances than country curates in general. He had an estate in Radnorshire of respectable value, and married the sister of Mr. Greenly, of Titley, in Herefordshire, who, being of so good a family, had probably a good fortune. He appears to have possessed some taste for letters, and his library was well provided with the professional literature of that age. Shobdon, though a remote place, gave him great opportunities of society: Lord Bateman resided there, in one of the finest midland situations that England affords; and a clergyman of companionable talents and manners was always a welcome guest at his table. Miss Tyler also became a favorite with Lady Bateman, and spent a great deal of time with her, enough to acquire the manners of high life, and too many of its habits and notions. Mrs. Bradford died a few years before her husband; not, however, till he was too far advanced in life, or too confirmed in celibate habits to think of marrying again. By that time he had become a victim to the gout. An odd accident happened to him during one of his severe fits, at a time when no persuasions could have induced him to put his feet to the ground, or to believe it possible that he could walk. He was sitting with his legs up, in the full costume of that respectable and orthodox disease, when the ceiling, being somewhat old, part of it gave way, and down came a fine nest of rats, old and young together, plump upon him. He had what is called an antipathy to these creatures, and, forgetting the gout in the horror which their visitation excited, sprung from his easy chair, and fairly ran down stairs.

Miss Tyler had the management of his house after his wife's death, and she had also, in no small degree, the management of the parish She had influence enough to introduce inoculation there, and I believe great merit in the exertions which she made on that occasion, and

* Here I was at intervals till my sixth year, and formed a delectable plan with two schoolmates for going to an island and living by ourselves. We were to have one mountain of gingerbread and another of candy. . . . I had a great desire to be a soldier: Colonel Johnson once gave me his sword; I took it to bed, and went to sleep in a state of most complete happiness: in the morning it was gone. Once I sat upon the grass in what we call a brown study; at last, out it came, with the utmost earnestness, to my aunt Mary: "Auntee Polly, I should like to have all the weapons of war, the gun, and the sword, and the halbert, and the pistol, and all the weapons of war." Once I got horsewhipped for taking a walk with a journeyman barber who lived opposite, and promised to give me a sword. This took a strange turn when I was about nine years old. I had been reading the historical plays of Shakspeare, and concluded there must be civil wars in my own time, and resolved to be a very great man, like the Earl of Warwick. Now it would be prudent to make partisans; so I told my companions at school that my mother was a very good woman, and had taught me to interpret dreams. They used to come and repeat their dreams to me, and I was artful enough to refer them all to great civil wars, and the appearance of a very great man who was to appear—meaning myself. I had resolved that Tom should be a great man too, and actually dreamed once of going into his tent to wake him the morning before a battle, so full was I of these ideas.—*Letter to G. C. Bedford, Esq., Sept.* 30, 1797.

the personal attention which she bestowed. It occurs to my recollection now also while I write, that she effected a wholesome and curious innovation in the poor-house, by persuading them to use beds stuffed with beech-leaves, according to a practice in some parts of France which she had heard or read of. It was Mr. Bradford who had placed my uncle Mr. Hill at Oxford, first at St. Mary's Hall, afterward at Christ Church, where he obtained a studentship, which must have been by means of some Shobdon connections. When Mr. Bradford died, which was in the year 1778, he left the whole of his property to Miss Tyler, except £50 to my mother, and a small provision, charged upon his estates, for my poor uncle William, as one utterly incapable of providing for himself.

Finding herself mistress of £1500 in money from Mr. Bradford's effects, besides the estate, and her own paternal portion of £600, she began to live at large, and to frequent watering places. At one of these (I think it was Weymouth) she fell in with Armstrong, the physician and poet, a writer deservedly respectable for his poem upon Health, and deservedly infamous for another of his productions. He recommended her to try the climate of Lisbon, less for any real or apprehended complaint than because he perceived the advice would be agreeable; and thus, before you and I were born, did Armstrong prepare the way for our friendship, as well as for the great literary labors of my life. To Lisbon accordingly she went, taking with her my uncle, who had lately entered into orders, and Mrs. ——— (a distant relation, the widow of a decayed Bristol merchant) as a sort of *ama*. Miss Palmer (sister of that Palmer who planned the mail coach system), one of her Bath acquaintances, joined the party. They remained about twelve months abroad, where some of your friends no doubt remember them, during the golden age of the factory, in 1774, the year of my birth. Miss Tyler was then thirty-four. She was remarkably beautiful, as far as any face can be called beautiful in which the indications of a violent temper are strongly marked.

LETTER VI.

DESCRIPTION OF MISS TYLER'S HOUSE AT BATH—INOCULATION—MISS TYLER'S FRIENDS AND ACQUAINTANCES.

April 7th, 1821.

On her return from Lisbon Miss Tyler took a house in Bath, and there my earliest recollections begin, great part of my earliest childhood having been passed there.

The house was in Walcot parish, in which, five-and-forty years ago, were the skirts of the city. It stood alone, in a walled garden, and the entrance was from a lane. The situation was thought a bad one, because of the approach, and because the nearest houses were of a mean description; in other respects it was a very desirable residence. The house had been quite in the country when it was built One of its fronts looked into the garden, the other into a lower garden, and over other garden grounds to the river, Bath Wick Fields (which are now covered with streets) and Claverton Hill, with a grove of firs along its brow, and a sham castle in the midst of their long, dark line. I have not a stronger desire to see the Pyramids than I had to visit that sham castle during the first years of my life. There was a sort of rural freshness about the place. The dead wall of a dwelling-house (the front of which was in Walcot Street) formed one side of the garden inclosure, and was covered with fine fruit-trees: the way from the garden door to the house was between that long house wall and a row of espaliers, behind which was a grass-plat, interspersed with standard trees and flower beds, and having one of those green rotatory garden seats shaped like a tub, where the contemplative person within may, like Diogenes, be as much in the sun as he likes. There was a descent by a few steps to another garden, which was chiefly filled with fragrant herbs, and with a long bed of lilies of the valley. Ground-rent had been of little value when the house was built. The kitchen looked into the garden, and opened into it; and near the kitchen door was a pipe, supplied from one of the fine springs with which the country about Bath abounds, and a little stone cistern beneath. The parlor door also opened into the garden; it was bowered with jessamine, and there I often took my seat upon the stone steps.

My aunt, who had an unlucky taste for such things, fitted up the house at a much greater expense than she was well able to afford. She threw two small rooms into one, and thus made a good parlor, and built a drawing-room over the kitchen. The walls of that drawing-room were covered with a plain green paper, the floor with a Turkey carpet: there hung her own portrait by Gainsborough, with a curtain to preserve the frame from flies and the colors from the sun; and there stood one of the most beautiful pieces of old furniture I ever saw—a cabinet of ivory, ebony, and tortoise shell, in an ebony frame. It had been left her by a lady of the Spenser family, and was said to have belonged to the great Marlborough. I may mention, as a part of the parlor furniture, a square screen with a foot-board and a little shelf, because I have always had one of the same fashion myself, for its convenience; a French writing-table, because of its peculiar shape, which was that of a Cajou nut or a kidney—the writer sat in the concave, and had a drawer on each side; an arm-chair made of fine cherry wood, which had been Mr. Bradford's, and in which she always sat—mentionable because, if any visitor who was not in her especial favor sat therein, the leathern cushion was always sent into the garden to be aired and purified before she would use it again; a mezzotinto print of Pope's Eloisa, in an oval black frame, because of its supposed likeness to herself; two prints in the same kind of engraving, from pictures by Angelica Kauffman, one of Hector and

Andromache, the other of Telemachus at the court of Menelaus: these I notice because they were in frames of Brazilian wood; and the great print of Pombal, *o grande marquez*, in a similar frame, because this was the first portrait of any illustrious man with which I became familiar. The establishment consisted of an old man-servant, and a maid, both from Shobdon. The old man used every night to feed the crickets. He died at Bath in her service.

Here my time was chiefly passed from the age of two till six. I had many indulgences, but more privations, and those of an injurious kind; want of playmates, want of exercise, never being allowed to do any thing in which by possibility I might dirt myself; late hours in company, that is to say, late hours for a child, which I reckon among the privations (having always had the healthiest propensity for going to bed betimes); late hours of rising, which were less painful, perhaps, but in other respects worse. My aunt chose that I should sleep with her, and this subjected me to a double evil. She used to have her bed warmed, and during the months while this practice was in season, I was always put into Molly's bed first, for fear of an accident from the warming-pan, and removed when my aunt went to bed, so that I was regularly wakened out of a sound sleep. This, however, was not half so bad as being obliged to lie till nine, and not unfrequently till ten in the morning, and not daring to make the slightest movement which could disturb her during the hours that I lay awake, and longing to be set free. These were, indeed, early and severe lessons of patience. My poor little wits were upon the alert at those tedious hours of compulsory idleness, fancying figures and combinations of form in the curtains, wondering at the motes in the slant sun-beam, and watching the light from the crevices of the window-shutters, till it served me, at last, by its progressive motion, to measure the lapse of time. Thoroughly injudicious as my education under Miss Tyler was, no part of it was so irksome as this.

I was inoculated at Bath at two years old, and most certainly believe that I have a distinct recollection of it as an insulated fact, and the precise place where it was performed. My mother sometimes fancied that my constitution received permanent injury from the long preparatory lowering regimen upon which I was kept. Before that time she used to say I had always been plump and fat, but afterward became the lean, lank, greyhound-like creature that I have ever since continued. She came to Bath to be with me during the eruption. Except the spots upon the arm, I had only one pustule; afraid that this might not be enough, she gave me a single mouthful of meat at dinner, and, before night, above a hundred made their appearance, with fever enough to frighten her severely. The disease, however, was very favorable. A year or two afterward I was brought to the brink of death by a fever, and still I remember the taste of one of my medicines (what it was I know not), and the cup in which it was administered. I remember, also, the doses of bark which followed. Dr. Schomberg attended me on both occasions. One of Schomberg's sons was the midshipman who was much talked of some forty years ago for having fought Prince William Henry, then one of his shipmates. I think he is the author of a history of our naval achievements. Alexander, another son, was a fellow of Corpus, and died in 1790 or 1791, having lost the use of his lower parts by a stroke of the palsy. I had the mournful office of going often to sit by him as he lay upon his back in bed, when he was vainly seeking relief at Bath. Boy as I was, and till then a stranger to him, he, who had no friend or relation with him, was glad of the relief which even my presence afforded to his deplorable solitude.

Miss Tyler had a numerous acquaintance, such as her person and talents (which were of no ordinary kind) were likely to attract. The circle of her Herefordshire acquaintance, extending as far as the sphere of the three music meetings in the three dioceses of Hereford, Worcester, and Gloucester, she became intimate with the family of Mr. Raikes, printer and proprietor of the Gloucester Journal. One of his sons introduced Sunday Schools* into this kingdom; others became India directors, bank directors, &c., in the career of mercantile prosperity. His daughter, who was my aunt's friend, married Francis Newberry, of St. Paul's Church-yard, son of that Francis Newberry who published Goody Two-shoes, Giles Gingerbread, and other such delectable histories in sixpenny books for children, splendidly bound in the flowered and gilt Dutch paper of former days. As soon as I could read, which was very early, Mr. Newberry presented me with a whole set of these books, more than twenty in number: I dare say they were in Miss Tyler's possession at her death, and in perfect preservation, for she taught me (and I thank her for it) never to spoil nor injure any thing. This was a rich present, and may have been more instrumental than I am aware of in giving me that love of books, and that decided determination to literature, as the one thing desirable, which manifested itself from my childhood, and which no circumstances in after life ever slackened or abated.

I can trace with certainty the rise and direction of my poetical pursuits. They grew out of my aunt's intimacy with Miss ——. Her father had acquired a considerable property as a wax and tallow-chandler at Bath, and vested great part of it in a very curious manner for an illiterate tradesman. He had a passion for the stage, which he indulged by speculating in theaters; one he built at Birmingham, one at Bristol, and one at Bath. Poor man, he outlived his reasonable faculties, and was, when I knew him, a pitiable spectacle of human weakness and de-

* I know not where or when they were first instituted; but they are noticed in an ordinance of Albert and Isabel, in the year 1608, as then existing in the Catholic Netherlands, the magistrates being enjoined to see to their establishment and support in all places where they were not yet set on foot.

cay, hideously ugly, his nose grown out in knobs and bulbs, like an under-ground artichoke, his fingers crooked and knotted with the gout, filthy, irascible, helpless as an infant, and feebler than one in mind. In one respect this was happy for him. His wife was a kind, plain-mannered, domestic woman; her clothes caught fire one day, she ran into the street in flames, and was burned to death. Mrs. Coleridge, who was then a girl of eight or nine years old, and lived in the same street, saw her in flames, and remembers how frightfully the dogs barked at the sight. Her husband, though in the house at the time, never knew what had befallen her. He survived her many years, and would frequently say she had been gone more than a week to Devizes, and it was time for her to come back. After this dreadful event he lived with his two daughters, Miss —— and Mrs. —— (a widow), in Galloway's Buildings, in a house at which I often visited with my aunt, during fifteen or sixteen years of my life, occasionally for weeks together. Sometimes I was taken to see this deplorable old man, whose sight always excited in me a mingled feeling of horror and disgust, not to be recalled without some degree of pain. In consequence of his incapacity, the property of the Bath and Bristol theaters devolved upon his children, and was administered by his son, who was, in truth, a remarkable and rememberable person.

Mr. —— must have been about five-and-thirty when I first remember him, a man of great talents and fine person, with a commanding air and countenance, kind in his manners and in his nature; yet there was an expression in his eyes which I felt, before I had ever heard of physiognomy, or could have understood the meaning of the word. It was a wild, unquiet look, a sort of inward emanating light, as if all was not as it ought to be within. I should pronounce now that it was the eye of one predisposed to insanity; and this I believe to have been the fact, though the disease manifested itself not in him, but in his children. They, indeed, had the double reason to apprehend such an inheritance, for their mother was plainly crazed with hypochondriacism and fantasticalness. She was a widow and an actress when he married her, and her humors soon made any place more agreeable to him than home. The children were my playmates at those rare times when I had any. The eldest son was taken from the Charter House because he was literally almost killed there by the devilish cruelty of the boys; they used to lay him before the fire till he was scorched, and shut him in a trunk with saw-dust till he had nearly expired with suffocation. The Charter House at that time was a sort of hell upon earth for the under boys. He was of weak understanding and feeble frame, very like his mother in person; he lived, however, to take orders, and I think I have heard that he died insane, as did one of his sisters, who perfectly resembled him. Two other sons were at Eton; the elder of the two had one of the most beautiful countenances I ever remember to have seen, only that it had his father's eyes, and a more fearful light in them. He was a fine generous, overflowing creature; but you could not look at him without feeling that some disastrous fate would befall one so rash, so inconsiderate, and, withal, so keenly susceptible. When he was at Cambridge he used to give orders to his gyp by blowing a French horn, and he had a tune for every specific command, which the gyp was trained to understand, till so noisy and unacademical a practice was forbidden. There he ran wild, and contracted debts in all imaginable ways, which his father, the most indulgent of fathers, again and again discharged. These habits clung to him after he had left college. On the last occasion, where his conduct had been deeply culpable, and a large sum had been paid for him, Mr. —— did not utter a single reproach, but in the most affectionate manner entreated him to put away all painful thoughts of the past, and look upon himself as if he were only now beginning life. The poor fellow could not bear his father's kindness, and knowing, perhaps, too surely, that he could not trust his resolutions to amend his life, he blew out his own brains.

I had not seen him for several years before his death. When we were boys I admired him for his wit, his hilarity, his open, generous temper, and his countenance, which might better be called *radiant* than described by any other epithet; but there was something which precluded all desire of intimacy. If we had been thrown together in youth, there would have been an intellectual attraction between us; but intellect alone has never been the basis of my friendships, except in a single instance, and that instance proved the sandiness of such a foundation. Yet we liked each other; and I never think of him without a hope, or rather a belief, an inward and sure persuasion, that there is more mercy in store for human frailty than even the most liberal creed has authorized us to assert.

The next letter will explain in what way my acquaintance with this family was the means of leading

> My favor'd footsteps to the Muses' hill,
> Whose arduous paths I have not ceased to tread,
> From good to better persevering still.

LETTER VII.

BATH AND BRISTOL THEATERS—REMOVED TO ANOTHER DAY SCHOOL—THENCE TO A BOARDING SCHOOL AT CORSTON—DESCRIPTION OF SCHOOL AND SCHOOLMASTER.

September 2d, 1821.

THE Bath and Bristol theaters were then, and for many years afterward, what in trade language is called *one concern*. The performers were stationed half the year in one city, half in the other. When they played on Mondays, Wednesdays, and Fridays at Bristol, they went to Bath on the Saturday in two immense coaches each as big as a caravan of wild beasts, and returned after the play. When the nights of performance at Bath were Tuesdays, Thursdays, and Saturdays, they played at Bristol on the Monday. Mondays and Saturdays were the fashionable nights. On Thursdays and Fridays they always played to thin, and very frequently to losing houses. The population of London is too large for a folly like this to show itself there.

Miss Tyler, through her intimacy with Miss ——, had the command of orders for free admission. She was exceedingly fond of theatrical representations, and there was no subject of which I heard so much from my earliest childhood. It even brought upon me once a most severe reprehension for innocently applying to the Church a phrase which, I then learned to my cost, belonged only to the play-house, and saying one Sunday, on our return from morning service, that it had been a very *full house.* When I was taken to the theater for the first time, I can perfectly well remember my surprise at not finding the pit literally a deep hole, into which I had often puzzled myself to think how or why any persons could possibly go. You may judge by this how very young I must have been. I recollect nothing more of the first visit, except that the play was the Fathers, a comedy of Fielding's, which was acted not more than one season, and the farce was Coxheath Camp. This recollection, however, by the help of that useful book, the Biographia Dramatica, fixes the date to 1778, when I was four years old.

A half sheet of reminiscences, written one-and-twenty years ago at Lisbon, has recalled to my recollection this and a few other circumstances, which might otherwise, perhaps, have been quite obliterated. Yet it surprises me to perceive how many things come to mind which had been for years and years forgotten! It is said that when earth is flung to the surface in digging a well, plants will spring up which are not found in the surrounding country, seeds having quickened in light and air which had lain buried during unknown ages—no unapt illustration for the way in which forgotten things are thus brought up from the bottom of one's memory.

I was introduced to the theater before it was possible for me to comprehend the nature of the drama, so as to derive any pleasure from it, except as a mere show. What was going on upon the stage, as far as I understood it, appeared real to me; and I have been told that one night, when the Critic was represented, and I heard that Sir Walter Raleigh's head was to be cut off, I hid mine in Miss Mary Delamere's lap, and could not be persuaded to look up till I was assured the dreaded scene was over. It was not long before I acquired a keen relish for the stage; but at this time my greatest pleasure was a walk in the fields, and the pleasure was heightened beyond measure if we crossed the river in the ferry-boat at Walcot or at the South Parade. Short as the passage was, I have not yet forgotten the delight which it used to give me. There were three points beyond all others which I was desirous of reaching, the sham castle on Claverton Hill, a summer-house on Beechen Cliffs, and the grave of a young man, whom a practiced gambler, by name (I think) Count Rice, had killed in a duel. The two former objects were neither of them two miles distant; but they were up hill, and my aunt regarded it as an impossibility to walk so far. I did not reach them, therefore, till I was old enough to be in some degree master of my own movements. The tomb of the unfortunate duelist was at Bath Weston, and we got there once, which was an extraordinary exertion; but the usual extent of our walks into the country (which were very rare) was to a cottage in an orchard about half way to that village. It was always a great joy to me when I was sent from home, though my father's house was in one of the busiest streets in a crowded city. I had more liberty then, and was under no capricious restrictions, and I had more walks into the fields, though still too few. My mother sometimes, and sometimes my aunt Mary, would walk with me to Kingsdown, to Brandon Hill, Clifton, or that bank of the river which is called the Sea Banks, and we often went to my grandmother's, where I liked best to be, because I had there a thorough enjoyment of the country.

Miss Tyler, whose ascendency over my mother was always that of an imperious elder sister, would not suffer me to be breeched till I was six years old, though I was tall of my age. I had a fantastic costume of nankeen for highdays and holidays, trimmed with green fringe: it was called a vest and tunic, or a *jam.* When at last I changed my dress, it was for coat, waistcoat, and breeches of foresters' green; at that time there was no intermediate form of apparel in use. I was then sent as a day scholar to a school on the top of St. Michael's or Mile Hill, which was then esteemed the best in Bristol, kept by Mr. Foot,* a dissenting minister of that community who are called General Baptists, in contradistinction to the Particular or Calvinistic Baptists. Like most of his denomination, he had passed into a sort of low Arianism, if indeed he were not a Socinian. With this, however, I had no concern, nor did my parents regard it. To a child, indeed, it could be of no consequence; but a youth might easily and imperceptibly have acquired from it an injurious bias, if his good conduct and disposition had made him a favorite with him. He was an old man, and if the school had ever been a good one, it had woefully deteriorated. I was one of the least boys there, I believe the very least, and certainly both as willing and as apt to learn as any teacher could have desired; yet it was the only school where I was ever treated with severity. Lessons in the grammar, which I did not comprehend, and yet could have learned well enough by rote under gentle discipline and a good-natured teacher, were frightened out of my head, and then I was shut up during play-time in a closet at the top of the stairs, where

* He published some letters to Bishop Hoadley. This I learn from Gregonne's *Sectes Religieuses.*

there was just light enough through some bars to see my lesson by. Once he caned me cruelly—the only time that any master ever laid his hand upon me—and I am sure he deserved a beating much more than I did. There was a great deal of tyranny in the school, from the worst of which I was exempted, because I went home in the evening; but I stood in great fear of the big boys, and saw much more of the evil side of human nature than I should ever have learned in the course of domestic education.

I had not been there more than twelve months when the master died. He was succeeded by John Prior Estlin, a Socinian minister, with whom in after years I was well acquainted, a good scholar and an excellent man. Had I continued at the school, he would have grounded me well, for he was just the kind of man to have singled me out and taken pleasure in bestowing careful culture where it would not have been lost. Unfortunately, my father (I know not for what reason) thought proper to remove me upon Mr. Foot's death, and placed me at a school nine miles from Bristol, in a village called Corston, about a mile from the Globe at Newton, a well-known public house on the road between Bath and Bristol. The stage was to drop me at that public house, and my father to accompany it on horseback, and consign me to the master's care. When the time for our departure drew nigh, I found my mother weeping in her chamber; it was the first time I had ever seen her shed tears. The room (that wherein I was born), with all its furniture, and her position and look at that moment, are as distinct in my memory as if the scene had occurred but yesterday; and I can call to mind with how strong and painful an effort it was that I subdued my own emotions. I allude to this in the Hymn to the Penates as

> The first grief I felt,
> And the first painful smile that clothed my front
> With feelings not its own.

What follows is also from the life:

> Sadly at night
> I sat me down beside a stranger's hearth,
> And when the lingering hour of rest was come,
> First wet with tears my pillow.

One of my earliest extant poems (the Retrospect) describes this school, and a visit which I made to it, after it had ceased to be one, in the year 1793. You have it, as it was originally written at that time, in the volume which I published with Robert Lovell, and as corrected for preservation, in the collection of my Minor Poems. The house had been the mansion of some decayed family, whose history I should like to trace if Collinson's Somersetshire were to fall in my way. There were vestiges of former respectability and comfort about it, which, young as I was, impressed me in the same manner that such things would do now—walled gardens, summer-houses, gate-pillars, surmounted with huge stone balls, a paddock, a large orchard, walnut-trees, yards, out-houses upon an opulent scale. I felt how mournful all this was in its fallen state, when the great walled garden was converted into a play-ground for the boys, the gateways broken, the summer-houses falling to ruin, and grass growing in the interstices of the lozenged pavement of the forecourt. The features within I do not so distinctly remember, not being so well able to understand their symbols of better days; only I recollect a black oaken stair-case from the hall, and that the school-room was hung with faded tapestry, behind which we used to have our hoards of crabs.

Here one year of my life was passed with little profit and with a good deal of suffering. There could not be a worse school in all respects. Thomas Flower, the master, was a remarkable man, worthy of a better station in life, but utterly unfit for that in which he was placed. His whole delight was in mathematics and astronomy, and he had constructed an orrery upon so large a scale that it filled a room. What a misery it must have been for such a man to teach a set of stupid boys, year after year, the rudiments of arithmetic. And a misery he seemed to feel it. When he came into his desk, even there he was thinking of the stars, and looked as if he were out of humor, not from ill nature, but because his calculations were interrupted. But, for the most part, he left the school to the care of his son Charley, a person who was always called by that familiar diminutive, and whose consequence you may appreciate accordingly. Writing and arithmetic were all they professed to teach; but twice in the week a Frenchman came from Bristol to instruct in Latin the small number of boys who learned it, of whom I was one. Duplanier was his name. He returned to France at the commencement of the Revolution, and a report obtained credit at Bristol, and got into the newspapers, that, having resumed his proper name, which for some reason or other he had thought fit to conceal in England, he went into the army, and became no less a personage than General Menou, of Egyptian notoriety. For Duplanier's sake, who was a very good-natured man, I am glad the story was disproved.

That sort of ornamental penmanship which now, I fear, has wholly gone out of use, was taught there. The father, as well as Charley, excelled in it. They could adorn the heading of a rule in arithmetic in a ciphering-book, or the bottom of a page, not merely with common flourishing, but with an angel, a serpent, a fish, or a pen, formed with an ease and freedom of hand which was to me a great object of admiration; but, unluckily, I was too young to acquire the art. I have seen, in the course of my life, two historical pieces produced in this manner; worthy of remembrance they are, as notable specimens of whimsical dexterity. One was David killing Goliath: it was in a broker's shop at Bristol, and I would have bought it if I could have afforded at that time to expend some ten shillings upon it. The other was a portrait of King Joam V. on horseback, in the bishop's palace at Beja. They taught the beautiful Italian, or lady's hand, used in the age of our parents; engrossing (which, I suppose, was devised to insure distinctness and legibility); and some varieties of German text, worthy for their square, massy, antique forms to have figured in an antiquarian's title-page.

Twice during the twelve months of my stay great interest was excited throughout the commonwealth by a grand spelling match, for which poor Flower deserves some credit, if it was a device of his own to save himself trouble and amuse the boys. Two of the biggest boys chose their party, boy by boy alternately, till the whole school was divided between them. They then hunted the dictionary for words unusual enough in their orthography to puzzle ill-taught lads; and having compared lists, that the same word might not be chosen by both, two words were delivered to every boy, and kept by him profoundly secret from all on the other side till the time of trial. On a day appointed we were drawn up in battle array, quite as anxious on the occasion as the members of a cricket club for the result of a grand match against all England. Ambition, that "last infirmity of noble minds," had its full share in producing this anxiety; and, to increase the excitement, each person had wagered a halfpenny upon the event. The words were given out in due succession on each side, from the biggest to the least; and for every one which was spelled rightly in its progress down the enemy's ranks, the enemy scored one; or one was scored on the other side if the word ran the gauntlet safely. The party in which I was engaged lost one of these matches and won the other. I remember that my words for one of them were Crystallization and Coterie, and that I was one of the most effective persons in the contest, which might easily be.

Charley and his father frequently saved themselves some trouble by putting me to teach bigger boys than myself. I got on with Latin here more by assisting others in their lessons than by my own, when the master came so seldom. This assistance was not voluntary on my part; it was a tax levied upon me by the law of the strongest, a law which prevails as much in schools as it did in the cabinets of Louis XIV. and the Emperor Napoleon, and does in that of the United States of America; but the effect was, that I made as much progress as if my lessons had been daily. At Mr. Foote's I read Cordery and Erasmus, each with a translation in a parallel column, which was doubled down at lesson time. Here I got into Phædrus without a translation, but with the help of an *ordo verborum*, indicated by figures in the margin. But I am at the end of my paper, and the slip beside me has items enough concerning Corston for another letter.

LETTER VIII.

RECOLLECTIONS OF CORSTON CONTINUED.

December 28th, 1821.

I REMEMBER poor Flower with compassion, and not without respect, as a man who, under more auspicious circumstances, might have passed his life happily for himself, and perhaps honorably as well as usefully for his country. His attainments and talents were, I have no doubt, very considerable in their kind; and I am sure that his temper and disposition were naturally good. I never saw so little punishment in any school. There was but one flogging during my stay there: it was for running away, which was considered the heaviest of all offenses. The exhibition was then made as serious as possible; the instrument was a scourge of packthread instead of a rod. But, though punishments in private schools were at that time, I believe, always much more severe than in public ones, I do not remember that this was remarkable for severity. We stood in awe and respect of him rather than fear. If there was nothing conciliating or indulgent about him, there was no rigor or ill nature; but his manner was what you might expect to find in one who was habitually thoughtful, and who, when not engaged in abstruse studies, had reason enough for unhappiness, because of his domestic circumstances. His school was declining. He was about fifty years of age; and having lost his first wife, had married one of his maids, who took to drinking; the house, therefore, was in disorder; the servants were allowed to take their own course, and the boys were sadly neglected. In every thing which relates to personal cleanliness, they were left to the care of themselves. I had a profusion of curly hair: just before the holidays, it was thought proper to examine into the state of its population, which was found to be prodigiously great; my head, therefore, was plastered with soap, and in that condition I was sent home, with such sores in consequence of long neglect that my mother wept at seeing them.

Our morning ablutions, to the entire saving of all materials, were performed in a little stream which ran through the barton, and in its ordinary state was hardly more than ankle deep. We had porridge for breakfast in winter, bread and milk in summer. My taste was better than my appetite; the green leeks in this uncleanly broth gave me a dislike to that plant, which I retain to this day (St. David forgive me!); and if it were swimming with fat, as it usually was, I could better fast till the hour of dinner than do violence to my stomach by forcing down the greasy and offensive mixture. The bread and milk reminds me of an anecdote connected with the fashion of those days. Because I was indulged with sugar in my bread and milk at home, when I went to school I was provided with a store carefully secured in paper. I had a cocked hat for Sundays; during the rest of the week it lay in my box upon the top of my clothes, and when the paper of brown sugar was reduced in bulk, I deposited it in the cock of the hat. As you may suppose, my fingers found their way there whenever I went to the box, and the box was sometimes opened for that purpose; thus the sugar was by little and little strewn over the hat. It was in a sweet, clammy condition the first time

I was sent for from school by my aunt Tyler, to visit her at Bath; and as the cocked hat was then in the last and lowest stage of its fashion, mine was dismissed to be rounded by the hatter, and I never wore one again till I was at Madrid, where round hats were prohibited.

One day in the week we had bread and cheese for dinner; or, when baking day came round, a hot cake, with cheese or a small portion of butter at our choice. This, to my liking, was the best dinner in the week. Some of the boys would split their cake, lay the cheese in thin layers between the halves, and then place it under a screw-press, so as to compress it into one mass. This rule of going without meat one day in the week was then, I believe, general in the country schools, and is still practiced in many, retained, perhaps, for motives of frugality, from Catholic times; and yet, so stupid is popular obstinacy, fish, even where it is most plentiful, is never used. One of the servants had the privilege of selling gingerbread and such things. We had bread and cheese for supper, and were permitted to raise salads for this meal, in little portions of ground, into which what had been in better times the flower border of the great pleasure garden was divided: these portions were our property, and transferable by sale. We raised mustard and cress, radishes and lettuce. When autumn came, we had no lack of apples, for it is a country of orchards. The brook, which has already been mentioned, passed through one immediately before it entered the barton where our ablutions were performed; the trees on one side grew on a steepish declivity, and in stormy weather we constructed dams across the stream to stop the apples which were brought down. Our master had an extensive orchard of his own, and employed the boys to gather in the fruit: there was, of course, free license to eat on that day, and a moderate share of pocketings would have been tolerated; but whether original sin was particularly excited by that particular fruit or not, so it was that a subtraction was made enormous enough to make inquiry unavoidable; the boxes were searched in consequence, and the whole plunder was thus recovered. The boys were employed also to *squail* at the *bannets*, that is, being interpreted, to throw at his walnuts when it was time to bring them down: there were four or five fine trees on the hill-side above the brook. I was too little to bear a part in this, which required considerable strength; but for many days afterward I had the gleaning among the leaves and broken twigs with which the ground was covered, and the fragrance of those leaves, in their incipient decay, is one of those odors which I can recall at will, and which, whenever it occurs, brings with it the vivid remembrance of past times.

One very odd amusement, which I never saw or heard of elsewhere, was greatly in vogue at this school. It was performed with snail shells, by placing them against each other, point to point, and pressing till the one was broken in, or sometimes both. This was called conquering; and the shell which remained unhurt acquired esteem and value in proportion to the number over which it had triumphed, an accurate account being kept. A great conqueror was prodigiously prized and coveted; so much so, indeed, that two of this description would seldom have been brought to contest the palm, if both possessors had not been goaded to it by reproaches and taunts. The victor had the number of its opponents added to its own; thus, when one conqueror of fifty conquered another which had been as often victorious, it became conqueror of a hundred and one. Yet even in this, reputation was sometimes obtained upon false pretenses. I found a boy one day who had fallen in with a great number of young snails, so recently hatched that the shells were still transparent, and he was besmearing his fingers by crushing these poor creatures one after another against his conqueror, counting away with the greatest satisfaction at his work. He was a good-natured boy, so that I, who had been bred up to have a sense of humanity, ventured to express some compassion for the snails, and to suggest that he might as well count them and lay them aside unhurt. He hesitated, and seemed inclined to assent, till it struck him as a point of honor or of conscience, and then he resolutely said no! that would not do, for he could not then fairly say he had conquered them. There is a surprising difference of strength in these shells, and that not depending upon the size or species; I mean, whether yellow, brown, or striped. It might partly be estimated by the appearance of the point or top (I do not know what better term to use): the strong ones were usually clear and glossy there, and white if the shell were of the large, coarse, mottled-brown kind. The top was then said to be petrified; and a good conqueror of this description would triumph for weeks or months. I remember that one of the greatest heroes bore evident marks of having once been conquered. It had been thrown away in some lucky situation, where the poor tenant had leisure to repair his habitation or, rather, where the restorative power of nature repaired it for him, and the wall was thus made stronger than it had been before the breach, by an arch of new masonry below. But, in general, I should think the resisting power of the shell depended upon the geometrical nicety of its form.

One of the big boys one day brought down a kite with an arrow from the play-ground: this I think a more extraordinary feat than Apollo's killing Python, though a Belvidere Jack Steel (this was the archer's name) would not make quite so heroic a statue. We had a boy there who wore midshipman's uniform, and whose pay must have more than maintained him at school; his father was a purser, and such things were not uncommon in those days. While I was at this school, the corporation of Bristol invited Rodney from Bath to a public dinner, after his great victory; and we, to do him honor in our way, were all marched down to the Globe at Newton, by the road side, that we might see him pass, and give him three cheers. They were heartily given, and were returned with great good humor from the carriage window. Another circumstance has made me remember the day well. Looking about for conquerors in Newton churchyard before we returned to school, I saw a slow-worm get into the ground under a tombstone; and in consequence, when I met, no long time afterward, with the ancient opinion that the spinal marrow of a human body generates a serpent, this fact induced me long to believe it without hesitation, upon the supposed testimony of my own eyes.

Though I had a full share of discomfort at Corston, I recollect nothing there so painful as that of being kept up every night till a certain hour, when I was dying with sleepiness. Sometimes I stole away to bed; but it was not easy to do this, and I found that it was not desirable, because the other boys played tricks upon me when they came. But I dreaded nothing so much as Sunday evening in winter: we were then assembled in the hall to hear the master read a sermon, or a portion of Stackhouse's History of the Bible. Here I sat at the end of a long form, in sight, but not within feeling of the fire, my feet cold, my eyelids heavy as lead, and yet not daring to close them, kept awake by fear alone, in total inaction, and under the operation of a lecture more soporific than the strongest sleeping dose. Heaven help the wits of those good people who think that children are to be edified by having sermons read to them!

After remaining there about twelve months, I was sent for home, upon an alarm that the itch had broken out among us. Some of the boys communicated this advice to their parents in letters which Duplanier conveyed for them; all others, of course, being dictated and written under inspection. The report, whether true or false, accelerated the ruin of the school. A scandalous scene took place of mutual reproaches between father and son, each accusing the other for that neglect, the consequences of which were now become apparent.

The dispute was renewed with more violence after the boys were in bed. The next morning the master was not to be seen; Charley appeared with a black eye, and we knew that father and son had come to blows! Most, if not all, the Bristol boys were now taken away, and I among them, to my great joy. But, on my arrival home, I was treated as a suspected person, and underwent a three days' purgatory in brimstone.

LETTER IX.

RECOLLECTIONS OF HIS GRANDMOTHER'S HOUSE AT BEDMINSTER—LOVE FOR BOTANY AND ENTOMOLOGY.

July, 1822.

THE year which I passed at Corston had been a mournful one for my mother. She lost my sweet little sister Louisa during that time; and being after a while persuaded to accompany Miss Tyler to London, where she had never before been, they were recalled by the tidings of my grandmother's sudden death. Miss Tyler had found it expedient to break up her establishment at Bath, and pass some time in visiting among her friends. She now took up her abode at Bedminster till family affairs should be settled, and till she could determine where and how to fix herself. Thither also I was sent, while my father was looking out for another school at which to place me.

I have so many vivid feelings connected with this house at Bedminster, that if it had not been in a vile neighborhood, I believe my heart would have been set upon purchasing it, and fixing my abode there, where the happiest days of my childhood were spent. My grandfather built it (about the year 1740, I suppose), and had made it what was then thought a thoroughly commodious and good house for one in his rank of life. It stood in a lane, some two or three hundred yards from the great western road. You ascended by several semicircular steps into what was called the fore-court, but was, in fact, a flower garden, with a broad pavement from the gate to the porch. That porch was in great part lined, as well as covered, with white jessamine; and many a time have I sat there with my poor sisters, threading the fallen blossoms upon grass stalks. It opened into a little hall, paved with diamond-shaped flags. On the right hand was the parlor, which had a brown or black boarded floor, covered with a Lisbon mat, and a handsome time-piece over the fire-place; on the left was the best kitchen, in which the family lived. The best kitchen is an apartment that belongs to other days, and is now no longer to be seen, except in houses which, having remained unaltered for the last half century, are inhabited by persons a degree lower in society than their former possessors. The one which I am now calling to mind, after an interval of more than forty years, was a cheerful room, with an air of such country comfort about it, that my little heart was always gladdened when I entered it during my grandmother's life. It had a stone floor, which I believe was the chief distinction between a best kitchen and a parlor. The furniture consisted of a clock, a large oval oak table with two flaps (over which two or three fowling-pieces had their place), a round tea-table of cherry wood, Windsor chairs of the same, and two large armed ones of that easy make (of all makes it is the easiest), in one of which my grandmother always sat. On one side of the fire-place the china was displayed in a buffet—that is, a cupboard with glass doors; on the other were closets for articles less ornamental, but more in use. The room was wainscoted and ornamented with some old maps, and with a long looking-glass over the chimney-piece, and a tall one between the windows, both in white frames. The windows opened into the fore-court, and were as cheerful and fragrant in the season of flowers as roses and jessamine which grew luxuriantly without, could make them. There was a passage between this apartment and the kitchen, long enough to admit of a large airy pantry, and a larder on the left hand, the windows of both opening into the barton, as did those of the kitchen; on the right was a door into the back court. There was a rack in the kitchen well furnished with bacon, and a mistletoe bush always suspended from the middle of the ceiling.

The green room, which was my uncle Edward's, was over the parlor. Over the hall was a smaller apartment, which had been my grandfather's office, and still contained his desk and his pigeon-holes: I remember it well, and the large-patterned, dark, flock paper, with its faded ground. The yellow room, over the best kitchen, was the visitor's chamber; and this my mother occupied whenever she slept there. There was no way to my grandmother's, the blue room over the kitchen, but through this and an intervening passage, where, on the left, was a store-room. The blue room had a thorough light, one window looking into the barton, the other into the back court. The squire slept in the garret; his room was on one side, the servants' on the other: and there was a large open space between, at the top of the stairs, used for lumber and stores.

A door from the hall, opposite to the entrance, opened upon the cellar stairs, to which there was another door from the back court. This was a square, having the house on two sides, the wash-house and brew-house on the third, and walled on the fourth. A vine covered one side of the house here, and grew round my grandmother's window, out of which I have often reached the grapes. Here also was the pigeon-house, and the pump, under which the fatal dipping* was performed. The yard or barton was of considerable size; the entrance to it was from the lane, through large folding gates, with a horse-chestnut on each side. And here another building fronted you, as large as the house, containing the dairy and laundry, both large and excellent in their kind, seed-rooms, stable, hay-lofts, &c. The front of this out-house was almost clothed with yew, clipped to the shape of the windows. Opposite the one gable-end were the coal and stick houses; and on the left side of the barton was a shed for the cart, and, while my grandfather lived, for an open carriage, which after his death was no longer kept. Here, too, was the horse-block, beautifully overhung with ivy, from an old wall against which it was placed. The other gable end was covered with fruit-trees, and at the bottom was a raised chamomile bed.

An old fashioned bird's-eye view, half picture, half plan, would explain all this more intelligibly than my description can do; and if I possessed the skill, I should delight in tracing one: my memory would accurately serve. If I have made myself understood, you will perceive that the back court formed a square with the house. Behind both was a piece of waste ground, left for the passage of carts from the barton to the orchard, but considerably wider than was necessary for that purpose. It was neatly kept in grass, with a good wide path from the court to the kitchen garden. This was large, excellently stocked, and kept in admirable order by my uncle Edward. It was inclosed from the waste ground by a wall about breast high, surmounted with white rails till it joined the out-houses. The back of these was covered with pear and plum trees—the green gages, I remember, were remarkably fine of their kind. One side was walled, and well clothed with cherry, peach and nectarine trees; the opposite one was separated by a hedge from the lane leading to the orchard, from which the garden was divided at the bottom. I have called it a kitchen garden, because that name was given it; but it was ornamental as well as useful, with grass walks, espaliers, and a profusion of fine flowers. The side of the house in the fore-court also was covered with an apricot-tree, so that every luxury of this kind which an English sun can ripen was there in abundance. Just by the orchard gate was a fine barberry-bush; and that peculiar odor of its blossoms, which is supposed to injure the wheat within its reach, is still fresh in my remembrance. Wordsworth has no sense of smell. Once, and once only in his life, the dormant power awakened: it was by a bed of stocks in full bloom, at a house which he inhabited in Dorsetshire, some five-and-twenty years ago; and he says it was like a vision of Paradise to him; but it lasted only a few minutes, and the faculty has continued torpid from that time. The fact is remarkable in itself, and would be worthy of notice, even if it did not relate to a man of whom posterity will desire to know all that can be remembered. He has often expressed to me his regret for this privation. I, on the contrary, possess the sense in such acuteness, that I can remember an odor and call up the ghost of one that is departed. But I must return to the barberry-bush. It stood at the entrance of a potato garden, which had been taken from the orchard. The orchard was still of considerable size. At the bottom was a broad wet ditch, with a little draw-bridge over it leading into the fields, through which was the pleasantest way to church and to Bristol. It was just one mile to the church, and two to my father's house in Wine Street.

It was very seldom indeed that my grandmother went to Bristol. I scarcely recollect ever to have seen her there. The extent of her walks was to church, which she never missed, unless the weather absolutely confined her to the house. She was not able to attend the evening service also, on account of the distance; but in the morning she was constant, and always in good time; for if she were not there before the absolution, she used to say that she might as well have remained at home. At other times she rarely went out of her own premises. Neighbors of her own rank there were none within her reach; her husband's acquaintance had mostly

* See page 24.

died off, and she had made no new ones since his death. Her greatest happiness was to have my mother there with some of the young fry; and we, on our part, had no pleasure so great as that of a visit to Bedminster. It was, indeed, for my mother, as well as for us, an advantage beyond all price to have this quiet country home at so easy a distance, abounding as it did with all country comforts. Bedminster itself was an ugly, dirty, poor, populous village, many of the inhabitants being colliers; but the coal-pits were in a different part of the parish, and the house was at a sufficient distance from all annoyances. If there was no beauty of situation, there was complete retirement and perfect comfort. The view was merely to a field and cottage on the other side the lane, on a rising ground belonging to the property. But the little world within was our own, and to me it was quite a different world from that in which I lived at other times. My father's house was in one of the busiest and noisiest streets of Bristol, and of course had no outlets. At Bath I was under perpetual restraint. But here I had all wholesome liberty, all wholesome indulgence, all wholesome enjoyments; and the delight which I there learned to take in rural sights and sounds has grown up with me, and continues unabated to this day.

My chief amusement was in the garden, where I found endless entertainment in the flowers and in observing insects. I had little propensity to any boyish sports, and less expertness in them. My uncles Edward and William used to reproach me with this sometimes, saying they never saw such a boy. One schoolboy's art, however, they taught me, which I have never read of, nor seen practiced elsewhere; it was that of converting a marble into a black witch, and thereby making it lucky. You know that if a marble be put in the fire, it makes a good detonating ball. I have sacrificed many a one so, to frighten the cook. But if the marble be wrapped up in brown paper (perhaps any paper may answer the purpose as well), with some suet or dripping round about it, it will not explode while the fat is burning, and when you take it out of the grate it is as black as jet.

But, if I was unapt at ordinary sports, a botanist or entomologist would have found me a willing pupil in those years; and if I had fallen in with one, I might, perhaps, at this very day, have been classifying mosses, and writing upon the natural history of snails or cock-chafers, instead of recording the events of the Peninsular War. I knew every variety of grass blossom that the fields produced, and in what situations to look for each. I discovered that snails seal themselves up in their shells during the winter, and that ants make their way into the cock-chafer through an aperture in the breast, and eat out its inside while it is yet alive. This gave me a great dislike to the ants, which even the delightful papers about them in the Guardian did not overcome. Two curious facts concerning these insects, which fell under my own observation in those days, are worthy of being noted. They spoiled the produce of some of our best currant-trees one year. The trees were trained against a wall; the ants walked over them continually and in great numbers (I can not tell why, but probably after the *aphides*, which, as Kirby and Spence tell us, they regularly *milk*), and thus they imparted so rank a smell to the fruit that it could not be eaten. The ants were very numerous that season, and this occasioned a just and necessary war upon them. They had made a highway through the porch, along the interstices of the flag-stones. The right of path, as you may suppose, was not acquiesced in; and when this road was as full as Cheapside at noonday, boiling water was poured upon it. The bodies, however, all disappeared in a few hours, carried away, as we supposed, by their comrades. But we know that some insects are marvelously retentive of life; and this circumstance has sometimes tempted me to suspect that an ant may derive no more injury from being boiled, than a fly from being bottled in Madeira, or a snail from having its head cut off, or from lying seven years in a collector's cabinet. Of the latter fact (which was already authenticated), my neighbor, Mr. Fryer, of Ormathwaite, had proof the other day.

There are three flowers which, to this day, always remind me of Bedminster. The Syringa, or Roman jessamine, which covered an arbor in the fore-court, and another at the bottom of the kitchen garden; the everlasting pea, which grew luxuriantly under the best kitchen windows; and the evening primrose—my grandmother loved to watch the opening of this singularly delicate flower—a flower, indeed, which in purity and delicacy seems to me to exceed all others. She called it mortality, because these beauties pass away so soon, and because, in the briefness of its continuance (living only for a night), it reminded her of human life.

The house was sold after her death, as soon as a purchaser could be found, there being no longer the means for supporting it. The reversion of her jointure had long ago been sold by John Tyler. The house was Edward's property, he having bought it when he came of age Her loss was deeply felt by him and the poor Squire; and, indeed, it was fatal to their happiness, for happy hitherto they had been, according to their own sense of enjoyment. In losing her they lost every thing. The Squire was sent to board in a village on the coast of the Bristol Channel, called Worle; and Edward Tyler, who was very capable of business, took a clerk's place in Bristol. But their stay was gone; and eventually, I have no doubt, both their lives were shortened by the consequences.

I went to look at the place some twenty years ago; it was a good deal altered: bow windows had been thrown out in the front, and a gazebo erected in the roof. After viewing about the front as much as I could without being noticed and deemed impertinent, I made my way round into the fields, and saw that the draw-bridge was still in existence. I have seen the gazebo since from the window of a stage-coach, and this is probably the last view I shall ever have of a place so dear to me. Even the recollections of it will soon be confined to my own breast, for my uncle and my aunt Mary are now the only living persons who partake them.

LETTER X.

IS PLACED AS A DAY BOARDER AT A SCHOOL IN BRISTOL—EARLY EFFORT OF AUTHORSHIP—LOVE FOR DRAMATIC AUTHORS—MISS PALMER—SCHOOL RECOLLECTIONS—OPINION OF PUBLIC AND PRIVATE EDUCATION.

January 10th, 1823.

I WAS now placed as a day boarder at a school in that part of Bristol called the Fort, on the hill above St. Michael's Church. William Williams, the master, was, as his name denotes, a Welshman. I find him satirized, or, to use a more accurate word, slandered, in the Miscellanies of my uncle's old master, Emanuel Collins, as an impudent pretender. This he certainly was not; for he pretended to very little, and what he professed to teach he taught well. The Latin he left wholly to an usher, Bevan by name, who was curate of the parish. The writing, ciphering, and merchant's accounts he superintended himself, though there was a writing-master who made and mended the pens, ruled the copy-books, and examined the slates. Williams was an author of the very humblest class. He had composed a spelling-book solely for the consumption of his own school: it was never published, and had not even a title-page. For love of this spelling-book, he exercised the boys in it so much that the thumbing and dog-leaving turned to good account. But he was, I verily believe, conscientiously earnest in making them perfect in the Catechism. The examination in this was always dreaded as the most formidable duty of the school, such was the accuracy which he exacted, and the severity of his manner on that occasion. The slightest inattention was treated as a crime.

My grandmother died in 1782, and, either in the latter end of that year or the ensuing January, I was placed at poor old Williams's, whom, as that expression indicates, I remember with feelings of good will. I had commenced poet before this, at how early an age I can not call to mind; but I very well recollect that my first composition, both in manner and sentiment, might have been deemed a very hopeful imitation of the Bell-man's verses. The discovery, however, that I could write rhymes gave me great pleasure, which was in no slight degree heightened when I perceived that my mother was not only pleased with what I had produced, but proud of it. Miss Tyler had intended, as far as she was concerned, to give me a systematic education, and for this purpose (as she afterward told me) purchased a translation of Rousseau's Emilius. That system being happily even more impracticable than Mr. Edgeworth's, I was lucky enough to escape from any experiment of this kind, and there good fortune provided for me better than any method could have done. Nothing could be more propitious for me, considering my aptitudes and tendency of mind, than Miss Tyler's predilection, I might almost call it passion, for the theater. Owing to this, Shakspeare was in my hands as soon as I could read; and it was long before I had any other knowledge of the history of England than what I gathered from his plays. Indeed, when first I read the plain matter of fact, the difference which appeared then puzzled and did not please me, and for some time I preferred Shakspeare's authority to the historian's.

It is curious that "Titus Andronicus" was at first my favorite play; partly, I suppose, because there was nothing in the characters above my comprehension; but the chief reason must have been that tales of horror make a deep impression upon children, as they do upon the vulgar, for whom, as their ballads prove, no tragedy can be too bloody: they excite astonishment rather than pity. I went through Beaumont and Fletcher also before I was eight years old: circumstances enable me to recollect the time accurately. Beaumont and Fletcher were great theatrical names, and therefore there was no scruple about letting me peruse their works. What harm, indeed, could they do me at that age? I read them merely for the interest which the stories afforded, and understood the worse parts as little as I did the better. But I acquired imperceptibly from such reading familiarity with the diction, and ear for the blank verse of our great masters. In general, I gave myself no trouble with what I did not understand; the story was intelligible, and that was enough. But the knight of the Burning Pestle perplexed me terribly; burlesque of this kind is the last thing that a child can comprehend. It set me longing, however, for Palmerin of England, and that longing was never gratified till I read it in the original Portuguese. My favorite play upon the stage was "Cymbeline," and next to that, "As You Like It." They are both romantic dramas; and no one had ever a more decided turn for music or for numbers than I had for romance.

You will wonder that this education should not have made me a dramatic writer. I had seen more plays before I was seven years old than I have ever since I was twenty, and heard more conversation about the theater than any other subject. Miss Tyler had given up her house at Walcot before I went to Corston; and when I visited her from school, she was herself a guest with Miss Palmer and her sister, Mrs. Bartlett, whose property was vested in the Bath and Bristol theaters. Their house was in Galloway's Buildings, from whence a covered passage led to the play-house, and they very rarely missed a night's performance. I was too old to be put to bed before the performance began, and it was better that I should be taken than left with the servants; therefore I was always of the party; and it is impossible to describe the thorough delight which I received from this habitual indulgence. No after enjoyment could equal or approach it; I was sensible of no defects either in the dramas or in the representation; better acting, indeed, could nowhere have been found: Mrs. Siddons was the heroine, Dimond and Murray would have done credit to any stage, and among the comic actors were Edwin and Blanchard—and Blisset, who, though never known to a London audience, was, of all comic actors whom I have ever seen, the most perfect. But I was happily insensible to that difference between good and bad acting, which in riper years takes off so much from the pleasure of dramatic representation; every thing answered the height of my expectations and desires. And I saw it in perfect comfort, in a small theater, from the front row of a box not too far from the center. The Bath theater was said to be the most comfortable in England, and no expense was spared in the scenery and decorations.

My aunt, who hoarded every thing except money, preserved the play-bills, and had a collection of them which Dr. Burney might have envied. As she rarely or never suffered me to be out of doors, lest I should dirt my clothes, these play-bills were one of the substitutes devised for my amusement instead of healthy and natural sports. I was encouraged to prick them with a pin, letter by letter; and, for want of any thing better, became as fond of this employment as women sometimes are of netting or any ornamental work. I learned to do it with great pleasure, pricking the larger types by their outline, so that when they were held up to the window they were bordered with spots of light. The object was to illuminate the whole bill in this manner. I have done it to hundreds; and yet I can well remember the sort of dissatisfied and damping feeling which the sight of one of these bills would give me a day or two after it had been finished and laid by. It was like an illumination when half the lamps are gone out. This amusement gave my writing-masters no little trouble; for, in spite of all their lessons, I held a pen as I had been used to hold the pin.

Miss Tyler was considered as an amateur and patroness of the stage. She was well acquainted with Henderson, but of him I have no recollection. He left Bath, I believe, just as my play-going days began. Edwin, I remember, gave me an ivory wind-mill when I was about four years old; and there was no family with which she was more intimate than Dimond's. She was thrown also into the company of dramatic writers at Mr. Palmer's, who resided then about a mile from Bath, on the Upper Bristol Road, at a house called West Hall. Here she became acquainted with Coleman and Sheridan, and Cumberland and Holcroft; but I did not see any of them in those years, and the two former, indeed, never. Sophia Lee was Mrs. Palmer's most intimate friend. She was then in high reputation for the first volume of the Recess, and for the Chapter of Accidents. You will not wonder, that hearing, as I continually did, of living authors, and seeing in what estimation they were held, I formed a great notion of the dignity attached to their profession. Perhaps in no other circle could this effect so surely have been produced as in a dramatic one, where ephemeral productions excite an intense interest while they last. Superior as I thought actors to all other men, it was not long before I perceived that authors were still a higher class.

Though I have not become a dramatist, my earliest dreams of authorship were, as might be anticipated, from such circumstances, of a dramatic form, and the notion which I had formed of dramatic composition was not inaccurate. "It is the easiest thing in the world to write a play!" said I to Miss Palmer, as we were in a carriage on Redcliffe Hill one day, returning from Bristol to Bedminster. "Is it, my dear?" was her reply. "Yes," I continued, "for you know you have only to think what you would say if you were in the place of the characters, and to make them say it." This brings to mind some unlucky illustrations which I made use of about the same time to the same lady, with the view of enforcing what I conceived to be good and considerate advice. Miss Palmer was on a visit to my aunt at Bedminster; they had fallen out, as they sometimes would do. These bickerings produced a fit of sullenness in the former, which was not shaken off for some days; and while it lasted, she usually sat with her apron over her face. I really thought she would injure her eyes by this, and told her so in great kindness; "for you know, Miss Palmer," said I, "that every thing gets out of order if it is not used. A book, if it is not opened, will become damp and moldy; and a key, if it is never turned in the lock, gets rusty." Just then my aunt entered the room. "Lord, Miss Tyler!" said the offended lady, "what do you think this child has been saying? He has been comparing my eyes to a rusty key and a moldy book." The speech, however, was not without some good effect, for it restored good humor. Miss Palmer was an odd woman with a kind heart; one of those persons who are not respected so much as they deserve, because their dispositions are better than their understanding. She had a most generous and devoted attachment to Miss Tyler, which was not always requited as it ought to have been. The earliest dream which I can remember related to her; it was singular enough to impress itself indelibly upon my memory. I thought I was sitting with her in her drawing-room (chairs, carpet, and every thing are now visibly present to my mind's eye) when the devil was introduced as a morning visitor. Such an appearance, for he was in his full costume of horns, black bat-wings, tail, and cloven feet, put me in ghostly and bodily fear; but she received him with perfect politeness, called him dear Mr. Devil, desired the servant to put him a chair, and expressed her delight at being favored with a call.

There was much more promise implied in my notion of how a play ought to be written than would have been found in any of my attempts.

The first subject which I tried was the continence of Scipio, suggested by a print in a pocket-book. Battles were introduced in abundance, because the battle in Cymbeline was one of my favorite scenes; and because Congreve's hero in the Mourning Bride finds the writing of his father in prison, I made my prince of Numantia find pen, ink, and paper, that he might write to his mistress. An act and a half of this nonsense exhausted my perseverance. Another story ran for a long time in my head, and I had planned the characters to suit the actors on the Bath stage. The fable was taken from a collection of tales, every circumstance of which has completely faded from my recollection, except that the scene of the story in question was laid in Italy, and the time, I think, about Justinian's reign. The book must have been at least thirty or forty years old then, and I should recognize it if it ever fell in my way. While this dramatic passion continued, I wished my friends to partake it, and, soon after I went to Williams's school, persuaded one of my schoolfellows to write a tragedy. Ballard was his name, the son of a surgeon at Portbury, a good-natured fellow, with a round face which I have not seen for seven or eight-and-thirty years, and yet fancy that I could recognize it now, and should be right glad to see it. He liked the suggestion, and agreed to it very readily, but he could not tell what to write about. I gave him a story. But then another difficulty was discovered; he could not devise names for the personages of the drama. I gave him a most heroic assortment of *propria quæ maribus et fœminis*. He had now got his *Dramatis Personæ*, but he could not tell what to make them say, and then I gave up the business. I made the same attempt with another schoolfellow, and with no better success. It seemed to me very odd that they should not be able to write plays as well as to do their lessons. It is needless to say that both these friends were of my own age; this is always the condition of school intimacies. The subject of the second experiment was a boy whose appearance prepossessed every body. My mother was so taken with the gentleness of his manners, and the regularity and mildness of his features, that she was very desirous I should become intimate with him. He grew up to be a puppy, sported a tail when he was fifteen, and at five-and-twenty was an insignificant withered *homunculus*, with a white face shriveled into an expression of effeminate peevishness. I have seen many instances wherein the promise of the boy has not been fulfilled by the man, but never so striking a case of blight as this.

The school was better than Flower's, inasmuch as I had a Latin lesson every day instead of thrice a week. But my lessons were solitary ones, so few boys were there in my station, and, indeed, in the station of life next above mine, who received a classical education in those days, compared with what is the case now. Writing and arithmetic, with at most a little French, were thought sufficient, at that time, for the sons of opulent Bristol merchants. I was in Phædrus when I went there, and proceeded through Cornelius Nepos, Justin, and the Metamorphoses. One lesson in the morning was all. The rest of the time was given to what was deemed there of more importance. Writing was taught very differently at this school from what it was at Corston, and much less agreeably to my inclinations. We did copies of capital letters there, and were encouraged to aspire at the ornamental parts of penmanship. But Williams, who wrote a slow, strong hand himself, admirable of its kind, put me back to the rudiments at once, and kept me at strokes, pot-hooks, and hangers; *u's*, *n's*, and *m's*, and such words as *pupil* and *tulip*, Heaven knows how long, with absurd and wearisome perseverance. Writing was the only thing in which any pains were ever taken, or any method observed, to ground me thoroughly, and I was universally pronounced a most unpromising pupil. No instruction ever could teach me to hold the pen properly; of course, therefore, I could make none of those full, free strokes, which were deemed essential to good writing, and this drew upon me a great deal of unavailing reproof, though not severity, for old Williams liked me, on the whole; and Mr. Foote was the only preceptor (except a dancing-master) who ever laid hands on me in anger. At home, too, my father and my uncle Thomas used to shake their heads at me, and pronounce that I should never write a decent hand. My ciphering-book, however, made some amends, in my master's eyes. It was in this that his pains and the proficiency of his scholars were to be shown. The books he used to sew himself, half a dozen sheets folded into the common quarto size; they were ruled with double red lines, and the lines which were required in the sums were also double ruled with red ink. When the book was filled, the pencil lines were carefully rubbed out; and Williams, tearing off the covers, deposited it in an envelope of fine cartridge paper, on which he had written, in his best hand, the boy's name to whom it belonged. When there were enough of these to form a volume, they were consigned to a poor old man, the inhabitant of an alms-house, who obtained a few comforts beyond what the establishment allowed him by binding them. Now, though I wrote what is called a stiff, cramp hand, there was a neatness and regularity about my books which were peculiar to them. I had as quick a sense of symmetry as of meter. My lines were always drawn according to some standard of proportion, so that the page had an appearance of order at first sight. I found the advantage of this when I came to be concerned with proof-sheets. The method which I used in my ciphering-book led me to teach the printers how to print verses of irregular length upon a regular principle; and Ballantyne told me I was the only person he ever met with who knew how a page would look before it was set up. I may add that it was I who set the fashion for black letter in title-pages and half titles, and that this arose from my admiration of German text at school.

I remained at this school between four and five years, which, if not profitably, were at least not unhappily spent. And here let me state the deliberate opinion upon the contested subject of public or private education, which I have formed from what I have experienced, and heard, and observed. A juster estimate of one's self is acquired at school than can be formed in the course of domestic instruction, and, what is of much more consequence, a better intuition into the characters of others than there is any chance of learning in after life. I have said that this is of more consequence than one's self-estimate, because the error upon that score which domestic education tends to produce is on the right side—that of diffidence and humility. These advantages a day scholar obtains, and he avoids great part of the evils which are to be set against them. He can not, indeed, wholly escape pollution, but he is far less exposed to it than if he were a boarder. He suffers nothing from tyranny, which is carried to excess in schools; nor has he much opportunity of acquiring or indulging malicious and tyrannical propensities himself. Above all, his religious habits, which it is almost impossible to retain at school, are safe. I would gladly send a son to a good school by day; but, rather than board him at the best, I would, at whatever inconvenience, educate him myself. What I have said applies to public schools as well as private; of the advantages which the former possess I shall have occasion to speak hereafter.

LETTER XI.

MRS. DOLIGNON—EARLY LOVE FOR BOOKS—MISS TYLER TAKES A HOUSE IN BRISTOL—FURTHER RECOLLECTIONS OF HIS UNCLE WILLIAM—HIS DEATH.

January 19th, 1823.

My home, for the first two years while I went to Williams's school, was at my father's, except that during the holidays I was with Miss Tyler, either when she had lodgings at Bath, or was visiting Miss Palmer there. The first summer holidays I passed with her at Weymouth, whither she was invited to join her friend Mrs. Dolignon.

This lady, whom I remember with the utmost reverence and affection, was a widow with two children, Louisa, who was three or four years older than me, and John, who was just my age. Her maiden name was Delamere, she and her husband being both of refugee race—an extraction of which I should be far more proud than if my family name were to be found in the Roll of Battle Abbey. I have heard that Mr. Dolignon, in some delirium, died by his own hand, and this, perhaps, may have broken her spirits, and given a subdued and somewhat pensive manner to one who was naturally among the gentlest, meekest, kindest of human beings. I shall often have to speak of her in these letters. She had known me at Bath in my earliest childhood; I had the good fortune then to obtain a place in her affections, and that place I retained, even when she thought it necessary to estrange me from her family.

Landor, who paints always with the finest touch of truth, whether he is describing external or internal nature, makes his Charoba disappointed at the first sight of the sea:

> "She coldly said, her long-lash'd eyes abased,
> 'Is this the mighty ocean? Is this all?'"

and this he designs as characteristic of a "soul discontented with capacity." When I went on deck in the Corunna packet the first morning, and for the first time found myself out of sight of land, the first feeling was certainly one of disappointment as well as surprise at seeing myself in the center of so small a circle. But the impression which the sea made upon me when I first saw it at Weymouth was very different; probably because not having, like Charoba, thought of its immensity, I was at once made sensible of it. The sea, seen from the shore, is still, to me, the most impressive of all objects, except the starry heavens; and if I could live over any hours of my boyhood again, it should be those which I then spent upon the beach at Weymouth. One delightful day we passed at Portland, and another at Abbotsbury, where one of the few heronries in this kingdom was then existing, and perhaps still may be. There was another at Penshurst, and I have never seen a third. I wondered at nothing so much as at the Chesil Bank, which connects Portland, like the Firm Island of Amadis, with the main land, the shingles whereof it is formed gradually diminishing in size from one end to the other, till it becomes a sand-bank. The spot which I recollect with most distinctness is the church-yard of an old church in the island, which, from its neglected state, and its situation near the cliffs—above all, perhaps, because so many shipwrecked bodies were interred there, impressed me deeply and durably.

The first book which I ever possessed beyond the size of Mr. Newberry's gilt regiment was given me soon after this visit by Mrs. Dolignon. It was Hoole's translation of the *Gerusalemme Liberata*. She had heard me speak of it with a delight and interest above my years. My curiosity to read the poem had been strongly excited by the stories of Olendo and Sophronia, and of the Enchanted Forest as versified by Mrs. Rowe. I read them in the volume of her Letters, and despaired, at the time, of ever reading more of the poem till I should be a man, from a whimsical notion that, as the subject related to Jerusalem, the original must be in Hebrew. No one in my father's house could set me right upon this point; but going one day with my mother into a shop, one side of which was fitted up with a circulating library, containing not more than three or four hundred volumes, almost all novels, I there laid my hand upon Hoole's version, a little before my visit to Weymouth. The copy which Mrs. Dolignon sent me is now in my sight, upon the shelf, and in excellent preservation, considering that when a schoolboy I perused it so often that I had no small portion of it by heart. Forty years have tarnished the gilding upon its back; but they have not effaced my remembrance of the joy with which I received it, and the delight which I found in its repeated perusal.

During the years that I resided in Wine Street, I was upon a short allowance of books. My father read nothing except Felix Farley's Bristol Journal. A small glass cupboard over the desk in the back parlor held his wine-glasses and all his library. It consisted of the Spectator, three or four volumes of the Oxford Magazine, one of the Freeholder's, and one of the Town and Country; these he had taken in during the Wilkes and Liberty epidemic. My brother Tom and I spoiled them by coloring, that is, bedaubing the prints; but I owe to them some knowledge of the political wit, warfare, and scandal of those days; and from one of them, that excellent poem, the Old Bachelor, was cut out, which I reprinted in the Annual Anthology. The other books were Pomfret's Poems, The Death of Abel, Aaron Hill's translation of Merope, with The Jealous Wife, and Edgar and Emmeline, in one volume; Julius Cæsar, the Toy Shop, All for Love, and a Pamphlet upon the Quack Doctors of George II.'s days, in another; the Vestal Virgins, the Duke of Lerma, and the Indian Queen, in a third. To these my mother had added the Guardian, and the happy copy of Mrs. Rowe's Letters which introduced me to Torquato Tasso.

The holidays made amends for this penury, and Bull's Circulating Library was then to me what the Bodleian would be now. Hoole, in his notes, frequently referred to the Orlando Furioso. I saw some volumes thus lettered on Bull's counter, and my heart leaped for joy. They proved to be the original; but the shopman, Mr. Cruett (a most obliging man he was), immediately put the translation into my hand, and I do not think any accession of fortune could now give me so much delight as I then derived from that vile version of Hoole's. There, in the notes, I first saw the name of Spenser, and some stanzas of the Faëry Queen. Accordingly, when I returned the last volume, I asked if that work was in the library. My friend Cruett replied that they had it, but it was written in old English, and I should not be able to understand it. This did not appear to me so much a necessary consequence as he supposed, and I therefore requested he would let me look at it. It was the quarto edition of '17, in three volumes, with large prints folded in the middle, equally worthless (like all the prints of that age) in design and execution. There was nothing in the language to impede, for the ear set me right where the uncouth spelling (orthography it can not be called) might have puzzled the eye; and the few words which are really obsolete were sufficiently explained by the context. No young lady of the present generation falls to a new novel of Sir Walter Scott's with keener relish than I did that morning to the Faëry Queen. If I had then been asked wherefore it gave me so much more pleasure than ever Ariosto had done, I could not have answered the question. I now know that it was very much owing to the magic of its verse; the contrast between the flat couplets of a rhymester like Hoole, and the fullest and finest of all stanzas, written by one who was perfect master of his art. But this was not all. Ariosto too often plays with his subject; Spenser is always in earnest. The delicious landscapes which he luxuriates in describing brought every thing before my eyes. I could fancy such scenes as his lakes and forests, gardens and fountains presented; and I felt, though I did not understand, the truth and purity of his feelings, and that love of the beautiful and the good which pervades his poetry.

When Miss Tyler had lived about among her friends as long as it was convenient for them to entertain her, and longer in lodgings than was convenient for herself, she began to think of looking out for a house at Bristol; and, owing to some odd circumstances, I was the means of finding one which precisely suited her. Mrs. Wraxall, the widow of a lawyer, had heard, I know not how, that I was a promising boy, very much addicted to books, and she sent to my mother requesting that I might drink tea with her one evening. The old lady was mad as a March hare after a religious fashion. Her behavior to me was very kind; but, as soon as tea was over, she bade me kneel down, and down she knelt herself, and prayed for me by the hour to my awful astonishment. When this was done she gave me a little book called Early Piety, and a coarse edition of the Paradise Lost, and said she was going to leave Bristol. It struck me immediately that the house which she was about to quit was such a one as my aunt wanted. I said so; and Mrs. Wraxall immediately answered, "Tell her that if she likes it, she shall have the remainder of my lease." The matter was settled in a few days, for this was an advantageous offer. The house at that time would have been cheap at £20 a year, and there was an unexpired term of five years upon it at only £11. This old lady was mother to Sir Nathaniel Wraxall, who had been bred up, and perhaps born, in that habitation. The owner was poor John Morgan's father. Mr. Wraxall, many years before, had taken it at a low rent upon a repairing lease, and had expended a great deal of money upon it at a time when it was rather a rural than a suburban residence. The situation had been greatly worsened, but it was still in the skirts of the city, and out of reach of its noise.

It stood in the avenue leading from Maudlin Lane to Horfield Lane or Road. When the plan of Bristol for Barrett's wretched history of that city was engraved, the buildings ended with Maudlin Lane, and all above was fields and gardens. That plan is dated 1780, but must have been drawn at least ten years earlier, for it marks St. Leonard's Church, which was pulled down in the beginning of 1771. The avenue is marked there by the name of Red Coat Lane; a mere lane it appears, running up between fields, and with a hedge on each side. It was now, however, known by the name of Terril Street. There were at the bottom four or five houses on the left hand, built like the commencement of a street, and these were there when the plan was taken. Where they ended the steeper ascent began; and some houses followed, which, though contiguous, stood each in its little garden, some thirty yards back from the street. There were five of these, and the situation was such that they must have been in good estimation before some speculator, instead of building a sixth, erected at right angles with them a row of five or six inferior dwellings. Above these was only a steep paved avenue between high walls, inaccessible for horses because of some flights of steps. The view was to a very large garden opposite, one of those which supplied the market with fruit and culinary vegetables.

The house upon which Miss Tyler now entered was small but cheerful; Sir Nathaniel would perhaps be ashamed to remember it, but to his father it had evidently been an object of pride and pleasure. As is usual in suburban gardens, he had made the most of the ground. Though no wider than the front of the house, there was a walk paved with lozenge-shaped stones from the gate, and two gravel walks. The side beds were allotted to currant and gooseberry bushes; the others were flower beds, and there were two large apple-trees and two smaller ones. In front of the house the pavement extended, under which was an immense cistern for rain water, so large as to be absurd: it actually seemed fitter for a fort than for a small private family. The kitchen was under ground. On one side the gate was a summer-house, with a sort of cellar, and another cistern below it.

As soon as my aunt was settled here, she sent for her brother William, who, since his mother's death, had been boarded at a substantial shop-keeper's in the little village of Worle, on the Channel, about twenty miles from Bristol. I look back upon his inoffensive and monotonous course of life with a compassion which I was then not capable of feeling. For one or two years he walked into the heart of the city every Wednesday and Saturday to be shaved, and to purchase his tobacco; he went, also, sometimes to the theater, which he enjoyed highly. On no other occasion did he ever leave the house; and as inaction, aided, no doubt, by the inordinate use of tobacco, and the quantity of small-beer with which he swilled his inside, brought on a premature old age, even this exercise was left off. As soon as he rose, and had taken his first pint of beer, which was his only breakfast, to the summer-house he went, and took his station in the bow-window as regularly as a sentinel in a watch-box. Here it was his whole and sole employment to look at the few people who passed, and to watch the neighbors, with all whose concerns at last he became perfectly intimate by what he could thus oversee and overhear. He had a nickname for every one of them. In the evening my aunt and I generally played at five-card loo with him, in which he took an intense interest; and if, in the middle of the day, when I came home to dinner, he could get me to play at marbles in the summer-house, he was delighted. The points to which he looked on in the week were the two mornings when Joseph came to shave him: this poor journeyman barber felt a sort of compassionate regard for him, and he had an insatiable appetite for such news as the barber could communicate. Thus his days passed in wearisome uniformity. He had no other amusement, unless in listening to hear a comedy read; he had not, in himself, a single resource for whiling away the time, not even that which smoking might have afforded him; and, being thus utterly without an object for the present or the future, his thoughts were perpetually recurring to the past. His affections were strong and lasting. Indeed, at his mother's funeral his emotions were such as to affect all who witnessed them. That grief he felt to the day of his death. I have also seen tears in his eyes when he spoke of my sisters, Eliza and Louisa, both having died just at that age when he had most delight in fondling them, and they were most willing to be fondled. Whether it might have been possible to have awakened him to any devotional feelings may be doubted; but he believed and trusted simply and implicitly, and more, assuredly, would not be required from one to whom so little had been given. He lived about four years after this removal. His brother Edward died a year before him, of pulmonary consumption. This event affected him deeply. He attended the funeral, described the condition of the coffins in the family vault in a manner which I well remember, and said that his turn would be next. One day, on my return from school at the dinner hour, going into the summer-house, I found him sitting in the middle of the room and looking wildly. He told me he had been very ill, that he had had a seizure in the head such as he had never felt before, and that he was certain something very serious ailed him. I gave the alarm; but it passed over; neither he himself, nor any person in the house, knew what such a seizure indicated. The next morning he arose as usual, walked down stairs into the kitchen, and, as he was buttoning the knees of his breeches, exclaimed, "Lord have mercy upon me!" and fell from the chair. His nose was bleeding when he was taken up. Immediate assistance was procured, but he was dead before it arrived. The stroke was mercifully sudden, but it had been preceded by a long and gradual diminution of vital strength; and I have never known any other case in which, when there were so few external appearances of disease or decay, the individual was so aware that his dissolution was approaching.

I often regret that my memory should have retained so few of the traditional tales and proverbial expressions which I heard from him, more certainly than from all other persons in the course of my life. Some of them have been lately recalled to my recollection by Grimm's Collection. What little his mind was capable of receiving it had retained tenaciously, and of these things it had a rich store. Upon his death Miss Tyler became the sole survivor of her paternal race.

LETTER XII.

HIS RECOLLECTIONS OF SCHOOL AT BRISTOL—HIS SCHOOLMASTER AND SCHOOLFELLOWS.

August 20th, 1823.

MY memory strengthens as I proceed in this task of retrospection; and yet, while some circumstances—a look, a sound, a gesture, though utterly unimportant, recur to me more vividly than the transactions of yesterday, others, which I would fain call to mind, are irrevocably gone. I have sometimes fancied, when dreaming upon what may be our future state, that in the next world we may recover a perfect recollection of all that has occurred to us in this, and in the prior stages of progressive existence, through which it is not improbable that our living principle has ascended. And yet the best and happiest of us must have something or other, *altâ mente repostum*, for which a draught of Lethe would be desired.

The pleasantest of my school years were those which I passed at Williams's, especially after I took up my abode at Terril Street, for I then went home to dinner, and found much more satisfaction there in my own pursuits from twelve o'clock till two than in his contracted playground. What I learned there, indeed, was worth little; it was just such a knowledge of Latin as a boy of quick parts and not without diligence will acquire under bad teaching. When I had gone through the Metamorphoses, Williams declared his intention of taking me from the usher and instructing me in Virgil himself, no other of his pupils having proceeded so far. But the old man, I suppose, discovered that the little classical knowledge which he ever possessed had passed away as irrevocably as his youth, and I continued under the usher's care, who kept me in the Eclogues so long that I was heartily sick of them, and I believe have never looked in them from that time. Over and over again did that fellow make me read them; probably because he thought the book was to be gone through in order, and was afraid to expose himself in the Georgics. No attempt was made to ground me in prosody; and as this defect in my education was never remedied (for when I went to Westminster I was too forward in other things to be placed low enough in the school for regular training in this), I am at this day as liable to make a false quantity as any Scotchman. I was fond of arithmetic, and have no doubt that, at that time, I should have proceeded with pleasure through its higher branches, and might have been led on to mathematics, of which my mind afterward became impatient, if not actually incapable.

Sometimes, when Williams was in good humor, he suspended the usual business of the school and exercised the boys in some uncommon manner. For example, he would bid them all take their slates, and write as he should dictate. This was to try their spelling; and I remember he once began with this sentence: "As I walked out to take the air, I met a man with red hair, who was heir to a good estate, and was carrying a hare in his hand." Another time he called upon all of a certain standing to write a letter, each upon any subject that he pleased. You will perhaps wonder to hear that no task ever perplexed me so woefully as this. I had never in my life written a letter, except a formal one at Corston before the holidays, every word of which was of the master's dictation, and which used to begin, "Honored Parents." Some of the boys produced compositions of this stamp; others, who were a little older and more ambitious, wrote in a tradesman-like style, soliciting orders, or acknowledging them, or sending in an account. For my part, I actually cried for perplexity and vexation. Had I been a blockhead, this would have provoked Williams; but he always looked upon me with a favorable eye, and, expressing surprise rather than anger, he endeavored both to encourage and shame me to the attempt. To work I fell at last, and presently presented him with a description of Stonehenge, in the form of a letter, which completely filled the slate. I had laid hands not long before upon the Salisbury Guide, and Stonehenge had appeared to me one of the greatest wonders in the world. The old man was exceedingly surprised, and not less delighted, and I well remember how much his astonishment surprised me, and how much I was gratified by his praise. I was not conscious of having done any thing odd or extraordinary, but the boys made me so; and to the sort of envy which it excited among them, I was indebted for a wholesome mortification. One morning, upon entering the school a few minutes before the master made his appearance, some half dozen of them beset me, and demanded whether I, with all my learning, could tell what the letters *i. e.* stood for. The question was proposed in the taunting tone of expected triumph, which I should well have liked to disappoint. But when I answered that I supposed it was for John the Evangelist, the unlucky guess taught me never again to be ashamed of acknowledging myself ignorant of what I really did not know. It was a useful lesson, especially as I was fortunate enough to perceive, early in life, that there were very many subjects of which I must of necessity be so.

Of all my schoolmasters, Williams is the one whom I remember with the kindliest feelings. His Welsh blood was too easily roused; and his spirit was soured by the great decline of his school. His numbers in its best days had been from seventy to a hundred; now they did not reach forty, when the times were dearer by all the difference which the American War had occasioned, and his terms could not be raised in proportion to the increased price of every thing, because schools had multiplied. When his ill circumstances pressed upon him, he gave way, perhaps more readily, to impulses of anger; because anger, like drunkenness, suspends the sense of care, and an irascible emotion is felt as a relief from painful thoughts. His old wig, like a bank of morning clouds in the east, used to indicate a stormy day. At better times both the wig and the countenance would have beseemed a higher station; and his anger was the more frightful, because at those better times there was an expression of good humor and animation in his features which was singularly pleasing, and I believe denoted his genuine character. He would strike with a ruler sometimes when his patience was greatly provoked by that incorrigible stupidity, which of all things, perhaps, puts patience to the severest trial. There was a hulking fellow (a Creole with negro features and a shade of African color in him), who possessed this stupidity in the highest degree; and Williams, after flogging him one day, made him pay a halfpenny for the use of the rod, because he required it so much oftener than any other boy in the school. Whether G—— was most sensible of the mulct or the mockery, I know not, but he felt it as the severest part of the punishment. This was certainly a tyrannical act; but it was the only one of which I ever saw Williams guilty.

There were a good many Creoles at this school, as, indeed, at all the Bristol schools. Cassava bread was among the things which were frequently sent over to them by their parents, so that I well knew the taste of manioc long before I heard its name. These Creoles were neither better nor worse than so many other boys in any respect. Indeed, though they had a stronger national cast of countenance, they were, I think, less marked by any national features of mind or disposition than the Welsh, certainly much less than the Irish.. One of them (evidently by his name of French extraction) was, however, the most thoroughly fiendish human being that I have ever known. There is an image in Kehama, drawn from my recollection of the devilish malignity which used sometimes to glow in his dark eyes, though I could not there give the likeness in its whole force, for his countenance used to darken with the blackness of his passion. Happily for the slaves on the family estate, he, though a second brother, was wealthy enough to settle in England; and an anecdote which I heard of him when he was about thirty years of age, will show that I have not spoken of his character too strongly. When he was shooting one day, his dog committed some fault. He would have shot him for this upon the spot, if his companion had not turned the gun aside, and, as he supposed, succeeded in appeasing him; but, when the sport was over, to the horror of that companion (who related the story to me), he took up a large stone and knocked out the dog's brains. I have mentioned this wretch, who might otherwise have better been forgotten, for a charitable reason; because I verily believe that his wickedness was truly an original, innate, constitutional sin, and just as much a family disease as gout or scrofula. I think so, because he had a nephew who was placed as a pupil with King, the surgeon at Clifton, and in whom, at first sight, I recognized a physiognomy which I hope can belong to no other breed. His nephew answered in all respects to the relationship, and to the character which Nature had written in every lineament of his face. He ran a short career of knavery, profligacy, and crimes, which led him into a prison, and there he died by his own hand.

Another of my then schoolfellows, who was also a Creole, came to a like fate, but from very different circumstances. He was the natural son of a wealthy planter by a woman of color, and went through the school with the character of an inoffensive, gentlemanly, quiet boy, who never quarreled with any body, nor ever did an ill-natured thing. When he became a young man, he was liberally supplied with money, and launched into expenses which such means tended to create and seemed to justify. The supplies suddenly ceased, I am not certain whether by an experiment of rigor, or owing to his father's dying without providing for him in his will; the latter I think was the case. Poor H——, however, was arrested for debt, and put an end to his hopeless prospects in prison, by suicide.

Colonel Hugh Baillie, who made himself conspicuous some few months ago by very properly resenting the unjust expulsion of his son from Christ Church (an act of the late dean's miserable misgovernment), was one of my cotemporaries at this school. My old Latin master, Duplanier, kept a French academy next door, and by an arrangement between the two masters, his boys came three mornings in the week to write and cipher with us. Among these intermitting schoolfellows was poor John Morgan, with whom Coleridge lived for several years; Gee, whom I have already mentioned; and a certain H—— O——, with whom I had an adventure in after-life well worthy of preservation.

This youth was about three years older than I; of course, I had no acquaintance with him, nor did I ever exchange a word with him, unless it were when the whole school were engaged in playing prison-base, in which he took the lead as the πόδας ὠκὺς of his side. His father was a merchant, concerned, among other things, in the Irish linen trade: my father had some dealings with him, and, in his misfortunes, found him—what, I believe, is *not* a common character—an unfeeling creditor. They were a proud family; and, a few years after my father's failure, failed themselves, and, as the phrase is, went to the dogs. This H—— O—— was bred to be an attorney, but wanted either brains or business to succeed in his calling—I dare say both. I had forgotten his person, and should never have thought of him again (except when the game of prison-base was brought to my mind), if, in the year 1798, I had not been surprised by hearing one day at Cottle's shop that he had been there twice or thrice to inquire for me, and had left a message requesting that, if I came into Bristol that day (it was during the year of my abode at Westbury), I would call on him at an attorney's office at a certain hour. Accordingly, thither I went, rung at the bell, inquired for Mr. O——, gave my name, and was ushered into a private room. Nothing could be more gracious than his recognition of a person whom he must have passed twenty times in the street during the last three months: "we had been schoolfellows at such a place, at such a time," &c., &c., all which I knew very well; but how we came to be acquaintances now was what I had to learn, and to explain this cost him a good deal of humming and hawing, plentifully intermixed with that figure of speech which the Irish call *blarney*, and which is a much more usual as well as useful figure than any of those, with the hard names of which poor boys used to be tormented in the Latin grammar. From the use which he made of this figure, he appeared to know that I was an author of some notoriety, and that one of my books was called Joan of Arc. The compliments which he laid on were intermingled with expressions of great regret for the deficiencies of his own education: he learned a little Latin, a little French, but there it had stopped; in short, I knew what must be the extent of his acquirements; "for you and I, Mr. Southey, you know, were schoolfellows." At last it came out that, from a consciousness of these deficiencies, he had been led to think that a glossary of the English language was a work very much wanted, and that no one could be more competent to supply such a *desideratum* than the gentleman whom he had the honor of addressing. I was as little able to guess what his deficiencies had to do with a glossary as you can be; and, not feeling any curiosity to get at a blockhead's meaning, endeavored to put an end to the interview by declaring at once my utter inability to execute such a work, for the very sufficient reason that I was wholly ignorant of several languages, the thorough knowledge of which was indispensable in such researches. This produced more *blarney*, and an explanation that my answer did not exactly apply to what his proposal intended. What he meant was this: there were a great many elegant words, which persons like himself, whose education had been neglected, would often like to use in conversation (he said this feelingly; it had often been his own case; he felt it, indeed, every day of his life); they would be glad to use these words if they only knew their meaning; and what he wanted was a glossary or dictionary of such words, a little book which might be carried in the pocket. It would certainly command an extensive sale: I could make the book; he had a large acquaintance, and could procure subscribers for it; and we might make a thriving partnership concern in this literary undertaking. Before he arrived at this point, the scene had become far too comical to leave any room in my feelings for anger. I kept my countenance (which has often been put to much harder trials than my temper, and is, moreover, a much more difficult thing to keep), declined his proposal decidedly but civilly, took my leave in perfect good humor, and hastened back to Cottle's, to relieve myself by telling him the adventure.

LETTER XIII.

VISITORS TO HIS SCHOOLMASTER.

May 27th, 1824.

NEARLY four years have elapsed since I began this series of reminiscences, and I have only written twelve letters, which bring me only into the twelfth year of my age. Alas! this is not the only case in which I feel that the remaining portion of my life, were it even to be protracted longer than there is reason to expect upon the most favorable calculation of chances, must be too short for the undertakings which I have sometimes dreamed of completing. It is, however, the case in which I can, with least inconvenience, quicken my speed; and frail as by humiliating experience I know my own resolutions to be, I will nevertheless endeavor to send off a letter from this time forth at the end of every month. Matter for one more will be afforded before I take leave of poor old William Williams; and that part of it which has no connection with myself, will not be the least worth relation.

It was a good feature in his character that he had a number of poor retainers, who used to drop in at school hours, and seldom went away empty handed. There was one poor fellow, familiarly called Dr. Jones, who always set the school in a roar of laughter. What his real history was I know not; the story was, that some mischievous boys had practiced upon him the dreadfully dangerous prank of giving him a dose of cantharides, and that he had lost his wits in consequence. I am not aware that it could have produced this effect, though it might very probably have cost him his life. Crazy, however, he was, or, rather, half crazed, and it was such a merry craziness that it would have been wishing him ill to have wished him otherwise. The bliss of ignorance is merely negative; there was a positive happiness in his insanity; it was like a perpetual drunkenness, sustained just at that degree of pleasurable excitement, which, in the sense of present enjoyment, is equally regardless of the future and of the past. He fancied himself a poet, because he could produce, upon demand, a rhyme in the sorriest doggerel; and the most celebrated *improvisatore* was never half so vain of his talent as this queer creature, whose little figure of some five feet two I can perfectly call to mind, with his suit of rusty black, his more rusty wig, and his old cocked hat. Whenever he entered the schoolroom he was greeted with a shout of welcome;

all business was suspended; he was called upon from all sides to give us a rhyme; and when the master's countenance offered any encouragement, he was entreated also to ask for half a holiday, which, at the price of some doggerel, was sometimes obtained. You will readily believe he was a popular poet.

The talent of composing imitative verses has become so common in our days, that it will require some evidence to make the next generation believe what sort of verses were received as poetry fifty years ago, when any thing in rhyme passed current. The magazines, however, contain proof of this, the very best of them abounding in such trash as would be rejected now by the provincial newspapers. Whether the progress of society, which so greatly favors the growth and development of imitative talent, is equally favorable to the true poetical spirit, is a question which I may be led to consider hereafter. But, as I had the good fortune to grow up in an age when poets, according to the old opinion, were born and not made, and as, at the time to which this part of my reminiscences relates, the bent of my nature had decidedly shown itself, I may here make some observations upon the grounds and consequences of that opinion.

In the earliest ages, certain it is, that they who possessed that gift of speech which enabled them to clothe ready thoughts in measured or elevated diction were held to be inspired. False oracles were uttered in verse, and true prophecies delivered in poetry. There was, therefore, some reason for the opinion. A belief akin to it, and not improbably derived from it, prevails even now among the ignorant, and was much more prevalent in my childhood, when very few of the lower classes could write or read, and when, in the classes above them, those who really were ignorant knew that they were so. Sleight of hand passed for magic in the Dark Ages, sleight of tongue for inspiration; and the ignorant, when they were no longer thus to be deluded, still looked upon both as something extraordinary and wonderful. Especially the power of arranging words in a manner altogether different from the common manner of speech, and of disposing syllables so as to produce a harmony which is felt by the dullest ear (a power which has now become an easy, and, therefore, is every day becoming more and more a common acquirement), appeared to them what it originally was in all poets, and always will be in those who are truly such; and even now, though there are none who regard its possessor with superstitious reverence, there are many who look upon him as one who, in the constitution of his mind, is different from themselves. As no madman ever pretended to a religious call without finding some open-eared listeners ready to believe in him and become his disciples; so, perhaps, no one ever composed verses with facility who had not some to admire and applaud him in his own little circle. This was the case even with so poor a creature as Dr. Jones. And to the intoxication of conceit, which the honest admiration of the ignorant has produced in half-crazed rhymers like him, it is owing that some marvelous productions have found their way to the press. Dr. Jones, by whom I have been led into this digression, was a doggerelist of the very lowest kind. One other such I once met with, when I was young enough to be heartily amused at an exhibition which, farcical as it was, would now make me mournful. He was a poor engraver, by name Coyte; very simple, very industrious, very poor, and completely crazed with vanity, because he could compose off-hand, upon any subject, such rhymes as the bell-man's used to be. Bedford's father used occasionally to relieve him, for he was married, and could earn but a miserable livelihood for his family. I saw him on one of his visits to Brixton, in the year 1793, when he was between forty and fifty years of age. His countenance and manner might have supplied Wilkie with a worthy subject. Mr. Bedford (there never lived a kinder-hearted man) loved merriment, and played him off, in which Grosvenor and Horace joined, and I was not backward. We gave him subjects upon which he presently wrote three or four sorry couplets. No creature was ever more elated with triumph than he was at the hyperbolical commendations which he received; and this, mingled with the genuine humility which the sense of his condition occasioned, produced a truly comic mixture in his feelings and gesticulations. What with pleasure, inspiration, exertion, and warm weather (for it was in the dog-days), he perspired as profusely, though I dare say not as fragrantly, as an elephant in love, and literally overflowed at eyes and mouth, frothing and weeping in a salivation of happiness. I think this poor creature published "A Cockney's Rambles in the Country" some twelve or fourteen years ago, for such a pamphlet I saw advertised by Joseph William Coyte; and I sent for it at the time, but it was too obscure to be found.

These are examples of the very humblest and meanest rhymesters, who nevertheless felt themselves raised above their companions because they could rhyme. I have been acquainted with poets in every intermediate degree between Jones and Wordsworth, and their conceit has almost uniformly been precisely in an inverse proportion to their capacity. When this conceit acts upon low and vulgar ignorance, it produces direct craziness, as in the instances of which I have been speaking. In the lower ranks of middle life I have seen it, without amounting to insanity, assume a form of such extravagant vanity that the examples which have occurred within my own observation would be deemed incredible if brought forward in a farce. Of these in due time. There is another more curious manifestation of the same folly, which I do not remember ever to have seen noticed, but which is well worthy of critical observation, because it shows in its full extent, and therefore *in puris naturalibus*, a fault which is found in by much the greater part of modern poetry—the use of words which have no signification where they are used, or which, if they mean any thing, mean nonsense—the substitution of sound for sense. I could show you passage after passage in cotemporary writers—the most popular writers, and some of them the most popular passages in their works, which, when critically, that is to say, strictly, but justly examined, are as absolutely nonsensical as the description of a moonlight night in Pope's Homer. Pope himself intended that for a fine description, and did not perceive that it was as absurd as his own "Song by a Person of Quality." Now there have been writers who have possessed the talent of stringing together couplet after couplet in sonorous verse, without any connection, and without any meaning, or any thing like a meaning, and yet they have had all the enjoyment of writing poetry, have supposed that this actually was poetry, and published it as such. I know a man who has done this, who made me a present of his poem; yet he is very far from being a fool; on the contrary, he is a lively, pleasant companion, and his talents in conversation are considerably above par. The most perfect specimen I ever saw of such verses was a poem called "The Shepherd's Farewell," printed in quarto some five-and-thirty years ago. Coleridge once had an imperfect copy of it. I forget the author's name; but when I was first at Lisbon, I found out that he was a schoolmaster, and that poor Paul Berthon had been one of his pupils. Men of very inferior power may imitate the manner of good writers with great success; as, for example, the two Smiths have done; but I do not believe that any imitative talent could produce genuine nonsense verses like those of "The Shepherd's Farewell." The intention of writing nonsensically would appear, and betray the purport of the writer. Pure, involuntary, unconscious nonsense is inimitable by any effort of sense.

Such writers as these, if they were cross-examined, would be found to imagine that they composed under the real influence of poetical inspiration; and were Taylor the pagan to set about *heathenizing* one of them, I am persuaded that he would not find it difficult to make him believe in the Muses. In fact, when this soul of conceit is in action, the man is fairly beside himself. An innate self-produced inebriety possesses him; he abandons himself to it, and while the fit lasts is as mad as a March hare. The madness is not permanent, because such inspiration, according to received opinion, only comes on when the rhymester is engaged in his vocation. And well it is when it shows itself in rhyme; for the case is very different with him who has the gift of uttering prose with the same fluency and the same contempt of reason. He in good earnest sets up for an inspired messenger; he has received *a call;* and there are not only sects, but societies, in this country ready to accredit him, and take him into employ, and send him forth with a roving commission, through towns and villages, to infect others with the most infectious of all forms of madness, disturb the peace of families, and prepare the way for another attempt to overthrow the Established Church—another struggle, which will shake these kingdoms to their center.

Dr. Jones has led me into a long digression, upon which I should not have entered if I had foreseen that it would have extended so far. Another of Williams's visitors, and an equally popular one, was a glorious fellow, Pullen by name, who, during the age of buckskin, made a fortune as a breeches maker in Thomas Street. If I could paint a portrait from memory, you should have his likeness. Alas! that I can only give it in words, and that that perfect figure should at this hour be preserved only in my recollections! *Sic transit gloria mundi!* His countenance expressed all that could be expressed by human features of thorough-bred vulgarity, prosperity, pride of purse, good living, coarse humor, and boisterous good nature He wore a white tie-wig. His eyes were of the hue and luster of scalded gooseberries, or oysters in sauce. His complexion was the deepest extract of the grape; he owed it to the Methuen treaty; my uncle, no doubt, had seen it growing in his rides from Porto; and Heaven knows how many pipes must have been filtered through the Pullenian system before that fine permanent purple could have been fixed in his cheeks. He appeared always in buckskins of his own making, and in boots. He would laugh at his own jests with a voice like Stentor, supposing Stentor to have been hoarse; and then he would clap old Williams on the back with a hand like a shoulder of mutton for breadth and weight. You may imagine how great a man we thought him. They had probably been boon companions in their youth, and his visits seldom failed to make the old man lay aside the schoolmaster. He was an excellent hand at demanding half a holiday, and when he succeeded, always demanded three cheers for his success, in which he joined with all his might and main. If I were a believer in the Romish purgatory, I should make no doubt that every visit that he made to that schoolroom was carried to the account of his good works. Some such set-off he needed, for he behaved with brutal want of feeling to a son who had offended him, and who, I believe, would have perished for want if it had not been for the charity of John Morgan's mother, an eccentric but thoroughly good woman, and one of those people whom I shall rejoice to meet in the next world. This I learned from her several years afterward. At this time Pullen was a widower between fifty and sixty; a hale, strong-bodied man, upon whom his wine-merchant might reckon for a considerable annuity during many years to come. He had purchased some lands adjacent to the Leppincott property near Bristol, in the pleasantest part of that fine neighborhood. Sir Henry Leppincott was elected member for the city at that election in which Burke was turned out. He died soon afterward; his son was a mere child; and Pullen, the glorious Pullen, in the plenitude of his pride, and no doubt in a new pair of buckskins, called on the widow, introduced himself as the owner of the adjacent estate, and upon that score, without further ceremony, proposed marriage as an arrangement of mutual fitness. Lady Leppincott, of course, rang the bell, and ordered the servants to turn him out of the house. This is a story which would be deemed too extravagant in a novel, and yet you would believe it without the slightest hesitation if you had ever seen the incomparable breeches maker.

Mrs. Estan, the actress, whom you must remember, was at that time preparing to make her first appearance on the stage at the Bristol Theater. The part she had chosen was Letitia Hardy, in "The Belle's Stratagem," and in that part she had to dance a *minuet de la cour*, to perfect herself in which, and perhaps for the sake of accustoming herself to figure away before an audience, she came to our school on two or three dancing days, and took lessons there—a circumstance too remarkable to be forgotten in a schoolboy's life. Walters, the dancing-master, was not a little proud of his pupil. That poor man was for three years the plague of my life, and I was the plague of his. In some unhappy mood, he prevailed on my mother to let me learn to dance, persuading himself as well as her that I should do credit to his teaching. It must have been for my sins that he formed this opinion: in an evil hour for himself and for me it was formed; he would have had much less trouble in teaching a bear, and far better success. I do not remember that I set out with any dislike or contempt of dancing, but the unconquerable incapacity which it was soon evident that I possessed produced both, and the more he labored to correct an incorrigible awkwardness, the more awkwardly, of course, I performed. I verily believe the fiddle-stick was applied as much to my head as to the fiddle-strings when I was called out. But the rascal had a worse way than that of punishing me. He would take my hands in his, and lead me down a dance; and then the villain would apply his thumb nail against the flat surface of mine, in the middle, and press it till he left the mark there. This species of torture I suppose to have been his own invention, and so intolerable it was that at last, whenever he had recourse to it, I kicked his shins. Luckily for me, he got into a scrape by beating a boy unmercifully at another school, so that he was afraid to carry on this sort of contest; and giving up, at last, all hope of ever making me a votary of the Graces or of the dancing Muse, he contented himself with shaking his head and turning up his eyes in hopelessness whenever he noticed my performance. I had always Tom Madge for my partner; a poor fellow long since dead, whom I remember with much kindness. He was as active as a squirrel, but every limb seemed to be out of joint when he began to dance. We were always placed as the last couple, and went through the work with the dogged determination of never dancing more when we should once be delivered from the dancing-master—a resolution which I have piously kept, even unto this day.

Williams, who read well himself, and prided himself upon it, was one day very much offended with my reading, and asked me scornfully who taught me to read. I answered my aunt. "Then," said he, "give my compliments to your aunt, and tell her that my old horse, that has been dead these twenty years, could have taught you as well." I delivered the message faithfully, to her great indignation. It was never forgotten or forgiven, and perhaps it accelerated the very proper resolution of removing me. My uncle made known his intention of placing me at Westminster. His connection with Christ Church naturally led him to prefer that to any other school, in the hope that I should get into college, and so be elected off to a studentship. But, as I was in feeble health, and, moreover, had been hitherto very ill taught, it was deemed advisable that I should be placed for twelve months under a clergyman competent to prepare me for a public school.

Before I take leave of Williams, two or three memoranda upon the slip of paper before me must be scored off. There was a washing tub in the play-ground, with a long towel on a reel beside it. This tub was filled every morning for the boarders to perform their ablutions, all in the same water, and whoever wished to wash hands or face in the course of the day, had no other. I was the only boy who had any repugnance to dip his hands in this pig-trough. There was a large cask near, which received the rain water; but there was no getting at the water, for the top was covered, and to have taken out the spigot would have been a punishable offense. I, however, made a little hollow under the spigot, to receive the drippings, just deep enough to wet the hands, and there I used to wash my hands with clean water when they required it. But I do not remember that any one ever followed my example. I had acquired the sense of cleanliness and the love of it, and they had not.

A time was remembered when there were wars of school against school, and a great battle which had taken place in the adjoining park between Williams's boys and Foot's, my first master. At both schools I heard of this, and the victory was claimed by both; for it was an old affair, a matter of tradition (not having been noticed in history), long before my generation, or any who were in the then school, but remembered as an event second only in importance, if second, to the war of Troy.

It was fully believed in both these schools, and at Corston, that no bastard could span his own wrist. And I have no doubt this superstition prevailed throughout that part of England.

LETTER XIV.

HE IS SENT AS A DAY SCHOLAR TO A CLERGYMAN IN BRISTOL—EARLY POETICAL EFFORTS.

June 29th, 1824.

In a former letter I have mentioned Mrs. S——, who had been Miss Tyler's schoolmistress. My aunt kept up an acquaintance with her as long as she lived, and after her death with her two daughters, who lived together in a house on Redclift Parade, the pleasantest situation in Bristol, if there had been even a tolerable approach to it. One of these sisters was unmarried; the other a widow with one son, who was just of my age: Jem Thomas was his name. Mr. Lewis, the clergyman under whom I was placed at the end of 1786 or the beginning of 1787, lodged and boarded with these sisters. He had been usher at the grammar school; and, having engaged to educate this boy, was willing to take a few more pupils from the hours of ten till two. When I went to him he had two others, C—— and R——, both my seniors by three or four years. The former I used to call Caliban: he might have played that character without a mask, that is, supposing he could have learned the part; for the resemblance held good in mind as well as in appearance, his disposition being somewhat between pig and baboon. The latter was a favorite with Lewis; his father had formerly practiced in Bristol as a surgeon, but had now succeeded to an estate of some value. He was little and mannish, somewhat vain of superficial talents, and with a spice of conceit both in his manners and in his dress; but there was no harm in him. He took an honorary Master's degree at the Duke of Portland's installation in 1793, which was the only time I ever saw him after we ceased to be fellow-pupils. He married about that time, and died young.

Caliban had a sister whom I shall not libel when I call her Sycorax. A Bristol tradesman, a great friend of S. T. C.'s, married her for her money; and the only thing I ever heard of Caliban in after life was a story which reached me of her every where proclaiming that her brother was a very superior man to Mr. Coleridge, and had confuted him one evening seven-and-twenty times in one argument. The word which Coleridge uses as a listener when he is expected to throw in something, with or without meaning, to show that he is listening, is, or used to be, as I well remember, *undoubtedly*. The foolish woman had understood this expletive in its literal meaning, and kept account with her fingers that he pronounced it seven-and-twenty times, while enduring the utterance of an animal in comparison with whom a centaur would deserve to be called human, and a satyr rational.

Jem Thomas was a commonplace lad, with a fine, handsome person, but by no means a good physiognomy, and I can not remember the time when I was not a physiognomist. He was educated for a surgeon, and ruined by having at his disposal, as soon as he came of age, something between two and three thousand pounds, which his grandfather unwisely left to him at once, instead of leaving it to his mother for her life. This he presently squandered; went out professionally to the East Indies, and died there. So much for my three companions, among whom it was not possible that I could find a friend. There came a fourth, a few weeks only before I withdrew: he was a well-minded boy, and has made a very respectable man. Harris was his name: he married Betsy Petrie, who was one of my fellow-travelers in Portugal.

I profited by this year's tuition less than I should have done at a good school. It is not easy to remedy the ill effects of bad teaching; and the further the pupil has advanced in it, the greater must be the difficulty of bringing him into a better way. Lewis, too, had been accustomed to the mechanical movements of a large school, and was at a loss how to proceed with a boy who stood alone. I began Greek under him, made nonsense-verses, read the *Electa ex Ovidio et Tibullo* and Horace's Odes advanced a little in writing Latin, and composed English themes.

C'est le premier pas qui coute. I was in as great tribulation when I had the first theme to write as when Williams required me to produce a letter. The text, of course, had been given me; but how to begin, what to say, or how to say it, I knew not. No one who had witnessed my perplexity upon this occasion would have supposed how much was afterward to be spun from these poor brains. My aunt, at last in compassion, wrote the theme for me. Lewis questioned me if it was my own, and I told him the truth. He then encouraged me sensibly enough; put me in the way of composing the commonplaces of which themes are manufactured (indeed, he caused me to transcribe some rules for themes, making a regular receipt as for a pudding); and he had no reason afterward to complain of any want of aptitude in his scholar, for when I had learned that it was not more difficult to write in prose than in verse, the ink dribbled as daintily from my pen as ever it did from John Bunyan's. One of these exercises I still remember sufficiently well to know that it was too much like poetry, and that the fault was of a hopeful kind, consisting less in inflated language than in poetical imagery and sentiment. But this was not pointed out as a fault, and luckily I was left to myself; otherwise, like a good horse, I might have been spoiled by being broken in too soon.

It was still more fortunate that there was none to direct me in my favorite pursuit, certain as it is that any instructor would have interfered with the natural and healthy growth of that poetical spirit which was taking its own course. That spirit was like a plant which required no forcing nor artificial culture; only air and sunshine, and the rains and the dews of heaven. I do not remember in any part of my life to have been so conscious of intellectual improvement as I was during the year and half before I was placed at Westminster: an improvement derived, not from books or instruction, but from constantly exercising myself in English verse; and from the development of mind which that exercise produced, I can distinctly trace my progress by help of a list, made thirty years ago, of all my compositions in verse which were then in existence, or which I had at that time destroyed.

Early as my hopes had been directed toward

the drama, they received a more decided and more fortunate direction from the frequent perusal of Tasso, Ariosto, and Spenser. I had read, also, Mickle's Lusiad and Pope's Homer. If you add to these an extensive acquaintance with the novels of the day, and with the Arabian and mock-Arabian tales, the whole works of Josephus (taken in by me with my pocket-money in threescore sixpenny numbers, which I now possess), such acquaintance with Greek and Roman history as a schoolboy picks up from his lessons and from Goldsmith's abridged histories, and such acquaintance with their fables as may be learned from Ovid, from the old Pantheon, and, above all, from the end of Littleton's Dictionary, you will have a fair account of the stock upon which I began. But Shakspeare, and Beaumont and Fletcher, must not be forgotten; nor Sidney's Arcadia; nor Rowley's Poems, for Chatterton's history was fresh in remembrance, and that story, which would have affected one of my disposition any where, acted upon me with all the force of local associations.

The first of my Epic Dreams was created by Ariosto. I meant to graft a story upon the Orlando Furioso, not knowing how often this had been done by Italian and Spanish imitators. Arcadia was to have been the title and the scene; thither I meant to carry the Moors under Marsilius after their overthrow in France, and there to have overthrown them again by a hero of my own, named Alphonso, who had caught the Hippogriff. This must have been when I was between nine and ten, for some verses of it were written on the covers of my Phædrus. They were in the heroic couplet. Among my aunt's books was the first volume of Bysshe's Art of Poetry, which, worthless as it is, taught me at that age the principle upon which blank verse is constructed, and thereby did me good service at a good time. I soon learned to prefer that meter, not because it was easier than rhyme (which was easy enough), but because I felt in it a greater freedom and range of language, because I was sensible that in rhyming I sometimes used expressions, for the sake of the rhyme, which were far-fetched, and certainly would not have occurred without that cause. My second subject was the Trojan Brutus; the defeat and death of King Richard, and the Union of the two Roses, was my third. In neither of these did I make much progress; but with the story of Egbert I was more persevering, and partly transcribed several folio sheets. The sight of these was an encouragement to proceed, and I often looked at them with delight in the anticipation of future fame. This was a solitary feeling, for my ambition or vanity (whichever it may deserve to be called) was not greater than the shyness which accompanied it. My port-folio was of course held sacred. One day, however, it was profaned by an acquaintance of my aunt's who called to pay a morning visit. She was shown into the parlor, and I, who was sent to say my aunt would presently wait upon her, found her with my precious Egbert in her hand. Her compliments had no effect in abating my deep resentment at this unpardonable curiosity; and, though she was a good-natured woman, I am afraid I never quite forgave her. Determining, however, never to incur the risk of a second exposure, I immediately composed a set of characters for my own use.

In my twelfth and thirteenth year, besides these loftier attempts, I wrote three heroic epistles in rhyme: the one was from Diomede to Egiale; the second from Octavia to Mark Antony; the third from Alexander to his father Herod, a subject with which Josephus supplied me. I made, also, some translations from Ovid, Virgil, and Horace, and composed a satirical description of English manners, as delivered by Omai, the Taheitean, to his countrymen on his return. On the thirteenth anniversary of my birth, supposing (by an error which appeared to be common enough at the end of the century) that I was then entering the first year of my teens instead of completing it, and looking upon that as an awful sort of step in life, I wrote some verses in a strain of reflection upon mortality grave enough to provoke a smile when I recollect them. Among my attempts at this time were two descriptive pieces entitled Morning in the Country and Morning in Town, in eight-syllable rhymes, and in imitation of Cunningham. There was also a satirical peep into Pluto's dominions, in rhyme. I remember the conclusion only, and that because it exhibits a singular indication how strongly and how early my heart was set upon that peculiar line of poetry which I have pursued with most ardor. It described the Elysium of the Poets, and that more sacred part of it in which Homer, Virgil, Tasso, Spenser, Camoens, and Milton were assembled. While I was regarding them, Fame came hurrying by with her arm full of laurels, and asking in an indignant voice if there was no poet who would deserve them? Upon which I reached out my hand, snatched at them, and awoke.

One of these juvenile efforts was wholly original in its design. It was an attempt to exhibit the story of the Trojan War in a dramatic form, laying the scene in Elysium, where the events which had happened on earth were related by the souls of the respective heroes as they successively descended. The opening was a dialogue between Laodamia and Protesilaus, in couplets: the best rhymes which I had yet written. But I did not proceed far, probably because the design was too difficult, and this would have been reason enough for abandoning it even if I had not entered with more than usual ardor upon a new heroic subject, of which Cassibelan was the hero. I finished three books of this poem, and had advanced far in the fourth before I went to Westminster. All this was written fairly out in my own private characters, and in my best writing, if one may talk of calligraphy in an unknown hand which looked something like Greek, but more like conjuration, from the number of trines and squares which it contained. These characters, however, proved fatal to the poem, for it was not possible for me to continue it at school for want of privacy; disuse made the cipher so difficult that I could not read it without almost spelling as I went on; and at last, in very vexation, I burned the manuscript.

I wonder whether Spurzheim could, at that time, have discovered an organ of constructiveness in my pericranium. The Elysian drama might seem to indicate that the faculty was there, but not a trace of it was to be found in any of the heroic poems which I attempted. They were all begun upon a mere general notion of the subject, without any prearrangement, and very little preconception of the incidents by which the catastrophe was to be brought about. When I sat down to write, I had to look as much for the incidents as for the thoughts and words in which they were to be clothed. I expected them to occur just as readily; and so, indeed, such as they were, they did. My reading in the old chivalrous romances has been sufficiently extensive to justify me in asserting that the greater number of those romances were written just in the same way, without the slightest plan or forethought; and I am much mistaken if many of the Italian romantic poems were not composed in the same inartificial manner. This I am sure—that it is more difficult to plan than to execute well, and that abundance of true poetical power has been squandered for want of a constructive talent in the poet. I have felt this want in some of the Spanish and Portuguese writers even more than their want of taste. The progress of my own mind toward attaining it (so far as I may be thought to have attained it) I am able to trace distinctly, not merely by the works themselves, and by my own recollections of the views with which they were undertaken and composed, but by the various sketches and memoranda for four long narrative poems, made during their progress, from the first conception of each till its completion. At present, the facility and pleasure with which I can plan a heroic poem, a drama, and a biographical or historical work, however comprehensive, is even a temptation to me. It seems as if I caught the bearings of a subject at first sight, just as Telford sees from an eminence, with a glance, in what direction his road must be carried. But it was long before I acquired this power—not fairly, indeed, till I was about five or six-and-thirty; and it was gained by practice, in the course of which I learned to perceive wherein I was deficient.

There was one point in which these premature attempts afforded a hopeful omen, and that was in the diligence and industry with which I endeavored to acquire all the historical information within my reach relating to the subject in hand. Forty years ago I could have given a better account of the birth and parentage of Egbert, and the state of the Heptarchy during his youth, than I could do now without referring to books; and when Cassibelan was my hero, I was as well acquainted with the division of the island among the ancient tribes, as I am now with the relative situation of its counties. It was, perhaps, fortunate that these pursuits were unassisted and solitary. By thus working a way for myself, I acquired a habit and a love for investigation, and nothing appeared uninteresting which gave me any of the information I wanted. The pleasure which I took in such researches, and in composition, rendered me, in a great degree, independent of other amusements; and no systematic education could have fitted me for my present course of life so well as the circumstances which allowed me thus to feel and follow my own impulses.

LETTER XV.

CHARACTER OF MISS TYLER—HIS MOTHER—SHADRACH WEEKS—HIS BROTHER HENRY PLACED WITH MISS TYLER—HIS SISTER'S DEATH.

July 17th, 1824.

Few boys were ever less qualified for the discipline of a public school than I was, when it was determined to place me at Westminster; for, if my school education had been ill conducted, the life which I led with Miss Tyler tended in every respect still more to unfit me for the new scenes, the new world almost it might be called, on which I was about to enter.

When my aunt settled at Bristol, she brought with her a proud contempt for Bristol society. In fact, she had scarcely any acquaintance there, and seldom saw any company except when some of her Bath friends came to Clifton for the summer, or when the players took up their abode in the city, for then Mr. Dimond used to visit her. He was a most gentlemanly and respectable man, as well as a good actor. Great is the delight which I have had in seeing him perform, and hardly less was that which I have felt in listening to his conversation. The days when he dined with us were almost our only gala days. At such times, and when she went out, Miss Tyler's appearance and manners were those of a woman who had been bred in the best society, and was equal to it; but if any stranger or visitor had caught her in her ordinary apparel, she would have been as much confused as Diana when Actæon came upon her bathing-place, and almost with as much reason, for she was always in a bed-gown and in rags. Most people, I suspect, have a weakness for old shoes; ease and comfort, and one's own fireside, are connected with them; in fact, we never feel any regard for shoes till they attain to the privileges of age, and then they become almost as much a part of the wearer as his corns. This sort of feeling my aunt extended to old clothes of every kind; the older and the raggeder they grew, the more unwilling she was to cast them off. But she was scrupulously clean in them; indeed, the principle upon which her whole household economy was directed was that of keeping the house clean, and taking more precautions against dust than would have been needful against the plague in an infected city. She labored under a perpetual *dusto-phobia*, and a comical disease it was; but whether I have been most amused or annoyed by it, it would be difficult to say. I had, however, in its consequences, an early lesson how fearfully the mind may be enslaved by indulging its own peculiarities and whimsies, innocent as they may appear at first.

The discomfort which Miss Tyler's passion for cleanliness produced to herself, as well as to her little household, was truly curious: to herself, indeed, it was a perpetual torment; to the two servants, a perpetual vexation; and so it would have been to me if Nature had not blessed me with an innate hilarity of spirit which nothing but real affliction can overcome. That the better rooms might be kept clean, she took possession of the kitchen, sending the servants to one which was under ground; and in this little, dark, confined place, with a rough stone floor, and a sky-light (for it must not be supposed that it was a best kitchen, which was always, as it was intended to be, a comfortable sitting-room; this was more like a scullery), we always took our meals, and generally lived. The best room was never opened but for company, except now and then on a fine day to be aired and dusted, if dust could be detected there. In the other parlor I was allowed sometimes to read, and she wrote her letters, for she had many correspondents; and we sat there sometimes in summer, when a fire was not needed, for fire produced ashes, and ashes occasioned dust, and dust, visible or invisible, was the plague of her life. I have seen her order the tea-kettle to be emptied and refilled because some one had passed across the hearth while it was on the fire preparing for her breakfast. She had indulged these humors till she had formed for herself notions of uncleanness almost as irrational and inconvenient as those of the Hindoos. She had a cup once buried for six weeks, to purify it from the lips of one whom she accounted unclean; all who were not her favorites were included in that class. A chair in which an unclean person had sat was put out in the garden to be aired; and I never saw her more annoyed than on one occasion, when a man, who called upon business, seated himself in her own chair: how the cushion was ever again to be rendered fit for her use, she knew not! On such occasions, her fine features assumed a character either fierce or tragic; her expressions were vehement even to irreverence; and her gesticulations those of the deepest and wildest distress—hands and eyes uplifted, as if she was in hopeless misery, or in a paroxysm of mental anguish.

As there are none who like to be upon ill terms with themselves, most people find out some device whereby they may be reconciled to their own faults; and in this propensity it is that much of the irreligion in the world, and much of its false philosophy, have originated. My aunt used frequently to say that all good-natured people were fools. Hers was a violent temper rather than an ill one; there was a great deal of kindness in it, though it was under no restraint. She was at once tyrannical and indulgent to her servants, and they usually remained a long while in her service, partly, I believe, from fear, and partly from liking: from liking, because she sent them often to the play (which is probably, to persons in that condition, as it is to children, the most delightful of all amusements), and because she conversed with them much more than is usual for any one in her rank of life. Her habits were so peculiar, that the servants became, in a certain degree, her confidants; she therefore was afraid to change them; and they even, when they wished to leave her, were afraid to express the wish, knowing that she would regard it as a grievous offense, and dreading the storm of anger that it would bring down. Two servants in my remembrance left her for the sake of marrying; and, although they had both lived with her many years, she never forgave either, nor ever spoke of them without some expression of bitterness. I believe no daughter was ever more afraid of disclosing a clandestine marriage to a severe parent than both these women were of making their intention known to their mistress, such was the ascendency that she possessed over them. She had reconciled herself to the indulgence of her ungoverned anger by supposing that a bad temper was naturally connected with a good understanding and a commanding mind.

Besides her servants, there were two persons over whom she had acquired the most absolute control. Miss Palmer was the one: a more complete example can not be imagined of that magic which a strong mind exercises over a weak one. The influence which she possessed over my mother was equally unbounded and more continual, but otherwise to be explained: it was the ascendency of a determined and violent spirit over a gentle and yielding one. There was a difference of twelve years between their ages, and the authority which Miss Tyler had first exerted as an elder sister she never relaxed. My mother was one of those few persons (for a few such there are) who think too humbly of themselves. Her only fault (I verily believe she had no other) was that of yielding submissively to this imperious sister, to the sacrifice of her own inclination and judgment, and sense of what was right. She had grown up in awe and admiration of her, as one who moved in a superior rank, and who, with the advantage of a fine form and beautiful person, possessed that, also, of a superior and cultivated understanding: withal, she loved her with a true sisterly affection which nothing could diminish, clearly as she saw her faults, and severely as at last she suffered by them. But never did I know one person so entirely subjected by another, and never have I regretted any thing more deeply than that subjection, which most certainly, in its consequences, shortened her life.

If my mother had not been disfigured by the small-pox, the two sisters would have strikingly resembled each other except in complexion, my mother being remarkably fair. The expression, however, of the two countenances was as opposite as the features were alike, and the difference in disposition was not less marked. Take her for all in all, I do not believe that any human being ever brought into the world, and carried through it, a larger portion of original goodness than my dear mother. Every one who knew her loved her, for she seemed made to be happy herself, and to make every one happy within her little sphere. Her understanding was as good as her heart: it is from her I have inherited that alertness of mind, and quickness of apprehension, without which it would have been impossible for me to have undertaken half of what I have performed. God never blessed a human creature with a more cheerful disposition, a more generous spirit, a sweeter temper, or a tenderer heart. I remember that when first I understood what death was, and began to think of it, the most fearful thought it induced was that of losing my mother; it seemed to me more than I could bear, and I used to hope that I might die before her. Nature is merciful to us. We learn gradually that we are to die; a knowledge which, if it came suddenly upon us in riper age, would be more than the mind could endure. We are gradually prepared for our departure by seeing the objects of our earliest and deepest affections go before us; and even if no keener afflictions are dispensed to wean us from this world, and remove our tenderest thoughts and dearest hopes to another, mere age brings with it a weariness of life, and death becomes to the old as natural and desirable as sleep to a tired child.

My father's house being within ten minutes' walk of Terril Street (or rather run, for I usually galloped along the by-ways), few days passed on which I did not look in there. Miss Tyler never entered the door, because there was an enmity between her and Thomas Southey. She had given just occasion to it. They hated each other cordially now, and took no pains to conceal it. My visits at home, therefore, were short, and I was seldom allowed to dine or pass the evening there. My brother Tom was at school; the difference of age between us made us at that time not very suitable companions when we were together. There was not a single boy of my own age, or near it, in any of the few families with whom either my mother or aunt were acquainted; and my only friend and companion was my aunt's servant-boy, Shadrach Weeks, her maid's brother. Shad, as we called him, was just my own age, and had been taken into her service soon after she settled in Bristol. He was a good-natured, active, handy lad, and became very much attached to me, and I to him. At this hour, if he be living, and were to meet me, I am sure he would greet me with a hearty shake by the hand; and, be it where it might, I should return the salutation. We used to work together in the garden, play trap in the fields, make kites and fly them, try our hands at carpentry, and, which was the greatest of all indulgences, go into the country to bring home primrose, violet, and cowslip roots; and sometimes to St. Vincent's Rocks, or, rather, the heights about a mile and a half further down the river, to search for the bee and fly orchis. Some book had taught me that these rare flowers were to be found there; and I sought for them year after year with such persevering industry, for the unworthy purpose of keeping them in pots at home (where they uniformly pined and died), that I am afraid botanists who came after me may have looked for them there in vain. Perhaps I have never had a keener enjoyment of natural scenery than when roaming about the rocks and woods on the side of the Avon with Shad and our poor spaniel Phillis. Indeed, there are few scenes in the island finer of their kind, and no other where merchant vessels of the largest size may be seen sailing between such rocks and woods—the shores being upon a scale of sufficient magnitude to supply all that the picturesque requires, and not upon so large a one as to make the ships appear comparatively insignificant.

Had it not been for this companion, there would have been nothing to counteract the effeminating and debilitating tendency of the habits to which my aunt's peculiarities subjected me. Pricking play-bills had been the pastime which she encouraged as long as I could be prevailed on to pursue it, and afterward she encouraged me to cut paper into fantastic patterns. But I learned a better use of my hands in Shad's company; and we became such proficients in carpentry, that, before I went to Westminster, we set about the enterprise of making and fitting up a theater for puppets. This was an arduous and elaborate work, of which I shall have more to say hereafter, as our design extended with our progress. At this time, little more had been done than to finish the body of the theater, where there were pit, boxes, and gallery, and an ornamented ceiling, which, when it was put on, made the whole look on the outside like a box of unaccountable form. The spectator was to look through a glass behind the gallery, which was intended to have been a magnifier, till, to our great disappointment, we were assured at the optician's that no single magnifier could produce any effect at the distance which this was required to act. The scenery and stage contrivances I shall speak of in due time, for this was an undertaking which called forth all our ingenuity, and continued for several years to occupy me during the holidays.

Before I went to Westminster, my brother Henry had been taken into Miss Tyler's household, when he was about five years old. In 1787 a daughter was born, and christened Margaretta. I remember her as well as it is possible to remember an infant—that is, without any fixed and discriminating remembrance. She was a beautiful creature, and I was old enough to feel the greatest solicitude for her recovery, when I set off for London early in the spring of 1788. A thoughtless nurse-maid had taken her out one day to the most exposed situation within reach, what is called the Sea Banks, and kept her there unusually long while a severe east wind was blowing. From that hour she drooped;

cough and consumption came on. I left her miserably and hopelessly ill, and never saw her more. This was the first death that I had ever apprehended and dreaded, and it affected me deeply.

LETTER XVI.

IS PLACED AT WESTMINSTER—SCHOOLFELLOWS—FIRST HOLIDAYS—ANECDOTE OF GEORGE THE THIRD—LATIN VERSES.

August 29th, 1824.

The business of placing me at Westminster afforded my aunt an excuse for going to London. Miss Palmer was easily persuaded to accompany her, and to hire a carriage for the season, and we set off in February, 1788. I had never before been a mile from Bath in that direction, and when my childish thoughts ever wandered into the *terra incognita* which I was one day to explore, this had been the road to it, simply because all the other outlets from that city were familiar to me. We slept at Marlborough the first night, at Reading the second, and on the third day we reached Salt Hill. Tom and Charles Palmer were summoned from Eton to meet their aunt there, and we remained a day for the purpose of seeing Windsor, which I have never seen since. Lodgings had been engaged in a small house in Pall Mall, for no situation that was less fashionable would content Miss Tyler, and she had a reckless prodigality at fits and starts, the effects of which could not be counteracted by the parsimony and even penuriousness of her usual habits. Mr. Palmer was at that time controller of the Post-office, holding the situation which he had so well deserved, and from which he was not long afterward most injuriously displaced. We visited him, and the Newberrys, and Mrs. Dolignon, and went often to the theaters; and my aunt appeared to be as happy as if she were not incurring expenses which she had no means of discharging. My father had given her thirty pounds for the journey, a sum amply sufficient for taking me to school and leaving me there, and, moreover, as much as he could afford; but she had resolved upon passing the season in town, as careless of all consequences as if she had been blind to them.

About six weeks elapsed before I was deposited at my place of destination. In the interval I had passed a few days with the Newberrys at Addiscombe, and with the Miss Delameres at Cheshunt. At the latter place I was happy, for they were excellent women, to whom my heart opened, and I had the full enjoyment of the country there, without any drawback. London I very much disliked: I was too young to take any pleasure in the companies to which I was introduced as an inconvenient appendage of my aunt's; nor did I feel half the interest at the theaters, splendid as they were, which I had been wont to take at Bath and Bristol, where every actor's face was familiar to me, and every movement of the countenance could be perceived. I wished for Shad, and the carpentry, and poor Phillis, and our rambles among the woods and rocks. At length, upon the first of April (of all ominous days that could be chosen), Mr. Palmer took me in his carriage to Dean's Yard, introduced me to Dr. Smith, entered my name with him, and, upon his recommendation, placed me at the boarding house, then called Otley's, from its late mistress, but kept by Mrs. Farren; and left me there, with Samuel Hayes, the usher of the house, and of the fifth form, for my tutor.

Botch Hayes, as he was denominated, for the manner in which he mended his pupil's verses, kept a small boarding house next door; but at this time a treaty of union between the two houses was going on, which, like the union of Castile and Aragon, was to be brought about by a marriage between the respective heads of the several states. This marriage took place during the ensuing Whitsun holidays; and the smaller flock was removed, in consequence, to our boarding house, which then took the name of Hayes's, but retained it only a few months, for Hayes, in disgust at not being appointed under master, withdrew from the school. His wife, of course, followed his fortunes, and was succeeded by Mrs. Clough, who migrated thither with a few boarders from Abingdon Street. But as Botch Hayes is a person who must make his appearance in the Athenæ Cantabrigienses (if my lively, happy, good-natured friend Mr. Hughes carries into effect his intention of compiling such a work), I will say something of him here.

He was a man who, having some skill and much facility in versifying, walked for many years over the Seatonian race-ground at Cambridge, and enjoyed the produce of Mr. Seaton's Kislingbury estate without a competitor. He was, moreover, what Oldys describes Nahum Tate to have been—"a free, good-natured, fuddling companion;" to all which qualities his countenance bore witness. With better conduct and better fortune, Hayes would have had learning and talents enough to have deserved and obtained promotion. His failings were so notorious, and the boys took such liberties with him (sticking his wig full of paper darts in school, and, indeed, doing or leaving undone whatever they pleased, in full reliance upon his easy and indolent good-nature), that it would have been a most unfit thing to have appointed him under master, in course of seniority, when Vincent succeeded Dr. Smith. Perhaps he would not have taken offense at being passed by, if a person thoroughly qualified had been chosen in his stead; but he could not bear to have an inferior usher, who was a man of no talents whatever, promoted over him, and therefore, to the great injury of his worldly affairs, which could ill bear such a sacrifice, he left the school altogether. Hayes it was who edited those sermons which Dr. Johnson is supposed to have written for his friend Dr. Taylor.

I was placed in the under fourth, a year lower than I might have been if I could have made

Latin verses, and yet more than a year too high for being properly trained to make them. The manner of introducing a boy into the ways of the school was by placing him for a week or ten days under the direction of one in the same remove, who is called his substance, the newcomer being the shadow; and, during this sort of novitiate, the shadow neither takes nor loses place by his own deserts, but follows the substance. A diligent and capable boy is, of course, selected for this service; and Smedley, the usher of the fourth, to my great joy, picked out George Strachey, the very individual on whom my physiognomical eyes would have rested if I might have made a choice throughout the whole school. Strachey and I were friends at first sight. But he boarded at home; and it is in the boarding house, more than in the school, that a friend is wanted; and there, God knows, I had, for some time, a solitary heart.

The present Lord Amherst was head of the house; a mild, inoffensive boy, who interfered with no one, and, having a room to himself (which no other boy had), lived very much to himself in it, liked and respected by every body. I was quartered in the room with ——, who afterward married that sweet creature, Lady ——, and never was woman of a dove-like nature more unsuitably mated, for ——, when in anger, was perfectly frantic. His face was as fine as a countenance could be which expressed so ungovernable and dangerous a temper; the finest red and white, dark eyes and brows, and black curling hair; but the expression was rather that of a savage than of a civilized being, and no savage could be more violent. He had seasons of good nature, and at the worst was rather to be dreaded than disliked, for he was plainly not master of himself. But I had cause to dread him, for he once attempted to hold me by the leg out of the window. It was the first floor, and over a stone area: had I not struggled in time, and clung to the frame with both hands, my life would probably have been sacrificed to this freak of temporary madness. He used to pour water into my ear when I was abed and asleep, fling the porter-pot or the poker at me, and in many ways exercised such a capricious and dangerous tyranny, merely by right of the strongest (for he was not high enough in the school to fag me), that at last I requested Mr. Hayes to remove me into another chamber. Thither he followed me; and, at a very late hour one night, came in wrapped in a sheet, thinking to frighten me by personating a ghost, in which character he threw himself upon the bed, and rolled upon me. Not knowing who it was, but certain that it was flesh and blood, I seized him by the throat, and we made noise enough to bring up the usher of the house, and occasion an inquiry, which ended in requiring ——'s word that he never would again molest me.

He kept his word faithfully, and left school a few months afterward, when he was about seventeen or eighteen, and apparently full grown—a singularly fine and striking youth; indeed, one of those figures which you always remember vividly. I heard nothing of him till the Irish rebellion: he served in the army there; and there was a story, which got into the newspapers, of his meeting a man upon the road, and putting him to death without judge or jury, upon suspicion of his being a rebel. It was, no doubt, an act of madness. I know not whether any proceedings took place (indeed, in those dreadful times, any thing was passed over); but he died soon afterward, happily for himself and all who were connected with him.

Miss Tyler returned to Bristol before the Whitsun holidays, having embarrassed herself, and had recourse to shifts of which I knew too much. To spare the expense of a journey so soon after my entrance at school, I was invited for the holidays by the good Miss Delameres to Cheshunt. I passed three weeks there very happily, having the use of an excellent microscope, and frequently taking my book into the greenhouse, and reading there for the sake of the temperature and the odor of the flowers. During part of the time there were two other guests in the house. The one was a nice, good-humored, warm-hearted girl, in the very flower of youth and feeling, who was engaged to a French or Swiss clergyman, Mercier by name. Her own was La Chaumette. She was of Swiss extraction, and, having passed the preceding year among her relations in the Pays de Vaud, had brought home something like a *maladie du pays*, if that phrase may be applied to a longing after any country which is not our own: it was, however, a very natural affection for one who was compelled to exchange Lausanne for Spitalfields. I used to abuse Switzerland as a land of bears and wolves, and ice and snow, for the sake of seeing the animation with which she defended and praised it. Not long afterward she married to her heart's content, and, to the very great regret of all who knew her, died in her first childbed. Poor Betsey la Chaumette! after a lapse of nine-and-twenty years, I thought of her in Switzerland, and when I was at Echichens with the Awdrys, met with a Swiss clergyman who knew her and remembered her visit to that country.

I have heard her mother relate an anecdote of herself which is well worthy of preservation, because of another personage to whom it relates also. She was a most lively, good-humored, entertaining woman; and her conversation was the more amusing because it was in broken English, intermingled plentifully with French interjections. In person she was strong-featured, large, and plain even to ugliness, if a countenance can be called ugly which was always brightened with cheerfulness and good nature. There was a Mr. Giffardiere, who held some appointment in the queen's household (I think he used to read French to her), and was one of those persons with whom the royal family were familiar. Mrs. La Chaumette was on a visit to him at Windsor, and it was insisted upon by the Giffardieres that she must have one of the Lunardi bonnets (immortalized by Burns) which were then in fashion, it being the first age of balloons. This she resisted most *womanfully*, pleading her time of life and ugliness with characteristic volubility and liveliness, but to no purpose. Her eloquence was overruled; and as nobody could appear without such a bonnet, such a bonnet she had. All this went to the palace; for kings and queens are sometimes as much pleased at being acquainted with small private affairs as their subjects are in conversing upon great public ones. Mrs. La Chaumette's conversation was worth repeating, even to a king; and she was so original a person, that the king knew her very well by character, and was determined to see her. Accordingly, he stopped his horse one day before Giffardiere's apartments, and, after talking a while with him, asked if Mrs. La Chaumette was within, and desired she might be called to the window. She came in all the agitation or *fluster* that such a summons was likely to excite. The king spoke to her with his wonted good nature, asked her a few questions, hoped she liked Windsor, and concluded by saying he was glad to hear she had consented at last to have a Lunardi bonnet. Trifling as this is, it is a sort of trifling in which none but a kind-hearted king would have indulged; and I believe no one ever heard the story without liking George III. the better for it: I am sure this was the effect it produced in the circle of her acquaintance. How well do I remember the looks, and tones, and gestures, and *mon Dieus!* with which she accompanied the relation.

James Beresford was the other visitor at Cheshunt; an unsuccessful translator of the Æneid into blank verse, but the very successful author of the Miseries of Human Life. He was then a young man, either just in orders, or on the point of being ordained. This story was then remembered of him at the Charter House: that he had been equally remarkable when a boy for his noisiness and his love of music; and having one day skipped school to attend a concert, there was such an unusual quietness in consequence of his absence, that the master looked round, and said, "Where's Beresford? I am sure he can not be in school!" and the detection thus brought about cost poor Beresford a flogging. Him also, like Betsey la Chaumette, I never saw after that visit; and, with all his pleasantness and good nature, he left upon me an unpleasant impression, from a trifling circumstance which I remember as indicative of my own moral temper at that time. Our holidays' exercise was to compose a certain number of Latin verses from any part of Thomson's Spring. I did my task doggedly, in such a manner that it was impossible any exercise could have been more unlike a good one, and yet the very best could not more effectually have proved the diligence with which it had been made. There was neither a false quantity, nor a grammatical fault, nor a decent line in the whole. The ladies made me show it to Beresford; and he, instead of saying, in good-natured sincerity, "You have never been taught to make verses, but it is plain that you have taken great pains in making these, and therefore I am sure the usher will give you credit for what you have done," returned them to me, saying, "Sir, I see you will be another Virgil one of these days." I knew that this was neither deserved as praise nor as mockery; and I felt then, as I have continued through life to do, that unmerited censure brings with it its own antidote in the sense of injustice which it provokes, but that nothing is so mortifying as praise to which you are conscious that you have no claim.

Smedley spoke to me sensibly and kindly about this exercise, and put me in training as far as could then be done. He had no reason to complain of my want of good will, for before the next holidays I wrote about fifty long and short verses upon the death of Fair Rosamund, which I put into his hands. The composition was bad enough, I dare say, in many respects, but it gave proofs of good progress. They were verses to the ear as well as to the fingers; and I remember them sufficiently to know that the attempt was that of a poet. It is worth remembering, as being the only Latin poem that I ever composed voluntarily; for there my ambition ended. When I was so far upon a footing with the rest of the remove that I could make verses decent enough to pass muster, I was satisfied. It was in English, and not in heathen Latin, that

> "The sacred Sisters for their own
> Baptized me in the springs of Helicon;"

and I also knew, though I did not know Lope de Vega had said it, that

> "Todo paxaro en su nido
> Natural canto mantiene,
> En que ser perfeto viene:
> Porque en el canto aprendido
> Mil imperfeciones tiene."

LETTER XVII.

RECOLLECTIONS OF WESTMINSTER CONTINUED.

March 16th, 1825.

The Christmas before my entrance at Westminster, I remember seeing in the newspapers the names of those boys who acted in the Westminster play that year (1787). For one who knew nothing of the school, nor of any person in it, it was something to be acquainted with three or four boys, even by name; and I pleased myself with thinking that they were soon to be my friends. This was a *vain* fancy in both senses of the word: by their being selected to perform in the play, I supposed they were studious and clever boys, with whom I should, of course, become familiar; and I had no notion of the inequality which station produces at a public school. It is such that, when I came to Westminster, I never exchanged a word with any of these persons. Oliphant, Twistleton, and Carey were three of them. Carey was a marked favorite with Vincent, and afterward with Cyril Jackson at Christ Church; he is now Bishop of Exeter, having been head master of the school where, at the time of which I am now writing, he was one of the monitors. It is said that he is indebted to Cyril Jackson for his promotion to the bench, the dean requesting a bishopric for him, or, rather, earnestly recommending him for one when he refused it for himself. Twistleton was remarkable for a handsome person, on which he prided himself, and for wearing his long hair loose and powdered in school, but tied and dressed when he went out; for in those days hobble-dehoys used to let their hair grow, cultivating it for a tail, which was then the costume of manhood. The Westminster play gave him a taste for private theatricals. Immediately after leaving school he married a girl with whom he had figured away in such scenes; she became an actress afterward in public of some pretensions and much notoriety, as being the wife of an honorable and a clergyman. For a while Twistleton figured in London as a popular preacher, which too frequently is but another kind of acting; he then went out to India, and died there lately as archdeacon in Ceylon, where he had latterly taken a very useful and becoming part in promoting the efforts which are made in that island for educating and converting the natives. Oliphant was the more remarkable person of the three, and would probably have risen to celebrity had he lived. He was from Liverpool, the son, I believe, of a tradesman, one of the queerest fellows in appearance that I ever remember to have seen; and so short-sighted, that we had stories of his walking into a grave in the cloisters, and running his head through a lamp-lighter's ladder in the street. The boys in the sixth form speak in public once a week, in rotation, three king's scholars and three town boys. Generally this is got through as a disagreeable task; but now and then an ambitious fellow mouths instead of mumbling it; and I remember Twistleton and Oliphant reciting the scene between Brutus and Cassius with good effect, and with voices that filled the school. After leaving Cambridge Oliphant tried his fortune as an author, and published a novel, which I never saw; but it had some such title as "Memoirs of a Wild Goose Philosopher." He died soon afterward.

His first efforts in authorship were, however, made as a periodical essayist before he left school. The Microcosm, which the Etonians had recently published, excited a spirit of emulation at Westminster; and soon after I went there, some of the senior king's scholars, of whom Oliphant was at the head, commenced a weekly paper called the Trifler. As the master's authority in our age of lax discipline could not prevent this, Smith contented himself, in his good-natured, easy way, with signifying his disapprobation by giving as a text for a theme, on the Monday after the first number appeared, these words, *scribimus indocti doctique*. There were two or three felicitous papers in the Microcosm which made a reputation for the book; indeed, Eton has never produced men of more genius than those who contributed to it. The Trifler may in general have been on a par with it; that is to say, neither of them could contain any thing better in serious composition than good schoolboy's exercises; but it had no lucky hits of a lighter kind; and when forty numbers had been published, more to the contentment of the writers than of any body else, the volume was closed and was forgotten. The only disgraceful circumstance attending it was that a caricature was put forth, representing Justice as weighing the Microcosm against the Trifler, and the former, with its authors, and the king as a make-weight on their side, was made to kick the beam. This was designed and etched by James Hook, then a junior king's scholar, and now the very Reverend Dean of Worcester. I do not suppose it was sold in the print-shops, but the boys were expected to subscribe for it at a shilling each.

My first attempt to appear in print was in the aforesaid Trifler. I composed an elegy upon my poor little sister's death, which took place just at that time. The verses were written with all sincerity of feeling, for I was very deeply affected; but that they were very bad I have no doubt; indeed, I recollect enough of them to know it. However, I sent them by the penny-post, signing them with the letter B.; and in the next number this notice was taken of the communication: "B.'s Elegy must undergo some alterations, a liberty all our correspondents must allow us to take." After this I looked for its appearance anxiously, but in vain; for no further mention was made of it, because no alteration could have rendered it fit for appearance, even among the compositions of elder schoolboys. Oliphant and his colleagues never knew from whence it came; I was far too much below them to be suspected, and, indeed, at that time, I was known out of my remove for nothing but my curly head.

Curly heads are not common; I doubt whether they can be reckoned at three per cent. upon the population of this country; but, luckily for me, the present Sir Charles Burrell (old Burrell, as we then called him, a very good-natured man) had one as well as myself. The space between Palace Yard and St. Margaret's Church-yard was at that time covered with houses. You must remember them, but I knew all the lanes and passages there; intricate enough they were, and afforded excellent cover, just in the most dangerous part, on the border, when we were going out of bounds, or returning home from such an expedition. The improvements which have laid all open there have done no service to the Westminster boys, and have deprived me of some of the pleasantest jogging-places for memory that London used to contain. In one of these passages was the door of a little schoolmaster, whose academy was announced by a board upon the front of a house, close to St. Margaret's Church-yard. Some of the day boys in my remove took it into their heads, in the pride of Westminster, to annoy this academician by beating up his quarters, and one day I joined in the party. The sport was to see him sally with a cane in his hand, and to witness the admiration of his own subjects at our audacity. He complained at last, as he had good cause, to Vincent; but no suspicion fell or could fall upon the real parties; for it so was, that the three or four ringleaders in these regular rows were in every respect some of the best boys in the school, and the very last to whom any such pranks would have been imputed. The only indication he could give was that one of the culprits was a curly-headed fellow. One evening, a little to my amusement, and not a little to my consternation, I heard old Burrell say that Vincent had just sent for him, and taxed him with making a row at a schoolmaster's in St. Margaret's Churchyard, and would hardly believe the protestations of innocence, which he reiterated with an oath when he told the story, and which I very well knew to be sincere. It was his curly head, he said, that brought him into suspicion. I kept my own counsel, and did not go near the academy again.

At a public school you know something of every boy in your own boarding house and in your own form; you are better acquainted with those in your own remove (which at Westminster means half a form); and your intimacies are such as choice may make from these chances of juxtaposition. All who are above you you know by sight and by character, if they have any: to have none indicates an easy temper, inclined rather to good than evil. Of those who are below you, unless they are in the same house, you are acquainted with very few, even by name. The number, however, of those with whom you are more or less brought in contact, is such, that after-life seldom or never affords another opportunity of knowing so many persons so well, and forming so fair an estimate of human nature. Is that estimate a favorable one? and what says my own experience? Of the three hundred boys who were my cotemporaries during four years (about fifty, perhaps, being changed annually), there were very few upon whose countenance Nature had set her best testimonials. I can call to mind only one wherein the moral and intellectual expression were in perfect accord of excellence, and had full effect given them by the features which they illuminated. Those who bore the stamp of reprobation, if I may venture to use a term which is to be abhorred, were certainly more in number, but not numerous. The great majority were of a kind to be whatever circumstances might make them; clay in the potter's hand, more or less fine; and as it is fitting that such subjects should be conformed to the world's fashion and the world's uses, a public school was best for them. But where there is a tendency to low pursuits and low vices, such schools are fatal. They are nurseries, also, for tyranny and brutality. Yet, on the other hand, good is to be acquired there, which can be attained in no other course of education.

Of my own cotemporaries there, a fair proportion have filled that place and maintained that character in the world which might have been expected from the indications of their boyhood. Some have manifested talents which were completely latent at that time; and others who put forth a fair blossom have produced no fruit. But, generally speaking, in most instances where I have had opportunity of observing, the man has been what the boy promised, or, as we should say in Cumberland, offered to be.

Our boarding house was under the tyranny of W. F——. He was, in Westminster language, a great beast; that is, in plain truth, a great brute—as great a one as ever went upon two legs. But there are two sorts of human brutes—those who partake of wolf-nature or of pig-nature, and F—— was of the better breed, if it be better to be wolfish than swinish. He would have made a good prize-fighter, a good buccaneer, or, in the days of Cœur de Lion or of my Cid, a good knight, to have cut down the misbelievers with a strong arm and a hearty good will. Every body feared and hated him; and yet it was universally felt that he saved the house from the tyranny of a greater beast than himself. This was a fellow by name B——, who was mean and malicious, which F—— was not. I do not know what became of him; his name has not appeared in the Tyburn Calendar, which was the only place to look for it; and if he has been hanged, it must have been under an *alias*, an observation which is frequently made when he is spoken of by his schoolfellows. He and F—— were of an age and standing, the giants of the house, but F—— was the braver, and did us the good office of keeping him in order. They hated each other cordially, and, the evening before we were rid of "Butcher B——," F—— gave the whole house the great satisfaction of giving him a good thrashing.

It was so obviously impossible to put Latin and Greek into F——, at either end, even if there had been any use in so doing, that no attempt was made at it. The Greek alphabet he must have known; but he could have known nothing more of Greek, nor, indeed, of any thing else, than just to qualify him for being crammed to pass muster, at passing from one form to another; and so he was floated up to the Shell, beyond which the tide carried no one. He never did an exercise for himself of any kind; they were done by deputy, whom the fist appointed; and, after a while, it was my ill fortune to be promoted to that office. My orders were that the exercises must always be bad enough; and bad enough they were. I believe, indeed, that the habit of writing bad Latin for him spoiled me for writing it well, when, in process of time, I had exercises of the same kind to compose in my own person. It was a great deliverance when he left school. I saw him once afterward, in the High Street at Oxford. He recognized me instantly, stopped me, shook me heartily by the hand, as if we had been old friends, and said, "I hear you became a devilish fine fellow after I left, and used to *row* Dodd (the usher of the house) famously!" The look and the manner with which these words were spoken I remember perfectly; the more so, perhaps, because he died soon afterward, and little as it was to have been expected, there was something in his death which excited a certain degree of respect as well as pity. He went into the army, and perished in our miserable expedition to St. Domingo, where, by putting himself forward on all occasions of service, and especially by exerting himself in dragging cannon when the soldiers were unequal to the fatigue, he brought on the yellow fever, and literally fell a victim to a generosity and good-nature which he had never been supposed to possess.

That fever proved fatal to a good many of my Westminster schoolfellows, who, some of them because they were fit for the army, and others because they were fit for nothing else, took to that profession at the commencement of the Revolutionary war. Rather a large proportion of them perished in the West Indies. "Who the devil would have thought of my burying old Blair!" was the exclamation of one who returned, and who of the two might better have been buried there himself. Blair was a cousin of the present Countess of Lonsdale, and I was as intimate with him as it was possible to be with one who boarded in another house, though it would not have been easy to have found a boy in the whole school more thoroughly unlike myself in every thing, except in temper. He was, as Lord Lonsdale told me, a spoiled child—idle, careless, fond of dogs and horses, of hunting rats, baiting badgers; and, above all, of driving stage-coaches. But there was a jovial hilarity, a perpetual flow of easy good spirits, a sunshine of good humor upon his countenance, and a merriment in his eye, which bring him often to my mind, and always make me think of him with a great deal of kindness. He was remarkably fat, and might have sat for the picture of Bacchus, or of Bacchus's groom; but he was active withal.

Blair spent one summer holidays with his mother, Lady Mary, at Spa, and used to amuse me greatly by his accounts of the place and the people, and the delight of traveling abroad, but, above all, by his description of the French postillions. He had brought back a postillion's whip, having learned to crack it in perfection; and that French flogger, as he called it, did all his exercises for him; for if Marsden, whom he had nominated to the office of secretary for this department, ever demurred when his services were required, crack went the French flogger, and the sound of what he never felt produced prompt obedience. The said Marsden was a person who could have poured out Latin verses, such as they were, with as much facility as an Italian *improvisatore* performs his easier task. I heard enough about Spa, at that time, to make me very desirous of seeing the place; and when I went thither, after my first visit to the field of Waterloo, it was more for the sake of poor Blair than for any other reason. Poor fellow, the yellow fever made short work with his plethoric frame, when he went with his regiment to the West Indies. The only station that he would thoroughly have become would have been that of abbot in some snug Benedictine abbey, where the rule was comfortably relaxed. In such a station, where the habit would just have imposed the restraint he needed, he would have made monks, tenants, dependents, and guests all as happy as indulgence, easy good-nature, and hearty hospitality could make them. As it was, flesh of a better grain never went to the land-crabs, largely as in those days they were fed.

There was another person in the remove, who, when he allowed himself time for such idle entertainment, was as fond of Blair's conversation as I was (our intercourse with him was only during school hours), but to whom I was attached by sympathies of a better kind. This was William Bean, the son of an apothecary at Camberwell, from which place he walked every day to school, a distance of more than three miles to and fro. He had a little of the Cockney pronunciation, for which Blair used to laugh at him and mimic him. His appearance was odd, as well as remarkable, and made the worse by his dress. One day, when he had gone into the boarding house with me, Dickenson (the present member for Somersetshire, a good-natured man) came into the room, and, fixing his eyes upon him, exclaimed, with genuine surprise, "O you cursed quiz, what is your name?" One Sunday afternoon, when with my two most intimate associates (Combe and Lambe) I had been taking a long ramble on the Surrey side of the river, we met Bean somewhere near the Elephant and Castle, returning home from a visit, in his Sunday's suit of dittos, and in a cocked hat to boot. However contented he might have been in this costume, I believe that, rather than have been seen in it by us, he would have been glad if the earth had opened, and he could have gone down for five minutes to Korah, Dathan, and Abiram. However, the next morning, when he threw himself upon our mercy, and entreated that we would not say that we had met him in a *cock and pinch*, my companions promised him, as willingly as I did, to be silent.

With this quizzical appearance, there were in Bean's swarthy face and in his dark eyes the strongest indications of a clear intellect, a steady mind, and an excellent heart all which he had in perfection. He had been placed at Westminster in the hope of his getting into college; but, being a day scholar, and having no connections acquainted with the school, he had not been put in the way of doing this, so that when the time came for what is called *standing out*, while all the other candidates were in the usual manner crammed by their helps, Bean stood alone, without assistance, and consequently failed. Had the mode of examination been what it ought to be, a fair trial of capacity and diligence, in which no cramming was allowed, his success would have been certain; and had he gone off from Westminster to either university, he would most certainly have become one of the most distinguished men there. Every thing might have been expected from him that could result from the best capacity and the best conduct. But he failed, and was immediately taken from school to learn his father's profession. I had too sincere a regard for him to lose sight of him thus, and several times, in summer afternoons, when the time allowed, walked to Camberwell Green just to see and shake hands with him, and hurry back; and this I continued to do as long as I remained at Westminster.

In 1797 or 1798, he stopped me one day in the street, saying he did not wonder that I should have passed without recognizing him, for he had had the yellow fever three times, and, not having long recovered, still bore strong vestiges of it in his complexion. He had gone into the army in his professional line, and had just then returned from the West Indies. I never saw him more; but, going along Camberwell Green some ten years ago, and seeing the name still over the door, I went in and inquired for him of his brother, who immediately remembered my name, and told me that William had been doing well in the East Indies, and that they soon hoped for his return; upon which I left a message for him, to be communicated in their next letter, and my direction, whenever he might arrive. Shortly after this I became acquainted with poor Nash, whose father's house was nearly opposite to Bean's; and, to my great pleasure, I found that Nash knew him well, had seen him at Bombay, and spoke of him as having proved just such a man as I should have expected, that is, of sterling sense and sterling worth. You may imagine how I was shocked at learning subsequently, through the same channel, what had been his fate. Tidings had been received, that, going somewhere by sea (about Malacca, I think) upon a short passage, with money for his regiment, of which he acted as paymaster at that time, for the sake of that money he had been murdered by the Malay boatmen.

He had saved about £5000 or £6000, which he left to his mother, an unhappy and unworthy woman, who had forsaken her family, but still retained a strong affection for this eldest son, and wished, when he was a boy, to withdraw him from his father. With that view she came one day to Westminster, and waited in the cloisters to waylay him when the school was over. A scene ensued which was truly distressing to those who felt as they ought to do, for he flew from her, and both were so much agitated as to act and speak as if there had been no spectators. I was not present, but what I heard of it strengthened my regard for him; and I had his situation with respect to his mother in my mind when certain passages in Roderick were written.

Dr. Pinckland has mentioned him with respect in his notes on the West Indies, as one of the assistants in some military hospital in which the doctor was employed. I was pleased at meeting with this brief and incidental notice of his name while he was yet living, though with a melancholy feeling that the abler man was in the subordinate station. That brief notice is the only memorial of one who, if he had not been thus miserably cut off, would probably have left some durable monument of himself; for, during twenty years of service in all parts of the globe, he had seen much, and I have never known any man who would more certainly have seen things in the right point of view, morally as well as intellectually. Had he returned, I should have invited him hither, and he would have come. We should have met like men who had answered each other's expectations, and whom years and various fortunes, instead of alienating, had drawn nearer in heart and in mind. That meeting will take place in a better world.

THE

LIFE AND CORRESPONDENCE

OF

ROBERT SOUTHEY.

CHAPTER I.

SCHOOL FRIENDSHIPS — THE FLAGELLANT — IS COMPELLED TO LEAVE WESTMINSTER—WRECK OF HIS FATHER'S AFFAIRS AND HIS DEATH—IS REFUSED ADMITTANCE AT CHRIST CHURCH, AND ENTERS AT BALIOL COLLEGE, OXFORD—COLLEGE LIFE—HIS STUDIES—PHILOSOPHICAL SPECULATIONS—EXCURSION TO HEREFORDSHIRE—VISIT TO BRIXTON—JOAN OF ARC—RETURN TO BRISTOL — LETTERS ON A UNIVERSITY LIFE, ETC.—FITS OF DESPONDENCY — POETRY AND PHILOSOPHY — MR. LOVEL—AMERICA — NUMBER OF VERSES DESTROYED AND PRESERVED—A.D. 1791–1793.

My father has entered so fully into the history of his family and the details of his early life, that it is only needful for me to take up the thread of the narrative where he has laid it down. I can not, however, but regret that he had not at least completed the account of his schoolboy days, and given us a little more insight into the course of his studies, feelings, and opinions at that period, and also into the origin of those more lasting friendships he formed during the latter part of his stay at Westminster.

But, while it may justly be regretted that he has not carried down his autobiography to a later date, it is not much to be wondered at that he found the task becoming more difficult and more painful. Recollections must have crowded upon his mind almost faster than he could arrange and relate them (as we perceive they had already done, from the many collateral histories into which he has diverged), and he was coming to that period of his life which of all others it would have been most difficult for him accurately to record. He had, indeed, in early life, often contemplated "writing the history of his own mind," and had imagined that it would be the most pleasing and the most profitable task he could engage in; but he probably found it was more agreeable in anticipation than in reality, and when once the thread was broken, he seems neither to have found time nor inclination to resume it.

He has spoken of his early Westminster acquaintances, but he has not mentioned the two chief friendships he formed there, apparently not having come to the time when they had commenced: these were with Mr. C. W. W. Wynn, and Mr. Grosvenor Charles Bedford (late of the Exchequer), with whom he seems at school to have been on terms of the closest intimacy, and who continued through life among his most valuable friends. That even long prior to his going to Westminster he had found his chief pleasure in his pen, and that he had both read and written largely, he has himself recorded, and he has also mentioned his having made an unsuccessful attempt to obtain admission for one of his youthful compositions in a Westminster Magazine called "The Trifler," which appears to have had only a brief existence. It was not long, however, before he found an opportunity of making his first essay in print, which proved not a little unfortunate in its results. Having attained the upper classes of the school, in conjunction with several of his more particular friends, he set on foot a periodical entitled "The Flagellant," which reached only nine numbers, when a sarcastic attack upon corporeal punishment, as then inflicted, it seems, somewhat unsparingly at Westminster, roused the wrath of Dr. Vincent, the head master, who immediately commenced a prosecution for libel against the publisher.

This seems to have been a harsh and extraordinary proceeding, for the master's authority, judiciously exercised, might surely have controlled or stopped the publication; neither was there any thing in the paper itself which ought to have made a wise man angry. Like most of the others, it is merely a schoolboy's imitation of a paper in the Spectator or Rambler. A letter of complaint from an unfortunate victim to the rod is supposed to have been called forth by the previous numbers, and the writer now comments on this, and enters into a dissertation on flogging with various quotations, ascribing its invention to the author of all evil. The signature was a feigned one; but my father immediately acknowledged himself the writer, and reluctantly apologized. The doctor's wrath, however, was not to be appeased, and he was compelled to leave the school.

Having quitted Westminster under these untoward circumstances early in the spring of the year 1792, he remained until the close of it, as usual, with his aunt, Miss Tyler, in the College Green, Bristol; and there, partly from want of regular employment and society, partly from his naturally excitable disposition, we find him in every imaginable mood of mind, now giving way to fits of despondency, revolving first one scheme of future life and then another, and again brightening up under the influence of a buoyant and happy temper, continually writing verses, and eager again to come before the public as an author, despite the unfortunate issue of his first attempt.

"The Flagellant is gone," he writes at this time to his schoolfellow and coadjutor in that luckless undertaking, Mr. Grosvenor Bedford; "still, however, I think that our joint productions may acquire some credit. The sooner we have a volume published, the better: 'The Medley,' 'The Hodge-podge,' 'The What-do-you-call-it,' or, to retain our old plan, 'Monastic Lucubrations;' any of these, or any better you may propose, will do. Shall we dedicate to Envy, Hatred, and Malice, and all Uncharitableness? Powerful arbitrators of the minds of men, who have already honored us with your marked attention, ye who can convert innocence into treason, and, shielded by the arm of power, remain secure, &c., &c., &c.; or shall we dedicate it to the doctor, or to the devil, or to the king, or to ourselves? Gentlemen, to you in whose breasts neither envy nor malice can find a place, who will not be biased by the clamors of popular prejudice, nor stoop to the authority of ignorance and power, &c., &c.

"I see no reason why we should not publish pretty soon; it will be at least four months before we can prepare it for the press, and, surely, by that time we may venture again upon the world.

"　.　.　.　.　.　We have ventured,
Like little wanton boys that swim on bladders,
These last nine numbers in a sea of glory,
But far above our depth; the high-blown bubble
At length burst under us, and now has left us
(Yet smarting from the rod of persecution
Though yet unwearied) to the merciless rage
Of the rude sea that swallowed Number Five."

These boyish schemes, however, were not to be carried into effect; and "the wreck of his father's affairs," to which he has alluded in the Autobiography, taking place at this time, he was occupied for a while by some of the more painful realities of life. "Since my last," he writes again to Mr. Bedford, "I have been continually going backward and forward upon business, which would not allow me to fix sufficient attention upon any thing else. It is now over. I have time to look about me; I hope, with fairer prospects for the future. One of my journeys was to my father's brother at Taunton, to request him to assist my father to recover that situation into which the treachery of his relations and injustice of his friends had thrown him. I had never seen this uncle, and you may guess how unpleasant so humiliating an errand must prove to so proud a spirit. He was absent. I left a letter, and two days ago received an answer and a refusal. Fortunately, my aunt had prevented the necessity; but her goodness does not extenuate his unnatural parsimony. He is single, and possessed of property to the amount of £100,000, without a child to provide for. That part of his fortune which he inherited must one day be mine; it will, I hope, enable me to despise the world and live independent."*

But his father's health was now completely broken by his misfortunes: he sank rapidly; and my father, having gone up to matriculate at Oxford, was only recalled in time to follow him to the grave.

It had been intended that he should enter at Christ Church, and his name had been put down there for some time; but the dean (Cyril Jackson), having heard of the affair of the Flagellant, refused to admit him, doubtless supposing he would prove a troublesome and disaffected under-graduate, and little dreaming the time would come when the University would be proud to bestow on him her highest honors.

Having been rejected at Christ Church, he entered at Baliol College,† and returned to his home at Miss Tyler's, to remain there till the time when his residence at Oxford should commence. The following letter will illustrate sufficiently his character at this period.

To Grosvenor C. Bedford, Esq.

(With a rude sketch of a church.)

"Nov. 20, 1792.

"MY DEAR BEDFORD,

"I doubt not but you will be surprised at my sending a church neither remarkable for beauty of design nor neatness of execution. Waiving, however, all apologies for either, if you are disposed at some future time to visit the 'Verdant House' of your friend when he shall be at supper—'not when he eats, but when he is eaten'—you will find it on the other side of this identical church. The very covering of the vault affords as striking an emblem of mortality as would even the moldering tenant of the tomb. Yesterday, I know not from what strange humor, I visited it for the second time in my life; the former occasion was mournful, and no earthly consideration shall ever draw me there upon a like. My pilgrimage yesterday was merely the result of a meditating moment when philosophy had flattered itself into apathy. I am really astonished when I reflect upon the indifference with which I so minutely surveyed the heaving turf, which inclosed within its cold bosom ancestors upon whom fortune bestowed rather more of her smiles than she has done upon their descendants—men who, content with an independent patrimony, lay hid from the world, too obscure to be noticed by it, too elevated to fear its insult. Those days are past. Three Ed-

* Oct. 21, 1792.

† The following is extracted from the Register of Admissions at Baliol College:

"Termino Michaelis, 1792, Nov. 3. Robertus Southey Filius natu maximus Roberti Southey Generosi de Civitate Bristol; Admissus est Commensalis."

ward Hills there sleep forever. I send the epitaph which, at present, is inscribed upon one of the cankered sides; perhaps the production of some one of my forefathers, who possessed more piety than poetry:

"'Farewell this world
With all Its Vanity;
We hope, through Christ,
To live eternally.'

"You have the exact orthography, and the inscription will probably cover the remains of one who has written so much for others, and must be content with so humble an epitaph himself, unless you will furnish him with one more characteristical.

"Were you to walk over the village (Ashton) with me, you would, like me, be tempted to repine that I have no earthly mansion here—it is the most enchanting spot that nature can produce. My rambles would be much more frequent were it not for certain reflections, not altogether of a pleasant nature, which always recur. I can not wander like a stranger over lands which once were my forefathers', nor pass those doors which are now no more open, without feeling emotions altogether inconsistent with pleasure and irreconcilable with the indifference of philosophy.

"What is there, Bedford, contained in that word of such mighty virtue? It has been sounded in the ear of common sense till it is deafened and overpowered with the clamor. Artifice and vanity have reared up the pageant, science has adorned it, and the multitude have beheld at a distance and adored. It is applied indiscriminately to vice and virtue, to the exalted ideas of Socrates, the metaphysical charms of Plato, the frigid maxims of Aristotle, the unfeeling dictates of the Stoics, and the disciples of the defamed Epicurus. Rousseau was called a philosopher while he possessed sensibility the most poignant. Voltaire was dignified with the name when he deserved the blackest stigma from every man of principle. Whence all this seeming absurdity? or why should reason be dazzled by the name when she can not but perceive its imbecility?

"So far I wrote last night; upon running it over, I think you will fancy you have a rhapsody for the Flagellant instead of a letter; and, really, had I continued it in the same mood, it would have been little different. If I had any knowledge of drawing, I would send you some of the most pleasing views you can conceive, whether rural, melancholy, pleasing, or grand. At some future period I hope to show you the place, and you will then judge whether I have praised it too lavishly. . . . . In the course of next summer the Duke of Portland will be installed at Oxford: the spectacle is only inferior to a coronation. I have rooms there, and am glad of the opportunity to offer them to you. We are permitted to have men in college upon the occasion: the whole University makes up the procession. It will be worth seeing, as perhaps coronations, like the secular games, will soon be as a tale that is told.

"Within this half hour I have received a letter from my uncle at Lisbon, chiefly upon a subject which I have been much employed upon since March 1. I will show it you when we meet. It is such as I expected from one who has been to me more than a parent—without asperity, without reproaches. . . . . To-morrow I answer it, and, as he has desired, send him the Flagellant. I then hope to drop the subject forever in this world; in the next all hearts are open, and no man's intentions are hid.

"I can now tell you one of the uses of philosophy: it teaches us to search for applause from within, and to despise the flattery and the abuse of the world alike; to attend only to an inward monitor; to be superior to fortune: why, then, is the name so prostituted? Do give me a lecture upon philosophy, and teach me how to become a philosopher. The title is pretty, and surely the philosophic S. would sound as well as the philosophic Hume or the philosopher of Ferney. Would it not be as truly applied? I am loth to part with my poor Flagellants; they have cost me very dear, and perhaps I shall never see them more.* One copy ought to be preserved, in order to contradict the inventions of future malice. Are you not ashamed of your idleness?

"R. SOUTHEY.

"P.S.—If I can one day have the honor of writing after my name Fellow of Baliol College, that will be the extent of my preferment. Sometimes I am tempted to think that I was sent into this world for a different employment; but, as the play says, beware of the beast that has three legs. Now, Bedford, as you might long puzzle to discover the genus of the beast, know that his grasp is always mortal; that, in short (here follows a sketch). But, as that drawing wants explanation as much, if not more, than the description, know it is—the gallows.

"About the 17th of January I began my residence at Oxford, where the prime of my life is to pass in acquiring knowledge, which, when I begin to have some ideas of, it will be cut short by the doctor, who levels all ranks and degrees. Is it not rather disgraceful, at the moment when Europe is on fire with freedom—when man and monarch are contending—to sit and study Euclid or Hugo Grotius? As Pindar says, a good button-maker is spoiled in making a king; what will be spoiled when I am made a fellow of Baliol? That question I can not resolve. I can only say I have spoiled a sheet of paper, and you fifteen minutes in reading it.

"N.B.—If you do not soon answer it, you will spoil my temper."

My father went up to reside at Baliol in January, 1793, being at this time ill suited to a college life both by his feelings and opinions. "My prepossessions," he writes, "are not very favor-

* This proved to be the case: he never saw the latter numbers of the Flagellant again. Mr. Hill preserved the copy which had been sent to him, but in after years kept it carefully from my father's knowledge, thinking he would destroy it. This copy is now before me, and is, perhaps, the only one in existence.

able. I expect to meet with pedantry, prejudice, and aristocracy, from all which, good Lord, deliver poor Robert Southey."* And almost immediately on his arrival: "Behold me, my friend, entered under the banners of science or stupidity—which you please—and, like a recruit got sober, looking to the days that are past, and feeling something like regret. Would you think it possible that the wise founders of an English university should forbid us to wear boots?† What matters it whether I study in shoes or boots? to me it is matter of indifference; but folly so ridiculous puts me out of conceit with the whole. When the foundation is bad, the fabric must be weak. None of my friends are yet arrived, and as for common acquaintance, I do not wish for them. Solitude I do not dislike, for I fear it not; but there is a certain demon called Reflection that accompanies it, whose arrows, though they rankle not with the poison of guilt, are yet pointed by melancholy. I feel myself entered upon a new scene of life, and, whatever the generality of Oxonians conceive, it appears to me a very serious one. Four years hence I am to be called into orders, and during that time (short for the attainment of the requisite knowledge) how much have I to learn! I must learn to break a rebellious spirit, which neither authority nor oppression could ever bow: it would be easier to break my neck. I must learn to work a problem instead of writing an ode. I must learn to pay respect to men remarkable only for great wigs and little wisdom."‡

He was, indeed, but little disposed to pay much deference either to the discipline or the etiquette of the college. It was usual for all the members to have their hair regularly dressed and powdered according to the prevailing fashion, and the college barber waited upon the "freshmen" as a matter of course. My father, however, peremptorily refused to put himself under his hands; and I well remember his speaking of the astonishment depicted in the man's face, and of his earnest remonstrances on the impropriety he was going to commit in entering the dining hall with his long hair,§ which curled beautifully, in its primitive state. A little surprise was manifested at first, but the example was quickly followed by others.

It does not appear what particular course of reading he pursued while at the University; but one of his college friends declares that he was a perfect "helluo librorum" then as well as throughout his life; and among his diversified writings there is abundant evidence that he had drunk deeply both of the Greek and Latin poets.

His letters, which at this time seem to have been exercises in composition, give evidence of his industry, and at the same time indicate a mind imbued with heathen philosophy and Grecian republicanism. They are written often in a style of inflated declamation, which, as we shall see, before many years had passed, subsided into a more natural and tranquil tone under the influence of his matured taste.

A few of these are here laid before the reader.

To G. C. Bedford, Esq.

"Friday, Jan. 25, 1793, 6 in the evening.

"Such is the hour when I begin this letter; when it will be finished is uncertain. Expecting Wynn to drink tea with me every moment, I have not patience to wait without employment, and know of none more agreeable than that of writing to you. My Mentor, while he prohibits my writing, must nevertheless allow an exception in your favor; and believe me, I look upon it as one great proof of my own reformation, or whatever title you may please to give, when I can pass a whole week without composing one word. Over the pages of the philosophic Tacitus the hours of study pass as rapidly as even those which are devoted to my friends, and I have not found as yet one hour which I could wish to have employed otherwise: this is saying very much in praise of a collegiate life; but remember that a mind disposed to be happy will find happiness every where; and why we should not be happy is beyond my philosophy to account for. Heraclitus certainly was a fool, and, what is much more rare, an unhappy one. I never yet met with any fool who was not pleased with the idea of his own sense; but for your whimpering sages, let sentiment say what it will, they are men possessed with more envy than wisdom."

To G. C. Bedford, Esq.

"Saturday, Feb. 12, 5 in the morning.

"Now, Bedford, this is more than you would do for me—quit your bed after only five hours' rest, light a fire, and then write a letter; really, I think it would not have tempted me to rise unless assisted by other inducements. To-day I am going to walk to Abingdon with three men of this college; and having made the pious resolution (your good health in a glass of red negus) of rising every morning at five to study, that the rest of the day may be at my own disposal, I procured an alarum clock and a tinder-box. This morning was the first. I rose, called up a neighbor, and read about three hundred lines of Homer, when I found myself hungry; the bread and cheese were called in as auxiliaries, and I made some negus: as I spiced it my eye glanced over the board, and the assemblage seemed so curious that I laid all aside for your letter—a lexicon, Homer, inkstand, candles, snuffers, wine, bread and cheese, nutmeg grater, and hour-glass. But I have given up time enough to my letter; the glass runs fast, and for once the expression is not merely figurative.

"Monday.

"How rapidly does Time hasten on when his wings are not clogged by melancholy! Perhaps no human being ever more forcibly experienced

* To Grosvenor C. Bedford, Dec., 1792.

† This law belongs to Baliol College, and is still, or was very lately, in force.

‡ To Grosvenor C. Bedford, Esq., Jan. 16, 1793.

§ There is a portrait of my father engraved in Mr. Cottle's Reminiscences, which shows the long hair, &c.

this than myself. Often have I counted the hours with impatience when, tired of reflection and all her unpleasant train, I wished to forget myself in sleep. Now I allow but six hours to my bed, and every morning, before the watchman rises, my fire is kindled and my bed cold : this is practical philosophy; but every thing is valued by comparison, and, when compared with my neighbor, I am no philosopher. Two years ago Seward drank wine, and ate butter and sugar; now, merely from the resolution of abridging the luxuries of life, water is his only drink, tea and dry bread his only breakfast. In one who professed philosophy this would be only practicing its tenets, but it is quite different with Seward. To the most odd and uncommon appearance he adds manners, which, as one gets accustomed to them, are the most pleasing. At the age of fourteen he began learning, and the really useful knowledge he possesses must be imputed to a mind really desirous of improvement. 'Do you not find your attention flag?' I said to him as he was studying Hutchinson's Moral Philosophy in Latin. 'If our tutors would but make our studies interesting, we should pursue them with pleasure.' 'Certainly we should,' he replied; 'but I feel a pleasure in studying them, because I know it is my duty.' This I take to be true philosophy, of that species which tends to make mankind happy, because it first makes them good. We had verses here upon the 30th of January to the memory of Charles the Martyr. It is a little extraordinary that you should quote those very lines to poor Louis which I prefixed to my ode: 'His virtues plead like angels, trumpet-tongued, against the deep damnation of his taking off.' . . . . Morose austerity and stern enthusiasm are the characteristics of superstition; but what is, in reality, more cheerful or happy than Religion? I have in my own knowledge more than one instance of this, and doubt not you have likewise. Ought not, therefore, that wretch who styles himself a philosopher to be shunned like pestilence, who, because Christianity has to him no allurement, seeks to deprive the miserable of their only remaining consolation? . . . . I keep a daily journal for myself, as an account of time which I ought to be strict in; but this, being only destined for my own eye, is uninteresting and unimportant. Boswell might compile a few quartos from the loose memorandums, but they would tire the world more than he has already done. Twenty years hence this journal will be either a source of pleasure or of regret; that is, if I live twenty years, and for life I have really a very strong predilection; not from Shakspeare's fearfully beautiful passage, 'Ay, but to die and go we know not whither,' but from the hope that my life may be serviceable to my family, and happy to myself; if it be the longer life the better, existence will be delightful, and anticipation glorious. The idea of meeting a different fate in another world is enough to overthrow every atheistical doctrine. The very dreadful trials under which virtue so often labors must surely be only trials. Patience will withstand the pressure, and faith will lead to hope. Religion soothes every wound, and makes the bed of death a couch of felicity. Make the contrast yourself: look at the warrior, the hypocrite, and the libertine, in their last moments, and reflection must strengthen every virtuous resolution. May I, however, practice what I preach. Let me have £200 a year and the comforts of domestic life, and my ambition aspires not further.

"Most sincerely yours,
"ROBERT SOUTHEY."

To G. C. Bedford, Esq.

"March 16, 1793.

"I am now sitting without fire in a cold day, waiting for Wynn to go upon the Isis, 'silver-slippered queen,' as Warton calls her; the epithet may be classical, but it certainly is ridiculous. Of all poetical figures, the prosopopœia is that most likely to be adopted by a savage nation, and which adds most ornament, but not to composition; but, in the name of common sense, what appropriate idea does 'silver-slippered' convey? Homer's Χρυσοπέδιλος* probably alludes to some well-known statue so habited. Nature is a much better guide than antiquity.

"Wednesday.

"On the water I went yesterday, in a little skiff, which the least deviation from the balance would overset. To manage two oars and yet unable to handle one!† My first setting off was curious. I did not step exactly in the middle; the boat tilted up, and a large barge from which I embarked alone saved me from a good ducking; my arm, however, got completely wet. I tugged at the oar very much like a bear in a boat; or, if you can conceive any thing more awkward, liken me to it, and you will have a better simile. . . . . When I walk over these streets, what various recollections throng upon me! what scenes fancy delineates from the hour when Alfred first marked it as the seat of learning! Bacon's study is demolished, so I shall never have the honor of being killed by its fall. Before my window Latimer and Ridley were burned, and there is not even a stone to mark the place where a monument should be erected to religious liberty. . . . . I have walked over the ruins of Godstow Nunnery with sensations such as the site of Troy or Carthage would inspire: a spot so famed by our minstrels, so celebrated by tradition, and so memorable in the annals of legendary, yet romantic truth. Poor Rosamond! some unskillful impostor has painted an epitaph upon the chapel wall, evidently within this century. The precise spot where she lies is forgotten, and the traces are still visible of a subterranean passage—perhaps the scene of many a deed of darkness; but we should suppose the best. Surely, among the tribe who

* "'Αργυρόπεζα" would have been nearer the mark. Warton was imitating Milton, who uses the term "tinsel-slippered."

† My father used to say he learned two things only at Oxford, to row and to swim.

were secluded from the world, there may have been some whose motives were good among so many victims of compulsion and injustice. Do you recollect Richardson's plan for Protestant nunneries?* To monastic foundations I have little attachment; but were the colleges ever to be reformed (and reformation will not come before it is wanted), I would have a little more of the discipline kept up. Temperance is much wanted; the waters of Helicon are far too much polluted by the wine of Bacchus ever to produce any effect. With respect to its superiors, Oxford only exhibits waste of wigs and want of wisdom; with respect to under-graduates, every species of abandoned excess. As for me, I regard myself too much to run into the vices so common and so destructive. I have not yet been drunk, nor mean to be so. What use can be made of a collegiate life I wish to make; but, in the midst of all, when I look back to Rousseau, and compare myself either with his Emilius or the real pupil of Madame Brulenck, I feel ashamed and humbled at the comparison. Never shall child of mine enter a public school or a university. Perhaps I may not be able so well to instruct him in logic or languages, but I can at least preserve him from vice.

"Yours sincerely,

"ROBERT SOUTHEY."

To Charles Collins, Esq.

"Ledbury, Herefordshire; Easter Sunday, 1793.

"Had I, my dear Collins, the pen of Rousseau, I would attempt to describe the various scenes which have presented themselves to me, and the various emotions occasioned by them. On Wednesday morning, about eight o'clock, we sallied forth. My traveling equipage consisted of my diary, writing-book, pen, ink, silk handkerchief, and Milton's Defense. We reached Woodstock to breakfast, where I was delighted with reading the Nottingham address for peace. Perhaps you will call it stupidity which made me pass the very walls of Blenheim without turning from the road to behold the ducal palace: perhaps it was so; but it was the stupidity of a democratic philosopher who had appointed a day in summer for the purpose. . . . . Evesham Abbey detained me some time: it was here where Edward defeated and slew Simon de Montfort. Often did I wish for your pencil, for never did I behold so beautiful a pile of ruins. I have seen the abbeys of Battle and Malmsbury, but this is a complete specimen of the simple Gothic: a tower, quite complete, fronts the church, whose roof is drooping down, and admits through the chasm the streaming light; the high, pointed window frames, where the high grass waves to the lonely breeze; and that beautiful moss, which at once ornaments and carpets the monastic pile, rapt me to other years. I recalled the savage sons of superstition, I heard the deep-toned mass, and the chanted prayer for those that fell in fight; but fancy soon recurred to a more enchanting scene—'The Blind Beggar of Bethnal Green and his Daughter:' you know how intimately connected with this now moldering scene that ballad is. Over this abbey I could detain you, Collins, forever, so many, so various are the reveries it caused. We reached Worcester to dinner the second day. . . . . Here we stayed three days; and I rode with Mr. Severn to Kidderminster, with intent to breakfast at ——, but all the family were out. We returned by Bewdley. There is an old mansion, once Lord Herbert's, now moldering away, in so romantic a situation, that I soon lost myself in dreams of days of yore—the tapestried room—the listed fight—the vassal-filled hall—the hospitable fire—the old baron and his young daughter: these formed a most delightful day-dream. How horrid it is to wake into common life from these scenes! at a moment when you are transported to happier times to descend to realities! Could these visions last forever! Yesterday we walked twenty-five miles over Malvern Hills to Ledbury, to Seward's brothers. Here I am before breakfast, and how soon to be interrupted I know not. Believe me, I shall return reluctantly to Oxford. These last ten days seem like years to look back—so crowded with different pictures. . . . . This peripatetic philosophy pleases me more and more; the twenty-six miles I walked yesterday neither fatigued me then nor now. Who, in the name of common sense, would travel stewed in a leathern box when they have legs, and those none of the shortest, fit for use? What scene can be more calculated to expand the soul than the sight of Nature, in all her loveliest works? We must walk over Scotland: it will be an adventure to delight us all the remainder of our lives. We will wander over the hills of Morven, and mark the driving blast, perchance bestrodden by the spirit of Ossian."

On his return to Baliol he writes to another friend thus characteristically, affording a curious picture of his own mind at this time.

"April 4, 1793.

"MY DEAR GROSVENOR,

"My philosophy, which has so long been of a kind peculiar to myself—neither of the school of Plato, Aristotle, Westminster, nor the Miller—is at length settled: I am become a peripatetic philosopher. Far, however, from adopting the tenets of any self-sufficient cynic or puzzling sophist, my sentiments will be found more enlivened by the brilliant colors of fancy, nature, and Rousseau than the positive dogmas of the Stagirite or the metaphysical refinements of his antagonist. I aspire not to the honorary titles of subtle disputant or divine doctor. I wish to found no school, to drive no scholars mad. Ideas rise up with the scenes I view; some pass away

* "Considering the condition of single women in the middle classes, it is not speaking too strongly to assert that the establishment of Protestant nunneries upon a wide plan and liberal scale would be the greatest benefit that could possibly be conferred upon these kingdoms. The name, indeed, is deservedly obnoxious, for nunneries, such as they exist in Roman Catholic countries, and such as at this time are being re-established in this, are connected with the worst corruptions of popery, being only nurseries of superstition and of misery."—*Southey's Colloquies*, vol. i., p. 338.

with the momentary glance, some are engraved upon the tablet of memory, and some impressed upon the heart. You have told me what philosophy is not, and I can give you a little more information upon the subject. It is not reading Johannes Secundus because he may have some poetical lines; it is not wearing the hair undressed, in opposition to custom, perhaps (this I feel the severity of, and blush for); it is not rejecting Lucan lest he should vitiate the taste, and reading without fear what may corrupt the heart; it is not clapped on with a wig, or communicated by the fashionable hand of the barber. It had nothing to do with Watson when he burned his books; it does not sit upon a wool-sack; honor can not bestow it, persecution can not take it away. It illumined the prison of Socrates, but fled the triumph of Octavius: it shrank from the savage murderer, Constantine; it dignified the tent of Julian. It has no particular love for colleges; in crowds it is alone, in solitude most engaged; it renders life agreeable, and death enviable. . . . . I have lately read the 'Man of Feeling:' if you have never yet read it, do now, from my recommendation; few works have ever pleased me so painfully or so much. It is very strange that man should be delighted with the highest pain that can be produced. I even begin to think that both pain and pleasure exist only in idea. But this must not be affirmed; the first twinge of the toothache, or retrospective glance, will undeceive me with a vengeance.

"Purity of mind is something like snow, best in the shade. Gibraltar is on a rock, but it would be imprudent to defy her enemies, and call them to the charge. My heart is equally easy of impression with Rousseau, and perhaps more tenacious of it. Refinement I adore, but to me the highest delicacy appears so intimately connected with it, that the union is like body and soul."

And again, a few weeks afterward, he says, in reference to some observations which had been made as to his not sufficiently cultivating his abilities: "Wynn accuses me of want of ambition; the accusation gave me great pleasure. He wants me to wish distinction, and to seek it. I want it not, I wish it not. The abilities which Nature gave me, which Fashion has not cramped, and which Vanity often magnifies, are never neglected. I will cultivate them with diligence, but only for my friends. If I can bring myself sometimes to their remembrance, I have attained the ne plus ultra of my ambition."*

The early part of the long vacation was spent in an excursion into Herefordshire to visit a college friend. "Like the Wandering Jew," he writes from thence, "you see I am here, and there, and every where; now tramping it to Worcester, now peripateticating it to Cambridge, and now an equestrian in the land of cider, traversing the shores of the Wye, and riding listlessly over the spot where Ariconium stood, walking above the dusty tombs of my progenitors in the Cathedral."†

* To G. C. Bedford, May 6, 1793.

† To Grosvenor C. Bedford, July 31, 1793.

In the following month (August) he went to visit his old schoolfellow and constant correspondent, Mr. Grosvenor Bedford, who then resided with his parent at Brixton Causeway, four miles on the Surrey side of the metropolis; and there, the day after completing his nineteenth year, he resumed, and in six weeks completed, his poem of Joan of Arc, the subject of which had been previously suggested to him in conversation with Mr. Bedford, and of which he had then written above three hundred lines. In one of the prefaces to the collected edition of his poems, he says, "My progress would not have been so rapid had it not been for the opportunity of retirement which I enjoyed there, and the encouragement I received. Tranquil, indeed, the place was, for the neighborhood did not extend beyond half a dozen families, and the London style and habits of life had not obtained among them. Uncle Toby might have enjoyed his rood and a half of ground there, and not have had it known. A fore-court separated the house from the foot-path and the road in front; behind these was a large and well-stocked garden, with other spacious premises, in which utility and ornament were in some degree combined. At the extremity of the garden, and under the shade of four lofty Linden-trees, was a summer-house, looking on an ornamented grass-plat, and fitted up as a conveniently habitable room. That summer-house was allotted to me, and there my mornings were passed at the desk."

Three months were most happily spent here in various amusements and occupations, of which writing Joan of Arc was the chief; but the poetical bow was not always bent; a war of extermination was carried on against the wasps, which abounded in unwonted numbers, and which they exercised their skill in shooting with horse-pistols loaded with sand, the only sort of sporting, I have heard my father say, he ever attempted.

The following amusing letter was written soon after this visit.

To Grosvenor Charles Bedford, Esq.

"Bristol, Oct. 26, 1793.

"Never talk to me of obstinacy, for, contrary to all the dictates of sound sense, long custom, and inclination, I have spoiled a sheet of paper by cutting it to the shape of your fancy. Accuse me not of irascibility, for I wrote to you ten days back, and, though you have never vouchsafed me an answer, am now writing with all the mildness and goodness of a philosopher.

"Call me Job, for I am without clothes, expecting my baggage from day to day; and much as I fear its loss unrepining, own I am modest in assuming no merit for all these good qualities. Know then, most indolent of mortals, that my baggage is not yet arrived, that I am fearful of its safety, and yet less troubled than all the rest of the family, who cry out loudly upon my puppet-show dress, and desire I will write to inquire concerning it. . . . .

"Now I am much inclined to fill this sheet, and that with verse, but I will punish myself to torment you: you shall have half a prose letter. The college bells are dinning the king's proclamation in my ear, the linings of my breeches are torn, you are silent, and all this makes me talkative and angrily communicative; so that, had you merited it, you would have received such a letter—so philosophic, poetical, grave, erudite, amusing, instructive, elegant, simple, delightful, simplex munditiis—in short, *το αγαθον και το αριστον, το βελτιστον*—such a letter, Grosvenor, full of odes, elegiacs, epistles, monodramas, comodramas, tragodramas, all sorts of dramas, though I have not tasted spirits to-day. Don't think me drunk, for if I am, 'tis with sobriety; and I certainly feel most seriously disposed to be soberly nonsensical. Now you wish I would dispose my folly to a short series; which sentence if you comprehend, you will do more than I can. You must not be surprised at nonsense, for I have been reading the history of philosophy, the ideas of Plato, the logic of Aristotle, and the heterogeneous dogmas of Pythagoras, Antisthenes, Zeno, Epicurus, and Pyrrho, till I have metaphysicized away all my senses, and so you are the better for it. . . . .

"Now good-night! Egregious nonsense, execrably written, is all you merit. O my clothes! O Joan!"*

"Sunday morning.

"Now, my friend, whether it be from the day itself, from the dull weather, or from the dream of last night, I know not, but I am a little more serious than when I laid down the pen. My baggage makes me very uneasy: the loss of what is intrinsically worth only the price of the paper would be more than ever I should find time, or perhaps ability, to repair; and even supposing some rascal should get them and publish them, I should be more vexed than at the utter loss. Do write immediately. I direct to you, that you may have this the sooner. Inform me when you receive it, and with what direction. It is almost a fortnight since I left Brixton, and I am equipped in such old shirts, stockings, and shoes, as have been long cast off, and have lost all this time, in which I should have transcribed half of Joan. . . . .

"Of the various sects that once adorned the republic of Athens, to me that of Epicurus, while it maintained its original purity, appears most consonant to human reason. I am not speaking of his metaphysics and atomary system; they are (as all cosmogonies must be) ridiculous; but of that system of ethics and pleasure combined, which he taught in the garden. When the philosopher declared that the ultimate design of life is happiness, and happiness consists in virtue, he laid the foundation of a system which might have benefited mankind. His life was the most temperate, his manner the most affable, displaying that urbanity which can not fail of attracting esteem. Plotinus, a man memorable for corrupting philosophy, was in favor with Gallienus, with whose imperial qualifications you are well acquainted: the enthusiast requested his *royal highness* would give him a ruined city in Campania, which he might rebuild and people with philosophers, governed by the laws of Plato, and from whom the city should be called Platonopolis. Gallienus, who was himself an elegant scholar, was pleased with the plan, but his friends dissuaded him from the experiment. The design would certainly have proved impracticable in that declining and degenerate age—most probably in any age. New visionary enthusiasts would have been continually arising, fresh sects formed, and each would have been divided and subdivided till all was anarchy. Yet I can not help wishing the experiment had been tried; it could not have been productive of evil, and we might, at this period, have received instruction from the history of Platonopolis. Under the Antonines or under Julian the request would have been granted: despotism is perhaps a blessing under such men. . . . . I could rhapsodize most delightfully upon this subject; plan out my city—her palaces, her hovels—all simplex munditiis (my favorite quotation); but if you were with me, Southeyopolis would soon be divided into two sects: while I should be governing with Plato (correcting a few of Plato's absurdities with some of my own), and almost deifying Alcæus, Lucan, and Milton, you (as visionary as myself) would be dreaming of Utopian kings possessed of the virtue of the Antonines, regulated by peers every one of whom should be a Falkland, and by a popular assembly where every man should unite the integrity of a Cato, the eloquence of a Demosthenes, and the loyalty of a Jacobite.

"Yours most sincerely,

"R. S."

For some reason which does not appear, he did not reside during the following term at Balliol, and the latter part of the year was consequently passed at Bristol at Miss Tyler's. Some extracts from his letters will sufficiently illustrate this period.

"For once in my life I rejoiced that Grosvenor Bedford's paper was short, and his letter at the end. To suppose that I felt otherwise than grieved and indignant at the fate of the unfortunate Queen of France was supposing me a brute, and to request an avowal of what I felt implied a suspicion that I did not feel. You seemed glad, when arguments against the system of republicanism had failed, to grasp at the crimes of wretches who call themselves Republicans, and stir up my feelings against my judgment."*

To another of his Westminster friends at Christ Church he writes: "Remember me to Wynn. . . . I have much for his perusal. Perhaps all my writings are owing to my acquaintance with him; he saw the first, and I knew the value of his praise too much to despise it. Wynn will like many parts of my Joan, but he will shake his head at the subject, and with propriety, if I had designed it for publication; but as the amuse-

* The first MS. of Joan of Arc was in his baggage.

* Oct. 29, 1793.

ment of my leisure, I heeded no laws but those of inclination. He will be better pleased to hear I have waded through the task of correcting and expunging my literary rubbish. There is something very vain in thus writing of myself, but I know that the regard which Wynn entertains for me, while he sees the vanity, will make him pleased with the intelligence."*

Soon afterward he again refers to the then all-engrossing topic of the day—the French Revolution, the heinous enormities of which were beginning a little to disturb his democratic views. "I am sick of this world, and discontented with every one in it. The murder of Brissot has completely harrowed up my faculties, and I begin to believe that virtue can only aspire to content in obscurity; for happiness is out of the question. I look round the world, and every where find the same mournful spectacle—the strong tyrannizing over the weak, man and beast. The same depravity pervades the whole creation; oppression is triumphant every where, and the only difference is, that it acts in Turkey through the anger of a grand seignior, in France of a revolutionary tribunal, and in England of a prime minister. There is no place for virtue. Seneca was a visionary philosopher; even in the deserts of Arabia, the strongest will be the happiest, and the same rule holds good in Europe and in Abyssinia. Here are you and I theorizing upon principles we can never practice, and wasting our time and youth—you in scribbling parchments, and I in spoiling quires with poetry. I am ready to quarrel with my friends for not making me a carpenter, and with myself for devoting myself to pursuits certainly unimportant, and of no real utility either to myself or to others."†

In a letter to another friend, Horace Bedford, that heavy depression which the objectless nature of his life at this time brought upon him is painfully shown.

"I read and write till my eyes ache, and still find time hanging as heavy round my neck as the stone round the neck of a drowning dog. . . . Nineteen years have elapsed since I set sail upon the ocean of life, in an ill-provided boat; the vessel weathered many a storm, and I took every distant cloud for land. Still pushing for the Fortunate Islands, I discovered that they existed not for me, and that, like others wiser and better than myself, I must be content to wander about and never gain the port. Nineteen years! certainly a fourth part of my life; perhaps how great a part; and yet I have been of no service to society. Why, the clown who scares crows for twopence a day is a more useful member of society; he preserves the bread which I eat in idleness. . . . . Yesterday is just one year since I entered my name in the vice-chancellor's book. It is a year of which I would wish to forget the transactions, could I only remember their effects. My mind has been very much expanded; my hopes, I trust, extinguished; so adieu to hope and fear, but not to folly."‡

* To Charles Collins, Esq., Bristol, Oct. 30, 1793.
† To Grosvenor Bedford, Nov. 11, 1793. ‡ Nov. 3, 1793.

To Horace Walpole Bedford, Esq.

(With verses.)

"College Green, Bristol, Nov. 13, 1793.

* * * * * * *

"I lay down Leonidas to go on with your letter. It has ever been a favorite poem with me. I have read it, perhaps, more frequently than any other composition, and always with renewed pleasure: it possesses not the "thoughts that breathe and words that burn," but there is a something very different from those strong efforts of imagination, that please the judgment and feed the fancy without moving the heart. The interest I feel in the poem is, perhaps, chiefly owing to the subject, certainly the noblest ever undertaken. It needs no argument to prove this assertion.

"Milton is above comparison, and stands alone as much from the singularity of the subject as the excellence of the diction: there remain Homer, Virgil, Lucan, Statius, S. Italicus, and V. Flaccus, among the ancients. I recollect no others, and among their subjects you will find none so interesting as the self-devoted Leonidas.

"Among the moderns we know Ariosto, Tasso, Camoens, Voltaire, and our own immortal Spenser; the other Italian authors in this line, and the Spanish ones, I know not. Indeed, that period of history upon which Glover's epics are founded is the grandest ever yet displayed. A constellation of such men never honored mankind at any other time, or, at least, never were called into the energy of action. Leonidas and his immortal band—Æschylus, Themistocles, and Aristides the perfect republican—even the satellites of Xerxes were dignified by Artemisia and the injured Spartan, Demaratus. To look back into the page of history—to be present at Thermopylæ, at Salamis, Platæa—to hear the songs of Æschylus and the lessons of Aristides—and then behold what Greece is—how fallen even below contempt—is one of the most miserable reflections the classic mind can endure. What a republic! what a province!

"If this world did but contain ten thousand people of both sexes visionary as myself, how delightfully would we repeople Greece and turn out the Moslem. I would turn Crusader, and make a pilgrimage to Parnassus at the head of my republicans (N.B., only lawful head), and there reinstate the Muses in their original splendor. We would build a temple to Eleutherian Jove from the quarries of Paros—replant the grove of Academus—ay, and the garden of Epicurus, where your brother and I would commence teachers; yes, your brother; for if he would not comb out the powder and fling away the poultice to embark in such an expedition, he deserves to be made a German elector or a West India planter. Charles Collins should occupy the chair of Plato, and hold forth to the Societas Scientium Literariorum Studiosorum (not unaptly styled the 'Society of Knowing Ones'); and we would actually send for —— to represent Euclid. Now, could I lay down my whole plan—build my house in the prettiest Doric style—

plant out the garden like Wolmer's, and imagine just such a family to walk in it, when here comes a rascal by crying 'Hare skins and rabbit skins,' and my poor house, which was built in the air, falls to pieces, and leaves me, like most visionary projectors, staring on disappointment. * * * * * * * * * * When we meet at Oxford, which I hope we shall in January, there are a hundred things better communicated in conversation than by correspondence. I have no object of pursuit in life but to fill the passing hour and fit myself for death; beyond these views I have nothing. To be of service to my friends would be serving myself most essentially; and there are few enterprises, however hazardous and however romantic, in which I would not willingly engage.

"It was the favorite intention of Cowley to retire with books to a cottage in America, and seek that happiness in solitude which he could not find in society. My asylum there would be sought for different reasons (and no prospect in life gives me half the pleasure this visionary one affords). I should be pleased to reside in a country where men's abilities would insure respect; where society was upon a proper footing, and man was considered as more valuable than money; and where I could till the earth, and provide by honest industry the meat which my wife would dress with pleasing care—redeunt spectacula mane—reason comes with the end of the paper.

"Yours most sincerely,

"R. Southey."

To a proposal from Mr. Grosvenor Bedford to join with him in some publication, something, I suppose, after the manner of the Flagellant, he replies:

"Your plan of a general satire I am ready to partake when you please. Pope, Swift, and Atterbury, you know, once attempted it, but malevolence intruded into the design, and Martin Scriblerus bore too strong a resemblance to Woodward. Swift's part is more leveled at follies than at vice: establish the empire of justice, and vice and folly will be annihilated together. Draw out your plan and send it me, if you have resolution for so arduous a task; you know mine.

"I have plans lying by me enough for many years or many lives. Yours, however, I shall be glad to engage in. Whether it be the devil or not, I know not, but my pen delights in lashing vice and folly."*

The following letters will conclude the year. In the latter one we have a curious picture of the marvelous industry with which he must have followed his poetical pursuits.

To Grosvenor C. Bedford, Esq.

"Bath, Dec. 14, 1793.

"The gentleman who brings this letter must occupy a few lines of it. His name is Lovel. I know him but very little personally, though long by report: you must already see he is eccentric. Perhaps I do wrong in giving him this, but I wish your opinion of him. Those who are superficially acquainted with him feel wonder; those who know him, love. This character I hear. He is on the point of marrying a young woman with whom I spent great part of my younger years. We were bred up together, I may almost say, and that period was the happiest of my life. Mr. Lovel has very great abilities: he writes well; in short, I wish his acquaintance myself; and, as his stay in town is very short, you will forgive the introduction. Perhaps you may rank him with Duppa, and, supposing excellence to be at 100, Duppa is certainly much above 50. Now, my dear Grosvenor, I doubt I am acting improperly; it was enough to introduce myself so rudely; but abilities always claim respect, and that Lovel has these I think very certain. Characters, if anyways marked, are well worth studying; and a young man of two-and-twenty, who has been his own master since fifteen, and who owes all his knowledge to himself, is so far a respectable character. My knowledge of him, I again repeat, is very confined. His intended bride I look upon as almost a sister, and one should know one's brother-in-law. . . . .

"What is to become of me at ordination, Heaven only knows! After keeping the strait path so long, the Test Act will be a stumbling-block to honesty; so chance and Providence must take care of that, and I will fortify myself against chance. The wants of man are so very few that they must be attainable somewhere, and, whether here or in America, matters little. I have long learned to look upon the world as my country.

"Now, if you are in the mood for a reverie, fancy only me in America; imagine my ground uncultivated since the creation, and see me wielding the ax, now to cut down the tree, and now the snakes that nestled in it. Then see me grubbing up the roots, and building a nice, snug little dairy with them: three rooms in my cottage, and my only companion some poor negro whom I have bought on purpose to emancipate. After a hard day's toil, see me sleep upon rushes, and, in very bad weather, take out my casette and write to you, for you shall positively write to me in America. Do not imagine I shall leave rhyming or philosophizing; so thus your friend will realize the romance of Cowley, and even outdo the seclusion of Rousseau; till at last comes an ill-looking Indian with a tomahawk, and scalps me—a most melancholy proof that society is very bad, and that I shall have done very little to improve it! So vanity, vanity will come from my lips, and poor Southey will either be cooked for a Cherokee, or oysterized by a tiger.

"I have finished transcribing Joan, and bound her in marble paper with green ribbon, and now am about copying all my remainables to carry to Oxford. Thence once more a clear field, and then another epic poem, and then another, and so on, till Truth shall write on my tomb, 'Here lies an odd mortal, whose life only benefited the paper manufacturers, and whose death will only hurt the post-office.'

* Nov. 22, 1793.

"Do send my great-coat, &c. My distresses are so great that I want words to express the inconvenience I suffer. So, as breakfast is not yet ready (it is almost nine o'clock), you shall have an ode to my great-coat. Excellent subject, excellent trifler—or blockhead, say you; but, Bedford, I must either be too trifling or too serious; the first can do no harm, and I know the last does no good. So come forth, my book of Epistles."

To Horace Bedford, Esq.

"Dec. 22, 1793.

"I have accomplished a most arduous task, transcribing all my verses that appear worth the trouble, except letters. Of these I took one list, another of my pile of stuff and nonsense, and a third of what I have burned and lost. Upon an average, 10,000 verses are burned and lost, the same number preserved, and 15,000 worthless. Consider that all my letters* are excluded, and you may judge what waste of paper I have occasioned. Three years yet remain before I can become anyways settled in life, and during that interval my object must be to pass each hour in employment. The million would say I must study divinity; the bishops would give me folios to peruse, little dreaming that to me every blade of grass and every atom of matter is worth all the Fathers. I can bear a retrospect; but when I look forward to taking orders, a thousand dreadful ideas crowd at once upon my mind. Oh, Horace, my views in life are surely very humble; I ask but honest independence, and that will never be my lot. . . . . .

"I have many epistolary themes in embryo. Your brother's next will probably be upon the advantages of long noses, and the recent service mine accomplished in time of need. Philosophy and folly take me by turns. I spent three hours one night last week in cleaving an immense wedge of old oaken timber without ax, hatchet, or wedges; the chopper was one instrument, one piece of wood wedged another, and a third made the hammer. Shad† liked it as well as myself, so we finished the job and fatigued ourselves. I amused myself, after writing your letter, with taking profiles; to-day I shall dignify my own and Shad's with pasteboard, marbled border, and a bow of green ribbon, to hang up in my collection room. . . . . The more I see of this strange world, the more I am convinced that society requires desperate remedies. The friends I have (and you know me to be cautious in choosing them), are many of them struggling with obstacles, which never could happen were man what Nature intended him. A torrent of ideas bursts into my mind when I reflect upon this subject. In the hours of sanguine expectation these reveries are agreeable, but more frequently the visions of futurity are dark and gloomy, and the only ray that enlivens the scene beams on America. You see I must fly from thought: to-day I begin Cowper's Homer, and write an ode; to-morrow read and write something else."

* Many of his early letters are written in verse, often on four sides of folio paper.

† A servant of his aunt's, Miss Tyler.

CHAPTER II.

OPINIONS, POLITICAL AND RELIGIOUS—SCHEMES OF FUTURE LIFE—FIRST ACQUAINTANCE WITH MR. COLERIDGE—PANTISOCRACY—QUARREL WITH MISS TYLER—LETTER TO THOMAS SOUTHEY.—A.D. 1794.

So passed the close of 1793. At the latter end of the following January my father was again in residence at Baliol. Before, however, we come to the events of the year, it is necessary to make a few preliminary remarks.

The expenses of my father's education, both at school and college, had been defrayed by his uncle, the Rev. Herbert Hill, at that time chaplain to the British Factory at Lisbon, whom he so touchingly addresses in the Dedication to the "Colloquies:"

"O friend! O more than father! whom I found
Forbearing always, always kind; to whom
No gratitude can speak the debt I owe."

And the kindness with which this was done had been the more perfectly judicious, as, although it had been both wished and hoped that my father would take holy orders, his uncle had never even hinted to him that he was educating him with that view. Other friends, however, had not shown the same judgment, and he had up to this time considered himself as "destined for the Church"—a prospect to which he had never reconciled himself, and which now began to weigh heavily upon him.

It is not to be concealed or denied that the state of my father's mind with respect to religion, and more especially with respect to the doctrines of the Church of England, was very different in very early life from the opinions and feelings which he held in the maturity of his later years. Neither is this much to be wondered at when we remember the sort of "bringing up" he had received, the state of society at that time, and the peculiar constitution of his own mind. His aunt, Miss Tyler, although possessing many good qualities, could hardly be said to have been a religiously-minded person. He had been removed from one school to another, undergoing "many of those sad changes through which a gentle spirit has to pass in this uneasy and disordered world;"* and he has said himself, doubtless from his own experience, that such schools are "unfavorable to devotional feelings, and destructive to devotional habits; that nothing which is not intentionally profane can be more irreligious than the forms of worship which are observed there; and that at no time has a schoolboy's life afforded any encouragement, any inducement, or any opportunity for devotion."† It must also be borne in mind that the aspect of the Church in this country at that time, as it presented itself to those who did not look below

* Life of Cowper, vol. i., p. 6. † Ibid., p. 12.

the surface, was very different from that which it now presents. A cloud, as it were, hung over it; if it had not our unhappy divisions, it had not, also, the spur to exertion, and the sort of spiritual freshness, which the storms of those dissensions have infused into it—good coming out of evil, as it so often does in the course of God's providence.

It is not so strange, therefore, that he should have entertained an invincible repugnance to taking holy orders. Enthusiastic and visionary in the extreme, imbued strongly with those political views* which rarely fail to produce lax and dangerous views in religion, as his uncle quietly observes in one of his letters to him—"I knew what your politics were, and therefore had reason to suspect what your religion might be"—viewing the Church only as she appeared in the lives and preaching of many of her unworthy, many of her cold and indolent ministers; never directed to those studies which would probably have solved his doubts and settled his opinions, and unfortified by an acquaintance with "that portion of the Church's history, the knowledge of which," as he himself says, "if early inculcated, might arm the young heart against the pestilent errors of these distempered times,"† it is little to be wondered at if he fell into some of these errors.

His opinions at this time were somewhat unsettled, although they soon took the form of Unitarianism, from which point they seem gradually to have ascended, without any abrupt transition, as the troubles of life increased his devotional feelings, and the study of religious authors informed his better judgment, until they finally settled down into a strong attachment to the doctrines of the Church of England. For the present he felt he could not assent to those doctrines, and therefore, although no man could possibly have been more willing to labor perseveringly and industriously for a livelihood, he began to feel much anxiety and distress of mind as to his future prospects, and to make several fruitless attempts to find some suitable profession.

These several projects are best narrated by himself:

"Once more am I settled at Baliol, once more among my friends, alternately studying and philosophizing, railing at collegiate folly, and enjoying rational society. My prospects in life are totally altered. I am resolved to come out Æsculapius secundus. . . . . Our society at Baliol continues the same in number. The freshmen of the term are not estimable (as Duppa says), and we are enough with the three Corpus men, who generally join us. The fiddle with one string is gone, and its place supplied with a harpsichord in Burnett's room. Lightfoot stil melodizes on the flute, and, had I but a Jews harp, the concert would be complete . . . . On Friday next my anatomical studies begin; they must be pursued with attention. Apollo has hitherto only received my devotion as the deity of poets; I must now address him as a physician. I could allege many reasons for my preference of physic. Some disagreeable circumstances must attend the study, but they are more than counterbalanced by the expansion it gives the mind, and the opportunities it affords of doing good. Chemistry I must also attend: of this study I have always been fond, and it is now necessary to pursue it with care."*

And again, a few days after, he writes to Mr. Grosvenor Bedford: "I purpose studying physic: innumerable and insuperable objections appeared to divinity: surely the profession I have chosen affords at least as many opportunities of benefiting mankind. . . . . In this country, a liberal education precludes the man of no fortune from independence in the humbler lines of life: he may either turn soldier, or embrace one of three professions, in all of which there is too much quackery. . . . . Very soon shall I commence my anatomical and chemical studies. When well grounded in these, I hope to study under Cruikshank to perfect myself in anatomy, attend the clinical lectures, and then commence—Doctor Southey!!!"

He accordingly attended, for some little time, the anatomy school, and the lectures of the medical professors, but he soon abandoned the idea as hastily as he had adopted it; partly from being unable to overcome his disgust to a dissecting-room, and partly because the love of literary pursuits was so strong within him, that, without his being altogether aware of it at the time, it prevented his applying his mind sufficiently to the requisite studies. His inclinations pointed ever to literature as the needle to the north; and however he might resolve, and however temporary circumstances led him for some years to attempt other objects and to frame other plans, an *invisible arm* seemed to draw him away from them, and place him in that path which he was finally destined to pursue, for which he had been fitted by Providence, and in which he was to find happiness, distinction, and permanent usefulness both to his country and to his kind.

Among other schemes which at this time crossed his mind was the possibility of selling the reversion of some property which he conceived he should inherit from his uncle, John Southey, of Taunton; and he now requests his friend, Mr. Grosvenor Bedford, to make some inquiries at Doctors Commons on the subject. "The information you may there receive," he writes, "will perhaps have some weight in my scale of destiny: it rests partly on the will of John Cannon Southey, who died in 1760. Hope and fear have almost lost their influence over m . If my reversion can be sold for any comfortable independence, I am sure you would advise me

* In the following passage, written with reference to the times of Charles I., my father has evidently in view the causes of his own early Republican bias: "And, at the same time, many of the higher classes had imbibed from their classical studies prejudices in favor of a popular government, which were as congenial to the generous temper of inexperienced youth as they are inconsistent with sound knowledge and mature judgment."—*Book of the Church*, vol. ii., p. 356.

† Book of the Church; Preface, p. 1.

* To Horace Bedford, Esq., Jan. 24, 1794.

to seize happiness with mediocrity than lose it in waiting for affluence. My wishes are not above mediocrity. . . . . Every day do I repine at the education that taught me to handle a lexicon instead of a hammer, and destined me for one of the drones of society. Add to this, that had I a sufficiency in independence, I have every reason to expect happiness. The most pleasing visions of domestic life would be realized. . . . . When I think on this topic, it is rather to cool myself with philosophy than to indulge in speculation. Twenty is young for a Stoic, you will say; but they have been years of experience and observation. . . . . They have shown me that happiness is attainable; but, withal, taught me by repeated disappointments never to build on so sandy a foundation. It will be all the same a hundred years hence, is a vulgar adage which has often consoled me. Now do I execrate a declamation which I must make. O for emancipation from these useless forms, this useless life, these haunts of intolerance, vice, and folly!"*

Respecting the reversion here mentioned no satisfactory information could be obtained, and he next turned his thoughts toward obtaining some official employment in London. "You know my objection to orders," he writes to Mr. Grosvenor Bedford, "and the obstacles to any other profession: it is now my wish to be in the same office with you. . . . . Do, my dear Grosvenor, give me some information upon this topic. I speak to you without apologizing; you will serve me if you can, and tell me if you can not: it would be a great object to be in the same office with you. In this plan of life, the only difficulty is obtaining such a place, and for this my hopes rest on Wynn and you. In case of success, I shall joyfully bid adieu to Oxford, settle myself in some economical way of life, and, when I know my situation, unite myself to a woman whom I have long esteemed as a sister, and for whom I now indulge a warmer sentiment. . . . . Write to me soon. I am sanguine in my expectations if you can procure my admission. Promotion is a secondary concern, though of that I have hopes. My pen will be my chief dependence. In this situation, where a small income relieves from want, interest will urge me to write, but independence secures me from writing so as to injure my reputation. Even the prospect of settling honestly in life has relieved my mind from a load of anxiety.

"In this plan of life every thing appears within the bounds of probability; the hours devoted to official attendance, even if entirely taken up by business, would pass with the idea that I was doing my duty and honestly earning my subsistence. If they should not be fully occupied, I can pursue my own studies; and should I be fortunate enough to be in the same office with you, it would be equally agreeable to both. What situation can be pleasanter than that which places me with all my dearest friends?"†

* May 11, 1794.

† May 28, 1794.

In reply to this, Mr. Bedford urges upon him all the objections to which such a situation would be liable, and begs him to reconsider his determination with respect to taking holy orders, probably thinking that a little time might calm his feelings and settle his opinions. His arguments, however, were of no avail. My father repeats his determination not to enter the Church, and continues: "Is it better that I should suffer inconvenience myself, or let my friends suffer it for me? Is six hours' misery to be preferred to wretchedness of the whole twenty-four? . . . . I have only one alternative—some such situation, or emigration. It is not the sally of a momentary fancy that says this; either in six months I fix myself in some honest way of living, or I quit my country, my friends, and every fondest hope I indulge forever."

But, before many steps had been taken in the matter, an obstacle appeared which had not previously occurred to my father's mind, and which at once put a stop to all further anticipations of the kind. It was evident that, before an official appointment of any kind, however trifling, could be procured, inquiry would be made at Oxford respecting his character and conduct; and, his political opinions once known, all chances of success would be destroyed. His Republican views were so strong and so freely expressed, that there was no possibility of any inquiry being made that would not place an insurmountable obstacle to his obtaining any employment under a Tory ministry. This being once suggested by a friend, was so apparent, that the scheme was as quickly abandoned as it had been hastily and eagerly conceived.*

"I think ——'s objection is a very strong one," he writes: "my opinions are very well known. I would have them so; Nature never meant me for a negative character: I can neither be good nor bad, happy nor miserable, by halves. You know me to be neither captious nor quarrelsome, yet I doubt whether the quiet, harmless situation I hoped for were proper for me: it certainly, by imposing a prudential silence, would have sullied my integrity. I think I see you smile, and your imagination turns to a strait waistcoat and Moorfields. Aussi bien.

"Some think him wondrous wise,
And some believe him mad."†

In the midst of his disappointment at the failure of these plans, upon which he seems to have set his hopes somewhat strongly, his first acquaintance commenced with Mr. Coleridge, and from this sprang a train of circumstances fraught with much importance to the after lives of both.

Mr. Coleridge was at this time an under-graduate of Jesus College, Cambridge, where he had entered in February, 1791, and he had already given proofs both of his great talents and his eccentricities. In the summer of that year he had gained Sir William Brown's gold medal for the Greek ode. It was on the slave trade, and its poetic force and originality were, as he said

* June 1, 1794.

† To Grosvenor Bedford, Esq., June 25, 1794.

himself, much beyond the language in which they were conveyed. In the winter of 1792–3 he had stood for the University (Craven) scholarship with Dr. Keats, the late head master of Eton, Mr. Bethell, of Yorkshire, and Bishop Butler, who was the successful candidate. In 1793 he had written without success for the Greek ode on astronomy, a translation of which is among my father's minor poems. In the latter part of this year, "in a moment of despondency and vexation of spirit, occasioned principally by some debts, not amounting to £100, he suddenly left his college and went to London," and there enlisted as a private in the 15th Light Dragoons, under an assumed name bearing his own initials. In this situation, than which he could not, by possibility, have chosen one more incongruous to all his habits and feelings, he remained until the following April, when the termination of his military career was brought about by a chance recognition in the street. His family were apprised of his situation; and, after some difficulty, he was duly discharged on the 10th of April, 1794, at Hounslow.*

In the following June Mr. Coleridge went to Oxford, on a visit to an old schoolfellow; and, being accidentally introduced to my father, an intimacy quickly sprung up between them, hastened by the similarity of the views they then held, both on the subjects of religion and politics. Each seems to have been mutually taken with the other. Coleridge was seized with the most lively admiration of my father's person and conversation; my father's impression of him is well told by himself. "Allen is with us daily, and his friend from Cambridge, Coleridge, whose poems you will oblige me by subscribing to, either at Hookham's or Edwards's. He is of most uncommon merit—of the strongest genius, the clearest judgment, the best heart. My friend he already is, and must hereafter be yours. It is, I fear, impossible to keep him till you come, but my efforts shall not be wanting."†

We have seen that in one or two of his early letters my father speaks of emigration and America as having entered his mind, and the failure of the plans I have just mentioned now caused him to turn his thoughts more decidedly in that direction, and the result was a scheme of emigration, to which those who conceived it gave the euphonious name of "Pantisocracy." This idea, it appears, was first originated by Mr. Coleridge and one or two of his friends, and he mentioned it to my father on becoming acquainted with him at Oxford. Their plan was to collect as many brother adventurers as they could, and to establish a community in the New World upon the most thoroughly social basis. Land was to be purchased with their common contributions, and to be cultivated by their common labor. Each was to have his portion of work assigned him; and they calculated that a large part of their time would still remain for social converse and literary pursuits. The females of the party—for all were to be married men—were to cook and perform all domestic offices; and having even gone so far as to plan the architecture of their cottages and the form of their settlement, they had pictured as pleasant a Utopia as ever entered an ardent mind.

The persons who at first entered into the scheme were my father; Robert Lovell, the son of a wealthy Quaker, who married one of the Misses Fricker; George Burnett, a fellow-collegian from Somersetshire; Robert Allen, then at Corpus Christi College; and Edmund Seward, of a Herefordshire family, also a fellow-collegian, for whom my father entertained the sincerest affection and esteem.

Seward, however, did not long continue to approve of the plan; his opinions were more moderate than those of his friends, although he was inclined to hold democratic views, and he was strongly attached to the doctrines of the Church of England, in which he intended to take orders. His letters on the subject of Pantisocracy are indicative of a very thoughtful and pious mind, and he expresses much regret that he should at first have given any encouragement to a scheme which he soon saw must fail, if attempted to be carried out.

He perceived that the two chief movers, my father and Mr. Coleridge, were passing through a period of feverish enthusiasm which could not last; and he especially expresses his fear that the views on religious subjects held by the party generally were not sufficiently fixed and practical, and that discussions and differences of opinion on these points would probably arise, which, more than on any other, would tend to destroy that perfect peace and unanimity they so fondly hoped to establish.

These apprehensions, however, were not participated in by the rest of the party. Mr. Coleridge quitted Oxford for a pedestrian tour in Wales; and from Gloucester he writes his *first* letter to my father: "You are averse," he says, "to gratitudinarian flourishes, else would I talk about hospitality, attention, &c., &c.; however, as I must not thank you, I will thank my stars. Verily, Southey, I like not Oxford, nor the inhabitants of it. I would say thou art a nightingale among owls; but thou art so songless and heavy toward night that I will rather liken thee to the matin lark; thy *nest* is in a blighted cornfield, where the sleepy poppy nods its red-cowled head, and the weak-eyed mole plies his dark work, but thy soaring is even unto heaven. Or let me add (for my appetite for similes is truly canine at this moment), that as the Italian nobles their new-fashioned doors, so thou dost make the adamantine gate of Democracy turn on its golden hinges to most sweet music."*

The long vacation having commenced, my father went down to his aunt at Bath, and from thence writes as follows:

* Coleridge's Biographia Literaria. Biographical Supplement, vol. ii., p. 336, 337.

† To Grosvenor Bedford, Esq., June 12, 1794.

* July 6, 1794.

To Grosvenor C. Bedford, Esq.

"Bath, July 20, 1794.

"Grosvenor, I believe nearly three weeks have elapsed since your last letter at Oxford damped my breakfast with disappointment. To see you at all times would be a source of much pleasure; but I should have been particularly glad to have introduced you to Allen and Coleridge; they shared in my disappointment, but that part of human unhappiness is not alleviated by partition. Coleridge is now walking over Wales. You have seen a specimen of Allen's poetry, but never of his friend's; take these; they are the only ones I can show, and were written on the wainscot of the inn at Ross, which was once the dwelling-house of Kyrle."

[Here follow the well-known lines to "The Man of Ross."]

"Admire the verses, Grosvenor, and pity that mind that wrote them from its genuine feelings. 'Tis my intention soon to join him in Wales, then proceed to Edmund Seward, seriously to arrange with him the best mode of settling in America. Yesterday I took my proposals for publishing Joan of Arc to the printer; should the publication be any ways successful, it will carry me over, and get me some few acres, a spade, and a plow. My brother Thomas will gladly go with us, and perhaps two or three more of my most intimate friends. In this country I must either sacrifice happiness or integrity: but when we meet I will explain my notions more fully.

"I shall not reside next Michaelmas at Oxford, because the time will be better employed in correcting Joan and overlooking the press. If I get fifty copies subscribed for by that time. . . . . Grosvenor, I shall inscribe Joan of Arc to you, unless you are afraid to have your name prefixed to a work that breathes some sentiments not perfectly in unison with court principles. Corrections will take up some time, for the poem shall go into the world handsomely: it will be my legacy to this country, and may, perhaps, preserve my memory in it. Many of my friends will blame me for so bold a step, but as many encourage me; and I want to raise money enough to settle myself across the Atlantic. If I have leisure to write there, my stock of imagery will be much increased. . . . . My proposals will be printed this evening. I remain here till to-morrow morning, for the sake of carrying some to Bristol. Methinks my name will look well in print. I expect a host of petty critics will buzz about my ears, but I must brush them off. You know what the poem was at Brixton; when well corrected, I fear not its success.

"I have a linen coat making, much like yours; 'tis destined for much service. Burnett ambulated to Bristol with me from Oxford; he is a worthy fellow, whom I greatly esteem. We have a wild Welshman, red hot from the mountains, at Baliol, who would please and amuse you much. He is perfectly ignorant of the world, but with all the honest, warm feelings of nature, a good head, and a good heart. Lightfoot is A.B.; old Baliol Coll. has lost its best inhabitants in him and Seward; Allen, too, resides only six weeks longer in the University; so it would be a melancholy place for me, were I to visit it again for residence. My tutor will much wonder at seeing my name;* but, as Thomas Howe is half a Democrat, he will be pleased. What miracle could illuminate him, I know not; but he surprised me much by declaiming against the war, praising America, and asserting the right of every country to model its own form of government. This was followed by, 'Mr. Southey, you won't learn any thing by my lectures, sir; so, if you have any studies of your own, you had better pursue them.' You may suppose I thankfully accepted the offer. Let me hear from you soon. You promised me some verses.

"Sincerely yours,

"ROBERT SOUTHEY.

"P.S.—How are the wasps this year? My dog eats flies voraciously, and hunts wasps for the same purpose. If he catches them, I fear he will follow poor Hyder.† I saved him twice to-day from swallowing them like oysters."

The Pantisocratic scheme seemed now to flourish; all were full of eager anticipation. "Every thing smiles upon me," says my father; "my mother is fully convinced of the propriety of our resolution; she admires the plan; she goes with us. Never did so delightful a prospect of happiness open upon my view before; to go with all I love; to go with all my friends, except your family and Wynn; to live with them in the most agreeable and most honorable employment; to eat the fruits I have raised, and see every face happy around me; my mother sheltered in her declining years from the anxieties which have pursued her; my brothers educated to be useful and virtuous."‡

In the course of this month (August), Mr. Coleridge, having returned from his excursion in Wales, came to Bristol; and my father, who was then at Bath, having gone over to meet him, introduced him to Robert Lovell, through whom, it appears, they both at this time became known to Mr. Cottle; and here, also, Mr. Coleridge first became acquainted with his future wife, Sarah Fricker, the eldest of the three sisters, one of whom was married to Robert Lovell, the other having been engaged for some time to my father. They were the daughters of Stephen Fricker, who had carried on a large manufactory of sugar-pans or molds at Westbury, near Bristol, and who, having fallen into difficulties in consequence of the stoppage of trade by the American war, had lately died, leaving his widow and six children wholly unprovided for.

During this visit to Bath, the tragedy entitled "The Fall of Robespierre"§ was written, the history of which is best explained by the following extract of a letter from my father to the late Henry Nelson Coleridge, Esq.: "It originated in sportive conversation at poor Lovell's, and

* As the author of Joan of Arc.

† A dog belonging to Mr. Bedford's father, which died from the sting of a wasp in the throat.

‡ To Grosvenor Bedford, Esq., August 1, 1794.

§ Printed in "Remains of S. T. Coleridge."

we agreed each to produce an act by the next evening—S. T. C. the first, I the second, and Lovell the third. S. T. C. brought part of his; I and Lovell, the whole of ours. But L.'s was not in keeping, and therefore I undertook to supply the third also by the following day. By that time S. T. C. had filled up his. A dedication to Mrs. Hannah More was concocted, and the notable performance was offered for sale to a bookseller in Bristol, who was too wise to buy it. Your uncle took the MSS. with him to Cambridge, and there rewrote the first act at leisure, and published it. My portion I never saw from the time it was written till the whole was before the world. It was written with newspapers before me as fast as newspapers could be put into blank verse. I have no desire to claim it now; but neither am I ashamed of it; and, if you think proper to print the whole, so be it."

From Bath Mr. Coleridge went up to London, apparently with the view of consulting some friend respecting the publication of the "Fall of Robespierre." From thence he thus writes to my father: "The day after my arrival I finished the first act: I transcribed it. The next morning Franklin (of Pembroke Coll., Cam., a *ci-devant Grecian* of our school—so we call the first boys) called on me, and persuaded me to go with him and breakfast with Dyer, author of 'The Complaints of the Poor,' 'A Subscription,' &c., &c. I went; explained our system. He was enraptured; pronounced it impregnable. He is intimate with Dr. Priestley, and doubts not that the doctor will join us. He showed me some poetry, and I showed him part of the first act, which I happened to have about me. He liked it hugely; it was 'a nail that would drive.' . . . . Every night I meet a most intelligent young man, who has spent the last five years of his life in America, and is lately come from thence as an agent to sell land. He was of our school. I had been kind to him: he remembers it, and comes regularly every evening to 'benefit by conversation,' he says. He says £2000 will do; that he doubts not we can contract for our passage under £400; that we shall buy the land a great deal cheaper when we arrive at America than we could do in England; 'or why,' he adds, 'am I sent over here?' That twelve men may *easily* clear 300 acres in four or five months; and that, for 600 dollars, a thousand acres may be cleared, and houses built on them. He recommends the Susquehanna, from its excessive beauty, and its security from hostile Indians. Every possible assistance will be given us: we may get credit for the land for ten years or more, as we settle upon it. That literary characters make *money* there, &c., &c. He never saw a *bison* in his life, but has heard of them: they are quite backward. The musquitoes are not so bad as our gnats; and, after you have been there a little while, they don't trouble you much."*

From London Mr. Coleridge returned to Cambridge, and writes from thence, immediately on his arrival, full of enthusiasm for the grand plan:

* September 6, 1794.

"Since I quitted this room, what and how important events have been evolved! America! Southey! Miss Fricker! . . . Pantisocracy! Oh! I shall have such a scheme of it! My head, my heart, are all alive. I have drawn up my arguments in battle array: they shall have the *tactitian* excellence of the mathematician, with the enthusiasm of the poet. The head shall be the mass; the heart, the fiery spirit that fills, informs, and agitates the whole." And then, in large letters, in all the zeal of Pantisocratic fraternity, he exclaims, "SHAD GOES WITH US: HE IS MY BROTHER!!" and, descending thence to less emphatical calligraphy, "I am longing to be with you: make Edith my sister. Surely, Southey, we shall be frendotatoi meta frendous—most friendly where all are friends. She must, therefore, be more emphatically my sister. . . . C——, the most excellent, the most Pantisocratic of aristocrats, has been laughing at me. Up I arose, terrible in reasoning. He fled from me, because 'he would not answer for his own sanity, sitting so near a madman of genius.' He told me that the strength of my imagination had intoxicated my reason, and that the acuteness of my reason had given a directing influence to my imagination. Four months ago the remark would not have been more elegant than just; now it is nothing."*

In the mean time, my father, though not quite so much carried away as Mr. Coleridge, was equally earnest in forwarding the plan as far as it could be forwarded without that which is the sinews of emigration as well as of war, and without which, though the "root of all evil," not even Pantisocracy could flourish. "In March we depart for America," he writes to his brother Thomas, then a midshipman on board the Aquilon frigate; "Lovell, his wife, brother, and two of his sisters; all the Frickers; my mother, Miss Peggy, and brothers; Heath, apothecary, &c.; G. Burnett, S. T. Coleridge, Robert Allen, and Robert Southey. Of so many we are certain, and expect more. Whatever knowledge of navigation you can obtain will be useful, as we shall be on the bank of a navigable river, and appoint you admiral of a cock-boat. . . .

"My aunt knows nothing as yet of my intended plan; it will surprise her, but not very agreeably. Every thing is in a very fair train, and all parties eager to embark. What do your common blue trowsers cost? Let me know, as I shall get two or three pairs for my working winter dress, and as many jackets, either blue or gray: so my wardrobe will consist of two good coats, two cloth jackets, four linen ones, six brown Holland pantaloons, and two nankeen ditto for dress. . . . .

"My mother says I am mad; if so, she is bit by me, for she wishes to go as much as I do. Coleridge was with us nearly five weeks, and made good use of his time. We preached Pantisocracy and Aspheteism every where. These, Tom, are two new words, the first signifying the equal government of all, and the other the gen-

* September 18, 1794.

eralization of individual property; words well understood in the city of Bristol. We are busy in getting our plan and principles ready to distribute privately. . . . . . The thoughts of the day and the visions of the night all center in America. Time lags heavily along till March, but we have done wonders since you left me. . . . . I hope to see you in January; it will then be time for you to take leave of the navy, and become acquainted with all our brethren, the Pantisocrats. You will have no objection to partake of a wedding dinner in February."* . . . .

By the middle of the following month the plan was still progressing favorably, but the main difficulty was beginning to occur to them. My father writes again to his brother: "Our plan is in great forwardness; nor do I see how it can be frustrated. We are now twenty-seven adventurers. Mr. Scott talks of joining us; and if so, five persons will accompany him. . . . . I wish I could speak as satisfactorily upon money matters. Money is a huge evil which we shall not long have to contend with. All well.

"Thank you for the hanger; keep it for me. You shall not remain longer in the navy than January. Live so long in hope; think of America! and remember that while you are only thinking of our plan, we are many of us active in forwarding it.

"Would you were with us! we talk often of you with regret. This Pantisocratic scheme has given me new life, new hope, new energy; all the faculties of my mind are dilated; I am weeding out the few lurking prejudices of habit, and looking forward to happiness. I wish I could transfuse some of my high hope and enthusiasm into you; it would warm you in the cold winter nights."† . . . .

Hitherto all had gone on pretty smoothly. The plan of emigration, as well as my father's engagement to marry, had been carefully concealed from his aunt, Miss Tyler, who, he was perfectly aware, would most violently oppose both; and now, when at last she became acquainted with his intention, her anger knew no bounds. The consequence can not be more graphically described than by himself.

To Thomas Southey.

"Bath, October 19, 1794.

"My dear Brother Admiral,

"Here's a row! here's a kick-up! here's a pretty commence! We have had a revolution in the College Green, and I have been turned out of doors in a wet night. Lo and behold, even like mine own brother, I was penniless. It was late in the evening; the wind blew and the rain fell, and I had walked from Bath in the morning. Luckily, my father's old great-coat was at Lovell's. I clapped it on, swallowed a glass of brandy, and set off. I met an old drunken man three miles off, and was obliged to drag him all the way to Bath, nine miles! Oh, Patience, Patience, thou hast often helped poor Robert Southey, but never didst thou stand him in more need than on Friday, the 17th of October, 1794.

"Well, Tom, here I am. My aunt has declared she will never see my face again, or open a letter of my writing. So be it; I do my duty, and will continue to do it, be the consequences what they may. You are unpleasantly situated; so is my mother; so were we all till this grand scheme of Pantisocracy flashed upon our minds, and now all is perfectly delightful.

"Open war—declared hostilities! the children are to come here on Wednesday, and I meet them at the Long Coach on that evening. My aunt abuses poor Lovell most unmercifully, and attributes the whole scheme to him; you know it was concerted between Burnett and me. But, of all the whole catalogue of enormities, nothing enrages my aunt so much as my intended marriage with Mrs. Lovell's sister Edith; this will hardly take place till we arrive in America; it rouses all the whole army of prejudices in my aunt's breast. Pride leads the fiery host, and a pretty kick-up they must make there.

"I expect some money in a few days, and then you shall not want; yet, as this is not *quite* certain, I can not authorize you to draw on me. Lovell is in London; he will return on Tuesday or Wednesday, and I hope will bring with him some ten or twenty pounds; he will likewise examine the wills at Doctors' Commons, and see what is to be done in the reversion way. Every thing is in the fairest train. Favell and Le Grice, two young Pantisocrats of nineteen, join us; they possess great genius and energy. I have seen neither of them, yet correspond with both. You may, perhaps, like this sonnet on the subject of our emigration, by Favell:

"'No more my visionary soul shall dwell
On joys that were; no more endure to weigh
The shame and anguish of the evil day,
Wisely forgetful! O'er the ocean swell,
Sublime of Hope, I seek the cottaged dell
Where Virtue calm with careless step may stray,
And, dancing to the moonlight roundelay,
The wizard passion wears a holy spell.
Eyes that have ached with anguish! ye shall weep
Tears of doubt-mingled joy, as those who start
From precipices of distemper'd sleep,
On which the fierce-eyed fiends their revels keep,
And see the rising sun, and feel it dart
New rays of pleasure trembling to the heart.'

"This is a very beautiful piece of poetry, and we may form a very fair opinion of Favell from it. Scott, a brother of your acquaintance, goes with us. So much for news relative to our private politics.

"This is the age of revolutions, and a huge one we have had on the College Green. Poor Shadrach is left there, in the burning fiery furnace of her displeasure, and a prime hot birth has he got of it: he saw me depart with astonishment. 'Why, sir, you be'nt going to Bath at this time of night, and in this weather! Do let me see you sometimes, and hear from you, and send for me when you are going.'

"We are all well, and all eager to depart. March will soon arrive, and I hope you will be with us before that time.

"Why should the man who acts from convic-

* September 20, 1794. † Bath, October 14, 1794.

tion of rectitude grieve because the prejudiced are offended? For me, I am fully possessed by the great cause to which I have devoted myself; my conduct has been open, sincere, and just; and, though the world were to scorn and neglect me, I should bear their contempt with calmness. Fare thee well.

"Yours in brotherly affection,

"ROBERT SOUTHEY."

It might have been hoped that this storm would have blown over, and that, when Pantisocracy had died a natural death, and the marriage had taken place, Miss Tyler's angry feelings might have softened down; but it was not so, and the aunt and nephew never met again!

One other incident belongs to the close of this year—the publication of a small volume of poems, the joint production of Mr. Lovell and my father. Many of them have never been republished. The motto prefixed to them was an appropriate one:

"Minuentur atræ
Carmine curae."

CHAPTER III.

PANTISOCRACY PROPOSED TO BE TRIED IN WALES—LETTERS TO MR. G. C. BEDFORD—DIFFICULTIES AND DISTRESSES—HISTORICAL LECTURES—DEATH OF EDMUND SEWARD—MR. COTTLE PURCHASES THE COPYRIGHT OF JOAN OF ARC—PANTISOCRACY ABANDONED—MISUNDERSTANDING WITH MR. COLERIDGE—LETTER TO MR. G. C. BEDFORD—MEETING WITH HIS UNCLE, MR. HILL—CONSENTS TO ACCOMPANY HIM TO LISBON—MARRIAGE—LETTERS TO MR. BEDFORD AND MR. COTTLE.—1794–1795.

MY father was now a homeless adventurer; conscious of great resources in himself, but not knowing how to bring them into use; full of hope and the most ardent aspirations, but surrounded with present wants and difficulties. America was still the haven of his hopes, and for a little while he indulged in the pleasing anticipation, "Would that March were over!" he writes at this time to Mr. Bedford. "Affection has one or two strong cords round my heart, and will try me painfully—you and Wynn! A little net-work must be broken here; that I mind not, but my mother does. My mind is full of futurity, and lovely is the prospect; I am now like a traveler crossing precipices to get home, but my foot shall not slip."*

The difficulty of raising sufficient funds for their purpose was now, however, becoming daily more and more evident; and it appears to have been next proposed by my father that the experiment of Pantisocracy should be first tried in some retired part of Wales, until some lucky turn of fortune should enable them to carry out their scheme of transatlantic social colonization. To this Mr. Coleridge at first strongly objects, and sees now more clearly the difficulties of the plan, which the roll of the Atlantic seemed to obscure from their sight. "For God's sake, my dear fellow," he writes in remonstrance to my father, "tell me what we are to gain by taking a Welsh farm? Remember the principles and proposed consequences of Pantisocracy, and reflect in what degree they are attainable by Coleridge, Southey, Lovell, Burnett, and Co., some five men *going partners* together! In the next place, supposing that we have found the preponderating utility of our aspheterizing in Wales, let us, by our speedy and united inquiries, discover the sum of money necessary. Whether such a farm, with so very large a house, is to be procured without launching our frail and unpiloted bark on a rough sea of anxieties. How much money will be necessary for *furnishing* so large a house. How much necessary for the maintenance of so large a family—eighteen people—for a year at least."

But the plan of going into Wales did not prosper any more than that of genuine Pantisocracy: the close of the year and the beginning of the next found matters still in the same unsatisfactory state. Mr. Coleridge had kept the Michaelmas Term at Cambridge—the last he kept; and, having gone from thence to London, remained there until early in the following January, when he returned to Bristol with my father, who had chanced to go up to town at that time.

The following letters will illustrate this period. In the latter one we have a vivid picture of the distresses and difficulties of his present position.

To Grosvenor C. Bedford, Esq.

"Bath, Jan. 5, 1795.

"MY DEAR GROSVENOR,

"If I were not very well acquainted with your disposition, I should apprehend, by your long silence, that you are offended with me. In one letter I spoke too warmly, but you know my affections are warm. I was sorry at having done so, and wrote to say so. The jolting of a rough cart over rugged roads is very apt to excite tumults in the intestinal canal; even so are the rubs of fortune prone to create gizzard grumblings of temper.

"Now, if you are not angry (and, on my soul, I believe you and anger to be perfectly heterogeneous), you will write to me very shortly; if you are, why, you must remain so for a fortnight: then, it is probable, I shall pass two days in London, on my way to Cambridge; and as one of them will be purely to be with you, if I do not remove all cause of complaint you have against Robert Southey, you shall punish him with your everlasting displeasure.

"From Horace, too, I hear nothing. Were I on the Alleghany Mountains, or buried in the wilds of Caernarvonshire, I could not have less intercourse with you. Perhaps you are weaning me, like a child. And now, Bedford, I shall shortly see G. S.,* if he be in London or at Trin-

* Oct. 19, 1794.

* A schoolfellow with whom he had once been very intimate.

ity. Two days in London: one with you, when I shall call on him; the other with some friends of Coleridge and correspondents of mine, admirable poets and Pantisocrats. How will G. S. receive me? is he altered? will he be reserved, and remember only our difference? or is there still the same goodness of heart in him as when we first met? I feel some little agitation at the thought. G. S. was the first person I ever met with who at all assimilated with my disposition. I was a physiognomist without knowing it. He was my *substance.* I loved him as a brother once: perhaps he is infected with *politesse;* is polite to all, and affectionate to none.

"Coleridge is a man who has every thing of ——— but his vices: he is what ——— would have been, had he given up that time to study which he consumed you know how lamentably.

"I will give you a little piece which I wrote, and which he corrected. 'Twas occasioned by the funeral of a pauper, without one person attending it.*

"I like this little poem, and there are few of mine of which I can say that.

"Bedford, I can sing eight songs: 1. The antique and exhilarating Bacchanalian, Back and Sides go Bare. 2. The Tragedy of the Mince-pie, or the Cruel Master Cook. 3. The Comical Jest of the Farthing Rush-light. 4. The Bloody Gardener's Cruelty. 5. The Godly Hymn of the Seven Good Joys of the Virgin Mary; being a Christmas Carol. 6. The Tragedy of the Beaver Hat; or, as newly amended, The Brunswick Bonnet; containing three apt Morals. 7. The Quaint Jest of the Three Crows. 8. The Life and Death of Johnny Bulan.

"Now I shall outdo Horace! . . . Farewell, and believe me always

"Your sincere and affectionate
"ROBERT SOUTHEY."

To Grosvenor C. Bedford, Esq.

"Bristol, Feb. 8, 1795.

"I have been reading the first four numbers of 'The Flagellant:' they are all I possess. My dearest Grosvenor, they have recalled past times forcibly to my mind, and I could almost weep at the retrospect. Why have I not written to you before? Because I could only have told you of uncertainty and suspense. There is nothing more to say now. The next six months will afford more variety of incidents. But, my dear Bedford, though you will not love me the less, you will shake your head, and lament the effects of what you call enthusiasm. Would to God that we agreed in sentiment, for then you could enter into the feelings of my heart, and hold me still dearer in your own.

"There is the strangest mixture of cloud and of sunshine! an outcast in the world! an adventurer! living by his wits! yet happy in the full conviction of rectitude, in integrity, and in the affection of a mild and lovely woman; at once the object of hatred and admiration; wondered at by all; hated by the aristocrats; the very oracle of my own party. Bedford! Bedford! mine are the principles of peace, of non-resistance; you can not burst our bonds of affection. Do not grieve that circumstances have made me thus; you ought to rejoice that your friend acts up to his principles, though you think them wrong.

"Coleridge is writing at the same table; our names are written in the book of destiny, on the same page.

"Grosvenor, I must put your brains in requisition. We are about to publish a magazine on a new plan. One of the prospectuses, when printed, will be forwarded to you. 'Tis our intention to say in the title-page, S. T. C. and R. S., Editors; and to admit nothing but what is good. A work of the kind must not be undertaken without a certainty of indemnification, and then it bids very fair to be lucrative, so the booksellers here tell us. To be called The Provincial Magazine, and published at Bristol if we settle here. We mean to make it the vehicle of all our poetry: will you not give us some essays, &c., &c.? We can undoubtedly make it the best thing of the kind ever published; so, Bedford, be very wise and very witty. Send us whole essays, hints, good things, &c., &c., and they shall cut a most respectable figure. The poetry will be printed so as to make a separate volume at the end of the year.

"What think you of this? I should say that the work will certainly express our sentiments, so expressed as never to offend; but, if truth spoken in the words of meekness be offense, we may not avoid it.

"I am in treaty with The Telegraph, and hope to be their correspondent. Hireling writer to a newspaper! 'Sdeath! 'tis an ugly title: but, *n'importe*, I shall write truth, and only truth. Have you seen, in Friday's Telegraph, a letter to Canning, signed Harrington? 'Twas the specimen of my prose.

"You will be melancholy at all this, Bedford; I am so at times, but what can I do? I could not enter the Church, nor had I finances to study physic; for public offices I am too notorious. I have not the gift of making shoes, nor the happy art of mending them. Education has unfitted me for trade, and I must, perforce, enter the muster-roll of authors."

"Monday morning.

"My days are disquieted, and the dreams of the night only retrace the past to bewilder me in vague visions of the future. America is still the place to which our ultimate views tend; but it will be years before we can go. As for Wales, it is not practicable. The point is, where can I best subsist? . . . London is certainly the place for all who, like me, are on the world. . . . . London must be the place. If I and Coleridge can only get a fixed salary of £100 a year between us, our own industry shall supply the rest. I will write up to 'The Telegraph:' they offered me a reporter's place, but nightly em-

* Here follows "The Pauper's Funeral," printed among my father's minor poems.

ployments are out of the question. My troublesome guest, called honesty, prevents my writing in The True Briton. God knows I want not to thrust myself forward as a partisan: peace and domestic life are the highest blessings I could implore. Enough! this state of suspense must soon be over: I am worn and wasted with anxiety, and, if not at rest in a short time, shall be disabled from exertion, and sink to a long repose. Poor Edith! Almighty God protect her!

"You can give me no advice, nor point out any line to pursue; but you can write to me, and tell me how you are, and of your friends. Let me hear from you as soon as possible: moralize, metaphysicize, pun, say good things, promise me some aid in the magazine, and shake hands with me as cordially by letter as when we parted in the Strand. I look over your letters, and find but little alteration of sentiment from the beginning of '92 to the end of '94. What a strange mass of matter is in mine during those periods! I mean to write my own life, and a most useful book it will be. You shall write the Paraleipomena; but do not condole too much over my mistaken principles, for such pity will create a mutiny in my sepulchred bones, and I shall break prison to argue with you, even from the grave. God love you! I think soon to be in London, if I can get a situation there: sometimes the prospect smiles upon me. I want but fifty pounds a year certain, and can trust myself for enough beyond that. . . . . . Fare you well, my dear Grosvenor! Have you been to court? quid Romæ facias? O thou republican aristocrat! thou man most worthy of republicanism! what hast thou to do with a laced coat, and a chapeau, and a bag wig, and a sword?

"Ah spirit pure
That error's mist had left thy purged eye!

* * * * * * *

"Peace be with you, and with all mankind, is the earnest hope of your

"R. S."

My father having ceased to reside at Oxford, and having no longer his aunt's house as a home, was compelled now to find some means of supporting himself; and Mr. Coleridge being in the same predicament, they determined upon giving each a course of public lectures. Mr. Coleridge selected political and moral subjects; my father, history, according to the following prospectus:

"Robert Southey, of Baliol College, Oxford, proposes to read a course of Historical Lectures, in the following order:

"1st. Introductory; on the Origin and Progress of Society.

"2d. Legislation of Solon and Lycurgus.

"3d. State of Greece from the Persian War to the Dissolution of the Achaian League.

"4th. Rise, Progress, and Decline of the Roman Empire.

"5th. Progress of Christianity.

"6th. Manners and Irruptions of the Northern Nations. Growth of the European States. Feudal System.

"7th. State of the Eastern Empire, to the Capture of Constantinople by the Turks; including the Rise and Progress of the Mohammedan Religion, and the Crusades.

"8th. History of Europe, to the Abdication of the Empire by Charles the Fifth.

"9th. History of Europe, to the Establishment of the Independence of Holland.

"10th. State of Europe, and more particularly of England, from the Accession of Charles the First to the Revolution in 1688.

"11th. Progress of the Northern States. History of Europe to the American War.

"12th. The American War.

"Tickets for the whole course, 10*s*. 6*d*., to be had of Mr. Cottle, bookseller, High Street."

Of these lectures I can find no trace among my father's papers. Mr. Cottle states that they were numerously attended, and "their composition greatly admired." My father thus alludes to them at the time in a letter to his brother Thomas: "I am giving a course of Historical Lectures at Bristol, teaching what is right by showing what is wrong; my company, of course, is sought by all who love good Republicans and odd characters. Coleridge and I are daily engaged. . . . . John Scott has got me a place of a guinea and a half per week, for writing in some new work called The Citizen, of what kind I know not, save that it accords with my principles. Of this I daily expect to hear more.

"If Coleridge and I can get £150 a year between us, we purpose marrying and retiring into the country, as our literary business can be carried on there, and practicing agriculture till we can raise money for America—still the grand object in view.

"So I have cut my cable, and am drifting on the ocean of life; the wind is fair, and the port of happiness, I hope, in view. It is possible that I may be called upon to publish my Historical Lectures; this I shall be unwilling to do, as they are only splendid declamation."*

The delivery of these lectures occupied several months; but the employment they furnished did not prevent occasional fits of despondency, although his naturally elastic mind soon shook them off. He seems to have purposed paying a visit to his friends at Brixton at this time, but it was not accomplished. To this he refers in the following curious letter:

To Grosvenor C. Bedford, Esq.

"May 27, 1795.

"My dear Grosvenor,

"You and Wynn could not more enjoy the idea of seeing me than I anticipated being with you; as for coming now, or fixing any particular time, it may not be. My mind, Bedford, is very languid; I dare not say I will go at any fixed period. If you knew the fearful anxiety with which I sometimes hide myself to avoid an invitation, you would perhaps pity, perhaps despise me. There is a very pleasant family here, lit-

* March 21, 1795.

erary and accomplished, that I have almost offended by never calling on. Coleridge is there three or four times in the course of the week; the effort to join in conversation is too painful to me, and the torpedo coldness of my *phizmahogany* has no right to chill the circle. By-the-by, my dear Grosvenor, if you know any artist about to paint a group of banditti, I shall be very fit to sit for a young cub of ferocity; I have put on the look at the glass so as sometimes to frighten myself. . . . .

"Well, but there is no difficulty in discovering the assiduities of affection; the eye is very eloquent, and women are well skilled in its language. I asked the question. Grosvenor, you will love your sister Edith. I look forward with feelings of delight that dim my eyes to the day when she will expect you, as her brother, to visit us—brown bread, wild Welsh raspberries—heigh-ho! this schoolboy anticipation follows us through life, and enjoyments uniformly disappoint expectation. * * * * * * * * * * * *

"Poetry softens the heart, Grosvenor. No man ever tagged rhyme without being the better for it. I write but little. The task of correcting Joan is a very great one; but as the plan is fundamentally bad, it is necessary the poetry should be good. The Convict, for which you asked, is not worth reading; I think of some time rewriting it. If I could be with you another eight weeks, I believe I should write another epic poem, so essential is it to be happily situated.

"I shall copy out what I have done of Madoc, and send you ere long; you will find more simplicity in it than in any of my pieces, and, of course, it is the best. I shall study three works to write it—the Bible, Homer, and Ossian. . . . .

"Some few weeks ago I was introduced to Mr. and Mrs. Perkins: they were on a visit, and I saw them frequently; he pleased me very much, for his mind was active and judicious, and benevolence was written in every feature of his face. I never saw a woman superior to her in mind, nor two people with a more rational affection for each other. On their quitting this place, they urged me to visit them at Bradford. A few days ago I was with my mother at Bath, and resolved to walk over to tea: it is but six miles distant, and the walk extremely beautiful. I got to Bradford, and inquiring for Mr. Perkins, was directed two miles in the country, to Freshford. My way lay by the side of the river; the hills around were well wooded, the evening calm and pleasant; it was quite May weather; and as I was alone, and beholding only what was beautiful, and looking on to a pleasant interview, I had relapsed into my old mood of feeling benevolently and keenly for all things. A man was sitting on the grass tying up his bundle, and of him I asked if I was right for Freshford; he told me he was going there. 'Does Mr. Perkins live there?' 'Yes; he buried his wife last Tuesday.' I was thunderstruck. 'Good God! I saw her but a few weeks ago.' 'Ay, sir, ten days ago she was as well as you are; but she is in Freshford church-yard now!'

"Grosvenor, I can not describe to you what I felt; the man thought I had lost a relation. It was with great difficulty I could resolve on proceeding to see him; however, I thought it a kind of duty, and went. Guess my delight on finding another Mr. Perkins, to whom I had been directed by mistake!

"You do not know what I suffered under the impression of her death, at the relief I felt at discovering the mistake. Strange selfishness! this man, too, had lost a wife, a young wife but lately married, whom perhaps he loved; and I —I rejoiced at his loss, because it was not my friend! yet, without this selfishness, man would be an animal below the orang outang. It is mortifying to analyze our noblest affections, and find them all bottomed on selfishness. I hear of thousands killed in battle — I read of the young, the virtuous, dying and think of them no more—when, if my very dog died, I should weep for him; if I lost you, I should feel a lasting affliction; if Edith were to die, I should follow her.

"I am dragged into a party of pleasure to-morrow* for two days. An hour's hanging would be luxury to me compared with these detestable schemes. Party of pleasure! Johnson never wrote a better tale than that of the Ethiopian king. Here is the fire at home, and a great chair, and yet I must be moving off for pleasure. Grosvenor, I will steal Cadman's† long pipe, chew opium, and learn to be happy with the least possible trouble.

"Coleridge's remembrances to you. He is applying the medicine of argument to my misanthropical system of indifference. It will not do; a strange dreariness of mind has seized me. I am indifferent to society, yet I feel my private attachments growing more and more powerful, and weep like a child when I think of an absent friend. God bless you."

A few weeks later he writes again in much affliction at the death of his friend Seward.

To Grosvenor C. Bedford, Esq.

"Bristol, June 15, 1795.

"Bedford—he is dead; my dear Edmund Seward! after six weeks' suffering.

"These, Grosvenor, are the losses that gradually wean us from life. May that man want consolation in his last hour who would rob the survivor of the belief that he shall again behold his friend! You know not, Grosvenor, how I loved poor Edmund: he taught me all that I have of good. When I went with him into Worcestershire, I was astonished at the general joy his return occasioned—the very dogs ran

* An account of this party of pleasure is given in Cottle's Reminiscences of Coleridge. Apparently the reality was not more agreeable than the anticipation.

† The name of a mutual acquaintance.

out to him. In that room where I have so often seen him, he now lies in his coffin!

"It is like a dream, the idea that he is dead—that his heart is cold—that he, whom but yesterday morning I thought and talked of as alive—as the friend I knew and loved—is dead! When these things come home to the heart, they palsy it. I am sick at heart; and, if I feel thus acutely, what must his sisters feel? what his poor old mother, whose life was wrapped up in Edmund? I have seen her look at him till the tears ran down her cheek.

"There is a strange vacancy in my heart. The sun shines as usual, but there is a blank in existence to me. I have lost a friend, and such a one! God bless you, my dear, dear Grosvenor! Write to me immediately. I will try, by assiduous employment, to get rid of very melancholy thoughts. I am continually dwelling on the days when we were together: there was a time when the sun never rose that I did not see Seward. It is very wrong to feel thus—it is unmanly. God bless you!

"Robert Southey.

"P.S.—I wrote to Edmund on receiving your last: my letter arrived the hour of his death, four o'clock on Wednesday last. Perhaps he remembered me at that hour.

"Grosvenor, I am a child; and all are children who fix their happiness on such a reptile as man: this great, this self-ennobled being called man, the next change of weather may blast him.

"There is another world where all these things will be amended.

"God help the man who survives all his friends."

The passionate grief to which this letter gave utterance did not pass lightly away. In the "Hymn to the Penates," first printed in 1796, he alludes touchingly to his dear friend departed; and the following very beautiful poem, which will be read with increased interest in connection with the subject which gave rise to it, was written four years later.

"THE DEAD FRIEND.

1.

"Not to the grave, not to the grave, my soul,
Descend to contemplate
The form that once was dear!
The spirit is not there
Which kindled that dead eye,
Which throbb'd in that cold heart,
Which in that motionless hand
Hath met thy friendly grasp.
The spirit is not there!
It is but lifeless, perishable flesh
That molders in the grave;
Earth, air, and water's ministering particles
Now to the elements
Resolved, their uses done.
Not to the grave, not to the grave, my soul,
Follow thy friend beloved,
The spirit is not there!

2.

"Often together have we talk'd of death;
How sweet it were to see
All doubtful things made clear;
How sweet it were with powers
Such as the Cherubim,
To view the depth of heaven!
O Edmund! thou hast first
Begun the travel of eternity!
I look upon the stars,
And think that thou art there,
Unfetter'd as the thought that follows thee.

3.

"And we have often said how sweet it were,
With unseen ministry of angel power,
To watch the friends we loved.
Edmund! we did not err!
Sure I have felt thy presence! Thou hast given
A birth to holy thought,
Hast kept me from the world unstain'd and pure.
Edmund! we did not err!
Our best affections here,
They are not like the toys of infancy;
The soul outgrows them not;
We do not cast them off;
Oh, if it could be so,
It were indeed a dreadful thing to die!

4.

"Not to the grave, not to the grave, my soul,
Follow thy friend beloved!
But in the lonely hour,
But in the evening walk,
Think that he companies thy solitude;
Think that he holds with thee
Mysterious intercourse;
And though remembrance wake a tear,
There will be joy in grief.

"*Westbury*, 1799."

In the midst of these griefs and perplexities, a bright spot showed itself in the laying of what I may call the foundation stone of my father's literary reputation.

His poem of Joan of Arc, as we have seen, had been written in the summer of 1793, and he had for some time ardently desired to publish it, but, for want of means, was unable to do so. Toward the close of the following year it had been announced for publication by subscription; but subscribers came slowly forward, and it seemed very doubtful whether a sufficient number could be obtained. Shortly afterward, his acquaintance with Mr. Cottle commenced. For the result I will quote his own words, as commemorating, in a very interesting manner, when he had almost arrived at the close of his literary career, that which may be called its commencement, and which was so important an epoch in his troubled early life.

"One evening I read to him part of the poem, without any thought of making a proposal concerning it, or expectation of receiving one. He, however, offered me fifty guineas for the copyright, and fifty copies for my subscribers, which was more than the list amounted to; and the offer was accepted as promptly as it was made. It can rarely happen that a young author should meet with a bookseller as inexperienced and as ardent as himself, and it would be still more extraordinary if such mutual indiscretion did not bring with it cause for regret to both. But this transaction was the commencement of an intimacy which has continued without the slightest shade of displeasure at any time on either side to the present day. At that time few books were printed in the country, and it was seldom, indeed, that a quarto volume issued from a provincial press. A font of new type was ordered for what was intended to be the handsomest book that Bristol had ever yet sent forth; and, when the paper arrived, and the printer was ready to commence his operations, nothing had been done toward preparing the poem for the press, except that a few verbal alterations had been made.

"I was not, however, without misgivings; and, when the first proof-sheet was brought me, the more glaring faults of the composition stared me in the face. But the sight of a well-printed page, which was to be set off with all the advantages that fine wove paper and hot pressing could impart, put me in spirits, and I went to work with good will. About half the first book was left in its original state; the rest of the poem was recast and recomposed while the printing went on. This occupied six months."*

In this work of correction my father was now occupied, having laid aside "Madoc," which had been commenced in the autumn of the previous year, for that purpose. Meantime the scheme of Pantisocracy was entirely abandoned, and the arrival from Lisbon of Mr. Hill changed the current of his thoughts. "My uncle is in England," he writes to Mr. Bedford: "I am in daily expectation of seeing him again. . . . . Grosvenor, when next I see you it will not be for a visit: I shall fix my residence near you to study the law! ! ! My uncle urges me to enter the Church; but the gate is perjury, and I am little disposed to pay so heavy a fine at the turnpike of orthodoxy. . . . . . On seeing my uncle, I shall communicate to him my intentions concerning the law. If he disapproves of them, I have to live where I can, and how I can, for fifteen months. I shall then be enabled to enter and marry. If he approves, why then, Grosvenor, my first business will be to write to you, and request you to procure me lodgings somewhere at Stockwell, or Newington, or any where as far from London, and as near your road, as possible. I can not take a house till my finances will suffer me to furnish it; and for this I depend upon my Madoc, to which, after Christmas, I shall apply with assiduity, always remembering John Doe and Richard Roe. And now will you permit me, in a volume of poems which go to the press to-morrow, to insert your 'Witch of Endor,' either with your name or initials, and to be corrector plenipotent? This is an office Coleridge and I mutually assume, and we both of us have sense enough, and taste enough, to be glad of mutual correction. His poems and mine will appear together; two volumes elegant as to type and hot-pressed paper, and for his, *meo periculo*, they will be of more various excellence* than any one volume this country has ever yet seen. I will rest all my pretensions to poetical taste on the truth of this assertion."†

It does not appear that this idea of publishing conjointly with Mr. Coleridge was carried into effect, probably owing to a temporary estrangement, which now took place between himself and my father, in consequence of the latter being the first to abandon the Pantisocratic scheme. This had greatly disturbed and excited Mr. Coleridge, who was by no means sparing in his reproaches, and manifested, by the vehemence of his language, that he must have felt for the time no common disappointment.

My father's next letter to Mr. Bedford gives an interesting sketch of the progress of his own mind.

To Grosvenor C. Bedford, Esq.

"Bath, October 1, 1795.

"I have been living over three years and a half in your letters, Grosvenor, with what variety of reflections you may imagine, from the date of the 'Flagellant,' through many a various plan! You asked Collins, when you first saw him after his residence at Oxford, if I was altered, and his 'No' gave you pleasure. I have been asking myself the same question, and, alas! in truth, must return the same answer. No, I am not altered. I am as warm-hearted and as open as ever. Experience never wasted her lessons on a less fit pupil; yet, Bedford, my mind is considerably expanded, my opinions are better grounded, and frequent self-conviction of error has taught me a sufficient degree of skepticism on all subjects to prevent confidence. The frequent and careful study of Godwin was of essential service. I read, and all but worshiped. I have since seen his fundamental error—that he theorizes for another state, not for the rule of conduct in the present. . . . . I can confute his principles, but all the good he has done me remains; 'tis a book I should one day like to read with you for our mutual improvement. When we have been neighbors six months, our opinions will accord—a bold prophecy, but it will be fulfilled.

"My poetical taste was much meliorated by Bowles, and the constant company of Coleridge. . . . . For religion, I can confute the Atheist, and baffle him with his own weapons; and can, at least, teach the Deist that the arguments in favor of Christianity are not to be despised; metaphysics I know enough to use them as defensive armor, and to deem them otherwise difficult trifles.

"You have made me neglect necessary business. I was busy with this huge work of mine when your letters tempted me, and gave me an appetite for the pen; somehow they have made me low-spirited, and I find a repletion of the lachrymal glands. Apropos: do kill some dozen men for me anatomically, any where except in the head or heart. Hang all wars! I am as much puzzled to carry on mine at Orleans as our admirable minister is to devise a plan for the next campaign. . . . . *Pardonnez moi!* my republican royalist! my philanthropic aristocrat.

"I am obliged to Nares for a very handsome review. It is my intention to write a tragedy;

* Preface to Joan of Arc, Collected Edition of the Poems, 1837.

† In one of Mr. Coleridge's letters to my father (Sept. 18, 1794), after some verbal criticism on several of his sonnets combined with much praise, he thus prefaces the quotation of one of his own: "I am almost ashamed to write the following, it is so inferior. Ashamed! no, Southey; God knows my heart. I am *delighted* to feel you superior to me in genius as in virtue." Here was an honorable rivalry of praise!

‡ August 22, 1795.

the subject from the Observer—the Portuguese accused before the Inquisition of incest and murder. Read the story.

"Madoc is to be the pillar of my reputation. How many a melancholy hour have I beguiled by writing poetry! * * * * * * * * * * * * *

"Friday, October 9.

"I found your letter on my arrival to-day. My uncle writes not to me, and I begin to think he is so displeased at my rejecting a good settlement, for the foolish prejudice I have against perjuring myself, that he gives me up. *Aussi bien!* so be it, any thing but this terrible suspense. Zounds, Grosvenor, suspense shall be the subject of my tragedy. Indeed, indeed, I have often the heartache. Can not you come to Bath for a week? I have so much to say to you, and I will never quit Edith: every day endears her to me. I am as melancholy here at Bath as you can imagine, and yet I am very little here—not two days in the week: the rest I pass with Cottle, that I may be near her. Cottle offered me his house in a letter which you shall see when we meet, and for which he will ever hold a high place in your heart. I bear a good face, and keep all uneasiness to myself: indeed, the port is in view, and I must not mind a little sickness on the voyage.

* * * * * * *

Bedford, I have beheld that very identical tiger. There's a grand hexameter for you!

"Bedford, I have beheld that very identical tiger who stopped the mail coach on the king's highway, not having the fear of *God* and the *king* before his eyes—no, nor of the *guard* and his *blunderbuss.* What a pity, Grosvenor, that that blunderbuss should be leveled at you! how it would have *struck* a Democrat! Never mind, 'tis only a *flash*, and you, like a fellow whose *uttermost upper grinder* is being torn out by the roots by a mutton-fisted barber, will *grin* and endure it.

"Gayety suits ill with me. The above extempore witticisms are as old as six o'clock Monday morning last, and noted down in my pocket-book for you.

"God bless you! Good night.

"Oct. 10.

"I visited Hannah More, at Cowslip Green, on Monday last, and seldom have I lived a pleasanter day. She knew my opinions, and treated them with a flattering deference. Her manners are mild, her information considerable, and her taste correct. There are five sisters, and each of them would be remarked in a mixed company. Of Lord Orford they spoke very handsomely, and gave me a better opinion of Wilberforce than I was accustomed to entertain. They pay for and direct the education of 1000 poor children; and for aristocracy, Hannah More is much such an aristocrat as a certain friend of mine.

* * * * * * *

"God love you, my dear friend!

"Robert Southey."

The long-expected and perhaps somewhat dreaded meeting with Mr. Hill soon took place; but there was no diminution of kindness on his part, notwithstanding the great disappointment he felt at his nephew's determination not to enter the Church, in which it would have been in his power immediately and effectually to have assisted him. He now seems to have given up all hope of prevailing upon him to change his resolution; and it was soon arranged that my father should accompany him to Lisbon for a few months, and then return to England, in order to qualify himself for entering the legal profession. Mr. Hill's object in this was partly to take him out of the arena of political discussion into which he had thrown himself by his lectures, and bring him round to more moderate views, and also to wean him, if possible, from what he considered an "imprudent attachment." In the former object he partly succeeded; in attempting to gain the latter, he had not understood my father's character. He was too deeply and sincerely attached to the object of his choice to be lightly turned from it; and the similarity of her worldly circumstances to his own would have made him consider it doubly dishonorable even to postpone the fulfillment of his engagement.

This matter, however, he does not appear to have entered into with his uncle. He consented to accompany him to Lisbon, and thus communicates his resolution to his constant correspondent:

To Grosvenor C. Bedford, Esq.

"Oct. 23, 1795.

"And where, Grosvenor, do you suppose the fates have condemned me for the next six months? to Spain and Portugal! Indeed, my heart is very heavy. I would have refused, but I was weary of incessantly refusing all my mother's wishes, and it is only one mode of wearing out a period that must be unpleasant to me any where.

"I now know neither when I go, nor where, except that we cross to Coruña, and thence by land to Lisbon. Cottle is delighted with the idea of a volume of travels. My Edith persuades me to go, and then weeps that I am going, though she would not permit me to stay. It is well that my mind is never unemployed. I have about 900 lines and half a preface yet to compose, and this I am resolved to finish by Wednesday night next. It is more than probable that I shall go in a fortnight.

"Then the advantageous possibility of being captured by the French, or the still more agreeable chance of going to Algiers. . . . Then to give my inside to the fishes on the road, and carry my outside to the bugs on my arrival; the luxury of sleeping with the mules, and if they should kick in the night. And to travel, Grosvenor, with a lonely heart! . . . When I am returned I shall be glad that I have been. The knowledge of two languages is worth acquiring, and perhaps the climate may agree with me, and counteract a certain habit of skeletonization, that, though I do not apprehend it will hasten me to the worms, will, if it continues, certainly cheat them of their supper. . . . We will write a good opera; my expedition will teach me the costume of Spain.

"By-the-by, I have made a discovery respecting the story of the 'Mysterious Mother.' Lord O. tells it of Tillotson: the story is printed in a work of Bishop Hall's, 1652; he heard it from Perkins (the clergyman whom Fuller calls an excellent chirurgeon at jointing a broken soul: he would pronounce the word 'damn' with such an emphasis as left a doleful echo in his auditors' ears a good while after. Warton-like, I must go on with Perkins, and give you an epigram. He was lame of the right hand: the Latin is as blunt as a good-humored joke need be:

"Dextera quantumvis fuerat tibi manca, docendi
Pollebas mirâ dexteritate tamen;

"Though Nature thee of thy *right* hand bereft,
Right well thou *writest* with thy hand that's *left:*

and all this in a parenthesis). Hall adds that he afterward discovered the story in two German authors, and that it really happened in Germany. If you have not had your transcription of the tragedy bound, there is a curious piece of information to annex to it. . . . I hope to become master of the two languages, and to procure some of the choicest authors; from their miscellanies and collections that I can not purchase, I shall transcribe the best or favorite pieces, and translate, for we have little literature of those parts, and these I shall request some person fond of poetry to point out, if I am fortunate enough to find one. *Mais hélas! J'en doute*, as well as you, and fear me I shall be friendless for six months!

"Grosvenor, I am not happy. When I get to bed, reflection comes with solitude, and I think of all the objections to the journey; it is right, however, to look at the white side of the shield. The Algerines, if they should take me, it might make a very pretty subject for a chapter in my Memoirs; but of this I am very sure, that my biographer would like it better than I should.

"Have you seen the 'Mœviad?' The poem is not equal to the former production of the same author, but the spirit of panegyric is more agreeable than that of satire, and I love the man for his lines to his own friends; there is an imitation of Otium Divos very eminently beautiful. Merry has been satirized too much and praised too much. . . . .

"I am in hopes that the absurd fashion of wearing powder has received its death-blow; the scarcity we are threatened with (and of which we have as yet experienced only a very slight earnest) renders it now highly criminal. I am glad you are without it. * * * * * * * * * * * * *

"God bless you!
"ROBERT SOUTHEY."

When the day was fixed for the travelers to depart, my father fixed that also for his wedding-day; and on the 14th of November, 1795, was united at Radclift church, Bristol, to Edith Fricker. Immediately after the ceremony they parted. My mother wore her wedding-ring hung round her neck, and preserved her maiden name until the report of the marriage had spread abroad. The following letters will explain these circumstances, and fill up the interval until his return:

To Grosvenor C. Bedford, Esq.

"Nov. 21, 1795. Nan Swithin near St. Columbs.

"Grosvenor, what should that necromancer deserve who could transpose our souls for half an hour, and make each the inhabitant of the other's tenement? There are so many curious avenues in mine, and so many closets in yours, of which you have never sent me the key.

"Here I am, in a huge and handsome mansion, not a finer room in the county of Cornwall than the one in which I write; and yet have I been silent, and retired into the secret cell of my own heart. This day week, Bedford! There is a something in the bare name that is now mine that wakens sentiments I know not how to describe: never did man stand at the altar with such strange feelings as I did. Can you, Grosvenor, by any effort of imagination, shadow out my emotion? . . . She returned the pressure of my hand, and we parted in silence. Zounds! what have I to do with supper!

"Nov. 22.

"I love writing, because to write to a dear friend is like escaping from prison. Grosvenor, my mind is confined here; there is no point of similarity between my present companions and myself. But, 'If I have freedom in,' &c.: you know the quotation.*

"This is a foul country: the tinmen inhabit the most agreeable part of it, for they live under ground. Above, it is most dreary—desolate. My *sans culotte*,† like Johnson's in Scotland, becomes a valuable piece of timber, and I a most dull and sullenly silent fellow; such effects has place! I wonder what Mr. Hoblyn thinks of me. He mentioned that he had seen my poems in the B. Critic. My uncle answered, 'It is more than I have.' Never had man so many relations so little calculated to inspire confidence. My character is open, even to a fault. Guess, Grosvenor, what a Kamtschatka climate it must be to freeze up the flow of my thoughts, which you have known more frisky that your spruce beer!

"My bones are very thinly cushioned with flesh, and the jolting over these rough roads has made them very troublesome. Bedford, they are at this moment uttering aristocracy, and I am silent. Two whole days was I imprisoned in stage-coaches, cold as a dog's nose, hungry, and such a sinking at the heart as you can little conceive. Should I be drowned on the way, or by

* "Stone walls do not a prison make,
Nor iron bars a cage
Minds innocent and quiet take
That for a hermitage.

"If I have freedom in my love,
And in my soul am free,
Angels alone, that soar above,
Enjoy such liberty."—*Lovelace's Poems.*

† His walking-stick.

any other means take possession of that house where anxiety never intrudes, there will be a strange page or two in your life of me.

"My Joan of Arc must by this time be printed: the first of next month it comes out. To me it looks like something that has concerned me, but from which my mind is now completely disengaged. The sight of pen and ink reminds me of it. You will little like some parts of it. For me, I am now satisfied with the poem, and care little for its success.

"You supped upon Godwin and oysters with Carlisle. Have you, then, read Godwin, and that with attention? Give me your thoughts upon his book; for, faulty as it is in many parts, there is a mass of truth in it that must make every man think. Godwin, as a man, is very contemptible. I am afraid that most public characters will ill endure examination in their private lives. To venture upon so large a theater, much vanity is necessary, and vanity is the bane of virtue—'tis a foul upas-tree, and no healing herb but withers beneath its shade: what, then, had I to do with publishing? This, Grosvenor, is a question to which I can give myself no self-satisfying solution. For my Joan of Arc there is an obvious reason; here I stand acquitted of any thing like vanity or presumption. Grosvenor, what motive created the F.? certainly it was not a bad one. . . . .

"The children in the next room are talking—a harpsichord not far distant annoys me grievously—but then there are a large company of rooks, and their croak is always in unison with what is going on in my thorax. I have a most foul pain suddenly seized me there. Grosvenor, if a man could but make pills of philosophy for the mind! but there is only one kind of pill that will cure mental disorders, and a man must be laboring under the worst before he can use that. . . . . I am waiting for the packet, and shall be here ten days. Direct to me at Miss Russell's, Falmouth: there I shall find your letters; and remember, that by writing you will give some pleasure to one who meets with very little. Farewell! Yours, R. S."

To Joseph Cottle, Esq.

"Falmouth, 1695.

"MY DEAR FRIEND,

"I have learned from Lovel the news from Bristol, public as well as private, and both of an interesting nature. My marriage is become public. You know my only motive for wishing it otherwise, and must know that its publicity can give me no concern. I have done my duty. Perhaps you may hardly think my motives for marrying at that time sufficiently strong. One, and that to me of great weight, I believe, was never mentioned to you. There might have arisen feelings of an unpleasant nature at the idea of receiving support from one not legally a husband; and (do not show this to Edith) should I perish by shipwreck or any other casualty, I have relations whose prejudices would then yield to the anguish of affection, and who would love, cherish, and yield all possible consolation to my widow. Of such an evil there is but a possibility; but against possibility it was my duty to guard. . . . . Farewell!

"Yours sincerely,

"ROBERT SOUTHEY."

To Grosvenor C. Bedford, Esq.

"29th Nov., 1795.

"Bedford, our summons arrived this morning, the vessel goes Tuesday, and when you receive this I shall be casting up my accounts with the fishes.

"Grosvenor, you have my will, if the ship founders, or any other chance sends me to supper. All my papers are yours: part are with my mother, and part with Edith. Relic worship is founded upon human feelings, and you will value them. There is little danger of accidents, but there can be no harm in these few lines. All my letters are at your disposal; and if I be drowned, do not you be surprised if I pay you a visit; for if permitted, and if it can be done without terrifying or any ways injuring you, I certainly will do it.

"But I shall visit you *in propriâ personâ* in the summer.

"Would you had been with me on the 14th! 'twas a melancholy day, yet mingled with such feelings!

"You will get a letter from Madrid—write you to Lisbon. I expect to find letters there, and this expectation will form the pleasantest thought I shall experience in my journey.

"I should like to find your Musæus at Bristol on my return. If you will direct it to Miss Fricker (heigh-ho! Grosvenor), at Mr. Cottle's, High Street, Bristol, he will convey it to her; and, I believe, next to receiving any thing from me, something for me and from my friend will be the most agreeable occurrence during my absence. I give you this direction, as it will be sure to reach her. Edith will be as a parlor boarder with the Miss Cottles (his sisters), two women of elegant and accomplished manners. The eldest lived as governess in Lord Derby's family a little while; and you will have some opinion of them when I say that they make even bigotry amiable. They are very religious, and the eldest (who is but twenty-three) wished me to read good books—the advice comes from the heart. She thinks very highly of me, but fancies me irreligious, because I attend no place of worship, and indulge speculations beyond reason.

"God bless and prosper you, and grant I may find you as happy on my arrival as I hope and expect to be. Yours sincerely,

"ROBERT SOUTHEY."

"Falmouth, Monday evening.

"Well, Grosvenor, here I am, waiting for a wind. Your letter arrived a few hours before me. . . . . Edith you will see, and know, and love; but her virtues are of the domestic order, and you will love her in proportion as you know her. I hate your daffydowndilly women, ay, and men too; the violet is ungaudy in the appearance, though a sweeter flower perfumes not the evening gale. 'Tis equally her wish to see you. Oh! Grosvenor, when I think of our winter evenings that will arrive, and then look at myself arrayed for a voyage in an inn parlor! I scarcely know whether the tear that starts into my eye proceeds from anticipated pleasure or present melancholy. I am never comfortable at an inn; boughten ospitalities are two ill-connected ideas. Grosvenor, I half shudder to think that a plank only will divide the husband of Edith from the unfathomed ocean! and, did I believe its efficacy, could burn a hecatomb to Neptune with as much devotion as ever burned or smoked in Phæacia. Farewell!

"ROBERT SOUTHEY."

CHAPTER IV.

LETTERS TO MR. LOVEL AND MR. BEDFORD FROM LISBON—RETURN TO ENGLAND—DEATH OF MR. LOVEL—LETTERS TO MR. BEDFORD—LITERARY EMPLOYMENTS AND INTENTIONS.—1796.

THE two following letters are the only ones written from Lisbon at this time that I shall lay before the reader. A series of descriptive letters, written during a subsequent and longer visit to that country, will appear in the next volume.

To Robert Lovel.

"Feb. 19, 1796.

"I have an invincible dislike to saying the same things in two different letters, and yet you must own it is no easy matter to write half a dozen different ones upon the same subject. I am at Lisbon, and therefore all my friends expect some account of Portugal; but it is not pleasant to reiterate terms of abuse, and continually to present to my own mind objects of filth and deformity. By way of improving your English cookery, take the Portuguese receipt for dressing rabbits. The spit is placed either above the fire, below the fire, by the side of the fire, or in the fire (this is when they have a spit, and that is little better than an iron skewer, for they *roast* meat in a *jug*, and *boil* it in a frying-pan); to know if it is done, they crack the joints with their fingers, and then lay it aside till it cools; then they seize the rabbit, tear it piecemeal with their fingers into rags, and fry it up with oil, garlic, and anise seed. I have attempted sausages made of nothing but garlic and anise seed. They cut off the rump of a bird always before they dress it, and neither prayers nor entreaties can save a woodcock from being drawn and quartered. R—— (who never got up till we were in sight of Corunna) lay in his bed studying what would be the best dinner when we landed; he at last fixed upon a leg of mutton, soles and oyster sauce, and toasted cheese, to the no small amusement of those who knew he could get neither, and to his no small disappointment when he sat down to a chicken fried in oil, and an omelet of oil and eggs. He leaped out of bed in the middle of his first night in Spain, in order to catch the fleas, who made it too hot for him.

Miss* remains in Lord Bute's stables in Madrid. She amused me on the road by devouring one pair of horse-hair socks, one tooth-brush, one comb, a pound of raisins, ditto of English beef, and one pair of shoes: Maber has as much reason to remember her. So you see Miss lived well upon the road. Tossed about as I have been by the convulsions of air, water, and earth, and enduring what I have from the want of the other element, I am in high health. My uncle and I never molest each other by our different principles. I used to work Maber sometimes, but here there is no one whom I am so intimate with, or with whom I wish intimacy. Here is as much visiting and as little society as you can wish, and a Bristol alderman may have his fill of good eating and drinking, yet is this metropolis supplied only from hand to mouth, and when the boats can not come from Alentejo, the markets are destitute: at this time there is no fuel to be bought! Barbary supplies them with corn, and that at so low a rate that the farmers do not think it worth while to bring their corn to market, so that the harvest of last year is not yet touched. They can not grind the Barbary corn in England: it is extremely hard, and the force and velocity of English mills reduce the husk as well as the grain to powder I learned all this from the vice-consul, who has written much to Lord Grenville on the subject, and proposed damping the corn previous to grinding it, so as to prevent the bran from pulverizing. Lord G. has even sent for grindstones to Lisbon, in hopes they might succeed better. It is melancholy to reflect on what a race possesses the fertile coasts of Barbary! Yet are these Portuguese not a degree above them. You may form some idea how things are managed in this country from the history of the present war. By treaty, the Portuguese were to furnish the English with a certain number of ships, or a certain sum of money; and the Spaniards with troops or money; the money was expected, but the secretary of state, Mello, argued that it was more politic to lay it out among their own countrymen, and make soldiers and sailors. The old boy's measures were vigorous. He sent for the general of one of the provinces, appointed him commander in Brazil, and ordered him to be ready at an hour's notice; but old Mello fell ill, and the general, after remaining three months at Lisbon (for during Mello's illness the other party managed affairs), found no more probability of departing than on the first day, and he accordingly sent for his furniture, wife, and family to Lisbon. Soon after they arrived the secretary recovered; every thing was hurried for the expedition, and the wife, family, and furniture sent home again. Mello fell ill again; every thing was at a stand, and the general once more called his family to Lisbon. The old fellow recovered, sent them all

* A favorite dog.

home again, put every thing in readiness, fell ill again, and died. The measures of the government have ever since been uniformly languid; and, though the stupid hounds sent ships to England and troops to Spain, they never believed themselves at war with France till the French took their ships at the mouth of the river!

"The meeting of the two courts at Badajos is supposed to have been political, and it was surmised that Spain meant to draw Portugal into an alliance with France: they, however, parted on bad terms. War with Spain is not improbable, and, if our minister knew how to conduct it, would amply repay the expenses of the execrable contest. The Spanish settlements could not resist a well-ordered expedition, and humanity would be benefited by the delivery of that country from so heavy a yoke. There is a very seditious Spaniard there now, preaching Atheism and Isocracy; one of Godwin's school; for Godwin has his pupils in Spain.

"I can see no paper here but the London Chronicle, and those every other day papers are good for nothing. Coleridge is at Birmingham, I hear; and I hear of his projected 'Watchman.' I send five letters by this post to Bristol, and two to London—a tolerable job for one who keeps no secretary. I shall send four by the Magician frigate, and four more by the next packet. This is pretty well, considering I read very hard, and spend every evening in company. . . . I know not why I have lost all relish for theatrical amusements, of which no one was once more fond. The round of company here is irksome to me, and a select circle of intimate friends is the *summum bonum* I propose to myself. I leave this country in April; and, when once I reach England, shall cross the seas no more. O the supercelestial delights of the road from Falmouth to Launceston! Yet I do believe that Christian, in the 'Pilgrim's Progress,' felt little more pleasure at his journey's end than I shall in traversing the lovely hills and plains of Cornwall. . . . . John Kett was of great service to me in Spain, and will return to England, where, as soon as I shall have pitched my tent, I purpose burning him a sacrifice to the household gods, and inurning his ashes with a suitable epitaph. Then shall *sans culotte* be hung upon the wall, and I will make a trophy of my traveling shoes and fur cap. I am now going out to dinner; then to see a procession; then to talk French; then to a huge assembly, from whence there is no returning before one o'clock. O midnight! midnight! when a man does murder thee, he ought at least to get something by it.

"Here are most excellent wines, which I do in no small degree enjoy: the best Port; Bucellas of exquisite quality; old Hock, an old gentleman for whom I have a very great esteem; Cape, and I have 'good hope' of getting some to-day; and Malmsey such as makes a man envy Clarence. * * * * * *
* * * * * * * *

"Farewell! Love to Mrs. L.

"ROBERT SOUTHEY."

To Grosvenor C. Bedford, Esq.

"Feb. 24, 1796, Lisbon, from which God grant me a speedy deliverance.

"I am bitterly disappointed at not finding 'The Flagellant' here, of which I sent my only copy to my uncle. It was my intention to have brought it home again with me. You see, Grosvenor, this relic is already become rare. Have you received the original Joan of Arc, written at Brixton, bound decently, &c.? I left it with Cottle, to send with your copy: he has the transcript of it himself, which he begged with most friendly devotion, and, I believe, values as much as a monk does the parings of his tutelary saint's great toe nail. Is not the preface a hodge-podge of inanity? I had written the beginning only before I quitted Bristol. The latter days of my residence there were occupied by concerns too nearly interesting to allow time for a collected mass of composition; and you will believe that, after quitting Edith on Sunday evening, I was little fit to write a preface on Monday morning. I never saw the whole of it together; and, I believe, after making a few hasty remarks on epic poems, I forgot to draw the conclusion for which only they were introduced. *N'importe;* the ill-natured critic may exercise malignity in dissecting it, and the friendly one his ingenuity in finding out some excuse.

"What has all this to do with Lisbon? say you. Take a sonnet for the ladies, imitated from the Spanish of Bartolomi Leonardo, in which I have given the author at least as many ideas as he has given me.

"Nay, cleanse this filthy mixture from thy hair,
And give the untrick'd tresses to the gale;
The sun, as lightly on the breeze they sail,
Shall gild the bright brown locks: thy cheek is fair,
Away then with this artificial hue,
This blush eternal! lady, to thy face
Nature has given no imitable grace.
Why these black spots obtruding on the view
The lily cheek, and these ear jewels too,
That ape the barbarous Indian's vanity!
Thou need'st not with that necklace there invite
The prying gaze; we know thy neck is white.
Go to thy dressing-room again, and be
Artful enough to learn simplicity.

"Could you not swear to the author if you had seen this in the newspaper? You must know, Bedford, I have a deadly aversion to any thing merely ornamental in female dress. Let the dress be as elegant (*i. e.*, as simple) as possible, but hang on none of your gewgaw eye-traps.

"Do write to me, and promise me a visit at Bristol in the summer; for, after I have returned to Edith, I will never quit her again, so that we shall remain there till I settle doggedly to law, which I hope will be during the next winter.
* * *

Friday, 24th.

"Timothy Dwight (Bedford, I defy you or Mr. Shandy to physiognomize that man's name rightly. What historian is it who, in speaking of Alexander's Feast, says they listened to *one Timothy*, a musician?) Timothy Dwight, an American, published, in 1785, an heroic poem on the conquest of Canaan. I had heard of it, and long wished to read it, in vain; but now the

American minister (a good-natured man, whose poetry is worse than any thing except his criticism) has lent me the book. There certainly is some merit in the poem; but, when Colonel Humphreys speaks of it, he will not allow me to put in a word in defense of John Milton. If I had written upon this subject, I should have been terribly tempted to take part with the Canaanites, for whom I can not help feeling a kind of brotherly compassion. There is a fine ocean of ideas floating about in my brain-pan for Madoc, and a high delight do I feel in sometimes indulging them till self-forgetfulness follows.

"'Tis a vile kind of philosophy, that for to-morrow's prospect glooms to-day; *àpropos*, sit down when you have no better employment, and find all the faults you can in 'The Retrospect'* against I return. It wants the pruning-knife before it be republished. . . . . . When I correct Joan, I shall call you in—not as plenipotent amputator—you shall mark what you think the warts, wens, and cancers, and I will take care you do not cut deep enough to destroy the life. The fourth book is the best. Do you know I have never seen the whole poem together, and that one book was printing before another was begun? The characters of Conrade and Theodore are totally distinct; and yet, perhaps, equally interesting. There is too much fighting; I found the battles detestable to write, as you will do to read; yet there are not ten better lines in the whole piece than those beginning, 'Of unrecorded name died the mean man, yet did he leave behind,' &c.†

"Do you remember the days when you wrote No. 3, at Brixton? We dined on mutton chops and eggs. I have the note you wrote for Dodd ‡ among your letters. I anticipate a very pleasant evening when you shall show the cedar box§ to Edith. 'Oh, pleasant days of fancy!' By-the-by, if ever you read aloud that part of the fifth book, mind that erratum in the description of the Famine,

"With jealous eye,
Hating a rival's look, the husband hides
His miserable meal."

After I had corrected the page and left town, poor Cottle, whose heart overflows with the milk of human kindness, read it over, and he was as little able to bear the picture of the husband as he would have been to hide a morsel from the hungry; and, suo periculo, he altered it to '*Each man conceals*,' and spoiled the climax. I was very much vexed, and yet I loved Cottle the better for it.

"No, Grosvenor, you and I shall not talk politics. I am weary of them, and little love politicians; for me, I shall think of domestic life, and confine my wishes within the little circle of friendship. The rays become more intense in proportion as they are drawn to a point. Heigh-ho! I should be very happy were I now in England. With Edith by the fireside, I would listen to the pelting rain with pleasure; now it is melancholy music, yet fitly harmonizing with my hanging mood.

"Farewell! write long letters.

"R. S.

"P.S.—In many parts of Spain they have female shavers: the proper name of one should be *Barbara*."

My father's visit to Lisbon did not exceed the anticipated time—six months; and his next letter to his friend is written in the first moments of joy on his return.

"Portsmouth, May 15, 1796.

"Thanks be to God, I am in England!

"Bedford, you may conceive the luxury of that ejaculation, if you know the miseries of a sea voyage; even the stoic who loves nothing, and the merchant whose trade-tainted heart loves nothing but wealth, would echo it. Judge you with what delight Robert Southey leaped on terra firma.

"To-night I go to Southampton; to-morrow will past pains become pleasant.

"Now, Grosvenor, is happiness a sojourner on earth, or must man be cat-o'-ninetailed by care until he shields himself in a shroud? My future destiny will not decide the problem, for I find a thousand pleasures and a thousand pains of which nine tenths of the world know nothing. . . . Come to Bristol; be with me there as long as you can. I almost add, advise me there; but your advice will come too late.

"I am sorry you could ask if you did wrong in showing Wynn my letter. I have not a thought secret from him. . . . My passage was very good, and I must be the best-tempered fellow in Great Britain, for the devil a drop of gall is there left in my bile bag. I intend a hymn to the Dii Penates. Write to me directly, and direct to Cottle. I have, as yet, no where to choose my place of rest. I shall soon have enough to place me above want, and till that arrives, shall support myself in ease and comfort, like a silk-worm, by spinning my own brains. If poor Necessity were without hands as well as legs, badly would she be off.

"Lord Somerville is dead—no matter to me, I believe, for the estates were chiefly copyhold, and Cannon Southey minded wine and women too much to think of renewing for the sake of his heirs. . . . . Farewell.

"We landed last night at eleven o'clock. Left

* "The Retrospect" was published, among some poems by my father and Mr. Lovel, in the autumn of 1794.

† "Of unrecorded name
The soldier died; and yet he left behind
One who then never said her daily prayers
Of him forgetful; who to every tale
Of the distant war lending an eager ear,
Grew pale and trembled. At her cottage door
The wretched one shall sit, and with fixed eye
Gaze on the path where on his parting steps
Her last look hung. Nor ever shall she know
Her husband dead, but cherishing a hope,
Whose falsehood inwardly she knows too well,
Feel life itself with that false hope decay;
And wake at night with miserable dreams
Of his return, and weeping o'er her babe,
Too surely think that soon that fatherless child
Must of its mother also be bereft."
Joan of Arc, 7th Book.

‡ One of the Westminster masters.

§ The depository of the contributions to "The Flagellant."

Lisbon on Thursday, the 5th, and were becalmed south of the rock till breakfast time on Saturday, so that our passage was remarkably good."

My father's visit to Lisbon seems chiefly to have been useful to him by giving him an acquaintance with the Spanish and Portuguese languages, and by laying the foundation of that love for the literature of those countries, which continued through life, and which he afterward turned to good account. These advantages, however, could not be perceived at the time; and as he returned to England with the same determination not to take orders, the same political bias, and the same romantic feelings as he left it, Mr. Hill felt naturally some disappointment at the result.

His comments on his nephew's character at this time are interesting: "He is a very good scholar," he writes to a friend, "of great reading, of an astonishing memory. When he speaks he does it with fluency, with a great choice of words. He is perfectly correct in his behavior, of the most exemplary morals, and the best of hearts. Were his character different, or his abilities not so extraordinary, I should be the less concerned about him; but to see a young man of such talents as he possesses, by the misapplication of them, lost to himself and to his family, is what hurts me very sensibly. In short, he has every thing you would wish a young man to have, excepting common sense or prudence."

Of this latter quality my father possessed more than his uncle here gives him credit for. In all his early difficulties (as well as through life), he never contracted a single debt he was unable promptly to discharge, or allowed himself a single personal comfort beyond his means, which, never abundant, had been, and were for many years, greatly straitened; and from them, narrow as they were, he had already begun to give that assistance to other members of his family which he continued to do until his latest years. It is probable, however, that Mr. Hill here chiefly alludes to his readiness to avow his peculiar views in politics and religion.

Immediately on his return, my father and mother fixed themselves in lodgings in Bristol, where they remained during the ensuing summer and autumn. My father's chief employment at this time was in preparing a volume of "Letters from Spain and Portugal" for the press, and also in writting occasionally for the Monthly Magazine. His own letters will describe the course of his occupations, opinions, and prospects during this period. The first of them alludes to the death of his brother-in-law, as well as brother-poet, Mr. Lovel, who had been cut off, in the early prime of youth, during my father's absence abroad. He had been taken ill with a fever while at Salisbury, and traveling home in hot weather, before he was sufficiently recovered, relapsed immediately, and died, leaving his widow and one child without any provision. She (who, during my father's life, found a home with him, and who now, at an advanced age, is a member of my household) is the sole survivor of those whose eager hopes once centered in Pantisocracy: one of the last of that generation so fast passing away from us!

To Grosvenor C. Bedford, Esq.

"May 27, 1796.

* * * * * * *

"Poor Lovel! I am in hopes of raising something for his widow by publishing his best pieces, if only enough to buy her a harpsichord. . . . . The poems will make a five-shilling volume, which I preface, and to which I shall prefix an epistle to Mary Lovel. Will you procure me some subscribers? . . . . Many a melancholy reflection obtrudes. What I am doing for him, you, Bedford, may one day perform for me. How short my part in life may be, He only knows who assigned it; I must be only anxious to discharge it well.

"How does time mellow down our opinions! Little of that ardent enthusiasm which so lately fevered my whole character remains. I have contracted my sphere of action within the little circle of my own friends, and even my wishes seldom stray beyond it. A little candle will give light enough to a moderate-sized room; place it in a church, it will only 'teach light to counterfeit a gloom;' and in the street, the first wind extinguishes it. Do you understand this, or shall I send you to Quarles's Emblems?

"I am hardly yet in order; and, while that last word was writing, arrived the parcel containing what, through all my English wanderings, have accompanied me—your letters. Ay, Grosvenor, our correspondence is valuable, for it is the history of the human heart during its most interesting stages. I have now bespoke a letter-case, where they shall repose in company with another series, now, blessed be God, complete—my letters to Edith. Bedford, who will be worthy to possess them when we are gone? 'Odi profanum vulgus?' must I make a funeral pile by my death-bed?

"Would that I were so settled as not to look on to another removal. I want a little room to arrange my books in, and some Lares of my own. Shall we not be near one another? Ay, Bedford, as intimate as John Doe and Richard Roe, with whose memoirs I shall be so intimately acquainted; and there are two other cronies—John a Nokes and Jack a Styles, always, like Gyas and Cloanthus, and the two kings of Brentford, hand in hand. Oh, I will be a huge lawyer. * * * * Come soon. My 'dearest friend' expects you with almost as much pleasure and impatience as

"Robert Southey."

To Grosvenor C. Bedford, Esq.

"June 12, 1796.

* * * * * * * *

"I have declared war against metaphysics, and would push my arguments, as William Pitt would his *successes*, even to the extermination of the enemy. 'Blessed be the hour I 'scaped the wrangling crew.'

"I think it may be proved that all the material and necessarian controversies are 'much ado about nothing;' that they end exactly where they began; and that all the moral advantages said to result from them by the illuminated are fairly and more easily deducible from religion, or even from common sense. * * * * * * * * * * * * What of Carlisle's wings? I believe my flying scheme—that of breaking in condors and riding them—is the best; or if a few *rocs* could be naturalized—though it might be a *hard* matter to *break* them. Seriously, I am very far from convinced that flying is impossible, and have an admirable tale of a Spanish bird for one of my letters, which will just suit Carlisle. . . . . Yes, your friends shall be mine, but it is we (in the dual number) who must be intimate. If Momus had made a window in my breast, I should by this time have had sense enough to add a window-shutter. London is not the only place for me: I have an unspeakable loathing for that huge city. 'God made the country, and man made the town.' Now, as God made me likewise, I love the country. Here I am in the skirts of Bristol; in ten minutes in a beautiful country; and in half an hour among rocks and woods, with no other company than the owls and jackdaws, with whom I fraternize in solitude; but London! it is true that you and Wynn will supply the place of the owls and jackdaws, but Brixton is not the country: the poplars of Pownall Terrace can not supply the want of a wild wood; and, with all my imagination, I can not mistake a mile stone for a rock; but these are among the *τα ουκ εφ' ἡμιν*. It is within doors, and not without, that happiness dwells, like a vestal watching the fire of the Penates. * *

"I have told you what I am about. Writing letters to the world is not, however, quite so agreeable as writing to you, and I do not love shaping a good thing into a good sentence. . . . Then for a volume of poems, and then for the Abridgment of the Laws, or the Lawyer's Pocket Companion, in fifty-two volumes folio! Is it not a pity, Grosvenor, that I should not execute my intention of writing more verses than Lope de Vega, more tragedies than Dryden, and more epic poems than Blackmore? The more I write, the more I have to write. I have a Helicon kind of dropsy upon me, and *crescit indulgens sibi*. The quantity of verses I wrote at Brixton is astonishing; my mind was never more employed: I killed wasps, and was very happy. And so I will again, Grosvenor, though employed on other themes; and, if ever man was happy because he resolved to be so, I will. * * Of Lightfoot it is long since I have heard any thing. * * * * * * * *

"'When blew the loud blast in the air,
So shrill, so full of woe,
Unable such a voice to bear,
Down fell Jericho.'

"Lightfoot, on the authority of some rum old book, used to assert the existence of a tune that would shake a wall down, by insinuating its sounds into the wall, and vibrating so strongly as to shake it down. Now, Grosvenor, to those lines in the fourth book of Joan that allude to Orlando's magic horn, was I going to make a note, which, by the help of you and Lightfoot, would have been a very quaint one, and by the help of Dr. Geddes, not altogether unlearned, not to mention great erudition in quotations from Boiardo, Ariosto, Archbishop Turpin, and Spenser.

"Farewell, Grosvenor! Have you read Count Rumford's Essays? I am ashamed to say that I have not yet. Have you read Fawcett's Art of War? With all the faults of Young, it possesses more beauties, and is, in many parts, in my opinion, excellent.

"R. S."

To Grosvenor C. Bedford, Esq.

"June 26, 1796.

* * * * * *

"Take the whole of the Spanish poem; it is by George of Montemayor, addressed by Sireno to a lock of Diana's hair, whom, returning after twelve months' absence, he finds married to another.

"'Ah me, thou relic of that faithless fair!
Sad changes have I suffered since that day,
When in this valley from her long loose hair
I bore thee—relic of my love—away.
Well did I then believe Diana's truth,
For soon true love each jealous care represses,
And fondly thought that never other youth
Should wanton with the maiden's unbound tresses.

"'There, on the cold clear Ezla's breezy side,
My hand amid her ringlets wont to rove,
She proffered now the lock, and now denied,
With all the baby playfulness of love.
There the false maid, with many an artful tear,
Made me each rising thought of doubt discover,
And vowed, and wept, till hope had ceased to fear,
Ah me! beguiling like a child her lover.

"'Witness thou, how that fondest, falsest fair,
Has sighed and wept on Ezla's sheltered shore,
And vowed eternal truth, and made me swear
My heart no jealousy should harbor more.
Ah! tell me, could I but believe those eyes,
Those lovely eyes with tears my cheek bedewing,
When the mute eloquence of tears and sighs
I felt and trusted, and embraced my ruin?

"'So false, and yet so fair! so fair a mien
Vailing so false a mind, who ever knew?
So true, and yet so wretched! who has seen
A man like me, so wretched and so true?
Fly from me on the wind! for you have seen
How kind she was, how loved by her you knew me.
Fly, fly! vain witness what I once have been,
Nor dare, all wretched as I am, to view me!

"'One evening, on the river's pleasant strand,
The maid, too well beloved! sat with me,
And with her finger traced upon the sand,
Death for Diana, not inconstancy.
And love beheld us from his secret stand,
And marked his triumph, laughing to behold me;
To see me trust a writing traced in sand,
To see me credit what a woman told me.'*

"If you can add any thing to the terseness of the conclusion or the simplicity of the whole, do it. The piece itself is very beautiful.

"My letters occupy more of my time and less of my mind than I could wish. Conceive

* Since copying this beautiful translation, I have found that my father had inserted it in his "Letters from Spain and Portugal." I think, notwithstanding, the reader will not be displeased to see it here.

Garagantua eating wood strawberries one at a time, or green peas, or the old dish—pap with a fork, and you will have some idea how my mind feels in dwelling on desultory topics. Joan of Arc was a whole—it was something to think of every moment of solitude, and to dream of at night; my heart was in the poem; I threw my own feelings into it in my own language, ay, and out of one part of it and another, you may find my own character. Seriously, Grosvenor, to go on with Madoc is *almost* necessary to my happiness: I had rather leave off eating than poetizing; but these things must be. I will feed upon law and digest it, or it shall choke me. Did you ever pop upon a seditious ode in the ludicrous style, addressed to the cannibals? It was in the Courier and Telegraph; a stray sheep marked Caius Gracchus, to which you may place another signature.

"Grosvenor, I do not touch on aught interesting to-night. I am conversing with you now in that easy, calm, good-humored state of mind, which is, perhaps, the *summum bonum;* the less we think of the world the better. . . . . My feelings were once like an ungovernable horse; now I have tamed Bucephalus; he retains his spirit and his strength, but they are made useful, and he shall not break my neck. . . . . This is, indeed, a change; but the liquor that ceases to ferment does not immediately become flat; the beer then becomes fine, and continues so till it is dead.

"To-morrow Wynn comes; shall I find him altered? Would that I were among you. If unremitting assiduity can procure me independence, that prize shall be mine. Christian went a long way to fling off his burden in the Pilgrim's Progress. . . . . I doubt only my lungs; I find my breath affected when I read aloud, but exercise may strengthen them.

"When do you come? It was wisely done of the old conjuror, who kept six princesses transformed into cats, to tie each of them fast, and put a mouse close to her nose without her being able to catch it; for the nearer we are to a good, the more do we necessarily desire it: the attraction becomes more powerful as we approach the magnet. . . . .

"Do not despise Godwin too much. . . . . He will do good by defending Atheism in print, because, when the arguments are known, they may be easily and satisfactorily answered. Tell Carlisle to ask him this question: If man were made by the casual meeting of atoms, how could he have supported himself without superior assistance? The use of the mucles is only attained by practice—how could he have fed himself? how know from what cause hunger proceeded? how know by what means to remedy the pain? The question appears to me decisive. . . . . Merry (of whose genius, erroneous as it was, I always thought highly) has published the 'Pains of Memory;' a subject once given me, and from which some lines in Joan of Arc are extracted. Farewell!

"R. S."

To Grosvenor C. Bedford, Esq.

"July 17, 1796.

* * * * * * * * *

"Besides my letters, I write for the Monthly Magazine. This is a new job: you may easily trace me there, if it be worth your while. They give five guineas a sheet, but their sheets are sixteen closely-printed pages. I manufacture up my old rubbish for them, with a little about Spanish literature. I shall be glad to get rid of all this.

"So you abuse Anna St. Ives, and commend the Pucelle of the detestable Voltaire. Now, Grosvenor, it was not I who said 'I *have not* read that book.' *I* said—God be thanked that I did say it, and plague take the boobies who mutilated it in my absence—I said, 'I have *never been guilty* of reading the Pucelle of Voltaire.' Report speaks it worthy of its author—a man whose wit and genius could only be equaled by his depravity. I will tell you what a man, not particularly nice in his moral opinions, said to me upon the subject of that book: 'I should think the worse of any man who, having read one canto of it, could proceed to a second.' . . . . Now, my opinion of Anna St. Ives is diametrically opposed to yours. I think it a book of consummate wisdom, and I shall join my forces to Mrs. Knowles, to whom I desire you would make my fraternal respects.

"Sunday.

"How has this letter been neglected! No more delays, however. I am continually writing or reading: the double cacoethes grows upon me every day; and the physic of John Nokes, by which I must get cured, is sadly nauseous. *N'importe.* I wish I were in London, for if industry can do any thing for any body, it shall for me. My plan is to study from five in the morning till eight, from nine to twelve, and from one to four. The evening is my own. Now, Grosvenor, do you think I would do this if I had a pig-sty of my own in the country?

"So goes the world! There is not a man in it who is not discontented. However, if no man had more reason for discontent than you and I have, it would be already a very good world; for, after all, I believe the worst we complain of is, that we do not find mankind as good as we could wish. . . . . Many of our mental evils—and God knows they are the worst—we make ourselves.

"If a young man had his senses about him when he sets out in life, he should seriously deliberate whether he had rather never be miserable or sometimes be happy. I like the up and down road best; but I have learned never to despise any man's opinion because it is different from my own. Surely, Grosvenor, our restlessness in this world seems to indicate that we are intended for a better. We have all of us a longing after happiness; and surely the Creator will gratify all the natural desires that he has implanted in us. If you die before me, will you visit me? I am half a believer in apparitions, and would purchase conviction at the expense of a tolerable fright.

"George Burnett's uncle was for three months terribly afflicted by the nightmare; so much so, that, by being constantly disturbed, his health was considerably impaired. One night he determined to lie awake and watch for HER.

"'Oh Bedford, Bedford,
If ever thou didst a good story love!'

One night, he says, he determined to lie awake and watch for HER. At the usual hour he heard HER coming up the stairs; he got up in the bed in a cold sweat; he heard HER come into the room; he heard HER open the curtain, and then —he leaped out of bed and caught HER by the hair before SHE—for SHE it was—could fall upon his breast. Then did this most incomparable hero bellow to John for a candle. They fought; she pulled and he pulled, and bellowed till John came with a light; and then—she vanished immediately, and he remained with a handful of HER hair.

"Now, Bedford, would you not have had that made into a locket? The tale, methinks, is no bad companion for your father's dream. The exploit of Mr. Burnett is far beyond that of St. Withold—though, by-the-by, he met the nine foals into the bargain—and *they made a bargain*.

"I have written you an odd letter, and an ugly one, upon very execrable paper. By-the-by, if you have a Prudentius, you may serve me by sending me all he says about a certain Saint Eulalia, who suffered martyrdom at Merida. I passed through that city, and should like to see his hymn upon the occasion; and if there be any good in it, put it in a note. How mortifying is this confinement of yours! I had planned so many pleasant walks, to be made so much more pleasant by conversation;

"For I have much to tell thee, much to say
Of the odd things we saw upon our journey,
Much of the dirt and vermin that annoyed us.

And you should have seen my letters before they went to press, and annotated them, and heard the plot of my tragedy; but now! I have a mortal aversion to all these disjunctive particles: *but*, and *if*, and *yet*, always herald some bad news. . . . I shall be settled in London, I hope, before Christmas. I do not remember a happier ten weeks than I passed at Brixton, nor, indeed, a better employed period. God grant me ten such weeks of leisure once more in my life, and I will finish Madoc. God bless you. R. S."

To Grosvenor C. Bedford, Esq.

"July 31, 1796.

"Oh that you could bring Bristol to the sea! for as for bringing the sea to Bristol, that could not be done, as Trim says, 'unless it pleased God;' and, as Toby says, how the devil should it? I must not ask you to come to me, and I can not come to you. . . . For your club, I grant you a few hours once a fortnight will not make me worse; but will they make me better? and if they will not, why should I quit the fireside? You will be in a state of requisition perpetually with me; and it seems you have bespoke a place in my heart for Carlisle, but I will not let in too many there, because I do not much like being obliged to turn them out.

"Lenora is partly borrowed from an old English ballad:

"Is there any room at your head, William?
Is there any room at your feet?
Is there any room at your side, William,
Wherein I may creep?

"There's no room at my head, Margerett,
There's no room at my feet
There's no room at my side, Margerett,
My coffin is made so meet!

But the other ballad of Bürger, in the Monthly Magazine, is most excellent. I know no commendation equal to its merit; read it again, Grosvenor, and read it aloud. The man who wrote that should have been ashamed of Lenora. Who is this Taylor? I suspected they were by Sayers.

"Have you read Cabal and Love? In spite of a translation for which the translator deserves hanging, the fifth act is dreadfully affecting. I want to write my tragedies of the Banditti:

"Of Sebastian,
"Of Iñez de Castro,
"Of the Revenge of Pedro.
"My epic poem, in twenty books, of Madoc.
"My novel, in three volumes, of Edmund Oliver.
"My romance of ancient history of Alcas.
"My Norwegian tale of —— Harfagne.
"My Oriental poem of The Destruction of the Dom Daniel.

And, in case I adopt Rousseau's system,
"My —— Pains of Imagination.

There, Grosvenor, all these I want to write!

"Οτοττοτοί!

"A comical Cornish curate, who saw me once or twice, has written me a quaint letter, and sent me a specimen of his Paradise Found!!!!

"Wynn wishes me to live near Lincoln's Inn, because, in a year's time, it will be necessary for me to be with a special pleader; but I wish to live on the other side of Westminster Bridge, because it will be much more necessary to be within an evening's walk of Brixton. To all serious studies I bid adieu when I enter upon my London lodgings. The law will neither amuse me, nor ameliorate me, nor instruct me; but, the moment it gives me a comfortable independence—and I have but few wants—then farewell to London. I will get me some little house near the sea, and near a country town, for the sake of the post and the bookseller; and you shall pass as much of the summer with me as you can, and I will see you in the winter—that is, if you do not come and live by me; and then we will keep mastiffs like Carlisle, and make the prettiest theories, and invent the best systems for mankind; ay, and become great philanthropists, when we associate only among ourselves and the fraternity of dogs, cats, and cabbages; for as for poultry, I do not like eating what I have *fed*, and as for pigs, they are too like the multitude. There, in the cultivation of poetry and potatoes I will be innocently employed; not but I mean to aspire to higher things; ay, Grosvenor, I will make cider and mead, and try more experiments upon wine than a London vintner; and perhaps, Grosvenor, the first Christmas day you pass with me after I am so settled, we may make a Christmas fire of all my law books. Amen, so be it. . . . .

"I hope to get out my Letters by Michaelmas day, and the Poems will be ready in six weeks after that time. That done, farewell to Bristol, my native place, my home for two-and-twenty years, where from many causes I have endured much misery, but where I have been very happy. . . . .

"No man ever retained a more perfect knowledge of the history of his own mind than I have done. I can trace the development of my character from infancy; for developed it has been, not changed. I look forward to the writing of this history as the most pleasing and most useful employment I shall ever undertake. This removal is not, however, like quitting *home*. I am never domesticated in lodgings; the hearth is unhallowed, and the Penates do not abide there. Now, Grosvenor, to let you into a secret: though I can not afford to buy a house, or hire one, I have lately built a very pretty castle, which is, being interpreted, if I can get my play of the 'Banditti' brought on the stage, and if it succeed —hang all those little conjunctions—well, these 'ifs' granted—I shall get money enough to furnish me a house. . . . God bless you! R. S."

To Grosvenor C. Bedford, Esq.

"Bristol, August 29, 1796, by the fireside.

". . . . Do not hurt the polypi for the sake of trying experiments; mangle the dead as much as you please, but let not Carlisle dissect dogs or frogs alive. Of all experimental surgeons, Spallanzani is the only fair one I ever heard of. He kept a kite, and gave him all his food in little bags tied to a long string, which he used to pull up again to see the process of digestion. Now this was using the kite very ill, but he served himself in the same manner.

"You will, perhaps, hear of me in Sussex, certainly if you go to Rye, which is only ten miles distant from Hastings. I wish you may see the Lambs. . . . . I was a great favorite there once, more so than I shall ever be any where again, for the same reason that people like a kitten better than a cat, and a kid better than the venerable old goat. . . . I have been very happy at Rye, Grosvenor, and love to remember it. You know the history of the seventeen anonymous letters that Tom and I sent down the day before we went ourselves.* There is a wind-mill on the bank above the house: with the glass, I used to tell the hour by Rye clock from the door; which clock, by-the-by, was taken among the spoils of the Spanish Armada.

"I hope you may go there. I wrote a good many bad verses in Sussex, but they taught me to write better, and you know not how agreeable it is to me to meet with one of my old lines, or old ideas, in Joan of Arc. . . . If we were together now, we would write excellent letters from Portugal. I have begun a hymn to the Penates, which will, perhaps, be the best of all my lesser pieces; it is to conclude the volume of poems. . . . . It is a great advantage to have a London bookseller: they can put off an edition of a book, however stupid; and, without great exertions in its favor, no book, however excellent, will sell. The sale of Joan of Arc in London has been very slow indeed. Six weeks ago Cadell had only sold three copies. . . . .

"Would I were with you! for, though I hate to be on the sea, I yet wish to pitch my tent on the shore. I do not know any thing more delightful than to lie on the beach in the sun, and watch the rising waves, while a thousand vague ideas pass over the mind, like the summer clouds over the water; then, it is a noble situation to Shandeize. Why is it salt? why does it ebb and flow? what sort of fellows are the mermen? &c., &c.: these are a thousand of the prettiest questions in the world to ask, on which you may guess away *ad secula seculorum;* and here am I tormented by Mr. Rosser's dilatory devils, and looking on with no small impatience to the time when I shall renounce the devil and all his works.

"I am about to leave off writing just when I have learned what to write and how to write. . . . I mean to attempt to get a tragedy on the stage, for the mere purpose of furnishing a house, which a successful play would do for me. I know I can write one; beyond this, all is mere conjecture; it is, however, worth trying, for I find lodgings very disagreeable. Lodge, however, I must in London, and you will be good enough to look out for me, I hope ere long, two rooms on the Brixton side the water.

"I have a thousand things to say to you. Long absence seems to have produced no effect on us, and I still feel that perfect openness in writing to you that I shall never feel to any other human being. Grosvenor, when we sit down in Shandy Hall, what pretty speculations shall we make! You shall be Toby, and amuse yourself by marching to Paris; I will make systems, and Horace shall be Doctor Slop.

"I have projected a useful volume, which would not occupy a month—specimens of the early English poets, with a critical account of all their works—only to include the less known authors and specimens never before selected. My essays would be historical and biographical as well as critical. I can get this printed without risking any thing myself. . . . .

"Yours sincerely, R. S."

To Grosvenor C. Bedford, Esq.

"Bristol, Oct., 1796.

"I know not even the day of the month, but October is somewhat advanced, and this is Friday evening. Why did I not write sooner? Excuses are bad things. I have much to employ me, though I can always make a little leisure. If you were married, Grosvenor, you would know the luxury of sitting indolently by the fireside;

* I can find no account of this excursion. It was probably during one of his Westminster holidays.

at present you only half know it. There is a state of complete mental torpor, very delightful, when the mind admits no sensation but that of mere existence; such a sensation I suppose plants to possess, made more vivid by the dews and gentle rains. To indulge in fanciful systems is a harmless solitary amusement, and I expect many a pleasant hour will be thus wore away, Grosvenor, when we meet. The devil never meddles with me in my unemployed moments; my day dreams are of a pleasanter nature. I should be the happiest man in the world if I possessed enough to live with comfort in the country; but in this world, we must sacrifice the best part of our lives to acquire that wealth which generally arrives when the time of enjoying it is past.

* * * * * * * * *

"I ardently wish for children; yet, if God shall bless me with any, I shall be unhappy to see them poisoned by the air of London.

"'Sir—I do thank God for it—I do hate
Most heartily that city.'

So said John Donne; 'tis a favorite quotation of mine. My spirits always sink when I approach it. Green fields are my delight. I am not only better in health, but even in heart, in the country. A fine day exhilarates my heart; if it rains, I behold the grass assume a richer verdure as it drinks the moisture: every thing that I behold is very good, except man; and in London I see nothing but man and his works. A country clergyman, with a tolerable income, is surely in a very enviable situation. Surely we have a thousand things to *transfuse* into each other, which the lazy language of the pen can not express with sufficient rapidity. Your illness was very unfortunate. I could wish once to show you the pleasant spots where I have so often wandered, and the cavern where I have written so many verses. You should have known Cottle, too, for a worthier heart you never knew.

"You love the sea. Whenever I pitch my tent, it shall be by it. When will that be? Is it not a villainous thing that poetry will not support a man, when the jargon of the law enriches so many? . . . . . I had rather write an epic poem than read a brief.

"Have you read St. Pierre? If not, read that most delightful work, and you will love the author as much as I do.

"I am as sleepy an animal as ever. The rain beats hard, the fire burns bright, 'tis but eight o'clock, and I have already begun yawning. Good-night, Grosvenor, lest I set you to sleep. My father always went to bed at nine o'clock. I have inherited his punctuality and his drowsiness. God bless you.

"ROBERT SOUTHEY.

"I am the lark that sings early, and early retires. What is that bird that sleeps in the morning and is awake at night, Grosvenor? Do you remember poor Aaron?"*

* Aaron was a tame owl, kept by either my father or Mr. Bedford, I forget which, at Westminster.

To Grosvenor C. Bedford, Esq.

"Nov. 21, 1796.

"When do I come to London? A plain question. I can not tell, is as plain an answer. My book will be out before Christmas, and I shall then have no further business in Bristol; yet, Bedford, this is not saying when I shall leave it. The best answer is, as soon as I can, and the sooner the better. I want to be there. I want to feel myself settled, and God knows when that will be, for the settlement of a lodging is but a comfortless one. To complete comfort, a house to one's self is necessary. . . . . However, I expect to be as comfortable as it is possible to be in that cursed city, 'that huge and hateful sepulcher of men.' I detest cities, and had rather live in the fens of Lincolnshire or on Salisbury Plain than in the best situation London could furnish. The neighborhood of you and Wynn can alone render it tolerable. I fear the air will wither me up, like one of the miserable myrtles at a town parlor window. . . . . Oh, for 'the house in the woods and the great dog!'

"I already feel intimate with Carlisle; but I am a very snail in company, Grosvenor, and pop into my shell whenever I am approached, or roll myself up like a hedgehog in my rough outside. It is strange, but I never approach London without feeling my heart sink within me; an unconquerable heaviness oppresses me in its atmosphere, and all its associated ideas are painful. With a little house in the country, and a bare independence, how much more useful should I be, and how much more happy! It is not talking nonsense, when I say that the London air is as bad for the mind as for the body, for the mind is a chameleon that receives its colors from surrounding objects. In the country, every thing is good, every thing in nature is beautiful. The benevolence of Deity is every where presented to the eye, and the heart participates in the tranquillity of the scene. In the town my soul is continually disgusted by the vices, follies, and consequent miseries of mankind.

"My future studies, too. Now, I never read a book without learning something, and never write a line of poetry without cultivating some feeling of benevolence and honesty; but the law is a horrid jargon—a quibbling collection of voluminous nonsense; but this I must wade through—ay, and I will wade through—and when I shall have got enough to live in the country, you and I will make my first Christmas fire of all my new books. Oh, Grosvenor, what a blessed bonfire! The devil uses the statutes at large for fuel when he gives an attorney his house warming.

"I shall have some good poems to send you shortly. Your two birth-day odes are printed; your name looks well in capitals, and I have pleased myself by the motto prefixed to them: it is from Akenside. Shall I leave you to guess it? I hate guessing myself.

"'Oh, my faithful friend!
Oh early chosen! ever found the same,

And trusted, and beloved; once more the verse,
Lond-destined, always obvious to thine ear,
Attend indulgent.'

"My Triumph of Woman is manufactured into a tolerable poem. My Hymn to the Penates will be the best of my minor pieces. The B. B. Eclogues may possibly become popular.

"Read St. Pierre, Grosvenor; and, if you ever turn pagan, you will certainly worship him for a demi-god. . . . . I want to get a tragedy out, to furnish a house with its profits. Is this a practicable scheme, allowing the merit of the drama? or would a good novel succeed better? Heigh-ho! ways and means! . . . .

"Yours sincerely, R. S."

CHAPTER V.

GOES TO LONDON TO STUDY THE LAW—LETTERS FROM THENCE—TAKES LODGINGS AT BURTON IN HAMPSHIRE—LETTERS TO MR. MAY AND MR. BEDFORD—GOES TO BATH—LINES BY CHARLES LAMB—RETURNS TO LONDON—LETTER TO MR. WYNN—VISIT TO NORFOLK—LETTERS FROM THENCE—TAKES A HOUSE AT WESTBURY, NEAR BRISTOL—EXCURSION INTO HEREFORDSHIRE.—1797.

MY father continued to reside in Bristol until the close of the year 1796, chiefly employed, as we have seen, in working up the contents of his foreign note-books into "Letters from Spain and Portugal," which were published in one volume early in the following year. This task completed, he determined to take up his residence in London, and fairly to commence the study of the law, which he was now enabled to do through the true friendship of Mr. C. W. W. Wynn, from whom he received for some years from this time an annuity of £160—the prompt fulfillment of a promise made during their years of college intimacy. This was indeed one of those acts of rare friendship—twice honorable—"to him that gives and him that takes it;" bestowed with pleasure, received without any painful feelings, and often reverted to as the staff and stay of those years when otherwise he must have felt to the full all the manifold evils of being, as he himself expressed it, "cut adrift upon the ocean of life."

How reluctantly he had looked forward to his legal studies, his past letters have shown; nor did the prospect appear more pleasing when the anticipation was about to be changed to the reality.

To Grosvenor C. Bedford, Esq.

"Jan. 1, 1797.

"So, Bedford, begins the year that will terminate our correspondence. I mean to spend one summer in North Wales, studying the country for Madoc, and do not intend writing to you then, because you shall be with me. And for all the rest of the days I look on to clearly, the view is bounded by the smoke of London. Methinks, like Camoens, I could dub it Babylon, and write lamentations for the 'Sion' of my birth-place, having, like him, no reason to regret the past, except that it is not the present: it is the country I want. A field thistle is to me worth all the flowers of Covent Garden.

"However, Bedford, happiness is a flower that will blossom any where; and I expect to be happy, even in London. You know who is to watch at my gate; and if he will let in any of your club, well and good.

"Time and experience seem to have assimilated us: we think equally ill of mankind, and, from the complexion of your last letters, I believe you think as badly as I do of their rulers. I fancy you are mounted above the freezing point of aristocracy, to the temperate degree where I have fallen. . . . Methinks, Grosvenor, the last two years have made me the *elder;* but you know I never allow the aristocracy of years.

"I have this day finished my Letters, and now my time is my own—my 'race is run;' and perhaps the next book of mine which makes its appearance will be my 'posthumous works!' . . . . I must be on the Surrey side of the water; this will suit me and please you. I am familiar with the *names* of your club—shall I ever be so with themselves? Naturally of a reserved disposition, there was a considerable period of my life in which high spirits, quick feelings, and principles enthusiastically imbibed, made me talkative; experience has taught me wisdom, and I am again as silent, as *self-centering* as in early youth.

"After the nine hours' law study, I shall have a precious fragment of the day at my own disposal. Now, Grosvenor, I must be a miser of time, for I am just as sleepy a fellow as you remember me at Brixton. You see I am not collected enough to write; this plaguy cough interrupts me, and shakes all the ideas in my brain out of their places.

"Jan. 7.

"A long interval, Grosvenor, and it has not been employed agreeably. I have been taken ill at Bristol. . . . I was afraid of a fever . . . . a giddiness of head, which accompanied the seizure, rendered me utterly unfit for any thing. I was well nursed, and am well. . . . When I get to London I have some comfortable plans; but much depends on the likeability of your new friends. You say you have engaged some of them to meet me: now, if you taught them to expect any thing in me, they must owe their disappointment to you. Remember that I am as reserved to others as I am open to you. You have seen a hedgehog roll himself up when noticed, even so do I shelter myself in my own thoughts. . . .

"I have sketched out a tragedy on the martyrdom of Joan of Arc, which is capable of making a good closet drama. My ideas of tragedy differ from those generally followed. There is seldom *nature* enough in the dialogue; even Shakspeare gets upon the stilts sometimes; the dramatist ought rather to display a knowledge of the workings of the human heart than his own imagination; high-strained metaphor can rarely be introduced with propriety—similes never. Do you think I shall strip tragedy of all its ornaments? this, time must discover. Yet look on the dramatic parts of Joan of Arc; they are the best; the dialogue is impassioned, but it is natural. John Doe and Richard Roe must, however, form the chief personages in the last act of my life. Grosvenor, will it be a tragedy or a comedy? However, I will not now think of the catastrophe, but rather look on to the pleasant scenes when we shall meet. Fare you well. . . .

"Yours affectionately, R. S."

In the course of the next month (February) my father went up to town for the purpose of fixing himself in some convenient situation for his legal studies. "Now, my dear Edith," he writes from there, "am I of Gray's Inn, where I this day paid twelve pounds fifteen shillings for admission.*. . . Edith, you must come to me. I am not merely uncomfortable, I am unhappy without you. I rise in the morning without expecting pleasure from the day, and I lie down at night without one wish for the morning. This town presents to me only a wilderness. . . . I am just returned from ——; they can receive us for £40 a year: two rooms, they are not large, but they are handsomely furnished, and there is a good book-case, and every thing looks clean. . . . Direct to me at Mr. Peacock's, No. 20 Prospect Place, Newington Butts, near London; but, my dear Edith, there is 'no prospect' in this vile neighborhood." . . . . And again, a few days later, he writes in that playful and affectionate strain in which all his letters to my mother are couched: "Grosvenor has just been talking of you. He was correcting an error in Musæus. I had laid down my pen, and begun one of my melodious whistles, upon which he cried for mercy for God's sake, and asked if you liked my whistling; adding that he would spirit you up to rebellion if ever I did any thing you did not like. I said you had often threatened to tell Grosvenor Bedford. Well, Edith, on the fifth day I shall see you once more; and you do not know with what comfort I think at night that one day more is gone. I do not misemploy the leisure I make here. Such books as, from their value, ought not to be lent from the library, I am now consulting, and appropriating such of their contents as may be useful to my red book.

". . . . Richards, I understand, was much pleased with me on Sunday. I was, as always in the company of strangers, thoughtful, reserved, and almost silent. God never intended that I should *make myself agreeable* to any body. I am glad he likes me. however; he can and will assist me in this ugly world."†

The following letters will show the course of his London life during the few months he resided there at this time.

* This letter is without date, but the receipt for these entrance fees, which I have before me, fixes the time, February 7, 1797.

† Feb. 16, 1797.

To Joseph Cottle.

"London, Feb., 1797.

"My dear Friend,

"I am now entered on a new way of life, which will lead me to independence. You know that I neither lightly undertake any scheme, nor lightly abandon what I have undertaken. I am happy because I have no wants, and because the independence I labor to obtain and of attaining which my expectations can hardly be disappointed, will leave me nothing to wish. I am indebted to you, Cottle, for the comforts of my latter time. In my present situation I feel a pleasure in saying thus much.

"As to my literary pursuits, after some consideration I have resolved to postpone every other till I have concluded Madoc. This must be the greatest of all my works. The structure is complete in my mind; and my mind is likewise stored with appropriate images. Should I delay it, these images may become fainter, and perhaps age does not improve the poet.

"Thank God! Edith comes on Monday next. I say thank God! for I have never, since my return, been absent from her so long before, and sincerely hope and intend never to be so again. On Tuesday we shall be settled; on Wednesday my legal studies begin in the morning, and I shall begin with Madoc in the evening. Of this it is needless to caution you to say nothing, as I must have the character of a lawyer; and, though I can and will unite the two pursuits, no one would credit the possibility of the union. In two years the poem shall be finished, and the many years it must lie by will afford ample time for correction. Mary* has been in the Oracle; also some of my sonnets in the Telegraph, with outrageous commendation. I have declined being a member of a Literary Club which meets weekly, and of which I have been elected a member. Surely a man does not do his duty who leaves his wife to evenings of solitude, and I feel duty and happiness to be inseparable. I am happier at home than any other society can possibly make me. . . . . God bless you!

"Yours sincerely,

"Robert Southey."

To Joseph Cottle.

"London, March 13, 1797.

* * * * * *

"Perhaps you will be surprised to hear that, of all the lions or *literati* that I have seen here, there is not one whose countenance has not some unpleasant trait. Mary Imlay's† is the best, infinitely the best: the only fault in it is an expression somewhat similar to what the prints of Horne Tooke display—an expression indicating superiority; not haughtiness, not sarcasm in Mary Imlay, but still it is unpleasant. Her eyes are light brown, and, though the lid of one of them is affected by a little paralysis, they are the most meaning I ever saw. * * * *

"When I was with George Dyer one morning

* His ballad of Mary, the Maid of the Inn.

† The daughter of Mary Wollstonecroft.

last week, Mary Hayes and Miss Christal entered, and the ceremony of introduction followed. Mary Hayes writes in the 'Monthly Magazine' under the signature of M. H., and sometimes writes nonsense there about *Helvetius*. She has lately published a novel—'Emma Courtenay;' a book much praised and much abused. I have not seen it myself, but the severe censures passed on it by persons of narrow mind have made me curious, and convinced me that it is at least an uncommon book. Mary Hayes is an agreeable woman, and a Godwinite. Now, if you will read Godwin's book with attention, we will consider between us in what light to consider that sectarian title. As for Godwin himself, he has large, noble eyes, and a *nose*—oh, most abominable nose! Language is not vituperatious enough to describe the effect of its downward elongation.* He loves London, literary society, and talks nonsense about the collision of mind; and Mary Hayes echoes him. But Miss Christal—have you seen her poems?—a fine, artless, sensible girl! Now, Cottle, that word sensible must not be construed here in its dictionary acceptation. Ask a Frenchman what it means, and he will understand it, though, perhaps, he can by no circumlocution explain its French meaning. Her heart is alive, she loves poetry, she loves retirement, she loves the country: her verses are very incorrect, and the literary circles say she has no genius; but she has genius, Joseph Cottle, or there is no truth in physiognomy. Gilbert Wakefield came in while I was disputing with Mary Hayes upon the moral effects of towns. He has a most critic-like voice, as if he had snarled himself hoarse. You see I like the women better than the men. Indeed, they are better animals in general, perhaps because more is left to nature in their education. Nature is very good, but God knows there is very little of it left.

"I wish you were within a morning's walk, but I am always persecuted by time and space. Robert Southey and Law and Poetry make up an odd kind of triunion. We jog on easily together, and I advance with sufficient rapidity in *Blackstone* and *Madoc*. I hope to finish my poem and to begin my practice in about two years. God bless you!

"Yours affectionately,
"ROBERT SOUTHEY."

To Thomas Southey.

"March 31, 1797.

"I have stolen time to write to you, though uncertain whether you may still be at Plymouth; but, if the letter should have to follow you, well and good; if lost, it matters little. I have a bookseller's job on my hands: it is to translate a volume from the French—about a month's work;* and the pay will be not less than five-and-twenty guineas, an employment more profitable than pleasant; but I should like plenty such. Three or four such jobs would furnish me a house. . . . . Your description of the Spanish coast about St. Sebastian has very highly delighted me. I intend to versify it, put the lines in Madoc, and give your account below in the note. To me, who had never seen any other but the tame shores of this island, the giant rocks of Galicia appeared stupendously sublime. They even derived a grandeur from their barrenness: it gives them a majestic simplicity that fills the undistracted mind. I have in contemplation another work upon my journey—a series of poems, the subjects occasioned by the scenes I passed, and the meditations which those scenes excited. Do you perceive the range this plan includes? History, imagination, philosophy, all would be pressed into my service. . . . A noble design! and it has met with some encouragement. But time is scarce; and I must be a lawyer—a sort of animal that might be made of worse materials than those with which nature tempered my clay.

* * * * * * *

Should I publish the series of poems I mentioned, it is my intention to annex prints from the sketches my uncle took upon our road. I sometimes regret that, after leaving the College Green, I have never had encouragement to go on with drawing. The evening when Shad and I were so employed was then the pleasantest part of the day, and I began at last to know something about it. I would gladly get those drawings; but my aunt never lets any thing go; and the greater part of my books, and all those drawings, and my coins, with a number of things of little intrinsic value, but which I should highly prize, are all locked up in the Green.

"The poor old theater is going to ruin, for which I have worked so many hours, and which so deeply interested me once. Such are the revolutions of private life, and such strange alterations do a few years produce!

"My aunt told Peggy† it was pretty well in me to write a book about Portugal who had not been there six months; for her part, she had been there twelve months, and yet she could not write a book about it—so apt are we to measure knowledge by time. I employed my time there in constant attention, seeing every thing and asking questions, and never went to bed without writing down the information I had acquired during the day. I am now tolerably versed in Spanish and Portuguese poetry, and am writing a series of essays upon the sub-

* Godwin's nose came in for no small share of condemnation. In another letter he says, "We dine with Mary Wollstonecroft (now Godwin) to-morrow. Oh, he has a foul nose, and I never see it without longing to cut it off. By-the-by, Dr. —— told me that I had exactly Lavater's nose; to my no small satisfaction, for I did not know what to make of that protuberance or promontory of mine. I could not compliment him. He has a very red, drinking face; and little, good-humored eyes, like cunning and short-sightedness united."—*To Joseph Cottle*, May, 1797.

* The work was tolerably hard. "I am running a race with the printers again," he writes to Mr. Cottle, April 5, "translating a work from the French (Necker on the Revolution, vol. ii.—Dr. Aiken and his son translate the first vol.). My time is now wholly engrossed by the race, for I run at the rate of sixteen pages a day, as hard going as sixteen miles for a hack horse."

† His cousin, Margaret Hill.

ject in the 'Monthly Magazine'—a work which, probably, you do not see.

"Farewell! I hope you may soon come to Portsmouth, that we may see you.

"Yours affectionately,

"ROBERT SOUTHEY."

"April 28, 1797.

"MY DEAR THOMAS,

"I have been regretting that you were not at Portsmouth in the great insurrection,* that I might have had a full, true, and particular account of that extraordinary business—a business at which every body is astonished. . . . . As I have no business in London (except, indeed, to dine at Gray's Inn once at the latter end of June) till November, we intend spending the summer and autumn somewhere by the sea; where is not yet determined, but most probably somewhere in Hampshire. . . . . London is a place for which I entertain a most hearty hatred, and Edith likes it as little as myself; and as for the sea, I like it very much when on shore.

"I had a letter from Lisbon yesterday. My uncle's family has been very unfortunate: his poor old woman is dead, and so is his dog Linda. His mare, which was lame, he had given away to be turned into the woods; she has not been seen lately, and he thinks the wolves have eaten her: it was an account that made me melancholy. I had been long enough an inhabitant of his house to become attached to every thing connected with it; and poor old Ursula was an excellent woman: he will never find her equal, and I shall never think of Lisbon again without some feelings of regret. . . . .

"My acquaintance here are more than are convenient, and I meet with invitations unpleasant to refuse, and still more unpleasant to accept. This is another motive to me to wish for a country residence as long as possible. I find the distance in this foul city very inconvenient; 'tis a morning's walk to call upon a distant friend, and I return from it thoroughly fatigued. We are going to dine on Wednesday next with Mary Wollstonecroft—of all the literary characters, the one I most admire. My curiosity is fully satisfied, and the greater part of these people, after that is satisfied, leave no other remaining. This is not the case with her. She is a first-rate woman, sensible of her own worth, but without arrogance or affectation.

"I have two reasons for preferring a residence near the sea: I love to pickle myself in that grand brine tub; and I wish to catch its morning, evening, and mid-day appearance for poetry, with the effect of every change of weather. Fancy will do much; but the poet ought to be an accurate observer of nature; and I shall watch the clouds, and the rising and setting sun, and the sea-birds with no inattentive eye. I have remedied one of my deficiencies, too, since a boy, and learned to swim enough to like the exercise. This I began at Oxford, and practiced a good deal in the summer of 1795. My last dip was in the Atlantic Ocean, at the foot of the Arrabida Mountain—a glorious spot. I have no idea of sublimity exceeding it. . . . . Have you ever met with Mary Wollstonecroft's letters from Sweden and Norway? She has made me in love with a cold climate, and frost and snow, with a northern moonlight. Now I am turned lawyer, I shall have no more books to send you, except, indeed second editions, when they are called for, and then my alterations will be enough, perhaps, to give one interested in the author some pleasure in the comparison. God bless you.

"Yours affectionately,

"ROBERT SOUTHEY."

As the spring advanced, my father began to pine more and more for country air, and, conceiving that his legal studies could be as well pursued by the sea-side as in the smoke of London, went down into Hampshire to look for some place to settle in for the summer months. Southampton was their first halting-place, and from thence he writes to Mr. Bedford complaining of their ill success.

"In every village of the Susquehanna Indians* there is a vacant dwelling called *the Strangers' House*. When a traveler arrives there at one of these villages, he stops and halloos; two of the elders of the tribe immediately go out to meet him; they lead him to this house, and then go round to tell the inhabitants that a stranger is arrived, fatigued and hungry.

"They do not order these things quite so well in England. We arrived at Southampton at six last evening. 'Lodgings' were hung out at almost every house, but some would not let less than eleven rooms, some seven, and so on, and we walked a very long and uncomfortable hour before we could buy hospitality, and that at a very dear rate. I mean to walk to-morrow through Lyndhurst and Lymington to Christ Church—that is, if Edith be better, for she is now very unwell. I hope and believe it is only the temporary effect of fatigue; but, Grosvenor, a single man does not know what anxiety is.

"Edith is not well enough to walk out. I therefore have seen only enough of this place to dislike it. . . . . I want a quiet, lonely place, in sight of something green. Surely in a walk of thirty miles this may be found; but if I find the whole coast infected by visitors, I will go to Bristol, where I shall have the printer on the one side, Charles Danvers on the other, Cottle

* The mutiny of the fleet at Spithead.

* "Here, with Cadwallon and a chosen band,
I left the ships. Lincoya guided us
A toilsome way among the heights; at dusk
We reach'd the village skirts; he bade us halt,
And raised his voice; the elders of the land
Came forth, and led us to an ample hut,
Which in the center of their dwellings stood,
The Strangers' House. They eyed us wondering,
Yet not for wonder ceased they to observe
Their hospitable rites; from hut to hut
The tidings ran that strangers were arrived,
Fatigued, and hungry, and athirst; anon,
Each from his means supplying us, came food
And beverage such as cheer the weary man."
Madoc, Book V.

in front, the woods and rocks of Avon behind, and be in the center of all good things.

"Our journey was hot and dusty, but through a lovely country. At one time the coach was full, and all but me asleep. Something fell off the roof, and I had the unutterable pleasure of waking all of them by bellowing out for the coachman to stop. . . . . Would we were settled, ay, and for life, in some little sequestered valley! I would be content never to climb over the hills that sheltered me, and never to hear music or taste beverage but from the stream that ran beside my door. Let me have the sea, too, and now and then some pieces of a wreck to supply me with fire-wood and remind me of commerce. This New Forest is very lovely; I should like to have a house in it, and dispeople the rest, like William the Conqueror. Of all land objects a forest is the finest. Gisborne has written a feeble poem on the subject. The feelings that fill me when I lie under one tree, and contemplate another in all the majesty of years, are neither to be defined nor expressed, and their indefinable and inexpressible feelings are those of the highest delight. They pass over the mind like the clouds of the summer evening —too fine and too fleeting for memory to detain.

"And now, Grosvenor, would I wager sixpence that you are regretting my absence, because you feel inclined to come to tea with us. I could upbraid you;* but this is one of the follies of man, and I have my share of it, though, thank God! but a small share. What we can do at any time is most likely not to be done at all. We are more willing to make an effort. Is this because we feel uneasy at the prospect of labor and something to be done? and we are stimulated to industry by a love of indolence. I am a self-observer, and, indeed, this appears to me the secret spring.† God bless you.

"R. Southey."

Having succeeded in finding lodgings at Burton, near Christ Church, my father and mother settled themselves there for the summer months, which passed very happily. Here his mother joined them from Bath, and his brother Thomas, then a midshipman on board the Phœbe frigate, who, having lately been taken by the French, had just been released from a short imprisonment at Brest. They had also at this time a young friend domesticated with them. Mr. Charles Lloyd, son of a banker at Birmingham, who had been living for some time with Mr. Coleridge at Nether Stowey, in Somersetshire, and who subsequently became known as an author, and coming to reside in Westmoreland, was classed among the lake poets. Here also Mr. Cottle visited them, and here my father first became acquainted with Mr. Rickman (late one of the clerks of the House of Commons), who will hereafter appear as one of his most constant correspondents and most valued friends.

The surrounding country seems to have afforded him great pleasure, keenly alive as he ever was to all natural beauties, and just at this time doubly inclined to enjoy them, coming from the "no prospect" of Prospect Place, Newington Butts. The sea he delighted in; the New Forest was near at hand, and "a congregation of rivers, the clearest you ever saw." The only drawbacks were his detested legal studies, and the idea of returning to London.

A few of his letters will fill up the present year. The first of these is addressed to Mr. May, whom he had met during his visit to Lisbon, and with whom he had already formed a friendship, as close as it was destined to be lasting. Mr. May, it seems, had promised to lend him the Pucelle of Chapelain.

To John May, Esq.

"Burton, June 26, 1797.

* * * * * * *

"Neither the best friends nor the bitterest enemies of Chapelain could have felt more curiosity than I do to see his poem. Good it can not be; for, though the habit of writing satire, as, indeed, the indulgence of any kind of wit, insensibly influences the moral character, and disposes it to sacrifice any thing to a good point, yet Boileau must have had some reason for the extreme contempt in which he held this unfortunate production. I am inclined to think it better, however, than it has always been represented. Chapelain stood high in poetical reputation when he published this, the work on which he meant to build his fame. He is said to have written good odes; certainly, then, his epic labors can not be wholly void of merit; and for its characteristic fault, extreme harshness, it is very probable that a man of genius, writing in so unmanly a language, should become harsh by attempting to be strong. The French never can have a good epic poem till they have republicanized their language. It appears to me a thing impossible in their meter; and for the prose of Fénélon, Florian, and Betaube, I find it peculiarly unpleasant. I have sometimes read the works of Florian aloud: his stories are very interesting and well conducted; but in reading them I have felt obliged to simplify as I read, and omit most of the similes and apostrophes; they disgusted me, and I felt ashamed to pronounce them. Ossian is the only book bearable in this style: there is a melancholy obscurity in the history of Ossian, and of almost all his heroes, that must please. Ninety-nine readers in a hundred can not understand Ossian, and therefore they like the book. I read it always with renewed pleasure.

"Have you read Madame Roland's Appel a l'impartiale Posterité? It is one of those books that make me love individuals, and yet dread, detest, and despise mankind in a mass. There was a time when I believed in the persuadibility of man, and had the mania of man-mending.

* The two friends seem to have had less intercourse when both were in London than they had anticipated. I find a not uncommon reason hinted at. Mr. Bedford had been unsuccessful in some attachment; and the sight of domestic happiness, just at that time, brought back painful thoughts.

† May 25, 1797.

Experience has taught me better. After a certain age the organs of voice can not accommodate themselves to the utterance of a foreign pronunciation; so it is with the mind: it grows stiff and unyielding, like our sinews, as we grow older. The ablest physician can do little in the great lazar-house of society: it is a pest-house that infects all within its atmosphere. He acts the wisest part who retires from the contagion; nor is that part either a selfish or a cowardly one: it is ascending the ark, like Noah, to preserve a remnant which may become the whole. As to what is the cause of the incalculable wretchedness of society, and what is the panacea, I have long felt certified in my own mind. The rich are strangely ignorant of the miseries to which the lower and largest part of mankind are abandoned. . . . . The savage and civilized states are alike unnatural, alike unworthy of the origin and end of man. Hence the prevalence of skepticism and Atheism, which, from being the effect, becomes the cause of vice. . . . .

"I have lived much among the friends of Priestley, and learned from them many peculiar opinions of that man, who speaks all he thinks. No man has studied Christianity more, or believes it more sincerely; he thinks it not improbable that *another revelation* may be granted us, for the obstinacy and wickedness of mankind call for no less a remedy. The necessity of another revelation I do not see myself. What we have, read with the right use of our own reasoning faculties, appears to me sufficient; but in a Millenarian this opinion is not ridiculous, and the many yet unfulfilled prophecies give it an appearance of probability. . . . .

"The slave trade has much disheartened me. That their traffic is supported by the consumption of sugar is demonstrable: I have demonstrated it to above fifty persons with temporary success, and not three of those persons have persevered in rejecting it. This is perfectly astonishing to me; and what can be expected from those who will not remedy so horrible an iniquity by so easy an exertion? The future presents a dreary prospect; but all will end in good, and I can contemplate it calmly without suffering it to cloud the present. I may not live to do good to mankind personally, but I will at least leave something behind me to strengthen those feelings and excite those reflections in others from whence virtue must spring. In writing poetry with this end, I hope I am not uselessly employing my leisure hours. God bless you. . . . .

"Affectionately yours,

"ROBERT SOUTHEY."

To John May, Esq.

"Burton, July 11, 1797.

"I thank you for Chapelain: I read his poem with the hope of finding something good, and would gladly have reversed the sentence of condemnation, which I must, in common honesty, confirm. It is very bad indeed, and can please only by its absurdity. . . . .

"I thank you, also, for your good opinion of me: I would fain be thought well of by the 'ten righteous men,' and communicate frequently with you as one of them. . . . . I suffer no gloomy presages to disturb the tranquil happiness with which God has blessed me now, and which I know how to value, because I have felt what it is to want every thing except the pride of a well-satisfied conscience.

"The sister and niece of Chatterton are now wholly destitute. On this occasion I appear as editor of all his works for their relief; this is a heinous sin against the world's opinion for a young lawyer, but it would have been a real crime to have refused it. We have a black scene to lay before the public: these poor women have been left in want, while a set of scoundrels have been reaping hundreds from the writings of Chatterton. I hope now to make the catastrophe to the history of the poor boy of Bristol: you shall see the proposals as soon as they are printed. Cottle has been with me a few days, and we have arranged every thing relative to this business: he is the publisher, and means to get the paper at prime cost, and not receive the usual profit from what he sells. The accounts will be published, and we hope and expect to place Mrs. Newton in comfort during the last years of her life.

"Cottle brought with him the new edition of Coleridge's poems: they are dedicated to his brother George in one of the most beautiful poems I ever read. . . . . It contains all the poems of Lloyd and Lamb, and I know no volume that can be compared to it. You know not how infinitely my happiness is increased by residing in the country. I have not a wish beyond the quietness I enjoy; every thing is tranquil and beautiful; but sometimes I look forward with regret to the time when I must return to a city which I so heartily dislike. . . . God bless you! Yours affectionately,

"ROBERT SOUTHEY."

To John May, Esq.

"July 15, 1799.

"MY DEAR FRIEND,

"I sincerely thank you for your letter. . . . . I am inclined to think, when my uncle blamed me for not doing my utmost to relieve my family, he must have alluded to my repeated refusal of entering orders; a step which undoubtedly would almost instantly have relieved them, and which occasioned me great anguish and many conflicts of mind. To this I have been urged by him and by my mother; but you know what my religious opinions are, and I need not ask whether I did rightly and honestly in refusing. Till Christmas last, I supported myself wholly by the profits of my writings. . . . . Thus you may see that the only means I have ever possessed of assisting my mother was by entering the Church. God knows I would exchange every intellectual gift which he has blessed me with for implicit faith to have been able to do this. . . . . I care not for the opinion of the world, but I would willingly be thought justly of by a few individuals. I labor at a study which I very much dislike to render myself independent, and I work for the bookseller whenever I can get employment, that I may have to spare for others. . . . . I now do all I can; perhaps I may some day be enabled to do all I wish; however, there is One who will accept the will for the deed. God bless you! ROBERT SOUTHEY."

The next letter refers to a proposal of Mr. Bedford's, that, when my father and mother came again to reside in London, they should occupy the same house with him.

"August 2, 1797.

"MY DEAR GROSVENOR,

"I like the plan you propose, and see no objection to it at present; but you know how feasible those things appear which we wish. One circumstance only may happen to prevent it. I have some hopes that my mother will come and live with me. This I very earnestly wish, and shall use every means to induce her, but it does not appear so probable as I could desire. This I shall know in a short time; and if then you have not changed your intentions, you know how gladly I should domesticate under the same roof with you. . . . .

"I think you would derive more good from Epictetus than from studying yourself. There is a very proud independence in the Stoic philosophy which has always much pleased me. You would find certain sentences in the Enchiridion which would occur to the mind when such maxims were wanted, and operate as motives; besides, when you are examining yourself, you ought to have a certain standard whereby to measure yourself; and, however far an old Stoic may be from perfection, he is almost a god when compared to the present race, who libel that nature which appeared with such exceeding luster at Athens, at Lacedæmon, and in Rome. I could send you to a better system than that of the bondsman Epictetus, where you would find a better model on which to form your conduct. But the mind should have arrived at a certain stage to profit properly by that book which few have attained: it should be cool and confirmed. . . . . God bless you!

"ROBERT SOUTHEY."

To Grosvenor C. Bedford, Esq.

"Bath, Sept. 22, 1797.

"Me voici then at Bath! And why had you not your birth-day poem? In plain, downright, sincere sincerity, I totally forgot it, till on the morning of the 11th of September, when I found myself on Poole Heath, walking through desolation,* with that gloomy capability which my nativity-caster marks as among the prominent features of my character. We left Burton yesterday morning. The place was very quiet, and I was very comfortable, nor know I when to expect again so pleasant a summer. We live in odd times, Grosvenor; and even in the best periods of this bad society, the straightest path is most cursedly crooked.

"I shall be with you in November. Send me my Coke, I pray you. I want law food, and, though not over hungry, yet must I eat and execrate like Pistol. . . . . Something odd came into my head a few hours since. I was feeling that the love of letter writing had greatly gone from me, and inquiring why: my mind is no longer agitated by hopes and fears, no longer doubtful, no longer possessed with such ardent enthusiasm: it is quiet, and repels all feelings that would disturb that state. When I write I have nothing to communicate, for you know all my opinions and feelings; and no incidents can occur to one settled as I am. . . .

"Yours sincerely,

"R. S."

"Bath, Nov. 19, 1797.

"Grosvenor, I have found out a better fence for our Utopia than Carlisle's plantation of vipers and rattlesnakes: it is—to surround it with a vacuum; for you know, Grosvenor, this would so puzzle the philosophers on the other side, and we might see them making experiments on the atmosphere, to the great annoyance of dogs, whom they would scientifically torture. Besides, if we had any refractory inmate, we might push him into the void.

". . . . I hate the journey; and yet, going to London, I may say with Quarles,

"'My journey's better than my journey's end.'

A little home, Grosvenor, near the sea, or in any quiet country where there is water to bathe in, and what should I wish for in this life? and how could I be so honorably or so happily employed as in writing?

"If Bonaparte should come before I look like Sir John Comyns! Oh, that fine chuckle-head was made for the law! I am too old to have my skull molded.

". . . . Why not trust the settled quietness to which my mind has arrived? It is wisdom to avoid all violent emotions. I would not annihilate my feelings, but I would have them under a most Spartan despotism. Grosvenor, Inveni portum, spes et fortuna valete.

"'Tu quoque, si vis
Lumine claro
Cernere rectum,
Gaudia pelle,
Pelle timorem,
Spemque fugato,
Nec dolor adsit.'

I have laid up the advice of Boëthius in my heart, and prescribe it to you; so fare you well.

"ROBERT SOUTHEY."

The beautiful and affecting lines found in the next letter would have found a fitting place in Mr. Justice Talfourd's "Final Memorials" of Charles Lamb, where all the circumstances of this domestic tragedy are detailed. I may here add that they would have been sent to him had they come into my hands prior to the publication of those most interesting volumes.

* See antè, p. 23.

To C. W. W. Wynn, Esq.

"Bath, Nov. 20, 1797.

"MY DEAR WYNN,

". . . . You will be surprised, perhaps, at hearing that Cowper's poem does not at all please me: you must have taken it up in some moment when your mind was predisposed to be pleased, and the first impression has remained; indeed, I think it not above mediocrity. I can not trace the author of the 'Task' in one line. I know that our tastes differ much in poetry, and yet I think you must like these lines by Charles Lamb. I believe you know his history, and the dreadful death of his mother.

"'Thou shouldst have longer lived, and to the grave
Have peacefully gone down in full old age;
Thy children would have tended thy gray hairs.
We might have sat, as we have often done,
By our fireside, and talked whole nights away,
Old time, old friends, and old events recalling,
With many a circumstance of trivial note,
To memory dear, and of importance grown.
How shall we tell them in a stranger's ear!

"'A wayward son ofttimes was I to thee:
And yet, in all our little bickerings,
Domestic jars, there was I know not what
Of tender feeling that were ill exchanged
For this world's chilling friendships, and their smiles
Familiar whom the heart calls strangers still.

"'A heavy lot hath he, most wretched man,
Who lives the last of all his family!
He looks around him, and his eye discerns
The face of the stranger; and his heart is sick.
Man of the world, what canst thou do for him?
Wealth is a burden which he could not bear;
Mirth a strange crime, the which he dares not act;
And generous wines no cordial to his soul.
For wounds like his, Christ is the only cure.
Go, preach thou to him of a world to come,
Where friends shall meet and know each other's face;
Say less than this, and say it to the winds.'

"I am aware of the danger of studying simplicity of language; but you will find in my blank verse a fullness of phrase when the subject requires it; these lines may instance:

"'It was a goodly sight
To see the embattled pomp, as with the step
Of stateliness the barbed steeds came on;
To see the pennons rolling their long waves
Before the gale; and banners broad and bright
Tossing their blazonry; and high-plumed chiefs,
Vidames, and seneschals, and castellans,
Gay with their bucklers' gorgeous heraldry,
And silken surcoats on the buoyant wind
Billowing.'

God bless you!

"Yours affectionately,
"R. SOUTHEY."

A few days after the date of this letter, my father and mother again took up their abode in London; but the plan of occupying lodgings conjointly with Mr. Bedford was not accomplished, chiefly on account of Charles Lloyd being still with them. From thence he writes to his brother Thomas.

To Thomas Southey.

"London, Dec. 24, 1797.

"MY DEAR TOM,

". . . . I have also another motive for wishing to live out of the town, to avoid the swarms of acquaintances who buzz about me and sadly waste my time—an article I can but little afford to throw away. I have my law, which will soon occupy me from ten in the morning till eight in an office, excepting the dinner-time. My Joan of Arc* takes up more time than you would suppose, for I have had a mine of riches laid open to me in a library belonging to the Dissenters, and have been disturbing the spiders; add to this that I write now for the 'Critical Review,' and you will see that I can not afford to keep levee days. . . . . I keep a large copy of my poems for you. They have sold uncommonly well; 1000 were printed, and I hear 750 are already gone. The Joan of Arc is scandalously delayed at Bristol. I have had only five proofs in all, and this delay, as the book is wanted, is a serious loss. A print of the Maid will be prefixed, solely for the sake of giving Robert Hancock some employment, and making his name known as an engraver. I have got a promise of having him introduced to Alderman Boydell, the great publisher of engravings; he is still at Bath, and I am in hopes I shall be the means of essentially serving him.

"You will be surprised to hear that I have been planning a charitable institution, which will, in all probability, be established. It was planned with John May and Carlisle, and the outline is simply this: Many poor victims perish, after they have been healed at the hospitals, by returning to unwholesome air, scanty and bad food, cold, and filth. We mean to employ them in a large garden, for many persons may be usefully employed in some manner there. When in good order, the produce of the garden will support the institution; in the long winter evenings the people will be employed in making nets, baskets, or matting, and the women in making sheeting—all things that will be wanted at home, and for the overplus a ready sale will be had among the supporters of the Convalescent Asylum. My name will not appear in the business: I leave the credit to lords and esquires. I will send you our printed plan as soon as it is ready. Six hours' labor is all that will be required from the strongest persons: for extra work they will be paid; then they may leave the Asylum with some little money, and with some useful knowledge.

"We are much pleased with this scheme, as it will make every body useful whom it benefits: a man with one leg may make holes for cabbages with his wooden leg, and a fellow with one arm follow and put in the plants. . . . .

"Would you were here to-morrow! we would keep holiday; but 'tis very long since Christmas has been a festival with us. God bless you.

"Yours affectionately,
"R. SOUTHEY."

My father remained in London only a very short time, when, finding it extremely prejudicial both to his own health and my mother's, he

* He was at present engaged in revising Joan of Arc for a second edition, in which all that part which had been written by Mr. Coleridge was omitted.

determined to seek some other place of residence, and went down to Bristol with that intention. Soon afterward he writes to his friend, Mr. Wynn, in somewhat depressed spirits.

To C. W. W. Wynn, Esq.

"Bath, Wednesday, April 4, 1798.

"MY DEAR WYNN,

"I should have thought you would have liked the Merida Inscription. It was designed for my Letters, but, on consideration, the point appears more applicable to our own country, and as one martyr is as good as another, Señora Eulalia must give place to old Latimer and Ridley. Its appearance in the Oracle makes me let out what I intended not to have told you till Christmas. I then thought to have taken you into a house of my own, and shown you the chairs and tables into which I had transmuted bad verses. Immediately before I left town I agreed to furnish the Morning Post with occasional verses without a signature.* My end in view was to settle in a house as soon as possible, which this, with the Review, would enable me at Christmas to do. I told no person whatever but Edith. I signed the Inscription because I meant to insert it in my letters. Of all the rest Lord William is the only piece that bears the mark of the beast. I did not tell you, because you would not like it now, and it would have amused you at Christmas: Lord William's is certainly a good story, and will, when corrected, make the best of my ballads. I am glad you like it. There is one other, which, if you have not seen, I will send you: it is ludicrous, in the Alonzo meter, called the 'Ring'†—a true story, and, like the 'Humorous Lieutenant,'‡ it is not good for much, and yet one or two stanzas may amuse you.

"I write this from Bath, where I was summoned in consequence of my mother's state of health. She is very ill, and I hope to remove her to Lisbon speedily. The climate would, I am certain, restore her, though I fear nothing else can.

"You call me lazy for not writing; is it not the same with you? Do you feel the same inclination for filling a folio sheet now, as when, in '90 and '91, we wrote to each other so fully and so frequently? The inclination is gone from me. I have nothing to communicate—no new feelings—no new opinions. We move no longer in the same circles, and no longer see things in the same point of view. I never now write a long letter to those who think with me: it is useless to express what they also feel; and as for reasoning with those who differ from me, I have never seen any good result from argument. I write not in the best of spirits; my mother's state of health depresses me—the more so, as I have to make her cheerful. Edith is likewise very unwell; indeed, so declining as to make me somewhat apprehensive for the future. A few months will determine all these uncertainties, and perhaps change my views in life—or rather destroy them. This is the first time that I have expressed the feelings that often will rise. Take no notice of them when you write.

"God bless you. If nothing intervene, I shall see you in May. I wish, indeed, that month were over. Few men have ever more subdued their feelings than myself, and yet I have more left than are consistent with happiness.

"Once more, God bless you.

"Yours affectionately,

"ROBERT SOUTHEY."

To C. W. W. Wynn, Esq.

"Bristol, May 5, 1798.

"MY DEAR WYNN,

". . . . You have seen my brother in the Gazette, I suppose—mentioned honorably, and in the wounded list. His wounds are slight, but his escape has been wonderful. The boatswain came to know if they should board the enemy forward, and was told, by all means. Tom took a pike and ran forward. He found them in great confusion, and, as he thought, only wanting a leader; he asked if they would follow him, and one poor fellow answered 'Ay.' On this Tom got into the French ship, followed, as he thought, by the rest, but, in fact, only by this man. Just as he had made good his footing, he received two thrusts with a pike in his right thigh, and fell. They made a third thrust as he fell, which glanced from his shoulder blade, and took a small piece of flesh out of his back. He fell between the two ships, and this saved his life, for he caught a rope and regained the deck of the Mars.* * * I do not know whether it would be prudent in Tom to accompany Lord Proby to Lisbon, as Lord Bridport has sent him word that he would not forget him when he has served his time, and offered him a berth on board his own ship. He will use his own judgment, and probably, I think, follow the fortunes of Butterfield, the first lieutenant. When I saw him so noticed by Butterfield, I felt, as he says of himself during the engagement, 'something that I never felt before.' I felt more proud of my brother when he received ten pounds prize-money, and sent his mother half; and yet it gave me something like exultation that he would now be respected by his acquaintance, though not for his best virtues. He is an excellent young man, and, moreover, a good seaman. God bless him, and you also.

"Yours affectionately,

"R. SOUTHEY."

Among my father's college friends, and as forming one of the enthusiastic party who were to have formed a "model republic" on the banks of the Susquehanna, has been mentioned George Burnett, who, of all the number, suffered most permanently from having taken up those visionary views. He had intended to enter the Church of

* For this he was to receive a guinea a week. A similar offer was made about this time by the editor of the Morning Chronicle to Burns, and refused.

† This ballad is called "King Charlemagne" in the later editions of his poems.

‡ This was probably one of his early poems, which was never republished.

* This was in the engagement between the Mars and L'Hercule.

England, and, had he not been tempted to quit the beaten track, would probably have become a steady, conscientious, and useful clergyman. Carried away by the influence chiefly of my father and Mr. Coleridge, he imbibed first their political and then their religious opinions; and thus, being led to abandon the intention with which he had entered Oxford, he became so completely unsettled as to render his short life a series of unsuccessful attempts in many professions. Much of this was, indeed, owing to the vacillating character of his mind; but it was not the less, through life, a subject of regret to my father, not unmixed with self-reproach.

At the present time he was minister to a Unitarian congregation at Yarmouth, whither my father now went for a short visit, having the additional motive of seeing his brother Henry, whom, some time previously, he had placed with Burnett as a private pupil. Through Burnett's means he was now introduced to William Taylor, of Norwich, with whose writings he was already acquainted, and toward whom he found himself immediately and strongly drawn by the similarity of their tastes and pursuits. This meeting led to a correspondence (chiefly upon literary subjects), which has been already given to the public, and to a friendship which would have been a very close one, had there not, unhappily, been a total want of sympathy between the parties on the most important of all subjects —William Taylor's religious opinions being of the most extravagant and rationalistic kind. This difference my father felt much in later life, as his own religious feelings deepened and strengthened, although he always entertained toward him the sincerest regard, and a great respect for his many good qualities.

The other incidents of this visit may be gathered from the following letters, the latter of which, if there is nothing particularly striking in the versification, yet affords too pleasing a picture of his mind to be omitted.

To Mrs. Southey.

"May 29, 1798.

. . . . "I am writing from Ormsby, the dwelling-place of Mr. Manning, distant six miles from Yarmouth. We came here yesterday to dinner, and leave it to-morrow evening. I have begun some blank verse to you and laid it aside, because, if I do not tell you something about this place now, I shall not do it at all. . . . . This part of England looks as if Nature had wearied herself with adorning the rest with hill and dale, and squatted down here to rest herself. You must even suppose a very Dutch-looking Nature to have made it of such pancake flatness. An unpromising country, and yet, Edith, I could be very happy with such a home as this. I am looking through the window over green fields, as far as I can see—no great distance; the hedges are all grubbed up in sight of the house, which produces a very good effect. A few fine acacias, white-thorns, and other trees are scattered about; a walk goes all round, with a beautiful hedge of lilachs, laburnums, the Guelder rose, Barbary shrubs, &c., &c. Edith, you would not wish a sweeter scene, and, being here, I wish for nothing but you; half an hour's walk would reach the sea-shore.

"I had almost forgot one with whom I am more intimate than any other part of the family, Rover—a noble dog, something of the spaniel, but huge as a mastiff, and his black and brindled hair curling close, almost like a lady's wig. A very sympathizing dog, I assure you, for he will not only shake hands, but, if I press his paw, return the pressure. Moreover, there is excellent Nottingham ale, sent annually by Mr. Manning's son-in-law from Nottingham; what my uncle would call 'fine stuff,' such as Robin Hood and his outlaws used to drink under the greenwood tree. Robin Hood's beverage! how could I choose but like it? It is sweet and strong—very strong: a little made me feel this. . . . The cows in this country have no horns; this, I think, a great improvement in the breed of horned cattle, and this kind is found more productive. Another peculiarity about Yarmouth is the number of arches formed by the jaw-bones of a whale: they trade much with Greenland there. The old walls and old gates of the town are yet standing, the town is certainly a pleasing one. I left it, however, with pleasure, to enjoy the society of Ormsby, and I shall leave Ormsby with pleasure for the society of Norwich. In short, every movement is agreeable, because it brings me homeward.

"Thursday.

"We went yesterday in the morning to the ruins of Caister Castle, once the seat of Fastolffe, where, after wasting a great part of his fortune in the French wars, and being defeated at Patay, and disgraced in consequence of his flight, he retired to quarrel with his neighbors. The ruin is by no means fine, compared with several I have seen, but all these things produce a pleasant effect upon the mind; and, besides, it is well, when I am writing about the man, to have some knowledge of every thing knowable respecting him. In the evening we returned with William Taylor to Norwich. On the way we left the chaise, and crossed a moor on foot, in hopes of hearing the bittern cry. It was not till we were just quitting the moor that one of these birds thought proper to gratify us; then he began, and presently we saw one, so that I re-entered the chaise highly satisfied. . . . . God bless you. Your affectionate

"ROBERT SOUTHEY."

To Mrs. Southey.

"June 4, 1798.

"Edith, it ever was thy husband's wish,
Since he hath known in what is happiness,
To find some little home, some low retreat,
Where the vain uproar of the worthless world
Might never reach his ear; and where, if chance
The tidings of its horrible strifes arrived,
They would endear retirement, as the blast
Of winter makes the sheltered traveler
Draw closer to the hearth-side, every nerve
Awake to the warm comfort. Quietness
Should be his inmate there; and he would live

To thee, and to himself, and to our God.
To dwell in that foul city—to endure
The common, hollow, cold, lip intercourse
Of life; to walk abroad and never see
Green field, or running brook, or setting sun!
Will it not wither up my faculties,
Like some poor myrtle that in the town air
Pines on the parlor window?

"Every where
Nature is lovely: on the mountain height,
Or where the imbosomed mountain glen displays
Secure sublimity, or where around
The undulated surface gently slopes
With mingled hill and valley: every where
Nature is lovely; even in scenes like these,
Where not a hillock breaks the unvaried plain,
The eye may find new charms that seeks delight.

"At eve I walk abroad; the setting sun
Hath softened with a calm and mellow hue
The cool fresh air; below, a bright expanse,
The waters of the *Broad** lie luminous.
I gaze around; the unbounded plain presents
Ocean immensity, whose circling line
The bending heaven shuts in. So even here
Methinks I could be well content to fix
My sojourn; grow familiar with these scenes
Till time and memory make them dear to me.
And wish no other home.

"There have been hours
When I have longed to mount the winged bark,
And seek those better climes, where orange groves
Breathe on the evening gale voluptuous joy.
And, Edith! though I heard from thee alone
The pleasant accents of my native tongue,
And saw no wonted countenance but thine,
I could be happy in the stranger's land,
Possessing all in thee. O best beloved!
Companion, friend, and yet a dearer name!
I trod those better climes a heartless thing,
Cintra's cool rocks, and where Arrabida
Lifts from the ocean its sublimer heights,
Thine image wandered with me, and one wish
Disturbed the deep delight.

"Even now that wish,
Making short absence painful, still recurs.
The voice of friendship, that familiar voice,
From which in other scenes I daily heard
First greeting, poorly satisfies the heart.
And wanting thee, though in best intercourse,
Such as in after years remembrance oft
Will love to dwell upon; yet when the sun
Goes down, I see his setting beams with joy,
And count again the allotted days, and think
The hour will soon arrive when I shall meet
The eager greeting of affection's eye,
And hear the welcome of the voice I love.

* * * * * *

"What have I to tell you? Can you be interested in the intercourse I have with people whose very names are new to you? On Sunday I went to dine with Sir Lambert Blackwell. . . . He has a very pretty house, and the finest picture I ever saw: it is St. Cecilia at the moment when the heads of her parents are brought in to terrify her into an abandonment of Christianity. I never saw a countenance so full of hope, and resignation, and purity, and holy grief: it is by Carlo Dolce. I have seen many fine pictures, but never one so perfect, so sublime, so interesting, irresistibly interesting, as this. . . . God bless you. Your ROBERT SOUTHEY."

Upon my father's return from this visit to Norfolk, he rejoined my mother at Bristol, and very shortly afterward he took a small house at Westbury, a beautiful village about two miles distant from thence. Here they resided for twelve months. "This," he says, in one of the prefaces to the collected edition of his poems, "was one of the happiest portions of my life.* I have never, before or since, produced so much poetry in the same space of time. The smaller pieces were communicated by letter to Charles Lamb, and had the advantage of his animadversions. I was then, also, in habits of the most frequent and familiar intercourse with Davy, then in the flower and freshness of his youth. We were within an easy walk of each other, over some of the most beautiful ground in that beautiful part of England. When I went to the Pneumatic Institution, he had to tell me of some new experiment or discovery, and of the views which it opened for him; and when he came to Westbury, there was a fresh portion of 'Madoc' for his hearing. Davy encouraged me with his hearty approbation during its progress; and the bag of nitrous oxyd with which he generally regaled me upon my visit to him was not required for raising my spirits to the degree of settled fair, and keeping them at that elevation."

In addition to "Madoc," my father was at this time preparing for the press a second volume of his minor poems, and a second edition of his "Letters from Spain and Portugal;" and he was also engaged in editing the first volume of the "Annual Anthology," which was published in Bristol in the course of the following year. Other literary employments are mentioned in his letters, but Blackstone, and Coke upon Littleton, seem to have been almost wholly thrown aside; the study of the law was daily becoming more and more distasteful to him, and he was beginning to find, that, however he might command his attention, and bring the full force of his understanding to bear upon the subject, the memory was not to be controlled by the will; and that the time and trouble so employed, *not* being upon a "labor of love," was purely "labor lost."

His mother was now residing with him, and also the "Cousin Margaret" mentioned in the Autobiography.

To Thomas Southey.

"Martin Hall, Westbury, June 27, 1798.

"MY DEAR TOM,

"Here we are, and you see have christened the house properly, I assure you, as the martins have colonized all round it, and doubly lucky must the house be on which they so build and bemire. We hesitated between the appropriate names of Rat Hall, Mouse Mansion, Vermin Villa, Cockroach Castle, Cobweb Cottage, and Spider Lodge; but, as we routed out the spiders, brushed away the cobwebs, stopped the rat holes, and found no cockroaches, we bethought us of the animals without, and dubbed it Martin Hall.

"I am sorry, Tom, you could not have seen

* So they call the wide spread of a river in the fens.

* "To me the past presents
No object for regret;
To me the present gives
All cause for full content.
The future? It is now the cheerful noon,
And on the sunny, smiling fields I gaze
With eyes alive to joy;
When the dark night descends,
I willingly shall close my weary lids
In sure and certain hope to wake again."
Minor Poems, Westbury, 1798.

us settled; you would like the old house; and the view from the *drawing-room* and garden is delightful: we have turned to most notably. But once the house was an inn, or ale-house, so we have had application to sell beer, and buy a stock of tobacco-pipes. Much has been done, and much is yet to do. The rooms are large, the garden well stocked; we cut our own cabbages, live upon currant puddings, and shall soon be comfortably settled.

* * * * * * *

"I wish you had been here, you might have been up to your eyes in dirt and rubbish. * * We have bespoke a cat—a great carroty cat."

To H. H. Southey.

"Martin Hall, July 14, 1798.

"My dear Harry,

"I thank you for your ode of Anacreon: the Greek meter in which you have translated it is certainly the best that could be chosen, but perhaps the most difficult, as the accent should flow so easily that a bad reader may not be able to spoil them. This is the case with your fourth and fifth lines: an old woman can't read them out of the proper cadence. * * * * I think this meter much improved to an English ear by sometimes ending a line with a long syllable instead of a trochee. This you will see regularly done in the following translation from the Spanish of Villegas. The original meter is that of Θελω λεγειν Ατρειδας, and the verses flow as harmoniously as those of Anacreon.

"'The maidens thus address me:
How is it, Don Esteban,
That you of love sing always,
And never sing of war?

"'I answer thus the question,
Ye bachelor* young damsels:
It is that men are ugly,
It is that you are fair.

"'For what would it avail me
To sing to drums and trumpets,
While marching sorely onward,
Encumbered by my shield?

"'Think you the tree of glory
Delights the common soldier;
That tree so full of blossoms
That never bears a fruit?

"'Let him who gains in battles
His glorious wounds, enjoy them;
Let him praise war who knows not
The happiness of peace.

"'I will not sing of soldiers,
I will not sing of combats,
But only of the damsels—
My combats are with them.'

* * * * * * *

* * "We are now tolerably settled at Martin Hall. I have labored much in making it comfortable, and comfortable it now is. Our sitting-room is large, with three windows and two recesses—once windows, but now converted into book-cases, with green baize hanging half way down the books, as in the College Green. The room is papered with cartridge paper, bordered with yellow vandykes edged with black. I have a good many books, but not all I want, as many of my most valuable ones are lying in London. I shall be very glad to get settled in a house at London, where I may collect all my chattels together, and move on contentedly for some dozen years in my profession. You will find little difficulty either in Anacreon or in Homer; the language will soon become familiar to you, and you will, I hope, apply yourself to it with assiduity. I remember William Taylor promising to give you some instruction in German when you were well enough acquainted with the ancient languages to begin the modern ones. I need not tell you how valuable such instruction would be, or how gladly I should avail myself of such an opportunity were it in my power. It is of very great advantage to a young man to be a good linguist: he is more respected, and may be more useful; his sources of pleasure are increased; and, what in the present state of the world is to be considered, in case of necessity, he has additional means of supporting himself. The languages, Harry—which I learned almost as an amusement—have considerably contributed and do contribute to my support.

"You will send me your other translations from Anacreon, and, in return, I will always send you some piece which you had not before seen. I wish you would sometimes, on a fine evening, walk out, and write as exact a description of the sunset, and the appearance of every thing around, as you can. You would find it a pleasant employment, and I can assure you it would be a very useful one. I should like you to send me some of these sketches; not of sunset only, but of any natural scene. If you have Ossian at hand, you may see what I mean in the description of night by five Scotch bards. Your neighborhood to the sea gives you opportunities of seeing the finest effects of sunrise—fine weather, or storms; or you may contrast it with inland views and forest scenery, of which I believe you will see much in Nottinghamshire.

"Let me hear from you soon, and often, and regularly. God bless you!

"Your affectionate brother,

"Robert Southey."

A few weeks spent in Herefordshire, and a pedestrian excursion into Wales, accompanied by his friend Mr. Danvers, were the chief variations in my father's life during this summer. In these journeys he found temporary relief from a state of ill health, which was beginning gradually to creep over him, partly induced, probably, by his ordinary sedentary habits, and intense mental application, and that anxiety about his "ways and means" which necessarily followed him through life, and of which he had already a full share, from the various relations who were wholly or chiefly dependent on him. The two following letters were written during these excursions.

To C. W. W. Wynn, Esq.

"Hereford, August 15, 1798.

"My dear Wynn,

"You will, I think, be somewhat amused at

* This is literal. The original is muchachas bachilleras – bachelor girls.

H

this copy of a note from a West-country farmer's daughter: it is genuine, I assure you:

"'Dear Miss,

"'The energy of the Races prompts me to assure you that my request is forbidden; the idea of which I had awkwardly nourished, notwithstanding my propensity to reserve. Mr. T. will be there; let me with confidence assure you that him and brothers will be very happy to meet you and brothers. Us girls can not go for reasons; the attention of the cows claims our assistance in the evening. Unalterably yours.'

Is it not admirable?

"I have seen myself Bedforized,* and it has been a subject of much amusement. Holcroft's likeness is admirably preserved. I know not what poor Lamb has done to be croaking there. What I think the worst part of the anti-Jacobin abuse is the lumping together men of such opposite principles: this was stupid. We should have all been welcoming the Director, not the Theophilanthrope. The conductors of the Anti-Jacobin will have much to answer for in thus inflaming the animosities of this country. They are laboring to produce the deadly hatred of Irish faction—perhaps to produce the same end. Such an address as you mention might probably be of great use; that I could assist you in it is less certain. I do not feel myself at all calculated for any thing that requires methodical reasoning; and though you and I should agree in the main object of the pamphlet, our opinions are at root different. The old systems of government I think must fall; but in this country, the immediate danger is on the other hand—from an unconstitutional and unlimited power. Burleigh saw how a Parliament might be employed against the people, and Montesquieu prophesied the fall of English liberty when the Legislature should become corrupt. You will not agree with me in thinking his prophecy fulfilled.

"Violent men there undoubtedly are among the Democrats, as they are always called, but is there any one among them whom the ministerialists will allow to be moderate? The Anti-Jacobin certainly speaks the sentiments of government.

"Heywood's Hierarchie is a most lamentable poem, but the notes are very amusing. I fancy it is in most old libraries. I do not see any thing that promises well for ballads. There are some fine Arabic traditions that would make noble poems. I was about to write one upon the Garden of Irem; the city and garden still exist in the deserts invisibly, and one man only has seen them. This is the tradition, and I had made it the ground-work of what I thought a very fine story; but it seemed too great for a poem of 300 or 400 lines.

"I do not much like Don Carlos: it is by far the worst of Schiller's plays.

"Yours affectionately,

"R. Southey."

To Thomas Southey.

"Hereford, Aug. 29, 1798.

"My dear Tom,

"Your letter was very agreeable, for we began to doubt whether or no you were in the land of the living. We have been a fortnight in this part of the world, part of the time at Dilwyn, the original seat of the Tylers; and Shobdon was one of the places we visited. Our absence from home will not exceed a month, and though the time has passed pleasantly, I shall not be sorry to sit quietly down once more at Martin Hall. . . . . I have heard high commendation of you, somewhat in a roundabout way, from a Taunton lady, who writes to a friend of hers, 'The gallant Southey for me.' Now, Tom, who the devil this Taunton damsel is, I could not find out, for the name was dropped by the way, so you must guess if you can.

"My Letters* are in the press, and my volume will soon—it will include the 'Vision.' I have begun my English Eclogues, and written two which I rather like. My Calendar also is greatly advanced since you left us: it now extends to some 1400 lines, and much of the remainder is planned out. I have learned to rise early when at home, and written two new books of 'Madoc' wholly, before any one else in the house was up.

"Do you know that I have been caricatured in the Anti-Jacobin Magazine, together with Lloyd, Lamb, the Duke of Bedford, Fox, &c., &c. The fellow has not, however, libeled my likeness, because he did not know it; so he clapped an ass's head on my shoulders.

"I have done a great deal in the planning way since I have been in Herefordshire. You would, I think, be pleased with the skeleton of a long poem upon the destruction of the Dom Daniel, of which the outline is almost completed; when it will get further, I know not. I have much on my hands: my Calendar will probably fill three volumes, and the more the work gets on, the better does it please me.

"Edith has learned to ride; she thinks of entering among the light horsewomen, and I hope to get her the rank of a corporella.

"Did you hear of the glorious take in about Bonaparte at Bristol? Oh, Tom, I saw the newspaper boy pass by Martin Hall with a paper cap, inscribed *Bonaparte taken!* and the bells rung Sunday, and all day Monday. Tuesday I was at Cottle's when the mail was expected. The volunteers were ready to strike up, and two men kneeling on the church and post-office with the flags ready to let fly. N.B.—It rained very hard. The four streets full of people, all assembled to see the triumphal entry of the mail-coach, as it was to be crowned with laurels: you never saw so total a blank as when all proved to be false. . . . .

"I shall now do better one year than the last; so, Tom, let us hope all things, for we have weathered worse times than we shall ever know again, I trust. God bless you. R. S."

To Mrs. Southey.

"Bwlch, Brecknockshire, Oct. 14, 1798.

"Without a map, my dear Edith will know

* This is explained in the next letter.

* Letters from Spain and Portugal, 2d edit.

nothing of the place I date from, and if she have a map to refer to, very probably she may miss the name. . . . . What have we seen? Woods, mountains, and mountain glens and streams. In those words are comprehended all imaginable beauty. Sometimes we have been winding up the dingle side, and every minute catching the stream below through the wood that half hid it, always hearing its roar; then over mountains, where nothing was to be seen but hill and sky, their sides rent by the winter streams; sometimes a little tract of cultivation appeared up some coomb-place, so lonely, so beautiful: they looked as though no tax-gatherer ever visited them. I have longed to dwell in these solitary houses in a mountain vale, sheltered by the hills and the trees that grow finely round the houses; the vale rich by the soil swept down the hills; a stream before the door, rolling over large stones—pure water, so musical, too! and a child might cross it; yet at wet seasons it must thunder down a torrent. In such scenes there is a simpleness of sublimity fit to feed imagination. . . . . Yesterday, at two, we reached Brecon, a distance of eighteen miles. A little but clean ale-house afforded us eight pennyworth of bread, cheese, and ale, and we departed for Crickhowel, a stage of thirteen more. A woman whom we met, and of whom we asked the distance, measured it by the 'great inn' at Bwlch, on the way, and we determined to halt there. Before we got there heavy rain overtook us, and we were wet the lower half when we reached the great inn at Bwlch, which is not quite so good as the memorable ale-house at Tintern. However, we have very good beds here; the cream was good, and the tea excellent.

"So we have ate, drank, dried ourselves, and grown comfortable; also we have had the pleasure of the landlord's company, who, being somewhat communicative and somewhat tipsy, gave us the history of himself and family. . . . I much like the appearance of the Welsh women: they have all a character in their countenances, an intelligence which is very pleasant. Their round, shrewd, national physiognomy is certainly better than that of the English peasantry, and we have uniformly met with civility. There is none of the insolence and brutality which characterize our colliers and milk-women.

"At Merthyr we witnessed the very interesting custom of strewing the graves. They are fenced round with little white stones, and the earth in the coffin shape planted with herbs and flowers, and strewn with flowers. Two women were thus decorating a grave—the one a middle-aged woman, and much affected. This affected me a good deal; the custom is so congenial to one's heart; it prolongs the memory of the dead, and links the affections to them. . . . . This part of Brecknockshire is most beautiful: the Usk rolling through a rich and cultivated vale, and mountains rising on every side. We feel no fatigue, and I get more comfortable every day now our faces are turned homeward.

"God bless you, my dear Edith. Farewell. Now for the Black Mountain and St. David's."

To John May, Esq.

"Westbury, Dec. 14, 1798.

"MY DEAR FRIEND,

"We are enduring something like a Kamtschatkan winter here. I am obliged to take my daily walk, and, though I go wrapped up in my great-coat, almost like a dancing bear in hirsute appearance, still the wind pierces me. We are very deficient in having no winter dress for such weather as this. I am busy upon the Grecian history, or, rather, it is the employment of all my leisure. The escape of my Pythoness* was in the early ages, and they, I believe, will suit me best. I must have the Pythian games celebrated; for the story, I have only invention to trust to. The costume of Greece will be new to the English drama, owing to the defects of our theaters; but I had rather get to some country and some people less known. Among the many thoughts that have passed over my mind upon this subject, I have had the idea of grounding stories upon the oppression exercised at different periods of time upon particular classes of people; the Helots, for instance, the Albigenses, or the Jews. The idea of a tragedy upon one of the early martyrs has for some years been among my crude plans; but it would not suit the stage, because it would not suit the times. There is something more noble in such a character than I can conceive in any other: firm to the defiance of death in avowing the truth, and patient under all oppression, without enthusiasm, supported by the calm conviction that this is his duty. Among the Helots, something may be made of the infernal Crypteia; but I am afraid to meddle with a Spartan; there is neither feeling, thinking, nor speaking like one who has been educated according to the laws of Lycurgus: knowledge of human nature is not knowledge of Lacedæmonian nature. The state of slavery among our own countrymen at an early period is better; the grievances of wardship, and the situation of a fief or villain. Dramatists and novelists have ransacked early history, and we have as many crusaders on the stage and in the circulating library as ever sailed to Palestine; but they only pay attention to the chronology, and not to the manners or mind of the period. * * * * * *

"Yours affectionately,

"ROBERT SOUTHEY."

With one brief extract referring to his health, I will conclude this chapter. It is from a letter to William Taylor, of Norwich, who had now become one of his regular correspondents, and to whom he was in the habit of submitting many of his minor pieces for criticism as he wrote them.

"I was very glad to see your hand-writing again. I have been much indisposed, and my recovery, I fear, will be slow. My heart is af-

* My father had been urged by several friends to try his hand at dramatic composition; and this refers to one of the subjects on which he had purposed to write a play.

fected, and this at first alarmed me, because I could not understand it; however, I am scientifically satisfied it is only a nervous affection. Sedentary habits have injured my health; the prescription of exercise prevents me from proceeding with the work that interests me, and only allows time for the task labor, which is neither pleasant to look at nor to remember. My leisure is quite destroyed: had it not been for this, I should, ere this, have sent you the remainder of my Eclogues.*

CHAPTER VI.

RESIDENCE AT WESTBURY—DRAMATIC PLANS—ILL HEALTH—GOES TO LONDON TO KEEP THE TERM AT GRAY'S INN—MADOC COMPLETED—EXCURSION INTO DEVONSHIRE—LETTERS FROM THENCE—GOES AGAIN TO RESIDE AT BURTON—SEVERE ILLNESS—RETURNS TO BRISTOL—THALABA—PROJECT OF ESTABLISHING BEGUINAGES—POEM IN HEXAMETERS, ON MOHAMMED, COMMENCED—CONTINUED ILL HEALTH—MAKES ARRANGEMENTS FOR GOING TO LISBON.—1799, 1800.

THE commencement of the year 1799 found my father still at Westbury, and still employed at some one or other of his many literary avocations. I have not thought it needful to notice particularly the reception which his writings had hitherto met with from the public, because it was not of that peculiarly marked character which materially influences an author's career. He had, however, been gradually "working his way up the hill," and the booksellers were ready enough to find him abundant periodical employment, which, though it "frittered away his time," and was but indifferently remunerated, he still found more profitable than any other way in which he could employ his pen. I can not but regret that no list of his many contributions to magazines and reviews, and other periodicals, during his early life, can be found. Although the articles themselves might not be worth preservation, still, could the number of them be added to the rest of his works, especially taking into account his very numerous writings in the Annual and Quarterly Reviews, he would unquestionably be found to have been one of the most voluminous writers of any age or of any country. The following letters will give some idea of his untiring industry:

To Thomas Southey.

"Jan. 5, 1799.

"MY DEAR TOM,

"Ever since you left us have I been hurried from one job to another. You know I expected a parcel of books when you went away. They came, and I had immediately to kill off one detachment; that was but just done, when down came a bundle of French books, to be returned with all possible speed. This was not only unexpected work, but double work, because all extracts were to be translated. Well, that I did, and by that time the end of the month came round, and I am now busy upon English books again. What with this and my weekly communications with Stuart,* and my plaguy regimen of exercise, I have actually no time for any voluntary employment. In a few days I hope to breathe a little in leisure.

"I am sorry it is low water with you, and that we can not set you afloat. We are heavily laden, and can, with hard work, barely keep above water. I have been obliged to borrow; by-and-by we shall do better; but we are just now at the worst, and these vile taxes will take twenty pounds from me, at the least.

"We had an odd circumstance happened to us on Wednesday. Just as we were beginning breakfast, a well-dressed woman, in a silk gown and muff, entered the room. 'I am come to take a little breakfast,' said she. Down she laid her muff, took a chair, and sat down by the fire. We thought she was mad; but she looked so stupid, that we soon found that was not the case. Sure enough, breakfast she did. I was obliged once to go down and laugh. My mother and Edith behaved very well, but Margery could not come into the room. When the good lady had done, she rose, and asked what she had to pay. 'Nothing, ma'am,' said my mother. 'Nothing! why, how is this?' 'I don't know how it is,' said my mother, and smiled; 'but so it is.' 'What, don't you keep a public?' 'No, indeed, ma'am;' so we had half a hundred apologies, and the servant had a shilling. We had a good morning's laugh for ourselves, and a good story for our friends, and she had a very good breakfast. I wish you had been here.

"Harry is going to a Mr. Maurice, a gentleman who takes only a few pupils, at Normanston, near Lowestoff, Suffolk. You may, perhaps, know Lowestoff, as the more easterly point of the island. It is a very fortunate situation for him.

"The frost has stopped the pump and the press. My letters are just done, but not yet published. Our bread has been so hard frozen, that no one in the house except myself could cut it, and it made my arm ache for the whole day.

"I do not know where Lloyd is; it is a long time since I have heard from him. Indeed, my own employments make me a vile correspondent.

"The Old Woman of Berkeley cuts a very respectable figure on horseback; and Beelzebub is so admirably done, that one would suppose he had sat for the picture.† . . . . . I know not how you exist this weather. My great-coat is a lovely garment, my mother says; and, but for it, I should, I believe, be found on Durdham Down in the shape of a great icicle. At home the wind comes in so cuttingly in the evenings, that I have taken to wear my Welsh wig, to the great improvement of my personal charms! Edith says I may say that.

* Westbury, Dec. 27, 1758.

* Editor of the Morning Post.

† This engraving was copied from the Nuremberg Chronicle.

"I shall make a ballad upon the story of your shipmate the marine,* who kept the fifth commandment so well. By the help of the devil, it will do; and there can be no harm in introducing him to the devil a little before his time. God bless you. Yours affectionately,

"ROBERT SOUTHEY.

"A happy new year."

To C. W. W. Wynn, Esq.

"Jan. 9, 1799.

"MY DEAR WYNN,

"As for the verses upon Mr. Pitt, I never wrote any. Possibly Lewis may have seen a poem by Coleridge, which I have heard of, but have never seen—a dialogue between Blood, Fire, and Famine, or some such interlocutors.† Strangers are perpetually confounding us.

"My Eclogues, varying in subject, are yet too monotonous, in being all rather upon melancholy subjects.

"I have some play plots maturing in my head, but none ripe. My wish is to make something better than love the main-spring; and I have one or two sketches, but all the plots seem rather calculated to produce one or two great scenes rather than a general effect. My mind has been turned too much to the epic, which admits a longer action, and passes over the uninteresting parts.

"The escape of the Pythoness with a young Thessalian seems to afford most spectacle. If you have Diodorus Siculus at hand, and will refer to lib. 16, p. 428, you may find all the story, for I know no more than the fact.

"Pedro the Just pleases me best. This is my outline: You know one of Inez's murderers escaped—Pacheco. This man has, by lightning or in battle, lost his sight, and labors under the agony of remorse. The priest, to whom he has confessed, enjoins him to say certain prayers where he committed the murder. Thus disfigured, he ran little danger of discovery; what he did run enhanced their merits. A high reward has been offered for Pacheco, and the confessor sends somebody to inform against him and receive it.

"Leonora, his daughter, comes to Coimbra to demand justice. Her mother's little property has been seized by a neighboring noble, who trusts to the hatred Pedro bears the family, and their depressed state, for impunity. This, too, may partly proceed from Leonora having refused to be his mistress. A good scene may be made when she sees the king, and he thinks she is going to entreat for her father; but Pedro was inflexibly just, and he summons the nobleman.

"Pacheco is thrown into prison. The nobleman, irritated at the king, is still attached to Leonora. He is not a bad man, though a violent one. He offers to force the prison, deliver Pacheco, and retire into Castille, if she will be his. The king's confessor intercedes for Pacheco, but his execution is fixed for the day when Inez is to be crowned. At the decisive moment, Leonora brings the children of Inez to intercede, and is successful. She refuses to marry the noble, and expresses her intention of entering a nunnery after her mother's death.

"This is a half plot—you see, capable of powerful scenes, but defective in general interest, I fear.

"I have thought of a domestic story, founded on the persecution under Queen Mary. To this my objection is, that I can not well conclude it without either burning my hero, or making the queen die very *à propos*—which is cutting the knot, and not letting the catastrophe necessarily arise from previous circumstances. However, the story pleases me, because I have a fine Catholic woman and her confessor in it.

"For feudal times, something may be made, perhaps, of a fief with a wicked lord, or of the wardship oppressions; but what will young Colman's play be? It may forestall me.

"Then I have thought of Sparta, of the Crypteia, and a Helot hero; but this would be interpreted into sedition. Of Florida, and the customary sacrifice of the first-born male: in this case, to have a European father, and an escape. Sebastian comes into my thoughts; and Beatrix of Milan, accused by Orombello on the rack, and executed. A Welsh or English story would be better; but, fix where I will, I will be well acquainted with country, manners, &c. God bless you. You have these views as they float before me, and will be as little satisfied with any as myself. Help me if you can.

"Yours affectionately,

"ROBERT SOUTHEY."

To Grosvenor C. Bedford, Esq.

"January 21, 1799.

"MY DEAR GROSVENOR,

"You ask me why the devil rides on horseback.* The Prince of Darkness is a gentleman, and that would be reason enough; but, moreover, the history doth aver that he came on horseback for the old woman, and rode before her, and that the color of the horse was black. Should I falsify the history, and make Apollyon a pedestrian? Besides, Grosvenor, Apollyon is cloven-footed; and I humbly conceive that a biped—and I never understood his dark majesty to be otherwise—that a biped, I say, would walk clumsily upon cloven feet. Neither hath Apollyon wings, according to the best representations; and, indeed, how should he? For, were they of feathers, like the angels, they would be burned in the everlasting fire; and were they of leather, like a bat's, they would be shriveled. I conclude, therefore, that wings he hath not. Yet do we find, from sundry reputable authors and

* This man persuaded his father to murder his mother, and then turned king's evidence, and brought his father to the gallows.

† "Fire, Famine, Slaughter," was the title of this poem.

* The allusion here is to the illustration of my father's "pithy and profitable" ballad of the "Old Woman of Berkeley," which is referred to in the last letter but one. It seems that Mr. Bedford, whose humor on such subjects tallied exactly with his own, had questioned the propriety of the portraiture.

divers histories, that he transporteth himself from place to place with exceeding rapidity. Now, as he can not walk fast or fly, he must have some conveyance. Stage-coaches to the infernal regions there are none, though the road be much frequented. Balloons would burst at setting out, the air would be so rarefied with the heat; but horses he may have of a particular breed.

"I am learned in Dæmonology, and could say more; but this sufficeth. I should advise you not to copy the ballad, because the volume will soon be finished. I expect to bring it with me on Ash-Wednesday to town. . . . . .

"I am better, but they tell me that constant exercise is indispensable, and that at my age, and with my constitution, I must either throw off the complaint now, or it will stick to me forever. Edith's health requires care: our medical friend dreads the effect of London upon both. When my time is out in our present house (at Midsummer), we must go to the sea a while. I thought I was like a Scotch fir, and could grow any where; but I am sadly altered, and my nerves are in a vile state. I am almost ashamed of my own feelings; but they depend not upon volition. These things throw a fog over the prospect of life. I can not see my way: it is time to be in an office, but the confinement would be ruinous. You know not the alteration I feel. I could once have slept with the seven sleepers without a miracle; now the least sound wakes me, and with alarm. However, I am better. . . . God bless you.

"Yours affectionately.

"R. Southey."

To John May, Esq.

"Jan. 22, 1799.

"My dear Friend,

"Since my last my dramatic ideas have been fermenting, and have now, perhaps, settled—at least, among my various thoughts and outlines, there is one which pleases me, and with which Wynn seems well satisfied. I am not willing to labor in vain, and before I begin I would consult well with him and you, the only friends who know my intention. The time chosen is the latter part of Queen Mary's reign; the characters—Sir Walter, a young convert to the Reformation; Gilbert, the man who has converted him; Stephen, the cousin of Sir Walter, and his heir in default of issue, a bigoted Catholic; Mary, the betrothed of Walter, an amiable Catholic; and her Confessor, a pious, excellent man. Gilbert is burned, and Walter, by his own enthusiasm, and the bigotry and interested hopes of his cousin, condemned, but saved by the queen's death. The story thus divides itself: 1. To the discovery of Walter's principles to Mary and the Confessor. 2. The danger he runs by his attentions to the accused Gilbert. 3. Gilbert's death. 4. Walter's arrest. 5. The death of the queen. In Mary and her Confessor I design Catholics of the most enlarged minds, sincere but tolerating, and earnest to save Walter, even to hastening his marriage, that the union with a woman of such known sentiments might divert suspicion. Gilbert is a sincere but bigoted man, one of the old Reformers, ready to suffer death for his opinions, or to inflict it. Stephen, so violent in his hate of heresy as half to be ignorant of his own interested motives in seeking Walter's death. But it is from delineating the progress of Walter's mind that I expect success. At first he is restless and unhappy, dreading the sacrifices which his principles require; the danger of his friend and his death excite an increasing enthusiasm; the kindness of the priest, and Mary's love, overcome him; he consents to temporize, and is arrested; then he settles into the suffering and steady courage of a Christian. To this I feel equal, and long to be about it. I expect a good effect from the evening hymn to be sung by Mary, and from the death of Gilbert. From the great window, Mary and the Confessor see the procession to the stake, and hear the *Te Deum*; they turn away when the fire is kindled, and kneel together to pray for his soul; the light of the fire appears through the window, and Walter is described as performing the last office of kindness to his martyred friend. You will perceive that such a story can excite only good feelings; its main tendency will be to occasion charity toward each other's opinions. The story has the advantage of novelty. The only martyrdom-plays I know are mixed with much nonsense: the best is Corneille's 'Polyeucte:' in English we have two bad ones from Massinger and Dryden. When I see you I will tell you more; the little thoughts for minute parts, which are almost too minute to relate formally in a letter.

"I come to town the week after next again: the thought of the journey is more tolerable, as I expect relief from the exercise, for very great exercise is necessary. I do not, and will not, neglect my health, though it requires a very inconvenient attention. My medical guide tells me that, with my habits, the disorder must be flung off now, or it will adhere to me through life. God bless you.

"Yours affectionately,

"Robert Southey."

My father's health still continued in a very unsatisfactory state, although he was less alarmed about it himself than he had been a short time previously. In reply to some anxious inquiries from his friend William Taylor, who, with a singular misapprehension of his character, tells him that he has a "mimosa sensibility, an imagination excessively accustomed to summon up trains of melancholy ideas, and marshal funeral processions; a mind too fond by half, for its own comfort, of sighs and sadness, of pathetic emotion and heart-rending woe;" he says: "Burnett has mistaken my complaint, and you have mistaken my disposition. I was apprehensive of some local complaint of the heart, but there is no danger of its growing too hard, and the affection is merely nervous. The only consequence which there is any reason to dread is, that it may totally unfit me for the confinement of London and a lawyer's office. I shall make the attempt somewhat heartlessly, and discouraged by the prognostics of my medical advisers. If my health suffer, I will abandon it at once. The world will be again before me, and the prospect sufficiently comfortable. I have no wants, and few wishes. Literary exertion is almost as necessary to me as meat and drink, and, with an undivided attention, I could do much.

"Once, indeed, I had a mimosa sensibility, but it has long ago been rooted out. Five years ago I counteracted Rousseau by dieting upon Godwin and Epictetus: they did me some good, but time has done more. I have a dislike to all strong emotion, and avoid whatever could excite it. A book like Werter gives me now unmingled pain. In my own writings you may observe I dwell rather upon what affects than what agitates."*

Notwithstanding the little encouragement my father found to continuing the study of the law, both from the state of his health, and the peculiar inaptitude of his mind to retain its technicalities, even though, at the time of reading, it fully apprehended them, he still thought it right to continue to keep his terms at Gray's Inn, and early in May went up to London for that purpose. Here his friends had now become numerous, and he had to hurry from one to another with so little cessation, that his visits there were always a source of more fatigue than pleasure. His great delight was the old book-stalls, and his chief anxiety to be at home again.

"At last, my dear Edith," he writes the day after his arrival, "I sit down to write to you in quiet and with something like comfort. . . . . My morning has been spent pleasantly, for it has been spent alone in the library; the hours so employed pass rapidly enough, but I grow more and more home-sick, like a spoiled child. On the 29th you may expect me. Term opens on the 26th. After eating my third dinner, I can drive to the mail, and thirteen shillings will be well bestowed in bringing me home four-and-twenty hours earlier: it is not above sixpence an hour, Edith, and I would gladly purchase an hour at home now at a much higher price. * * * * * * * * *
My stall-hunting, the great and only source of my enjoyment in London, has been tolerably successful. I have picked up an epic poem in French, on the Discovery of America, which will help out the notes of Madoc; another on the American Revolution, the Alaric, and an Italian one, of which I do not know the subject, for the title does not explain it; also I have got Astræa, the whole romance, a new folio, almost a load for a porter, and the print delightfully small—fine winter evenings' work; and I have had self-denial enough—admire me, Edith!—to abstain from these books till my return, that I may lose no time in ransacking the library.

"I met Stuart one day, luckily, as it saved me a visit. To-morrow must be given up to writing for him, as he has had nothing since I came to town. The more regularly these periodical works are done, the easier they are to do. I have had no time since I left home—in fact, I can do nothing as it should be done any where else.

"* * * * Do not suppose I have forgotten to look out for a book for you; to-day I saw a set of Florian, which pleases me, unless a better can be found. * * *
Do you know that I am truly and actually learning Dutch, to read Jacob Cats. You will, perhaps, be amused at a characteristic trait in that language: other people say, I pity; but the Dutch verb is, I pity myself."

The two following letters were also written during this absence from home.

To Mrs. Southey.

Brixton, May 9, 1799.

"Your letter, my dear Edith, reached me not till late last evening, and it could hardly have arrived more opportunely, for it was on my return from a visit to Mr. —— that I found it. We had dined there; B., and C., and I, with fourteen people, all of whom were completely strange to me, and most of whom I hope and trust will remain so. There were some blockheads there, one of whom chose to be exposed by engaging in some classical and historical disputes with me; another gave as a toast General Suwarrow, the man who massacred men, women, and children for three successive days at Warsaw, who slew at Ockzakow thirty thousand persons in cold blood, and thirty thousand at Ismael. I was so astonished at hearing this demon's name as only to repeat it in the tone of wonder; but, before I had time to think or to reply, C. turned to the man who gave the toast, and said he would not drink General Suwarrow, and off we set, describing the man's actions till they gave up all defense, and asked for some substituted name; and Carlisle changed him for Count Rumford. It was a hateful day; the fellows would talk politics, of which they knew nothing. * * * * * *
After being so put to the torture for five hours, your letter was doubly welcome.

* * * * * * *

"G. Dyer is foraging for my Almanac, and promises pieces from Mrs. Opie, Mr. Mott of Cambridge, and Miss Christall. I then went to Arch's, a pleasant place for half an hour's book news: you know he purchased the edition of the Lyrical Ballads: he told me he believed he should lose by them, as they sold very heavily. . . . . My books sell very well. Other book news have I none, except, indeed, that John Thelwall is writing an epic poem, and Samuel Rogers is also writing an epic poem; George Dyer, also, hath similar thoughts. * * * *
William Taylor has written to me from Norwich, and sent me Bodmer's Noah, the book that I wanted to poke through and learn German by. He tempts me to write upon the subject, and

* March 12, 1799.

take my seat with Milton and Klopstock; and in my to-day's walk, so many noble thoughts for such a poem presented themselves, that I am half tempted, and have the Deluge floating in my brain with the Dom Daniel and the rest of my unborn family.

" * * * * * * *

As we went to dinner yesterday, a coachful of women drew up to the door at the moment we arrived there: it rained merrily, and Carlisle offered his umbrella; but the prim gentry were somewhat rudely shy of him, and me too, for his hair was a little ragged, and I had not silk stockings on. He made them ashamed of this at dinner. Never did you see any thing so hideous as their dresses: they were pink muslin, with round little white spots, waists ever so far down, and buttoned from the neck down to the end of the waist. * * * * * *

* * * * * * * *

Horne Tooke's letter to the Income Commissioners has amused me very much: he had stated his under sixty pounds a year; they said they were not satisfied; and his reply begins by saying he has much more reason to be dissatisfied with the smallness of his income than they have.

* * * * * * *

"God bless you.

"Yours affectionately,

"Robert Southey."

My father was now, much to his regret, compelled to quit his house at Westbury; and Burton, in Hampshire, being the place which, next to Bristol, he had found in all respects best suited to him, he went thither to look for a house, and with some difficulty succeeded in procuring one; but, not being able to obtain immediate possession, the intervening time, after a short interval, was passed in an excursion into Devonshire. Of these movements the following letters give an account:

To Grosvenor Bedford, Esq.

"Bristol, June 5, 1799.

"My dear Grosvenor,

"Here is de koele June—we have a March wind howling, and a March fire burning: it is *diabolus diei*. On my journey I learned one piece of information, which you may profit by: that on Sunday nights they put the new horses into the mail always, because, as they carry no letters, an accident is of less consequence as to the delay it occasions. This nearly broke our necks, for we narrowly escaped an overturn; so I travel no more on a Sunday night in the mail.

" * * * * * * *

I am the better for my journey, and inclined to attribute it to the greater quantity of wine I drank at Brixton than I had previously done; therefore I have supplied the place of æther by the grape-juice, and supplied the place of the table-spoon by the cork-screw. I find printer's faith as bad as Punic faith. New types have been promised from London for some weeks, and are not yet arrived; therefore I am still out of the press. I pray you to send me the old woman who was circularized,

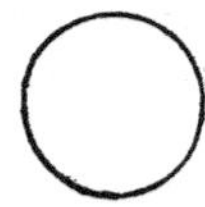

who saw her own back, whose head was like the title-page of a Jew's prayer-book, who was an emblem of eternity, the omikron of old women. You will make a good ballad of this quaint tale: it is for subjects allied to humor or oddity that you possess most power. * * * Find such subjects, and you will find pleasure in writing in proportion as you feel your own strength. I will, at my first leisure, transcribe for you St. Anthony and the Devil.

"The time of removal is so near at hand, that I begin to wish every thing were settled and over. This is a place which I leave with some reluctance after taking root here for twenty-five years, and now our society is so infinitely mended.

"Davy, the Pneumatic Institution experimentalist, is a first-rate man, conversable on all subjects, and learnable-from (which, by-the-by, is as fine a Germanly compounded word as you may expect to see). I am going to breathe some wonder-working gas, which excites all possible mental and muscular energy, and induces almost a delirium of pleasurable sensations without any subsequent dejection.

" * * * * * * *

I was fortunate enough to meet Sharpe, of whom you said so much, on the Sunday that I left Brixton. I was with Johnson in the King's Bench when he came in. I missed his name as he entered, but was quite surprised at the novelty and good sense of all his remarks. He talked on many subjects, and on all with a strength and justness of thought which I have seldom heard: the meeting pleased me much. I wish much to see more of Sharpe; he seems a man whom it would be impossible not to profit by. He talked of Combe, who is in the King's Bench. You said that Combe wrote books which were not known to be his. Sharpe mentioned as his, Lord Lyttleton's Letters, many of Sterne's Letters, and Æneas Anderson's Account of China. God bless you! Yours affectionately,

"Robert Southey."

To Thomas Southey.

"Friday, July 12, 1799.

"My dear Tom,

"I write to you from Danvers's, where we are and have been since we left Westbury. I have been to Biddlecombe's,* and surveyed Southey Palace that is to be. We shall not get possession till Michaelmas. The place will be comfortable; the garden is large, but unstocked, with a fish-pond and a pigeon-house. My mother is in the College Green. Edith and I are going into Devonshire, first to the north coast,

* The name of a friend residing at Christ Church, Hampshire.

Minehead, the Valley of Stones, and Ilfracombe, the wildest part of the country; perhaps we may cross over to the south on our way to Burton. I wish to see Lightfoot at Kingsbridge, and there would be a likelihood of seeing you.

"My miscellaneous volume, which is to be christened Annual Poems, comes on rapidly; they are now striking off the eleventh sheet.

"Yesterday I finished Madoc, thank God! and thoroughly to my own satisfaction; but I have resolved on one great, laborious, and radical alteration. It was my design to identify Madoc with Mango Capac, the legislator of Peru: in this I have totally failed, therefore Mango Capac is to be the hero of another poem; and instead of carrying Madoc down the Marãnon, I shall follow the more probable opinion, and land him in Florida: here, instead of the Peruvians, who have no striking manners for my poem, we get among the wild North American Indians. On their customs and superstitions, facts must be grounded, and woven into the work, spliced so neatly as not to betray the junction. These alterations I delay. . . . So much for Madoc: it is a great work done, and my brain is now ready to receive the Dom Daniel, the next labor in succession. Of the meter of this poem I have thought much, and my final resolution is to write it irregularly, without rhymes: for this I could give you reasons in plenty; but, as you can not lend me your ear, we will defer it till you hear the poem. This work is intended for immediate publication.

"My first poems are going to press for a third edition; by the time they are completed, I shall probably have a second volume of the Annual Poems ready; and so I and the printers go merrily on.

"Oh, Tom! such a gas has Davy discovered, the gaseous oxyd! Oh, Tom! I have had some; it made me laugh and tingle in every toe and finger tip. Davy has actually invented a new pleasure, for which language has no name. Oh, Tom! I am going for more this evening; it makes one strong, and so happy! so gloriously happy! and without any after-debility, but, instead of it, increased strength of mind and body. Oh, excellent air-bag! Tom, I am sure the air in heaven must be this wonder-working gas of delight!

Yours, ROBERT SOUTHEY."

To John May, Esq.

"Stowey, August, 1799.

"MY DEAR FRIEND,

" * * * * * * *

My walk to Ilfracombe led me through Lynmouth, the finest spot, except Cintra and the Arrabida, that I ever saw. Two rivers join at Lynmouth. You probably know the hill streams of Devonshire: each of these flows down a coombe, rolling down over huge stones like a long waterfall; immediately at their junction they enter the sea, and the rivers and the sea make but one sound of uproar. Of these coombes the one is richly wooded, the other runs between two high, bare, stony hills. From the hill between the two is a prospect most magnificent; on either hand, the coombes and the river before the little village. The beautiful little village, which, I am assured by one who is familiar with Switzerland, resembles a Swiss village—this alone would constitute a view beautiful enough to repay the weariness of a long journey; but, to complete it, there is the blue and boundless sea, for the faint and feeble line of the Welsh coast is only to be seen on the right hand if the day be perfectly clear. Ascending from Lynmouth up a road of serpentining perpendicularity, you reach a lane which by a slight descent leads to the Valley of Stones, a spot which, as one of the greatest wonders indeed in the West of England, would attract many visitors if the roads were passable by carriages. Imagine a narrow vale between two ridges of hills somewhat steep; the southern hill turfed; the vale, which runs from east to west, covered with huge stones and fragments of stones among the fern that fills it; the northern ridge completely bare, excoriated of all turf and all soil, the very bones and skeleton of the earth; rock reclining upon rock, stone piled upon stone, a huge and terrific mass. A palace of the Preadamite kings, a city of the Anakim, must have appeared so shapeless, and yet so like the ruins of what had been shaped after the waters of the flood subsided. I ascended with some toil the highest point; two large stones inclining on each other formed a rude portal on the summit: here I sat down; a little level platform, about two yards long, lay before me, and then the eye immediately fell upon the sea, far, very far below. I never felt the sublimity of solitude before. . .

"Of Beddoes you seem to entertain an erroneous opinion. Beddoes is an experimentalist in cases where the ordinary remedies are notoriously and fatally inefficacious. If you will read his late book on consumption, you will see his opinion upon this subject; and the book is calculated to interest unscientific readers, and to be of use to them. The faculty dislike Beddoes, because he is more able, and more successful, and more celebrated than themselves, and because he labors to reconcile the art of healing with common sense, instead of all the parade of mystery with which it is usually enveloped. Beddoes is a candid man, trusting more to facts than reasonings. I understand him when he talks to me, and, in case of illness, should rather trust myself to his experiments than be killed off *secundem artem*, and in the ordinary course of practice. . . . .

"God bless you.

"Yours affectionately, R. SOUTHEY."

To Joseph Cottle.

"Exeter, Sept. 22, 1799.

"MY DEAR COTTLE,

"You will, I hope, soon have a cargo to send me of your own (for the 2d vol. of the Anthology), and some from Davy. If poor Mrs. Yearsley were well, I should like much to have her name there. . . . . As yet, I have only Coleridge's pieces and my own, amounting, in the whole, to some eighty or one hundred pages.

"Thalaba the Destroyer is progressive. There is a poem called '*Gebir*,' of which I know not whether my review be yet printed (in the Critical), but in that review you will find some of the most exquisite poetry in the language. The poem is such as Gilbert,* if he were only half as mad as he is, could have written. I would go a hundred miles to see the anonymous author.

"My other hard work now is gutting the libraries here, and laying in a good stock of notes and materials, arranged in a way that would do honor to any old bachelor. Thalaba will be very rich in notes. . . . . .

"There are some *Johnobines* in Exeter, with whom I have passed some pleasant days. It is the filthiest place in England: a gutter running down the middle of every street and lane. We leave it on Monday week, and I shall rejoice to taste fresh air and feel settled. Exeter, however, has the very best collection of books for sale of any place out of London; and that made by a man who some few years back was worth nothing: Dyer—not Woolmer, whose catalogue you showed me. Dyer himself is a thinking, extraordinary man, of liberal and extraordinary talents for his circumstances. I congratulate you on being out of bookselling: it did not suit you. Would that we authors had one bookseller at our direction, instead of one bookseller directing so many authors!

"My list of title-pages increases. I have lately made up my mind to undertake one great historical work, the History of Portugal; but for this, and for many other noble plans, I want uninterrupted leisure time, wholly my own, and not frittered away by little periodical employments. . . . . . God bless you.

"Yours affectionately,

"Robert Southey."

To S. T. Coleridge.

"Exeter, Oct. 3, 1799.

"Bonaparte was remarkably studious, and mathematics his particular study. He associated little, or not at all, with the other officers, and in company was reserved and silent. This is Mrs. Keenan's account, to whom I looked up with more respect, because the light of his countenance had shone upon her. Banfill tells me that the mathematical tutor of Bonaparte is in Exeter—an emigrant. He says that he was an excellent mathematician—in the military branch chiefly—and that he was always the great man, always the first, always Bonaparte. . . .

"Jackson has taste to a certain extent. . . . His music I take for granted; his pictures are always well conceived, the creations of a man of genius; but he can not execute; his trees are like the rustic work in a porter's lodge, seaweed landscapes, cavern drippings chiseled into ramifications—cold, cramp, stiff, stony. I thank him for his 'Four Ages.' A man with a name may publish such a book; but when a book is merely a lounging collection of scraps, the common-place book printed, one wishes it to hold more than half an hour's turning over, a little turtle soup and a little pine-apple; but one wants a huge basin of broth and plenty of filberts. . . . I soon talked of Bampfylde,* and Jackson rose in my esteem, for he talked of him till I saw the tears. I have copied one ode, in imitation of Gray's Alcaic, and nineteen sonnets. After I had done, Jackson required a promise that I would communicate no copy, as he was going to publish them. He read me the preface: it will tell you what a miraculous musician Bampfylde was, and that he died insane; but it will not tell you Bampfylde's history.

"His wish was to live in solitude and write a play. From his former lodging near Chudley, often would he come to town in winter before Jackson was up—and Jackson is an early riser—ungloved, open-breasted, with a pocket-full of music, and poems, to know how he liked them. His *friends*—plague on the word—his relations, I mean, thought this was a sad life for a man of family, so they drove him to London. 'Poor fellow!' said Jackson; 'there did not live a purer creature; and if they would have let him alone, he might have been alive now. In London his feelings took a wrong course, and he paid the price of debauchery.'

"His sixteen printed sonnets are dedicated to Miss Palmer, now Lady Inchiquin, a niece of Sir Joshua Reynolds. Her he was madly in love with. Whether Sir J. opposed this match on account of Bampfylde's own irregularities in London, or of the hereditary insanity, I know not; but this was the commencement of his madness. On being refused admittance at Sir Joshua's, he broke the windows, and was taken to Newgate! Some weeks after, Jackson, on knowing of what had passed, went to London, and inquired for Bampfylde. Lady B., his mother, said she knew little of him; she had got him out of Newgate; he was in some beggarly place. 'Where?' In King Street, Holborn, she believed, but did not know the number. Away went Jackson, and knocked at every door till he found the right. It was a miserable place. The woman of the house was one of the worst class of women in London. She knew B. had no money, and that he had been there three days without food. Jackson found him with the levity of derangement—his shirt-collar black and ragged, his beard of two months' growth. He said he was come to breakfast, and turned to a harpsichord in the room, literally, he said, to let B. gorge himself without being noticed. He took him away, gave his mother a severe lecture, and left him in decent lodgings and with a decent allowance, earnestly begging him to write. He never wrote. The next news was his confinement, and Jackson never saw him more. Almost the last time they met, he showed him several poems; among others, a ballad on the murder

* Author of "The Hurricane."

* I might have hesitated in publishing this melancholy account of poor Bampfylde's private history, had it not already been related in the Autobiography of Sir Egerton Brydges.

of David Rizzio. 'Such a ballad!' said J. He came to J. to dinner, and was asked for copies. 'I burned them,' was the reply; 'you did not seem to like them, and I wrote them to please you, so I burned them.' After twenty years' confinement his senses returned, but he was dying in a consumption. He was urged by his apothecary to leave the house in Sloane Street, where he was well treated, and go into Devonshire. 'Your Devonshire friends will be very glad to see you.' He immediately hid his face. 'No, sir,' said he; 'they who knew me what I was, shall never see me what I am.'

* * * * * * *

"Yours affectionately, R. S."

To S. T. Coleridge.

"Christ Church. [No date.]

* * * * * * *

"I went to the Chapter Coffee-house Club. A man read an essay upon the comparative evils of savage and civilized society; and he preferred the first, because it had not the curses of government and religion! He had never read Rousseau. What amused me was to find him mistaken in every fact he adduced respecting savage manners. I was going to attack him, but perceived that a visitor was expected to be silent. They elected me a member of one of these meetings, which I declined. . . . .

"A friend of Wordsworth's has been uncommonly kind to me—Basil Montague. He offered me his assistance as a special pleader, and said, if he could save me 100 guineas, it would give him more than 100 guineas' worth of pleasure. I did thank him, which was no easy matter; but I have been told that I never thank any body for a civility, and there are very few in this world who can understand silence. However, I do not expect to use his offer: his papers which he offered me to copy will be of high service. Tell Wordsworth this.

"I commit willful murder on my own intellect by drudging at law, but trust the guilt is partly expiated by the candle-light hours allotted to Madoc. That poem advances very slowly. I am convinced that the best way of writing is to write rapidly, and correct at leisure. Madoc would be a better poem if written in six months, than if six years were devoted to it. However, I am satisfied with what is done, and my outline for the whole is good. . . . .

"God bless you. R. S."

To Thomas Southey.

Sylph Brig.

"Burton, October 25, 1799.

"MY DEAR TOM,

"For these last three weeks you have been 'poor Tom,' and we have been lamenting the capture of the Sylph, and expecting a letter from you, dated 'Ferrol.' The newspapers said you had been captured and carried in there; and I have written word to Lisbon, and my uncle was to write to Jardine, at Corunna; and my mother has been frightened lest you should have been killed in an action previous to your capture—and, after all, it is a lie!

"Five weeks were we at Exeter. I wrote to you, directing Torbay, and I walked round Torbay. You cruised at an unlucky time. However, if you have picked up a hundred pounds, I am glad we did not meet. We are in Hampshire, and shall get into our palace on Wednesday next. You will direct as formerly—Burton, near Ringwood. So much hope had I of seeing you when I walked down to Dartmouth, and round by Brixham and the bay, that I put the Annual Anthology and the concluding books of Madoc in my knapsack for you.

"Our dwelling is now in a revolutionary state, and will, I hope, be comfortable. Small it is, and somewhat quaint, but it will be clean; and there is a spare bed-room, and a fish-pond, and a garden, in which I mean to work wonders; and then my book-room is such a room, that, like the Chapter House at Salisbury, it requires a column to support the roof.

* * * * * * *

"But you ought to have been taken, Tom; for consider how much uneasiness has been thrown away; and here were we, on seeing your handwriting, expecting a long and lamentable, true and particular, account of the loss of the Ville de Paris, the lapelles, the new shirts, books, and all the lieutenant paraphernalia; and then comes a pitiful account of a cruise, and £100 prize-money, instead of all these adventures!

"There was my mother working away to make a new shirt, thinking you would come home shirtless, breechesless, all oil, one great flea-bite, and able to talk Spanish.

"I have no news to tell, except that we expect Harry home for the Christmas holidays. Concerning my own employment, the Dom Daniel romance is rechristened, anabaptized Thalaba the Destroyer, and the fifth book is begun; this I should like to show you. . . . . God bless you.

"Yours affectionately,

"ROBERT SOUTHEY."

My father had now, as he hoped, fairly settled himself for a time. He had revolutionized two adjoining cottages into a dwelling-house, and, at some inconvenience, had got his books about him, for already he had collected far more than were easily either moved or accommodated, though far fewer than he either wished or required. In this respect, indeed, the old proverb of "a rolling stone" was wholly inapplicable to him, and the number that accumulated made every new movement more troublesome and more expensive.

But he was not yet destined to find a "rest for the sole of his foot." Hardly was his new home cleared from "the deal shavings and the brick and mortar," than he was laid prostrate by severe illness—"so reduced by a nervous fever as to be able neither to read nor write;" and, on partially recovering from this attack, the uneasy feelings about his heart, which he had before experienced, returned with so much force as to compel him at once to repair to Bristol for abler advice than the retired neighborhood of Burton afforded. From thence he writes to Mr. Bedford and Mr. Coleridge:

To Grosvenor C. Bedford, Esq.

"Kingsdown, Bristol, Dec. 21, 1799.

"Grosvenor, I think seriously of going abroad. My complaint, so I am told by the opinion of many medical men, is wholly a diseased sensibility (mind you, physical sensibility), disordering the functions, now of the heart, now of the intestines, and gradually debilitating me. Climate is the obvious remedy. In my present state, to attempt to undergo the confinement of legal application were actual suicide. I am anxious to be well, and to attempt the profession: *much* in it I shall never do: sometimes my principles stand in my way, sometimes the want of readiness which I felt from the first—a want which I always know in company, and never in solitude and silence. Howbeit, I will make the attempt; but mark you, if by stage writing, or any other writing, I can acquire independence, I will not make the sacrifice of happiness it will inevitably cost me. I love the country, I love study—devotedly I love it; but in legal studies it is only the subtlety of the mind that is exercised. However, I need not philippicize, and it is too late to veer about. In '96 I might have chosen physic, and succeeded in it. I caught at the first plank, and missed the great mast in my reach; perhaps I may enable myself to swim by-and-by. Grosvenor, I have nothing of what the world calls ambition. I never thought it possible that I could be a great lawyer; I should as soon expect to be the man in the moon. My views were bounded—my hopes to an income of £500 a year, of which I could lay by half to effect my escape with. *Possibly* the stage may exceed this. . . . . I am not indolent; I loathe indolence; but, indeed, reading law is laborious indolence—it is thrashing straw. I have read, and read, and read, but the devil a bit can I remember. I have given all possible attention, and attempted to command volition. No! The eye read, the lips pronounced, I understood and re-read it; it was very clear; I remembered the page, the sentence; but close the book, and all was gone! Were I an independent man, even on less than I now possess, I should long since have made the blessed bonfire, and rejoiced that I was free and contented. . . . . . .

"I suffer a good deal from illness, and in a way hardly understandable by those in health. I start from sleep as if death had seized me. I am sensible of every pulsation, and compelled to attend to the motion of my heart till that attention disturbs it. The pain in my side is, I think, lessened, nor do I at all think it was consumption; organic affection it could not have been, else it had been constant; and a heart disease would not have been perceived *there*. I must go abroad, and recruit under better skies. Not to Lisbon: I will see something new, and something better than the Portuguese. Ask Duppa about Italy, about Trieste, and the way through Vienna, and say something to him on my part expressive of respect—of a wish one day to see more of him.

"But of these plans you shall know more when they are more molded into form. In the mean time I must raise the supplies, and for this purpose there is Thalaba. My expedition will not be a ruinous one, and it shall be as economical as it ought. I will at least return wiser, if not better.

"But now for more immediate affairs. The Anthology prospers. Send me something. O for another parody, such as 'The Rhedycinian Barbers'—a ballad good as 'The Circular Old Woman.'* There is a poem called Gebir, written by God knows who, sold for a shilling: it has miraculous beauties; and the Bishop of St. Giles's said the best poems in the Anthology were by Mrs. Opie and George Dyer! and he writes reviews!

"I expect to see my brother Henry to-morrow, after twenty months' absence. He is now sixteen, and promises much. If I go abroad, I shall make every effort to take him with me. Tom is cruising, and, I think, likely to rise in his profession.

* * * * * * *

"Yours, ever the same,

"ROBERT SOUTHEY."

To S. T. Coleridge, Esq.

"Bristol, Dec. 27, 1799.

"Geese were made to grow feathers, and farmers' wives to pluck them. I suspect booksellers and authors were made with something of the like first cause. With Thalaba I must make sure work and speedy, for abroad I *must* go. Complaints of immediate danger I have none, but increased and increasing nervous affections threaten much remote. I have rushes of feeling nightly, like fainting or death, and induced, I believe, wholly by the dread of them. Even by day they menace me, and an effort of mind is required to dispel them. . . . . So I *must* go, and I *will* go. Now, then, the sooner the better. Some progress is made in the sixth book of Thalaba; my notes are ready for the whole—at least there is only the trouble of arranging and seasoning them. If the bargain were made, it would be time to think of beginning to print, for the preliminaries are usually full of delays, and time with me is of importance. I must have the summer to travel in, and ought to be in Germany by the beginning of June. Treat, therefore, with Longman, or any man, for me.

"The W.'s† are at Clifton: if they saw the probable advantages of a journey to Italy—of the *possible reach* to Constantinople, the Greek Islands, and Egypt—in a light as strong as I do, they would, I think, wish to delay the new birth of Lessing; but this is, on your part, a matter of feeling; and when I spoke of your joining us,

* There is no trace of this ballad to be found. Who can tell the history of this mysterious rotundity? See p. 112.

† The Messrs. Wedgewood.

it was with the conviction that it was a vain wish, but it is a very earnest one. Together we might do so much; and we could leave the women for excursions—now into Hungary, now into Poland, and see the Turks. Zounds! who knows but, like Sir John Maundeville, we might have gone where the devil's head is always above ground! Go I must, but it would be a great satisfaction to have a companion. . . . .

"But Lessing's life—and I half wish he had never lived—how long after the first of April (an ominous day) will that confine you? Or, if you come here to do it, can not I raise mortar and carry bricks to the edifice? . . . . For Stuart I *must* make out another quarter. I have huge drains, like the Pontic marshes—a leech hanging on every limb. . . . .

"God bless you.

"Yours, R. SOUTHEY."

To G. C. Bedford, Esq.

"Bristol, Jan. 1, 1800.

"We shall be very glad to see you, my dear Grosvenor, if you can come. There is a bed in the house, and I am of necessity an idle man, and can show you all things worth seeing, and get you a dose of the beatifying gas, which is a pleasure worth the labor of a longer journey. . .

"I have often thought of the Chancery line. . . . . —— did not seem to like it: he is ambitious for me, and perhaps hardly understands how utterly I am without that stimulus. I shall write to him a serious letter about it. Do not suppose that I feel burdened or uneasy; all I feel is, that were I possessed of the same income in another way, I would never stir a finger to increase it in a way to which self-gratification was not the immediate motive, instead of self-interest. It is enough for all my wants, and just leaves motive enough not to be idle, that I may have to spare for my relatives. This, Grosvenor, I do feel; practically I know my own wants, and can therefore speculate upon them securely.

"Come to Bristol, I pray and beseech you. Winter as it is, I can show you some fine scenes and some pleasant people. You shall see Davy, the young chemist, the young every thing, the man least ostentatious, of first talent that I have ever known; and you may experimentalize, if you like, and arrange my Anthology papers, and be as boyish as your heart can wish . . . . and I can give you Laver for supper. O rare Laver! . . . .

"Perhaps the closest friendships will be found among men of inferior intellect, for such most completely accord with each other. There is scarcely any man with whom the whole of my being comes in contact; and thus with different people I exist another and yet the same. With ——, for instance, the school-boy feelings revive; I have no other associations in common with him. With some I am the moral and intellectual agent; with others I partake the daily and hourly occurrences of life. You and I, when we would see alike, must put on younger spectacles. Whatever is most important in society, appears to us under different points of view. The man in Xenophon blundered when he said he had two souls—my life for it he had twenty! God bless you.

"Yours affectionately,

"ROBERT SOUTHEY."

To S. T. Coleridge, Esq.

"Jan. 8, 1800.

"MY DEAR COLERIDGE,

"I have thought much, and talked much, and advised much about Thalaba, and will endeavor to travel without publishing it; because I am in no mood for running races, and because I like what is done to be done so well, that I am not willing to let it go raggedly into the world. Six books are written, and the two first have undergone their first correction.

"I have the whim of making a Darwinish note at the close of the poem, upon the effects produced in our globe by the destruction of the Dom Daniel. *Imprimis*, the sudden falling in of the sea's roots necessarily made the maelstrom; then the cold of the north is accounted for by the water that rushed into the caverns putting out a great part of the central fire; the sudden generation of steam shattered the southern and south-east continents into archipelagos of islands; also the boiling spring of Geyser has its source here —who knows what it did not occasion!

"Thomas Wedgewood has obtained a passport to go to France. I shall attempt to do the same, but am not very anxious for success, as Italy seems certainly accessible, or at least Trieste is. Is it *quite impossible* that you can go? Surely a life of Lessing may be as well written in Germany as in England, and little time lost. I shall be ready to go as soon as you please: we should just make a carriage-full, and you and I would often make plenty of room by walking. You can not begin Lessing before May, and you allow yourself ten months for the work. Well, we will be in Germany before June. At the towns where we make a halt of any time, something may be done, and the actual traveling will not consume more than two months; thus three months only will be lost, and it is worth this price: we can return through France, and, in the interim, Italy offers a society almost as interesting. Duppa will fortify me with all necessary directions for traveling, &c.; and Moses* will be a very mock-bird as to languages: he shall talk German with you and me, Italian with the servants, and English with his mother and aunt; so the young Israelite will become learned without knowing how.

"* * * * * * *

Beddoes advertised, at least six weeks ago, certain cases of consumption treated in a cow-house, and the press has been standing till now in expectation of—what think you? only waiting till the patients be cured! This is beginning to print a book sooner than even I should venture. Davy is in the high career of experience, and

* This appellation was given to Hartley Coleridge in his infancy and childhood.

will soon new-christen (if the word be a chemical one) the calumniated azote. They have a new palsied patient, a complete case, certainly recovering by the use of the beatifying gas.

"Perhaps, when you are at a pinch for a paragraph,* you may manufacture an anti-ministerial one out of this passage in Bacon's Essays:

"'You shall see a *bold fellow* many times do Mohammed's miracle. Mohammed made the people believe that he would call a hill to him, and from the top of it offer up his prayers for the observers of his law. The people assembled; Mohammed called the hill to come to him again and again, and when the hill stood still, he was never a bit abashed, but said, If the hill will not come to Mohammed, Mohammed will go to the hill. So these men, when they have promised great matters and failed most shamefully, yet (if they have the perfection of *boldness*) they will but slight it over, make a turne, and no more adoe.'

"I am glad I copied the passage, for in so doing I have found how to make this a fine incident in the poem.†

"Maracci's Refutation of the Koran, or, rather, his preliminaries to it, have afforded me much amusement and much matter. I am qualified in doctrinals to be a mufti. The old father groups together all the Mohammedan miracles: some, he says, are nonsense; some he calls lies; some are true, but then the devil did them; but there is one that tickled his fancy, and he says it must be true of some Christian saint, and so stolen by the Turks. After this he gives, by way of contrast, a specimen of Christian miracles, and chooses out St. Januarius's blood and the Chapel of Loretto! God bless you.

"ROBERT SOUTHEY."

It has already been mentioned that, during my father's residence at Burton, in Hampshire, he had made the acquaintance of Mr. Rickman, at that time residing there. This had soon ripened into an intimacy, and a friendship and correspondence had now commenced which continued through life, Mr. Rickman being not only, as Mr. Justice Talfourd well names him, "the sturdiest of jovial companions,"‡ and, as Charles Lamb equally well describes him, "fullest of matter with least verbosity," but also a man of vast and varied practical knowledge upon almost all subjects, of the kindest heart, and unwearied in offices of friendship.

Two men more different in most respects than Mr. Rickman and my father could hardly be found—and yet the points of agreement proved stronger than the points of difference—both were pre-eminently *straightforward* men; and they had what is perhaps the closest bond of real friendship—a high respect for each other's talents, an admiration of each other's character, and a similarity of opinion on almost all the leading questions of the day. Mr. Rickman had, however, been cast in somewhat the rougher mold of the two, and was made of "sterner stuff," and consequently sympathized less with his friend in his "poetic fancies" than on other subjects; and, in now writing to urge him to take up a subject in which he had always felt much interested, he commences by a recommendation which was acted upon fully to his satisfaction in after years. I quote the greater part of this letter, that the reply to it may be the better understood:

"Poetry has its use and its place, and, like some human superfluities, we should feel awkward without it; but when I have sometimes considered, with some surprise, the facility with which you compose verse, I have always wished to see that facility exerted to more useful purpose. The objects I propose for your investigation are, therefore, the employment and consequent amelioration of woman-kind, the consequences on the welfare of society, and some illustration of the possibility of these things. You think it too good an alteration to be expected—and so do I, from virtue; but if the vanity of any leading women could be interested, it might become *fashionable* to promote certain establishments for this purpose, and then it might go down. Besides, the glory of the *proposal* will remain; and if Mary Woolstonecroft had lived, she would have recommended something like this to the world. *Magnis tamen excidit ausis!* Are you aware that female *fraternities* exist (or did exist) in all the great towns of Holland and Flanders, called Beguinages? Employment enough would be found for females: I would take upon me to furnish you with an ample list. Any dry deductions on the head of political economy which might occur, I would also attempt in the service. This is my favorite study, and nothing could there operate more beneficially than an increased utility of the fair half of our species. You like women better than I do, therefore I think it likely that you may take as much trouble to benefit the sex, as I to benefit the community by their means. For all this, I have been in love these ten years. . . . .

"How do you and Bonaparte agree at present? I never liked the Corsican, and now he has given me new offense by his absurd misnomers, which go to confound all the fixed ideas of consuls, tribunes, and Senate. . . . .

"I begin to be almost tired of staying in this obscure place so long; I imagine I was born for better purposes than to vegetate at Christ Church. . . . . I long to see you in prose; I think your conscience would keep you careful, and your imagination make you rapid, and, consequently, easy and fluent, in composition. I suppose you are in the enjoyment of much enlightened society at Bristol. I do not understand your taste for retirement; no man's contemplation can be so spirited as when encouraged by the information and applause of literary friends."* . . . .

* For the Morning Post, to which Mr. C. was then a contributor. † See p. 119.

‡ Final Memorials of Charles Lamb, vol. ii., p. 206.

* J. R. to R. S., Jan. 4, 1800.

To John Rickman, Esq.

"Bristol, Jan. 9, 1800.

"The subject of your letter is important. I had considered it cursorily, for my mind has been more occupied by the possible establishment of a different state of society than by plans for improving the present. To my undertaking the work you propose, I wish there were no obstacles, but a very important one exists in the nature of my own powers. The compositions in which I have indulged have encouraged rapidity of feeling, a sudden combination of ideas, but they have been unfavorable to regular deduction and methodical arrangement. Another objection arises from my present plans. . . . . However, I am impressed by your letter, and should much like to talk with you upon the subject, and map out the country before us. Have you not leisure for a visit to Bristol? . . .

"Poetry does not wholly engross my attention; the history of Spanish and Portuguese literature is a subject on which I design to bestow much labor, and in which much useful matter may be conveyed. But poetry is my province, and at present no unimportant one; it makes its way where weightier books would not penetrate, and becomes a good mental manure.

"I shall be selfishly sorry if you leave Christ Church: the prospect of having you my neighbor considerably influenced me in taking the Burton House. However, if I recover my health, London must be my place of residence; and you probably will be drawn into that great vortex—a place which you and I see with widely different eyes. Much as I enjoy society, rather than purchase it by residing in that huge denaturalized city, I would prefer dwelling on Poole Heath. Bristol allows of country enjoyments and magnificent scenery, and an open *sky view*, for in London you neither see earth, air, nor water, undisguised. We have men of talent here also, but they are not gregarious—at least not regularly so as in Norwich and London. I mingle among them, and am in habits of intimacy with Davy, by far the first in intellect: with him you would be much pleased. . . . . Certainly this place has in my memory greatly advanced; ten years ago, Bristol man was synonymous with Bœotian in Greece, and now we are before any of the provincial towns.

"The Corsican has offended me, and even his turning out the Mamelukes will not atone for his rascally constitution. The French are children, with the physical force of men; unworthy, and therefore incapable, of freedom. Once I had hopes; the Jacobins might have done much, but the base of morality was wanting, and where could the corner-stone be laid? They have retarded our progress for a century to come. Literature is suspected and discouraged; Methodism, and the Catholic system of persecution and slavery, gaining ground. Our only hope is from more expeditions, and the duke commander; new disgrace and new taxes may bring the nation to their senses, as bleeding will tame a madman. Still, however, the English are the first people, the only men. Bonaparte has made me Anti-Gallican; and I remember Alfred, and the two Bacons, and Hartley, and Milton, and Shakespeare, with more patriotic pride than ever.

"The Beguines I had looked upon as a religious establishment, and the only good one of its kind. When my brother was a prisoner at Brest, the sick and wounded were attended by nuns, and these women had made themselves greatly beloved and respected. I think they had been regularly professed, and were not of the lay order. I think I see the whole importance of your speculation. Mary Woolstonecroft was but beginning to reason when she died; her volume is mere feeling, and its only possible effect to awaken a few female minds more excitable than the common run. The one you propose would go on different grounds and enter into detail: the more my mind dwells upon it, the stronger interest it takes; I could work under your directions, and would work willingly at least, if not well. Come, I pray you, to Bristol; talk over the plan, and map it out, and methodize my rambling intellect. I will submit to any drilling that shall discipline it to good purpose. . . . . Farewell.

"Yours, with respect and esteem,

"Robert Southey."

The two following months were passed in lodgings at Bristol, in a very unsettled state as to his future movements. Meantime he was engaged in editing another volume of the Annual Anthology, in pursuing the composition of Thalaba with unabated ardor, and in making various attempts in English hexameters. In this measure he had contemplated a "long and important poem," Mohammed the subject, of the plan of which he thus speaks at this time in one of his published letters to Mr. William Taylor, to whom he had sent a portion for his criticism: "From Coleridge I am promised the half, and we divided the book according as the subject suited us; but I expect to have nearly the whole work! His ardor is not lasting, and the only inconvenience that his dereliction can occasion will be that I shall write the poem in fragments, and have to seam them together at the last. The action ends with the capture of Mecca; the mob of his wives are kept out of sight, and only Mary, the Egyptian, introduced. Ali is of course my hero; and if you will recollect the prominent characters of Omar, and Abubeker, and Hamza, you will see variety enough. Among the Koreish are Amrou and Caled. From Maracci's curious prolegomena to his Refutation of the Koran I have collected many obscure facts for the narrative. Still, however, though the plan is well formed and interesting, I fear it would not give the hexameters a fair chance. A more popular story, and one requiring not the elevation of thought and language which this demands, would probably succeed better; a sort of pastoral epic, which is one of my boy-plans yet unexecuted."*

A fragment only of "Mohammed" was ever

* Feb 3, 1800.

written, which may be found in the *latest* edition of the Poems.

My father's health still continuing in a most unsatisfactory state, and change of climate being both the prescription of his physician (Dr. Beddoes) and the remedy in which he had himself the greatest faith, he was very desirous of again visiting Lisbon, and had written to his uncle on the subject, whose residence there, and his own desire to collect materials for a History of Portugal, combined to fix his choice. To this, as well as to other subjects of interest, he alludes in the following letter.

To John May, Esq.

"Feb. 18, 1800.

"My dear Friend,

"Your last letter entered into an interesting subject. A young man entering into the world is exposed to hourly danger—and what more important than to discover the best preservative? To have a friend dear enough, and respectable enough, to hold the place of a confessor, would assuredly be the best; and if the office of confessor could always be well filled, I would give up half the Reformation to restore it. In my moments of reverie I have sometimes imagined myself such a character—the obscure instrument in promoting virtue and happiness; but it is obvious that more evil than good results from the power being, like other power, often in improper hands. I have wandered from the subject. It is not likely I shall ever gain the confidence of my brothers to the desired extent. Whatever affection they may feel for me, a sort of fear is mixed with it; I am more the object of their esteem than love: there has been no equality between us; we have been rarely domesticated together, and when that has been the case, they have been accustomed, if they were faulty, to understand my silent disapprobation.* No; —— will never intrust his feelings to me; and as to precepts of warning, indeed, I doubt their propriety; I doubt lest, from the strange perverting power of the mind, they should be made to minister to temptation. Indirect admonition, example—are not these better means? Feelings almost romantically refined were my preservation, and with these I amalgamated afterward an almost stoical morality. * *

"My health fluctuates, and the necessity of changing climate is sadly and sufficiently obvious, lest, though my disease should prove of no serious danger, the worst habits of hypochondriasm fasten upon me and palsy all intellectual power. I look with anxiety for my uncle's letter, and think so much of Lisbon that to abandon the thought would be a considerable disappointment. It would highly gratify me to see my uncle, and I have associations with Lisbon that give me a friendship for the place—recollected feelings and hopes, pleasures and anxieties—all now mellowed into remembrances that endear the associated scenes. But that my uncle should approve—that is, perhaps, little probable; a few weeks will decide; and if I do not go to Portugal, I have no choice but Italy, for Madeira is a prison, and the voyage to the West Indies of a terrifying length. This detestable war! if they would make peace upon motives as light as they made war, there would be cause enough, because I want to cross from Dover to Calais: it would save me some sea-sickness, and the wealth and blood of the nation into the bargain.

"I have busied myself in idleness already in the History of Portugal, and the interest which I take in this employment will make me visit the field of Ourique, and the banks of Mondeyo, and the grave of Inez. The Indian transactions are too much for an episode, and must be separately related. The manners and literature of the country should accompany the chronological order of events. I should disturb the spiders of the Necessidades, and leave no convent library unransacked. Should Italy be my destination, no definite object of research presents itself: the literature of that country is too vast a field to be harvested by one laborer; the history split into fifty channels; the petty broils of petty states infinitely perplexed, infinitely insignificant.

"You have heard me mention Rickman as one whose society was my great motive for taking the cottage at Burton. He is coming to Bristol to assist me in an undertaking which he proposed and pressed upon me—an essay upon the state of women in society, and its possible amelioration by means, at first, of institutions similar to the Flemish beguinages. You will feel an interest in this subject. I shall be little more than mason in this business, under the master architect. Rickman is a man of uncommon talents and knowledge, and political economy has been his favorite study: all calculations and facts requiring this knowledge he will execute. The part intended to impress upon the reader the necessity of alleviating the evil which he sees enforced, will be mine, for Rickman would write too strictly and too closely for the public taste. You probably know the nature of the beguinages: they were female fraternities, where the members were engaged in some useful employments, and bound by no religious obligations. The object is to provide for the numerous class of women who want employment the means of respectable independence, by restoring to them those branches of business which the men have mischievously usurped, or monopolized, when they ought only to have shared.

"O! what a country might this England become, did its government but wisely direct the strength, and wealth, and activity of the people! Every profession, every trade is overstocked; there are more adventurers in each than possibly can find employment; hence poverty and crime.

* In later life, in his intercourse with his children, to whom he was indeed "the father, teacher, playmate," his own beautifully expressed wish was fully realized:

"And should my youth, as youth is apt, I know,
Some harshness show,
All vain asperities I day by day
Would wear away,
Till the smooth temper of my age should be
Like the high leaves upon the holly-tree."

The Holly Tree: Poems, p. 129.

Do not misunderstand me as asserting this to be the sole cause, but it is the most frequent one. A system of colonization, that should offer an outlet for the superfluous activity of the country, would convert this into a cause of general good; and the blessings of civilization might be extended over the deserts that, to the disgrace of man, occupy so great a part of the world! Assuredly, poverty and the dread of poverty are the great sources of guilt. . . . . That country can not be well regulated where marriage is imprudence, where children are a burden and a misfortune. A very, very small portion of this evil our plan, if established, will remove; but of great magnitude if separately considered. I am not very sanguine in my expectations of success, but I will do my best in examining the evil and proposing a remedy. God bless you!

"Yours affectionately,

"ROBERT SOUTHEY."

In the course of the following month a letter from his uncle reached him, cordially approving of his wish to try the effect of Lisbon air, and urging him to leave England as soon as possible. His arrangements were quickly completed, and in the following letter to Mr. Coleridge he provides against all possible contingencies:

To S. T. Coleridge, Esq.

"Bristol, April 1, 1800.

"MY DEAR COLERIDGE,

"The day of our departure is now definitely fixed. We leave Bristol next week, on Thursday. I do not wish to see you before we go; the time is too short, and, moreover, the company of a friend who is soon to be left for a long absence is not desirable. A few words upon business. For the Third Anthology Davy and Danvers will be my delegates: should you be in Bristol, of course the plenipotentiaryship is vested in you. The Chatterton subscription will not fill in less than twelve months: if illness or aught more cogent detain me beyond that period, I pray you to let that duty devolve upon you; there will be nothing but the task of arrangement. Danvers has a copy of Madoc. The written books of Thalaba will be left with Wynn. A man, when he goes abroad, should make his will; and this is all my wealth: be my executor in case I am summoned upon the grand tour of the universe, and do with them, and with whatever you may find of mine, what may be most advantageous for Edith, for my brothers Henry and Edward, and for my mother.

"There is not much danger in a voyage to Lisbon; my illness threatens little, and faith will probably render the proposed remedy efficacious. In Portugal I shall have but little society; with the English there I have no common feeling. Of course, I shall enjoy enough leisure for all my employments. My uncle has a good library, and I shall not find retirement irksome.

"Our summer will probably be passed at Cintra, a place which may be deemed a cool paradise in that climate. I do not look forward to any circumstance with so much emotion as to hearing again the brook which runs by my uncle's door. I never beheld a spot that invited to so deep tranquillity. My purposed employments you know. The History will be a great and serious work, and I shall labor at preparing the materials assiduously. The various journeys necessary in that pursuit will fill a journal, and grow into a saleable volume. On this I calculate: this is a harvest which may be expected; perhaps, also, a few mushrooms may spring up.

"If peace will permit me, I shall return along the south of Spain and over the Pyrenees. Edith little likes her expedition. She wants a female companion; but this can not be had, and she must learn to be contented without one; moreover, there is at Lisbon a lady of her own age, for whom I have a considerable regard, and who will not be sorry to see once more an acquaintance with more brains than a calf. She will be our neighbor. My uncle, also, is a man for whom it is impossible not to feel affection. I wish we were there: the journey is troublesome, and the voyage shockingly unpleasant, from sickness and the constant feeling of insecurity; however, if we have but mild weather, I shall not be displeased at one more lesson in sea scenery.

* * * * * * *

"I should willingly have seen Moses again: when I return he will be a new being, and I shall not find the queer boy whom I have been remembering. God bless him! We are all changing: one wishes, sometimes, that God had bestowed upon us something of his immutability. Age, infirmities, blunted feelings, blunted intellect, these are but comfortless expectancies! but we shall be boys again in the next world.

"Coleridge, write often to me. As *you* must pay English postage, write upon large paper; as *I* must pay Portuguese by weight, let it be thin. My direction need only be, with the Rev. Herbert Hill, Lisbon; he has taken a house for us. We shall thus govern ourselves, and the plea of illness will guarantee me from cards, and company, and ball-rooms! No! no! I do not wear my old cocked hat again! it can not, certainly, fit me now.

"I take with me for the voyage your poems, the Lyrics, the Lyrical Ballads, and Gebir; and, except a few books designed for presents, these make all my library. I like Gebir more and more. If you ever meet its author, tell him I took it with me on a voyage.

* * * * * * *

"God bless you!

"Yours affectionately,

"R. S."

CHAPTER VII.

LETTERS FROM PORTUGAL.

VOYAGE AND ARRIVAL—VISITS—ANECDOTES—DESCRIPTION OF LISBON—ROMISH CUSTOMS—DESCRIPTION OF THE COUNTRY, PROCESSIONS, ETC.—ACCOUNT OF A BULL-FIGHT—PROPOSED

MONUMENT TO FIELDING—THALABA FINISHED—LETTERS FROM CINTRA—LENT PLAYS—WINE—LAWS—MONASTIC SUPERSTITIONS—BAD ROADS—ADVICE TO HIS BROTHER HENRY AS TO HIS STUDIES—ATTACHMENT TO CINTRA—ACCOUNT OF MAFRA; ITS CHURCH, CONVENT, AND LIBRARY—PESTILENCE AT CADIZ—DESCRIPTION OF CINTRA; SCENERY, ETC.—DIRECTIONS FOR THE PUBLICATION OF THALABA—PROJECTED HISTORY OF PORTUGAL—EXCURSION TO COSTA—FISHERMEN—IMAGE BY THE ROAD SIDE—JOURNEY TO POMBAL—TORRES VEDRAS, ETC.—ENGLISH POLITICS—THALABA—MADOC—KEHAMA—PROBABLE INVASION OF PORTUGAL—ACCOUNT OF JOURNEY TO FARO.—1800, 1801.

MY father had at one time intended to publish a second volume of "Letters from Spain and Portugal;" and, among some fragmentary preparations for these, I find a description of his embarkation and voyage, with which the following series of letters may be fitly prefaced. They are so complete in themselves as to render any remarks on my part needless.

"MY DEAR T.,

"I parted from you at Liskeard with a heavy heart. The thought of seeing you upon the way was a pleasure to look on to when we took our departure from Bristol; but, having left you, we had taken leave of the last friend before our voyage. Falmouth was not a place to exhilarate us: we were in the room where I met poor Lovel on my former journey; he was the last person with whom I shook hands in England as I was stepping into the boat to embark, and the first news on my return, when, within three hours, I expected to have been welcomed by him, was, that he was in his grave. Few persons bear about with them a more continual feeling of the uncertainty of life, its changes and its chances, than I do. Well! well! I bear with me the faith also, that though we should never meet again in this world, we shall all meet in a better.

"Thanks to the zephyrs, Capt. Yescombe was yet in the harbor. I went on board, chose our berths, passed the custom-house, and then endeavored to make poor Time as easy as he could be upon the rack of expectation. Six days we watched the weather-cock, and sighed for north-easterns. I walked on the beach, caught soldier-crabs, and loitered to admire the sea-anemones in their ever-varying shapes of beauty; read Gebir, and wrote half a book of Thalaba. There was a sight on the Monday, but the rain kept me within doors: six boys ate pap for a hat, and six men jumped in sacks for a similar prize; in the evening there was an assembly, and the best dancer was a man with a wooden leg. A short account of six days; if, however, I were to add the bill, you would find it a long one!

"We embarked at four on Thursday afternoon. As we sailed out of the harbor, the ships there and the shore seemed to swim before my sight like a vision. Light winds and favorable; but we were before the wind, and my poor inside, being obliged to shift every moment with the center of gravity, was soon in a state of insurrection. There is a pleasure in extracting matter of jest from discomfort and bodily pain; a wholesome habit if it extends no further, but a deadly one if it be encouraged when the heart is sore. I lay in my berth, which always reminded me of a coffin whenever I got into it, and, when any one come near me with inquiries, uttered some quaint phrase or crooked pun in answer, and grunted in unison with the intestinal grumbling which might have answered for me. * * * * * * * We saw the Berlings* on Tuesday night; on Wednesday, Edith and I went on deck at five o'clock: we were off the rock, and the sun seemed to rest upon it for a moment as he rose behind. Mafra was visible; presently we began to distinguish the heights of Cintra and the Penha Convent. The wind blew fresh, and we were near enough the shore to see the silver dust of the breakers, and the sea-birds sporting over them in flocks. A pilot-boat came off to us: its great sail seemed to be as unmanageable as an umbrella in a storm; sometimes it was dipped half over in the water, and it flapped all ways, like a woman's petticoat in a high wind. We passed the church and light-house of Nossa Senhora de Guia†, the Convent of St. Antonio with a few trees behind it, and the town of Cascaes. Houses were now scattered in clusters all along the shore. The want of trees in the landscape was scarcely perceived, so delightful was the sight of land, and so cheerful does every thing look under a southern sun.

"Our fellow-traveler was much amused by the numerous wind-mills which stood in regiments upon all the hills. A large building he supposed to be an inn, and could see the sign and the great

* Some rocks on the coast of Portugal.

† I find some verses upon this light-house, translated from Vieira the painter, which were intended to go in a note to this letter:

"Now was the time, when in the skies,
Night should have shown her starry eyes;
But those bright orbs above were shrouded,
And heaven was dark and over-clouded.
And now the beacon we espied,
Our blessed Lady of the Guide;
And there, propitious, rose her light,
The never-failing star of night.
The seaman, on his weary way,
Beholds with joy that saving ray,
And steers his vessel, from afar,
In safety o'er the dangerous bar.
A holy impulse of delight
Possess'd us at that well-known sight;
And, in one feeling all allied,
We blessed Our Lady of the Guide.
'Star of the sea, all hail!' we sung,
And praised her with one heart and tongue;
And, on the dark and silent sea,
Chanted Our Lady's Litany."

From a letter to Lieut. Southey, July 11, 1808.

The reader may perhaps be reminded of Sir Walter Scott's beautiful impromptu on a similar subject:

"PHAROS *loquitur.*

"Far in the bosom of the deep,
O'er these wild shelves my watch I keep,
A ruddy gem of changeful light,
Bound on the dusky brow of Night;
The seaman bids my luster hail,
And scorns to strike his timorous sail."

Lockhart's Life of Scott, vol. ii., p. 184.

gateway for the stage-coaches: the glass enabled him to find out that it was a convent door, with a cross before it. An absence of four years had freshened every object to my own sight, and perhaps there is even a greater delight in recollecting these things than in first beholding them. It is not possible to conceive a more magnificent scene than the entrance of the Tagus, and the gradual appearance of the beautiful city upon its banks.

"The Portuguese say of their capital,

'*Quem naõ ha visto Lisboa*
Naõ ha visto cousa boa.'

'He who has not seen Lisbon has not seen a fine thing.'

"It is indeed a sight, exceeding all it has ever been my fortune to behold in beauty, and richness, and grandeur: Convents and Quintas, gray olive-yards, green orange-groves, and greener vineyards; the shore more populous every moment as we advanced, and finer buildings opening upon us; the river, bright as the blue sky which illuminated it, swarming with boats of every size and shape, with sails of every imaginable variety; innumerable ships riding at anchor far as the eye could reach, and the city extending along the shore, and covering the hills to the furthest point of sight."

To S. T. Coleridge, Esq.

"Lisbon, May-day, 1800.

"Here, then, we are, thank God! alive, and recovering from dreadful sickness. I never suffered so much at sea, and Edith was worse than I was. We scarcely ate or slept at all; but the passage was very fine and short; five days and a half brought us to our port, with light winds the whole of the way. The way was not, however, without alarm. On Monday morning, between five and six, the captain was awakened with tidings that a cutter was bearing down upon us, with English colors, indeed, but apparently a French vessel; we made a signal, which was not answered; we fired a gun, she did the same, and preparations were made for action. We had another Lisbon packet in company, mounting six guns; our own force was ten; the cutter was a match, and more, for both, but we did not expect to be taken. You may imagine Edith's terror, awakened on a sick bed—disturbed I should have said—with these tidings! The captain advised me to surround her with mattresses in the cabin; but she would not believe herself in safety there, and I lodged her in the cock-pit, and took my station on the quarter-deck with a musket. How I felt I can hardly tell; the hurry of the scene, the sight of grape-shot, bar-shot, and other ingenious implements of this sort, made an undistinguishable mixture of feelings. . . . . The cutter bore down between us. I saw the smoke from her matches, we were so near, and not a man on board had the least idea but that an immediate action was to take place. We hailed her; she answered in broken English, and passed on. 'Tis over! cried somebody. Not yet! said the captain; and we expected she was coming round as about to attack our comrade vessel. She was English, however, manned chiefly from Guernsey, and this explained her Frenchified language. You will easily imagine that my sensations at the ending of the business were very definable—one honest, simple joy that I was in a whole skin! I laid the musket in the chest with considerable more pleasure than I took it out. I am glad this took place; it has shown me what it is to prepare for action.

"Four years' absence from Lisbon have given every thing the varnish of novelty, and this, with the revival of old associations, makes me pleased with every thing. Poor Manuel, too, is as happy as man can be to see me once more; here he stands at breakfast, and talks of his meeting me at Villa Franca, and what we saw at this place and at that, and hopes that whenever I go into the country he may go with me. It even amused me to renew my acquaintance with the fleas, who opened the campaign immediately on the arrival of a foreigner. We landed yesterday about ten in the morning, and took possession of our house the same night. Our house is very small, and thoroughly Portuguese; little rooms all doors and windows—odd, but well calculated for coolness. From one window we have a most magnificent view over the river—Almada Hill, and the opposite shore of Alentejo, bounded by hills about the half mountain height of Malvern.

* * * * * * *

"To-day is a busy day we are arranging away our things, and seeing visitors: these visits must all be returned; there ends the ceremony, and then I may choose retirement. I hurry over my letters for the sake of feeling at leisure to begin my employments. The voyage depriving me of all rest, and leaving me too giddy to sleep well, will, with the help of the fleas, break me in well for early rising. The work before me is almost of terrifying labor: folio after folio to be gutted, for the immense mass of collateral knowledge which is indispensable; but I have leisure and inclination.

"Edith, who has been looking half her time out of the window, has just seen 'really a decent-looking woman;' this will show you what cattle the passers-by must be. She has found out that there are no middle-aged women here, and it is true; like their climate, it is only summer and winter. Their heavy cloaks of thick woolen, like horsemen's coats in England, amuse her in this weather, as much as her clear muslin would amuse them in an English winter. * *

"Thalaba will soon be finished. Rickman is my plenipotentiary with the booksellers for this. Pray send me your Plays. . . . . Thalaba finished, all my poetry, instead of being wasted in rivulets and ditches, shall flow into the great Madoc Mississippi river. I have with me your volume, Lyrical Ballads, Burns, and Gebir. Read Gebir again: he grows upon me.

"My uncle's library is admirably stocked with foreign books. . . . . My plan is this: immediately to go through the chronicles in order, and then make a skeleton of the narrative; the timbers put together, the house may be furnished at leisure. It will be a great work, and worthy of all labor.

"I am interrupted momentarily by visitors, like fleas infesting a new-comer! Edith's spirits are mending: a handful of roses has made her forgive the stink of Lisbon, and the green pease, the oranges, &c., are reconciling her to a country for which nature has done so much. We are transported into your midsummer, your most luxuriant midsummer! Plague upon that heart-stop, that has reminded me that this is a voyage of prescription as well as of pleasure. But I will get well; and you must join us, and return with us over the Pyrenees, and some of my dreams must be fulfilled!

"God bless you! Write to me, and some long letters; and send me your Christabell and your Three Graces, and finish them on purpose to send them. Edith's love. I reach a long arm, and shake hands with you across the seas.

"Yours, ROBERT SOUTHEY."

To Lieutenant Southey, H.M.S. Bellona.

"Lisbon, May 8, 1800.

* * * * * * *

"The English, when strangers here, are so suspicious of the natives as to be very rash in misinterpreting them. A young man, whom I knew, fired at the watch one night when they accosted him: the ball passed through the watchman's hat; he was seized and confined, and it required interest and money to excuse him for what was inexcusable. My uncle, walking one night with a midshipman, was stopped by persons bearing a young man who had been run through the body by a lieutenant. They had stopped him, seeing his companion's uniform, but, knowing my uncle, suffered him to pass after telling the circumstances. The lieutenant was drunk; the young man was a gentleman, who, seeing him staggering about the streets, took him by the arm to lead him home; the Englishman did not understand what he said, and ran him through.

"As yet, we have not done receiving all our visits of ceremony. We are going, the first night we are at liberty, to the Portuguese play. The court have shown a strange caprice about the Opera: they permitted them to have a few female singers, and the proprietors of the Opera sent to Italy for more and better ones. They came. No! they would not license any more; the present women might act, but not the new-comers. You must not expect me to give you any reason for this inconsistency: 'tis the sheer whim of authority; but an odd reason was assigned for permitting two, who still act—one because she is very religious, the other because she is Portuguese and of a certain age.

"On Sunday a princess was christened. In the evening the guns fired a signal for all persons to illuminate. It was a pleasing sight from our window: the town all starred, and the moving lights of the shipping. . . . . But the river, seen by moonlight from hence, is a far finer spectacle than art can make. It lies like a plain of light under the heaven, the trees and houses now forming a dark and distinct foreground, and now undistinguishable in shade as the moon moves on her way—Almada stretching its black isthmus into the waters, that shine like midnight snow. . . . . A magnificent equipage passed our window on Monday: it was a nobleman either going to be married or to court. The carriage was drawn by four horses, each covered with a white netting, and crested with white plumes: they were very restive—indeed, but half broke in. I had seen them breaking in before, and on these occasions they always fill the carriage with servants to make it heavy, so that their necks also run a chance of being broken in. It was like the pomp of romance. They bury in covered buildings that adjoin the church: the graves are built in divisions, like tanners' pits: you may, perhaps, remember such at Bristol, at St. Paul's, which I saw building. Quicklime is thrown in with every body, which, of course, is soon consumed; still the bones accumulate, and occasionally these places are cleared out. . . . .

"They have a singular mode of fishing at Costa, a sort of wigwam village on the sands south of the bar. The gang of fishermen to each net is about fifty, all paid and fed by the captain regularly—not according to their success. Half hold one end of a rope, the other is carried off in the boat: the rope is about half a mile in length, the net in the middle. A high surf breaks on the shore; the men then thrust off the boat, themselves breast-deep, and stooping under every wave that meets them; the others row round to shore, and then they all haul in. This place is about nine miles only from Lisbon, and yet criminals run away there and are safe. Sometimes a magistrate goes down, but they always know that he is coming, and away to the woods for the day. It is common to go there from town, and dine upon the sands. The people are civil and inoffensive; indeed, generally so over Portugal, except among the boatmen, who have enough intercourse with foreigners to catch all their vices.

"Lord Somerville went by the last packet. I did not see him; he would have called one evening, but my uncle, knowing him pressed for time, begged him to waive the ceremony. I have been very industrious, and continue so—rise early, and never waste a minute. If I am at home without visitors, I go from book to book; and change is more relief than idleness. The American minister called on me after supper on Tuesday: this was somewhat familiar, and, I apprehend, was meant as civility. God bless you.

"R. S."

To Lieutenant Southey, H.M.S. Bellona.

"Lisbon, May 23, 1800.

"Lisbon has twice been clean since the creation. Noah's flood washed it once, and the fire after the earthquake purified it. When it will be clean again will be difficult to say; probably not till the general conflagration. A house, at which I called yesterday, actually has a drain running round one of the sides, which empties all the filth before the entrance. . . . . Government will neither cleanse the city themselves, nor suffer any one else to do it. An English merchant applied lately for permission to clean the street in which he lived, and it was refused. This is one of the curious absurdities of the P. government. An English invalid, who was terribly shaken in his carriage by the ragged pavement in his street, applied to the proper officers to allow him to have it mended : they would not do it. He was a man of fortune.

"The filthiest offices in the place are performed by negroes. . . . These poor people were brought as slaves into Portugal, till Pombal prohibited all future importation, still leaving those already in the country slaves, that property might not be invaded. Once since, a petition was presented that the country wanted negroes, and a few were imported in consequence. When they have grown old in service and slavery, the trick of Portuguese generosity is to give them their liberty; that is as if, in England, a man, when his horse was grown old, should turn him adrift, instead of giving the old animal the run of his park. Of course, black beggars are numerous. Gray-headed, and with gray beards, they look strangely; and some, that have the leprosy, are the most hideous objects imaginable. The old women wear nothing on their heads, and, what with their woolly hair and their broad features, look sometimes so fearfully ugly that I do not wonder at the frequency of negresses in romance. A priest in this country *sold his own daughter* by a negress. The Portuguese despise the negroes, and by way of insult sneeze at them as they pass : this is their strongest mark of contempt. Our phrase, 'a fig for him,' is explained by an amulet in use here against witchcraft, called a *figa :* the mules and asses wear it. It is the figure of a hand closed, the thumb cocked out between the fore and middle fingers. I first saw it mentioned in a curious poem by Vieira, the famous, and, indeed, only good Portuguese painter. He had one given him when a child to save him from an evil eye, for he was in more danger on account of his being handsome and quick; as we say, a child is too clever to live. The 'gift of the gab' must also be of Portuguese extraction : *gaban* is to praise, to coax.

"No doubt this is a regular government; it is an old monarchy, and has an Established Church. . . . A lawyer in England wrote a book to prove that our monarchy was absolute also; and Hughes, the clergyman at Clifton, whom you may have seen at my aunt's, lamented in a pamphlet that that *awful tribunal, the Inquisition, had relaxed its vigilance;* but you may not forge and murder with impunity. An acquaintance of mine (Tennant, well known for some famous chemical experiments on the diamond) met an Irishman in Switzerland who had been at Rome. He said it was the most *laineant* government in the world : you might kill a man in the streets, and nobody would take the *laist* notice of it. This also is a *laineant* government : a man stabs his antagonist, wipes the knife in his cloak, and walks quietly away. It is a point of honor in the spectators to give no information. If one servant robs his master, it is a point of honor in his fellow-servants never to inform of him. Both these points of honor are inviolable from prudence, for a stab would be the consequence. One method of revenge used in the provinces is ingeniously wicked : they beat a man with sand-bags. These do not inflict so much immediate pain as a cane would do, but they so bruise all the fine vessels, that, unless the poor wretch be immediately scarified, a lingering death is the consequence. My uncle has known instances at Porto. For all useful purposes of society, this is a complete anarchy : in the police every individual is interested; security is the object of political institutions, and here every man is at the mercy of every ruffian he meets. These things make no noise here. A man was murdered this week within thirty yards of our house, and we only heard it ten days afterward by mere accident; yet all goes on smoothly, as the Tagus flows over the dead bodies that are thrown into it. . . . In England you will imagine that this insecurity must occasion perpetual disquiet. Not so. As I do not quarrel, and nobody has any interest in sending me to the next world, there is no danger. We are, indeed, safer than in England, because there is not so much ingenuity exerted in villainy. Instruments for picking pockets and breaking open houses have not yet been introduced. The country is not civilized enough to produce coiners. A man may as easily escape being assassinated here, as he can fighting a duel in England.

"On Sunday, some boys, dressed like bluecoat boys, went under our window, with baskets, begging provisions or money. A man has set up this charity school on speculation, and without funds, trusting to chance alms. The 'Emperor of the Holy Ghost' also passed us in person : his flags are new, and his retinue magnificent in their new dresses of white and scarlet. His musicians were all negroes. Before him went a grave and comely personage, carrying a gilt wand of about ten feet high. The emperor is about six years old, exceedingly thin, dressed like a man in full dress, silk stockings, large buckles, a sword, and an enormous cocked hat, bigger than yours, edged with white fringe. On either side marched a gentleman usher, from time to time adjusting his hat, as its heavy corners preponderated. The attendants carried silver salvers, on which they had collected much copper money : few poor people passed who did not give something.

"Lately a negro went along our street with a Christ in a glass case, which he showed to every one whom he met. They usually kissed the glass and gave him money. Pombal, in his time, prohibited such follies. These images have all been blessed by the pope, and are therefore thus respected. I was in a shop the other day waiting for change, when a beggar woman came in. As I did not give her any thing, she turned to an image of Our Lady, prayed to it and kissed it, and then turned round to beg again.

"Religion is kept alive by these images, &c., like a fire perpetually supplied with fuel. They have a saint for every thing. . . . One saint preserves from lightning, another from fire, a third clears the clouds, and so on—a salve for every sore. It is a fine religion for an enthusiast—for one who can let his feelings remain awake, and opiate his reason. Never was goddess so calculated to win upon the human heart as the Virgin Mary; and devotees, Moravians as well as Catholics, not unfrequently mingle the feelings of earthly and spiritual love, as strangely as our Bible has mixed the language in Solomon's Song. We have an instance in Crashaw the poet's hymn to St. Theresa.

"One of the new convent towers is miserably disfigured by a projecting screen of wood. The man who rings the bell stands close by it, and the ugly thing is put there, lest he should see the nuns walking in the garden, or lest they should see him, for a nun has nothing but love to think of, and a powder magazine must be guarded warily. A million sterling has been expended upon this convent: it is magnificent within, wholly of marble, and the color well disposed. A million sterling! and the great square is unfinished, and the city without flagstones, without lamps, without drains!

"I meet the galley slaves sometimes, and have looked at them with a physiognomic eye, to see if they differed from the rest of the people. It appeared to me that they had been found out, the others had not. The Portuguese face, when fine, is very fine, and it rarely wants the expression of intellect.

"The gardens have usually vine-covered walks, stone pillars supporting the trellis poles. Some you see in the old-fashioned style—box cut into patterns like the zigzag twirling of a Turkey carpet pattern. The Convent of the Necessidades has a very large and fine garden, open to men, but not to women. This is laid out in shady walks, like the spokes of wheels, that center into fountains; the space between the walks occupied with oranges, lemons, and other fruit-trees. Every where innumerable lizards are to be seen sporting in the sun, gray or green, from two inches to twenty in length, nimble, harmless, beautiful animals. . . . . God bless you. R. S."

To Mrs. Southey, Senr.

Lisbon, May 23, 1800.

"My dear Mother,

"Our trunk arrived by the last packet: a joyful arrival, for I was beginning to be as bare as a plucked ostrich. . . . . We go on comfortably; as clean as an English house up stairs, as dirty as a Portuguese one below. Edith, like Mr. Pitt, is convinced of the impossibility of reform. Manuel will clean the kitchen, indeed, but immediately he will scrape the fish-scales all over it. These people have no foresight. We, however, are very well off; and, for a Portuguese, our Maria Rosa is extraordinarily tidy.

"—— is here, the Wine Street man, and he goes to market himself; and I am going to cultivate his acquaintance, in order to find out what good things may have escaped my appetite here. Nothing like a Bristol pointer at an eatable thing. . . . . My uncle has enough to do with burying and christening among the soldiers, though the priests poach among his flock sadly. We profit somewhat by the war, getting most excellent pieces of the sirloin from the rations. The summer we pass at Cintra, whither, however, we shall not go till July, for in June we have to see the procession of the 'Body of God,' of St. Anthony, and the royal family with the knight of the new convent; and we must also wait to see a bull-fight, which, being a cool summer amusement, only takes place in the hottest weather.

* * * * * * * *

"I read nothing but Spanish and Portuguese. Edith knows enough of the common words to get all needful things done about the house. We have had an infinite number of visitors, and our debt is not yet paid off. * * * *

"Edith has seen the aqueduct. Even after having seen it, I was astonished at its magnitude. Shakspeare's 'lessen'd to a crow' seemed hardly hyperbolical when I looked down from the middle arch upon the brook of Alcantara: the women washing there would have escaped my sight if I had not seen them moving as they walked. It is a work worthy of Rome in the days of her power and magnificence. The Portuguese delight in water; the most luscious and cloying sweetmeats first—for instance, preserved yolk of egg—and then a glass of water, and this is excellent which comes by the aqueduct. The view from the top is wonderfully fine: a stony, shallow brook below, a few women washing in it, bare-kneed, the sides sprinkled with linen drying in the sun; orange, and vine, and olive yards along the line of fertility that runs below the hills, and houses scattered in the little valley, and bare, dark hills and wind-mills, and houses far beyond, and distant mountains. She has also seen the new convent. The inside of the church is of marble, and the color very well disposed. You will remember that a marble room, chilling as it would be in England, is here only cool and comfortable. It is dedicated to the Heart of Jesus, which is the subject of more than one picture in the church. In one, the queen (for she built it) is represented adoring the heart. You would not like the Roman Catholic religion quite so well if you saw it here in all its naked nonsense—could you but see the mummery and smell the friars! There is no dying in peace for these fellows: they kill more than even the country apothecaries. When a man is given over, in they come, set up singing, which they never cease till the poor wretch is dead; build an altar in the room, light their candles, and administer extreme unction, which has much the same effect as if in England you measured a sick man for his coffin and dressed him in his shroud. They watch after the dying like Bristol undertakers. My uncle is always obliged to mount guard, and yet last week they smuggled off an officer; got at him when his senses were gone, stuck a candle in his hand, and sung 'O be joyful' for a convert.

"We have had three illuminations for the new pope. . . . . We had another illumination for the christening of a princess. These things are not, as in England, at the will of the mob. An illumination is proclaimed; at a proper hour, the guns fire to say, 'Now light your candles;' at ten they fire again to give notice you may put them out; and if you do not illuminate, you are fined about thirty shillings—but no riots, no mobbing, no breaking windows. . . . .

"The literature of this place takes up much of my time. I am never idle, and, I believe, must set at Thalaba in good earnest to get it out of my way. God bless you.

"Your affectionate son,

"Robert Southey."

To Lieut. Southey, H.M.S. Bellona.

"Lisbon, May 30, 1800.

"The country immediately adjoining Buenos Ayres, the hill on which we live, is very unpleasant; bare, burned hills, bearing nothing but wind-mills. The Valley of Alcantara, over which the great aqueduct passes, is indeed very striking: it winds among these hills, and perhaps owes much of its beauty to the contrast, like the villages in the South Downs, and that beautiful valley on the left of the road from Salisbury to Deptford. In rich countries they would not be noticed, but here they are like water in the deserts. The whole road to Cintra is thus ugly and uninteresting. The road paved all the way—a very devil's bowling-alley—you can imagine no scenery more wearying; but eastward of Lisbon it is totally different; there all is rich and beautiful—exquisitely beautiful, now that the green corn and the vineyards give it all the fresh verdure of an English landscape. Yesterday evening I took a long ride there with my uncle about the Valley of Chellas, the gardens of which delightful spot chiefly supply Lisbon. The place is intersected by a thousand by-lanes, unenterable by carriage, and as intricate as one of the last propositions in Euclid, all angles and curves. In this scenery there is scarcely an English feature. Orange-trees in the gardens, and vine-covered trellis-walks; olive-trees growing in the corn-fields, and now in full blossom: the blossom is somewhat like the old-man's-beard of our hedges; not so striking at a distance as when looked into, but it gives a grayness to the tree, a sober blossom, in character with the dusty foliage; fig-trees, their broad leaves so green and rich, and a few broad-headed pine-trees here and there, and cherries, apricots, &c., in the gardens, varying the verdure. In the gardens is usually a water-wheel, and the garden is veined with little aqueducts. These wheels creak eternally; and such is the force of association, that the Portuguese reckon this creaking among the delights of the country: they think of water, and the garden revived by it.

"The country looks covered with wood; not, indeed, of forest size, but large enough for beauty, and all useful. The fences are either walls—and the walls are soon covered with luxuriant vegetation in this country—or aloe-guarded banks; and the aloe is magnificent: the stem of the blossom looks almost like a piece of timber; and the fennel grows finely as a weed: you know its handsome leaf, fine as vegetable threads, or like hair fine and curled, its blossom growing tall, a fine yellow flower, distinguishable at a considerable distance from its size; and the acanthus, the plant that gave a man of genius the idea of the Corinthian capital, which he in consequence invented—blend these with wild roses and woodbines, more profusely beautiful than I ever saw them elsewhere, and you have the idea of these bank-fences. Our way was up and down steep hills, whence we looked over the valleys, its scattered houses, and here and there a convent, always a beautiful object, and sometimes the river, and its far shore like a low cloud. It was dusk before we returned, and the fire-flies were awake, flashing about the banks, and then putting out their candles, and again in light, like fairy fire-works. My uncle, when first in this country, had lost himself in a lane at Cintra: it was evening; he had heard nothing of these fire-flies and some hundreds rose at once before him: he says he thought there was a volcano beginning under his feet.

"The warm weather is come. We shut our windows to exclude the heated air, and our shutters to darken the room. If half the money expended upon the souls in purgatory were employed in watering the street, we should be relieved from the torment of burning. Yet is the heat more endurable than the intense light; this is insufferably painful: the houses are white, the stones in the street white, the very dust bleached, and all reflect back upon us the scorching sun. The light is like the quivering of a furnace fire: it dazzles and makes the eyes ache, and blindness is very common. At evening the sea breeze rises; a sudden change! tremendous for an invalid, but it purifies the town, and then, owl-like, we come out of our nests. At Cintra we shall be cool. We wait only for the processions of the Body of God, and St. Anthony, the 12th and 13th of June, and the Heart of Jesus on the 28th, and the first bull-fight, which will be about that time.

"The butchers annually pay a certain sum to government, like tax or turnpike-men in England. Veal is prohibited; there are, however, smugglers who carry on a contraband trade in veal, and better mutton than is to be procured in the legal way: one of these was taken up near our door a few days since; a public calamity, I assure you. The Portuguese servants do not like mutton, and they mutinied in an English family the other day on this account. A tax of one real per pound on all meat sold in Lisbon raises the fund for the aqueduct; a light tax (about the fifth of a halfpenny) for so great a benefit. The water is indeed purchased from the Gallegos, who are water-carriers by trade; but you may send to the fountains if you please; and the great aqueduct is known by a name expressive of this—they call it the free waters. The number of Gallegos employed here is disgraceful both to Spain and Portugal: to their own country, that these industrious people can not find employment at home; to this, that the Portuguese are lazy enough to let foreigners do their work, who annually drain Lisbon of its specie.

"The mules and goats have a most ugly, cup-shaped bell, from six to twelve inches long, hanging from their neck, with a clapper as rude as the rude cup in which it clinks. Manuel is at war with my uncle's mule, and, like worse people than himself, adopts the system of coercion when conciliation has been advised, and the effects of force experienced. 'You should coax the mule,' said my uncle, 'and never go near her without carrying her something in your hand.' 'No, senhor,' said Mambrino, 'that is the way with *horned cattle*, I know, but not with beasts like mules and horses; nothing but beating will do.' One day there was a hallaballoo (I never saw that word in a dictionary, so pardon the spelling if it be wrong) in the stables, which alarmed my uncle; out he went, and there was Manuel, discomfited by the mule, and crawled up under the manger in bodily fear.

"Friday, June 6th.

"Your letter has just reached me: a welcome visitant. Here a letter is of ten-fold more value than in England. Our friends are, perhaps, like our daily comforts—their value hardly understood till we are deprived of them. I go on comfortably. The weather makes me lazy, and yet I have read enormously, and digested much. Laziness is the influenza of the country. The stone-cutter will lay his head upon the stone at which he has worked, and sleep, though it be hot enough to broil a beef-steak. The very dogs are lazy: it was but yesterday I saw a great son of a bitch (literally) let a mule step upon him, from sheer laziness; and then he rose, howling, and *walked* away. The fellows lie sleeping every where in the streets; they seem to possess the power of sleeping when they will. Everlasting noise is another characteristic of Lisbon. Their noonday fire-works, their cannonading on every fool's pretext, their bells to every goat in a flock and every mule in a drove, prove this; above all, their everlasting bell-ding-donging — for bell-ringing would convey the English idea of music, and here it is only noise. A merchant, not far from my uncle's, has a private chapel, from whence his bells annoy the whole neighborhood. The English hotel, till lately, was near him, and the invalids were disturbed, and of course injured, by the noise. They sent to state this, and request that he would have the goodness to dispense with the bell-ringing; he returned for answer that the prince had given him leave to have a private chapel, and his bells should ring in spite of any body! I would have this fellow hung up by the heels, as a clapper to Great Tom of Lincoln, and punish him in kind.

"We often heard a noise below which puzzled us; it was like damping linen, but so often, that all the linen in Lisbon could not have supplied the sound. At last, when Maria was cleaning the adjoining room, we heard it. She was laying the dust, and in the same way as she damps the clothes in ironing—by taking a great mouthful of water, and then spirting it out: this is the Portuguese way, and the mouth makes a very good watering-pot.

"I have heard a good anecdote to illustrate the personal insecurity in this kingdom. Did you ever see old H——? He was a Porto merchant, and had a quarrel with a Portuguese, in consequence of which he and his antagonist always went out with guns, each watching for the first shot; but the Portuguese used to attack his house at night, and fire through the windows at him, till Mrs. H——, who did not like this chance-shooting, prevailed on her husband to quit the kingdom. The gallows here has a stationary ladder; and, God knows, if the hangman did all that was necessary, he would have a hard place.

"My uncle has purchased charts of all the coasts and ports of Spain and its islands, with the intention of giving them to you. Should you ever get on this station, they will be eminently useful. Lord St. Vincent has a copy, but the copies are so rare and so expensive that there can be very few in the navy.

"God bless you! Edith's love.

"Yours affectionately,

"Robert Southey."

To Lieut. Southey, H.M.S. Bellona.

"Sunday, June 15, 1800, Lisbon.

"My dear Tom,

"On Tuesday Rundell goes. To-morrow I have an engagement for the day, and lack of paper has till now prevented me from preparation; so now for a galloping letter!

"Thursday last we saw the long-looked-for procession of the Body of God. The pix is carried in all other processions empty; in this only it has the wafer—this is the only *Real Presence*. The pix is a silver vessel; and our vulgarism, 'please the pigs,' which has sometimes puzzled me, is only a corruption, and that an easy one, of 'please the pix'—the holiest church utensil. So much for the object of this raree-show. On the night preceding, the streets through which it is to pass are cleaned. The only miracle I ever knew the wafer perform is that of cleaning the streets of Lisbon: they are strewn with sand, and the houses hung with crimson damask from top to bottom. When the morning arrived, the streets were lined with soldiers; they marched on, filing to the right and left: their new uniforms are put on this day, and their appearance was very respectable: this alone was a fine sight. We were in a house in one of the new streets, where the houses are high and handsome, and perfectly regular, and the street longer than Redcliffe Street, every window and balcony crowded, and the Portuguese all in full dress; and of the finery of Portuguese full dress you can have but very inadequate ideas: not a jewel in Lisbon but was displayed—the rainbow would have been ashamed to be seen. The banners of the city and its various corporate trades led the way. I never saw banners so clumsily carried: they were stuck out with bars—not suffered to play freely and wave with the wind, and roll out their beauties in light and shade. Sticks were stuck at right angles in the poles to carry them by; nothing could be more awkward or more laborious for the bearers, some of whom were walking backward like lobsters, and others crab-sidling along. Then came a champion in armor, carrying a flag: God knows, his armor was heavy enough; and as both his arms were employed upon the flag, his horse was led. Here, also, I saw St. George, but not St. George of England! This was a Portuguese wooden St. George, his legs stiff and striding like a boot-jack, a man walking on each side to hold him on by the feet; his house, when he is at home, is the Castle, from whence he goes to the Duke of Cadaval's, where they dress his hat up with all their magnificent jewels for the procession, which he calls and returns on his way back. When the late king was dying, he had all the saints in Lisbon sent for, and this St. George was put to bed to him. The consultation produced no good effect.

"Scarcely any part of the procession was more beautiful than a number of very fine led horses, their saddles covered with rich escutcheons. All the brotherhoods then walked—an immense train of men in red or gray cloaks; and *all* the friars. Zounds, what a regiment! many of them fine young men, some few 'more fat than friars became,' and others, again, as venerable figures as a painter could wish. Among the bearded monks were many so old, so meager, so hermit-like in look, of such a bread-and-water diet appearance, that there needed no other evidence to prove they were indeed penitents, as austere as conscientious folly could devise. The knights of the different orders walked in their superb dresses—the whole patriarchal church in such robes! and after the pix came the prince himself, a group of nobles round him closing the whole. I never saw aught finer than this: the crowd closing behind, the whole street, as far as the eye could reach, above and below, thronged, flooded with people—and the blaze of their dresses! and the music! I pitied the friars: it was hot, though temperate for the season; yet the sun was painful, and on their shaven heads; they were holding up their singing-books, or their hands, or their handkerchiefs, or their cowls, to shade them. I have heard that it has been death to some of them in a hot season. Two years ago, at this very procession, a stranger received a stroke of the sun, and fell down apparently dead. The Irish friars got hold of him, and carried him off to be buried. The coffins here are like a trunk, and the lid is left open during the funeral service; before it was over, the man moved. What then did the Paddies? Oh, to be sure, and they could not bury him then! but they locked him in the church instead of calling assistance, and the next day the man was dead enough, and they finished the job!

"Had this been well managed, it would have been one of the finest conceivable sights; but it was a long procession broken into a number of little pieces, so irregularly they moved. On the prince, and the group about the Body of God—I like to translate it, that you may see the nakedness of the nonsensical blasphemy—they showered rose-leaves from the windows. The following day St. Anthony had a procession, and the trappings of the houses were ordered to remain for him: this was, like the Lent processions, a perfect puppet-show—the huge idols of the people carried upon men's shoulders. There were two negro saints, carried by negroes: I smiled to think what black angels they must make. We have got another raree-show to see in honor of the Heart of Jesus: this will be on Friday next; and then we think of Cintra.

"This has been a busy time for the Catholics. Saturday, the 7th of this month, as the Eve of Trinity Sunday, was a festival at the emperor's* head-quarters; his mountebank stage was illuminated, and pitch barrels blazing along the street, their flames flashing finely upon the broad flags that floated across the way. It was somewhat terrible; they were bonfires of superstition, and I could not help thinking how much better the spectators would have been pleased with the sight had there been a Jew, or a heretic like me, in every barrel. The scene was thronged with spectators, and, to my great surprise, I saw women walking in safety; nothing like personal insult was attempted: the boys had their bonfires and fire-works, but they seemed to have no idea that mischief was amusement. The succeeding day, Trinity Sunday, was the termination of the emperor's reign. His train was increased by a band of soldiers: he was crowned, and dined in public. The emperor for the ensuing year was elected; and thus ends the mummery, till Lent, and feasting, and folly come round again. At Cascaes the emperor is a man, and the farce more formal. There was a brother of John V., who delighted in blackguard mischief. He went to the emperor, then on the throne, with the intention of kicking him down, or some such practical jest. The emperor knew him, sat like an old senator when the Gauls approached, and held out his hand for the prince to kiss: it effectually disconcerted him, and he growled out as he retired, 'The rascal plays his part better than I expected.'

"In the course of a conversation, introduced by these processions, I said to a lady, who remembers the auto-da-fés, 'What a dreadful day it must have been for the English when one of these infernal executions took place!' 'No,' she said, 'not at all; it was like the processions, expected as a fine sight, and the English, whose houses overlooked the streets through which they

* The Emperor of the Holy Ghost, as he is called; see antè, p. 125.

passed, kept open house as now, and made entertainments!!' They did not, indeed, see the execution—that was at midnight; but they should have shut up their houses, and, for the honor of their own country, have expressed all silent abhorrence. Did such an event take place now, I should shake the dust from my feet, and curse the city, and leave it forever! What is it that has prevented these Catholic bonfires? I do not understand. The Constitution and the people never were more bigoted; and the dislike of Pombal would, after his disgrace, have only been a motive for reviving them. Is it that the priests themselves and the nobles have grown irreligious? Perhaps the books of Voltaire may have saved many a poor Jew from the flames.

"Portugal is certainly improving, but very, very, very slowly. The factories have been long declining in opulence; and the Portuguese, who had some years since no merchants of note, have now the most eminent and wealthy in the place. They are beginning to take the profits themselves, which they had suffered us to reap. This is well, and as it should be; but they have found out that Cintra is a fine place, and are buying up the houses there as they are vacant, so that they will one day dispossess the English, and this I do not like. Cintra is too good a place for the Portuguese. It is only fit for us Goths—for Germans or English.

"Your Thalaba is on the stocks. You will have it some six months before it can possibly be printed, and this is worth while. I this morning finished the tenth book—only two more; and at the end of a journey Hope always quickens my speed. Farewell. I am hurried, and you must and may excuse (as Rundell is postman extraordinary) a sheet not quite filled. God bless you! Edith's love.

"R. S."

To Lieut. Southey, H.M.S. Bellona.

"June 22, 1800.

"My dear Tom,

"We are just returned from a bull-feast, and I write to you while the feelings occasioned by this spectacle are fresh. I had never before seen one. The buffoonery of teazing bullocks at Madrid was rather foolish than cruel, and its extreme folly excited laughter, as much at the spectators as the thing itself. This is widely different. The hand-bill was pompous: 'Antonio de Cordeiro, who had so distinguished himself last year, was again to perform. The entertainment would deserve the approbation of a generous public. Ten bulls were to be killed, four to be tormented: they were picked bulls, of the Marquis de ——'s breed (I forget his name), and chosen out for their courage and ferocity.' Yesterday the bull-fighters paraded the streets, as you may have seen rope-dancers and the 'equestrian troop' at Bristol fair. They were strangely disfigured with masques: one fellow had a paunch and a Punch-humpback, and all were dressed in true tawdry style. Hot weather is always the season, and Sunday always the day, the amusement being cool and devout! At half after four it began: the hero was on horseback, and half a dozen men on foot to assist him; about ten more sat with pitchforks to defend themselves, ready when wanted. The bulls were all in the area till the amusement opened. They were not large, and not the same breed as in England; they had more the face of the cow than the short, sulky look of gentlemen—quiet, harmless animals, whom a child might safely have played with, and a woman would have been ashamed to fear. So much for their *ferocity!* Courage, indeed, they possessed; they attacked only in self-defense, and you would, like me, have been angry to see a fellow with a spear provoking a bull whose horns were tipped with large balls, the brave beast, all bleeding with wounds, still facing him with reluctant resistance. Once I saw crackers stuck into his neck to irritate him, and heard them burst in his wounds: you will not wonder that I gave the Portuguese a hearty and honest English curse. It is not an affair of courage; the horse is trained, the bull's horns muffled, and half a dozen fellows, each ready to assist the other, and each with a cloak, on which the poor animal wastes his anger: they have the rails to leap over, also, and they know that when they drop the cloak he aims always at that; there is, therefore, little danger of a bruise, and none of any thing else. The amusement is, therefore, as cowardly as cruel. I saw nine killed; the first wound sickened Edith, and my own eyes were not always fixed upon the area. My curiosity was not, perhaps, strictly excusable, but the pain which I endured was assuredly penalty enough. The fiercest of the whole was one of the four who were only tormented: two fellows on asses attacked him with goads, and he knocked them over and over with much spirit; two more came on, standing each in the middle of a painted horse, ridiculously enough—and I fancy those fellows will remember him for the next fortnight whenever they turn in bed—and their sham horses were broken to pieces. Three dogs were loosed at another bull, and effectually sickened. I hate bull-dogs; they are a surly, vicious breed, ever ready to attack, mischievous and malicious enough to deserve Parliamentary praise from Mr. Wyndham and Mr. Canning. A large theater was completely full; men, women, and children were clapping their hands at every wound, and watching with delight the struggles of the dying beasts. It is a damnable sport! and, much to the honor of the English here, they all dislike it: very rarely does an Englishman or Englishwoman witness it a second time.

"You will find in Thalaba one accurate image which I observed this evening: a death-sweat *darkening the dun hide* of the animal. This amusement must have mischievous effects: it makes cruelty familiar; and as for the assertion that bull-baiting or bull-butchering keeps up the courage of the nation, only Wyndham and Canning could have been absurd enough and unfeeling enough to believe it; if it were true, the Spaniards ought to be the bravest nation in the world, because their amusement is the most cruel, and a butcher ought to make the best soldier.

"On Thursday we go to Cintra; this, therefore, will be my last letter of Lisbon anecdote. In Africa a Portuguese saw an orang-outang, the most human beast that has yet been discovered, walking quietly with a stick in his hand; he had the wickedness to shoot him, and was not, as he ought to have been, hung for willful murder. The head and hands were sent here: I have seen them in the Museum, in spirits. I have seen many an uglier fellow pass for a man, in spite of the definition that makes him a reasoning animal: he has eyebrows, and a woolly head, almost like a negro's, but the face not black.

"Fielding died and was buried here. By a singular fatality, four attempts have been made to erect a monument, and all have miscarried. A Frenchman set on foot a subscription for this purpose, and many of the factory engaged for one, two, or three moidores: circumstances took him from Lisbon, and this droppod. Another Frenchman had a monument made at his own expense, and paid for it; there was a fine French inscription, that, as his own countrymen had never given the great Fielding a monument, it was reserved for a Frenchman to honor his country by paying that respect to genius: he also went away, and is now following the French Pretender; and his monument lies among masonry and rubbish, where I have sought for it in vain. Then De Visme undertook the affair; and the bust of Fielding, designed for this purpose, is still in the house which belonged to him here. I know not what made this scheme abortive. Last, the Prince of Brazil went to work, and the monument was made. The Lady Abbess of the New Convent wished to see it: it was sent to her; she took a fancy to it, and there it has remained ever since; and Fielding is still without a monument.

"De Visme introduced the present fashion of painting rooms in stucco, with landscapes on the walls, and borders of flowers or arabesque: the fashion is, I believe, Italian. The workmen whom he employed had taste enough to be pleased with it, and it is general in all new houses. The ceilings are now painted: thus, instead of the huge layer of boards which was usual, nothing can look more cool, or be more convenient, for a cloth and soap cleans it.

"In the larger old houses, here and in Spain, in the country, there is usually a room with no windows, but, instead, arches quite open to the air. The appearance is strange and picturesque, and I should esteem it one of the inconveniences of Lisbon that the intolerable dust prevents the enjoyment of these open rooms there: the dust is a huge evil. * * * * * We had the hot wind for three days this week: a detestable burning blast, a bastard sort of siroc, tamed by crossing the sea and the land, but which parches the lips, and torments you with the Tantalus plague of fanning your cheek and heating it at the same time. The sea breeze is, on the other hand, as delightful: we feel it immediately; it cools the air, and freshens up all our languid feelings. In the West Indies they call this wind the doctor—a good seamanly phrase for its healing and comfortable effect.

"At the time the aqueduct was built, a large reservoir was made for its waste water. In winter, much water runs to waste; in summer, more is wanted, and the waterman wait a long time round the fountain before they can in turn fill their barrels; but these people, in building the reservoir, never calculated the weight of the water till the building was finished: so it stands still uncovered, a useless pile, and a rare monument of the national science. I saw a funeral from the country pass the window at night, the attendants holding torches, and the body in the trunk coffin carried upon a litter (that is, like a sedan chair carried by mules instead of men).

"The servants here, in marketing, think it a part of their fair profits to cheat you as much as they can, and have no idea that this is dishonesty: it is a sort of commission they think they are entitled to. This is so much the case, that one of these fellows, when he was stipulating about wages, thought them too little, and inquired if he was to go to market; he was told yes, and then he said he would come. . . . . .

"The queen's stables serve as an asylum. Rogues and murderers go there, and do the work for nothing. They are safe by this means, and the people, whose business it is to hire and pay the servants, pocket the money, so that they infest the neighborhood. They quarreled with our dragoons, who broke into the stables, and thrashed them heartily, to the great satisfaction of the people near.

"God bless you! Edith's love.

"Yours, R. S."

To C. W. W. Wynn, Esq.

"Cintra, July 23, 1800.

"MY DEAR WYNN,

"You must, long ere this have received my second letter. I continue in comfortable health, and spirits that cast a sunshine upon every thing. I pray you make peace, that I may return in the spring over the Pyrenees. The cause would certainly be good, and so would the effects.

"Thalaba is finished, and I am correcting it; the concluding books you shall shortly receive. Giantly is not a coinage; it is sterling English of the old mint: I used it to avoid the sameness of sound in the *Giant Tyrant* as it stood at first. You object to the 'fowls of *the air*,'* and do not remember the elision. You object, likewise, to a license which I claim as lawful, that of making two short syllables stand for one long one. The eighth book explains enough what Azrael had been doing. The previous uncertainty is well. You will, I trust, find the Paradise a rich poetical picture, a proof that I can employ magnifi-

* "I had written at first 'fowls of heaven,' but heaven occurs a few lines above. But the line is wholly altered this way."

cence and luxury of language when I think them in place. The other faults you point out are removed. Thank you for —— letters. I shall inclose one to him when next I write, the only mode of conveyance with which I am acquainted. —— and I, both of us, were sent into the world with feelings little likely to push us forward in it. One overwhelming propensity has formed my destiny, and marred all prospects of rank or wealth; but it has made me happy, and it will make me immortal. ——, when I was his shadow, was almost my counterpart; but his talents and feelings found no center, and perforce thus have been scattered; he will probably succeed in worldly prospects far better than I shall do, but he will not be so happy a man, and his genius will bring forth no fruits. I love him dearly, and I know he never can lose the instinctive attachment which led to our boyish intimacy. Yet —— shrunk from me in London. I met him at your rooms; he was the same immutable character. I walked home with him at night; our conversation was unreserved, and, in silence and solitude, I rejoiced even with tears that I had found again the friend that was lost. From that time, a hasty visit is all I saw of him: it was his indolence; I know he esteems me. Our former coolness I remember among my follies; you were with me when I atoned for it by a voluntary letter, and you saw an answer such as I had reason to expect. I wrote again to him, a common young man's letter; he never answered it: the fact was, I had the disease of epistolizing, and he had not. Our future intercourse can not be much; by the time he returns to London, I trust I shall have retired from it, and pitched my tent near the church-yard in which I shall be buried. Of the East Indies I know not enough to estimate the reason and reasonableness of his dislike. Were I single, it is a country which would tempt me, as offering the shortest and most certain way to wealth, and many curious subjects of literary pursuit. About the language, —— is right; it is a baboon jargon not worth learning; but were I there, I would get the Vedams and get them translated. It is rather disgraceful that the most important acquisition of Oriental learning should have been given us by a Frenchman; but Anquetil du Perron was certainly a far more useful and meritorious Orientalist than Sir Wm. Jones, who disgraced himself by enviously abusing him. Latterly, Sir William's works are the dreams of dotage. I have some distant view of manufacturing a Hindoo romance, wild as Thalaba; and a nearer one of a Persian story, of which see the germ of vitality. I take the system of the Zendavesta for my mythology, and introduce the powers of darkness persecuting a Persian, one of the hundred and fifty sons of the great king; every evil they inflict becomes the cause of developing in him some virtue which his prosperity had smothered: an Athenian captive is a prominent character, and the whole warfare of the evil power ends in exalting a Persian prince into a citizen of Athens. I pray you be Greek enough to like that catastrophe, and forget France when you think of Attic republicanism.

"I have written no line of poetry here, except the four books of Thalaba, nor shall I till they are corrected and sent off, and my mind completely delivered of that subject. Some credit may be expected from the poem; and if the booksellers will not give me £100 for a 4to edition of 500 copies, or £140 for a pocket one of 1000, why, they shall not have the poem.

"I long to see the face of a friend, and hunger after the bread-and-butter comforts and green fields of England. Yet do I feel so strongly the good effects of climate—and I am now perspiring in my shirt while I write, in the coolness of Cintra, a darkened room, and a wet floor—that I certainly wish my lot could be cast somewhere in the south of Europe. The spot I am in is the most beautiful I have ever seen or imagined. I ride a jackass, a fine, lazy way of traveling: you have even a boy to beat old Dapple when he is slow. I eat oranges, figs, and delicious pears—drink Colares wine, a sort of half-way excellence between port and claret—read all I can lay my hands on—dream of poem after poem, and play after play—take a siesta of two hours, and am as happy as if life were but one everlasting to-day, and that to-morrow was not to be provided for.

"Here is a long letter about myself, and not a word about Portugal. My next shall be a brimming sheet of anecdotes.

"I am sorry —— is so disgusted with India, though I can not wish he were otherwise. From all accounts, an English East Indian is a very bad animal: they have adopted by force the luxury of the country, and its tyranny and pride by choice. A man who feels and thinks must be in solitude there. Yet the comfort is, that your wages are certain; so many years of toil for such a fortune at last. Is a young man wise who devotes the best years of his life to such a speculation? Alas! if he is, then am I a pitiable blockhead. But to me, the fable of the ant and grasshopper has long appeared a bad one: the ant hoards and hoards for a season in which he is torpid; the grasshopper—there is one singing merrily among the canes—God bless him! I wish you could see one, with his wings and his vermilion legs.

"God bless you! Write often, and let me have a very long letter upon short paper, as postage is by weight. Remember me to Elmsley; and pray pull Bedford's ears till *I* hear him bray: I wish my *burro boy* could get at him!"

To Mrs. Southey, Sen.

"Cintra, August 21, 1800.

"MY DEAR MOTHER,

"You will have known, before this can arrive, that your Bristol dispatches reached me. That I have not written sooner is the fault of the wind. We have been three weeks without a packet; and, now we have one, my letters may probably be detained for want of a convey ance to Lisbon. Poor Peggy !* I am impatient for letters: your last was a troubling one, and undid half that Portugal had done for me. However, I am materially amended. Tom writes that she is better; but I know the nature of the disease too well to hope so easily, perhaps, as you and he may have done. However, other diseases there are, undistinguishably similar in their symptoms, which are sometimes mistaken for this, and the patient is said to have recovered from a consumption when his lungs have been sound all the while.

"We have been here about two months, living alone, and riding jackasses. My uncle is sadly confined in Lisbon: the soldiers' children die as fast as they are born, from inattention or bad management, one of the million war-evils! and he must bury them. We have acquaintance out of number, but no friends: of course, I go among these people no oftener than absolute decorum requires. Patty Collins's niece has more brains than three parts of the factory: her I like hugely; but she is never at Cintra. I want Danvers here, and Davy, and Rickman, and Cottle, and you, and some fresh butter, and the newspaper: howbeit, I am very comfortable, and very busy. I want you to eat melons: we get them for about three farthings a pound; and grapes—oh! what grapes! Our desserts are magnificent.

"We have three servants here, a man, and maid, and a boy—all good servants for the country. * * * * * *

"The Roman Catholics have contrived to rank nastiness among Christian virtues, and they practice no other so universally. The poor Moriscoes in Spain were forbidden to use their baths, because it was a Turkish custom. Certain of the austerer monks would think it wicked to kill any of their vermin; others wear no linen, and sleep in their woolen dress from one year to another—fine, fat, frying friars, looking as oily as Aaron's beard in the sun. I should like to catch a Quaker, and bring him here among filth and finery.

"Since we left Lisbon I have written scarcely any letters, and have a week's work to settle my accounts with Tom: tell him that Thalaba has monopolized me; that by the King George, in her next voyage (about three weeks hence), I send over his copy, together with that for the press. Except to Bristol and to Tom, I have neglected all my other correspondents. Actually I have not time: I *must ride;* I am visited; and the correcting Thalaba and transcribing it is a very serious job.

"The French! You are probably alarmed for us, and, perhaps, not without cause; but we are in the dark, and only know that the situation is very critical. We are quite easy about the matter. The house is on fire! 'Och! and is that all?' said the Paddy; 'now, why did you disturb me? I am but a lodger!' In my own opinion, no attempt will be made on Portugal; it is not worth the trouble. Why make a dust by pulling down a house that must fall? We shall have peace!

"By the next packet I shall write, and send to Biddlecombe his year's rent. When we return, I shall immediately take a house in London, or near it: for a summer or two, Burton may do; but if Rickman leaves Christ Church, I must look for a situation where there is better society. I wish I could settle here; the climate suits me so well, that I could give up society, and live like a bear by sucking my own paws. You like the Catholics: shall I give you an account of one of their Lent plays upon transubstantiation, which is lying on the table? It begins by the Father turning Adam out of doors. 'Get out of my house, you rascal!' Adam goes a begging, and bitterly does he complain that he can find no house, no village, nobody to beg of. At last he meets the Four Seasons, and they give him a spade, and a plow, &c., but nothing to eat. Then comes Reason, and tells him to go to law with his Father, who is obliged to find him in victuals. Adam goes to law; an angel is his counsel, and the devil pleads against him. He wins his cause; and the Father settles upon him oil—for extreme unction; *lamb;* and bread and wine. Up comes the Sacrament, and there is an end of the play. This is written by a priest, one of the best Spanish writers, who has written seventy-two of these plays, all upon the body and blood, and all in the same strain of quaint and pious blasphemy. In another, Christ comes in as a soldier to ask his reward of my Lord World for serving him, and he produces the testimonials of his service: that, on the eighth day of his enlisting, he was wounded with a knife; that he had a narrow escape when the *infantry* were all cut off; that he went as a spy among the enemies, and even got into their Temple; that he stood a siege of forty days, and would not capitulate, though without provisions, and, after three assaults, put the enemy to flight; that he succored Castle Magdalen when the enemy had got possession; that he supplied a camp consisting of more than 5000 persons with food, who would all have been starved; that he did good service at sea in a storm; therefore, for him and his twelve followers, he asked his reward. I could fill sheet after sheet with these Bunyanisms, and send you miracles as strange as any in Thalaba.

"But you are crying out already, and are satisfied with the specimen. Farewell! We are going on well; only Edith's burro fell with her, and threw her overhead down hill, and she is now lame with a bruised knee. She excels in ass-womanship; and I am hugely pleased with riding sideways, and having a boy to beat the John and guide him.

"Harry must forgive me. I do not forget him, and will write very soon; but the interruption it occasions, and the time it takes up, make letter-writing a serious evil. God bless you.

"Your affectionate son,

"ROBERT SOUTHEY."

* His cousin, Margaret Hill, at this time in very ill health.

To John Rickman, Esq.

Cintra, August 22, 1800.

"MY DEAR RICKMAN,

"In the long space of three months since I wrote to you (or rather four!), you will expect I have done much. In truth, I have not been idle. For the great history, I have only collected the knowledge of *what* documents to reach, and *where* to seek them. The public library books are not removable; and I, like all the English, am driven to the cool retirement of Cintra. I have the general facts already in my memory, and I think a fair and accurate opinion of the chief personages, differing very considerably from their received characters, and a map of the method to be pursued. The ground is well manured, and the seed is in. I speak the language, not, indeed, grammatically, but fluently; and Portuguese, *from a familiar voice*, is almost as intelligible to me as English. I know the progress of their language, step by step, and have written materials toward the literary history, of collateral and incidental information—such anecdotes as paint the manners and character of a people. My collection would fill half an octavo volume.

"But Thalaba: it has taken up a greater portion of my time than I expected or wished. I have been polishing and polishing, adding and adding, and my unlearned readers ought to thank me very heartily for the toil, unpleasant and unproductive, of translating so many notes. By the King George packet I shall send it over, which will probably sail from Lisbon in about three weeks. . . . . The MS. (if the French waylay it not) may reach you the beginning of October at the latest; and, if the booksellers fall into my terms, a London printer will dispatch one quarto in a month, or two pocket volumes in a fortnight: £100 I will have for 400 4to copies, £130 for 1000 of the smaller size. The whole property I will not sell, because I expect the poem will become popular, and of course productive.

* * * * * * *

"Our house stands here in a lemon-garden of somewhat less than half an acre. Its fruit usually sells for twenty moidores; this year, owing to its failure, it produced only ten. These orchards, you see, are wonderfully productive, but they require more attention than any English crops. They are watered regularly. Here there is a large tank in every garden, whence the water is conveyed by little channels, which the man conducts round the roots of every tree, loosening the soil with a hoe: by this the leaves, as they fall, are sooner mingled with the soil, and afford a constant manure. Wages are as high as eighteen pence a day, *with* wine. The price of bread, of course, can differ little from its price in England; all other provisions are rather dearer, in some respects owing to actual scarcity, still more to the paper money, as every tradesman will have his profit upon the discount. The wine owes its advance to the enormous taxes in England. As the English tax it so highly, said the government here, we will tax it too; and they laid on the very moderate duty of a six-and-thirty per pipe. If people will give £75 a pipe, said the Porto merchants, no doubt they will give £80, and we will have our profit. They therefore laid on the five, and are making fortunes. *More* wine is imported than before the new duties, because the excise, to which it is subject, so materially checks the home-brewed; still much is manufactured. By an accident I happened to *know* that one merchant made his own Lisbon. . . . .

"No debtor is imprisoned here: shame, shame to our own laws! There is a Board of Bankruptcy—an institution, perhaps, of unequaled absurdity, so is it managed. Any debtor who will surrender all his effects to the board receives 10 per cent. It has been established about thirty years, and *they have never made one dividend.* Where goes the money? There is a fund for cleaning and lighting the city. There are no lamps and no scavengers. Where goes the fund?

* * * * * * *

"The number of monastics decreases; not from any dearth of laziness or fanaticism, but because the revenues are not now equal to the support of the original number. Sometimes the monks desert; in that case they pursue them. They took one poor fellow at work in a garden, where, for three months, he had been usefully employed, and enjoying freedom. . . . .

"Here is a fine soil of folly, and a plentiful crop do the friars reap! Some little good they do in return. They are good landlords, and the Church lands are the only lands that are tolerably cultivated. The ruin of Spain and Portugal is the fashion that all the wealthy have of residing wholly in the metropolis, where they spend to the uttermost, vex their tenants, and never pay their debts. Portugal, you say, *must* have bad roads. It will be very difficult to make them good. In winter the very heavy rains wash away all the smaller parts, and leave only the larger stones; in summer the sun dries them up, and the wind sweeps the stones bare. Brentford stones would be thought a fine road here. Hence slow and little traveling, and bad inns; in country towns no booksellers! scarcely any reading any where. Like beasts and savages, the people can bear total indolence. Their delight is to look into the street, put somebody to hunt their heads at the same time, and it is happiness! Even in their garden walls they have grates to look into the road. . . . .

"I lack society sadly. The people here know much of their own business, very little of the country they live in, and nothing of any thing else except cards. My uncle, indeed, is a man of extensive knowledge; and here is one family, of which the master is a man of some science, and where I can open my flood-gates. I want you and Davy, and a newspaper, and bread and butter, and a green field for me and the horse: it would do his old English heart as much good as it would mine. But I have ample and pleasant employment—curiosity forever on the hunt—a situation the most beautiful that I have ever seen, and a climate for which Nature seems to have destined me, only, blessed be God, she dropped me the other side of the bay. . . . . Edith's remembrance. Farewell!

"Yours, R. SOUTHEY."

To Henry Southey.

"Cintra, August 25, 1800.

"MY DEAR HARRY,

* * * * * * *

"On my return to England in the next spring, I shall take a house in or near London, where you shall live with me, and study anatomy at the Westminster Hospital, under Carlisle, whom you know to be a man of genius and my friend. By the time you have acquired enough previous knowledge, I trust some of my eggs will have hatched, so that you may graduate either at Edinburgh or in Germany, as shall appear best. Till my return you will remain where you are; you are well employed, and evidently improving rapidly. Nor is there any home to which you possibly could remove! On my return you will have one, and, I trust, more comfortable than any you have yet had. We are rising in the world: it is our turn, and will be our own faults if we do not, all of us, attain that station in the world to which our intellectual rank entitles us.

"Attend to prose particularly; excellence in that is acquirable. You know the value of literature, and may, perhaps, one day find it, as I have done, a resource as well as a delight. In your course of history, Gibbon must be read: it is the link that connects ancient with modern history. For the history of Portugal you must wait; there is none but that in the Universal History. It is a fine subject, and you will see, on my return, a skeleton—I hope half-musiled.

"Thalaba has taken up too much of my time, and I am eager to send it off, and wash my hands of all that could have been written in England: it is finished, and half ready for the press. I am polishing and polishing, and hewing it to pieces with surgeon severity. Yesterday I drew the pen across six hundred lines, and am now writing to you instead of supplying their place. It goes over for publication very shortly—I trust in three weeks. Rickman is my agent and supervisor of the press. I am sorry you do not know Rickman. I esteem him among the first men of my knowledge. * * * * * * * * For six weeks we have been at Cintra—a spot the most beautiful that I have ever seen, and which is probably unique. Eighteen miles distant, at Lisbon, the sun is insupportable. Here we are cool, with woods and water. The wealthier English are all here; still, however, I lack society, and, were it not for a self-sufficiency (like the bear, who sucks his paws when the snow shuts him up in his den), should be in a state of mental famine. My uncle is little here: people will die, and must be buried. He is a man of extensive information; his library very well furnished, and he very well acquainted with its contents. One Englishman here only talks politics with me: his taste in French is every thing, and in all else mine is right English and Antigallican. The English here know very little of the country they live in, and nothing of the literature. Of Camoens they have heard, and only of Camoens. By the help of my uncle I have acquired an extensive knowledge, and am almost as well acquainted with Portuguese literature as with that of my own country. It is not worth much; but it is not from the rose and the violet only that the bee sucks honey.

"You would be amused could you see Edith and myself on ass-back—I sitting sideways, gloriously lazy, with a boy to beat my Bayardo, as well adapted to me as ever that wild courser was to Rinaldo. In this climate there is no walking: a little exercise heats so immoderately; but their cork woods or fir woods, and mountain glens, and rock pyramids, and ever-flowing fountains, and lemon groves ever in flower and in fruit, want only society to become a Paradise. Could I but colonize Cintra with half a dozen familiars, I should wish never to leave it. As it is, I am comfortable, my health establishing itself, my spirits everlastingly partaking the sunshine of the climate; yet I *do* hunger after the bread and butter, and the fireside comforts, and the intellect of England. You will, I think, whenever my library is at hand, learn Portuguese, because I have got the history of Charlemagne and the Twelve Paladins in that language, and Palmerin of England. I have only laid hands on half an old Spanish romance, Don Florisel, son of Amadis of Greece, who was a perfect Jack the Giant Killer, and has taught me to forgive Don Quixote for knocking knight-errantry on the head. Bad poetry I find in abundance. . . . . The Portuguese Academy published a book in honor of the victories of the Empress-Queen Maria Theresa. My literary history will have a chapter upon the follies of literature, in which this work will furnish my best example. Every possible form of acrostic is there; poems to read up and down, and athwart and across; crosses, and circles, and wheels. Literature is almost dead here. More books are published annually at Bristol than in Portugal. There are no books to induce a love of reading—no Arabian Tales or Seven Champions. * * * * * * In case of peace—and surely, surely, it must come—we shall return through Spain and France. I am anxious to see Biscay. Our man Bento, who served in the Spanish army against France, has given me a curious account of that province, where the people are clean, industrious, and free, and speak Welsh or something very like it. On entering France, one of the Spanish generals ordered his company to kill man, woman, and child: in Roncesvalles (where Orlando and the Paladins were slain) a little boy of about six years was playing on a wall; he stopped to look at the troops; Bento saw one of his fellow-soldiers, in obedience to these orders, cut off the child's head. 'I have seen a thousand men killed,' said he, when he told the story, 'but I never felt any pain except when I saw that poor child murdered.'

What is to be the fate of Portugal? We know not. Much is going on, but all in secrecy. I expect peace every where. Bonaparte ought not to have risked that battle—to stake so much on one game! Moreau would not have done it: it was a prodigality of human blood merely to please the Parisians. . . . .

"God bless you!

"Yours affectionately, R. S."

To Lieutenant Southey, H.M.S. Bellona.

"October 6, 1800.

"You saw Mafra from the sea, a magnificent object, but, like every thing in Portugal, it looks best at a distance: its history you know from the last letter in my first edition.* . . . . We yesterday went there from Cintra, a distance of three leagues (twelve miles). A quinta of the Marquis Pombal, on the way, forms a pleasing object, from the olives which are planted to screen the vines, the gray foliage and the lively sunshine, as it were, of the vines contrasting very well. The quarries are near where the first stone is dug for the Lisbon buildings. Two columns are now lying by the road, which in the great Pombal's time were hewn for the Square of Lisbon, each of a single stone: a foolish waste of labor, only becoming barbarian pride; for columns whose parts are put together upon the spot look as well, and are in reality as firm: there they lie, like the square itself, and the half-finished streets, monuments to the memory of Pombal.

"Two leagues on the way lies a place called Cheleinas: it may contain fifty scattered houses—I assuredly speak on the outside of its number—but the place is a *town*, and its inhabitants strangely jealous of its title. Some lads, lately passing through, inquired the name of the *village;* the man replied, angrily, it was a town; and as they, not believing it, laughed at him, he raised an uproar, and they were actually in danger of being stoned by the offended townsmen. A bridge has been lately built here over a valley, and a great work it is: it happens to be in the prince's road from Queluz to Mafra, and on that account this improvement has been made. The valley in which Cheleinas stands would not be noticed for beauty in a cultivated country, but here it appears beautiful from the contrast of vine and olive yards with naked and sun-burned hills. The people are in fault, not the climate: trees will grow wherever they will plant them; but planting indicates foresight, and Portuguese never think of the future. A stream runs through it, which in the rainy season must be wide and rapid: this sweeps down the soil from the mountains, and fertilizes the bottom. A circuitous road round the hill top, to avoid a steep descent, leads to Mafra: there is a by-path, nearer by two miles, which I advise none but a pedestrian to take. Mafra itself is a small place, the estalagem rather better than usual, and not worse than a dirty English ale-house. Saturday had been the day of St. Francisco—a holiday in all Franciscan communities, more especially there because the prince conceives himself under great obligations to St. Francisco, and regularly attends his festival at Mafra. Of course the country was assembled there, food and fruit exposed for sale in the Plaza, and all the women equipped in all their finery. We went to mass; the prince followed the Host as it was carried round the church: in the evening there was a procession, and the prince paraded with it; and thus the regent of Portugal passes his time, dangling after saints, and assisting at puppet-shows, and no doubt he lay down last night thoroughly satisfied that he had done his duty.

"The church, and convent, and palace are one vast building, whose front exhibits a strange and truly Portuguese mixture of magnificence and meanness; in fact, it has never been faced with stone—a mud plaster is in its place; the windows are not half glazed, red boards filling up the workhouse-looking casements. The church is beautiful; the library the finest book-room I ever saw, and well stored. The friar who accompanied us said 'it would be an excellent room to eat and drink in, and go to play afterward;' and 'if we liked better to play in the dark, we might shut the windows!' He heard the servant remark to me that there were books enough for me to read there, and asked if I loved reading. 'And I,' said he, 'love eating and drinking.' Honest Franciscan! He told us, also, that the dress of their order was a barbarous dress, and that dress did not change the feelings. I suspect this man wishes he had professed in France. A Portuguese of some family was a nun in France: after the dissolution of the monasteries, her brother immediately engaged with a Portuguese abbess to receive her, and wrote in all haste for the distressed nun; she wrote, in answer, that she was much obliged to him, but she was married.

"'You have a superb convent here,' said I. 'Yes,' said the monk; 'but it is a wretched place in winter, we suffer so from the cold; the rheumatism kills many: we have no fire in our cells, only in the kitchen.' Such is Mafra: a library, whose books are never used; a palace, with a mud-wall front; and a royal convent, inhabited by monks who loathe their situation. The monks often desert: in that case they are hunted like deserters, and punished, if caught, with confinement and flogging. They take the vows young—at fourteen: those who are most stupidly devout may be satisfied with their life; those who are most abandoned in all vice may do well also; but a man with any feeling, any conscience, any brains, must be miserable. The old men, whose necks are broken to their yoke, whose feelings are all blunted, and who are, by their rank or age, exempt from some services, and indulged with some privileges—these men are happy enough. A literary man would be well off, only that literature would open his eyes.

"The library was not originally a part of the foundation: the Franciscan order excluded all

* Letters from Spain and Portugal.

art, all science; no pictures might profane their churches; but when Pombal turned them out of this palace, he removed to it the regular canons of St. Vincent, an order well born and well educated, wealthy enough to support themselves, and learned enough to instruct others. His design was to make Mafra a sort of college for the education of the young Portuguese; the library was formed with this intention: in what manner this plan was subverted by the present prince, you may see in the old 'Letters.' Incredibly absurd as the story may appear, it is nevertheless strictly true.

"The Franciscan is by far the most numerous monastic family. A convent that subsists upon its revenues must necessarily be limited in its numbers, but every consecrated beggar gets more than enough for his own support; so the more the merrier. . . . . . . God bless you! I conclude in haste.

"Yours affectionately,

"R. Southey."

To Lieutenant Southey, H.M.S. Bellona.

"Cintra, Oct. 7, 1800.

"My dear Tom,

". . . . You have probably heard enough of the infection at Cadiz to be anxious for information. Our accounts agree in nothing but in the extent of the calamity: one day we are assured it is the black vomit, another day the yellow fever, and now it is ripened into the plague. This only is certain, that for the last ten or twelve days of our accounts, from 240 to 260 persons have died daily in Cadiz. Whether it has extended beyond that city is also uncertain; some reports say that it has spread to the south—to Malaga and Alicante; others bring it to the frontier town, within 200 miles of us. We all think and talk seriously of our danger, and forget it the moment the conversation is changed. Whenever it actually enters Portugal, we shall probably fly to England. I hope the rains, which we may soon expect, will stop the contagion.

"So much have I to tell you, that it actually puzzles me where to begin. My Cintra memorandums must be made; and more than once have I delayed the task of describing this place, from a feeling of its difficulty. There is no scenery in England which can help me to give you an idea of this. The town is small, like all country towns of Portugal, containing the Plaza or square, and a number of narrow, crooked streets, that wind down the hill: the palace is old—remarkably irregular—a large, rambling, shapeless pile, not unlike the prints I have seen in old romances of a castle—a place whose infinite corners overlook the sea: two white towers, like glass-houses exactly, form a prominent feature in the distance, and with a square tower mark it for an old and public edifice. From the valley the town appears to stand very high, and the ways up are long, and winding, and weary; but the town itself is far below the summit of the mountain. You have seen the *Rock of Lisbon* from the sea—that rock is the *Sierra*, or Mountain of Cintra: above, it is broken into a number of pyramidal summits of rock piled upon rock; two of them are wooded completely, the rest bare. Upon one stands the Penha convent; a place where, if the Chapel of Loretto had stood, one might have half credited the lying legend, that the angels or the devil had dropped it there—so unascendable the height appears on which it stands, yet is the way up easy. On another point the ruins of a Moorish castle crest the hills. To look down from hence upon the palace and town, my head grew giddy, yet is it further from the town to the valley than from the summit to the town. The road is like a terrace, now with the open heath on the left, all purple with heath flowers, and here and there the stony summits and coombs winding to the vale, luxuriantly wooded, chiefly with cork-trees. Descending as you advance toward Colares, the summits are covered with firs, and the valley appears in all the richness of a fertile soil under this blessed climate.

"The cork is perhaps the most beautiful of trees: its leaves are small, and have the dusky color of evergreens, but its boughs branch out in the fantastic twistings of the oak, and its bark is of all others the most picturesque; you have seen deal curl under the carpenter's plane: it grows in such curls; the wrinkles are of course deep; one might fancy the cavities the cells of hermit fairies. There is one tree in particular here which a painter might well come from England to see, large and old; its trunk and branches are covered with fern—the yellow, sun-burned fern—forming so sunny a contrast to the dark foliage! a wild vine winds up and hangs in festoons from the boughs, its leaves of a bright green, like youth—and now the purple clusters are ripe. These vines form a delightful feature in the scenery; the vineyard is cheerful to the eyes, but it is the wild vine that I love, matting over the hedges, or climbing the cork or the tall poplar, or twisting over the gray olive in all its unpruned wantonness. The chestnut also is beautiful; its blossoms shoot out in *rays* like stars, and now its hedge-hog fruit stars the dark leaves. We have yet another tree of exquisite effect in the landscape—the fir; not such as you have seen, but one that shoots out no branches, grows very high, and then spreads broad in a mushroom shape exactly, the bottom of its head of the brown and withered color that the yew and the fir always have, and the surface of the brightest green. If a mushroom serves as the Pantheon Dome for a faëry hall, you might conceive a giant picking one of these pines for a parasol: they have somewhat the appearance in distance that the palm and cocoa have in a print.

"The English are numerous here, enough to render it a tolerable market, for sellers will not be wanting where purchasers are to be found; yet, last year, the magistrate of the place was idiot enough to order that no Englishman should be served till all the Portuguese were satisfied—one of those laws which carries its antidote in its own absurdity. Among this people the English are in high favor; they are liberal, or, if you will, extravagant, and submit to imposition: now a Portuguese fights hard for a farthing—servants love to be in an English family. If a Portuguese mistress goes out, she locks up her maids for fear of the men: the relations of the servants often insist that this shall be done. Oftentimes the men and women of a family do not know each other. All kitchen work is done by men, who sleep and live below; the females are kept above —a precious symptom of national morals! calculated to extend the evil it is designed to prevent; but I wander from Cintra. The fire-flies were abundant when we first came here: it was like faëry land to see them sparkling under the trees at night; the glow-worms were also numerous—their light went out at the end of July; but we have an insect which almost supplies their places—a winged grasshopper, in shape like our own; in color a gray ground hue, undistinguishable from the soil on which they live till they leap up, and their expanded wings then appear like a purple. We hear at evening the grillo: it is called the cricket, because its song is like that animal, but louder; it is, however, wholly different—shaped like a beetle, with wings like a bee, and black: they sell them in cages at Lisbon by way of singing birds.

"We ride asses about the country: you would laugh to see a party thus mounted; and yet soon learn to like the easy pace and sure step of the John *burros*. At the southwestern extremity of the rock is a singular building which we have twice visited—a chapel to the Virgin (who is omnipresent in Portugal), on one of the stony summits, far from any house: it is the strangest mixtures you can imagine of art and nature; you scarcely, on approaching, know what is rock and what is building, and from the shape and position of the chapel itself, it looks like the ark left by the waters upon Mount Ararat. Long flights of steps lead up, and among the rocks are many rooms, designed to house the pilgrims who frequent the place. A poor family live below with the keys. From this spot the coast lies like a map below you to Cape Espichel with the Tagus. 'Tis a strange place, that catches every cloud, and I have felt a tempest there when there has been no wind below. In case of plague it would be an excellent asylum. At the northwestern extremity is a rock which we have not yet visited, where people go to see fishermen run the risk of breaking their necks, by walking down a precipice. I have said nothing to you of the wild flowers, so many and so beautiful: purple crocuses now cover the ground; nor of the flocks of goats that morning and evening pass our door; nor of the lemon venders—of these hereafter.

"Our Lady of the Incarnation will about fill the sheet. Every church has a fraternity attached to its patron saint; for the anniversary festival they beg money; what is deficient the chief of the brotherhood supplies; for there are four days preceding the holiday: thus people parade the country with the church banner, taking a longer or a shorter circuit according to the celebrity of the saint, attacking the sun with sky-rockets, and merry-making all the way. Those of whom I now speak traveled for five days. I saw them return; they had among them four *angels on horseback*, who, as they took leave of the Virgin at her church door, each alternately addressed her, and reminded her of all they had been doing to her honor and glory, and requested her to continue the same devout spirit in *her* Portuguese, which must infallibly render them *still* invincible; this done, the angels went into the Plaza to see the fire-works! * * * * * * * * * *

"Yours truly, R. S."

To John Rickman, Esq.

"October, 1800.

"MY DEAR RICKMAN,

"At last the opportunity is arrived of sending my important parcel.* My private instructions must be vague—to make the best bargain you can, and on no terms to sell the copyright. . . . . Longman will probably offer to advance the expense of publishing, and share the profits: this is not fair, as brains ought to bear a higher interest than money. If you are not satisfied with his terms, offer it to Arch, in Grace Church Street, or to Philips of the Monthly Magazine, a man who can afford to pay a good price, because he can advertise and puff his own property every month. The sale of the book is not doubtful; my name would carry it through an edition, though it were worthless. * * * * *

"In literature, as in the play-things of schoolboys and the frippery of women, there are the ins and outs of fashion. Sonnets, and satires, and essays have their day, and my Joan of Arc has revived the epomania that Boileau cured the French of 120 years ago; but it is not every one who can shoot with the bow of Ulysses, and the gentlemen who think they can bend the bow because I made the string twang, will find themselves somewhat disappointed. Whenever that poem requires a new edition, I think not of correcting it; the ore deserves not to be new cast; but of prefixing a fair estimate of its merits and defects. * * * * * *

"Foreign Jews are tolerated in Lisbon—that is, they are in no danger from the Inquisition, though forbidden to exercise the ceremonials of their faith. The intercourse with Barbary brings a few Moors here, so that the devout Portuguese are accustomed to the sight of Jews, Turks, and heretics. You remember Davy's story of the Cornishman's remark when his master said, 'Now, John, we are in Devonshire:' 'I don't see but the pigs have got tails the same as along o' we.' If the natives here have sense enough to make a similar inference, they will be one degree wiser than their forefathers. Lisbon grows; many a corn-field, in which I have walked five years ago, is now covered with houses: this is a short-lived increase of population—a fine February day—for the English tenant these habita-

* The MS. of Thalaba.

tions; and when the army shall be recalled, the houses will be desolate; but the city exhibits an unequivocal sign of recovering industry and opulence. The gaps in the new streets, that have stood vacant since the disgrace of Portal, are now filled up, or filling: these are not nests for passage-birds, but large and magnificent houses for the merchants.

"But commerce will for a long, long while be, as in America, a sordid, selfish, money-getting drudgery, encouraging no art, and ignorant of every science. It is not genius that is wanted in Portugal—genius exists every where; but encouragement, or the hope of encouragement, must waken it to action; and here no ambition can exist, except the desire of place and court pageantry. A man of letters, a philosopher, would starve here; a fine singer and a female dancer are followed as in London. * * * * * * The Italian opera is, in my mind, only high treason against common sense: nothing is attended to but the music; the drama is simply a substratum for the tune, and the mind lies fallow while the sensual ear is gratified. The encouragement of a national theater may call up talents that shall confer honor upon the nation.

"My first publication will probably be the literary part of the History, which is too important to be treated of in an appendix, or in separate and interrupting chapters. Lisbon is rich in the books which suit my purpose; but I, alas! am not rich, and endure somewhat of the tortures of Tantalus. The public library is, indeed, more accessible than our Museum, &c., in England; but the books are under wire cases, and the freedom of research is miserably shackled by the necessity of asking the librarian for every volume you wish to consult: to hunt a subject through a series of authors is thus rendered almost impossible. The Academy, however, have much facilitated my labor by publishing many of their old chronicles in a buyable shape, and also the old laws of Portugal. There is a Frenchman here busy upon the history of Brazil. His materials are excellent, and he is indefatigable; but I am apprehensive for his papers, even if his person should escape. The ministry know what he is about, and you need not be told with what an absurd secrecy they hide from the world all information respecting that country: the population of Brazil is said to double that of the mother, and now dependent, country. So heavy a branch can not long remain upon so rotten a trunk. God bless you.

"Yours truly, R. SOUTHEY."

To Mrs. Southey, Sen.

"Lisbon [no date].

"MY DEAR MOTHER,

" * * * * * * * * * * * * About Harry, it is necessary to remove him; his room is wanted for a more profitable pupil, and he has outgrown his situation. I have an excellent letter from him, and one from William Taylor, advising me to place him with some provincial surgeon of eminence, who will, for a hundred guineas, board and instruct him for four or five years. A hundred guineas! well, but, thank God! there is Thalaba ready, for which I ask this sum. I have, therefore, thus eat my calf, and desired William Taylor to inquire for a situation; and so once more goes the furniture of my long-expected house in London.* * * * * * * * * * * * The plague, or the yellow fever, or the black vomit, has not yet reached us, nor do we yet know what the disease is, though it is not three hundred miles from us, and kills five hundred a day at Seville! Contagious by clothes or paper it can not be, or certainly it would have been here. A man was at Cintra who had recovered from the disease, and escaped from Cadiz only seventeen days before he told the story in a pot-house here. In Cadiz it might have been confined, because that city is connected by a bridge with the main land; but once beyond that limit, and it must take its course—precautions are impossible; the only one in their power they do not take—that of suffering no boat to come from the opposite shore. Edith is for packing off to England; but I will not move till it comes, and then away for the mountains.

"Our weather is most delightful—not a cloud, cool enough to walk, and warm enough to sit still; purple evenings, and moonlight more distinct than a November noon in London. We think of mounting jackasses and rambling some two hundred miles in the country. I shall laugh to see Edith among the dirt and fleas, who, I suspect, will be more amused with her than she will with them. She is going in a few days to visit the nuns: they wanted to borrow some books of an English woman: 'What book would you like?' said Miss Petre, somewhat puzzled by the question, and anxious to know. 'Why, we should like novels: have you got Ethelinde, or the Recluse of the Lake? We have had the first volume, and it was so interesting! and it leaves off in such an interesting part! We used to hate to hear the bell for prayers while we were reading it.' And after a little pause she went on, 'And then it is such *a good* book: we liked it, because the characters are so *moral and virtuous.*' By-the-by, they have sent Edith some cakes.

"We are afraid the expedition under Sir Ralph Abercrombie is coming here: his men are dying of the scurvy, and have been for some time upon a short allowance of salt provisions: they will starve us if they come. What folly, to keep five-and-twenty thousand men floating about so many months! horses and soldiers both dying for want of fresh food. * * * * * * * * * * *

"God bless you.

"Your affectionate son,

"ROBERT SOUTHEY."

---

* The sum ultimately received for the first edition of Thalaba (£115) was not required for this purpose, the fee for his brother's surgical education being paid by Mr. Hill.

To Lieut. Southey, H.M.S. Bellona.

"Thursday, Feb. 12, 1801, Lisbon.

"On Tuesday we crossed the river to Casilhas Point, procured jackasses, and proceeded to a place called Costa to dinner. You know the castle in the mouth of the Tagus, the state prison, where the man is confined that beat the king? The Costa is a collection of fishermen's huts on the sand, in a line with it, on the south side of the river: the ride is about seven miles, over a hilly country, that every where displayed novel and striking views; for the foreground, huge aloes and the prickly pear, the broom and furze in blossom; broad-headed firs every where where the sandy soil was not cultivated for vines or olives; the sweep of the bay southward skirted by the pine-covered plains and the mountain boundary; behind us Lisbon on its heights, and the river blue and boundless as a sea. Through a cleft in a sand-bank, a winter ravine way for the rains, we first saw the Costa at about half a mile below us—the most singular view I ever beheld—huts all of thatch scattered upon the sand: we descended by a very steep way cut through the sand-hill, the sand on either side fretted by the weather, like old sculpture long weather-worn: all below belongs to the sea; but on the bare sands, a numerous tribe have fixed their habitations, which exactly resemble the wigwams of the Nootka savages—a wooden frame all thatched is all; most commonly the floor descends for warmth, and the window often on a level with the ground without; two only symptoms showed us that we were in a civilized country—a church, the only stone building, and a party stretched upon the sand at cards. The men live by fishing, and a stronger race I never saw, or more prolific, for children seemed to swarm. As parties from Lisbon are frequent here, there are two or three hovels of entertainment. Ours had ragged rhymes upon its walls, recommending us to drink by the barrel and not by the quart.

"In riding to Odwellas, I saw something curious: it was a Padroña by the road side—we have no other word in English, and it occurs often in romance, for a place raised by the way side—where a station or inscription is placed: there was an image of Christ there, and some unaccountable inscriptions about robbery, and hiding heaven in the earth, which a series of pictures in tiles behind explained. A hundred years ago, the church of Odwellas was robbed of the church plate, and of the sacrament. Then I saw the thief playing at skittles when the sacristan of the church passed by, whom he followed in and hid himself; then I saw him robbing the altar; next, he hides the church dresses in the house of a woman; and here he is burying the sacrament plate in a vineyard upon this very spot; here he is examined upon suspicion, and denies all, and says who ever did the sacrilege ought to have his hands cut off; here he is taken in the act of stealing the fowls of the convent, and he confesses all; here they dig up the hidden treasure, and carry it back in a solemn procession; here he is going to execution; here you see his hands cut off, according to his own sentence, and here he is strangled and burned. It is remarkable that in almost all these tiles, the face of the criminal is broken to pieces, probably in abhorrence of his guilt. The loss of the wafer has been ever regarded as a national calamity, to be lamented with public prayer, and fasts, and processions. It happened at Mexico in the Conqueror's days, and Cortez himself paraded with the monks and the mob.

Sat., March 28.

"In the long interval that has elapsed since this letter was begun, we have traveled about three hundred and fifty miles. Waterhouse and I took charge of Edith and three ladies: a doctor at Alvea da Cruz, of whom we besought house-room one night in distress, told us, with more truth than politeness, that four women were a mighty inconvenience. We did not find them so: they made our chocolate in the morning, laughed with us by day, enjoyed the scenery, packed our provisions basket, and at night endured flea-biting with a patience that entitles them to an honorable place in the next martyrology. All Lisbon, I believe, thought us mad when we set out; and they now regard our return with equal envy, as only our complexions have suffered. To detail the journey would be too long. We asked at Santarem if they had rooms for us; they said plenty: we begged to see them: they had two rooms—four men in bed in one, one fellow in bed in the other. At Pombal, Waterhouse and I slept in public, in a room that served as a passage for the family. Men and women indiscriminately made the ladies' beds. One night we passed through a room wherein eight men were sleeping, who rose up to look at us, something like a picture of the resurrection. These facts will enable you to judge of the comforts and decencies of the Portuguese. They once wanted us, four women and two men, to sleep in two beds in one room. Yet, bad as these places are, the mail coach has made them still worse; that is, it has rendered the people less civil, and made the expenses heavier.

"We crossed the Zezere, a river of importance in the history of Portugal, as its banks form the great protection of Lisbon: it is the place where a stand might most effectually be made against an invading army. The river is fine, about the width of our Avon at Rownham, and flowing between hills of our Clifton and Leigh height, that are covered with heath and gum-cistus; the water is beautifully clear, and the bottom sand: like all mountain streams, the Zezere is of irregular and untamable force. In summer, horsemen ford it; in winter, the ferry price varies according to the resistance of the current, from one vintem to nine—that is, from a penny to a shilling. It then enters the Tagus with equal waters, sometimes with a larger body; for, as the rains may have fallen heavier east or north, the one river with its rush almost stagnates the other.

"At Pombal we saw Our Lady's oven, where annually a fire is kindled, a wafer baked, and a man, the Shadrach of the town, walks round the glowing oven, and comes out unhurt and unsinged by special miracle of Our Lady of Cardal. At Thomar is a statue of St. Christofer on the bridge: three grains of his leg, taken in a glass of water, are a sovereign cure for the ague; and poor St. Christofer's legs are almost worn out by the extent of the practice. Torres Vedras is the place where Father Anthony of the wounds died—a man suspected of sanctity. The pious mob attacked his body, stripped it naked, cut off all his hair, and tore up his nails to keep for relics. I have seen relics of all the saints—yea, a thorn from the crown of crucifixion, and a drop of the Redemption blood. All this you shall hereafter see at length in the regular journal.

"A more interesting subject is our return. My uncle will, I think, return with us, or, at least, speedily follow. We look forward to the expulsion of the English as only avoidable by a general peace, and this so little probable that all preparations are making for removal. My uncle is sending away all his books, and I am now in the dirt of packing. In May I hope to be in Bristol; eager enough, God knows, to see old friends, and old, familiar scenes, but with no pleasant anticipation of English taxes, and English climate, and small beer, after this blessed sun, and the wines of Portugal. My health has received all the benefit I could and did expect: a longer residence would, I think, render the amendment permanent; and, with this idea, the prospect of a return hereafter, to complete the latter part of my History, is by no means unpleasant.

"God bless you, and keep you from the north seas. I have written in haste, being obliged to write many letters on my return. Edith's love. I know not when or where we shall meet; but, when I am on English ground, the distance between us will not be so impassable. Farewell!

"Yours truly,

"ROBERT SOUTHEY."

To C. W. W. Wynn, Esq.

"Lisbon, Feb. 21, 1801.

"MY DEAR WYNN,

"Your letter gave me the first detail of the great news. A passage of four days made it as fresh as possible, and we are here cursing winds and water that we must wait a fortnight before another mail can reach us. What will happen? the breach is made; and this lath and plaster can not long keep out the weather. Will the old administration be strong enough to force their plans upon the crown? Possibly. Equally so, that the art of alarming, in which they were so proficient, may now be turned successfully against them. Yet, on this point, the whole body of opposition is with them, and the whole intellect of the country. I rather expect, after more inefficient changes, the establishment of opposition—and peace. The helm requires a strong hand.

"Decidedly as my own principles lead to toleration, I yet think in the sufferance of converts and proselytism it has been carried too for. You might as well let a fire burn, or a pestilence spread, as suffer the propagation of popery. I hate and abhor it from the bottom of my soul, and the only antidote is poison. Voltaire and such writers cut up the wheat with the tares. The monastic establishments in England ought to be dissolved; as for the priests, they will, for the most part, find their way into France; they who remain should not be suffered to recruit, and would soon die away in peace. I half fear a breach of the Union—perhaps another rebellion—in that wretched country.

"I do not purpose returning till the year of my house-rent be complete, and shall then leave Lisbon with regret, in spite of English house-comforts and the all-in-all happiness of living among old friends and familiar faces. This climate so completely changes my whole animal being, that I would exchange every thing for it. It is not Lisbon; Italy, or the south of Spain or of France, would, perhaps, offer greater inducements, if the possibility of a foreign settlement existed.

"On my History no labor shall be spared. Now I only heap marble: the edifice must be erected in England; but I must return again to the quarry. You will find my style plain and short, and of condensed meaning—plain as a Doric building, and, I trust, of eternal durability. The notes will drain off all quaintness. I have no doubt of making a work by which I shall be honorably remembered. You shall see it, and Elmsly, if he will take the trouble, before publication. Of profit I must not be sanguine; yet, if it attain the reputation of Robertson, than whom it will not be worse, or of Roscoe and Gibbon, it will procure me something more substantial than fame. My price for Thalaba was, for 1000 copies £115, twelve copies being allowed me; the booksellers would have bargained for a quarto edition also, but it would have been ill judged to have glutted the public.

"I expect, in the ensuing winter, to be ready with my first volume: to hurry it would be injudicious, and historic labor will be relieved by employing myself in correcting Madoc. My intention is therefore to journey through North Wales next summer to the lakes, where Coleridge is settled, and to pass the autumn (their summer) there. For a Welsh map of the roads, and what is to be seen, you must be my director; perhaps, too, you might in another way assist Madoc, by pointing out what manners or superstition of the Welsh would look well in blank verse. Much may have escaped me, and some necessarily must. Long as this poem (from the age of fourteen) has been in my head, and long as its sketch has now lain by me, I now look on at no very distant date to its publication, after an ample revision and recasting. You will see it and scrutinize it when corrected.

"Thalaba is now a whole and unembarrassed story: the introduction of Laila is not an episode, it is so connected with the murder of Hodeirah and the after actions of Thalaba, as to be essentially part of the tale. Thalaba has certainly and inevitably the fault of Samson Agonistes—its parts might change place; but, in a romance, epic laws may be dispensed with; its faults now are verbal. Such as it is, I know no poem which can claim a place between it and the Orlando. Let it be weighed with the Oberon; perhaps, were I to speak out, I should not dread a trial with Ariosto. My proportion of ore to dross is greater. Perhaps the anti-Jacobin criticasters may spare Thalaba: it is so utterly innocent of all good drift, it may pass through the world like Richard Cromwell, notwithstanding the sweet savor of its father's name. Do you know that they have caricatured me between Fox and Norfolk—worshiping Bonaparte? Poor me—at Lisbon—who have certainly molested nothing but Portuguese spiders! Amen! I am only afraid my company will be ashamed of me; one, at least—he is too good for me; and, upon my soul, I think myself too good for the other.

"The Spanish embassador trundled off for Madrid this morning: he is a bad imitation of a hogshead in make. All is alarm here, and I sweat in dreadfully cold weather for my books, creditors—alas! for many a six-and-thirty! We have two allies, more faithful than Austria the honest or Paul the magnanimous—famine and the yellow fever; but the American gentleman is asleep till summer, and as for famine, she is as busy in England as here. I rejoice in the eventual effects of scarcity—the cultivation of the wastes; the population bills you probably know to be Rickman's, for which he has long been soliciting Rose, and the management is his, of course, and compliment. It is of important utility.

"Of the red wines I spoke in my last. Will you have Bucellas as it can be got? It should be kept rather in a garret than a cellar, a place dry and warm; but ample directions shall be sent with it. You may, perhaps, get *old* now, when so just an alarm prevails; *new* is better than none, because it will improve even in ideal value should Portugal be closed to England; its price will little, if at all, differ from Port or Lisbon; it is your vile taxes that make the expense; and, by-the-by, I must vent a monstrous oath against the duty upon foreign books. *Sixpence per pound weight* if bound—it is abominable!

"Farewell, and God bless you.

"Yours affectionately,

"R. Southey."

To S. T. Coleridge, Esq.

"Lisbon, March 28, 1801.

"The sight of your handwriting did not give me much pleasure: 'twas the leg of a lark to a hungry man—yet it was your handwriting. *

"I have been more than once tottering on the brink of a letter to you, and more than once the glimpse at some old Spaniard, or the whim of a walk, or an orange, or a bunch of grapes, has tempted me either to industry or idleness. I return rich in materials: a twelvemonth's work in England will produce a first volume of my History, and also of the Literary History. Of success I am not sanguine, though sufficiently so of desert; yet I shall leave a monument to my own memory, and perhaps, which is of more consequence, procure a few life-enjoyments.

"My poetizing has been exclusively confined to the completion of Thalaba. I have planned a Hindoo romance of original extravagance, and have christened it 'The Curse of Keradon;' but it were unwise to do any thing here which were as well done in England; and, indeed, the easy business of hunting out every thing to be seen has taken up no small portion of my time. I have ample materials for a volume of miscellaneous information: my work in England will be chiefly to arrange and tack together; here I have been glutting, and go home to digest. In May we return; and, on my part, with much reluctance. I have formed local attachments, and not personal ones: this glorious river, with its mountain boundaries, this blessed winter sun, and the summer paradise of Cintra. I would gladly live and die here. My health is amended materially, but I have seizures enough to assure me that our own unkindly climate will blight me, as it does the myrtle and oranges of this better land; howbeit, business must lead me here once more for the after volumes of the History. If your ill health should also proceed from English skies, we may, perhaps, emigrate together at last. One head full of brains, and I should ask England nothing else.

"Meantime, my nearer dreams lay their scenes about the lakes.* Madoc compels me to visit Wales; perhaps we can meet you in the autumn; but for the unreasonable distance from Bristol and London, we might take up our abiding near you. I wish you were at Allfoxen†—there was a house big enough: you would talk me into a healthy indolence, and I should spur you to profitable industry.

" * * * * * * * *
* * * * * * * *

We are threatened with speedy invasion, and the critical hour of Portugal is probably arrived No alarm has been so general: they have sent for transports to secure us a speedy retreat; nor is it impossible that all idlers may be requested to remove before the hurry and crowd of a general departure. Yet I doubt the reality of the danger. Portugal *buys respite:* will they kill the goose that lays golden eggs? Will Spain consent to admit an army through that will shake her rotten throne? Will Bonaparte venture an army where there is danger of the yellow fever? to a part whence all plunder will be removed, where that army will find nothing to eat after a march of 1000 miles, through a starved country? On the other hand, this country may turn round, may join the coalition, seize on English

* Mr. Coleridge was at this time residing at Keswick.

† A house in Somersetshire, where Mr. Wordsworth resided at one time.

property, and bid us all decamp: this was apprehended; and what dependence can be placed upon utter imbecility? Were it not for Edith, I would fairly see it out, and witness the whole boderation. There is a worse than the Bastile here, over whose dungeons I often walk. * * * * * * * * * But this is not what is to be wished for Portugal—this conquest which would excite good feelings against innovation; if there was peace, the business would probably be done at home. England is now the bedarkening power; she is in politics what Spain was to religion at the Reformation. Change here involves the loss of their colonies, and an English fleet would cut off the supplies of Lisbon. * * * * * * * The monastic orders will accelerate revolution, because the begging friars, mostly young, are mostly discontented, and the rich friars every where objects of envy. I have heard the people complain of monastic oppression, and distinguish between the friars and the religion they profess. I even fear, so generally is that distinction made, that popery may exist when monkery is abolished.

"In May I hope to be in Bristol, and if it can be so arranged, in September at the lakes. I should like to winter there; then I might labor at my History; and we might, perhaps, amuse ourselves with some joint journeyman work, which might keep up winter fires and Christmas tables. Of all this we will write on my return. I now long to be in England, as it is impossible to remain and root here at present. We shall soon and inevitably be expelled, unless a general peace redeem the merchants here from ruin. England has brought Portugal into the scrape, and with rather more than usual prudence, left her in it: it is understood that this country may make her own terms, and submit to France without incurring the resentment of England. When the Portuguese first entered this happy war, the phrase of their ministers was, that they were going to be pall-bearers at the funeral of France. Fools! they were digging a grave, and have fallen into it.

"Of all English doings I am quite ignorant. Thomas Dermody, I see, has risen again, and the Farmer's Boy is most miraculously overrated. The Monthly Magazine speaks with shallow-pated pertness of your Wallenstein: it interests me much; and, what is better praise, invited me to a frequent reperusal of its parts: will you think me wrong in preferring it to Schiller's other plays? it appears to me more dramatically true. Max may, perhaps, be overstrained, and the woman is like all German heroines; but in Wallenstein is that greatness and littleness united which stamp the portrait. William Taylor, you see, is making quaint theories of the Old Testament writers; how are you employed? Must Lessing wait for the Resurrection before he receives a new life?

"So you dipped your young pagan* in the Derwent, and baptized him in the name of the river! Should he be drowned there, he will get into the next edition of Wanley's Wonders, under the head of God's Judgments. And how comes on Moses, and will he remember me? God bless you!

"Yours, ROBERT SOUTHEY."

* The Rev. Derwent Coleridge, principal of St. Mark's College, Chelsea.

To Mrs. Southey.

"Faro, April 17, 1801.

"By the luckiest opportunity, my dear Edith, I am enabled to write and ease myself of a load of uneasiness. An express is about to leave Faro, otherwise till Tuesday next there would have been no conveyance. We are at Mr. Lempriere's, hospitably and kindly received, and for the first time resting after ten days' very hard labor. At Cassillas our letter to Kirwan was of no use, as he was absent. For mules they asked too much, and we mounted burros to Azectão; there no supply was to be found, and the same beasts carried us to Setubal, which we did not reach till night. The house to which we had an introduction was deserted, and we lost nothing by going to an excellent estalagem. Next day it rained till noon, when we embarked, and sailed through dull and objectless shores to Alcacere: mules to Evora, the distance nine leagues. At the end of the first it set in a severe rain, and the coldest north wind we ever experienced: the road was one infinite charreca, a wilderness of gum cistus. We would have stopped any where: about six in the evening we begged charity at a peasant's house, at the Monte dos Moneros, three leagues short of Evora, dripping wet and deadly cold, dreading darkness, and the effects of so severe a wetting, and the cold wind; we got admittance, and all possible kindness; dried ourselves and baggage, which was wet also; supped upon the little round curd cheeses of the country, olives, and milk, and slept in comfort. The morning was fine, but the same wind continued till yesterday, and has plagued us cruelly by day and by night.

"At Evora we remained half a day; there our night sufferings began: from thence till we reached Faro we have never slept in one ceiled room: all tiled so loosely that an astrologer would find them no bad observatories; and by no possible means could we keep ourselves warm. Waterhouse I taught, indeed, by Niebuhr's example in Arabia, to lie with his face under the sheets, but it suffocated me. From Evora we took burros to Beja—a day and a half; we slept at Villa Ruina; from Viana to that little town is a lovely track of country, and, except that little island of cultivation, we have seen nothing but charrecas till we reached Tavira. The bishop gave us cheese and incomparable wine, and a letter to Father John of the Palm at Castro: to Castro a day's journey. On the road there was a monumental cross, where a man had been eaten by the wolves. John of the Palm is a very blackguard priest, but he was useful. We had a curious party there of his friends, drinking wine with us in the room, or, rather, between the four walls where we were pounded, not housed, for the night: a deputy judge, with a great sword, old as the Portuguese monarchy, smoking, and handing round his cigar out of his own mouth to the rest of the company; our muleteer, that was to be, hand and glove with the priest and the magistrate; and another pot companion. Next day across the field of Ourique, and seven long leagues of wilderness: there was no estalagem; in fact, we were in the wilds of Alentejo, where hardly any traveler has penetrated; we were again thrown on charity, and kindly received: this was Tuesday. On Wednesday we crossed the mountains to Tavira, seven leagues; in the bishop's language, long leagues, terrible leagues, infinite leagues: the road would be utterly impassable were it not that the Host is carried on horseback in these wilds, and therefore the way must be kept open. As we passed one ugly spot, the guide told us a man broke his neck there lately. This day's journey, however, was quite new: wherever we looked was mountain—waving, swelling, breasting, exactly like the sea-like prints of the Holy Hand which you see in old travels. At last the sea appeared, and the Guadiana, and the frontier towns Azamonte and Castro Marini. We descended, and entered the garden, the Paradise of Algarve: here our troubles and labor were to end; we were out of the wilderness. Milk and honey, indeed, we did not expect in this land of promise, but we expected every thing else. The sound of a drum alarmed us, and we found Tavira full of soldiers. The governor examined our pass, and I could not but smile at the way in which he eyed Roberto Southey, the negociente, of ordinary stature, thin and long face, a dark complexion, &c., and squinted at Waterhouse's lame legs. For a man in power he was civil, and sent us to the Corregidor to get our beasts secured. This second inspection over, we were in the streets of Tavira, to beg a night's lodging—and beg hard we did for some hours. At last, induced by the muleteer, whom she knew, and by the petition of some dozen honest people, whom our situation had drawn about us, a woman, who had one room unoccupied by the soldiers, turned the key with doubt and delay, for her husband was absent, and we wanted nothing but a ceiling. Yesterday we reached Faro, and to-day remain here to rest. * * * * * *

"Our faces are skinned by the cutting wind and sun: my nose has been roasted by a slow fire—burned alive by sunbeams: 'tis a great comfort that Waterhouse has no reason to laugh at it; and even Bento's* is of a fine carbuncle color. Thank God! you were not with us; one room is the utmost these hovels contain; the walls of stone, unmortared, and the roofs what I have described them.

"Yet we are well repaid, and have never faltered either in health or spirits. At Evora, at Beja, at the Ourique field, was much to interest; and here we are in a lovely country, to us a little heaven. * * * * * *

I have hurried over our way, that you may know simply where we have been, and where we are: the full account would be a week's work. You will be amused with the adventures of two Irish and one Scotch officers, who came from Gibraltar to Lagos, with a fortnight's leave of absence, to amuse themselves: they brought a Genoese interpreter, and understood from him that it was eleven leagues to Faro, and a good *turnpike* road. I write their own unexaggerated account: they determined to ride there to dinner, and they were three days on the way, begging, threatening, drawing their swords to get lodged at night—all in vain; the first night they slept in the fields; afterward they learned an humbler tone, and got, between four of them, a shelter, but no beds; here they waited six weeks for an opportunity of getting back; and one of them was paymaster at Gibraltar: they were utterly miserable for want of something to do—billiards eternally; they even bought birds, a cat, a dog, a fox, for playthings; yesterday embarked, after spending a hundred pieces here in six weeks, neither they nor any one else knowing how, except that they gave six testoons a piece for all the Port wine in the place. * * * * * *

"God bless you! I have a thousand things to tell you on my return, my dear Edith.

"Yours affectionately,

"ROBERT SOUTHEY."

* His servant.

CHAPTER VIII.

RETURN TO ENGLAND—THINKS OF GOING DOWN TO CUMBERLAND—LETTER FROM MR. COLERIDGE, DESCRIBING GRETA HALL—THOUGHTS OF A CONSULSHIP—THE LAW—LYRICAL BALLADS—CONSPIRACY OF GOWRIE—MADOC—DIFFICULTY OF MEETING THE EXPENSE OF THE JOURNEY TO KESWICK—LETTER TO MR. BEDFORD—UNCHANGED AFFECTION—GOES DOWN TO KESWICK—FIRST IMPRESSIONS OF THE LAKES—EXCURSION INTO WALES—APPOINTMENT AS PRIVATE SECRETARY TO MR. CORRY—GOES TO DUBLIN—LETTERS FROM THENCE—GOES TO LONDON—ACCOUNT OF HIS OFFICIAL DUTIES.—1801.

IN the course of the following June my father and mother returned to England, and for a short time again took up their residence at Bristol. His sojourn abroad had in all respects been a most satisfactory as well as a most enjoyable one: the various unpleasant, and, indeed, alarming symptoms under which he had previously labored, had proved to be rather of nervous than of organic origin; and as they seemed to have owed their rise to sedentary habits and continued mental exertion, they had readily given way, under the combined influence of change of scene and place, a more genial climate, and the healthful excitement of travel in a foreign land, and scenes full alike of beauty and of interest. He had not, indeed, been idle the while, for he had laid up large stores for his projected History of Portugal (never, alas! destined to be completed); and he had finished Thalaba, a transcript of which had been sent to England, and its publication negotiated for with the Messrs. Longman, by his friend Mr. Rickman. He had now entirely abandoned all idea of continuing the study of the law, and his thoughts and wishes were strongly turned toward obtaining some appointment which would enable him to reside in a southern climate. In the mean time, having no especial reason for wishing to remain in Bristol, he had for some time contemplated a journey into Cumberland, for the double purpose of seeing the lakes and visiting Mr. Coleridge, who was at this time residing at Greta Hall, Keswick, having been tempted into the north by the proximity of Mr. Wordsworth, and to whom he had written concerning this intention some months before leaving Lisbon. Mr. Coleridge's answer waited his return, and a portion of it may not unfitly be transcribed here, describing, as it does, briefly yet very faithfully, the place destined to be my father's abode for the longest portion of his life—the birth-place of all his children (save one), and the place of his final rest.

To Robert Southey, Esq.

"Greta Hall, Keswick, April 13, 1801.

"MY DEAR SOUTHEY,

"I received your kind letter on the evening before last, and I trust that this will arrive at Bristol just in time to rejoice with them that rejoice. Alas! you will have found the dear old place sadly *minus*ed by the removal of Davy. It is one of the evils of long silence, that when one recommences the correspondence, one has so much to say that one can say nothing. I have enough, with what I have seen, and with what I have done, and with what I have suffered, and with what I have heard, exclusive of all that I hope and all that I intend—I have enough to pass away a great deal of time with, were you on a desert isle, and I your *Friday*. But at present I purpose to speak only of myself relatively to Keswick and to you.

"Our house stands on a low hill, the whole front of which is one field and an enormous garden, nine tenths of which is a nursery garden. Behind the house is an orchard, and a small wood on a steep slope, at the foot of which flows the River Greta, which winds round and catches the evening lights in the front of the house. In front we have a giant's camp—an encamped army of tent-like mountains, which by an inverted arch gives a view of another vale. On our right the lovely vale and the wedge-shaped lake of Bassenthwaite; and on our left Derwentwater and Lodore full in view, and the fantastic mountains of Borrodale. Behind us the massy Skiddaw, smooth, green, high, with two chasms and a tent-like ridge in the larger. A fairer scene you have not seen in all your wanderings. Without going from our own grounds, we have all that can please a human being. As to books, my landlord, who dwells next door,* has a very respectable library, which he has put with mine—histories, encyclopedias, and all the modern gentry. But then I can have, when I choose, free access to the princely library of Sir Guilfred Lawson, which contains the noblest collection of travels and natural history of perhaps any private library in England; besides this, there is the Cathedral library of Carlisle, from whence I can have any books sent to me that I wish; in short, I may truly say that I command all the libraries in the county. * * * * *

"Our neighbor is a truly good and affectionate man, a father to my children, and a friend to me. He was offered fifty guineas for the house in which we are to live, but he preferred me for a tenant at twenty-five; and yet the whole of his income does not exceed, I believe, £200 a year. A more truly disinterested man I never met with; severely frugal, yet almost carelessly generous; and yet he got all his money as a common carrier,† by hard labor, and by pennies and pennies. He is one instance among many in this country of the salutary effect of the love of knowledge—he was from a boy a lover of learning. * * The house is full twice as large as we want: it hath more rooms in it than Allfoxen: you might have a bed-room, parlor, study, &c., &c., and there would always be rooms to spare for your or my visitors. In short, for situation and convenience—and when I mention the name of Wordsworth, for society of men of intellect—I know no place in which you and Edith would find yourselves so well suited."

The remainder of this letter, as well as another of later date, was filled with a most gloomy account of his own health, to which my father refers in the commencement of his reply.

To S. T. Coleridge, Esq.

"Bristol, July 11, 1801.

"Yesterday I arrived, and found your letters; they did depress me, but I have since reasoned or dreamed myself into more cheerful anticipations. I have persuaded myself that your complaint is gouty; that good living is necessary, and a good climate. I also move to the south; at least so it appears; and if my present prospects ripen, we may yet live under one roof.

* * * * * * *

"You may have seen a translation of Persius, by Drummond, an M.P. This man is going embassador, first to Palermo, and then to Constantinople: if a married man can go as his secretary, it is probable that I shall accompany him. I daily expect to know. It is a scheme of Wynn's to settle me in the south, and I am returned to look about me. My salary will be small—a very trifle; but after a few years I look on to something better, and have fixed my mind on a consulship. Now, if we go, you must

* Greta Hall was at this time divided into two houses, which were afterward thrown together.

† This person, whose name was Jackson, was the "master" in Mr. Wordsworth's poem of "The Wagoner," the circumstances of which are accurately correct.

join us as soon as we are housed, and it will be marvelous if we regret England. I shall have so little to do that my time may be considered as wholly my own: our joint amusements will easily supply us with all expenses. So no more of the Azores, for we will see the Great Turk, and visit Greece, and walk up the Pyramids, and ride camels in Arabia. I have dreamed of nothing else these five weeks. As yet every thing is so uncertain, for I have received no letter since we landed, that nothing can be said of our intermediate movements. If we are not embarked too soon, we will set off as early as possible for Cumberland, unless you should think, as we do, that Mohammed had better come to the mountain; that change of all externals may benefit you; and that, bad as Bristol weather is, it is yet infinitely preferable to northern cold and damp. Meet we must, and will.

"You know your old Poems are a third time in the press; why not set forth a second volume? * * * * Your Christabel, your Three Graces, which I remember as the very consummation of poetry. I must spur you to something, to the assertion of your supremacy; if you have not enough to muster, I will aid you in any way—manufacture skeletons that you may clothe with flesh, blood, and beauty; write my best, or what shall be bad enough to be popular; we will even make plays *à-la-mode* Robespierre. . . . . Drop all task-work; it is ever unprofitable; the same time, and one twentieth part of the labor, would produce treble emolument. For Thalaba I received £115: it was just twelve months' *intermitting* work, and the after editions are my own.

* * * * * * *

"I feel here as a stranger—somewhat of Leonard's feeling. God bless Wordsworth for that poem!* What tie have I to England? My London friends? There, indeed, I have friends. But if you and yours were with me, eating dates in a garden at Constantinople, you might assert that we were in the best of all possible places; and I should answer, Amen; and if our wives rebelled, we would send for the chief of the black eunuchs, and sell them to the Seraglio. Then should Moses learn Arabic, and we would know whether there was any thing in the language or not. We would drink Cyprus wine and Mocha coffee, and smoke more tranquilly than ever we did in the Ship in Small Street.

"Time and absence make strange work with our affections; but mine are ever returning to rest upon you. I have other and dear friends, but none with whom the whole of my being is intimate—with whom every thought and feeling can amalgamate. Oh! I have yet such dreams! Is it quite clear that you and I were not meant for some better star, and dropped, by mistake, into this world of pounds, shillings, and pence?

* * * * * * *

"God bless you!

"Robert Southey."

* "The Brothers" is the title of this poem.

To S. T. Coleridge, Esq.

"July 25.

"In about ten days we shall be ready to set forward for Keswick, where, if it were not for the rains, and the fogs, and the frosts, I should probably be content to winter; but the climate deters me. It is uncertain when I may be sent abroad, or where, except that the South of Europe is my choice. The appointment hardly doubtful, and the probable destination Palermo or Naples. We will talk of the future, and dream of it, on the lake side. * * * * * I may calculate upon the next six months at my own disposal; so we will climb Skiddaw this year, and scale Ætna the next; and Sicilian air will keep us alive till Davy has found out the immortalizing elixir, or till we are very well satisfied to do without it, and be immortalized after the manner of our fathers. My pocket-book contains more plans than will ever be filled up; but, whatever becomes of those plans, this, at least, is feasible. * * * * * * * * * * * Poor H——, he has literally killed himself by the law; which, I believe, kills more than any disease that takes its place in the bills of mortality. Blackstone is a needful book, and my Coke is a borrowed one; but I have one law book whereof to make an auto-da-fé; and burned he shall be; but whether to perform that ceremony, with fitting libations, at home, or fling him down the crater of Ætna directly to the devil, is worth considering at leisure.

"I must work at Keswick; the more willingly, because with the hope, hereafter, the necessity will cease. My Portuguese materials must lie dead, and this embarrasses me. It is impossible to publish any thing about that country now, because I must one day return there—to their libraries and archives; otherwise I have excellent stuff for a little volume, and could soon set forth a first vol. of my History, either civil or literary. In these labors I have incurred a heavy and serious expense. I shall write to Hamilton, and review again, if he chooses to employ me. * * * * * * It was Cottle who told me that your Poems were reprint*ing* in a *third* edition: this can not allude to the Lyrical Ballads, because of the number and the participle present. * * * I am bitterly angry to see one new poem smuggled into the world in the Lyrical Ballads, where the 750 purchasers of the first can never get at it. At Falmouth I bought Thomas Dermody's Poems, for old acquaintance' sake; alas! the boy wrote better than the man! * * * Pyes Alfred (to distinguish him from Alfred the Pious*) I have not yet inspected, nor the willful murder of Bonaparte, by Anna Matilda, nor the high treason committed by Sir James Bland Burgess, Baronet, against our lion-hearted Richard. Davy is fallen stark mad with a play, called the Conspiracy of Gowrie, which is by Rough; an imitation of Gebir, with some poetry; but mis-

* This alludes to Mr. Cottle's "Alfred."

erably and hopelessly deficient in all else: every character reasoning, and metaphorizing, and metaphysicking the reader most nauseously. By-the-by, there is a great analogy between hock, laver, pork pie, and the Lyrical Ballads: all have a *flavor*, not beloved by those who require a *taste*, and utterly unpleasant to dram-drinkers, whose diseased palates can only *feel* pepper and brandy. I know not whether Wordsworth will forgive the stimulant tale of Thalaba—'tis a turtle soup, highly seasoned, but with a flavor of its own predominant. His are sparagrass (it ought to be spelled so) and artichokes, good with plain butter, and wholesome.

"I look on Madoc with hopeful displeasure; probably it must be corrected, and published now. This coming into the world at seven months is a bad way; with a Doctor Slop of a printer's devil standing ready for the forced birth, and frightening one into an abortion. * * * * * * Is there an emigrant at Keswick who may make me talk and write French? And I must sit at my almost forgotten Italian, and read German with you; and we must read Tasso together. * * *

"God bless you!

"Yours, R. S."

To S. T. Coleridge, Esq.

"Bristol, August 3, 1801.

"Following the advice of the Traumatic Poet,* I have been endeavoring to get money—and to get it honestly. I wrote to ——, and propounded to him Madoc, to be ready for the press in six months, at a price equivalent to that of Thalaba, in proportion to its length; and I asked for fifty pounds *now*, the rest on *publication*. —— writes to beat down the price. * * * * * And I have answered, that the difference about terms sets me at liberty from my proposal.

"And so, how to raise the wind for my long land voyage? Why, I expect Hamilton's account daily (for whom, by-the-by, I am again at work!), and he owes me I know not what—it may be fifteen pounds, it may be five-and-twenty: if the latter, off we go, as soon as we can get an agreeable companion in a post-chaise; if it be not enough, why I must beg, borrow, or steal. I have once been tempted to sell my soul to Stuart for three months, for thirteen guineas in advance; but my soul mutinied at the bargain * * * * * Madoc has had a miraculous escape! it went against my stomach and my conscience—but *malesuada fames*.

"Your West India plan is a vile one. Italy, Italy. I shall have enough leisure for a month's journey. Moses, and the young one with the heathenish name, will learn Italian as they are learning English—an advantage not to be overlooked; society, too, is something; and Italy has never been without some great mind or other, worthy of its better ages. When we are well tired of Italy, why, I will get removed to Portugal, to which I look with longing eyes as the land of promise. But, in all sober seriousness, the plan I propose is very practicable, very pleasant, and eke also very *prudent*. My business will not be an hour in a week, and it will enable me to afford to be idle—a power which I shall never wish to exert, but which I do long to possess. * * * * * * Davy's removal to London extends his sphere of utility, and places him in affluence; yet he will be the worse for it. Chameleon-like, we are all colored by the near objects; and he is among metaphysical sensualists: he should have remained a few years longer here, till the wax cooled, which is now passive to any impression. I wish it was not true, but it unfortunately is, that experimental philosophy always deadens the feelings; and these men who 'botanize upon their mothers' graves' may retort and say that cherished feelings deaden our usefulness; and so we are all well in our way.

"* * * * * * * Do not hurry from the baths for the sake of meeting me, for when I set out is unpleasantly uncertain; and as I suppose we must be Lloyd's guests a few days, it may as well or better be before your return. My mother is very unwell, perhaps more seriously so than I allow myself to fully believe. If Peggy* were—what shall I say?—released is a varnishing phrase; and death is desirable, when recovery is impossible. I would bring my mother with me for the sake of total change, if Peggy could be left, but that is impossible; recover she can not, yet may; and I believe will, suffer on till winter. Almost I pre-feel that my mother's illness will, at the same time, recall me. * * * * The summer is going off, and I am longing for hot weather, to bathe in your lake; and yet am I tied by the leg. Howbeit, Hamilton's few days can not be stretched much longer; and when his account comes, I shall draw the money, and away. God bless you!

"R. SOUTHEY."

A letter from Mr. Bedford, containing some reproaches for a much longer silence than was his wont, called forth the following reply:

To Grosvenor C. Bedford, Esq.

"August 19, 1801.

"MY DEAR GROSVENOR,

"The tone and temper of your letter left me in an uncomfortable mood—certainly I deserved it, as far as negligence deserves reproof so harsh—but indeed, Grosvenor, you have been somewhat like the Scotch judge, who included all rape, robbery, murder, and horse-stealing under the head of sedition; so have you suspected negligence of cloaking a cold, and fickle, and insin-

* The "Traumatic Poet" was a Bristol acquaintance of my father's and Mr. Coleridge, who somewhat overrated his own powers of poetical composition; two choice sonnets of his, on "Metaphor" and "Personification," were printed in the first volume of the Annual Anthology.

* His cousin, Margaret Hill, to whom he was grealy attached, then dying in a consumption.

cere heart. Dear, dear Grosvenor, if by any magic of ear you could hear how often your name passes my lips! or could you see how often I see your figure in my walks—the recollections—and the wishes—but what are these? A hundred times should I have begun a letter if there had been enough to fill it—if I could have sent you the exquisite laugh when I again saw St. Augustine and his load, or the smile when I read Saunders's death in the newspaper; but these are unwritable things—the gossip, and the playfulness, and the boyishness, and the happiness: I was about to write, however—in conscience and truth I was—and for an odd reason. I heard a gentleman imitate Henderson; and there was in that imitation a decisiveness of pronunciation, a rolling every syllable over the tongue, a force and pressure of lip and of palate, that, had my eyes been shut, I could have half believed you had been reading Shakspeare to me—and I was about to tell you so, because the impression was so strong.

"With Drummond it seems I go not, but he and Wynn design to get for me—or try to get—a better berth—that of secretary to some Italian legation, which is permanent, and not personally attached to the minister. Amen. I love the south, and the possibility highly pleases me, and the prospect of advancing my fortunes. To England I have no strong tie; the friends whom I love live so widely apart that I never see two in a place; and for acquaintance, they are to be found every where. Thus much for the future; for the present I am about to move to Coleridge, who is at the lakes; and I am laboring, somewhat blindly indeed, but all to some purpose, about my ways and means; for the foreign expedition that has restored my health, has at the same time picked my pocket; and if I had not good spirits and cheerful industry, I should be somewhat surly and sad. So I am—I hope most truly and ardently for the last time—pen-and-inking for supplies, not from pure inclination. I am rather heaping bricks and mortar than building—hesitating between this plan and that plan, and preparing for both. I rather think it will end in a romance, in meter Thalabian—in mythology Hindoo—by name the Curse of Kehama, on which name you may speculate; and if you have any curiosity to see a crude outline, the undeveloped life-germ of the egg, say so, and you shall see the story as it is, and the poem as it is to be, written piece-meal.

"Thus, then, is my time employed, or thus it ought to be; for how much is dissipated by going here and there—dinnering, and tea-taking, and suppering, traying, or eveninging, take which phrase of fashion pleases you—you may guess.

"Grosvenor, I perceive no change in myself, nor any symptoms of change; I differ only in years from what I was, and years make less difference in me than in most men. All things considered, I feel myself a fortunate and happy man; the future wears a better face than it has ever done, and I have no reason to regret that indifference to fortune which has marked the past. By-the-by, it is unfortunate that you can not come to the sacrifice of one law book—my whole proper stock—whom I design to take up to the top of Mount Ætna, for the express purpose of throwing him down straight to the devil. Huzza, Grosvenor! I was once afraid that I should have a deadly deal of law to forget whenever I had done with it; but my brains, God bless them! never received any, and I am as ignorant as heart could wish. The tares would not grow.

"You will direct to Keswick, Cumberland. I set off on Saturday next, and shall be there about Tuesday; and if you could contrive to steal time for a visit to the lakes, you would find me a rare guide.

"If you have not seen the second volume of Wordsworth's Lyrical Ballads, I counsel you to buy them, and read *aloud* the poems entitled The Brothers, and Michael, which, especially the first, are, to my taste, excellent. I have never been so much affected, and so *well*, as by some passages there.

"God bless you. Edith's remembrance.

"Yours as ever,

"ROBERT SOUTHEY."

My father's first impression of the lake country was not quite equal to the feelings with which he afterward regarded it; and he dreaded the climate, which, even when long residence had habituated him to it, he always considered as one of the greatest drawbacks to the north of England. "Whether we winter here or not," he writes, immediately on his arrival at Keswick, "time must determine; inclination would lead me to, but it is as cold as at Yarmouth, and I am now growling at clouds and Cumberland weather. The lakes at first disappointed me—they were diminutive to what I expected; the mountains little, compared to Monchique; and for beauty, all English, perhaps all existing scenery, must yield to Cintra, my last summer's residence. Yet, as I become more familiar with these mountains, the more is their sublimity felt and understood: were they in a warmer climate, they would be the best and most desirable neighbors."

To Grosvenor C. Bedford, Esq.

"Keswick, Sept. 6, 1801.

" * * * * * * * * * * * De Anthologiâ, which is of or concerning the Anthology. As I hope to be picking up lava from Ætna, I can not be tying up nosegays here in England; but blind Tobin, whom you know—God bless him for a very good fellow!—but Tobin the blind is very unwilling that no more anthologies should appear; wherefore there will be more volumes, with which all I shall have to do will be to see that large-paper copies be printed to continue sets, becoming myself only a gentleman contributor, to which ingenious publication I beg your countenance, sir, and support. * * * * * * You ask me questions about my future plans which I can not readily answer, only that if I got a decent salary abroad, even should my health take a fancy to this queer climate, I have no estate to retire to at home, and so shall have a good prudential reason for remaining there. My dreams incline to Lisbon as a resting-place: I am really attached to the country, and, odd as it may seem, to the people. In Lisbon they are, like all metropolitans, roguish enough, but in the country I have found them hospitable, even to kindness, when I was a stranger and in want. The consulship at Lisbon would, of all possible situations, best delight me—better than a grand consulship—'tis a good thousand a year. But when one is dreaming, you know, Grosvenor—

"These lakes are like rivers; but oh for the Mondego and Tagus! And these mountains, beautifully indeed are they shaped and grouped; but oh for the great Monchique! and for Cintra, my paradise! the heaven on earth of my hopes; and if ever I should have a house at Cintra, as in earnest sincerity I do hope I shall, will not you give me one twelvemonth, and eat grapes, and ride donkeys, and be very happy? In truth, Grosvenor, I have lived abroad too long to be contented in England: I miss southern luxuries—the fruits, the wines; I miss the sun in heaven, having been upon a short allowance of sunbeams these last ten days; and if the nervous fluid be the galvanic fluid, and the galvanic fluid the electric fluid, and the electric fluid condensed light, zounds! what an effect must these vile, dark, rainy clouds have upon a poor nervous fellow, whose brain has been in a state of high illumination for the last fifteen months!

"God bless you! I am going in a few days to meet Wynn at Liverpool, and then to see the Welsh lions. * * * * * * Grosvenor Bedford, I wish you would write a history, for, take my word for it, no employment else is one thousandth part so interesting. I wish you would try it. We want a Venetian history. I would hunt Italy for your materials, and help you in any imaginable way. Think about it, and tell me your thoughts.

"Yours affectionately,

"R. SOUTHEY."

On my father's arrival at Llangedwin, the residence of his friend Mr. C. W. W. Wynn, he found a letter awaiting him, offering him the appointment of private secretary to Mr. Corry, at that time Chancellor of the Exchequer for Ireland: the terms "prudently limited to one year, lest they should not suit each other;" the proffered salary £400 Irish (about £350 English), of which the half was specified as traveling expenses. This had been brought about through his friend Mr. Rickman, who was at that time secretary to Mr. Abbot, and, in consequence, residing in Dublin—an additional inducement to my father to accept the appointment, as he would have to reside there himself during half the year.

His immediate services being required, after hurrying back for a few days to Keswick, he lost no time in taking possession of his new office.

To Mrs. Southey.

"Dublin, Wednesday, Oct. 14, 1801.

* * * * * * *

"On Sunday, after delaying till the latest possible moment for the chance of passengers, we dropped down the River Dee. The wind almost immediately failed us; I never saw so dead a calm; there was not a heaving, a ripple, a wrinkle on the water; the ship, though she made some way with the tide, was as still as a house, to our feelings. Had the wind continued as when we embarked, eighteen hours would have blown us to Dublin. I saw the sun set behind Anglesea; and the mountains of Carnarvonshire rose so beautifully before us, that, though at sea, it was delightful. The sunrise on Monday was magnificent. Holyhead was then in sight, and in sight on the wrong side it continued all day, while we tacked and retacked with a hard-hearted wind. We got into Beaumaris Bay, and waited there for the midnight tide: it was very quiet; even my stomach had not provocation enough, as yet, to be sick. In the night we proceeded. About two o'clock a very heavy gale arose: it blew great guns, as you would say; the vessel shipped water very fast; it came pouring down into the cabin, and both pumps were at work—the dismallest thump, thump, I ever heard: this lasted about three hours. As soon as we were clear of the Race of Holyhead the sea grew smoother, though the gale continued. On Tuesday the morning was hazy; we could not see land, though it was not far distant; and when at last we saw it, the wind had drifted us so far south that no possibility existed of our reaching Dublin that night. The captain, a good man and a good sailor, who never leaves his deck during the night, and drinks nothing but butter-milk, therefore readily agreed to land us at Balbriggen; and there we got ashore at two o'clock. Balbriggen is a fishing and bathing town, fifteen miles from Dublin—but miles and money differ in Ireland from the English standard, eleven miles Irish being as long as fourteen English. * * *

"To my great satisfaction, we had in our company one of the most celebrated characters existing at this day; a man whose name is as widely known as that of any human being, except, perhaps, Bonaparte!

"He is not above five feet, but, notwithstanding his figure, soon became the most important personage of the party. 'Sir,' said he, as soon as he set foot in the vessel, 'I am a unique; I go any where, just as the whim takes me: this morning, sir, I had no idea whatever of going to Dublin; I did not think of it when I left home; my wife and family know nothing of the trip. I have only one shirt with me besides what I have on; my nephew here, sir, has not another shirt to his back; but money, sir, money—any thing may be had at Dublin.' Who the devil is this fellow? thought I. We talked of rum—he had just bought 100 puncheons, the weakest drop 15 above proof: of the west of England—out he pulls an Exeter newspaper from his pocket: of bank paper—his pocket-book was stuffed with notes, Scotch, Irish, and English; and I really am obliged to him for some clews to discover forged paper. Talk, talk, everlasting: he could draw for money on any town in the United Kingdoms, ay, or in America. At last he was made known for Dr. Solomon. At night I set upon the doctor, and turned the discourse upon disease in general, beginning with the Liverpool flux—which remedy had proved most effectual—nothing like the Cordial Balm of Gilead. At last I ventured to touch upon a tender subject: did he conceive Dr. Brodum's medicine to be at all analogous to his own? 'Not in the least, sir; color, smell, all totally different. As for Dr. Brodum, sir—all the world knows it—it is manifest to every body—that his advertisements are all stolen, *verbatim et literatim*, from mine. Sir, I don't think it worth while to notice such a fellow.' But enough of Solomon, and his nephew and successor that is to be—the Rehoboam of Gilead—a cub in training.

"Mr. Corry is out of town for two days, so I have not seen him. The probability is, Rickman tells me, that I shall return in about ten days: you shall have the first intelligence. At present I know no more of my future plans than that I am to dine to-day with the secretary of the lord lieutenant, and to look me out a lodging first.

"But you must hear all I have seen of Ireland. The fifteen miles that we crossed are so destitute of trees, that I could only account for it by a sort of instinctive dread of the gallows in the natives. I find they have been cut down to make pikes. Cars instead of carts or wagons; women without hats, shoes, or stockings. One little town we passed, once famous—its name Swords: it has the ruins of a castle and a church, with a round tower adjoining the steeple, making an odd group: it was notoriously a pot-walloping borough; and for breeding early ducks for the London market, the manufactory of ducks appeared to be in a flourishing state. Post-chaises very ugly, the doors fastening with a staple and chain; three persons going in one, paying more than two. The hotel here abominably filthy. I see mountains near Dublin most beautifully shaped, but the day is too hazy. You shall hear all I can tell you by my next. I am quite well, and, what is extraordinary, was never once sick the whole way. * * * *
* * * * * * * *
Edith, God bless you! I do not expect to be absent from you above a fortnight longer.

"Yours affectionately,

"R. Southey."

To Mrs. Southey.

"Dublin, Oct. 16, 1801.

"Dear Edith,

"In my last no direction was given. You will write under cover, and direct thus:

Right Honble
Isaac Corry,
&c., &c., &c.,
Dublin.

This said personage I have not yet seen, whereby I am kept in a state of purportless idleness. He is gone to his own country, playing truant from business among his friends. To-morrow his return is probable. I like his character; he does business well, and with method, but loves his amusement better than business, and prefers books better than official papers. It does not appear that my work will be any ways difficult—copying and letter-writing, which any body could do, if any body could be confidentially trusted.

"John Rickman is a great man in Dublin and in the eyes of the world, but not one jot altered from the John Rickman of Christ Church, save only that, in compliance with an extorted promise, he has deprived himself of the pleasure of scratching his head by putting powder in it. He has astonished the people about him. The government stationer hinted to him, when he was giving an order, that if he wanted any thing in the pocket-book way, he might as well put it down in the order. Out he pulled his own: 'Look, sir, I have bought one for two shillings.' His predecessor admonished him not to let himself down by speaking to any of the clerks. 'Why, sir,' said John Rickman, 'I should not let myself down if I spoke to every man between this and the bridge.' And so he goes on in his own right way. He has been obliged to mount up to the third story before he could find a room small enough to sleep in; and there he led me, to show me his government bed, which, because it is a government bed, contains stuff enough to make a dozen; the curtains being completely double, and mattress piled upon mattress, so that tumbling out would be a dangerous fall. About our quarters here, when we remove hither in June, he will look out. The filth of the houses is intolerable—floors and furniture offending you with Portuguese nastiness; but it is a very fine city—a magnificent city—such public buildings, and the streets so wide! For these advantages Dublin is indebted to the prodigal corruption of its own government. Every member who asked money to make improvements got it; and if he got £20,000, in decency spent five for the public, and pocketed the rest. These gentlemen are now being hauled a little over the coals, and they have grace enough to thank God the Union did not take place sooner.

"The peace was not welcome to the patricians; it took away all their hopes of 'any fun' by the help of France. The government, acting well and wisely, control both parties—the Orangemen and the United Irishmen—and command respect from both; the old fatteners upon the corruption are silent in shame: the military, who must be kept up, will be well employed in making roads: this measure is not yet announced to the public. It will be difficult to civilize this people. An Irishman builds him a turf stye, gets his fuel from the bogs, digs his patch of potatoes, and then lives upon them in idleness: like a true savage, he does not think it worth while to work that he may better himself. Potatoes and butter-milk—on this they are born and bred; and whisky sends them to the third heaven at once. If Davy had one of them in his laboratory, he could analyze his flesh, blood, and bones into nothing but potatoes, and butter-milk, and whisky: they are the primary elements of an Irishman. Their love of 'fun' eternally engages them in mischievous combinations, which are eternally baffled by their own blessed instinct of blundering. The United Irishmen must have obtained possession of Dublin but for a bull. On the night appointed, the mail-coach was to be stopped and burned about a mile from town, and that was the signal: the lamplighters were in the plot; and oh! to be sure! the honeys would not light a lamp in Dublin that evening, for fear the people should see what was going on. Of course, alarm was taken, and all the mischief prevented. Modesty characterizes them as much here as on the other side of the water. A man stopped Rickman yesterday: 'I'll be oblaged to you, sir, if you'll plaise to ask Mr. Abbot to give me a place of sixty or seventy pounds a year.' Favors, indeed, are asked here with as unblushing and obstinate a perseverance as in Portugal. This is the striking side of the picture—the dark colors that first strike a stranger; their good qualities you can not so soon discover. Genius, indeed, immediately appears to characterize them; a love of saying good things, which 999 Englishmen in a thousand never dream of attempting in the course of their lives. When Lord Hardwicke came over, there fell a fine rain, the first after a long series of dry weather. A servant of Dr. Lindsay's heard an Irishman call to his comrade in the street, 'Ho, Pat! and we shall have a riot'—of course, a phrase to quicken an Englishman's hearing—'this rain will breed a riot: the little potatoes will be pushing out the big ones.'

"Did I send, in my last, the noble bull that Rickman heard? He was late in company, when a gentleman looked at his watch, and cried, 'It is *to-morrow morning!* I must wish you good *night*.'

"I have bought no books yet, for lack of money. To-day Rickman is engaged to dinner, and I am to seek for myself some ordinary or chop-house. This morning will clear off my letters, and I will make business a plea hereafter for writing fewer—'tis a hideous waste of time. My love to Coleridge, &c., if, indeed, I do not write to him also.

"Edith, God bless you!

"Yours affectionately,

"ROBERT SOUTHEY."

To S. T. Coleridge, Esq.

"Dublin, Oct. 16, 1801.

"DEAR COLERIDGE,

"The map of Ireland is a beautiful map—mountains, and lakes, and rivers, which I hope one day to visit with you. St. Patrick's Purgatory and the Giant's Causeway lie in the same corner. Where 'Mole, that mountain hoar,' is, I can not find, though I have hunted the name in every distortion of possible orthography. A journey in Ireland has, also, the great advantage of enabling us to study savage life. I shall be able to get letters of introduction, which, as draughts for food and shelter in a country where whisky-houses are scarce, will be invaluable. This is in the distance: about the present, all I know has been just written to Edith; and the sum of it is, that I am all alone by myself in a great city.

"From Lamb's letter to Rickman I learn that he means to print his play, which is the lukewarm John,* whose plan is as obnoxious to Rickman as it was to you and me; and that he has been writing for the Albion, and now writes for the Morning Chronicle, where more than two thirds of his materials are superciliously rejected. Stuart would use him more kindly. Godwin, having had a second tragedy rejected, has filched a story from one of De Foe's novels for a third, and begged hints of Lamb. * * * * * * * * * *

Last evening we talked of Davy. Rickman also fears for him; something he thinks he has (and excusably, surely) been hurt by the attentions of the great: a worse fault is that vice of metaphysicians—that habit of translating right and wrong into a jargon which confounds them—which allows every thing and justifies every thing. I am afraid, and it makes me very melancholy when I think of it, that Davy never will be to me the being that he has been. I have a trick of thinking too well of those I love—better than they generally deserve, and better than my cold and containing manners ever let them know. The foibles of a friend always endear him, if they have coexisted with my knowledge of him; but the pain is, to see beauty grow deformed—to trace disease from the first infection. These scientific men are, indeed, the victims of science; they sacrifice to it their own feelings, and virtues, and happiness.

"Old and ill-suited moralizings, Coleridge, for a man who has left the lakes and the mountains to come to Dublin with Mr. Worldly Wisdom! But my moral education, thank God! is pretty well completed. The world and I are only about to be acquainted. I have outgrown the age for forming friendships. * * *

"God bless you! R. SOUTHEY.

My father's presence seems only to have been required in Dublin for a very short time, and after rejoining my mother at Keswick, they went at once to London, Mr. Corry's duties requiring his residence there for the winter portion of the year. Here, when fairly established in his "scribe capacity," he appears to have experienced somewhat of the truth of the saying, "When thou doest well to thyself, men shall

* The name of this play is "John Woodvil."

speak good of thee." "I have been a week in town," he writes to Mr. William Taylor, "and in that time have learned something. The civilities which already have been shown me discover how much I have been abhorred for all that is valuable in my nature: such civilities excite more contempt than anger, but they make me think more despicably of the world than I could wish to do. As if this were a baptism that purified me of all sins—a regeneration; and the one congratulates me, and the other visits me, as if the author of Joan of Arc and of Thalaba were made a great man by scribing for the Irish Chancellor of the Exchequer.

"I suppose," he continues, "my situation, by all these symptoms, to be a good one; for a more ambitious man, doubtless very desirable, though the ladder is longer than I design to climb. My principles and habits are happily enough settled; my objects in life are, leisure to do nothing but write, and competence to write at leisure; and my notions of competence do not exceed £300 a year. Mr. Corry is a man of gentle and unassuming manners: fitter men for his purpose he doubtless might have found in some respects, none more so in regularity and dispatch."* * * * * *

These qualities, however, which my father might truly say he possessed in a high degree, were not called into much exercise by the duties of his secretaryship, which he thus humorously describes:

To John Rickman, Esq.

"London, Nov. 20, 1801.

"The chancellor and the scribe go on in the same way. The scribe has made out a catalogue of all books published since the commencement of '97 upon finance and scarcity; he hath also copied a paper written by J. R., containing some Irish alderman's hints about oak bark; and nothing more hath the scribe done in his vocation. Duly he calls at the chancellor's door; sometimes he is admitted to immediate audience; sometimes kicketh his heels in the ante-chamber (once he kicked them for cold, but now there is a fire); sometimes a gracious message emancipates him for the day. Secrecy hath been enjoined him as to these state proceedings. On three subjects he is directed to read and research—corn-laws, finance, tithes, according to their written order. Alas! they are heathen Greek to the scribe! He hath, indeed, in days of old, read Adam Smith, and remembereth the general principle established; he presupposeth that about corn, as about every thing else, the fewer laws the better: of finance he is even more ignorant: concerning the tithes, something knoweth he of the Levitical law, somewhat approveth he of a commutation for land, something suspecteth he why they are to be altered; gladly would the people buy off the burden, gladly would the government receive the purchase money—the scribe seeth objections thereunto. Meantime, sundry are the paragraphs that have been imprinted respecting the chancellor and the scribe: they have been compared (in defiance of the Butleraboo statute) to Empson and Dudley; and Peter Porcupine hath civilly expressed a hope that the poet will make no false *numbers* in his new work. Sometimes the poet is called a Jacobin; at others it is said that his opinions are revolutionized. The chancellor asked him if he would enter a reply in that independent paper whose lying name is the True Briton, a paper over which the chancellor implied he had some influence; the poet replied 'No; that those flea-bites itched only if they were scratched.' The scribe hath been courteously treated, and introduced to a Mr. Ormsby; and this is all he knoweth of the home politics.

* * * * * * *

* * * * * * *

Ευρηκα. Ευρηκα. Ευρηκα.

You remember your heretical proposition *de Cambro-Britannis*—that the Principality had never produced, and never could produce, a great man; that I opposed Owen Glendower and Sir Henry Morgan to the assertion in vain. But I have found the great man, and not merely the great man, but the *maximus homo*, the μεγιστος ἀνθρωπος, the μεγιστοτατος—we must create a super-superlative to reach the idea of his magnitude. I found him in the Strand, in a shop-window, laudably therein exhibited by a Cambro-Briton; the engraver represents him sitting in a room, that seems to be a cottage, or, at best, a farm, pen in hand, eyes uplifted, and underneath is inscribed

'The Cambrian Shakespear.'

But woe is me for my ignorance! the motto that followed surpassed my skill in language, though it doubtless was a delectable morsel from that great Welshman's poems. You must, however, allow the justice of the name for him, for all his writings are in Welsh; and the Welshmen say that he is as great a man as Shakspeare, and they must know, because they can understand him. I inquired what might be the trivial name of this light and luster of our dark age, but it hath escaped me; but that it meant, being interpreted, either Thomas Denbigh, or some such every-day baptismal denomination. And now I am no prophet if you have not, before you have arrived thus far, uttered a three-worded sentence of malediction. * * * * *

To-day I dine with Lord Holland. Wynn is intimate with him, and my invitation is for the sake of Thalaba. The sale of Thalaba is slow—about 300 only gone.

* * * * * * *

"Yours truly,

"R. Southey."

* Nov. 11, 1801.

CHAPTER IX.

HIS MOTHER'S DEATH—MELANCHOLY THOUGHTS—RESIGNS HIS SECRETARYSHIP—EDITION OF CHATTERTON'S WORKS—THOUGHTS OF RESIDING AT RICHMOND—AT KESWICK—WELL-KNOWN PERSONS MET IN LONDON—NEGOTIATES FOR A HOUSE IN WALES—CHRONICLE OF THE CID—REVIEW OF THALABA IN THE "EDINBURGH"—NEGOTIATION FOR HOUSE BROKEN OFF—WANT OF MORE BOOKS—ALARM OF WAR—EDINBURGH REVIEW—HAYLEY'S LIFE OF COWPER—RECOLLECTIONS OF BRIXTON—EARLY DIFFICULTIES—AMADIS OF GAUL—THE ATLANTIC A GOOD LETTER-CARRIER—HOME POLITICS—SCOTTISH BORDER BALLADS—CUMBERLAND'S PLAYS—PLAN FOR A BIBLIOTHECA BRITANNICA.—1802, 1803.

So passed the close of the year. The commencement of a new one was saddened by his mother's last illness. She had joined them in London, and a few weeks only elapsed before very alarming symptoms appeared. The best advice availed not; she sank rapidly, and was released on the 5th of January, 1802, being in the fiftieth year of her age. My father was deeply affected at her death; for though in childhood he had experienced but little of her care and attention, having been so early, as it were, adopted by his aunt, he had had the happiness of adding much to her comfort and support during her later years. "In her whole illness," he writes to his brother Henry, "she displayed a calmness, a suppression of complaint, a tenderness toward those around her, quite accordant with her whole life. It is a heavy loss. I did not know how severe the blow was till it came."*

The following letter communicates the tidings of her death to his friend Mr. Wynn; and, though presenting a painful picture, is yet one of those which let in so much light upon the character of the writer, that the reader will not wish it to have been withheld.

To C. W. W. Wynn, Esq.

"Saturday, Jan. 9, 1802.

"MY DEAR WYNN,

"You will not be surprised to learn that I have lost my mother. Early on Tuesday morning there came on that difficulty of breathing which betokened death. Till then all had been easy; for the most part she had slept, and, when waking, underwent no pain but that wretched sense of utter weakness; but then there was the struggle and sound in the throat, and the deadly appearance of the eyes, that had lost all their tranquillity. She asked for laudanum: I dropped some, but with so unsteady a hand that I knew not how much; she saw the color of the water, and cried, with a stronger voice than I had heard during her illness, 'That's nothing, Robert! thirty drops—six-and-thirty!'

"It relieved her. She would not suffer me to remain by her bedside; that fearful kindness toward me had, throughout, distinguished her. 'Go down, my dear; I shall sleep presently!' She knew, and I knew, what that sleep would be. However, I bless God the last minutes were as easy as death can be: she breathed without effort—breath after breath weaker, till all was over. I was not then in the room; but, going up to bring down Edith, I could not but look at her to see if she was indeed gone: it was against my wish and will, but I did look.

"We had been suffering for twelve hours, and the moment of her release was welcome. Like one whose limb has just been amputated, he feels the immediate ceasing of acute suffering; the pain of the wound soon begins, and the sense of the loss continues through life. I calmed and curbed myself, and forced myself to employment; but at night there was no sound of feet in her bed-room, to which I had been used to listen, and in the morning it was not my first business to see her. I had used to carry her her food, for I could persuade her better than any one else to the effort of swallowing it.

"Thank God, it is all over! Elmsley called on me, and offered me money if I needed it: it was a kindness that I shall remember. Corry had paid me a second quarter, however.

"I have now lost all the friends of my infancy and childhood. The whole recollections of my first ten years are connected with the dead. There lives no one who can share them with me. It is losing so much of one's existence. I have not been yielding to, or rather indulging, grief; that would have been folly. I have read, written, talked: Bedford has been often with me, and kindly.

"When I saw her after death, Wynn, the whole appearance was so much that of utter death, that the first feeling was as if there could have been no world for the dead. The feeling was very strong, and it required thought and reasoning to recover my former certainty, that as surely we must live hereafter as all here is not the creation of folly or of chance.

"God bless you!

"Yours affectionately, R. SOUTHEY."

The next few months passed by without the occurrence of any circumstance worthy of record, his official "duties," which appear to have been more nominal than real, being only varied by a short visit to Mr. William Taylor at Norwich. His spirits had not recovered the shock they received from his mother's death; and it was plain that, however easy and profitable was the appointment he held, it was not sufficiently suited to him to induce him long to retain it, although it afforded him a large share of time for his literary pursuits. Of the present course of these the following letter will give sufficient information:

To Grosvenor C. Bedford, Esq.

"London, March 30, 1802.

"DEAR GROSVENOR,

"I had wondered at your silence, which Cor-

* Jan. 6, 1802.

ry's servant made longer than it else had been, bringing me your letter only yesterday. * * * * * * * The Southey Gazette is happily barren of intelligence, unless you will hear with interest that I yesterday bought the Scriptores Rerum Hispanicarum, after a long search; that the day before, my boots came home from the cobbler's; that the gold leaf which Carlisle stuffed into my tooth is all come out; and that I have torn my best pantaloons. So life is passing on, and the growth of my History satisfies me that it is not passing altogether unprofitably. One acquaintance drops in to-day, another to-morrow; the friends whom I have here look in often, and I have rather too much society than too little. Yet I am not quite the comfortable man I should wish to be; the lamentable rambling to which I am doomed, for God knows how long, prevents my striking root any where—and we are the better as well as the happier for local attachment. Now do I look round, and can fix upon no spot which I like better than another, except for its mere natural advantages. 'Tis a *res damnabilis*, Bedford, to have no family ties that one cares about. And so much for the Azure Fiends, whom I shall now take the liberty of turning out of the room. I am busy at the Museum, copying unpublished poems of Chatterton, the which forthwith go to press. Soon I go with Edith to pass two or three days at Cheshunt; and, by the close of next month, I make my bow and away for my holidays to Bristol, that I may be as near Danvers and his mother as possible: my strongest family-like feeling seems to have grown there.

" * * * * * * * * I wish I were at Bath with you; 'twould do me good all over to have one walk over Combe Down. I have often walked there, before we were both upon the world. * * * * * * * Oh! that I could catch Old Time, and give him warm water, and antimonial powder, and ipecacuanha, till he brought up again the last nine years! Not that I want them all; but I do wish there was a house at Bath wherein I had a home-feeling, and that it were possible ever again to feel as I have felt returning from school along the Bristol road. *Eheu fugaces, Posthume, Posthume!* The years may go; but I wish so many good things did not go with them, the pleasures, and the feelings, and the ties of youth. Blessings on the Moors, and the Spaniards, and the Portuguese, and the saints! I yet feel an active and lively interest in my pursuits. I have made some progress in what promises to be a good chapter about the Moorish period; and I have finished the first six reigns, and am now more than half way through a noble black-letter chronicle of Alonzo the XIth, to collate with the seventh. The Life of the Cid will be a fit frame for a picture of the manners of his time, and a curious picture it will be: putting all that is important in my text, and all that is quaint in my notes, I shall make a good book.

"Ride, Grosvenor, and walk, and bathe, and drink water, and drink wine, and eat, and get well, and grow into good spirits, and write me a letter. ROBERT SOUTHEY."

In this letter my father speaks of passing his holidays in Bristol. A very short time, however, only elapsed before he emancipated himself altogether from the trammels of his official duties. Mr. Corry, it seems, having little or no employment for him as secretary, wished him to undertake the tuition of his son; but as this was neither "in the bond," nor at all suited to my father's habits and inclinations, he resigned his appointment, losing thereby, to use his own words, "a foolish office and a good salary." I may add, however, that this circumstance only somewhat hastened his resignation, for a situation which was "all pay and no work" was by no means suited either to his taste or his conscience.

He now took up his abode once more in Bristol. "Here," he writes to Mr. Coleridge, "I have meantime a comfortable home, and books enough to employ as much time as I can find for them; my table is covered with folios, and my History advances steadily, and to my own mind well. No other employment pleases me half so much; nevertheless, to other employment I am compelled by the most cogent of all reasons. I have a job in hand for Longman and Rees, which will bring me in £60, a possibility of £40, and a chance of a further £30; this is an abridgment of Amadis of Gaul into three duodecimos, with an essay—anonymously and secretly: if it sell, they will probably proceed through the whole library of romance. * * * * * * In poetry I have, of late, done very little, some fourscore lines the outside; still I feel myself strong enough to open a campaign, and this must probably be done to find beds, chairs, and tables for my house when I get one."*

But the various works here alluded to are not the only ones upon which my father had been lately engaged. A native of Bristol himself, he had always taken a strong interest in Chatterton's writings and history:

> . . . . "The marvelous boy,
> That sleepless soul that perish'd in his pride:"†

so much so, that the neglect of his relatives, who were in distressed circumstances, forms the subject of some indignant stanzas in one of his earliest unpublished poetical compositions; and, during his last residence in Bristol, his sympathies had been especially enlisted by Mr. Cottle in behalf of Mrs. Newton, Chatterton's sister.

Some time previously, Sir Herbert Croft had obtained possession from Mrs. Newton of all her brother's letters and MSS., under promise of speedily returning them; instead of which, some months afterward, he incorporated and published them in a pamphlet entitled "Love and Madness." At the use thus surreptitiously made of her brother's writings, Mrs. Newton more than once remonstrated; but, beyond the sum of £10, she could obtain no redress. Mr. Cottle and

* July 25, 1802.

† Wordsworth.

my father now took the matter up, and the former wrote to Sir H. Croft, pointing out to him Mrs. Newton's reasonable claim, and urging him, by a timely concession, to prevent that publicity which otherwise would follow. He received no answer; and my father then determined to print by subscription all Chatterton's works, including those ascribed to Rowley, for the benefit of Mrs. Newton and her daughter. He accordingly sent proposals to the "Monthly Magazine," in which he detailed the whole case between Mrs. Newton and Sir Herbert Croft, and published their respective letters. The public sympathized rightly on the occasion, for a handsome subscription followed. Sir Herbert Croft was residing in Denmark at the time these proposals were published, and he replied to my father's statement by a pamphlet full of much personal abuse.

It was now arranged that a new edition of Chatterton's works should be jointly edited by Mr. Cottle and my father, the former undertaking the consideration of the authenticity of Rowley, the latter the general arrangement of the work. It was published, in three vols. octavo, at the latter end of the present year (1802), and the editors had the satisfaction of paying over to Mrs. Newton and her daughter upward of £300, a sum which was the means of rescuing them from great poverty in their latter days.

To Grosvenor C. Bedford, Esq.

"Kingsdown, July 25, 1802.

"Grosvenor, I do not like the accounts which reach me of your health. Elmsley says you look ill; your friend Smith tells me the same tale; and I know you are not going the way to amendment. Instead of that office and regular business, you ought to be in the country, with no other business than to amuse yourself: a longer stay at Bath would have benefited you. If the waters were really of use to you, you ought to give them a longer trial. * * * * * * * * * * As for 'It can't be,' and 'I must be at the office,' and such like phrases, when a man is seriously ill they mean nothing.*

"Tom is with me, and has been here about a fortnight, and kept me in as wholesome a state of idleness as I wish you to enjoy.

"Since the last semi-letter I wrote, my state affairs have been settled, and my unsecretaryfication completed—a good sinecure gone; but, instead of thinking the loss unlucky, I only think how lucky it was I ever had it. A light heart and a thin pair of breeches—you know the song; and it applies, for, breeches being the generic name, pantaloons are included in all their modifications, and I sit at the present writing in a pair of loose jean trowsers without lining.

"So many virtues were discovered in me when I was Mr. Secretary, that I suppose nothing short of sedition, privy conspiracy, and rebellion will be found possible reasons for my loss of office. The old devil will be said to have entered, having taken with him seven other evil spirits, and the last state of that man (meaning me) will be worse than the first.

"But I hope I am coming to live near London—not in its filth. If John May can find me a good snug house about Richmond, there I will go, and write my History, and work away merrily; and I will drink wine when I can afford it, and when I can not, strong beer shall be the nectar—nothing like stingo! and if that were to fail too, laudanum is cheap: the Turks have found that out; and while there are poppies, no man need go to bed sober for want of his most gracious majesty's picture. And there will be a spare bed at my Domus—mark you that, Grosvenor Bedford! and Tom's cot into the bargain; and, from June till October, always a cold pie in the cupboard; and I have already got a kitten and a dog in remainder—but that is a contingency; and you know there is the contingency of another house animal, whom I already feel disposed to call whelp and dog, and all those vocables of vituperation by which a man loves to call those he loves best.

"Eblis's angels sometimes go up to peep at the table of fate, and then get knocked on the head with stars, as we see; only foolish people, such as we are, mistake them for shooting stars. I should like one look at the table, just to see what will happen before the end of the year—not to the world in general, nor to Europe, nor to Napoleon, nor to King George, but to the center to which these great men and these great things are very remote radii—to my own microcosm—hang the impudence of that mock-modesty phrase!—'tis a megalocosm, and a megistocosm, and a megistatocosm too to me; and I care more about it than about all the old universe, with Mr. Herschel's new little planets to boot. Vale, vale, mi sodales. R. S."

To S. T. Coleridge, Esq.

"Bristol, Aug. 4, 1802.

"In reply to your letter, there are so many things to be said that I know not where to begin. First and foremost, then, about Keswick, and the pros and cons for domesticating there. To live cheap—to save the crushing expense of furnishing a house; sound, good, mercantile motives! Then come the ghosts of old Skiddaw and Great Robinson—the whole eye-wantonness of lakes and mountains, and a host of other feelings, which eight years have modified and molded, but which have rooted like oaks, the stronger for their shaking. But then your horrid latitude! and incessant rains! * * * and I myself one of your green-house plants, pining for want of sun. For Edith, her mind's eyes are squinting about it; she wants to go, and she is afraid for my health. * * * Some time hence I must return to Portugal, to complete and correct my materials and outlines: whenever that may be, there will be a hinderance and a loss in disposing of furniture, supposing I

* "Have you time to die, sir?" was the home question of a London physician to a patient, a lawyer in full practice, who was making similar excuses for not taking his prescription of rest and freedom from anxious thought; and it admitted but of one reply.

had it. Now I am supposing that this I should find at Keswick, and this preponderance would fall like a ton weight in the scale.

" * * * * * * * *

As to your Essays, &c., &c., you spawn plans like a herring; I only wish as many of the seed were to vivify in proportion. * * * * * * * * * * *

Your Essays on Cotemporaries I am not much afraid of the imprudence of, because I have no expectation that they will ever be written; but if you were to write, the scheme projected upon the old poets would be a better scheme, because more certain of sale, and in the execution nothing invidious. Besides, your sentence would fall with greater weight upon the dead: however impartial you may be, those who do *not* read your books will think your opinion the result of your personal attachments, and that very belief will prevent numbers from reading it. Again, there are some of these living poets to whom you could not fail of giving serious pain—Hayley, in particular; and every thing about that man is good except his poetry. Bloomfield I saw in London, and an interesting man he is—even more than you would expect. I have reviewed his Poems with the express object of serving him; because, if his fame keeps up to another volume, he will have made money enough to support him comfortably in the country; but in a work of criticism, how could you bring him to the touchstone? and to lessen his reputation is to mar his fortune.

"We shall probably agree altogether some day upon Wordsworth's Lyrical Poems. Does he not associate more feeling with particular phrases, and you also with him, than those phrases can convey to any one else? This I suspect. Who would part with a ring of a dead friend's hair? and yet a jeweler will give for it only the value of the gold: and so must words pass for their current value.

* * * * * * * *

"I saw a number of notorious people after you left London. Mrs. Inchbald—an odd woman, but I like her. Campbell * * who spoke of old Scotch ballads with contempt! Fuseli * * Flaxman, whose touch is better than his feeling. Bowles * * Walter Whiter, who wanted to convert me to believe in Rowley. Perkins, the Tractorist,* a demure-looking rogue. Dr. Busby—oh! what a Dr. Busby!—the great musician! the greater than Handel! who is to be the husband of St. Cecilia in his seraph state, * * * and he set at me with a dead compliment! Lastly, Barry, the painter: poor fellow! he is too mad and too miserable to laugh at.

* * * * * * * *

"Heber sent certain volumes of Thomas Aquinas to your London lodgings, where peradventure they still remain. I have one volume of the old Jockey, containing quaint things about angels, and one of Scotus Erigena; but if there be any pearls in those dunghills, you must be the cock to scratch them out—that is not my dunghill. What think you of thirteen folios of Franciscan history? I am grown a great Jesuitophilist, and begin to think that they were the most enlightened personages that ever condescended to look after this 'little snug farm of the earth.' Loyola himself was a mere friar * but the missionaries were made of admirable stuff. There are some important questions arising out of this subject. The Jesuits have not only succeeded in preaching Christianity where our Methodists, &c., fail, but where all the other orders of their own church have failed also: they had the same success every where, in Japan as in Brazil. * * * * * * My love to Sara, if so it must be * * however, as it is the casting out of a Spiritus Asper—which is an evil spirit—for the omen's sake, Amen! Tell me some more, as Moses says, about Keswick, for I am in a humor to be persuaded—and if I may keep a jackass there for Edith! I have a wolf-skin great-coat, so hot that it is impossible to wear it here. Now, is not that a reason for going where it may be useful? Vale. R. S."

The following month, September, was marked by the birth of his first child, a daughter, named after her paternal grandmother, Margaret; and, ardently as he had always wished for children, the blessing was most joyfully and thankfully welcomed. But the hopes thus raised were doomed in this case to be soon blasted.

My father was now becoming weary of being a wanderer upon the face of the earth, and having now a nursery as well as a library to remove, a permanent residence was becoming almost a matter of necessity. His thoughts, as we have seen, had at one time turned toward settling at Richmond, and latterly more strongly toward Cumberland; but for a while he gave up this scheme, attracted by the greater conveniences of Wales, and he now entered into treaty for a house in Glamorganshire, in the Vale of Neath, "one of the loveliest spots," he thought it, in Great Britain. "There," he says, "I mean to remain, and work steadily at my History till it be necessary for me to go to Portugal, to correct what I shall have done, and hunt out new materials. This will be two years hence; and if the place answer my wishes, I shall not forsake it then, but return there as to a permanent residence. One of the motives for fixing there is the facility afforded of acquiring the Welsh language."*

To Grosvenor C. Bedford, Esq.

"Nov. 28, 1802.

"Dear Grosvenor,

"I thought you would know from Wynn that I trespass on my eyes only for short letters, or from Rickman, to whom my friend Danvers will have carried the latest news of me this day. If

* This alludes to Perkins's magnetic Tractors.

* To William Taylor, Esq., Nov. 21, 1802.

those unhappy eyes had been well, you would, ere this, have received Kehama. They have been better, and are again worse, in spite of *lapis calaminaris*, goulard, Cayenne pepper, and the surgeon's lance; but they will soon be well, so I believe and trust. You have seen my Cid, and have not seen what I wrote to Wynn about its manner. Every where possible the story is told in the very phrase of the original chronicles, which are almost the oldest works in the Castilian language. The language, in itself poetical, becomes more poetical by necessary compression; if it smack of romance, so does the story: in the notes, the certain will be distinguished from the doubtful passages quoted, and references to author and page uniformly given. Thus much of this, which is no specimen of my historical style: indeed, I do not think uniformity of style desirable; it should rise and fall with the subject, and adapt itself to the matter. Moreover, in my own judgment, a little peculiarity of style is desirable, because it nails down the matter to the memory. You remember the facts of Livy; but you remember the very phrases of Tacitus and Sallust, and the phrase reminds you of the matter when it would else have been forgotten. This may be pushed, like every thing, too far, and become ridiculous; but the principle is true.

"As a different specimen, I wish you could see a life of St. Francisco, a section upon Mohammedanism, and a chapter upon the Moorish period. Oh, these eyes! these eyes! to have my brain in labor, and this spell to prevent delivery like a cross-legged Juno! Farewell till to-morrow; I must sleep, and *laze*, and play whist till bed-time.

" * * * * * * Snakes have been pets in England: is it not Cowley who has a poem upon one?

> 'Take heed, fair Eve, you do not make
> Another tempter of the snake.'

They *ought* to be tamed and taken into our service, for snakes eat mice, and can get into their holes after them; and, in our country, the venomous species is so rare, that we should think them beautiful animals were it not for the recollection of the Old Serpent. *When* I am housed and *homed* (as I shall be, or hope to be, in the next spring; not that the negotiation is over yet, but I expect it will end well, and that I shall have a house in the loveliest part of South Wales, in a vale between high mountains; and an onymous house too, Grosvenor, and one that is down in the map of Glamorganshire, and its name is Maes Gwyn; and so much for that, and there's an end of my parenthesis), *then* do I purpose to enter into a grand confederacy with certain of the animal world: every body has a dog, and most people have a cat; but I will have, moreover, an otter, and teach him to fish, for there is salmon in the River Neath (and I should like a hawk, but that is only a vain hope, and a gull or an osprey to fish in the sea), and I will have a snake if Edith will let me, and I will have a toad to catch flies, and it shall be made murder to kill a spider in my domains: then, Grosvenor, when you come to visit me—N.B., you will arrive per mail between five and six in the morning at Neath; *ergo*, you will find me at breakfast about seven—you will see puss on the one side, and the otter on the other, both looking for bread and milk, and Margery in her little great chair, and the toad upon the tea-table, and the snake twisting up the leg of the table to look for his share. These two pages make a letter of decent length from such a poor blind Cupid as

"ROBERT SOUTHEY."

To C. W. W. Wynn, Esq., M.P.

"Dec. 22, 1802.

"*Vidi* the Review of Edinburgh. The first part is designed evidently as an answer to Wordsworth's Preface to the second edition of the Lyrical Ballads; and, however relevant to me, *quoad* Robert Southey, is certainly utterly irrelevant to Thalaba. In their account of the story they make some blunders of negligence: they ask how Thalaba knew that he was to be the Destroyer, forgetting that the Spirit told him so in the text; they say that the inscription of the locust's forehead teaches him to read the ring, which is not the case; and that Mohareb tries to kill him at last, though his own life would be destroyed at the same time, without noticing that that very 'though' enters into the passage, and the reason why is given. I added all the notes for the cause which they suspect: they would have accused me of plagiarism where they could have remembered the original hint; but they affirm that all is thus borrowed—without examining, when all that belongs to another is subtracted, what quantity of capital remains. This is dishonest, for there is no hint to be found elsewhere for the best parts of the poem, and the most striking incidents of the story.

"The general question concerning my system and taste is one point at issue, the meter another. These gentlemen who say that the meter of the Greek choruses is difficult to understand at a first reading, have, perhaps, made it out at last, else I should plead the choruses as precedent, and the odes of Stolberg in German, and the Ossian of Cesarotti in Italian; but this has been done in the M. Magazine's review of Thalaba. For the question of taste, I shall enter into it when I preface Madoc. I believe we are both classics in our taste; but mine is of the Greek, theirs of the Latin school. I am for the plainness of Hesiod and Homer, they for the richness and ornaments of Virgil. They want periwigs placed upon bald ideas. A narrative poem must have its connecting parts: it can not be all interest and incident, no more than a picture all light, a tragedy all pathos. * * * The review altogether is a good one, and will be better than any London one, because London reviewers always know something of the authors who appear before them, and this inevitably affects the judgment. I, myself, get the worthless poems of some good-natured person whom I know. I am aware of what review-phrases go for, and contrive to give that person no pain, and deal out such milk-and-water praise as will do no harm: to speak of smooth versification, and moral tendency, &c., &c., will take in some to buy the book, while it serves as an emollient mixture for the patient. I have rarely scratched without giving a plaster for it, except, indeed, where a fellow puts a string of titles to his name, or such an offender as ——— appears, and then my inquisitorship, instead of actually burning him, only ties a few crackers to his tail.

"But when any Scotchman's book shall come to be reviewed, then see what the Edinburgh critics will say. * * * Their philosophy appears in their belief in Hindoo chronology! and when they abuse Parr's style, it is rather a knock at the dead lion, old Johnson. A first number has great advantages; the reviewers say their say upon all subjects, and lay down the law: that contains the Institutes; by-and-by they can only comment.

"God bless you! R. S."

In the mean time, my father's pleasant anticipations of living in Wales were suddenly all frustrated; for, just as the treaty was on the point of being concluded, it occurred to him that some small additions were wanting in the kitchen department, and this request the landlord so stoutly resisted, that the negotiation was altogether broken off in consequence.

Upon this slight occurrence, he used to say, hinged many of the outward circumstances of his future life; and much and deeply as he afterward became attached to the lakes and mountains of Cumberland, he would often speak with something like regret of Maes Gwyn and the Vale of Neath.

Meanwhile his literary labors were proceeding much in their usual course, notwithstanding the complaint in his eyes. "I am reviewing for Longman," he says at this time; "reviewing for Hamilton; translating, perhaps about again to versify for the Morning Post: drudge—drudge —drudge. Do you know Quarles's emblem of the soul that tries to fly, but is chained by the leg to earth? For myself I could do easily, but not easily for others, and there are more claims than one upon me."*

From some cause or other, his correspondence seems somewhat to have diminished at this time; the few letters, however, that I am able to select relating to this period are not devoid of interest.

To John Rickman, Esq.

"Jan. 30, 1803.

"My dear Rickman,

" * * * * * * * * * * * * * * *

I am rich in books, considered as plain and poor Robert Southey, and in foreign books considered as an Englishman; but, for my glutton appetite and healthy digestion, my stock is but small, and the historian feels daily and hourly the want of materials. I believe I must visit London for the sake of the Museum, but not till the spring be far advanced, and warm enough to write with tolerable comfort in their reading-room. My History of Monachism can not be complete without the Benedictine History of Mabillon. There is another book in the Museum which must be noticed literally or put in a note—the Book of the Conformities of St. Francis and Jesus Christ! I have thirteen folios of Franciscan history in the house, and yet want the main one, Wadding's Seraphic Annual, which contains the original bulls.

"Of the Beguines I have, as yet, found neither traces nor tidings, except that I have seen the name certainly among the heretic list; but my monastic knowledge is very far from complete. I know only the outline for the two centuries between Francisco and Luther, and nothing but Jesuit history from that period.

"Do not suspect me of querulousness. Labor is my amusement, and nothing makes me growl but that the kind of labor can not be wholly my own choice—that I must lay aside old chronicles, and review modern poems; instead of composing from a full head, that I must write like a schoolboy upon some idle theme on which nothing can be said or ought to be said. I believe the best thing will be as you hope, for, if I live and do well, my History shall be done, and that will be a fortune to a man economical from habit, and moderate in his wants and wishes from feeling and principle.

"Coleridge is with me at present: he talks of going abroad, for, poor fellow, he suffers terribly from this climate. You bid me come with the swallows to London! I wish I could go with the swallows in their winterly migration. * * * * * *

"Yours affectionately, R. S."

To S. T. Coleridge, Esq.

"Bristol, March 14, 1803.

"Dear Coleridge,

"It is nearly a week now since Danvers and I returned from Rownham, and now the burden will soon fall off my shoulders, and I shall feel as light as old Christian when he had passed the directing post: forty guineas' worth of reviewing has been hard work. * * * * * * * * * * * *

The very unexpected and extraordinary alarm brought by yesterday's papers may in some degree affect my movements, for it has made Tom write to offer his services; and if the country arm, of course he will be employed. But *quid Diabolus* is all this about? Stuart writes well upon the subject, yet I think he overlooks some circumstances in Bonaparte's conduct which justify some delay in yielding Alexandria and Malta: that report of Sebastiani's was almost a declaration that France would take Egypt as soon as we left it. You were a clearer-sighted politician than I. If war there must be, the St. Domingo business will have been the cause, though not the pretext, and that rascal will set the poor

* To William Taylor, Esq., January 23, 1803.

negroes cutting English throats instead of French ones. It is true, country is of less consequence than color there, and these black gentlemen can not be very wrong if the throat be a white one; but it would be vexatious if the followers of Toussaint should be made the tools of Bonaparte.

"Meantime, what becomes of your scheme of traveling? If France goes to war, Spain must do the same, even if the loss of Trinidad did not make them inclined to it. You must not think of the Western Islands or the Canaries; they are prisons from whence it is very difficult to escape, and where you would be cut off from all regular intercourse with England; besides, the Canaries will be hostile ports. In the West Indies you ought not to trust your complexion. When the tower of Siloam fell, it did not give all honest people warning to stand from under. How is the climate of Hungary? Your German would carry you there, and help you there till you learned a Sclavonic language; and you might take home a profitable account of a country and a people little known. If it should be too cold a winter residence, you might pass the summer there, and reach Constantinople or the better parts of Asia Minor in the winter. This looks like a tempting scheme on paper, and will be more tempting if you look at the map; but, for all such schemes, a companion is almost necessary.

"The Edinburgh Review will not keep its ground. It consists of pamphlets instead of critical accounts. There is the quantity of a three shilling pamphlet in one article upon the Balance of Power, in which the brimstone-fingered son of oatmeal says that wars now are carried on by *the sacrifice of a few useless millions and more useless lives*, and by a few sailors fighting *harmlessly* upon the barren ocean: these are his very words. * * * * He thinks there can be no harm done unless an army were to come and eat up all the sheep's trotters in Edinburgh. If they buy many books at Gunville,* let them buy the Engleish metrical romancces published by Ritson: it is, indeed, a treasure of true old poetry: the expense of publication is defrayed by Ellis. Ritson is the oddest, but most honest of all our antiquarians, and he abuses Percy and Pinkerton with less mercy than justice. With somewhat more modesty than Mister Pinkerton, as he calls him, he has mended the spelling of our language, and, without the authority of an act of Parliament, changed the name of the very country he lives in into Engleland. The beauty of the common stanza will surprise you.

"Cowper's Life is the most pick-pocket work, for its shape and price, and author and publisher, that ever appeared. It relates very little of the man himself. This sort of delicacy seems quite groundless toward a man who has left no relations or connections who could be hurt by the most explicit biographical detail. His letters are not what one does expect, and yet what one ought to expect, for Cowper was not a strong-minded man even in his best moments. The very few opinions that he gave upon authors are quite ludicrous; he calls Mr. Park

> .... 'that comical spark,
> Who wrote to ask me for a Joan of Arc.'

'One of our best hands' in poetry. Poor wretched man! the Methodists among whom he lived made him ten times madder than he could else have been. * * * * * *

"God bless you! R. S."

To Grosvenor C. Bedford, Esq.

"Bristol, April 3, 1803.

"I have been thinking of Brixton, Grosvenor, for these many days past, when more painful thoughts would give me leave. An old lady, whom I loved greatly, and have for the last eight years regarded with something like a filial veneration, has been carried off by this influenza. She was mother to Danvers, with whom I have so long been on terms of the closest intimacy. * * * * Your ejection from Brixton has very long been in my head as one of the evil things to happen in 1803, though it was not predicted in Moore's Almanac. However, I am glad to hear you have got a house, * * * and still more, that it is an old house. I love old houses best, for the sake of the odd closets, and cupboards, and good thick walls that don't let the wind blow in, and little out-of-the-way polyangular rooms with great beams running across the ceiling—old heart of oak, that has outlasted half a score generations; and chimney-pieces with the date of the year carved above them, and huge fire-places that warmed the shins of Englishmen before the house of Hanover came over The most delightful associations that ever made me feel, and think, and fall a dreaming, are excited by old buildings—not absolute ruins, but in a state of decline. Even the clipped yews interest me; and if I found one in any garden that should become mine, in the shape of a peacock, I should be as proud to keep his tail well spread as the man who first carved him. In truth, I am more disposed to connect myself by sympathy with the ages which are past, and by hope with those that are to come, than to vex and irritate myself by any lively interest about the existing generation.

"Your letter was unusually interesting, and dwells upon my mind. I could, and perhaps will, some day, write an eclogue upon leaving an old place of residence. What you say of yourself impresses upon me still more deeply the conviction that the want of a favorite pursuit is your greatest source of discomfort and discontent. It is the pleasure of *pursuit* that makes every man happy, whether the merchant, or the sportsman, or the collector, the philobibl, or the *reader-o-bibl*, and *maker-o-bibl* like me: pursuit at once supplies employment and hope. This is what I have often preached to you, but perhaps I never told you what benefit I myself have de-

* The seat of Mr. Wedgewood.

rived from resolute employment. When Joan of Arc was in the press, I had as many legitimate causes for unhappiness as any man need have—uncertainty for the future, and immediate want, in the literal and plain meaning of the word. I often walked the streets at dinner-time for want of a dinner, when I had not eighteen pence for the ordinary, nor bread and cheese at my lodgings. But do not suppose that I thought of my dinner when I was walking—my head was full of what I was composing. When I lay down at night, I was planning my poem; and when I rose up in the morning, the poem was the first thought to which I was awake. The scanty profits of that poem I was then anticipating in my lodging-house bills for tea, bread and butter, and those little &cs., which amount to a formidable sum when a man has no resources; but that poem, faulty as it is, has given me a Baxter's shove into my right place in the world.

"So much for the practical effects of Epictetus, to whom I hold myself indebted for much amendment of character. Now—when I am not comparatively, but positively, a happy man, wishing little, and wanting nothing—my delight is the certainty that, while I have health and eyesight, I can never want a pursuit to interest. Subject after subject is chalked out. In hand I have Kehama, Madoc, and a voluminous history; and I have planned more poems and more histories; so that, whenever I am removed to another state of existence, there will be some *valde lacrymabile hiatus* in some of my posthumous works.

"We have all been ill with La Gripe. But the death of my excellent old friend is a real grief, and one that will long be felt: the pain of amputation is nothing; it is the loss of the limb that is the evil. She influenced my everyday thought, and one of my pleasures was to afford her any of the little amusements which age and infirmities can enjoy. * * * * *
* * * * * * * *
When do I go to London? If I can avoid it, not so soon as I had thought. The journey, and some unavoidable weariness in tramping over that overgrown metropolis, half terrifies me; and then the thought of certain pleasures, such as seeing Rickman, and Duppa, and Wynn, and Grosvenor Bedford, and going to the old bookshops, half tempts me. I am working very hard to fetch up my lee-way; that is, I am making up for time lost during my ophthalmia. Fifty-four more pages of Amadis, and a preface—no more to do—huzza! land! land!

* * * * * * *
* * * * * * *

"God bless you! R. S."

To Lieutenant Southey, H.M.S. Galatea.

"Bristol, April 22, 1803.

"My dear Tom,

"Huzza! huzza! huzza! The bottle is a good post, and the Atlantic delivers letters according to direction.

"Yours of May 23, 1802 . Lat. 33° 46′ N., Lon. 64° 27′ W., was found by Messrs. Calmer and Seymour, of St. Salvador's, Dec. 18, 1802, on the N.W. of that island . . . . . Lat. 23° 30′ N., Lon. 73° 30′ W., very civilly inclosed by some Mr. Aley Pratt, Feb. 10, sent per Betsey Cains, Capt. Wilmott, and has this day reached me from Ramsgate, to my very great surprise and satisfaction. You had sealed it so clumsily that some of the writing was torn, and the salt water had got at it, so that the letter is in a ruinous state; but it shall be preserved as the greatest curiosity in my collection. I shall send the account to Stuart.

"I did heartily regret that you were not here. We would have drawn a cork in honor of Messrs. Calmer and Seymour, and Aley Pratt, who, by keeping the letter two months, really seem to have been sensible that the letter was of value. When I consider the quadrillion of chances against such a circumstance, it seems like a dream—the middle of the Atlantic, thrown in there! cast on a corner of St. Salvador's, and now here, at No. 12 St. James's Place, Kingsdown, Bristol—hunting me through the ocean to the Bahamas, and then to this very individual spot. Oh, that the bottle had kept a log-book! If the Bottle-conjurer had been in it, now!

"I think this letter decisive of a current: chance winds would never have carried it 600 miles in less than seven months; and, if I recollect right, by theory there ought to be a current in that direction. Supposing the bottle to have been found the very day it landed, it must have sailed at the rate of three knots in a day and night: it was picked up 209 days after the post set off. More letters should be thrown overboard about the same latitude; and then, when we have charts of all the currents, some dozen centuries hence, that particular one shall be called Southey's Current. * * * *
The news is all pacific, and I fully expect you will be paid off ere long. All goes on as usual here. Margaret screams as loud as the parrot; that talent she inherited. * * *

"God bless you! R. Southey."

To Lieutenant Southey, H.M.S. Galatea.

"Bristol, May 30, 1803.

"Why, Tom! you must be mad—stark, staring mad—jumping mad—horn mad, to be lying in port all this time! For plain or stark madness I should prescribe a simple strait waistcoat; staring madness may be alleviated by the use of green spectacles; for jumping madness I have found a remedy in a custom used by the Siamese: when they take prisoners, they burn their feet to prevent them from running away; horn madness is, indeed, beyond my skill; for that, Doctor's Commons is the place. I am vexed and provoked for you to see prizes brought in under your nose. * * * * * *
* * * * * * * *
My books have had an increase since you left. I have bought a huge lot of Cody, tempted by the price—books of voyages and travels, and the Asiatic Researches. The Annual Review is not

yet published. Amadis still goes on slowly, but draws near an end. . . . . Do you see— and if you have seen the Morning Post, you will have seen—that a poem upon Amadis is advertised? This is curious enough. It seems by the advertisement that it only takes in the first book. If the author have either any civility or any brains, he will send me a copy; the which I am not so desirous of as I should be, as it will cost me twenty shillings to send him one in return. However, I shall like to see his book: it may make a beautiful poem, and it looks well that he has stopped at the first book, and avoided the length of story; but, unless he be a very good poet indeed, I should prefer the plain dress of romance.

"I have been very hard at history, and have almost finished, since your departure, that thick folio chronicle which you may remember I was about skin-deep in, and which has supplied me with matter for half a volume. This war terrifies and puzzles me about Portugal. I think of going over alone this next winter, while I can. I have fifteen quartos on the way from Lisbon; and, zounds! if they should be taken! . . . . Next month I shall go to London. The hard exercise of walking the streets will do me good. My picture in the Exhibition* pleases every body, I hear: I wish you had seen it.

"* * * * * * *

Remember my advice about all Dutch captains in your cruise: go always to the bottom in your examination: tin cases will sound if they be kicked, and paper will rustle; to you it may be the winning a prize: the loss is but a kick, and that the Dutchman gains. Do you know that I actually must learn Dutch! that I can not complete the East Indian part of my history without it. Good-by. R. S."

To C. W. W. Wynn, Esq.

"June 9, 1803.

"I have just gone through the Scottish Border Ballads. Walter Scott himself is a man of great talent and genius; but, wherever he patches an old poem, it is always with new bricks. Of the modern ballads, his own fragment is the only good one, and that is very good. I am sorry to see Leyden's good for so little. Sir Agrethorn is flat, foolish, Matthewish, Gregoryish, Lewisish. I have been obliged to coin vituperative adjectives on purpose, the language not having terms enough of adequate abuse. I suppose the word Flodden Field entitles it to a place here, but the scene might as well have been laid in El Dorado, or Tothill Fields, or the country of Prester John, for any thing like costume which it possesses. It is odd enough that almost every passage which Scott has quoted from Froissart should be among the extracts which I had made.

"In all these modern ballads there is a modernism of thought and language-turns to me very perceptible and very unpleasant, the more so for its mixture with antique words—polished steel and rusty iron! This is the case in all Scott's ballads. His Eve of St. John's is a better ballad in story than any of mine, but it has this fault. Elmsley once asked me to versify that on the Glenfinlas—to try the difference of style; but I declined it, as waste labor and an invidious task. Matthew G. Lewis, Esq., M.P., sins more grievously in this way; he is not enough versed in old English to avoid it: Scott and Leyden are, and ought to have written more purely. I think, if you will look at Q. Orraca, you will perceive that, without being a canto from our old ballads, it has quite the ballad character of language.

"Scott, it seems, adopts the same system of meter with me, and varies his tune in the same stanza from iambic to anapæstic *ad libitum*. In spite of all the trouble that has been taken to torture Chaucer into heroic meter, I have no doubt whatever that he wrote upon this system, common to all the ballad writers. Coleridge agrees with me upon this. The proof is, that, read him thus, and he becomes every where harmonious; but expletive syllables, en's, and y's, and e's, only make him halt upon ten lame toes. I am now daily drinking at that pure well of English undefiled, to get historical manners, and to learn English and poetry.

"His volume of the Border Songs is more amusing for its prefaces and notes than its poetry. The ballads themselves were written in a very unfavorable age and country; the costume less picturesque than chivalry, the manners more barbarous. I shall be very glad to see the Sir Tristram which Scott is editing: the old Cornish knight has been one of my favorite heroes for fifteen years. Those Romances that Ritson published are fine studies for a poet. This I am afraid will have more Scotch in it than will be pleasant. I never read Scotch poetry without rejoicing that we have not Welsh-English into the bargain, and a written brogue.

" * * * * * * *

Rickman tells me there will be no army sent to Portugal; that it is understood the French may overrun it at pleasure, and that then we lay open Brazil and Spanish America. If, indeed, the Prince of Brazil could be persuaded to go over there, and fix the seat of his government in a colony fifty times as large, and five hundred fold more valuable than the mother country, England would have a trade opened to it far more than equivalent to the loss of the Portuguese and Spanish ports. But if he remains under the protection of France, and is compelled to take a part against England, any expedition to Brazil must be for mere plunder. Conquest is quite impossible.

"Most likely I shall go up to town in about a week or ten days. God bless you! R. S."

To Grosvenor C. Bedford, Esq.

"June 12, 1803.

"Why, Grosvenor, that is an idle squeamishness of yours, that asking a previous leave to

* This picture was by Opie.

speak. Where my conscience becomes second to your challenge, the offense shall be amended; where we differ, mine is the voice potential. But, in truth, I will tell you that I am out of humor with Kehama, for half a hundred reasons: historical composition is a source of greater, and quieter, and more continuous pleasure; and that poem sometimes comes into my head with a—shall I sit down to it? and this is so easily turned out again, that the want of inclination would make me half suspect a growing want of power, if some rhymes and poemets did not now and then come out and convince me to the contrary. * * * Abuse away *ad libitum*.

"If Cumberland must have a Greek name, there is but one that fits him—Aristophanes—and that for the worst part of his character. If his plays had any honest principle in them, instead of that eternal substitution of honor for honesty, of a shadow for a substance—if his novels were not more profligate in their tendency than Matthew Lewis's unhappy book—if the perusal of his Calvary were not a cross heavy enough for any man to bear who has ever read ten lines of Milton—if the man were innocent of all these things, he ought never to be forgiven for his attempt to blast the character of Socrates. Right or wrong, no matter; the name had been canonized, and, God knows! wisdom and virtue have not so many saints that they can spare an altar to his clumsy pick-ax. I am no blind bigot to the Greeks, but I will take the words of Plato and greater Xenophon against Richard Cumberland, Esq.

" * * * * * * * * * * * * * * *

The Grenvilles are in the right, but they got right by sticking in the wrong: they turned their faces westward in the morning, and swore the sun was there; and they have stood still and sworn on, till, sure enough, there the sun is. But they stand upon the strong ground now, and have the argument all hollow; yet what is to come of it, and what do they want—their country asks that question. War? They have it: every man in the country says Amen, and they whose politics are most democratic say Amen most loudly and most sincerely. In spite of their speeches, I can not wish them in; and, when change of ministry is talked of, can not but feel, with Fox, that, little as I may like them, ten to one I shall like their successors worse, and sure I am that worse war ministers than the last can not curse this country. * * * * These men behaved so well upon Despard's business, and have shown such a respect to the liberties and feelings of this country, that they have fully won my good will. I believe they will make a sad piecemeal patchwork administration. * * * It does seem that, by some fatality, the best talents of the kingdom are forever to be excluded from its government. Fox has not done well—not what I could have wished; but yet I reverence that man so truly, that whenever he appears to me to have erred. I more than half suspect my own judgment.

"I am promised access to the king's library by Heber; and, indeed, it is a matter of considerable consequence that I should obtain it. Morning, noon, and night, I do nothing but read chronicles, and collect from them; and I have traveled at a great rate since the burden of translating and reviewing has been got rid of; but this will not last long; I must think by-and-by of some other job-work, and turn to labor again, that I may earn another holiday.

"I call Margaret, by way of avoiding all commonplace phraseology of endearment, a worthy child and a most excellent character. She loves me better than any one except her mother. Her eyes are as quick as thought; she is all life and spirit, and as happy as the day is long; but that little brain of hers is never at rest, and it is painful to see how dreams disturb her. A Dios!

"R. S."

Soon after the date of the letter, my father paid a short visit to London, the chief purpose of which was to negotiate with Messrs. Longman and Rees respecting "the management of a Bibliotheca Britannica upon a very extensive scale, to be arranged chronologically, and made a readable book by biography, criticism, and connecting chapters, to be published like the Cyclopædia in parts, each volume 800 quarto pages." "The full and absolute choice of all associates, and the distribution of the whole," to be in his hands. And, in order to be near the publisher, as well as for the convenience of communicating with the majority of those whom he hoped to associate with him in the work—of whom the chief were Mr. Sharon Turner, Mr. Rickman, Captain Burney, Mr. Carlisle,* Mr. William Taylor, Mr. Coleridge, Mr. Duppa, and Mr. Owen—he purposed removing very shortly to Richmond, where, indeed, he had already obtained the refusal of a house.

Upon concluding his agreement with Messrs. Longman and Rees, he seems to have communicated at once with Mr. Coleridge, whose letter in reply the reader will not be displeased to have laid before him, containing, as it does, the magnificent plan of a work almost too vast to have been conceived by any other person. Alas! that the plans of such a mind should have been but splendid dreams.

S. T. Coleridge to R. Southey.

"Keswick, July, 1803.

"My dear Southey,

" * * * * * * *

I write now to propose a scheme, or, rather, a rude outline of a scheme, of your grand work. What harm can a proposal do? If it be no pain to you to reject it, it will be none to me to have it rejected. I would have the work entitled Bibliotheca Britannica, or a History of British Literature, bibliographical, biographical, and critical. The two *last* volumes I would have to be a chronological catalogue of all noticeable or

* Afterward Sir Anthony Carlisle.

extant books; the others, be the number six or eight, to consist entirely of separate treatises, each giving a critical biblio-biographical history of some one subject. I will, with great pleasure, join you in learning Welsh and Erse; and you, I, Turner, and Owen, might dedicate ourselves for the first half year to a complete history of all Welsh, Saxon, and Erse books that are not translations, that are the native growth of Britain. If the Spanish neutrality continues, I will go in October or November to Biscay, and throw light on the Basque.

"Let the next volume contain the history of *English* poetry and poets, in which I would include all prose truly poetical. The first half of the second volume should be dedicated to great single names, Chaucer and Spenser, Shakspeare, Milton, and Taylor, Dryden and Pope; the poetry of witty logic—Swift, Fielding, Richardson, Sterne: I write *par hazard*, but I mean to say all great names as have either formed epochs in our taste, or such, at least, as are representative; and the great object to be in each instance to determine, first, the true merits and demerits of the *books;* secondly, what of these belong to the age—what to the author *quasi peculium.* The second half of the second volume should be a history of poetry and romances, every where interspersed with biography, but more flowing, more consecutive, more bibliographical, chronological, and complete. The third volume I would have dedicated to English prose, considered as to style, as to eloquence, as to general impressiveness; a history of styles and manners, their causes, their birth-places and parentage, their analysis. * * * *

"These three volumes would be so generally interesting, so exceedingly entertaining, that you might bid fair for a sale of the work at large. Then let the fourth volume take up the history of metaphysics, theology, medicine, alchemy, common, canon, and Roman law, from Alfred to Henry VII.; in other words, a history of the dark ages in Great Britain. The fifth volume —carry on metaphysics and ethics to the present day in the first half; the second half, comprise the theology of all the Reformers. In the fourth volume there would be a grand article on the philosophy of the theology of the Roman Catholic religion. In this (fifth volume), under different names—Hooker, Baxter, Biddle, and Fox—the spirit of the theology of all the other parts of Christianity. The sixth and seventh volumes must comprise all the articles you can get, on all the separate arts and sciences that have been treated of in books since the Reformation; and, by this time, the book, if it answered at all, would have gained so high a reputation, that you need not fear having whom you liked to write the different articles—medicine, surgery, chemistry, &c., &c., navigation, travelers, voyagers, &c., &c. If I go into Scotland, shall I engage Walter Scott to write the history of Scottish poets? Tell, me, however, what you think of the plan. It would have one prodigious advantage: whatever accident stopped the work, would only prevent the future good, not mar the past; each volume would be a great and valuable work *per se.* Then each volume would awaken a new interest, a new set of readers, who would buy the past volumes of course; then it would allow you ample time and opportunities for the slavery of the catalogue volumes, which should be, at the same time, an index to the work, which would be, in very truth, a pandect of knowledge, alive and swarming with human life, feeling, incident. By-the-by, what a strange abuse has been made of the word encyclopædia! It signifies, properly, grammar, logic, rhetoric, and ethics and metaphysics, which last, explaining the ultimate principles of grammar—log., rhet., and eth.—formed a circle of knowledge. * * * To call a huge unconnected miscellany of the *omne scibile*, in an arrangement determined by the accident of initial letters, an encyclopædia, is the impudent ignorance of your Presbyterian book-makers. Good-night!

"God bless you! S. T. S."

To S. T. Coleridge, Esq.

Bristol, Aug. 3, 1803.

"DEAR COLERIDGE,

"I meant to have written sooner; but those little units of interruption and preventions, which sum up to as ugly an aggregate as the items in a lawyer's bill, have come in the way. * * * * * * * * * * Your plan is too good, too gigantic, quite beyond my powers. If you had my tolerable state of health, and that love of steady and productive employment which is now grown into a necessary habit with me—if you were to execute and would execute it, it would be, beyond all doubt, the most valuable work of any age or any country; but I can not fill up such an outline. No man can better feel where he fails than I do; and to rely upon you for whole quartos! Dear Coleridge, the smile that comes with that thought is a very melancholy one; and if Edith saw me now, she would think my eyes were weak again, when, in truth, the humor that covers them springs from another cause.

"For my own comfort, and credit, and peace of mind, I must have a plan which I know myself strong enough to execute. I can take author by author as they come in their series, and give his life and an account of his works quite as well as ever it has yet been done. I can write connecting paragraphs and chapters shortly and pertinently, in my way; and in this way the labor of all my associates can be more easily arranged. * * * * * * * * And, after all, this is really nearer the actual design of what I purport by a Bibliotheca than yours would be—a book of reference, a work in which it may be seen what has been written upon every subject in the British language: this has elsewhere been done in the dictionary form; whatever we get better than that form, *ponemus lucro.*

"The Welsh part, however, should be kept completely distinct, and form a volume, or half a volume, by itself; and this must be delayed till the last in publication, whatever it be in order, because it can not be done till the whole of the Archæology is printed, and by that time I will learn the language, and so, perhaps, will you. George Ellis is about it; I think that, with the help of Turner and Owen, and poor Williams, we could then do every thing that ought to be done.

"The first part, then, to be published is the Saxon: this Turner will execute, and to this you and William Taylor may probably both be able to add something from your stores of northern knowledge. The Saxon books all come in sequence chronologically; then the mode of arrangement should be by centuries, and the writers classed as poets, historians, &c., by *centuries*, or by *reigns*, which is better. * * * * * * * * * *

Upon this plan the Schoolmen will come in the first volume.

"The historical part of the theology, and the bibliographical, I shall probably execute myself, and you will do the philosophy. By-the-by, I have lately found the book of John Perrott the Quaker, who went to convert the pope, containing all his epistles to the Romans, &c., written in the Inquisition at Rome; for they allowed him the privilege of writing, most likely because his stark madness amused them. This fellow (who turned rogue at last, wore a sword, and persecuted the Quakers in America to make them swear) made a schism in the society against George Fox, insisting that hats should be kept on in meeting during speaking (has not this prevailed?), and that the Friends should not shave. His book is the most frantic I ever saw—quite Gilbertish; and the man acted up to it. * * *

"God bless you! R. S."

CHAPTER X.

DEATH OF HIS LITTLE GIRL—ARRIVAL AT KESWICK—POSTPONEMENT OF THE BIBLIOTHECA BRITANNICA—STAGNATION OF TRADE—MADOC—SCENERY OF THE LAKES—HISTORY OF PORTUGAL—HASLITT'S PICTURES OF MR. COLERIDGE AND MR. WORDSWORTH—WANTS INFORMATION CONCERNING THE WEST INDIES—LITERARY OCCUPATIONS AND PLANS—THE ANNUAL REVIEW—POLITICS—THE YELLOW FEVER—NEW THEORY OF SUCH DISEASES—DESCRIPTION OF SCENERY REFLECTED IN KESWICK LAKE—SPECIMENS OF ENGLISH POETS PROJECTED—COURSE OF LIFE AT KESWICK—VISIT FROM MR. CLARKSON—HABITS OF MIND—MADOC—MR. COLERIDGE AND MR. GODWIN—DIRECTIONS TO MR. BEDFORD ABOUT SPECIMENS—REGRET AT MR. COLERIDGE LEAVING ENGLAND—MODERN CRITICS—MR. COLERIDGE'S POWERS OF MIND—LETTER TO MR. BEDFORD ON HABITS OF PROCRASTINATION—LITERARY EMPLOYMENTS—SPECIMENS OF ENGLISH POETS—GOES TO LONDON—LETTERS FROM THENCE—RETURN—SPANISH BOOKS—THE MABINOGION—SIR H. DAVY—MR. SOTHEBY—WILLIAM OWEN, ETC.—CHANGE OF ADMINISTRATION—PROGRESS OF HISTORICAL LABORS.—1804.

SUCH were my father's plans at the commencement of the month—to take up his abode at Richmond, and to devote himself almost wholly to this great work; and, had nothing interfered to prevent this scheme being carried into effect, his future life would probably have taken, in some respects, a very different course. He was now, as it were, about to cast anchor (as he used himself to phrase it), and, as it proved even against probabilities, the place where he now fixed himself was to be his permanent abode. But the Bibliotheca Britannica was not to be the turning point of his life, nor were the banks of the Thames and the fair and fertile scenes of Richmond to inspire his verse. Public troubles and private griefs combined to disarrange his present plans and to influence his future ones. The little girl whose birth had been so joyfully hailed barely a twelvemonth before, of whom he was "foolishly fond" beyond the common love of fathers for mere infants, who had hitherto shown "no sign of disease save a somewhat unnatural quickness and liveliness," now suddenly began to manifest unequivocal tokens of the presence of one of those diseases most fatal to children (and often worse than fatal, as permanently affecting the intellect), "hydrocephalus" produced by teething; and, after happily a brief period of suffering, she was laid to her early rest, and the fond parents were again childless.

Bristol was now a place only recalling painful sensations, and Mr. and Mrs. Coleridge being still resident at Keswick, my father and mother hastened down thither.

To Lieut. Southey, H.M.S. Galatea.

"Greta Hall, Keswick, Sept. 8, 1803.

"DEAR TOM,

"We arrived yesterday. Yours reached me to-day. I was glad to hear from you; a first letter after such a loss is always expected with some sort of fear—it is the pulling off the bandage that has been put upon a green wound. * * * * * * *

"Edith was very ill at Bristol. On the way we stayed five days with Miss Barker, in Staffordshire—one of the people in the world whom I like. To escape from Bristol was a relief. The place was haunted, and it is my wish never to see it again. Here my spirits suffer from the sight of little Sara,* who is about her size. However, God knows that I do not repine, and that in my very soul I feel that his will is best. These things do one good: they loosen, one by one, the roots that rivet us to earth; they fix and confirm our faith, till the thought of death becomes so inseparably connected with the hope of meeting those whom we have lost, that death itself is no longer considered as an evil.

* Mr. Coleridge's only daughter.

"Did I tell you that, in this universal panic and palsy, Longman has requested me to delay the Bibliotheca? This is a relief to me. I feel freer and easier. In consequence, I do not go to Richmond, but remain here, where I can live for half the expense. My design is to finish and print Madoc, that by the profits I may be enabled to go to Portugal. But my plans have been so often blasted that I look upon every thing as quite vague and uncertain. This only you may know, that while I am well I am actively employed; and that now, not being happy enough for the quiet half-hours of idleness, I must work with double dispatch.

"I hope you will see the Annual Review. There are some admirable things by William Taylor in it; my own part is very respectable, and one article, I hear, is by Harry. I shall probably do more in the next volume. You could have helped me in the maritime books. Do you know Harry is an ensign in the Norwich Volunteers?

"Edward has written to me; he was to go on board the following day. I could not at that time see to his fitting out as I should have done; but, when once fairly quit of her,* the boy shall not want as far as my means will go. It is you and I who have fared the worst; the other two will have fewer difficulties to cope with, yet perhaps they will not go on so well. Men are the better for having suffered; of that every year's experience more and more convinces me.

"Edith suffers deeply and silently. She is kept awake at night by recollections, and I am harassed by dreams of the poor child's illness and recovery; but this will wear away. Would that you could see these lakes and mountains! How wonderful they are! how awful in their beauty. All the poet-part of me will be fed and fostered here. I feel already in tune, and shall proceed to my work with such a feeling of power as old Samson had when he laid hold of the pillars of the Temple of Dagon. The Morning Post will somewhat interrupt me. Stuart has paid me so well for doing little, that in honesty I must work hard for him. Edith will copy you some of my rhymes.

"Amadis is most abominably printed; never book had more printer's blunders: how it sells is not in my power to say—in all likelihood, badly; for all trade is suspended, to a degree scarcely credible. I heard some authentic instances at Bristol. Hall, the grocer, used to have tea and sugar weighed out in pounds and half pounds, &c., on a Saturday night, for his country customers. Thirty years' established business enabled him to proportion the quantity to this regular demand almost to a nicety. He has had as much as twenty *pounds'* WORTH uncalled for. Mrs. Morgan, on a Saturday, used to take, upon the average, £30 in her shop; she now does not take £5. But this will wear away. I am quite provoked at the folly of any man who can feel a moment's fear for this country at this time.

* Miss Tyler.

"We look to the Morning Post, with daily disappointment, for news of the Galatea. Stuart has sold the paper, having thus realized £25,000. While his advice and influence upholds it, little difference will be perceived; but whenever that be withdrawn, I prophesy a slow decline and downfall. How comes on the Spanish? You will find it useful before the war is over, I fear—*fear*, because the Spaniards are a good and honorable people; and, in spite of the plunder which will fall to the share of the sailors, I can not but wish they may be spared from suffering in a war to which they assuredly are averse.

"God bless you, Tom. You must inquire of Danvers for Joe;* he will look after him, and drop a card occasionally at his door. Poor fellow, I was sorry to leave him: 'twas a heart-breaking day, that of our departure. Can't you contrive to chase some French frigate through the race of Holyhead up to the Isle of Man, engage her there, and bring her into Whitehaven? Edith's love. R. S."

To Lieut. Southey, H.M.S. Galatea.

"Keswick, Oct. 29, 1803.

"DEAR TOM,

"Your letter did not reach me till yesterday, eight days after its date, so that, though this be the earliest reply, perhaps it may not arrive at Cork till after your departure. This place is better suited for me than you imagine: it tempts me to take far more exercise than I ever took elsewhere, for we have the loveliest scenes possible close at hand; and I have, therefore, seldom or never felt myself in stronger health. And as for good spirits, be sure I have the outward and visible sign, however it may be for the inward and spiritual grace.

"My reviewing, more than ordinarily procrastinated, stands still. I began Clarke's book, and, having vented my gall there, laid the others all by till the first of November, that I might be free till then for work more agreeable. My main work has been Madoc. I am now arrived at the old fifth book, and at the twelfth of the booklings into which it is now divided. I mean to call them neither books, cantos, nor any thing else, but simply 1, 2, 3, &c., entitling each part from its peculiar action: thus, 1. The Return; 2. Cadwallon; 3. The Voyage; 4. Lincoya; 5. The War; 6. The Battle; 7. The Peace; 8. Emma; 9. Mathraval; 10. The Gorsedd, *i. e.*, the Meeting of the Bards; 11. Dinevawr; 12. Bards—and so on. The eleven divisions finished, which bring it down to the end of the old fourth book, contain 2536 lines—an increase, on the whole, of 731; but, of the whole, not one line in five stands as originally written. About 9000 lines will be the extent; but the further I proceed, the less alteration will be needed. When I turn the half way, I shall then say to my friends, 'Now get me subscribers, and I will publish Madoc.' In what is done there is some of my

* A favorite terrier.

best workmanship. I shall get by it less money than fame, and less fame than envy, but the envy will be only life-long; and when that is gone and the money spent—you know the old rhyme.

"It seems we are to have war with poor Portugal. If this be the case, my uncle must of course settle in England. This would be very pleasant to me, were it not so deeply and rootedly my own desire to settle in Portugal; but, *adonde não he remedio, então paciencia*, as I learned from the Portuguese. This war has affected me in every possible shape: in the King George packet I lost a whole cargo of books, for which I had been a year and a half waiting, and my uncle searching.

"I must go to work for money; and that also frets me. This hand-to-mouth work is very disheartening, and interferes cruelly with better things—more important they can not be called, for the bread and cheese is the business of the first necessity. But from my History I do expect permanent profit, and such a perpetual interest as shall relieve me. I shall write the volume of letters which you have heard me talk of—an omnium gatherum of the odd things I have seen in England.

"Whenever you are at a decent distance, and can get leave of absence, do come. Get to Liverpool by water, or, still better, to Whitehaven. You will be thoroughly delighted with the country. The mountains, on Thursday evening, before the sun was quite down, or the moon bright, were all of one dead-blue color; their rifts, and rocks, and swells, and scars had all disappeared; the surface was perfectly uniform; nothing but the outline distinct; and this even surface of dead blue, from its unnatural uniformity, made them, though not transparent, appear transvious—as though they were of some soft or cloudy texture through which you could have passed. I never saw any appearance so perfectly unreal. Sometimes a blazing sunset seems to steep them through and through with red light; or it is a cloudy morning, and the sunshine slants down through a rift in the clouds, and the pillar of light makes the spot whereon it falls so emerald green, that it looks like a little field of Paradise. At night you lose the mountains, and the wind so stirs up the lake that it looks like the sea by moonlight. Just behind the house rises a fine mountain, by name Latrigg: it joins Skiddaw. We walked up yesterday—a winding path of three quarters of an hour, and then *rode down on our own burros*, in seven minutes. Jesu-Maria-Jozè! that was a noble ride! but I will have a saddle made for my burro next time. The path of our slide is still to be seen from the garden—so near is it. One of these days I will descend Skiddaw in the same manner, and so immortalize myself.

"There is a carpenter here, James Lawson by name, who is become my Juniper* in the board-making way. He has made me a pair, of walnut, the large size, and of a reddish wood, from Demerara the small, and is about to get me some yew. This, as you may suppose, is a consolation to me, and it requires all Edith's powers of prudential admonition to dissuade me from having a little table with a drawer in it. His father* asked Derwent yesterday who made him? *D.:* James Lawson. *Father:* And what did he make you of? *D.:* The stuff he makes wood of. When Derwent had got on thus far in his system of Derwentogony, his imagination went on, and he added, 'He sawed me off, and I did not like it.'

"We began to wonder uneasily that there was no news of you. Edith's love. God bless you!

"R. S."

To Grosvenor C. Bedford, Esq.

"Greta Hall, Keswick, Nov. 10, 1803.

"Dear Grosvenor,

"You will have guessed why I have not written: to say any thing about a painful subject is painful; I do not love to write concerning what I never mention. I am very well, very cheerful, and very actively employed; and yet, with all this, *hæret lateri.* * * * * *

"You asked me some questions about the Bibliotheca. Longman wrote to me to postpone it, he being infected with the universal panic. I was no ways averse to the delay of the scheme, the discontinuance being optional with me. In truth, I have plans enough without it, and begin to think that my day's work is already sufficiently cut out for me. I am preparing Madoc for publication, and have so far advanced in the correction as to resolve upon trying my fortune at a subscription. I will print it for a guinea, in one quarto, if possible at that price; if not, in three small volumes. I will not *print* my intention till the success of a subscription has been tried privately—that is, without being published—because, if it fails, I can better go to a bookseller. If you can procure me some names, do; but never make yourself uncomfortable by asking. Of course, no money till the delivery of the book.

"It is now fifteen years since the subject first came into my occiput, and I believe Wynn was made acquainted with it almost at the time. It has been so much the subject of my thoughts and dreams, that in completing it, in sending off what has been so peculiarly and solely my own, there is a sort of awfulness and feeling, as if one of the purposes of my existence will then be accomplished. * * * * * *

"I am growing old, Bedford—not so much by the family Bible, as by all external and outward symptoms: the gray hairs have made their appearance; my eyes are wearing out; my shoes, the very cut of my father's, at which I used to laugh; my limbs not so supple as they were at Brixton in '93; my tongue not so glib; my heart quieter; my hopes, thoughts, and feelings, all of the complexion of a sunny autumn evening. I have a sort of presage that I shall live to finish Madoc and my History. God grant it, and that then my work will be done.

"God bless you! R. S."

* A carpenter at Bristol.

* Mr. Coleridge.

To John Rickman, Esq.

"Nov. 18, 1803.

"DEAR RICKMAN,

"I am manufacturing a piece of Paternoster Row goods, value three guineas, out of Captain Burney's book; and not very easy work, it being always more difficult to dilate praise than censure: however, by help of Barros, I have been able to collate accounts with him in the great voyage of Magelhaens (for he has misnamed him), and so to eke out my pages by additions. About the other worthy, Sir Francis, I have invented a quaint rhyme, which I shall insert as ancient, and modestly wonder that, as the author has a genuine love for all quaint things, it should have escaped his researches:

'Oh Nature, to Old England true,
Continue these mistakes;
Give us for our kings such queens,
And for our Dux such Drakes.'

" * * * * * * *

My History goes on well; I am full sail in the Asiatic Channel, and have found out some odd things. The Christians of St. Thomas worshiped the Virgin Mary, which throws back that superstition to an earlier date than is generally allowed it. The astrolabe, the quadrant, the compass, were found in the East, *quomodo diabolus?* Martin Behaim invented the sea astrolabe at Lisbon, by express direction of Joam II., and behold! within ten or a dozen years Vasco da Gama finds it in India.

"They had gunpowder there—espingards, what shall I call them?—and cannon; but the Portuguese owed their success to the great superiority of their artillery: in fact, the main improvements in sea artillery were invented by Joam II. himself. But the great intercourse between India and the Old World is most remarkable in the first voyage of Gama: he met with a Moor of Fez, a Moor of Tunis, a *Venetian* and a Polish Jew. The world was not so ignorant as has been supposed; individuals possessed knowledge which there were no motives for communicating. No sooner was it known that K. Joam II. would reward people for intelligence respecting the East, than two of his own Jew subjects came, and told him they had been there. The commercial spirit of the Moors is truly astonishing: Dutchmen or East India directors could not be more jealous of their monopolies. The little kingdoms which Gama found resemble Homer's Phæacia. Every city had its monarch, and he was the great merchant; his brothers were captains of ships. Spice, spice, was what the Europeans wanted; and for what could they require it in such quantities and at such a cost? Spiced wines go but a little way in answering this. The Hindoos, too, wanted coral from the Portuguese—odd fellows! when it grows in their own seas. I believe the Portuguese conquests to have been the chief cause that barbarized the Mohammedans; their spreading commerce would else have raised up a commercial interest, out of which an enlightened policy might have grown. The Koran was a master-piece of policy, attributing sanctity to its language. Arabic thus became a sort of Free-mason's passport for every believer—a bond of fraternity. * * * *

"God bless you! R. S."

To Richard Duppa, Esq.

"Greta Hall, Keswick, Dec. 14, 1803.

"DEAR DUPPA,

"I have not had the heart to write to you, though the long silence has lain like a load upon my conscience. When we parted I had as much present happiness as man could wish, and was full of all cheerful hopes: however, no man, if he be good for any thing, but is the better for suffering. It has long been my habit to look for the good that is to be found in every thing, and that alchemy is worth more than the grand secret of all the adepts.

"I had almost completed my arrangements for removing to Richmond at Christmas, and here we are at the uttermost end of the north, and here for some time we shall probably remain—how long, God knows I am steady in my pursuits, for they depend upon myself; but my plans and fortunes, being of the τὰ οὐκ ἐφ' ἡμῖν, are more mutable: they are fairly afloat, and the winds are more powerful than the steersman. Longman caught the alarm—the Bonaparte ague or English influenza—after I left town, and sent to me to postpone my Bibliotheca, at the very time when I wished the engagement off my mind, not being in a state of mind to contemplate it with courage. He shall now wait my convenience, and I shall probably finish off my own works of choice here, where, living cheaper, I have more leisure. My History is in a state of rapid progression. The last time I saw Mr. —— in town he gave me a draft for fifty pounds as his subscription, he said, to this work. I tell you this because you know him, and, therefore, not to tell you would make me feel ungrateful for an act of uncommon liberality, done in the handsomest way possible. I little thought, at the time, how soon an unhappy circumstance would render the sum needful This work I am alternating and relieving by putting Madoc to the press, and my annual job of reviewing interrupts both for a while; but, happily, this job comes, like Christmas, but once a year, and I have almost killed off my cotemporaries.

"Haslitt, whom you saw at Paris, has been here—a man of real genius. He has made a very fine picture of Coleridge for Sir George Beaumont, which is said to be in Titian's manner. He has also painted Wordsworth, but so dismally, though Wordsworth's face is his idea of physiognomical perfection, that one of his friends, on seeing it, exclaimed, 'At the gallows—deeply affected by his deserved fate—yet determined to die like a man;' and if you saw the picture, you would admire the criticism. We have a neighbor here who also knows you—Wilkinson, a clergyman, who draws, if not with much genius, with great industry and most useful fidelity. I have learned a good deal by examining his collection of etchings.

"Holcroft, I hear, has discovered, to his own exceeding delight, prophetic portraits of himself and Coleridge among the damned in your Michael Angelo. I have found out a more flattering antetype of Coleridge's face in Duns Scotus. Come you yourself and judge of the resemblances. Coleridge and our lakes and mountains are worth a longer journey. Autumn is the best season to see the country, but spring, and even winter, is better than summer, for in settled fine weather there are none of those goings on in heaven which at other times give these scenes such an endless variety. * * * You will find this house a good station for viewing the lakes; it is, in fact, situated on perhaps the very finest single spot in the whole lake country, and we can show you things which the tourists never hear of. * * * * * * * * * * * * * *

"Edith desires to be remembered to you: she is but in indifferent health. I myself am as well as I ever was. The weather has been, and is, very severe, but it has not as yet hurt me: however, it must be owned the white bears have the advantage of us in England, and still more the dormice. If their torpor could be introduced into the human system, it would be a most rare invention. I should roll myself up at the end of October, and give orders to be waked by the chimney-sweeper on May-day.

"God bless you.

"Yours affectionately,

"R. Southey."

To Lieut. Southey, H.M.S. Galatea.

"Dec. 17, 1803.

"Dear Tom,

"The news in your letter has vexed me, and, after my manner, set me upon discovering all the consolations that can be extracted from it. First and foremost, that if you go as convoy, you will not be stationed there; and, therefore, to sail at this season into warm weather is no such bad thing. If you go to Jamaica you will find a whole lot of letters, unless they have been burned at the post-office. As you will keep a keen look-out for all imaginable things, I need give you only one commission, which is, that you do use your best endeavors to bring home a few live land-crabs for me, that I may endeavor to rear a breed in England.

"Do not send off Henry, because it will be lost at the custom-house. Keep it till you yourself come to England, and can safely get it ashore: 'tis a good book for a long voyage; very dull, but full of matter, and trustworthy as far as the author's information goes.

"My review of Miss Baillie was for the Critical; that in the Annual I suspect to be by Mrs. Barbauld, who wrote the review of Chateaubriand's Beauties of Christianity, and that infamous account of Lamb's Play, for infamous it is. Harry's only article is Soulavie's Memoirs, and I have never seen the book since this was told me. The rules you lay down will always point out Wm. Taylor.

"I think it possible, Tom, that you might collect some interesting information from the negroes, by inquiries of any who may wait upon you, if they be at all intelligent, concerning their own country; principally, what their superstitions are: as, Whom do they worship? Do they ever see apparitions? Where do the dead go? What are their burial, their birth, their marriage ceremonies? What their charms or remedies for sickness? What the power of their priests; and how the priests are chosen, whether from among the people, or if a separate breed, as the Levites and Bramins? You will easily see with what other questions these might be followed up; and by noting down the country of the negro, with what information he gave, it seems to me very likely that a very valuable account of their manners and feelings might be collected. Ask, also, if they know any thing of Timbuctoo, the city which is sought after with so much curiosity as being the center of the internal commerce of Africa. This is the way to collect facts respecting the native Africans and their country. I would engage, in twelve months, were I in the West Indies, to get materials for a volume that should contain more real importances than all travelers have yet brought home. Ask, also, what beasts are in their country. They will not know English names for them, but can describe them so that you will know them: the unicorn is believed to exist by me as well as by many others—you will not mistake the rhinoceros for one. Inquire, also, for a land crocodile, who grows to the length of six, eight, or ten feet, having a tongue slit like a snake's: my Portuguese speak of such animals in South Africa; they may exist in the western provinces.

"You would have been very useful to me if you had been at the table when I was reviewing Clarke's book, and Captain Burney's. Indeed, I often want a sailor to help me out. In the process of my History some curious facts respecting early navigation have come to light. I find the needle and the quadrant used in the Indian Seas before any European vessel had ever reached them; and, what surprises me more, the same knowledge of soundings in our own seas in 1400 as at present, which is very strange, for that practice implies a long series of registered experiences. The more I read, the more do I find the necessity of going to old authors for information, and the sad ignorance and dishonesty of our boasted historians. If God do but give me life, and health, and eyesight, I will show how history should be written, and exhibit such a specimen of indefatigable honesty as the world has never yet seen. I could make some historical triads, after the manner of my old Welsh friends, of which the first might run thus: The three requisites for an historian—industry, judgment, genius; the patience to investigate, the discrimination to select, the power to infer and to enliven.

"Edith's love. God bless you!

"R. Southey."

To John Rickman, Esq.

"Dec. 23, 1803.

"DEAR RICKMAN,

" * * * * * * * *

I am about a curious review of the Mission at Otaheite. Capt. Burney will find his friends rather roughly handled, for I look upon them as the most degraded of the human species. * * * * * They have induced me to think it probable that the Spaniards did less evil in Hispaniola than we suppose. Coleridge's scheme to mend them is by extirpating the bread-fruit from their island, and making them live by the sweat of their brows. It always grieves me when I think you are no friend to colonization. My hopes fly further than yours; I want English knowledge and the English language diffused to the east, and west, and the south.

"Can you get for me the evidence upon the Slave Trade as printed for the House of Commons? I want to collect all materials for speculating upon the negroes. That they are a fallen people is certain, because, being savages, they have among them the forms of civilization. It is remarkable that, in all our discoveries, we have never discovered any people in a state of progression except the Mexicans and Peruvians. That the Otaheitans are a degraded race, is proved by their mythology, which is physical allegory—*ergo*, the work of people who thought of physics. I am very desirous to know whether the negro priests and jugglers be a caste, or if any man may enter into the fraternity; and if they have a sacred language. We must continue to grope in darkness about early history till some strong-headed man shall read the hieroglyphics for us. Much might yet be done by comparison of languages: some hundred words of the most common objects—sun, moon, and stars, the parts of the body, the personal pronouns, the auxiliary verbs, &c.—if these were collected, as occasion could be found, from every different tribe, such languages as have been diffluent we should certainly be able to trace to their source. In New Holland, language is said to be confluent, every tribe, and almost every family, having its own; but that island is an odd place—coral above water, and coal; new birds, beasts, and plants; and such a breed of savages! It looks like a new country, if one could tell where the animals came from.

"Do you know that the Dodo is actually extinct, having been, beyond doubt, too stupid to take care of himself. * * * * There is no hope of recovering the species, unless you could get your friend —— to sit upon a gander's egg. God bless you.

"R. S."

To Lieut. Southey, H.M.S. Galatea.

"Dec. 31, 1803.

"DEAR TOM,

"I have just received yours, and regret that I did not write sooner, upon a reasonable calculation that convoys are even more uncertain than packets. A letter, per bottle, I see by the newspapers, thrown in on the way to the West Indies, if I recollect right, in latitude 47°, has found its way to the Isle of Sky, having traveled five miles per day *against* prevalent winds; therefore a current is certain. I will send into town for the paper, and send you the particulars in this or my next. Do not spare bottles in your passage; and be sure that I have a letter from the Western Isles.

"For God's sake adapt your mode of living to the climate you are going to, and abstain almost wholly from wine and spirits. General Peche, an East Indian officer here, with whom we dined on Christmas day, told me that, in India, the officers who were looking out for preferment, as a majority, &c., and who kept lists of all above them, always marked those who drank any spirits in a morning with an X, and reckoned them for nothing. 'One day,' said he, 'when we were about to march at daybreak, I and Captain —— were in my tent, and we saw a German of our regiment, so I said we'd try him; we called to him, said it was a cold morning, and asked him if he would drink a glass to warm him. I got him a full beaker of brandy and water, and, egad! he drank it off. When he was gone, I said, 'Well, what d'ye think; we may cross him, mayn't we? Oh yes, said he, cross him by all means. And the German did not live twelve months.' Spice is the stimulus given by nature to hot countries, and, eaten in whatever quantities, can do no harm. But the natives of all hot countries invariably abstain from spirits as deadly. Eat fruits plentifully, provided they do not produce flux; animal food sparingly in the hot season: fish will be better than meat. Do not venture to walk or ride in the heat of the sun; and do not be ashamed of a parasol: it has saved many a man's life. I am sure all this is very physical and philosophical sense. But I will desire King, who knows the West Indies, to write out to you a letter of medical advice. This is certain, that bilious people fare worst, and nervous people, for fear predisposes for disease: from these causes you are safe.

"Edith will go on with Madoc for you, and a letter full shall go off for Barbadoes this week. My last set you upon a wide field of inquiry. I know not what can be added unless you should be at St. Vincent's, where the Caribs would be well worthy attention, making the same queries of and to them as to the negroes. Of course, there are no Spanish books except at the Spanish islands. Oh! that I were at Mexico for a hunt there! Could you bring home a live alligator? a little one, of course from his hatching to six feet long: it would make both me and Carlisle quite happy, for he should have him. And pray, pray, some live land-crabs, *that they may breed;* and any other monsters. Birds lose their beauty; and I would not be accessory to the death of a humming-bird, for the sake of keeping his corpse in a cabinet; but with crocodiles, sharks, and land-crabs it is fair play—you catch them, or they you. Your own eyes will do all that I can direct them. How unfortunate that neither of us can draw! I want drawings of the trees.

"Thompson, the friend of Burns, whose correspondence with him about songs fills the whole fourth volume, has applied to me to write him verses for Welsh airs: of course I have declined it, telling him that I could as soon sing his songs as write them, and referring him to Harry, whom he knows, for an estimate of that simile of disqualification. Still I am at reviewing; but ten days will lighten me of that burden, and then huzza for history, and huzza for Madoc, for I shall be a free man again! I have bought Pinkerton's Geography, after all, for the love of the maps, having none: it is a useful book, and will save me trouble.

"We shall not think of holding any part of St. Domingo. What has been done can only have been for the sake of what plunder was to be found, and perhaps, also, to save the French army from the fate which they so justly deserved. God forbid that ever English hand be raised against the negroes in that island! Poor wretches! I regard them as I do the hurricane and the pestilence, blind instruments of righteous retribution and divine justice; and sure I am that whatever hand be lifted against them will be withered. Of Spanish politics I can say nothing, nor give even a surmise. Here, at home, we have the old story of invasion, upon which the types naturally range themselves into a very alarming and loyal leading paragraph. Let him come, say I; it will be a fine thing for the bell-ringers and the tallow-chandlers.

"I trust this will reach you before your departure. Write immediately on your arrival, and afterward by every packet, for any omission will make me uneasy. I will not be remiss on my part.

"God bless you! Edith's love. A happy new year, and many returns! R. S."

To Grosvenor C. Bedford, Esq.

"Greta Hall, Keswick, Jan. 9, 1804.

"*Infailix homo! infailix homo!* said a German to Coleridge, who did not understand for whom he was inquiring by the name of Tŏctŏr Tŏd; *infailix homo! suspensus a patibulo!* Without any patibulary reflection, *infailix homo* is the soul of exclamation that your letter prompts. Zounds! if Giardini were in your inside, what an admirable solo he might play upon guts that must, by this time, have been fretted to fiddle-strings! I verily believe that your gripes must be organic, and not, as in all other men, bag-pipical.

"The plain English of all this is, that your metaphysics, as you call them, are to your mind what a regular course of drastic physic would be to your body—very disagreeable, and very weakening; that, being neither a man of business, nor of fashion, nor of letters, you want object and occupation in the world; and that, if you would study Arabic, Welsh, or Chinese, or resolve to translate Tristram Shandy into Hebrew, you would soon be a happy man.

" * * * * * * * *

Here we live as regularly as clock-work—indeed, more regularly than our own clocks, which go all paces. The old Barber has been at work for some days. I take Horace's liberty to personify the sky, and then simply barbarize the prosopopœia.

"Of the only three visitable families within reach, one is fled for the winter, and the others flying. *N'importe*, our dog Dapper remains, and he is as intimate with me as heart could wish. I want my books, and nothing else; for, blessed be God! I grow day by day more independent of society, and feel neither a want nor a wish for it. Every thing at present looks, from the window, like the confectioners' shops at this season in London; and Skiddaw is the hugest of twelfth cakes; but when I go down by the lake-side, it would puzzle all my comparison-compounding fancy to tell you what it looks like there: the million or trillion forms of beauty soon baffle all description.

"Coleridge is gone for Devonshire, and I was going to say I am alone, but that the sight of Shakspeare, and Spenser, and Milton, and the Bible on my table, and Castanheda, and Barros, and Osorio at my elbow, tell me I am in the best of all possible company. Do not think of getting any subscribers for Madoc. I am convinced the plan of publishing it by subscription was foolish, and shall doubtless convince those who induced me to think of it. Have you seen the Critical Reviewal of Thalaba? I wish to see it, for it comes not only from one of my best friends, but from one of the most learned, most able, and most excellent men within the circle of my knowledge. * * * * * * *
My brother Harry is at Edinburgh, distinguishing himself as a disputant in the Medical Society. Poor Tom is going for the West Indies! What are our dunces sending troops there for? I could find in my heart to set at them; for, to tell you the truth, a set-to at the Methodists in this Review has put me in a very pamphleteering mood.

* * * * * * *

"God bless you! R. S."

To John Rickman, Esq.

"January 20, 1804.

"Dear Rickman,

"* * * * * * *

Arthur Aikin writes me that 1200 of the Annual Review have sold of 2000 that were printed, and that the demand continues unabated. He is in high spirits at its success, and wishes me to come to London—looking upon me, I suppose, as one of his staff-officers—as, in fact, William Taylor and I constitute his main strength. It is clear enough that, if I regarded pen-and-ink-manship solely as a trade, I might soon give in an income of double the present amount; but I am looking forward to something better, and will not be tempted from the pursuit in which I have so long and so steadily persevered. * * This vile reviewing still bird-limes me. I do it slower than any thing else—yawning over tiresome work; and parcel comes down after parcel, so that I have already twice whooped before I was out of the wood. Yesterday Malthus received, I trust, a mortal wound from my hand; to-day I am at the Asiatic Researches. Godwin's Life of Chaucer is on the road to me: by-the-by, the philosopher came in for a hard rap over the knuckles with Mr. Malthus. These things keep me from better employment, but they whet the desire for it, and I shall return to my Portuguese society with double zest.

"In the Dark Ages, medicine was in the hands of the Jews. Why was this? Am I right in supposing it was because they traveled, and brought with them the wisdom and experience, as well as folly of the East? Christians could not travel safely; but Hebrew, like Arabic, was a passport, for synagogues and mosques were every where. A decree of the Lateran Council, that the sacrament should be *first prescribed* to the sick, seems leveled against Jew physicians.

"Have you read the Institutes of Menu, translated by Sir W. Jones? I should be very glad to see your corollaries from that book. Hindostan, indeed the whole of civilized Asia, puzzles me, and provokes me that we should have so few documents to reason from. As far as their history can be unraveled from fable, nothing is discoverable but the war of *sects*, not of religions; and how so ridiculous a religion should have been so blended with astronomy, how allegory should put on so ugly a mask, is a puzzle.

" * * * * * * *

I am well, but have an ominous dimness of sight at times, which makes me think of Tobin; that would, indeed, be a sore visitation! but I will feed while the summer lasts, that my paws may be fat enough to last licking through the dark winter, if it must come.

"Vale! R. S."

To Messrs. Longman and Rees.

"Jan. 26, 1804.

"DEAR SIRS,

"If Mr. ——'s little tale (which reached me last night) be long enough for publication, I should think it possesses sufficient interest to be salable. The author is, in my judgment, a man of very considerable, and, indeed, extraordinary talents. This —— he has probably written hastily, and, I fear, upon the spur of want.

"Having myself sought after information respecting the countries on the Mississippi, I can say that the descriptions and natural history are, as far as my knowledge goes, accurate, and therefore it is fair to presume that such circumstances as were new to me are equally true to nature.

"I know nothing of —— but from his Travels; from that he appears to be a self-taught man, who has all his life-long been struggling with difficulties; and the book left upon me a melancholy impression, that, however much adversity had quickened his talents, it had injured his moral feelings. Pride and vanity are only defensive vices in a poor and neglected man of talents, and being defensive, they cease to be vices. Something of the same palliation may be pleaded for an evident libertinism of heart and thought which is every where too manifest in his book: in this he resembles Smollett and Defoe, which last truly great man he resembles also in better things.

"Should you execute your design of the Collection of Voyages and Travels, which I hope and trust you will, this man might be made exceedingly useful to you. Being himself a sailor, and having seen and observed many countries, you will rarely find one so well qualified to digest many travels into one full account. I had begun a letter to you upon the subject of the Collection some months ago, but laid it aside when the alarm of invasion seemed to suspend all literary, and, indeed, all other speculation. Should you resume the scheme, I will willingly send you an outline of what seems to me to be the most advisable plan.

" * * * * * * * *

It has occurred to me that I could make a good companion to Ellis's very excellent book, under the title of Specimens of the Modern English Poetry, beginning exactly where he leaves off, and following exactly his plan—coming down to the present time, and making death the time where to stop. Two volumes would comprise it, perhaps. Let me know if you like the scheme: it would require more trouble and more *search* than you will be at first aware of, but, with Ellis's work, it would form such a series of arranged selections as no other country can boast. I could do it well, and should do it willingly. If it should be taken by the public as a supplement, it would be a good speculation. Should you see Coleridge, show him this. I would, of course, affix my name."

To Lieutenant Southey, H.M.S. Galatea.

"Keswick, Jan. 31, 1804.

"DEAR TOM,

"From this uttermost end of the north it will not be easy, or indeed possible, to send any thing to the West Indies, except what will go in the compass of a letter, else you should have the Iris's* bundled up for you. * * * My plan for Madoc stands, then, at present, that Longman shall risk all expenses, and share the eventual profits; printing it in quarto, and with engravings, for I am sure the book will sell the better for being made expensive. * * Having now cleared off all my Annual Reviewing (oh, Tom, such a batch! almost as much as last year's rabble), I am now, for a while, at full leisure, and of course direct it principally to Madoc, that it may be off my hands, for I should not be willing to leave the world till I have left that in a fair state behind me. I am now finishing

* A Norwich newspaper, edited by Mr. William Taylor.

the 14th section. * * * * * They tell me that Walter Scott has reviewed Amadis in the Edinburgh Review; to what purport I know not, but probably a favorable one, if it be his doing, for he is a man whose taste accords with mine, and who, though we have never seen each other, knows that I respect him, as he, on his part, respects me. The same friendly office has been performed in the Critical at last for Thalaba, by William Taylor: this, too, I have not seen.

"As for politics, Tom, we that live among the mountains, as the old woman said, do never hear a word of news. This talk of war with Spain I do not believe, and I am at last come round to the opinion that no invasion is intended, but that the sole object of Bonaparte is to exhaust our finances. Booby! not remembering that a national bankruptcy, while it ruins individuals, makes the state rich. * * * * * How long the present Duncery may go on, God knows; I am no enemy to them, for they mean well, but in this broil with the Volunteers they are wrong, and dangerously wrong as regards their own popularity. I wish every Volunteer would lay down his arms, being fully persuaded that in case of necessity he would take them up again; but this attempt to increase the system of patronage, by depriving them of their covenanted right of electing their own officers, is rascally and abominable. The elections universally made show that the choice always falls upon men who have either the claim of property, character, or talents. Of more permanent political importance will be a circumstance of which there is no talk of at all. Inquiries are making into the actual state of the poor in England; an office has been established for the purpose, and the superintendence, by Rickman's recommendation, assigned to Poole, Coleridge's friend, of whom you must have heard me speak—a man of extraordinary powers, more akin in mind to Rickman than any man I know. This is a very gratifying circumstance to me, to see so many persons, with whom I became acquainted before the world did, rising in the world to their proper stations. * * * * * *

"God bless you! R. S."

To Lieutenant Southey, H.M.S. Amelia.

"Feb. 11, 1804.

"Dear Tom,

"It is not possible that my letters can give you more pleasure than yours give me. You have always reason to suppose that all is well with me when you hear nothing to the contrary. I am only exposed to the common accidents of life, but you are in the way of battle and slaughter, pestilence and hurricanes, and every letter that arrives from you relieves me from a certain kind of apprehension. * * * * As this letter was not finished at a heat, it has lain two or three weeks; to own the truth fairly, I had such a fear about me of the yellow fever, because you mentioned indisposition on the night preceding the date of your last, that I had not heart to go on with it. Once I received a letter from a poor fellow three months after he was dead: it excited a most painful feeling; and it is little less unpleasant to address one to a person whom you fear may not be among the living; however, yours of Dec. 4 has just come to hand. You do not tell me whether the fever is out of the ship; but I conclude it must almost have done its work, and will go out like a fire when it no longer finds any thing it can destroy. I have a sort of theory about such diseases which I do not understand myself, but somebody or other will, some of these days. They are so far analogous to vegetables as that they take root, grow, ripen, and decay. Those which are eruptive, blossom and seed; for the pustule of the smallpox, &c., is, to all intents and purposes, the flower of the disease, or the fructification by which it is perpetuated. Now these diseases, like vegetables, choose their own soil: some plants like clay, others sand, others chalk; so the yellow fever will not take root in a negro, nor the yaws in a white man. There is a hint for a new theory; you will see the truth of the analogy at once, and I can no more explain it than you can, but so it is. * * * * * * * We have been dreadfully shocked here by the fate of Wordsworth's brother, captain of the Abergavenny East Indiaman, which has just been lost in Portland Bay—almost as shocking as the Halsewell—300 lives. * * * * Bonaparte wants peace; a continental war is a far more probable event. What will become of Portugal, Heaven knows; and till that be decided, I can as little tell what will become of me. Meantime, I shall continue to work hard and to economize. * * * * *

"God bless you!

"Yours very affectionately, R. S."

To Grosvenor C. Bedford, Esq.

"Greta Hall, Feb. 16, 1804.

"Dear Grosvenor,

"I have seen a sight more dreamy and wonderful than any scenery that fancy ever yet devised for Faëry Land. We had walked down to the lake side: it was a delightful day, the sun shining, and a few white clouds hanging motionless in the sky. The opposite shore of Derwentwater consists of one long mountain, which suddenly terminates in an arch, thus ‿, and through that opening you see a long valley between mountains, and bounded by mountain beyond mountain; to the right of the arch the heights are more varied and of greater elevation. Now, as there was not a breath of air stirring, the surface of the lake was so perfectly still that it became one great mirror, and all its waters disappeared; the whole line of shore was represented as vividly and steadily as it existed in its actual being—the arch, the vale within, the single houses far within the vale, the smoke from their chimneys, the furthest hills, and the shadow and substance joined at their bases so indivisibly, that you could make no separation even in your judgment. As I stood on the shore, heaven and the clouds seemed lying under me. I was looking down into the sky, and the whole range of mountains, having one line of summits under my feet, and another above me, seemed to be suspended between the firmaments. Shut your eyes and dream of a scene so unnatural and so beautiful. What I have said is most strictly and scrupulously true; but it was one of those happy moments that can seldom occur, for the least breath stirring would have shaken the whole vision, and at once unrealized it. I have before seen a partial appearance, but never before did, and perhaps never again may, lose sight of the lake entirely, for it literally seemed like an abyss of sky before me; not fog and clouds from a mountain, but the blue heaven spotted with a few fleecy pillows of cloud, that looked placed there for angels to rest upon them.

"I am treating with my bookseller to publish a supplementary or companion work to Ellis's Specimens, beginning where he leaves off, and coming down to the present time, exclusive of the living poets, so that my work, with his, should contain a brief notice of all the English poets, good, bad, and indifferent, with specimens of each, except the dramatic writers. If this take place, it will cost me a journey to London, and a month's hard work there; the main part can be done here. You know Ellis's book, of course, and if you do not, Nicholl can show it you (who, by-the-by, will go to the devil for charging half a guinea a volume for it, unless he can send Ellis instead). Now, if I should make this work, of which there is little doubt, you may, if so disposed, give me an opportunity of acknowledging my obligations for assistance to my friend Mr. G. C. Bedford in the preface, and perhaps find some amusement in the task. So tell me your lordship's pleasure, and I will prescribe to you what to do for me; and if you shall rouse yourself to any interest in the pursuit, it may prove really a good prescription. By doing something to assist me, you may learn to love some pursuit for yourself.

"With what can Isaac Reid have filled his one-and-twenty volumes? Comments upon Shakspeare seem to keep pace with the National Debt, and will at last become equally insufferable and out of fashion; yet I should like to see his book, and would buy it if I could. There must be a mass of English learning heaped together, and his Biog. Dramatica is so good a work that I do not think old age can have made him make a bad one; besides, this must have been the work or amusement of his life. * *

"I live almost as recluse a life as my neighbor, the Bassenthwaite Toad, whose history you have seen in the newspapers; only if he finds it dull I do not, for I have books, and Port wine, and a view from my window. I feel as much pleasure in having finished my reviewing as ever I did at school when my Bible exercise was done, and what sort of pleasure that was you may judge by being told that one of the worst dreams that ever comes athwart my brain is that I have those Latin verses to make. I very often have this dream, and it usually ends in a resolution to be my own master, and not make verses, and not stay any longer at school, because I am too old. It is odd that school never comes pleasantly in my dreams: it is always either thus, or with a notion that I can not find my book to go on with. I never dream of Oxford; perhaps my stay was not long enough to make an impression sufficiently deep.

"God bless you!

"Yours affectionately, R. S."

To Lieut. Southey, H.M.S. Galatea.

"Keswick, Friday, Feb. 17, 1804.

"DEAR TOM,

"When I remember how many letters I wrote to you on your last West Indies station, and that you never received one of the number, it seems as if this, too, was to be sent upon a forlorn hope. However, I will now number what I send, that you may see if any be missing, and make inquiry for them.

"I have wanted you to help me in weighing anchor for Madoc, and for want of you have been obliged to throw into shade what else should have been brought out in strong light. Had you been at my elbow, he should have set sail in a very seaman-like manner; if this reaches you, it may yet be in time for you to tell me what I should say to express that the sails are all *ready* for sailing next day. I am afraid *bent* is not the word, and have only put it in just to keep the place, designing to omit it and clap some general phrase in, unless you can help me out in time. The whole first part of the poem is now finished; that is, as far as Madoc's return to America, 3600 lines; the remaining part will be longer. As my guide once told me in Portugal, we have got half way, for we have come two short leagues, and have two long ones to go; and upon his calculation I am half through the poem.

"Of my own goings on I know not that there is any thing which can be said. Imagine me in this great study of mine from breakfast till dinner, from dinner till tea, and from tea till supper, in my old black coat, my corduroys alternately with the long worsted pantaloons and gaiters in one, and the green shade, and sitting at my desk, and you have my picture and my history. I play with Dapper, the dog, down stairs, who loves me as well as ever Cupid did, and the cat, up stairs, plays with me; for puss, finding my room the quietest in the house, has thought proper to share it with me. Our weather has been so wet that I have not got out of doors for a walk once in a month. Now and then I go down to the river, which runs at the bottom of the orchard, and throw stones till my arms ache, and then saunter back again. James Lawson, the carpenter, serves me for a Juniper: he has made boards for my papers, and a screen, like those in the frame, with a little shelf to hold my ivory knife, &c., and is now making a little table for Edith, of which I shall probably make the most use. I rouse the house to breakfast every morning, and qualify myself for a boatswain's place by this practice; and thus one day passes like another, and never did the days appear to pass so fast. Summer will make a difference. Our neighbor, General Peche, will return in May; Harry, also, will come in May. Sir George and Lady Beaumont are expected to visit Mrs. Coleridge. Danvers is to come in the autumn. The Smiths of Bownham (who gave me Hayley's Life of Cowper) will probably visit the lakes this year, and most likely Duppa will stroll down to see me and the mountains. I am very well—never better. Edith tolerable. God bless you! If you do not henceforward receive a letter by every packet, the fault will not be mine. R. S."

To S. T. Coleridge, Esq.

"Greta Hall, Feb. 19, 1804.

"*Parson*-son,* the Piscis Piscium sive Piscissimus, left us to-day. * * * * He is piping hot from Bristol, and brimful of admiration for Beddoes, who, indeed, seems to have done so much for Mrs. C. that there are good hopes of her speedy recovery. He is in high spirits about the Slave Trade, for the West India merchants will not consent to its suspension for five years, to prevent the importation of hands into the newly-conquered islands; and what from that jealousy, and from the blessed success of the St. Domingo negroes, I believe we may hope to see the traffic abolished. * * * * * * * *

"If I were a single man and a Frenchman, I would go as a missionary to St. Domingo, where a world of good might be done in that way: the climate may be defied by any man in a high state of mental excitement. I know not whether I sent you some curious facts respecting vivaciousness, but I have met with enough to lead to important physiological conclusions, and, in particular, to explain the sufficiently common fact of sick persons fixing the hour of their death, and living exactly to that time: the simple solution is, that they would else have died *sooner*. In proceeding with my History, I continually find something that leads to interesting speculation: it would, perhaps, be better if there were always some one at hand to whom I could communicate these discoveries, and who should help me to hunt down the game when started; not that I feel any wish for such society, but still it would at times be useful. It is a very odd, but a marked characteristic of my mind—the very nose in the face of my intellect—that it is either utterly idle or uselessly active without its tools. I never enter into any regular train of thought unless the pen be in my hand; they then flow as fast as did the water from the rock in Horeb, but without that wand the source is dry. At these times conversation would be useful. However, I am going on well—never better. The old cerebrum was never in higher activity. I find daily more and more reason to wonder at the miserable ignorance of English historians, and to grieve with a sort of despondency at seeing how much that has been laid up among the stores of knowledge has been neglected and utterly forgotten.

"Madoc goes on well; the whole detail of the alteration is satisfactorily completed, and I shall have it ready for the press by midsummer. I wish it could have been well examined first by you and William Taylor; however, it will be well purged and purified in the last transcription, and shall go into the world, not such as will obtain general approbation now, but such as may content most men to read. I am not quite sure whether the story will not tempt me to have a cross in the title-page, and take for my motto, *In hoc signo*. * * * *

"If Μακρος Ανθρωπος agrees with me about the Specimens, it will oblige me to go to London. Perhaps we may contrive to meet. *

"I am sorry, sir, to perceive by your letter that there is a scarcity of writing-paper in London; perhaps, the next time you write, Mr. Rickman or Mr. Poole* will have the goodness to accommodate you with a larger sheet, that you may have the goodness to accommodate me with a longer letter; and if, sir, it be owing to the weakness of your sight that you write so large a hand, and in lines so far apart, there is a very excellent optician, who lives at Charing Cross, where you may be supplied with the best spectacles, exactly of the number which may suit your complaint.

"I am, sir, your obedient humble servant,

"ROBERT SOUTHEY."

To S. T. Coleridge, Esq.

"Feb., 1804.

"I am not sorry that you gave Godwin a dressing, and should not be sorry if he were occasionally to remember it with the comfortable reflection '*in vino veritas;*' for, in plain truth, already it does vex me to see you so lavish of the outward and visible signs of friendship, and to know that a set of fellows whom you do not care for and ought not to care for, boast every where of your intimacy, and with good reason, to the best of their understanding. You have accustomed yourself to talk affectionately and write affectionately to your friends, till the expressions of affection flow by habit in your conversation and in your letters, and pass for more than they are worth; the worst of all this is, that your letters will one day rise up in judgment against you (for be sure that hundreds which you have forgotten are hoarded up for some Curl or Philips of the next generation), and you will be convicted of a double dealing, which, though you do not design, you certainly do practice. And now that I *am* writing affectionately *more meo*, I will let out a little more. You say in yours to Sara that you love and honor me. Upon my soul I believe you; but if I did not thoroughly believe it before, your saying so is the thing of all things that

* Mr. Clarkson.

* Of Nether Stoway, Somersetshire; at that time officially employed in superintending an inquiry into the state of the poor in England and Wales.

would make me open my eyes and look about me to see if I were not deceived. Perhaps I am too intolerant to these kind of phrases; but, indeed, when they are true, they may be excused, and when they are not, there is no excuse for them.

"—— was always looking for such things, but he was a foul feeder, and my moral stomach loathes any thing like froth. There is a something outlandish in saying them, more akin to a French embrace than an English shake by the hand, and I would have you leave off saying them to those whom you actually do love, that if this should not break off the habit of applying them to indifferent persons, the disuse may at least make a difference. Your feelings go naked; I cover mine with a bear-skin: I will not say that you harden yours by your mode, but I am sure that mine are the warmer for their clothing. * * * It is possible, or probable, that I err as much as you in an opposite extreme, and may make enemies where you would make friends; but there is a danger that you may sometimes excite dislike in persons of whose approbation you would yourself be desirous. You know me well enough to know in what temper this has been written, and to know that it has been some exertion; for the same habit which makes me prefer sitting silent to offering contradiction, makes me often withhold censure when, perhaps, in strictness of moral duty, it ought to be applied. The medicine might have been sweetened, perhaps; but, dear Coleridge, take the simple bitters, and leave the sweetmeats by themselves.

"That ugly-nosed Godwin has led me to this. I dare say he deserved all you gave him; in fact, I have never forgiven him his abuse of William Taylor, and do now regret, with some compunction, that in my reviewal of his Chaucer I struck out certain passages of well-deserved severity * * * Two days of S. T. C.'s time given to ——. Another Antonio! If we are to give account for every idle hour, what will you say to this lamentable waste? Or do you expect to have them allowed to you in your purgatory score? * * * If he had not married again, I would have still have had some bowels of compassion for him; but to take another wife with the picture of Mary Woolstonecroft in his house! Agh! I am never ashamed of letting out my *dislikes*, however, and what is a good thing, never afraid; so let him abuse me, and we'll be at war.

"I wish you had called on Longman. That man has a kind heart of his own, and I wish you to think so: the letter he sent me was a proof of it. Go to one of his Saturday evenings: you will see a coxcomb or two, and a dull fellow or two; but you will perhaps meet Turner and Duppa, and Duppa is worth knowing. Make yourself known to him in my name, and tell him how glad I should be to show him the lakes. I have some hope, from Rickman's letter, that you may see William Taylor in town: that would give me great pleasure, for I am very desirous that you should meet. For universal knowledge, I believe he stands quite unrivaled: his conversation is a perpetual spring of living water; and then, in every relation of life, so excellent is he, that I know not any man who, in the circle of his friends, is so entirely and deservedly beloved."

To Grosvenor C. Bedford, Esq.

"March 8, 1804.

"I have not the Spanish Gil Blas. Such a book exists, but, if I remember rightly, with the suspicious phrase *restored* to the Spaniards, which may imply a retranslation of what they say is translated. Yet it is very likely that the story is originally Spanish, and, indeed, if the Spaniards claim it, I am ready to believe them, they being true men, and Le Sage's being a Frenchman strong reason for suspecting him to be a thief; however, if he has stolen, there can be no doubt that he has tinkered old metal into a better shape, and I should think your time ill employed in Englishing what every body reads in French.

"And now let me tell you what to do for me, and how to do it.*

"Take half a quatrain, or a whole one doubled; write, as a title, the name of the poet in question; then, under that, the time or *place* of his birth, when discoverable, and the time of his death. After that, a brief notice of his life and works to the average length of a Westminster theme, as much shorter as his demerits deserve, as much longer as apt anecdotes or the humor of pointed and rememberable criticism may tempt your pen. * * * * * * Now for a list of those whom I can turn over to your care at once:

"Henderson—this you will do *con amore*.

"Garrick—Tom D'Urfey—Tom Browne.

"Cary, the author of Chrononhotonthologus —see if his namby-pamby be of suitable brevity; the Biographia and a Biog. Dictionary will be sufficient guides. Lady M. W. Montague, Stephen Duck—kill off these, and put them by till I see you; and kill them off, the faster the better, that you may fall upon more; for so much labor as you do, so much am I saved, which is very good for both of us, says Dr. Southey.

"Great news at Keswick: a firing heard off the Isle of Man at four o'clock in the morning yesterday! The French are a coming, a coming, a coming—and what care we? We, who have eighteen volunteers, and an apothecary at their head! Did I ever tell you of De Paddy, one of the 'United,' who was sent to serve on board Tom's ship last war? The first day of his service, he had to carry the plum pudding for the dinner of his mess, and the Patrician had never seen a plum pudding before; he came holding it up in triumph, and exclaimed, in perfect ecstasy, 'Och! your sowls! look here! if dis be war, may it never be paice!' * * * *

"No time for more; farewell!

"R. SOUTHEY."

---

* See p. 173.

To S. T. Coleridge, Esq.

"Greta Hall, March 12, 1804.

"Your going abroad appeared to me so doubtful, or, indeed, so improbable an event, that the certainty comes on me like a surprise, and I feel at once what a separation the sea makes. When we get beyond the reach of mail coaches, then, indeed, distance becomes a thing perceptible. I shall often think, Coleridge, *Quanto minus est cum reliquis versari quam tui meminisse!* God grant you a speedy passage, a speedy recovery, and a speedy return! I will write regularly and often; but I know by Danvers how irregularly letters arrive, and at how tedious a time after their date. Look in old Knolles before you go, and read the Siege of Malta: it will make you feel that you are going to visit sacred ground. I can hardly think of that glorious defense without tears. * * * * * *

"You would rejoice with me were you now at Keswick, at the tidings that a box of books is safely harbored in the Mersey, so that for the next fortnight I shall be more interested in the news of Fletcher* than of Bonaparte. It contains some duplicates of the lost cargo; among them, the collection of the oldest Spanish poems, in which is a metrical romance upon the Cid. I shall sometimes want you for a Gothic etymology. Talk of the happiness of getting a great prize in the lottery! What is that to the opening a box of books! The joy upon lifting up the cover must be something like what we shall feel when Peter the Porter opens the door up stairs, and says, Please to walk in, sir. That I shall never be paid for my labor according to the current value of time and labor, is tolerably certain; but if any one should offer me £10,000 to forego that labor, I should bid him and his money go to the devil, for twice the sum could not purchase me half the enjoyment. It will be a great delight to me in the next world to take a fly and visit these old worthies, who are my only society here, and to tell them what excellent company I found them here at the lakes of Cumberland two centuries after they had been dead and turned to dust. In plain truth, I exist more among the dead than the living, and think more about them, and, perhaps, feel more about them. * * * * * * * Moses has quite a passion for drawing, strong enough to be useful were he a little older. When I visit London I will set him up in drawing-books. He was made quite happy yesterday by two drawings of Charles Fox, which happened to be in my desk, and to be just fit for him. The dissected map of England gives him his fill of delight, and he now knows the situation of all the counties in England as well as any one in the house, or, indeed, in the kingdom. I have promised him Asia: it is a pity that Africa and America are so badly divided as to be almost useless, for this is an excellent way of learning geography, and I know by experience that what is so learned is never forgotten. * * * You would be amused to see the truly Catholic horror he feels at the Jews, because they do not eat pork and ham, on which account he declares he never will be an old clothes man. Sara is as fond of me as Dapper is, which is saying a good deal. As for Johnny Wordsworth, I expect to see him *walk* over very shortly: he is like the sons of the Anakim. No M. Post yesterday, none to-day—vexatious after the last French news. I should not suppose Moreau guilty; he is too cautious a general to be so imprudent a man. * * * *

"God bless you! R. S."

To S. T. Coleridge, Esq.

"Greta Hall, March 14, 1804.

"Your departure hangs upon me with something the same effect that the heavy atmosphere presses upon you—an unpleasant thought, that works like yeast, and makes me feel the animal functions going on. As for the manner of your going, you will be, on the whole, better off than in a king's ship. Now you are your own master; there you would have been a *guest*, and, of course, compelled to tolerate the worst of all possible society, except that of soldier-officers.

"I had hopes of seeing you in London; for almost as soon as Edith is safe in bed, if safe she be (for my life has been so made up of sudden changes that I never even mentally look to what is to happen without that if, and the optative *utinam*)—as soon, I say, as that takes place, I shall hurry to town, principally to put to press this book of Specimens, which can only be finished there, for you will stare at the catalogue of dead authors whom I shall have to resurrectionize. This will be a very curious and useful book of mine: how much the worse it will be for your voyage to Malta, few but myself will feel. If it sells, I shall probably make a supplementary volume to Ellis's, to include the good pieces which he has overlooked, for he has not selected well, and, perhaps, to analyze the epics and didactics, which nobody reads. Had I conceived that you would think of transcribing any part of Madoc, you should have been spared the trouble; but, in writing to you, it has always appeared to me better to *write* than to *copy*, the mere babble having the recommendation that it is exclusively your own, and created for you, and in this the feeling of exclusive property goes for something. The poem shall be sent out to you, if there be a chance of its reaching you; but will you not have left Malta by the time a book to be published about New Year's Day can arrive there?

"Had you been with me, I should have talked with you about a preface; as it is, it will be best simply to state, and as briefly as possible, what I have aimed at in my style, and wherein, in my own judgment, I have succeeded or failed. Longman has announced it, in his Cyclopædic List, under the title of an epic poem, which I assuredly shall not affix to it myself: the name, of which I was once over-fond, has nauseated me, and, moreover, should seem to render me ame-

* The name of a Keswick carrier.

nable to certain laws which I do not acknowledge.

"If I were at Malta, the siege of that illustrious island should have a poem, and a good one too; and you ought to think about it, for of all sieges that ever have been or ever will be, it was the most glorious, and called forth the noblest heroism. Look after some modern Greek books; in particular, the poem from which the Teseide of Boccaccio and the Knight's Tale are derived; if, indeed, it be not a translation from the Italian. Could you lay hand on some of these old books, and on *old* Italian poetry, by selling them at Leigh and Sotheby's you might lmost pay your travels.

"More manuscripts of Davis come down today. I have run through his Life of Chatterton, which is flimsy and worthless. I shall *not* advise Longman to print it, and shall *warn* the writer to expunge an insult to you and to myself, which is not to be paid for by his praise. We formed a just estimate of the man's moral stamina, most certainly, and as for man-mending, I have no hopes of it. The proverb of the silk purse and the sow's ear comprises my philosophy upon that subject.

"I write rapidly and unthinkingly, to be in time for the post. Why have you not made Lamb declare war upon Mrs. Bare-bald? He should singe her flaxen wig with squibs, and tie crackers to her petticoats till she leaped about like a parched pea for very torture. There is not a man in the world who could so well revenge himself. The Annual Review (that is, the first vol.) came down in my parcel to-day. My articles are wickedly misprinted, and, in many instances, made completely nonsensical. If I could write Latin even as I could once, perhaps I should talk to Longman of publishing a collection of the best modern Latin poets: they were *dulli canes* many of them, but a poor fellow who has spent years and years in doing his best to be remembered, does deserve well enough of posterity to be reprinted once in every millennium, and, in fact, there are enough good ones to form a collection of some extent.

"God bless you! prays your old friend and brother, R. SOUTHEY."

To John Rickman, Esq.

"Keswick, March 30, 1804.

"MY DEAR RICKMAN,

"Turner wrote to me and complained heavily of Scotch criticism, which he seems to feel too much. Such things only provoke me to interject Fool! and Booby! seasoned with the participle damnatory; but as for being vexed at a review—I should as soon be fevered by a flea-bite! I sent him back a letter of encouragement and stimulant praise, for these rascals had so affected him as to slacken his industry. I look upon the invention of reviews to be the worst injury which literature has received since its revival. People formerly took up a book to learn from it, and with a feeling of respectful thankfulness to the man who had spent years in acquiring that knowledge, which he communicates to them in a few hours; now they only look for faults. Every body is a critic; that is, every reader imagines himself superior to the author, and reads his book that he may censure it, not that he may improve by it. * *

"You are in great measure right about Coleridge; he is worse in body than you seem to believe; but the main cause lies in his own management of himself, or, rather, want of management. His mind is in a perfect St. Vitus's dance—eternal activity without action. At times he feels mortified that he should have done so little; but this feeling never produces any exertion. I will begin to-morrow, he says, and thus he has been all his life-long letting to-day slip. He has had no heavy calamities in life, and so contrives to be miserable about trifles. Poor fellow! there is no one thing which gives me so much pain as the witnessing such a waste of unequaled power. I knew one man resembling him, save that with equal genius he was actually a vicious man.

"If that man had common prudence, he must have been the first man in this country, from his natural and social advantages, and as such, we who knew him and loved him at school used to anticipate him. I learned more from his conversation than any other man ever taught me, because the rain fell when the young plant was just germinating and wanted it most; and I learned more morality by his example than any thing else could have taught me, for I saw him wither away. He is dead and buried at the Cape of Good Hope, and has left behind him nothing to keep his memory alive. A few individuals only remember him with a sort of horror and affection, which just serves to make them melancholy whenever they think of him or mention his name. This will not be the case with Coleridge; the *disjecta membra* will be found if he does not die early; but, having so much to do, so many errors to weed out of the world which he is capable of eradicating, if he does not die without doing his work, it would half break my heart, for no human being has had more talents allotted.

"Wordsworth will do better, and leave behind him a name unique in his way. He will rank among the very first poets, and probably possesses a mass of merits superior to all, except only Shakspeare. This is doing much, yet would he be a happier man if he did more.

"I am made very happy by a re-enforcement of folios from Lisbon, and I shall feel some reluctance in leaving them, and breaking off work to go for London to a more trifling employment; however, my History is to be considered as the capital laid by—the savings of industry; and you would think me entitled to all the praise industry can merit, were you to see the pile of papers. * * * * *

"Vale! R. S."

To Grosvenor C. Bedford, Esq.

"Greta Hall, March 31, 1804.

"DEAR GROSVENOR,

"* * * I am bound for London,

chiefly to complete these Specimens and put them to press. Alas! for your unhappy habit of procrastination! 'Don't delay,' you write in your postscript, and this in answer to a letter which had lain above a fortnight in your desk! Here it happens to be of no moment; but you tell me the habit has produced and is producing worse consequences. I would give you advice if it could be of use; but there is no curing those who choose to be diseased. A good man and a wise man may at times be angry with the world, at times grieved for it; but be sure no man was ever discontented with the world if he did his duty in it. If a man of education who has health, eyes, hands, and leisure, wants an object, it is only because God Almighty has bestowed all those blessings upon a man who does not deserve them. Dear Grosvenor, I wish you may feel half the pain in reading this that I do in writing it. * * * * * *

"There!

"And what shall I say after this? for this bitter pill will put your mouth out of taste for whatever insipidities I might have had to offer; only the metaphor reminds me of a scheme of mine, which is to improve cookery by *chemical tuning*, making every dish prepare the palate for that which is to come next; and this reminds me that I have discovered most poignant and good galvanism in drinking water out of an iron cup: how far this may improve fermented liquors remains to be experimented. The next time you see a pump with an iron ladle thereunto appended, stop, though it be on Cornhill, and drink and try.

"I am very happy, having this week received the oldest poem in the Castilian language, and the oldest code of Gothic laws, and a re-enforcement of folios besides, containing the history of Portugal from the Creation down to 1400 A.D. God bless you!

"Yours very affectionately, R. S."

To John Rickman, Esq.

"March, 1804.

"Dear Rickman,

"* * * * * * *

I have more in hand than Bonaparte or Marquis Wellesley—digesting Gothic law, gleaning moral history from monkish legends, and conquering India, or rather Asia, with Albuquerque; filling up the chinks of the day by hunting in Jesuit chronicles, and compiling Collectanea Hispanica et Gothica. Meantime Madoc sleeps, and my lucre of gain compilation* goes on at night, when I am fairly obliged to lay history aside, because it perplexes me in my dreams. 'Tis a vile thing to be pestered in sleep with all the books I have been reading in the day jostled together. God bless you! R. S."

To Grosvenor C. Bedford, Esq.

"April 23, 1804.

"Dear Grosvenor,

"I thought to have seen you before this time, and am daily, indeed hourly, in anticipation of being able to say when I set out. You know that I design to take up with me the first part of Madoc, and leave it with the printer. Now have I been thinking that your worship would, perhaps, be not unwilling to stand man-midwife upon the occasion, and be appointed grand plenipotentiary over commas, semicolons, and periods. My books have all suffered by misprinting. In fact, there is a lurking hope at the bottom of this request, that when you have once been brought into a habit of dealing with the devil on my account, you may be induced to deal with him on your own.

"I shall bring up with me as much toward the Specimens as can be supplied by Anderson's Collection, Cibber's Lives, and an imperfect series of the European Magazine. The names omitted in these may, beyond all doubt, be supplied from the obituary in the Gentleman's Magazine, *alias* the Oldwomania, a work which I have begun to take in here at Keswick, to enlighten a Portuguese student among the mountains, and which does amuse me by its exquisite inanity, and the glorious and intense stupidity of its correspondents; it is, in truth, a disgrace to the age and the country. My list of names is already long enough to prove that there will be some difficulty in getting at all the volumes requisite, not that it is or can be a matter of conscience to read through all the dull poetry of every rhymester. The language of vituperation or criticism has not yet been so systematized as to afford terms for every shade of distinction. I had an idea of applying the botanical nomenclature to novels, and dividing them into monogynia, monandria, cryptogamia, &c., but for poems the pun will not hold good.

"'Tis a long way to London! I wish I were on my way, and then shall I wish myself arrived, and then be wishing myself back again; for complete rest, absolute, unprospective, rooted rest, is the great object of my desires. Near London must be my final settlement, unless any happy and unforeseen fortune should enable me to move to the south, and thus take a longer lease of life; in fact, if I could afford the money sacrifice, I would willingly make the other, and keep my History unpublished all my life, that I might pass it in Portugal. Society, connections, native language—all these are weighty things; but what are they to the permanent and perpetual exhilaration of a climate that not merely prolongs life, but gives you double the life while it lasts? I have actually felt a positive pleasure in breathing there; and even here, in this magnificent spot, the recollection of the Tagus, and the Serra de Ossa; of Coimbra, and its cypresses, and orange groves, and olives, its hills and mountains, its venerable buildings, and its dear river; of the Vale of Algarve, the little islands of beauty amid the desert of Alentejo, and, above all, of Cintra, the most blessed spot in the habitable globe, will almost bring tears into my eyes.

"Vale!

R. S."

* Specimens of English Poets.

To Mrs. Southey.

"Palace Yard, May 10, 1804.

"MY DEAR EDITH,

"Safe, sound, and rested sufficiently—this is the best information; and if you can send me as complete an 'all's well' in return, heartily glad shall I be to receive it.

"On Friday I dined with * * At six that evening got into the coach; slept at Warrington; breakfasted at Stowe; dined at Birmingham; slept at Stratford-upon-Avon: in the dark we reached that place, so that I could not see Shakspeare's grave, but I will return that road on purpose. At five, on Sunday morning, we arrived in Oxford, and I walked through it at that quiet and delightful hour, and thought of the past and the present. We did not reach London till after five last evening, so that I was forty-eight hours in the coach. I landed at the White Horse Cellar: no coach was to be procured, and I stood in all the glory of my filth beside my trunk, at the Cellar door, in my spencer of the cut of 1798 (for so long is it since it was made), and my dirty trowsers, while an old fellow hunted out a porter for me. For about five minutes I waited; the whole mob of Park loungers and Kensington Garden buckery, male and female, were passing by in all their finery, and all looked askance on me. Well, off I set at last, and soon found my spencer was the wonderful part of my appearance. I stopped at the top of St. James's Street, just before a group, who all turned round to admire me, pulled it off, and gave it to my dirty porter, and exhibited as genteel a black coat as ever Joe Aikin made. * * * * * * They have inserted my account of Malthus instead of William Taylor's, for which, as you know, I am sorry, and also preferred my account of poor Ritson's romance to one which Walter Scott volunteered. Scott, it seems, has shown his civility by reviewing Amadis here and in the Edinburgh, which I had rather he had left alone; for, though very civil, and in the right style of civility, he yet denies my conclusion respecting the author, without alleging one argument, or shadow of argument, against the positive evidence adduced. * * * Bard Williams is in town, so I shall shake one honest man by the hand whom I did not expect to see.

"God bless you!

"Yours affectionately, R. SOUTHEY."

To Mrs. Southey.

"London, May 16, 1804.

"MY DEAR EDITH,

"A. Aikin had need send me certain complimentary sugar-plums: he has cut out some of my bitterest and best sentences, and has rejected my reviewal of his father's Letters on the English Poets, to make room for something as Bare-bald* as the book itself. However, no wonder; there must be a commander-in-chief, and the Annual Review has at least as good, or better, than either army, navy, or government in England.

"You should have seen my interview with Hyde. I was Eve, he the tempter: could I resist Hyde's eloquence? A coat, you know, was predetermined; but my waistcoat was *shameful.* I yielded; and yielded also to a calico under-waistcoat, to give the *genteel fullness* which was requisite. This was not all. Hyde pressed me further: delicate patterns for pantaloons—they make gaiters of the same; it would not soil, and it would wash. I yielded, and am to-morrow to be completely hyded in coat, waistcoat, under-waistcoat, pantaloons, and gaiters, and shall go forth, like ——, conquering and to conquer. If Mrs. —— should see me! and in my new hat —for I have a new hat—and my new gloves. O Jozé! I will show myself to Johnny Cockbain* for the benefit of the North. Davy talks of going to the lakes with Sir G. Beaumont, probably, and, in that case, soon. Elmsley talks of going in the autumn, and wishes me to accompany him to Edinburgh. Wynn wants me in Wales, and would fetch me. I can not be in two places at once, and must not be cut in half, for to Solomon's decision I have an objection. * * * * * * * * * I shall desire A. Aikin, my commander, to ship me down a huge cargo, that I may get at least fifty pounds for next year, and look to that for a supply in April. In the foreign one which he proposes, I will not take any active part: it will take more time, and yield less money in proportion. The whole article upon Peter Bayley is in, in all its strength. * * * * I perfectly long to be at home again, and home I will be at the month's end, God willing, for business *shall not* stand in my way. I will do all that is possible next week and the beginning of the following, and then lay such a load upon Dapple's back as he never trudged under before. He shall work, a lazy, long-eared animal, he shall work, or the printer's devil shall tease him out of his very soul.† * * * *

"Dear Edith, how weary I am! God bless you! R. S."

To Mrs. Southey.

"London, May, 1804.

" * * * * * * * * * The Thames is ebbing fast before the window, and a beautiful sight it is, dear Edith; but I wish I were upon the banks of the Greta! I will not remain an hour longer than can be helped. You have no notion of the intolerable fatigue it is to walk all day and not get to bed till after midnight. * * * * * * I have lost a grand triumph over you, Edith. Had you seen me in my Hyde when I tried it, you would never have sent me to a London hyde-maker again. The sleeves are actually as large as the thighs of my pantaloons, and cuffs to them like what old men wear in a comedy. I am sure, if I were a country farmer, and caught such

* See page 177.

* A Keswick tailor.

† These kind intentions refer to the Specimens of the English poets, and were directed toward Mr. Bedford, who had long borne very patiently the flattering appellation here given him.

a barebones as myself in such a black sack, I would stick him up for a scarecrow.

"I saw Longman yesterday, who was very glad to see me. I am trying to make him publish a collection of the scarce old English poets, which will be the fittest thing in the world for Lamb to manage, if he likes it; or, perhaps, to manage with my co-operation. The Amadis sells not amiss; the edition, they say, will go off. Thalaba goes off slowly, but is going. They got me W. Taylor's review, which is very characteristic of his style, talents, and good will for the author. I will bring down the number.

* * * * * * *

"On Thursday Carlisle gives me a dinner. There must be one day for Turner; and as for all my half a thousand acquaintances, they may ask till they are blind, for I won't go. I might live all the year here by being invited out as a show, but I will not show myself. I write you very unsatisfactory letters, dear Edith, but you know how like a bear with a sore head this place makes me; and never was I more uncomfortable in it, though with a pleasanter house over my head than ever, and better company.

"God bless you! R. S."

To John Rickman, Esq.

"Keswick, June 6, 1802.

"Dear Rickman,

"Here I am at length, at least all that remains of me—the skin and bones of Robert Southey. Being now at rest, and, moreover, egregiously hungry, the flesh which has been expended in stage-coaches and in London streets will soon be replaced. *Dulce est actorum meminisse—laborum* will not so fully conclude the line as my meaning wishes. Labor enough I had; but there are other things besides my labor in London to be remembered—more pleasurable in themselves, but not making such pleasurable recollections, because they are to be wished for again.

"However, I found excellent society awaiting me at home: Florian de Ocampo and Ambrosio Novales—thirteen of the little quartos, bringing down Spanish history to the point where Prudencio de Sandoval takes it up, and where I also begin the full tide of my narration. Novales was the correspondent of Reserdius, into whose work you once looked, and was, like him, an excellent Latinist, and a patient, cautious, martyr-murdering antiquary, an excellent weeder of lies wherever they were to be found. In company with these came the four folios of the Bibliotheca Hispanica: there is affixed a portrait of the late king, so exquisitely engraved and so exquisitely ugly, that I know not whether it be most honorable to Spain to have advanced so far in the arts, or disgraceful to have exercised them upon such a fool's pate. I am sure Duppa would laugh at his Catholic majesty, but whether an interjection of admiration at that print, or the laugh (which is the next auxiliary part of speech to the ohs and ahs, interjections), will come first, is only to be decided by experiment.

* * * * * * *

"You will read the Mabinogion, concerning which I ought to have talked to you. In the last, that most odd and Arabian-like story of the Mouse, mention is made of a begging scholar, that helps to the date; but where did the Kimbri get the imagination that could produce such a tale! That enchantment of the basin hanging by the chain from heaven is in the wildest spirit of the Arabian Nights. I am perfectly astonished that such fictions should exist in Welsh: they throw no light on the origin of romance, every thing being utterly dissimilar to what we mean by that term; but they do open a new world of fiction; and if the date of their language be fixed about the twelfth or thirteenth century, I can not but think the mythological substance is of far earlier date, very probably brought from the East by some of the first settlers or conquerors. If William Owen will go on and publish them, I have hopes that the world will yet reward him for his labors. Let Sharon* make his language grammatical, but not alter their idiom in the slightest point. I will advise him about this, being about to send him off a parcel of old German or Theotistic books of Coleridge's, which will occasion a letter. * * *

"God bless you! R. S."

To S. T. Coleridge, Esq.

"June 11, 1804, Keswick.

"Dear Coleridge,

"The first news of you was from Lamb's letter, which arrived when I was in London. I saw, also, your letter to Stuart, and heard of one to Tobin, before I returned and found my own. Ere this you are at Malta. What an infectious thing is irregularity! Merely because it was uncertain when a letter could set off, I have always yielded to the immediate pressure of other employment; whereas, had there been a day fixed for the mail, to have written would then have been a fixed business, and performed like an engagement.

"All are well—Sara and Sariola, Moses and Justiculus, Edith and the Edithling. Mary is better.

"I was worn to the very bone by fatigue in London—more walking in one day than I usually take in a month; more waste of breath in talking than serves for three months' consumption in the country; add to this a most abominable cold, affecting chest, head, eyes, and nose. It was impossible to see half the persons whom I wished to see, and ought to have seen, without prolonging my stay to an inconvenient time, and an unreasonable length of absence from home. I called upon Sir George† unsuccessfully, and received a note that evening, saying he would be at home the following morning; then I saw him, and his lady, and his pictures, and afterward met him the same day at dinner at Davy's. As he immediately left town, this was all our intercourse, and as it is not likely that he will visit the lakes this year, probably will be all.

* Sharon Turner, Esq. † Sir George Beaumont.

"I went into the Exhibition merely to see your picture, which perfectly provoked me. Hazlitt's does look as if you were on your trial, and certainly had stolen the horse; but then you did it cleverly: it had been a deep, well-laid scheme, and it was no fault of yours that you had been detected. But this portrait by Northcote looks like a grinning idiot; and the worst is, that it is just like enough to pass for a good likeness with those who only know your features imperfectly. Dance's drawing has that merit at least, that nobody would ever suspect you of having been the original. Poole's business will last yet some weeks. As the Abstract is printed, I can give you the very important result: one in eight throughout Great Britain receives permanent parish pay;* what is still more extraordinary and far more consolatory, one in nine is engaged in some benefit society—a prodigious proportion, if you remember that, in this computation, few women enter, and no children.

"I dined with Sotheby, and met there Henley, a man every way to my taste. Sotheby was very civil, and as his civility has not that smoothness so common among the vagabonds of fashion, I took it in good part. He is what I should call a clever man. Other lions were Price, the picturesque man, and Davies Giddy, whose face ought to be perpetuated in marble for the honor of mathematics. Such a forehead I never saw. I also met Dr. —— at dinner, who, after a long silence, broke out into a discourse upon the properties of the conjunction *Quam*. Except his quamical knowledge, which is as profound as you will imagine, he knows nothing but bibliography, or the science of title-pages, impresses, and dates. It was a relief to leave him, and find his brother, the captain, at Rickman's, smoking after supper, and letting out puffs at the one corner of his mouth and puns at the other. The captain hath a son—begotten, according to Lamb, upon a mermaid; and thus far is certain, that he is the queerest fish out of water. A paralytic affection in childhood has kept one side of his face stationary, while the other has continued to grow, and the two sides form the most ridiculous whole you can imagine; the boy, however, is a sharp lad, the inside not having suffered.

"William Owen lent me three parts of the Mabinogion, most delightfully translated into so Welsh an idiom and syntax that such a translation is as instructive (except for etymology) as an original. I was, and am, still utterly at a loss to devise by what possible means fictions so perfectly like the Arabian Tales in character, and yet so indisputably of Cimbric growth, should have grown up in Wales. Instead of throwing light upon the origin of romance, as had been surmised, they offer a new problem, of almost impossible solution. Bard Williams communicated to me some fine arcana of bardic mythology, quite new to me and to the world, which you will find in Madoc. I have ventured to lend Turner your German Romances, which will be very useful to him, and which will be replaced on your shelves before your return, and *used*, not *abused*,* during your absence. I also sent him the Indian Bible, because I found him at the Indian grammar, for he is led into etymological researches. That is a right worthy and good man; and, what rarely happens, I like his wife as well as I do him. Sir, all the literary journals of England will not bring you more news than this poor sheet of Miss Crosthwaite's letter paper. I have proposed to Longman to publish a collection of the scarcer and better old poets, beginning with Pierce Ploughman, and to print a few only at a high price, that they may sell as rarities. This he will determine upon in the autumn. If it be done, my name must stand to the prospectus, and Lamb shall take the job and the emolument, for whom, in fact, I invented it, being a fit thing to be done, and he the fit man to do it.

"The Annual Review succeeds beyond expectation: a second edition of the first volume is called for. Certain articles respecting the Methodists and Malthus are said to have contributed much to its reputation. By-the-by, that fellow has had the impudence to marry, after writing upon the miseries of population. In the third volume I shall fall upon the Society for the Suppression of Vice.

"Thus far had I proceeded yesterday, designing to send off the full sheet by that night's post, when Wordsworth arrived, and occasioned one day's delay. I have left him talking to Moses, and mounted to my own room to finish. What news, you will wish to ask, of Keswick? The house remains *in statu quo*, except that the little parlor is painted, and papered with cartridge paper. Workmen to plaster this room could not be procured when Jackson sent for them, and so unplastered it is likely to remain another winter. A great improvement has been made by thinning the trees before the parlor window. Just enough of the lake can be seen through such a framework, and such a fretted canopy of foliage as to produce a most delightful scene, and utterly unlike any other view of the same subject. The lakers begin to make their appearance, though none have, as yet, reached us; but Sharpe has announced his approach in a letter to W. We are in hourly expectation of Harry; and in the course of the year I expect Duppa to be my guest, and probably Elmsley.

"God bless you! R. S."

To Lieut. Southey, H.M.S. Galatea.

"June 27, 1804, Keswick.

"'Tis a heartless thing, dear Tom, to write from this distance, and at this uncertainty, the more so when I recollect how many letters of mine were sent to the West Indies when you were last there, which never reached you. Two packets, say the papers, have been taken; and

* This seems almost incredible.

* This was a gentle hint to Mr. Coleridge, who valued books none the less for being somewhat ragged and dirty, and did not take the same scrupulous care as my father to prevent their becoming so.

if so, two of my epistles are now deeper down than your sounding-lines have ever fathomed—unless, indeed, some shark has swallowed and digested bags and bullets. We are uneasy at receiving no letter since that which announced your arrival at Barbadoes. I conceived you were at the Surinam expedition, and waited for the Gazette to-day with some unavoidable apprehensions. It has arrived, and I can find no trace of the Galatea, which, though so far satisfactory as that it proves you have not been killed by the Dutchman, leaves me, on the other hand, in doubt what has become of you and your ship. * *

"About the changes in the Admiralty, I must tell you a good thing of W. T. in the Isis: he said it was grubbing up English oak, and planting Scotch fir in its place, for the use of the navy. An excellent good thing! If, however, I am not pleased that Lord Melville should be in, I am heartily glad that his predecessor is out, for no man ever proved himself so utterly unfit for the post. Our home politics are becoming very interesting, and must ultimately lead to the strongest administration ever seen in England. Pitt has played a foolish game in coming in alone: it has exasperated the prince, who is the rising sun to look to, and is playing for the regency.

"The lakers and the fine weather have made their appearance together. As yet we have only seen Sharpe, whose name I know not if you will remember: he is an intimate of Tuffin, or Muffin, whose name you can not forget, and, like him, an excellent talker—knowing every body, remembering every thing, and having strong talents besides. Davy is somewhere on the road. He is recovering from the ill effects of fashionable society, which had warped him. Rickman told me his mind was in a healthier tone than usual, and I was truly rejoiced to find it so. Wordsworth came over to see me on my return, and John Thelwall, the lecturer on elocution, dined with us on his travels. But the greatest event of Greta Hall is, that we have had a jack of two-and-twenty pounds, which we bought at threepence a pound. It was caught in the lake with a hook and line. We dressed it in pieces, like salmon, and it proved, without exception, one of the finest fish I had ever tasted; so, if ever you catch such a one, be sure you boil it instead of roasting it in the usual way. I am in excellent good health, and have got rid of my sore eyes—for how long God knows. The disease, it seems, came from Egypt, and is in some mysterious manner contagious, so that we have naturalized another curse.

"Madoc is in the printer's hands: Ballantyne, of Edinburgh, who printed the Minstrelsy of the Scottish Border—if you remember the book. Next week I expect the first proof. Do not be frightened to hear after this that I have not done a stroke further in correcting and filling up the MSS. since my return. Reviewing is coming round again: I have a parcel upon the road, and groan in spirit at the prospect; not but of all trades it is the least irksome, and the most like my own favorite pursuits, which it certainly must, in a certain degree, assist, as well as, in point of time, retard. There is much of mine in the second volume,* and of my best; some of which you will discover, and some perhaps not. A sixth of the whole is mine—pretty hard work. I get on bravely with my History, and have above three quarto volumes done —quartos as they ought to be, of about 500 *honest* pages each. It does me good to see what a noble pile my boards make.

"My dog Dapper is as fond of me as ever Cupid was: this is a well-bred hound of my landlord's, who never fails to leap upon my back when I put my nose out of doors, and who, never having ventured beyond his own field till I lately tempted him, is the most prodigious coward you ever beheld. He almost knocked Edith down in running away from a pig; but I like him, for he is a worthy dog, and frightens the sauntering lakers as much as the pig frightened him.

"The Scotch reviewers are grown remarkably civil to me, partly because Elmsley was, and partly because Walter Scott is, connected with them. My Amadis and the Chatterton have been noticed very respectfully there. I told you in my last that Amadis sold well—as much in one year as Thalaba in three! But I feel, and my booksellers feel, that I am getting on in the world, and the publication of Madoc will set me still higher.

"How goes on the Spanish? keep to it by all means, for it is not an impossible nor an improbable thing that you and I may one day meet in Portugal, and, if so, take a journey together. You will then find it useful, for it turns readily into Portuguese. My uncle and I keep up a pretty regular intercourse. I am trying to set his affairs here in order. A cargo of books, value about eleven pounds, which were lost for twelve months, have been recovered, and I am feeding upon them. God bless you, Tom! Lose no opportunity of writing. Edith's love.

"R. S."

CHAPTER XI.

FAMILY DETAILS—POLITICS—HE WISHES TO EDIT SIR PHILIP SIDNEY'S WORKS—DR. VINCENT—THE WEST INDIES—SPANISH WAR—WISHES TO GO TO PORTUGAL WITH SIR JOHN MOORE—USE OF REVIEWING—EARLY POEMS, WHY WRITTEN—TRAVELS IN ABYSSINIA—STEEL MIRRORS—SIR W. SCOTT'S NEW POEM—MADOC—THE COMPASS, WHEN FIRST USED—THE DIVING BELL—USES OF PRINTING—CHANGES IN THE CRITICAL REVIEW—LOSS OF THE ABERGAVENNY—ENDOWMENT OF THE ROMISH CHURCH IN IRELAND—TRANSLATION FROM THE LATIN—REASONS FOR NOT GOING TO LONDON—ENGLISH POETRY—PUBLICATION OF MADOC—DUTY UPON FOREIGN BOOKS A GREAT HARDSHIP—STORY

* Of the Annual Review.

OF PELAYO—THE BUTLER—MADOC CRITICISED AND DEFENDED—REVIEWING—LITERARY REMARKS—LORD SOMERVILLE—SUGGESTION TO HIS BROTHER THOMAS TO COLLECT INFORMATION ABOUT THE WEST INDIES—THE MORAVIANS—VISIT TO SCOTLAND AND TO SIR W. SCOTT AT ASHIESTIEL—REVIEWALS OF MADOC—ESPRIELLA'S LETTERS.

To Lieut. Southey, H.M.S. Galatea.

"Greta Hall, July 30, 1804.

"DEAR TOM,

"Your three letters have arrived all together this evening, and have relieved me from very considerable anxiety. Mine, I find, are consigned to the Atlantic without bottles; and three books of Madoc, which Edith copied in them, gone to edify the sharks—gentlemen who will digest them far more easily than the critics. However, there must be yet some other letters on the way, and I trust you will have learned before this can reach you that I have two Ediths in the family—the Edithling (who was born on the last of April) continuing to do well, only that I am myself somewhat alarmed at that premature activity of eye and spirits, and those sudden startings, which were in her poor sister the symptoms of a dreadful and deadly disease. However, I am on my guard. * * * * * I did not mean to trust my affections again on so frail a foundation; and yet the young one takes me from my desk, and makes me talk nonsense as fluently as you perhaps can imagine.

"Both Edith and I are well; indeed, I have weathered a rude winter and a ruder spring bravely. Harry is here, and has been here about three weeks, and will remain till the end of October. He is a very excellent companion, and tempts me out into the air and the water when I should else be sitting at home. We have made our way well in the world, Tom, thus far, and, by God's help, we shall yet get on better. Make your fortune, and Joe may yet live to share its comforts, as he stands upon his majesty's books in my name, though degraded by the appellation of mongrel. Madoc is in a Scotch press: Ballantyne's, who printed the Minstrelsy of the Scottish Borders—a book which you may remember I bought at Bristol.

"You ask of Amadis: it has been well reviewed, both in the Annual and Edinburgh, by Walter Scott, who in both has been very civil to me. Of all my later publications, this has been the most successful, more than 500 of the 1000 having sold within the year, so that there is a fair chance of the £50 dependent upon the sale of the whole. Thalaba has been very admirably reviewed in the Critical by William Taylor; but it does not sell, and will not for some years reach a second edition. Reviewing is coming round again! one parcel arrived! another on the road! a third ready to start! I grudge the time thus to be sold sorely; but patience! it is, after all, better than pleading in a stinking court of law, or being called up at midnight to a patient; it is better than being a soldier or a sailor; better than calculating profits and loss on a counter; better, in short, than any thing but independence. * * * *

"July is, indeed, a lovely month at the lakes, and so the lakers seem to think, for they swarm here. We have been much interrupted by visitors—among others, young Roscoe—and more are yet to come. These are not the only interruptions: we have been, or rather are, manufacturing black currant jam for my uncle, and black currant wine for ourselves—Harry and I chief workmen—pounding them in a wooden bowl with a great stone, as the acid acts upon a metal mortar. We have completed a great work in bridging the River Greta at the bottom of the orchard, by piling heaps of stones so as to step from one to another—many a hard hour's sport, half-knee deep in the water. Davy has been here—stark mad for angling This is our history—yours has been busier. As for news, the packet which conveys this will convey later intelligence than it is in my power to communicate. Sir Francis may, and probably will, lose his election, but it is evident he has not lost his popularity. Pitt will go blundering on till every body, by miserable experience, think him what I always did. * * * * Whensoever the great change of ministry, to which we all look on with hope, takes place, I shall have friends in power able to serve me, and shall, in fact, without scruple, apply to Fox through one or two good channels: this may be very remote, and yet may be very near. When Madoc is published, I mean to send Fox a copy, with such a note as may be proper for me to address to such a man. * * * *

"God bless you, Tom! It grows late, and I have two proofs to correct for to-night's post. Once more, God bless you! R. S."

To Lieutenant Southey, H.M.S. Galatea.

"Keswick, Sept. 12, 1804.

"DEAR TOM,

"It is a heartless and hopeless thing to write letter after letter, when there seems so little probability of their ever reaching you. How is it that all your letters seem to find me, and none of mine to find you? I can not comprehend. I write, and write, and write, always directing Barbadoes or elsewhere, and suppose that, according to direction, they go any where elsewhere than to the Galatea.

"My intention is, God willing, to remain here another year, and in the autumn of 1805 to go once more to Lisbon, and there remain one, two, or three years, till my History be well and effectually completed. Meantime, these are my employments: to finish the correcting and printing of Madoc; to get through my annual work of reviewing; and bring my History as far onward as possible. In the press I have, 1. Metrical Tales and other Poems, being merely a corrected republication of my best pieces from the Anthology. 2. Specimens of the later English Poets, *i. e.*, of all who have died from 1685 to 1800:

this is meant as a supplement to George Ellis's Specimens of the Early Poets—a book which you may remember at Bristol: it will fill two vols. in crown octavo, the size of Ritson's Engleish Romanceës, if you recollect them. 3. Madoc, in quarto, whereof twenty-two sheets are printed; one more finishes the first part.

"Harry has been here since the beginning of July, and will yet remain about six weeks longer. We mountaineerify together, and bathe together, and go on the lake together, and have contrived to pass a delightful summer. I am learning Dutch, and wish you were here to profit by the lessons at the breakfast-table, and to mynheerify with me, as you like the language. My reason for attaining the language is, that as the Dutch conquered, or rather destroyed, the Portuguese empire in Asia, the history of the downfall of that empire is, of course, more fully related by Dutch than by Portuguese historians.

"You ask for politics. I can tell you little. The idea of invasion still continues the same humbug and bugbear as when it was first bruited abroad, to gull the people on both sides of the water. Bonaparte dares not attempt it—would to God he did! Defeat would be certain, and his ruin inevitable: as it is, he must lose reputation by threatening what he can not execute; and I believe that the Bourbons will finally be restored. At home, politics look excellently well; the coalition of Fox and the Grenvilles has been equally honorable to all parties, and produced the best possible effects in rooting out the last remains of that political violence which many years so divided the country. The death of the king, or another fit of madness, which is very probable; or his abdication, which most persons think would be very proper; or the declining health of Pitt, or the actual strength of the opposition, are things of which every one is very likely to bring the coalition into power, and in that case neither you nor I should want friends. So live in hope, as you have good cause to do. Steer clear of the sharks and the land-crabs, and be sure that we shall both of us one day be as well off as we can wish.

"The H——'s are visiting Colonel Peachy, whose wife was also of Bishop Lydiard—a Miss Charter: both she and her sister knew you well by name. We are getting upon excellently good terms; for they are very pleasant and truly womanly women, which is the best praise that can be bestowed upon a woman. Will you not laugh to hear that I have actually been employed all the morning in making arrangements for a subscription ball at Keswick? I! very I! your brother, R. S.! To what vile purposes may we come! It was started by Harry and Miss Charter at the theater (for we have a strolling company at an ale-house here), and he, and I, and General Peche have settled it; and all Cumberland will now envy the gayeties of Keswick. Mrs. General insisted upon my opening the ball with her. I advised her, as she was for performing impossibilities, to begin with turning the wind before she could hope to turn me; so I shall sip my tea, and talk with the old folks some hour or so, and then steal home to write Madoc, drink my solitary glass of punch, and get to bed at a good Christian-like hour, as my father, and no doubt his father, did before me. Oh, Tom, that you were but here! for, in truth, we lead as pleasant a life as heart of man could wish. I have not for years taken such constant exercise as this summer. Some friend or acquaintance or other is perpetually making his appearance, and out then I go to lackey them on the lake or over the mountains. I shall get a character for politeness!

"I have so far altered my original plan of the History as to resolve upon not introducing the life of St. Francisco, and the chapters therewith connected, but to reserve them for a separate history of Monachism, which will make a very interesting and amusing work: a good honest quarto may comprise it. My whole historical labors will then consist of three separate works: 1. Hist. of Portugal—the European part, 3 vols. 2. Hist. of the Portuguese Empire in Asia, 2 or 3 vols. 3. Hist. of Brazil. 4. Hist. of the Jesuits in Japan. 5. Literary History of Spain and Portugal, 2 vols. 6. History of Monachism. In all, ten, eleven, or twelve quarto volumes; and you can not easily imagine with what pleasure I look at all the labor before me. God give me life, health, eyesight, and as much leisure as even now I have, and done it shall be. God bless you!

"R. S."

To Messrs. Longman and Rees.

"Keswick, Nov. 11, 1804.

"Dear Sirs,

" * * * * * * * *

I should like to edit the works of Sir Philip Sidney, who is, in my judgment, one of the greatest men of all our countrymen. I would prefix a Life, an Essay on the Arcadia, his greatest work, and another on his Meters. It would make three octavo volumes: to the one there should be his portrait prefixed; to the second a view of Penshurst, his birth-place and residence; to the third, the print of his death, from Mortimer's well-known etching. Perhaps I overrate the extent of the work; for, if I recollect right, Burton's Anatomy, which is such another folio, was republished in two octavos. His name is so illustrious, that an edition of 500 would certainly sell: the printer might begin in spring. I could write the Essays here. In the autumn I shall most likely be in London, and would then complete the Life, and the book might be published by Christmas of 1805. If you approve the scheme, it may be well to announce it, as we may very probably be forestalled, for this is the age of editors. I design my name to appear, for it would be a pleasure and a pride to have my name connected with that of a man whom I so highly reverence.

Mr. Longman promised me a visit in September. I have not found him so punctual as he will always find me. Believe me, yours truly,

"Robert Southey."

To G. C. Bedford, Esq.

"Keswick, Dec. 1, 1804.

"DEAR GROSVENOR,

"Sir Roger l'Estrange is said, in Cibber's Lives, to have written a great number of poetical works, which are highly praised in an extract from Winstanley. *Ubi sunt?* God knows, among all the titles to his works, I do not see one which looks as if it belonged to a poem; perhaps Hill or Heber may help you out; but the sure store-house in all desperate cases will be the Museum. He has the credit of having written the famous song, 'Cease, rude Boreas,' when in prison: this, however, is only a tradition, and wants evidence sufficient for our purpose. There, sir, is a pussagorical answer to your pussechism. * * * * * If you are in the habit of calling on Vincent, you may do me a service by inquiring whether a MS. of Giraldus Cambrensis, designated by Cave, in his Historia Litteraria, as the Codex Westmonast, be in the Dean and Chapter Library; for this MS. contains a map of Wales as subsisting in his time, and that being the time in which Madoc lived, such a map would form a very fit and very singular addition to the book; and if it be there I would wish you to make a formal application on my part for permission to have it copied and engraved. These bodies corporate are never very accommodating; but Vincent is bound to be civil on such an occasion, if he can, lest his refusal should seem to proceed from personal dislike toward one whom he must be conscious that he has used unhandsomely, and to the utmost of his power attempted to injure. God knows I forgive him—*ex imo corde.* I am too well satisfied with my own lot, with my present pursuits, and the new and certain hopes which they present, not to feel thankful to all those who have in any way contributed to make me what I am. If he and I had been upon friendly terms, it might have interested him, who has touched upon Portuguese history himself, to hear of my progress, and my knowledge might possibly have been of some assistance to him. I have no kindly feelings toward him. He made a merit of never having struck me, whereas that merit was mine for never having given him occasion so to do. It is my nature to be sufficiently susceptible of kindness, and I remember none from him. Here is a long rigmarole about nothing: the remembrance of old times always makes me garrulous, and the failing is common to most men. * * *

"God bless you! R. S."

To Lieut. Southey, Barbadoes.

"Keswick, Dec. 26, 1804.

"DEAR TOM,

"I have made some use of your letters in the third Annual Review. M'Kinnan has published a Tour through the British West Indies—a decent book, but dull. In reviewing it, I eked out his account with yours, and contrasted his words upon the slave trade with a passage from your letters. In doing this, I could not help thinking what materials for a book you might bring home if you would take the trouble; as thus: describe the appearance of all the islands you touch at, from the sea—their towns, how situated, how built—what public buildings, what sort of houses—the inside of the houses, how furnished—what the mode of life of the towns-people, of the planter, in different ranks, and of the different European settlers—in short, all you see and all you hear, looking about the more earnestly and asking questions. Many anecdotes of this and the last war you have opportunities of collecting, particularly of Victor Hughes; something also of St. Domingo, or Hayti, as it must now be called, which I find means *asperosa* in Spanish, *rugged.* If you would bring home matter for a picture of the islands as they now are, I could delineate what they were from the old Spaniards, and there would be a very curious book between us. *

"Hamilton is broke, whereby I shall lose from £20 to £30, which he owes me for critical work, and which I shall never get; rather hard upon one whose brains and eyesight have quite enough to do by choice, and are never overpaid for what they do by necessity. For meaner matter, my little girl is not pretty, but she is a sweet child, so excellently good-tempered—as joyous as a skylark in a fine morning, and so quick of eye, of action, and of intellect, that I have a sad feeling about me of the little chance there is of rearing her; so don't think too much about her.

"Whether this war with Spain will involve one with Portugal is what we are all speculating about at present. I think it very likely that Bonaparte will oblige the Portuguese to turn the English out—a great evil to me in particular; though, should my uncle be driven to England, my settling will the sooner take place. At present I am as unsettled as ever, at a distance from my books, perpetually in want of them, wishing and wanting to be permanently fixed, and still prevented by the old cause. Make a capital prize, Tom, and lend me a couple of hundreds, and you shall see what a noble appearance my books will make. N.B.—I have a good many that wait for your worship to letter them. This Spanish war may throw something in your way; but I don't like the war, and think it is unjust and ungenerous to quarrel with an oppressed people because they have not strength to resist the French. You know I greatly esteem the Spaniards. As for France, I am willing to pay half my last guinea to support a contest for national honor against him; but it began foolishly, and well will it be if we do not end it even more foolishly than we began.

"God bless you! R. S."

My father, as the reader is well aware, had long been desirous of again visiting Spain and Portugal, chiefly for the sake of obtaining still further materials for the two great historical works he was engaged upon—the History of Portugal and the History of Brazil. It seems that Mr. Bedford, through some of his friends, had at this time an opportunity of furthering these views, and had inquired of my father what situation he felt himself equal to undertake. His reply explains the rest sufficiently, and the next letter shows that the scheme soon fell to the ground.

To Grosvenor C. Bedford, Esq.

"Keswick, Jan. 20, 1805.

"DEAR GROSVENOR,

"* * * * There is a civil office for the inspection of accounts, and I am adequate to be inspector; so, if you can not learn that there be any thing more proper, let that be the thing asked—but consult Rickman. I have only proceeded on newspaper authority; and, if the expedition be not going to Portugal, would not take the best office any where else. Actual work I expect, and have seen enough of the last army at Lisbon to know that commissaries and inspectors have plenty of leisure. Thus much General Moore must know, whether we are to send forces to Portugal or not; for it depends upon his report, if the papers lie not. If we do, the place where all the civil operations are carried on is Lisbon; there the commissaries, &c., remain, if the army takes the field; there I want to go, you know for what purpose. To say that I do not wish to make money would be talking nonsense; but the mere object of making money would not take me from home. I can inspect accounts, I can make contracts (for beef and oats are soon understood), and, doing these, can yet have leisure for my own pursuits. What efforts I make are more because the thing is prudent than agreeable. * * *

"Madoc is provokingly delayed. Job once wished that his enemy had written a book: if he himself had printed one, it would have tried his patience. I am every day expecting the Great Snake* in a frank from Duppa. My emblem of the cross, prefixed to the poem, with the *In hoc signo*, and what I have said in the poem of the Virgin Mary, is more liable to misconstruction than could be wished. In what light I consider these things may be seen in the reviews of the Missions to Bengal and Otaheite. I have just finished another article for the year upon the South African Missions. The great use of reviewing is, that it obliges me to think upon subjects on which I had been before content to have very vague opinions, because there had never been any occasion for examining them; and this is a very important one.

"It will do me a world of good to see the first proof sheet under favor of the Grand Parleur: I shall begin to think seriously of the preface. You will find it worth while to go to Longman, for the sake of seeing the new publications, which all lie on his table—a good way of knowing what is going on in the world of typography.

"God bless you! R. S."

To John Rickman, Esq.

"Feb. 16, 1805.

"DEAR RICKMAN,

"The motto† to those Metrical Tales is strictly true; but there is a history belonging to them which will show that it was not trifling when I wrote them. With the single exception of Gualberto (the longest and best), all the others were written expressly for the Morning Post; and this volume-full is a selection from a large heap, by which I earned £149 4*s*., and is now published for the very same reason for which it was originally composed. Besides the necessity for writing such things, there was also a great fitness, inasmuch as, by so doing, a facility and variety of style was acquired, to be converted to better purposes, and I had always better purposes in view. * * * * * * *

"I have been reading the earliest travels in Abyssinia, namely, the History of the Portuguese Embassy in 1520, by Francisco Alvares, the chaplain—a book exceedingly rare, my copy, which is the Spanish translation, a little 24mo volume, having cost a moidore. As I can not bear to lose any thing, I shall draw up just such an abstract as if for a review, and throw whatever is not essential to the main narrative among the works of supererogation, which will be enough for a volume. The king, or, to give him his proper title, the Neguz, dwelt like an Arab in his tent. * * * What every where surprises me in the history of these discoveries is, that so little should be known of the East in Europe, when so many Europeans were to be found in the East, for the Neguz was never without some straggler or other; still more that in Europe such idle dreams about Ethiopia should prevail, when Abyssinians so often found their way to Rome. The opportunities lost by foolish ministers and foolish kings makes me swear for pure vexation. If Albuquerque had lived, I verily believe he would have expelled the Mamelukes from Egypt, by the help of the African Christians, and have made that country a Christian instead of a Turkish conquest. I should like to give Egypt to the Spaniards: they are good colonists. * * * * * * * * * * * * *
Do you know that reflecting mirrors of steel were used instead of spectacles for weak or dim-eyed persons to read in? This must have been so troublesome and so expensive that it never can have been common. But that it was used, I have found in an old book, purchased when I was first your guest in London—the 400 questions proposed by the Admiral of Castille and his friends to a certain Friar Minorita; 1550 the date of the book, some thirty years after it had been written. I am in the middle of this most quaint book, and have found, among the most whimsical things that ever delighted the quaintness of my heart, some of more consequence. * * The probabilities of my seeing you this year seem to increase. I begin to think that the mountain may come to Mohammed; in plain English, that, instead of my going to Lisbon, my uncle may come to England, in which case I shall meet him in London. The expedition to Portugal seems given up. Coleridge is confidential secretary to Sir A—— Ball, and has been taking some pains

* An engraving of one of the incidents in Madoc.
† I am unable to refer to this edition.

to set the country right as to its Neapolitan politics, in the hope of saving Sicily from the French. He is going with Capt. —— into Greece, and up the Black Sea to purchase corn for the government. Odd, but pleasant enough—if he would but learn to be contented in that state of life into which it has pleased God to call him: a maxim which I have long thought the best in the Catechism. * * * * *

"God bless you! R. S."

To C. W. W. Wynn, Esq.

"March 5, 1805.

"DEAR WYNN,

" * * * * * * *

I have read Scott's poem* this evening, and like it much. It has the fault of mixed language which you mentioned, and which I expected; and it has the same obscurity, or, to speak more accurately, the same want of perspicuousness, as his Glenfinlas. I suspect that Scott did not write poetry enough when a boy,† for he has little command of language. His vocabulary of the obsolete is ample; but, in general, his words march up stiffly, like half-trained recruits—neither a natural walk, nor a measured march which practice has made natural. But I like his poem, for it is poetry, and in a company of strangers I would not mention that it had any faults. The beginning of the story is too like Coleridge's Christobell, which he had seen; the very line, 'Jesu Maria, shield her well!' is caught from it. When you see the Christobell, you will not doubt that Scott has imitated it; I do not think designedly, but the echo was in his ear, not for emulation, but *propter amorem.* This only refers to the beginning, which you will perceive attributes more of magic to the lady than seems in character with the rest of the story.

"If the sale of Madoc should prove that I can afford to write poetry, Kehama will not lie long unfinished. After lying fallow since the end of October, I feel prolific propensities that way. * * * * *

"My book ought to be delivered before this, upon the slowest calculation. I pray you compare the conscientious type of my notes with that of Scott's; and look in his title-page,‡ at the cruelty with which he has actually split Paternoster Row.

"God bless you! R. S."

To John Rickman, Esq.

"Keswick, March 22, 1805.

"I never learned the Memoria Technica, but if ever I have a son he shall. Where is the earliest mention of the mariner's compass? I have no better reference than a chronological table at the end of a worn-out dictionary, which says, invented or improved by Gicia of Naples, A.D. 1302. Now I have just found it mentioned in the Laws of Alonzo the Wise, which laws were begun A.D. 1251, and finished in seven years; and it is not mentioned as any thing new, but made use of as an illustration. You can understand the Spanish:

"'Assi como les marineros sequian en le nocte, escura por el aguja que les es mediarnera entre la piedra e la estrella, e les muestra por lo vayar.'

"I suspect that this implies a belief in some specific virtue in the north star, as if the magnetic influence flowed from it. This, however, is matter for more inquiry, and I will one day look into it in Raymond Lully and Albertus Magnus—likely authors. The passage certainly carries the use of the needle half a century further back than the poor chronology; but whether I have made what antiquarians call a discovery, is more than I can tell. Robertson ought to have found it; for to write his introduction to Charles V. without reading these laws, is one of the thousand and one omissions for which he ought to be called rogue as long as his volumes last.

"These Partidas, as they are called, are very amusing. I am about a quarter through them some way, as they fill three folios by help of a commentary. They are divided into seven parts, for about seven times seven such reasons as would have delighted Dr. Slop; and King Alfonzo has ingeniously settled the orthography of his name by beginning each of the seven parts with one of the seven letters which compose it, in succession. His majesty gives directions that no young princes should dip their fingers into the dish in an unmannerly way, so as to grease themselves, and expatiates on the advantages to be derived from reading and writing—if they are able to learn those arts. He was himself an extraordinary man; too fond of study to be a good king in a barbarous age, but therefore not only a more interesting character to posterity, but a more useful one in the long run.

"You will see in the Madociana a story how Alexander went down in a diving-bell to see what was going on among the fishes—remarkable, because it is found in Spanish, German, and *Welsh* romances of the Middle Ages. I have since found a similar story of somebody else among the Malays, who certainly did not get it from Europe, or Alexander (Iscander) would have been their hero also. The number of good stories of all kinds which are common to the Orientals and Europeans are more likely to have been brought home by peaceable travelers than by the Crusaders. I suspect the Jew peddlers were the great go-betweens. They always went every where. All the world over you found Jew merchants and Jew physicians; wherever there is any thing to be got, no danger deters a Jew from venturing. I myself saw two fellows at Evora, under the very nose of the Inquisition, who, if they had any noses, could not have mistaken their game. I knew the cut of their jibs at once; and, upon inquiring what they had for sale, was told—green spectacles. A History of

* The Lay of the Last Minstrel.

† This would seem, from Sir W. Scott's Life, to be true. He mentions, in his Autobiography, having been a great reader of poetry, especially old ballads, but does not speak of having written much, if any, in boyhood.

‡ My father used to pride himself upon his *title-pages*, and upon his knowledge of *typography* in general; being, as one of his printers said, the only person he ever knew who could tell how a page would look before it was set up.

the Jews since their dispersion, in the shape of a Chronological Bibliotheca, would be a very valuable work. I want an academy established to bespeak such works, and reward them well, according to the diligence with which they shall be executed.

"The abuses, or main abuses, of printing, spring from one evil—it almost immediately makes authorship a trade. Per-sheeting was in use as early as Martin Luther's time, who mentions the price—a curious fact. The Reformation did one great mischief: in destroying the monastic orders, it deprived us of the only bodies of men who could not possibly be injured by the change which literature had undergone. They could have no *peculium;* they labored hard for amusement; the society had funds to spare for printing, and felt a pride in thus disposing of them for the reputation of their orders. We laugh at the ignorance of these orders, but the most worthless and most ignorant of them produced more works of erudition than all the English and all the Scotch universities since the Reformation; and it is my firm belief that a man will at this day find better society in a Benedictine monastery than he could at Cambridge—certainly better than he could at Oxford.

"You know I am no friend to popery or to monachism; but if the Irish Catholics are to be emancipated, I would let them found convents, only restricting them from taking the vows till after a certain age, as Catharine did in Russia—though perhaps it may be as well to encourage any thing to diminish the true Patric-ian breed. The good would be, that they would get the country cultivated, and serve as good inns, and gradually civilize it. As the island unluckily is theirs, and there is no getting the devil to remove it any where else, we had better employ the pope to set it to rights.

" * * * * * * *

William Taylor has forsaken the Critical, because it has fallen into the hands of ——, an orthodox, conceited, preferment-hunting Cambridge fellow: such is the character he gives of him. My book will suffer by the change. The Annual is probably delayed by the insurrection among the printers. Authors are the only journeymen who can not combine—too poor to hold out, and too useless to be bought in.

"Vale! R. S."

To C. W. W. Wynn, Esq., M.P.

"April 3, 1805.

"Dear Wynn,

"I have been grievously shocked this evening by the loss of the Abergavenny,* of which Wordsworth's brother was captain. Of course the news came flying up to us from all quarters, and it has disordered me from head to foot. At such circumstances I believe we feel as much for others as for ourselves—just as a violent blow occasions the same pain as a wound, and he who breaks his shin feels as acutely at the moment as the man whose leg is shot off. In fact, I am writing to you merely because this dreadful shipwreck has left me utterly unable to do any thing else. It is the heaviest calamity Wordsworth has ever experienced, and, in all probability, I shall have to communicate it to him, as he will very likely be here before the tidings can reach him. What renders any near loss of the kind so peculiarly distressing is, that the recollection is perpetually freshened when any like event occurs, by the mere mention of shipwreck, or the sound of the wind. Of all deaths it is the most dreadful, from the circumstances of terror which accompany it.

"I have to write the history of two shipwrecks—that of Sepulveda and his wife, which is mentioned by Camoens, and that of D. Paulo de Lina, one of the last Portuguese who distinguished himself favorably in India. Both these, but especially the first, are so dreadfully distressful, that I look on to the task of dwelling upon all the circumstances, and calling them up before my own sight, and fixing them in my own memory, as I needs must do, with very great reluctance. Fifteen years ago, the more melancholy a tale was, the better it pleased me, just as we all like tragedy better than comedy when we are young. But now I as unwillingly encounter this sort of mental pain as I would any bodily suffering. * * * * * *
* * * * * * * *

"God bless you! R. S."

To C. W. W. Wynn, Esq., M.P.

"April 6, 1805.

"Dear Wynn,

"I am startled at the price of Madoc; not that it is dear compared with other books, but it is too much money; and I vehemently suspect that, in consequence, the sale will be just sufficient for the publisher not to lose any thing, and for me not to gain any thing. What will be its critical reception I can not anticipate. There is neither meter nor politics to offend any body, and it may pass free for any matter that it contains, unless, indeed, some wiseacre should suspect me of favoring the Roman Catholic religion.

"And this catch-word leads me to the great political question. A Catholic establishment would be the best, perhaps the only means of civilizing Ireland. Jesuits and Benedictines, though they would not enlighten the savages, would humanize them, and bring the country into cultivation. A petition that asked for this, saying plainly we are papists, and will be so, and this is the best thing that can be done for us, and for you too—such a petition I could support, considering what the present condition of Ireland is, how wretchedly it has always been governed, and how hopeless the prospect is.

"You will laugh at me, but I believe there is more need to check popery in England than to encourage it in Ireland. It was highly proper to let the immigrant monastics associate together

* An allusion to this shipwreck is made in a published letter of an earlier date: which of the two dates is correct, I can not at this time ascertain.

here, and live in their old customs, but it is not proper to let them continue their establishments, nor proper that the children of Protestant parents should be inveigled into nunneries. You will tell me their vows are not binding in England; but they are binding *in foro conscientiæ;* and, believe me, whatever romances have related of the artifices of the Romish priesthood, does not and can not exceed the truth. This, by God's blessing, I will one day prove irrefragably to the world. The Protestant Dissenters will die away. Destroy the Test Act, and you kill them. They affect to appeal wholly to reason, and bewilder themselves in the miserable snare of materialism. Besides, their creed is not reasonable: it is a vile mingle mangle which a Catholic may well laugh at. But Catholicism, having survived the first flood of reformation, will stand, perhaps, to the end of all things. It would yield either to a general spread of knowledge (which would require a totally new order of things), or to the unrestrained attacks of infidelity, which would be casting out devils by Beelzebub, the prince of the devils. But if it be tolerated here—if the old laws of prevention be suffered to sleep, it will gain ground, perhaps to a dangerous extent. You do not know what the zeal is, and what the power of an army of priests, having no interest whatever but that of their order. * * * * You will not carry the question now; what you will do in the next reign, Heaven knows! * * * * * *

"Coleridge is coming home full of Mediterranean politics. Oh, for a vigorous administration! but that wish implies so much, that Algernon Sidney suffered for less direct high treason. If I were not otherwise employed, almost I should like to write upon the duty and policy of introducing Christianity into our East Indian possessions, only that it can be done better at the close of the Asiatic part of my History. Unless that policy be adopted, I prophesy that by the year 2000 there will be more remains of the Portuguese than of the English empire in the East. * * * * * * * *

"We go on badly in the East, and badly in the West. You will see in the Review that I have been crying out for the Cape. We want a port in the Mediterranean just now; for, if Gibraltar is to be besieged, certainly Lisbon will be shut against us. Perhaps Tangiers could be recovered: that coast of Africa is again becoming of importance; but, above all things, Egypt, Egypt. This country is strong enough to conquer, and populous enough to colonize; conquest would make the war popular, and colonization secure the future prosperity of the country, and the eventual triumph of the English language over all others. It would amuse you to hear how ambitious of the honor of England and of the spread of her power I am become. If we had a king as ambitious as Napoleon, he could not possibly find a privy counselor more after his own heart. Heaven send us another minister ——! How long is the present one to fool away the resources of the country? If I were superstitious, I could believe that Providence meant to destroy us because it has infatuated us.

"God bless you! R. S."

In later life my father held very different opinions respecting the effect likely to be produced by the establishment of popery in Ireland to those which he expresses in the foregoing letter. Increased knowledge of the past history of that country, and of its present condition, dispossessed him altogether of the idea that the Roman Catholic Church, set up in her full power, would be the most effective means of civilizing and humanizing the people. He affirms, indeed (Colloquies with Sir Thomas More, vol. i., p. 289), after quoting Bishop Berkeley's admirable exhortation to the Romish priests, that, "had they listened to it, and exerted themselves for improving the condition of the people with half the zeal that they display in keeping up an inflammatory excitement among them, the state of Ireland would have been very unlike what it now is, and they themselves would appear in a very different light before God and man." "They might," he continues, "have wrought as great a change in Ireland as the Jesuits effected among the tribes of Paraguay and California;" and this "without opposition, without difficulty, in the strict line of their duty, in the proper discharge of their sacerdotal functions * * * to the immediate advancement of their own interests, and so greatly to the furtherance of those ambitious views which the ministers of the Romish Church must ever entertain, that I know not how their claims, if supported by such services, could have been resisted." * * * "I would not dissemble the merits of the Romish clergy," he continues, "nor withhold praise from them when it is their due; they attend sedulously to the poor, and administer relief and consolation to them in sickness and death with exemplary and heroic devotion. Many among them undoubtedly there are whose error is in opinion only, and whose frame of mind is truly Christian, and who, according to the light which they possess, labor faithfully in the service of the Lord. But the condition of Ireland affords full evidence for condemning them as a body. In no other country is their influence so great, and in no other country are so many enormities committed." * * * *

To Grosvenor C. Bedford, Esq.

"April 13, 1805.

"DEAR GROSVENOR,

"There is a translation of Sallust by Gordon. I have never seen it, but, having read his Tacitus, do not think it likely that any new version would surpass his, for he was a man of great powers. It is not likely that Longus Homo, or any other Homo, would pay for such a translation, because the speculation is not promising, every person who wishes to read Sallust being able to read the original. * * * * * * There are some Greek authors which we want in English, Diodorus Siculus in particular; but why not choose for yourself, and venture upon original composition? In my conscience I do not think any man living has more of Rabelais in his nature than you have. A grotesque satire *à la Garagantua* would set all the kingdom staring, and place you in the very first rank of reputation. * * * * You ask if I shall come to town this summer? Certainly not, unless some very material accident were to render it necessary. I do not want to go, I should not like to go, and I can't afford to go—solid reasons, Mr. Bedford, as I take it, for not going. This is an inconvenient residence for many reasons, and I shall move southward as soon as I have the means, either to the neighborhood of London or Bath. When that may be, Heaven knows, for I have not yet found out the art of making more money than goes as fast as it comes, in bread and cheese, which these ministers make dearer and dearer every day, and I am one of that class which feels every addition. However, I am well off as it is, and perfectly contented, and ten times happier than half those boobies who walk into that chapel there in your neighborhood, and when they are asked if I shall give sixteen pence for tenpenny-worth of salt, say yes—for which the devil scarify them with wire whips, and then put them in brine, say I.

"* * * I shall endeavor to account for the decline of poetry after the age of Shakspeare and Spenser, in spite of the great exceptions during the Commonwealth, and to trace the effect produced by the restorers of a better taste, of whom Thomson and Gilbert West are to be esteemed as the chief, before the Wartons, with this difference, that what he did was the effect of his own genius; what they, by a feeling of the genius of others. This reign will rank very high in poetical history. Goldsmith, Cowper, Burns, are all original, and all unequaled in their way. Falconer is another whose works will last forever. * * * * *

"God bless you! R. S."

To C. W. W. Wynn, Esq., M.P.

"April 16, 1805.

"Dear Wynn,

"Madoc has reached Keswick. I am sorry to see Snowdon uniformly misspelled, by what unaccountable blunder I know not. It is a beautiful book, but I repent having printed it in quarto. By its high price, one half the edition is condemned to be furniture in expensive libraries, and the other to collect cobwebs in the publishers' warehouses. I foresee that I shall get no solid pudding by it: the loss on the first edition will eat up the profits of the second, if the publishers, as I suppose they will, should print a second while the quarto hangs upon hand. However, after sixteen years it is pleasant, as well as something melancholy, to see it, as I do now for the first time, in the shape of a book. Many persons will read it with pleasure, probably no one with more than you; for, whatever worth it may have, you will feel that, had it not been for you, it could never possibly have existed. It is easy to quit the pursuit of fortune for fame; but had I been obliged to work for the necessary comforts instead of the superfluities of life, I must have sunk, as others have done before me. Interrupted just when I did not wish it, for it is twilight—just light enough to see that the pen travels straight—and I am tired with a walk from Grasmere, and was in a mood for letter-writing—but here is a gentleman from Malta with letters from Coleridge. God bless you! R. S."

To C. W. W. Wynn, Esq., M.P.

June 25, 1805.

"Dear Wynn,

"Madoc is doing well: rather more than half the edition is sold, which is much for so heavy a volume. The sale, of course, will flag now, till the world shall have settled what they please to think of the poem; and if the reviews favor it, the remainder will be in a fair way.* In fact, books are now so dear that they are becoming rather articles of fashionable furniture than any thing else; they who buy them do not read them, and they who read them do not buy them. I have seen a Wiltshire clothier, who gives his bookseller no other instructions than the dimensions of his shelves; and have just heard of a Liverpool merchant who is fitting up a library, and has told his bibliopole to send him Shakspeare, and Milton, and Pope, and if any of those fellows should publish any thing new, to let him have it immediately. If Madoc obtain any celebrity, its size and cost will recommend it among these gentry—libros *consumere nati*—born to buy quartos and help the revenue. * * * * * * * * * * * You were right in your suspicious dislike of the introductory lines. The *ille ego* is thought arrogant, as my self-accusing preface would have been thought mock modesty. For this I care little: it is saying no more, in fact, than if I had said author of *so and so* in the title-page; and, moreover, it is not amiss that critics who will find fault with something, should have these straws to catch at. I learn from Sharpe very favorable reports of its general effect, which is, he says, far greater than I could have supposed.

"* * * This London Institution is likely to supply the place of an academy. Sharpe has had most to do with the enlistment, and perhaps, remotely, I may have had something, having conversed last year with him upon the necessity of some association for publishing such extensive national works as booksellers will not undertake, and individuals can not, such as the Scriptores Rerum Britan., Saxon Archaiologies, &c., &c. Application will be made to

* "I think Southey does himself injustice in supposing the Edinburgh Review, or any other, could have hurt Madoc, even for a time. But the size and price of the work, joined to the frivolity of an age which must be treated as nurses humor children, are sufficient reasons why a poem, on so chaste a model, should not have taken immediately. We know the similar fate of Milton's immortal work in the witty age of Charles II., at a time when poetry was much more fashionable than at present."—*Letter from Sir W. Scott to Miss Seward, Life*, vol. iii., p. 21.

Coleridge to lecture on Belles-Lettres. Some such application will perhaps be made to me one day or other; indeed, a hint to that effect was given me from the Royal Institution last year. My mind is made up to reject any such invitations, because I have neither the acquirements nor the wish to be a public orator. *

"Your letter has got the start of mine. I believe I told you that both Lord and Lady Holland had left invitations for me with my uncle to Holland House, and that he had offered me the use of his Spanish collection. Did Fox mention to you that I had sent him a copy of Madoc? I did so because Sharpe desired me to do so, who knows Fox; and I prefaced it with a note, as short as could be, and as respectful as ought to be. I am much gratified by what you tell me of the poem's reception: there was a strong and long fit of dejection upon me about the time of its coming out. I suspected a want of interest in the first part, and a want every where of such ornament as the public have been taught to admire. And still I can not help feeling that the poem looks like the work of an older man—that all its lights are evening sunshine. This would be ominous if it did not proceed from the nature of the story, and the key in which it is pitched, which was done many years since, before Thalaba was written or thought of. * *

"God bless you! R. S."

To C. W. W. Wynn, Esq., M.P.

"July 5, 1805.

"DEAR WYNN,

"Fox has written me a very civil letter of thanks; saying, however, that he had not yet had time to read the poem, so his praise can of course only have been of detached parts.

"They tell me the duty upon foreign works is not worth collecting, and that it might be repealed if any member thought it worth his while to take up the matter. If this be the case, I pray you take into consideration the case of your petitioner; there is now a roomful of books lying for me at Lisbon, all of use to me, and yet literally and truly such, the major part, that, were they to be sold in England, they would not yield the expense of the duty. I can not smuggle them all in, to my sorrow, being obliged to get over only a box at a time, of such a smuggleable size that a man can easily carry it, and this I can not do at London, where I wish to have them. What my uncle has sent over, and fairly paid for, has cost about a hundred pounds freight and duty—the freight far the smaller part. Now, if this barbarous tax can be repealed, whoever effects its repeal certainly deserves to be esteemed a benefactor to literature, and it may also be taken into the account that you would save me from the sin of smuggling, which else, assuredly, I have not virtue enough to resist. Seriously, if the thing could be done, it would be some pride to me, as well as some profit, that you should be the man to do it. * * * * * I have just received a good and valuable book from Lisbon, the Barbarorum Leges Antiquæ, well and laboriously edited by a monk at Venice, in five folios, the last published in 1792. An excellent work it appears to me, upon the slight inspection I have yet given it—one that by its painful and patient labor reminds one of old times; such a book as monasteries do sometimes produce, but universities never. My books here are few but weighty, and every day I meet with something or other so interesting to me, that a wish arises for some friend to drop in, to whom and with whom I could talk over the facts which have appeared, and the speculations growing out of them. What profit the History may ultimately produce, Heaven knows; but I would not, for any thing that rank or fortune could give, forego the pleasure of the pursuit.

"The story of Pelayo, the restorer of the Gothic or founder of the Spanish monarchy, has been for some time in my thoughts as good for a poem. I would rather it were a Portuguese than a Spanish story; that, however, can not be helped. The historical facts are few and striking—just what they should be; and I could fitly give to the main character the strong feelings and passions which give life and soul to poetry, and in which I feel that Madoc is deficient. There is yet half an hour's daylight, enough to show you what my ideas are upon the subject, in their crude state. Pelayo revolted because his sister was made by force the concubine of a Moorish governor, or by consent; and because his own life was attempted by that governor, in fear of his resentment, he retreated to the mountains, where a cavern was his strong-hold; and from that cavern miraculously defeated an army of unbelievers: the end is, that he won the city or castle of Gijon, and was chosen king. There are for characters, Pelayo himself; the young Alphonso, who married his daughter, and succeeded to his throne; Orpas, the renegade archbishop, killed in the battle of the Cave; Count Julian; his daughter Florinda, the innocent cause of all the evil, who killed herself in consequence; and, lastly, King Rodrigo himself, who certainly escaped from the battle, and lived as a hermit for the remainder of his days. If I venture upon machinery, of all subjects here is the most tempting one. What a scene would the famous Cave of Toledo furnish, and what might not be done with the ruined monasteries, with the relics and images which the fugitives were hiding in the woods and mountains! I forgot to mention among the historical characters the wife of Rodrigo, who married one of the Moorish governors. Monks and nuns (the latter not yet cloistered in communities), persecuted Arians, and Jews, and slaves, would furnish fictitious and incidental characters in abundance. You see the raw materials: if English history could supply me as good a subject, it would on every account be better; but I can find none. That of Edmund Ironside is the best, which William Taylor threw out to me as a lure in the Annual Review; but when an historical story is taken, the issue ought to be of permanent importance.

"I have never thought so long at one time about Pelayo as while thus talking to you about him; but Madoc does not fully satisfy me, and I should like to produce something better—something pitched in a higher key. A Spanish subject has one advantage, that it will cost me no additional labor of research; only, indeed, were I to choose Pelayo, I would see his cave, which is fitted up as a chapel, has a stream gliding from it, and must be one of the finest things in Spain. God bless you! R. S."

The following letter requires some explanation. The Butler, and his man William, to whom allusion will from this time occasionally be found in the letters to Mr. Bedford, were mythological personages, the grotesque creation of his fertile imagination. The idea, which was a standing jest among the intimate friends of the originator, was of a hero possessing the most extraordinary powers—with something like the combined qualities of Merlin, Garagantua, and Kehama, to be biographized in a style compounded of those of Rabelais, Swift, Sterne, and Baron Munchausen.

Mr. Bedford, however, was not to be induced by all his friend's entreaties to immortalize the Butler, and no relic of him consequently remains, except the occasional allusions in these letters, which, although they can afford amusement to but few persons, are inserted here as showing the extreme elasticity of my father's mind, which delighted to recreate itself in pure unmitigated nonsense—a property shared in common with many wise men.

To Grosvenor C. Bedford, Esq.

"Greta Hall, July 6, 1805.

" * * * * * * * *

Butler denotes the sensual principle, which is subject or subordinate to the intellectual part of the internal man; because every thing which serves for drinking or which is drunk (as wine, milk, water) hath relation to truth, which is of the intellectual part, thus it hath relation to the intellectual part; and whereas the external sensual principle, or that of the body, is what subministers, therefore by *Butler* is signified that subministering sensual principle, or that which subministers of things sensual.

"Read that paragraph again, Grosvenor. Don't you understand it? Read it a third time. Try it backward.

"See if you can make any thing of it diagonally. Turn it upside down.

"Philosophers have discovered that you may turn a polypus inside out, and it will live just as well one way as the other. It is not to be supposed that Nature ever intended any of its creatures to be thus inverted, but so the thing happens. As you can make nothing of this Butler any other way, follow the hint, and turn the paragraph inside out. That's a poozzle.

"Now, then, I will tell you what it is in plain English. It is Swedenborgianism, and I have copied the passage verbatim from a Swedenborgian dictionary. Allow, at least, that it would make an excellent chapter in your book, if thou hadst enough grace in thee ever to let such a book come forth. Nonsense, sublime nonsense, is what this book ought to be; such nonsense as requires more wit, more sense, more reading, more knowledge, more learning, than go to the composition of half the wise ones in the world. I do beseech you, do not lightly or indolently abandon the idea; for, if you will but Butlerize in duodecimo, if you fail of making such a reputation as you would wish, then will I pledge myself to give one of my ears to you, which you may, by the hands of Harry, present to the British Museum. The book ought only to have glimpses of meaning in it, that those who catch them may impute meaning to all the rest by virtue of faith.

"God bless you! I wish you could come to the lakes, that we might talk nonsense and eat gooseberry pie together, for which I am as famous as ever. R. S."

Madoc having now been published some months, the opinions of his various friends began to reach him. That of Mr. Rickman was a somewhat unfavorable one, and, as may be well supposed, he had no false delicacy in expressing it, my father being well used to this sort of masculine freedom, ready to use it himself to others, and wholly incapable of taking any umbrage at it himself. His defense of his poetical offspring will be the better understood by the quotation here of his friend's remarks: "About Madoc I am very glad to hear that the world admires it and buys it, though in reading it, I confess I can not discover that it is in any degree so good as your two former poems, which I have read lately by way of comparison. The result has been, that I like them the more, and Madoc the less. The Virgilian preface, very oddly (as I think), sets forth the planting of Christianity in America. It is the license of poetry to vary circumstances and to invent incidents, but, surely, not to predicate a result notoriously false. Thus Virgil embellishes the origin of the Roman empire; but he does not tell you that Judaism was established in it, or that in his own time republican Rome remained unfettered by emperors. Historically speaking, the Spaniards introduced Christianity into America. Besides this, I much dislike the sort of nameless division you have adopted, and the want of numbering the lines. How is the poem to be referred to? Neither do I like the metaphysical kind of preachings produced by your Welshman for the instruction of savages. * * * I am very glad the public admire Madoc so much more than I do, and also that many persons knowing so much more of poetry do so too. No doubt I am wrong, but it would not be honest to conceal my error."*

To John Rickman, Esq.

"July, 1805.

"Dear Rickman,

" * * * Your objections to the ex-

* June 27, 1805.

ordial lines are not valid. I say there of what the subject is to treat, not affirming that it is historically true. Just as I might have said, in an introduction to Thalaba, that he destroyed the Dom Daniel, and so put an end to all sorcery. The want of numerals is a fault, I confess; not so the namelessness of the divisions; nor, indeed, are they nameless, for in the notes they are regarded as *sections;* and that each has not its specific name from its subject-matter affixed to it, is, you know, the effect of your own advice. However, call them sections, cantos, canticles, chapters, what you will, and then consider in what way is this mode of division objectionable.

"I am not surprised at your little liking the poem; on the contrary, I am more surprised at those who like it, because what merit it has is almost wholly of execution, which is infinitely better than the subject. Now every body can feel if a story be interesting or flat, whereas there are very few who can judge of the worth of the language and versification. I have said to somebody, perhaps it was to you, that, had this been *written* since Thalaba (for, as you know, the plan was formed, and the key pitched, before Thalaba was begun or dreamed of), I should have thought it ominous of declining powers, it is in so sober a tone, its coloring so autumnal, its light every where that of an evening sun, but as only the last finish of language, the polishing part, is of later labor, the fair inference is, that instead of the poet's imagination having grown weaker, he has improved in the mechanism of his art. A fair inference it is, for I am no self-flatterer, Heaven knows. Having confessed thus much, I ought to add, that the poem is better than you think it. * * * Compare it with the Odyssey, not the Iliad; with King John or Coriolanus, not Macbeth or the Tempest. The story wants unity, and has, perhaps, too Greek, too stoical a want of passion; but, as far as I can see, with the same eyes wherewith I read Homer, and Shakspeare, and Milton,* it is a good poem, and must live. You will like it better if ever you read it again. * * * *"

To John May, Esq.

"Keswick, August 5, 1805.

"MY DEAR FRIEND,

"I am much gratified with your praises of Madoc, and disposed to acquiesce in some of your censure. * * * * It pleased me that you had selected for praise the quieter passages, those in an under key, with which the feeling has the most, and the fancy the least to do. * * * * * * *

"My History would go to press this winter if my uncle were in England, and probably will not till he and I have met, either in that country or in this. Believe me, it is an act of forbearance to keep back what has cost me so many hours of labor: the day when I receive the first proof sheet will be one of the happiest of my life. The work may or may not succeed; it may make me comfortably independent, or obtain no credit till I am in a world where its credit will be of no effect; but that it will be a good book, and one which, sooner or later, shall justify me in having chosen literature for my life pursuit, I have a sure and certain faith. If I complained of any thing, it would be of the necessity of working at employments so worthless in comparison with this great subject. However, the reputation which I am making, and which, thank God! strengthens every year, will secure a sale for these volumes whenever they appear. Roscoe's Leo is on the table—*sub judice.* One great advantage in my subject is that it excites no expectations: the reader will be surprised to find in me a splendor of story which he will be surprised not to find in the miserable politics of Italian princelings.

"I can not answer your question concerning the cotemporary English historians; Bishop Nicholson will be your best guide. Of English history we have little that is good—I speak of modern compilers, being ignorant, for the most part, of the monkish annalists. Turner's Hist. of the Anglo-Saxons ought to be upon your shelves * * * so much new information was probably never laid before the public in any one historical publication; Lord Lyttleton's Henry II. is a learned and honest book. Having particularized these two, the 'only faithful found,' it may safely be said, that of all the others, those which are the oldest are probably the best. What Milton and Bacon have left, have, of course, peculiar and first-rate excellence.

"I beg of you to thank young Walpole for his book. * * * I wish he were to travel any where rather than in Greece; there is too much hazard and too little reward; nor do I think much can be gleaned after the excellent Chandler. Hungary, Bohemia, Poland, are the countries for an able and inquisitive traveler. I should, for myself, prefer a town in Ireland to a town in Greece, as productive of more novelty.

"I should be much obliged if you could borrow for me Beausobre's Histoire du Manicheisme, which, for want of catalogues, I can not get at by any other channel. The book is said to be of sterling value, and the subject so connected with Christian and Oriental superstition, that my knowledge of both is very imperfect till I have read it. Besides, I think I have discovered that one of the great Oriental mythologies was borrowed from Christianity—that of Budda, the Fo

* I may here, not inappropriately, quote Sir Walter Scott's opinion of Madoc, as corroborating what my father himself here allows, that the execution is better than the subject, and also that the poem will well bear one of the surest tests of merit of all kinds—an intimate knowledge: "As I don't much admire compliments, you may believe me sincere when I tell you that I have read Madoc three times since my first cursory perusal, and each time with an increased admiration of the poetry. But a poem, whose merits are of that higher tone, does not immediately take with the public at large. It is even possible that during your own life—and may it be as long as every real lover of literature can wish—you must be contented with the applause of the few whom nature has gifted with the rare taste for discriminating in poetry; but the mere *readers of verse* must one day come in, and then Madoc will assume his real place at the feet of Milton. Now this opinion of mine was not that (to speak frankly) which I formed on reading the poem at first, though I then felt much of its merit."—*W. S. to R. S.*, Oct. 1, 1807.

of the Chinese; if so, what becomes of their chronology?

"God bless you! R. S."

To Lieutenant Southey, H.M.S. Amelia.

"Keswick, August 22, 1805.

"My dear Tom,

"I wrote to you as soon as the letter, by favor of old Neptune, arrived. As both seem to have taken the same course, it will now be desirable to have others thrown over in that track, and if half a dozen should in half a century follow one another, it would prove the existence of a current.

"Our neighbor, General Peachy, invited us lately to meet Lord Somerville at dinner. * * * From hence he went into Scotland, and there saw ——, who was on the point of coming here to visit Wordsworth and me. To —— he spoke of the relationship with us: he said of me and Wordsworth that, however we might have got into good company, he might depend upon it we were still Jacobins at heart, and that he believed he had been instrumental in having us looked after in Somersetshire. This refers to a spy who was sent down to Stowey to look after Coleridge and Wordsworth; the fellow, after trying to tempt the country people to tell lies, could collect nothing more than that the gentlemen used to walk a good deal upon the coast, and that they were what they called poets. He got drunk at the inn, and told his whole errand and history, but we did not till now know who was the main mover. * * *

"Continue, I beseech you, to write your remarks upon all you see and all you hear, but do not trust them to letters, lest they should be lost. Keep minutes of what you write. Such letters as your last would make a very interesting and very valuable volume. Little is known here of the West Indies, except commercially: the moral and physical picture would have all the effect of novelty. In particular, look to the state of the slaves. If you were now in England, it is very possible that your evidence might have considerable weight before the House of Lords, now that the question of abolition is again coming on. Keep your eye upon every thing; describe the appearance of the places you visit, as seen from the ship—your walks on shore—in short, make drawings in writing. Nothing is so easy as to say what you see, if you will but disregard how you say it, and think of nothing but explaining yourself fully. Write me the history of a planter's day—what are his meals—at what hours—what his dress—what his amusements—what the employments, pleasures, education, &c., of his children and family. Collect any anecdotes connected with the French expeditions—with the present or the last war; and depend upon it, that by merely amusing yourself thus, you may bring home excellent and ample materials, to which I will add a number of curious historical facts, gleaned from the Spanish historians and travelers.

"The seas are clear for you once more, and I hope, by this time, you have picked up some more prizes. Your climate, too, is now getting comfortable: I envy you as much in winter as you can envy me in summer. * * *

"God bless you!"

To C. W. W. Wynn, Esq.

"1805.

"My dear Wynn,

"Whenever the encouragement of literature is talked of again in the House, I should think a motion for letting proof sheets pass as franks would not be opposed: they can not produce £100 a year to the post-office, probably not half the sum; but it is a tax of some weight on the few individuals whom it affects, and a good deal of inconvenience is occasioned to the printers by waiting for franks, while their presses stand still. Few persons have greater facility for getting franks than myself, yet the proofs which come without them, and those which are over-weight from being damp, or which are misdated, do not cost me less than 30*s.* a year. The proofs of Madoc cost me 50*s.*—rather too much out of five-and-twenty pounds profit.

"I have by me Bishop Lavington's Tracts concerning the Moravians; and as I can in great part vouch for the accuracy of his Catholic references, there seems no reason to suspect him in the others. At first these tracts left upon my mind the same impression which has been made upon yours; nor have I now any doubt that Zinzendorff was altogether a designing man, and that the absurdities and obscenities charged upon them in their outset are in the main true. But it is so in the beginning of all sects, and it seems to be a regular part of the process of fanaticism. Devotion borrows its language from carnal love. This is natural enough; and the consequences are natural enough also, when one who is more knave than enthusiast begins to talk out of Solomon's Song to a sister in the spirit. But this sort of leaven soon purges off; the fermentation ceases, and the liquor first becomes fine, then vapid, and at last you come to the dregs. Moravianism is in its second stage; its few proselytes fall silently in, led by solitary thought and conviction, not hurried on by contagious feelings, and the main body of its members have been born within the pale of the society. They do not live up to the rigor of their institutions in England; even here, however, it is certain that they are a respectable and respected people, and, as missionaries, they are meritorious beyond all others. No people but the Quakers understand how to communicate Christianity so well, and the Quakers are only beginning, whereas the Moravians have for half a century been laboring in the vineyard. Krantz's History of what they have done in Greenland is a most valuable book; there is also a History of their American Missions which I want to get. Among the Hottentots they are doing much good. The best account of the society, as it exists here, is to be found, I believe, in a novel called Wanley Penson. A great deal concerning their early history is to be found in Wesley's Journals. He was at one time closely connected with them, but, as there could not be two popes, a separation unluckily took place—I say unluckily, because Methodism is far the worst system of the two.

"If you have not read Collins's book on Bantry Bay, I recommend you to get it before the business comes on in Parliament. It is unique in its kind; the minute history of a colony during the first years of difficulty and distress. There was one man in power there precisely fit for his situation—Governor King, and if it had been possible to induce him to stay there, governor he ought to have been for life, with discretionary powers. One thing is plain respecting this colony, and that is, that no more convicts ought to be sent to the establishments already made. Send them to new settlements, and let the old ones purify: at present the stock of vice is perpetually renewed. Instead of doing this, the fresh convicts should be sent at once to new points along the coast; for new settlements must necessarily consume men, and these are the men who are fit to be consumed.

"Are you right in thinking that Sallust has the advantage in subject over Tacitus? To me it appears that the histories which Sallust relates excite no good feeling, treating only of bad men in bad times; but that the sufferings of good men in evil days form the most interesting and improving part of human history. I prefer Tacitus to all other historians—infinitely prefer him, because no other historian inculcates so deep and holy a hatred of tyranny. It is from him that I learned my admiration of the Stoics. God bless you! R. S."

The autumn of this year was varied by a short excursion to Scotland, accompanied by his friend, the Rev. Peter Elmsley (afterward principal of St. Alban Hall, Oxford). Edinburgh was their destination; and a few days were passed in a visit to Sir Walter Scott, at Ashestiel. The following letter, written during this absence from home, is too characteristic to be omitted. Mr. Thomas Moore, indeed, in his life of Lord Byron, seems very desirous of proving the incompatibility of genius with any comfortable habits or domestic tastes; declares that immortality has never thus been struggled for or won;* and appears to think that true poets must necessarily be as untamed as Mazeppa's steed. But, nevertheless, I am in nowise afraid that the possession of more amiable qualities will deprive my father of his claim to be remembered hereafter.

To Mrs. Southey.

"October 14, 1805.

"I need not tell you, my own dear Edith, not to read my letters aloud till you have first of all seen what is written only for yourself. What I have now to say to you is, that having been eight days from home, with as little discomfort, and as little reason for discomfort as a man can reasonably expect, I have yet felt so little comfortable, so great sense of solitariness, and so many homeward yearnings, that certainly I will not go to Lisbon without you; a resolution which, if your feelings be at all like mine, will not displease you. If, on mature consideration, you think the inconvenience of a voyage more than you ought to submit to, I must be content to stay in England, as on my part it certainly is not worth while to sacrifice a year's happiness; for, though not unhappy (my mind is too active and too well disciplined to yield to any such criminal weakness), still, without you, I am not happy. But for your sake as well as my own, and for little Edith's sake, I will not consent to any separation; the growth of a year's love between her and me, if it please God that she should live, is a thing too delightful in itself, and too valuable in its consequences, both to her and me, to be given up for any light inconveniences either on your part or mine. An absence of a year would make her effectually forgot me. * * * But of these things we will talk at leisure; only, dear, dear Edith, we must not part. * * * * * * * * * *

Last night we saw the young Roscius in Douglas: this was lucky and unexpected. He disappointed me. I could tell you precisely how, and how he pleased me on the other hand, but that this would take time,* and the same sort of thought as in reviewing; and in letter writing I love to do nothing *more* than just say what is uppermost. This evening I meet Jeffrey and Brougham at Thomson's rooms. I know not if Harry knows him: he is the person who reviewed Miss Seward, and is skillful in manuscripts. Among the books I have bought is a little work of Boccaccio, for which my uncle has been looking many years in vain, so extremely rare is it. Its value here was not known, and it cost me only three shillings, being, I conceive, worth as many guineas. I have likewise found the old translation of Camoens.

" * * * * * * *

The third sitting will finish the letter. Thomson brought with him the review of Madoc (which will be published in about ten days), sent to me by Jeffrey, who did not like to meet me till I had seen it. There was some sort of gentleman-like decency in this, as the review is very unfair and very uncivil, though mixed up with plenty of compliments, and calculated to serve the book in the best way, by calling attention to it and making it of consequence. Of course I shall meet him with perfect courtesy, just giving him to understand that I have as little respect for his opinions as he has for mine; thank him for sending me the sheets, and then turn to other subjects. * * * * Since breakfast we have been walking to Calton Hill and to the Castle, from which heights I have seen the city and the neighboring country to ad-

* Life and Works of Lord Byron, vol. iii., p. 129.

* In another letter he says, "Though a little disappointed, still I must say he is incomparably the best actor I have ever seen."

vantage. I am far more struck by Edinburgh itself than I expected, far less by the scenery around it. * * * *

"God bless you, my own dear Edith.

"R. S."

To Grosvenor C. Bedford, Esq.

"Keswick, Nov. 13, 1805.

"Dear Grosvenor,

"Here has been as great a gap in our correspondence as I have seen in the seat of my brother Sir Dominie's pantaloons, after he has been sliding down Latrigg. Sir, I shall be very happy to give you a slide down Latrigg also, if you will have the goodness to put it in my power to do so, and then you will understand the whole merits of the simile.

"Will you Butlerize, Mr. Bedford? By the core of William's heart, which I take to be the hardest of all oaths, and therefore the most impossible to break, I will never cease persecuting you with that question and that advice till you actually set that good ship afloat, in which you are to make as fair a voyage to the port of Fame as ever Englishman accomplished. Mr. Bedford, it appears to me that Englishmen accomplish that said expedition better by sea than by land, and that, therefore, the metaphor is a good one, and a sea-horse better than Pegasus. Do, do begin; and begin by writing letters to me, which may be your first crude thoughts; and I will unpack my memory of all its out-of-the-way oddities, and give them to you for cargo and ballast.

"Elmsley will have told you of our adventures in Scotland, if the non-adventures of a journey in Great Britain at this age of the world can deserve that name. I am returned with much pleasant matter of remembrance; well pleased with Walter Scott, with Johnny Armstrong's Castle on the Esk, with pleasant Teviotdale, with the Tweed and the Yarrow; astonished at Edinburgh, delighted with Melrose, sick of Presbyterianism, and, above all things, thankful that I am an Englishman and not a Scotchman. The Edinburgh Reviewers I like well as companions, and think little of as any thing else. Elmsley has more knowledge and a sounder mind than any or all of them. I could learn more from him in a day than they could all teach me in a year. Therefore I saw them to disadvantage, inasmuch as I had better company at home; and, in plain English, living as I have done, and, by God's blessing, still continue to do, in habits of intimate intercourse with such men as Rickman, William Taylor, Wordsworth, and Coleridge, the Scotchmen did certainly appear to me very pigmies—literatuli.

"I go to Portugal next year, if politics permit me, and expect to take Edith and the Edithling with me, for at least a two years' residence. Bating the voyage and the trouble of removal, this is a pleasant prospect. I love the country, and go well prepared to look for every thing that I can want. My winter will be fully employed, and hardly. I am at my reviewing, of which this year I take my leave forever. It is an irksome employment, over which I lose time, because it does not interest me. A good exercise certainly it is, and such I have found it; but it is to be hoped that the positive immorality of serving a literary apprenticeship in censuring the works of others will not be imputed wholly to me. In the winter of 1797, when I was only twenty-three and a half, I was first applied to to undertake the office of a public critic! Precious criticism! And thus it is that these things are done. I have acquired some knowledge, and much practice in prose, at this work, which I can safely say I have ever executed with as much honesty as possible; but, on the whole, I do and must regard it as an immoral occupation, unless the reviewer has actually as much knowledge at least of the given subject as the author upon whom he undertakes to sit in judgment.

"When will your worship call upon me for my preface? May I inform you that *Patres nostri* frequently remind me that we are losing time, thereby hinting that loss of time is loss of money.

"What a death is Nelson's! It seems to me one of the characteristics of the sublime that its whole force is never perceived at once. The more it is contemplated, the deeper is its effect. When this war began, I began an ode, which almost I feel now disposed to complete; take the only stanza:

"O dear, dear England! O my mother isle!
 There was a time when, woe the while!
In thy proud triumphs I could take no part;
 And even the tale of thy defeat
In those unhappy days was doom'd to meet
Unnatural welcome in an English heart:
For thou wert leagued in an accursed cause,
O dear, dear England! and thy holiest laws
Were trampled under foot by insolent power.
Dear as my own heart's blood wert thou to me,
But even thou less dear than liberty!

I never ventured on more, for fear lest what followed should fall flat in comparison. Almost I could now venture, and try at a funeral hymn for Nelson.

"God bless you! R. S."

To Lieutenant Southey.

"Nov. 15, 1805.

"My dear Tom,

"You will have heard of Nelson's most glorious death. The feeling it occasioned is highly honorable to the country. He leaves a name above all former admirals, with, perhaps, the single exception of Blake, a man who possessed the same genius upon great occasions. We ought to name the two best ships in the navy from these men.

"My trip to Edinburgh was pleasant. I went to accompany Elmsley. We stayed three days with Walter Scott at Ashestiel, the name of his house on the banks of the Tweed. I saw all the scenery of his Lay of the Last Minstrel, a poem which you will read with great pleasure when you come to England; and I went salmon-spearing on the Tweed, in which, though I struck at no fish, I bore my part, and managed one end of the boat with a long spear. Having had neither new coat nor hat since the Edithling was born, you may suppose I was in want of both; so at Edinburgh I was to rig myself, and, moreover, lay in new boots and pantaloons. Howbeit, on considering the really respectable appearance which my old ones made for a traveler, and considering, moreover, that as learning was better than house or land, it certainly must be much better than fine clothes, I laid out all my money in books, and came home to wear out my old wardrobe in the winter. My library has had many additions since you left me, and many gentlemen in parchment remain with anonymous backs till you come and bedeck them.

"From your last letter, I am not without hopes that you may have taken some steps toward getting to Europe, and in that case it is not absolutely impossible that you may yet reach this place before we quit it, and that you may make the circumnavigation of the lakes in my company. I am an experienced boatman, and, what is better, recline in the boat sometimes like a bashaw, while the women row me. Edith is an excellent hand at the oar. Her love. God bless you! R. S."

To Grosvenor C. Bedford, Esq.

"Dec. 6, 1805.

"William's iron-gray had his advantages and disadvantages. He never required shoeing; for, as the hoof is harder than the flesh, so, in just proportion to his metallic muscles, he had hoofs of adamant; but, then, he was hard-mouthed. There was no expense in feeding him; but he required scouring, lest he should grow rusty. Instead of spurs, William had a contrivance for touching him with aquafortis. It was a fine thing to hear the rain hiss upon him as he galloped. * * * The Butler wears a chest of drawers—sometimes a bureau.

"Bedford, I will break off all acquaintance with you if you do not publish the Butler. Who would keep a Phœnix with a spaniel's ear, a pig's tail, C——'s nose, and W——'s wig, all naturally belonging to him, in a cage only for his own amusement, when he might show it for five shillings a piece, and be known all over the world as the man who hatched it himself?

" * * By the 1st of January, send me the first chapter, being the mythology of the Butler, or else—I will for evermore call you *sir* when I speak *to* you, and *Mr.* Bedford when I speak *of* you; and, moreover, will always pull off my hat when I meet you in the streets.

"I perceive that the reviewals of Madoc have in a certain degree influenced you, which they will not do if you will look at them when they are three months old, or if you recollect that a review is the opinion of one man upon the work of another, and that it is not very likely that any man who reviews a poem of mine should know quite as much of the mechanism of poetry, or should have thought quite so much upon the nature of poetry, as I have done. The Monthly is mere malice, and is beneath all notice; but look at the Edinburgh, and you will see that Jeffrey himself does not know what he is about. He talks of Virgil, and Pope, and Racine as what I have set up against. I told him Pope was a model for satire. That, he said, was a great concession. 'No,' said I; 'if his style be a model for satire, how can it be for serious narrative?' And he did not attempt to hold up his Homer for imitation, but fairly and unequivocally declared he did not like it. And yet Jeffrey attacks me for not writing in Madoc like Pope! The passages which he has quoted, for praise or for censure, may just as well change places; they are culled capriciously, not with any sense of selection. The real faults of Madoc have never been pointed out. William Taylor has criticized it for the Annual very favorably and very ably: there are remarks in his critiques to set one thinking and considering; but W. Taylor is a man who fertilizes every subject he touches upon.

"Don Manuel—how could you not understand it was a secret? Do you not remember how covertly I inquired of you the text in Field's Bible? * * The use of secrecy is to excite curiosity, and, perhaps, to pass through the reviews under cover. Rickman particularly recommended the foreign cast of remarks through the whole of the journey. Thus do doctors differ. As for the queerities, let them stay: it is only they who know me pretty nearly that know what a queer fish I am; others conceive me to be a very grave sort of person. Besides, I have not the least intention of keeping the thing concealed after the purpose of secrecy has answered.

"That wretch Mack has very likely spoiled my voyage to Lisbon. If there be not peace, Bonaparte will show himself master of the Continent and turn us out of Portugal, if only to show that he is more powerful in that peninsula than Charlemagne was. I am afraid of France, and wish for single-handed war carried on steadily and systematically. We ought to have Egypt, Sicily, and the Cape; if we do not, France will. But nothing good ever will be done while that wretched minister is at the head of affairs. *

"Tui favoris studiosissimus, R. S."

To Lieut. Southey, H.M.S. Amelia.

"Keswick, Dec. 7, 1805.

"DEAR TOM,

"I was preparing last night to write to you; but the newspaper came, and seeing therein that a mail was arrived, I waited till this evening for a letter, and have not been disappointed. Thank you for the turtle, and thank Heaven it has never reached me. In bodily fear lest it should, I wrote off immediately to Wynn, and if he had not been in town, should have given it to any body who would have been kind enough to have eased me of so inconvenient a visitor. How, Tom, could you think of sending me a turtle! When, indeed, I come to be lord mayor, it may be a suitable present; but now! its carriage down would not have been less than forty shillings. Nobody would have known how to kill it, how to cut it up, or how to dress it; there would have been nobody here to help us eat it, nobody to whom we could have given it. Whether Wynn has got it I can not tell, but most likely it has been eaten upon the way.

"Your extracts are very interesting, but several have miscarried: the devil seems to be post-master-general on that station. Go on as you have begun, and you will soon collect more, and more valuable materials than you are aware of. Describe a West Indian tavern—its difference from ours. Go to church one Sunday, to describe church and congregation. Inquire at every town if there be any schools there—any Dissenters; how the Methodists get on; collect some Jamaica newspapers—and, if you can, the Magazine which is printed there. Your Tortola letter is a very delightful one. Put down all the stories you hear. When you go ashore, take notice of the insects that you see, the birds, &c.—all make parts of the picture. Lose nothing that a Creole, or any man acquainted with the islands, tells you concerning them. Send me all the stories about Pompey—he must be a curious character: ask him his history. What sort of church-yards have they? any epitaphs? Where do they bury the negroes? Is there any funeral service for them?

"You talk of invasion: depend upon it, it never will and never can be attempted while our fleet is what it is; and poor Nelson has left its name higher than ever. What a blaze of glory has he departed in! The Spaniards, you will see, behaved most honorably to the men who were wrecked, and who fell into their hands—and about our wounded, and the French very ill. Continental politics are too much in the dark for me to say any thing. It is by no means clear that Prussia will take part against France, though highly probable, and now highly politic. If she should, I think Bonaparte's victories may prove his destruction.

"No further news of the sale of Madoc. The reviews will probably hurt it for a time; that is in their power, and that is all they can do. Unquestionably the poem will stand and flourish. I am perfectly satisfied with the execution—now, eight months after its publication, in my cool judgment. William Taylor has said it is the best English poem that has left the press since the Paradise Lost; indeed, this is not exaggerated praise, for, unfortunately, there is no competition.

"I want you grievously to tell Espriella stories about the navy, and give him a good idea of its present state, which, of course, I can not venture to do except very slightly and very cautiously, fully aware of my own incompetence. Some of your own stories you will recognize. The book will be very amusing, and promises more profit than any of my former works. Most praise I have had for Amadis, for the obvious reason that it excited no envy; they who were aiming at distinction as poets, &c., without success, had no objection to allow that I could translate from the Spanish. But praise and fame are two very distinct things. Nobody thinks the higher of me for that translation, or feels a wish to see me for it, as they do for Joan of Arc and Thalaba. Poor Thalaba got abused in every review except the Critical; and yet there has not any poem of the age excited half the attention, or won half the admiration that that kind has. I am fairly up the hill.

"Little Edith looks at the picture of the ships in the Cyclopedia, and listens to the story how she has an uncle who lives in a ship, and loves her dearly, and sends her a kiss in a letter. Poor Cupid* has been hung at last for robbing a hen-roost! Your three half-crown sticks, you see, were bestowed upon him in vain. He is the first of all my friends who ever came to the gallows, and I am very sorry for him. Poor fellow! I was his godfather. Of Joe the last accounts were good. Thus have I turned my memory inside out, to rummage out all the news for you, and little enough it is. We live here in the winter as much out of the way of all society as if we were cruising at sea. From November till June not a soul do we see, except perhaps Wordsworth once or twice during the time. Of course it is my working season, and I get through a great deal. Edith's love. God bless you, Tom.

"R. S."

CHAPTER XII.

ADVANTAGES OF KESWICK AS A RESIDENCE—OPINIONS POLITICAL, SOCIAL, AND RELIGIOUS—THE LANGUAGE OF MADOC DEFENDED—FOREIGN POLITICS—CURIOUS CASE OF MENTAL DERANGEMENT AMELIORATED—HOBBES'S THEORY OF A STATE OF NATURE COMBATED—MR. COLERIDGE—MR. WORDSWORTH—MR. DUPPA'S LIFE OF MICHAEL ANGELO—DETAILS OF HIMSELF AND HIS LITERARY PURSUITS AND OPINIONS—POLITICAL CHANGES—LITERARY LABORS—CONGRATULATIONS TO MR. WYNN ON THE BIRTH OF A CHILD—REMARKS ON THE EFFECTS OF TIME—BRISTOL RECOLLECTIONS—BEAUSOBRE'S HISTORY OF MANICHEISM—GOES TO NORWICH—THE ANNUAL REVIEW—JESUITISM IN ENGLAND—BRIEF VISIT TO LONDON AND RETURN—QUAINT THEORY OF THE ORIGIN OF LANGUAGES—THALABA—URGES MR. BEDFORD TO VISIT HIM AT KESWICK—DIRECTIONS ABOUT SPECIMENS OF ENGLISH POETS—KEHAMA—DEATH OF HIS UNCLE JOHN SOUTHEY—LINES UPON THAT EVENT—MOUNTAIN EXCURSIONS—REVIEWS OF MADOC—EPIC SUBJECTS SUGGESTED—TRANSLATION OF PALMERIN OF ENGLAND—PAPERS CONCERNING SOUTH AMERICA—MEMOIRS OF COLONEL HUTCHINSON.—1806.

My father was now a settled dweller among the mountains of Cumberland; and although for some years he again and again refers to Lisbon as a place he earnestly desired to revisit, still this was a project which would probably have assumed a very different aspect, had it come more immediately before him: he would never have

* Cupid was a dog, of what kind does not appear, belonging to Mr. Danvers.

removed his family abroad, and he was far too much attached to, and, indeed, too dependent upon, home comforts and domestic relations, to have made up his mind to leave them even for the furtherance of his chief literary pursuits.

A more thoroughly domestic man, or one more simple in his mode of living, it would be difficult to picture; and the habits into which he settled himself about this time continued through life, unbroken regularity and unwearied industry being their chief characteristics. Habitually an early riser, he never encroached upon the hours of the night; and finding his highest pleasure and his recreation in the very pursuits necessary for earning his daily bread, he was, probably, more continually employed than any other writer of his generation. "My actions," he writes about this time to a friend, "are as regular as those of St. Dunstan's quarter-boys. Three pages of history after breakfast (equivalent to five in small quarto printing); then to transcribe and copy for the press, or to make my selections and biographies, or what else suits my humor, till dinner-time; from dinner till tea I read, write letters, see the newspaper, and very often indulge in a siesta—for sleep agrees with me, and I have a good, substantial theory to prove that it must; for as a man who walks much requires to sit down and rest himself, so does the brain, if it be the part most worked, require its repose. Well, after tea I go to poetry, and correct, and rewrite, and copy till I am tired, and then turn to any thing else till supper; and this is my life—which, if it be not a very merry one, is yet as happy as heart could wish. At least I should think so if I had not once been happier; and I do think so, except when that recollection comes upon me. And then, when I cease to be cheerful, it is only to become contemplative—to feel at times a wish that I was in that state of existence which passes not away; and this always ends in a new impulse to proceed, that I may leave some durable monument and some efficient good behind me."

The place of abode which he had chosen for himself, or, rather, which a variety of circumstances had combined to fix him in, was, in most respects, well suited to his wishes and pursuits. Surrounded by scenery which combines in a rare degree both beauty and grandeur, the varied and singularly striking views which he could command from the windows of his study were of themselves a recreation to the mind, as well as a feast to the eye, and there was a perpetual inducement to exercise which drew him oftener from his books than any other cause would have done, though not so often as was advisable for due relaxation both of mind and body. Uninterrupted leisure for a large portion of the year was absolutely essential; and that the long winter of our northern clime, which may be said generally to include half the autumnal and nearly all the spring months, was well calculated to afford him. With the swallows the tourists began to come, and among them many friends and acquaintances, and so many strangers bearing letters of introduction, that his stores of the latter were being continually increased, and sometimes pleasing and valuable additions made to the former class. During several years his brother Henry, while a student of medicine at Edinburgh, spent his vacations at Keswick, and occasionally some of his more intimate friends came down for a few weeks. These were his golden days; and on such occasions he indulged himself in a more complete holiday, and extended his rambles to those parts of the mountain country which were beyond the circle lying immediately within reach of his own home. These happy times left a permanent memory behind them, and the remembrance of them formed many anecdotes for his later years.

The society thus obtained, while occasionally it was a heavy tax upon his time (to whom time was all his wealth), was, on the whole, more suited to his habits than constant intercourse with the world would have been, and more wholesome than complete seclusion. "London," he writes at this time to his friend Mr. Rickman, who was urging him to make a longer visit than usual, "disorders me by over stimulation. I dislike its society more from reflection than from feeling. Company, to a certain extent, intoxicates me. I do not often commit the fault of talking too much, but very often say what would be better unsaid, and that, too, in a manner not to be easily forgotten. People go away and repeat single sentences, dropping all that led to them, and all that explains them; and very often, in my hearty hatred of assentation, I commit faults of the opposite kind. Now I am sure to find this out myself, and to get out of humor with myself; what prudence I have is not ready on demand; and so it is that the society of any except my friends, though it may be sweet in the mouth, is bitter in the belly."

As concerns his social and political opinions, it may be said that they were for many years in a transition state—rather settling and sobering than changing; indeed, if fairly examined, they altered through life, not so much in the objects he had in view, as in the means whereby those objects were to be gained. He had begun in early youth with those generous feelings toward mankind, which made him believe almost in their perfectibility, but these soon passed away. "There was a time," he wrote, six years earlier, "when I believed in the persuadibility of man, and had the mania of man-mending. Experience has taught me better." But before experience had finished her lessons, he had another stage to pass through; and from having too good an opinion of human nature, he, for a time, entertained far too low a one. Many of his early letters are full of the strongest misanthropical expressions; and in his earliest published prose work, the letters from Spain and Portugal, he gives emphatic utterance to the same feelings. "Man is a beast," he exclaims, "and an ugly beast, and Monboddo libels the orang-outangs by suspecting them to be of the same family;" but this, again, was naturally a transition state, and his mature mind judged more justly and much more charitably, being removed alike from the visionary enthusiasm of his young life, and the self-concentered apathy which succeeded it.

With respect to particular questions of politics, it will be seen, in the course of this volume, that on certain prominent subjects his feelings became strongly enlisted on the same side which the Tory politicians advocated, and in direct opposition to those who professed to be the leaders of Liberal opinions; agreement on some points elicited agreement on others, and, in like manner, disagreement naturally had for its fruits dislike and complete estrangement.

His religious views, also, during middle life, were settling down into a more definite shape, and were drawing year after year nearer to a conformity with the doctrines of the Church of England. However vague and unsettled his thoughts on such subjects were in early youth, he had never doubted the great truths of Revelation; and how rarely this was the case at that period, especially among men of cultivated minds, at least of that stirring democratic school into whose society he had been thrown, the memories of many of the passing generation will bear testimony. "I knew no one who believed," is the startling expression of one of my father's cotemporaries, himself a man of intellect and well-stored mind, when speaking of his own passage through that "Valley of the Shadow of Death," and referring to the friends of his own age and standing; and he goes on to say that he took up the study of the grounds and evidences of Christianity with the full expectation that he should find no difficulty whatever in refuting to his own satisfaction what so many others considered as hardly worthy the serious consideration of reasonable men. Many of those persons whose mental and social qualifications my father most admired were at best but unsettled in their faith; and though, almost without exception in later life, they sought and found the only sure resting-place for their hopes and fears, still the frequent intercourse with such men was an ordeal not to be passed through without difficulty or without danger. But he was blessed with a pure and truthful heart, strong in the rejection of evil principles; and this, through God's mercy, was confirmed by his solitary, laborious, and dutiful life, united as it was with the constant study of the Holy Scriptures, and at a rather later period, by an acquaintance with the works of most of the great English theologians.

The reader has seen from my father's letters the reception which Madoc had hitherto met with, and that many of the reviews had been somewhat unfavorable, and had not failed to take full advantage of those defects in the structure of the story of which the author himself seems to have been well aware.

These hostile criticisms, however, had not always their intended effect. Mr. Bedford asks him at the close of the past year, "I should like to know what *you call* the real *faults* of Madoc? Wyndham told Wynn that from what he had seen of the abusive reviews, he was inclined to like the poem exceedingly, and from those specimens speaks of it in high terms: this would make Godwin's nose three times as horrid as ever we thought it."

To this my father replies:

To Grosvenor C. Bedford, Esq.

"Jan. 1, 1806.

"DEAR GROSVENOR,

"You use Godwin's name as if he had maliciously reviewed Madoc, which I do not by any means suspect or believe, though he has all the ill will in the world to make me feel his power. The Monthly was rather more dull than he would have made it. I should well like to know who the writer is; for, by the Living Jingo—a deity whom D. Manuel* conceives to have been worshiped by the Celts—I would contrive to give him a most righteous clapper-clawing in return.

"Thalaba is faulty in its language. Madoc is not. I am become what they call a Puritan in Portugal with respect to language, and I dare assert that there is not a single instance of illegitimate English in the whole poem. The faults are in the management of the story and the conclusion, where the interest is injudiciously transferred from Madoc to Yuhidthiton; it is also another fault to have rendered *accidents* subservient to the catastrophe. You will see this very accurately stated in the Annual Review: the remark is new, and of exceeding great value. I acknowledge no fault in the execution of any magnitude, except the struggle of the women with Amalahta, which is all clumsily done, and must be rewritten. Those faults which are inherent in and inseparable from the story, as they could not be helped, so are they to be considered as defects or *wants* rather than faults. I mean the division of the poem into two separate stories and scenes, and the inferior interest of the voyage, though a thing of such consequence. But as for unwarrantable liberties of language—there is not a solitary sin of the kind in the whole 9000 lines. Let me be understood: I call it an unwarrantable liberty to use a verb deponent, for instance, actively, or to form any compound contrary to the strict analogy of the language—such as *tameless* in Thalaba, applied to the tigress. I do not recollect any coinage in Madoc except the word *deicide;* and that such a word exists I have no doubt, though I can not lay my finger upon an authority, for depend upon it the Jews have been called so a thousand times. That word is unobjectionable. It is in strict analogy—its meaning is immediately obvious, and no other word could have expressed the same meaning. Archaisms are faulty if they are too obsolete. *Thewes* is the only one I recollect; that also has a peculiar meaning, for which there is no equivalent word. But, in short, so very laboriously was Madoc re-

* The fictitious name of the writer of "Espriella's Letters."

written and corrected, time after time, that I will pledge myself, if you ask me in any instance why one word stands in the place of another which you, perhaps, may think the better one, to give you a reason (most probably, *euphoniæ gratiâ*), which will convince you that I had previously weighed both in the balance. Sir, the language and versification of that poem are as full of profound mysteries as the Butler; and he, I take it, was as full of profundity as the great deep itself.

"I do not know any one who has understood the main merit of the poem so nearly as I wished it to be understood as yourself: the true and intrinsic greatness of Madoc, the real talents of his enemies, and (which I consider as the main work of skill) the feeling of respect for them—of love even for the individuals, yet with an abhorrence of the *national* cruelties that perfectly reconcile you to their dreadful overthrow. You have very well expressed this.

" * * * * * * *

I have written this at two days—many sittings—under the influence of influenza and antimony. I am mending, but very weak, and sufficiently uncomfortable. R. S.

"Jan. 1. Multos et felices."

To Lieut. Southey, H.M.S. Amelia.

"Jan. 1, 1806. (Many happy returns.)

"MY DEAR TOM,

* * * * * * *

"Don't be cast down, Tom: were I to make laws, no man should be made master and commander till he was thirty years of age. Made you will be at last, and will get on at last as high as your heart can wish: never doubt that, as I never doubt it.

"Don't send me another turtle till I am lord mayor, and then I shall be much obliged to you for one; but, for Heaven's sake, not till then. I consigned over all my right and title in the green fat to Wynn, by a formal power sent to Coutts the banker, who was to look out for him; but of his arrival not a word yet—ten to one ut he is digested. When you are coming home, if you could *bring* a cargo of dried tamarinds, I should like them, because they are very seldom to be got in England: I never saw them but once. *Dried*, mark you, in the husk—not preserved. The acid is exceedingly delightful. Now remember, the words are *when you are coming home*, and *bring:* do not attempt to send them, or there will be trouble, vexation, unnecessary expense, and, most likely, the loss of the thing itself.

"My daughter never sees a picture of ship or boat but she talks of her uncle in the ship, and as regularly receives the kiss which he sent in the letter. You will be very fond of her if she goes on as well when you come home as she does at present. Harry is hard at work for the last season at Edinburgh, preparing to pass muster and be be-doctored in July. Most likely he will go to Lisbon with me in the autumn—at least I know not how he can be better employed for a few months than in traveling and spoiling his complexion.

"The extraordinary success of Bonaparte, or, rather, the wretched misconduct of Austria, has left the Continent completely under the control of France. Our plan should be to increase our cruisers and scour the seas effectually—to take all we can, and keep all we take—professing that such is our intention, and that we are ready to make peace whenever France pleases, upon the simple terms of leaving off with our winnings. Meantime we ought to take the Cape, the French islands in the East (those in the West would cost too many lives, and may be left for the blacks), Minorca, Sicily, and Egypt. If France chooses to have the main-land, the islands should be ours. I suppose we shall go upon some such plan. As for invasion, the old story will begin again in the spring; but it is a thing impossible, and you sailors best know this. Lord St. Vincent used to say, when it was talked of, 'I don't say they can't come; I only say that they can't come by sea.' What will affect me is the fate of Portugal; for it is now more than ever to be expected that Bonaparte will turn us out, merely to show he can do it. This will be to me a grievous annoyance. It is not unlikely that he will propose peace after these splendid victories, and it is not impossible that Pitt may accept it, to keep his place. Heaven forbid! To give up Malta now would be giving up the national honor: it would be confessing that we had lost the game, whereas we can play the single-handed game forever. Our bad partners ruin us. The ultimate consequences of the success of France may not be so disastrous to Europe as is generally supposed. Suppose that the Continent be modeled as Bonaparte pleases—which it will be—and that it remains so in peace for twenty or thirty years: he will have disabled Austria, it is true, but all the other powers will be strengthened, and a new state created in Italy which did not exist before. Then she will be under French direction: true, but still not French; the difference of language effectually prevents that. Bonaparte will not be a long-lived man; he can not be, in the ordinary course of nature; there has been, and will be too much wear and tear of him. His successor, if the succession go regularly on, as I suppose it will, will certainly not inherit his talents, and the first-born emperor will have all the benefit of imperial education, which is quite sure to make him upon a level with all other sovereign princes. By that time the French generals will have died off, and we must not forget that it is the Revolution which made these men generals, and that men no longer rise according to their merit.

"Jan. 5.

"I have just received the following news: 'Sir—Am extremely sorry to be obliged to inform you, that a turtle, that I flattered myself would have survived home, from the excessive long passage and performance of quarantine at Cork, Falmouth, and Sea Reach died in the former port, with every one on board the ship. Respectfully, y[r] much obliged and obedient servant, STEPHEN T. SELK.' So much for the turtle! I think, if government will make such beasts perform quarantine, they ought to pay for the loss. Surfeits and indigestions they may bring into the city, but of the yellow fever there can be no danger. The Court of Aldermen should take it into consideration.

"And now, to finish this letter of gossip, I am in the midst of reviewing, which will be over by the time this reaches you, even if, contrary to custom, it should reach you in regular course. Espriella also will, by that time, be gone to press. This, and the History of the Cid, I shall have to send you in the summer. No further news of the sale; in fact, if the edition of 500 goes off in two years, it will be a good sale for so costly a book. I hope it will not be very long before Thalaba goes to press a second time. God bless you! R. S."

To Messrs. Longman and Rees.

"Jan. 5, 1806.

"DEAR SIRS,

"A gentleman in this neighborhood, Mr. ——, is printing some poems at his own expense, which Faulder is to publish; and he has applied to me to request that your name also may appear in the title-page. In such cases, the only proper mode of proceeding is to relate the plain state of the matter. His verses are good for nothing, and not a single copy can possibly sell, except what his acquaintance may purchase; but he has been laboring under mental derangement—the heaviest of all human calamities—and the passion which he has contracted for rhyming has changed the character of his malady, and made him, from a most miserable being, a very happy one. Under these circumstances you will not, perhaps, object to gratifying him, and depositing copies of his book in your ware-room, for the accommodation of the spiders. He tells me his MS. is at ——, if you think fit to inspect it: this trouble you will hardly take: the poems are as inoffensive as they are worthless. I shall simply tell him that I have made the application, without giving him any reason to expect its success. You will, of course, use your own judgment, only I will beg you to signify your assent or dissent to him himself. * * *

"Believe me, yours truly,

"ROBERT SOUTHEY."

The following curious letter needs some explanation. My father had sent the MS. of his letters, under the assumed character of Espriella, to his friend Mr. Rickman for his remarks, who was anxious that some strong condemnation of pugilism should not appear, as he considered it acted as a sort of *safety-valve* to the bad passions of the lower orders, and in some cases prevented the use of the knife; and he goes on to say, "The abstract love of bloodshed is a very odd taste, but I am afraid very natural; the increase of gladiatorial exhibitions at Rome is not half so strong a proof of this as the Mexican sacrifices, which I think commenced not till about A.D. 1300—and by a kind of accident or whim—and lasted above 200 years, with a horrible increase, and with the imitation of all the neighboring states. This last circumstance is a wonderful proof of the love of blood in the human mind. Without that, the practice must have raised the strongest aversion around Mexico. I believe Leviathan Hobbes says 'that a state of nature is a state of war, *i. e.*, bloodshed.' I begin to think so too; else why has Nature made such a variety of offensive as well as defensive armor in all her animal and vegetable productions? It seems a perverted industry, and is unexplainable, unless we believe Hobbes."*

My father's reply shows he was of a different opinion.

To John Rickman, Esq.

"Jan. 15, 1806.

"DEAR RICKMAN,

"Before I speak of myself, let me say something upon a more important subject. Nature has given *offensive* armor for two reasons: in the first place, it is defensive because it serves to intimidate; a better reason is, that claws and teeth are the tools with which animals must get their living; and that the general system of one creature eating another is a benevolent one, needs little proof; there *must* be death, and what can be wiser than to make death subservient to life? As for a state of nature, the phrase, as applied to man, is stark naked nonsense. Savage man is a degenerated animal. My own belief is, that the present human race is not much more than six thousand years old, according to the concurrent testimony of all rational history. The Indian records are good for nothing. But add as many millenniums as you will, the question, 'How came they here at first?' still occurs. The infinite series is an infinite absurdity; and to suppose them growing like mushrooms or maggots in mud, is as bad. Man must have been *made* here, or *placed* here with sufficient powers, bodily and mental, for his own support. I think the most reasonable opinion is, that the first men had a knowledge of language and of religion; in short, that the accounts of a golden or patriarchal age are, in their foundation, true. How soon the civilized being degenerates under unfavorable circumstances, has been enough proved by history. Free-will, God, and final retribution solve all difficulties. That Deity can not be understood, is a stupid objection; without one we can understand nothing. I can not put down my thoughts methodically without much revision and re-arrangement; but you may see what I would be at: it is no difficult matter to harpoon the Leviathan, and wound him mortally.

" * * * * * * *

You may account by other means for the spread of the Mexican religion than by the love of blood. Man is by nature a religious animal; and if the

* J. R. to R. S., Jan. 9, 1806.

elements of religion were not innate in him, as I am convinced they are, sickness would make him so. You will find that all savages connect superstition with disease—some cause, which they can neither comprehend nor control, affects them painfully, and the remedy always is to appease an offended Spirit, or drive away a malignant one. Even in enlightened societies, you will find that men more readily believe what they *fear* than what they hope: * * * religions, therefore, which impose privations and self-torture, have always been more popular than any other. How many of our boys' amusements consist in bearing pain? grown children like to do the same from a different motive. You will more easily persuade a man to wear hair-cloth drawers, to flog himself, or swing upon a hook, than to conform to the plain rules of morality and common sense. I shall have occasion to look into this subject when writing of the spirit of Catholicism, which furnishes as good an illustration as the practices of the Hindoos. Here, in England, Calvinism is the popular faith. . . . Beyond all doubt, the religion of the Mexicans is the most diabolical that has ever existed. It is not, however, by any means so mischievous as the Brahminical system of caste, which, wherever it exists, has put a total stop to the amelioration of society. The Mexicans were rapidly advancing. Were you more at leisure, I should urge you to bestow a week's study upon the Spanish language, for the sake of the mass of information contained in their travelers and historians. * *

"God bless you! R. S."

To Walter Scott, Esq., Advocate.

"Greta Hall, Keswick, Feb. 4, 1806.

"MY DEAR SIR,

"We are under considerable uneasiness respecting Coleridge, who left Malta early in September to return overland from Naples, was heard of from Trieste, and has not been heard of since. Our hope is, that, finding it impracticable to proceed, he may have returned, and be wintering at Naples or in Sicily.

"Wordsworth was with me last week; he has of late been more employed in correcting his poems than in writing others; but one piece he has written, upon the ideal character of a soldier, than which I have never seen any thing more full of meaning and sound thought. The subject was suggested by Nelson's most glorious death, though having no reference to it. He had some thoughts of sending it to the Courier, in which case you will easily recognize his hand.

"Having this occasion to write, I will venture to make one request. My friend Duppa is about to publish a Life of Michael Angelo: the book will be a good book, for no man understands his art better. I wish, when it comes in course of trial, you would save it from Judge Jeffrey, or intercede with him for as favorable a report as it may be found to deserve. Duppa deserves well of the public, because he has, at a very considerable loss, published those magnificent heads from Raffaelle and Michael Angelo, and is publishing this present work without any view whatever to profit; indeed, he does not print copies enough to pay his expenses.

"Mrs. Southey and her sister join me in remembrance to Mrs. Scott. I know not whether I shall ever again see the Tweed and the Yarrow, yet should be sorry to think I should not. Your scenery has left upon me a strong impression—more so for the delightful associations which you and your country poets have inseparably connected with it. I am going in the autumn, if Bonaparte will let me, to streams as classical and as lovely—the Mondego of Camoens, the Douro, and the Tagus; but I shall not find such society on their banks.

"Remember me to my two fellow-travelers. Heaven keep them and me also from being the subject of any further experiments upon the infinite compressibility of matter.

"Believe me, yours very truly,

"ROBERT SOUTHEY.

"If Hogg should publish his poems, I shall be very glad to do what little I can in getting subscribers for him."

To the Rev. Nicholas Lightfoot.

"Keswick, Feb. 8, 1806.

"MY DEAR FRIEND,

"You tell me to write as an egotist, and I am well disposed so to do; for what else is it that gives private letters their greatest value, but the information they bring us of those for whom we are interested? I saw your marriage in the papers, and perhaps one reason why my letter has remained so long unfinished in my desk is a sort of fear lest I should mention it after death might have dissolved it—a sort of superstitious feeling to which I am subject. I wish you—being a father myself—as large a family as you can comfortably bring up, and if you are not provided with a godfather upon the next occasion, I beg you to accept of me, as an old and vary affectionate friend; 'tis a voluntary kind of relationship, in which it would gratify me to stand to a child of yours, and which I should consider as a religious pledge on my part for any useful, kind, and fatherly offices which it might ever happen to be in my power to perform.

"I have for some time looked on with pleasure to the hope of seeing you next autumn, when, in all probability, if the situation of affairs abroad does not prevent me, I shall once more visit Portugal, not for health's sake, but to collect the last materials for my history, and to visit those parts of the kingdom which I have not yet seen. In this case my way will lie through Devonshire, and I will stop a day or two at Crediton, and talk over old times.

"You inquire of the wreck of the Seward family—a name as dear to my inmost heart as it can be to yours. No change has taken place among them for some years, as I understand from Duppa, who was my guest here the autumn before last, and with whom I have an occasional correspondence.

"I passed through Oxford two years ago, and walked through the town at four o'clock in the morning; the place never before appeared to me half so beautiful. I looked up at my own windows, and as you may well suppose, felt as most people do when they think of what changes time brings about.

"If you have seen or should see the Annual Review, you may like to know that I have borne a great part in it thus far, and I may refer you for the state of my opinions to the Reviewals of the Periodical Accounts of the Baptist Mission, vol. i., of Malthus's Essay on Population, Miles's History of the Methodists, and the Transactions of the Missionary Society, vol. ii. and iii., and of the Report of the Society for the Suppression of Vice, vol. iii. In other articles you may trace me from recollections of your own, by family likeness, by a knowledge of Spanish literature, and by a love of liberty and literature freely and warmly expressed. I was ministerial under Addington, regarded his successor with the utmost indignation, and am exceedingly well pleased at the present changes. Time, you say, moderates opinions as it mellows wine. My views and hopes are certainly altered, though the heart and soul of my wishes continues the same. It is the world that has changed, not I. I took the same way in the afternoon that I did in the morning, but sunset and sunrise make a different scene. If I regret any thing in my own life, it is that I *could* not take orders, for of all ways of life that would have best accorded with my nature; but I could not get in at the door.

"In other respects time has not much altered me. I am as thin as ever, and to the full as noisy: making a noise in any way whatever is an animal pleasure with me, and the louder it is the better. Do you remember the round hole at the top of the stair-case, opposite your door?*

"Coleridge is daily expected to return from Malta, where he has been now two years for his health. I inhabit the same house with his wife and children—perhaps the very finest single spot in England. We overlook Keswick Lake, have the Lake of Bassenthwaite in the distance on the other side, and Skiddaw behind us. But we only sojourn here for a time. I may, perhaps, be destined to pass some years in Portugal—which, indeed, is my wish—or, if otherwise, must ultimately remove to the neighborhood of London, for the sake of the public libraries.

"My dislike was not to schoolmasters, but to the rod, which I dare warrant you do not make much use of. Here is a long letter, and you have in it as many great I's as your heart can wish. It will give me much pleasure to hear again from you, and to know that your family is increased. If I can not be godfather now, let me put in a claim in time for the next occasion; but I hope you will write to tell me that three things have been promised and vowed in *my* name by proxy. No man can more safely talk of defying the world, the flesh, and the devil. With the world my pursuits are little akin; the flesh and I quarreled long ago, and I have been nothing but skin and bone ever since; and as for the devil, I have made more ballads in his abuse than any body before me.

"God bless you, Lightfoot!

"Yours very affectionately,

"ROBERT SOUTHEY."

* See p. 219.

To John Rickman, Esq.

"Feb. 11, 1806.

"MY DEAR RICKMAN,

" * * * * * * * * * It seems to me that the Grenvilles get into power just as they could wish, but that it is otherwise with Fox and Grey. They are pledged to parliamentary reform, and in this their other colleagues will not support them. It will be put off at first with sufficient plausibility, under the plea of existing circumstances; but my good old friend Major Cartwright (who is as noble an old Englishman as ever was made of extra best superfine flesh and blood) will find that existing circumstances have no end; there must come a time when it will appear, that if the question be not honestly brought forward, it has been given up as the price of their admission to power; and in that case, Fox had better for himself have died, instead of the other minister who had nothing to lose in the opinion of wise men; so that I am not sure that Fox's friends ought to rejoice at his success.

"But *quoad* Robert Southey, things are different. I have a chance of getting an appointment at Lisbon (this, of course, is said to yourself only); either the Secretaryship of Legation or the Consulship—whichever falls vacant first—has been asked for me, and Lord Holland has promised to back the application. * * * I shall follow my own plans—relying upon nobody but myself, and shall go to Lisbon in the autumn: if Fortune finds me there, so much the better, but she shall never catch me on the wild goose chase after her.

"I want Tom to be an admiral, that when he is fourscore he may be killed in a great victory and get a monument in St. Paul's; for this reason, I have some sort of notion that one day or other I may have one there myself, and it would be rather awkward to get among so many sea captains, unless one had a friend among them to introduce one to the mess-room. It is ridiculous giving the captains the honors—a colonel in the army has the same claim; better build a pyramid at once, and insert their names as they fall in this marble gazette. * * * *

"God bless you! R. S."

To Lieutenant Southey, H.M.S. Amelia.

"Keswick, February 15, 1806.

"A world of events have taken place since last I wrote—indeed, so as almost to change the world here. Pitt is dead, Fox and the Grenvilles in place, Wynn Under Secretary of State in the Home Office. I have reason to expect something; of the two appointments at Lisbon which would suit me, whichever falls vacant first is asked for me; both are in Fox's gift, and Lord as well as Lady Holland speak for me. It is likely that one or other will be vacated ere long, and if I should not succeed, then Wynn will look elsewhere. Something or other will certainly turn up ere it be very long. I hope, also, something may some way or other be done for you; you shall lose nothing for want of application on my part.

"St. Vincent supersedes Cornwallis in the Channel fleet: Sir Samuel was made admiral in the last list of promotions. As for peace or war, one knows not how to speculate. If I were to guess any thing, it would be, that by way of getting all parties out of the way with credit, Bonaparte may offer us Malta, which he can not take, as an indemnification for Hanover, which we must lose. I should be glad this compromise were made. You have news enough here to set you in a brown study for the rest of the day. I will only add an anecdote, which I believe is not in the papers, and which sailors will like to know. The flag of the Victory was to be buried with Nelson; but the sailors, when it was lowering into the grave, tore it in pieces to keep as relics. His reward has been worthy of the country—a public funeral of course, and a monument, besides monuments of some kind or other in most of the great cities by private subscriptions. His widow made countess with £2000 a year, his brother an earl with an adequate pension, and £200,000 to be laid out in the purchase of an estate, never to be alienated from the family. Well done, England!

"As several of my last letters have been directed to St. Kitt's, I conclude that by this time one or other may have reached you. Yours is good news so far as relates to your health, and to the probability of going to Halifax—better summer-quarters than the Islands. If you should go there, such American books as you may fall in with will be curiosities in England. The New York publications I conclude travel so far north; reviews and magazines, novels or poetry—any thing of real American growth I shall be glad to have. Keep a minute journal there, and let nothing escape you. * * *

"Did I tell you that I have promised to supply the lives of the Spanish and Portuguese authors in the remaining volumes of Dr. Aikin's great General Biography? This will not interfere with my own plans; where it does, it is little more than printing the skeleton of what is hereafter to be enlarged. I can tell you nothing of the sale of Madoc, except that Longman has told me nothing, which is proof enough of slow sale; but if the edition goes off in two years, or indeed in three, it will be well for so costly a book. There is a reaction in these things; my poems make me known first, and then I make the poems known: as I rise in the world, the books will sell. I have occasional thoughts of going on with Kehama now, when my leisure time approaches, to keep my hand in, and to leave it for publication next winter. Not a line has been added to it since you left me.

"No news yet of Coleridge. We are seriously uneasy about him. It is above two months since he ought to have been home. Our hope is, that, finding the Continent overrun by the French, he may have returned to Malta. Edith's love.

"God bless you, Tom! R. S."

To Richard Duppa, Esq.

"Feb. 23, 1806.

"DEAR DUPPA,

"Nicholson, I see, sets up a new review. Carlisle ought to get you well taken care of there. Need you be told the history of all reviews? If a book falls into the hands of one who is neither friend nor enemy—which for a man known in the world is not very likely—the reviewer will find fault to show his own superiority, though he be as ignorant of the subject upon which he writes as an ass is of metaphysics, or John Pinkerton of Welsh antiquities and Spanish literature. As your book, therefore, has little chance of fair play, get it into the hands of your friends. Have you any access to the Monthly?

"For politics. As far as the public is concerned, God be praised! How far I may be concerned, remains to be seen. My habits are now so rooted, that every thing not connected with my own immediate pursuit seems of secondary consequence, and as far as relates to myself, hardly worth a hope or fear. So far as any thing can be given me which will facilitate that pursuit, I greatly desire it, and have good reason to expect the best. But nothing that can happen will in any way affect my plan of operations for the present year. I go to London in a month's time; I go to Lisbon in the autumn, and in the interim must work like a negro. By-the-by, can not you give me a letter to Bartolozzi? He will like to see an Englishman who can talk to him of the persons with whom he was acquainted in England.

"I am reading an Italian History of Heresies in four folios, by a certain Domenico Bernino. If there be one thing in the world which delights me more than another, it is ecclesiastical history. This book of Bernino's is a very useful one for a man who knows something of the subject, and is aware how much is to believed, and how much is not.

"My reviewing is this day finished forever and ever, amen. Our Fathers who are in the Row will, I dare say, wish me to continue at the employment, but I am weary of it. Seven years have I been, like Sir Bevis, preying upon 'rats and mice, and such small deer,' and for the future will fly at better game. It is best to choose my own subjects.

"You mentioned once to me certain prophetical drawings by a boy. Did you see them, or can you give me any particulars concerning them? for I find them connected with Joanna Southcote, of whose prophecies I have about a dozen pamphlets, and about whom Don Manuel is going to write a letter. I like our friend Huntingdon's Bank of Faith so well on a cooler perusal, that I shall look for two other of his works at the shop of his great friend, Baker, in Oxford Street. That man is a feature in the age, and a great man in his way. People who are curious to see extraordinary men, and go looking after philosophers and authors only, are something like the good people in genteel life, who pay nobody knows what for a cod's head, and don't know the luxury of eating sprats. Oh! Wordsworth sent me a man the other day who was worth seeing; he looked like a first assassin in Macbeth as to his costume, but he was a rare man. He had been a lieutenant in the navy, was scholar enough to quote Virgil aptly, had turned Quaker or semi-Quaker, and was now a dealer in wood somewhere about twenty miles off. He had seen much and thought much, his head was well stored, and his heart in the right place.

"It is five or six-and-twenty years since he was at Lisbon, and he gave me as vivid a description of the Belem Convent as if the impression in his memory was not half a day old. Edridge's acquaintance, Thomas Wilkinson, came with him. They had both been visiting an old man of a hundred in the Vale of Lorton, and it was a fine thing to hear this Robert Foster describe him. God bless you!

"R. S."

To C. W. W. Wynn, Esq.

"Feb. 28, 1806.

"My dear Wynn,

"The intelligence* in your letter has given me more pleasure than I have often felt. In spite of modern philosophy, I do not believe that the first commandment is an obsolete statute yet, and I am very sure that man is a better being, as well as a happier one, for being a husband and a father. May God bless you in both relations of life!

"I shall be in London about the time when you are leaving it. * * It is long since we have met, and I shall be sorry to lose one of those opportunities of which life does not allow very many. It will be nearly two years since you were here, and if our after meetings are to be at such long intervals, there are not many to look on to. Many things make me feel old—ten years of marriage; the sort of fatherly situation in which I have stood to my brother Henry, now a man himself; the premature age at which I commenced author; the death of all who were about me in childhood; a body not made of lasting materials, and some wear and tear of mind. You once remarked to me how time strengthened family affections, and, indeed, all early ones: one's feelings seem to be weary of traveling, and like to rest at home. I had a proof the other night in my sleep how the mere lapse of time changes our disposition; I thought, of all men in the world, ——† called upon me, and that we were heartily glad to see each other. They who tell me that men grow hard-hearted as they grow older, have had a very limited view of this world of ours. It is true with those whose views and hopes are merely and vulgarly worldly; but when human nature is not perverted, time strengthens our kindly feelings, and abates our angry ones. * * * *

"God bless you!

"Yours affectionately, R. S."

* Of the birth of a child.

† A Westminster school-fellow, from whom he had received much brutal treatment.

To Grosvenor C. Bedford, Esq.

"Keswick, March 6, 1806.

"I am writing, Grosvenor, as you know, the History of Portugal—a country of which I probably know more than any foreigner, and as much as any native. Now has it come athwart me, this afternoon, how much more accurate, and perhaps, a thousand years hence, more valuable, a book it would be, were I to write the History of Wine Street below the Pump, the street wherein I was born, recording the revolutions of every house during twenty years. It almost startles me to see how the events of private life, within my own knowledge, *et quorum pars maxima, etc.*, equal or outdo novel and comedy; and the conclusion to each tale—the *mors omnibus est communis*—makes me more serious than the sight of my own gray hairs in the glass; for the hoar frosts, Grosvenor, are begun with me. Oh, there would be matter for moralizing in such a history beyond all that history offers. The very title is a romance. You, in London, need to be told that Wine Street is a street in Bristol, and that there is a pump in it, and that by the title I would mean to express that the historian does not extend his subject to that larger division of the street which lies above the pump. You, I say, need all these explanations, and yet, when I first went to school, I never thought of Wine Street and of that pump without tears, and such a sorrow at heart as, by Heaven! no child of mine shall ever suffer while I am living to prevent it; and so deeply are the feelings connected with that place rooted in me, that perhaps, in the hour of death, they will be the last that survive. Now this history it is most certain that I, the Portuguese historiographer, &c., &c., &c., shall never have leisure, worldly motive, nor perhaps heart to write; and yet, now being in tune, I will give you some of the recollections whereof it would be composed, catching them as they float by me; and as I am writing, forms enough thicken upon me to people a solitary cell* in Bedlam, were I to live out the remainder of a seventy years' lease.

"Let me begin with the church at the corner. I remember the *old* church: a row of little shops were built before it, above which its windows re-

* Baron Trenck, in his account of his long and wretched imprisonment, says, "I had lived long and much in the world; vacuity of thought, therefore, I was little troubled with." May not this give some clew to the cause why solitary confinement makes some insane and does not affect others? I have read somewhere of a man who said, if his cell had been *round* he must have gone mad, but there was a *corner* for the eye to rest upon.—Ed.

ceived light; and on the leads which roofed them, crowds used to stand at the chairing of members, as they did to my remembrance when peace was proclaimed after the American war. I was christened in that old church, and at this moment vividly remember our pew under the organ, of which I certainly have not thought these fifteen years before. —— was then the rector, a humdrum somnificator, who, God rest his soul for it! made my poor mother stay at home Sunday evenings, because she could not keep awake after dinner to hear him. A worldly-minded man succeeded, and effected, by dint of begging and impudence, a union between the two parishes of Christ Church and St. Ewins,* for no other conceivable reason than that he might be rector of both. However, he was a great man; and it was the custom once a year to catechize the children, and give them, if they answered well, a good plum-cake apiece in the last day of the examination, called a cracknell, and honestly worth a groat; and I can remember eating my cracknell, and being very proud of the praise of the curate (who was a really good man), when he found that I knew the etymology of *Decalogue;* for be it known to your worship that I did not leave off loving plum-cake when I began my Greek, nor have I left it off now when I have almost forgotten it. But I must turn back to the *pew*, and tell you how, in my very young days, a certain uncle Thomas, who would make a conspicuous figure in the history of Wine Street below the pump, once sentenced me to be deprived of my share of pie on Sunday for some misdemeanor there committed—I forget what—whether talking to my brother Tom, or reading the Revelations there during the sermon, for *that* was my favorite part of the Christian religion, and I always amused myself with the scraps from it after the collects whenever the prayer-book was in my hand.

"There were quarter-boys to this old church clock, as at St. Dunstan, and I have many a time stopped with my satchel on my back to see them strike. My father had a great love for these poor quarter-boys, who had regulated all his movements for about twenty years; and when the church was rebuilt, offered to subscribe largely to their re-establishment; but the Wine Streeters had no taste for the arts, and no feeling for old friends, and God knows what became of the poor fellows; but I know that when I saw them represented in a pantomine, which was called Bristol, and got up to please the citizens, I can not say whether I felt more joy at seeing them, or sorrow in thinking they were only represented—only stage quarter-boys, and not the real ones.

"The church was demolished, and sad things were said of the indecencies that occurred in removing the coffins for the new foundation to be laid. We had no interest in this, for our vault was at Ashton. I sent you once, years ago, a drawing of this church. It is my only freehold —all the land I possess in the world—and is now full—no matter! I never had any feeling about a family grave till my mother was buried in London, and that gave me more pain than was either reasonable or right. My little girl lies with my dear good friend Mrs. Danvers. I, myself, shall lie where I fall; and it will be all one in the next world. Once more to Christ Church. I was present in the heart of a crowd when the foundation stone was laid, and read the plates wherein posterity will find engraved the name of Robert Southey—for my father was church-warden—by the same token that that year he gave me a penny to go to the fair instead of a shilling as usual, being out of humor or out of money; and I, referring to a common phrase, called him a *generous* church-warden. There was money under the plate. I put some half-pence which I had picked out for their good impressions; and Winter, the bookseller, a good medal of the present king. * * * * * * * * * * Shame on me for not writing on foolscap! Vale!

"ROBERT SOUTHEY."

To John Rickman, Esq.

"March 15, 1806.

"MY DEAR RICKMAN,

"My last week has been somewhat desultorily employed in going through Beausobre's History of Manicheism, and in sketching the life of D. Luisa de Carvajal, an extraordinary woman of high rank, who came over to London in James the First's time, to make proselytes to the Catholic religion, under the protection of the Spanish embassador. It is a very curious story, and ought to be related in the history of that wretched king, who beheaded Raleigh to please the Spaniards.

"Beausobre's book is one of the most valuable that I have ever seen; it is a complete Thesaurus of early opinions, philosophical and theological. It is not the least remarkable circumstance of the Catholic religion that it has silently imbibed the most absurd parts of most of the heresies which it opposed and persecuted. I do not conceive Manes to have been a fanatic: there is too much philosophy in the whole of his system, even in the mythology, for that. His object seems to have been to unite the superstitions of the East and West; unluckily, both priests and magi united against the grand scheme—the Persians flayed him alive, and the Catholics roasted his disciples whenever they could catch them. Beausobre, as I expected, has perceived the similarity between Buddas and the Indian impostor; but he supposes that he came from the East. I am inclined to think otherwise, because I have found elsewhere that the Adam whose footstep is shown in Ceylon was a Manichæan traveling disciple, though both Moors and Portugese very naturally attributed this story to their old acquaintance. A proof this that the immediate disciples of Manes

* These are still held by one person; but as the population of the latter is stated at fifty-five only in the Clergy List, and the income of the two under £400, it would seem to be an unobjectionable union.—ED.

were successful; besides, the Asiatic fables are full of resemblances to Christianity. * *

"If there be any one thing in which the world has decidedly degenerated, it is in the breed of Heresiarchs: they were really great men in former times, devoting great knowledge and powerful talents to great purposes. In our days they are either arrant madmen or half rogues. * * * I am about to be the St. Epiphanius of Richard Brothers and Joanna Southcote; what say you to paying these worthies a visit some morning? the former is sure to be at home, and we might get his opinion of Joanna. I know some of his witnesses, and could enter into the depths of his system with him. As for Joanna, though tolerably well versed in the history of human credulity, I have never seen any thing so disgraceful to common sense as her precious publications. * *

"Metaphysicians have become less mischievous, but a good deal more troublesome. There was some excuse for them when they believed their opinions necessary to salvation; and it was certainly better for plain people like you and I that they should write by the folio than talk by the hour. * * * * * *

"God bless you! R. S."

To Mrs. Southey.

"Norwich, April 12, 1806.

"My dear Edith,

* * * * * * *

"My adventures here are such as you might guess—a mere repetition of visits and dinners. * * * Yesterday a sumptuous dinner with Joseph Gurney. The two impossibilities for a stranger at Norwich are, to find his way about the city, and to know the names of the Gurneys. They talked about Clarkson, and seemed to fear his book would not sell as he expected it to do, not more than twenty subscribers having been procured among the Quakers there. * * * To-morrow I sup at Newmarket on my way to London, and sleep in the coach; and there you have my whole history thus far.

"King Arthur has, I see, been playing his usual editorial tricks with me, and has lopped off a defense of Bruce against Pinkerton because he did not like to have Mr. Pinkerton contradicted; and some remarks upon the infamous blunders of the printer, because he did not choose to insert any thing that was not agreeable to the bookseller. And yet Miss Lucy Aikin says her brother is by nature of an intrepid character, and alleges as a proof of his intrepidity that he puts his name to the Annual Review!

"I have got a clew to the state of the Catholics here, of which some use may be made by D. Manuel. —— is the head of the sect here, and loves to talk about them, and from him I have borrowed a sort of Catholic almanac, which explains their present state. I shall purchase one in London, and turn it to good account. He tells me the Jesuits exist in England as a separate body, and have even a chapel in Norwich; but how they exist, and whence their funds are derived, is a secret to himself. This is a highly curious fact, and to me, particularly, a very interesting one: I shall make further inquiry. St. Winifred has lately worked a miracle at her Well, and healed a paralytic woman. These Catholics want only a little more success to be just as impudent as they were three centuries ago. * *

"God bless you, my dear Edith! R. S."

From Norwich my father went on to London, where, however, he remained only a very short time, and then returned home through Herefordshire, where he had some affairs to look after concerning his uncle, Mr. Hills, living in that county.

A letter to Mr. Bedford on his return commences with one of those quaint fancies with which he delighted to amuse himself.

To Grosvenor C. Bedford, Esq.

"Greta Hall, May 27, 1806.

"A discovery of the original language propounded to the consideration of the worshipful Master Bedford.

"There was in old times a King of Egypt, who did make a full politic experiment touching this question, as is discoursed of by sundry antique authors. Howbeit to me it seemeth that it falleth short of that clear and manifest truth which should be the butt of our inquiry. Now, methinks, if it could be shown what is the very language which Dame Nature, the common mother of all, hath implanted in animals whom we, foolishly misjudging, do term dumb, that were, indeed, a hit palpable and of notable import. To this effect I have noted what that silly bird, called of the Latins Anser, doth utter in time of affright; for it then thinketh of the water, inasmuch as in the water it findeth its safety; and while its thoughts be upon the water so greatly desired of, it crieth *qua—a-qua—a-qua*; wherefore it is to be inferred that *aqua* is the very natural word for water, and the Latin, therefore, the *primitive, natural, and original tongue*.

"Etymology is of more value when applied to the elements of language, and it must be acknowledged that I have here hit upon an elementary word. One of those critics, I forget which, who thought proper to review Thalaba without taking the trouble to understand the story, noticed, as one of the absurdities of the book, that Thalaba was enabled to read some unintelligible letters on a ring by others equally unintelligible upon the head of a locust—an absurdity existing only in their own stupid and careless misconception, for the thing is clear enough. I remember giving myself credit for putting a very girlish sort of thing into Oneiza's mouth when I made her call those locust's lines 'Nature's own language;' for I have heard unthinking people talk of a natural language; and you know the story of the woman with child by a Dutchman, who was afraid to swear the child to an Englishman, because the truth would be found out when the child came to speak Dutch.

"I beseech you to come to me this season: we

shall see more of each other in one week when once housed together, than during a seven years' intercourse in London. And if you do not come this year, the opportunity may be gone forever, and you will never see this country so well nor so cheerfully after I have left it. *If* he were here, would be the thought to damp enjoyment, you would come as a mere laker, and pay a guide for telling you what to admire. When I go abroad it will be to remain there for a considerable time, and you and I are now old enough to feel the proportion which a few years bear to the not very many that constitute the utmost length of life.

"This feeling is the stronger upon me just now, as, in arranging my letters, I have seen those of three men now all in their graves, each of whom produced no little effect upon my character and after life — Allen, Lovell, and poor Edmund Seward — whom I never remember without the deepest love and veneration. Come you to Keswick, Bedford, and make sure of a few weeks' enjoyment while we are both alive.

"I wish you would get the Annual Reviews, because without them my operas are very incomplete: my share there is very considerable, and you would see in many of the articles more of the tone and temper of my mind than you can otherwise get at. * * * * * You must be my biographer if I go first. * * Documents you shall have in plenty, if, indeed, you need more than our correspondence already supplies. This is a subject on which we will talk some evening when the sun is going down, and has tuned us to it. If the harp of Memnon had played in the evening instead of at the sunrise, it would have been a sweet emblem of that state of mind to which I now refer, and which, indeed, I am at this minute enjoying. But it is supper-time.

"God bless you, Grosvenor!"

To Grosvenor C. Bedford, Esq.

"Keswick, June 17, 1806.

"DEAR GROSVENOR,

"There are two poets who must come into our series, and I do not remember their names in your list: Sir John Moore, of whom the only poem which I have ever seen should be given. It is addressed to a lady, he himself being in a consumption. If you do not remember it, Wynn will, and I think can help you to it, for it is very beautiful. The other poor rhymer is poor old Botch Hayes, whom we are in duty bound not to forget, and of whom you may say what you will, only let it be in the best good humor; because poor Botch's heart was always in the right place, which certainly his wig was not. And you may say, that though his talent at producing common-place English verses was not very convenient for his competitors at Cambridge for the Seatonian prize, that his talent of producing common-place Latin ones was exceedingly so for his pupils at Westminster. I don't say that I would wish to plant a laurel upon old Hayes's grave; but I could find in my heart to plant a vine there (if it would grow), as a more appropriate tree, and to pour a brimming libation of its juice, if we had any reason to think that the spirit of the grape could reach the spirit of the man. Poor fellow! that phrase of 'being no one's enemy but his own' is not admitted as a set-off on earth, but in the other world, Grosvenor!

"Our last month has been so unusually fine that the farmers want rain. July will probably give them enough. September and October are the safest months to come down in; though, if you consider gooseberry-pie as partaking of the nature of the *summum bonum* (to speak modestly of it), about a fortnight hence will be the happiest time you can choose. If Tom and Harry should be with me in time for the feat, I have thoughts of challenging all England at a match at gooseberry-pie: barring Jack the Giganticide's leathern bag, we are sure of the victory. Thank God! Tom has escaped the yellow fever; and if ever he lives to be an admiral, Grosvenor — as by God's blessing he may — he shall give you and me a good dinner on board the flag-ship. We shall be so much the older by that time, that I fear good fortune would make neither of us much the happier.

"I have been inserting occasional rhymes in Kehama, and have in this way altered and amended about six hundred lines. When what is already written shall be got through in this manner, I shall think the poem in a way of completion: indeed, it will most likely supply my ways and means for the next winter, instead of reviewing. Elmsley advised me to go on with it; and the truth is, that my own likings and dislikings to it have been so equally divided, that I stood in need of somebody's encouragement to settle the balance. It gains by rhyme, which is to passages of no inherent merit what rouge and candle-light are to ordinary faces. Merely ornamental parts, also, are aided by it, as foil sets off paste. But where there is either passion or power, the plainer and more straightforward the language can be made, the better. Now you will suppose that upon this system I am writing Kehama. My proceedings are not quite so systematical; but what with revising and re-revising over and over again, they will amount to something like it at last.

"God bless you. R. S."

To Grosvenor C. Bedford, Esq.

July 5, 1806.

"MY DEAR GROSVENOR,

"I thought it so likely you would hear from Wynn the particulars concerning John Southey's will,* that I felt no inclination to repeat the story to you, which would not have been the case had the old man done as he ought to have done. Good part of his property, consisting of a newly-purchased estate, is given to a very distant relative of his mother's family, and, of course, gone forever. About £2000 in legacies: the rest falls to his brother, as sole executor and re-

* An uncle of my father's, a wealthy solicitor of Taunton. See p. 18.

siduary legatee. Neither my own name nor either of my brothers' is mentioned. Thomas Southey apprised me of this the day of the old man's death. With him I am on good terms—that is, if we were in the same town, we should dine together, for the sake of relationship, about once a month; and if any thing were to happen to me, of any kind of family importance—such as the birth of a child—I should write a letter to him, beginning 'Dear Uncle.' He invites me to the 'Cottage,' and I shall go there on my way to Lisbon. I think it likely that he will leave his property rather to Tom than to me, for the name's sake, but not likely that he will leave it out of the family. He is about three or four-and-fifty, a man of no education, nor, indeed, of any thing else. And so you have all that I can tell you about the matter, excepting that there's an end of it. Some people, they say, are born with silver spoons in their mouths, and others with wooden ladles. I will hope something for my daughter, upon the strength of this proverb, inasmuch as she has three silver cups; but, for myself, I am of the fraternity of the wooden ladle.

" * * * Last night I began the Preface*—huzza! And now, Grosvenor, let me tell you what I have to do. I am writing, 1. The History of Portugal; 2. The Chronicle of the Cid; 3. The Curse of Kehama; 4. Espriella's Letters. Look you, all these *I am* writing. The second and third of these must get into the press, and out of it before this time twelve months, or else I shall be like the Civil List. By way of interlude comes in this Preface. Don't swear, and bid me do one thing at a time. I tell you I can't afford to do one thing at a time—no, nor two neither; and it is only by doing many things that I contrive to do so much; for I can not work long together at any thing without hurting myself, and so I do every thing by heats; then, by the time I am tired of one, my inclination for another is come round.

"Dr. Southey is arrived here. He puts his degree in his pocket, summers here, and will winter in London, to attend at an hospital. About this, of course, I shall apply to Carlisle; and, if it should so happen that you do not see him here, shall give him a direction to you when he goes to London. R. S."

The following lines, written immediately after hearing of the event mentioned in the commencement of this letter, and preserved accidentally by a friend to whom he had sent them, may be appropriately inserted here.

"So thou art gone at last, old John,
And hast left all from me:
God give thee rest among the bless'd—
I lay no blame to thee.

"Nor marvel I, for though one blood
Through both our veins was flowing,
Full well I know, old man, no love
From thee to me was owing.

"Thou hadst no anxious hopes for me,
In the winning years of infancy,
No joy in my up-growing;
And when from the world's beaten way
I turned mid rugged paths astray,
No fears where I was going.

"It touched thee not if envy's voice
Was busy with my name;
Nor did it make thy heart rejoice
To hear of my fair fame.

"Old man, thou liest upon thy bier,
And none for thee will shed a tear!
They'll give thee a stately funeral,
With coach and hearse, and plume and pall;
But they who follow will grieve no more
Than the mutes who pace with their staves before.
With a light heart and a cheerful face
Will they put mourning on,
And bespeak thee a marble monument,
And think nothing more of Old John.

"An enviable death is his,
Who, leaving none to deplore him,
Hath yet a joy in his passing hour,
Because all he loved have died before him.
The monk, too, hath a joyful end,
And well may welcome death like a friend,
When the crucifix close to his heart is press'd,
And he piously crosses his arms on his breast,
And the brethren stand round him and sing him to rest,
And tell him, as sure he believes, that anon,
Receiving his crown, he shall sit on his throne,
And sing in the choir of the bless'd.

"But a hopeless sorrow it strikes to the heart,
To think how men like thee depart.
Unloving and joyless was thy life,
Unlamented was thine end;
And neither in this world nor the next
Hadst thou a single friend:
None to weep for thee on earth—
None to greet thee in heaven's hall;
Father and mother, sister and brother—
Thy heart had been shut to them all.

"Alas, old man, that this should be!
One brother had raised up seed to thee;
And hadst thou, in their hour of need,
Cherished that dead brother's seed,
Thrown wide thy doors, and called them in,
How happy thine old age had been!
Thou wert a barren tree, around whose trunk,
Needing support, our tendrils should have clung;
Then had thy sapless boughs
With buds of hope and genial fruit been hung;
Yea, with undying flowers,
And wreaths forever young."

* To the "Specimens of English Poets."

To Lieutenant Southey, H.M.S. Amelia.

"Monday, July 28, 1806.

"My dear Tom,

"For many days I have looked for a letter from you, the three lines announcing your arrival in England being all which have yet reached me. Yesterday the Dr. and I returned home after a five days' absence, and I was disappointed at finding no tidings of you. We were two days at Lloyd's; and have had three days' mountaineerning—one on the way there, two on our return—through the wildest parts of this wild country, many times wishing you had been with us. One day we lost our way upon the mountains, got upon a summit where there were precipices before us, and found a way down through a fissure, like three sides of a chimney, where we could reach from side to side, and help ourselves with our hands. This chimney-way was considerably higher than any house, and then we had an hour's descent afterward over loose stones. Yesterday we mounted Great Gabel—one of the highest mountains in the country—and had a magnificent view of the Isle of Man, rising out of a sea of light, for the water lay like a sheet of silver. This was a digression from our straight road, and exceedingly fatiguing it was; however, after we got down we drank five quarts of milk between us, and got home as fresh as larks after a walk of eleven hours. You will find it harder service than walking the deck when you come here.

"Our landlord, who lives in the house adjoining us, has a boat, which is as much at our service as if it were our own; of this we have voted you commander-in-chief whenever you shall arrive. The lake is about four miles in length, and something between one and two in breadth. However tired you may be of the salt water, I do not think you will have the same objection to fresh when you see this beautiful basin, clear as crystal, and shut in by mountains on every side except one opening to the northwest. We are very frequently upon it, Harry and I being both tolerably good boatmen; and sometimes we sit in state and the women row us—a way of manning a boat which will amuse you. The only family with which we are on familiar terms, live, during the summer and autumn, on a little island here—one of the loveliest spots in this wide world. They have one long room, looking on the lake from three windows, affording the most beautiful views; and in that room you may have as much music, dancing, shuttle-cocking, &c., as your heart can desire. They generally embargo us on our water expeditions. I know not whether you like dining under a tree, as well as with the conveniences of chairs and table, and a roof over your head—which I confess please me better than a seat upon any moss, however cushiony, and in any shade, however romantic; if, however, you do, here are some delightful bays at the head of the lake, in any of which we may land; and if you love fishing, you may catch perch enough on the way for the boat's company, and perhaps a jack or two into the bargain.

"One main advantage which this country possesses over Wales is, that there are no long tracks of desolation to cross between one beautiful spot and another. We are sixteen miles only from Winandermere, and three other lakes are on the way to it. Sixteen only from Wastwater, as many from Ulswater, nine from Buttermere and Crummock. Lloyd expects you will give him a few days—a *few* they must be; for though I shall be with you, we will not spare you long from home; but his house stands delightfully, and puts a large part of the finest scenery within our reach. You will find him very friendly, and will like his wife much—she is a great favorite with me. The Bishop of Llandaff lives near them, to whom I have lately been introduced. God bless you! R. S."

To Joseph Cottle, Esq.

"Keswick, Aug. 11, 1806.

"MY DEAR COTTLE,

"Madoc has not made my fortune. By the state of my account in May last—that is, twelve months after its publication—there was a balance due to me (on the plan of dividing the profits) of £3 19*s.* 1*d.* About 180 then remained to be sold, each of which will give me 5*s.*; but the sale will be rather slower than distillation through a filtering stone. We mean to print a small edition in two vols. without delay, and without alterations, that the quarto may not lose its value.

"Of the many *reviewings* of this poem I have only seen the Edinburgh, Monthly, and Annual. I sent a copy to Mr. Fox, and Lady Holland told me it was the rule at St. Ann's Hill to read aloud till eleven, and then retire; but that when they were reading Madoc they often read till the clock struck twelve. In short, I have had as much *praise* as heart could desire, but not quite so much of the more solid kind of remuneration. * * * * * * I am preparing for the press the Chronicle of the Cid—a very curious monument of old Spanish manners and history, which will make two little volumes, to the great delight of about as many readers as will suffice to take off an edition of 750.

"You suggest to me three epic subjects, all of them striking, but each liable to the same objection, that no entire and worthy interest can be attached to the conquering party in either. 1st. William of Normandy is less a hero than Harold. The true light in which that part of our history should be regarded was shown me by William Taylor. The country was not thoroughly converted. Harold favored the pagans, and the Normans were helped by the priests. 2dly. Alaric is the chief personage of a French poem by Scudery, which is notoriously worthless. The capture of Rome is in itself an event so striking that it almost palsies one's feelings; yet nothing resulted which could give a worthy purport to the poem. In this point Theodoric is a better hero: the indispensable requisite, however, in a subject for me is, that the end—the ultimate end—must be worthy of the means. 3dly. The expulsion of the Moriscoes. This is a dreadful history, which I will never torture myself by reading a second time. Besides, I am convinced, in opposition to the common opinion, that the Spaniards did wisely in the act of expelling them, though most wickedly in the way of expelling them. One word more about literature, and then to other matters. How goes on the Fall of Cambria, and what are you about?

"My little girl is now two years and a quarter old—a delightful play-fellow, of whom I am somewhat more fond than is fitting. * * * * Edith is in excellent health; I myself the same barebones as ever, first cousin to an anatomy, but with my usual good health and steady good spirits; neither in habits nor in any thing else different from what I was, except that if my *upper story* is not better furnished, a great deal of good furniture is thrown away.

" * * * * * * * *

In spite of the slow sale of Madoc, I can not but think that it may answer as well for the year's ways and means to finish the 'Curse of Kehama,' and sell the first edition, as to spend the time in criticising other people's books. * * *

"God bless you! R. SOUTHEY."

To John Rickman, Esq.

"Oct. 13, 1806.

"MY DEAR RICKMAN,

"You will be glad to hear that my child proves to be of the more worthy gender.

"I would do a great deal to please poor Tobin (indeed, it is doing a good deal to let him inflict an argument upon me), but to write an epilogue is doing too much for any body. Indeed, were I ever so well disposed to misemploy time, paper, and rhymes, it would be as much out of my reach as the moon is; and I bless my stars for the incapacity, believing that a man who can do such things well can not do any thing better.

"I am also thoroughly busy. Summer is my holiday season, in which I lay in a store of exercise to serve me for the winter, and leave myself, as it were, lying fallow to the influences of heaven. I am now very hard at Palmerin—so troublesome a business, that a look before the leap would have prevented the leap altogether. I expected it would only be needful to alter the *Propria quæ maribus* to their original orthography, and restore the costume where the old translators had omitted it, as being to them foreign or obsolete; but they have so mangled, mutilated, and massacred the manners—vulgarized, impoverished, and embeggared the language—so lopped, cropped, and docked the ornaments, that I was fain to set my shoulder stiffly to the wheel, and retranslate about the one half. As this will not produce me one penny more than if I had reprinted it with all its imperfections on its head, the good conscience with which it is done reconciles me to the loss of time; and I have, moreover, such a true love of romance that the labor is not irksome, though it is hard. To correct a sheet—sixteen pages of the square-sized black letter—is a day's work; that is, from breakfast till dinner, allowing an hour's walk, and from tea till supper; and the whole is about sixty sheets.

"Secondly, Espriella is regulated by the printer, who seems as little disposed to hurry me as I am to hurry him. * * *

"Thirdly, the reviewing is come round, of which, in the shape of Missionaries, Catholic Miracles, Bible and Religious Societies, Clarkson, and little Moore (not forgetting Captain Burney), I have more to do than I at first desired, yet not more than will make a reasonable item on the right side of the King of Persia's* books.

"Fourthly, I have done half the Cid, and, whenever I seem sufficiently ahead of other employment to lie-to for a while, this is what I go to.

"Lastly, for the Athenæum—*alias* Foolæum, for I abominate such titles—I am making some preparations, meaning, among other things, to print there certain collections of unemployed notes and memoranda, under the title of Omniana. * * * By God's blessing I shall have done all this by the end of the winter, and come to town early in the spring, to inspect certain books for the Cid at the Museum and at Holland House. God bless you! R. S."

* Artaxerxes, surnamed Longimanus—Longman.

To John Rickman, Esq.

"Dec. 23, 1806.

"MY DEAR RICKMAN,

" * * * * * * *

I am left alone to my winter occupations, and truly they are quite sufficient to employ me. Two months, however, if no unlucky interruption prevent, will be sufficient to clear all off, and send Espriella and Palmerin into the world. I have an additional and weighty motive for dispatch. The times being South American mad, my account of Brazil, instead of being the last work in the series, must be the first. There are in the book-case down stairs at your house sixteen bundles of sealed papers. Those papers contain more information respecting South America than his majesty's agents have been able to obtain at Lisbon—more, in all probability, than any other person in Europe possesses except one Frenchman, now returned to Paris: he has seen them, and is very likely to get the start of me, unless, which is not improbable, Bonaparte choose to withhold from the world information which would be of specific use to England.

"Concerning these papers, of whose contents I was till last week ignorant, my uncle has written to me, urging me to make all possible speed with this part of the book, and desiring me to offer the information to government. I inclosed the letter to Wynn, and it may be he will advise me to come up to London upon this business. I hope not. I should rather wash my hands of all other business first, and then can certainly, in half a year, accomplish a large volume, for on this subject there is no collateral information to hunt for. A very few books contain all the printed history, and there will be more difficulty in planning the work than in executing it. There will be business of some consequence in the way of map-making, which will delight Arrowsmith. My uncle has very valuable materials for a map of Brazil.

"This is of so much consequence that it will perhaps be advisable to let the Palmerin sleep, and so have a month's time. * * * Wynn's letter will instruct me whether to set to work for myself or for the government; giving them information is, God knows, throwing pearls you know to whom, but, so the pearls be paid for, well. The best thing they could do for me and for them, if they really want information about South America, is to send me to Lisbon for that specific purpose, without any ostensible charge.

"There is nothing in the world like resolute, straightforward honesty; it is sure to conquer in the long run. I have been reading Quaker history, which is worth reading because it proves this, and proves also that institutions can completely new-model our nature; for, if the instinct of self-defense be subdued, nothing else is so powerful.

"Fox's death is a loss to me, who had a promise from him, but I will not affect to think it a loss to the country: he lived a year too long. England can not fall yet, blessed be God! because its inhabitants are Englishmen; but, if any thing could destroy a country, it would be the incurable folly of such governors.

"Have you seen the Memoirs of Colonel Hutchinson? If not, by all means read it: it is the history of a right Englishman; and the sketch of English history which it contains from the time of the Reformation is so admirable, that it ought to make even Scotchmen ashamed to mention the name of Hume. I have seldom been so deeply interested by any book as this. * * * * * * "R. S."

CHAPTER XIII.

HE UNDERTAKES TO EDIT "KIRKE WHITE'S REMAINS"—DETAILS OF HIS SETTLING AT GRETA HALL—GRANT OF A SMALL PENSION—OPINIONS ON THE CATHOLIC QUESTION—PROGRESS OF "KIRKE WHITE'S REMAINS"—HEAVY DEDUCTIONS FROM HIS PENSION—MODERN POETRY—POLITICS—PREDICTS SEVERE CRITICISMS ON THE "SPECIMENS OF ENGLISH POETRY"—RECOLLECTIONS OF COLLEGE FRIENDS—REMARKS ON CLASSICAL READING—THE CATHOLIC QUESTION—SPANISH PAPERS WANTED—MR. DUPPA'S "LIFE OF MICHAEL ANGELO"—MOTIVES FOR EDITING "KIRKE WHITE'S REMAINS"—BEST SEASON FOR VISITING THE LAKES—EFFECT UPON THEM OF CLOUD AND SUNSHINE—THEORY OF EDUCATING CHILDREN FOR SPECIFIC LITERARY PURPOSES—PROBABLE ESTABLISHMENT OF A NEW EDINBURGH REVIEW—PLAYFUL LETTER TO THE LATE HARTLEY COLERIDGE—NEW EDITION OF DON QUIXOTE PROJECTED—PLAN OF A CRITICAL CATALOGUE—PALMERIN OF ENGLAND—LAY OF THE LAST MINSTREL—CHRONICLE OF THE CID—MORTE D'ARTHUR—PECUNIARY DIFFICULTIES—SALE OF ESPRIELLA'S LETTERS—SPECIMENS OF ENGLISH POETRY—OVERTURES MADE TO HIM TO TAKE PART IN THE EDINBURGH REVIEW—REASONS FOR DECLINING TO DO SO.—1807.

AMID all my father's various and multiplied occupations, he was yet one of those of whom it might be truly said, that

> "They can make who fail to find
> Brief leisure even in busiest days"

for any kindly office; and needful as was all his time and all his labor to provide for the many calls upon him, he was never grudging of a portion of it to assist another. "Silver and gold" he had little to bestow, but "such as he had" he "gave freely."

We have already seen how materially he had assisted, in conjunction with his friend Mr. Cottle, in establishing the reputation of Chatterton, and in procuring for his needy relatives some profit from his writings; he now engaged himself in a task not dissimilar, except in the perfect and unalloyed satisfaction with which the whole character of the subject of it could be drawn out and contemplated.

In the spring of the year 1804, he had observed in the Monthly Review what he considered a most harsh and unjust reviewal of a small volume of poems by Henry Kirke White; and having also accidentally seen a letter which the author had written to the reviewers, explaining the peculiar circumstances under which these poems were written and published, he understood the whole cruelty of their injustice. In consequence of this, he wrote to Henry to encourage him: told him that, though he was well aware how imprudent it was in young poets to publish their productions, his circumstances seemed to render that expedient from which it would otherwise be right to dissuade him; advised him, therefore, if he had no better prospects, to print a larger volume by subscription, and offered to do what little was in his power to serve him in the business.

This letter, which I regret has not been preserved, produced a reply full of expressions of gratitude both for the advice and offers of assistance it contained; but, in consequence of Kirke White's going very soon afterward to Cambridge, but little further communication took place, and his untimely and lamented death, in October, 1806, caused by the severe and unrelenting course of study he pursued, acting upon a frame already debilitated by too great mental exertion, put an end to the hopes my father had cherished both of enjoying his friendship and of witnessing his fame.

On his decease, one of his friends wrote to my father, informing him of the event, as one who had professed an interest in his fortunes. This led to an inquiry what papers he had left behind him, to a correspondence with his brother Neville, and, ultimately, to the publication, under my father's editorship, of two volumes of his "Remains," accompanied with a brief Memoir of his Life.

To the preparation of these the three following letters refer; others, relating to the same subject, as well as to more general matters, addressed to Kirke White's two brothers, with whom, especially the elder, the acquaintance thus begun ripened into an intimate and life-long friendship, will appear in their proper places.

To Mr. Neville White.

"Keswick, Dec. 20, 1806.

"DEAR SIR,

"Your letter and parcel arrived yesterday, just as I had completed the examination of the former papers. I have now examined the whole.

"What account of your brother shall be given it rests with you, sir, and his other nearest friends, to determine. I advise and *entreat* that it may be as full and as minute as possible. The example of a young man winning his way against great difficulties, of such honorable ambition, such unexampled industry, such a righteous and holy confidence of genius, ought not to be withheld. A full and faithful narrative of his difficulties, his hopes, and his eventual success, till it pleased God to promote him to a higher state of existence, will be a lasting encouragement to others who have the same up-hill path to tread; he will be to them what Chatterton was to him, and he will be a purer and better example. If it would wound the feelings of his family to let all and every particular of his honorable and admirable life be known, those feelings are, of course, paramount to every other consideration. But I sincerely hope this may not be the case. It will, I know, be a painful task to furnish me with materials for this, which is the most useful kind of biography, yet, when the effort of beginning such a task shall have been accomplished, the consciousness that you are doing for him what he would have wished to be done, will bring with it a consolation and a comfort.

"Let me beg of you and of your family, when you can command heart for the task, to give me all your recollections of his childhood and of every stage of his life. Do not fear you can be too minute; I will arrange them, insert such poems as will best appear in that place, and add such remarks as grow out of the circumstances. The narrative itself can not be told too plainly; all ornament of style would be misplaced in it: that which is meant to tickle the ear will never find its way either to the understanding or the heart.

"Respecting the mode of publication, you had better consult Mr. ——. The booksellers will, beyond a doubt, undertake to publish them on condition of halving the eventual profits, which are the terms on which I publish. The profit, I fear, will not be much, unless the public should be taken with some unusual fit of good feeling; and, indeed, this is not unlikely, for they are more frequently just to the dead than to the living.

"I shall be glad to see all his magazine publications; possibly some of the pieces marked by me for transcription may be found among them. There is one poem, printed in the Globe for Feb. 11, 1803, which I remember noticing when it appeared, and which may be more easily copied from the newspaper than from the manuscript. Whether any of his prose writings should be inserted, I shall better be able to judge after having seen the magazines. But the most valuable materials which could be intrusted to me would be his letters—the more that could be said of him in his own words, the better.

"I have been affected at seeing my own name among your brother's papers; there is a defense of Thalaba, a part of which I regard as the most discriminating and appropriate praise which I have received.* It seems to have been published in some magazine. These are the highest gratifications which a writer can receive; for that class of readers who call themselves the public, I have as little respect as need be; but to interest and influence such a mind as Henry White's is the best and worthiest object which any poet could propose to himself—the fulfillment of his dearest hopes.

"Yours truly, ROBERT SOUTHEY."

To Mr. Neville White.

"Keswick, Feb. 3, 1807.

"DEAR SIR,

" * * * It will be well to print the Melancholy Hours, and some other of the prose compositions. They mark the character, as well as the powers, of your brother's mind, and should, therefore, be preserved. The No. 10 which you mention is, I believe, that criticism upon Thalaba the Destroyer, of which I spoke in a former letter. I may be permitted to expunge from it, or to soften, a few epithets, of which it gratifies me that your brother should have thought me worthy, but which it is not decent that I should edit myself. * * Believe me, sir, if I were not now proving the high respect which I feel for your brother, it would give me pain to think what value he assigned to the mere expression of it. How deeply I regret that the little intercourse we ever had should have ended where it did, it is needless now to say. I should have begged him to have visited me here but for this reason: when he told me he was going to Cambridge, there were some circumstances which made me believe he was under the patronage of Mr. Henry Thornton, or of some other persons of similar views; that his opinions had taken what is called an evangelical turn, and that he was designed for that particular ministry. My own religious opinions are not less zealous and not less sincere, but they are totally opposite. I would not run the risk of disturbing his sentiments, and therefore delayed

* It may not be uninteresting to the reader to see here that portion of Kirke White's remarks on Thalaba which is thus referred to. After saying that "an innovation so bold as that of Mr. Southey is sure to meet with disapprobation and ridicule," he continues: "Whoever is conversant with the writings of this author, will have observed and admired that greatness of mind and comprehension of intellect by which he is enabled, on all occasions, to throw off the shackles of habit and prepossession. Southey never treads in the beaten track: his thoughts, while they are those of nature, carry that cast of originality which is the stamp and testimony of genius. He views things through a peculiar phasis; and while he has the feelings of a man, they are those of a man almost abstracted from mortality, and reflecting on and painting the scenes of life as if he were a mere spectator, uninfluenced by his own connection with the objects he surveys. To this faculty of bold discrimination I attribute many of Mr. Southey's excellences as a poet. He never seems to inquire how other men would treat a subject, or what may happen to be the usage of the times; but, filled with that strong sense of fitness, which is the result of bold and unshackled thought, he fearlessly pursues that course which his own sense of propriety points out.
" * * * * * * * * * * * *
At first, indeed, the verse may appear uncouth, because it is new to the ear; but I defy any man, who has any feeling of melody, to peruse the whole poem without paying tribute to the sweetness of its flow and the gracefulness of its modulation.

"In judging of this extraordinary poem, we should consider it as a genuine lyric production—we should conceive it as recited to the harp, in times when such relations carried nothing incredible with them. Carrying this idea along with us, the admirable art of the poet will strike us with ten-fold conviction; the abrupt sublimity of his transitions, the sublime simplicity of his manner, and the delicate touches by which he connects the various parts of his narrative, will then be more strongly observable; and we shall, in particular, remark the uncommon felicity with which he has adapted his versification, and, in the midst of the wildest irregularity, left nothing to shock the ear or offend the judgment."—*Remains*, vol. ii., p. 285, 286.

forming that personal friendship with him, to which I looked on with pleasure, till his mind should have outgrown opinions through which it was well that it should pass.

"In reading and re-reading the poem, I have filled up a few of the gaps with conjectural words of correction, which shall be printed in italics, and to which, therefore, there can be no objection. The more I read them, the more is my admiration; they are as it should be—of very various merit, and show the whole progress of his mind. Many of them are excellently good—so good that it is impossible they could be better, and all together certainly exceed the productions of any other young poet whatsoever. I do not except Chatterton from the number; and I have a full confidence that, sooner or later, the public opinion will confirm mine. Perhaps this may be immediately acknowledged.

"I am greatly in hopes that many of his letters may be fit for publication. Till these arrive, it is not possible to judge to what extent the proposed introductory account (in which they would probably be inserted, or after it) will run; but as soon as this is ascertained, the volumes may be divided, and the second go to press. Will you have the goodness to copy for me that abominable criticism in the Monthly Review upon Clifton Grove, and also the notice they took of your brother's letter? That criticism must be inserted; and if you remember any other reviewal in which he was treated with illiberality, I shall be glad to hold up such criticism to the infamy which it deserves.

"It will give me great pleasure if a likeness can be recovered—very great pleasure. Your brother Henry, sir, is not to be lamented. He has gained that earthly immortality for which he labored, and that heavenly immortality of which he was worthy. I say this with tears, but they are tears of admiration as well as of human regret. If you knew me, sir, and how little prone I am to let such feelings as these appear upon the surface, you would understand these words in their literal sense and in their full meaning.

"Yours very truly,

"ROBERT SOUTHEY."

To Mr. Neville White.

"March 3, 1807.

"MY DEAR SIR,

"Your parcel reached me on Sunday evening, and I have perused every line of its contents with deep and painful interest. The letters, and your account (of which I should say much were I writing to any other person), have made me thoroughly acquainted with one of the most amiable and most admirable human beings that ever was ripened upon earth for heaven. Be assured that I will not insert a sentence which can give pain or offense to any one. There will come a time (and God only knows how soon it may come) when some one will perform that office for me which I am now performing for your incomparable brother, and I shall endeavor to show how that office ought to be performed. I will be scrupulously careful; and if, when the papers pass through your hands, you should think I have not been sufficiently so, I beg you will, without hesitation, expunge whatever may appear exceptionable.

* * * * * * *

"When I obeyed the impulse which led me to undertake this task, it was from a knowledge that Henry White had left behind him an example, which ought not to be lost, of well-directed talents, and that, in performing an act of respect to his memory, I should at the same time hold up the example to others who have the up-hill paths of life to tread. No person can be more thoroughly convinced that goodness is a better thing than genius, and that genius is no excuse for those follies and offenses which are called its eccentricities.

"The mention made in my last of any difference in religious opinions from your brother was merely incidental; nor is it by any means my intention to say any more upon the subject than simply to state that those opinions are not mine, lest it should be supposed they were, from the manner in which I speak of him.

"I shall now proceed as speedily as I can with the work.

"Yours truly, and with much esteem,

"ROBERT SOUTHEY."

To Richard Duppa, Esq.

"March 27, 1807.

"DEAR DUPPA,

"The ministry—by this time, perhaps, no longer a ministry—have made a very pretty kettle of fish of it; which phrase, by-the-by, would look well in literal translation into any other language. Perhaps you will be surprised to hear that on the Catholic Question I am as stiffly against them as his majesty himself. Of all my friends, Coleridge is perhaps the only one who thinks with me upon this subject; but I am clear in my own mind. I am, however, sorry for the business—more to think what a rabble must come in, than for any respect for those who are going out—though the *Limited Service* and the Abolishment of the Slave Trade are great things. As for any effect upon my own possible fortunes, you need not be told how little any such *possibilities* ever enter into my feelings: they have entered into my calculations just enough to keep me unsettled, and nothing more. And here I am now planting garden inclosures, rose-bushes, currants, gooseberries, and resolute to become a mountaineer—perhaps forever—unless I should remove for final settlement at Lisbon. My study is to be finished—my books gathered together; and if you do not come down again, the very first summer you are not otherwise engaged, why—you may stay and be smoke-dried in London for your good-for-nothingness. I have a man called Willy, who is my Juniper in this business. We are going to have laburnums and *lilacs*, syringas, barberry bushes, and a pear-tree to grow up by your window against the wall, and *white* curtains in my library, and to dye the old ones in the parlor blue, and to put fringe to them, Mr. Duppa, and to paper the room, Mr. Duppa, and I am to have a carpet in my study, Mr. Duppa, and the chairs are to be new bottomed, and we are to buy some fenders at the sale of the general's things, and we have bought a new hearth-rug. And then the outside of the house is to be rough-cast as soon as the season will permit, and there is a border made under the windows, and there is to be a gravel walk there, and turf under the trees beyond *that*, and beyond *that* such peas and beans! Oh! Mr. Duppa, how you will like them when you come down, and how fine we shall be, if all this does not ruin me!

"The reason of all this is, that some arrangements of Coleridge's made it necessary that I should either resolve upon removing speedily, or remaining in the house. The one I could not do, and was, not unwillingly, forced to the other. Indeed, the sense of being unsettled was the only uneasiness I had; and these little arrangements for future comfort give me, I am sure, more solid satisfaction and true enjoyment than his great Howickship can possibly have felt upon getting into that Downing Street, from whence he will so reluctantly get out—like a dog on a wet day out of the kitchen, growling as he goes, with his tail between his legs, and showing the teeth with which he dares not bite. Jackson—God bless him—is as well pleased about it as I am; and that excellent good woman, Mrs. Wilson, is rejoiced at heart to think that we are likely to remain here for the remainder of her days.

"Sir, it would surprise you to see how I dig in the garden. I am going to buy the 'Complete Gardener;' and we do hope to attain one day to the luxuries of currant wine, and such like things, which I hope will meet your approbation, after you and I have been up Causey Pike again, and over the Fells to Blea Tarn—expeditions to the repetition of which I know you look on with great pleasure.

"I shall miss Harry this summer—an excellent boatman, and a companion whose good spirits and good humor never fail. If T. Grenville would make Tom a captain, and send him down to grass for the summer, he would do a better thing than he has done yet since he went to the Admiralty. Wynn did mention my brother to him; but we had no borough interest to back us, and fourteen years' hard service go for nothing, with wounds, blowing up, honorable mention, and excellent good conduct. Still I have a sort of faith (God willing) that he will be an admiral yet.

"I am hurrying my printer with Espriella, for fear another translation should appear before mine, which, you know, would be very unlucky. Ten sheets of the second volume are done. I much wish it were out, having better hopes of its sale than the fate of better books will perhaps warrant. But this is a good book in its way, and its way ought to be, in book-selling phrase, a taking one.

"God bless you! R. S."

At the commencement of the preceding letter, my father alludes to the tottering condition of the Grenville ministry, of which his friend Mr. Wynn was a member, who had been for some time looking out for an opportunity of serving him; and under the impression that their resignation had taken place, without any having occurred, he now writes: "When you have it in your power again, let the one thing you seek for me be the office of Historiographer, with a decent pension. If £300, it would satisfy my wishes—if £400, I should be rich. I have no worldly ambition: a man who lives so much in the past and the future can have none. * * * * When you are in, do not form higher wishes for me than I have for myself. I *am* in that state of life to which it has pleased God to call me, *for* which I am formed, *in* which I am contented; nor is it likely that I could be in any other so usefully, so worthily, or so happily employed. If what I now receive shall in the future come from the Treasury, I shall not then have any serious wish for any change of fortune; nor would this be one, if you were wealthier. What more is necessary I get—hardly enough, it is true, but still in my own way; and it is not impossible but that some day or other one of my books should, by some accident, hit the fashion of the day, and, by a rapid sale, place me in comparative affluence. I must be a second time cut off if I do not still inherit an independence; and if, after all, I should go out of the world as poor a man as I am at this present—the moment it comes to be 'poor Southey,' my name becomes a provision for my wife and children, even though I had not that reliance upon individual friendship which experience makes me feel."*

The next letter shows that his friend had succeeded in obtaining for him a small pension, which, though it really diminished his income instead of increasing it, was very acceptable, for the reasons he here states.

To John May, Esq.

"Keswick, March 30, 1807.

"MY DEAR FRIEND,

"I am just now enabled to give you some intelligence concerning myself. In this topsy-turvying of ministers, Wynn was very anxious, as he says, 'to pick something out of the fire for me.' The registership of the Vice-Admiralty Court in St. Lucia was offered, worth about £600 a year. He wrote to me, offering this, or, as an alternative, the only one in his power, a pension of £200; but, before my answer could arrive, it was necessary that he should choose for me, and he judged rightly in taking the latter. Fees and taxes will reduce this to £160,† the precise sum for which I have hitherto been indebted to him, so that I remain with just the same income as before. The different source from which it is derived is, as you may suppose, sufficiently grateful; for though Wynn could till

* March 27, 1807.

† The deduction proved to be £56, reducing it to £144

now well afford this, and I had no reluctance in accepting it from one who is the oldest friend I have in the world (we have been intimate for nineteen years), he has now nearly doubled his expenditure by marrying. * * This, I suppose, is asked for and granted to me as a man of letters, in which character I feel myself fully and fairly entitled to receive it; and you know me too well to suppose that it can make me lose one jot of that freedom, both of opinion and speech, without which I should think myself unworthy, not of this poor earthly pittance alone, but of God's air and sunshine, and my inheritance in heaven.

"I sent you the Specimens, and shall have to send you, owing to some omissions of Bedford's, a supplementary volume hereafter, which will complete its bibliographical value. Of its other merits and defects, hereafter. It will not be long before, I trust, you will receive Espriella: the printer promises to quicken his pace, and I hurry him, anticipating that this book will give you and my other friends some amusement, and deserve approbation on higher grounds. Thank you for all your kindness to Harry. * * This change of ministry—I am as hostile to the measure which was the pretext for it as the king himself; but, having conceded that measure, the king's conduct is equally unexceptionable. Neither the country nor the Commons called for the change, and they were getting credit, and deserving it, by the 'Arms Bill,' the blessed 'Abolition of the Slave Trade,' the projected reforms, and the projected plan for educating the poor. And now their places are to be filled by a set of men of tried and convicted incapacity, with an old woman at their head! But I must refer you to my friend, Don Manuel Alvarez, for the reason why there is *always* a lack of talents in the English government.

"God bless you!

"Yours in haste, R. S."

To C. W. W. Wynn, Esq.

"April, 1807.

"My dear Wynn,

"And so I am a Court Pensioner! It is well that I have not to kiss hands upon the occasion, or, upon my soul, I do not think I could help laughing at the changes and chances of this world! O dear, dear Wynn, when you and I used to hold debates with poor Bunbury over a pot of porter, how easily could your way of life have been predicted! And how would his and mine have mocked all foresight! And yet mine has been a straight-onward path! Nothing more has taken place *in* me than the ordinary process of beer or wine—of fermenting—and settling—and ripening.

"If Snowdon will come to Skiddaw in the summer, Skiddaw will go to Snowdon at the fall of the leaf. I shall work hard to get the Cid ready for publication, and must go with it to London. In that case my intention is to go first to Bristol, and perhaps to Taunton, and Wales will not be out of my way. But I wish to show you those parts of the country which you have not seen, and which I have since you were here; and to introduce you to the top of Skiddaw, which is an easy morning's walk.

"The mystery of this wonderful history of the change in administration is certainly explained; but who are the king's advisers? Are they his sons, or old Lord Liverpool? Mr. Simeon's wise remark, that 'the new ministry was better than no ministry at all,' put me in mind of a story which might well have been quoted in reply. One of the German electors, when an Englishman was introduced to him, thought the best thing he could say to him was to remark that 'it was bad weather;' upon which the Englishman shrugged up his shoulders and replied, 'yes—but it was *better than none!*' Would not this have *told* in the House? You do not shake my opinion concerning the Catholics. Their religion regards no national distinctions—it teaches them to look at Christendom and at the Pope as the head thereof—and the interests of that religion will always be preferred to any thing else. Bonaparte is aware of this, and is aiming to be the head of the Catholic party in Germany.

"These people have been increasing in England of late years, owing to the number of seminaries established during the French Revolution. It is worth your while to get their Almanac—the 'Lay Directory' it is called, and published by Brown and Keating, Duke Street, Grosvenor Square. They are at their old tricks of miracles here and every where else. St. Winifred has lately worked a great one, and is in as high odor as ever she was.

"I am for abolishing the test with regard to every other sect—Jews and all—but not to the Catholics. They *will not tolerate:* the proof is in their whole history—in their whole system—and in their present practice all over Catholic Europe: and it is the nature of their principles *now* to spread in this country; Methodism, and the still wilder sects preparing the way for it. You have no conception of the zeal with which they seek for proselytes, nor the power they have over weak minds; for their system is as well the greatest work of human wisdom as it is of human wickedness. It is curious that the Jesuits exist in England as a body, and have possessions here; a Catholic told me this, and pointed out one in the streets of Norwich, but he could tell me nothing more, and expressed his surprise at it, and his curiosity to learn more. Having been abolished by the Pope, they keep up their order secretly, and expect their restoration, which, if he be wise, Bonaparte will effect. Were I a Catholic, that should be the object to which my life should be devoted—I would be the second Loyola.

"Concessions and conciliations will not satisfy the Catholics; vengeance and the throne are what they want. If Ireland were far enough from our shores to be lost without danger to our own security, I would say establish the Catholic religion there, as the easiest way of civilizing it; but Catholic Ireland would always be at the command of the Pope, and the Pope is now at the command of France. It is dismal to think of the state of Ireland. Nothing can redeem that country but such measures as none of our statesmen, except perhaps Marquis Wellesley, would be hardy enough to adopt—nothing but a system of Roman conquest and colonization, and shipping off the refractory to the colonies.

"England condescends too much to the Catholic religion, and does not hold up her own to sufficient respect in her foreign possessions; and the Catholics, instead of feeling this as an act of indulgence to their opinions, interpret it as an acknowledgment of their superior claims, and insult us in consequence. This is the case at Malta. In India the want of an established church is a crying evil. Nothing but missionaries can secure in that country what we have won. The converts would immediately become English in their feelings; for, like Mohammed, we ought to make our language go with our religion—a better policy this than that of introducing pig-tails, after our own home-plan of princely reform, for which ——, with all due respect to him, or whoever else was the agent in this inconceivable act of folly, ought to be gibbeted upon the top of the highest pagoda in Hindostan. God bless you! R. S."

To Mr. Neville White.

"April 7, 1807.

"My dear Sir,

" * * * * * * *

The preliminary account is nearly finished. I have inserted in it such poems as seem best suited to that place, because they refer to Henry's then state of mind, and thus derive an interest from the narrative, and in their turn give it also. After the introduction I purpose to insert a selection of his letters, or, rather, of extracts from them, in chronological order. Upon mature consideration, and upon trial as well, I believe this to be better than inserting them in the account of his life. If the reader feel for Henry that love and admiration which I have endeavored to make him feel, he will be prepared to receive these epistolary fragments as the most authentic and most valuable species of biography; and if he does not feel that love, it is no matter how he receives them, for his heart will be in fault, and his understanding necessarily darkened.

"I have, to the best of my judgment, omitted every thing of which the publication could occasion even the slightest unpleasant feeling to any person whatever; and if any thing of this kind has escaped me, you will, of course, consider your own opinion as decisive, and omit it accordingly, without any regard to mine. Assuredly we will not offend the feelings of any one; but there are many passages which, though they can give no pain to an individual, you perhaps may think will not interest the public. If this fear come across you, take up Chatterton's letters to his mother and sister, and see if the very passages which will excite in you the greatest interest are not of the individual and individualizing character, and then remember that Henry's is to be a name equally dear to the generation which will come after us. * * * * * * * * *

"My heart has often ached during this employment.

"Yours very truly and respectfully,

"Robert Southey."

One extract from a letter written to Mr. Neville White at the close of the year I will place here, as it speaks of the completion of my father's grateful office.

"The sight of the books now completed gave me a melancholy feeling, and I could not help repeating some lines of Wordsworth's:

"'Thou soul of God's best earthly mold,
Thou happy soul, and can it be
That this * * * *
Is all that must remain of thee?'

But this is not all: so many days and nights of unrelenting study, so many hopes and fears, so many aspirations after fame, so much genius, and so many virtues, have left behind them more than this—they have left comfort and consolation to his friends, an honorable remembrance for himself, and for others a bright and encouraging example.

"Our intercourse will not be at an end. When I visit London, which will certainly be during the winter, and probably very soon, I shall see you. We shall have, it is to be hoped and expected, to communicate respecting after editions; and at all times it will give me great pleasure to hear from you."

To Grosvenor C. Bedford, Esq.

"April 21, 1807.

"Whether, Grosvenor, you will ascribe it to the cut of my nose, I can not tell; nor whether it be a proof of the natural wickedness of the heart, but so it is, that I am less disposed to be very much obliged to the Treasury for giving me £200 a year, than I am to swear at the Taxes for having the impudence to take £56 of it back again. And if it were a pull Devil pull Baker between that loyalty which, as you know, has always been so predominant in my heart, and that Jacobinism of which, you know how vilely, I have been suspected, I am afraid the 56 would give a stronger pull on the Baker's side than the 144 on the Devil's. Look you, Mr. Bedford of the Exchequer, it is out of all conscience. Ten in the hundred has always, in all Christian states, been thought damnable usury; and to say that a man took ten in the hundred was the same as saying that he would go to the Devil.* But this is eight-and-twenty in the

* So says the epigram attributed to Shakspeare, upon his friend Mr. Combe, an old gentleman noted for his wealth and usury:

"Ten in the hundred lies here ingraved;
'Tis a hundred to ten his soul is not saved.
If any man ask, 'Who lies in this tomb?'
'Oh! oh!' quoth the Devil, ''tis my John-a-Combe.'"

It must be added that Mr. Knight strenuously opposes the tradition that Shakspeare wrote these lines.—*Knight's Shakspeare, a Biography*, p. 488.

hundred, for which may eight-and-twenty hundred Devils * * * * * * I am a little surprised to hear you speak so contemptuously of modern poetry, because it shows how very little you must have read, or how little you can have considered the subject. The improvement during the present reign has been to the full as great in poetry as it has been in the experimental sciences, or in the art of raising money by taxation. What can you have been thinking of? Had you forgotten Burns a second time? had you forgotten Cowper, Bowles, Montgomery, Joanna Baillie, Walter Scott? to omit a host of names which, though inferior to them, are above those of any former period except the age of Shakspeare, and not to mention Wordsworth and another poet, who has written two very pretty poems in my opinion, called Thalaba and Madoc. * * * I am as busy in my household arrangements as you can be. My tent is pitched at last, and I am thankful that my lot has fallen in so goodly a land.

"Politics are very amusing, and go to the tune of *Tantara-rara*. The king has been fighting for a *veto* upon the initiation of laws, and he has won it. I had got into good humor with the late ministry because of the Limited Service Bill, the Abolishment of the Slave Trade, and their wise conduct with regard to the Continent. As for their successors, they have given a pretty sample of their contempt for all decency by their reinstatement of Lord Melville, the attempt at giving Percival the place for life, and the threat held out by Canning of a dissolution. The Grenvilles now find the error of their neglecting Scotland at the last election, an error which I heard noticed with regret at the time. What is it has made them so unpopular in the city? It is to me incomprehensible why the memory of Pitt should be held in such idolatrous reverence—a man who was as obstinate in every thing wrong as he was ready to give up any thing good, and who, except in the Union and in the Scarcity, was never by any accident right during his long administration.

"I finish poor Henry White's papers to-morrow. One volume of Palmerin still remains to do, and then there will be nothing to impede my progress in S. America. Our Fathers wrote to me about the same time that you did; they were then in pursuit of the culprits Hinchcliffe and Gildon. I'll tell you what I would have done had I been in town and could not have found them. I would have made them a present of verses of my own, just enough in number to fill the gap, and dull enough to suit them. Nobody would have suspected it, and it would have been a very pious fraud to save trouble.

"It consoles me a little when I think of the reviewing* that is to take place: how much more you will feel it than I shall. I am case-hardened; but you—oh, Mr. Bedford, how your back and shoulders *will* tingle! how you *will* perspire! how you *will* bite your nails and gnash your teeth! how you *will* curse the reviewers, and the printers, and the poor poets, with now and then a remembrance of me and yourself. Why, man, there never was so bad a book before! If I were to take any twenty pages, and enumerate all the faults in them—do you remember Duppa, when he came from the Installation at Oxford, all piping hot? even to that degree of heat would the bare enumeration excite you, and your shirt would be as wet as if you had tumbled into a bath. I tell you my opinion as a friend, just to prepare you for what is to come, and am actually laughing at the conceit of how you will look when you take up the first review! Farewell! R. S."

* Of the Specimens of English Poets.

To the Rev. Nicholas Lightfoot.

"Keswick, April 24, 1807.

"MY DEAR LIGHTFOOT,

"Circumstances have prevented me going to Portugal so soon as I intended. I am, however, likely (God willing, I may say certain, as far as human intentions can be so) to procure a whole holiday for your boys in the month of November next. Business will then lead me to London, and when I am so far south I have calls into the west, having an uncle and aunt near Taunton. The Barnstaple coach will carry me to Tiverton; and for the rest of the way I have shoulders to carry a very commodious knapsack, and feet to carry myself, being a better walker than when we were at Oxford.

"Your last letter is fourteen months old, and they may have brought forth so many changes that I almost fear to ask for my godchild Fanny. During that time I have had a son born into the world, and baptized into the Church by the name of Herbert, who is now six months old, and bids fair to be as noisy a fellow as his father—which is saying something; for be it known that I am quite as noisy as ever I was, and should take as much delight as ever in showering stones through the hole of the stair-case against your room door, and hearing with what hearty good earnest 'you fool!' was vociferated in indignation against me in return. O, dear Lightfoot, what a blessing it is to have a boy's heart! it is as great a blessing in carrying one through this world, as to have a child's spirit will be in fitting us for the next.

"If you are in the way of seeing reviews and magazines, they will have told you some of my occupations; the main one they can not tell you, for they do not know it, nor is it my intention that they shall yet a while. I am preparing that branch of the History of Portugal for publication first which would have been last in order, had not temporary circumstances given it a peculiar interest and utility—that which relates to Brazil and Paraguay. The manuscript documents in my possession are very numerous, and of the utmost importance, having been collected with unwearied care by my uncle during a residence of above thirty years in Portugal.

"Burnett is about to make his appearance in the world of authors with, I trust, some credit to himself. When we meet I will tell you the whole course of his eventful history, for more eventful it has been than any one could have prognosticated on his entrance at old Baliol.

"Elmsley, I am sorry to say, is fatter than ever he was: he is one of my most intimate and most valuable friends. I hear from Duppa, or of him, frequently. His visit to Oxford at the Installation has been the occasion of throwing him quite into the circle of my friends in London. I sometimes think with wonder how few acquaintances I made at Oxford; except yourself and Burnett, not one whom I should feel any real pleasure in meeting. Of all the months in my life (happily they did not amount to years), those which were passed at Oxford were the most unprofitable. What Greek I took there I literally left there, and could not help losing; and all I learned was a little swimming (very little the worse luck) and a little boating, which is greatly improved, now that I have a boat of my own upon this delightful lake. I never remember to have dreamed of Oxford—a sure proof how little it entered into my moral being; of school, on the contrary, I dream perpetually.

"C—— is become a great disciplinarian. Some friend of Dr. Aikin's dined one day at Baliol, and I was made the subject of conversation in the common room; poor C—— was my only friend: I believe he allowed that I must be damned for all my heresies, that was certain, but that it was a pity; he remembered me with a degree of affection which neither a dozen years, nor that heart-deadening and uncharitable atmosphere had effaced. I should be glad to shake hands with him again. * * Let me hear from you, and believe me,

"Yours very truly, ROBERT SOUTHEY."

To Grosvenor C. Bedford, Esq.

"Keswick, May 5, 1807.

"MY DEAR GROSVENOR,

"When I wished you never to read the classics again, it was because, like many other persons, *you read nothing else*, and were not likely ever to get more knowledge out of them than you had got already, especially as you chiefly (I may say exclusively) read those from whom least is to be got, which is also another sin of the age. Your letter contains the usual blunders which the ignorance of the age is continually making, and upon which, and nothing else, rests the whole point at issue between such critics as Jeffrey and myself: you couple Homer and Virgil under the general term of classics, and suppose that both are to be admired upon the same grounds. A century ago this was better understood; the critics of that age did read what they wrote about, and understood what they read, and they knew that whoever thought the one of these writers a good poet must upon that very principle hold the other to be a bad one. Greek and Latin poets, Grosvenor, are as opposite as French and English (excepting always Lucretius and Catullus), and you may as well suppose it possible for a man equally to admire Shakspeare and Racine as Homer and Virgil; that is, provided he knows why and wherefore he admires either. Elmsley will tell you this, and I suppose you will admit him to be authority upon this subject.

"You ask me about the Catholic question. I am against admitting them to power of any kind, because the immediate use that would be made of it would be to make proselytes, for which Catholicism is of all religions best adapted. Every ship which had a Catholic captain would have a Catholic chaplain, and in no very long time a Catholic crew: so on in the army; just as every rich Catholic in England at this time has his mansion surrounded with converts fairly purchased—the Jerningham family in Norfolk for instance. I object to any concessions, because no concession can possibly satisfy them; and I think it palpable folly to talk or think of tolerating any sect (beyond what they already enjoy) whose first principle is that their Church is infallible, and, therefore, bound to persecute all others. This is the principle of Catholicism every where, and when they can they avow it and act upon it.

"If our statesmen (God forgive me for degrading the word)—if our traders in politics—had better information of how things are going on abroad, they would not talk of the distinction between Catholic and Protestant as political parties being extinct. But for that distinction Prussia could not have retained its conquests from Austria; and that distinction Bonaparte is at this time endeavoring to profit by. This is a regular conspiracy—a system carrying on to propagate popery in the North of Germany, of which Coleridge could communicate much if he would, he knowing the main directors of the new propaganda at Rome. The mode of doing it is curious: they bring the people first to believe in Jacob Behmen, and then they may believe in any thing else. All fanaticism tends to this point. You will hear something that bears upon this subject from Espriella when he makes his appearance; and you will also see more of the present history of enthusiasm in this country than any body could possibly suspect who has not, as I have done, cast a searching eye into the holes and corners of society, and watched its under currents, which carry more water than the upper stream.

"I have a favor to ask of Horace, which is, that he will do me the kindness to send me the titles of such Portuguese manuscripts as are in the Museum. There can not be so many as to make this a thing of much trouble; and there are some of great value, which were, I believe, part of the plunder of Osorio's library carried off from Sylvas by Sir F. Drake. I wish to know what they are, for the purpose of ascertaining how many among them are not to be found in their own country, and either taking myself, or causing to be taken, if a fit transcriber can be found, copies to present to some fit library at Lisbon: in so doing I shall render the literature of that country a most acceptable service, which it would most highly gratify me to do, and for which I should receive very essential services in return. There are, I believe, in particular, some papers of Geronimo Lobos concerning Abyssinia, and a MS. of which Vincent has made some use. I am particularly desirous of effecting this, not merely because I could do nothing which would be more essentially useful to my own views there, but also because of the true and zealous love which I feel for Portuguese literature, in which I am now as well versed as in that of my own country, and into which (whenever the reign of priestcraft is at an end) I hope to be one day adopted.

"I pray you remember that what I think upon the Catholic question by no means disposes me in favor of the new ministry. I, Mr. Bedford, am, as you know, a court pensioner, and have, as you well know, deserved to be so for my great and devoted attachment to the person of his majesty and the measures of his government. Nevertheless, Mr. Bedford, his ministers are men of tried and convicted incapacity; they have *always* been the contempt of Europe; whether they can be more despised than their predecessors have uniformly and deservedly been, I know not. I can not tell how far below nothing the political barometer can sink till it has been tried.

"God bless you! R. S."

To Richard Duppa, Esq.

"May 23, 1807.

"MY DEAR DUPPA,

"Your book and your letter reached me at the same time. I have cut the leaves, collated the prints, and observe many valuable additions and some great typographical improvements. It was accompanied by a note from Mr. Murray of a very complimentary kind. I like to be complimented in my authorial character, and best of all by booksellers, because their good opinion gets purchasers, and so praise leads to pudding, which I consider to be the solid end of praise.

"I have Walter Scott's promise to do what he can for M. Angelo in the Edinburgh, with this sort of salvo—that Jeffrey is not a very practicable man, but he would do his best with him. My acquaintance with Scott is merely an *acquaintance;* but I had occasion *once* to write to him respecting the sale of a MS. intrusted to me, and bought by him for the Advocate's Library, and in that letter I introduced the subject. I was greatly in hopes, and indeed expected, that Wordsworth would have done as much in the Critical, by means of his brother, who writes there. Had it not been for this, I might, perhaps, have done something by applying to Fellowes, the anti-Calvinist, a very interesting man —such a one, indeed, that, though I never met him but once, I could without scruple have written to him. Wonderful to tell, he bears a part in that Review, though his opinions are as opposite to *Hunt's*, and all his other steeple-hunting whippers-in, as light is to darkness. The hostile article I have not seen; one of the advantages of living here is, that I never see these things till their season is over, and then, like wasps in winter, their power of stinging is at an end. I should have been angry at seeing your book abused when the abuse could do any hurt, and should have felt that sort of heat in my cheek which denotes the moral temperature of the minute to be above temperate. Now, whenever it falls in my way, which, very likely, never may be the case, it will come as a matter of literary history—as what was said by some malevolent and ignorant person when a good book first appeared, and so it will furnish me an anecdote to relate when I speak of the book; or if I should ever live to old age, and have leisure to leave behind me that sort of transcript from recollections which would make such excellent materials for the literary history of my own times.

"You are mistaken about Henry White; the fact is briefly this: at the age of seventeen he published a little volume of poems of very great merit, and sent with them to the different Reviews a letter stating that his hope was to raise money by them to pursue his studies and get to college. Hamilton, then of the Critical, showed me this letter. I asked him to let me review the book, which he promised; but he sent me no books after the promise. Well, the M. Review noticed this little volume in the most cruel and insulting manner. I was provoked, and wrote to encourage the boy, offering to aid him in a subscription for a costlier publication. I spoke of him in London, and had assurances of assistance from Sotheby, and, by way of Wynn, from Lord Carysfort. His second letter to me, however, said he was going to Cambridge, under *Simeon's* protection. I plainly saw that the Evangelicals had caught him; and as he did not want what little help I could have procured, and I had no leisure for new correspondences, ceased to write to him, but did him what good I could in the way of reviewing, and getting him friends at Cambridge. He died last autumn, and I received a letter informing me of it. It gave me a sort of shock, because, in spite of his evangelicism, I always expected great things, from the proof he had given of very superior powers; and, in replying to this letter, I asked if there were any intention of publishing any thing which he might have left, and offered to give an opinion upon his papers, and look them over. Down came a boxful, the sight of which literally made my heart ache and my eyes overflow, for never did I behold such proofs of human industry. To make short, I took the matter up with interest, collected his letters, and have, at the expense of more time than such a poor fellow as myself can very well afford, done what his family are very grateful for, and what I think the world will thank me for too. Of course I have done it gratuitously. His life will affect you, for he fairly died of intense application. Cambridge finished him. When his nerves were already so overstrained that his nights were utter misery, they gave him medicines to enable him to hold out during examination for a prize! The horse won, but he died after the race! Among his letters there is a great deal of Methodism: if this procures for the book, as it very likely may, a sale among the righteous over-much, I shall rejoice for the sake of his family, for whom I am very much interested. I have, however, in justice to myself, stated, in the shortest and most decorous manner, that my own views of religion differ widely from his. Still, that I should become, and that, too, voluntarily, an editor of methodistical and Calvinistic letters, is a thing which, when I think of it, excites the same sort of smile that the thoughts of my pension does, and I wonder, like the sailor, what is to be done next.

"Want of room has obliged me to reserve most of your letters, which I meant for the latter end of Espriella's remarks;* but when I came to the latter end, the printing had got beyond my calculation of pages so much that I was fain to stop. I have good hopes of such a sale as may induce my friend to travel again, my own stock of matter not being half exhausted, nor, indeed, my design half completed. The book ought to be published in a month. Palmerin will appear nearly at the same time, and, perhaps, tend to remove suspicion, if any should subsist. The reception of this book will determine whether it is to be followed up or not; but if it be, be assured that you shall have ample revenge upon Fuseli.

"I know nothing of botany, and every day regret that I do not. It is a settled purpose of my heart, if my children live, to make them good naturalists. If you come either into Yorkshire or Northumberland, you must not return to the south without touching at Greta Hall, and seeing me in my glory. We have papered the parlor this very day. It is not so fine a room as yours, Mr. Duppa, but it is very beautiful, I assure you—and the masons are at this time making a ceiling to my study—and I have got curtains for it, the color of nankeen—and there is to be a carpet, and a new fender, and all sorts of things that are proper. Miss Barker tells me she has seen you. I am in good hope of persuading her to come down this summer, and if she comes she shall not go till I have a set of drawings for the parlor.

"I want to hear, in spite of great trouble and little profit, that you have fixed upon a new subject, and are again at work. There is no being happy without having some worthy occupation in hand.

"Farewell! R. S."

To John Rickman, Esq.

"May 27, 1807.

"My dear Rickman,

"The pleasantest season in the country for one who lives in it is undoubtedly the month of blossoms and beauty, when we have not only immediate enjoyment, but summer before us. The best season for seeing a country, and especially this country, is during the turn of the leaf. September and October are our best months. We have usually long and delightful autumns, extending further into the winter than they do in the south of England. Our harvests, such as they are, are sometimes not in till the end of October, every thing with us being proportionably late.

"Mrs. Rickman has seen all that water colors can do for our lakes, in seeing them as delineated by Glover, who is of all our artists the truest to nature. But I will show her sights beyond all reach of human coloring—such work as nature herself makes with traveling clouds, and columns of misty sunshine, falling as if from an eye of light in Heaven, like that upon Guy Fawkes in the prayer-book. *Every* point of sight is beautiful, and Derwentwater can only be judged by a panorama, such as you will have from our boat. Do not wait for another year for the sake of including your Scotch journey. God knows what another year may produce, either of good or evil, to both of us. There is always so much chance of being summoned off on the grand tour of the universe, that a man ought not, without good reason, to delay any little trip he may wish to take first upon our microcosm. * * * * * * What you say about breeding up a boy to understand the Keltic language has often been in my mind. Have you seen a good book in reply to Malthus by Dr. Jarrold? This disjointed question comes in, because he shows how animals that are the most highly finished are most apt, like looking-glasses, to break in the making; and I have always the fear of too much sensorial power in my children so before my eyes, as never willingly to shape any plan about them which might occasion more cause for disappointment. How easy would it be for the London Institution, or any society, to look out promising lads, and breed them up for specific literary purposes. Should Herbert live, I should more incline (as more connected with my own pursuits) to let him pass two or three years in Biscay, and so procure all that is to be found of Cantabrian antiquity—a distinct stock, I learn, from the Keltic; but I believe that one part of our population came from those shores, of which the prevalence of dark hair and dark complexions is to me physical proof. Nothing can be so little calculated to advance our stock of knowledge as our inveterate mode of education, whereby we all spend so many years in learning so little. I was from the age of six to that of twenty learning Greek and Latin, or, to speak more truly, learning nothing else. The little Greek I had sleepeth, if it be not dead, and can hardly wake without a miracle, and my Latin, though abundant enough for all useful purposes, would be held in great contempt by those people who regard the classics as the scriptures of taste. * *

"God bless you! R. S."

Some differences having arisen between the Messrs. Longman and Co. and the editor of the Edinburgh Review, it was at this time in contemplation to carry on the work under a different management; and on this supposition they wrote to my father, requesting him to furnish them with certain articles "in his best manner,"

* Mr. Duppa had been furnishing him with some information for this book.

and offering payment at a higher rate than he had received for the Annual Review. His reply shows that his principle was, "whatsoever his hand found to do, to do it with his might."* The contemplated separation of the editor from the Review did not, however, take place, and the articles were consequently transferred to the Annual, my father stating that nothing but the circumstance of the Review having changed hands, and their needing a ready writer, would induce him to have any thing to do with it, disapproving as he did the principles upon which it was conducted.

To the Messrs. Longman and Co.

"June 5, 1807.

"DEAR SIRS,

"I will review the books as soon as they arrive, and as well as I can, but I can not do them better for an Edinburgh Review than for an Annual one. There are many articles which are valued precisely in proportion to the time and labor bestowed upon them, and which, therefore, can be accurately fixed accordingly; these articles are not of that description. The worst reviewals you have ever had from me have cost me more time and labor than the best. When the subject is good, and I am acquainted with it, the pen flows freely; otherwise it is tilling an ungrateful soil. I can promise you a better review of Clavigero than any other person could furnish; upon the other books, I will do my best. All reviewals, however, which are not seasoned either with severity or impertinence, will seem flat to those whose palates have been accustomed to ——'s sauce-damnable.

"Some time ago, the Bishop of Llandaff observed to me that few things were more wanted than a regular collection of translations of the ancient historians, comprising the whole of them in their chronological order. It is worth thinking of; and if you should think of it, modern copyright need not stand in your way. Littlebury's Herodotus is better than Beloe's, and Gordon's Tacitus far superior to Murphy's. Such a collection, well annotated, &c., could not fail to sell, and might best be published volume by volume; if it were carried to the end of the Byzantine history, so much the better both for the public and the publishers. This is not a plan in which I could bear any part myself, but it is worth your consideration.

* * * * * * *

"The Spanish Joinville, I fear, perished at Hafod. If, however, by good fortune, it should have been returned to you before the fire, have the goodness to inclose it in the next parcel. I wait the arrival of one, expected by every carrier, to make up a bundle for Dr. Aikin: the reason is this; one of the books which I sent for implies by the title that I have been deceived in one of the Omniana articles, and I ordered the book for the sake of ascertaining the truth and correcting the error.

"Is there not a new edition of Whitehead's Life of Wesley? If you will send me it, and with it the life published by Dr Coke for the conference, I will either review it for you, or make a life myself for the Athenæum, having Thompson's here, and also a complete set of Wesley's journals, which I have carefully read and marked for the purpose.

"Yours truly, R. SOUTHEY.

"I hope you will accommodate matters with Jeffrey; for if there should be two Edinburgh Reviews, or if he should set up another under a new title, you would probably be the sufferer, even though yours should manifestly be the best —such is the force of prejudice."

The following playful effusion was addressed to Hartley Coleridge, who is often referred to in the earlier letters by the name of Moses, it being my father's humor to bestow on his little playfellows many and various such names. When those allusions and this letter were selected for publication, my cousin was yet among us, and I had pleasantly anticipated his half-serious, half-playful remonstrances for thus bringing his childhood before the public. *Now* he is among the departed; and those only who knew him intimately can tell how well-stored and large a mind has gone with him, much less how kind a heart and how affectionate a disposition. He has found his last peaceful resting-place (where Dr. Arnold so beautifully expresses a wish that he might lie) "beneath the yews of Grasmere church-yard, with the Rotha, with its deep and silent pools, passing by;" but his name will long be a "living one" among the hill-sides and glens of our rugged country,

"Stern and wild,
Meet nurse for a poetic child."

To Hartley Coleridge.

"Keswick, June 13, 1807.

"NEPHEW JOB,

"First, I have to thank you for your letter and your poem; and, secondly, to explain why I have not done this sooner. We were a long time without knowing where you were, and, when news came from Miss Barker that you were in London, by the time a letter could have reached you you were gone; and, lastly, Mr. Jackson wrote to you to Bristol. I will now compose an epistle which will follow you further west.

"Bona Marietta hath had kittens; they were remarkably ugly, all taking after their father Thomas, who there is reason to believe was either uncle or grandsire to Bona herself, the prohibited degrees of consanguinity which you will find at the end of the Bible not being regarded by cats. As I have never been able to persuade this family that catlings, fed for the purpose and smothered with onions, would be rabbits to all eatable purposes, Bona Marietta's ugly progeny no sooner came into the world than they were sent out of it; the river nymph Greta conveyed them to the river god Derwent; and if neither

* Ecclesiastes, ix., 10.

the eels nor the ladies of the lake have taken a fancy to them on their way, Derwent hath consigned them to the Nereids. You may imagine them converted into sea-cats by favor of Neptune, and write an episode to be inserted in Ovid's Metamorphoses. Bona bore the loss patiently, and is in good health and spirits. I fear that if you meet with any of the race of Mrs. Rowe's cat at Ottery, you will forget poor Marietta. Don't bite your arm, Job.

"We have been out one evening in the boat —Mr. Jackson, Mrs. Wilson, and the children— and kindled our fire upon the same place where you drank tea with us last autumn. The boat has been painted, and there is to be a boat-house built for it. Alterations are going on here upon a great scale. The parlor has been transmogrified. That, Hartley, was one of *my* mother's words; your mother will explain it to you. The masons are at work in my study; the garden is inclosed with a hedge; some trees planted behind it, a few shrubs, and abundance of currant-trees. We must, however, wait till the autumn before all can be done that is intended in the garden. Mr. White, the Belligerent, is settled in the general's house. Find out why I give him that appellation.

"There has been a misfortune in the family. We had a hen with five chickens, and a gleed has carried off four. I have declared war against the gleed, and borrowed a gun; but since the gun has been in the house, he has never made his appearance. Who can have told him of it? Another hen is sitting, and I hope the next brood will be luckier. Mr. Jackson has bought a cow, but he has had no calf since *you* left him. Edith has taken your place in his house, and talks to Mrs. Wilson by the hour about *her* Hartley. She grows like a young giantess, and has a disposition to bite her arm, which, you know, is a very foolish trick. Herbert is a fine fellow; I call him the Boy of Basan, because he roars like a young bull when he is pleased; indeed, he promises to inherit his father's vocal powers.

"The weather has been very bad—nothing but easterly winds, which have kept every thing back. We had one day hotter than had been remembered for fourteen years: the glass was at 85° in the shade, in the sun in Mr. Calvert's garden at 118°. The horses of the mail died at Carlisle. I never remember to have felt such heat in England, except one day fourteen years ago, when I chanced to be in the mail-coach, and it was necessary to bleed the horses, or they would have died then. In the course of three days the glass fell forty degrees, and the wind was so cold and so violent that persons who attempted to cross the Fells beyond Penrith were forced to turn back.

"Your friend Dapper, who is, I believe, your god-dog, is in good health, though he grows every summer graver than the last. This is the natural effect of time, which, as you know, has made me the serious man I am. I hope it will have the same effect upon you and your mother, and that, when she returns, she will have left off that evil habit of quizzing me and calling me names: it is not decorous in a woman of her years.

"Remember me to Mr. Poole, and tell him I shall be glad when he turns laker. He will find tolerable lodgings at the Hill; a boat for fine weather, good stores of books for a rainy day, and as hearty a shake by the hand on his arrival as he is likely to meet with between Stowey and Keswick. Some books of mine will soon be ready for your father. Will he have them sent any where? or will he pick them up himself when he passes through London on his way northward? Tell him that I am advancing well in South America, and shall have finished a volume by the end of the year. The Chronicle of the Cid is to go to press as soon as I receive some books from Lisbon, which must first be examined. This intelligence is for him also.

"I am desired to send you as much love as can be inclosed in a letter: I hope it will not be charged double on that account at the post-office; but there is Mrs. Wilson's love, Mr. Jackson's, your Aunt Southey's, your Aunt Lovell's, and Edith's; with a purr from Bona Marietta, an open-mouthed kiss from Herbert, and three wags of the tail from Dapper. I trust thev will all arrive safe, and remain,

"Dear nephew Job,

"Your dutiful uncle,

"ROBERT SOUTHEY."

To the Messrs. Longman and Co.

"June 29, 1807.

"DEAR SIRS,

"I have been told by persons most capable of judging, that the old translation of Don Quixote is very beautiful. The book has never fallen in my way. If it be well translated, the language of Elizabeth's reign must needs accord better with the style of Cervantes than more modern English would do, and I should think it very probable that it would be better to correct this than to translate the work anew. As for my undertaking any translation, or, indeed, any revision, which might lead to the labor, or half the labor, which Palmerin cost me, it is out of the question; but if Mr. Heber can lend you this translation, I will give you my opinion upon it; and I will do for you, if you want it, what you would find much difficulty in getting done by any other person—add to a Life of Cervantes an account of all his other writings, and likewise of the books in Don Quixote's library, as far as my own stores will reach, and those which we may find access to, and make such notes upon the whole book as my knowledge of the history and literature of Spain can supply. I believe a new translation has been announced by Mr. ——, whose translation of Yriarte proved that either he did not understand the original, or that of all translators he is the most impudent. Such preliminaries as these which I propose might fill half a volume, or extend to a whole one, just as might be judged most expedient. It gives me very great pleasure to hear that you have engaged for a genuine version of the Arabian Nights, which I consider as one of the greatest desideratums in modern Oriental literature. We have a number of imitations in our language, which I am still boy enough to delight in; and were you, as the French have done, to publish a complete collection of them, I, for one, should be glad of the opportunity of buying them. If you published them volume by volume, with good prints, like your Theatre, school-boys would take off half an edition.

"As the new Joinville is, beyond all comparison, the most unreasonably dear book I ever saw, so is your Holinshed the cheapest; and I shall keep the copy you have sent accordingly. Dear books may not deter the rich from purchasing, but here is proof for you that cheap ones tempt the poor.

"To-morrow I will make up my parcel for the Athenæum. At Dr. Aikin's request, I have undertaken (long since) the Spanish and Portuguese literary part of his Biography. Some articles appeared in the last volume, and, few as they are, I suppose they entitle me to it. Will you ask Dr. A. if this be the case?

"Yours truly, R. SOUTHEY."

To the Messrs. Longman and Co.

"August 25, 1807.

"DEAR SIRS,

"The motives which induced me to propose selling an edition of the Cid may be very soon explained. I have been settling myself here in a permanent place of abode, and, in consequence, many unavoidable expenses have been incurred. Among others, that of removing from Bristol a much larger library than perhaps any other man living, whose means are so scanty, is possessed of. I thank you for the *manner* in which you have objected to purchasing it, and am more gratified by it than I should have been by your acceptance. The sale of this book can not be so doubtful as that of a poem. A part of it shall be sent up in a few days, and the sooner it is put to press the better. If it suit you, I should much like to let Pople print it. He has not made all the haste he could with Palmerin, but he has taken great pains with it; for never had printer a more perplexed copy to follow, and he has been surprisingly correct.

"I do not know what the state of my account with you is. Mr. Aikin has sent me no returns either for this year's reviewing or the last. I suppose, however, that the edition of Espriella will about balance it; and if I may look to you for about £150 between this and the end of the year, my exigencies will be supplied. Meantime I am desirous that my exertions should be proportionate to my wants. The old edition of Don Quixote, if carefully collated and corrected, will, I believe, be very superior to any other. As soon as the original arrives, with the remainder of my books, from London, I shall be able to speak decisively; but I have little or no doubt but it will prove as I expect. If this be the case, I am ready to undertake it, to supply such preliminaries as I formerly stated, and to add notes.

"The 'Catalogue Raisonné' can not be executed by a single person. I could do great part of it—probably all except the legal and scientific departments. Upon this matter I will think, and write to you in a few days.

"What is this History of South America which I am told is announced? I am getting on with my own Brazil and the River Plata, and it is not possible that any man in England can have one tenth part of the materials which I possess for such a work. Were you to see the manuscripts which I possess you would be fully convinced of this, and without seeing them you can hardly form an estimate of their value and importance. * * * * * *

"Yours truly, R. SOUTHEY."

To the Messrs. Longman and Co.

"Sept. 20, 1807.

"DEAR SIRS,

"I have been considering and reconsidering the plan of a Critical Catalogue. On the scale which you propose, it approaches so nearly to what we had formerly projected as a complete Bibliotheca Britannica, that I should be loth to go so near it and yet stop short. On the present scale (and were you disposed to extend it to the original extent, it would be quite impossible for me till my historical labors are closed), the opinions given must necessarily be so short, that in most instances the main business would be to copy title-pages. Now it would take an amanuensis more time ten-fold to hunt out the book than to do this; and yet, as you say, my time may be employed more satisfactorily for myself, and probably more to your advantage as well as my own, than in mere transcription.

"Of the possible size of such a work I can not form even a decent conjecture. Scarce books are more numerous than good ones, have longer titles, and require sometimes a long description. Perhaps the best way would be to begin with a chronological list of all that have been printed before the accession of Henry VIII., when printing may be said to have become common. All these books have a great value from their scarcity—indeed, their main value—and had better be classed together than under any separate heads. A complete list might be furnished by Mr. Dibdin, who must already have collected all the necessary knowledge for his edition of Ames. Mr. Park could supply the poets, and, indeed, manage the whole better than any other person. I could give a better opinion of works than he could, and believe that I *know* more of them; but there is a sort of title-page and colophon knowledge—in one word, bibliology—which is exactly what is wanted for this purpose, and in which he is very much my superior. The way in which I could be best employed would be in looking over the MS., adding to it any thing in my knowledge, if any thing there might be, which had escaped him, and supplying a brief criticism where it was wanted, and I could give it.

"Any such assistance I should willingly give; but upon slow and frequent consideration, I certainly think the whole may be better executed in London than here, and by many others than by me, for of all sorts of work, it is that in which there must be most transcription, and in which it will be most inconvenient to employ an amanuensis.

"The extent of such a book will probably be wholly immaterial to its sale. None but those who have libraries will buy it, and those may almost be calculated upon. There will also be some sale for it abroad, more than is usual for English books. The one thing in which it seems possible to improve upon the best catalogue is, by arranging the books in every subdivision chronologically, according to the time when they were written.

* * * * * * *

"Yours truly, R. SOUTHEY."

To Walter Scott, Esq.

"Keswick, Sept. 27, 1807.

"MY DEAR SIR,

"I have desired Longman to send you a copy of Palmerin of England, knowing that you, who love to read as well as to sing of knights' and gentle ladies' deeds, will not be dismayed at the sight of four volumes more corpulent than volumes are wont to be in these degenerate days. The romance, though not so good as Amadis, is a good romance, and far superior to any other of the Spanish school that I have yet seen. I know not whether you will think that part of the preface satisfactory, in which it is argued that Moraes is the author. It is so to myself.*

"I rejoice to hear that we are to have another Lay, and hope we may have as many Last Lays of the Minstrel as our ancestors had Last Words of Mr. Baxter. My own lays are probably at an end. That portion of my time which I can afford to employ in laboring for fame is given to historical pursuits; and poetry will not procure for me any thing more substantial. This motive alone would not, perhaps, wean me from an old calling, if I were not grown more attached to the business of historical research, and more disposed to instruct and admonish mankind than to amuse them.

"The Chronicle of the Cid is just gone to press—the most ancient and most curious piece of chivalrous history in existence—a book after your own heart. It will serve as the prologue to a long series of labors, of which, whenever you will take Keswick in your way to or from London, I shall be very glad to show you some samples. I am now settled here, and am getting my books about me; you will find a boat for fine weather, and a good many out-of-the-way books for a rainy day.

"I beg to be remembered to Mrs. Scott.

"Yours very truly,

"ROBERT SOUTHEY."

* It has since been proved that the real author of Palmerin was Luis Hurtado, a Spaniard. See Quarterly Review, vol. lxxii., p. 10.

To Messrs. Longman and Co.

"Nov. 13, 1807.

"DEAR SIRS,

"We have certainly some reason to complain of Cadell and Davies; poor Cervantes, however, has more. * * * Their splendid edition will be sure to sell for its splendor. I would have made such a work as should have been reprinted after the plates were worn out. I thank you for offering to engage in it, but my nature is as little disposed to this kind of warfare as yours; and I have as many plans to execute as I shall ever find life to perform. Let it pass. Morte d'Arthur is a book which I shall edit with peculiar pleasure, because it has been my delight since I was a school-boy. There is nothing to be done in it but to introduce it with a preface and accompany it with notes. No time need be lost. As soon as you can meet with a copy, it may be put into Pople's hands; and by the time he has got through it, the introduction and annotations will be ready. I will send back Heber's books (which I have detained, expecting to use them for the D. Quixote). For the Athenæum, it will be sufficient to say that I am preparing an edition of Morte d'Arthur, with an introduction and notes.

"I have materials for a volume of Travels in Portugal, which the expulsion of the English from that country, and the consequent impossibility of my returning there to visit the northern provinces, as was my intention, induces me to think of preparing for the press. In what form are such works most profitable? If in quarto with engravings, I can procure some sketches and some finished drawings. If you judge it expedient to reprint my former volume, it must undergo some corrections; for, though it has pleased the public to receive my first publications far more favorably than my later ones, I am fully sensible of their faults, and look upon them with sufficient humiliation.

" * * * * * * *

The D. Quixote shall be returned in my first parcel. The only reason I have for regretting that Mr. Balfour has elbowed me out of an office to which he certainly has no pretensions whatever is, that I wished to do something, the emolument of which should be certain, for I can not be anticipating uncertain profits without feeling some anxiety. I have translations enough almost to make a little volume like Lord Strangford's, but then I am not a lord. I have ballads enough for half a volume, but people are more ready to ask copies of them now than they would be to buy them; and were I to write as many more, according to all likelihood I should not get more by publishing them than any London newspaper would give me for any number of verses, good, bad, or indifferent, sold by the yard, and without the maker's name to warrant them. What I feel most desirous to do is to send Espriella again on his travels, and so complete my design; but this must not be unless he hits the fancy of the public.

"Yours truly, R. SOUTHEY."

To Grosvenor C. Bedford, Esq.

"Nov. 15, 1807.

"MY DEAR GROSVENOR,

"I do not know that I should have taken up my pen with the intention of inflicting a letter upon you, if it had not been for a suspicion, produced by your last letter, that you expect me in London sooner than it is any ways possible for me to be there, and that peradventure, therefore, you may think it is not worth while to look after my pension till I arrive in proper person to receive it. Now, Mr. Bedford, touching this matter there are two things to be said. My going to London seems to me no very certain thing. It depends something on my uncle's movements, of whose arrival from Lisbon I daily expect to hear; and, of course, if I go, my journey must be so timed as to meet him. It depends, also, something on my finances; and I begin to think that I can not afford the expense of the journey, for I have had extraordinary goings-out this year in settling myself, and no extraordinary comings-in to counterbalance them. The Constable is a leaden-heeled rascal, and if I do not take care, will be left confoundedly behind. I must work like a negro the whole winter to set things right, and the nearer the time for my projected journey approaches, the less likely is it that I can spare it. My object in going would be to consult certain books for the preliminaries and notes for the Cid; and these books I should assuredly feel myself bound to consult if it required no other sacrifices than those of time and trouble. But if the necessary expense can not prudently and justifiably be afforded, I must be content to do the best I can, which will be quite good enough to satisfy every body except myself. In the second place, if you can, by any interest, get my pension paid, I pray you exert it. I foresee that I shall be kept in hot water by it till I am lucky enough to get some little prize in the lottery of life, which will enable me to wait without inconvenience for arrears. At present, the only chance for this is in the sale of Espriella. Should that go through two or three editions, it will set me fairly afloat.

"I thought to have brought up my lee-way by doing a specific piece of job-work, of which I have been rather unhandsomely disappointed. The story is simply this: Smirke has projected a splendid edition of Don Quixote with Cadell and Davies. They proposed to Longman to take a share in it, and he was authorized by them to ask me to translate it. While I was corresponding with them upon the fitness of revising the first translation in preference, and forming such a plan for preliminaries and annotations as would have made a great body of Spanish learning, Cadell and Davies, unknown to them, struck a bargain with a Mr. Balfour, who is no more able to translate Don Quixote than he would have been to write it. This is some disappointment to me, as I should have been paid a specific sum for my work, and could have calculated upon it. The Longmans behave as they ought to do in the business. They refuse to take any share in the work in consequence of this unhandsome dealing toward me, and offer to publish my edition upon our ordinary terms of halving the profits. This, however, would not serve my purpose.

"My affairs are not in a bad train, except for the present. The profits of the current edition of Espriella, and of the unborn one of the Cid, are anticipated and gone. Those of the Specimens, of the small edition of Madoc, and of Palmerin, are untouched. But if the three send me in £100 at the end of the year's sale, it will be more than I expect. The first volume of Brazil will be ready for the press next summer. I think also of publishing my travels in Portugal, for which good materials have long lain by me, and we are now talking of editing Morte d'Arthur. Reviewing comes among the ordinaries of the year; in my conscience I do not think any body else does so much and gets so little for it. Have I told you that my whole profits upon Madoc up to Midsummer last amount to £25? and the whole it is likely to be, unless the remaining 134 copies be sold as waste paper.

"I shall do yet; and if there be any thing like a dispirited tone in this letter, it is more because my eyes are weak than for any other cause. It is likely that Espriella will bear me out—I must be more than commonly unlucky if it does not—and if it does not, I will seek more review employment, write in more magazines, and scribble verses for the newspapers. As long as I can keep half my time for labors worthy of myself and of posterity, I shall not feel debased by sacrificing the other, however unworthily it may be employed. You will say, why do you not write for the stage? The temptations to it are so strong, and I have made the resolution so often, that not to have done it yet is good proof of a self-conviction that it would not be done well; besides, I have not leisure from present urgencies.

"Now do not fancy me bent double like the Pilgrim, under this load upon my back; I am as bolt upright as ever, and in as wholesome good spirits, and, as soon as this letter is folded and sent off, shall go on with reviewing Buchanan's Travels, and forget every thing except what I know concerning Malabar.

"God bless you! R. S."

To Richard Heber, Esq.

"Keswick, Nov. 16, 1807.

"MY DEAR SIR,

"I am now about to edit Morte d'Arthur. My Round-table knowledge is as extensive as that of any, perhaps, but my Round-table library is scanty: of old books it contains none except the English Geoffrey of Monmouth and the two long Poems of Luigi Alemanni. My plan is, to give the history of Arthur, and collect, by the aid of Turner, Owen, and Edward Williams, all that the Welsh themselves can supply, and then the critical bibliography of the Round Table. The notes will refer to the originals from which this delightful book has been compiled, and give all the illustrations that I can supply. Once more, therefore, I must beg your assistance, and ask you to send me as many books as you have which bear upon this subject. A Mr. Goldsmid sent me a list of his romances some time ago, and his collection will probably contain what yours may want. Will you add to them your copy of Oviedo's History of the New World?

"The printer's copy of Palmerin was, I hope, returned to you, according to your desire and my directions. It will show you that I am not an idle editor, whatever those unhappy Specimens may have induced you to think. Should this Palmerin sell, I would gladly follow it with the third part, if the original could be procured; but the only chance of meeting with one would be in the king's library, and there, of course, it would be useless.

"I have many things in hand. The Chronicle of the Cid will be likely to please you. It will soon be followed by the History of Brazil, and that by the other part of the History of Portugal and its Conquests. With poetry I must have done, unless I could afford another Madoc for five-and-twenty pounds, which is all that it has pleased the public to let me get by it. I feel some pride in having done well, but it is more than counterbalanced by the consciousness that I could do better, and yet am never likely to have an opportunity. St. Cecilia herself could not have played the organ if there had been nobody to blow the bellows for her. Drafts upon posterity will not pass for current expenses. My poems have sold exactly in an inverse ratio to their merit; and I can not go back to boyhood, and put myself again upon a level with the taste of the book-buying readers. My numerous plans and collections for them will figure away when I am dead, and afford excellent occasion for exclamations of edifying regret from those very persons who would have traduced what they will think it decorous to lament.

"You will see, in the preface to Palmerin, that I have tracked Shakspeare, Sydney, and Spenser to Amadis of Greece. I have an imperfect copy of Florisel of Nequea, the next in the series, and there I find the mock execution of Pamela and Philoclea, and Amoret with her open wound.

"Yours very truly, ROBERT SOUTHEY."

To Grosvenor C. Bedford, Esq.

"Keswick, Nov. 24, 1807.

"MY DEAR GROSVENOR,

"Mine is a strong spirit, and I am very desirous that you should not suppose it to be more severely tried than it is. The temporary inconvenience which I feel is solely produced by unavoidable expenses in settling myself, which will not occur again; and if Espriella slides into a good sale, or if one edition of our deplorable Specimens should go off, I shall be floated into smooth water. Bear this in mind, also, that I can command an income, fully equivalent to all my wants, whenever I choose to write for money, and for nothing else. Our Fathers in the Row would find me task-work to any amount which I might wish to undertake, and I could assuredly make £300 a year as easily as I now make half that sum, simply by writing anonymously, and doing what five hundred trading authors could do just as well. This is the worst which can befall me.

"Old John Southey dealt unjustly by me; but it was what I expected, and his brother will, without doubt, do just the same. In case of Lord Somerville's death without a son, a considerable property devolves to me or my representatives—encumbered, however, with a lawsuit to recover it; and, as I should be compelled to enter into this, I have only to hope his lordship will have the goodness to live as long as I do, and save me from the disquietude which this would occasion. I used to think that the reputation which I should establish would ultimately turn to marketable account, and that my books would sell as well as if they were seasoned with slander or obscenity. In time they will—it will not be in my time. I have, however, an easy means of securing some part of the advantage to my family, by forbearing to publish any more corrected editions during my lifetime, and leaving such corrections as will avail to give a second lease of copyright, and make any book-seller's editions of no value. As for my family, I have no fears for them; they would find friends enough when I am gone; and having this confidence, you may be sure that there is not a lighter-hearted man in the world than myself.

"Basta—or, as we say in Latin, Ohe jam satis est. My eyes are better, which I attribute to an old velvet bonnet of Edith's, converted without alteration into a most venerable studying cap for my worship: it keeps my ears warm, and I am disposed to believe that having the sides of my head cold, as this Kamtschatka weather needs must make it, affected the eyes. Mr. Bedford, you may imagine what a venerable, and, as the French say, *penetrating* air this gives me. Hair, forehead, eyebrows, and eyes are hidden; nothing appears but nose; but that is so cold that I expect every morning when I get out of bed to see the snow lie on the summit of it. This complaint was not my old Egyptian* plague, but pure weakness, which makes what I have said probable. * * * *

"We had an interesting guest here a few evenings ago, who came to visit Tom—Captain Guillem, Nelson's first lieutenant at Trafalgar, a sailor of the old Blake and Dampier breed, who has risen from before the mast, was in Duncan's action, and at Copenhagen, &c. He told us more of Nelson than I can find time to write. * * * * * * * * * *

"God bless you! R. S."

To Grosvenor C. Bedford, Esq.

"Dec 5, 1807.

"MY DEAR GROSVENOR,

" * * * * * * * Our Fathers inform me that about 300 copies of Espriella remain unsold, and that probably it would be expedient to begin reprinting it in

* A species of ophthalmia, from which he formerly suffered.

about a month. You may have heard or seen that D. Manuel has a friend in the Courier and in the Morning Post. This is Stuart's doing, who will befriend him still more by giving me some facts for what further is to be added to complete the object of the book. As for the Specimens, I am perfectly satisfied that it will be very easy to metamorphose them into a good book, if ever there should be a second edition.

"I have seen only one reviewal of it, which was in the Monthly Magazine some months ago, and then the author contrived to invalidate all the censure which he had cast upon it by abusing me *in toto* as a blockhead, coxcomb, &c., &c.

"I am a good deal surprised at your saying that the dunces of 1700 were like the dunces of 1800. Surely you have said this without thinking what you were saying: they are as different as the fops of the two periods. You are wrong, also, in your praise of Ellis's book: his is a very praiseworthy book, as far as matter of fact, history, and arrangement go; but the moment that ends, and the series of specimens begins, all views of manner, and all light of history, disappear, and you have little else than a collection of amatory pieces selected with little knowledge and less taste.

* * * * * * *

"Captain Guillem is at home in the Isle of Man, having realized from ten to fifteen thousand pounds. He has no chance of being employed, having no interest to get a ship, and, what is better, no wish to have one. Yet he is precisely such a man as ought to be employed—a true-bred English sailor. Let him be at sea forty years, and there would be no mutiny on board his ship; boy-captains are the persons who make mutinies. Oh, Grosvenor Bedford, what a pamphlet would I write about the navy if my brother were not in it!

"I do not send you Henry White's Remains, because, though as many copies were offered me as I should choose to take, I declined taking any more than one for myself. I hope they will sell, and believe so; his piety will recommend the book to the Evangelicals, and his genius to men of letters.

"God bless you! R. S."

My father's acquaintance with Sir Walter Scott, commenced by the short visit he had made to Ashestiel in the autumn of 1805, and continued, as we have seen, by letter, now began to assume a closer character, and, through his friendly mediation, some overtures were now made to him to take service in the corps of his opponent Jeffrey, in the Edinburgh Review. "As you occasionally review," Sir Walter wrote to him at this time (November, 1807), "will you forgive my suggesting a circumstance for your consideration, to which you will give exactly the degree of weight you please? I am perfectly certain that Jeffrey would think himself both happy and honored in receiving any communications which you might send him, choosing your books and expressing your own opinions. The terms of the Edinburgh Review are ten guineas per sheet, and will shortly be advanced considerably. I question if the same unpleasant sort of work is any where else so well compensated. The only reason which occurs to me as likely to prevent your rendering the Edinburgh some critical assistance, is the severity of the criticisms upon Madoc and Thalaba. I do not know if this will be at all removed by my assuring you, as I do upon my honor, that Jeffrey has, notwithstanding the flippancy of these attacks, the most sincere respect both for your person and talents. The other day I designedly led the conversation on that subject, and had the same reason I always have had to consider his attack as arising from a radical difference in point of taste, or, rather, feeling of poetry, but by no means from any thing approaching either to enmity or a false conception of your talents. I do not think that a difference of this sort should prevent you, if you are otherwise disposed to do so, from carrying a portion, at least, of your critical labors to a better market than the Annual. Pray think of this; and, if you are disposed to give your assistance, I am positively certain that I can transact the matter with the utmost delicacy toward both my friends. I am certain you may add £100 a year, or double that sum, to your income in this way, with almost no trouble; and, as times go, that is no trifle."

In this letter (which is published in Sir Walter Scott's Life) he speaks also of his intention of publishing a small edition of the Morte d'Arthur, which, as the reader has seen, was ground already preoccupied by my father, who, in his reply, explains this, as well as answers at length his friend's proposal.

To Walter Scott, Esq.

"Keswick, Dec. 8, 1807.

"My dear Scott,

"I am very much obliged to you for the offer which you make concerning the Edinburgh Review, and fully sensible of your friendliness, and the advantages which it holds out. I bear as little ill-will to Jeffrey as he does to me, and attribute whatever civil things he has said of me to especial civility, whatever pert ones (a truer epithet than severe would be) to the habit which he has acquired of taking it for granted that the critic is, by virtue of his office, superior to every writer whom he chooses to summon before him. The reviewals of Thalaba and Madoc do in no degree influence me. Setting all personal feelings aside, the objections which weigh with me against bearing any part in this journal are these: I have scarcely one opinion in common with it upon any subject. Jeffrey is for peace, and is endeavoring to frighten the people into it: I am for war as long as Bonaparte lives. He is for Catholic emancipation: I believe that its immediate consequence would be to introduce an Irish priest into every ship in the navy. My feelings are still less in unison with him than my opinions. On subjects of moral or political importance, no man is more apt to speak in the very gall of bitterness than I am, and this habit is likely to go with me to the grave; but that sort of bitterness in which he indulges, which tends directly to wound a man in his feelings, and injure him in his fame and fortune (Montgomery is a case in point), appears to me utterly inexcusable. Now, though there would be no necessity that I should follow this example, yet every separate article in the Review derives authority from the merit of all the others; and, in this way, whatever of any merit I might insert there would aid and abet opinions hostile to my own, and thus identify me with a system which I thoroughly disapprove. This is not said hastily. The emolument to be derived from writing at ten guineas a sheet, Scotch measure, instead of seven pounds, Annual, would be considerable; the pecuniary advantage resulting from the different manner in which my future works would be handled, probably still more so. But my moral feelings must not be compromised. To Jeffrey as an individual I shall ever be ready to show every kind of individual courtesy; but of Judge Jeffrey of the Edinburgh Review I must ever think and speak as of a bad politician, a worse moralist, and a critic, in matters of taste, equally incompetent and unjust.

"Your letter was delayed a week upon the road by the snow. I wish it had been written sooner, and had traveled faster, or that I had communicated to you my own long-projected edition of Morte d'Arthur. I am sorry to have forestalled you, and you are the only person whom I should be sorry to forestall in this case, because you are the only person who could do it certainly as well, and perhaps better, with less labor than myself. My plan is to give the whole bibliology of the Round Table in the preliminaries, and indicate the source of every chapter in the notes.

"The reviewal of Wordsworth I am not likely to see, the Edinburgh very rarely lying in my way. My own notions respecting the book agree in the main with yours, though I may probably go a step further than you in admiration. There are certainly some pieces there which are good for nothing (none, however, which a bad poet could have written), and very many which it was highly injudicious to publish. That song to Lord Clifford, which you particularize, is truly a noble poem. The Ode upon Pre-existence is a dark subject darkly handled. Coleridge is the only man who could make such a subject luminous. The Leech-gatherer is one of my favorites; there he has caught Spenser's manner, and, in many of the better poemets, has equally caught the best manner of old Wither, who, with all his long fits of dullness and prosing, had the heart and soul of a poet in him. The sonnets are in a grand style. I only wish Dundee had not been mentioned. James Grahame and I always call that man Claverhouse, the name by which the devils know him below.

"Marmion is expected as impatiently by me as he is by ten thousand others. Believe me, Scott, no man of real genius was ever yet a puritanical stickler for correctness, or fastidious about any faults except this own. The best artists, both in poetry and painting, have produced the most. Give me more lays, and correct them at leisure for after editions—not laboriously, but when the amendment comes naturally and unsought for. It never does to sit down doggedly to correct.

"The Cid is about half through the press, and will not disappoint you. It is much in the language of Amadis, both books having been written before men began to think of a fine style. This is one cause why Amadis is so far superior to Palmerin. There are passages of a poet's feeling in the Cid, and some of the finest circumstances of chivalry. I expect much credit from this work.

"To recur to the Edinburgh Review, let me once more assure you that, if I do not grievously deceive myself, the criticisms upon my own poems have not influenced me; for, however unjust they were, they were less so, and far less uncourteous, than what I meet with in other journals; and, though these things injure me materially in a pecuniary point of view, they make no more impression upon me than the bite of a sucking flea would do upon Garagantua. The business of reviewing, much as I have done in it myself, I disapprove of, but, most of all, when it is carried on upon such a system as Jeffrey's. The judge is criminal who acquits the guilty, but he is far more so who condemns the innocent. In the Annual I have only one coadjutor, all the other writers being below contempt. In the Edinburgh I should have had many with whom I should have felt it creditable to myself to have been associated, if the irreconcilable difference which there is between Jeffrey and myself upon every great principle of taste, morality, and policy did not occasion an irremovable difficulty. Meantime, I am as sincerely obliged to you as if this difference did not exist, and I could have availed myself of all its advantages, to the importance of which I am fully sensible.

"I am very curious for your Life of Dryden, that I may see how far your estimate of his merits agrees with my own. In the way of editing, we want the yet unpublished metrical romances from the Auchinleck MS., of which you have just given such an account as to whet the public curiosity, and a collection of the Scotch poets. K. James, who is the best, has not been well edited; Blind Harry but badly; Dunbar, and many others, are not to be procured. Your name would make such a speculation answer, however extensive the collection might be. I beg my respects to Mrs. Scott, and am,

"Yours very truly,

Robert Southey."

CHAPTER XIV.

BRAZILIAN AFFAIRS—DISLIKE OF LEAVING HOME—CONDEMNS THE IDEA OF MAKING PEACE WITH BONAPARTE—THE INQUISITION—THE SALE OF

HIS WORKS—GRATEFUL FEELINGS TOWARD MR. COTTLE—THOUGHTS ON THE REMOVAL OF HIS BOOKS TO KESWICK—MEETING WITH THE AUTHOR OF GEBIR—REMARKS ON MARMION—POLITICAL OPINIONS—KEHAMA—HIS POSITION AS AN AUTHOR—ON METERS—POPULATION OF SPAIN—CONDUCT OF THE FRENCH AT LISBON—REMARKS ON DISEASES—PHYSICAL PECULIARITIES—SPANISH AFFAIRS—PRESENT OF BOOKS FROM MR. NEVILLE WHITE—ACCOUNT OF FLOATING ISLAND IN DERWENTWATER—HE PREDICTS THE DEFEAT OF THE FRENCH IN THE PENINSULA—PORTUGUESE LITERATURE—INFANCY OF HIS LITTLE BOY—POETICAL DREAMS—CHRONICLE OF THE CID—DOUBTS ABOUT GOING TO SPAIN—ANECDOTE OF AN IRISH DUEL—LITERARY EMPLOYMENTS—ADVICE TO A YOUNG AUTHOR—THE CONVENTION OF CINTRA—SPANISH BALLADS—POLITICS OF THE EDINBURGH REVIEW—THE QUARTERLY REVIEW SET ON FOOT—THE CHRONICLE OF THE CID—KEHAMA—ARTICLES IN THE QUARTERLY REVIEW—SPANISH AFFAIRS.—1808.

To Grosvenor C. Bedford, Esq.

"Jan. 11, 1808.

"MY DEAR GROSVENOR,

" * * * * * * * * I have seen both the Scotch and the more rascally British Reviews of our Specimens—both a good deal worse than the book itself, which is a great consolation; for they have really not discovered its defects, and have imputed faults to it which it does not possess. If the first edition can be got off, I will make it a curious and good book.

"How soon I may see you, Heaven knows: the sooner the better. My uncle is in town, and applications are made to him from all quarters for that information which Lord G. rejected last year, as relating to the *wrong side* of South America—a strong fact, between you and I, against his statesmanship. I am in hopes he will draw up an account of the present state of Brazil (which no other person living can do so well), while I proceed with the history. This removal of the Braganza family is a great event, though it has been done not merely without that dignity which might have been given to it, but even meanly and pitifully. * * * Still, the event itself is a great one; and if I could transfuse into you all the recollections, &c., which it brings with it to me, you would feel an interest in it which it is not very easy to describe.

"I am hard at work, and shall be able to send my first volume to press as soon as I return from London. Meanwhile, the thought of the journey plagues me—the older I grow the more do I dislike going from home. Oh dear! oh dear! there is such a comfort in one's old coat and old shoes, one's own chair and own fireside, one's own writing-desk and own library, with a little girl climbing up to my neck, and saying, 'Don't go to London, papa; you must stay with Edith;' and a little boy, whom I have taught to speak the language of cats dogs, cuckoos, and jackasses, &c., before he can articulate a word of his own—there is such a comfort in all these things, that *transportation* to London for four or five weeks seems a heavier punishment than any sins of mine deserve. Nevertheless, I shall be heartily glad to see Grosvenor Bedford, provided Grosvenor Bedford does not look as if his liver were out of order. * * * *

"God bless you! R. S."

To Walter Scott, Esq.

"Keswick, Feb. 11, 1808.

"MY DEAR SCOTT,

"I should long ago have thanked you for your offer of Sir Lancelot, but as I had written to Heber requesting from him all his Round-table books, I waited, or rather have been waiting, to see whether or not it would be among them. It is above two months since news came that Heber would look them out for me; but as they are not yet arrived, and my appearance in London has been expected for the last two or three weeks, it is probable that he is waiting to let me look them out for myself. I go for London next week, my family having just been increased by the birth of another girl—an event for which I have been waiting.

"Wordsworth has completed a most masterly poem upon the fate of the Nortons; two or three lines in the old Ballad of the Rising in the North gave him the hint. The story affected me more deeply than I wish to be affected; young readers, however, will not object to the depth of the distress—and nothing was ever more ably treated. He is looking, too, for a narrative subject, to be pitched in a lower key. I have recommended to him that part of Amadis wherein he appears as Beltenebros—which is what Bernardo Tasso had originally chosen, and which is in itself as complete as could be desired. This reminds me that to-day I met with the name of Amadis as a Christian name in Portugal, in the age between Lobeira and Montaloo. Having found Oriana, Briolania, Grimanesa, and Lisuarte there before, they may be looked upon as five good witnesses that the story is originally Portuguese.

"My Chronicle of the Cid is printed, and waits for the introduction and supererogatory notes, both which will be of considerable length, and must be completed at Holland House, where I shall find exactly those books which were out of reach of my means. The History of Brazil will be in the press as soon as this is out of it. What an epoch in history will this emigration of the Braganzas prove, if we are not frightened by cowardly politicians into making peace, and cajoling them back again to Portugal! Such men as these have long since extinguished all political morality and political honesty among us, and now they would extinguish national honor, which is all we have left to suppy their place! My politics would be, to proclaim to France and to the world that England will never make peace with Napoleon Bonaparte, because he has proved himself to be one whom no treaties and no ties can bind, and still more because he is notoriously a murderer, with whom it is infamous to treat. Send this language into France, and let nothing else go into it that our ships can keep out, and the French themselves would, in no very long time, rid the world of a tyrant. The light of Prince Arthur's shield would bring Orgoglio to the ground. God bless you!

"Yours very truly, R. SOUTHEY."

To S. T. Coleridge, Esq.

"Feb. 12, 1808.

"MY DEAR COLERIDGE,

"De Origine et Progressu Officii S. Inquisitionis, ejusque dignitate et utilitate, Antone Ludovico a Panamo, Boroxense, Archidiaconio et Canonico Legionense. . . . 1598, folio. The book is in the Red Cross Street Library. I read it six years ago, and sent up an account of it within the last six weeks for Dr. Aikin's Biography, where it will be in villainously bad company. You will find there that God was the first Inquisitor, and that the first Auto da Fé was held upon Adam and Eve. You will read enough to show you that Catholic writers defend the punishment of heretics, and quite sufficient to make your blood run cold. I have the History of the Portuguese Inquisition to write, and look on to the task with absolute horror. I am decidedly hostile to what is called Catholic Emancipation, as I am to what is called peace.

"I have had a correspondence with Clarkson concerning the best mode of publishing my Brazilian history; and what he points out as the best plan is little better than the half-and-half way, and involves a great deal of trouble, and, what is worse, a great deal of solicitation. I am a bad trading author, and doomed always to be so, but it is not the bookseller's fault; the public do not buy poetry unless it be made fashionable; mine gets reviewed by enemies who are always more active than friends; one reviewer envies me, another hates me, and a third tries his hand upon me as fair game. Thousands meantime read the books, but they borrow them; even those persons who are what they call my friends, and who know that I live by these books, never buy them themselves, and then wonder that they do not sell. Espriella has sold rapidly, for which I have to thank Stuart; the edition is probably by this time exhausted, and, I verily believe, half the sale must be attributed to the puffs in the Courier. The sale of a second edition would right me in Longman's books. Puff me, Coleridge! if you love me, puff me! Puff a couple of hundreds into my pocket!

"As for the booksellers, I am disposed to distinguish between Long*man* and Trades*man* nature (setting hu*man* nature out of the question): now Trades*man* nature is very bad, but Long*man* nature is a great deal better, and I am inclined to believe that it will get the better of the evil principle, and that liberal dealing may even prove catching. It is some proof of this that his opinion of me and conduct toward me alter not, notwithstanding the spiders spin their webs so securely over whole piles of Madoc and Thalaba. * * * *

"I am strongly moved by the spirit to make an attack upon Jeffrey along his whole line, beginning with his politics. Stuart would not be displeased to have half a dozen letters. Nothing but the weary work it would be to go through his reviews for the sake of collecting the blunders in them, prevents me. He, and other men who are equally besotted and blinded by party, will inevitably frighten the nation into peace, the only thing which can be more mischievous and more dishonorable than our Danish expedition. I wish to God you would lift up your voice against it. Alas! Coleridge, is it to be wondered at that we pass for a degenerated race, when those who have the spirit of our old worthies in them let that spirit fret itself away in silence?

"Lamb's book I have heard of, and know not what it is. If co-operative labor were as practicable as it is desirable, what a history of English literature might he, and you, and I set forth! * * * * *

"God bless you! R. S."

To Joseph Cottle, Esq.

"Greta Hall, April 20, 1808.

"MY DEAR COTTLE,

"On opening a box to-day, the contents of which I had not seen since the winter of 1799, your picture made its appearance. Of all Robert Hancock's performances it is infinitely the best. I can not conceive a happier likeness. I have been thinking of you and of old times ever since it came to light. I have been reading your Fall of Cambria, and in the little interval that remains before supper must talk to you in reply to your letter.

"What you say of my copyrights affected me very much. Dear Cottle, set your heart at rest on that subject. It ought to be at rest. These were yours, fairly bought, and fairly sold. You bought them on the chance of their success, which no London bookseller would have done; and had they not been bought, they could not have been published at all. Nay, if you had not purchased Joan of Arc, the poem never would have existed, nor should I, in all probability, ever have obtained that reputation which is the capital on which I subsist, nor that power which enables me to support it.

"But this is not all. Do you suppose, Cottle, that I have forgotten those true and most essential acts of friendship which you showed me when I stood most in need of them? Your house was my house when I had no other. The very money with which I bought my wedding-ring and paid my marriage fees was supplied by you. It was with your sisters I left Edith during my six months' absence, and for the six months' after my return it was from you that I received, week by week, the little on which we lived, till I was enabled to live by other means. It is not the settling of a cash account that can cancel obligations like these. You are in the habit of preserving your letters, and if you were not, I would entreat you to preserve *this*, that it might be seen hereafter. Sure I am, there never was a more generous or a kinder heart than yours; and you will believe me when I add that there does not live that man upon earth whom I remember with more gratitude and more affection. My head throbs and my eyes burn with these recollections. Good-night! my dear old friend and benefactor. R. S."

To Grosvenor C. Bedford, Esq.

"Keswick, April 26, 1808.

"Dear Grosvenor,

"From one scene of confusion to another. You saw me in London everlastingly at work in packing my books, and here they are now lying in all parts about me, up to my knees in one place, up to my eyes in another, and above head and ears in a third. I can scarcely find stepping-places through the labyrinth, from one end of the room to the other. Like Pharaoh's frogs, they have found their way every where, even into the bed-chambers. * * * * And now, Grosvenor, having been married above twelve years, I have for the first time collected all my books together. What a satisfaction this is you can not imagine, for you can not conceive the hundredth part of the inconvenience and vexation I have endured for want of them. But the joy which they give me brings with it a mingled feeling—the recollection that there are as many materials heaped up as I shall ever find life to make use of; and the humiliating reflection how little knowledge can be acquired in the most laborious life of man, that knowledge becoming every age less and less, in proportion to the accumulation of events. For some things I have been born too late. Under the last reign, for instance, as in the first half of this, my pension would have been an income adequate to my wants, and my profits as a writer would have been at least quadrupled. On the other hand, bad as these times are, they are better than those which are coming.

"At Bristol I met with the man of all others whom I was most desirous of meeting—the only man living of whose praise I was ambitious, or whose censure would have humbled me. You will be curious to know who this could be. Savage Landor, the author of Gebir, a poem which, unless you have heard me speak of it, you have probably never heard of at all. I never saw any one more unlike myself in every prominent part of human character, nor any one who so cordially and instinctively agreed with me on so many of the most important subjects. I have often said, before we met, that I would walk forty miles to see him, and, having seen him, I would gladly walk fourscore to see him again. He talked of Thalaba, and I told him of the series of mythological poems which I had planned—mentioned some of the leading incidents on which they were to have been formed, and also told him for what reason they were laid aside—in plain English, that I could not afford to write them. Landor's reply was, 'Go on with them, and I will pay for printing them, as many as you will write, and as many copies as you please' I had reconciled myself to my abdication (if the phrase may be allowable), and am not sure that this princely offer has not done me mischief; for it has awakened in me old dreams and hopes which had been laid aside, and a stinging desire to go on, for the sake of showing him poem after poem, and saying, 'I need not accept your offer, but I have done this because you made it.' It is something to be praised by one's peers; ordinary praise I regard as little as ordinary abuse. God bless you! R. S."

To Walter Scott, Esq.

"Keswick, April 22, 1808.

"My dear Scott,

"Your letter followed me to London. The hope which it held out that we might meet here, and the endless round of occupations in which I was involved during the whole nine weeks of my absence, prevented me from thanking you for Marmion so soon as I ought, and should otherwise have done.

"Half the poem I had read at Heber's before my own copy arrived. I went punctually to breakfast with him, and he was long enough dressing to let me devour so much of it. The story is made of better materials than the Lay, yet they are not so well fitted together. As a whole, it has not pleased me so much; in parts it has pleased me more. There is nothing so finely conceived in your former poem as the death of Marmion; there is nothing finer in its conception any where.

"The introductory epistles I did not wish away, because as poems they gave me great pleasure, but I wished them at the end of the volume or at the beginning—any where except where they were. My taste is perhaps peculiar in disliking all interruptions in narrative poetry. When the poet lets his story sleep, and talks in his own person, it is to me the same sort of unpleasant effect that is produced at the end of an act; you are alive to know what follows, and lo—down comes the curtain, and the fiddlers begin with their abominations. The general opinion, however, is with me in this particular instance.

"I am highly gratified by the manner in which you speak of Kirke White's Remains. That book has been received to my heart's desire. The edition (750) sold in less than three months, and there is every probability that it will obtain a steady sale, so as to produce something considerable to his mother and sisters.

"I saw Frere in London, and he has promised to let me print his translations from the Poema del Cid. They are admirably done—indeed, I never saw any thing so difficult to do, and done so excellently, except your supplement to Sir Tristrem. I do not believe that many men have a greater command of language and versification than myself, and yet this task of giving a specimen of that wonderful poem I shrunk from, fearing the difficulty. At present I am putting together the materials of my introduction, which, with the supplementary notes, will take about three months in printing; at least, it will be as long before the book can be published. The price of paper stops all my other press-work for the present.

"So much of my life passes in this blessed retirement, that when I go to London the effect is a little like what Nourjahad used to find after one of his long naps. I find a woeful difference of political opinion between myself and most of those persons who have hitherto held the same feelings with me; and yet it should seem that they have been sleeping over the great events of these latter years, not I. There is a base and cowardly feeling abroad, which would humble this country at the feet of France. This feeling I have every where been combating with vehemence; but, at the same time, I have execrated with equal vehemence the business of Copenhagen: Ishmael-like, my hand has been against every body, and every body's hand against me. Wordsworth is the only man who agrees with me on both points. I require, however, no other sanction to convince me that I am right. Coleridge justifies the attack on Denmark, but he justifies it upon individual testimony of hostile intentions on the part of that court, and that testimony by no means amounts to proof in my judgment. But what is done is done; and the endless debates upon the subject, which have no other meaning and can have no other end than that of harassing the ministry, disgust me, as they do every one who has the honor of England at heart. Such a system makes the publicity of debate a nuisance, and will terminate in putting a stop to it.

"Is there any hope of seeing you this year at the Lakes? I should much like to show you Kehama. During my circuit I fell in with Savage Landor, the author of Gebir, to whom I spoke of my projected series of mythological poems, and said also for what reason the project had been laid aside. He besought me to go on with them, and said he would print them at his expense. Without the least thought of accepting this princely offer, it has stung me to the very core; and as the bite of the tarantula has no cure but dancing, so will there be none but singing for this. Great poets have no envy; little ones are full of it. I doubt whether any man ever criticised a good poem maliciously, unless he had written a bad one himself.

"Yours truly,

R. SOUTHEY."

To Walter Savage Landor, Esq.

"May 2, 1808.

"I have sent you all that is written of the Curse of Kehama: you offered to print it for me; if ever I finish the poem it will be because of that offer, though without the slightest intention of accepting it. Enough is written to open the story of the poem, and serve as a specimen of its manner, though much of what is to follow would be in a wilder strain. Tell me if your ear is offended with the rhymes when they occur, or if it misses them when they fail. I wish it had never been begun, because I like it too well to throw it behind the fire, and not well enough to complete it without the 'go on' of some one whose approbation is worth having.

"My history as an author is not very honorable to the age in which we live. By giving up my whole time to worthless work in reviews, magazines, and newspapers, I could thrive, as by giving up half my time to them I contrive to live. In the time thus employed every year I could certainly produce such a poem as Thalaba, and if I did I should starve. You have awakened in me projects that had been laid asleep, and recalled hopes which I had dismissed contentedly, and, as I thought, forever. If you think Kehama deserves to be finished, I will borrow hours from sleep, and finish it by rising two hours before my customary time; and when it is finished I will try whether subscribers can be procured for five hundred copies, by which means I should receive the whole profit to myself. The bookseller's share is too much like the lion in the fable: 30 or 33 per cent. they first deduct as booksellers, and then half the residue as publishers. I have no reason to complain of mine: they treat me with great respect and great liberality, but I wish to be independent of them; and this, if it could be effected, would make me so.

"The will and the power to produce any thing great are not often found together. I wish you would write in English, because it is a better language than Latin, and because the disuse of English as a living and literary language would be the greatest evil that could befall mankind. It would cost you little labor to write perspicuously, and thus get rid of your only fault. *

* * * * *

"Literary fame is the only fame of which a wise man ought to be ambitious, because it is the only lasting and living fame. Bonaparte will be forgotten before his time in purgatory is half over, or but just remembered like Nimrod, or other cut-throats of antiquity, who serve us for the common-places of declamation. If you made yourself King of Crete, you would differ from a hundred other adventurers only in chronology, and in the course of a millennium or two, nothing more would be known of your conquest than what would be found in the stereotype Gebir prefixed as an account of the author. Pour out your mind in a great poem, and you will exercise authority over the feelings and opinions of mankind as long as the language lasts in which you write.

* * * * * * *

"Farewell! I wish you had purchased Loweswater instead of Llantony. I wish you were married, because the proverb about a rolling stone applies to a single heart, and I wish you were as much a Quaker as I am. Christian stoicism is wholesome for all minds; were I your confessor, I should enjoin you to throw aside

Rousseau, and make Epictetus your manual. Probatum est.

"Yours truly, ROBERT SOUTHEY."

To Walter Savage Landor, Esq.

"May 20, 1808.

"You have bound me to the completion of Kehama, and, if I have health and eyesight, completed it will be within twelve months. Want of practice has not weakened me: I have ascertained this, and am proceeding.

"I will use such materials as have stood the test; those materials are the same in all languages, and we know what they are. With respect to meter it is otherwise: there we must look to English only, and in English we have no other great poem than the Paradise Lost. Blank verse has long appeared to me the noblest measure of which our language is capable, but it would not suit Kehama. There must be quicker, wilder movements; there must be a gorgeousness of ornament also—Eastern gem-work, and sometimes rhyme must be rattled upon rhyme, till the reader is half dizzy with the thundering echo. My motto must be,

Ποικίλον εἶδος ἔχων, ὅτι ποικίλον ὕμνον ἀφάσσω.

This is not from any ambition of novelty, but from the nature and necessity of the subject. I am well aware that novelty in such things is an obstacle to success; Thalaba has proved it to be so. The mass of mankind hate innovation: they hate to unlearn what they have learned wrong, and they hate to confess their ignorance by submitting to learn any thing right. I would tread in the beaten road rather than get among thorns by turning out of it; but the beaten road will not take me where I want to go. What seems best to be done is this, to write mostly in rhyme, to slip into it rather than out of it, and then generally into some meter so strongly marked as to leave the ear fully satisfied.

"One inference, I think, must be drawn from the obscurity of Pindar's meter—that, be it what it may, the pleasure which it gave did not result from rhythm. Indeed, the whole system of classical meters seems to have been that of creating difficulty for the sake of overcoming it. We mis-read Sapphics without making them worse; we mis-read Pentameters and make them better; and the Hexameter remains the most perceptible of all measures, though in our pronunciation we generally distort four feet out of the six.

"A great deal more may be done with rhyme than has yet been done with it. There is a crypto-rhyme, which may often be introduced with excellent effect: the eye has nothing to do with it, but the ear feels it, without, perhaps, perceiving any thing more than the general harmony, and not knowing how that harmony is produced. Sometimes the sparing intermixture of rhymes in a paragraph may be so managed as to satisfy the ear, and give greater effect to their after profusion. These are not things which one thinks of in composition, but they are thought of in correcting; they are the touches in finishing off, when a little alteration produces a great difference.

"Your dislike to the ballad meter is, perhaps, because you are sick of a tune which has been sung so often and so badly. It is not incapable of dignity, but there is a sort of language that usually goes with it, and has the effect of making it so. Kehama is pitched in too high a key for it; I shall weed out all uncouth lines, and leave the public nothing to abuse except the strangeness of the fable, which you may be sure will be plentifully abused. The mythology explains itself as it is introduced; yet, because the names are not familiar, people will fancy there is a difficulty in understanding it. Sir William Jones has done nothing in introducing it so coldly and formally as he has done. They who read his poems do not remember them, and none but those who have read them can be expected to have even heard of my Divinities. But for popularity I care only as regards profit, and for profit only as regards subsistence. The praise of ten would have contented you; often have I said that you did not underrate the number of men whose praise was truly desirable. Ten thousand persons will read my book; if five hundred will promise to buy it, I shall be secure of all I want. You shall have it in large portions as fast it is written.

"Yours, ROBERT SOUTHEY."

To S. T. Coleridge, Esq.

"June 13, 1808.

"DEAR COLERIDGE,

"I have the last census of Spain here, and perhaps you may like to give the Courier a statement of the population of the Northern Provinces, as taken in 1797, and published in 1801.

		Population.	Males from the Age of 16 to 50.
These Provinces are what we call Biscay.	Asturias ..	364,238	80,554
	Galicia ...	1,142,630	225,454
	Alava	67,523	15,367
	Guipuzcoa	104,491	23,343
	Vizcaya ..	111,436	25,801
			400,519

"These are the provinces which have asked assistance; but there is probably a French force at Ferrol, which may, for a while, keep part of Galicia in awe. The people are a hardy race, and most of them good shots, because there are no game laws, plenty of game, and wolves in the country. Probably every man has his gun. One hardly dares indulge a hope; but if Europe is to be redeemed in our days, you know it has always been my opinion that the work of deliverance would begin in Spain. And now that its unhappy government has committed suicide, the Spaniards have got rid of their worst enemy.

"This account of Lisbon, which has just reached me, may also fitly appear in the Courier, for the edification of Roscoe and such politicians: 'Every private family has a certain number of French officers and soldiers quartered upon them, who behave with their accustomed insolence and brutality. The ladies of one family very naturally, upon the intrusion of these unwelcome guests, retired to their own apartments, where they proposed remaining; but these civilized Frenchmen required their presence, and would admit of no excuse. *Il faut que les dames viennent* was the only reply which they made; and, of course, the women were compelled to be subject to their ribaldry and impertinence. Whole families of the middling class are seen begging at the corners of the streets; and women, who had till now borne an unblemished reputation, prostitute themselves publicly to gain wherewithal to buy bread. The soldiers and the flower of the peasantry are sent to recruit the French armies in distant parts.' Nothing can exceed the misery and the despondency of the people.

"Were I minister, I would send half the regular army without delay to Spain; the distance is nothing—a week would be but an average passage; and these seas are not like the German Ocean, where so many brave men have been sacrificed in useless expeditions during stormy seasons.

"Of public affairs enough! We have had a bilious fever in the house, which was epidemic among the children of the place. Herbert has suffered severely from it; I thought we should lose him. The disease has reduced him very much, and left him in a state of great debility. Keswick is scarcely ever without some kind of infectious fever, generally among the children. When these things get into a dirty house, they hardly ever get out of it; and I attribute this more to the want of cleanliness than to the climate. But ague is beginning to reappear, which had scarcely been heard of during the last generation: this is the case over the whole kingdom, I believe. What put a stop to it then, or what brought it back now, is beyond the reach of our present knowledge. You love the science of physic; and Nature, who seems to have meant you for half a dozen different things when she made you, meant you for a physician among the rest. I will tell you, therefore, two odd peculiarities of my constitution; the slightest dose of laudanum acts upon me as an aperient; if I am at any time exposed to the sun bareheaded for two minutes, I infallibly take cold. This probably shows how soon I should be subject to a stroke of the sun, and indicates the same over-susceptibility which the nitrous oxyd did, a smaller dose affecting me than any other person who ever breathed it.

"I have read that play of Calderon's since my return: its story is precisely as you stated it, and in the story the wonder lies. Are we not apt to do with these things as naturalists do with insects? put them in a microscope, and exclaim how beautiful! how wonderful! how grand! when all the beauty and all the grandeur are owing to the magnifying medium? A shaping mind receives the story of the play and makes it *terrific;* in Calderon it is *extravagant*. The machinery is certainly most extraordinary; and most extraordinary must the state of public opinion be, where such machinery could be received with the complacency of perfect faith—as undoubtedly this was, and would be still in Spain.

"At last I have got all my books about me, and right rich I am in them—above 4000 volumes. With your Germans, &c., there is probably no other house in the country which contains such a collection of foreign literature. My Cid will be published in about six weeks. Brazil is not yet gone to press—the price of paper has deterred me; and yet there is little likelihood of any reduction—indeed, no possibility, till the North is again open to us.

"This is the moment for uniting Spain and Portugal; and the greater facility of doing this in a commonwealth than in a monarchy would be reason enough for preferring that form of government, were there no other. Portugal loses something in importance and in feeling by being incorporated in the Spanish monarchy; it would preserve its old dignity by uniting in a federal republic—a form which the circumstances of Spain more especially require, and its provincial difference of laws and dialects. Each province should have its own cortes, and the general congress meet at Madrid, otherwise that city would soon waste away. No nation has ever had a fairer opportunity for reforming its government and modeling it anew. But I dare say this wretched cabinet will be meddling too much in this, and too little in the desperate struggle which must be made; that we shall send tardy and inefficient aid—enough to draw on a heavier French force, and not enough to resist the additional force which it will occasion.

"The crown, like the Ahrimanes of the earth, will sacrifice any thing rather than see the downfall of royalty.

"That best of all good women, Mrs. Wilson, has borne the winter better than any former one since we have known her.

"I am thinking about a poem upon Pelajo, the restorer of Spain. Do you wish to serve me? Puff Espriella, in the Courier, as the best guide to the lakes. All well. God bless you!

"R. S."

To Mr. Neville White.

"Keswick, June 20, 1808."

"MY DEAR NEVILLE,

"The box arrived about an hour ago. Sir William Jones's works are placed opposite my usual seat, and on the most conspicuous shelf in the room. * * * I have retired to my library to thank you for the most splendid set of books it contains. I thank you for them, Neville, truly and heartily; but do not let it hurt you if I say that so costly a present gives me some pain as well as pleasure. Were you a rich man, you could not give me more books than I would joyfully accept, for I delight in accumulating such treasures as much as a miser does in keeping together gold; but, as things are at present, no proof was needed of your generous spirit, and, from the little you have to spare, I can not but feel you are giving me too much. You will not be offended at my expressing this feeling, nor will you impute it to any unjust pride, which, blessed be God, I am too poor a man, and too wise a one, to be guilty of in any, even the smallest degree. Be assured that I shall ever value the books far more than if they had come from a wealthier donor, and that I write the donor's name in them with true respect and esteem. You will be pleased to hear they are books of immediate use to me. Seven years ago I began a long poem, which Sir William Jones, had he been living, would have liked to see, because it has the system of Hindoo mythology for its basis. I believe you heard me mention it at Mr. Hill's. I have been stimulated by the approbation of one of the few men living whose approbation could stimulate me, to go on with this poem, and am winning time for it by rising earlier than was my custom, because I will not allow any other part of the day to an employment less important than writing history, and far less profitable than that of writing any thing else, how humble or how worthless soever. In the hours thus fairly won for the purpose, I get on steadily and well. Now, though I had long ago gone through those works of Sir William, and made from them such extracts as were necessary for my purpose, it was still very desirable that I should have them at hand. Lord Teignmouth's Life also is new to me.

"I have not seen the Scotch review of Marmion, but I have heard that on its appearance Walter Scott showed Jeffrey the letter in which I had refused to bear a part in his review. * * * I do not know whether Scott may have shown him another letter, in which I spoke of the 'Remains.' Scott may perhaps review them himself, unless this affair of Marmion, or, what is more likely, their utter and irreconcilable difference of political opinion, should make him withdraw from the journal altogether.

"Henceforward we shall have little business to write about. You may supply the place by telling me of what you read, and I may sometimes be able to direct you to books which will supply further, or, perhaps, better information upon the subjects which interest you, and sometimes save you time in acquiring knowledge by telling you the shortest and nearest road to it. God bless you! R. SOUTHEY."

To John Rickman, Esq.

"July, 1808.

"MY DEAR RICKMAN,

"I very much wish you were here. You may have heard that there is an island which sometimes comes up in this lake, and, after a while, goes down again. Five years have I been expecting this appearance, and now, sure enough, it is above water. It may stay there for some weeks—sometimes six or eight—it may already have sunk. But Davy *ought* to put himself in the first mail-coach; and perhaps curiosity may induce you to expedite your journey for the sake of seeing the oddest thing you are ever likely to see.

"How it is effected is for Davy to discover; but as much of the bottom of the lake as is equal to the area of your house has been forced up to the surface in several pieces, and in other parts you plainly see that there are rents in the bottom where parts have sunk in, for it is not a deep part of the lake. The gas which follows the immersion of a pole stinks, and over one part of the water a thin steam was plainly discernible when I was there. As no person was there when it rose, we can not tell whether it was accompanied by any great agitation of the water, or any noise; but the noise, if any, can not have been very great, or it would have been heard here. It is possible that the cause may have some connection with the sulphureous springs in the neighborhood, almost certain that it is the same which occasions our bottom winds.*

"A Portuguese sermon has just helped me to a discovery which will amuse you. Who was the first man that doubled the Cape of Good Hope? The Prophet Jonah. Examine his track in the whale, and this proves to be the case; and you will observe that this magnifies the miracle prodigiously, for what a passage he had from the Mediterranean to the Persian Gulf!

"My friends the Spaniards and Portuguese are justifying the opinion which I have long given of them to the astonishment of those who heard me. Bonaparte will, I suppose, pour in upon them with his whole force; so let him. You know how little respect I have for what is called the spirit of history, or the philosophy of history, by those people who want to have every thing given them in extracts and essences; but the truth of the present history is, that a great military despotism, in its youth and full vigor—like that of France—will and must beat down corrupt establishments and worn-out governments, but that it can not beat down a true love of liberty and a true spirit of patriotism, unless there be an overwhelming superiority of physical force, which is not the case here. * * In Spain the fire has burst out which will consume. Well done! my friend William Bryan the Prophet; you certainly did prophesy to me in St. Stephen's court concerning Spain as truly as Francis Moore did, in his almanac last year, concerning the Grand Turk. * * *

"God bless you! R. S."

To Richard Duppa, Esq.

"Keswick, July 11, 1808.

"DEAR DUPPA,

"The thought of writing to you—or, rather, the thought that I had not written—has very often risen in my conscience heavily. Joanna Southcote has been the cause. Her books, with Sharp's dirty treasure, are now on their way to London. It is so much better to say I *have done* a thing than I *will do* it, that I really have defer-

* The floating island still appears at intervals. There is said to be a bottom wind, when the lake is violently agitated without any disturbance in the atmosphere—a phenomenon which does not seem yet to have been satisfactorily accounted for

red writing for the sake of saying these books were actually gone.

"For the last three weeks I have suffered from a blinding and excoriating catarrh—always with me a very obstinate disease, and more violent than I have ever seen it in any person except one of my own family. Diseases are the worst things a man can inherit, and I am never likely to inherit any thing else. That father's brother of mine in Somersetshire—whom I would so gladly sell at half price—received me as cordially as was in his nature last April, and gave me £25—an act of great generosity in a man of £1200 a year, and remarkable as being all I ever have had, or ever shall have, from him, for he has now turned his sister out of doors, and desired never to see any of the family again. Duppa, my breeches' pockets will never be so full as to make me stick in Heaven's gate. Three lines of that fellow's pen will cut me off from more than all the pens I shall ever wear to the stump will gain for me, and yet I hope many is the goose egg yet unlaid which is to produce quills for my service.

"The Lakers are coming in shoals, and some of them find their way here. Among others, I have had the satisfaction of seeing Joanna Baillie: she drank tea with us, and very much pleased we were with her—as good-natured, unaffected, and sensible a woman as I have ever seen.

"A month ago you might, perhaps, have been gratified by knowing what were my thoughts of the state of Spain; now, I suppose, every body thinks alike. But I have always said that, if the deliverance of Europe were to take place in our days, there was no country in which it was so likely to begin as Spain; and this opinion, whenever I expressed it, was received with wonder, if not with incredulity. But there is a spirit of patriotism, a glowing and proud remembrance of the past, a generous shame for the present, and a living hope for the future, both in the Spaniards and Portuguese, which convinced me that the heart of the country was sound, and that those nations are likely to rise in the scale, perhaps, Duppa, when we are sunk. Not that England will sink yet, but there is more public virtue in Spain than in any other country under Heaven. I have no fears nor doubts concerning that country; the spirit of liberty is not to be extinguished: nothing but that spirit could possibly check the progress of Bonaparte; this will check, and, it is my firm conviction, eventually destroy him. William Bryan prophesied a happy termination in Spain when I saw him in London, and I dare say, if ever we meet again, he will not fail to remind me of it. I expect his corrected copy of Espriella with some curiosity.

"God bless you!

"Yours, ROBERT SOUTHEY."

To John Adamson, Esq.

"Keswick, Aug. 6, 1808.

"SIR,

"I have never seen the name of Nicola Luiz except in Murphy; and the title of the Portuguese Plautus which he gives him, being generally applied to Gil Vicente, thought it not unlikely that he might have written Richard for Robert, as he is apt to do so. Barbosa's great Bibliotheca is not in my possession, and I have referred in vain to Nicolas Antonio, to the Mappa de Portugal, which contains a copious list of poets, and to the Catalogue of Authors which the Academy printed as the sources from which their dictionary was to be compiled. How it should be that this name is not to be found in either, is to me altogether unaccountable.

"It is possible that Antonio Ferreira's play may have been originally published under this fictitious name. I have no other reason for supposing so than that it seems almost certain, if the name of Nicola Luiz were a real one, it would have been included in one or all of the works which I have consulted; and Ferreira did in one instance practice an artifice of this kind, yet I think you must have seen his play. It begins:

'Colhey, colhey alegres,
Donzellas minhas, mil cheirosas flores.'

Should this be the tragedy in question, I will, with great pleasure, transmit you an account of the author, or send you my copy of his works (should that be more agreeable), which, when you have completely done with it, may be returned through my brother Dr. Southey, of Durham.

"The tragedy of Domingos dos Reis Quita, upon the same story, has been Englished by Benjamin Thompson. There are two Spanish ones by Geronimo Bermudez (published originally under the name of Antonio de Silva), in the sixth volume of the Parnaso Español. Henry K. White had merely begun the first scene of his projected play, and that, as was evident from the handwriting, at a very early age.

"The Portuguese have two poems upon the same story, the Penasco de las Lagrimas, written in Spanish by Francisco de França da Costa, and the Saudades de D. Ignes de Castro, by Manoel de Azevedo. This latter I have myself planned a play upon, The Revenge of Pedro: whether it will ever be executed, is very doubtful, but this part of the story is far fitter for dramatic poetry than the foregoing.

"I am, sir, yours with respect,

"ROBERT SOUTHEY."

To John Adamson, Esq.

"Aug. 12, 1808.

"DEAR SIR,

"I thank you for your translation, and will, by the first carrier, send off the plays of Ferreira and Quita, and the Saudades.

"You have mistaken the meaning of *Xarifalte*. Portuguese orthography is very loose in any but modern authors, and it is sometimes necessary to hunt a word through every possible mutation of labial or guttural letters. Under gérafalte it is to be found, which is the ger-falcon of our ancestors.

"The story of Iñez is, in any point of view,

sufficiently atrocious, but the poets have not been true to history. It is expressly asserted by Fernan Lopez that Pedro denied his marriage during his father's life, and never affirmed it till some years afterward; what is still worse, that Affonso repeatedly asked him if she were his wife, and said that if she were he would acknowledge her as such. I am myself decidedly of opinion that she was not. The arguments against the fact of the marriage which Joam das Regas used at the election of King Joam I., are to me as satisfactory as those which he brought against its legality, if the fact had been proved, would have been in these days. I am sorry, also, to disbelieve the coronation of the dead body: there is not a word of it in the Chronicler, though he fully describes its removal from Coimbra, and the Portuguese nobles were not men who would have submitted to such a ceremony.

"If your play be of modern date, Nicola Luiz is probably a modern author, and that removes all difficulty concerning him. There was a tragedy upon the same subject, published by Dr. Simmonds about ten years ago, which obtained considerable praise.

"Your translation, I dare say, does justice to the original; had it been still unprinted, I would have noticed a few instances in which the proper names are mis-accented. What pleases me best in the play is to perceive that the author has avoided the fault of Camoens, and not made his heroine talk about Hyrcanian tigers, and such other common-places which pass current for passion and for poetry.

"I have seen the Fonte das Lagrimas: Link omits to mention that two beautiful cedars brush its surface with their boughs. I have also seen the tombs of Iñez and Pedro: they are covered with bass-relief, which ought to be accurately copied and engraved.

"There is a shocking story of one of the children of Iñez—the Infant D. Joam, who murdered his wife: it is a worse story than even the murder of his mother. If at any time chance should bring you this way, I shall have great pleasure in showing you all those facts of Portuguese history relating to your subject which have occurred to me in the course of long and laborious employment upon the history and literature of Portugal.

"I am, sir, yours respectfully,

"ROBERT SOUTHEY."

To Lieutenant Southey, H.M.S. Dreadnought.

"Aug. 16, 1808.

"MY DEAR TOM,

"—— is gone to Spain! to fight as a private in the Spanish army, and he has found two Englishmen to go with him. A noble fellow! This is something like the days of old, as we poets and romancers represent them—something like the best part of chivalry: old honors, old generosity, old heroism are reviving, and the cancer of that nation is stopped, I believe and fully trust, now and forever. A man like —— can not long remain without command; and, of all things in this world, I should most rejoice to hear that King Joseph had fallen into his hands; he would infallibly hang him on the nearest tree, first, as a Bonaparte by blood; secondly, as a Frenchman by adoption; thirdly, as a king by trade.

"Miss Seward's criticism has appeared in the Gentleman's Magazine. Her verses have not been inserted in the Courier, which is rather odd. She reads Madoc to all her acquaintance, and must be the means of selling several copies.

"Another island came up on Saturday last, which I shall visit the first fine day—probably with Jackson and Jonathan Ottley, who is going to measure it and catch a bottle of the gas, Jonathan being, as you know, our Keswick philosopher. We are now having a spell of wind and rain.

"We have got the prettiest kitten you ever saw—a dark tabby—and we have christened her by the heathenish name of Dido. You would be very much diverted to see her hunt Herbert all round the kitchen, playing with his little bare feet, which she just pricks at every pat, and the faster he moves back the more she paws them, at which he cries 'Naughty Dido!" and points to his feet and says, "Hurt, hurt, naughty Dido.' Presently he feeds her with comfits, which Dido plays with a while, but soon returns to her old game. You have lost the amusing part of Herbert's childhood—just when he is trying to talk, and endeavoring to say every thing.

" * * * * I have been in the water very seldom since you went; but the last time I accomplished the great job of fairly swimming on my back, which is a step equal to that of getting one's first commission.

"I hope that the opening of Pelayo is pretty well arranged, but I will not begin upon it till I come to a stop in Kehama. You will not, perhaps, be surprised to hear that two of my old dreams are likely to be introduced, with powerful effect, in this poem—good proof that it was worth while to keep even the imperfect register that I have. The fear is, that what happened to Nebuchadnezzar is perpetually happening to me. I forget my dreams, and have no Daniel to help out my recollection; and if by chance I do remember them, unless they are instantly written down, the impression passes away almost as lightly as the dream itself. Do you remember the story of Mickle the poet, who always regretted that he could not remember the poetry which he composed in his sleep? it was, he said, so infinitely superior to any thing which he produced in his waking hours. One morning he awoke, and repeated the lamentation over his unhappy fortune, that he should compose such sublime poetry, and yet lose it forever! 'What!' said his wife, who happened to be awake, 'were you writing poetry?' 'Yes,' he replied, 'and such poetry that I would give the world to remember it.' 'Well, then,' said she, 'I did luckily hear the last lines, and I am sure I remember them exactly: they were,

"By Heaven, I'll wreak my woes
Upon the cowslip and the pale primrose."'

This is one of Sharpe's stories: it is true, and an excellently good one it is. I am not such a dreamer as Mickle, for what I can remember is worth remembering, and one of the wildest scenes in Kehama will prove this. God bless you! R. S."

To Grosvenor C. Bedford, Esq.

"August 16, 1808.

"Are you not half ready to suspect, Grosvenor, that I have forsworn letter writing? I write as seldom to any of my friends as I do to you, and yet letters of business and of common courtesy accumulate upon me so fast that they occasion a very considerable and even inconvenient expense of time, especially to a man who, in the summer, is troubled with an influenza called laziness, and all the year round with the much more troublesome disease of poverty.

"It is not to be told how I rejoice at seeing my friends the Spaniards and Portuguese proving themselves to the eyes of the world to be what I have so long said they were. Huzza! Santiago and St. George! Smite them, as my Cid said, for the love of charity.

"Grosvenor! the most deserving of his majesty's pensioners thinketh of his pension—it is low water with him.

"Have you seen a defense, or rather eulogium, of Madoc, in the last Gentleman's Magazine, by Miss Seward? who preaches up its praise wherever she goes.

"You will have the Cid in about a fortnight. The translations in the appendix are by Frere, and they are, without any exception, the most masterly I have seen. The introduction, to be what it ought to be, and what I could have made it, would have required a volume to itself, for my reading is far more extensive on these subjects than almost any person can suppose. It is a rapid sketch—just sufficient to introduce the Chronicle, by giving the reader a summary view of the previous history and present state of Spain. The Chronicle is well done; and the translation improves so much on the original, by incorporating matter from other sources, as to be unique in its kind. There is a good deal of miscellaneous matter brought together in the notes. The intrinsic value of the work is of a very high order. Romance has nothing finer than all the proceedings at Zamora, and poetry nothing superior to the living pictures which you will find every where. The Cid's speech at the cortes is perfect eloquence of its kind. If it be remembered that all this was written, in all probability, before the year 1200 (certainly within half a century sooner or later), I think it must be considered as one of the most curious and valuable specimens of early literature—certainly as the most beautiful, beyond all comparison.

"Tom has been lucky in his Admiralty appointment, being first in a flag-ship, the Dreadnought. He says, and very justly, that our troops to Spain might have been conveyed in half the time, at half the expense, and without any risk at all, by putting as many on board some of our large ships of war as they could take (800 or 1000 they could carry very well), and letting each ship make the best of her way to the port nearest the scene of action. A convoy may be wind-bound for months, and any single transport which parts company would fall to the first privateer, whereas a ship of the line could beat down, take advantage of every start of wind, and defy all upon the ocean. There is very good sense in this. But transports imply jobs, and every thing must be a job in England.

"Farewell! I am getting on with South America.

"My son is the oddest fellow in the world: I wish you could see his bright eyes. * *

"God bless you! R. S."

To Grosvenor C. Bedford, Esq.

"September 9, 1808.

"My dear Grosvenor,

"Had I been a single man, I should long ere this have found my way into Spain.* I do not perceive any possibility of my going now—for this plain reason, my pension would not support my family during my absence, and there is no reason to suppose that any salary which might be allotted me would be more than sufficient for my own expenses abroad. So much the better; for if it were otherwise, and the offer were made me, I believe I ought to accept it, and this could not be done without a great sacrifice. Three children, and a fourth in prospect, are not easily left, and ought not to be left unless some important advantage were to be obtained by leaving them. I am obliged to Gifford—very much obliged to him: it is likely that Frere, from his knowledge of my uncle, would be disposed to listen to him; but that enough could be obtained to render my acceptance of it prudent, or even practicable, seems out of the question.

"So far was written last night, immediately on the receipt of your letter. In matters of any import this is my way—to reply from the instantaneous feeling, and then let the reply lie quietly for cooler judgment. You see what my thoughts are upon the subject. I should accept an advantageous offer, but am so certain of being desperately home-sick during the whole time of absence, that I am glad there is so little probable chance of any offer sufficiently advantageous. Yet, had I £500 to dispose of, I would go in the first packet for Lisbon, expressly to purchase books. The French have, without doubt, sold off the convent libraries, and perhaps the public ones, and such a collection may now be made as could never at any other time be within reach.

"As for a history of the Spanish Revolution, Landor is in the country, and if he is disposed to do it, there never was that man upon earth who could do it better.

"God bless you! R. S."

* This letter was in reply to one from Mr. Bedford, conveying an offer from Gifford to endeavor to procure him an appointment in Spain, that he might write an account of the transactions then going forward there.

To John Rickman, Esq.

"Keswick, Sept. 13, 1808.

"MY DEAR RICKMAN,

"Your estimate of Spain is right.* The difference between our age and that of Elizabeth is, that the bulk of the people are better in no respect, and worse in some. The middle classes are veneered instead of being heart of oak, and the higher ones are better classics, and worse in every other possible point of view. Ours is a degrading and dwarfing system of society. I believe, as you do, that the Spaniards have displayed more spirit than we should have done, and that the peacemongers were ready to have sacrificed the honor of England for their looms and brew-houses; yet, in the end, we should have beaten France. Religion has done much for Spain; in what light I regard it, you will see by the introduction to the Cid, written six years ago, and only remodeled now, and that before these late events took place. But much has also been done by those awakening recollections of the deeds of their forefathers, which every Spaniard felt and delighted to feel. The very ballads of the Cid must have had their effect.

* * * * * * *

"I am very idle—boating and walking about, and laying in health and exercise for the next season of hibernation. Right glad shall I be when you come and help me in this laudable and needful part of my year's work. The last odd thing that has turned up in my reading is, that the Merino sheep were originally English, and transported from hence into Spain; *ergo*, the quality of the wool depends upon the climate and pasture, and a few generations may be expected to bring it back to what it originally was. * * * * * * * * * * * * *

"God bless you! R. S."

To Lieutenant Southey, H.M.S. Dreadnought.

"Greta Hall, Oct. 13, 1808.

"DEAR TOM,

"An Irishman who was abroad came in one day and said that he had seen that morning what he had never seen before—a fine crop of anchovies growing in the garden. 'Anchovies?' said an Englishman, with a half laugh and a tone of wonder. And from this the other, according to the legitimate rules of Irish logic, deduced a quarrel, a challenge, and a duel, in which the poor Englishman, who did not believe that anchovies grew in the garden, was killed on the spot. The moment he fell, the right word came into the challenger's head. 'Och! what a pity!' he cried, 'and I meant capers all the while!' Mr. Spence knew the parties, and told this story the other day at Calvert's, from whence it traveled to me.

"What, think you, was announced the other day in the Keswick play-bill? A tale in verse, by R. Southy, Esq., to be recited by Mr. Deans. There's fame for you! What the tale was I have not heard—most likely the Maid of the Inn, which is right worthy of such recitation.

"It occurred to me last night, I know not how, that I have never, to the best of my recollection, seen one of the large house-snails in this country, and very few indeed of the smaller kind, which are so numerous, and of such beautiful varieties, in our part of the kingdom. You know what a collector of snail shells I was in my time, hoarding up all the empty ones I could find. The rocks used to be my hunting-place. That amusement has made me familiar with every variety in that neighborhood, and certain I am that the greater number are not to be found here. Slugs we have in plenty. By-the-by, I have lately seen it mentioned in an old French book that frogs eat snails, shells and all.

"I wish you had the Cid to have shown the Spaniards: they would have been pleased to see that the Campeador was beginning to have his fame here in England, 700 years after his death. Unquestionably that Chronicle is one of the finest things in the world, and so I think it will be admitted to be. Coleridge is perfectly delighted with it. Frere, passionately as he admired the poem, had never seen the Chronicle, which is remarkable enough. You will see, by comparing the Dumb-ee scene in both, that the Chronicle is sometimes the most poetical of the two.* I am so fond of this kind of cotemporary history, and so persuaded of the good which it is likely to do, by giving us a true knowledge of other times, and reviving those high and generous feelings which all modern habits of life tend to counteract, that I think seriously of translating the works of Fernan Lopez as soon as my history is completed. There is the Chronicle of Pedro the Just, which is a very small volume, my great MS., and the Chronicle of Joam I. The whole would fill three such quartos as the Cid. I should like to do it for the pleasure of the thing, as the man said when he was to shoot Shepherd's goat. * * * *

"I am getting on with my Letters from Portugal. The evenings close in by tea-time, and fire and candle bring with them close work at the desk, and nothing to take me from it. The Long-man of the Row recommends the small size in preference to quarto, as producing greater profits, in consequence of its readier sale. To this I willingly assent. They will probably extend to three such volumes as Espriella. When they are done, the fresh letters of Espriella will come in their turn; and so I go on. Huzza! two-and-twenty volumes already; the Cid, when reprinted, will make two more; and, please God, five a year in addition as long as I live.

"Edith has just been in with her kiss—as regular as the evening gun. She wants to know when uncle will come home. Sooner, perhaps, than he himself thinks for the glorious revolution

* "I do not know whether you allow credit to my opinion that the Spanish resistance is all from religion. * * * You know I reckon the state of Spain to be about like that of England under Elizabeth and James the First * * *—*J. R. to R. S., Sept.* 10, 1808.

* Cid, book ix., c. xiii.

in Spain will bring Bonaparte down. It is morally impossible that such a nation can be subdued. If King Joseph should fall into their hands, I pray that —— may be on the spot; he will take care that no mischief shall happen by keeping him prisoner.

* * * * * * *

"God bless you! R. S."

To Mr. Ebenezer Elliott.

"October 13, 1808.

"Sir,

"A recommendation to the booksellers to look at a manuscript is of no use whatever. In the way of business they glance at every thing which is offered them, and no persons know better what is likely to answer their purpose. Poetry is the worst article in the market; out of fifty volumes which may be published in the course of a year, not five pay the expense of publication: and this is a piece of knowledge which authors in general purchase dearly, for in most cases these volumes are printed at their risk.

"From that specimen of your productions which is now in my writing desk, I have no doubt that you possess the feeling of a poet, and may distinguish yourself; but I am sure that premature publication would eventually discourage you. You have an example in Kirke White; his Clifton Grove sold only to the extent of the subscription he obtained for it; and the treatment which it experienced drove him, by his own account, almost to madness. My advice to you is, to go on improving yourself, without hazarding any thing: you can not practice without improvement. Feel your way before you with the public, as Montgomery did. He sent his verses to the newspapers, and, when they were copied from one to another, it was a sure sign they had succeeded. He then communicated them, as they were copied from the papers, to the Poetical Register; the Reviews selected them for praise; and thus, when he published them in a collected form, he did nothing more than claim, in his own character, the praise which had been bestowed upon him under a fictitious name. Try the newspapers. Send what you think one of your best short poems (that is, any thing short of 100 lines) to the Courier or the Globe. If it is inserted, send others, with any imaginary signature. If they please nobody, and nobody notices them for praise, nobody will for censure, and you will escape all criticism. If, on the contrary, they attract attention, the editor will be glad to pay you for more—and they still remain your property, to be collected and reprinted in whatever manner you may think best hereafter.

"If, however, you are bent upon trying your fortune with the Soldier's Love, can you not try it by subscription? 250 names will indemnify you for the same number of copies. I will give you a fair opinion of your manuscript if you will direct Longman to forward it to me, and will willingly be of what little use I can. But be assured that the best and wisest plan you can pursue is to try your strength in the London newspapers.

"Believe me, with the best wishes for your welfare and success, yours sincerely,

"Robert Southey."

To Humphrey Senhouse, Esq.

"Keswick, Oct. 15, 1808.

"My dear Sir,

"I have had a visit this morning from S—— and C—— upon the subject of this convention in Portugal. They, and some of their friends, are very desirous of bringing before the country, in some regular form, the main iniquity of the business—which has been lost sight of in all the addresses—and of rectifying public opinion by showing it in its true light.* A military inquiry may or may not convict Sir Hugh Dalrymple of military misconduct. This is the least part of his offense, and no legal proceedings can attach to the heinous crime he has committed; the high treason against all moral feeling, in recognizing Junot by his usurped title, and deadening that noble spirit from which, and which only, the redemption of Europe can possibly proceed—by presuming to grant stipulations for the Portuguese which no government ever pretended to have power to make for an independent ally—covenanting for the impunity of the traitors, and guaranteeing the safety of an army of ruffians, all of whom, without his intervention, must soon have received their righteous reward from the hands of those whom they had oppressed. He has stepped in to save these wretches from the vengeance of an injured people; he has been dealing with them as fair and honorable enemies, exchanging compliments and visits, dining with them in the palaces from which they had driven the rightful lords, and upon the plate which they had stolen. He, therefore, has abandoned our vantage ground, betrayed the cause of Spain and Portugal, and disclaimed, as far as his authority extends, the feelings which the Spaniards are inculcating, and in which lie their strength and their salvation, by degrading into a common and petty war between soldier and soldier, that which is the struggle of a nation against a foreign usurper, a business of natural life and death, a war of virtue against vice, light against darkness, the good principle against the evil one.

"It is important to make the country feel this; and these sentiments would appear with most effect if they were embodied in a county address, of which the ostensible purport might be to thank

* The feeling of the country seems to have been more generally roused on this occasion than almost on any other: "The London newspapers joined in one cry of wonder and abhorrence. On no former occasion had they been so unanimous, and scarcely ever was their language so energetic, so manly, so worthy of the English press. The provincial papers proved that from one end of the island to the other the resentment of this grievous wrong was the same. Some refused to disgrace their pages by inserting so infamous a treaty; others surrounded it with broad black lines, putting their journals into mourning for the dismal information it contained."—*Edinburgh Annual Register*, 1808, p. 368.

his majesty for having instituted an inquiry, and to request that he would be pleased to appoint a day of national humiliation for this grievous national disgrace. This will not be liable to the reproof with which he thought proper to receive the city address, because it prejudges nothing—military proceedings are out of the question: what is complained of is a breach of the law of nations, and an abandonment of the moral principle which the words of the convention prove, and which can not be explained away by any inquiry whatsoever.

" * * * * * * * *

S—— and C—— know many persons who will come forward at such a meeting. Coleridge or Wordsworth will be ready to speak, and will draw up resolutions to be previously approved, and brought forward by some proper person. We will prepare the way by writing in the county papers. Here ends my part of the business, and not a little surprised am I to find myself even thus much concerned in any county affairs, when the sole freehold I am ever likely to possess is a tenement six feet by three, in Crosthwaite church-yard.

* * * * * * *

" Believe me, yours very truly,

" ROBERT SOUTHEY."

To Walter Scott, Esq.

" Keswick, Nov. 6, 1808.

" MY DEAR SCOTT,

" I have sometimes thought of publishing translations from the Spanish and Portuguese, with the originals annexed, but there was no prospect of profit to tempt me; and as certainly, if I live, it is my intention to enter fully into the literary history of both countries. That made me lay aside the thought of any thing on a lesser scale. Another reason, perhaps, may have been this, that it is not more difficult to compose poetry than to translate it, and that, in my own opinion, I can make as good as I can find. Very, very few of the Spanish ballads are good; they are made in general upon one receipt, and that a most inartificial one; they begin by describing the situation of somebody who makes a speech which is the end. Nothing like the wildness or the character of our ballads is to be found among them. It is curious, and at present inexplicable to me, how their prose should be so exquisitely poetical as it is in the Cid, and their poetry so completely prosaical as it is in their narrative poems. Nevertheless, I might be tempted. Some translations I have by me, and many of my books are marked for others. There are some high-toned odes in the Spanish, and a good many beautiful sonnets. Many of their epics would afford good extracts; and I am competent to give critical sketches of biography, formed not at second-hand, but from full perusal of the authors themselves. My name, however, is worth nothing in the market, and the booksellers would not offer me any thing to make it worth my while to interrupt occupations of greater importance. I thank you heartily for your offer of aid, and should the thing be carried into effect, would gladly avail myself of it.

" I am planning something of great importance, a poem upon Pelayo, the first restorer of Spain: it has long been one of my chosen subjects; and those late events, which have warmed every heart that has right British blood circulating through it, have revived and strengthened old resolutions. It will be in regular blank verse, and the story will naturally take rather a higher tone than Madoc.

" It gives me great pleasure to hear that you have done with the Edinburgh Review. Of their article respecting Spain, I heard from Coleridge. That subject is a fair touchstone whether a man has any generous sympathies in his nature. There is not in history such another instance of national regeneration and redemption. I have been a true prophet upon this subject, and am not a little proud of the prophecy. Of the eventual issue I have never felt a moment's doubt. Such a nation, such a spirit, are invincible. But what a cruel business has this convention of Cintra been. Junot clearly expressed his own feelings of our commander-in-chief when he recommended him to take up his quarters at Quintella's house as he had done: "the man," he said, " kept a very good table, and he had seldom had reason to find fault with it." My blood boils to think that there should be an English general to whom this rascal could venture to say this! In one of the Frenchmen's knapsacks, among other articles of that property which they bargained to take away with them, was a delicate female hand with rings upon the fingers.

" Our ministers do not avail themselves as they might do of their strong cause. They should throw away the scabbard and publish a manifesto, stating why this country never will make peace with Bonaparte, and on what plain terms it will at any moment make peace with France under any other ruler. I fully believe that it would be possible to overthrow his government by this means at this time.

" A reviewal of my Cid by you will be the best aid that it can possibly receive. Five hundred only were printed, and in spite of the temporary feeling and the wonderful beauty of the book, I dare say they will hang upon hand.

" It will rejoice me to see you here, and show you my treasures, and talk of the days of the shield and the lance. We have a bed at your service, and shall expect you to be our guest. Wordsworth, who left me to-day, desires his remembrances. He is about to write a pamphlet upon this precious convention, which he will place in a more philosophical point of view than any body has yet done. I go to press in a few weeks with my History of Brazil, and have Thalaba at present in Ballantyne's hands—that poem having just reached the end of its seven years' apprenticeship. And I have got half way through my Hindoo poem, which, it is to be hoped, will please myself, inasmuch as it is not likely to please any body else. It is too strange, too much beyond all human sympathies; but I shall go on, and as, in such a case, I have usually little but my labor for my pains, the certainty that it never can be popular will not deter me from gratifying my own fancy.

"Mrs. Southey joins me in remembrances to Mrs. Scott.

"Believe me, yours very truly,

"ROBERT SOUTHEY."

The autumn of this year was marked by a circumstance which exercised considerable influence over my father's future literary labors—the setting on foot of the Quarterly Review, in which, up to the last few years of his life, he bore so constant and prominent a part. At this time the Edinburgh Review had the field all to itself; and though it had commenced upon principles of "neutrality," or something of the kind as to party politics,* its "Whiggery" had gradually increased until it had become of the deepest dye. We have seen that in the preceding year Sir Walter Scott (at that time himself a contributor) had endeavored also to enlist my father under its banners, with what success the reply has shown. *Now* he had not only himself withdrawn his aid, but also his name from the subscribers' list,† so highly did he disapprove of the political tone it had assumed; and viewing the matter as one of great importance from its large circulation (9000 copies being then printed quarterly), from there being no periodical to compete with it in literary criticism, and from the impression which the "flashy and bold character of the work" was likely to make upon youthful minds, he was especially desirous that some counteracting influence should be established. In him, therefore, the idea originated. The first intimation of it my father received was from his friend Mr. Bedford, who was intimately acquainted with Gifford, the appointed future editor, and who, knowing how decidedly he was opposed to the principles advocated in the Edinburgh, especially as respected "the base and cowardly spirit with which they set forth the invincible power of France, and the necessity of sacrificing every thing that is dear and honorable to obtain her forbearance," now wrote to him, giving him an account of the plan upon which it was proposed to conduct this Review, and wishing him to draw up an account of the affairs of Spain for the first number. His reply was as follows:

To Grosvenor C. Bedford, Esq.

"Keswick, Nov. 9, 1808.

"MY DEAR GROSVENOR,

"I am ready, desirous, and able to bear a part in this said Review. You will, however, think it odd, that the very subject on which you think me most able is one which I should rather avoid. I have not the sort of talent requisite for writing a political pamphlet upon the state of Spain; these things require a kind of wire-drawing which I have never learned to perform, and a method of logical reasoning to which my mind has never been habituated, and for which it has no natural aptitude. What I feel about Spain you know; what I think about it is this—the country has much to suffer, in all probability there will be many and dreadful defeats of the patriots, and such scenes as have never been witnessed in Europe since the destruction of Saguntum and Numantia may perhaps be renewed there. Joseph will very likely be crowned at Madrid, and many of us may give up the cause of Spanish independence as lost. But so surely as God liveth, and as the spirit of God liveth and moveth in the hearts of men, so surely will that country eventually work out its own redemption.

"Now, Grosvenor, understand me clearly. I could not fill half a score of pages by dilating and diluting this—that is, I should be a sorry pamphleteer; but I believe myself to be a good reviewer in my own way, which is that of giving a succinct account of the contents of the book before me, extracting its essence, bringing my own knowledge to bear upon the subject, and, where occasion serves, seasoning it with those opinions which in some degree leaven all my thoughts, words, and actions. If you had read the Annual Reviews, you would comprehend this better by example than I can make you in a letter. Voyages and travels I review better than any thing else, being well read in that branch of literature; better, indeed, than most men. Biography and history are within my reach; upon any of these topics I will do my best. * * * * * * You know my way of thinking upon most subjects. I despise all parties too much to be attached to any. I believe that this country must continue the war while Bonaparte is at the head of France, and while the system which he has perfected remains in force; I therefore, from my heart and soul, execrate and abominate the peacemongers. I am an enemy to any further concessions to the Catholics; I am a friend to the Church establishment. I wish for reform, because I can not but see that all things are tending toward revolution, and nothing but reform can by any possibility prevent it.

"Thus much is said to you that it may be said through you. To yourself I add that the pay proposed will be exceedingly suitable to my poor finances, and that the more books of travels they send me the better. I had almost forgotten to say, that if a fit text be sent me, the subject of converting the Hindoos is one upon which I am well prepared.

"Farewell, and God bless you! R. S."

Very shortly after the date of this letter, some further doubts crossed my father's mind as to the projected Review being sufficiently independent in its politics for him to contribute to it with perfect satisfaction. The circumstance of there being reason to expect "political information to be communicated from authentic sources" seemed to him to imply that silence would be observed on such points as it might be unpleasing

* See Life of Sir Walter Scott, 2d edit., vol. iii., p. 65.
† Ibid., 126–129.

to the ministry to have strongly animadverted upon, and he consequently expresses these fears to Mr. Bedford in the strong language he naturally used to a familiar correspondent. This produced a further exposition of the principles upon which the Review was to be conducted; and his reply will show that, notwithstanding these passing doubts, he entered at the first heartily and zealously into the plan.

It is, however, right to state, that at no period could the Quarterly Review be said *fairly* to represent my father's opinions, political or otherwise, and great injustice was often done him both by imputing articles to him which he never wrote, and also by supposing that, in those known to be his, *all* his mind had appeared. The truth was, as his letters will show, that his views on most subjects, while from this time they gradually drew nearer to those of the Tory party, yet occasionally differed widely from them, and most certainly were never those of a blind, time-serving, and indiscriminating allegiance. In his contributions to the Quarterly Review these differences of opinion were broadly stated, and measures often recommended of a very different character to those which that party adopted. This might be, and probably was, sometimes done in a manner which admitted, and, perhaps, required the editor's correction; but it would seem that Gifford had a heavy and unsparing hand in these matters, and my father frequently and bitterly complains of the mutilation of his papers, and of their being tamed down to the measure of the politics the Review was intended to represent, and gauged often by ministerial timidity. This, it appears, from the following letter, he apprehended would sometimes be the case, but *not* to the extent to which it was subsequently carried.

To Grosvenor C. Bedford, Esq.

"Nov. 17, 1808.

"MY DEAR GROSVENOR,

"You have taken what I said a little too seriously; that is, you have given it more thought than it deserved. The case stands thus: you wish to serve the public, ministers wish to serve themselves; and so it happens that, just at this time, the two objects are the same. I am very willing to travel with them as far as we are going the same way, and, when our roads separate, shall of course leave them. Meantime, that suppression which there certainly will be upon certain points is of little consequence to me, who shall have nothing to do with those points. Murray has sent me materials for the missionary article, in which Gifford wishes me to enter upon the subject generally. My intent was to have confined myself to the Hindoo question; but I am master of the whole subject, and will therefore take the wider view. There are three reviewals of mine upon this very topic in the three first Annuals, and these were the first which ever appeared concerning them. I am strong here, and shall do well, God willing; yet how much better could I do if nobody but Robert Southey were responsible for the opinions expressed.

"I know from Walter Scott that he reviews the Cid; it is not a text for entering directly upon the present Spanish affairs, though a fine one for *touching* upon them. Two things are required for the review of that book which will not be found in one person—a knowledge of Spanish literature, and of the manners of chivalry, so as to estimate the comparative value of my Chronicle. The latter knowledge Scott possesses better than any body else.

"About Cevallos you best know your own stock of materials. Authors may be divided into silk-worms and spiders—those who spin because they are full, and those who spin because they are empty. It is not likely that there are any facts of importance which are not known to the public; and, indeed, if I undertook the task, I should have little to do with the past history of *these* transactions, but state as summarily and strongly as I could what the conduct of France had been; hold up the war as a crusade on the part of us and the Spaniards (I love and vindicate the Crusades); show why I expected this from their character, and also why I now expect in full faith a glorious termination at last, though prepared to hear of heavy reverses for a time, possibly the recoronation of Joseph at Madrid. Finally, I would represent the thought of peace with Bonaparte as high treason against all honorable feelings and all liberty. Of the Spanish frigates I would say nothing; would to God that they who issued orders for their capture were buried in the deep with them! There is a sort of methodical writing, carrying with it an air of official imposingness which does better in such cases than better things (though I would not be supposed to imply that it necessarily excludes them); and of this style I should guess that Herries is master.

"Elmsley may be applied to, and, I think, with success. As for Davy, I know not whether the prize which he received from Bonaparte sticks to his fingers or no; I would sooner have cut mine off than accepted it. It is likely to co-operate with some of his Royal Institution associates in making him cry out for peace: yet Davy's heart is sound at the core, and his all-grasping, all-commanding genius must have redeemed him. The best channel to him is through Sotheby, a man on whom you may calculate. I am particularly anxious that my hint about Poole should be adopted. One article from him about the poor will be worth its weight in gold. I hope Malthus will not be a contributor. By that *first* book moral restraint was pronounced impracticable; by his *second* it is relied upon as his remedy for the poors' rates, which are to be abolished to prevent the poor from marrying; and moral restraint and the parson are to render them contented in celibacy. His main principle is that God makes men and women faster than He can feed them, and he calls upon government to stop the breed. As if we did not at this moment want men for our battles! Rickman's name should stand in the place of his. Rickman has ten-fold his knowledge and his ability. There is no man living equal to Rickman upon the subject of political economy. He, too, is a Crusader as to this war. Malthus will prove a peace-monger.

"It would attract much notice, and carry with it much recommendation, if an account of the Welsh Archæology could be procured. Turner may be asked for it; I am afraid he is too busy: William Owen, alas! is one of Joanna Southcote's four-and-twenty elders; and Bard Williams is, God knows where, and nothing is to be got out of him except by word of mouth. There is, however, the chance of Turner; there is Davies of Olveston, the author of the Celtic Researches; there is Wynn's Welshman—Peter Roberts.

"Farewell! I finish my Annualizing in a few days, and shall then set about the Missions.

"God bless you! R. S.

"Let not Gifford suppose me a troublesome man to deal with, pertinacious about trifles, or standing upon punctilios of authorship. No, Grosvenor, I am a quiet, patient, easy-going hack of the mule breed; regular as clock-work in my pace, sure-footed, bearing the burden which is laid on me, and only obstinate in choosing my own path. If Gifford could see me by this fireside, where, like Nicodemus, one candle suffices me in a large room, he would see a man in a coat 'still more threadbare than his own' when he wrote his 'Imitation,' working hard and getting little—a bare maintenance, and hardly that; writing poems and history for posterity with his whole heart and soul; one daily progressive in learning, not so learned as he is poor, not so poor as proud, not so proud as happy. Grosvenor, there is not a lighter-hearted nor a happier man upon the face of this wide world.

"Your godson thinks that I have nothing to do but to play with him, and any body who saw what reason he has for his opinion would be disposed to agree with him. I wish you could see my beautiful boy!"

To John Rickman, Esq.

"Nov. 20, 1808.

"My dear Rickman,

"The earliest chronicle in French is that of Geoffrey Vilhardouin, so often quoted by Gibbon, which relates the capture of Constantinople by the Latins, and is, therefore, long subsequent to My Cid. I believe the earliest histories of the Normans are in Latin, and believe, also, that all Latin chronicles will be found either as you describe them, or florid and pedantic. Men never write with feeling in any language but their own; they never write well upon subjects with which they do not sympathize; and what sympathy could there ever be between monks and chivalry? My Cid is the finest specimen of chivalrous history: it is so true a book that it bespeaks belief for the story of his victory after death, and it requires arguments and dates to prove that this part is not authentic.

"I am brimful of this kind of knowledge, and much more of it will appear in the first volume of Portuguese History than in the Cid. There are two other subjects on which I am as well informed as those for which you give me credit*—savage manners and monastic history; and the latter, not the least curious of the whole, certainly the most out-of-the-way. It is a little unlucky that the least interesting of all my histories must come out first.

"The Saxon language, you say, ousted the Welsh as completely as its possessors. But there is reason to believe that a part only of our prior population was Celtic, and that we had previously hived Teutonic and Cantabrian swarms. A Basque dictionary would be a treasure; none of our etymologists have had recourse to it. I was told by the only person I ever met with who had studied this language, that there was far more of it than had been supposed both in the Spanish and Portuguese—about as much, probably, as we have of Welsh. Bilboa would be the place to get Basque books; but I will try to obtain a dictionary through Frere, who has offered his services to my uncle in this line—a new species of diplomacy of more use than the old.

"In one point, and only in one, does China offer an exception to the evil consequences of polygamy,† and that is, it has remained an undivided empire. This, I suppose, is owing to the unique circumstance of its having a literary aristocracy, all subordinate authority being in the hands of men whose education and whose habits of life make them averse to war. Robbers are the only rebels there; the demoralizing effects of the system are the same there as every where. Shuey-ping-sin‡ exemplifies that. I have not asserted that it is a barrier to intellectual improvement otherwise than as that must be checked by public disturbances and private voluptuousness. The want of an alphabet in China is certainly cause sufficient; but it is a supererogatory cause, for those Orientals who have one are not advanced a step further. For an effect so general there must be some general cause, operating under so many varieties of climate and religion; and this is the only one which has universally existed.

"I recommend and exhort you to read Captain Beaver's African Memoranda; you will find a book and a man after your own heart: I would walk to the Land's End to have the satisfaction of shaking hands with him. * * *

"God bless you! R. S."

* "Two out-of-the-way things you certainly know better than all other men—Eastern fable and European chivalry and romance; and this nobody will dispute who has read the annotations to Thalaba and My Cid."—*J. R. to R. S.*

† "In your introduction to My Cid, I was not surprised that you insist largely on the evils of polygamy, knowing that to be your particular aversion. I myself do not admire polygamy, nor much more that idea of Dr. Johnson's, that happiness would not be less in quantity if all marriages were made by law without consulting the inclinations of the couples. However, in taking a general view, we must not forget that the largest and most populous empire in the world, China, goes on pretty well under both these inconveniences, for I think in fairness you will allow that the want of an alphabet accounts sufficiently for the frozen limits of Chinese science, without calling in the aid of polygamy or of aught else."—*J. R. to R. S., Oct.* 12, 1808.

‡ The title of a Chinese novel.

To Lieutenant Southey, H.M.S. Dreadnought.

"Keswick, Nov. 22, 1808.

"MY DEAR TOM,

"I am not quite sure which deserves the severest cart's-tailing, you or your admiral; you for what you say of Frere's translation, he for what he says of mine. A translation is good precisely in proportion as it faithfully represents the matter, manner, and spirit of its original: this is equally well done in his verse and my prose, and I will venture to say never has been, and never will be, better done elsewhere. You do not like it at all! With what notion have you been reading it? Not, I am sure, with the recollection that it is part of the oldest poem extant in any modern language, being of the time of our William the Conqueror, the manner and the meter of which have been represented as accurately as possible. In fact, his translation had long been the admiration of all who had seen it, and I had heard wonders of it from Walter Scott, Harry, Heber, and the Hollands, before I saw it. Your phrase of 'eking out' is cart's-tailable without benefit of clergy. Instead of wanting materials, I suppressed half a drawerful of notes, besides my own King Ramiro and Garci Ferrandez.

"Now to the admiral's criticism. He seems to suppose that a book ought always to be rendered into English of the newest fashion; and, if not, that it then should be given in the English of its own age—a book of the fifteenth century (sixteenth he means) in that of the fifteenth. He did not recollect that in the thirteenth century there was no such thing as English, which is, I think, answer enough. But the fact is, that, both in this Chronicle and in Amadis, I have not formed a style, but followed one. The original, when represented as literally as possible, ran into that phraseology, and all I had to do was to avoid words, and forms of words, of modern creation, and also such as were unintelligibly obsolete. There is, as you must have heard Wordsworth point out, a language of pure intelligible English, which was spoken in Chaucer's time, and is spoken in ours; equally understood then and now; and of which the Bible is the written and permanent standard, as it has undoubtedly been the great means of preserving it. To that beautiful manner of narration which characterizes the best Chronicles, this language is peculiarly adapted; and, in fact, it is *appropriated* to such narration by our books of chivalry, and, I might almost say, *consecrated* to it by the historical parts of Scripture. It so happens that, of all the things which I have ever done, the only one for which all the Reviews with one accord commended me, was for the manner in which I had rendered Amadis. I wish he may steer as clear of all mischief as I shall of them upon this occasion. The fault which he finds is, that I have translated the Chronicle of the Cid instead of writing his History.

"The new Review is to appear in April. Among the persons who are calculated upon to write in it, there are Frere; G. Ellis; your admiral's brother, a man of more than common talents, and well to be liked; Heber; Coplestone, the Oxford Poetry Professor (a great admirer of Madoc); Miss Baillie; Sharon Turner; and Captain Burney. A good many of these persons, I know, have the same thorough conviction of the destructive folly it would be to make peace that I and Walter Scott have; for, to do Scott justice, all his best and bravest feelings are alive upon that subject. I think we shall do good, and will do my part with a hearty good-will. What I said to Bedford was, that as long as this government caravan was traveling my road, I was content to travel with it; and that, though all my opinions hang together, all the hanging which they imply does not immediately appear. One good thing is, that I shall be pretty sure of civil treatment here, and the Review will carry great weight with it.

"—— has not written to me. There will be such a tremendous campaign that the chances are much against any individual, especially one who will seek the hottest service, as he will do. In the field he is but one, and as obnoxious to a ball as the merest machine of a soldier; but, should he be in a besieged town, such a man is worth a whole regiment there.

"God protect him, wherever he be!

"God bless you! R. S."

To Walter Savage Landor, Esq.

"Keswick, Nov. 26, 1808.

"In the height of our indignation here at the infamy in Portugal, one of our first thoughts was what yours would be. We in England had the consolation to see that the country redeemed itself by the general outcry which burst out. Never was any feeling within my recollection so general; I did not meet a man who was not boiling over with shame and rage.

"The Spaniards *will* be victorious. I am prepared to hear of many reverses, but this has from the beginning been as much a faith as an opinion with me; and you, who know the Spaniards, will understand on what ground it has been formed. I am glad you know them, their country, and their language, which, in spite of your Romanized ears, becomes a man's mouth better than any other in present use, except, perhaps, our own. Come and see me when you have nothing to call you elsewhere, and the wind of inclination may set in this way, and we will talk about Spain, and retravel your route, a part of which I remember as vividly as I do my father's house.

"Find out a woman whom you can esteem, and love will grow more surely out of esteem than esteem will out of love. Your soul would then find anchorage. There are fountain springs of delight in the heart of man, which gush forth at the sight of his children, though it might seem before to be hard as the rock of Horeb, and dry as the desert sands. What I learned from Rousseau, before I laid Epictetus to my heart, was, that Julia was happy with a husband whom she had not loved, and that Wolmer was more to be admired than St. Preux. I bid no man beware of being poor as he grows old, but I say to all men, beware of solitariness in age. Rest is the object to be sought. There is no other way of attaining it here, where we have no convents, but by putting an end to all those hopes and fears to which the best hearts are the most subject. *Experto crede Roberto.* This is the holy oil which has stilled in me a nature little less tempestuous than your own.

"I have 1800 lines of Kehama to send you as soon as they can be transcribed, which will be with all convenient speed. Seven sections, cantos, or canticles more will finish the poem. The sight of the goal naturally quickens one's speed, and I have good hope of completing it before the spring. Pelayo, whereof I wrote in my letter to Coruña, is not yet begun, the materials not having quite settled into satisfactory order. It is a grand subject, and I feel myself equal to it in every thing except topographical knowledge. I ought to have seen Gijon and Covadonga. Asturian scenery, however, must resemble that of the contiguous parts of Leon and Galicia, and I have the whole road from Lugo to Astorga in my eye and in my heart.

"We used our endeavors here to obtain a county meeting and send in a petition which should have taken up the Convention upon its true grounds of honor and moral feeling, keeping all pettier considerations out of sight. Wordsworth—who left me when we found the business hopeless—went home to ease his heart in a pamphlet, which I daily expect to hear he has completed. Courts of Inquiry will do nothing, and can do nothing. But we can yet acquit our own souls, and labor to foster and keep alive a spirit which is in the country, and which a cowardly race of hungry place-hunters are endeavoring to extinguish.

"The ill news is just come, and ministers are quaking for Sir John Moore, for whom I do not quake, as he and his army will beat twice their number of French. The fall of Madrid must be looked for, and, perhaps, Zaragoza may be the Saguntum of modern history. *That* may God forbid! but Spain is still unconquerable, and will still be victorious, though there should be a French garrison in every one of its towns. We, as usual, are in fault; thirty thousand English at Bilboa would have secured that side, and England ought to have supplied thrice that number if she supplied any.

* * * * * * *

"God bless you! R. S."

To Grosvenor C. Bedford, Esq.

"Dec. 20, 1808.

"My dear Grosvenor,

"Here is my vindication of the Indian Mission packed up on the table; but, unluckily, too late for to-day's coach, so it can not reach London before Monday. It is written with hearty goodwill, and requires no signature to show whence it comes. Now I wish you would ask Mr. Gifford—if he thinks it expedient to use the pruning-knife—to let the copy be returned to me when the printer has done with it, because it is ten to one that the passages which he would curtail—being the most Robert Southeyish of the whole—would be those that I should like best myself; and, therefore, I would have the satisfaction of putting them in again for my own satisfaction, if for nobody's else. I must still confess to you, Grosvenor, that I have my fears and suspicions as to the freedom of the Review, and this article will, in some measure, put it to the proof; for it is my nature and my principle to speak and write as earnestly, as plainly, and as straight to the mark as I think and feel. If the editor understands his own interest, he will not restrict me. A Review started against the Edinburgh will instantly be suspected of being a ministerial business, and a sprinkling of my free and fearless way of thinking will win friends for it among those very persons most likely to be prejudiced against it, and to be misled by the Scotchmen. The high orthodox men, both of Church and State, will always think as they are told: there is no policy in writing to them; the Anti-Jacobin and British Critic are good enough for their faces of brass, brains of lead, and tongues of bell-metal. I shall not offend them, though my reasonings appeal to better hearts and clearer understandings. I would say this to him if I knew him; but I do not desire you to say it, because I do not know how far it might suit the person to whom it relates.

"Spain! Spain! * * * were the resources of the nation at my command, I would stake my head upon the deliverance of that country, and the utter overthrow of Bonaparte. But, good God! what blunders, what girlish panics, what absolute cowardice are there in our measures! Disembarking troops when we ought to be sending ship after ship as fast as they could be put on board. It is madness to wait for transports; send ships of the line, and let them run singly for Lisbon, and Cadiz, and Catalonia. Nothing can ruin the Spaniards unless they feel the misconduct of England as I am grieved to say I feel it. It is the more heart-breaking because the heart of England is with those noble people. We are not only ready, willing, and able to make every effort for them, but even eager to do it; and yet all is palsied by plans so idiotic that the horse-whip were a fitter instrument of punishment for them than the halter, if it were not for their deadly consequences. God bless you! R. S."

CHAPTER XV.

COWPER'S TRANSLATION OF MILTON'S LATIN AND ITALIAN POEMS—KEHAMA—HISTORY OF BRAZIL—POLITICS—LITERARY ADVICE—SKETCH OF MR. RICKMAN'S CHARACTER—PLEASURE AT SEEING HIS WRITINGS IN PRINT—SPANISH AFFAIRS—THE QUARTERLY REVIEW—EXCURSION TO DURHAM—FREEDOM OF HIS OPINIONS—THE CID—SENSITIVE FEELINGS—GEBIR—BAD EF-

FECT OF SCIENTIFIC STUDIES—ANXIETY ABOUT HIS LITTLE BOY—MR. CANNING WISHES TO SERVE HIM—APPLICATION FOR STEWARDSHIP OF GREENWICH HOSPITAL ESTATES—MR. WORDSWORTH'S PAMPHLET ON THE CONVENTION OF CINTRA—ECLOGUE OF THE ALDERMAN'S FUNERAL—THE QUARTERLY REVIEW—SIR JOHN MOORE'S RETREAT—DEATH OF HIS LANDLORD—MR. CANNING'S DUEL—MORTE D'ARTHUR—ECLECTIC AND QUARTERLY REVIEWS—DR. COLLYER'S LECTURES—MR. COLERIDGE'S "FRIEND"—THE SOLDIER'S LOVE—KEHAMA FINISHED—PFLAYO—WAR IN THE PENINSULA.—1809.

In the following letter my father refers to one he had lately received from Miss Seward, partly on the subject of Hayley's edition of Cowper's Milton. The reader will probably, therefore, not be displeased to see it prefaced by the quotation of her remarks.

"To Mr. Hayley's quarto, which he calls Cowper's Milton, I six years past subscribed, and have sedulously perused my copy. Far from proving what its editor expects—the consummation of Milton's and his translator's glory—it appears to me utterly incapable of adding to that of either. If Milton's Latin and Italian compositions are rich in poetic matter, they have met with no justice from Cowper, in whose dress they strike me as pedantic, tuneless, and spiritless. Of the Damonides Langhorne formed a sweet and touching poem, one of the darlings of my youthful years. Cowper is as hard as iron in comparison, and almost all the pathos vanishes in the stiff and labored expression; yet Hayley, for his idol, *challenges* the comparison, alleging also his conviction that, if the spirit of Milton could have directed the choice of a translator from all living men, he would have selected Cowper, and that from the parity in their genius, their style, their character, and their fortunes. To this imaginary choice I am more than skeptical. *Rhyme* was not Cowper's *forte:* nothing which he has written in it, except by sudden gleams, is above mediocrity. He not only wanted ear to form its harmony, but rejected that harmony systematically. The numbers of its great master were displeasing to him. He says in his letters, 'Pope set his ideas to a tune which *any one* may catch;' hence, when Cowper wrote in *rhyme*, provided he could cram his thoughts into the couplets, he chose rather that they should be rough than harmonious, that they should stumble rather than that they should glide. His blank verse is the sheet-anchor of his poetic fame. The Task, and the fragment on Yardley Oak, will be coeval with our language; and, if his other works live, it will be for that they were written by the author of these two compositions. As for the quarto, seldom did a great book issue from the press whose contents were of less consequence to the literature of the country. The critical remarks which they contain on the Paradise Lost are few and trivial. T. Warton's notes, copied from that able writer's edition of Milton's lesser poems, are the most valuable part of the work.

"Hayley is quite insane upon the subject of imputed similitude between Milton and Cowper as poets and men. He broaches it again and again, to the perfect nausea of all who can understand the writings of either, or who ever made a remark on their characters and destiny. To *such* it must be evident that only one point of similitude exists—that the best works of each are in *blank* verse. Between the *Paradise Lost* and the *Task* there is no *other* shadow of resemblance. The subject of the first, grave, dignified, regular, unbroken, and genuinely epic; that of the other, originally light and comic. Meantime, the poet floats through the pages of his desultory song, without rudder, without compass or anchor; yet he makes a varied and very interesting voyage, pleasing even to the most learned reader, and far more pleasing to the generality of readers than poetry of a higher order, because it presents objects familiar to their observation, and level with their capacity, and in numbers suited to the theme—sufficiently spirited and harmonious, but bearing no likeness to Milton's rich maze of alternately grand and delicate verse."

It appears that Mr. Bedford had been urged by Gifford to review this book, which he objected to do upon the plea of being a "very poor Italian scholar, and not at all read in Milton, whom," he continues, "I freely confess I do not understand sufficiently to be in the same raptures with, which our countrymen, in general, think it a national duty to feel."

To this my father replies:

To Grosvenor C. Bedford, Esq.

"Jan. 6, 1809.

"My dear Grosvenor,

"You make a confession respecting Milton which nine hundred and ninety-nine persons out of the thousand would make if they were honest enough; for his main excellences are like M. Angelo's, only to be thoroughly appreciated by an artist. This, however, by no means incapacitates you from reviewing Hayley's book, in which your business lies with Cowper and with his biographer, one of whose works (his Animal Ballads) I once reviewed by quoting from O'Keefe's song—*Hayley*, gaily, gamborally, higgledy, piggledy, galloping, draggle-tail, dreary dun. Hayley, as Miss Seward has just remarked to me in a letter, is perfectly insane upon the subject of Cowper's resemblance to Milton; there is no other resemblance between them than that both wrote in blank verse—but blank verse as different as possible. You may compare Cowper's translations (which, I suppose, are very bad, as many of his lesser pieces are, and as Miss Seward tells me) with Langhorne's; and you may estimate Cowper himself as a poet, as a man of intellect, and as a translator of Homer, showing that he is not overvalued; but that his popularity is owing to his piety, not his poetry, and that that piety was craziness. I like his letters, but think their so great popularity one of the very many proofs of the imbecility of the age. By-the-by, a very pretty piece of familiar verse, by Cowper, appeared, about two years ago, in the Monthly Magazine.

"Ah, Grosvenor! the very way in which you admire that passage in Kehama* convinces me that it ought not to be there. Did I not tell you it was clap-trappish? you are clapping as hard as you can to prove the truth of my opinion. That it grew there naturally is certain, but does it suit with the poem? is it of a piece or color with the whole? Is not the poet speaking in himself, whereas the whole character of the poem requires that he should be out of himself? I know very well that three parts of the public will agree with you in calling it the best thing in the poem, but my poem ought to have no things which do not necessarily belong to it. There will be a great deal to do to it, and a good deal is already done in the preceding parts.

"I have long expected a schism between the Grenvilles and the Foxites. Jeffrey has been trying to unite the Opposition and the Jacobins, as they are called. He *hurts* the Opposition, and he wrongs the Jacobins; he hurts the former by associating them with a name that is still unpopular, and he wrongs the friends of liberty by supposing that they are not the deadliest enemies of Bonaparte. Walter Scott, whom I look upon as as complete an anti-Jacobin as need be, does not sing out more loudly, 'Fight on, my merry men all!' than I do. General Moore must feel himself stronger than we have supposed him to be, or he would not advance into the plains of Castille. If he have 40,000, he will beat twice the number; and, for my own part, superior as he is in cavalry and artillery (ours being the best in the world), I do not see what we have to fear from numbers against him, for nothing can withstand our cavalry in a flat country. You know, Grosvenor, I never felt a fear till it was said he was retreating, and now that he is marching on, all my apprehensions are over. Huzza! it will be Rule Britannia by land as well as by sea.

"I have had a grievous cold, which has prevented me from rising as soon as it is light, and thereby, for a while, stopped Kehama. This evening I have corrected the fourth sheet of Brazil: the volume will be ready in the spring. I am now busy in filling up some skeleton chapters in the middle of the volume. This will be as true a history, and as industriously and painfully made, as ever yet appeared; yet I can not say that I expect much present approbation for it. It is deficient in fine circumstances; and as for what is called fine writing, the public will get none of that article from me; sound sense, sound philosophy, and sound English I will give them.

"I was beginning to wonder what was become of Wynn. Can you procure for me a copy of the report of the Court of Inquiry, or will you ask Rickman if he can? I do not write to him till the season of franking returns. I shall want it hereafter as one of my documents. Lord Moira has risen in my estimation; he is the only person who seems to have had any thing like a feeling of the moral strength which was on our side, and which we completely gave up by the convention. God bless you! R. S."

To Lieut. Southey, H.M.S. Dreadnought.

"Keswick, Jan. 10, 1809.

"MY DEAR TOM,

"I have corrected five sheets of the Brazil, and am now hard at work in transcribing and filling up skeleton chapters; that, in particular, which contains every thing concerning my friends the Tupinambas that has not inadvertently been said before. I wish you were here to hear it, as it gets on. There is a great pleasure in reading these things to any one who takes an interest in them—and, like our toast at breakfast, they seem the better for coming in fresh and fresh. I made an important discovery relative to De Lery—one of my best printed authorities—this morning. This author, who, though a Frenchman, was a very faithful writer, translated his own French into Latin, and I used the Latin edition in De Boy's collection—you remember the book with those hideous prints of the savages at their cannibal feasts—William Taylor laid hands on the French book, and sent it me; it arrived last Thursday only; and I, in transcribing with my usual scrupulous accuracy, constantly referred to this original, because I knew that when an author translates his own book, he often alters it, and therefore it was probable that I might sometimes find a difference worthy of notice. Well, I found my own references to the number of the chapter wrong; for the first time it passed well enough for a blunder, though I wondered at it a little, being remarkably exact in these things; the second time I thought it very extraordinary; and a third instance made me quite certain that something was wrong, but that the fault was not in me. Upon examination, it appeared that a whole chapter, and that chapter the most important as to the historical part of the volume, had been omitted by De Boy, because he was a Catholic, De Lery a Huguenot, and this chapter exposed the villainy of Villegagnon, who went to Brazil expressly to establish an asylum for the Huguenots; when there, was won over by the Guises, apostatized, and thus ruined a colony, which must else inevitably have made Rio de Janeiro now the capital of a French instead of a Portuguese empire. The main facts I had collected before, and clearly understood; but the knavery of a Roman Catholic editor had thus nearly deprived me of my best and fullest authority, and of some very material circumstances, for no one has ever yet suspected this collection of being otherwise than faithful, though it is now more than two hundred years old. See here the necessity of tracing every thing to the fountain-head when it is possible.

"What you said about transports I repeated to Bedford: he made inquiry, and understood the

* See Curse of Kehama, Canto x., verse 20, commencing,

"They sin who tell us love can die."

objection came from the navy captains, who did not like to have their ships encumbered, or to *feel* as if they were transports. I repeated it to Coleridge and Wordsworth, and through them it has reached Stuart, and got into the Courier, whether or not with effect time will show; but there is nothing like sending so obvious a truth afloat: it will find its way sooner or later. I see the captains are petitioning for an increase of pay: they will get it, to be sure, and then the increase must extend to you also.

"Things in Spain look well. Bonaparte's bulletins prove beyond all doubt that every heart is against him, and his threat of taking the crown himself is the perfect phrensy of anger. Sir John Moore's movements backward and forward have been mere moves at chess to gain time, and wait for a blunder on the part of the adversary—so Bedford tells me; and his intelligence is good, coming from Herries, who is Perceval's secretary, and Gifford, who is in Canning's confidence. Moore is a very able man, and is acting with a boldness which gives every body confidence that knows him. He will beat twice his own number of Frenchmen; and I do not think greater odds can be brought against him. It looks well, that in this fresh embarkation, the officers are desired not to take more baggage than they can carry themselves. At him, Trojan! We shall beat him, Tom, upon Spanish ground. Let but our men fairly see the faces of the French in battle, and they will soon see their backs too.

"The Grenvilles and Foxites are likely to separate upon the question of peace. Canning hankers after the Grenvilles, and would do much to bring them in with him instead of his wretched associates. They are not popular; but, if they had courage to make a home charge upon the Duke of York, and insist upon his removal as a preliminary and *sine quâ non* to their going in, that measure would win them a popularity which would carry them in in spite of every obstacle. God bless you!

"Yours, R. S."

To Lieut. Southey, H.M.S. Dreadnought.

"Keswick, Feb. 3, 1809.

"We want a Nelson in the army. Poor Sir John Moore was too cautious a man. He waited, in distrust of the Spaniards, to see what course the war would take, instead of being on the spot to make it take the course he wished. When Hope was at the passes of the Guadarrama Mountain, he and the rest of the army should have been at Samosierra, the other key to Madrid. There would have been re-enforcements sent if he had not positively written to have empty transports, and the men were therefore disembarked. Had there been twenty thousand fresh troops at Corunna to have met the French, what a victory should we have obtained, when even with the wreck of an army, foot-sore, broken-hearted, and half starved, we defeated them so completely at the last! One thing results from this action—the fear of invasion must be at rest forever. We can beat the French under every possible disadvantage, and with two, almost, indeed, three to one against us. Come, then, Bonaparte! the sooner the better.

"Ministers are jarring with each other. It is Canning who stands up for Spain; and I learn from Walter Scott that they will stand by the Spaniards to the last, cost what it may. But they paralyze one another, and the rest of the cabinet—by meeting him half way, doing *half* what he proposes—utterly undoes every thing. Still, if we had a few such men as Cochrane in the army—men who would have the same faith in British bottom by land as we have at sea, that faith would redeem us. To be upon the defensive in the field is ruin. Men never can win a battle unless they are determined to win it, and expect to win it; and that can not be the case when they wait to be attacked. 100,000 men in Spain would overthrow and destroy Bonaparte; but we send them in batches to be cut up. We squander the strength of the country, we waste the blood of the country, we sacrifice the honor of the country, and bring upon ourselves a disgrace, which Bonaparte, were he ten times more powerful than he is, could never inflict upon us, were there but true wisdom and right courage in our rulers.

"But, though Bonaparte may take the country, he can not keep it. He would not have done what he has if the Spaniards had proclaimed a republic, for which, you may remember, I pointed out the peculiar fitness which their separate states afforded.

"The new review is to be called the Quarterly, and will, I suppose, soon start. I fancy W. Scott has taken care of the Cid there. Of the new edition of Thalaba, nine books are printed. It would be convenient if I could borrow from my Hindoo gods a few of their supernumerary heads and hands, for I find more employment than my present complement can get through.

"Holding that my face will 'carry off a drab,' I have a new coat of that complexion just come home from Johnny Cockbains, the king of the tailors.

"God bless you! R. S."

To Mr. Ebenezer Elliott.

"Keswick, Feb. 3, 1809.

"SIR,

"Yesterday I received your note inclosing the specimen of your poems. I have perused that specimen, but my advice can not be comprised in a few words.

"A literary as well as a medical opinion, Mr. Elliott, must needs be blindly given, unless the age and circumstances of the person who requires it are known. When I advised Henry White to publish a second volume of poems, it was because he had fixed his heart upon a University education, and this seemed to be a feasible method of raising funds for that end, his particular circumstances rendering that prudent which would otherwise have been very much the reverse; for poetry is not a marketable article unless there be something strange or peculiar to give it a fashion; and in his case, what money might possibly have been raised would, in almost every instance, have been considered rather as given to the author than paid for his book. Your poem would not find purchasers except in the circle of your own friends; out of that circle not twenty copies would be sold. I believe not half that number.

"You are probably a young man, sir, and it is plain from this specimen that you possess more than one of those powers which form the poet, and those in a far more than ordinary degree. Whether your plans of life are such as to promise leisure for that attention (almost, it might be said, that devotement), without which no man can ever become a great poet, you yourself must know. If they should, you will in a very few years have outgrown this poem, and would then be sorry to see it in print, irrecoverably given to the public, because you would feel it to be an inadequate proof of your own talents. If, on the other hand, you consider poetry as merely an amusement or an ornament of youth, to be laid aside in riper years for the ordinary pursuits of the world, with still less indulgence will you then regard the printed volume, for you will reckon it among the follies of which you are ashamed. In either case it is best not to publish.

"It is far, very far from my wish to discourage or depress you. There is great promise in this specimen: it has all the faults which I should wish to see in the writings of a young poet, as the surest indications that he has that in him which will enable him to become a good one. But no young man can possibly write a good narrative poem, though I believe he can not by any other means so effectually improve himself as by making the attempt. I myself published one at the age of twenty-one: it made a reputation for me—not so much by its merits, as because it was taken up by one party, and abused by another, almost independently of its merits or demerits, at a time when party spirit was more violent than it is to be hoped it will ever be again. What has been the consequences of this publication? That the poem from beginning to end was full of incorrect language and errors of every kind; that all the weeding of years could never weed it clean; and that many people at this day rate me, not according to the standard of my present intellect, but by what it was fourteen years ago. Your subject, also, has the same disadvantage with mine, that it is anti-national; and believe me, this is a grievous one; for, though we have both been right in our feelings, yet to feel *against* our own country can only be right upon great and transitory occasions, and none but our cotemporaries can feel with us—none but those who remember the struggle and took part in it. And you are more unfortunate than I was, for America is acting at this time unnaturally against England; and every reader will feel this; and his sense of what the Americans are now, will make him fancy that you paint falsely in describing them as they were then. There is yet another reason—criticism is conducted upon a different plan from what it was when I commenced my career. You live near the Dragon of Wantley's den; but you will provoke enemies as venomous if you publish; and Heaven knows whether or no you are gifted with armor of proof against them. Nor is it the effect that malicious censure and ridicule might produce upon your own feelings which is of so much importance, as what would be produced upon your friends. They who are so only in name will derive a provoking pleasure from seeing you laughed at and abused; they who love you will feel more pain than you yourself, because you will and must have a higher confidence in yourself, and a stronger conviction of injustice than they can be supposed to possess.

"The sum of my advice is, do not publish this poem; but if you can, without grievous imprudence, afford to write poetry, continue so to do, because, hereafter, you will write it well. As yet you have only green fruit to offer; wait a season, and there will be a fair and full gathering when it is ripe.

'ROBERT SOUTHEY."

To Walter Savage Landor, Esq.

"Keswick, Feb. 9, 1809.

"You have a bill coming before Parliament. The speaker's secretary happens to be one of my very intimate friends, and one of the men in the world for whom I have the highest respect. It may be some convenience to you on this occasion to know him, because he can give you every necessary information respecting Parliamentary business, and thus, perhaps, spare you some needless trouble; and there needs no other introduction than knocking at his door and sending up your name, with which he is well acquainted. Rickman is his name; and you will find it over his door, in St. Stephen's Court, New Palace Yard, next door to the speaker's. I will tell you what kind of man he is. His outside has so little polish about it, that once having gone from Christ Church to Pool in his own boat, he was taken by the press-gang, his robust figure, hard-working hands, and strong voice all tending to deceive them. A little of this is worn off. He is the strongest and clearest-headed man that I have ever known. 'Pondere, numero et mensurâ' is his motto; but to all things he carries the same reasoning and investigating intellect as to mathematical science, and will find out in Homer and the Bible facts necessarily to be inferred from the text, and which yet have as little been supposed to be there intimated as the existence of metal was suspected in potash before Davy detected it there. I have often said that I learned how to see for the purposes of poetry from Gebir, how to read for the purposes of history from Rickman. His manners are stoical: they are like the husk of the cocoa-nut, and his inner nature is like the milk within its kernel. When I go to London I am always his guest. He gives me but half his hand when he welcomes me at the door, but I have his whole heart—and there is not that thing in the world which he thinks would serve or gratify me that he does not do for me, unless it be something which he thinks I can as well do myself. The subject which he best understands is political economy. Were there but half a dozen such men in the House of Commons, there would be courage, virtue, and wisdom enough there to save this country from that revolution to which it is so certainly approaching.

"I should not have written just now had it not been to mention Rickman, thinking that you may find it useful to know him; for I wished, when writing, to tell you of Kehama: a good many interruptions have occurred to delay my progress, indispositions of my own or of the children—the latter the only things concerning which I am anxious over much. At present my wife is seriously ill, and when I shall be sufficiently at rest to do any thing, God knows. Another heat will finish the poem.

"Coleridge's essay* is expected to start in March.

"My uncle, Mr. Hill, is settled at his parsonage, at Staunton-upon-Wye—in that savage part of the world to which your cedar plantation will give new beauty, and your name new interest, when those cedars shall have given place to their offspring: it is probable that you have no other neighbor so well informed within the same distance. Next year, God willing, I shall travel to the south, and halt with him; it is likely I may then find you out, either at Llantony or somewhere in the course of a wide circuit. Meantime I will still hope that some fair breeze of inclination may send you here to talk about Spain, to plan a great poem, and to cruise with me about Derwentwater. God bless you!

"R. SOUTHEY."

To Grosvenor C. Bedford, Esq.

"Feb. 12, 1809.

"MY DEAR GROSVENOR,

"How shall I thank you for the pleasure and delight of your excellent and pretty letter, inclosing the half quarter of my poor mutilated pension? That pension makes me disposed to swear every time it comes.

"I have been busy in using borrowed books, which were to be returned with great speed, and which were like woodcocks, all trail. They cost me three weeks' incessant application—that is, all the application I could command. I waited to begin a new article for the Quarterly till the first number was published; and as that is so near at hand, will begin to-morrow. But if Gifford likes my pattern-work, he should send me more cloth to cut; he should send me Travels, which I review better than any thing else. I am impatient to see the first number. Young lady never felt more desirous to see herself in a new ball-dress, than I do to see my own performance in print, often as that gratification falls to my lot. The reason is, that in the multiplicity of my employments, I forget the form and manner of every thing as soon as it is out of sight, and they come to me like pleasant recollections of what I wish to remember. Besides, the thing looks differently in print. In short, Mr. Bedford, there are a great many philosophical reasons for this fancy of mine, and one of the best of all reasons is, that I hold it good to make every thing a pleasure which it is possible to make so. And these sort of Claude's spectacles are very convenient things for a man who lives in a land of rain and clouds: they make an artificial sunshine for what some people would call gloomy weather. * * * *

"God bless you! In a few days I will create leisure for another number of Kehama. I have not written a line of it these last two months: first, I was indisposed myself; then the children were: lastly, my wife. Anxiety unfits me for any thing that requires feeling as well as thought. I can labor, I can think—thought and labor will not produce poetry.

"In haste, yours, ROBERT SOUTHEY."

To John May, Esq.

"Keswick, Feb. 16, 1809.

"MY DEAR FRIEND,

" * * * * * * *

What is your Lisbon news? Notwithstanding the Duke of York and Mrs. Clarke, I think of those countries; and notwithstanding the disasters which our gross misconduct could not fail to bring on, my confidence in the ultimate success of a good cause remains undiminished. I could have wished, indeed, that the work of reformation, which Joseph Bonaparte is beginning, had been begun by the junta that they had called the principle of liberty as well as of loyalty to their aid, and made freedom their watchword as well as the Virgin Mary, for she may be on both sides. Certainly it was not easy to do this; and I have always suspected that those leaders, such as Palafox, who might have wished to do it, bore in mind the first great struggle of the Portuguese against Castille, when the Infante Don João, a prisoner and in chains, served as João the First's stalking-horse, and was painted upon his banner, till he found he could safely assume the crown himself. The convenience of such a name as Ferdinand, and the stain which France has brought upon the very name of Republicanism, were causes which might well induce a timid, and, therefore, a feeble line of conduct. * * * Why is Bonaparte gone to Paris at such a time? If any change in the north should call him into Germany, with only part of his army, the tide will roll back, and King Joseph be forced a second time to decamp. Meantime I expect a desperate resistance about the southern coast, wherever our ships can be of use. Is it possible we can leave Elvas without seeing it well garrisoned? the place is absolutely impregnable. Moore would have done wisely had he fallen back upon the frontier, where there was a double line of fortified towns, into which he might have thrown his troops whenever he felt it necessary to leave the mountains;

* The Friend.

and against those fortresses the French would have wasted, and must have divided their force, allowing us time to send out another army. Regular armies in such wars as this must always be successful in the field, but they have always met their chief disasters before fortified towns; tactics are nothing there, individual courage every thing; and women and children fight by the side of their husbands or their fathers, from the windows, on the house-tops, or on the walls.

"Have you seen William Taylor's Defense of the Slave Trade in Bolinbroke's Voyage to the Demerary? It is truly William Taylorish; thoroughly ingenious, as usual, but not ingenuous; he weakens the effect of his own arguments by keeping the weak side of his cause altogether out of sight. In defending the slave trade, as respects the duty of man toward man, he has utterly failed; he has succeeded in what you and I shall think of more consequence—in showing what the probable end is for which wise Providence has so long permitted the existence of so great an evil. * * * * *

"Believe me, yours affectionately,

"Robert Southey."

To W. Gifford, Esq.

"Keswick, March 6, 1809.

"Sir,

"Your letter, and its inclosed draft, reached me this afternoon. I have to acknowledge the one, and thank you for the other. It gratifies me that you approve my defense of the missionaries, because I am desirous of such approbation; and it will gratify me if it should be generally approved, because I wrote from a deep and strong conviction of the importance of the subject. With respect to any alteration in this or any future communication, I am perfectly sensible that absolute authority must always be vested in the editor. The printer has done some mischief by misplacing a paragraph in p. 225, which ought to have followed the quotation in the preceding page. The beginning of the last paragraph is made unintelligible by this dislocation; and, indeed, you have omitted the sarcasm which it was designed to justify. I could have wished that this Review had less resembled the Edinburgh in the tone and temper of its criticisms. That book of Miss Owenson's is, I dare say, very bad both in manners and morals; yet, had it fallen into my hands, I think I could have told her so in such a spirit, that she herself would have believed me, and might have profited by the censure. The same quantity of rain which would clear a flower of its blights, will, if it falls heavier and harder, wash the roots bare, and beat the blossoms to the ground. I have been in the habit of reviewing more than eleven years, for the lucre of gain, and not, God knows, from any liking to the occupation; and of all my literary misdeeds, the only ones of which I have repented have been those reviewals which were written with undue asperity, so as to give unnecessary pain. I propose to continue the subject of the Missions through two other articles, neither of which will probably be half so long as the first—one respecting the South Sea Islands, the other South Africa. Lord Valentia's book I shall be glad to receive, and any others which you may think proper to intrust to me. Two things I can promise—perfect sincerity in what I write, without the slightest assumption of knowledge which I do not possess, and a punctuality not to be exceeded by that of Mr. Murray's opposite neighbors at St. Dunstan's.

"I am sir, yours very respectfully,

"Robert Southey."

To Lieut. Southey, H.M.S. Dreadnought.

"Keswick, March 14, 1809.

"My dear Tom,

"Yesterday I returned from a visit to Henry and his bride. * * * * * He lives in a street called by the unaccountable name of Old Elvet. A lucky opening on the opposite side of the way leaves him a good view of the Cathedral on the hill, and the river is within a stone's throw of his back door. Durham stands upon a peninsula—that is to say, the main part of it—a high bank, on which is the Cathedral, and the castle, and the best houses; and there are delightful walks below, such as no other city can boast, through fine old trees on the river's bank, from whence you look to the noble building on the opposite side, and see one bridge through the other. Harry is well off there, getting rapidly into practice, and living among all sorts of people—prebends and Roman Catholics, fox-hunters and old women, with all of whom he seems to accord equally well. * * * It is a place where any person might live contentedly. Among all these thousand and one acquaintances there are some whom one might soon learn to love, and a great many with whom to be amused, and none that are insufferable. One day I dined with Dr. Zouch, who wrote the Life of Sir P. Sidney. I never saw a gentler-minded man; the few sentences of bigotry which he has written must have cost him strange efforts to bring forth, for I do not think a harsh expression ever could pass his lips, nor a harsh feeling ever enter his heart. In spite of his deafness, I contrived to have a good deal of talk with him. Dr. Bell was there, the original transplanter of that Hindoo system of teaching which Lancaster has adopted. He is a great friend of Coleridge's; a man pleasant enough, *certes* a great benefactor to his country, but a little given to flattery, and knowing less about India than a man ought to know who has lived there. Another day I dined with Dr. Fenwick, the ex-physician of the place. There we drank the Arch-duke Charles's health in Tokay, a wine which I had never before tasted. This is the first victory by which I ever got any thing. The Tokay proved prolific. Harry's next door neighbor was one of the party, and fancied some unknown wine which had been presented to him might be the same as this; and he proposed, as we walked home, to bring in a bottle and sup with us. I, nowever, recognized it for Old Sack—itself no bad thing.

* * * * * * *

"On Monday last, after a week's visit, I took coach where I had appointed, to pass a day with James Losh, whom you know I have always mentioned as coming nearer the ideal of a perfect man than any other person whom it has ever been my good fortune to know; so gentle, so pious, so zealous in all good things, so equal-minded, so manly, so without speck or stain in his whole habits of life. I slept at his house, which is two miles from Newcastle, and the next day took the mail to Carlisle. It is an interesting road, frequently in sight of the Tyne before you reach Hexham, and then as frequently along the Eden. We reached Carlisle at ten o'clock. Yesterday I rose at five, and walked to Hesket to breakfast, fourteen miles; a mile lost on the way made it fifteen. There was many a gentle growl within for the last five miles. From thence another stage of fourteen brought me home by half after two—a good march, performed with less fatigue than any other of equal length in the whole course of my pedestrian campaigns.

"I found all well at home, God be praised! Your letter was waiting for me, and one from Gifford, containing £16 8*s.* for my article in the second Quarterly, with *quant. suff.* of praise, which I put down to the account of due desert. He has a reviewal of Holmes's American Annals in his hands for the third number. I am about the Polynesian Mission, and am to have Lord Valencia's Travels as soon as they appear. He requested me to choose any subjects I pleased. I have named Barlow's Columbiad, Elton's Hesiod, and Whitaker's Life of St. Neots; and I have solicited the office of justifying Frere against Sir John Moore's friends. * * * * Send for Wordsworth's pamphlet:* the more you read it the higher will be your admiration. * * * * *

"God bless you! R. S."

To Richard Duppa, Esq.

"March 31, 1809.

"MY DEAR DUPPA,

"I am sorry for your loss—a heavy one under any circumstances, and particularly so to one who, being single at your time of life, will now feel more entirely what it is to have no person who intimately loves him. It is not in the order of nature that there should ever be a void in the heart of man—the old leaves should not fall from the tree till the young ones are expanding to supply their place.

"I have now three girls living, and as delightful a play-fellow in the shape of a boy as ever man was blessed with. Very often, when I look at them, I think what a fit thing it would be that Malthus should be hanged.

"You may have known that I have some dealings, in the way of trade, with your bookseller, Murray. One article of mine is in his first Quarterly, and he has bespoken more. Whenever I shall have the satisfaction of seeing you once more under this roof, it will amuse you to see how dexterously Gifford emasculated this article of mine of its most forcible parts. I amused myself one morning with putting them all in again, and restoring vigor, consistency, and connection to the whole. It is certainly true that his majesty gives me a pension of £200 a year, out of which his majesty deducts £60 and a few shillings; but, if his majesty trebled or decupled the pension, and remitted the whole taxation, it would be the same thing. The treasury should never bribe, nor his judges deter me from delivering a full and free opinion upon any subject which seems to me to call for it. If I hate Bonaparte, and maintain that this country never ought to accept of any peace while that man is Emperor of France, it is precisely upon the same principle that I formerly disliked Pitt, and maintained that we never ought to have gone to war.

"I am glad you have been interested by the Cid; it is certainly the most curious chronicle in existence. In the course of the summer—I hope early in it—you will see the first volume of my History of Brazil, of which nine-and-twenty sheets are printed. This book has cost me infinite labor. The Cid was an easy task; of that no other copy was made than what went to the press; of this every part has been twice written, many parts three times, and all with my own hand. For this I expect to get a sufficient quantity of abuse, and little else; money is only to be got by such productions as are worth nothing more than what they fetch per sheet. I could get my thousand a year if I would but do my best endeavors to be dull, and aim at nothing higher than Reviews and Magazines

"God bless you!

"Yours very truly,

"R. SOUTHEY."

To Walter Savage Landor, Esq.

"April 23, 1809.

"I shall send three sections of Kehama to meet you in London; three more will complete it, and would have so done before this time had all things been going on well with me. I had a daughter born on the 27th of last month; a few days after the birth her mother was taken ill, and for some time there was cause of serious alarm. This, God be thanked, is over. The night before last we had another alarm of the worst kind, though happily this also is passing away. My little boy went to bed with some slight indications of a trifling cold. His mother went up as usual to look at him before supper; she thought he coughed in a strange manner, called me, and I instantly recognized the sound of the croup. We have a good apothecary within three minutes' walk, and luckily he was at home. He immediately confirmed our fears. The child was taken out of bed and bled in the jugular vein, a blister placed on the throat next

* On the Convention of Cintra.

morning, and by these vigorous and timely remedies we hope and trust the disease is subdued. But what a twelve hours did we pass, knowing the nature of the disease, and only hoping the efficacy of the remedy. Even now I am far, very far, from being at ease. There is a love which passeth the love of women, and which is more lightly alarmed than the wakefullest jealousy.

"Landor, I am not a stoic at home: I feel as you do about the fall of an old tree; but, O Christ! what a pang it is to look upon the young shoot and think it will be cut down. And this is the thought which almost at all times haunts me; it comes upon me in moments when I know not whether the tears that start are of love or of bitterness. There is an evil, too, in seeing all things like a poet; circumstances which would glide over a healthier mind sink into mine; every thing comes to me with its whole force—the full meaning of a look, a gesture, a child's imperfect speech, I can perceive, and can not help perceiving; and thus am I made to remember what I would give the world to forget.

"Enough, and too much of this. The leaven of anxiety is working in my whole system; I will try to quiet it by forcing myself to some other subject.

"What prevented Gebir from being read by the foolish? I believe the main reason was, that it is too hard for them; more than that, it was too good. That they should understand its merits was not to be expected; but they did not find meaning enough upon the surface to make them fancy they understood it. Why should you not write a poem as good, and more intelligible, and display the same powers upon a happier subject? Yet certain it is that Gebir excited far more attention than you seem to be aware of. Two manifest imitations have appeared, Rough's Play of the Conspiracy of Gowrie, and the first part of Sotheby's Saul. When Gifford published his Juvenal, one of the most base attacks that ever disgraced a literary journal was made upon it in the Critical Review by some one of the heroes of his Baviad. Gifford wrote an angry reply, in which he brought forward all the offenses of the Review for many years back: one of those offenses was its praise of Gebir. I laughed when I heard this, guessing pretty well at the nature of Gifford's feelings, for I had been the reviewer of whose partiality he complained. Gebir came to me with a parcel of other poems which I was to kill off. I was young in the trade, and reviewed it injudiciously, so that every body supposed it to be done by some friend of the author; for I analyzed the story; studded it with as many beautiful extracts as they would allow room for; praised its merits almost up to the height of my feelings, and never thought of telling the reader that if he went to the book itself he would find any more difficulty in comprehending it than he found in that abstract. Thus, instead of serving the poem, I in reality injured it. The world, nowadays, never believes praise to be sincere; men are so accustomed to hunt for faults, that they will not think any person can honestly express unmingled admiration.

"I once passed an evening with Professor Young at Davy's. The conversation was wholly scientific, and, of course, I was a listener. But I have heard the history of Thomas Young, as he is still called by those who knew him when he was a Quaker, and believe him to be a very able man. Generally speaking, I have little liking for men of science: their pursuits seem to deaden the imagination and harden the heart; they are so accustomed to analyze and anatomize every thing—to understand, or fancy they understand whatever comes before them, that they frequently become mere materialists, account for every thing by mechanism and motion, and would put out of the world all that makes the world endurable. I do not undervalue their knowledge, nor the utility of their discoveries; but I do not like the men. My own nature requires something more than they teach; it pants after things unseen; it exists upon the hope of that better futurity which all its aspirations promise and seem to prove.

"God bless you! R. S."

To Grosvenor C. Bedford, Esq.

"April 30, 1809.

"MY DEAR GROSVENOR,

"It would not be easy to tell you all I have suffered since Tuesday night, when Herbert was seized with the croup. God be praised! the disease seems to be subdued; but he is still in a state to make us very anxious: pale with loss of blood, his neck blistered, and fevered by the fretfulness the blister occasions. The poor child has been so used to have me for his play-fellow, that he will have me for his nurse, and you may imagine with what feelings I endeavor to amuse him. But, thank God! he is living, and likely to live.

"Almost the only wish I ever give utterance to is that the next hundred years were over. It is not that the uses of this world seem to me weary, stale, flat, and unprofitable—God knows, far otherwise! No man can be better contented with his lot. My paths are paths of pleasantness. I am living happily, and, to the best of my belief, fulfilling, as far as I am able, the purposes for which I was created. Still the instability of human happiness is ever before my eyes; I long for the certain and the permanent; and, perhaps, my happiest moments are those when I am looking on to another state of being, in which there shall be no other change than that of progressing in knowledge, and thereby in power and enjoyment.

"I have suffered some sorrow in my time, and expect to suffer much more; but, looking into my own heart, I do not believe that a single pang could have been spared. My Herbert says to me, 'O, you are very naughty,' when I hold his hands while his neck is dressed. I have as deep a conviction that whatever affliction I have ever endured, or yet have to endure, is dispensed to me in mercy and in love, as he will have for my motives for inflicting pain upon him now—if it should please God that he should ever live to understand them.

"It is three months before the third Quarterly will appear, and by that time present topics will have become stale; but I wish you would let Gifford know, that if the subject is not out of time, and it be thought fit to notice it, I will right zealously and fearlessly undertake a justification of Frere's conduct, which we in this part of the country do entirely approve. God bless you! R. S."

To Lieut. Southey, H.M.S. Dreadnought.

"Keswick, Monday, May 22, 1809.

"MY DEAR TOM,

"My last letter told you of Herbert's danger and his recovery. You will be a little shocked at the intelligence in this. We lost Emma yesterday night. Five days ago she was in finer health than we had ever seen her, and I repeatedly remarked it. For a day or two she had been ailing; on Saturday night breathed shortly, and was evidently ill. Edmondson repeatedly saw her, thought her better at ten o'clock, and assured us he saw no danger. In half an hour she literally fell asleep without a struggle. Edith is as well as should be expected, and I, perhaps, better. You know how I take toothache and tooth-drawings, and I have almost learned to bear moral pain, not, indeed, with the same levity, but with as few outward and visible signs. In fact, God be thanked for it, there never was a man who had more entirely set his heart upon things permanent and eternal than I have done; the transitoriness of every thing here is always present to my feeling as well as my understanding. Were I to speak as sincerely of my family as Wordsworth's little girl, my story—that I have five children; three of them at home, and two under my mother's care in heaven—No more of this; and, to convince you that I am not more unhappy than I profess, I will fill up the sheep, instead of sending you a mere annotation of this loss. It is well you left her such an infant, for you are thus spared some sorrow.

"Ballantyne has just sent me a present of Campbell's new poem, and inclosed the last Edinburgh Review in the parcel. They have taken occasion there, under cover of a Methodist book, to attempt an answer to my Missionary Defense. I hear from all quarters that this article of mine has excited much notice, and produced considerable effect. It had the great advantage of being in earnest, as well as thoroughly understanding the subject. The Edinburgh reviewer knew nothing of Hindoo history except what newspapers and pamphlets had taught him. * * * No wonder, therefore, that I should have the upper hand of such a man in the argument.

"Campbell's poem has disappointed his friends, Ballantyne tells me. It is, however, better than I expected, except in story, which is meager. This gentleman, also, who is one of Wordsworth's abusers, has been nibbling at imitation, and palpably borrowed from the two poems of Ruth and The Brothers. 'Tis amusing envy! to see how the race of borrowers upon all occasions abuse us who do not borrow. The main topic against me is, that I do not imitate Virgil in my story, Pope in my language, &c., &c.

"Scott is still detained in London, and this will prevent me from going with him to Edinburgh. Indeed, if engagements had not existed, I could not have left home now, for Edith will find it melancholy enough for some time to come with me, and without me it would be worse. Herbert, thank God! seems well; *seems* is all one dares say: of all precarious things, there is nothing so precarious as life. You would have been delighted with your eldest niece if you could have seen the sorrow she was in this morning for fear her mother should die for grief, and then she said she should die too, and then her papa would die for grief about her. Just now, Tom, it might have been happier for you and me if we had gone to bed as early as John and Eliza; a hundred years hence the advantage will be on our side. * * My notions about life are much the same as they are about traveling—there is a good deal of amusement on the road, but, after all, one wants to be at rest. Evils of this kind—if they may be called evils—soon cure themselves; the wound smarts, in a little while it heals, and, if the scar did not sometimes renew the recollection of the smart, it would, perhaps, be forgotten.

"My History gets on; the proof before me reaches to page 336: I look at it with great pleasure. Whether I may live to complete the series of works which I have projected, and, in good part, executed, God only knows; be that as it may, in what is done I shall, to the best of my power, have on all occasions enforced good opinions upon those subjects which are of most importance to mankind.

"God bless you! It is long since I have heard from you: what can you be cruising after? Things go on well in Spain, and will go on better when the Wellesleys get there. Once more, God bless you! R. S."

In the preceding letter my father refers to an intention of accompanying Sir Walter Scott to Edinburgh, which could not be carried into effect, owing to the latter having been detained in London. While there, with characteristic friendliness, he had been using his influence in my father's behalf with his friends connected with the government, and he now thus communicates to him his expectations of success, expressing his hope that they would still be able to travel in company to Scotland.

"I have much to say to you about the Quarterly Review, Rhadamanthus,* &c. I do not apprehend that there is any great risk of our

* This refers to a scheme of my father's (which Ballantyne was at one time anxious to engage in) for a Review "to exclude all cotemporary publications, and to select its subjects from all others." The plan, however, was never matured.

politics differing when there are so many strings in unison, but it may doubtless happen. Meanwhile, every one is grateful for your curious and invaluable article; and this leads me to a subject which I would rather have spoken than written upon, but the doubt of seeing you obliges me to touch upon it. George Ellis and I have both seen a strong desire in Mr. Canning to be of service to you in any way within his power that could be pointed out, and this without any reference to political opinions. An official situation in his own department was vacant, and, I believe, still is so; but it occurred to George Ellis and me that the salary—£300 a year—was inadequate for an office occupying much time, and requiring constant attendance. But there are professors' chairs both in England and Scotland frequently vacant; and there is hardly one, except such as are absolutely professional, for which you are not either fitted already, or capable of making yourself so on a short notice. There are also diplomatic and other situations, should you prefer them to the groves of Academus. * * * Mr. Canning's opportunities to serve you will soon be numerous, or they will be gone altogether, for he is of a different mold from the rest of his colleagues, and a decided foe to those half measures which I know you detest as much as I do. It is not his fault that the cause of Spain is not at this moment triumphant. This I know, and there will come a time when the world will know it too. * * * Think over the thing in your own mind, and let it, if possible, determine you on your northern journey. What would I not give to secure you a chair in our northern metropolis! * * * * * I ought in conscience to have made ten thousand pretty detours about all this, and paid some glowing compliments both to the minister and the bard; but they may all be summed up by saying, in one sober word, that Mr. C. could not have entertained a thought more honorable to himself, and, knowing him as I do, I must add, more honorable and flattering to your genius and learning."*

My father's reply was as follows:

To Walter Scott, Esq.

"Keswick, June 16, 1809.

"Dear Scott,

"My friends leave Bristol on Monday next, on their way hither; you thus perceive how impossible it is that I can now accompany you to Edinburgh, as I should else willingly have done.

"The latter part of your letter requires a confidential answer. I once wished to reside in Portugal, because the great object of my literary life related to that country: I loved the country, and had then an uncle settled there. Before Fox came into power this was told him by Charles Wynn, and, when he was in power, he was asked by Wynn to send me there. It so happened that John Allen wanted something which was in Lord Grenville's gift, and this was given him on condition that Fox, in return, provided for me. There were two things in Portugal which I could hold—the consulship, or the secretaryship of legation. The former was twice given away, but that Fox said was too good a thing for me; the latter he promised if an opportunity occurred of promoting Lord Strangford, and that never took place. Grey was reminded of his predecessor's engagement, and expressed no disinclination to fulfill it. The party got turned out; and one of the last things Lord Grenville did was to give me a pension of £200. Till that time I had received one of £160 from Charles W. Wynn, my oldest surviving friend. The exchange leaves me something the poorer, as the Exchequer deducts above sixty pounds. This is all I have. Half my time I sell to the booksellers; the other half is reserved for works which will never pay for the paper on which they are written, but on which I rest my future fame. I am, of course, straitened in circumstances; a little more would make me easy. My chance of inheritance is gone by: my father's elder brother was worth £40,000, but he cut me off without the slightest cause of offense.

"You will see by this that I would willingly be served, but it is not easy to serve me. Lisbon is too insecure a place to remove to with a family, and nothing could repay me for going without them. I have neither the habits nor talents for an official situation; nor, if I had, could I live in London—that is, I should soon die there. I have said to Wynn that one thing would make me at ease for life—create for me the title of Royal Historiographer for England (there is one for Scotland), with a salary of £400: the reduction would leave a net income of £278; with that I should be sure of all the decent comforts of life, and, for every thing beyond them, it would then be easy to supply myself. Of course, my present pension would cease. Whether Mr. Canning can do this, I know not; but, if this could be done, it would be adequate to all I want, and beyond that my wishes have never extended. I am sorry we are not to meet, but it would be unreasonable to expect it now; and, at some more convenient season, I will find my way to you and to the Advocate's Library. You will hear from Ballantyne what my plan is for Rhadamanthus, concerning which I shall think nothing more till I hear from him upon the subject. Since last you heard from me, I have lost one of my children; the rest, thank God! are well. Edith desires to be remembered to you and Mrs. Scott.

"Believe me, yours very truly,

"Robert Southey."

To Walter Scott, Esq.

"Keswick, July 6, 1809.

"My dear Scott,

"I have just been informed that the stewardship for the Derwentwater estates (belonging to Greenwich Hospital), now held by a Mr. Walton, is expected soon to be vacated by his death. It

* London, June 14, 1809.

is a situation which would give me a respectable income, perfectly suit my present place of abode, and not impose upon me more business than I could properly perform with comfort to myself. Mr. Sharp tells me this, and from him I learn that Mr. Long is one of the directors. Could this be obtained for me, I should be well provided for, and in a pleasant way; so I have thought it right to mention it, in consequence of your last letter, and, having so done, shall dismiss the subject from my thoughts. *Pelle timorem, spemque fugato*, is a lesson which I learned early in life from Boëthius, and have been a good deal the happier for practicing.

"The second Quarterly is better than the first. The affairs of Austria are treated with great power, great spirit, and clear views. I expected the utter overthrow of the house of Austria, and my fears have happily been disappointed. They have profited by experience, and, though every thing is now upon the balance, and one can not open the newspaper without great anxiety and many doubts, still it does appear that the chances are in our favor. One defeat will not destroy the emperor, if he is only true to himself, but one defeat would destroy Bonaparte. His authority, out of France, is maintained wholly by force; in France, by the opinion of his good fortune and the splendor of his successes. One thorough defeat will dissolve the spell. His colossal power then falls to pieces, like the image in Nebuchadnezzar's dream. I am afraid our expedition will be too late to turn the scale. If it were now in Germany it might do wonders; but we are always slow in our measures, and game so timorously that we are sure to lose. Why not twice forty thousand men? It has been proved that we can always beat the French with equal numbers, or at any time when we are not previously outnumbered. Why then send a force that can so easily be doubled or trebled by the enemy? For allied armies can not act together, and whatever battle we have to fight must be fought alone. Marlborough was the only general who could wield a confederacy.

"I have made offer of my services to Gifford to undertake Frere's justification against the friends of Sir John Moore, if it be thought advisable. I have offered also to provide for the fourth number a paper upon Methodism, which would be in all things unlike Sidney Smith's, except in having as much dread of its progress. I should examine the causes of its progress, the principles in human nature to which it appeals and by which it succeeds; its good and its evil; the means of preventing the one, and of obtaining the other at less risk; and instead of offending the whole religious public, as they call themselves, by indiscriminate ridicule, I should endeavor to show of what different parties that public is composed; how some of them may be conciliated and made useful, and others suppressed—for there are limits which common sense must appoint to toleration.

"I have finished an English Eclogue, which is at Ballantyne's service, either for his Annual Register or his Minstrelsy, and which shall be transcribed and sent him forthwith. I have never yet thanked you for Lord Somers, a very acceptable addition to my library—a very valuable collection, and made far more so by your arrangement and additions. I am sorry my life of D. Luisa de Carvajal is printed, or I would have offered it you, as worthy of being inserted among the Tracts of James I.'s time.

"Believe me, yours very truly,

"ROBERT SOUTHEY."

To C. W. W. Wynn, Esq., M.P.

"Keswick, July 8, 1809.

MY DEAR WYNN,

"You will be a little surprised to hear that Canning has expressed a wish to serve me, and that, in consequence, Walter Scott has been asked to communicate this to me, and find out in what manner it can be done conformably to my own inclinations. There was a situation of £300 a year in his own department which he would have offered, but that was rightly judged by himself, Scott, and Ellis to be inadequate to the expense of time and attendance which it required. So Scott wrote to mention to me professorships at the Universities, diplomatic situations, or any other thing which could be pointed out.

"Professorships in England are fenced about with subscription, and therefore unattainable by me. In Scotland I would accept one, if nothing more suitable could be found. The secretaryship in Portugal is now no longer desirable. My uncle has left that country, and the salary would not support me there. I am too old to begin the pursuit of fortune in that line, and nothing but the desire of becoming independent ever made me desirous of a situation for which I know myself in many points to be exceedingly unfit. The truth is that I have found my way in the world, and am in that state of life to which it has pleased God to call me, and for which it has pleased him to qualify me. At the same time, my means are certainly so straitened that I should very gladly obtain an addition to them, if it could be obtained without changing the main stream of my pursuits.

"Now Sharp has told me that the stewardship to Greenwich Hospital for the Derwentwater estates is expected soon to be vacated by the death of a Mr. Walton, and has advised me to apply for it. I have therefore written to Scott to tell him this; and I now write to you, well knowing that if you can be of use to me in this application, you will. What the value of this appointment is I do not know—Sharp fancies from £600 to £800 a year. If this be thought 'too good a thing for me,' as I dare say it will, the Cumberland estates might be divided from the Northumberland ones. Certes I should rather have the whole than half, but better half a loaf than no bread. And now I have done all that is in my power to do, having thus found out a specific thing, asked for it, and written to you for your assistance, if you can give me any. Having done this, I dismiss the subject altogether from my thoughts. In this respect I have been truly a philosopher, that no hopes or fears, with respect to worldly fortune, have ever given me an hour's anxiety. God bless you!

"R. S."

My father was the more desirous of obtaining this office, because the property included a large portion of country in the immediate vicinity of Keswick; and "it would give him the care of the woods, and the power of planting and beautifying." He accordingly did not cease his efforts with the foregoing letter, but through several other friends secured still further interest, and all appeared to be in a fair train for ultimate success, when a further inquiry into the nature and extent of the duties required at once put a stop to the matter. Indeed, a more practical man would at once have perceived that literary tastes and pursuits were hardly compatible with the management of a large and widely-scattered property. The following pleasant account of the nature of the office from his friend, Mr. Bedford, seems almost ludicrous, from the Protean qualities required.

"The present possessor, with all his knowledge, assiduity, and rapidity in the mode of transacting business, has always been employed for seventeen or eighteen hours out of twenty-four, together with his first clerk. The salary is about £700 a year. The place of residence varies over a tract of country of about eighty miles. The steward must be a perfect agriculturist, surveyor, mineralogist, and the best lawyer that, competently with these other characters, can be found; and lest his various duties should leave him any time for frivolous pursuits, it is in contemplation to raise up to him the seeds of controversy and quarrel, by associating with him some other person, who, under the pretense of sharing his labors, shall differ with him in all his opinions, without, perhaps, relieving him in any degree from the responsibility attached to the management of a revenue of £40,000 per annum. Would you, if you might have it on demand, accept a place with all these circumstances attached to it? For my own part, I would rather live in a hollow tree all the summer, and die when the cold weather should set in, than undertake such an employment."

This, as might be expected, was a complete damper to my father's wishes, and, with one exception, here ended his attempts to obtain official employment.

To Walter Scott, Esq.

"Keswick, July 30, 1809.

"My dear Scott,

"Wordsworth's pamphlet will fail of producing any general effect, because the sentences are long and involved; and his friend, De Quincey, who corrected the press, has rendered them more obscure by an unusual system of punctuation. This fault will outweigh all its merits. The public never can like any thing which they feel it difficult to understand. They will affect to like it, as in the case of Burke, if the reputation of the writer be such that not to admire him is a confession of ignorance; but, even in Burke's case, the public admiration was merely affected: his finer beauties were not remarked, and it was only his party politics that were generally understood, while the philosophy which he brought to their aid was heathen Greek to the multitude of his readers. I impute Wordsworth's want of perspicuity to two causes—his admiration of Milton's prose, and his habit of dictating instead of writing; if he were his own scribe, his eye would tell him where to stop; but in dictating his own thoughts are to himself familiarly intelligible, and he goes on, unconscious either of the length of the sentence, or the difficulty a common reader must necessarily find in following its meaning to the end, and unraveling all its involutions.

"A villainous cold, which makes me sleep as late as I possibly can in the morning, because the moment I wake it wakes with me, has prevented me finishing Kehama: it would else, ere this, have been completed. I think of publishing it on my own account, in a pocket volume of about 350 pages; but this is not yet determined. One of the pleasures which I had promised myself in seeing you was that of showing you this wildest of all wild poems, believing that you will be one of the few persons who will relish it. The rhymes are as irregular as your own, but in a different key, and I expect to be abused for having given the language the freedom and strength of blank verse, though I pride myself upon the manner in which this is combined with rhyme.

"The Eclogue* which I have sent Ballantyne has suffered a little by having all its local allusions cut out. This was done lest what was intended as a general character should have been interpreted into individual satire. The thing was suggested by my accidentally crossing such a funeral some years ago at Bristol; and had I been disposed to personal satire, the hero of the procession would have afforded ample scope for it. As soon as he knew his case was desperate, he called together all the persons to whom he was indebted in his mercantile concerns: 'Gentlemen,' said he, 'I am going to die, and my death will be an inconvenience to you, because it will be some time before you can get your accounts settled with my executors; now, if you will allow me a handsome discount, I'll settle them myself at once.' They came into the proposal, and the old alderman turned his death into nine hundred pounds' profit.

"If Queen Orraca is not too long for the English Minstrelsy, I will with great pleasure send off a corrected copy for it.

"Yours very truly, Robert Southey."

To Walter Scott, Esq.

"August 6, 1809.

"My dear Scott,

"The quest is over; I believe the steward-

* The Alderman's Funeral.

ship would have been promised to me had I been fit for it. All, therefore, that I have to regret is having relied so implicitly upon Sharp's information as to apply for the post before I had thoroughly ascertained my own competency for it. This was only one blunder. Another was in supposing there was no English Historiographer: old Dutens has had the office, with a salary of £400, for many years—upon what plea, they who gave it him can best tell. My aim must now be to succeed him, whenever he pleases to move off, obtaining, if possible, an increase of salary, so as to make it equivalent to what it originally was; and toward this I hope some way is gained by what has already been done. I go to Lowther this day week, and according as I feel my footing, will contrive to have my views and wishes explained.

"There came last night a letter from Ellis, communicating the result of his conversation with Canning: I have thanked him for his friendly interference, and told him how things stand.

"I will do my best for Ballantyne;* and going to work with clear views of the subject, and a thorough knowledge of the Spanish and Portuguese character, I shall come to it with great advantages. That lamentable ground over which poor Sir J. Moore retreated (as one of his own officers expresses it) 'faster than flesh and blood could follow him,' I paced on foot, loitering along that my foot-pace might not outstrip a lazy coach and six, and my recollection of passes where five hundred Englishmen could have stopped an army is as vivid as if I had just seen them. Bonaparte owes more to the blunders of his enemies than to his own abilities; and he has no surer allies than those writers who prepare our very generals to fear him, by constantly representing him as not to be conquered. Oh, for Peterborough! Oh, for a 'single hour of Dundee!' Sir John Moore was as brave a man as ever died in battle, but he had that fear upon him—his imagination was cowed and intimidated, though his heart was not. And now, because the Galicians did not turn out and expose themselves to certain destruction by attempting to protect an army whom he would not suffer to protect themselves, a party in this country are laboring to prove that we ought to abandon the Spaniards! Assuredly, if I am to write the history of his campaign, not a syllable shall be set down in malice, but by Heaven I will nothing extenuate; the retreat shall be painted in its true colors of shame and horror, accurately to the very life, or, rather, the very death, for death it was, not only to the wretched women and children, who never should have been permitted to enter Spain, but to man and beast—both marched till flesh and blood failed them, and the men broken-hearted to think that their lives were thus ignominiously wasted.

"If I thought you repeated the retainer's wish in sober earnest, I could not in conscience wish your old Man of the Sea were off your shoulders; but I believe, whenever he is laid down, doing what you please will be doing much, and that we shall have more Marmions and Williams of Deloraines. Lord Byron's waggery was new to me, and I can not help wishing you may some day have an opportunity of giving him the retort as neatly as you have given it to Cumberland.

"I have fixed myself here by a lease of one-and-twenty years, which, after many weary procrastinations, was executed a few days ago.

"I had nearly forgotten to say something concerning Morte d'Arthur. It is now more than a year that I have been playing the dog in the manger toward you; but the fault is not in me. Longman has been to blame in adjourning the printing the work *sine die*. I will in my next letter state to him that he is making me use you ill, and that, if there be any further delay, I shall feel myself bound to throw up the business.

"Yours very truly, ROBERT SOUTHEY."

To Lieut. Southey, H.M.S. Dreadnought.

"Sept. 19, 1809.

"MY DEAR TOM,

"Poor Jackson is gone at last, after a cruel illness. I followed him to the grave to-day. A good man, to whom the town of Keswick and many of its inhabitants are greatly beholden. He has left Hartley £50, to be paid when he comes of age. Had he thought of bequeathing him his books, it would have been a more suitable remembrance. Never had man a more faithful, anxious, and indefatigable nurse than he has had in Mrs. Wilson—always ready, always watchful, always willing, never uttering a complaint, never sparing herself; with the most disinterested affection; acting so entirely from the feelings of a good heart, that I do not believe even the thought of duty ever entered it. The night after his death we made her take a little spirit and water: it was not a tea-cupful, but upon her it acted as medicine; and she told me the next day that, for the first time during two years, she had slept through the night. He never turned in his bed during that whole time that she did not hear, nor did he make the slightest unusual sound or motion that she was not up to know what could be done for him. As you will readily suppose, I have long since told her never to think of quitting the place, but to remain here as long as she lives with people to whom she is attached (she dotes upon Edith and Herbert), and who can understand her worth.

"Busy as it is usually my fortune to be, I was never so busy as now. Three mornings more will finish my transcribing task for the first volume of my History of Brazil, including a long chapter, which, I fear, can hardly be got into the volume, though I much wish to insert it. Then come the notes—supplementary—which might, with great pleasure to myself and profit to my reader, be extended to another volume as large; but I shall not allow them much more than fifty pages. The book, as a whole, is more amusing than was to be expected. About a fortnight's morning work will complete my work

* See the beginning of the next chapter.

for it: 448 pages are printed; the whole will not be less than 660.

"Last night we had a prodigious flood, higher in some places than can be remembered; I say in some places, because the lake was previously low, and the force of the waters was spent before they found their way to it. Do you know the little bridge over what is usually a dry ditch at the beginning of the Church Lane? The water was over it, and three feet deep in the lane. Half Slack's Bridge is gone, a chaise-driver and horses lost between this place and Wigton, and the corn washed away to a heavy amount. It was a tremendous night.

"I must not wish you to be paid off unless you could be sure of a better appointment than you have at present, or of not being appointed at all. As for peace, I see no hope of it—no fear of it would be the better phrase. The Junta have mismanaged, and so have we; I know not whose mismanagement has been the worst. The army which has been wasted at Flushing would have recovered Spain; the Spaniards will now be left to do it their own way, by detail. What these changes at home will produce, one can not guess till it is known who is going out and who coming in. If Marquis Wellesley comes in, we may expect something. If Canning goes out, the candle will be taken out of the dark lantern. God bless you!

"R. S."

To Walter Scott, Esq.

"Keswick, Oct. 9, 1809.

"My dear Scott,

"Before I had leisure to thank you for your own letter and for Ellis's, and for all that there is therein, a new game of puss-catch-corner has been commenced at Westminster, and Canning has done the most foolish thing he ever did in his life. He should have remembered that Lord Castlereagh was an Irishman, and that, as the Union abolished the Irish Parliament, so ought the ill customs of that Parliament—dueling being one—to have been abolished with it; that, holding his rank and station in the country, it was as much a breach of decency in him to accept a challenge as it would have been in an archbishop; and that he might have done more by his example toward checking a mischievous and absurd practice than has ever been done yet. He got much credit by replying to the Russian manifesto, and he would have got more by a proper reply to Castlereagh. A single combat had some sense in it; there you relied upon your own heart and hand: there was some pleasure in hewing and thrusting, and the bravest came off best; but as for our duels, all that has been said against villainous gunpowder holds true against them.

"I wish to see Marquis Wellesley in power, because we want an enterprising minister—one who would make the enemy feel the mighty power of Great Britain, and not waste our force so pitifully as it has always hitherto been wasted. I wish to see him in power, because he has not been tried, and all the other performers upon the Westminster stage have. But I confess there is but little hope in my wishes. It appears to me that the very constitution of our cabinet necessarily produces indecision, half measures, and imbecility: it seems to me that a government so constituted is just like an army, all whose operations are guided by a council of war instead of a general. I am for ministerial dictatorships.

"Your views about the Morte d'Arthur are wiser ones than mine. I do most formally and willingly resign it into your hands. My intent was that the book should be read; but people are not disposed to read such things generally, or the Cid would not hang upon hand. Now a very limited edition is sure to find purchasers, and nothing need be sacrificed to insure success. I was not, by-the-by, aware that the book had been reformed by the godly critics whose worthy descendants have lately set forth a Family Shakspeare, and will, it is to be hoped, in due time present us with an Edition Expurgate of the Bible, upon the plan by Matthew Lewis. I have a bill of indictment against those Eclectics and Vice-Society men, whenever Murray will send me the needful documents, for be it known unto you that in one of the Eclectic Reviews there is a grand passage describing the *soul of Shakspeare in hell*. If I do not put some of those Pharisees into purgatory for this, for the edification of our Quarterly readers, then may my right hand forget its cunning.

"I have not seen the last Review, which makes me suppose that Murray is still on his journey. These Quarterly Reviews lose much by giving up all those minor publications, which served to play shuttlecock with, and were put to death with a pun, or served up in the sauce of their own humorous absurdity. Hence, too, they are less valuable as materials for the history of literature. The old Annual's was the best plan, if it had not been starved by scanty pay, and, moreover, choked with divinity.

"My next missionary article, when I have time to write it, will be singularly curious: it will relate to South Africa; and I shall obtain from my uncle a manuscript of D'Anville's concerning the Portuguese possessions there, and his plan for establishing a communication by land between them.

"I want to hear that you have planned another poem, and commenced it. For myself, I shall begin with Pelayo, the Spaniard, as soon as I can make up my mind in what meter to write it. That of Kehama, though in rhyme, is almost as much my own as Thalaba, and will, I dare say, excite as much censure.

"Yours very truly, R. Southey."

To Mr. Neville White.

"Keswick, October 10, 1809.

"My dear Neville,

"Thank you for the books; they arrived yesterday, and I have gone through about three fourths of Dr. Collyer's lectures. I have more respect for the Independents than for any other body of Christians, the Quakers excepted. * * * * Their English history is without a blot. Their American has, unhappily, some bloody ones, which you will see noticed in the next number of the Quarterly, if my reviewal of Holmes's American Annals should appear there in an unmutilated state. Dr. Collyer's is certainly an able book; yet he is better calculated to produce effect from the pulpit than in the study. Those parts of his lectures which are most ornamental, and, doubtless, the most popular in delivery, are usually extraneous to the main subject in hand. All his congregations would fairly say, 'What a fine discourse!' to every sermon; but, when the whole are read collectively, they do not exhibit that clear and connected view of prophecy which is what he should have aimed at. There is, perhaps, hardly any subject which requires so much erudition, and so constant an exertion of sound judgment. The doctor's learning is not extensive; he quotes from books of little authority, and never refers to those which are of most importance. Indeed, he does not appear to know what the Germans have done in Biblical criticism.

" * * * * * * *

It has occurred to me that it would add to the interest of the Remains if the name under the portrait were made a fac-simile of Henry's handwriting. Since I wrote to you, I fell in with Dr. Milner, the Dean of Carlisle, who talked to me about Henry; how little he had known of him, and how much he regretted that he should not have known him more. I told him what you were doing with James, expressing a hope that he might find friends at Cambridge, for his brother's sake as well as his own, which he thought would certainly be the case.

* * * * * * *

"We thank you for Miss Smith's book—a very, very interesting one. There are better translations of some of Klopstock's odes in the Monthly Magazine, where, also, is to be found a full account of the Messiah, with extracts translated by my very able and excellent friend, William Taylor, of Norwich. Coleridge and Wordsworth visited Klopstock in the year 1797: he wore a great wig. Klopstock in a wig, they said, was something like *Mr.* Milton. His Life will always retain its interest; his fame as a poet will not be lasting. * * * * In Germany, his day of reputation is already passing away. There is no other country where the principle of criticism is so well understood. But one loves Klopstock as well as if he had been really the poet that his admirers believe him to be; and his wife was as much an angel as she could be while on earth. * * *

"God bless you! R. S."

Mr. Coleridge, who was at this time residing at Grasmere, had lately commenced the publication of *The Friend*, which came out in weekly numbers; and, becoming apprehensive that it was not altogether well calculated to find favor with the class of readers likely to take in a periodical work, he now wrote to my father, requesting him to address such a letter to him in his *Friendly* character as might afford him a good plea for justifying the form and style of the paper in question.

Both the request and the reply to it will be interesting to the reader, especially as the Friend, however unattractive to the popular mind as a periodical, has, like the Spectator and the Rambler, taken a permanent place among the works of its author and the literature of the nation.

S. T. Coleridge to R. Southey.

"October 20, 1809.

"My dear Southey,

" * * * * * * *

What really makes me despond is the daily confirmation I receive of my original apprehension, that the plan and execution of *The Friend* is so utterly unsuitable to the public taste as to preclude all rational hopes of its success. Much, certainly, might have been done to have made the former numbers less so, by the interposition of others written more expressly for general interest; and, if I could attribute it wholly to any removable error of my own, I should be less dejected. I will do my best, will frequently interpose tales and whole numbers of amusement, will make the periods lighter and shorter; and the work itself, proceeding according to its plan, will become more interesting when the foundations have been laid. Massiveness is the merit of a foundation; the gilding, ornaments, stucco-work, conveniences, sunshine, and sunny prospects will come with the superstructure. Yet still I feel the deepest conviction that no efforts of mine, compatible with the hope of effecting any good purpose, or with the duty I owe to my permanent reputation, will remove the complaint. No real information can be conveyed, no important errors radically extracted, without demanding an effort of thought on the part of the reader; but the obstinate and now contemptuous aversion to all energy of thinking is the mother evil, the cause of all the evils in politics, morals, and literature, which it is my object to wage war against; so that I am like a physician who, for a patient paralytic in both arms, prescribes, as the only possible cure, the use of the dumb-bells. Whatever I publish, and in whatever form, this obstacle will be felt. The Rambler, which, altogether, has sold a hundred copies for one of the Connoisseur, yet, during its periodical appearance, did not sell one for fifty, and was dropped by reader after reader for its dreary gravity and massiveness of manner. Now what I wish you to do for me—if, amid your many labors, you can find or make a leisure hour—is, to look over the eight numbers, and to write a letter to The Friend in a lively style, chiefly urging, in a humorous manner, my Don Quixotism in expecting that the public will ever pretend to understand my lucubrations, or feel any interest in subjects of such sad and unkempt antiquity, and contrasting my style with the cementless periods of the modern Anglo-Gallican style, which not only are understood *beforehand*, but, being free from all connections of logic, all the hooks and eyes of intellectual memory, never oppress the mind by any after recollections, but, like civil visitors, stay a few moments, and leave the room quite free and open for the next comers. Something of this kind, I mean, that I may be able to answer it so as, in the answer, to state my own convictions at full on the nature of obscurity, &c. * * * *

"God bless you! S. T. COLERIDGE."

To S. T. Coleridge, Esq.

"TO THE FRIEND.

[Without date.]

"SIR,

"I know not whether your subscribers have expected too much from you, but it appears to me that you expect too much from your subscribers; and that, however accurately you may understand the diseases of the age, you have certainly mistaken its temper. In the first place, sir, your essays are too long. 'Brevity,' says a cotemporary journalist, 'is the humor of the times; a tragedy must not exceed fifteen hundred lines, a fashionable preacher must not trespass above fifteen minutes upon his congregation. We have short waistcoats and short campaigns; every thing must be short—except lawsuits, speeches in Parliament, and tax-tables.' It is expressly stated, in the prospectus of a collection of extracts, called the Beauties of Sentiment, that the extracts shall always be complete sense, and *not very long*. Secondly, sir, though your essays appear in so tempting a shape to a lounger, the very fiends themselves were not more deceived by the *lignum vitæ* apples, when

"'They, fondly thinking to allay
Their appetite with gust, instead of fruit
Chew'd bitter ashes,'

than the reader is who takes up one of your papers from breakfast table, parlor window, sofa, or ottoman, thinking to amuse himself with a few minutes' light reading. We are informed, upon the authority of no less a man than Sir Richard Phillips, how 'it has long been a subject of just complaint among the lovers of English literature, that our language has been deficient in lounging or parlor-window books;' and to remove the opprobrium from the language, Sir Richard advertises a list, mostly ending in *ana*, under the general title of 'Lounging Books or Light Reading.' I am afraid, Mr. Friend, that your predecessors would never have obtained their popularity unless their essays had been of the description, Ὅμοιον ὁμοίῳ φίλον—and this is a light age.

"You have yourself observed that few converts were made by Burke; but the cause which you have assigned does not sufficiently explain why a man of such powerful talents and so authoritative a reputation should have produced so little an effect upon the minds of the people. Was it not because he neither was nor could be generally understood? Because, instead of endeavoring to make difficult things easy of comprehension, he made things which were easy in themselves, difficult to be comprehended by the manner in which he presented them, evolving their causes and involving their consequences, till the reader, whose mind was not habituated to metaphysical discussions, neither knew in what his arguments began nor in what they ended? You have told me that the straightest line must be the shortest; but do not you yourself sometimes nose out your way, hound-like, in pursuit of truth, turning and winding, and doubling and running, when the same object might be reached in a tenth part of the time by darting straightforward like a greyhound to the mark? Burke failed of effect upon the people for this reason—there was the difficulty of mathematics without the precision in his writings. You looked through the process without arriving at the proof. It was the fashion to read him because of his rank as a political partisan; otherwise he would not have been read. Even in the House of Commons he was admired more than he was listened to; not a sentence came from him which was not pregnant with seeds of thought, if it had fallen upon good ground; yet his speeches convinced nobody, while the mellifluous orations of Mr. Pitt persuaded his majorities of whatever he wished to persuade them; because they were easily understood, what mattered it to him that they were as easily forgotten?

"The reader, sir, must think before he can understand you; is it not a little unreasonable to require from him an effort which you have yourself described as so very painful a one? and is not this effort not merely difficult, but in many cases impossible? All brains, sir, were not made for thinking: modern philosophy has taught us that they are galvanic machines, and thinking is only an accident belonging to them. Intellect is not essential to the functions of life; in the ordinary course of society it is very commonly dispensed with; and we have lived, Mr. Friend, to witness experiments for carrying on government without it. This is surely a proof that it is a rare commodity; and yet you expect it in all your subscribers!

"Give us your moral medicines in a more 'elegant preparation.' The Reverend J. Gentle administers his physic in the form of tea; Dr. Solomon prefers the medium of a cordial; Mr. Ching exhibits his in gingerbread nuts; Dr. Barton in wine; but you, Mr. Friend, come with a tonic bolus, bitter in the mouth, difficult to swallow, and hard of digestion.

"MY DEAR COLERIDGE,

"All this, were it not for the sir and the Mr. Friend, is like a real letter from me to you: I fell into the strain without intending it, and would not send it were it not to show you that I have attempted to do something. From jest I got into earnest, and, trying to pass from earnest to jest, failed. It was against the grain, and would not do. I had re-read the eight last numbers, and the truth is, they left me no heart for jesting or for irony. In time they will do their work; it is the form of publication only that is unlucky, and that can not now be remedied. But this evil is merely temporary. Give two or three amusing numbers, and you will hear of admiration from every side. Insert a few more poems —any that you have, except Christabel, for that is of too much value. There is scarcely any thing you could do which would excite so much notice as if you were *now* to write the character of Bonaparte, announced in former times for 'to-morrow,' and to-morrow, and to-morrow; and I think it would do good by counteracting that base spirit of condescension toward him, which I am afraid is gaining ground; and by showing the people what grounds they have for hope.

"God bless you! R. S."

To Mr. Ebenezer Elliott.

"Keswick, Nov. 22, 1809.

"MY DEAR SIR,

"I have had your poem little more than a week: yesterday I carefully perused it (not having had leisure before), and should this evening have written to you, even if your letter had not arrived.

"There are in this poem (which appears to me an alteration of that whereof you formerly sent me an extract) unquestionable marks both of genius and the power of expressing it. I have no doubt that you will succeed in attaining the fame after which you aspire; but you have yet to learn how to plan a poem; when you acquire this, I am sure you will be able to execute it.

"This is my advice to you. Lay this poem aside as one whose defects are incurable. Plan another, and be especially careful in planning it. See that your circumstances naturally produce each other, and that there be nothing in the story which could be taken away without dislocating the whole fabric. Ask yourself the question, is this incident of any use? does it result from what goes before? does it influence what is to follow? is it a fruit or an excrescence? Satisfy yourself completely with the plan before you begin to execute it. I do not mean to say that the detail must be filled up, only make the skeleton perfect. There is no danger of your getting into the fault of common-place authors, otherwise I would recommend you to read some of the bad epic writers, for the sake of learning what to avoid in the composition of a story.

"In your execution you are too exuberant in ornament, and resemble the French engravers, who take off the attention from the subject of their prints by the flowers and trappings of the foreground. This makes you indistinct; but distinctness is the great charm of narrative poetry: see how beautifully it is exemplified in Spenser, our great English master of narrative, whom you can not study too much, nor love too dearly. Your first book reminded me of an old pastoral poet—William Brown: he has the same fault of burying his story in flowers; it is one of those faults which are to be wished for in the writings of all young poets. I am satisfied that your turn of thought and feeling is for the higher branch of the art, and not for the lighter subjects. Your language would well suit drama: have your thoughts ever been turned to it?

* * * * * * *

"If, when you have planned another poem, you think proper to send me the plan, I will comment upon it, while it may be of use to point out its defects. It would give me great pleasure to be of any service to a man of genius, and such I believe you to be. If business ever brings you this way, let me see you. Should I ever travel through Rotherham, I will find you out. I have spoken so plainly and freely of your defects, that you can have no doubt of my sincerity when I conclude by saying go on and you will prosper.

"Yours respectfully, and with the best wishes,

"R. SOUTHEY.

"One thing more: forget this poem while you are planning another, lest you spoil that for the sake of appropriating materials from this."

To Lieut. Southey, H.M.S. Lyra.

"Nov. 25, 1809.

"MY DEAR TOM,

"I write to you for two reasons * * * *; the other, a more interesting one, is to tell you that I have this day finished Kehama, having written two hundred lines since yesterday morning. Huzza, Aballiboozobanganorribo!* It is not often in his lifetime a man finishes a long poem, and as I have nobody to give me joy, I must give myself joy. 24 sections, 4844 lines; 200 or 300 more will probably be added in course of correction and transcription; all has been done before breakfast (since its resumption) except about 170 lines of the conclusion. Huzza! better than lying abed, Tom; and, though I am not quite ready to begin another, I will rise as usual to-morrow, and work at the plans of Pelayo and Robin Hood. And now I am a little impatient that you should see the whole, and shall feel another job off my hands when your copy is completed. By beginning earlier with the next poem, I shall be able to keep pace with it, and send it to you as fast as it proceeds.

* * * * * * *

"Very, very few persons will like Kehama: every body will wonder at it; it will increase my reputation without increasing my popularity: a general remark will be, what a pity that I have wasted so much power. I care little about this, having in the main pleased myself, and all along amused myself; every generation will afford me some half dozen admirers of it, and the everlasting column of Dante's fame does not stand upon a wider base. There will be a good many minor ornaments to insert, the meter will in many places be enriched, and the story, perhaps, sometimes be rendered more perspicuous. Now that the whole is before me, I can see where to add and alter. If it receives half the

* See the Doctor, &c.

improvements which Thalaba did, I shall be well content.

"Pelayo is to be in blank verse: where the whole interest is to be derived from human character and the inherent dignity of the story, I will not run the hazard of enfeebling the finer parts for the sake of embellishing the weaker ones. I shall pitch Robin Hood in a different key—such as the name would lead one to expect—a wild pastoral movement, in the same sort of plastic meter as Garci Ferrandez.* I shall aim it at about 2000 lines, and endeavor not to exceed 3000.

"The state of home politics is perfectly hopeless. Bonaparte seems thoroughly to despise all we can do; all that we have done he is certainly entitled to despise; but if we had Marlborough or Peterborough alive again, six months would close his career forever even now. It remains to be seen whether he despises the Spaniards enough to let things go on in their present course, or if he will enter Spain again and overrun the open country. In that case there is a line of large towns between Barcelona and Cadiz, along the coast, some of which may be expected to hold out like Zaragoza and Gerona, which we could assist by sea, and which would afford opportunities for such men as Cochrane or Sir S. Smith grievously to annoy the besiegers—indeed, to cut them off if they had a good force. There ought to be four flying squadrons of 5000 men, each ready to land wherever they were wanted; under Cochrane they would keep five times their number of French in continual alarm. The only possible hope from the Marquis Wellesley is, that he may insist on a vigorous effort. What we are doing now is just worse than nothing; our men drink themselves to death; our officers learn to despise the Spaniards and Portuguese, because they do not dress, eat, and drink like themselves; and their opinions pass current here in England; and the consequence is, that never were a people so cruelly and basely calumniated as this nation, which has done more against the powers of France, and under every possible disadvantage, than all the rest of Europe conjointly. What a different story Sir Robert Wilson would tell, who has kept the field with his legion of Portuguese through all the perilous season!

* * * * * * * *

"God bless you! R. S."

CHAPTER XVI.

ENGAGEMENT WITH BALLANTYNE FOR THE EDINBURGH ANNUAL REGISTER—RODERIC BEGUN—PROFESSOR WILSON—DE QUINCEY—THE FRIEND—POLITICS—MADOC DEFENDED—MONTHLY REVIEW—LORD BYRON—WILLIAM ROBERTS—REVIEW OF THE MISSIONARIES—HISTORY OF BRAZIL—DECLINING LOVE OF POETICAL COMPOSITION—THE LADY OF THE LAKE—ROMANISM IN ENGLAND—POEM OF MR. ELLIOTT'S CRITICISED—PORTUGUESE LITERATURE—EDINBURGH ANNUAL REGISTER—SPANISH AFFAIRS—DOUBTS ABOUT THE METER OF KEHAMA—OLIVER NEWMAN PROJECTED—KEHAMA—COMPARATIVE MERITS OF SPENSER AND CHAUCER—EVIL OF LARGE LANDED PROPRIETORS—REMARKS ON WRITING FOR THE STAGE—LANDOR'S COUNT JULIAN—POLITICAL VIEWS—GIFFORD WISHES TO SERVE HIM—PROGRESS OF THE REGISTER—L. GOLDSMID'S BOOK ABOUT FRANCE—PASLEY'S ESSAY—NEW REVIEW PROJECTED—DEATH OF HIS UNCLE THOMAS SOUTHEY—LUCIEN BONAPARTE—DOMESTIC HAPPINESS—SPANISH WAR—LOVE FOR FLOWERS—1810–1811.

THE reader may probably have observed that for a considerable period comparatively but little mention has occurred in my father's letters of his long-projected History of Portugal, the materials for which had been collected with so much pains and expense, and which he had fondly hoped to make one of the chief pillars of his reputation.

For this there were several causes; but the chief one, and the one which lasted till his labors closed, was the necessity of his giving up the chief of his time to periodical writing—the only literary labour which could be said to be in any way adequately and fairly remunerated. The Quarterly Review had taken the place of the Annual, and he now entered upon another engagement of much greater magnitude.

At the close of the year 1808, James Ballantyne, the Edinburgh publisher, with whom he had previously had some communication, sent him the prospectus of an Annual Register, which was about to be commenced under favorable auspices, and with a fair list of literary contributors, soliciting his co-operation both in verse and prose.

He accordingly sent some trifling contributions of the former kind, and the matter rested thus until the following August, when Ballantyne again wrote to him, at first wishing him to write the history of Spanish affairs for the past year, and very shortly afterward, being disappointed by the person who had engaged to write the History of Europe, he urged him to take the historical department generally, at the annual payment of £400.

This was a work of no small labor, and the year already so far advanced that more than common industry and speed were required; on this head, however, the publishers had no cause to complain, and, indeed, they appeared well satisfied with their "historiographer" in every way, though sometimes a little startled with the fearless manner in which he expressed his opinions on the various political subjects that came before him; and they were very desirous of securing his further services in the miscellaneous volume.

This engagement, while it lasted, was the most profitable which had yet been offered to him; neither was it as distasteful to him then as

* Poems, p. 441.

it would have been in less stirring times, the events in Spain being a subject in which he took "as deep an interest as the heart of man is capable of;" and he moreover contemplated the compilation of an accurate body of cotemporaneous history, which might hereafter become a standard work of reference, and which would thus have a value far beyond that of the ordinary periodical literature of the day.

Still, however this might be, he could not but feel that, with works demanding far deeper research, admitting the fullest exercise of his powers, and requiring literary stores which at that time he alone possessed, lying on his shelves half finished, the time thus taken up was but unworthily occupied. But he lived in hope—in hopes that in time he would be enabled to live by the worthier labors of his busy pen, that works of solid and lasting merit would take their fitting place in the estimation of the public, and that his unrelenting studies would at length find their reward. How far these hopes were fulfilled or disappointed we have yet to see.

To John Rickman, Esq.

"Jan. 21, 1810.

"MY DEAR RICKMAN,

"I am one of those lucky people who find their business their amusement, and contrive to do more by having half a dozen things in hand at once than if employed upon any single one of them. * * * You will like what I have said concerning the Catholic question,* and not dislike the way in which I have discharged a little of my gall upon the Foxites, the place-mongers, and Mr. Whitbread. This is a very profitable engagement. They give me £400 for it; and if it continues two or three years (which I believe rests wholly with myself), it will make me altogether at ease in my circumstances, for by that time my property in Longman's hands will have cleared itself, the constable will come up with me, and we shall travel on, I trust, to the end of our journey cheek by jowl, even if I should not be able to send him forward like a running footman.

"The Quarterly pays me well—ten guineas per sheet: at the same measure, the Annual was only four. I have the bulky Life of Nelson in hand, and am to be paid double. This must be for the sake of saying they give twenty guineas per sheet, as I should have been well satisfied with ten, and have taken exactly the same pains. * * * * * *

"The next news of my gray goose quill is, that I have one quarto just coming out of the press for you. I have another just going in for Mrs. Rickman, though I suspect it will be less to her taste than any of my former poems. Kehama has been finished these two months, is more than half transcribed, and the first part ought to have reached Ballantyne's a month ago, but those rascally carriers have delayed or lost it. The days are now sufficiently lengthened to give me some half hour before breakfast, and I have begun Pelayo, conquered the difficulty of the opening, and am fairly afloat. Add to all this, that from the overflowings of my notes and notanda I am putting together some volumes of *Omniana* (which will, I have no doubt, pay better than any of the works of which they are in the main, as it were, the crumbs and leavings), and then you will have the catalogue of my works in hand. * *

"*Mathetes* is not De Quincey, but a Mr. Wilson. De Quincey is a singular man, but better informed than any person almost that I ever met at his age. The vice of the Friend is its roundaboutness. Sometimes it is of the highest merit both in matter and manner: more frequently its turnings, and windings, and twistings, and doublings provoke my greyhound propensity of pointing straightforward to the mark.

"The Coalition* which you seem to look on is likely enough to take place; if it should, and Dutens were to die, I might be the better for it; the country would not. The journey to Falmouth seems the best prospect; and yet, at my time of life (the gray hairs are coming), and with my habits, it would be much more agreeable to me to stay at home. I have no hope from chopping and changing, while the materials must remain the same. It signifies little who plays the first fiddle. Tantararara will always be the tune till there be an entirely new set of performers.

"God bless you! R. S."

To Mr. Ebenezer Elliott.

"Keswick, Feb. 9, 1810.

"The objections which have been made to the style of Madoc are ill founded. It has no other peculiarity than that of being pure English, which, unhappily, in these times, renders it peculiar. My rule of writing, whether for prose or verse, is the same, and may very shortly be stated. It is, to express myself, 1st, as perspicuously as possible; 2d, as concisely as possible; 3d, as impressively as possible. This is the way to be understood, and felt, and remembered. But there is an obtuseness of heart and understanding which it is impossible to reach; and if you have seen the reviewals of Madoc, after having read the poem, you will perceive that almost in every part or passage which they have selected for censure, they have missed the meaning. For instance, the Edinburgh sneers at the beginning of the third section, part ii.,†

* In the Edinburgh Annual Register.

* "If Lord Grenville consent to leave the experiment (of establishing Romanism in Ireland) untried, I do not see what should hinder him from joining with Lord Wellesley, Perceval, and Canning in forming a stronger government than the present; and I should the less wonder at it, as one may suppose that all the Tantarararas * * are bodily frightened at the remarkable progress of Cobbetism, built on the late disasters of our armies, though I can not consent to wish the battle of Talavera unfought, that having established that there is some truth in the old opinion of the bravery of the British, who that day, even by confession of the enemy, were not half their numbers."—*J. R. to R. S.*, Jan. 14, 1810.

† "'Not yet at rest, my sister!' quoth the prince,
As at her dwelling door he saw the maid,

and the words 'my own dear mother's child,' as inane.

"Now, as for the speech itself, if —— had not good feeling enough in his nature to feel its dramatic truth and fitness in that place, it is his misfortune; but that particular expression would, to any person who reflected upon its meaning with a moment's due attention, give it peculiar force; for in that state of society, most of the king's children were by different mothers. Of course, when Madoc addressed his sister as his mother's child, more affecting remembrances and more love were implied in that single expression than a whole speech could convey with equal expressiveness. The Eclectic ridicules 'Wilt thou come hither, prince, and let me feel thy face?'* I am utterly ignorant of the nature and essence of true poetry if that be not one of the finest scenes that I have ever been able to produce.

"The meter has been criticised with equal incapacity on the part of the critics. Milton and Shakspeare are the standards of blank verse: in these writers every variety of it is to be found, and by this standard I desire to be measured. The redundant verses (when the redundant syllable is any where but at the end of a line) are formed upon the admitted principle that two short syllables are equal in time to one long one. The truth is, that though the knack of versifying is a gift, the art is an acquirement. I versified more rapidly at the age of sixteen than now at six-and-thirty. But it requires a knowledge of that art to criticise upon the structure of verse; nor is it sufficient to understand the regular turn of the meter: a parrot might be taught that. In the sweep of blank verse, the whole paragraph must be taken into consideration before the merit or demerit of a single line, or sometimes of a single word, can be understood. Yet these critics are everlastingly picking out single lines, and condemning their cadence as bad. This might be true if the line could possibly stand alone. But were I to cut off one of the critic's fingers, and tell him it was only fit for a tobacco-stopper, that would be true also, because the act of amputation made it so.

"You appreciate the story with true judgment, and have laid your finger upon the faulty parts. This it is to have the inborn feeling of a poet. Of the language you are not so good a judge, because you have not mastered the art, and are not well read in the poets of Shakspeare's age. You can not read Shakspeare, Spenser, Milton, and the Elizabethan dramatists too much. There is no danger of catching their faults.

"Yours very truly,

"R. Southey."

Sit gazing on that lovely moonlight scene;
'To bed, Goervyl! Dearest, what hast thou
To keep thee wakeful here at this late hour,
When even I shall bid a truce to thought,
And lay me down in peace? Good night, Goervyl,
Dear sister mine, my own dear mother's child!'"

* Madoc, Part I., Section 3. This passage is too long for extraction here.

To Mr. Neville White.

"Keswick, March 11, 1810.

"My dear Sir,

"Your account of the Monthly Review interested me very much. If they rest the truth of their criticism upon that school poem in plain, direct, *tangible* language, I will most assuredly favor them with a few lines, first through the medium of as many magazines as we can get access to, and ultimately in a note to the Life. With regard to my own works, I am a perfect Quaker, and fools and rogues may misrepresent and libel them in perfect security; but upon the subject of Henry, the M. Review shall find me a very Tartar.

"Till you informed me of it, I did not know that Lord Byron had amused himself with lampooning me. It is safe game, and he may go on till he is tired. Every apprentice in satire and scandal for the last dozen years has tried his hand upon me. I got hold of the Simpliciad the other day, and wrote as a motto in it these lines, from one of Davenant's plays which I happened to have just been reading:

"'Libels of such weak fancy and composure,
That we do all esteem it greater wrong
To have our names extant in such paltry rhyme
Than in the slanderous sense.'

"The manner in which these rhymesters and prosesters misunderstand what they criticise, would be altogether ludicrous, if it did not proceed as often from want of feeling as from want of intellect.

"I want your assistance in a business in which I am sure it will interest you to give it. A youth of Bristol, by name William Roberts, died of consumption about two years ago, at the age of nineteen. He was employed in a bank, and his salary, £70 a year (I believe), was materially useful in assisting toward the support of his father and mother, and a grandmother, and one only sister. The family had known better days * * * * and one calamity following another, has reduced them very greatly. Yet still there remains that feeling which, if I call it pride, it is only for want of a better word to express something noble in its nature. William was a youth of great genius, and a few days before his death he bequeathed his poems in trust to his two intimate friends to be published for the benefit of his sister, that being all he had to bequeath, and his passionate desire (like that of Chatterton) was to provide for her. You must remember that at that time he did not foresee the subsequent distresses of his father and mother. These friends were a young physician of the name of Hogg, settled somewhere near London, and James, a banker of Birmingham, an acquaintance of mine, the author of that sweet poem upon the Otaheitean Girl, of which some stanzas were quoted in the third Quarterly Review. James has arranged the poems and letters of the poor fellow for the press, and will draw up a biographical memoir. He has consulted me upon the subject, and the plain statement which I have here made of the circumstances has interested me very deeply * * My opinion is, that great things might have been done by William Roberts; that every one will acknowledge this; but that his Remains will not obtain a general sale. Of Henry's I foresaw the success as much as such a thing could be foreseen. But Roberts has left nothing so good as Henry's best pieces; in fact, he died younger, and was precluded from the possibility of advancing himself as Henry did, in choosing a learned profession, because his salary was wanted at home. There is another reason, too, against their general sale; though he was most exemplary in all his duties, and, as far as I can discover, absolutely without a spot or blemish upon his character, and a regular and sincere churchman, there is nothing of that kind of piety in his writings to which the Remains are mostly indebted for their popularity.

* * * * * * *

"My hope is that such a sum may be raised as will be sufficient to place Eliza Roberts in a situation respectably to support herself and her parents. I do not yet know what extent the publication will run to, but as soon as this is settled, I will beg you to *beg* subscriptions. * * This whole account is written with such a cautious fear of saying too much, that I fear I have said too little, and may unwittingly have led you to think slightingly of what poor William Roberts has left behind him. If I have done this I have done wrong, for certainly he was a youth of great genius and most uncommon promise, which it is my firm belief, founded upon the purity of his life and principles, and the rectitude of his feelings, that he would amply have fulfilled, if it had not pleased God to remove him so early from this sphere of existence.

"God bless you!

"Yours affectionately,

ROBERT SOUTHEY."

To Sharon Turner, Esq.

"March 20, 1810.

"DEAR TURNER,

"I thank you for your little volume, which I have read with pleasure, as the faithful transcript of a good man's mind. It contains ample proof that you possess the perceptions of a poet; and if the diction in which they are clothed has sometimes its defects, it is because you have been too laboriously employed in more dignified pursuits to have had leisure for maturing the mechanical part of an art which, of all other trades or professions, requires the longest apprenticeship.

"What I have written upon the missionaries I well knew would accord with your feelings and opinions. I have not yet done with the subject, meaning, so soon as my many occupations will allow, to prepare an article upon the South African missions; and, perhaps, to go on at intervals till I have given a view of all the existing Protestant missions; proved my own firm belief that there are but two methods of extending civilization—conquest and conversion—the latter the only certain one; entered fully into the difficulties which oppose the reception of Christianity; and, finally, connected this subject with that of civilization.

"I had given Canning credit for the Austrian article, though half suspecting that it was giving him credit for too much, because there was a reference to the principles of human nature and a sense of its dignity rarely, or never, to be found in a politician by trade. The Quarterly does well; but it would do far better if it was emancipated from the shackles of party. It wants, also, some recondite learning: you should give them an account of the Welsh Archaiology; or, if that be too laborious, should take some of the Welshmen's publications, Davies or Roberts, for your text, and pour out from your full stores. * * * * *

"You will receive the first volume of my greatest labors very shortly; for, after many provoking delays, it has at last got out of the printer's hands. It is less interesting, perhaps, than the second volume will prove, or than the history of the mother country; but it will repay perusal, and you will find many valuable hints respecting savage life. I have a poem also in the press, which you will wonder at and abuse. It is, in my own judgment, a successful attempt at giving to rhyme the whole freedom, and more than the variety, of blank verse. But in all its structure and story it is so wholly unlike any thing else, that I expect to have very few admirers. This has been a sort of episode to my main employments. * * * What I am busied upon most intently is the historical part of Ballantyne's new Annual Register. The perfect freedom and perfect sincerity with which I am discharging this task has astonished Ballantyne, and I dare say he will find his account in it; for, sure I am, the veriest knave will feel that it is written with honesty. * * * * This evening I have finished the siege of Zaragoza, and my pulse has not yet recovered its usual regularity. The death of Sir John Moore will conclude the volume. * * *

"Believe me, yours very truly,

"ROBERT SOUTHEY."

To Walter Savage Landor, Esq.

"March 26, 1810.

"Is it a mark of strength or of weakness, of maturity or of incipient decay, that it is more delightful to me to compose history than poetry? not, perhaps, that I feel more pleasure in the act of composition, but that I go to it with more complacency, as to an employment which suits my temperament. I am loth to ascribe this lack of inclination to any deficiency of power, and certainly am not conscious of any; still I have an ominous feeling that there are poets enough in the world without me, and that my best chance of being remembered will be as an historian. A proof-sheet of Kehama, or a second sight scene in Pelayo, disperses this cloud; such, however, is my habitual feeling. It did not use to be the case in those days when I thought of nothing but poetry, and lived, as it were, in an atmosphere of nitrous oxyd—in a state of perpetual excitement, which yet produced no exhaustion.

"The first volume of my History of Brazil makes its appearance in a few days; perhaps at this time it may have been published. This is the commencement of a long series; the History of Portugal is to follow, then that of Portuguese Asia, then a supplementary volume concerning the African possessions. Lastly, if I have life, health, and eye-sight permitted me, the history of the Monastic Orders; sufficient employment for a life, which I should think well employed in completing them. * * * *

"God bless you! R. S."

To Walter Scott, Esq.

"Durham, May 11, 1810.

"MY DEAR SCOTT,

"Yesterday evening, on my return from the race-ground, I found your poem* lying on the table. A provoking engagement called me from it for two or three hours; but, notwithstanding this, and my obstinate habit of getting early to bed, I did not go to rest till I finished the book. Every reader's first thought, when he begins to think at all, will be to compare you with yourself. If I may judge from my own feelings, the Lady will be a greater favorite than either of her elder brethren. There is in all, the same skillful inscrutability of story till the artist is pleased to touch the spring which lays the whole machine open; but, while the plot is thus well wound up in the new poem, I think the narrative is more uniformly perspicuous than in the two former. There is in all, the like originality and beauty of circumstances. I am not willing to admit that some of the situations in the Lay and Marmion *can* be outdone; and if I thought they *were* outdone last night, and still incline to think so, it is probably because new impressions are more vivid than the strongest recollection.

"I wished most of the songs away on the first perusal; on recurring to them, I was glad they were there; yet, wherever they interrupt the narrative, without in any way tending to carry on the business of the story, my admiration of the things themselves does not prevent me from thinking them misplaced. Your title is likely to be a popular one; and for that very reason, I wish it had not been chosen. Of course it led me to expect some tale of Merlin or King Arthur's days; but what is of real consequence to one who loves old lays is, that whenever hereafter the Lady of the Lake will be mentioned, most readers will suppose your Ellen is intended; and in this way a sort of offense against antiquity has been committed. This is something in the manner of Momus's criticism, to find fault with the trinkets of the Lady and with her name. But I heartily give you joy of the poem, and congratulate you with perfect confidence upon the success which you have a right to expect, which you deserve, and which you will find. The portrait seems more like the more I look at it; and my friend Camp is now doubly immortalized. This reminds me of the dog in the poem—an incident so fine that it bears as well as courts comparison with one of the most affecting passages in Homer.

"Longman was instructed to send you my Brazil. I hope to get a long spell at the concluding volume before it is necessary to fall seriously to work upon the second Register. What you will think of Kehama I am not quite sure; of what the public will think, I can have, and never have had, the slightest doubt. No subject could have been devised more remote from human sympathies; and there are so few persons who are capable of standing aloof from them, that the subject must be admitted to have been imprudently chosen, if in choosing it I had any other motive than that of pleasing myself and some half a dozen others. If it had been my intention to provoke censure, I could not have done it more effectually; for, without intending any innovation, or being at first sensible of any, I have fallen into a style of versification as unusual as the ground-work of the story; with this, however, I am well satisfied. I have written the first canto of Pelayo in blank verse, and without machinery. This promises to be a striking poem, and, if it were ready now, might perhaps, in some degree, be a useful one.

"The meter of the Lady is to me less agreeable than the more varied measure. There is an advantage in writing in a meter to which one has been little accustomed; it necessarily induces a certain change of style, and thus enables the writer to clothe his old conceptions in so different a garb that they appear new even to himself. The alteration which you have made is not sufficiently great to obtain this advantage; and there is a loss of variety, from which I should have predicted a loss of freedom and a loss of power. This, however, is amply confuted by the poem, which certainly is never deficient either in force or freedom.

"I shall return home in the course of a fortnight; a short interval of idleness makes me feel impatient to get once more to my books and my desk. Pray remember me to Mrs. Scott, and believe me,

"Very affectionately yours,

"ROBERT SOUTHEY."

To the Rev. Herbert Hill.

"Keswick, May 30, 1810.

"MY DEAR UNCLE,

" * * * * * * *

My Register work was finished before I left home. * * * * An interval of idleness, which is to me more wearisome than any labor, has given me new appetite for employment, and I am now busily occupied with my second volume,* to which, with such alternations of work for the Review as are always wholesome as well as convenient (for over-application to any one sub-

* The Lady of the Lake.

* Of the "History of Brazil."

ject disturbs my sleep, and I have long learned, by neutralizing, as it were, one set of thoughts with another, to sleep as sweetly as a child), I shall devote the next three months uninterruptedly. My first volume seems to be well liked by my friends; they all speak of it as amusing, which I was at one time apprehensive it would not be.

"Murray the bookseller, with whom the Quarterly had led me into correspondence, promises to procure for me a MS. history of Lima, written by one of its viceroys. I shall be glad to see it, and am a good deal obliged by this mark of attention on his part; but those books upon Paraguay would be far more useful at this time, for I have no other guides than Charlevoix, and the mutilated translation of Techo, in Churchill. Luckily, a very brief summary of events is all that I am called upon, or, indeed, consistently with the main purpose and plan of the work, ought to give; still it is impossible to do this to my own satisfaction unless I feel myself thoroughly acquainted with the whole series of events. * * * * * *

"Scott sent me his poem to Durham. I like it better than eitheir Marmion or the Lay, though its measure is less agreeable; but the story has finer parts, and is better conceived. The portraits both of Camp and his master are remarkably good. He talks of a journey to the Hebrides; but, if that does not take place, of a visit southward; in which case, Keswick will be taken on his way, and we are to concoct some plan for employing Ballantyne's press.

"The old Douay establishment is removed to England, to a place called Ushaw, about four miles from Durham. They began it upon a Bank of Faith system, after Huntingdon's manner, having only £2000 to begin with. The £2000 have already been expended, and pretty near as much more will go before it is completed. There are 100 students there already, chiefly boys; and preparations are making for doubling the number. I rode over with Henry, and one of his Catholic friends, to look after the library. The philosophical tutor showed me a volume of the Acta Sanct. Benedictorum—'Saints, as they choose to call them,' said he. In the evening, however, the Ecclesiastical Antiquities of the Anglo-Saxons, by this very Mr. ——, were put into my hands; and there he relates miracles, and abuses Turner for what he calls *his* Romance of St. Dunstan! These fellows are all alike. I asked what the number of the English Catholics was supposed to be, and was told 300,000. This is most likely exaggerated. I should not have guessed them at half. God bless you! R. S."

To John May, Esq.

"Keswick, August 5, 1810.

MY DEAR FRIEND,

"Whatever you may think of my part in the Register in other respects, you will, I am sure, be well pleased with the perfect freedom which inspires it. It will offend many persons, and will please no party; but my own heart is satisfied, and that feeling would always be to me a sufficient reward. And even if it should injure me in a political point of view (as it probably may), by cutting off the prospect of obtaining any thing from government beyond the pension * * * * still I believe that even the balance of selfish prudence, though Mr. Worldy-wiseman himself were to adjust the scales, would prove in my favor; for I confidently expect that this work will materially increase my reputation among the booksellers; and, indeed, as long as I continue to be engaged in it, I shall need no other means of support. In the second part of the volume you will see me abundantly praised and most respectfully censured. I know not who the critic is, nor can I guess; he is very showy and sufficiently shallow. * * * As for my contempt of the received rules of poetry, I hold the same rules which Shakspeare, Spenser, and Milton held before me, and desire to be judged by those rules; nor have I proceeded upon any principle of taste which is not to be found in all the great masters of the art of every age and country wherein the art has been understood. When the critic specifies parts of my writings to justify his praise, he overlooks every thing which displays either a knowledge of human nature, or a power of affecting the passions, and merely looks for a specimen of able versification. *

"God bless you!

"Yours very affectionately, R. S."

To Walter Scott, Esq.

"Keswick, Sept. 17, 1810.

"MY DEAR SCOTT,

"In the Courier of the 15th (which has this evening reached us) is an article pretending to exhibit imitations from your poems, and signed S. T. C. At the first sight of this I was certain that S. T. Coleridge had nothing to do with it; and, upon putting the paper into his hands, his astonishment was equal to mine. What may be the motive of this dirty trick, Heaven knows. I can only conjecture that the fellow who has practiced it designs in some other paper or magazine to build up a charge of jealousy and envy in Coleridge, founded upon his own forgery. Coleridge declares he will write to the Courier disavowing the signature. I know he means to do it; but his actions so little correspond to his intentions, that I fear he will delay doing it, very probably, till it is too late. Therefore I lose no time in assuring you that he knows nothing of this petty and paltry attack, which I have no doubt, from whatever quarter it may have come, originates more in malice toward him than toward you.

"I was not without hopes of seeing you in this land of lakes, on your way from the Yorkshire Greta; but, happening to see Jeffrey about a fortnight ago, he told me that you were settled at Ashiestiel for the autumn. I say happening to see him, because his visit was to Coleridge, not to me; and he told C. that he had not called immediately on me, as he did not know what my feelings might be toward him, &c.

"You have probably seen my labors in the Register. Upon almost all points of present politics I believe there is little difference of opinion between us; and every where, I think, you will give me credit for fair dealing as well as plain speaking. At present I am working very hard upon the second volume; it is an employment which interests me very much, and I complain of nothing but the want sometimes of sufficient documents respecting the Spanish war. Particularly I regret the want of detailed accounts of the second siege of Zaragoza and the siege of Gerona, that I might be enabled to present a full record of those glorious events. I suppose you know the whole secret history of the Register, otherwise I would tell you how liberally the Ballantynes have behaved to me. They will probably find their account in having engaged a man who writes with such perfect freedom; for, though parts of the work may, and indeed will, offend all parties in turn, still there is a decided character of impartiality about it, which will prove the surest recommendation.

"Kehama has traveled so slowly through the press, that, instead of appearing at the end of one season, it will be ready about the beginning of the next. I expect every body to admire my new fashion of printing (though unfortunately the printers did not fall into it for the first three or four sheets); if any thing else is admired—*ponamus lucro*. My unknown critic in the Register will think that I am going against wind and tide with a vengeance, instead of sailing, according to his advice, with the stream. But if he or any body else should imagine that I purposely set myself in opposition to public opinion, they are very much mistaken. I do not think enough about public opinion for this to be possible. In planning and executing a poem, no other thought ever occurs to me than that of making it as good as I can. When it is finished, the ostrich does not commit her eggs with more confidence to the sand and the sun, and to Mother Nature, than I 'cast it upon the waters'—sure if it be good that it will be found after many days.

"It gratified me much to hear that you had been interested with my first volume of Brazil. The second will contain more stimulating matter; but it is from the history of Portugal that I think you will derive most amusement, so full will it be of high chivalrous matter and beautiful costume. Pelayo comes on slow and sure, thoroughly to my own mind as far as it has advanced.

"Yours very truly, R. SOUTHEY."

To Walter Savage Landor, Esq.

"Keswick, Jan. 11, 1811.

"I am brooding a poem upon Philip's War with the New Englanders, which was the decisive struggle between the red and white races in America. Nothing can be more anti-heroic than stiff Puritan manners; but these may be kept sufficiently out of sight; and high Puritan principles are fine elements to work with. One of my main characters is a Quaker, an (ideal) son of Goffe the regicide. A good deal of original conception is floating in my mind, and there is no subject in which my own favorite feelings and opinions could be so fully displayed. It has taken strong hold on me, and if my mind was but made up as to the fittest form of meter, I should probably begin it forthwith, and continue it and Pelayo together, having the one to turn to when the way was not plain before me in the other. Hexameters would not be more difficult than any other meter, but they will not allow of the necessary transition from the narrative to the dramatic style without too great a discrepancy. The manner of Kehama would not do: the narrative is pitched too high, the dialogue too low, for a poem in which the circumstances will be less elevated than the passion. For this very reason, rhyme, I fear, is required.

"You have done wonders with C. Julian. 1200 lines in a week were the quickest run (in sailors' phrase) that I ever made. But this is nothing to what you have accomplished; and your manner involves so much thought (excess of meaning being its fault), that the same number of lines must cost thrice as much expense of passion and of the reasoning faculty to you than they would to me. I am impatient to see this tragedy. I hear nothing of Kehama except that forty copies have been sold at Edinburgh, and that Scott has reviewed it for the next Quarterly.

"What is the meaning of the monogram in the title-page of your Ode to Gustavus? I never read your Latin without wishing it were English, and regretting that you were ever taught a language so much inferior to your own.

"Your abhorrence of Spenser is a strange heresy. I admit that he is inferior to Chaucer (who for variety of power has no competitor except Shakspeare), but he is the great master of English versification, incomparably the greatest master in our language. Without being insensible to the defects of the Fairy Queen, I am never weary of reading it. Surely Chaucer is as much a poet as it was possible for him to be when the language was in so rude a state. There seems to be this material point of difference between us—you think we have little poetry which was good for any thing before Milton; I, that we have little since, except in our own immediate days. I do not say there was much before, but what there was was sterling verse in sterling English. It had thought and feeling in it. At present, the surest way to become popular is to have as little of either ingredient as possible.

"Have you read Captain Pasley's book? I take it for my text in the next Quarterly, and would fain make it our political Bible.

"God bless you! R. S."

To John Rickman, Esq.

"Jan. 25, 1811.

"MY DEAR RICKMAN,

"Thank you for the East India Report and for the Burdett papers. Your notes upon Parliamentary Reform are now lying in my desk, to be introduced immediately after the foolish plan which he proposed in 1805—a plan which could do no possible good. It is downright absurdity to suppose that the House of Commons can be a pure representative body, when there is always a regular party organized against the government of the country, and consequently in semi-alliance with the enemy. Such a state of things (which never existed any where else, and, as you will say, could not exist here but by favor of old Neptune) was unknown to our old laws of Parliament; and it is therefore a manifest fallacy to argue from those laws against practices which are rendered necessary by the existing system, and without which there could be no government. The evil which I wish to see remedied is the aggregation of landed property, which gives to such a man as —— the command of whole counties, and enables such men as —— to sing 'we are seven,' like Wordsworth's little girl, into the ear of a minister, and demand for himself situations which he is unfit for. This is a worse evil than that which our mortmain statutes were enacted to remedy, for it is gradually rooting out the yeomanry of the country, and dwindling the gentry into complete political insignificance. It is not parliamentary reform which can touch this evil: some further limitation of entail, or a proper scheme of income taxation, might. Concerning parliamentary reform, indeed, my views are much changed; and Sir F. Burdett's scheme has not a little contributed to the alteration, elucidated as it is by all his subsequent conduct. The phrase, indeed, like Catholic Emancipation, is *vox et prœterea nihil.*

"God bless you! R. S."

To Mr. Ebenezer Elliott.

"Keswick, Feb. 7, 1811.

"I will willingly find fault with your play when you can find means of sending it me; that is, I will gladly, if it be in my power, point out in what manner it may be fitted for representation, should it require alteration, and appear capable of being so altered. Of managers and green-rooms I know nothing. Old Cumberland once said to me in his characteristic way, 'Whatever you do, sir, never write a play! the torments of the damned are nothing to it.' I myself suspect that if a man suffers any thing like purgatory in a green-room, it must be his own fault. I would send my play there, and if it was accepted they might mutilate it as they pleased, because the actors, generally speaking, must be the best judges of what will *tell* on the stage, and because the author can always restore the piece to its original state when he prints it.

"I am sorry you should have suspected any thing like a reproach upon 'single blessedness' in women in what is said of Lorrinite.* Nothing could be further from my thoughts. The passage has nothing beyond an individual reference to the witch herself, therein described as a '*cankered* rose.' You may find abundant proof in my writings, and would require none if you knew me, that no man can be more innocent of such opinions as you seem to have suspected. So far am I from not regarding continence as a virtue.

"Those unaccountable *clicks*, as you call them, in the middle of the lines, are, as you must have seen, too frequent to be accidental. I went upon the system of rhyming to the ear regardless of the eye, and have throughout availed myself of the power which this gave me. The verse was no bondage to me. If I do not greatly deceive myself, it unites the advantages of rhyme with the strength and freedom of blank verse in a manner peculiar to itself. As far as I can judge (which is, of course, and must be, from very imperfect and partial means), the story seems not to have shocked people as much as I expected, but that it should become popular is impossible. Many years must elapse before the opinion of the few can become the law of the many.

"I have fallen in love with the American subject which did not strike your fancy, and have half mounted it into a story of which a primitive Quaker is the hero; a curious character, you will say, for heroic poetry—certainly an original one.

"If ever you think upon political subjects, I beseech you read Captain Pasley's Essay on Military Policy—a book which ought to be not only in the hands, but in the heart of every Englishman. Farewell!

"Yours very truly. R. SOUTHEY."

To Walter Savage Landor, Esq.

'Keswick, Feb. 12, 1811.

"I am not disappointed in Count Julian; it is too Greek for representation in these times, but it is altogether worthy of you. The thought and feeling which you have frequently condensed in a single line is unlike any thing in modern composition. The conclusion, too, is Greek. I should have known this play to be yours had it fallen in my way without a name. There was one written ten years ago by Rough which *aimed* at being what this *is;* this has the profundity which was attempted there. I see nothing to be expunged, but I see many of what a schoolboy would call *hard* passages. Sometimes they are like water, which, however beautifully pellucid, may become dark by its very depth. Your own vase of tarnished gold is a better illustration; the very richness of the metal occasions its darkness. Sometimes they are like pictures—unless you get them in precisely the right point of view, their expression is lost. I can not tell how this is to be remedied if it is remediable; it is what makes the difference between difficult and easy authors. I will not yet specify what the passages are which are obscure, because, upon every fresh perusal, some of them will flash upon me.

"Never was a character more finely conceived than Julian. That image of his seizing the horses is in the very first rank of sublimity; it is the grandest image of power that ever poet produced.

* Curse of Kehama, canto xi. verse 3.

"You could not have placed the story in a finer dramatic light; but it has made you elevate some vile renegadoes into respectability. In my plan Sisabert will die by Florinda's hand, and Orpas will be cut down by Rodrigo's own hand. I go on very slowly; what I have done is too good to be sacrificed; but it will make the poem as faulty in structure as Shakspeare's Julius Cæsar; and I shall be a third of the way through it before Pelayo appears. My pace will soon be quickened; the way opens before me; hitherto there has been but one personage in view; tomorrow I introduce others, and shall soon get into the business of the poem. You wonder that I can think of two poems at once; it proceeds from weakness, not from strength. I could not stand the continuous excitement which you have gone through in your tragedy: in me it would not work itself off in tears; the tears would flow while in the act of composition, and would leave behind a throbbing head and a whole system in the highest state of nervous excitability, which would soon induce disease in one of its most fearful forms. From such a state I recovered in 1800 by going to Portugal, and suddenly changing climate, occupation, and all internal objects; and I have kept it off since by a good intellectual regimen.

"When I have read Count Julian again and again, I will then make out a list of the passages which appear so difficult that ordinary readers may be supposed incapable of understanding them. When you perceive that they may be difficult to others, it will be easy, in most instances, to make the meaning more obvious. Then you must print the tragedy. It will not have many more admirers than Gebir; but they will be of the same class and cast; and with Gebir it will be known hereafter, when all the rubbish of our generation shall have been swept away.

"What will you do next? Narrative is better than dramatic poetry, because it admits of the highest beauties of the drama: there are two characters in Roman history which are admirably fit for either; but in both cases their history suits the drama better than the epic—Sertorious and Spartacus. When I was a boy, the abortive attempt at restoring the republic by Caligula's death was one of my dramatic attempts. Another was that impressive story in Tacitus of 300 slaves (I think that was the number) put to death for not preventing the murder of their master, whom one of them had killed. The Emperor Majorian is a fine character. I wish I could throw out a subject that would tempt you, but rather to a poem than a play; for, though your powers for both are equal, and the play the more difficult work of the two, yet in my judgment the poem is the preferable species of composition.

"God bless you! R. S."

To Grosvenor C. Bedford, Esq.

"Keswick, Feb. 16, 1811.

'MY DEAR GROSVENOR,

"If I had not heard of you from Gifford at the beginning of the month, I should have been very uneasy about you. Thank you for your letter, and for your serviceable interpolation of the review,* which is just what it should be—that is to say, just what I should wish it, only I wish you would not call me the most sublime poet of the age, because, in this point, both Wordsworth and Landor are at least my equals. You will not suspect me of any mock-modesty in this. On the whole, I shall have done greater things than either, but not because I possess greater powers.

"My abode under Skiddaw will have been more unfavorable to my first year's Annals than to any other, because I had fewer channels of information opened, and because of home politics I was very ignorant, never liking them well enough to feel any interest beyond that of an election feeling. Now that it becomes my business to be better informed, I have spared no pains to become so; and the probability is, that I learn as much political news to my purpose by letters, as I should do by that intercourse which would be compatible with my way of life. Of three points I have now convinced myself, that the great desideratum in our government is a premier instead of a cabinet—that a regular opposition is an absurdity which could not exist any where but in an island without destroying the government—and that parliamentary reform is the shortest road to anarchy.

"I am sincerely obliged to Gifford for his desire to serve me, and sincerely glad that I stand in need of no services—not that I am by any means above being served, or feel any ways uncomfortable under an obligation. On the contrary, I should hold myself in the highest degree obliged to any person who would promote Tom for my sake; but for this we must wait till the First Lord is in power. For myself, I am in a fair way of wanting nothing; and if great men will but give me their praise,† they may keep their promises for others; their praise would prove actual puddings: let them only make it the fashion to buy my books, and in seven years' time I will purchase a house and ground enough for the use of a dairy within a day's journey of London. Scott had 2000 guineas for the Lady of the Lake. If Canning would but compare Bonaparte to Kehama in the House of Commons, I might get half as much by my next poem.

"I am reviewing Pasley's book—the most important political work that ever appeared in any country. The minister who shall first become a believer in that book, and act upon its unanswerable principles, will obtain a higher reputation than ever statesman did before him.

* This refers to a reviewal of Kehama, which Mr. Bedford had written for the Quarterly, not knowing that Sir Walter Scott had one in preparation. The latter was the one inserted.

† "Your article on the Evangelical Sects is much admired, and a few days ago, Perceval mentioned it in terms of the highest praise at his own table. Herries, who was present, told him that you were the author of it, and he did not praise it one whit the less on that account, but said it was the fairest, most candid, and comprehensive view he had ever seen of any subject."—*G. C. B. to R. S., Feb. 6, 1811.*

My review will be conciliatory toward the husbanding politicians, that is, it will endeavor to make them ashamed without making them angry. The blistering plaster for Whitbread goes all into the Register.

"Abella supplies me well with Spanish papers. I have found him excellently useful. He writes to me in —issimos of esteem, and I outstep a little the usual pace of English compliments in return, and am his friend and servant in superlatives—with a good conscience, believe me, for I really like him, and am very sensible of his services. Of course I have sent him my best works, and no doubt my name will soon be in high odor in the Isle of Lisbon. It was a mortification to me to hear he was about to return before I could see him in London. * *

"I have again taken to Pelayo, after a long interval, and the third section is nearly finished. It will bring me into busier scenes, and the story will begin to open. I am afraid that, having thus begun *ab ovo*, I must change the title of the poem, and call it Spain restored, for Pelayo can not appear till I have got on a thousand lines. If I cared about rules, this would be a fault; but the structure must depend upon the materials, and I have not too much of Roderic in the beginning, considering the part he has to play in the end.

"The capture of the Isle of France is a good thing. We must now look to the Persian Gulf and the Red Sea, and take especial care to keep the French out of those important points—important as to the means they afford of annoying us in their hands, or of spreading civilization in ours. Next year I purpose to give a whole chapter to the French intrigues with Persia, and their views in that quarter. I have neither time nor room for it in the present volume.

"I most heartily rejoice that the Outs are Outs still. R. S."

To John Rickman, Esq.

"Feb. 20, 1811.

"MY DEAR RICKMAN,

* * * * * * *

"I have it under the hand of —— that any new ministry *must* recall our troops from Spain and Portugal—to which I replied by praying that he might stay out of place so long as he thought so.

* * * * * * *

"When I read L. Goldsmid's* book about France, the impression it made upon me was, that he was sent over by Bonaparte to further his purposes here. God knows by what other means, but specially by publishing such outrageous and absurd stories *against* him as should give his good friends a plea for disbelieving any thing against a man who was so palpably calumniated. For instance, that B., when at the military college, poisoned a woman who was with child by him; that this *is* a lie, *I* know, because I happen to know a person resident in the same town at whose house B. was in the habit of visiting, and from whom I learned that his character was exactly what you would suppose—very studious and very correct. That it *must* be a lie is obvious, because such things could not be done with more impunity in France than in England; and to say that it might have been concealed, leads to the obvious question, 'If so, how came L. Goldsmid to know it?' A still grosser and more ridiculous story is, that Bonaparte makes his poison by giving arsenic to a pig, and tying the pig up by the hind legs, and collecting what runs from his mouth. *

"Now the man is no fool, and it is not possible that he can believe this himself, or that he can suppose it can be believed by any person of common sense. For what purpose, then, can he publish such lies?

"If he be the rascal which I take him to be, his newspaper shows what is the main purpose for which he has been sent over—to put the Bourbons into Bonaparte's hands. He recommends a Bourbon to be at the head of the army in Spain—a Bourbon to land in France. Now there can be no doubt this is what B. would above all things desire. * * *

"Farewell! R. S."

* L. Goldsmid was editor of the Argus in 1801, and was at this time editing the Antigallican Monitor.

To Walter Scott, Esq.

'Keswick, April 2, 1811.

"MY DEAR SCOTT,

'You can probably tell me how I could transmit a copy of Kehama to your friend Leyden, for whom, though I do not personally know him, I have always felt a very high respect, regarding him, with one only exception (which might be more properly expressed to any person than to you), as a man of more true genius and far higher promise than any of his cotemporary countrymen.

"No doubt you have seen Pasley's Essay. It will be, in the main, a book after your own heart, as it is after mine. He talks sometimes of conquest when he should talk of emancipation. A system of unlimited conquest leads at last to the consequences which we have seen exemplified in the fate of the Roman empire. For ourselves, I would wish no other accession of dominion than Danish Zealand and Holland in the North, with as many islands as you please in the Mediterranean; Italy to be formed into one independent state under our protection, as long as it needed it. I believe that the ministry do not want the inclination to act vigorously; but they want public opinion to go before, and protect them against the opposition. These men, and their coadjutors, the Morning Chronicle and the Edinburgh Review, have neither patriotism, nor principle, nor feeling, nor shame, to stand in their way. They go on predicting the total conquest of the Peninsula with as much effrontery as if they had not predicted it two years ago —nay, even asserted that it was then completed; and they deliver their predictions in such a way, that it requires more charity than I possess not to believe that they wish to see them fulfilled;

for this is the last and worst, yet the necessary effect of party spirit, when carried so far as these politicians carry it. I do not know that I ever regretted being alone so much as when the news of Graham's victory arrived. It gave me more delight than I could well hold, and I wanted somebody to share it with me. We shall have great news, too, from Portugal. Massena has no lines to fall back upon; and if Lord Wellington can but bring him to action, we know what the result must be. How happy his retreat must make Lord Grenville, who had just delivered so wise an opinion upon the state of Portugal in the House of Lords!

"Longman's new Review will interfere with the Quarterly; and, so far as it succeeds, so far will it prevent the extension of our sale. I have not learned who are the proprietors of it—not Longman himself, for he wrote to me some eight or ten weeks ago, wishing me to bear a part in it, and giving me to understand that it was set on foot by some independent M.P's.—so at least I understood his language. Of course I returned a refusal, upon the ground of my previous connection with the Quarterly. They have set out better than we did, though they have a considerable portion of heavy matter, and their first article ought to have been in a very different tone.

"Yours ever truly, R. SOUTHEY."

To Grosvenor C. Bedford, Esq.

"Keswick, April 21, 1811.

"MY DEAR GROSVENOR,

"I have some news to tell you of my own family. Mr. T. Southey is dead: about half his property he has left to the son of a friend of his at Bristol, and the rest to his man Tom, and a few other such objects of his regard. This conduct toward me and my brothers is neither very surprising nor very blamable: we lived at a distance from him, and, when he did see us, he saw animals of so very different a nature from himself, that the wonder would have been if he had taken any pleasure in their society. But he has a sister, now advanced in life, and ill provided for; and she kept his house till he turned her out of it, for no other reason than that she discovered some regret at seeing the foot-boy Tom preferred to her nephews; and he has not left her any thing. This is wicked and unnatural conduct. My account comes from her. She says nothing of herself, and, I verily believe, thinks nothing upon that score; but her letter is an affecting one. 'I hope God will forgive him (these are her concluding words). John made himself a slave to get this trash; Thomas has made himself a fool to give it away.* I hope neither you nor yours will ever want it.' The property thus disposed of is about £1000 a year. An estate of half that value was left by the elder brother to a farmer's son, whom the father used to send sometimes with a hare.

"You know me well enough to know that no man living more thoroughly understands what Shenstone called the flocci-nauci-nihili-pilification of money. I had no expectations, and, consequently, have experienced no disappointment. God be praised for it! I have, also, no want. My employment (provided I write prose) is sufficiently paid; I have plenty of it; and like it as well as if it were merely the amusement of leisure hours. And, in case of my death before I shall have been able to make a provision for my family, my life is insured for £1000; and the world must be worse than I believe it to be if my operas should not produce enough in addition to that. * * * * * *

"I have another piece of news, which did surprise me. Brougham has been commissioned to apply to my uncle for the purpose of discovering whether I would undertake to translate Lucien Bonaparte's poem. My uncle replied, he supposed not, but referred the plenipotentiary to me; and no further proceedings have taken place. When I hear from B. I shall recommend Elton for the task, who translates well, and will, probably, be glad of a task which is likely to be so well paid. This has amused me very much; but it has rather lowered Lucien in my opinion, by the vanity which it implies. If his poem be good for any thing, he may be sure it will find translators: it looks ill to be so impatient for fame as to look about for one, and pay him for his work. From whom the application to my worship came I do not know; Lucien has probably applied to some friend to recommend him to the best hand; and, dispatch being one thing required, the preference has, perhaps, on this score, been given to me over Mr. Thomas Campbell; by which, no doubt, I am greatly flattered. To Grosvenor Bedford I may say that, if the poem in question be a bad one, it will not be worth translating; and if it be otherwise, I humbly conceive that the time which would be required to translate it may quite as worthily be bestowed upon some work of my own.

"God bless you! R. S."

To Grosvenor C. Bedford, Esq.

"Keswick, June 9, 1811.

"MY DEAR GROSVENOR,

"I completed the Register last night. Its enormous length has cost me at least three months' labor more than the former volume, the whole of which is dead loss of the only capital I possess in the world. This is considerably inconvenient; half that time would have sufficed for the Life of Nelson, the other half have set me forward for the next three numbers of the Quarterly. My ways and means, therefore, are considerably deranged. * * * *

"So —— lectures to-morrow upon the Curse of Kehama! I like —— for the same reason for which Dr. Johnson liked Mrs. Mary Cobb. 'I love Moll,' said he; 'I love Moll Cobb for her impudence.' I like ——, however, for something else; for, though he is impudentissimus homo and the very emperor of coxcombs, yet, neverthleess, —— —— is an honest fellow, and has a good heart. He is a clever fellow, too, in

* This property had been left to Thomas Southey by his elder brother John.

the midst of his quackery. And so, partly because I like him for the aforesaid reasons, partly because half an hour's conversation with him will afford mirth for half a year afterward, I will certainly call upon —— when I go to town, and shake hands with him once more. Ah, Grosvenor! people may say what they will about good company, or what Sharpe, *more suo*, denominates the '*very best*' society—the 'VERY BEST'—there is no company like that of an old fellow you can laugh *with*, and laugh *at*, and laugh *about* till your eyes overflow with the very oil of gladness.

"God bless you! R. S."

To Walter Savage Landor, Esq.

"London, July 15, 1811.

"It is utterly unaccountable to me why you of all men should care either for good or evil report of your poems, certain as you must be of their sterling value. I look upon Gebir as I do upon Dante's long poem in the Italian, not as a good poem, but as containing the finest poetry in the language; so it is with Count Julian, and so, no doubt, it was with the play which you have so provokingly destroyed.

"In about three weeks I hope to see you in your turret. We leave London this day week, and I will write from Bristol as soon as I can say when we shall depart from it. I was at Llanthony in 1798, and forded the Hondy on foot because I could not find the bridge. Have you found St. David's cavern, which Drayton places there, and for which I inquired in vain?

"I am no botanist; but, like you, my earliest and deepest recollections are connected with flowers, and they always carry me back to other days. Perhaps this is because they are the only things which affect our senses precisely in the same manner as they did in childhood. The sweetness of the violet is always the same, and when you rifle a rose, and drink, as it were, its fragrance, the refreshment is the same to the old man as to the boy. We see with different eyes in proportion as we learn to discriminate, and, therefore, this effect is not so certainly produced by visual objects. Sounds recall the past in the same manner, but do not bring with them individual scenes, like the cowslip-field or the bank of violets, or the corner of the garden to which we have transplanted field flowers. Oh, what a happy season is childhood, if our modes of life and education will let it be so! It were enough to make one misanthropical when we consider how great a portion of the evil of this world is man's own making, if the knowledge of this truth did not imply that the evil is removable; and, therefore, the prime duty of a good man is by all means in his power to assist in removing it. God bless you! R. S."

CHAPTER XVII.

SCOTT'S VISION OF DON RODERIC—ADVICE TO A YOUNG FRIEND ON GOING TO CAMBRIDGE—BELL AND LANCASTER CONTROVERSY—PLAN OF THE BOOK OF THE CHURCH—WISHES TO ASSIST MR. W. TAYLOR IN HIS DIFFICULTIES—PROSPECT OF BEING SUMMONED TO THE BAR OF HOUSE OF COMMONS—SHELLEY AT KESWICK—UGLY FELLOWS—OXFORD—HERBERT MARSH—TESTAMENTARY LETTER—APPLICATION FOR THE OFFICE OF HISTORIOGRAPHER—CATHOLIC CONCESSIONS—MURDER OF MR. PERCEVAL—STATE OF ENGLAND—EDINBURGH ANNUAL REGISTER—EXCURSION INTO DURHAM AND YORKSHIRE—VISIT TO ROKEBY—THE QUARTERLY REVIEW—THE REGISTER.—1811–1812.

To Walter Scott, Esq.

"Keswick, Sept. 8, 1811.

"MY DEAR SCOTT,

"You will have thought me very remiss in not thanking you sooner for the Vision, if you did not remember that I had been traveling from Dan to Beersheba, and take into consideration how little opportunity can be found for the use of pen and ink in the course of a series of runaway visits, during a journey of nine hundred miles. It was given me at the Admiralty the very day that it arrived there. I opened it on the spot, discovered that a letter to Polwhele had been inclosed to me, in time for Croker to rectify the mistake by making a fair exchange, and thus saving mine from a journey to the Land's End. If, however, I have not written to you about D. Roderic, I have been talking to every body about him. The want of plan and unity is a defect inherent in the very nature of your subject, and it would be just as absurd to censure the Vision for such a defect as it is to condemn Kehama because all the agents are not human personages. The execution is a triumphant answer to those persons who have supposed that you could not move with ease in a meter less loose than that of your great poems. To me it appears, on the whole, better written than those greater works, for this very reason—you have taken fewer licenses of language, and have united with the majesty of that fine stanza (the most perfect that ever was constructed) an ease which is a perfect contrast to the stiffness of Gertrude of Wyoming.

"It is remarkable that three poets should at once have been employed upon Roderic. I have a tragedy of Landor's in my desk, of which Count Julian is the hero: it contains some of the finest touches, both of passion and poetry, that I have ever seen. Roderic is also the pre-eminent personage of my own Pelayo, as far as it has yet proceeded. Differing so totally as we do in the complexion and management of the two poems, I was pleased to find one point of curious comparison, in which we have both represented Roderic in the act of confession, and both finished the picture highly. Our representations are so totally different as to form a perfect contrast, yet each so fitted to the temper in which the confession is made, that it might be sworn, if you had chosen my point of time, you could have written as I have done, and that, if I had written of the unrepentant king, I should have conceived of him exactly like yourself. I copy my own lines, because I think you will be gratified at seeing a parallel passage, which never can be produced except to the honor of both:

"'Then Roderic knelt
Before the holy man, and strove to speak:
"Thou see'st," he cried; "thou see'st—" But memory
And suffocating thoughts repress'd the word,
And shudderings, like an ague fit, from head
To foot convulsed him. Till at length subduing
His nature to the effort, he exclaimed,
Spreading his hands, and lifting up his face,
As if resolved in penitence to bear
A human eye upon his shame, "Thou see'st
Roderic the Goth." That name would have sufficed
To tell its whole abhorred history.
He not the less pursued—"the ravisher!
The cause of all this ruin!" Having said,
In the same posture motionless he knelt,
Arms straightened down, and hands dispread, and eyes
Raised to the monk, like one who from his voice
Expected life or death.'

"I saw but little of Gifford in town, because he was on the point of taking wing for the Isle of Wight when I arrived. The Review seems to have shaken the credit of the Edinburgh, and might shake it still more. The way to attack the enemy with most effect is to take up those very subjects which he has handled the most unfairly, and so to treat them as to force a comparison which must end in our favor. I am about to do this upon the question of Bell and Lancaster—a question on which —— has grossly committed himself.

"You may well suppose that three months' idleness has brought upon me a heavy accumulation of business. Meantime, good materials for the third year's Register have reached me from Cadiz, and I have collected others respecting Sicily and the Ionian Islands. I saw the last volume on my road, and there I could trace your hand in a powerful but too lenient essay upon Jeffrey's journal.

"Believe me, yours very truly,
"R. Southey."

To Mr. James White.

"Keswick, Oct. 25, 1811.

"My dear James,

"By this time you are settled at Pembroke, know your way to your rooms, the faces of your fellow-collegians, and enough, I dare say, of a college life to find its duties less formidable, and its habits less agreeable than they are supposed to be. Those habits are said to have undergone a great reformation since I was acquainted with them; in my time they stood grievously in need of it, but even then a man who had any good moral principles might live as he pleased, if he dared make the trial; and, however much he might be stared at at first for his singularity, was sure ere long to be respected for it.

"Some dangers beset every man when he enters upon so new a scene of life; that which I apprehend for you is low spirits. * * * * * Walk a stated distance every day; and that you may never want a motive for walking, make yourself acquainted with the elements of botany during the winter, that as soon as the flowers come out in the spring you may begin to herbalize. A quarter of an hour every day will make you master of the elements in the course of a very few months. I prescribe for you mentally also, and this is one of the prescriptions; for it is of main importance that you should provide yourself with amusement as well as employment. Pursue no study longer than you can without effort attend to it, and lay it aside whenever it interests you too much: whenever it impresses itself so much upon your mind that you dream of it or lie awake thinking about it, be sure it is then become injurious. Follow my practice of making your latest employment in the day something unconnected with its other pursuits, and you will be able to lay your head upon the pillow like a child.

"One word more, and I have done with advice. Do not be solicitous about taking a high degree, or about college honors of any kind. Many a man has killed himself at Cambridge by overworking for mathematical honors: recollect how few the persons are who, after they have spent their years in severe study at this branch of science, ever make any use of it afterward. Your wiser plan should be to look on to that state of life in which you wish and expect to be placed, and to lay in such knowledge as will then turn to account. * * * * *

"Believe me, my dear James,
"Your affectionate friend,
"R. Southey."

To John May, Esq.

"Nov. 2, 1811.

"My dear Friend,

"* * * Since our return a larger portion of my time than is either usual or convenient has been taken up by the chance society of birds of passage; this place abounds with them during the traveling season; and as there are none of them who find their way to me without some lawful introduction, so there are few who have not something about them to make their company agreeable for the little time that it lasts.

"You have seen my article upon Bell and the Dragon in the Quarterly. It is decisive as to the point of originality, and would have been the heaviest blow the Edinburgh has ever received if all the shot of my heavy artillery had not been drawn before the guns were fired. I am going to reprint it separately with some enlargement, for the purpose of setting the question at rest, and making the public understand what the new system is, which is very little understood, and doing justice to Dr. Bell, whom I regard as one of the greatest benefactors to his species. * * * * The case is not a matter of opinion, but rests upon recorded and stated facts. I tread, therefore, upon sure ground, and, taking advantage of this, I shall not lose the opportunity of repaying some of my numerous obligations to the Edinburgh Review.

* * * * * * *

"Probably you have seen the manner in which the Edinburgh Annual Register is twice noticed in their last number. * * * When the first year's volume appeared it was not even suspected who was the historian; and Jeffrey, a day or two after its publication, went for the first time into the publisher's shop expressly to tell him how much he admired the history, saying that, though he differed from the writer on many, indeed on most points, he nevertheless must declare that it was liberal, independent, and spirited throughout, the best piece of cotemporary history which had appeared for twenty years. When the second volume appeared he knew who was the author!

"Believe me, very affectionately yours,

"R. SOUTHEY."

To the Rev. Herbert Hill.

"Dec. 31, 1811.

"MY DEAR UNCLE,

"The hint which I threw out concerning our English martyrs in writing upon the evangelical sects is likely to mature into something of importance. I conceived a plan which Dr. Bell and the Bishop of Meath took up warmly, and the former has in some degree bound me to execute it by sending down Fox's Book of Martyrs as soon as he reached London. The projected outline is briefly this: Under the title of the Book of the Church, to give what should be at once the philosophy and the anthology of our Church History, so written as to be addressed to the hearts of the young and the understandings of the old; for it will be placed on the establishment of the national schools. It begins with an account of the various false religions of our different ancestors, British, Roman, and Saxon, with the mischievous temporal consequences of those superstitions, being the evils from which the country was delivered by its conversion to Christianity. 2dly, A picture of popery, and the evils from which the Reformation delivered us. 3dly, Puritanism rampant, from which the restoration of the Church rescued us. Lastly, Methodism, from which the Establishment preserves us. These parts to be connected by an historical thread, containing whatever is most impressive in the acts and monuments of the English Church. How beautiful a work may be composed upon such a plan (which, from its very nature, excludes whatever is uninviting or tedious), you will at once perceive. The civil history would form a companion work upon a similar plan, called the Book of the Constitution, showing the gradual but uniform amelioration of society; and the direct object of both would be to make the rising generation feel and understand the blessings of their inheritance.

* * * * * * *

"I am well stored with materials, having all the republished chronicles and Hooker—the only controversial work which it will be at all necessary to consult. The other books which I want I have ordered: they are Burnett and the Church Histories of Fuller, and of the stiff old non-juror, Jeremy Collier. I will send the manuscript to you before it goes to the press, for it will require an inspecting eye. Meantime, if any thing occur to you which would correct or improve the plan, such as you here see it, do not omit to communicate your advice and opinion. I have a strong persuasion that both these works may be made of great, extensive, and permanent usefulness.

* * * * * * *

"R. S."

To Dr. Gooch.

"Keswick, Dec. 15, 1811.

"MY DEAR GOOCH,

"I have a letter from William Taylor of a dismal character. After stating the sum of their losses, he says, 'we can not subsist upon the interest of what remains. The capital will last our joint lives, but I shall be abandoned to a voluntary interment in the same grave with my parents. O! that nature would realize this most convenient doom!'

"Now my reason for transcribing this passage to you is, because it made a deep impression on me, and haunts me when I lie down at night. You know more of Norwich than I do, and more of William Taylor's connections. Who is most in his confidence? is it ——? I thought of writing directly to him. * * * But what I would say to the person who may be most likely to enter into my wishes is, that William Taylor's friends should raise such an annuity as would secure him from penury, and at once relieve his mind from the apprehensions of it; either raising a sum sufficient to purchase it (the best way, because the least liable to accidents), or by yearly contributions; Dr. Sayers (or any other the fittest person) receiving, and regularly paying it; and he never knowing particularly from whence it comes, but merely that it is his. The former plan is the best, because, in that case, there would be only to purchase the annuity, and put the security into his hands; and this might be done without any person appearing in it, the office transmitting him the necessary documents. This, of course, is a thing upon which the very wind must not blow. Ten years hence—or perhaps five—if the least desirable of these plans should be found most practicable, you and Harry may be able to co-operate in it. I am ready now, either with a yearly ten pounds, or with fifty at once. If more were in my power, more should be done; but, if his friends do not love him well enough to secure him at least £100 a year, one way or other, the world is worse than I thought it.

"You do not say whether you have seen Sharon Turner. That introduction was the best I could give you, because I think it would give you a friend. You could not fail to esteem and love Turner when you knew him. He is the happiest man I have ever known; and that could not be the case if he were not a very wise as well as a very good one.

"God bless you! R. SOUTHEY."

It has been already noticed that the Edinburgh Review had recommended the Annual Register for government prosecution, on account of the boldness of its language on the Spanish question, and also, especially, with respect to some remarks on Mr. Whitbread. It appears that there was some likelihood of this "friendly" hint being taken, and to this the following letter refers.

To Grosvenor C. Bedford, Esq.

"Keswick, Jan. 4, 1812.

"My dear Grosvenor,

"Concerning Whitbread, I believe, in every instance, the text of his speech will justify the comment. You have heard of taking the wrong sow by the ear: he had better take a wild boar by the ear than haul me up to London upon this quarrel. I should tell him it was true that I had said his speeches were translated into French, and circulated through all the departments of France, but I had not said—what has since come to my knowledge—that, when they were thus circulated, nobody believed them genuine; nobody believed it possible that such speeches could have been uttered by an Englishman. I should ask the House (that is, his side of the House; and, of course, in that *humble* language becoming a person at the bar) at what time they would be pleased to let their transactions become matter for history; and I should give the party a gentle hint not to delay that time too long, for reputations, like every thing else, find their level; and if he, and such as he, do not get into history soon, they may run a risk of not getting into it at all. I should speak of the situation in which Spain and England stand to each other, and contrast my own feelings with those which he has continually expressed. I should appeal to the whole tenor of the book whether the design of the writer was to vilify Parliament, or to bring the government into contempt; and, as an Englishman, a man of letters, and an historian, I should claim my privileges.

"Phillidor has made his appearance, and shall be returned in the first parcel, with the reviewal of Azara. Out of pure conscience, I have promised Gifford to take all these South American travelers myself, because I can not bear that the Edinburgh should gain credit upon this subject, when I am so much better versed in it than any other man in England possibly can be. I am heartily glad the state of South America is in Blanco's hands; it will be highly useful to the Review, and, I hope, to himself also; for he works hard, with little benefit, and, when he has once tried his strength in the Review, it will not be difficult to find other appropriate subjects for him. I have a high respect for this man's moral and intellectual character, and earnestly wish it were possible to obtain a pension, which never could be more properly bestowed. Canning has smitten the Quarterly with a dead palsy upon the Catholic Question, or else Blanco could supply such an exposition upon that subject as would entitle him to any thing that Mr. Perceval could give.

"Here is a man at Keswick, who acts upon me as my own ghost would do. He is just what I was in 1794. His name is Shelley, son to the member for Shoreham; with £6000 a year entailed upon him, and as much more in his father's power to cut off. Beginning with romances of ghosts and murder, and with poetry at Eton, he passed, at Oxford, into metaphysics; printed half a dozen pages, which he entitled 'The Necessity of Atheism;' sent one anonymously to Coplestone, in expectation, I suppose, of converting him; was expelled in consequence; married a girl of seventeen, after being turned out of doors by his father; and here they both are, in lodgings, living upon £200 a year, which her father allows them. He is come to the fittest physician in the world. At present he has got to the Pantheistic stage of philosophy, and, in the course of a week, I expect he will be a Berkeleyan, for I have put him upon a course of Berkeley. It has surprised him a good deal to meet, for the first time in his life, with a man who perfectly understands him, and does him full justice. I tell him that all the difference between us is that he is nineteen and I am thirty-seven, and I dare say it will not be long before I shall succeed in convincing him that he may be a true philosopher, and do a great deal of good with £6000 a year, the thought of which troubles him a great deal more at present than ever the want of a sixpence (for I have known such a want) did me. * * * God help us! the world wants mending, though he did not set about it exactly in the right way. God bless you, Grosvenor! R. S."

To Grosvenor C. Bedford, Esq.

"Keswick, Jan. 17, 1812.

"Dear Grosvenor,

"My household is affected with a complaint which I take at this time to be epidemic—the fear of ugly fellows. In Mrs. Coleridge, perhaps, this may have originated in her dislike to you, but the newspapers have increased it. Every day brings bloody news from Carlisle, Cockermouth, &c.; last night half the people in Keswick sat up, alarmed by two strangers, who, according to all accounts, were certainly 'no beauties,' and I was obliged to take down a rusty gun, and manfully load it for the satisfaction of the family. The gun has been properly cleaned to-day, and woe betide him who may be destined to receive its contents. But, in sober truth, the ugly fellows abound here as well as in London; we are indebted for them partly to the manufactories at Carlisle, and partly to that distinguished patriot ——, who encourages the importation of Irishmen. I am looking for a dog, and I want you to provide me with more convenient arms than this old Spanish fowling-piece. Buy for me, therefore, a brace of pistols, the plainer and cheaper the better, so they are good—that is, so they will stand fire without danger of bursting. Sights and hair-triggers may be dispensed with, as they are neither for show nor for dueling. And I have leave from my governess—

nay, more than that, she has desired me—to send for

A Watchman's Rattle!

Think of that, G. C. B.!!!—think of that!—designed by her to give the alarm when the ugly fellows come. But oh, Grosvenor, the glorious tunes, the solos and bravuras, that I shall play upon that noble musical instrument before any such fellow makes his appearance!* God bless you! R. S."

To Mr. James White

"Keswick, Feb. 16, 1812.

"MY DEAR JAMES,

"I was glad to hear from Neville that you were comfortably settled, and growing attached to college; and glad to hear afterward from yourself that you begin to feel your ground. There is no part of my own life which I remember with so little pleasure as that which was passed at the University; not that it has left behind it any cause of self-reproach, but I had many causes of disquietude and unhappiness—some imaginary, and some, God knows, real enough. And I can not think of the place without pain, because of the men with whom I there lived in the closest intimacy of daily and almost hourly intercourse; those whom I loved best are dead, and there are some whom I have never seen since we parted there, and possibly never shall see more. It is with this feeling I believe, more or less, that every man who has any feeling always remembers college. Seven years ago I walked through Oxford on a fine summer morning, just after sunrise, while the stage was changing horses: I went under the windows of what had formerly been my own rooms; the majesty of the place was heightened by the perfect silence of the streets, and it had never before appeared to me half so majestic or half so beautiful. But I would rather go a day's journey round than pass through that city again, especially in the day-time, when the streets are full. Other places in which I have been an inhabitant would not make the same impression; there is an enduring sameness in a university like that of the sea and mountains. It is the same in our age that it was in our youth; the same figures fill the streets, and the knowledge that they are not the same persons brings home the sense of change, which is of all things the most mournful.

"I see your name to the Bible Society, concerning which I have read Herbert Marsh's pamphlet and Dr. Clarke's reply. Marsh may possibly be fond of controversy, because he knows his strength. He is a clear, logical writer, and in these days a little logic goes a great way, for of all things it is that in which the writers of this generation are most deficient. His reasoning is to me completely satisfactory as to these two points—that where Christians of all denominations combine for the purpose either of spreading Christianity or distributing Bibles in other countries, the cause of the general church is promoted thereby; but that when they combine together at home, as that condition can only be effected by a concession on the part of the churchmen, by that concession the Church of England is proportionally weakened. Nothing can be clearer. But, though the Margaret Professor is perfectly right in his views, and his antagonists are mere children when compared to him, I think he has been injudicious in exciting the controversy, because upon that statement of the case which his opponents will make, and which appears at first sight to be a perfectly fair one, every body must conclude him to be in the wrong, and very few persons will take the trouble of looking further. And I think his object might have been effected by a little management without much difficulty—by an arrangement among the Church members of the Society that the Liturgy should be appended to the Bibles which they distributed at home, or by a Prayer-book Society. A man should be very careful how he engages in a controversy, in which, however right he may be, he is certain to appear wrong to the multitude; and he ought to be especially careful when he thus exposes not his own character alone, but that of the body to which he belongs. Besides, the mischief which Marsh perceives is not very great, because I apprehend that at least nine tenths of the business of B. Society relates to foreign countries. But I agree with him entirely as to the mischief that lurks under the name of liberality, by which is meant not an indulgence to the opinions of other communities, but an indifference to your own.

"Do you attend the Divinity Lectures? Herbert Marsh is likely to be a good lecturer, being a thorough master of his subject, and a reasoner of the old school.

"Give me a letter when you feel inclined; and believe me, my dear James, your affectionate friend, ROBERT SOUTHEY."

To C. W. W. Wynn, Esq.

"Keswick, April 15, 1812.

"MY DEAR WYNN,

"What a number of recollections crowd upon me when I think of ——! Of all our school companions, how very few of them are there whose lots in life have proved to be what might have been expected for them. You and Bedford have gone on each in your natural courses, and are to be found just where and what I should have looked to find, if I had waked after a Nourjahad sleep of twenty years. The same thing might be said of me if my local habitation were not here at the end of the map. I am leading the life which is convenient for me, and following the pursuits to which, from my earliest boyhood, I was so strongly predisposed. A less troubled youth would probably have led to a less happy manhood. I should have thought less and studied less, felt less and suffered less. Now, for all that I have felt and suffered, I know that I am the better; and God knows that I have yet

* These musical anticipations were fully realized, and the performance of them was one of the amusements of my childhood.

much to think, and to study, and to do. It is now eighteen years since you and I used to sit till midnight over your claret in Skeleton Corner—half your life and almost half mine. During that time we have both of us rather grown than changed, and accident has had as little to do with our circumstances as with our character.

"Your godson Herbert, who is just old enough to be delighted with the Old Woman of Berkeley, tells me he means, when he is a man, to be a poet like his father. It will be time enough ten years hence, if we live so long, to take thought as to what he shall be; the only care I need take at present is what should be done, in case of my death, for the provision of my family. I have insured my life for £1000. I had calculated upon my copy-rights as likely to prove valuable when it would become the humor of the day to regret me; but, to my great surprise, I find the booksellers interpret the terms of their taking the risk and sharing the profit as an actual surrender to them of half the property in perpetuity. Townsend, the traveler, who was as much deceived in this case as I have been, was about to try the point with them. I know not what prevented him. * * * This is a flagrant and cruel injustice. * * * If I live, and preserve my health and faculties, I have no doubt of realizing a decent competency in twenty years; but twenty years is almost as much as my chances of life would be reckoned at in tables of calculation. * * *

"One thing which I will do whenever I can afford leisure for the task, will be, to write and leave behind me my own Memoirs: they will contain so much of the literary history of the times as to have a permanent value on that account. This would prove a good post obit, for there can be no doubt I shall be sufficiently talked of when I am gone.

"Such are my ways and means for the future; but if I should not live to provide more than the very little which is already done, then, indeed, the exertion of some friends would be required. An arrangement might be made with Longman to allow of a subscription edition of my works: this would be productive in proportion to the efforts that were used. I should hope, also, in such a case, that the continuance of my pension might be looked for from either of the present parties in the state, through Perceval, or Canning, or yourself.

"This is a sort of testamentary letter. It is fit there should be one; and to whom, my dear Wynn, could it so properly be addressed? By God's blessing, I may yet live to make all necessary provision myself. My means are now improving every year. I am up the hill of difficulty, and shall very soon get rid of the burden which has impeded me in the ascent. I have some arrangements with Murray, which are likely to prove more profitable than any former speculations; and should I succeed in obtaining the office which the old Frenchman fills at present so properly—and which is the only thing for which I have the slightest ambition—it would soon put me in possession of the utmost I could want or wish for, inasmuch as I could lay by the whole income, and the title would be, in a great degree, productive.

"Hitherto I have been highly favored. A healthy body, an active mind, and a cheerful heart are the three best boons nature can bestow; and, God be praised, no man ever enjoyed them more perfectly. My skin and bones scarcely know what an ailment is; my mind is ever on the alert, and yet, when its work is done, becomes as tranquil as a baby; and my spirits invincibly good. Would they have been so, or could I have been what I am, if you had not been for so many years my stay and support? I believe not; yet you had been so long my familiar friend, that I felt no more sense of dependence in receiving my main, and at one time sole, subsistence from you, than if you had been my brother: it was being done to as I would have done.

"R. S."

The appointment of Historiographer, to which my father refers in the letter, appears to have fallen vacant almost immediately. Application was at once made for it in his behalf in several influential quarters, but it seems to have been filled up with extraordinary haste, having been bestowed upon Dr. Stanier Clarke, Librarian to the Prince Regent. It turned out ultimately that there was no salary attached to the office, the appointment being merely honorary.

The next letter was written immediately on hearing of the murder of Mr. Perceval.

To Grosvenor C. Bedford, Esq.

"Keswick, May 14, 1812.

"My dear Grosvenor,

"In spite of myself, I have been weeping; this has relieved the throbbings of my head; but my mind is overcharged, and must pour itself out. I am going to write something upon the state of popular feeling, which will probably appear in the Courier, where it will obtain the readiest and widest circulation. Enough to alarm the people I shall be able to say; but I would fain alarm the government, and if this were done in public they would think it imprudent, and, indeed, it would be so.

"I shall probably begin with what you say of the sensation occasioned by this most fatal event, and then give the reverse of your account as I have received it from Coleridge; what he heard in a pot-house into which he went on the night of the murder, not more to quench his thirst than for the purpose of hearing what the populace would say. Did I not speak to you with ominous truth upon this subject in one of my last letters? This country is upon the brink of the most dreadful of all conceivable states—an insurrection of the poor against the rich; and if, by some providential infatuation, the Burdettites had not continued to *insult* the soldiers, the existing government would not be worth a week's purchase, nor any throat which could be supposed to be worth cutting, safe for a month longer.

"You know, Grosvenor, I am no aguish politician, nor is this a sudden apprehension which has seized me. Look to what I have said of the effect of Mrs. Clarke's business upon the public in the last year's Register, and look to the remarks upon the tendency of manufactures to this state in Espriella, written five years ago. Things are in that state at this time that nothing but the army preserves us: it is the single plank between us and the red sea of an English Jacquerie—a Bellum Servile; not provoked, as both those convulsions were, by grievous oppression, but prepared by the inevitable tendency of the manufacturing system, and hastened on by the folly of a besotted faction, and the wickedness of a few individuals. The end of these things is full of evil, even upon the happiest termination; for the loss of liberty is the penalty which has always been paid for the abuse of it. But we must not now employ our thoughts upon the danger of our own victory; there is but too much yet to be done to render the victory certain.

"The first step should be the immediate renewal of associations for the protection of our lives and properties, and of the British Constitution; with the re-establishment to the utmost possible extent of the volunteers—as effective a force against a mob of united Englishmen as they would be inefficient in the first shock of an invasion. This may be safely said and pressed upon the government and the people; what I dare not say publicly is that there is yet danger from the army—that horrid flogging, for the abolition of which Burdett has been suffered to appear as the advocate! Oh that Perceval had prevented this popularity, by coming forward himself as the soldier's friend! He has good works enough for his good name, as well as for his soul's rest; but this would have remained for his colleagues and for the country.

"This, of course, can not be touched upon immediately, for it would be too obviously an act of fear; but if I knew the ministers, I would urgently press upon them the wisdom of granting some boon to the soldiers—something which, at little cost to the nation, would yet come home to the feelings of every individual in the army. The mere institution of honorary rewards would do this—fifty pounds in copper medals would go farther than as many thousands in bounties toward recruiting it hereafter. But I would couple it with something more; for instance, ten or twenty of the oldest men, or oldest soldiers, in every regiment which distinguished itself in the two late assaults, should have their discharge, with full pay for life, or an increase of pay if they chose to serve on. Do not think that these things are inefficacious or beneath the notice of statesmen. Why is it that poets move the heart of men, but because they understand the feelings of men, and it is by their feelings that they may be best governed? Look at the agitators; they address themselves to the passions of the mob, and who does not perceive with what tremendous effect!

"I wish you would read this to Gifford or to Herries, because I am sure that these cheap and easy measures would go far toward winning the affections of the soldiers at these perilous times. Other topics I shall speak of elsewhere—the establishment of a system of parochial education, and the necessity of colonial schemes as opening an issue in the distempered body politic. This will be for the Quarterly. Vigorous measures, I trust in God, will be taken while the feelings of the sound class are in a state to favor them. This murder, though committed publicly by a madman, has been made the act and deed of the populace. Shocking as this appears, so it is and so it must be considered. With timely vigor, the innocent blood which has been shed may prove an acceptable sacrifice, and save us; otherwise it is but the opening of the flood-gates.

"I thought of poor Herries as soon as I could think of any thing. The loss which the country has sustained I can scarcely dare to contemplate. There seems nothing to look to but the Wellesleys, with Canning, Huskisson for Chancellor of the Exchequer, and, in all likelihood, Sir James Mackintosh, who is sure to take the strongest side, and his talents will make him a powerful support to any party. Yet in this train there seems to follow a long catalogue of dangers: Catholic concessions, and next, by aid of all the admitted enemies of the Church, the sale of tithes to supply the necessities of the government—a measure which will be as certainly popular as it will be ultimately ruinous to the Church and most fatal to the country. There will be a glorious war to console us; but, under such circumstances, I shall look to that war with the painful thought that we may be repaid for our services to the Spaniards by finding an asylum in Spain when England will have lost all that our fathers purchased for us so dearly!

"God bless you! R. SOUTHEY.

"Tell Gifford I shall be ready for him with the French Biography, which will be a sketch of the Revolution, introducing an examination of our own state as tending toward the same gulf. Would to God it were not so well timed! What has passed seems like a dream to me—a sort of nightmare that overlays and oppresses my thoughts and feelings!"

To Grosvenor C. Bedford, Esq.

"Keswick, May 16, 1812.

"MY DEAR GROSVENOR,

"I have myself so strong a sense of Mr. Perceval's public merits, that I can not help writing to you to say how much I wish that a statue might be erected to him. This could only be done by subscription; but surely such a subscription might soon be filled, if his friends think it advisable. Suggest this to Herries; and if the thing should be begun, when the list has the proper names to begin with, put mine down for five guineas, which could not at this time be better employed.

"The fit place for this statue would be the spot where he fell. Permission to place it there would no doubt be obtained, and the opposition made to it would only recoil upon his political enemies.

"I have often been grieved by public events, but never so depressed by any as by this. It is not the shock which has produced this, nor the extent of private misery which this wretched madman has occasioned, though I can scarcely refrain from tears while I write. It is my deep and ominous sense of danger to the country, from the Burdettites on one hand, and from Catholic concessions on the other. You know I am no High-Church bigot: it would be impossible for me to subscribe to the Church Articles. Upon the mysterious points I rather withhold assent than refuse it, not presuming to define in my own imperfect conceptions what has been left indefinite. But I am convinced that the overthrow of the Church establishment would bring with it the greatest calamities for us and for our children. If any man could have saved it, it was Mr. Perceval. The repeal of the Test Act will let in Catholics and invite more Dissenters. When the present Duke of Norfolk dies, you will have Catholic members for all his boroughs. All these parties will join in plundering the Church. No man is more thankful for the English Reformation than I am; but nearly a century and a half elapsed before the evils which it necessarily originated had subsided.

"As for conciliating the wild Irish by such concessions, the notion is so preposterous, that when I know a man of understanding can maintain such an opinion, it makes me sick at heart to think upon what sandy foundations every political fabric seems to rest!

"I have strayed on unintentionally. Go to Herries, and if he will enter into my feelings about the statue, let no time be lost. God bless you! R. S."

To Grosvenor C. Bedford, Esq.

"May 17, 1812.

"My dear Grosvenor,

"I received a note from Lord Lonsdale on Saturday, inclosing a reply from Lord Hertford to his application, which reply states that a previous arrangement had been made for the office of historiographer. Thinking you would be likely to know this as soon as myself, I did not write to you. My interest was better than I expected. Upon Lord Lonsdale I had reckoned; but Scott wrote for me to Lord Melville, and seemed to depend upon success. I have now done with the state lottery. Of all things possible, I most desired an appointment at Lisbon; if it had been given me when it was desired, and when it would have been honorable in Fox so to have given it, knowing as he did my motive for wishing it, it would have involved me (owing to the subsequent troubles) in pecuniary difficulties which perhaps I should never have surmounted. That hope having failed, I looked to that good ship the Historiographer, believing myself better qualified for the post than most men, and, more than any other man, ambitious of fulfilling its duties; but that good ship, it seems, is still destined to be so ill manned as to be perfectly useless.

"This evening I have a letter from Canning, couched in the most handsome and friendly terms. He does not know that the office is disposed of, but hints at difficulties in the way of his obtaining it (even supposing he were in power), which Gifford has explained. He concludes with expressions and professions of good will, which I doubt not are sincere. But there is nothing to which I can look forward.

"Say to Gifford that I must beg him to end with my article instead of beginning with it. I am close pressed with the Register, which this week will bring, I hope and trust, to a conclusion. Mr. Ballantyne's historiographer is well paid, but the office is no sinecure.

"I wish you were here to see the country in full beauty. Your godson has just learned to read Greek, and I expect in my next parcel a grammar and vocabulary for him. He promises well, if it please God that he should live. God bless you! R. S."

To J. Rickman, Esq.

"May 18, 1812.

"My dear Rickman,

"The fate of poor Perceval has made me quite unhappy ever since I heard of it, not merely from the shock and the private misery which it is quite impossible to put out of mind, but from the whole train of evils to which this is but the beginning. I would fain have believed the report that Mr. Abbott was to take his place in the House of Commons, because, if he could have found tongue, I knew where whatever else might have been wanting was to be found. But it was not likely that he should quit a better situation for one of so much anxiety and labor. W—— and C——, I doubt not, ratted upon the Catholic question because they expected the prince upon that ground would eject Perceval, and then they should have a better chance than the *Early Friends*. If they come in, as I fear they will, we may have the war carried on, but we shall have Catholic concessions, after which the Church property is not worth seven years' purchase; they will sell the tithes; and the next step will be to put the Establishment to sale in the way of contracts; the minds of the people (which, God knows, need no further poison) will then be totally unsettled, and the ship will part from her last cable on a lee shore in the height of the storm. At this moment the army is the single plank between us and destruction; and I believe the only thing doubtful is whether we shall have a military despotism *before* we go through the horrors of a *bellum servile* or *after* it. This I am certain of, that nothing but an immediate suspension of the liberty of debate and the liberty of the press can preserve us. Were I minister, I would instantly suspend the Habeas Corpus, and have every Jacobin journalist confined, so that it should not be possible for them to continue their treasonable vocation. There they should stay till it would be safe to let them out, which it might be in some seven years. I would clear the gallery whenever one of the agitators rose to speak, and if the speech were printed, I would teach him that his privilege of attempting to excite rebellion did not extend beyond the walls of Parliament; that he might talk treason to those walls as long as he pleased, but that if he printed treason he was then answerable to the vengeance of his country. I did not forget* the main question about reading. One mouth suffices for a dozen or a score pair of ears in the tap-rooms and pot-houses, where Cobbett and Hunt are read as the evangelists of the populace. There is no way of securing the people against this sort of poison but by the old receipt of Mithradates—dieting them from their childhood with antidotes, and making them as ready to for for their church and state as the Spaniards. We are beginning to attempt this when it is too late. A judicial fatuity seems to have been sent among us. Romanists, sectarians of every kind, your liberality men, and your philosophers of every kind and of every degree of folly and emptiness, are united for the blessed purpose of plucking up old principles by the roots, each for their own separate ends, but all sure of meeting with the same end if they are successful. We who see this danger have no power to prevent it, and they who have the power can not be made to see it. * * *

"This is a melancholy strain. We must, however, work the ship till it sinks; and a vigorous minister might take advantage of the feelings of the sound part of the country at the moment, and the avowal which the Burdettites have made for strong measures of prevention. * * * * * I would give the poor gratuitous education in parochial schools—a boon which all among them who care for their children would rightly estimate; and if the work of coercion kept pace with that of conciliation, we might hold on till our battle in Spain ended in the overthrow of the enemy. But where is the dictator who is to save the commonwealth? Perceval had a character which was worth as much as his talents. The only statesman who has these advantages in any approaching degree is Lord Sidmouth, but he wants those abilities which in Perceval seemed always to grow according to the measure of the occasion. Yet he would be the best head of a ministry, for the weight which his good intentions would give him. Vansittart would do for Chancellor of Exchequer, if there were any other efficient minister in the Commons.

"I am going to write upon the French Revolution for the Quarterly Review—a well-timed subject: the evil is, that it is writing to those readers who are in the main of the same way of thinking. Our cotemporaries read, not in the hope of being instructed, but to have their opinions flattered. Yours truly, R. S."

The only recreation my father permitted himself during this summer consisted of an excursion into the neighboring county of Durham, where he had now two brothers residing, and a pedestrian tour from thence home through part of Yorkshire. His account of a visit to Rokeby will be read with interest.

To Mrs. Southey.

"Settle, July 23, 1812.

"MY DEAR EDITH,

"We left St. Helen's after an early breakfast on Tuesday, with Tom in company; looked at Raby and Bernard Castle, and made our way to the porter's lodge at Rokeby. * * * A sturdy old woman, faithful to her orders, refused us admittance, saying that if we were going to the Hall we might go in, but if not we must not enter the grounds; nor would she let us in till we had promised to call at the Hall. Accordingly, against the grain, in observance of this promise, to the house I went, and having first inquired if Sir Walter Scott was there, requested permission to see the grounds. Mr. Morritt was not within, but the permission was granted; and in ten minutes after, the footman came running to say we might see the house also, and we might fish if we pleased. I excused myself from seeing the house, saying we were going on, and returning a due number of thanks, &c. But presently we met Mr. and Mrs. M. in the walk by the river side, and were, as you may suppose, obliged to dine and sleep there, their hospitality being so pressed upon us that I could not continue to refuse it without rudeness. Behold the lion, then, in a den perfectly worthy of him, eating grapes and pears, and drinking claret. The grounds are the finest things of the kind I have ever seen. A little in the manner of Downton, more resembling Lowther, but the Greta at Rokeby affords finer scenery than either. There is a summer-house overlooking it, the inside of which was ornamented by Mason the poet: one day he set the whole family to work in cutting out ornaments in colored paper from antique designs, directing the whole himself. It is still in good preservation, and will, doubtless, be preserved as long as a rag remains. This river, in 1771, rose in the most extraordinary manner during what is still called the great flood. There is a bridge close by the summer-house at least sixty feet above the water; against this bridge and its side the river piled up an immense dam of trees and rubbish, which it had swept before it; at length, down comes a stone of such a size that it knocked down Greta Bridge by the way, knocked away the whole mass of trees, carried off the second bridge, and lodged some little way beyond it upon the bank, breaking into three or four pieces. Playfair the other day estimated the weight of this stone at about seventy-

* "What shall I say of the unhappy event which has happened here? I expected Mr. Perceval to be murdered, but I had expected it from the Burdettites and others rendered infuriate by the poison they imbibe from sixteen newspapers, emulous in violence and mischief. In reading your little book about Lancaster, I do not find that you discuss the main question, whether the mob can be conveniently taught reading while the liberty of the press exists as at present. Every one who reads at all reads a Sunday newspaper, not the Bible; and if any man before doubted the efficacy of that prescription, the behavior of the mob upon Mr. P.'s death may teach them better knowledge."—*J. R. to R. S., May* 16, 1812.

eight tons; the most wonderful instance, he said, he had ever heard of of the power of water. Before this stone came down, one of the trees had blocked up an old man and his wife who inhabited a room under the summer-house; the branches broke their windows, and a great bough barred the door; meantime the water, usually some twenty feet below, was on a level with it. The people of the house came to their relief, and sawed the bough off to let them out, and the windows remain as they were left, a memorial of this most extraordinary flood.

"Mr. Morritt's father bought the house of Sir Thomas Robinson, well known in his day by the names of Long Robinson and Long Sir Thomas. You may recollect a good epigram upon this man:

"'Unlike to Robinson shall be my song,
It shall be witty—and it sh'a'nt be long.'

Long Sir Thomas found a portrait of Richardson in the house: thinking Mr. Richardson a very unfit personage to be suspended in effigy among lords, ladies, and baronets, he ordered the painter to put him on the star and blue ribbon, and then christened the picture Sir Robert Walpole. You will easily imagine Mr. Morritt will not suffer the portrait to be restored. This, however, is not the most extraordinary picture in the room. That is one of Sir T.'s intended improvements, representing the river, which now flows over the finest rocky bed I ever beheld, metamorphosed by four dams into a piece of water as smooth and as still as a canal, and elevated by the same operation so as to appear at the end of a smooth shaven green. Mr. M. shows this with great glee. He has brought there from our country the stone fern and the Osmunda regalis.* Among his pictures is a Madonna by Guido; he mentioned this to a master of a college, whose name I am sorry to say that I have forgotten, for the gentleman in reply pointed to a picture above representing an aunt of Mr. Morritt's (I believe), dressed in the very pink of the mode, and asked if that lady was the Madonna!

"I am sorry, too, that I forgot to ask if this was the lady whose needle-work is in the house. Mr. M. had an aunt who taught Miss Linwood. Wordsworth thought her pictures quite as good. In one respect they may be better, for she made her stitches athwart and across, exactly as the strokes of the original pictures. Miss L. (Mr. M. says) makes her stitches all in one way. This lady had great difficulty about her worsted, and could only suit herself by buying damaged quantities, thus obtaining shades which would else have been unobtainable. The colors fly, and, in order to preserve them as long as possible, prints are fitted in the frames to serve as screens. The art cost her her life, though at an advanced age; it brought on a dead palsy, occasioned by holding her hands so continually in an elevated position working at the canvas. Her last picture is hardly finished; the needle, Mr. M. says, literally dropped from her hands. Death had been creeping on her for twelve years. God bless you! R. S."

To John May, Esq.

"Keswick, Aug. 14, 1812.

"My dear Friend,

"Let me trouble you with a commission which, if it be successful, will essentially enrich my store of historical documents. I have just learned, by accident, that there is in High Holborn a set of Muratori's great collection of the Italian historians, which, wanting one volume, is on that account offered for sale at a very low price—some five or six pounds, for a collection which I should joyfully purchase at the price of five-and-twenty, were it entire. * * * The three great works which I want are the Acta Sanctorum, the Byzantine Historians, and Muratori; and it would be folly not to purchase this set, notwithstanding it is imperfect, when the loss of one volume so materially diminishes the price, without lessening the utility of the other volumes. I should think it, at half a guinea a volume, a cheap purchase.

"My article upon the French Revolutionists in the last Quarterly is a good deal the worse for the mutilation which, as usual, it has undergone, but which I regard less than I do the alteration of one single word. Speaking of 'the pilot that weathered the storm,' I wrote 'whatever may have been his merits,' and this word is altered into 'transcendant as'—an alteration of which I shall certainly complain. Had the article been printed entire, it would have done me credit: the hint with which it concludes relates to an essay upon the state of the lower classes, which I have undertaken for the last number.

"I had yesterday the pleasure of cutting open the last volume of the Register—a greater delight to me than it will be to any other person, I dare be sworn. This is the last and greatest of an author's pleasures. The London proprietors urge an alteration in the plan, and want it to be brought out in a single volume, like the London Annual Register; the Edinburgh proprietors very wisely negative this proposal, and determine to carry it on upon the present plan, even if they are left to themselves. The change, I think, would have been fatal to the work: whether perseverance may preserve it, is very doubtful. I go to work, however, upon the year 1811, with great good will. You will find, in the second part of this new volume, a life of Lope de Aguirre, written as a chapter for the history of Brazil, but cut out as an excrescence, for which room could not be afforded. The narrative is an extraordinary piece of history, whole and entire of itself, and so little connected with that of any other country, that it would appear equally as an excrescence in the history of Peru or of Venezuela as in that of Brazil; so it is as well where it is as it could be any where else. * * * * * The ballad of the Inchcape Rock, in the same volume, is mine also, written many years ago, when I was poet to the Morn-

* The largest of the fern tribe, growing to the height of five and six feet—a rare plant even in its own districts. The finest specimens are on the River Rotha.

ing Post. I know not to whom it is obliged for its present situation, neither do I know who has been tinkering it. It lay uncorrected among my papers, because I had no use for it, unless I should ever publish a miscellaneous volume of verse. The Life of Nelson is sent to the press. I expect the first proof every day, and hope to finish the manuscript by the beginning of next month. Since my return from my late excursion, I have made good progress with Pelayo, or rather with Roderic, as the poem ought to be called. It pleases me so well, that I begin to wish other persons should be pleased with it as well as myself.

"Believe me, ever, your affectionate friend,

"ROBERT SOUTHEY."

The "sketch" referred to in the following letter was a very curious production. It consisted of a series of parallelisms between the events and characters in Thalaba and certain portions of the Scriptures, drawn out with great ingenuity and at considerable length. The view taken was as if the poem had been intended as an allegorical representation of the power and virtues of Faith.

To the Rev. John Martyn Longmire.

"Keswick, Nov. 4, 1812.

"I am truly sensible, sir, of the honor you have conferred upon me by your letter of October 29th, and shall be still farther gratified by a communication of the sketch which is there mentioned. My aim has been to diffuse through my poems a sense of the beautiful and good (τὸ καλὸν καὶ ἀγαθὸν) rather than to aim at the exemplification of any particular moral precept. It has, however, so happened, that both in Thalaba and Kehama, the nature of the story led me to represent examples of faith. At a very early age, indeed, when I was a school-boy, my imagination was strongly impressed by the mythological fables of different nations. I can trace this to the effect produced upon me, when quite a child, by some prints in the Christian's Magazine, copied, as I afterward discovered, from the great work of Picart. I got at Picart when I was about fifteen, and soon became as well acquainted with the gods of Asia and America as with those of Greece and Rome. This led me to conceive a design of rendering every mythology, which had ever extended itself widely, and powerfully influenced the human mind, the basis of a narrative poem. I began with the religion of the Koran, and consequently founded the interest of the story upon that resignation, which is the only virtue it has produced. Had Thalaba been more successful, my whole design would by this time have been effected; for prepared as I was with the whole materials for each, and with a general idea of the story, I should assuredly have produced such a poem every year. For popular praise, *quoad* praise, I cared nothing; but it was of consequence to me, inasmuch as it affected those emoluments with which my worldly circumstances did not permit me to dispense. The sacrifice, therefore, was made to prudence, and it was not made without reluctance. Kehama lay by me in an unfinished state for many years, and but for a mere accident, might, perhaps, forever have remained incomplete.

"Whether the design may ever be accomplished is now doubtful. The inclination and the power remain, but the time has passed away. My literary engagements are numerous and weighty, beyond those of any other individual; and though, by God's blessing, I enjoy good health, never-failing cheerfulness, and unwearied perseverance, there seems to be more before me than I shall ever live to get through.

* * * * * * *

"Believe me, sir, yours, with due respect,

"ROBERT SOUTHEY.

"My next mythological poem, should I ever write another, would be founded upon the system of Zoroaster. I should represent the chief personage as persecuted by the evil powers, and make every calamity they brought upon him the means of evolving some virtue, which would never else have been called into action, in the hope that the fables of false religion may be made subservient to the true, by exalting and strengthening Christian feelings."

CHAPTER XVIII.

PRESENT HAPPINESS — AFFAIRS OF THE EDINBURGH ANNUAL REGISTER EMBARRASSED — LIFE OF NELSON—RODERIC—THANKS SIR W. SCOTT FOR ROKEBY — REGRETS BEING COMPELLED TO PERIODICAL WRITING—POLITICS—MR. COLERIDGE'S TRAGEDY BROUGHT OUT — REMARKS ON THE LOSS OF YOUTHFUL HOPES—DESTRUCTION OF THE FRENCH ARMY IN RUSSIA—LIFE OF NELSON COMPLETED—LITERARY PLANS—REASONS FOR SUBMITTING TO GIFFORD'S CORRECTIONS—LETTERS CONCERNING MR. JAMES DUSAUTOY — GLOOMY POLITICAL FOREBODINGS—PAPER IN THE QUARTERLY REVIEW ON THE STATE OF THE POOR—NAVAL REVERSES IN THE WAR WITH AMERICA—EXPECTED DEATH OF HIS BROTHER-IN-LAW, MR. FRICKER — MONTGOMERY'S DELUGE — ANIMATED HORSE-HAIR—PLAY BY MR. W. S. LANDOR —VISIT TO LONDON—APPOINTMENT AS POET LAUREATE.—1813.

THE period of my father's life to which the following letters relate, may be said, upon the whole, to have been the busiest and most stirring portion of it, comprising, as it does, the maturest fruits of his poetical genius, with the most extensive engagements as a prose writer. His position in literature had been long no dubious one; and it had now become evident to him that he must rely upon literature alone as his profession, and trust to it wholly for his support. It might seem indeed, with the chances, the friends, and the interest he possessed, he had been singularly unfortunate in not obtaining some employment which would have secured him a regular income, and thus rendered him dependent upon authorship rather for the superfluities than the necessaries of life. If, however, there was any "tide in his affairs" which might have "led to fortune," he did not "take it at the flood;" and having made those two applications which have been noticed (for the Stewardship of the Greenwich Hospital Estates, and for the office of Historiographer Royal), he became wearied with the trouble and annoyance of solicitation, and was, perhaps, too ready to abandon the advantages which he might have obtained. But he was himself very unwilling to take any office which would allow him only a small portion of time for the only pursuit in which he took any pleasure, and it must be admitted that it would not have been easy for his best friends (and warmer friends no man ever possessed) to find any situation or employment which could possibly have suited a man whose tastes and habits were so completely fixed and devoted to a literary life.

The first few years to which we are now coming were the happiest of his life. Settled to his heart's content at Keswick, having found a few friends in the neighborhood and country, and having many distant ones most highly esteemed; finding in his labors and in his library (which was rapidly becoming one of the best ever possessed by any person of such limited means) ceaseless occupation and amusement that never palled, he had for the present all his heart's desire, so far, at least, as was compatible with a doubtful and hardly-earned subsistence.

His principal source of income latterly, as the reader has seen, had been derived from the Edinburgh Annual Register; but this, from the beginning, had been a losing concern, though started with the most sanguine anticipations of success. Indeed, it appears, from the Life of Sir W. Scott (vol. iv., p. 77), that the actual loss upon it had never been less than £1000 per annum, and it was therefore not to be wondered at that some considerable irregularities occurred in the publisher's payments, and that my father now found it prudent to declare his intention of withdrawing from it when the current volume should be concluded, having already suffered much inconvenience and some embarrassment from this cause.

The defalcation of £400 a year from his income was, however, a very serious matter, and he found it needful, without delay, to cast about for means of supplying its place. The establishment of the Quarterly Review had thus occurred at a fortunate time, both as affording him regular and tolerably profitable employment, and also as giving him scope for expressing earnest thoughts in vigorous language, which made themselves felt, despite the editor's merciless hand.

This was, indeed, in most respects a far better vehicle than the Register, affording a far wider range of subjects, and speaking to a different and much more numerous class of readers; and, however distasteful to him was the task of reviewing, his objections to it hardly applied to papers upon political, moral, or religious topics, and he felt and acknowledged that his reputation rose higher from his writings in the Quarterly Review than from any of his other works. It is true, indeed, that on its first establishment he wished rather to have books submitted to him for ordinary criticism than for the purpose of writing political essays; but that was simply because in mere reviewing he was well practiced, and knew his strength, whereas the other, though a higher department of art, was new to him, and was also less safe ground with reference to those persons whom he believed to influence the publication.

He had also, at this time, and for a few years longer, a constant source of deep and heartfelt delight in the endearing qualities of his only boy, now little more than six years old, who possessed a singularly beautiful and gentle disposition, and who was just beginning to manifest an intellect as quick, and an aptitude for study as remarkable, as his own. This was the head and front of his happiness, the crowning joy of his domestic circle; and while that circle remained unbroken, and he himself head and heart-whole to labor for his daily bread, the sun shone not upon a happier household. He might, indeed, had he been so disposed, have found enough in the precarious nature of his income to cause him much disquietude; but on such points his mind was imbued with a true philosophy; and while he labored on patiently and perseveringly, he yet took no undue thought for the morrow, being well persuaded of the truth of the saying, that "sufficient for the day is" both the good and "the evil thereof."

To John May, Esq.

"Keswick, Jan. 3, 1813.

"My dear Friend,

"Many happy new years to you, and may those which are to come prove more favorable to you in worldly concerns than those which are past! I have been somewhat unwell this Christmas; first with a cold, then with a sudden and unaccountable sickness, which, however, has not returned, and I now hope I have been physicked into tolerable order. The young ones are going on well: little Isabel thrives, your god-daughter is old enough to figure at a Christmas dance, and Herbert will very soon be perfect in the regular Greek verb. A Testament is to come for him in my next parcel, and we shall begin upon it as soon as it arrives. No child ever promised better, morally and intellectually. He is very quick of comprehension, retentive, observant, diligent, and as fond of a book and as impatient of idleness as I am. Would that I were as well satisfied with his bodily health; but, in spite of activity and bodily hilarity, he is pale and puny: just that kind of child of whom old women would say that he is too clever to live. Old women's notions are not often so well founded as this; and having this apprehension before my eyes, the uncertainty of human happiness never comes home to my heart so deeply as when I look at him. God's will be done! I must sow the seed as carefully as if I were sure that the harvest would ripen. My two others are the most perfect contrast you ever saw. Bertha, whom I call Queen Henry the Eighth, from her likeness to King Bluebeard, grows like Jonah's gourd, and is the very picture of robust health; and little Kate hardly seems to grow at all, though perfectly well—she is round as a mushroom-button. Bertha, the bluff queen, is just as grave as Kate is garrulous; they are inseparable play-fellows, and go about the house hand in hand. Shall I never show you this little flock of mine? I have seen almost every one of my friends here except you, than whom none would be more joyfully welcomed.

"I shall have two interesting chapters in this volume for 1811,* upon Sicily and South America. My Life of Nelson, by a miscalculation, which lies between Murray and the printer, will appear in two volumes instead of one, which will materially, beyond all doubt, injure the sale. Murray has most probably ordered a large impression, calculating upon its going off as a midshipman's manual, which design is thus prevented. If, however, this impression can pass off, I shall have no fear of its answering his purpose when printed in a suitable form; for, though the subject was not of my own choice, and might be reasonably thought to be out of my proper line, I have satisfied myself in the execution far more than I could have expected to do. The second sheet of the second volume is now before me. I have just finished the battle of Copenhagen, which makes an impressive narrative. Two chapters more will complete it, and I hope to send you the book by the beginning of March. My labor with it will be completed much before that time, probably in ten days or a fortnight, and then the time which it now occupies will be devoted to the *indigesta moles* of Mr. Walpole's papers. I find the day too short for the employment which it brings; however, if I can not always get through what is before me as soon as could be wished, in process of time I get through it all. My poem† comes on well; about 2700 lines are written; the probable extent is 5000; but the last half is like going down hill—the difficulty is over, and your progress accelerates itself. The poem is of a perfectly original character. What its success may be I can not guess.

'Yours very affectionately,

"ROBERT SOUTHEY."

To Walter Scott, Esq.

"Keswick, Jan. 13, 1813.

"MY DEAR SCOTT,

"I received Rokeby on Monday evening, and you need not be told that I did not go to bed till I had read the poem through. It is yours all over, and, like its brethren, perfectly original. I have only to congratulate you upon its appearance, upon its life and spirit, and (with sure and certain anticipation) upon its success. Let me correct an error in your last note, in time for the second edition. Robin the Devil lived not upon one of our islands, but on Curwen's in Winandermere, which then belonged to the Philipsons'. You may find the story in Nicholson and Burns's History of Westmoreland, p. 185–6.

"I enjoyed your poem the more, being for the first time able to follow you in its scenery. My introduction at Rokeby* was a very awkward one; and if the old woman who would not let me through the gate till I had promised her to call at the house, had been the porter or the porter's wife on the day of your story, Edmund might have sung long enough before he could have got in. However, when this awkwardness was over, I was very much obliged to her for forcing me into such society, for nothing could be more hospitable or more gratifying than the manner in which I and my companions were received. The glen is, for its extent, more beautiful than any thing I have seen in England. If I had known your subject, I could have helped you to some Teesiana for your description—the result of the hardest day's march I ever yet made; for we traced the stream from its spring-head, on the summit of Crossfell, about a mile from the source of the Tyne, all the way to Highforce.

"In the course of next month I hope you will receive my Life of Nelson, a subject not self-chosen—and out of my way, but executed *con amore.* Some of my periodical employment I must ere long relinquish, or I shall never complete the great historical works upon which so many years have been bestowed, in which so much progress has been made, and for which it is little likely that any other person in the country will ever so qualify himself again. Yonder they are lying unfinished, while I suffer myself to be tempted to other occupations of more immediate emolument indeed, but in all other respects of infinitely less importance. Meanwhile time passes on, and I, who am of a short-lived race, and have a sense of the uncertainty of life more continually present in my thoughts and feelings than most men sometimes reproach myself for not devoting my time to those works upon which my reputation, and perhaps the fortunes of my family, must eventually rest, while the will is strong, the ability yet unimpaired, and the leisure permitted me. If I do not greatly deceive myself, my History of Portugal will be one of the most curious books of its kind that has ever yet appeared; the matter is in itself so interesting, and I have hunted out so much that is recondite, and have so much strong light to throw upon things which have never been elucidated before.

"Remember us to Mrs. Scott, and believe me,

'My dear brother bard,

"Yours most truly,

"ROBERT SOUTHEY."

* Edinburgh Annual Register.

† Roderic, the Last of the Goths.

* See p. 285.

To C. W. W. Wynn, Esq.

"Keswick, Jan. 17, 1813.

"MY DEAR WYNN,

"It is somewhat late to speak of Christmas and the New Year; nevertheless, I wish you as many as you may be capable of enjoying, and the more the better. Winter is passing on mildly with us; and if it were not for our miry soil and bad ways, I should not wish for pleasanter weather than January has brought with it. Ailments rather than inclination have led me of late to take regular exercise, which I was wont to think I could do without as well as a Turk; so I take two or three of the children with me, and, giving them leave to call upon me for their daily walk, their eagerness overcomes my propensities for the chair and the desk; we now go before breakfast, for the sake of getting the first sunshine on the mountains, which, when the snow is on them, is more glorious than at any other season. Yesterday I think I heard the wild swan, and this morning had the finest sight of wild-fowl I ever beheld: there was a cloud of them above the lake, at such a height that frequently they became invisible, then twinkled into sight again, sometimes spreading like smoke as it ascends, then contracting as if performing some military evolution—once they formed a perfect bow; and thus wheeling and charging, and rising and falling, they continued to sport as long as I could watch them. They were probably wild ducks.

"Your godson is determined to be a poet, he says; and I was not a little amused by his telling me this morning, when he came near a hollow tree which has caught his eye lately, and made him ask me sundry questions about it, that the first poem he should make should be about that hollow tree. I have made some progress in rhyming the Greek accidence for him—an easier thing than you would perhaps suppose it to be; it tickles his humor, and lays hold of his memory.

"This last year has been full of unexpected events; such, indeed, as mock all human foresight. The present will bring with it business of importance at home, whatever may happen abroad.

"There is one point in which most men, however opposite in their judgments about the affairs of the Peninsula, have been deceived—in their expectations from the Cortes. There is a lamentable want of wisdom in the country; among the peasantry, its place is supplied by their love of the soil, and that invincible perseverance which so strongly marks the Spanish character. Bonaparte never can subdue them, even if his power had received no shock, and his whole attention were exclusively directed toward Spain: his life, though it should be prolonged to the length of Aurengzebe's (as great a villain as himself), would not give him time to wear out their perseverance and religious hatred. I have never doubted the eventual independence of Spain; but concerning the government which may grow out of the struggle my hopes diminish, and I begin to think that Portugal has better prospects than Spain, because the government there may be induced to reform itself.

"If Gifford prints what I have written, and lets it pass unmutilated, you will see in the next Quarterly some remarks upon the moral and political state of the populace, and the alarming manner in which Jacobinism (disappearing from the educated classes) has sunk into the mob—a danger far more extensive and momentous than is generally admitted. Very likely a sort of cowardly prudence may occasion some suppressions, which I should be sorry for. Wyndham would have acknowledged the truth of the picture, and have been with me for looking the danger in the face. It is an odd fact that the favorite song among the people in this little town just now (as I have happened to learn) is upon Parker the mutineer: it purports to have been written by his wife, and is in meter and diction just what such a woman would write.

"What part do you take in the East Indian question? I perceive its magnitude, and am wholly incapable of forming an opinion.

"Coleridge's tragedy,* which Sheridan and Kemble rejected fifteen years ago, will come out in about a fortnight at Drury Lane.

"God bless you! R. S."

To Dr. Gooch.

"Keswick, Jan. 20, 1813.

"MY DEAR GOOCH,

" * * * * * * *

Wordsworth refers, in more than one of his poems, with a melancholy feeling of regret, to the loss of youthful thoughts and hopes. In the last six weeks he has lost two children, one of them a fine boy of seven years old. I believe he feels, as I have felt before him, that 'there is healing in the bitter cup'—that God takes from us those we love as hostages for our faith (if I may so express myself)—and that to those who look to a reunion in a better world, where there shall be no separation, and no mutability except that which results from perpetual progressiveness, the evening becomes more delightful than the morning, and the sunset offers brighter and lovelier visions than those which we build up in the morning clouds, and which disappear before the strength of the day. The older I grow—and I am older in feeling than in years—the more I am sensible of this: there is a precious alchemy in this faith, which transmutes grief into joy, or, rather, it is the true and heavenly euphrasy which clears away the film from our mortal sight, and makes affliction appear what, in reality, it is to the wise and good—a dispensation of mercy.

"God bless you!

"Yours affectionately, R. SOUTHEY."

---

* After the successful appearance of this tragedy, which was entitled "Remorse," my father wrote, "I never doubted that Coleridge's play would meet with a triumphant reception. Be it known now and remembered hereafter, that this self-same play, having had no other alterations made in it now than C. was willing to have made in it then, was rejected in 1797 by Sheridan and Kemble. Had these sapient caterers for the public brought it forward at that time, it is by no means improbable that the author might have produced a play as good every season: with my knowledge of Coleridge's habits, I verily believe he would."—*To G. C. B., Jan.* 27, 1813.

To Mr. Neville White.

"Keswick, Jan. 25, 1813.

"MY DEAR NEVILLE,

"Before I say any thing of my own doings, let me rejoice with you over these great events in the North. Never in civilized Europe had there been so great an army brought together as Bonaparte had there collected, and never was there so total and tremendous a destruction. I verily think that this is the fourth act of the Corsican, and that the catastrophe of the bloody drama is near. May his fall be as awful as his crimes! The siege of Dantzic, and the accession of Prussia to our alliance, will probably be our next news. Saxony will be the next government to emancipate itself, for there the government is as well disposed as the people. I wish I could flatter myself that Alexander were great enough to perform an act of true wisdom as well as magnanimity, and re-establish Poland, not after the villainous manner of Bonaparte, but with all its former territory, giving up his own portion of that infamously acquired plunder, and taking Prussia's part by agreement, and Austria's by force; for Austria will most likely incline toward the side of France, in fear of Russia, and in hatred of the house of Brandenburgh. May this vile power share in his overthrow and destruction, for it has cursed Germany too long!

"Was there ever an infatuation like that of the party in this country who are crying out for peace? as if this country had not ample cause to repent of having once before given up the vantage ground of war, at a peace forced upon the state by a faction! Let us remember Utrecht, and not suffer the Whigs of this day to outdo the villainy of the Tories of that. There can be no peace with Bonaparte, none with France, that is not dictated at the edge of the sword. Peace, I trust, is now not far distant, and one which France must kneel to receive, not England to ask.

"The opening of the Baltic will come seasonably for our manufactures, and, if it set the looms to work again, we may hope that it will suspend the danger which has manifested itself, and give time for measures which may prevent its recurrence. You will see in the next Quarterly a paper upon the State of the Poor—or, rather, the populace—wherein I have pointed out the causes of this danger, and its tremendous extent, which, I believe, few persons are aware of. I shall be sorry if it be mutilated from any false notions of prudence. It may often be necessary to keep a patient ignorant of his real state, but public danger ought always to be met boldly, and looked in the face. I impute the danger to the ignorance of the poor, which is the fault of the state, for not having seen to their moral and religious instruction; to the manufacturing system, acting upon persons in this state of ignorance, and vitiating them; and to the anarchist journalists (Cobbett, Hunt, &c.) perseveringly addressing themselves to such willing and fit recipients of their doctrines.

"In the last number I reviewed D'Israeli's Calamities of Literature, the amusing book of a very good-natured man.

"The poem goes on slow and sure. Twenty years ago nothing could equal the ardor with which I pursued such employments. I was then impatient to see myself in print: it was not possible to long more eagerly than I did for the honor of authorship. This feeling is quite extinct; and, allowing as much as may be allowed for experience, wiser thoughts, and, if you please, satiety in effecting such a change, I can not but believe that much must be attributed to a sort of autumnal or evening tone of mind, coming upon me a little earlier than it does upon most men. I am as cheerful as a boy, and retain many youthful or even boyish habits; but I am older in mind than in years, and in years than in appearance; and, though none of the joyousness of youth is lost, there is none of its ardor left. Composition, where any passion is called forth, excites me more than it is desirable to be excited; and, if it were not for the sake of gratifying two or three persons in the world whom I love, and who love me, it is more than probable that I might never write a verse again. God bless you!

"Yours affectionately,

"ROBERT SOUTHEY."

To the Rev. Herbert Hill.

"Keswick, Feb. 1, 1813.

"MY DEAR UNCLE,

"The Life of Nelson* was completed this morning. The printer began with it before it was half written, but I have distanced him by ten sheets. Do not fear that I have been proceeding too fast: it is he who, after the manner of printers, has given me plenty of time by taking his own. This is a subject which I should never have dreamed of touching, if it had not been thrust upon me. I have walked among sea terms as carefully as a cat does among crockery; but, if I have succeeded in making the narrative continuous and clear—the very reverse of what it is in the lives before me—the materials are, in themselves, so full of character, so picturesque, and so sublime, that it can not fail of being a good book. * * * I am very much inclined to attempt, under some such title as the Age of George III., a sketch of the revolutions which, almost every where and in all things, have taken place within the last half century. Any comparison which it might induce with Voltaire would rather invite than deter me. When I come to town I shall talk with Murray about this.

"You wonder that I should submit to any expurgations in the Quarterly. The fact is, that there must be a power expurgatory in the hands

* This, which was, perhaps, upon the whole, the most popular of any of my father's works, originated in an article in the fifth number of the Quarterly Review, which was enlarged at Murray's request. My father received altogether £300 for it: £100 for the Review, £100 when the Life was enlarged, and £100 when it was published in the Family Library.

of the editor; and the misfortune is, that editors frequently think it incumbent on them to use that power merely because they have it. I do not like to break with the Review, because Gifford has been something more than merely civil to me, and offered me services which I had no reason to expect, because the Review gives me (and shame it is that it should be so) more repute than any thing else which I could do, and because there is no channel through which so much effect can be given to what I may wish to impress upon the opinion of the public. * *

"My aim and hope are, ere long, to support myself by the sale of half my time, and have the other half for the completion of my History. When I can command £500 for the same quantity that Scott gets £3000 for, this will be accomplished, and this is likely soon to be the case. God bless you! R. S."

My father's publication of Kirk White's Remains very naturally drew upon him many applications for similar assistance; and curious indeed would be the collections of verses, good, bad, and indifferent, which from time to time were transmitted to him by youthful poets. But few of these, as may well be imagined, gave sufficient promise to warrant his giving any encouragement to their writers to proceed in the up-hill path of authorship; others, however, showed such proofs of talent, that he could not but urge its cultivation, though he invariably gave the strongest warnings against choosing literature as any thing but recreation, or a possible assistance while following some other profession. In the case of Ebenezer Elliott, this led to an interesting correspondence with a man of great genius. Many of the applications he received do not admit of any particular account; but among them are some which give us glimpses of youthful minds whose loss the world has cause to lament. Such was William Roberts; and such, also, was one whose story now comes before me.

It seems that at the beginning of the year a youth of the name of Dusautoy, then about seventeen years of age, the son of a retired officer residing at Totness, Devon, and one of a numerous family, had written to my father, inclosing some pieces of poetry, and requesting his opinion and advice as to their publication. Neither the letter nor the reply to it have been preserved; but in Dusautoy's rejoinder, he expresses his grateful thanks for the warning given him; against the imprudence of prematurely throwing himself upon the cold judgment of the public; and asks in what degree it was probable or possible that literature would assist him in making his way to the bar, the profession to which at that time he was most inclined. Being one of a large family, his laudable object was as far as possible to procure the means for his own education.*

My father's reply was as follows:

To James Dusautoy, Esq.

"Keswick, Feb. 12, 1813.

"MY DEAR SIR,

"Your talents will do every thing for you in time, but nothing in the way you wish for some years to come. The best road to the bar is through the University, where honors of every kind will be within your reach. With proper conduct, you would obtain a fellowship by the time you were one or two-and-twenty, and this would enable you to establish yourself in one profession or another, at your own choice.

"This course is as desirable for your intellectual as for your worldly advancement. Your mind would then have time and opportunity to ripen, and bring forth its fruits in due season. God forbid that they should either be forced or blighted! A young man can not support himself by literary exertions, however great his talents and his industry. Woe be to the youthful poet who sets out upon his pilgrimage to the temple of fame with nothing but hope for his viaticum! There is the Slough of Despond, and the Hill of Difficulty, and the Valley of the Shadow of Death upon the way!

"To be called to the bar, you must be five years a member of one of the inns of court; but if you have a university degree, three will suffice. Men who during this course look to their talents

* It appears that two years before writing to my father, young Dusautoy, then a schoolboy of fifteen, had made a similar application to Sir Walter Scott, whose reply, which is now before me, is very characteristic of the kind-hearted frankness and sound judgment of the writer. Some portion of it will, I think, interest the reader, as it is now published for the first time. After saying that "though in general he had made it a rule to decline giving an opinion upon the verses so often sent him for his criticism, this application was so couched that he could not well avoid making an exception in their favor," he adds, "I have only to caution you against relying very much upon it: the friends who know me best, and to whose judgment I am myself in the constant habit of trusting, reckon me a very capricious and uncertain judge of poetry; and I have had repeated occasions to observe that I have often failed in anticipating the reception of poetry from the public. Above all, sir, I must warn you against suffering yourself to suppose that the power of enjoying natural beauty and poetical description are necessarily connected with that of producing poetry. The former is really a gift of Heaven, which conduces inestimably to the happiness of those who enjoy it. The second has much more of a knack in it than the pride of poets is always willing to admit; and, at any rate, is only valuable when combined with the first. * * * I would also caution you against an enthusiasm which, while it argues an excellent disposition and feeling heart, requires to be watched and restrained, though not repressed. It is apt, if too much indulged, to engender a fastidious contempt for the ordinary business of the world, and gradually to render us unfit for the exercise of the useful and domestic virtues, which depends greatly upon our not exalting our feelings above the temper of well-ordered and well-educated society. No good man can ever be happy when he is unfit for the career of simple and common-place duty; and I need not add how many melancholy instances there are of extravagance and profligacy being resorted to under pretense of contempt for the common rules of life. Cultivate then, sir, your taste for poetry and the belles-lettres as an elegant and most interesting amusement; but combine it with studies of a more severe and solid cast, and such as are most intimately connected with your prospects in future life. In the words of Solomon, 'My son, get knowledge.'"

The remainder of the letter consists of some critical remarks upon the pieces submitted to him, which, he says, appear to him "to have all the merits and most of the faults of juvenile composition; to be fanciful, tender, and elegant; and to exhibit both command of language and luxuriance of imagination."—*Ashiestiel, May* 6, 1811.

for support, usually write for newspapers and reviews: the former is destructively laborious, and sends many poor fellows prematurely to the grave; for the latter branch of employment there are always too many applicants. I began it at the age of four-and-twenty, which was long before I was fit for it.

"The stage, indeed, is a lottery where there is more chance of a prize; but there is an evil attending success in that direction which I can distinctly see, though you, perhaps, may not be persuaded of it. The young man who produces a successful play is usually the dupe of his own success; and being satisfied with producing an immediate and ephemeral effect, looks for nothing beyond it. You must aim at something more. I think your path is plain. Success at the University is not exclusively a thing of chance or favor; you are certain of it if you deserve it.

"When you have considered this with your friends, tell me the result, and rest assured that my endeavors to forward your wishes in this, or in any other course which you may think proper to pursue, shall be given with as much sincerity as this advice; meantime read Greek, and write as many verses as you please. By shooting at a high mark you will gain strength of arm, and precision of aim will come in its proper season.

"Ever yours very truly,

"ROBERT SOUTHEY."

Upon further consideration, it was determined that Dusautoy should enter at Cambridge; and my father having taken some trouble in the matter, he was very soon admitted a member of Emanuel College. In the following year (1814) he was an unsuccessful competitor for the English poetical prize,* the present Master of Trinity, Dr. Whewell, being the successful one. In the college examination he stood high, being the first man of his year in classics and fourth in mathematics. He also obtained several exhibitions, and had the promise of a scholarship as soon as a vacancy occurred. In the midst, however, of high hopes and earnest intentions, he fell a victim, among many others, to a malignant fever, which raged at Cambridge with such violence that all lectures were stopped, and the men who had escaped its influence permitted to return home. As an acknowledgment of his talents and character, he was buried in the cloisters of his college; a mark of respect, I understand, never before paid to any under-graduate.

My father had at one time intended publishing a selection from Dusautoy's papers, which were sent to him for that purpose; but further reflection convinced him that his first inspection of them "had led him to form too hasty a conclusion, not as to the intellectual power which they displayed, but as to the effect which they were likely to produce if brought before the public. To me," he continues, "the most obvious faults of these fragments are the most unequivocal proofs of genius in the author, as being efforts of a mind conscious of a strength which it had not yet learned to use—exuberance which proved the vigor of the plant and the richness of the soil. But common readers read only to be amused, and to them these pieces would appear crude and extravagant, because they would only see what *is*, without any reference to what might have been."

* The subject was Boadicea; and Dusautoy's composition an ode, "injudiciously written in Spenser's stanza."

To C. W. W. Wynn, Esq.

"Keswick, March 12, 1813.

"MY DEAR WYNN,

"Do not be too sure of your victory in the House of Commons. It is not unlikely that when the securities come to be discussed, you will find yourselves in a minority there, as well as in the country at large. The mischief, however, is done. It is like certain bodily complaints, trifling in themselves, but of infinite import as symptomatic of approaching death. The more I see, the more I read, and the more I reflect, the more reason there appears to me to fear that our turn of revolution is hastening on. In the minds of the busy part of the public it is already effected. The save-all reformers have made them suspicious; the opposition has made them discontented; the anarchists are making them furious. Methodism is undermining the Church, and your party, in league with all varieties of opinionists, have battered it till you have succeeded in making a breach. I give you all credit for good intentions; but I know the Dissenters and the philosophists better than you do, and know that the principle which they have in common is a hatred of the Church of England, and a wish to overthrow her. This they will accomplish, and you will regret it as much as I do—certainly not the less for having yourself contributed to its destruction.

"The end of all this will be the loss of liberty, for that is the penalty which, in the immutable order of things, is appointed for the abuse of it. What we may have to go through, before we sit down quietly in our chains, God only knows.

"Have you heard of the strange circumstance about Coleridge? A man hanging himself in the Park with one of *his* shirts on, marked at full length! Guess C.'s astonishment at reading this in a newspaper at a coffee-house. The thing is equally ridiculous and provoking. It will alarm many persons who know him, and I dare say many will always believe that the man was C. himself, but that he was cut down in time, and that his friends said it was somebody else in order to conceal the truth. As yet, however, I have laughed about it too much to be vexed.

"I have just got General Mackinnon's Journal:* never was any thing more faithful than his account of the country and the people. We have, I fear, few such men in the British army. I knew a sister of his well some years ago, and should rejoice to meet with her again, for she was one of the cleverest women I ever knew. When they lived in France, Bonaparte was a frequent visitor at their mother's house. Mackinnon

* See Inscription, xxxv., p. 178, one vol. edit.

would have made a great man. His remarks upon a want of subordination, and proper regulations in our army, are well worthy of Lord Wellington's consideration. It was by thinking thus, and forming his army, upon good moral as well as military principles, that Gustavus became the greatest captain of modern times: so he may certainly be called, because he achieved the greatest things with means which were apparently the most inadequate. God bless you!

"R. SOUTHEY."

In a former letter my father speaks of an article he had written for the forthcoming number of the Quarterly Review, on the state of the poor, and he there mentions briefly the heads of the general view he had taken of the subject. This had appeared, and Mr. Rickman now comments on it, whose practical and sensible remarks I quote here, as showing his frankness in stating differences of opinion, and his friend's willingness to hear and consider them:

"I have read your article on the poor with great satisfaction, for the abundance of wit it contains, and the general truth of its statements and reflections. With some things you know I do not agree—for instance, not in your dislike of manufactures to the same degree—especially I do not find them guilty of increasing the poor. For instance, no county is more purely agricultural than Sussex, where *twenty-three* persons, parents and children, in *one hundred* receive parish relief; no county more clearly to be referred to the manufacturing character than Lancashire, where the persons relieved by the parish are *seven in one hundred*—not a third part of the agricultural poverty. An explanation of this (not in a letter) will perhaps lead you to different views of the poor's-rate plan of relief, which in agricultural counties operates as a mode of equalizing wages according to the number of mouths in a family, so that the single man receives much less than his labor is worth, the married man much more. I do not approve of this, nor of the Poor Laws at all; but it is a view of the matter which, in your opinion more, perhaps, than in mine, may lessen the amount of the mischief. *

"I am afraid nothing will settle my mind about your wide education plan—a great *good* or a great *evil* certainly, but which I am not sure while the liberty of the press remains. I believe that more seditious newspapers than Bibles will be in use among your pupils.

"We go on badly in the House of Commons. * * * The Ministry considers nothing, forsooth, as a cabinet question—that is, they have no opinion collectively. I can not imagine any thing in history more pitiful than their junction and alliance with the high and mighty mob against the East India Company—an establishment second only, if second, to the English government, in importance to mankind. As to the Catholics, they will gain little from the House of Commons, and nothing from the Lords."*

* J. R. to R. S., March 12, 1813.

To John Rickman, Esq.

"March, 1813.

"MY DEAR RICKMAN,

"You and I shall agree about general education. Ignorance is no preventive in these days, if, indeed, it ever were one which could be relied on. All who have ears can hear sedition, and the more ignorant they are, the more easy is it to inflame them. My plan is (I know not whether Gifford has ventured to give it) to make transportation the punishment for seditious libeling. This, and this only, would be an effectual cure. The existence of a press in the state in which ours is in, is incompatible with the security of any government.

"About the manufacturing system as affecting the poor-rates, doubtless you are best informed. My argument went to show that, under certain circumstances of not unfrequent occurrence, manufactures occasioned a sudden increase of the craving mouths, and that the whole previous discipline of these persons fitted them to become Luddites. It is most likely there may be some ambiguity in that part of the article, from the vague use of the word poor, which ought to be distinguished from pauper—a distinction I never thought of making till your letter made me see the necessity for so doing.

"You give me comfort about the Catholics, and strengthen my doubts about the East India question. I have written on the former subject in the forthcoming Register, very much to the purport of Mr. Abbot's speech. Mr. Perceval should have given the Catholics what is right and proper they should have, by a bill originating with himself. What but ruin can be expected when a government comes to capitulate with the factious part of its subjects! * * *

"God bless you! R. S."

To Grosvenor C. Bedford, Esq.

"Keswick, May 26, 1813.

"MY DEAR GROSVENOR,

"Tom is made quite unhappy by these repeated victories of the Americans; and for my own part, I regard them with the deepest and gloomiest forebodings. The superior weight of metal will not account for all. I heard a day or two ago from a Liverpoolian, lately in America, that they stuff their wadding with bullets. This may kill a few more men, but will not explain how it is that our ships are so soon demolished, not merely disabled. Wordsworth and I agreed in suspecting some improvement in gunnery (Fulton is likely enough to have discovered something) before I saw the same supposition thrown out in the 'Times.' Still there would remain something more alarming to be resolved, and that is, how it happens that we injure them so little? I very much fear that there may be a dreadful secret at the bottom, which your fact about the cartridges* of the Macedonian points at. Do

* "H. Sharp is just arrived from Lisbon; he has been in America, where he went on board the Macedonian and the United States.[1] He says the captured ship was pierced

[1] The name of the vessel that took the Macedonian.

you know, or does Henry know, a belief in the navy which I heard from Ponsonby, that the crew of the —— loaded purposely in this manner, in order that by being made prisoners they might be delivered from ——'s tyranny? When Coleridge was at Malta, Sir A. Ball received a round-robin from ——'s crew, many of whom had served under him, and who addressed him in a manner which made his heart ache, as he was, of course, compelled to put the paper into ——'s hands. One day Coleridge was with him when this man's name was announced, and turning, he said to him in a low voice, 'Here comes one of those men who will one day blow up the British navy.'

"I do not know that the captain of the Macedonian was a tyrant. Peake certainly was not; he is well known here, having married a cousin of Wordsworth's; his ship was in perfect order, and he as brave and able a man as any in the service. Here it seems that the men behaved well; but in ten minutes the ship was literally knocked to pieces, her sides fairly staved in; and I think this can only be explained by some improvements in the manufactory of powder, or in the manner of loading, &c. But as a general fact, and of tremendous application, I verily believe that the sailors prefer the enemy's service to our own. It is in vain to treat the matter lightly, or seek to conceal from ourselves the extent of the evil. Our naval superiority is destroyed!

"My chief business in town will be to make arrangements for supplying the huge deficit which the termination of my labors in the Register occasions. I wish to turn to present account my Spanish materials, and still more the insight which I have acquired into the history of the war in the Peninsula; and to recast that portion of the Register, carry it on, and bring it forth in a suitable form. This can not be done without the consent of the publishers—Ballantyne, Longman, and Murray. To the two latter I have written, and am about to write to James Ballantyne. Should the thing be brought to bear, I must procure an introduction to Marquis Wellesley—that is, to the documents which I doubt not he would very readily supply; and I should have occasion for all the assistance from the Foreign Office which my friends could obtain. To the marquis I have means of access through Mr. Littleton, and probably, also, *viâ* Gifford, through Canning. It may be of use if you make known my wishes in that quarter. R. S."

To Mr. Neville White.

"Keswick, June 14, 1813.

"MY DEAR NEVILLE,

"Josiah Conder had told me, though less particularly, the circumstances of your sister's happy death, for happy we must call it. The prayer in the Litany against *sudden* death I look upon as a relic of Romish error, the only one remaining in that finest of all human compositions—death without confession and absolution being regarded by the Romanist as the most dreadful of all calamities, naturally is one of the evils from which they pray to be delivered. I substitute the word *violent* in my supplications; for since that mode of dissolution which, in the Scriptures, is termed falling asleep, and which should be the natural termination of life passed in peace, and innocence, and happiness, has become so rare, that it falls scarcely to the lot of one in ten thousand, instantaneous and unforeseen death is the happiest mode of our departure, and it is even more desirable for the sake of our surviving friends than for our own. I speak feelingly, for at this time my wife's brother is in the room below me, in such a state of extreme exhaustion, that, having been carried down stairs at two o'clock, it would not in the least surprise me if he should expire before he can be carried up again. He is in the last stage of consumption—a disease which at first affected the liver having finally assumed this form; his recovery is impossible by any means short of miracle. I have no doubt that he is within a few days of his death, perhaps a few hours; and sincerely do I wish, for his sake and for that of four sisters who are about him, that the tragedy may have closed before this reaches you. According to all appearance, it will.

"Your letter, my dear Neville, represents just that state of mind which I expected to find you in. The bitterness of the cup is not yet gone, and some savor of it will long remain; but you already taste the uses of affliction, and feel that ties thus broken on earth are only removed to heaven.

"Montgomery's poem came in the same parcel with your letter. I had previously written about it to the Quarterly, and was told, in reply, that it was wished to pass it by there, because it had disappointed every body. I wish I could say that I myself did not in some degree feel disappointed also; yet there is so much that is really beautiful, and which I can sincerely praise, and the outline of the story will read so well with the choicest passages interspersed, that I shall send up a reviewal, and do as a Frenchman would say, *my possible.* Of what is good in the poem I am a competent judge; of what may be defective in it, my judgment is not, perhaps, so properly to be trusted, for having once planned a poem upon the Deluge myself, I necessarily compare my own outline with Montgomery's. The best part is the death of Adam. Oh! if the whole had been like that! or (for that is impossible) that there had been two or three passages equal to it! Montgomery has crippled himself by a meter which, of all others, is the worst for long and various narrative, and which most certainly betrays a writer into the common track and common-places of poetical language. He has thought of himself in Javan, and the character of Javan is hardly prominent enough to be

through and through, and full of shot, while in the American vessel scarcely any have been lodged. Our ship seems to have been very badly fought; the captors declared that they found many of the guns with the cartridges put in the wrong way."—*G. C. B. to R. S., May* 24, 1813.

made the chief personage. Yet there is much, very much to admire and to recur to with pleasure.

"God bless you! Remember me to your mother, and tell James I shall always be glad to hear from him as well as of him.

"Yours most truly,

"R. SOUTHEY."

To Dr. Southey.

"Keswick, June 6, 1813.

"MY DEAR HARRY,

"Do you want to make your fortune in the philosophical world? If so, you may thank Owen Lloyd for the happiest opportunity that was ever put into an aspirant's hands. You must have heard the vulgar notion that a horse-hair, plucked out by the root and put in water, becomes alive in a few days. The boys at Brathay repeatedly told their mother it was true, that they had tried it themselves and seen it tried. Her reply was, show it me, and I will believe it. While we were there last week, in came Owen with two of these creatures in a bottle. Wordsworth was there; and to our utter and unutterable astonishment did the boys, to convince us that these long, thin black worms were their own manufactory by the old receipt, lay hold of them by the middle while they writhed like eels, and stripping them with their nails down on each side, actually lay bare the horse-hair in the middle, which seemed to serve as the back-bone of the creature, or the substratum of the living matter which had collected round it.

"Wordsworth and I should both have supposed that it was a collection of animalculæ round the hair (which, however, would only be changing the nature of the wonder), if we could any way have accounted for the motion upon this theory; but the motion was that of a snake. We could perceive no head; but something very like the root of the hair. And for want of glasses, could distinguish no parts. The creature, or whatever else you may please to call it, is black or dark brown, and about the girth of a fiddle-string. As soon as you have read this, draw upon your horse's tail and mane for half a dozen hairs; be sure they have roots to them; bottle them separately in water, and when they are alive and kicking, call in Gooch, and make the fact known to the philosophical world.* Never in my life was I so astonished as at seeing, what even in the act of seeing I could scarcely believe, and now almost doubt. If you verify the experiment, as Owen and all his brethren will swear must be the case, you will be able to throw some light upon the origin of your friend the tape-worm, and his diabolical family.

"No doubt you will laugh and disbelieve this, and half suspect that I am jesting. But indeed I have only told you the fact as it occurred; and you will at once see its whole importance in philosophy, and the use which you and Gooch may derive from it, coming forth with a series of experiments, and with such deductions as your greyhound sight and his beagle scent will soon start and pursue.

"And if the *horse's* hair succeeds, Sir Domine, by parallel reasoning you know, try one of your own. R. S."

* "The Cyclopædia says that the Gordius Aquaticus is vulgarly supposed to be animated horse-hair; the print of the creature represents it as much smaller than Owen Lloyd's manufactory, which is as large as the other Gordii upon the same plate, and very like them. But I distinctly saw the hair when the accretion was stripped off with the nail."—*R. S. to J. R., August* 2, 1813.

To Walter Savage Landor, Esq.

"Keswick, June 30, 1813.

"Your comedy came to hand a fortnight ago. * * * The charitable dowager is drawn from the life. At least it has all the appearance of a portrait. As a drama there is a want of incident and of probability in that upon which the catastrophe depends; but the dialogue abounds with those felicities which flash from you in prose and verse more than from any other writer. I remember nothing which at all resembles them except in Jeremy Taylor: he has things as perfect and as touching in their kind, but the kind is different; there is the same beauty, the same exquisite fitness, but not the point and poignancy which you display in the comedy and in the commentary, nor the condensation and strength which characterize Gebir and Count Julian.

"I did not fail to notice the neighborly compliment which you bestow upon the town of Abergavenny. Even out of Wales, however, something good may come besides Welsh flannel and lamb's-wool stockings. I am reading a great book from Brecknock; for from Brecknock, of all other places under the sun, the fullest Mohammedan history which has yet appeared in any European language, has come forth. Without being a good historian, Major Price is a very useful one; he amuses me very much, and his volumes are full of facts which you can not forget, though the Mohammedan *propria quæ maribus* render it impossible ever accurately to remember any thing more than the great outlines. A dramatist in want of tragic subjects never need look beyond these two quarto volumes.

"What Jupiter means to do with us, he himself best knows; for as he seems to have stultified all parties at home and all powers abroad, there is no longer the old criterion of his intentions to help us in our foresight. I think this campaign will lead to a peace: such a peace will be worse than a continuance of the war, if it leaves Bonaparte alive; but the causes of the armistice are as yet a mystery to me; and if hostilities should be renewed, which, on the whole, seems more probable than that they should be terminated, I still hope to see his destruction. The peace which would then ensue would be lasting, and during a long interval of exhaustion and rest perhaps the world will grow wiser, and learn a few practical lessons from experience. * * God bless you!

'R. S."

At the beginning of September my father went for a visit of a few weeks to London and the vicinity, and his letters from thence detail fully all the circumstances connected with his appointment to the office of poet laureate. These have been several times related, but never so accurately as here by himself. Mr. Lockhart, in his Life of Sir Walter Scott, gives the main facts, but was probably not acquainted with them all. My father, in the preface to the collected edition of his poems, corrects that account in a few minor details, but for obvious reasons omits to mention that the offer of the office to Sir Walter was made without the prince's knowledge.

There is now, however, no reason for suppressing any of the circumstances, and no further comments of mine are needful to elucidate what the reader will find so clearly explained.

To Mrs. Southey.

"Streatham, Sunday, Sept. 5, 1813.

"MY DEAR EDITH,

" * * * * * * *

One of the letters which you forwarded was from James Ballantyne; my business in that quarter seems likely to terminate rather better than might have been expected. I wish you had opened the other, which was from Scott. It will be easier to transcribe it than to give its contents; and it does him so much honor that you ought to see it without delay. 'My dear Southey,—On my return home, I found, to my no small surprise, a letter tendering me the laurel vacant by the death of the poetical Pye. I have declined the appointment as being incompetent to the task of annual commemoration, but chiefly as being provided for in my professional department, and unwilling to incur the censure of engrossing the emolument* attached to one of the few appointments which seems proper to be filled by a man of literature who has no other views in life. Will you forgive me, my dear friend, if I own I had you in my recollection? I have given Croker the hint, and otherwise endeavored to throw the office into your *choice* (this is not Scott's word, but I can not decipher the right one). I am uncertain if you will like it, for the laurel has certainly been tarnished by some of its wearers, and, as at present managed, its duties are inconvenient and somewhat liable to ridicule. But the latter matter might be amended, and I should think the regent's good sense would lead him to lay aside these biennial commemorations; and as to the former point, it has been worn by Dryden of old, and by Warton in modern days. If you quote my own refusal against me, I reply, 1st, I have been luckier than you in holding two offices not usually conjoined. 2dly, I did not refuse it from any foolish prejudice against the situation, otherwise how durst I mention it to you, my elder brother in the muse? but from a sort of internal hope that they would give it to you, upon whom it would be so much more worthily conferred; for I am not such an ass as not to know that you are my better in poetry, though I have had (probably but for a time) the tide of popularity in my favor. I have not time to add ten thousand other reasons, but I only wished to tell you how the matter was, and to beg you to think before you reject the offer which I flatter myself will be made you. If I had not been, like Dogberry, a fellow with two gowns already, I should have jumped at it like a cock at a gooseberry. Ever yours most truly, W. S.'

"I thought this was so likely to happen, that I had turned the thing over in my mind in expectation. So as soon as this letter reached me, I wrote a note to Croker to this effect—that I would not write odes as boys write exercises, at stated times and upon stated subjects, but that if it were understood that upon great public events I might either write or be silent as the spirit moved, I should now accept the office as an honorable distinction, which under those circumstances it would become. To-morrow I shall see him. The salary is but a nominal £120; and, as you see, I shall either reject it, or make the title honorable by accepting it upon my own terms. The latter is the most probable result.

* * * * * * *

"No doubt I shall be the better on my return for this course of full exercise and full feeding, which follows in natural order. By good fortune this is the oyster season, and when in town I devour about a dozen in the middle of the day; so that in the history of my life this year ought to be designated as the year of the oysters, inasmuch as I shall have feasted on them more than in any other year of my life. I shall work off the old flesh from my bones, and lay on a new layer in its place—a sort of renovation which makes meat better, and therefore will not make me the worse. Harry complains of me as a general disturber of all families. I am up first in the house here and at his quarters; and the other morning, when I walked from hence to breakfast with Grosvenor, I arrived before any body except the servants were up. This is as it should be. * * *

"God bless you! R. S."

To C. W. W. Wynn, Esq.

"Streatham, Sept. 20, 1813.

"MY DEAR WYNN,

"I saw your letter about the Laurel, and you will not be sorry to hear how completely I had acted in conformity with your opinion.

"Pye's death was announced a day or two before my departure from Keswick, and at the time I thought it so probable that the not-very-desirable succession might be offered me, as to bestow a little serious thought upon the subject, as well as a jest or two. On my arrival in town Bedford came to my brother's to meet me at breakfast; told me that Croker had spoken with him about it, and he with Gifford; that they

* Sir Walter Scott seems to have been under the impression that the emoluments of the laureateship amounted to £300 or £400 a year.—See *Life of Scott*, vol. iv., p. 118.

supposed the *onus* of the office would be dropped, or if it were not, that I might so execute it as to give it a new character; and that as *detur digniori* was the maxim upon which the thing was likely to be bestowed, they thought it would become me to accept it. My business, however, whatever might be my determination, was to call without delay at the Admiralty, thank C. for what was actually intended well, and learn how the matter stood.

"Accordingly, I called on Croker. He had spoken to the prince; and the prince, observing that I had written 'some good things in favor of the Spaniards,' said the office should be given me. You will admire the reason, and infer from it that I ought to have been made historiographer because I had written Madoc. Presently Croker meets Lord Liverpool, and tells him what had passed; Lord Liverpool expressed his sorrow that he had not known it a day sooner, for he and the Marquis of Hertford had consulted together upon whom the vacant honor could most properly be bestowed. Scott was the greatest poet of the day, and to Scott, therefore, they had written to offer it. The prince was displeased at this; though he said he ought to have been consulted, it was his pleasure that I should have it, and have it I should. Upon this, Croker represented that he was Scott's friend as well as mine; that Scott and I were upon friendly terms; and, for the sake of all three, he requested that the business might rest where it was.

"Thus it stood when I made my first call at the Admiralty. I more than half suspected that Scott would decline the offer, and my own mind was made up before this suspicion was verified. The manner in which Scott declined it was the handsomest possible; nothing could be more friendly to me, or more honorable to himself. God bless you!

"Yours very affectionately,

"ROBERT SOUTHEY."

To Mrs. Southey.

"Tuesday night, Sept. 28, 1813.

"MY DEAR EDITH,

"I have stolen away from a room full of people, that I might spend an hour in writing to you instead of wasting it at the card-table. Sunday I went by appointment to Lord William Gordon, who wanted to take me to see a young lady. Who should this prove to be but Miss Booth, the very actress whom we saw at Liverpool play so sweetly in Kotzebue's comedy of the Birth-day. There was I taken to hear her recite Mary the Maid of the Inn! and if I had not interfered in aid of her own better sense, Lord W. and her mother and sisters would have made her act as well as recite it. As I know you defy the monster, I may venture to say that she is a sweet little girl, though a little spoiled by circumstances which would injure any body; but what think you of this old lord asking permission for me to repeat my visit, and urging me to 'take her under my protection,' and show her what to recite, and instruct her how to recite it? And all this upon a Sunday! So I shall give her a book, and tell her what parts she should choose to appear in. And if she goes again to Edinburgh, be civil to her if she touches at the Lakes; she supports a mother and brother, and two or three sisters. When I returned to Queen Anne Street from the visit, I found Davy sitting with the doctor, and awaiting my return. I could not dine with him to-morrow, having an engagement, but we promised to go in the evening and take Coleridge with us, and Elmsley, if they would go. It will be a party of lions, where the doctor must for that evening perform the part of Daniel in the lion's den.

"I dined on Sunday at Holland House, with some eighteen or twenty persons. Sharp was there, who introduced me with all due form to Rogers and to Sir James Mackintosh, who seems to be in a bad state of health. In the evening Lord Byron came in.* He had asked Rogers if I was 'magnanimous,' and requested him to make for him all sorts of amends honorable for having tried his wit upon me at the expense of his discretion; and in full confidence of the success of the apology, had been provided with a letter of introduction to me in case he had gone to the Lakes, as he intended to have done. As for me, you know how I regard things of this kind; so we met with all becoming courtesy on both sides, and I saw a man whom in voice, manner, and countenance I liked very much more than either his character or his writings had given me reason to expect. Rogers wanted me to dine with him on Tuesday (this day): only Lord Byron and Sharp were to have been of the party, but I had a pending engagement here, and was sorry for it.

"Holland House is a most interesting building. The library is a sort of gallery, one hundred and nine feet in length, and, like my study, serves for drawing-room also. The dinner-room is paneled with wood, and the panels emblazoned with coats of arms, like the ceiling of one room in the palace at Cintra. The house is of Henry the Eighth's time. Good night, my dear Edith.

"We had a very pleasant dinner at Madame de Staël's. Davy and his wife, a Frenchman whose name I never heard, and the Portuguese embassador, the Conde de Palmella, a gentlemanly and accomplished man. I wish you had seen the animation with which she exclaimed against Davy and Mackintosh for their notions about peace.

"Once more farewell!

"R. SOUTHEY."

The following poetical announcement of his being actually installed may excite a smile:

* The following is Lord Byron's account of this meeting: "Yesterday, at Holland House, I was introduced to Southey, the best looking bard I have seen for some time. To have that poet's head and shoulders I would almost have written his Sapphics. He is certainly a prepossessing-looking person to look at, and a man of talent and all that, and—*there* is his eulogy."—*Life of Byron*, vol. ii., p. 244

"I have something to tell you, which you will not be sorry at,
'Tis that I am sworn in to the office of laureate.
The oath that I took there could be nothing wrong in,
'Twas to do all the duties to the dignity belonging.
Keep this, I pray you, as a precious gem,
For this is the laureate's first poem.

"There, my dear Edith, are some choice verses for you. I composed them in St. James's Park yesterday, on my way from the chamberlain's office, where a good old gentleman usher, a worthy sort of fat old man, in a wig and bag, and a snuff-colored full-dress suit with cut steel buttons and a sword, administered an oath." *

To Walter Scott, Esq.

"London, Nov. 5, 1813.

"MY DEAR SCOTT,

"If you have not guessed at the reason why your letter has lain ten weeks unanswered, you must have thought me a very thankless and graceless fellow, and very undeserving of such a letter. I waited from day to day that I might tell you all was completed, and my patience was nearly exhausted in the process. Let me tell you the whole history in due order, before I express my feelings toward you upon the occasion. Upon receiving yours I wrote to Croker, saying that the time was past when I could write verses upon demand, but that if it were understood that, instead of the old formalities, I might be at liberty to write upon great public events or to be silent, as the spirit moved—in that case the office would become a mark of honorable distinction, and I should be proud of accepting it. How this was to be managed he best knew; for, of course, it was not for me to propose terms to the prince. When next I saw him, he told me that, after the appointment was completed, he or some other person in the prince's confidence would suggest to him the fitness of making this reform in an office which requires some reform to rescue it from the contempt into which it had fallen. I thought all was settled, and expected every day to receive some official communication, but week after week passed on. My head-quarters at this time were at Streatham.* Going one day into town to my brother's, I found that Lord William Gordon, with whom I had left a card on my first arrival, had called three times on me in as many days, and had that morning requested that I would call on him at eleven, twelve, one, or two o'clock. I went accordingly, never dreaming of what this business could be, and wondering at it. He told me that the Marquis of Hertford was his brother-in-law, and had written to him, as being my neighbor in the country—placing, in fact, the appointment at his (Lord William's) disposal, wherefore he wished to see me to know if I wished to have it. The meaning of all this was easily seen; I was very willing to thank one person more, and especially a good-natured man, to whom I am indebted for many neighborly civilities. He assured me that I should now soon hear from the chamberlain's office, and I departed accordingly, in full expectation that two or three days more would settle the affair. But neither days nor weeks brought any further intelligence; and if plenty of employments and avocations had not filled up my mind as well as my time, I should perhaps have taken dudgeon, and returned to my family and pursuits, from which I had so long been absent.

"At length, after sundry ineffectual attempts, owing sometimes to his absence, and once or twice to public business, I saw Croker once more, and he discovered for me that the delay originated in a desire of Lord Hertford's that Lord Liverpool should write to him, and ask the office for me. This calling in the prime minister about the disposal of an office, the net emoluments of which are about £90 a year, reminded me of the old proverb about shearing pigs. Lord Liverpool, however, was informed of this by Croker; the letter was written, and in the course of another week Lord Hertford wrote to Croker that he would give orders for making out the appointment. A letter soon followed to say that the order was given, and that I might be sworn in whenever I pleased. My pleasure, however, was the last thing to be consulted. After due inquiry on my part, and some additional delays, I received a note to say that if I would attend at the chamberlain's office at one o'clock on Thursday, November 4, a gentleman usher would be there to administer the oath. Now it so happened that I was engaged to go to Woburn on the Tuesday, meaning to return on Thursday to dinner, or remain a day longer, as I might feel disposed. Down I went to the office, and solicited a change in the day; but this was in vain; the gentleman usher had been spoken to, and a poet laureate is a creature of a lower description. I obtained, however, two hours' grace; and yesterday, by rising by candle-light and hurrying the post-boys, reached the office to the minute. I swore to be a faithful servant to the king, to reveal all treasons which might come to my knowledge, to discharge the duties of my office, and to obey the lord chamberlain in all matters of the king's service, and in his stead the vice-chamberlain. Having taken this upon my soul, I was thereby inducted into all the rights, privileges, and benefits which Henry James Pye, Esq., did enjoy, or ought to have enjoyed.

"The original salary of the office was 100 marks. It was raised for Ben Jonson to £100 and a tierce of Spanish Canary wine, now wickedly commuted for £26; which said sum, unlike the Canary, is subject to income-tax, land-tax, and heaven knows what taxes besides. The whole net income is little more or less than £90. It comes to me as a God-send, and I have vested it in a life-policy: by making it up £102, it covers an insurance for £3000 upon my own life. I have never felt any painful anxiety as to providing for my family—my mind is too buoyant, my animal spirits too good, for this care ever to have affected my happiness; and I may add that a not unbecoming trust in Providence has ever supported my confidence in my-

* His uncle, Mr. Hill, was then rector of that parish.

self. But it is with the deepest feeling of thanksgiving that I have secured this legacy for my wife and children, and it is to you that I am primarily and chiefly indebted.

"To the manner of your letter I am quite unable to reply. We shall both be remembered hereafter, and ill betide him who shall institute a comparison between us. There has been no race; we have both got to the top of the hill by different paths, and meet there, not as rivals, but as friends, each rejoicing in the success of the other.

"I wait for the levee, and hope to find a place in the mail for Penrith on the evening after it, for I have the Swiss malady, and am home-sick. Remember me to Mrs. Scott and your daughter; and believe me, my dear Scott,

"Most truly and affectionately yours,

"ROBERT SOUTHEY."

CHAPTER XIX.

THE LAUREATE'S FIRST ODE — RESTRICTIONS UPON HIS FREEDOM OF SPEECH—COMPLAINTS OF GIFFORD'S CORRECTIONS—BONAPARTE—CONDUCT OF THE AUSTRIAN GOVERNMENT TOWARD HOFER — ANXIETY RESPECTING HIS CHILDREN'S HEALTH—THINKS OF AN ODE ON THE EXPECTED MARRIAGE OF THE PRINCESS CHARLOTTE — REPULSE OF THE BRITISH AT BERGEN-OP-ZOOM—QUOTATION FROM GEORGE GASCOIGNE CONCERNING THE DUTCH—FEELINGS ON THE NEWS OF THE SUCCESS OF THE ALLIED ARMIES—POETICAL PLANS—LORD BYRON'S ODE TO BONAPARTE — REMARKS ON MATHEMATICAL STUDIES—ON CLERICAL DUTIES—RIDICULOUS POEM—PORTRAIT AND MEMOIR WANTED — LAUREATE ODES — SPANISH AFFAIRS — HUMBOLDT'S TRAVELS — RODERIC —MR. COLERIDGE—DOMESTIC ANXIETIES—ADVICE ON COLLEGE STUDIES — CHILDREN'S JOY—HOSPITALS BADLY CONDUCTED—POLITICAL SPECULATIONS—BARNARD BARTON—MR. WORDSWORTH'S LAST POEM—LITERARY PLANS —THE ETTRIC SHEPHERD—LAUREATE ODES STILL REQUIRED — FOREIGN POLITICS — MR. CANNING — HISTORY OF BRAZIL — EXPECTS NOTHING FROM GOVERNMENT—A CRAZY COMPOSITOR — GRAVE OF RONSARD AT TOURS — RODERIC — OLIVER NEWMAN — THOUGHT OF DEATH—BONAPARTE—HISTORY OF BRAZIL—NEW YEAR'S ODE EXPECTED—THE PROPERTY-TAX — THE SQUID HOUND — LORD BYRON — RODERIC — DIFFICULTIES OF REMOVAL — INSCRIPTIONS AND EPITAPHS — EVIL OF GOING TO INDIA—MURAT—HISTORY OF PORTUGAL—HIS SON'S STUDIES—DR. BELL'S LUDUS LITERARIUS — QUESTION OF MARRIAGE WITH A WIFE'S SISTER—REJOICINGS AT THE NEWS OF THE BATTLE OF WATERLOO.—1814–1815.

MY father had now received that title which, insignificant as it has usually been in literary history, and, even in the case of its worthiest holders, little thought of, seemed, if I do not err, with him to acquire a new importance, and—whether for good or evil, whether in honor or in opprobrium—to live in the mouths of men.

The new laureate, notwithstanding his wishes and intentions of emancipating the office from its thraldom, was bound precisely by the same rules and etiquette as his predecessors. He had, indeed, as he has stated, expressed a wish to Mr. Croker that it might be placed upon a footing which would exact from the holder nothing like a schoolboy's task, but leave him to write when and in what manner he thought best, and thus render the office as honorable as it was originally designed to be; and it had been replied that some proper opportunity might be found for representing the matter to the prince in its proper light. This, however, probably from various causes, was never done; and, in the very first instance of official composition, he was doomed to feel the inconvenience of writing to meet the taste of those in power. The time, indeed, was most favorable to him: he could combine a work intended as a specimen of his fulfillment of the laureate's duties with the expression of his warmest feelings of patriotic exultation. But there was a drawback: his feelings, on one point at least, far outran the calmness of the temperament authorized in high places. It appeared that he might rejoice for England, and Spain, and Wellington, but he must not pour out the vials of his wrath upon France and Bonaparte.

This he had done liberally in the first draft of his first ode, the Carmen Triumphale for the commencement of the new year; but, having sent it, in MS., to Mr. Rickman, his cooler judgment suggested that there might be an impropriety in some parts of it appearing as the poet laureate's production. "I am not sure," he says, "that you do not forget that *office* imposes upon a man many restraints besides the one day's bag and sword at Carlton House. Put the case that, through the mediation of Austria, we make peace with Bonaparte, and he becomes, of course, *a friendly power*—can you stay in office, this Carmen remaining on record?"

To John Rickman, Esq.

"Keswick, Dec. 17, 1813.

"MY DEAR RICKMAN,

"I thank you for your letter, and, in consequence of it, immediately transcribed the Carmen, and sent it to Mr. Croker. It had never occurred to me that any thing of an official character could be attached to it, or that any other reserve was necessary than that of not saying any thing which might be offensive to the government; *e. g.*, in 1808 the poet laureate would be expected not to write in praise of Mrs. Clarke and the resignation of the Duke of York. I dare say you are right, and I am prepared to expect a letter from Mr. Croker, advising the suppression of any thing discourteous toward Bonaparte. In that case, I shall probably add something to that part of the poem respecting Hanover and Holland, and send the maledictory stanzas to the

Courier without a name. By-the-by, if the government did not feel as I do, the Courier would not hoist Bourbon colors, as it has lately done. *

"As for the Morning Chronicle, I defy the devil and all his works. My malice has —— and —— for its objects, and the stanza was intended as a peg upon which to hang certain extracts from the Edinburgh Review, and a remark upon the happy vein of prophecy which these worthies have displayed. With respect to attacks from that quarter, I shall be abused of course, and if there is a certain portion of abuse to be bestowed upon any body, it may better fall upon me than almost any other person; for, in the first place, I shall see very little of it, and, in the next, care no further for what I may happen to see than just mentally to acknowledge myself as so much in debt. * * * *

"Farewell! R. S."

To the Rev. Herbert Hill.

"Keswick, Dec. 28, 1813.

"MY DEAR UNCLE,

* * * * * * *

"I am sorely out of humor with public affairs. One of our politicians (Mr. Canning, I believe) called Bonaparte once the child of Jacobinism; but, whether Jacobinism or any thing worse bred him, it is this country that has nursed him up to his present fortunes. After the murders of the Duc d'Enghien and Palm—avowed, open, notorious as they were—we ought to have made the war personal against a wretch who was under the ban of humanity. Had this been our constant language, he would long since have been destroyed by the French themselves; nor do I think that Austria would ever have connected itself by marriage with a man so branded. But it is impossible to make the statesmen of this country feel where their strength lies. It will be no merit of theirs if peace is not made, morally certain as every man, who sees an inch before his nose, must be, that it would last no longer than it serves this villain's purpose. He will get back his officers and men, who are now prisoners upon the Continent; he will build fleets; he will train sailors; he will bring sailors from America, and send ships there, and we shall have to renew the contest at his time, and with every advantage on his side.

"I spoiled my poem, in deference to Rickman's judgment and Croker's advice, by cutting out all that related to Bonaparte, and which gave strength, purport, and coherence to the whole. Perhaps I may discharge my conscience by putting these rejected parts together,* and letting them off in the Courier before it becomes a libelous offense to call murder and tyranny by their proper names.

"You will see that I have announced a series of inscriptions recording the achievements of our army in the Peninsula. Though this is not exactly *ex officio*, yet I should not have thought of it if it had not seemed a fit official undertaking. This style of composition is that to which I am more inclined than to any other. My local knowledge will turn to good account on many of these epigrammata.

"I had a letter a day or two ago from Kinder, who is at this time forming a commercial establishment at St. Andero. The Spanish troops, he says, had behaved so ill that Lord W. had ordered them all within their own frontier. From the specimens which he had seen, he thought they combined a blacker assemblage of diabolical qualities than any set of men whom he ever before had an opportunity of observing. Now Kinder is a cool, clear-headed man, disposed to see things in their best colors, and, moreover, has been in Brazil and Buenos Ayres. The truth seems to be that, though there never was much law in Spain, there has been none during the last six years, and the ruffian-like propensities of the brute multitude have had their full swing. Kinder had been to the scene of action, and dined frequently at head-quarters. He finds Biscay more beautiful than he expected, but has seen nothing to equal the Vale of Keswick. I shall make use of him to get books from Madrid. My friend Abella is one of the deputies for Aragon to the New Cortes.

"The South Sea missionaries have done something at last besides making better books than their Jesuit forerunners. They have converted the King of Otaheité. His letters are in my last Evangelical Magazine, and very curious they are. If he should prove conqueror in the civil war which is desolating the island, this conversion may, very probably, lead to its complete civilization. Human sacrifices would, of course, be abolished, and schools established. His majesty himself writes a remarkably good hand. *

"God bless you! R. S."

To C. W. W. Wynn, Esq.

"Jan. 15, 1814.

"MY DEAR WYNN,

"One of our poets says, 'A dram of sweet is worth a pound of sour,' which, if it be not good poetry, is sound practical wisdom. I assure you you have gone far toward reconciling me to the Carmen, by praising the Dutch stanza, of which I had conceived the only qualification to be, that it was as flat as the country of which it treated, as dead as the water of the ditches, and as heavy astern as the inhabitants. How often have I had occasion to remember the old apologue of the painter, who hung up his picture for public criticism! The conclusion also, laus Deo! has found favor in your eyes.

"I have added three stanzas to the five which were struck out, and made them into a whole, which is gone, *sine nomine*, to the Courier, where you will be likely to see it sooner than if I were to transcribe the excerpts.

"There was another stanza, which I expunged myself, because it spoke with bitterness of those

"Who deemed that Spain
Would bow her neck before the intruder's throne;

* These, with some additions, are published in the collected edition of his poems, under the title of an "Ode written during the Negotiations with Bonaparte in Jan., 1814."

and I should have been sorry to have had it applied in a manner to have wounded you, its direction being against the Edinburgh Review. Upon this point your remarks have in no degree affected my opinion, either as to the propriety of the attack itself, or of the place for it. However rash I may be, you will, I think, allow that my disposition is sufficiently placable. I continued upon courteous terms with Jeffrey, till that rascally attack upon the Register, in which he recommended it for prosecution. As for the retaliation of which you are apprehensive, do not suppose, my dear Wynn, that one who has never feared to speak his opinions sincerely can have any fear of being confronted with his former self? I was a Republican; I should be so still, if I thought we were advanced enough in civilization for such a form of society; and the more my feelings, my judgment, my old prejudices might incline me that way, the deeper would necessarily be my hatred of Bonaparte. Do you know that the Anti-Jacobin treats my Life of Nelson as infected with the leaven of Jacobinism?

"If I were conscious of having been at any time swayed in the profession of my opinions by private or interested motives, then indeed might I fear what malice could do against me. True it is that I am a pensioner and poet laureate. I owe the pension to you, the laurel to the Spaniards. Whether the former has prevented me from speaking as I felt upon the measures of government, where I thought myself called upon to speak at all, let my volumes of the Register bear witness. The Whigs who attack me for celebrating our victories in Spain, ought to expunge from the list of their toasts that which gives 'The cause of Liberty all the world over.' The Inscriptions are for the battles we have won, the towns we have retaken, and epitaphs for those who have fallen—that is, for as many of them as I can find any thing about whose rank or ability distinguished them.

"God bless you! R. S."

To Grosvenor C. Bedford, Esq.

"Keswick, Jan. 29, 1814.

"My dear Grosvenor,

"I hope you have secured the manuscript of my article on the Dissenters, in which I suspect Gifford has done more mischief than usual. Merely in cutting open the leaves, I perceived some omissions which one would think the very demon of stupidity had prompted. You may remember the manner in which I had illustrated Messrs. Bogue and Bennet's mention of Paul and Timothy. He has retained the quotation, and cut out the comment upon it. I believe the article has lost about two pages in this way. The only other instances which caught my eye will show you the spirit in which he has gone to work. Bogue and Bennet claim Milton, Defoe, &c., as Dissenters. I called them blockheads for not perceiving that it was 'to their *catholic* and *cosmopolite* intellect' that these men owed their immortality, not to their *sectarian* opinions, and the exterminating pen has gone through the words catholic and cosmopolite. There is also a foolish insertion stuck in, to introduce the last paragraph, which at once alters it, and says, 'Now I am going to say something fine,' instead of letting the feeling rise at once from the subject. It is well, perhaps, that the convenience of this quarterly incoming makes me placable, or I should some day tell Gifford, that though I have nothing to say against any omission which may be made for political or prudential motives, yet when the question comes to be a mere matter of opinion in regard to the wording of a sentence, my judgment is quite as likely to be right as his. You will really render me a great service by preserving my manuscript reviewals: for some of these articles may most probably be reprinted whenever my operas come to be printed in a collected form after I am gone, and these rejected passages will then be thought of most value.

"I wish you would, as soon as you can, call on Gifford, and tell him—not what I have been saying, for I have got rid of my gall in thus letting you know what I feel upon the subject—but that I will review Duppa's pamphlet about Junius, and the Memoirs, for his next number. Perhaps I may succeed in this, as, in approaching Junius, I shall take rather a wider view of political morality than he and his admirers have done.

"Some unknown author has sent me a poem called the Missionary, not well arranged, but written with great feeling and beauty. I shall very likely do him a good turn in the Quarterly. It is Ercilla's ground-work, with a new story made to fit the leading facts.

"God bless you! R. S."

To Walter Savage Landor, Esq.

"Keswick, March 9, 1814.

"Did you see my ode in the Courier, beginning,

'Who calls for peace at this momentous hour?' &c.:

it grew out of the omitted portion of the Carmen Triumphale, wherein I could not say all I wished and wanted to say, because a sort of official character attached to it. For five years I have been preaching the policy, the duty, the necessity of declaring Bonaparte under the ban of human nature; and if this had been done in 1808, when the Bayonne iniquity was fresh in the feelings of the public, I believe that the Emperor of Austria could never have given him his daughter in marriage; be that as it may, Spain and Portugal would have joined us in the declaration; the terms of our alliance would have been never to make peace with him; and France, knowing this, would, ere this, have delivered herself from him. My present hope is that he will require terms of peace to which the allies will not consent: a little success is likely enough to inflate him, for he is equally incapable of bearing prosperous or adverse fortunes. As for the Bourbons, I do not wish to see them restored, unless there were no other means of effecting his overthrow. Restorations are bad things, when the expulsion has taken place from internal causes and not by foreign forces. They have been a detestable race, and the adversity which they have undergone is not of that kind which renovates the intellect, or calls into life the virtues which royalty has stifled. I used to think that the Revolution would not have done its work till the houses of Austria and Bourbon were both destroyed—a consummation which the history of both houses has taught me devoutly to wish for. Did I ever tell you that Hofer got himself arrested under a false name and thrown into prison at Vienna, and that he was actually turned out of this asylum by the Austrian government? If any member of that government escapes the sword or the halter, there will be a lack of justice in this world. The fact is one of the most shocking in human history, but a fact it is, though it has not got abroad. Adair told it me.

"I shall rejoice to see your Idyllia. The printer is treading close on my heels, and keeping me close to work with this poem. I shall probably send you two sections more in a few days.

"R. S."

To Mr. Neville White.

"Keswick, March 18, 1814.

"MY DEAR NEVILLE,

"I am afraid I have been silent for a longer time than has ever before passed without a letter since our communication began. How truly has it been said that the first twenty years of life are the longest part of it, let it be ever so long extended. Days, weeks, and months now pass away so rapidly and yet so imperceptibly, that I am scarcely sensible of the sum of time which has gone by, till some business stares me in the face which has been left undone.

"It is not, however, from uniformity of happiness that time of late has passed so speedily with me. We have had ailments enough among the children to keep me perpetually anxious for the last eight or ten weeks. These are things which a man hardly understands till they have happened to himself, and even then some are affected more by them and some less; but it is one of the weak parts of my nature to feel them more, perhaps, than the occasion always justifies. I myself have had my share, though not a very heavy one, of the complaints which the unusual length and obstinacy of the winter scattered so plentifully in these parts. And though I have not been idle, and what I have done might be deemed a sufficient quantity for one who had less to do, the last four months have perhaps produced less than any former ones. I readily acknowledge that it may be fortunate for me to be under the necessity of continually bestirring my faculties in composition, otherwise the pleasure of acquiring knowledge, and continually supplying those deficiencies in my own acquirements, of which they who know most are most sensible in themselves, is so much more delightful than the act of communicating what I already know, that very probably I might fall into this kind of self-indulgence.

"My great poem will not be out before June. I am working hard at it. For the Quarterly I have done little—only Montgomery's poem, and a little Moravian book about the Nicobar Islands. I shall be vexed if the former be either delayed or mutilated.

"This evening's newspaper brings great news. The old desire of my heart—that of seeing peace dictated before the walls of Paris—seems about to be fulfilled. But what a dreadful business has this been at Bergen-op-Zoom!* This is the consequence of government deferring to popular opinion when founded upon false grounds. Graham was extolled and rewarded for the battle of Barrosa—a battle which he ought not to have fought, and which was worse than useless. Government knew this, and felt concerning it as I am now expressing myself. Yet they, of course, were glad to raise a cry of success, and the Opposition joined it in extolling Graham for the sake of abusing the Spaniards; whereas, in truth, he was infinitely more in fault than La Peña. After the battle he never ought to have been trusted with command.

"Believe me, my dear Neville,

"Ever yours with the truest regard,

"ROBERT SOUTHEY."

To John Rickman, Esq.

"Keswick, March 23, 1814.

"MY DEAR RICKMAN,

"Your letter† operated well. Like a good boy, I began my task immediately after its arrival, and have now completed one part and begun the second, of a poem which is to consist of three. Can you give me a better title than *Carmen Maritale?* I distrust my own Latinity, which has long been disused and never was very good. The poem is in six-lined stanzas; first a proem, so called rather than introduction, that the antiquated word may put the reader in tune for what follows. It is a poet's egotism making the best of the laurel, and passing to the present subject by professing at first an unfitness for it; the second part will be a vision, wherein allegorical personages give good advice; and the concluding part a justification of the serious strain which has been chosen; something about the king; and a fair winding up with a wish that it may be long before the princess be called upon to exercise the duties of which she has been here reminded. The whole poem 300 to 400 lines —on which, when they are completed, I will request you to bestow an hour's reading, with a pencil in your hand.

"In George Gascoigne's poem there are many things about the Dutch, showing that the English despised them and despaired of their cause, just as in our days happened to the Spaniards:

"'And thus, my lord, your honor may discerne
Our perils past; and how, in our annoy,

* "The attempt by the English force under Graham to carry Bergen-op-Zoom (a place of extraordinary strength, but inadequately garrisoned) by a coup-de-main, was repulsed, March 8, 1814, with a loss of 900 killed and wounded, and 1800 prisoners: a bloody check, which paralyzed the operations of the English."—*Alison.*

† My father had been in doubt as to the likelihood of the Princess Charlotte's marriage with the Prince of Orange, and hesitated whether to commence a poem on that subject.

God saved me (your lordship's bound forever),
Who else should not be able now to tell
The state wherein this country doth persever,
Ne how they seem in careless minds to dwell
(So did they erst, and so they will do ever).
And so, my lord, for to bewray my mind,
Methinks they be a race of bull-beef borne,
Whose hearts their butter mollyfieth by kind,
And so the force of beef is clear outworne.
And eke their brains with double beer are lined,
Like sops of browasse puffed up with froth;
When inwardly they be but hollow geer,
As weak as wind which with one puff up goeth.
And yet they brag, and think they have no peer,
Because Harlem hath hitherto held out;
Although in deed (as they have suffered Spain)
The end thereof even now doth rest in doubt.'

"I dearly love a piece of historical poetry like this, which shows how men thought and felt, when history only tells me how they acted.

"R. S."

To John May, Esq.

"Keswick, April 25, 1814.

"MY DEAR FRIEND,

"If the King of France has any stray *cordon bleu* to dispose of here, Herbert has a fair claim to one, having been the first person in Great Britain who mounted the white cockade. He appeared with one immediately upon the news from Bordeaux, and wore it till the news from Paris.* My young ones were then all as happy as paper cockades could make them; and, to our great amusement, all the white ribbon in Keswick was bought up to follow their example. My own feelings, on the first intelligence, were unlike any thing that I ever experienced before or can experience again. The curtain had fallen after a tragedy of five-and-twenty years. Those persons who had rejoiced most enthusiastically at the beginning of the Revolution, were now deeply thankful for a termination which restored things, as nearly as can be, to the state from which they set out. What I said, with a voice of warning, to my own country, is here historically true—that 'all the intermediate sum of misery is but the bitter price which folly pays for repentance.' The mass of destruction, of wretchedness, and of ruin which that revolution has occasioned, is beyond all calculation. Our conception of it is almost as vague and inadequate as of infinity. This, however, occurred to me at the time less than my own individual history; for I could not but remember how materially the course of my own life had been influenced by that tremendous earthquake, which seemed to break up the great deeps of society, like a moral and political deluge. I have derived nothing but good from it in every thing except the mere consideration of immediate worldly fortune, which is to me as dust in the balance. Sure I am that under any other course of discipline I should not have possessed half the intellectual powers which I now enjoy, and perhaps not the moral strength. The hopes and the ardor, and the errors and the struggles, and the difficulties of my early life crowded upon my mind; and, above all, there was a deep and grateful sense of that superintending goodness which had made all things work together for good in my fortunes, and will, I firmly believe, in like manner uniformly educe good from evil upon the great scale of human events.

"I fear we shall make a bad peace. Hitherto the people have borne on their governors (I except Prussia, where prince and people have been worthy of each other). The rulers are now left to themselves, and I apprehend consequences which will fall heavy upon posterity, though not, perhaps, upon ourselves. I had rather the French philosophy had left any other of its blessings behind it than its *candor* and its *liberality*. It was very natural that the Emperor of Austria should not choose to have his son-in-law hanged. But here is Alexander breakfasting with Marshal Ney, who, if he had more necks than the Hydra or my Juggernaut,* owes them all to the gallows for his conduct in Galicia and in Portugal. Caulincourt is to have an asylum in Russia, and no doubt will be permitted to choose his latitude there. *Candor* is to make us impute all the enormities which the French have committed to Bonaparte. All the horrors, absolutely unutterable as they are, which you know were perpetrated in Portugal, and which I know were perpetrated in Spain, but which I literally can not detail in history, because I dare not outrage human nature and common decency by such details—all these must in *candor* be put out of remembrance. All was Bonaparte's doing, and the most amiable of nations were his victims rather than his agents—so this most veracious of nations tells us, and so we are to believe. But if the Devil could not have brought about all the crimes without the Emperor Napoleon, neither could the Emperor Napoleon have discharged the Devil's commission without the most amiable of nations to act up to the full scope of his diabolical desires. At present, I admit, our business is to conciliate and consolidate the counter-revolution. But no visitings to Marshal Ney, no compliments to his worthy colleagues, no asylums for the murderers of the Duc d'Enghien. In treating for peace, liberality will not fail to be urged by the French negotiators as a reason for granting them terms which are inconsistent with the welfare of Europe. Alexander is a weak man, though a good one; and our ministers will be better pleased to hear themselves called liberal by the Opposition, than to be called wise by posterity.

* * * * * * * *

"R. SOUTHEY."

To Walter Scott, Esq.

"Keswick, April 27, 1814.

"MY DEAR SCOTT,

"Thank God, we have seen the end of this long tragedy of five-and-twenty years! The curtain has fallen; and though there is the afterpiece of the Devil to Pay to be performed, we have nothing to do with that: it concerns the performers alone. I wish we had been within

* Of the occupation of Paris by the allied armies, and the restoration of the Bourbons.

* See Curse of Kehama, sect. xiv.

reach of a meeting upon the occasion; and yet the first feeling was not a joyous one. Too many recollections crowded upon the mind; and the sudden termination putting an end at once to those hopes, and fears, and speculations which, for many years past, have made up so large a part of every man's intellectual existence, seemed like a change in life itself. Much as I had desired this event, and fully as I had expected it, still, when it came, it brought with it an awful sense of the instability of all earthly things; and when I remembered that that same newspaper might as probably have brought with it intelligence that peace had been made with Bonaparte, I could not but acknowledge that something more uniform in its operations than human councils had brought about the event. I thought he would set his life upon the last throw, and die game; or that he would kill himself, or that some of his own men would kill him; and though it had long been my conviction that he was a mean-minded villain, still it surprised me that he should live after such a degradation—after the loss, not merely of empire, but even of his military character. But let him live; if he will write his own history, he will give us all some information, and if he will read mine, it will be some set-off against his crimes.

"I desired Longman to send you the Carmen Triumphale. In the course of this year I shall volunteer verses enough of this kind to entitle me to a fair dispensation for all task-work in future. I have made good way through a poem upon the princess's marriage in the olden style, consisting of three parts—the Proem, the Dream, and L'Envoy; and I am getting on with the series of Military Inscriptions. The conclusion of peace will, perhaps, require another ode, and I shall then trouble Jeffrey with a few more notes. As yet I know nothing more of his reply than what some sturdy friend in the Times has communicated to me; but I shall not fail to pay all proper attention to it in due season. He may rest assured that I shall pay all my obligations to him with compound interest. The uses of newspapers will for a while seem flat and unprofitable, yet there will be no lack of important matter from abroad; and for acrimonious disputes at home, we shall always be sure of them. I fear we shall be too liberal in making peace. There is no reason why we should make any cessions for pure generosity. It is very true that Louis XVIII. has not been our enemy; but the French nation has, and a most inveterate and formidable one. They should have their sugar islands, but not without paying for them—and that a good round sum—to be equally divided between Greenwich and Chelsea, or to form the foundation of a fund for increasing the pay of army and navy.

"I am finishing Roderic, and deliberating what subject to take up next; for as it has pleased you and the prince to make me laureate, I am bound to keep up my poetical character. If I do not fix upon a tale of Robin Hood, or a New England story connected with Philip's war, and Goffe the regicide, I shall either go far north or far east for scenery and superstitions, and pursue my old scheme of my mythological delineations. Is it not almost time to hear of something from you? I remember to have been greatly delighted when a boy with Amyntor and Theodora, and with Dr. Ogilvie's Rona. The main delight must have been from the scenes into which they carried me. There was a rumor that you were among the Hebrides. I heartily wish it may be true.

"Remember us to Mrs. Scott and your daughter. These children of ours are now growing tall enough and intelligent enough to remind us forcibly of the lapse of time. Another generation is coming on. You and I, however, are not yet off the stage; and, whenever we quit it, it will not be to men who will make a better figure there.

"Yours very affectionately,

"ROBERT SOUTHEY."

To Mr. Neville White.

"Keswick, April 29, 1814

"MY DEAR NEVILLE,

"My main employment at present is upon Roderic. The poem is drawing toward its completion; in fact, the difficulty may be considered as over, and yet a good deal of labor remains, for I write slowly and blot much. However, land is in sight, and I feel myself near enough the end of this voyage to find myself often considering upon what course I shall set sail for the next. Something of magnitude I must always have before me to occupy me in the intervals of other pursuits, and to think of when nothing else requires attention. But I am less determined respecting the subject of my next poem than I ever was before when a vacancy was so near. The New England Quaker story is in most forwardness, but I should prefer something which in its tone of feeling would differ more widely from that on which I am at present busied. As to looking for a *popular* subject, this I shall never do; for, in the first place, I believe it to be quite impossible to say what would be popular, and, secondly, I should not willingly acknowledge to myself that I was influenced by any other motive than the fitness of my story to my powers of execution.

"The laureateship will certainly have this effect upon me, that it will make me produce more poetry than I otherwise should have done. For many years I had written little, and was permitting other studies to wean me from it more and more. But it would be unbecoming to accept the only public mark of honor which is attached to the pursuit, and at the same time withdraw from the profession. I am, therefore, reviving half-forgotten plans, forming new ones, and studying my old masters with almost as much ardor and assiduity as if I were young again. Some of Henry's papers yonder strikingly resemble what I used to do twenty years ago, and what I am beginning to do again.

"Thank you for Lord Byron's Ode:* there is

* Ode to Napoleon Bonaparte.

in it, as in all his poems, great life, spirit, and originality, though the meaning is not always brought out with sufficient perspicuity. The last time I saw him he asked me if I did not think Bonaparte a great man in his villainy. I told him no—that he was a mean-minded villain. And Lord Byron has now been brought to the same opinion. But of politics in my next. I shall speedily thank Josiah Conder for his review, and comment a little upon its contents. Some of his own articles please me exceedingly. I wish my coadjutors in the Quarterly had thought half as much upon poetry, and understood it half as well.

"God bless you!

"Yours affectionately,

"R. Southey."

To Mr. James White.

"Keswick, May 2, 1814.

"My dear James,

"I am glad to hear from Neville that you are improved in health and spirits. What you say of the inconvenience of mathematical studies to a man who has no inclination for them, no necessity for them, no time to spare for acquiring them, and no use for them when they are acquired, is perfectly true; and I think it was one of the advantages (Heaven knows they were very few) which Oxford used to possess over Cambridge, that a man might take his degree, if he pleased, without knowing any thing of the science. A tenth or a fiftieth part of the time employed upon Euclid, would serve to make the under-graduate a good logician, and logic will stand him in good stead, to whatever profession he may betake himself.

"Your repugnance to the expense of time which this fatiguing study requires is very natural and very reasonable, and the best comfort I can offer is to remind you that the time will soon come when you will have the pleasure of forgetting all you have learned. Your apprehensions of deficiency in more important things are not so well founded. The Church stands in need of men of various characters and acquirements. She ought to have some sturdy polemics, equally able to attack and to defend. One or two of these are as many as she wants, and as many as she produces in a generation; she can not do without them, and yet sometimes they do evil as well as good. Horsley was the militant of the last generation, Herbert Marsh of the present. Next to these stiff canonists and sound theologians, she requires some who excel in the *literæ humaniores*, and who may keep up that literary character which J. Taylor, South, Sherlock, Barrow, &c., have raised, and which of late days has certainly declined. Of these a few also are sufficient. There are hardly more than half a dozen pulpits in the kingdom in which an eloquent preacher would not be out of his place. Every where else, what is required of the preacher is to be plain, perspicuous, and in earnest. If he feels himself, he will make his congregation feel. But it is not in the pulpit that the minister may do most good. He will do infinitely more by living with his parishioners like a pastor; by becoming their confidential adviser, their friend, their comforter; directing the education of the poor, and, as far as he can, inspecting that of all, which it is not difficult for a man of good sense and gentle disposition to do as an official duty, without giving it, in the slightest degree, the appearance of officious interference. Teach the young what Christianity is; distinguish by noticing and rewarding those who distinguish themselves by their good conduct; see to the wants of the poor, and call upon the charity of the rich, making yourself the channel through which it flows; look that the schools be in good order, that the work-house is what it ought to be, that the overseers do their duty; be, in short, the active friend of your parishioners. Sunday will then be the least of your labors, and the least important of your duties; and you will very soon find that the time employed in making a sermon would be better employed in adapting to your congregation a dozen, which your predecessors did not deliver to the press for no other purpose than that they should stand idle upon the shelves of a divinity library. The pulpit is a clergyman's parade, the parish is his field of active service.

"Believe me, my dear James,

"Yours very affectionately,

"Robert Southey."

To Grosvenor C. Bedford, Esq.

"May 9, 1814.

"My dear Grosvenor,

"Here is a choice poem for you—the production of a man who keeps a billiard-table at Carlisle, and who, having a genius for poetry, and not daring to show his productions to his wife and daughters, has pitched upon Calvert for his confidant. I give it to you *literatim*, and shall content myself with desiring you not to imagine, from the lyrical abruptness of the beginnings, that the poem is imperfect. It is a whole, and perfect in its kind.

"'Not forgetting Lord Wellington,
When he to Beaudeux came,
The most noble lord was received
With great honor to his name.
The Bourbon cry caled aloud so high,
That it made Paris shake and trimble.
May we all se that shock to be
And make Bonaparte to trimble.
Rise Paris and let us se
Shake off that yoke for liberty.
There is a shake now begun,
Tear it up and pull it down!
May we all united be
In this most noble cause,
To protect our king,
Our country, and our laws.
Louis haste, heare is a call,
Paris crie is one and all.
Blucher, by his great power,
Will protect the every hour.
May France rejoice and sing,
Long life to Louis our king.
We Britons will rejoice
To see Louis made their choice.'

* * *

"God bless you! R. Southey."

To Grosvenor C. Bedford, Esq.

"June 5, 1814.

"MY DEAR GROSVENOR,

"Another *homo, cui nomen* Colburn, lord of the New Monthly Magazine, has written for my portrait. Now, according to all rules of arithmetic (of which I know little) and algebra (of which I know nothing), if a portrait in one magazine be to do me yeoman's service, portraits in two will do the service of two yeomen. So do you answer for me to the European, either by note or letter, offering your drawing, and I will send the *alter homo* to the doctor to make use of the bust. *Quoad* the biographical sketch, nothing more need be mentioned than that I was born at Bristol, Aug. 12, 1774—prince and poet having the same birth-day—was of Westminster and afterward of Baliol College, Oxford, and that my maternal uncle being chaplain of the British Factory at Lisbon, my studies were by that circumstance led toward the literature and history of Portugal and Spain. This is what I shall tell Colburn, and his merry men may dress it up as he pleases.

"But O Grosvenor! I have this day thought of a third 'Portrait of the author,' to be prefixed to the delectable history of Dr. D. D——, to which history I yesterday wrote the preface with a peacock's pen. It is to be the back of the writer, sitting at his desk with his peacock's pen in his hand. As soon as Roderic is finished, which it will very soon be, I think the spirit will move me to spur myself on with his delicious book by sending it piecemeal to you. Will you enter into a commercial treaty with me, and send Butler in return? R. S."

To John Rickman, Esq.

"Keswick, June 16, 1814.

"MY DEAR RICKMAN,

"It came into my head that it might peradventure be a fit thing for the poet laureate to write certain verses upon the peace to the personages who are now dragging all London after their horses' heels. I was very well inclined to put the thought out of my head, if some of the very few persons whom I see here had not shown me by their inquiries that it would come into other heads as well as mine. The subjects for their kind were the best possible; so I fell to in good earnest, and have written three odes* in Thalaba's verse. The Carmen was an oration in rhyme. These are odes without rhyme, but in manner and matter altogether lyric. I shall have no time even to correct the press. I have written to Croker, saying that it may be proper to present copies to the persons be-oded, or that such presentations might be improper, and that, in my ignorance of such things, I requested him to act for me. * * * * *

"I am in some trouble about my old correspondent, Don Manual Abella, a man of letters and a stanch friend of the old Cortes, though no admirer of the head-over-heels activity of the new ones. I think he is in some danger of coming under a proscription, which seems to make little distinction of persons. That Ferdinand and the Constitution could long coexist was not possible. The king was a mere log, and must soon have been treated as such. But he has gone vilely to work; and I will not condemn him *in toto* till it be seen what sort of Constitution he means to give the people (*encore une Constitution!*). I very much fear that the old system of favoritism will return, and that abominations of every kind will be restored as well as the Inquisition, which blessed office, you see, has been re-established, in compliance with the popular cry, as a boon!

"An officer of Suchet's army, who served at the siege of Tarragona, and was afterward taken by Eroles, was brought here last week by Wordsworth, to whom he had letters of recommendation from France—a young man, and apparently one of the best of these Frenchmen. He had grace enough to acknowledge that the Spanish business was an unjust one, which he said all the officers knew; and he amused me by complaining that the Spaniards were very hard-hearted. To which I replied that they had not invited him and his countrymen. He said, 'They did make beautiful defense;' and I gathered from him some information upon points of consequence.

* * * * * * *

"I have sent to the Courier a doggerel March to Moscow, written months ago to amuse the children, and chiefly upon the provocation of an irresistible rhyme, which is *not* to be printed. I give you the suppressed stanza; for I am sure, if you happen to see the song, you will wonder how such a hit could have been missed.*

"The Emperor Nap, he talked so loud,
That he frightened Mr. Roscoe;
John Bull, he cries, if you'll be wise,
Ask the Emperor Nap if he will please
To grant you peace upon your knees,
Because he's going to Moscow!
He'll make all the Poles come out of their holes,
And eat the Prussians, and beat the Russians;
The fields are green, and the sky is blue,
Morblue! Parblue!
He'll certainly get to Moscow!

"There is some good doggerel in the rest, and Morbleu, &c., is the burden of the song.

* * * * * * *

"Yours most truly, R. S."

To Messrs. Longman and Co.

"Keswick, Sept. 3, 1814.

"DEAR SIRS,

" * * * I have had a visit from Mr. Canning to-day, who has offered me his good offices in Portugal, and to be the means of any communication with Henry Wellesley at Madrid. This new opening is so much the more acceptable, as my main source of information has been cut off, Abella, I fear, being at this time in prison.

"The restoration of the Jesuits is a most important measure, and not the least extraordinary

* To the Prince Regent, the Emperor of Russia, and the King of Prussia.

* This stanza is now printed with the rest of the poem.

of the great events which have lately taken place. This concluding volume of Brazil will be the only single work which contains the whole history of their empire in South America, and of their persevering struggle against the Indian slave-trade, which was the remote but main cause of their overthrow. I am working at this from manuscript documents, some of which fatigue the sight.

"Murray sent me the other day the two first and two last volumes of your translation of Humboldt, which I shall review. This traveler has so encumbered his volumes with science, that I think you would do well to extract his travels, insert in them the readable part of his other works in their proper place, and thus put the generally interesting part within reach of the reading public. This is what Pinkerton ought to have done. Can you lend me Humboldt's Essay on the Geography of Plants? It must, doubtless, contain some Brazilian information.

"Yours very truly,

"ROBERT SOUTHEY."

To Joseph Cottle, Esq.

"Keswick, Oct. 17, 1814.

"MY DEAR COTTLE,

"It is not long since I heard of you from De Quincey, but I wish you would let me sometimes hear *from you.* There was a time when scarcely a day passed without my seeing you, and in all that time I do not remember that there ever was a passing coldness between us. The feeling, I am sure, continues; do not, then, let us be so entirely separated by distance, which in cases of correspondence may almost be considered as a mere abstraction. * * * * * * * * * * * *

"Longman will send you my poem. It has been printed about two months, but he delays its publication till November, for reasons of which he must needs be the best judge. I am neither sanguine about its early, nor doubtful about its ultimate, acceptation in the world. The passion is in a deeper tone than in any of my former works; I call it a tragic poem for this reason; and also that the reader may not expect the same busy and complicated action which the term heroic might seem to promise. The subject has the disadvantage of belonging to an age of which little or no costume has been preserved. I was, therefore, cut off from all adornments of this kind, and had little left me to relieve the stronger parts but description, the best of which is from the life.

* * * * * * *

"Can you tell me any thing of Coleridge? A few lines of introduction for a son of Mr. ——, of St. James's (in your city), are all that we have received since I saw him last September twelvemonth in town. The children being thus entirely left to chance, I have applied to his brothers at Otley concerning them, and am in hopes through their means, and the aid of other friends, of sending Hartley to college. Lady Beaumont has promised £30 a year for this purpose, Poole £10. I wrote to Coleridge three or four months ago, telling him that unless he took some steps in providing for this object I must make the application, and required his answer within a given term of three weeks. He received the letter, and in his note by Mr. —— promised to answer it, but he has never taken any further notice of it. I have acted with the advice of Wordsworth. The brothers, as I expected, promise their concurrence, and I daily expect a letter, stating to what amount they will contribute. * *

"Believe me, my dear Cottle,

"Ever your affectionate old friend,

"ROBERT SOUTHEY."

To Mr. Neville White.

"Keswick, Nov. 8, 1814.

"MY DEAR NEVILLE,

"* * * I was *not* sorry that we did not meet at Ambleside merely to take leave. It is one of those things which, since my schoolboy days, I always avoid when I can; there are but too many of these long good-by's in life; and to one who has experienced in the losses you have sustained that fearful uncertainty of life which only experience makes us fully feel and understand, they are very painful. Our repast upon Kirkston* wore a good face of cheerfulness; but I could not help feeling how soon we were to separate, and how doubtful it was that the whole of the party would ever be assembled together again. * * * * * * * * * * * * * After our return Isabel was seized with a severe attack, and was brought to the very brink of the grave. I so verily expected to lose her, that I thought at one moment I had seen her for the last time. There are heavier afflictions than this, but none keener; and the joy and thankfulness which attend on recovery are proportionately intense. She has not yet regained her strength; but every day is restoring her, God be thanked.

"I am glad you have seen these children. * * If, by God's blessing, my life should be prolonged till they are grown up, I have no doubt of providing for them; and if Herbert's life be spared, he has every thing which can be required to make his name a good inheritance to him. * * * * * *

"O dear Neville! how unendurable would life be if it were not for the belief that we shall meet again in a better state of existence. I do not know that person who is happier than myself, and who has more reason to be happy; and never was man more habitually cheerful; but this belief is the root which gives life to all, and holds all fast. God bless you!

"Yours very affectionately,

"ROBERT SOUTHEY."

To Mr. James White.

"Keswick, Nov. 11, 1814.

"MY DEAR JAMES,

"I am grieved to learn from Neville that you

* A mountain pass leading from Ambleside to Patterdale.

are distressing yourself about what I could find in my heart to call these cursed examinations.* There are few things of which I am more thoroughly convinced, than that the system of feeding-up young men like so many game cocks for a sort of intellectual *long-main* is every way pernicious.

"University honors are like provincial tokens, not current beyond the narrow limits of the district in which they are coined; and even where they pass current they are not the only currency, nor the best. Doubtless there are many men at Cambridge in high repute, who have taken no honors and gained no prizes; and should you yourself stand for a fellowship or take pupils, you will find the opinion of what you *might have done* will act as well in your favor as if your acquirements had received the seal and stamp of approbation in the Senate House. Content yourself with graduating among the many; and remember that the first duty which you have to perform is that of keeping yourself, as far as it can depend upon yourself, in sound health of body and mind, both for your own sake and for the sake of those who are most dear to you. If I were near you I would rid you of these blue devils. When I was about eighteen I made Epictetus literally my manual for some twelve months, and by that wholesome course of stoicism counteracted the mischief which I might else have incurred from a passionate admiration of Werter and Rousseau. His tonics agreed with me; and if the old Grecian could know how impassible I have ever since felt myself to the τὰ οὐκ ἐφ' ἡμῖν, he would be well satisfied with the effect of his lessons. It is not your fault that these university distinctions have a local and temporary value, but it is your fault if you do not consider how local and how temporary that value is; and if you suffer yourself to be agitated by any losses and fears concerning what is worth so little. My dear James, in this matter, follow, in the strict interpretation of the words, the advice of Boëthius,

'Pelle timorem,
Spemque fugato.'

Remember that you only want your degree as a passport; content yourself with simply taking it; and if you are disposed to revenge yourself afterward by burning your mathematical books and instruments, bring them with you to Keswick when next you make us a visit, and I will assist at the auto-da-fè. We will dine by the side of the Lake, and light our fire with Euclid.

"Neville was more fortunate than you in his excursion to this land of loveliness. He had delightful weather, and he made the most of it. Never had we a more indefatigable guest, nor one who enjoyed the country more heartily. Since his return, Neville-like, he has loaded us with presents; and no children were ever happier than these young ones were when the expected box made its appearance. I happened to be passing the evening at the island with General Peachey when it arrived, and they one and all laid their injunctions upon their mother not to tell me what each had received, that they might surprise me with the sight in the morning. Accordingly, no sooner was my door opened in the morning than the whole swarm were in an uproar, buzzing about me. In an evil moment I had begun to shave myself; before the operation was half over, Edith with her work-box was on one side, Herbert with his books on the other; Bertha was displaying one treasure, Kate another, and little Isabel, jigging for delight in the midst of them, was crying out *mine—mine—Mitter White*—and holding up a box of Tunbridge ware. My poor chin suffered for all this, and the scene would have made no bad subject for Wilkie or Bird. God bless you!

"Your affectionate friend,

"ROBERT SOUTHEY."

To Dr. Gooch.

"Keswick, Nov. 30, 1814.

"MY DEAR GOOCH,

"Your letter reminds me that I have something to ask of you. You may remember telling me of a sailor in Yarmouth Hospital, after Nelson's battle at Copenhagen (if I recollect rightly), whom you attended, and who died in consequence of neglect after you had ceased to attend him, but expressed his delight at seeing you before he died. Though I have not forgotten, and could not forget the circumstances, I have acquired a sort of passion for authenticity upon all points where it is attainable, and you will oblige me by relating the particulars. I am about to compose a paper for the Quarterly, the text for which will be taken from the Reports of the *Poor Society*, and the object of which is to show what has been done in this country toward lessening the quantum of human suffering, and what remains to do. In treating of prevention, correction, and alleviation, I shall have to treat of schools, prisons, and hospitals; and respecting hospitals, must quote the saying of a Frenchman whom Louis XVI. sent over to England to inquire into the manner in which they were conducted. He praised them as they deserved, but added, *Mais il y manque deux choses, nos curés, et nos hospitalières.* And here, with due caution respecting *place*, &c., I wish to tell your story.

"I am fully convinced that a gradual improvement is going on in the world, has been going on from its commencement, and will continue till the human race shall attain all the perfection of which it is capable in this mortal state. This belief grows out of knowledge; that is, it is a corollary deduced from the whole history of mankind. It is no little pleasure to believe that in no age has this improvement proceeded so rapidly as in the present, and that there never was so great a disposition to promote it in those who have the power. The disposition, indeed, is alloyed with much weakness and much superstition; and God knows there are many disturbing

* This is strong language; but it might well be used to the brother of poor Kirke White, who, urged by exhortations, and kept up by stimulants, won in the race, and—died.

powers at work. But much has been done, more is doing, and nothing can be of more importance than giving this disposition a good direction. Perceval's death was one of the severest losses that England has ever sustained. He was a man who not only desired to act well, but desired it ardently; his heart always strengthened his understanding, and gave him that power which rose always to the measure of the occasion. Lord Liverpool is a cold man: you may convince his understanding, but you can only obtain an inert assent where zealous co-operation is wanted. It is, however, enough for *us* to know *what* ought to be done: the *how* and the *when* are in the hands of One who knows when and how it may be done best. Oh! if this world of ours were but well cultivated, and weeded well, how like the garden of Eden might it be made! Its evils might almost be reduced to physical suffering and death; the former continually diminishing, and the latter, always indeed an awful thing, but yet to be converted into hope and joy.

"I am much better pleased with ——'s choice than if he had made a more ambitious alliance. Give me neither riches nor poverty, said the Wise Man. Lead us not into temptation is one of the few petitions of that prayer which comprises all that we need to ask: riches always lead that way.

"Why have you not been to visit Joanna Southcote? If I had been less occupied, I should have requested you to go, not for the sake of a professional opinion (Dr. Simms having satisfied me upon that score), but that you might have got at some of the mythology, and ascertained how much was imposture and how much delusion. Gregoire has published a Histoire des Sectes, in two volumes, beginning with the last century. I shall review it as a second part to the article upon the Dissenters.

"You have in Roderic the best which I have done, and, probably, the best that I shall do, which is rather a melancholy feeling for the author. My powers, I hope, are not yet verging upon decay, but I have no right to expect any increase or improvement, short as they are of what they might have been, and of what I might have hoped to make them. Perhaps I shall never venture upon another poem of equal extent, and in so deep a strain. It will affect you more than Madoc, because it is pitched in a higher key. I am growing old, the gray hairs thicken upon me, my joints are less supple, and, in mind as well as body, I am less enterprising than in former years. When the thought of any new undertaking occurs, the question, Shall I live to complete what I have already undertaken? occurs also. My next poem will be, 'A Tale of Paraguay,' about a thousand lines only in length. Its object will be to plant the grave with flowers, and wreathe a chaplet for the angel of death. If you suspect, from all this, that I suffer any diminution of my usual happy spirits, you will be mistaken. God bless you!

"R. S."

To Bernard Barton, Esq.

"Keswick, Dec. 19, 1814.

"My dear Sir,

"You will wonder at not having received my thanks for your metrical effusions; but you will acquit me of all incivility when you hear that the book did not reach me till this morning, and that I have now laid it down after a full perusal.

"I have read your poems with much pleasure, those with most which speak most of your own feelings. Have I not seen some of them in the Monthly Magazine?

"Wordsworth's residence and mine are fifteen miles asunder, a sufficient distance to preclude any frequent interchange of visits. I have known him nearly twenty years, and for about half that time intimately. The strength and the character of his mind you see in the Excursion, and his life does not belie his writings, for in every relation of life, and every point of view, he is a truly exemplary and admirable man. In conversation he is powerful beyond any of his cotemporaries; and as a poet—I speak not from the partiality of friendship, nor because we have been so absurdly held up as both writing upon one concerted system of poetry, but with the most deliberate exercise of impartial judgment whereof I am capable, when I declare my full conviction that posterity will rank him with Milton. * *

"You wish the metrical tales were republished; they are at this time in the press, incorporated with my other minor poems, in three volumes. *Nos hæc novimus esse nihil* may serve as motto for them all.

"Do not suffer my projected Quaker poem to interfere with your intentions respecting William Penn; there is not the slightest reason why it should. Of all great reputations, Penn's is that which has been most the effect of accident. The great action of his life was his turning Quaker; the conspicuous one his behavior upon his trial. In all that regards Pennsylvania, he has no other merit than that of having followed the principles of the religious community to which he belonged, when his property *happened* to be vested in colonial speculations. The true champion for religious liberty in America was Roger Williams, the first consistent advocate for it in that country, and, perhaps, the first in any one. I hold his memory in veneration. But, because I value religious liberty, I differ from you entirely concerning the Catholic question, and never would intrust any sect with political power whose doctrines are inherently and necessarily intolerant.

"Believe me, yours with sincere respect,

"Robert Southey."

To Grosvenor C. Bedford, Esq.

"Keswick, Dec. 22, 1814.

"My dear Grosvenor,

"If Murray were to offer me £500 for a Register, I certainly should not for a moment hesitate. Indeed, I know not whether I ought not gladly to catch at the £400, circumstanced as I am. In that case I should advise him to begin with the Peace, for many reasons. First, because it would be so tremendous an undertaking to bring up the lee-way from the beginning of 1812; and, secondly, because there is a great advantage in commencing with a new era in history. It might be worth while at leisure (if I could possibly procure it) to write the volumes for 1812–13, for the sake of connecting the former volumes with these; but this I should despair of. My history of the Peninsula will include what is to me the most interesting portion, and the only portion which I can do thoroughly as it ought to be done. And, more than all, however I might spirit myself up to the undertaking, flesh and blood are not equal to it. I can not get through more than at present, unless I give up sleep, or the little exercise which I take (and I walk to the Crag* before breakfast); and, that hour excepted, and my meals (barely the meals, for I remain not one minute after them), the pen or the book is always in my hand.

"Had you not better wait for Jeffrey's attack upon Roderic? I have a most curious letter upon this subject from Hogg, the Ettric Shepherd, a worthy fellow, and a man of very extraordinary powers. Living in Edinburgh, he thinks Jeffrey the greatest man in the world—an intellectual Bonaparte, whom nobody and nothing can resist. But Hogg, notwithstanding this, has fallen in liking with me, and is a great admirer of Roderic. And this letter is to request that I will not do any thing to *nettle* Jeffrey while he is deliberating concerning Roderic, for he seems favorably disposed toward me! Morbleu! it is a rich letter! Hogg requested that he himself might review it, and gives me an extract from Jeffrey's answer, refusing him. 'I have, as well as you, a great respect for Southey,' he says; 'but he is a most provoking fellow, and at least as conceited as his neighbor Wordsworth.' But he shall be happy to talk to Hogg upon this and other *kindred* subjects, and he should be very glad to give me a lavish allowance of praise, if I would afford him occasion, &c.; but he must do what he thinks his duty, &c.! I laugh to think of the effect my reply will produce upon Hogg. How it will make every bristle to stand on end like quills upon the fretful porcupine!

"God bless you! R. S.

"What can I call the ode? Can you find any thing to stand with Carmen? Annuum I will not use, nor will I call it Ode for the New Year, for I will do nothing that I can avoid toward perpetuating the custom. How would Carmen Hortatorium do, if there be such a word?"

To Walter Scott, Esq.

"Keswick, Dec. 24, 1814.

"MY DEAR SCOTT,

"Are you still engaged with the Lord of the Isles, or may I give you joy of a happy deliverance? There are few greater pleasures in life than that of getting fairly through a great work of this kind, and seeing it when it first comes before us in portly form. I envy you the advantage which you always derive from a thorough knowledge of your poetical ground; no man can be more sensible of this advantage than myself, though I have in every instance been led to forego it.

"Longman was to take care that Roderic should be duly conveyed to you. Remember that if you do not duly receive every book which has the name of R. S. in the title-page, the fault lies among the booksellers. My last employment has been an *Odeous* one. I was in good hope that this silly custom had been dispensed with, but on making inquiry through Croker, the reply was that an ode I must write. It would be as absurd in me to complain of this, as it is in the higher powers to exact it. However, I shall no longer feel myself bound to volunteer upon extraordinary service. I had a ridiculous disappointment about the intended marriage of the Princess Charlotte, which was so mischievously broken off. Willing to be in time, as soon as I was assured that the marriage was to be, I fell to work, and produced some fifty six-lined stanzas, being about half of a poem in the old manner, which would have done me credit.

"I do not like the aspect of affairs abroad. We make war better than we make peace. In war John Bull's bottom makes amends for the defects of his head; he is a dreadful fellow to take by the horns, but no calf can be more easily led by the nose. Europe was in such a state when Paris was taken, that a commanding intellect, had there been such among the allies, might have cast it into whatever form he pleased. The first business should have been to have reduced France to what she was before Louis XIV.'s time; the second to have created a great power in the north of Germany with Prussia at its head; the third to have consolidated Italy into one kingdom or commonwealth. A fairer opportunity was given us than at the peace of Utrecht, but *moderation* and *generosity* were the order of the day, and with these words we have suffered ourselves to be fooled. Here at home the Talents, with that folly which seems to pursue all their measures like a fatality, are crying out in behalf of Poland and Saxony—the restoration of which would be creating two powerful allies for France; and in America we have both lost time and credit. Of Sir G. Prevost, from his former conduct, I have too good an opinion to condemn him until I have heard his defense; but there has evidently been misconduct somewhere; and at Baltimore I can not but think that the city would have been taken if poor Ross had not been killed. Confidence is almost every thing in war.

"Jeffrey, I hear, has written what his admirers call a *crushing* review of the Excursion. He might as well seat himself upon Skiddaw, and fancy that he crushed the mountain. I heartily wish Wordsworth may one day meet with him, and lay him alongside, yard-arm and yard-arm in argument.

"I saw Canning for an hour or two when he was in this country, and was far more pleased with him than I had expected. He has played

* A promontory jutting out into Derwentwater, about a mile from Greta Hall.

his cards ill. In truth, I believe that nature made him for something better than a politician. He is gone to a place where I wish I could go. Indeed, I should think seriously of going to Spain, if the country were not evidently in a very insecure state. Some of my old Guerilla friends, for want of other occupation, might employ a cartridge upon me. I have still a communication with Madrid, but of course we get no information concerning the real state of things; nor can I guess who is the mover of this mischief; for Ferdinand is a fool, and is, moreover, exceedingly popular, which seems as if he were a good-natured fool. And a change of ostensible counselors has produced no change of system. I am much gratified by the compliment the Academy have paid me, and if the Lisbon Academy should follow the example, I should desire no other mark of literary honor. The concluding volume of my Brazil is in the press, and I am closely employed upon it. You will find in it some warfare of the old hearty character, the whole history of the Jesuits in Paraguay, and much curious information respecting the savages. Remember me to Mrs. Scott and your daughter, and believe me,

"Yours very affectionately,

"ROBERT SOUTHEY."

To Grosvenor C. Bedford, Esq.

"Dec. 29, 1814.

"*Laus Deo!* Peace with America. All difficulty about the ode is thus terminated, and instead of singing O be joyful! I must set about another. So I shall pen one for the fiddlers, and alter the other, either to be published separately or with it. Coming extra-officially, it can not be offensive, and being in the press, it can not be suppressed without losing the price of the printer's labor.

"As for any such possibilities as those at which you hint, they are so very like impossibilities that I do not know how to distinguish them; for, in the first place, you may be sure that if the men in power were ever so well disposed toward me, they would think me already liberally remunerated for my literary merits; they can not know that by gaining a pension of £200 I was actually a loser of £20 a year; they, if they thought about it at all, would needs suppose that it was a clear addition to my former means, and that, if I lived decently before, the addition would enable me to live with ease and comfort. Secondly, they are never likely to think about me further than as I may, in pursuing my own principles, happen to fall in with their view of things. This happened in the Spanish war, and would have happened in the Catholic question if the Quarterly had not been under Canning's influence. Thirdly, I am neither enthusiast nor hypocrite, but a man deeply and habitually religious in all my feelings.

"No, Grosvenor, I shall never get more from government than has already been given me, and I am and ought to be well contented with it; only they ought to allow me my wine in kind, and dispense with the odes. When did this fool's custom begin? Before Cibber's time? I would have made the office honorable, if they would have let me. If they will not, the dishonor will not be mine. And now I am going to think about my rhymes, so farewell for the night.

"Friday, Dec. 30.

"I have been rhyming as doggedly and as dully as if my name had been Henry James Pye. Another dogged fit will, it is to be hoped, carry me through the job; and as the ode will be very much according to rule, and entirely good for nothing, I presume it may be found unobjectionable. Meantime the poor Mus. Doc. has the old poem to mumble over. As I have written in regular stanzas, I shall dispatch him one by this post to set him his tune. It is really my wish to use all imaginable civility to the Mus. Doc., and yet I dare say he thinks me a troublesome fellow as well as an odd one.

"God bless you! R. SOUTHEY."

To Walter Savage Landor, Esq.

"Keswick, Feb. 3, 1815.

"In one of the first books which I published, a crazy compositor took it into his head to correct the proofs after me; and this he did so assiduously, that it cost me no fewer than sixteen cancels to get rid of the most intolerable of his blunders. One of his principles was, that in printing verse, wherever the lines were so indented that two in succession did not begin in the same perpendicular, there was to be a full stop at the end of the former; and upon this principle he punctuated my verses. I discovered it at last in the printing office, upon inquiring how it happened that the very faults for which a leaf was canceled appeared most perseveringly in the reprint. The man then came forward, quite in a fit of madness, told me I should have made a pretty book of it if he had not corrected it for me, and it was as much as the master of the office could do to pacify him.

"You have, I think, at Tours, the grave of Ronsard, who would have been a great poet if he had not been a Frenchman. I have read his works in those odds and ends of time which can be afforded to such reading, and have so much respect for him, Frenchman as he was, that I shall not visit Tours without inquiring for his grave. Never did man more boldly promise immortality to himself—never did man more ardently aspire after it; and no Frenchman has ever impressed me with an equal sense of power; but poetry of the higher order is as impossible in that language as it is in Chinese. And this reminds me of a certain M. le Mierre, interprète, traducteur, &c., who has written to tell me that many of my *compatriotes, distingués par leur goût et leurs connoissances*, have spoken to him with great eulogies of my poem of Roderic; whereupon he, not having seen the poem, has resolved to translate it, and found a bookseller who will undertake to print the translation. I wrote him, as courtesy required, a civil reply, but expressed my doubts whether such a poem would accord with the tastes of a French public, and recommended him, if he should persist in his intention when he had read the work, to render it in prose rather than in verse.

"I have begun my Quaker poem, and written the first book in irregular rhyme—a measure which allows of a lower key than any structure of rhymeless verse, and may be laid aside, when the passion requires it, for dialogue. The principal character is rather a Seeker (in the language of that day) than a Quaker, a son of Goffe, the king's judge, a godson of Cromwell, a friend of Milton, a companion of William Penn. The plan is sufficiently made out; but I have no longer that ardor of execution which I possessed twenty years ago. I have the disheartening conviction that my best is done, and that to add to the bulk of my works will not be to add to their estimation. Doubtless I shall go on with the poem, and complete it if I live; but it will be to please others, not myself; and will be so long in progress, that in all likelihood I shall never begin another. You see I am not without those autumnal feelings which your stanza expresses, and yet the decline of life has delights of its own—its autumnal odors and its sunset hues. My disposition is invincibly cheerful, and this alone would make me a happy man, if I were not so from the tenor of my life; yet I doubt whether the strictest Carthusian has the thought of death more habitually in his mind.

"I hope to see you in the autumn, and will, if it be possible. God bless you! R. S."

To Mr. J. Neville White.

"Keswick, Feb. 16, 1815.

"MY DEAR NEVILLE,

"Since you heard from me, I have scarcely seen a face but those of my own family, nor been further from home than Friars' Crag, except one fine day, which tempted me to Lord William Gordon's. The weeks and months pass by as rapidly as an ebb tide. The older we grow, the more we feel this. The hour-glass runs always at the same rate; but when the sands are more than half spent, it is then only that we perceive how rapidly they are running out. I have been close at the desk this winter. The Quarterly takes up a heavy portion of my time. You would see in the last number two articles of mine—one upon the History of English Poetry, the other upon Forbes's Travels, both deplorably injured by mutilation. The next number will have a pretty full abstract of Lewis and Clarke's Travels. All these things cost me more time than they would any other person, for upon every subject I endeavor to read all such books relating to it as I had before left unread.

"I know not that there is any thing further to tell you of myself, unless it be that I have written the first book of Oliver Newman, and that it is in irregular rhymes. We are all, thank God, tolerably well. Herbert goes on stoutly with his Greek, and last week he began to learn German, which I shall acquire myself in the process of teaching him.

"How is James going on? This I am anxious to hear. The Income Tax was laid on with great injustice; it is taken off, not because it pressed with a cruel weight upon those of small fortune, but because it took in a proper proportion from the great landholders and capitalists, who can not be got at in an equal degree by any other manner. For instance, Lord —— pays probably £10,000 a year to this tax. Nothing that can be substantiated for it can by possibility take from him a tenth part of that sum. The tax ought not to be continued; but I would have given it one year longer, that government might have been enabled, with as much facility as possible, to wind up the accounts of a long war, unexampled alike in its duration, importance, and expense. Not to have done this will lower the English people in the eyes of other nations; but of all people under Heaven who have any country to boast of, we are the least patriotic.

"Believe me, my dear Neville,

"Very affectionately yours,

"ROBERT SOUTHEY."

To Dr. Southey.

"Keswick, Feb. 16, 1815.

"MY DEAR HARRY,

"I have got scent of the squid-hound, for whom I inquired in the Omniana. Cartwright heard of a sort of cuttle-fish of this enormous size; there is a beast of this family on the coast of Brazil, which twines its suckers round a swimmer and destroys him; and Langsdorff, who relates this, refers with disbelief to a book, which I wish you would examine for me. In the Histoire Naturelle des Mollusques, par Denys Montfort, Paris, An. 10, under the head of Le Poulpe Colossal, there must be an account of a fellow big enough to claw down a large three-masted vessel. Being a modern work of natural history, I dare say the book will be at the Royal Institution, and I pray you to extract the account for me. I shall make use of it in an article about Labrador for the Quarterly. Cartwright says, he is told they grow to a most enormous size, as big as a large whale, and he evidently does not disbelieve it. He was not a credulous man, and knew upon what sort of authority he was speaking. The description of the Kraken accords perfectly with this genus. You know, doctor, that I can swallow a Kraken. You know, also, that I am a mortal enemy to that sort of incredulity which is founded upon mere ignorance.

"Several weeks have elapsed since this letter was begun; and in the interim, to my no small satisfaction, I have found one of these monsters dead, and literally floating many a rood. The Frenchman, De Menonville, met with it between the Gulf of Mexico and St. Domingo (see Pinkerton's Coll., vol. xiii., p. 873), and knew not what to make of it.

"I have heard from many quarters of Lord Byron's praise, and regard it just as much as I did his censure. Nothing can be more absurd than thinking of comparing any of my poems with the Paradise Lost. With Tasso, with Virgil, with Homer, there may be fair grounds of comparison; but my mind is wholly unlike Milton's, and my poetry has nothing of his imagination and distinguishing character; nor is there any poet who has, except Wordsworth: he possesses it in an equal degree. And it is entirely impossible that any man can understand Milton, and fail to perceive that Wordsworth is a poet of the same class and of equal powers. Whatever my powers may be, they are not of that class. From what I have seen of the minor poems, I suspect that Chiabrera is the writer whom, as a poet, I most resemble in the constitution of my mind. His narrative poems I have never seen.

"The sale of Roderic is what I expected, neither better nor worse. It is also just what I should desire, if profit were a matter of indifference to me; for I am perfectly certain that great immediate popularity can only be obtained by those faults which fall in with the humor of the times, and which are, of course, ultimately fatal to the poems that contain them. God bless you! R. S."

To C. W. W. Wynn, Esq.

"Keswick, March 9, 1815.

"My dear Wynn,

"It would be needless to say that I am much gratified by your general opinion of Roderic. To most of your objections I can reply satisfactorily to my own judgment. The eleven syllable lines (by which we must here understand those which have the redundant syllable any where *except at the end*) I justify upon principle and precedent, referring to the practice of Shakspeare and Milton, as authorities from which there can be no appeal. The blending two short syllables into the time of one is as well known in versification as what are called binding-notes are in music.

"The descriptive passages are the relief of the poem, the time in which the action took place not affording me any costume available for this purpose; and relief was especially required in a work wherein the passion was pitched so high.

"I can not abbreviate the first scene between Julian and Roderic without destroying the connection; and for the blinding of Theodofred, where else could it have been introduced with so much effect as in its present place, where it is so related as at once to mark the character of Rusilla?

"The words to which you object are, one and all, legitimate English words; and I believe, in those places where they are used, the same meaning could not be expressed without a periphrasis. The account of the Spanish towns, &c., was for the double purpose of relief and of distinctly marking the geography. The auriphrygiate is the only piece of pedantry that I acknowledge, and I was tempted to it by the grandiloquence of the word. You need not be told how desirable it often is to connect blank verse with sonorous words.

"The image of the clouds and the moon* I saw from my chamber window at Cintra when going to bed, and noted it down with its application the next morning. I have it at this moment distinctly before my eyes, with all the accompanying earth-scenery. Thus much for Roderic. Shall I ever accomplish another work of equal magnitude? I am an older man in feelings than in years, and the natural bent of my inclinations would be never again to attempt one.

"The last Register was not mine, nor do I know by whom it was written. I have not seen it. For the former volume I have never been wholly paid, and have lost from £300 to £400 altogether—to me a very serious loss.* At present my time is divided at fits between the History of the Spanish War and that of Brazil: the latter is in the press, and will be published about the close of the year. I shall follow it immediately with the History of Portugal, which will be by far the most interesting of my historical works.

"Your godson bids fair to walk in the ways of his father. He is now in his ninth year, and knows about as much Greek as a boy in the under-fifth. His Latin consists in a decent knowledge of the grammar, and a tolerable *copia verborum*. His sister teaches him French, and he and I have lately begun to learn German together. Do not fear that we are over-doing him, for he has plenty of play, and, indeed, plays at his lessons. He takes it for granted that he must be a poet in his turn; and in this respect, as far as it is possible to judge, nature seems to agree with him. Be that as it may, there is not a happier creature upon this earth, nor could any father desire a child of fairer promise as to moral and intellectual qualities.

"When shall I see you? Alas! how little have we seen of each other for many, many years! I might also say, since we used to sit till midnight over your claret at Ch. Ch. The first term of my lease expires in two years, and some reasons would induce me to come near London, if I could encounter the expense; but, though my History of the War might possibly enable me to make the arduous removal, the increased costs of housekeeping would probably be more than I could meet. I know not whether I shall be in London this year; if I go, it will be shortly; but I can ill afford the time, and for weighty reasons ought not to afford it. On the other hand, my uncle is advancing in years and declining in health; and if my visits are to be at such long intervals as they have hitherto been, there can be very few more, even upon the most favorable chances of life.

"God bless you! R. S."

* Methinks if ye would know
How visitations of calamity
Affect the pious soul, 'tis shown ye there!
Look yonder at that cloud, which through the sky,
Sailing alone doth cross in her career
The rolling moon! I watched it as it came,
And deemed the bright opaque would blot her beams;
But, melting like a wreath of snow, it hangs
In folds of wavy silver round, and clothes
The orb with richer beauties than her own;
Then passing, leaves her in her light serene.
Roderic, sect. xxi.

* Part of this was ultimately paid, but not for several years.

To C. W. W. Wynn, Esq

"Keswick, May 20, 1815.

"MY DEAR WYNN,

"It is surprising to me that men whose fortunes are not absolutely desperate at home will go to India to seek them; that is, men who have any feelings beyond what is connected with the sense of touch. Fourteen years' transportation is a heavy sentence; Strachey, I think, has been gone seventeen. What a portion of human life is this, and of its best years! After such an absence, the pain of returning is hardly less severe, and perhaps more lasting, than that of departure. He finds his family thinned by death; his parents, if he finds them at all, fallen into old age, and on the brink of the grave; the friends whom he left in youth so changed as to be no longer the same. What fortune can make amends for this! It is indeed *propter vitam vivendi perdere causas!* I grieve to think sometimes that you and I, who were once in such daily habits of intimate intercourse, meet now only at intervals of two or three years; though, besides our communication by letter (too seldom, I *confess*, rather than *complain*), what we do in public serve to keep us in sight of each other. However indifferent may be the matter of the debate, I always look to see if Mr. C. Wynn has spoken. But Strachey must almost feel himself in another world.

"I thought that rascal Murat might have done more mischief. The proper termination of his career would be that the Sicilian Bourbons should catch him and send him to Madrid; and I think Louis the Eighteenth would now be fully justified in sending Prince Joseph to the same place. The contest in France can not surely be long; if Bonaparte could have acted with vigor on the offensive, he would have found perilous allies in Saxony, and little resistance from the Belgians. But the internal state of France paralyzes him; and if he acts on the defensive, he can derive no advantage from the injustice of the great German powers. Two things were wanting last year—the British army did not get to Paris, and the French were neither punished as they deserved, nor humbled as the interests of the rest of the world required. It will, I trust, now be put beyond all doubt that they have been conquered, and that their metropolis has been taken.

"The second edition of Roderic is selling well. It will probably soon reach to a third, and then fall into the slow steady sale of its predecessors. The sale will become of importance when by the laws of literary property it will no longer benefit the author in his family. This is an abominable injustice, and will, I suppose, one day be redressed, but not in our times. I am misemploying much time in reviewing for the lucre of gain, which nothing but filthy lucre should make me do. My History of Brazil, however, gets on in the press, and you would be surprised were you to see the materials which I have collected for it. I did not think it right to postpone this second volume till my History of the Spanish War was done, for it had already been postponed too long. But it is a considerable sacrifice which I thus have been making. As soon as this work is off my hands, I shall be able to put the History of Portugal to press without impeding the more profitable work. It is on this that I should wish to rest my reputation. As a poet, I know where I have fallen short; and did I consult only my own feelings, it is probable that I should write poetry no more; not as being contented with what I have done, but as knowing that I can hope to do nothing better. I might, were my whole heart and mind given to it, as they were in youth; but they are no longer at my own disposal. As an historian I shall come nearer my mark. For thorough research, indeed, and range of materials, I do not believe that the History of Portugal will ever have been surpassed.

"God bless you, my dear Wynn!

"Yours very affectionately, R. S."

To the Rev. Nicholas Lightfoot.

"Keswick, June 18, 1815.

"MY DEAR LIGHTFOOT,

"You can not think of me more frequently nor more affectionately than I do of you. These recollections begin to have an autumnal shade of feeling; and habitually joyous as my spirits are, I believe that if we were now to meet, my first impulse would be to burst into tears. I was not twenty when we parted, and one-and-twenty years have elapsed since that time. Of the men with whom I lived at Oxford, Wynn, Elmsley, and yourself are all that are left. Seward is dead, Charles Collins is dead, Robert Allen is dead, Burnett is dead. I have lost sight of all the rest.

"My family continue in number the same as when you heard from me last. I am my son's schoolmaster, and, in the process, am recovering my Greek, which I had begun to forget at Baliol. How long I may continue to abide here is uncertain: the first term of my lease will expire in 1817; if I do not remove then, I must remain for another seven years, and I am far too sensible of the insecurity of life to look beyond that time. Having many inducements to remove nearer London, and many to remain where I am, the trouble and enormous expense of moving (for I have not less than 5000 books) will probably turn the scale; certainly they will weigh heavy in it. It is not that I have any business in London as poet laureate; that office imposes upon me no such necessity; it only requires, as a matter of decorum, that when I happen to be there I should sometimes attend a levee, especially on the birth-day, but it is not expected that I should make a journey for this purpose, and accordingly I have never been at court since I kissed hands upon my appointment. * * * *

"I have just been reading the Ludus Literarius of my friend Dr. Bell: happy is the schoolmaster who profits by it, and reforms his school upon the Madras system. I pray you give the subject a serious consideration. The only real obstacle is the want of initiatory books, but they would be very easily made; and I believe that very few pieces of literary labor would be so largely repaid. It is *quite certain* that his system removes 99 parts in 100 of the miseries of the schoolboys and the schoolmaster.

* * * * * * *

"Thus, Lightfoot, my life passes as uniformly and as laboriously as yours. There is one difference in your favor: you, perhaps, look on to an end of your labors, which I never must do till 'my right hand forget its cunning.' But I am very happy, and I dare say so are you. 'The cheerful man's a king,' says the old song; and if this be true, both you and I are royal by nature.

"God bless you, my dear Lightfoot!

"Believe me, most truly and affectionately, your old friend, R. SOUTHEY."

To C. W. W. Wynn, Esq., M.P.

"Keswick, June 18, 1815.

"MY DEAR WYNN,

"You have done many things which have given me great pleasure since your last letter. I never was more rejoiced than when Lord Grenville gave his full and manly support to a war which, beyond all others in which we have been involved, is necessary and inevitable. I am very glad, also, to see that you are doing something to promote vaccination. Much may be done toward the cure and prevention of diseases by wise legislative interference; and this is one of the points in which the state of society is susceptible of great improvement. * * *

"The question of incest was touched upon, and you very properly recommended that the case of —— should rest upon the existing law, rather than make it the subject of a specific (and superfluous) clause in the act of divorce. But has it never occurred to you, my dear Wynn, that this law is an abominable relic of ecclesiastical tyranny? Of all second marriages, I have no hesitation in saying that these are the most natural, the most suitable, and likely to be the most frequent, if the law did not sometimes prevent them. It is quite monstrous to hear judges and lawyers speaking, as they have done of late, upon this subject, and confounding natural incest with what was only deemed to be incestuous, in order that the Church might profit by selling dispensations for its commission—a species of marriage, too, which was not only permitted by the Levitical law, but even enjoined by it. I should be glad to know in what part of the Christian dispensation it is prohibited as a crime. The probable reason why the law was not swept away in this country at the Reformation was, because it involved the *cause* of that event; but surely we owe no such respect to the memory of Henry the Eighth, that it should still continue to disgrace a reformed country.

"Longman was to send you my poems. You will perceive how very few have been written since I was twenty-five, and that may account for the numberless and incorrigible faults, and the good-for-nothingness of a great part of them, which, had they been my own property, would have gone behind the fire.

"They have made me member of another academy at Madrid—the R. A. *of History*—a body which have rendered most efficient service to the literature of that country. This gives me some privileges,* which I should be very glad to profit by, if I could afford a journey to Spain, for I should have better access to archives and manuscripts than any foreigner has ever enjoyed.

"You will see in the next Quarterly a picture, which I found in M. Larrey's book—Bonaparte sleeping in the Desert by a fire of human bodies and bones—the remains of travelers who had perished there, and been dried by the sun and sands! It is one of the most extraordinary and appropriate situations that ever fancy conceived. * * * *

"God bless you, my dear Wynn!

"Yours most affectionately,

"ROBERT SOUTHEY."

The important question of marriage with a wife's sister, touched upon in the foregoing letter, is far too summarily disposed of; for, first of all, the ecclesiastical prohibition is traced back to the primitive ages of Christianity, so that it can not be accounted for by the supposition that it originated in the wish to multiply dispensations. (See the printed evidence of Dr. Pusey, and of the Hon. and Rev. A. P. Perceval.)

Secondly, the Levitical law nowhere authorizes, much less enjoins, this particular union. The prohibited degrees are, in Leviticus, in most cases, stated only on one side, and the Church has supplied the other; as, if a man must not marry his father's wife, a woman must not marry her mother's husband. By this mode of interpretation, if a man must not marry his brother's wife (*Lev.*, xviii., 16, and xx., 21), a woman must not marry her sister's husband. The former of these connections is twice forbidden, the latter is not mentioned, but is inferred. My father's notion is, I suppose, based upon the other passage (*Deut.*, xxv., 5), where a brother is enjoined to take to him his brother's wife. This, however, is only an exceptional case, ordered for a special purpose, and can not be set against the general law stated in Leviticus, nor authorize the like exception in the case of the woman, the case not applying. It is not my wish to say any thing more upon this subject than seems called for by the opinion given in this letter. If I had not printed it, I might, perhaps, have been supposed by some who are acquainted with what my father's sentiments were, to have suppressed a statement upon a topic of more than common interest at the present time.

To Grosvenor C. Bedford, Esq.

"Keswick, June 24, 1815.

"MY DEAR GROSVENOR,

" * * * * * * *

Our bells are ringing as they ought to do; and

* The same privileges as if he had been a member of the royal household. "I do not know," he says in another letter, "how this will accord with the English privilege which I must use of speaking my free opinion of Ferdinand's conduct."

I, after a burst of exhilaration at the day's news,* am in a state of serious and thoughtful thankfulness for what, perhaps, ought to be considered as the greatest deliverance that civilized society has experienced since the defeat of the Moors by Charles Martel. I never feared or doubted the result; but if we had been thus thoroughly defeated in the first battle, the consequences would have been too fatal to think of with composure. Perhaps enough has been done to excite a revolt in Paris; but I have a strong impression, either upon my imagination or my judgment, that that city will suffer some part of its deserved chastisement. The cannon should be sent home and formed into a pillar to support a statue of Wellington in the center of the largest square in London.

"I am expecting the Review daily. Your hint respecting Marlborough does not accord with my own opinion of the subject. I could make nothing of a life of Marlborough. A battle can only be made tolerable in narration when it has something picturesque in its accidents, scenes, &c., &c., which is not the case with any of Marlborough's. The only part which I could make valuable would be what related to Louis XIV. and the peace of Utrecht. But if the Bibliopole of Albemarle Street were to propound sweet remuneration for the Egyptian story, he would do wisely. With all his sagacity, he turned a deaf ear to the most promising project which ever occurred to me—that of writing the age of George III. This I will do whenever (if ever) I get free from the necessity of raising immediate supplies by temporary productions. The subject, as you may perceive, is nothing less than a view of the world during the most eventful half century of its annals—not the *history*, but a philosophical summary, with reference to the causes and consequences of all these mighty revolutions. There never was a more splendid subject, and I have full confidence in my own capacity for treating it.

"Did I tell you of the Yankee's pamphlet, to abuse me for an article in the Quarterly which I did not write, and (between ourselves) would not have written? He talks of my getting drunk with my sack. One especial (and just) cause of anger is the expression that 'Washington, we believe, was an honest man;' and I am reviled for this in America, when I was consternating the lord chamberlain by speaking of Washington with respect in a New Year's Ode! Has Longman sent you the Minor Poems? The newspapers ought to reprint that ode upon Bonaparte. * * * * *

"God bless you! R. S."

To John Rickman, Esq.

"July 10, 1815.

"My dear R.,

"I could wish myself in London to be three-and-forty hours nearer the news. Was there ever such a *land* battle in modern times! The wreck has been as complete as at the Nile. Murray propounds me sweet remuneration to bring it into his next number, which, as I have a French history of Massena's campaign before me, it will be easy to do, the object of that book being to prove that the French beat us wherever they met us, and that Lord Wellington is no general, and, moreover, exceedingly afraid of them. The battle of Waterloo is a good answer to this. The name which Blucher has given it will do excellently in verse—the field of Fair Alliance! but I do not like it in prose, for we gave them such an English thrashing, that the name ought to be one which comes easily out of an English mouth. If you can help me to any information, I shall know how to use it.

"If Bonaparte comes here, which is very likely, I hope no magnanimity will prevent us from delivering him up to Louis XVIII.; unless, indeed, we could collect evidence of the murder of Captain Wright, and bring him to trial and condemnation for that offense. This would be the best finish.

"I am sorry La Fayette has opened his mouth in this miserable Assembly. As for the rest of them—gallows, take thy course. * * * * They should all be hanged in their robes for the sake of the *spectacle*, and the benefit of *M. Jean Quetch*. What a scene of vile flattery shall we have when the Bourbons are restored!

"Yours truly, R. S."

To Dr. Southey.

"Keswick, Aug. 23, 1815.

"My dear Harry,

"According to all form, I ought to write you a letter of congratulation;* but some unlucky ingredient in my moral, physical, and intellectual composition has all my life long operated upon me with respect to forms, like that antipathy which some persons feel toward cats, or other objects equally inoffensive. I get through them so badly at all times, that, whenever I am obliged to the performance, my chief concern is, how to slink out of it as expeditiously as possible. I have, moreover, a propensity which may seem at first not very well to accord with that constitutional hilarity which is my best inheritance. Occasions of joy and festivity seem rather to depress the barometer of my spirits than to raise it; birth-days and wedding-days, therefore, pass uncelebrated by me; and with the strongest conviction of the good effects of national holidays, and with a feeling toward them which men, who are incapable of understanding what is meant by the imaginative faculty, might call superstition, I yet wish, if it were possible, that Christmas and New Year's Day could be blotted from my calendar. It might not be difficult to explain why this is, but it would be somewhat metaphysical, which is bad, and somewhat sentimental, which is worse.

* Of the battle of Waterloo.

* On his marriage. On some similar occasion, my father remarks, "I never wish people joy of their marriage; that they will find for themselves: what I wish them is—patience."

"Monday, the 21st of August, was not a more remarkable day in your life than it was in that of my neighbor Skiddaw, who is a much older personage. The weather served for our bonfire,* and never, I believe, was such an assemblage upon such a spot. To my utter astonishment, Lord Sunderlin rode up, and Lady S., who had endeavored to dissuade *me* from going as a thing too dangerous, joined the walking party. Wordsworth, with his wife, sister, and eldest boy, came over on purpose. James Boswell arrived that morning at the Sunderlins. Edith, the Senhora,† Edith May, and Herbert were my convoy, with our three maid-servants, some of our neighbors, some adventurous lakers, and Messrs. Rag, Tag, and Bobtail, made up the rest of the assembly. We roasted beef and boiled plum-puddings there; sung 'God save the king' round the most furious body of flaming tar-barrels that I ever saw; drank a huge wooden bowl of punch; fired cannon at every health with three times three, and rolled large blazing balls of tow and turpentine down the steep side of the mountain. The effect was grand beyond imagination. We formed a huge circle round the most intense light, and behind us was an immeasurable arch of the most intense darkness, for our bonfire fairly put out the moon.

"The only mishap which occurred will make a famous anecdote in the life of a great poet, if James Boswell, after the example of his father, keepeth a diary of the sayings of remarkable men. When we were craving for the punch, a cry went forth that the kettle had been knocked over, with all the boiling water! Colonel Barker, as Boswell named the Senhora, from her having had the command on this occasion, immediately instituted a strict inquiry to discover the culprit, from a suspicion that it might have been done in mischief, water, as you know, being a commodity not easily replaced on the summit of Skiddaw. The persons about the fire declared it was one of the gentlemen—they did not know his name; but he had a red cloak on; they pointed him out in the circle. The red cloak (a maroon one of Edith's) identified him; Wordsworth had got hold of it, and was equipped like a Spanish Don—by no means the worst figure in the company. He had committed this fatal *faux pas*, and thought to slink off undiscovered. But as soon as, in my inquiries concerning the punch, I learned his guilt from the Senhora, I went round to all our party, and communicated the discovery, and getting them about him, I punished him by singing a parody, which they all joined in: ''Twas *you* that kicked the kettle down! 'twas you, sir, you!'

"The consequences were, that we took all the cold water upon the summit to supply our loss. Our myrmidons and Messrs. Rag and Co. had, therefore, none for their grog; they necessarily drank the rum pure; and you, who are physician to the Middlesex Hospital, are doubtless acquainted with the manner in which alcohol acts upon the nervous system. All our torches were lit at once by this mad company, and our way down the hill was marked by a track of fire, from flambeaux dropping the pitch, tarred ropes, &c. One fellow was so drunk that his companions placed him upon a horse, with his face to the tail, to bring him down, themselves being just sober enough to guide and hold him on. Down, however, we all got safely by midnight; and nobody, from the old lord of seventy-seven to my son Herbert, is the worse for the toil of the day, though we were eight hours from the time we set out till we reached home.

* * * * * * * * *

"God bless you. R. S."

"I heard of your election from your good and trusty ally, Neville White. If that man's means were equal to his spirit, he would be as rich as Crœsus."

CHAPTER XX.

FEELINGS OF REJOICING AT THE TERMINATION OF THE WAR WITH FRANCE — JOURNEY TO WATERLOO — ACCOUNT OF BEGUINAGES AT GHENT — NOTICES OF FLANDERS — OF THE FIELD OF BATTLE — PURCHASE OF THE ACTA SANCTORUM—DETENTION BY THE ILLNESS OF HIS DAUGHTER AT AIX-LA-CHAPELLE — RETURN HOME—PICTURE OF HIS DOMESTIC HAPPINESS IN THE PILGRIMAGE TO WATERLOO—MULTITUDE OF CORRESPONDENTS — MEETING WITH SPANISH LIBERALES IN LONDON—RAPID FLIGHT OF TIME — DECLINING FACILITY OF POETICAL COMPOSITION—POLITICS—REGRETS FOR THE DEATH OF YOUNG DUSAUTOY—THE PILGRIMAGE TO WATERLOO—SCOTT'S LORD OF THE ISLES—THE HISTORY OF BRAZIL—EVILS IN SOCIETY—WANT OF ENGLISH BEGUINAGES —EARLY ENGLISH POETRY — DEATH OF HIS SON—POETICAL CRITICISM—FEELINGS OF RESIGNATION — CIRCUMSTANCES OF HIS EARLY LIFE—GEOLOGY AND BOTANY BETTER STUDIES THAN CHEMICAL AND PHYSICAL SCIENCE—THOMSON'S CASTLE OF INDOLENCE—YOUTHFUL FEELINGS—OWEN OF LANARK—REMARKS ON HIS OWN FORTUNES AND CHARACTER — COLLEGE LIFE—WORDSWORTH'S POEMS.—1815–1816.

How deep an interest my father had taken in the protracted contest between France and England, the reader has seen; nor will he, I think, if well acquainted with the events of those times, and the state of feeling common among young men of the more educated classes at the close of the last century, be apt to censure him as grossly inconsistent, because he condemned the war at its outset, and augured well at the commencement of Bonaparte's career, and yet could earnestly desire that war, in its later stages, "to be carried on with all the heart, and all the soul, and all the strength of this mighty empire," and could rejoice in the downfall

* In honor of the battle of Waterloo.

† Miss Barker, a lady with whom my father first became acquainted at Cintra.

"Of him who, while Europe crouched under his rod,
Put his trust in his fortune, and not in his God;"

for the original commencement of the war in 1792–3 had been the combination of other European powers against revolutionary France—a direct act of aggression supported by England, which would now be condemned by most men, and was then naturally denounced by all those who partook, in any degree, of Republican feeling.* But in the lapse of years the merits of the contest became quite altered; and from about the time when Bonaparte assumed the imperial crown, all his acts were marked by aggressiveness and overbearing usurpation. Not to speak of those personal crimes which turned my father's feelings toward the man into intense abhorrence, his political measures with respect to Switzerland, Holland, Egypt, and Malta were those of an unscrupulous and ambitious conqueror; and the invasion of Portugal, with his insolent treachery toward the Spanish royal family, made his iniquity intolerable. The real difference between my father and the mass of writers and speakers in England at that time was, that he never laid aside a firm belief that the Providence of God would put an end to Napoleon's wicked career, and that it was the office of Great Britain to be the principal instrument of that Providence.

But in addition to the national feelings of joy and triumph at the successful termination of this long and arduous warfare, my father had some grounds for rejoicing more peculiar to himself. When one large and influential portion of the community, supported by the Edinburgh Review, prognosticated constantly the hopelessness of the war, the certain triumph of Bonaparte, and especially the folly of hoping to drive him out of Spain—when their language was, "France has conquered Europe; this is the melancholy truth; shut our eyes to it as we may, there can be no doubt about the matter; for the present, peace and submission must be the lot of the vanquished;" he had stood forth among the boldest and most prominent of those who urged vigorous measures and prophesied final success. And well might he now rejoice—kindle upon Skiddaw the symbol of triumph; and when contrasting the language he had held with that of those persons, exclaim, "Was I wrong? or has the event corresponded to this confidence?"

Ἀμέραι ἐπίλοιποι
Μάρτυρες σοφώτατοι.

Bear witness, Torres Vedras, Salamanca, and Vittoria! Bear witness, Orthies and Thoulouse! Bear witness, Waterloo!

With these feelings it was very natural that he should have been among the crowd of English who hastened over to view the scene of that "fell debate," on the issue of which had so lately hung the fate of Europe.

To quote his own words:

"And as I once had journeyed to survey
Far off Ourique's consecrated field,
Where Portugal, the faithful and the bold,
Assumed the symbols of her sacred shield.
More reason now that I should bend my way,
The field of British glory to survey.

"So forth I set upon this pilgrimage,
And took the partner of my life with me,
And one dear girl, just ripe enough of age
Retentively to see what I should see;
That thus, with mutual recollections fraught,
We might bring home a store for after thought."

Of this journey, as was his custom, he kept a minute and elaborate journal; but it is of too great length, and not possessing sufficient novelty, to be inserted here. The following letters, however, may not be without interest:

To John Rickman, Esq.

"Brussels, Oct. 2, 1815.

"MY DEAR RICKMAN,

"I wish you had been with me at Ghent, where the Beguines have their principal establishment. The Beguinage is a remarkable place, at one end of the city, and entirely inclosed. You enter through a gateway, where there is a statue of S. Elizabeth of Hungary, the patroness of the establishment. The space inclosed is, I should think, not less than the area of the whole town of Keswick or of Christ Church; and the Beguinage itself, unlike alms-house, college, village, or town: a collection of contiguous houses of different sizes, each with a small garden in front, and a high brick wall inclosing them all; over every door the name of some saint under whose protection the house is placed, but no opening through which any thing can be seen. There are several streets thus built, with houses on both sides. There is a large church within the inclosure, a burying-ground without any grave-stones; and a branch from one of the innumerable rivers with which Ghent is intersected, in which the washing of the community is performed from a large boat; and a large piece of ground, planted with trees, where the clothes are dried. One, who was the second person in the community, accosted us, showed us the interior, and gave us such explanation as we desired, for we had with us a lady who spoke French. It is curious that she knew nothing of the origin of her order, and could not even tell by whom it was founded; but I have purchased here the Life of S. Bega, from whom it derived its name, and in this book I expect to find the whole history.

"There are about 6000 Beguines in Brabant and Flanders, to which countries they are confined; 620 were residents in the Beguinage. They were rich before the Revolution. Their lands were then taken from them, and they were obliged to lay aside the dress of the order; but this was only done in part, because they were supported by public opinion; and being of evident utility to all ranks, few were disposed to injure them. They receive the sick who come to them, and support and attend them as long as

* He himself says of the Peace of Amiens: "No act of amnesty ever produced such conciliatory consequences as that peace. It restored in me the English feeling which had long been deadened, and placed me in sympathy with my country; bringing me thus into that natural and healthy state of mind, upon which time, and knowledge, and reflection were sure to produce their proper and salutary effects."—*From a MS. Preface to the Peninsular War.*

the illness requires. They are bound by no vow, and my informant assured me, with evident pride, that no instance of a Beguine leaving the establishment had ever been known. She herself had entered it after the death of her husband; and I suppose their numbers are generally, if not wholly, filled up by women who seek a retreat, or need an asylum from the world. The property which a Beguine brings with her reverts to her heir-at-law. At the Revolution, the church of the Beguinage was sold, as confiscated religious property. This sale was a mere trick, or, in English phrase, a job to accommodate some partisan of the ruling demagogues with ready money. Such a man bought it, and in the course of two or three weeks resold it to two sisters of the community for 300 Louis d'ors, and they made it over again to the order. There is a refectory, where they dine in common if they please, or, if they please, have dinner sent from thence to their own chambers. We went into three chambers —small, furnished with little more than necessary comforts, but having all these, and remarkably clean. In one, a Beguine, who had been bedridden many years, was sitting up and knitting. We were taken into the chamber, because it amused her to see visitors. She was evidently pleased at seeing us, and remarkably cheerful. In another apartment two sisters were spinning, one of eighty-five, the other of eighty-three years of age. In all this there is less information than I should have given you, if my tongue had not been the most anti-Gallican in the world, and the Flemish French not very intelligible to my interpreter. The dress is convenient, but abominably ugly. I shall endeavor to get a doll equipped in it. The place itself I wish you could see; and, indeed, you would find a visit to Bruges and Ghent abundantly overpaid by the sight of those cities (famous as they are in history), and of a country, every inch of which is well husbanded.

"Bruges is, without exception, the most striking place I ever visited, though it derives nothing from situation. It seems to have remained in the same state for above 200 years; nothing has been added, and hardly any thing gone to decay. What ruin has occurred there was the work of frantic revolutionists, who destroyed all the statues in the niches of the Stadt House, and demolished an adjoining church, one of the finest in the town. The air of antiquity and perfect preservation is such, that it carries you back to the age of the Tudors or of Froissart; and the whole place is in keeping. The poorest inhabitants seem to be well lodged; and if the cultivation of the ground and the well-being of the people be the great objects of civilization, I should almost conclude that no part of the world was so highly civilized as this. At Ghent there is more business, more inequality, a greater mixture of French manners, and the alloy of vice and misery in proportion. Brussels, in like manner, exceeds Ghent, and is, indeed, called a second Paris. The modern part of the city is perfectly Parisian; the older, and especially the great square, Flemish.

* * * * * * *

"We have seen the whole field of battle, or rather all the fields, and vestiges enough of the contest, though it is almost wonderful to observe how soon nature recovers from all her injuries The fields are cultivated again, and wild flowers are in blossom upon some of the graves.* The Scotchmen—'those men without breeches' —have the credit of the day at Waterloo.

"The result of what I have collected is an opinion that the present settlement of these countries is *not* likely to be durable. The people feel at present pretty much as a bird who is rescued from the claw of one eagle by the beak of another. The Rhine is regarded as a proper boundary for Prussia; and it is as little desired that she should *pass* that river as that France should reach it. There is a spirit of independence here, which has been outraged, but from which much good might arise if it were conciliated. This, I am inclined to think, would be best done by forming a wide confederacy, leaving to each of the confederates its own territory, laws, &c.; and this might be extended from the frontiers of France to the Hanseatic cities. One thing I am certain, that such arrangements would satisfy every body, except those sovereigns who would lose by it. I am aware how short a time I have been in the country, and how liable men, under such circumstances, are to be deceived; but I have taken the utmost pains to acquire all the knowledge within my reach, and have been singularly fortunate in the means which have fallen in my way. The merest accident brought me acquainted with a Liegois, a great manufacturer, &c., and I have not found that men talk to me with the less confidence because I am not a Free-mason. * * * * *

"We turn our face homeward to-morrow, by way of Maestricht and Louvaine to Brussels. The delay here will possibly oblige us to give up Antwerp. However, on the whole, I have every reason to be pleased with the journey. No month of my life was ever better employed. God bless you! R. S."

To John May, Esq.

"Liege, Oct. 6, 1815, 6 P.M.

"MY DEAR FRIEND,

"I have a happy habit of making the best of all things; and being just at this time as uncomfortable as the dust and bustle, and all the disagreeables of an inn in a large, filthy manufacturing city can make me, I have called for pen, ink, and paper, and am actually writing in the bar, the door open to the yard opposite to this unwiped table, the doors open to the public room, where two men are dining and talking French, and a woman servant at my elbow lighting a fire for our party. Presently the folding-doors are to be shut, the ladies are to descend

* "The passing season had not yet effaced
The stamp of numerous hoofs impressed by force,
Of cavalry, whose path might still be traced.
Yet Nature every where resumed her course;
Low pansies to the sun their purple gave,
And the soft poppy blossomed on the grave."
Pilgrimage to Waterloo.

from their chambers, the bar will be kept appropriated to our house, the male part of the company will get into good humor, dinner will be ready, and then I must lay aside the gray goose-quill. As a preliminary to these promised comforts, the servant is mopping the hearth, which is composed (like a tesselated pavement) of little bricks about two inches long by half an inch wide, set within a broad black stone frame. The fuel is of fire-balls, a mixture of pulverized coal and clay. I have seen a great deal, and heard a great deal — more, indeed, than I can keep pace with in my journal, though I strive hard to do it; but I minute down short notes in my pencil-book with all possible care, and hope, in the end, to lose nothing. As for Harry and his party, I know nothing more of them than that they landed at Ostend a week before us, and proceeded the same day to Bruges. To-morrow we shall probably learn tidings of them at Spa. Meantime, we have joined company with some fellow-passengers, Mr. Vardon, of Greenwich, with his family, and Mr. Nash, an artist, who has lived many years in India. Flanders is a most interesting country. Bruges, the most striking city I have ever seen, an old city in perfect preservation. It seems as if not a house had been built during the last two centuries, and not a house suffered to pass to decay. The poorest people seem to be well lodged, and there is a general air of sufficiency, cleanliness, industry, and comfort, which I have never seen in any other place. The cities have grown worse as we advanced. At Namur we reached a dirty city, situated in a romantic country; the Meuse there reminded me of the Thames from your delightful house, an island in size and shape resembling that upon which I have often wished for a grove of poplars, coming just in the same position. From thence along the river to this abominable place, the country is, for the greater part, as lovely as can be imagined, especially at Huy, where we slept last night, and fell in with one of the inhabitants, a man of more than ordinary intellect, from whom I learned much of the state of public opinion, &c.

"Our weather hitherto has been delightful. This was especially fortunate at Waterloo and at Ligny, where we had much ground to walk over. It would surprise you to see how soon nature has recovered from the injuries of war. The ground is plowed and sown, and grain, and flowers, and seeds already growing over the field of battle, which is still strewn with vestiges of the slaughter, caps, cartridges, boxes, hats, &c. We picked up some French cards and some bullets, and we purchased a French pistol and two of the eagles which the infantry wear upon their caps. What I felt upon this ground, it would be difficult to say: what I saw, and still more what I heard, there is no time at present for saying. In prose and in verse you shall some day hear the whole. At Les Quatre Bras I saw two graves, which probably the dogs or the swine had opened. In the one were the ribs of a human body, projecting through the mold; in the other, the whole skeleton exposed. Some of our party told me of a third, in which the worms were at work, but I shrunk from the sight. You will rejoice to hear that the English are as well spoken of for their deportment in peace as in war. It is far otherwise with the Prussians. Concerning them there is but one opinion: their brutality is said to exceed that of the French, and of their intolerable insolence I have heard but too many proofs. That abominable old Frederic made them a military nation, and this is the inevitable consequence. This very day we passed a party on their way toward France —some hundred or two. Two gentlemen and two ladies of the country, in a carriage, had come up with them; and these ruffians would not allow them to pass, but compelled them to wait and follow the slow pace of foot soldiers! This we ourselves saw. Next to the English, the Belgians have the best character for discipline.

"I have laid out some money in books—four or five-and-twenty pounds—and I have bargained for a set of the Acta Sanctorum to be completed and sent after me—the price 500 francs. This is an invaluable acquisition. Neither our time nor money will allow us to reach the Rhine. We turn back from Aix-la-Chapelle, and take the route of Maestricht and Louvaine to Antwerp, thence to Ghent again, and cross from Calais. I bought at Bruges a French History of Brazil, just published by M. Alphouse de Beauchamp, in three volumes octavo. He says, in his Preface, that having finished the two first volumes, he thought it advisable to see if any new light had been thrown upon the subject by modern authors. Meantime, a compilation upon this history had appeared in England, but the English author, Mr. Southey, had brought no new lights; he had promised much for his second volume, but the hope of literary Europe had been again deceived, for this second volume, so emphatically promised, had not appeared. I dare say no person regrets this delay so much as M. Beauchamp, he having stolen the whole of his two first volumes, and about the third part of the other, from the very Mr. Southey whom he abuses. He has copied my references as the list of his own authorities (manuscripts and all), and he has committed blunders which prove, beyond all doubt, that he does not understand Portuguese. I have been much diverted by this fellow's impudence.

"The table is laid, and the knives and forks rattling a pleasant note of preparation, as the woman waiter arranges them.

"God bless you! I have hurried through the sheet, and thus pleasantly beguiled what would have been a very unpleasant hour. We are all well, and your god-daughter has seen a live emperor at Brussels. I feel the disadvantage of speaking French ill, and understanding it by the ear worse. Nevertheless, I speak it without remorse, make myself somehow or other understood, and get at what I want to know. Once more, God bless you, my dear friend!

"Believe me always most affectionately yours,

"R. S."

To John May, Esq.

"Brussels, Friday, Oct. 20, 1815.

"MY DEAR FRIEND,

"I wrote to you from Liege, up to which time all had gone on well with us. Thank God, it is well with us at present; but your god-daughter has been so unwell, that we were detained six days at Aix-la-Chapelle in a state of anxiety which you may well imagine, and at a hotel where the Devil himself seemed to possess the mistress and the greater part of the domestics. Happily, I found a physician who had graduated at Edinburgh, who spoke English, and pursued a rational system; and happily, also, by this painful and expensive delay I was thrown into such society, that, now the evil is over, I am fully sensible of the good to which it has conduced. The day after my letter was written we reached Spa, and remained there Sunday and Monday—a pleasant and necessary pause, though the pleasure was somewhat interrupted by the state of my own health, which was somewhat disordered there—perhaps the effect of the thin Rhenish wines and the grapes. Tuesday we would have slept at Verones (the great clothing town) if we could have found beds. An English party had preoccupied them, and we proceeded to Herve, a little town half way between Liege and Aix-la-Chapelle, in the old principality of Limbourg.

* * * * *

"When we arrived at Aix-la-Chapelle, your god-daughter was so ill that, after seeing her laid in bed (about one o'clock in the afternoon), I thought it necessary to go to the banker's, and request them to recommend me to a physician. You may imagine how painful a time we passed. It was necessary for her to gargle every hour, even if we waked her for it; but she never slept an hour continuously for the three first nights. Thank God, however, she seems thoroughly recovered, and I can estimate the good with calmness. While I acted as nurse and cook (for we were obliged to do every thing ourselves), our party dined at the *table d'hote*, and there, as the child grew better, I found myself in the company of some highly distinguished Prussian officers. One of these, a Major Dresky, is the very man who was with Blucher at Ligny, when he was ridden over by the French; the other, Major Petry, is said by his brother officers to have won the battle of Donowitz for Blucher. Two more extraordinary men I never met with. You would have been delighted to hear how they spoke of the English, and to see how they treated us, as representatives of our country. Among the toasts which were given, I put this into French: 'The Belle-alliance between Prussia and England—may it endure as long as the memory of the battle.' I can not describe to you the huzzaing, and hob-nobbing, and hand-shaking with which it was received. But the chief benefit which I have received was from meeting with a certain Henry de Forster, a major in the German Legion, a Pole by birth, whose father held one of the highest offices in Poland. Forster, one of the most interesting men I ever met with, has been marked for misfortune from his birth. Since the age of thirteen he has supported himself, and now supports a poor brother of eighteen, a youth of high principles and genius, who has for two years suffered with an abscess of the spleen. Forster entered the Prussian service when a boy, was taken prisoner and cruelly used in France, and escaped, almost miraculously, on foot into Poland. In 1809 he joined the Duke of Brunswick, and was one of those men who proved true to him through all dangers, and embarked with him. The duke was a true German in patriotism, but without conduct, without principle, without gratitude. Forster entered our German Legion, and was in all the hot work in the Peninsula, from the lines of Torres Vedras till the end of the war. The severe duty of an infantry officer proved too much for his constitution, and a fall of some eighty feet down a precipice in the Pyrenees brought on a hæmorrhage of the liver, for which he obtained unlimited leave of absence, and came to Aix-la-Chapellle. I grieve to say that he had a relapse on the very day that we left him. I never saw a man whose feelings and opinions seemed to coincide more with my own. When we had become a little acquainted, he shook hands with me in a manner so unlike an ordinary greeting, that I immediately understood it to be (as really it was) a trial whether I was a Free-mason. This gave occasion to the following sonnet, which I put into his hands at parting:

"The ties of secret brotherhood, made known
By secret signs, and pressure of link'd hand
Significant, I neither understand
Nor censure. There are countries where the throne
And altar, singly, or with force combined,
Against the welfare of poor human kind
Direct their power perverse: in such a land
Such leagues may have their purpose; in my own,
Being needless, they are needs but mockery.
But to the wise and good there doth belong,
Ordained by God himself, a surer tie;
A sacred and unerring sympathy:
Which bindeth them in bonds of union strong
As time, and lasting as eternity.

"He has promised me to employ this winter in writing his memoirs—a task he had once performed, but the paper was lost in a shipwreck. He has promised, also, to come with the MSS. (if he lives) to England next summer, when I hope and expect that the publication will be as beneficial to his immediate interests as it will be honorable to his memory.

"We left Aix on Tuesday for Maestricht, slept the next night at St. Tron, Thursday at Louvaine, and arrived here to-day. To-morrow I go again with Nash to Waterloo, for the purpose of procuring drawings of Hougoumont. On Sunday we go for Antwerp, rejoin the Vardons on Monday night at Ghent, and then make the best of our way to Calais and London. God bless you, my dear friend!

"Yours most affectionately, R. S."

To John May, Esq.

"Keswick, Wednesday, Dec. 6, 1815.

"MY DEAR FRIEND,

"You will be glad to hear that we arrived safely this day, after a less uncomfortable journey than might have been apprehended from the season of the year. We found all well, God be thanked, and Edith, who complained a little the first day, got better daily as we drew nearer home. She complains of a headache now; but that is the natural effect of over-excitement, on seeing her brother and sisters and her cousin, and displaying the treasures which we have brought for them. We reached Wordsworth's yesterday about seven o'clock. Three hours more would have brought us home, but I preferred passing the night at his house; for, had we proceeded, we should have found the children in bed, and a return home, under fortunate circumstances, has something the character of a triumph, and requires daylight. Never, I believe, was there seen a happier household than this when the chaise drew up to the door. I find so many letters to answer, that to-morrow will be fully employed in clearing them off.

"God bless you, my dear friend!

"Yours most affectionately,

"ROBERT SOUTHEY."

I can not resist here quoting from the Pilgrimage to Waterloo the account of the return home. Many readers will not have seen it before. Those who have will not be displeased to see it again, giving, as it does, so vivid, so true a picture of his domestic happiness.

"O joyful hour, when to our longing home
The long-expected wheels at length drew nigh!
When the first sound went forth, 'They come, they come!'
And hope's impatience quicken'd every eye!
Never had man whom Heaven would heap with bliss
More glad return, more happy hour than this.

"Aloft on yonder bench, with arms dispread,
My boy stood, shouting there his father's name,
Waving his hat around his happy head;
And there, a younger group, his sisters came:
Smiling they stood with looks of pleased surprise,
While tears of joy were seen in elder eyes.

"Soon all and each came crowding round to share
The cordial greeting, the beloved sight;
What welcomings of hand and lip were there!
And when those overflowings of delight
Subsided to a sense of quiet bliss,
Life hath no purer, deeper happiness.

"The young companion of our weary way
Found here the end desired of all her ills;
She who in sickness pining many a day
Hunger'd and thirsted for her native hills,
Forgetful now of sufferings past and pain,
Rejoiced to see her own dear home again.

"Recover'd now, the home-sick mountaineer
Sat by the playmate of her infancy,
The twin-like comrade—render'd doubly dear
For that long absence: full of life was she,
With voluble discourse and eager mien
Telling of all the wonders she had seen.

"Here silently between her parents stood
My dark-eyed Bertha, timid as a dove;
And gently oft from time to time she woo'd
Pressure of hand, or word, or look of love,
With impulse shy of bashful tenderness,
Soliciting again the wish'd caress.

"The younger twain in wonder lost were they,
My gentle Kate and my sweet Isabel:
Long of our promised coming, day by day
It had been their delight to hear and tell;
And now, when that long-promised hour was come,
Surprise and wakening memory held them dumb.

* * * * * * * * * * *

"Soon they grew blithe as they were wont to be;
Her old endearments each began to seek:
And Isabel drew near to climb my knee,
And pat with fondling hand her father's cheek,
With voice, and touch, and look reviving thus
The feelings which had slept in long disuse.

"But there stood one whose heart could entertain
And comprehend the fullness of the joy;
The father, teacher, playmate, was again
Come to his only and his studious boy;
And he beheld again that mother's eye,
Which with such ceaseless care had watch'd his infancy.

"Bring forth the treasures now—a proud display—
For rich as Eastern merchants we return!
Behold the black Beguine, the sister gray,
The friars whose heads with sober motion turn,
The ark well fill'd with all its numerous hives,
Noah, and Shem, and Ham, and Japhet, and their wives.

"The tumbler, loose of limb; the wrestlers twain;
And many a toy beside of quaint device,
Which, when his fleecy troops no more can gain
Their pasture on the mountains hoar with ice,
The German shepherd carves with curious knife,
Earning with easy toil the food of frugal life.

"It was a group which Richter, had he view'd,
Might have deem'd worthy of his perfect skill;
The keen impatience of the younger brood,
Their eager eyes and fingers never still;
The hope, the wonder, and the restless joy
Of those glad girls, and that vociferous boy!

"The aged friend* serene with quiet smile,
Who in their pleasure finds her own delight;
The mother's heart-felt happiness the while;
The aunts, rejoicing in the joyful sight;
And he who in his gayety of heart,
With glib and noisy tongue perform'd the showman's part.

"Scoff ye who will! but let me, gracious Heaven,
Preserve this boyish heart till life's last day!
For so that inward light by Nature given
Shall still direct, and cheer me on my way,
And, brightening as the shades of life descend,
Shine forth with heavenly radiance at the end.

Pilgrimage to Waterloo; PROEM

To C. W. W. Wynn, Esq.

"Keswick, Dec. 15, 1815.

"MY DEAR WYNN,

" * * * * * * *

The infrequency of my letters, my dear Wynn, God knows, is owing to no distaste. The pressing employments of one who keeps pace with an increasing expenditure by temporary writings —the quantity which, from necessity as well as inclination, I have to read, and the multiplicity of letters which I have to write, are the sufficient causes. You do not know the number of letters which come to me from perfect strangers, who seem to think a poet laureate has as much patronage as the lord chancellor. Not unfrequently the writers remind me so strongly of my own younger days, that I have given them the best advice I could, with earnestness as well as sincerity; and more than once been thus led into an occasional correspondence. The laureateship itself with me is no sinecure. I am at work in consequence of it at this time. Do not suppose that I mean to rival Walter Scott. My poem will be in a very different strain. * * * * *

"During my stay in London I scarcely ever went out of the circle of my private friends. I dined in company with Mina and some other Liberals—a set of men who (while I can not but respect them as individuals, and feel that under

* Mrs. Wilson, who is referred to occasionally in this volume.

the late administration I myself might probably have felt and acted with them) do certainly justify Ferdinand, not in his capricious freaks of favor and disfavor, but in the general and decided character of his measures. They are thorough atheists, and would go the full length of their principles, being, I believe, all of them (as is, indeed, the character of the nation) of the same iron mold as Cortes and Pizarro. Mina is a finer character—young and ardent, and speaking of his comrades with an affection which conciliates affection for himself.

* * * * * * *

"There is but one point in your letter in which I do not agree with you, and that regards the army. The necessity of maintaining it appears to me manifest, and the contingent danger imaginary. Our danger is not from that quarter. If we are to suffer from the army, it will be by their taking part against the government (as in France), and siding in a mob revolution. In my judgment, we are tending this way insensibly to our rulers and to the main part of the people, but I fear inevitably. The foundations of government are undermined. The props may last during your lifetime and mine, but I can not conceal from myself a conviction that, at no very distant day, the whole fabric must fall! God grant that this ominous apprehension may prove false.

"God bless you, my dear Wynn!

"Yours affectionately, R. S."

To Mr. Neville White.

"Keswick, Jan. 8, 1816.

"My dear Neville,

"Did you ever watch the sands of an hour-glass? When I was first at Oxford, one of these old-fashioned measurers of time was part of my furniture. I rose at four o'clock, and portioned out my studies by the hour. When the sands ran low, my attention was often attracted by observing how much faster they appeared to run. Applying this image to human life, which it has so often been brought to illustrate (whether my sands run low or not, is known only to Him by whom this frail vessel was made, but assuredly they run fast), it seems as if the weeks of my youth were longer than the months of middle age, and that I could get through more in a day then than in a week now. Since I wrote to you, I have scarcely done any thing but versify; and certain it is that twenty years ago I could have produced the same quantity of verses in a fourth part of the time. It is true they would have been more faulty; but the very solicitude to avoid faults, and the slow and dreaming state which it induces, may be considered as indications that the season for poetry is gone by—that I am falling into the yellow leaf, or, to use a more consoling metaphor, and perhaps a more applicable one, that poetry is but the blossom of an intellect so constituted as mine, and that with me the fruit is set—in sober phrase, that it would be wisely done if henceforth I confined myself to sober prose. And this I could be well content to do, from a conviction in my own mind that I shall ultimately hold a higher place among historians (if I live to complete what is begun) than among poets. * * * *

"The affair of Lavalette, in France, pleases me well, except as far as regards the treatment of his wife for having done her duty. The king ought not to have pardoned him, and the law ought to have condemned him: both did as they ought, and, as far as depended upon them, his civil life was at an end. I should have had no pity for him if the ax had fallen; but a condemned criminal making his escape becomes a mere human creature striving for life, and the Devil take him, say I, who would not lend a hand to assist him, except in cases of such atrocious guilt as make us abhor and execrate the perpetrator, and render it unfit that he should exist upon earth.

"Of home politics, I grieve to say that the more I think of them, the worse they appear. All imaginable causes which produce revolution are at work among us; the solitary principle of education is the only counteracting power; and God knows this is very partial, very limited, and must be slow in its effects, even if it were upon a wider scale and a more permanent foundation. If another country were in this state, I should say, without hesitation, that revolution was at hand there, and that it was inevitable. If I hesitate at predicting to myself the same result here, it is from love or from weakness, from hope that we may mercifully be spared so dreadful a chastisement for our follies and our sins, and from fear of contemplating the evils under which we should be overwhelmed. God bless you!

"Yours most affectionately,

"R. Southey."

To Grosvenor C. Bedford, Esq.

"Keswick, Feb. 4, 1816.

"My dear G.,

"I have an official from the Treasury this evening, telling me, as you anticipated, that the prayer of my petition* is inadmissible. To be sure, it is much better they should repeal the duty than grant an exemption from it *speciali gratià;* but if they will do neither the one nor the other, it is too bad.

"Is it true that the Princess Charlotte is likely to be married? You will guess why I wish to know; though, if I had not written half a marriage poem, I certainly would not begin one, for, between ourselves, I have not been well used about the laureateship. They require task verses from me—not to keep up the custom of having them befiddled, but to keep up the task—instead of putting an end to this foolery in a fair and open manner, which would do the court credit, and save me a silly expense of time and trouble. I shall complete what I have begun, because it is begun, and to please myself, not to obtain favor with any body else; but when these things are done, if they continue to look for New Years' Odes from the laureate, they shall have nothing else.

* A petition that some foreign books might come in duty free.

"Tom has been here for the last fortnight, looking about for a house. I can not write verses in the presence of any person except my wife and children. Tom, therefore, without knowing it, has impeded my Pilgrimage; but I can prosify, let who will be present, and Brazil is profiting by this interruption.

"Were you not here when poor Lloyd introduced M. Simond? and have you seen the said M. Simond's Travels in England, by a native of France? You will like the liveliness and the pervading good sense; and you will smile at the complacency with which he abuses Handel, Raphael, and Milton. He honors me with a couple of pages—an amusing mixture of journalizing, personal civility, and critical presumption. My poems and Milton's, he says, have few readers, although they have many admirers. He applies to me the famous speech of the cardinal to Ariosto, Dove Diavolo, &c., and thinks I write nonsense. However, it is better than Milton's, both Milton's love and theology being coarse and material, whereas I have tenderness and spirituality!!! He sets down two or three things which I told him, states my opinions as he is pleased to suppose, and concludes that the reason why I disapprove of Mr. Malthus's writings is that I do not understand them. Bravo, M. Simond! Yet, in the main, it is a fair and able book, and I wonder how so sensible a man can write with such consummate self-assurance upon things above his reach.

"I long to have my Brazilian History finished, that that of the war may go to press in its stead; and could I abstain from reviewing, three months would accomplish this desirable object; but 'I must live,' as the French libeler said to Richelieu, and, unlike the cardinal, I know you will see the necessity for my so doing. However, I am in a fair train, and verily believe that after the present year I and the constable shall travel side by side in good fellowship. You will be glad to hear that I have got the correspondence of the Portuguese committee, with the official details of the conduct of Massena's army, and the consequent state of the people and the country. If I live to complete this work, I verily believe it will tend to mitigate the evils of war hereafter, by teaching men in command what ineffaceable infamy will pursue them if they act as barbarians.

"God bless you! R. S."

To Chauncey Hare Townshend, Esq.

"Keswick, Feb. 10, 1816.

"A natural but melancholy association reminds me of you. Between three and four years ago, a youth, as ardent in the study of poetry as yourself, but under less favorable circumstances of fortune, sent me some specimens of his poems, and consulted me concerning the course of life which he should pursue. He was the eldest of a very large family, and the father a half-pay officer. He wished to go to London, and study the law, and support himself while studying it by his pen. I pointed out to him the certain misery and ruin in which such an event would involve him, and recommended him to go to Cambridge, where, with his talents and acquirements, he could not fail of making his way, unless he was imprudent. I interested myself for him at Cambridge; he was placed at Emmanuel, won the good-will of his college, and was in the sure road both to independence and fame, when the fever of last year cut him off. I do not think there ever lived a youth of higher promise. His name was James Dusautoy. This evening I have been looking over his papers, with a view of arranging a selection of them for the press. In seeking to serve him, I have been the means of sending him prematurely to the grave. I will at least endeavor to preserve his memory.*

"Of the many poets, young and old, whom I have known only by letter, Kirke White, Dusautoy, and yourself have borne the fairest blossom. *In* the blossom *they* have been cut off. May *you* live to bring forth fruit!

"I think you intimated an intention of going to Cambridge. The fever has broken out there again; physicians know not how to treat it; it has more the character of a pestilence than any disease which has for many years appeared in this island; and unless you have the strongest reasons for preferring Cambridge, the danger and the *probability* of the recurrence of this contagion are such, that you would do well to turn your thoughts toward Oxford on this account alone.

"Your sonnets have gratified me and my family. Study our early poets, and avoid all imitation of your cotemporaries. You can not read the best writers of Elizabeth's age too often. Do you love Spenser? I have him in my heart of hearts.

"God bless you, sir!

"ROBERT SOUTHEY."

To Walter Scott, Esq.

"Keswick, March 17, 1816.

"MY DEAR SCOTT,

"I have a debt upon my conscience which has been too long unpaid. You left me a letter of introduction to the Duchess of Richmond, which I was graceless enough to make no use of, and, still more gracelessly, I have never yet thanked you for it. As for the first part of the offense, my stay at Brussels was not very long. I had a great deal to see there; moreover, I got among the old books; and having a sort of instinct which makes me as much as possible get out of the way of drawing-rooms, because I have an awkward feeling of being in the way when in them, I was much more at my ease when looking at emperors and princes in the crowd, than I should have been in the room with them.

"How I should have rejoiced if we had met at Waterloo! This feeling I had and expressed upon the ground. You have pictured it with your characteristic force and animation. My poem will reach you in a few weeks: it is so

* See antè, p. 293.

different in its kind, that, however kindly malice may be disposed, it will not be possible to institute a comparison with yours. I take a different point of time and a wider range, leaving the battle untouched, and describing the field only such as it was when I surveyed it. * *

"Mountaineer as I am, the cultivated scenery of Flanders delighted me. I have seen no town so interesting as Bruges—no country in a state so perfect as to its possible production of what is beautiful and useful, as the environs of that city and the Pays de Waes. Of single objects, the finest which I saw were the market-place at Brussels and at Ypres, and the town-house at Louvain; the most extraordinary, as well as the most curious, the cathedral at Aix-la-Chapelle, which is, perhaps, the most curious church in existence. The most impressive were the quarries of Maestricht. I found a good deal of political discontent, particularly in the Liege country—a general sense of insecurity—a very prevalent belief that England had let Bonaparte loose from Elba, which I endeavored in vain to combat; and a very proper degree of disappointment and indignation that he had not been put to death as he deserved—a feeling in which I heartily concurred.

"Did I ever thank you for the Lord of the Isles? There are pictures in it which are not surpassed in any of your poems, and in the first part especially, a mixture of originality, and animation, and beauty, which is seldom found. I wished the Lord himself had been more worthy of the good fortune which you bestowed upon him. The laurel which it has pleased you, rather than any other person, to bestow upon me, has taken me in for much dogged work in rhyme; otherwise, I am inclined to think that my service to the Muses has been long enough, and that I should, perhaps, have claimed my discharge. The ardor of youth is gone by; however I may have fallen short of my own aspirations, my best is done, and I ought to prefer those employments which require the matured faculties and collected stores of declining life. You will receive the long-delayed conclusion of my Brazilian History in the course of the summer. It has much curious matter respecting savage life, a full account of the Jesuit establishments, and a war in Pernambuco, which will be much to your liking.

"Remember me to Mrs. Scott and your daughter, who is old enough to be entitled to these courtesies, and believe me, my dear Scott,

"Yours very affectionately,

"ROBERT SOUTHEY."

To Sharon Turner, Esq.

"Keswick, April 2, 1816.

"MY DEAR TURNER,

"You will shortly, I trust, receive my Pilgrimage, the notes and title-page to which would have been at this time in the printer's hands, if I had not been palsied by the severe illness of my son, who is at this time in such a state that I know not whether there be more cause for fear or for hope. In the disposition of mind which an affliction of this kind induces, there is no person whom I feel so much inclined to converse with as with you.

"I have touched, in the latter part of my poem, upon the general course of human events, and the prospects of society. But perhaps I have not explained myself as fully and as clearly as if I had been writing in prose. The preponderance of good, and the progressiveness of truth, and knowledge, and general well-being, I clearly perceive; but I have delivered an opinion that this tendency to good is not an overruling necessity, and that that which *is*, is not necessarily the best that might have been, for this, in my judgment, would interfere with that free agency upon which all our virtues, and, indeed, the great scheme of Revelation itself, are founded.

"Time, my own heart, and, more than all other causes, the sorrows with which it has been visited (in the course of a life that, on the whole, has been happy in a degree vouchsafed to few, even among the happiest), have made me fully sensible that the highest happiness exists, as the only consolation is to be found, in a deep and habitual feeling of devotion. Long ere this would I have preached what I feel upon this subject, if the door had been open to me; but it is one thing to conform to the Church, preserving that freedom of mind which in religion, more than in all other things, is especially valuable, and another to subscribe solemnly to its articles. Christianity exists nowhere in so pure a form as in our own Church; but even there it is mingled with much alloy, from which I know not how it will be purified. I have an instinctive abhorrence of bigotry. When Dissenters talk of the Establishment, they make me feel like a High-Churchman; and when I get among High-Churchmen, I am ready to take shelter in dissent.

"You have thrown a new light upon the York and Lancaster age of our history, by showing the connection of those quarrels with the incipient spirit of Reformation. I wish we had reformed the monastic institutions instead of overthrowing them. Mischievous as they are in Catholic countries, they have got this good about them, that they hold up something besides worldly distinction to the respect and admiration of the people, and fix the standard of virtues higher than we do in Protestant countries. Would that we had an order of Beguines in England! There are few subjects which have been so unfairly discussed as monastic institutions: the Protestant condemns them in the lump, and the Romanist crams his legends down your throat. The truth is, that they began in a natural and good feeling, though somewhat exaggerated—that they produced the greatest public good in their season, that they were abominably perverted, and that the good which they now do, wherever they exist, is much less than the evil. Yet, if you had seen, as I once did, a Franciscan of fourscore, with a venerable head and beard, standing in the cloister of his convent, where his brothers la-

beneath his feet, and telling his beads, with a countenance expressive of the most perfect and peaceful piety, you would have felt with me how desirable it was that there should be such institutions for minds so constituted. The total absence of religion from our poor-houses, alms-houses, and hospitals, is as culpable in one way as the excess of superstition is in another. I was greatly shocked at a story which I once heard from Dr. Gooch. A woman of the town was brought to one of the hospitals, having been accidentally poisoned. Almost the last words which she uttered were, that this was a blasted life, and she was glad to have done with it! Who will not wish that she had been kissing the crucifix, and listening in full faith to the most credulous priest! I say this more with reference to her feelings at that moment, and the effect upon others, than as to her own future state, however awful that consideration may be. The mercy of God is infinite; and it were too dreadful to believe that they who have been most miserable here, should be condemned to endless misery hereafter.

"But I will have done with these topics, because I wish to say something respecting your second volume. You have surprised me by the additions you have made to our knowledge of our own early poetry. I had no notion that the Hermit of Hampole was so considerable a personage, nor that there remained such a mass of inedited poetry of that age. The Antiquarian Society would do well to publish the whole, however much it may be. You are aware how much light it would throw upon the history of our language, of our manners, and even of civil transaction; for all these things I should most gladly peruse the whole mass. St. Francisco Xavier is not the Xavier who wrote the Persian Life of Christ. In p. 3 you mention some novel verses which relate to Portuguese history. If the Scald Halldon's poem be not too long, may I request you to translate it for me, as a document for my history. Observe, that this request is purely conditional, as regarding the extent of the poem. If it is more than a half hour's work, it would be unreasonable to ask for time which you employ so well, and of which you have so little to spare.

"Remember us to Mrs. Turner, Alfred, and your daughter. We are in great anxiety, and with great cause, but there is hope. My wish at such time is akin to Macbeth's, but in a different spirit—a longing that the next hundred years were over, and that we were in a better world, where happiness is permanent, and there is neither change nor evil.

"God bless you!

"Yours very affectionately,

"R. SOUTHEY."

In the foregoing letter, my father speaks of his being at that time in a state of great anxiety, on account of the illness of his only boy Herbert, then ten years old, and in all respects a child after his father's own heart. Having been not only altogether educated by his father, but also his constant companion and play-fellow, he was associated with all his thoughts, and closely connected with all the habits of his daily life.

He seems, indeed, with all due allowance for parental partiality, to have been one of those children, of only too fair a promise, possessing a quietness of disposition hardly natural at that active age, and generally indicative of an innate feebleness of constitution, and evincing a quickness of intellect and a love of study which seem to show that the mind has, as it were, outgrown the body.

This I gather, not merely from my father's own letters, but from those who well remember the boy himself, and who speak of him as having been far beyond his age in understanding, and as bearing this painful and fatal illness with a patience and fortitude uncommon even in riper years.

This illness had now lasted for several weeks, and being of a strange and complicated nature, the want of that medical skill and experience which is only to be found in large towns, added much to the parents' anxiety and distress.

Subsequent examination however (showing a great accumulation of matter at the heart), proved that no skill could have availed. After a period of much suffering, he was released on the 17th of April. The following letters have a painful interest:

To Grosvenor C. Bedford, Esq.

"Wednesday, April 17, 1816.

"MY DEAR BEDFORD,

"Here is an end of hope and of fear, but not of suffering. His sufferings, however, are over, and, thank God! his passage was perfectly easy. He fell asleep, and is now in a better state of existence, for which his nature was more fitted than for this. You, more than most men, can tell what I have lost, and yet you are far from knowing how large a portion of my hopes and happiness will be laid in the grave with Herbert. For years it has been my daily prayer that I might be spared this affliction.

"I am much reduced in body by this long and sore suffering, but I am perfectly resigned, and do not give way to grief.

"In his desk there are the few letters which I had written to him, in the joy of my heart. I will fold up these and send them to you, that they may be preserved when I am gone, in memory of him and of me.* Should you survive me, you will publish such parts of my correspondence as are proper, for the benefit of my family. My dear Grosvenor, I wish you would make the selection while you can do it without sorrow, while it is uncertain which of us shall be left to regret the other. You are the fit person to do this; and it will be well to burn in time what is to be suppressed.

"I will not venture to relate the boy's conduct during his whole illness. I dare not trust my-

* These letters have not come into my hands. It does not appear that they have been preserved.

self to attempt this. But nothing could be more calm, more patient, more collected, more dutiful, more admirable.

"Oh! that I may be able to leave this country! The wound will never close while I remain in it. You would wonder to see me, how composed I am. Thank God, I can control myself for the sake of others; but it is a life-long grief, and do what I can to lighten it, the burden will be as heavy as I can bear. R. S.

"I wish you would tell Knox* what has happened. He was very kind to Herbert, and deserves that I should write to him."

To Grosvenor C. Bedford, Esq.

"April 18, 1816.

"My dear Grosvenor,

"Wherefore do I write to you? Alas! because I know not what to do. To-morrow, perhaps, may bring with it something like the beginning of relief. To-day I hope I shall support myself, or rather that God will support me, for I am weak as a child, in body even more than in mind. My limbs tremble under me; long anxiety has wasted me to the bone, and I fear it will be long before grief will suffer me to recruit. I am seriously apprehensive for the shock which my health seems to have sustained; yet I am wanting in no effort to appear calm and to console others; and those who are about me give me credit for a fortitude which I do not possess. Many blessings are left me—abundant blessings, more than I have deserved, more than I had ever reason to expect or even to hope. I have strong ties to life, and many duties yet to perform. Believe me, I see these things as they ought to be seen. Reason will do something, Time more, Religion most of all. The loss is but for this world; but as long as I remain in this world I shall feel it.

"Some way my feelings will vent themselves. I have thought of endeavoring to direct their course, and may, perhaps, set about a monument in verse for him and for myself, which may make our memories inseparable.

"There would be no wisdom in going from home. The act of returning to it would undo all the benefit I might receive from change of circumstance for some time yet. Edith feels this; otherwise, perhaps, we might have gone to visit Tom in his new habitation. Summer is at hand. While there was a hope of Herbert's recovery, this was a frequent subject of pleasurable consideration; it is now a painful thought, and I look forward with a sense of fear to the season which brings with it life and joy to those who are capable of receiving them. You, more than most men, are aware of the extent of my loss, and how, as long as I remain here, every object within and without, and every hour of every day, must bring it fresh to recollection. Yet the more I consider the difficulties of removing, the greater they appear; and perhaps by the time it would be possible, I may cease to desire it.

"Whenever I have leisure (will that ever be?) I will begin my own memoirs, to serve as a post-obit for those of my family who may survive me. They will be so far provided for as to leave me no uneasiness on that score. My life insurance is £4000; my books (for there is none to inherit them now) may be worth £1500; my copyrights, perhaps, not less; and you will be able to put together letters and fragments, which, when I am gone, will be acceptable articles in the market. Probably there would, on the whole, be £10,000 forthcoming. The whole should be Edith's during her life, and afterward divided equally among the surviving children. I shall name John May and Neville White for executors—both men of business, and both my dear and zealous friends. But do you take care of my papers, and publish my remains. I have, perhaps, much underrated the value of what will be left. A selection of my reviewals may be reprinted, with credit to my name and with profit. You will not wonder that I have fallen into this strain. One grave is at this moment made ready; and who can tell how soon another may be required? I pray, however, for continued life. There may be, probably there are, many afflictions for me in store, but the worst is past. I have more than once thought of Mr. Roberts; when he hears of my loss, it will for a moment freshen the recollection of his own.

"It is some relief to write to you, after the calls which have this day been made upon my fortitude. I have not been found wanting; and Edith, throughout the whole long trial, has displayed the most exemplary self-control. We never approached him but with composed countenances and words of hope; and for a mother to do this, hour after hour, and night after night, while her heart was breaking, is perhaps the utmost effort of which our nature is capable. Oh! how you would have admired and loved him, had you seen him in these last weeks! But you know something of his character. Never, perhaps, was child of ten years old so much to his father. Without ever ceasing to treat him as a child, I had made him my companion, as well as playmate and pupil, and he had learned to interest himself in my pursuits, and take part in all my enjoyments.

"I have sent Edith May to Wordsworth's. Poor child, she is dreadfully distressed; and it has ever been my desire to save them from all the sorrow that can be avoided, and to mitigate, as far as possible, what is inevitable. Something it is to secure for them a happy childhood. Never was a happier than Herbert's. He knew not what unkindness or evil was, except by name. His whole life was passed in cheerful duty, and love and enjoyment. If I did not hope that I have been useful in my generation, and may still continue to be so, I could wish that I also had gone to rest as early in the day; but my childhood was not like his.

"Let me have some money when you can, that these mournful expenses may be discharged. For five weeks my hand has been palsied, and this

* A school-fellow of my father's at Westminster, who was afterward one of the masters there.

brings with it a loss of means—an evil inseparable from my way of life. To-morrow I shall endeavor to resume my employments. You may be sure, also, that I shall attend to my health; nothing which exercise and diet can afford will be neglected; and whenever I feel that change of air and of scene could benefit me, the change shall be tried. I am perfectly aware how important an object this is; the fear is, lest my sense of its moment should produce an injurious anxiety. God bless you! R. S.

"You would save me some pain by correcting the remaining proofs,* for the sight of that book must needs be trying to me."

To Grosvenor C. Bedford, Esq.

"Saturday, April 20, 1816.

"MY DEAR GROSVENOR,

"Desire Gifford to reserve room for me in this number: I will not delay it beyond the first week in May; he may rely upon this: I am diligently at work; the exertion is wholesome for me at this season, and I want the money. It is the La Vendée article.

"A proof has reached me, so your trouble on that score may be spared.

"I am in all respects acting as you would wish to see me, not unmindful of the blessings which are left and the duties which I have to perform. But indeed, Grosvenor, it is only a deep, heartfelt, and ever-present faith which could support me. If what I have lost were lost forever, I should sink under the affliction. Throughout the whole sorrow, long and trying as it has been, Edith has demeaned herself with a strength of mind and a self-control deserving the highest admiration. To be as happy ever again as I have been, is impossible; my future happiness must be of a different kind, but the difference will be in kind rather than degree; there will be less of this world in it, more of the next, therefore will it be safe and durable.

"God bless you! R. S."

To John May, Esq.

"Keswick, April 22, 1816.

"MY DEAR FRIEND,

"I thank you for your letter, for your sympathy, and for your prayers. We have been supported even beyond my hopes, and according to our need. I do not feel any return of strength, but it will soon be restored; anxiety has worn me to the bone. While that state continued I was incapable of any employment, and my time was passed day and night alternately in praying that the worst might be averted, and in preparing for it if it might take place.

"Three things I prayed for—the child's recovery, if it might please God; that, if this might not be, his passage might be rendered easy; and that we might be supported in our affliction. The two latter petitions were granted, and I am truly thankful. But when the event was over, then, like David, I roused myself, and gave no way to unavailing grief, acting in all things as I should wish others to act when my hour also is come. I employ myself incessantly, taking, however, every day as much exercise as I can bear without injurious fatigue, which is not much. My appetite is good, and I have now no want of sleep. Edith is perfectly calm and resigned. Her fortitude is indeed exemplary to the highest degree, but her employments do not withdraw her from herself as mine do, and therefore I fear she has more to struggle with. Perhaps we were too happy before this dispensation struck us. Perhaps it was expedient for us that our hearts should be drawn more strongly toward another world. This is the use of sorrow, and to this use I trust our sorrow will be sanctified.

"Believe me, my dear friend, ever most truly and affectionately yours,

"ROBERT SOUTHEY."

To William Wordsworth, Esq.

"Monday, April 22, 1816.

"MY DEAR WORDSWORTH,

"You were right respecting the nature of my support under this affliction; there is but one source of consolation, and of that source I have drunk largely. When you shall see how I had spoken of my happiness but a few weeks ago, you will read with tears of sorrow what I wrote with tears of joy. And little did I think how soon and how literally another part of this mournful poem was to be fulfilled, when I said in it,

'To earth I should have sunk in my despair,
Had I not clasped the Cross, and been supported there.'

"I thank God for the strength with which we have borne this trial. It is not possible for woman to have acted with more fortitude than Edith has done through the whole sharp suffering; she has rather set an example than followed it. My bodily frame is much shaken. A little time and care will recruit it, and the mind is sound. I am fully sensible of the blessings which are left me, which far exceed those of most men. I pray for continued life, that I may fulfill my duties toward those whom I love. I employ myself, and I look forward to the end with faith and with hope, as one whose treasure is laid up in Heaven; and where the treasure is, there will the heart be also.

"At present it would rather do me hurt than good to see you. I am perfectly calm and in full self-possession; but I know my own weakness as well as my strength, and the wholesomest regimen for a mind like mine is assiduous application to pursuits which call forth enough of its powers to occupy without exhausting it. It is well for me that I can do this. I take regular exercise, and am very careful of myself.

"Many will feel for me, but none can tell what I have lost: the head and flower of my earthly happiness is cut off. But I am *not* unhappy.

"God bless you! R. S."

* Of the Pilgrimage to Waterloo.

To Grosvenor C. Bedford, Esq.

"Wednesday, April 24, 1816.

"MY DEAR GROSVENOR,

"You remember the two remedies for grief of which Pelayo speaks.* I practice what I preach, and have employed myself with a power of exertion at which I myself wonder, taking care so to vary my employments as not for any one to possess my mind too fully. I take regular exercise; I take tonics; I eat, drink, and sleep. See if this be not doing well. I converse as usual, and can at times be cheerful, but my happiness can never again be what it has been. Many blessings do I possess, but the prime blessing, the flower of my hopes, the central jewel of the ring, is gone. An early admiration of what is good in the stoical philosophy, and an active and elastic mind, have doubtless been great means of supporting me; but they would have been insufficient without a deeper principle; and I verily believe that were it not for the consolations which religion affords—consolations which in time will ripen into hope and joy—I should sink under an affliction which is greater than any man can conceive. You best can judge what the privation must be, and you can but judge imperfectly.

"Enough of this. I shall soon find a better mode of at once indulging and regulating these feelings. Upon this subject I have thoughts in my head which will, by God's blessing, produce good and lasting fruit.

"At present one of my daily employments is the Carmen Nuptiale, which is now nearly completed. It will extend to about a hundred and ten stanzas, the same meter as the Pilgrimage, which, printed in the same manner, may run to seventy pages—say three sheets. Its English title the Lay of the Laureate, which is not only a *taking* title for an advertisement, but a remarkably good one. It is for Longman to determine in what form he will print it, and what number of copies: quarto pamphlets, I think, are not liked, for their inconvenient size.

"There must be a presentation copy bound for the princess. Through what channel shall I convey it? Lord William Gordon would deliver it for me if I were to ask him. Can you put me in a better way? Would Herries like to do it, or is it proper to ask him?

"In a few days I shall send you the MSS.; the printing will be done presently. It comes too close upon the Pilgrimage; but, whatever may be thought of it at court, it will do me credit now and hereafter. I am very desirous of completing it, that I may have leisure for what lies nearer my heart.

"I will have a copy for Edith bound exactly like the court copy. What would it cost to have both these printed upon vellum? more, I suspect, than the fancy is worth.

"Press upon Gifford my earnest desire that the article of which the first portion accompanies this note may appear in the present number. It is of consequence to me, and the subject is in danger of becoming stale if it be delayed: dwell upon this point. It will be as interesting a paper as he has ever received from me.

"God bless you! R. S."

To Grosvenor C. Bedford, Esq.

"Keswick, April 26, 1816.

"MY DEAR GROSVENOR,

"Herbert died on the 17th, and he was in the tenth year of his age; say nothing more than this. How much does it contain to me, and to the world how little!

"I have great power of exertion, and this is of signal benefit at this time. My mind is closely employed throughout the whole day. I do more in one day than I used to do in three: hitherto the effect is good, but I shall watch myself well, and be careful not to exact more than the system will endure. I have certainly gained strength; but, as you may suppose, every circumstance of spring and of reviving nature brings with it thoughts that touch me in my heart of hearts. Do not, however, imagine that I am unhappy. I know what I have lost, and that no loss could possibly have been greater; but it is only for a time; and you know what my habitual and rooted feelings are upon this subject.

"It is not unlikely that Gifford will do *for* me in this number what he has done *by* me in others—displace some other person's article to make room for mine. He will act wisely if he does so, for the freshness of the subject will else evaporate. I shall finish it with all speed upon this supposition. It would surprise you were you to see what I get through in a day.

"The remainder of the proofs might as well have been sent me. Surrounded as I am with mementoes, there was little reason for wishing to keep them at a distance. And however mournful it must ever be to remember the Proem, and the delight which it gave when the proof-sheet arrived, I am glad that it was written, and Edith feels upon this point as I do. The proofs had better come to me, if it is not too late. I can verify the quotations, which it is impossible for you to do, and may, perhaps, add something.

"Tell Pople I shall be obliged to him if he will make some speed with the History of Brazil; that I find it impossible to comprise it in two volumes; a third there must be, but it will go to press as soon as the second is printed; and that there will be no delay on my part (that is, as far as man can answer for himself) till the whole is completed. I send a portion of copy in the frank which covers this. If I mistake not, this second volume will be found very amusing as well as very curious.

"Edith May returned from Wordsworth's this morning; we missed her greatly, and yet her return was a renewal of sorrow. Her mother behaves incomparably well: it is not possible that any mother could suffer more, or support

---

* "Nature hath assigned
Two sovereign remedies for human grief:
Religion—surest, firmest, first, and best;
And strenuous action next."

Roderic, canto xiv.

her sufferings better. She knows that we have abundant blessings left, but feels that the flower of all is gone; and this feeling must be for life. Bitter as it is, it is wholesome.

"God bless you! R. S."

To Grosvenor C. Bedford, Esq.

"April 30, 1816.

"MY DEAR GROSVENOR,

"Time passes on. I employ myself, and have recovered strength; but in point of spirits I rather lose ground. The cause, perhaps, is obvious. At first, we make great efforts to force the mind from thoughts which are intolerably painful; but as, from time, they become endurable, less effort is made to avoid them, and the poignancy of grief settles into melancholy. Both with Edith and myself, this seems to be the case. Certain I am that nothing but the full assurance of immortality could prevent me from sinking under an affliction which is greater than any stranger could possibly believe; and thankful I am that my feelings have been so long and so habitually directed toward this point. You probably know my poems better than most people, and may perceive how strongly my mind has been impressed upon this most consoling subject.

"Yesterday I finished the main part of the Lay. There remain only six or eight stanzas as a L'Envoy, which I may, perhaps, complete this night; then I shall send you the whole in one packet through Gifford. I have said nothing about it to Longman, for I think it very probable that you may advise me not to publish the poem now it is written, lest it should give offense; and having satisfied myself by writing it, it is quite indifferent to me whether it appears now or after my decease. The emolument to be derived from it is too insignificant to be thought of, and the credit which I should gain I can very well do without. So take counsel with any body you please, and remember that I, who am easily enough persuaded in any case, am in this perfectly unconcerned; for were it a thing of course that I should produce a poem on this occasion, there is at this time, God knows, sufficient reason why I might stand excused.

"Do not imagine that the poem has derived the slightest cast of coloring from my present state of mind. The plan is precisely what was originally formed. William Nichol is likely to judge as well as any man whether there be any unfitness in publishing it. You are quite aware that I neither wish to court favor nor to give offense, and that the absurdity of taking offense (if it were taken) would excite in me more pity than resentment.

"Good night! I am going to the poem in hope of completing it. I can not yet bear to be unemployed, and this I feel severely. You know how much I used to unbend, and play with the children, in frequent intervals of study, as though I were an idle man. Of this I am quite incapable, and shall long continue so. No circumstance of my former life ever brought with it so great a change as that which I daily and hourly feel, and perhaps shall never cease to feel. Yet I am thankful for having possessed this child so long; for worlds I would not but have been his father. Of all the blessings which it has pleased God to vouchsafe me, this was and *is* the greatest. R. S."

To Grosvenor C. Bedford, Esq.

"Friday, May 3, 1816.

"MY DEAR GROSVENOR,

"You will have seen by my last letters, that I am not exhausting myself by over-exertion. On the contrary, for many days I have been forcing myself to the more difficult necessity of bearing my own recollections. Time will soften them down; indeed, they now have, and always have had, all the alleviation which an assured hope and faith can bestow; and when I give way to tears, which is only in darkness or in solitude, they are not tears of unmingled pain. I begin to think that change of place would not be desirable, and that the pain of leaving a place where I have enjoyed so many years of such great happiness, is more than it is wise to incur without necessity. Nor could I reconcile either Edith or myself to the thought of leaving poor Mrs. Wilson,* whose heart is half broken already, and to whom our departure would be a death-stroke. Her days, indeed, must necessarily be few, and her life-lease will probably expire before the end of the term to which we are looking on.

"Murray has sent me £50 for the La Vendée article, which makes me indifferent when it appears; and proposes to me half a dozen other subjects at £100 each, at which rate I suppose in future I shall supply him with an article every quarter. This will set me at ease in money matters, about which, thank God and the easy disposition with which he has blessed me, I have never been too anxious.

"It is needless to say I shall be glad to see you here, but rather at some future time, when you will find me a better companion, and when your company would do me more good. Nor, indeed, must you leave your mother; her deliverance from the infirmities of life can not be long deferred by any human skill, or any favorable efforts of nature. Whenever that event takes place, you will need such relief as change of scene can afford; and whenever it may be, I hold myself ready to join you and accompany you to the Continent, for as long a time as you can be spared from your office, and as long a journey as that time may enable us to take. Remember this, and look to it as a fitting ar-

* Mrs. Wilson (the "aged friend" mentioned in the stanzas quoted from the Pilgrimage to Waterloo) had been housekeeper to Mr. Jackson, the former owner of Greta Hall, and she continued to occupy part of one of the two houses, which, though altogether in my father's occupation, had not been wholly thrown together as was afterward done. She had once been the belle of Keswick, and was a person of a marvelous sweetness of temper and sterling good sense, as much attached to the children of the family as if they had been her own, and remembered still by every surviving member of it with respect and affection.

rangement which will benefit us both. God bless you! R. S."

To Chauncey Hare Townshend, Esq.

"Keswick, May 16, 1816.

" * * * The loss which I have sustained is, I believe, heavier than any like affliction would have proved to almost any other person, from the circumstance of my dear son's character, and the peculiar habits of my life. The joyousness of my disposition has received its death-wound; but there are still so many blessings left me, that I should be most ungrateful did I not feel myself abundantly rich in the only treasures which I have ever coveted. Three months ago, when I looked around, I knew no man so happy as myself—that is, no man who so entirely possessed all that his heart desired, those desires being such as bore the severest scrutiny of wisdom. The difference now is, that what was then the flower of my earthly happiness is now become a prominent object of my heavenly hopes—that I have this treasure in reversion instead of actually possessing it; but the reversion is indefeasible, and when it is restored to me it will be forever; the separation which death makes is but for a time.

"These are my habitual feelings, not the offspring of immediate sorrow, for I have felt sorrow ere this, and, I hope, have profited by it.

"The Roman Catholics go too far in weaning their hearts from the world, and fall, in consequence, into the worst practical follies which could result from Manicheism. We lay up treasure in heaven when we cherish the domestic charities. 'They sin who tell us love can die,'* and they also err grievously who suppose that natural affections tend to wean us from God. Far otherwise! They develop virtues, of the existence of which in our own hearts we should else be unconscious; and binding us to each other, they bind us also to our common Parent.

"Let me see your poem when you have finished it, and tell me something more of yourself, where your home is, and where you have been educated. Any thing that you may communicate upon this subject will interest me. In my communication with Kirke White and with poor Dusautoy, I have blamed myself for repressing the expression of interest concerning them when it has been too late. Perhaps they have thought me cold and distant, than which nothing can be further from my nature; but may your years be many and prosperous. God bless you!

"Your affectionate friend,

"R. Southey."

To the Rev. Nicholas Lightfoot.

"May, 1816.

"My dear Lightfoot,

"I thank you for your letter. You may remember that in my youth I had a good deal of such practical philosophy as may be learned from Epictetus; it has often stood me in good stead; it affords strength, but no consolation; consolation can be found only in religion, and there I find it. My dear Lightfoot, it is now full two-and-twenty years since you and I shook hands at our last parting. In all likelihood, the separation between my son and me will not be for so long a time; in the common course of nature it can not possibly be much longer, and I may be summoned to rejoin him before the year, yea, before the passing day or the passing hour be gone. Death has so often entered my doors, that he and I have long been familiar. The loss of five brothers and sisters (four of whom I remember well), of my father and mother, of a female cousin who grew up with me, and lived with me; of two daughters, and of several friends (among them two of the dearest friends that ever man possessed), had very much weaned my heart from this world, or, more properly speaking, had fixed its thoughts and desires upon a better state wherein there shall be no such separation, before this last and severest affliction. Still it would be senseless and ungrateful to the greatest degree if I were not to feel and acknowledge the abundant blessings that I still possess, especially believing, trusting, *knowing*, as I do, in the full assurance of satisfied reason and settled faith, that the treasure which has been taken from me now is laid up in heaven, there to be repossessed with ample increase.

"Whenever I see Crediton, I must journey into the West for that sole purpose. My last ties with my native city were cut up by the roots two years ago, by the death of one of my best and dearest friends, and I shall never have heart to enter it again. Will you not give me one of your summer holidays, and visit, not only an old friend, but the part of England which is most worth visiting, and which attracts visitors from all parts? * * * *

"God bless you!

"Yours affectionately,

"R. Southey."

To the Rev. Herbert Hill.

"Keswick, May 4, 1816.

"My dear Uncle,

"My estimate of human life is more favorable than yours. If death were the termination of our existence, then, indeed, I should wish rather to have been born a beast, or never to have been born at all; but considering nothing more certain than that this life is preparatory to a higher state of being, I am thankful for the happiness I have enjoyed, for the blessings which are left me, and for those to which I look with sure and certain hope. With me the enjoyments of life have more than counterbalanced its anxieties and its pains. No man can possibly have been happier; and at this moment, when I am suffering under almost the severest loss which could have befallen me, I am richer both in heart and hope than if God had never given me the child whom it hath pleased him to take away. My heart has been exercised with better feelings during his life, and is drawn nearer toward Heaven by his removal.

* Kehama, canto ii., v. 10.

I do not recover spirits, but my strength is materially recruited, and I am not unhappy.

"I have employed myself with more than ordinary diligence. You will receive portions of my History in quick succession. I find abundant materials for a third volume, and have therefore determined not to injure a work which has cost me so much labor, by attempting to compress it because the public would prefer two volumes to three. * * * You will see that the story of Cardenas* is not an episode: it is the beginning of the great struggle with the Jesuits. This volume will bring the narrative down to the beginning of the last century, and conclude with the account of the manners of Brazil at that time, and the state of the country, as far as my documents enable me to give it. *

"You see I have not been idle; indeed, at present there is more danger of my employing myself too much than too little. * *

"God bless you! R. S."

To Mr. Neville White.

"Keswick, May 4, 1816.

"MY DEAR NEVILLE,

"Thank you for your letter. I have had the prayers and the sympathy of many good men, and perhaps never child was lamented by so many persons of ripe years, unconnected with him by ties of consanguinity. But those of my friends who knew him loved him for his own sake, and many there are who grieve at his loss for mine. I dare not pursue this subject. My health is better, my spirits are not. I employ myself as much as possible; but there must be intervals of employment, and the moment that my mind is off duty, it recurs to the change which has taken place: that change, I fear, will long be the first thought when I wake in the morning, and the last when I lie down at night. Yet, Neville, I feel and acknowledge the uses of this affliction. Perhaps I was too happy; perhaps my affections were fastened by too many roots to this world; perhaps this precarious life was too dear to me.

"Edith sets me the example of suppressing her own feelings for the sake of mine. We have many blessings left—abundant ones, for which to be thankful. I know, too, to repine because Herbert is removed, would be as selfish as it would be sinful. Yea, I believe that, in my present frame of mind, I could lay my children upon the altar, like Abraham, and say, 'Thy will be done.' This I trust will continue, when the depressing effects of grief shall have passed away. I hope in time to recover some portion of my constitutional cheerfulness, but never to lose that feeling with which I look on to eternity. I always knew the instability of earthly happiness; this woeful experience will make me contemplate more habitually and more ardently that happiness which is subject neither to chance nor change.

"Do not suppose that I am indulging in tears, or giving way to painful recollections. On the contrary, I make proper exertions, and employ myself assiduously for as great a portion of the day as is compatible with health. For the first week I did as much every day as would at other times have seemed the full and overflowing produce of three. This, of course, I could not continue, but at the time it was salutary. God bless you, my dear Neville!

"Yours most affectionately,

"R. SOUTHEY."

To Grosvenor C. Bedford, Esq.

"May 15, 1816.

"MY DEAR G.,

" * * * * * * *

If egotism* in poetry be a sin, God forgive all great poets! But perhaps it is allowable in them when they have been dead a few centuries, and therefore they may be permitted to speak of themselves and appreciate themselves, provided they leave especial orders that such passages be not made public until the statute of critical limitation expires. Who can be weak enough to suppose that the man who wrote that third stanza would be deterred from printing it by any fear of reprehension on the score of vanity? Who is to reprehend him? None of his peers assuredly; not one person who will sympathize with him as he reads; not one person who enters into his thoughts and feelings; not one person who can enter into the strain and enjoy it. Those persons, indeed, may who live wholly in the present; but I have taken especial care to make it known, that a faith in hereafter is as necessary for the intellectual as for the moral character, and that to the man of letters (as well as the Christian) the *present* forms but the slightest portion of his existence. He who would leave any durable monument behind him, must live in the past and look to the future. The poets of old scrupled not to say this; and who is there who is not delighted with these passages, whenever time has set his seal upon the prophecy which they contain?

* * * * * * *

"My spirits do not recover: that they should again be what they have been, I do not expect; that, indeed, is impossible. But, except when reading or writing, I am deplorably depressed: the worst is, that I can not conceal this. To affect any thing like my own hilarity, and that presence of joyous feelings which carried with it a sort of perpetual sunshine, is, of course, impossible; but you must imagine that the absence of all this must make itself felt. The change in my daily occupations, in my sports, my relaxations, my hopes, is so great, that it seems to have changed my very nature also. Nothing is said, but I often find anxious eyes fixed upon me, and watching my countenance. The best thing I can say is, that time passes on, and sooner or later remedies every thing.

* * * * * * *

* Hist. of Brazil., ch. xxv.

* This refers to some observations which had been made upon the Proem to the marriage song for the Princess Charlotte.

"I will have the books bound separately, because a book is a book, and two books are worth as much again as one; and if a man's library comes to the hammer, this is of consequence; and whenever I get my knock-down blow, the poor books will be knocked down after me. But why did I touch upon this string? Alas! Grosvenor, it is because all things bear upon one subject, the center of the whole circumference of all my natural associations. * * * * *

"God bless you! R. S."

To Chauncey Hare Townshend, Esq.

"Keswick, June 5, 1816.

"Thank you for both your letters. The history of your school-boy days reminds me of my own childhood and youth. I had a lonely childhood, and suffered much from tyranny at school, till I outgrew it, and came to have authority myself. In one respect, my fortune seems to have been better than yours, or my nature more accommodating. Where intellectual sympathy was not to be found, it was sufficient for me if moral sympathy existed. A kind heart and a gentle disposition won my friendship more readily than brighter talents, where these were wanting. *

"I left Westminster in a perilous state—a heart full of feeling and poetry, a head full of Rousseau and Werter, and my religious principles shaken by Gibbon: many circumstances tended to give me a wrong bias, none to lead me right, except adversity, the wholesomest of all discipline. An instinctive modesty, rather than any purer cause, preserved me for a time from all vice. A severe system of stoical morality then came to its aid. I made Epictetus, for many months, literally my manual. The French Revolution was then in its full career. I went to Oxford in January, 1793, a Stoic and a Republican. I had no acquaintance at the college, which was in a flagitious state of morals. I refused to wear powder, when every other man in the University wore it, because I thought the custom foolish and filthy; and I refused even to drink more wine than suited my inclination and my principles. Before I had been a week in the college, a little party had got round me, glad to form a sober society, of which I was the center. Here I became intimate with Edmund Seward, whose death was the first of those privations which have, in great measure, weaned my heart from the world. He confirmed in me all that was good. Time and reflection, the blessings and the sorrows of life, and I hope I may add, with unfeigned humility, the grace of God, have done the rest. Large draughts have been administered to me from both urns. No man has suffered keener sorrows, no man has been more profusely blessed. Four months ago no human being could possibly be happier than I was, or richer in all that a wise heart could desire. The difference now is, that what was then my chief treasure is now laid up in Heaven.

"Your manuscript goes by the next coach. I shall be glad to see the conclusion, and any other of your verses, Latin or English. Is any portion of your time given to modern languages? If not, half an hour a day might be borrowed for German, the want of which I have cause to regret. I was learning it with my son, and shall never have heart to resume that as a solitary study which in his fellowship was made so delightful. The most ambitious founder of a family never built such hopes upon a child as I did on mine; and entirely resembling me as he did, if it had been God's will that he should have grown up on earth, he would have shared my pursuits, partaken all my thoughts and feelings, and have in this manner succeeded to my plans and papers as to an intellectual inheritance. God bless you!

"ROBERT SOUTHEY."

To John May, Esq.

"Keswick, June 12, 1816.

"MY DEAR FRIEND,

"I have not written to you for some weeks. Time passes on, and the lapse of two months may perhaps enable me now to judge what permanent effect this late affliction may produce upon my habitual state of mind. It will be long before I shall cease to be sensible of the change in my relaxations, my pleasures, hopes, plans, and prospects; very long, I fear, will it be before a sense of that change will cease to be my latest thought at night and my earliest in the morning. Yet I am certainly resigned to this privation; and this I say, not in the spirit with which mere philosophy teaches us to bear that which is inevitable, but with a Christian conviction that this early removal is a blessing to him who is removed. We read of persons who have suddenly become gray from violent emotions of grief or fear. I feel in some degree as if I had passed at once from boyhood to the decline of life. I had never ceased to be a boy in cheerfulness till now. All those elastic spirits are now gone; nor is it in the nature of things that they should return. I am still capable of enjoyment, and trust that there is much in store for me; but there is an end of that hilarity which I possessed more uninterruptedly, and in a greater degree, than any person with whom I was ever acquainted. You advised me to write down my recollections of Herbert while they were fresh. I dare not undertake the task. Something akin to it, but in a different form, and with a more extensive purpose, I have begun; but my eyes and my head suffer too much in the occupation for me to pursue it as yet; and as these effects can not be concealed, I must avoid as much as possible all that would produce them. This, believe me, is an effort of forbearance, for my heart is very much set upon completing what I have planned. The effect upon Edith will be as lasting as upon myself; but she had not the same exuberance of spirits to lose, and therefore it will be less perceptible. The self-command which she has exercised has been truly exemplary, and commands my highest esteem. Your god-daughter, thank God! is well. Her daily lesson will long be a melancholy task on my part, since it will be a solitary one. She is now so far advanced that I can make some of her exercises of use, and set her to translate passages for my notes from French, Spanish, or Portuguese. Of course this is not done without some assistance and some correction. Still, while she improves herself she is assisting me, and the pleasure that this gives me is worth a great deal. She is a good girl, with a ready comprehension, quick feelings, a tender heart, and an excellent disposition. I pray God that her life may be spared to make me happy while I live, and some one who may be worthy of her when it shall be time for her to contract other ties and other duties.

"I suppose you will receive my Lay in a few days. God bless you, my dear friend!

"Yours most affectionately,

"ROBERT SOUTHEY."

In this series of melancholy letters there have been several allusions to a monument in verse which my father contemplated raising to the memory of his dear son. This design was never completed, but several hints and touching thoughts were noted down, and about fifty lines written, which seem to be the commencement. The latter part of these I quote here:

"Short time hath passed since, from my pilgrimage
To my rejoicing home restored, I sung
A true thanksgiving song of pure delight.
Never had man whom Heaven would heap with bliss
More happy day, more glad return than mine.
Yon mountains with their wintry robe were clothed
When, from a heart that overflow'd with joy,
I poured that happy strain. The snow not yet
Upon those mountain sides hath disappeared
Beneath the breath of spring, and in the grave
Herbert is laid, the child who welcomed me
With deepest love upon that happy day.
Herbert, my only and my studious boy;
The sweet companion of my daily walks;
Whose sports, whose studies, and whose thoughts I shared,
Yea, in whose life I lived; in whom I saw
My better part transmitted and improved.
Child of my heart and mind, the flower and crown
Of all my hopes and earthly happiness."

These fragments are published in the latest edition of his poems.

To Chauncey Hare Townshend, Esq.

"Keswick, July 22, 1816.

"MY DEAR CHAUNCEY,

" * * * It will be unfortunate if chance should not one day bring me within reach of you; but I would rather that chance should bring you to Cumberland, when you can spare a few weeks for such a visit. You will find a bed, plain fare, and a glad welcome; books for wet weather, a boat for sunny evenings; the loveliest parts of this lovely county within reach and within sight; and myself one of the best guides to all the recesses of the vales and mountains. As a geologist, you will enjoy one more pleasure than I do, who am ignorant of every branch of science. Mineralogy and botany are the only branches which I wish that I had possessed, not from any predilection for either, but because opportunities have fallen in my way for making observations (had I been master of the requisite knowledge) by which others might have been interested and guided. These two are sciences which add to our out-door enjoyments, and have no injurious effects. Chemical and physical studies seem, on the contrary, to draw on very prejudicial consequences. Their utility is not to be doubted; but it appears as if man could not devote himself to these pursuits without blunting his finer faculties.

"This county is very imperfectly visited by many of its numerous guests. They take the regular route, stop at the regular stations, ascend one of the mountains, and then fancy they have seen the lakes, in which, after a thirteen years' residence, I am every year discovering new scenes of beauty. Here I shall probably pass the remainder of my days. Our church, as you may perhaps recollect, stands at a distance from the town, unconnected with any other buildings, and so as to form a striking and beautiful feature in the vale. The church-yard is as open to the eye and to the breath of heaven as if it were a Druid's place of meeting. There I shall take up my last abode, and it is some satisfaction to think so—to feel as if I were at anchor, and should shift my berth no more. A man whose habitual frame of mind leads him to look forward, is not the worse for treading the church-yard path, with a belief that along that very path his hearse is one day to convey him.

"Do not imagine that I am of a gloomy temper; far from it; never was man blessed with a more elastic spirit or more cheerful mind; and even now the liquor retains its body and its strength, though it will sparkle no more.

"Your comments upon the Castle of Indolence express the feeling of every true poet; the second part must always be felt as injuring the first. I agree with you, also, as respecting the Minstrel, beautiful and delightful as it is. It still wants that imaginative charm which Thomson has caught from Spenser, but which no poet has ever so entirely possessed as Spenser himself. Among the many plans of my ambitious boyhood, the favorite one was that of completing the Faëry Queen. For this purpose I had collected every hint and indication of what Spenser meant to introduce in the progress of his poem, and had planned the remaining legends in a manner which, as far as I can remember after a lapse of four or five-and-twenty years, was not without some merit. What I have done as a poet falls far short of what I had hoped to do; but in boyhood and in youth I dreamed of poetry alone; and I suppose it is the course of nature, that the ardor which this pursuit requires should diminish as we advance in life. In youth we delight in strong emotions, to be agitated and inflamed with hope, and to weep at tragedy. In maturer life we have no tears to spare; it is more delightful to have our judgment exercised than our feelings.

"God bless you! Come and visit me when you can. I long to see you. R. S."

To Chauncey Hare Townshend, Esq.

"Keswick, August 17, 1816.

"MY DEAR CHAUNCEY,

"I was from home for a few days' absence

when your letter arrived. I have seen too many instances of unjust prepossession to be surprised at them now. Much of my early life was embittered by them when I was about your age; and in later years I have been disinherited by two uncles in succession, for no other assignable or possible reason than the caprice of weak minds and misgoverned tempers. In this manner was I deprived of a good property, which the ordinary course of law would have given me. These things never robbed me of a moment's tranquillity—never in the slightest degree affected my feelings and spirits, nor ever mingled with my dreams. There is little merit in regarding such things with such philosophy. I suffered no loss, no diminution of any one enjoyment, and should have despised myself if any thing so merely external and extraneous could have disturbed me. It is not in the heel, but in the heart, that I am vulnerable; and in the heart I have now been wounded: how deeply, He only who sees the heart can tell.

"Whenever you come I shall rejoice to see you. Do not, however, wind up your expectations too high. In many things I may, in some things I must, disappoint the ideal which you have formed. No man has ever written more faithfully from his heart; but my manners have not the same habitual unreserve as my pen. A disgust at the professions of friendship, and feeling, and sentiment in those who have neither the one nor the other, has, perhaps, insensibly led me to an opposite extreme; and in wishing rather *esse quam videri*, I may sometimes have appeared what I am not.

"I would not have you look on to the University with repugnance or dread. My college years were the least beneficial and the least happy of my life; but this was owing to public and private circumstances, utterly unlike those in which you will be placed. The comfort of being domesticated with persons whom you love, you will miss and feel the want of. In other respects, the change will bring with it its advantages. To enter at college is taking a degree in life, and graduating as a man. I am not sure that there would be either schools or universities in a Utopia of my creation; in the world as it is, both are so highly useful, that the man who has not been at a public school and at college feels his deficiency as long as he lives. You renew old acquaintances at college; you confirm early intimacies. Probably, also, you form new friendships at an age when they are formed with more judgment, and are therefore likely to endure. And one who has been baptized in the springs of Helicon is in no danger of falling into vice, in a place where vice appears in the most disgusting form.

"There is a paper of mine in the last Quarterly upon the means of bettering the condition of the poor. You will be interested by a story which it contains of an old woman upon Exmoor. In Wordsworth's blank verse it would go to every heart. Have you read The Excursion? and have you read the collection of Wordsworth's other poems, in two octavo volumes? If you have not, there is a great pleasure in store for you. I am no blind admirer of Wordsworth, and can see where he has chosen subjects which are unworthy in themselves, and where the strength of his imagination and of his feeling is directed upon inadequate objects. Notwithstanding these faults, and their frequent occurrence, it is by the side of Milton that Wordsworth will have his station awarded him by posterity. God bless you! R. S."

To John Rickman, Esq.

"Keswick, Aug. 25, 1816.

"MY DEAR RICKMAN,

"I have been long in your debt; my summers are more like those of the grasshopper than of the ant. Wynn was here nearly a week, and when he departed I rejoined him with my friend Nash at Lowther. * * * This, and a round home by way of Wordsworth's, employed a week; and what with the King of Prussia's librarian, the two secretaries of the Bible Society, and other such out-of-the-way personages who come to me by a sort of instinct, I have had little time and less leisure since my return.

"The last odd personage who made his appearance was Owen of Lanark,* who is neither more nor less than such a Pantisocrat as I was in the days of my youth. He is as ardent now as I was then, and will soon be cried down as a visionary (certainly he proposes to do more than I can believe practicable in this generation); but I will go to Lanark to see what he has done. I conversed with him for about an hour, and, not knowing any thing about him, good part of the time elapsed before I could comprehend his views—so little probable did it appear that any person should come to me with a leveling system of society, and tell me he had been to the Archbishop of Canterbury, and the ministers, &c. But he will be here again in a day or two, and meantime I have read a pamphlet which is much more injudicious than his conversation, and will very probably frustrate the good which he might by possibility have produced.

"To this system he says we must come *speedily*. * * * What he says of the manufacturing system has much weight in it; the machinery which enables us to manufacture for half the world has found its way into other countries; every market is glutted; more goods are produced than can be consumed; and every improvement in mechanism that performs the work of hands, throws so many mouths upon the public—a growing evil, which has been increasing by the premature employment of children, bringing them into competition with the grown workmen when they should have been at school or at play. He wants government to settle its paupers and supernumerary hands in villages upon waste lands, to live in community, urging that we must go to the root of the evil at once. He talks of what he has done at Lanark (and

* On this subject see Colloquies, vol. i., p. 132, &c.

this, indeed, has been much talked of by others); but his address to his people there has much that is misplaced, injudicious, and reprehensible. Did you see him in London? Had we met twenty years ago, the meeting might have influenced both his life and mine in no slight degree. During those years he has been a practical man, and I have been a student; we do not differ in the main point, but my mind has ripened more than his.

"You talk of brain transfusion, and placing one man's memory upon another man's shoulders. That same melancholy feeling must pass through the mind of every man who labors hard in acquiring knowledge; for, communicate what we can, and labor as assiduously as we may, how much must needs die with us? This reflection makes me sometimes regret (as far as is allowable) the time which I employ in doing what others might do as well, or what might as well be left undone. The Quarterly might go on without me, and should do so if I could go on without it. But what would become of my Portuguese acquirements and of yonder heap of materials, which none but myself can put in order, if I were to be removed by death?

"For the two voted monuments, I want one durable one, which should ultimately pay itself—a pyramid not smaller than the largest in Egypt, the inside of which should serve London for Catacombs: some such provision is grievously wanted for so huge a capitol. God bless you!

"R. S."

CHAPTER XXI.

CHANGES IN HIS POLITICAL OPINIONS—CAUSES WHICH MADE HIM A POLITICAL WRITER—HE IS REQUESTED TO GO TO LONDON TO CONFER WITH THE GOVERNMENT—REASONS FOR DECLINING TO DO SO—GLOOMY ANTICIPATIONS—MEASURES NECESSARY FOR PREVENTING A REVOLUTION—HE IS HATED BY THE RADICALS AND ANARCHISTS—THOUGHTS CONCERNING HIS SON'S DEATH—PLAN OF A WORK UPON THE STATE OF THE COUNTRY—PROPOSED REFORMS—EFFORT TO ASSIST HERBERT KNOWLES TO GO TO CAMBRIDGE—LETTER FROM HIM—HIS DEATH—FEARS OF A REVOLUTION—LITERARY EMPLOYMENT AND HOPES—SYMPATHY WITH A FRIEND'S DIFFICULTIES—MOTIVES FOR THANKFULNESS—MELANCHOLY FEELINGS—BLINDNESS OF MINISTERS.—1816.

THE cessation of the war, as it put an end to some of the great public interests which had for so long a time filled my father's thoughts and imagination, so left him more free to brood over a new class of subjects, not less important in themselves, and pressing, if possible, still more closely upon his personal hopes and fears. He viewed with great alarm the internal condition of England, and the danger arising from anarchical principles among the poor. Upon this subject, as we have seen, he had already written in the Quarterly Review, and his letters to Mr. Rickman have shown in brief some of his reflections. I conceive that no one who reads the records of his mind given in this work, can need be told that in all expressed opinions he was sincerity itself. That changes took place in his political views, no man was more ready to acknowledge; but they were not so many nor of such importance as has been fancied and pretended by his opponents. In his youth he was an abstract Republican, theoretically conceiving (I know not with what limitations) that men ought to be equal in government and rank, but practically caring very little for his own share in such things, leaving government to take care of itself, and devoting himself almost entirely to other pursuits. It is plain, from the whole course of the letters of his early life, that political discussion made no part of his every-day existence; and it is more than probable that, had he not been impelled by necessity to employ himself in periodical writings, after his first feverish enthusiasm had passed away, he would have continued tranquilly employed in his poetical or historical labors, and have left the field of politics to busier and more ambitious spirits than himself.

At a period much earlier than that which we are now speaking of, he had contracted a gloomy, misanthropical way of speaking, because circumstances had forced upon his unwilling mind the fact that human nature was not so good as he had fancied it—that, in short, men in general were not qualified to be worthy members of his Republic. Like many other ardent spirits, he had been dreaming of a *Respublica Platonis*, and, waking, he had found himself in *fæce Romuli*. In a letter of January, 1814, he says, "I was a Republican; I should be so still, if I thought we were advanced enough in civilization for such a form of society." His whole habit of mind was changed in the progress from youth to middle age; but on many of the details of political questions which occupied his pen, he can not be said to have undergone alteration, because they had not presented themselves at all to him during his youthful and enthusiastic state.

The thoughts which made him a political writer were roused wholly by a fear of revolution in England. This feeling was not an unnatural one. He was deeply impressed with the horrors of the French Revolution, and having contemplated the progress and operation in England of the same causes which had led to those horrors in France, he inferred that similar consequences must ensue at home, unless prompt measures were taken to avert them. He accordingly devoted himself to the task of using that power which he had obtained as a periodical writer for this object—a higher object could hardly be named—of exposing the evils in the social condition of the poor; of rousing his countrymen to acknowledge them; of patiently seeking out and suggesting, where practicable, the proper remedies: among the first and foremost of which may be named, the general education of the lower classes, based upon sound religious principles, of which he was one of the earliest and most active advocates.

As one of these evils which he wrote against was the incessant corrupting of men's minds by the revolutionary, the infidel, and the immoral part of the press, he unavoidably stirred up a host of enemies. But the work itself upon which he was engaged, taken as a whole, places him in the front rank of those who have labored for the benefit of mankind; and very many of the particular measures he labored to bring about are now generally acknowledged to be undoubted improvements. In uttering his sentiments, he was then, as we see, a leader of men in power instead of a follower; and in later days his services were amply acknowledged by men whose good opinion was praise indeed.

In the summer of this year (1816) a circumstance occurred which showed he had not written wholly in vain, and which, had he been less scrupulous, he might doubtless have turned to good account as respected his worldly circumstances, whatever might have been the effect upon his present comfort or his permanent reputation.

It appears that some of his papers in the Quarterly Review had attracted the especial notice of the ministry of that day, and a communication was privately made to him through various channels, and finally by Mr. Bedford, to the effect that Lord Liverpool wished to have an interview with him, for which purpose he was requested to go immediately to London.

This was certainly as high a compliment as could be paid to his powers as a political writer. He was, however, as the reader will see, too prudent hastily to catch at what most persons would have deemed a golden opportunity, and too independent to place himself unreservedly under the orders of the government. He was, indeed, ready enough, at any risk of unpopularity, to state the line of policy and the sort of measures he considered necessary at that time; but he preferred, like the bold Smith in "the Fair Maid of Perth," to "fight for his own hand;" and he took care not to afford the shadow of a foundation for those accusations which were often falsely brought against him, of "purchased principles and hireling advocacy."

To Grosvenor C. Bedford, Esq.

"Sept. 8, 1816.

"My Dear Grosvenor,

"I have seldom taken up a pen with so little knowledge of what was to proceed from it as on this occasion; for after sleeping upon your letters, and thinking on them, and breakfasting upon them, I am at a loss how to reply or how to act. If it be necessary, I will certainly go to London. Do you, after what I may say, talk with Herries, and determine whether it be so. * *

"It is very obvious that a sense of danger has occasioned this step. Look at my first Paper upon the Poor in the 16th Quarterly; had the ministry opened their eyes four years ago, had they seen what was passing before their eyes, the evil might then have been checked. The events of a successful war would have enabled them to pursue a vigorous policy at home. It will be more difficult now, and requires more courage. And less is to be done by administering antidotes than by preventing the distribution of the poison. Make, by all means, the utmost use of the press in directing the public opinion, but impose some curb upon its license, or all efforts will be in vain.

"In any way that may be thought desirable, I will do my best; but alas! Grosvenor, what *can* I do that I have not been doing? A journal with the same object in view as the Anti-Jacobin, but conducted upon better principles, might be of service. I could contribute to it from a distance. But to *you* it must be obvious, that as my head and hands are not, like Kehama's, multipliable at pleasure, I can exert myself only in one place at a time, and government would gain nothing by transferring me from the Quarterly to any thing else which they might be willing to launch. It may be said that the Q. R. is established; that this engine is at work, and will go on, and that it is desirable to have more engines than one. I admit this. * * * In short, whatever ought to be done I am ready to do, and to do it fearlessly. The best thing seems to write a small book or large pamphlet upon the state of the nation.

"In all this I see nothing which would require a change of residence; that measure would induce a great sacrifice of feeling, of comfort, and of expense, and draw on a heavily increased expenditure. They would provide for this; but in what manner? A man is easily provided for who is in a profession, or is capable of holding any official character; this is not my case. *

"You will understand that I will hasten to London if it be thought necessary, but that in my own calm judgment it is quite unnecessary, and I even believe that any conversation which the men in power might have with me would operate to my disadvantage. I should appear confused and visionary—an impracticable sort of man. On the whole, too, I do not think I *could* leave this country, where I am now, in a manner, attached to the soil by a sort of moral and intellectual serfage, which I could not break if I would, and would not if I could; and Edith is to be considered even more than myself.

"It is better that I should write either to you or Herries a letter to be shown, than that I should show myself. Good may undoubtedly be done by exposing the anarchists, and awakening the sound part of the country to a sense of their danger. This I can do; but it will be of no avail unless it be followed by effective measures. * * * * The immediate distress can best be alleviated by finding employment for the poor. * * * * I am very desirous that Mr. Owen's plan for employing paupers in agriculture should be tried: he writes like a madman, but his practice ought not to be confounded with his metaphysics; the experiment is worth trying. I do not doubt its success; and the consequences which he so foolishly anticipates will triumph should be regarded as the dreams of an enthusiast, not as reasons to deter government from the most plausible means of abolishing the poor-rates which has been (or in my judgment can be) proposed. I have seen Owen, and talked with him at great length.

"God bless you! R. S."

To John Rickman, Esq.

"Sept. 9, 1816.

"MY DEAR R.,

"About manufactures we shall not differ much, when we fully understand each other. I have no time now to explain; there are strangers coming to tea, and I seize the interval after dinner to say something relative to your prognostics—a subject which lies as heavy at my heart as any public concerns can do, for I fully and entirely partake your fears.*

"Four years ago I wrote in the Q. R. to explain the state of Jacobinism in the country, and with the hope of alarming the government. At present they are alarmed; they want to oppose pen to pen, and I have just been desired to go up to town and confer with Lord Liverpool. God help them, and is it come to this! It is well that the press should be employed in their favor; but if they rely upon influencing public opinion by such means, it becomes us rather to look abroad where we may rest our heads in safety, or to make ready for taking leave of them at home.

"I wish to avoid a conference which will only sink me in Lord Liverpool's judgment: what there may be in me is not payable at sight; give me leisure, and I feel my strength. So I shall write to Bedford (through whom, *via* Herries, the application has been made) such a letter as may be laid before him, and by this means I shall be able to state my opinion of the danger in broader terms than I could well do, perhaps, in conversation. The only remedy (if even that be not too late) is to check the press; and I offer myself to point out the necessity in a manner which may waken the sound part of the country from their sleep. My measures would be to make transportation the punishment for sedition, and to suspend the Habeas Corpus; and thus I would either have the anarchists under way for Botany Bay or in prison within a month after the meeting of Parliament. Irresolution will not do.

"I suppose that they will set up a sort of Anti-Jacobin journal, and desire me to write upon the state of the nation before the session opens. If they would but act as I will write—I mean as much in earnest and as fearlessly—the country would be saved, and I would stake my head upon the issue, which very possibly may be staked upon it without my consent.

"Of course no person knows of this application except my wife. By the time my letter (which will go to-morrow) can be answered, I shall be able to start for London, if it be still required. Most likely it will be. Meantime I should like to know your opinion of my views. They want you for their adviser. They who tremble must inevitably be lost. R. S."

To the Rev. James White.

"Keswick, Sept. 17, 1816.

"MY DEAR JAMES,

"Never, I entreat you, think it necessary to apologize for, or to explain any long interval of correspondence on your part, lest it should seem to require a like formality on mine, and make that be regarded in the irksome character of a debt which is only valuable in proportion as it is voluntary. We have both of us business always to stand in our excuse, nor can any excuses ever be needed between you and me. I thank you for your letter and your inquiries. Time is passing on, and it does its healing work slowly, but will do it effectually at last. As much as I was sensible of the happiness which I possessed, so much must I unavoidably feel the change which the privation of that happiness produces. My hopes and prospects in life are all altered, and my spirits never again can be what they have been. But I have a living faith, I am resigned to what is (if I know my own heart, truly and perfectly resigned), thankful for what has been, and happy in the sure and certain hope of what will be, when this scene of probation shall be over.

"I shall be glad to receive your communications upon the distresses of the manufacturers; they might probably have been of great use had they reached me when the last Quarterly was in the press. But I may, perhaps, still turn them to some account. There is another paper of mine upon the poor in the sixteenth number of the Quarterly, written when the Luddites, after their greatest outrages, seemed for a time to be quiet. In that paper I had recommended, as one means of employing hands that were out of work, the fitness of forming good foot-paths along the road side, wherever the nature of the soil was not such as to render it unnecessary. This was (foolish enough) cut out by the editor; but when the great object is to discover means of employing willing industry, the hint might be of some service wherever it is applicable. In the way of palliating an evil of which the roots lie deeper than has yet, perhaps, been stated, your efforts should be directed toward finding employment, and making the small wages that can be afforded go as far as possible; the reports of the Bettering Society show what may be done by saving the poor from the exactions of petty shop-keepers; and as winter approaches, great relief may be given by obtaining through the London Asso-

* "I am in a bad state of mind, sorely disgusted at the prevalence of that mock humanity, which is now becoming the instrument of dissolving all authority, government, and, I apprehend, human society itself. Again we shall have to go through chaos and all its stages. It is of no use to think, or to try to act for the benefit of mankind, while this agreeable poison is in full operation, as at present. I retire hopeless into my nut-shell till I am disturbed there, which will not be long if the humanity men prevail; the revolution will not, I expect, be less tremendous or less mischievous than that of France—the mock humanity being only a mode of exalting the majesty of the people, and putting all things into the power of the mob. I wish I may be wrong in my prognostics on this subject."—*J. R. to R. S., Sept.* 7, 1816.

ciation supplies of fish. Believe me, that person who should instruct the poor how to prepare cheap food in the most savory manner would confer upon them a benefit of the greatest importance, both to their comfort, health, and habits; for comforts produce good habits, unless there be a strong predisposition to evil. I have much yet to say upon this subject, which may, perhaps, furnish matter for a third paper in the Review. Sooner or later, I trust, we shall get the national schools placed upon a national establishment; this measure I shall never cease to recommend till it be effected.

"I believe I have never congratulated you on your emancipation from mathematics, and on your ordination. This latter event has placed you in an active situation; you have duties enough to perform, and no man who performs his duty conscientiously can be unhappy. He may endure distress of mind as well as of body, but under any imaginable suffering he may look on to the end with hope and with joy.

"Believe me, my dear James,
"Yours very truly,
"Robert Southey."

To Grosvenor C. Bedford, Esq.

"Keswick, Sept. 11, 1816.

"My dear Bedford,

"Upon mature deliberation, I am clearly of opinion that it would be very imprudent and impolitic for me to receive any thing in the nature of emolument from government at this time, in any shape whatsoever. Such a circumstance would lessen the worth of my services (I mean it would render them less serviceable), for whatever might come from me would be received with suspicion, which no means would be spared to excite. As it concerns myself personally, this ought to be of some weight; but it is entitled infinitely to greater consideration if you reflect how greatly my influence (whatever it may be) over a good part of the public would be diminished, if I were looked upon as a salaried writer. I must, therefore, in the most explicit and determined manner, decline all offers of this kind; but, at the same time, I repeat my offer to exert myself in any way that may be thought best. The whole fabric of social order* in this country is in great danger; the revolution, should it be effected, will not be less bloody nor less ferocious than it was in France. It *will* be effected unless vigorous measures be taken to arrest its progress; and I have the strongest motives, both of duty and prudence, say even self-preservation, for standing forward to oppose it. Let me write upon the State of Affairs (the freer I am the better I shall write), and let there be a weekly journal established, where the villainies and misrepresentations of the Anarchists and Malignants may be detected and exposed. But all will be in vain unless there be some check given to the licentiousness of the press, by one or two convictions, and an adequate (that is to say), an effectual punishment.

"It would be superfluous to assure you that, in declining any immediate remuneration, I act from no false pride or false delicacy. Proof enough of this is, that at first I was willing to accept it. But I feel convinced that it would (however undeservedly) discredit me with the public. Every effort, even now, is making to discredit me, as if I had sold myself for the laureateship. While I am as I am, these efforts recoil upon the enemy, and I even derive advantage from them. Do not argue that I suffer them to injure me if I refuse what might be offered me for fear of their censures. It is not their censures; it is the loss of ostensible independence, however really independent I should be. At present, in defiance of all that malignity can effect, I have a weight of character, and the rascals fear me while they hate me.

"God bless you! R. S."

To John Rickman, Esq.

"Sept. 20, 1816.

"My dear R.,

"If I am again desired to come to London, it will be very foolish, after the letters I have written. They are to this purport, to express my full opinion upon the real state of things, and expose the actual danger in broad terms; to recommend, as the only means of averting it, that the batteries which are now playing in breach upon the government be silenced; in other words, that the punishment for sedition be made such as to prevent a repetition of the offense. * * I have endeavored to make the necessity of these measures felt, and show that, for my own part, I can not be better employed any where than here; and that if it be thought advisable that I should either covertly or openly give up some time to political writing, it would counteract, in great measure, the effect of any thing, if I were to accept of any thing in shape of office or augmented pension. This, therefore, I have decidedly declined, but have offered to employ my pen zealously in recommendation and defense of vigorous measures. Should I therefore be again desired to visit London, my journey will pass as an ordinary occurrence, and nothing extraordinary will occur in it, except that I shall be introduced to some of the first officers of government instead of the second, to whom my acquaintance has hitherto been limited, and this may pass for a very natural occurrence. I can only repeat in conversation what I have already said in writing, and perhaps concur in arranging a journal, of which most certainly I will not undertake the management. That office is beneath me, and would require a sacrifice of character as well as time. The matter of danger is one which could not fail to present itself; and for that matter, I know very well what I have at stake in the event of a revolution, were the Hunts and Hazlitts to have the upper hand. There is no man whom the Whigs and the Anarchists hate more inveterately, because there is none whom

* What think you of a club of atheists meeting twice a week at an ale-house in Keswick, and the landlady of their way of thinking?—*To C. W. W. Wynn, Esq., Sept. 11, 1816.*

they fear so much. Nothing that I could do could increase the good disposition toward me, and it would be folly to dream of abating it. If the government will but act vigorously and promptly, all may yet be well; if they will not, I shall have no time to spare from my History of Brazil.

* * * * * * *

"I heartily wish you were in an *efficient* situation. Every thing may be done with foresight and intention; without them, every thing must go to ruin.

"God bless you! R. S."

To John Rickman, Esq.

"Keswick, Oct. 2, 1816.

"MY DEAR R.,

"I have received no further communication from Bedford, which is very well, as I must finish some few things, and rid my hands of them, before I set seriously to work in the good cause. Meantime the subject occupies my mind in all intervals of employment. * * I shall take a wide range; and I feel just now as if it were in my power to produce a work which, whatever might be its immediate effect, should be referred to hereafter as a faithful estimate of these times.

"Davy was here last week, and told me a valuable fact. A friend of his, who, applying philosophical knowledge to practical purposes, has turned manufacturer at Clitheroe, went abroad immediately after the peace, not to seek for orders, but to examine with his own eyes the state of the manufacturers on the Continent. He returned with a conviction that it was necessary to draw in; reduced his produce in time, and, in consequence, is doing well, while his neighbors are breaking all around. Certain it is that manufactures depending upon machinery advanced very rapidly during the last war. No prohibition or penalties, however severe, *can* prevent machinery and workmen from finding their way abroad; to this we must make up our mind, and it is better that it should be so. A little time sets these things to rights.

"I incline to think there will come a time when public opinion will no more tolerate the extreme of poverty in a large class of the community, than it now tolerates slavery in Europe. Meantime it is perfectly clear that the more we can improve the condition of the lower classes, the greater number of customers we procure for the home market; and that, if we can make people pay taxes instead of claiming poor-rates, the wealth as well as security of the state is increased. The poor-rates are a momentous subject, and I have long believed you were the only man who could grapple with it. I see, or think I see, palliatives and alteratives, in providing the laborers with garden and grass land, in establishing savings' banks, in national education, and in affording all possible facilities and encouragement for emigration, and in colonizing at home upon our waste lands.

"The state of the Church is another important question, assailed as it is on all sides. I think it would be possible to take in the Methodists as a sort of Cossacks, or certainly to employ those persons henceforward in aid of the Establishment, who, if not thus employed, will swell the numbers of the Methodists and act against it. There are no differences of doctrine in the way; it is but to let the license come from the clergyman instead of the magistrate, to invent some such name as coadjutor for those who have a 'call;' let them catechise the children, *convert* the women, reclaim the reprobates, and meet on week days, or at extra hours on Sundays in the church, to expound or sing psalms a little condescension, a little pay, and a little flattery.

"By nature I am a poet, by deliberate choice an historian, and a political writer I know not how—by accident, or the course of events. Yet I think I can do something toward awakening the country, and that I can obtain the confidence of well-disposed minds by writing honestly and sincerely upon things in which all persons are concerned.

"Were I to accept a good berth, which is held out to me, it would very much counteract the impression which I am aiming to produce. Instead of attempting to answer my arguments and assertions, the anarchists would then become the assailants, and attack me as one who had sold himself. God bless you! R. SOUTHEY."

To Grosvenor C. Bedford, Esq.

"Keswick, Oct. 5, 1816.

"MY DEAR GROSVENOR,

"I have not looked with impatience for further news from you, because, whatever news you might have to send, I must needs finish a paper in time for the present number—for the love of £100. I have no intention of going to London unless there be a necessity for it. Application was made to me, some months ago, to revise a great book by Raffles upon the Island of Java before it goes to press; I lent ear to it for the lucre of gain, but have heard nothing more. Had it come to any thing, it might have brought me to town in November; but if I could be as well employed, *quoad* money, at home (which seems likely), in other respects home employment would be better. I could wish myself independent of such considerations, if it were worth a wish as long as our necessities are supplied. It is my fate to have more claimants upon me than usually fall to the share of a man who has a family of his own; and if Tom's circumstances could be mended by a lift in his profession, it would be a relief to me as well as to him.

"That I shall make an appeal to the good sense of the country upon the existing state of things, and the prospect before us, is very likely, since my attention has been thus called to it. Indeed, if there be a probability of doing good, there seems little reason for any further stimulus, and the thing may be done certainly as well, and perhaps more becomingly, without any further intimation from the powers above. I incline at present to write anonymously, or under some fictitious name; for, were the book to attract notice (and if it does not it will be useless), a mystery about the author would very much increase its sale. In that case a change of publishers would contribute to keep the secret; and, if I seek a new one, Nicoll would obviously be the man. In meditating upon this work I grow ambitious, and think of presenting such a view of things as, whether it produce immediate benefit or not, may have a permanent value both for matter and composition.

"Pray inform me with the least possible delay whether, as P. L., I am exempt from serving parish offices, the people of Keswick having this day thrust honor upon me in the office of surveyor (what it means they best know); my appeal against the appointment must be made on the 12th of this month. Whatever the office be, I have neither knowledge, leisure, nor inclination for it.

"Abuse does good, and of that I have plenty· but praise is more useful, and is not so liberally bestowed. I have seen a number of the Champion, in which my name stands for text to a sermon nothing relating to me; but at the conclusion it is said that the change in my opinions, as implied in my last writings, is that I recommend implicit submission; hence it should appear that the said Champion had not read those writings. Hunt and Hazlitt, I know, incessantly attack me; this barking makes a noise, and noise calls attention; so that as long as they have it not in their power to pass sentence upon me as a counter-revolutionist, such enmity is in its degree useful.

"The children, thank God! are well, and so am I, as far as the husk is concerned; but the interior is as unlike what it was twelve months ago, as the darkest November day is unlike the bright sunshine of a genial May morning; and, whenever I relapse into recollections of what has been (and every hour brings with it something that calls up these thoughts), it is an effort to refrain from tears. I go about my business as usual, perform the ordinary functions of life, see company, go out visiting, take Nash up the mountains, talk, reason, jest, but my *heart*, meanwhile, is haunted; and though, thank God! I neither undervalue the uses of this world, nor wish in any way to shrink from my part in it, I could be right willing to say *Valete.*

"This is too deep a strain. Give me my cap and bells! * * * * * *

"Can you send me some money? I am *pauper et inops.* The next number will float me. I have a thousand things to say to you if you were here, and have planned many expeditions into the vales and up the mountains when next you come. Remember me to all at home. God bless you!

"R. SOUTHEY."

To John Rickman, Esq.

"Keswick, Nov. 20, 1816.

"MY DEAR R.,

" * * * * * * * *

About the poor I am very anxious to be informed thoroughly, and very sensible how deficient I am in the right sort of knowledge on this subject; that is, how the great evil is to be remedied—that of the poor-rates. My present views can reach no further than to the slow alterations and preventives, of good instruction in youth and encouragement to frugality and industry afterward by means of hope. Concerning immediate alleviations, I entirely agree with you in the great advantage of undertaking great public works, and stated it strongly some years ago in the first paper about the poor, which is in some respects better than the last, and which, if it had wrought duly upon the men in power, would have prevented all danger now. The anarchists felt its force, and for that reason have been spitting their venom at me ever since. * * *

"My scheme is something of this kind (but, though I am always long, even to dilatoriness, in planning whatever I write, the plan is very much altered in the course of execution): 1st. State in which the war has left us, political and moral. 2d. Necessity of that war, and Bonaparte drawn to the life, as the Perfect Emperor of the English friends of freedom. 3d. Sketch of the history of anarchical opinions in this country from Charles the First's time. Wilkes and Junius the root in modern times—the first fruit was the American war; the French Revolution the second. This leads to, 4th. A view of the united reformers, *i. e.*, the enemies of government, under their several classes; their modes of operation; their various plans of reform, and the sure consequences of each.

* * * * * * *

"All this will be well liked, and if I looked for favor it would be prudent to stop here; but it is not from any such motive that I put myself in the front of the battle. But here I wish to begin upon an exposure of the evils which exist in our state of society, and which it is the duty and interest of government, as far as possible, to mitigate and remove. Some things should be got rid of as matters of scandal. To destroy influence in elections would be neither wise if it were possible, nor possible if it were wise; but it is not fit that men should sell seats in Parliament, though very fit that they should be bought. I would have these bought openly, like commissions in the army, and the money applied to form a fund for public works, either national or provincial; a scandal is got rid of and a good produced, and the species of property which would be touched by it is one which ought not to have existed, as having always been contrary to positive law. I think, too, that the few great sinecures which still exist should be given up, and applied during the lives of the present incumbents to some purposes of public splendor, that they may give them up with a grace. I would also give members to the great towns which have none, restricting the voters by such qualifications as should, as far as may be, disqualify the mere mob. I would lay no stress on these things further than as depriving the anarchists of the only topics which give a shadow of plausibility to their harangues.

"The great evil is the state of the poor, which, with our press and our means of communication, constantly exposes us to the horrors of a *bellum servile*, and sooner or later, if not remedied, will end in one. * * * * * *

"There are also great evils in the delays of law, which are surely capable of remedy, and in the expense of criminal law. * * * A greater still in the condition of women; here we are upon your old ground; and passing from morals to religion, I think I could show how a great comprehension is practicable—that is, how the Church might employ those who would else be enlisted against her. And if there be a mode by which the tithes could be placed upon such a footing, or so commuted as to get rid of that perpetual cause of litigation, you are, of all men, most likely to point it out.

"One topic more, which is not introduced here in its proper place, may conclude this long outline. All professions, trades, and means of getting a livelihood among us are overstocked. We must create a new layer of customers at home by bettering the condition of the lower classes, and giving them more wants, with more means of gratifying them. We must extend establishments instead of diminishing them—more clergymen, more colleges, more courts of law; and, lastly, we must colonize upon the true principle of colonization, and cultivate every available acre at home. God bless you!

"Yours very truly, R. S."

To Grosvenor C. Bedford, Esq.

"Nov. 23, 1816.

"MY DEAR GROSVENOR,

"I want to raise £30 a year for four years from this time, and for this purpose:

"There is a lad at Richmond school (Yorkshire), by name Herbert Knowles, picked out from a humble situation for his genius (he has neither father nor mother), and sent to this school (a very excellent one) by Dr. Andrews, dean of Canterbury, and a clergyman, by name D'Oyle (so the name is written to me); if it should turn out to be D'Oyley, of the Bartlett's Building Society and the Quarterly, so much the better. From these and another clergyman he was promised £20 a year, his relations promised £30, and Tate the schoolmaster, a good and an able man, gave him the run of his school (more he could not do, for this valid reason, that he has a wife and ten children); so his boarding, &c., were to be provided for. The plan was, that when qualified here, he was to go as a sizar to St. John's; and this has been defeated by the inability of his relations to fulfill their engagements, owing to unforeseen circumstances, connected, I suppose, with the pressure of the times.

"In this state of things, Herbert Knowles, God help him! thought the sure way to help himself was to publish a poem. Accordingly, he writes one, and introduces himself by letter to me, requesting leave to dedicate it to my worship, if, upon perusal, I think it worthy, and so forth. Of course I represented to him the folly of such a scheme, but the poem is brimful of power and of promise. I have written to his master, and received the highest possible character of him both as to disposition and conduct; and now I want to secure for him that trifling assistance, which may put him in the right path, and give him at least a fair chance of rendering the talents, with which God has endowed him, useful to himself and beneficial to others.

"Of the £30 which are wanting for the purpose, I will give £10, and it is not for want of will that I do not supply the whole. Perhaps if you were to mention the circumstance to —— and to ——, it might not be necessary to go further. He must remain where he is till October next, and by that time will be qualified for St. John's. God bless you! R. S."

It does not appear that Mr. Bedford's applications were successful, and my father then applied to Mr. Rogers, with whose willingness to give assistance to struggling genius he was well acquainted, and who promptly and most kindly expressed his pleasure at this opportunity being afforded him, and also conveyed the promise of the third portion of the sum required from Lord Spencer, whose guest he chanced to be at the time my father's letter reached him. All difficulties now seemed removed, and the tidings were gladly communicated by my father to Herbert Knowles, whose grateful and sensible reply will, I think, not be deemed misplaced here.

Herbert Knowles to R. Southey, Esq.

"Gomersal, near Leeds, Dec. 28, 1816.

"MY DEAR SIR,

"I have duly received your two last letters, both of which have filled me with pleasure and gratitude, not so much for the solid advantage which your kindness affords and has obtained for me, as for the tender manifestation which it gives me of your concern for my welfare.

"And now, my dear sir, I will freely state to you my feelings and my sentiments at the present hour. Upon reading the Life of Kirke White, I was struck with surprise at the distinguished success which he met with at the University; and from his inordinate anxiety and immoderate exertions* to obtain it, I was insensibly led into

* I extract here the melancholy record of some of these exertions. "During his first term, one of the university scholarships became vacant; and Henry, young as he was in college, and almost self-taught, was advised by those who were best able to estimate his chance of success to offer himself as a competitor for it. He passed the whole term in preparing himself for this; reading for college subjects in bed, in his walks, or, as he says, where, when, and how he could; never having a moment to spare, and often going to his tutor without having read at all. His strength sunk under this; and though he had declared himself a candidate, he was compelled to decline: but this was not the only misfortune. The general college examination came on; he was utterly unprepared to meet it, and believed that a failure here would have ruined his prospects forever. He had only about a fortnight to read what other men had been the whole term reading. Once more he exerted himself beyond what his shattered health could bear; the disorder returned; and he went to his tutor, Mr. Catton, with tears in his eyes, and told him that he could not go into the hall to be examined. Mr. Catton, however, thought his success here of so much

the opinion, not that his success at college was considered as a *sine quâ non* for the benevolence of his patrons, but that that benevolence was given under the impression, and accompanied with the expectation, that he would make a corresponding compensation in the credit reflected upon them from his distinction at college.

"I will not deceive. If I thought the bounty of my friends was offered under the same impression, I would immediately decline it. Far be it from me to foster expectations which I feel I can not gratify. My constitution is not able to bear half the exertion under which Kirke White sunk; double those exertions would be insufficient to obtain before October next his attainments, or insure his success at St. John's. Two years ago I came to Richmond, totally ignorant of classical and mathematical literature. Out of that time, during three months and two long vacations, I have made but a retrograde course; during the remaining part of the time, having nothing to look forward to, I had nothing to exert myself for; and, wrapped in visionary thought, and immersed in cares and sorrows peculiarly my own, I was diverted from the regular pursuit of those qualifications which are requisite for University distinction. * * * * I need not say much more. If I enter into competition for University honors, I shall kill myself. Could I twine (to gratify my friends) a Laurel with the Cypress, I would not repine; but to sacrifice the little inward peace which the wreck of passion has left behind, and relinquish every hope of future excellence and future usefulness in one wild and *unavailing* pursuit, were indeed a madman's act, and worthy of a madman's fate.

"Yet will I not be idle; but, as far as health and strength allow, I will strive that my passage through the University, if not splendid, shall be respectable; and if it reflect no extraordinary credit on my benefactors, it will, I trust, incur them no disgrace.

* * * * * * *

"I am at a loss to convey to you the high sense I feel of your proffered kindness, and that of your friends. The common professions of gratitude all can use, and extraordinary ones are unnecessary. Suffice it, then, to say, *I thank you from my heart;* let time and my future conduct tell the rest.

"I know not how I should act with respect to Lord Spencer and Mr. Rogers. Will you direct me? Should I write to them? If so, will you give me their respective addresses? * * With the highest esteem for your character, profound veneration for your talents, and the warmest gratitude for your kindness, I have the honor to be,

"My dear sir, affectionately yours,

"HERBERT KNOWLES."

Alas! as in the case of Kirke White and young Dusautoy, the fair promise which high principle, talent, and good sense combined, seemed to hold forth, was blighted in the bud, and not two months from the date of this letter, Herbert Knowles was laid in his early grave. Too truly had he prognosticated that his feeble body and ardent mind could not have borne the requirements of hard study, for the mere excitement of his improved and now hopeful prospects seems to have hastened the close of a life which, we might suppose, under no circumstances, could have been a long one.

His kind friend, Mr. Tate, communicated the event to my father; and after speaking of him with the greatest affection, and saying that all that the kind attention of friends and medical skill could do, had been done, he adds, "But with ardor and genius, encouraged by the most flattering patronage, the stamina of his constitution could not support the anxious energies of such a mind; and before we were well aware of the danger that impended, the lamp was consumed by the fire which burned in it. * * * Poor Herbert had in prospect commenced his academical career. He died grateful to all his friends, and had longed for recovery the more earnestly, that he might redeem his unwilling silence by the expression of his gratitude."

To C. W. W. Wynn, Esq., M.P.

"Keswick, Dec. 7, 1816.

"MY DEAR WYNN,

" * * * * * * * Is there not something monstrous in taking such a subject as the Plague in a Great City?* Surely it is out-Germanizing the Germans. It is like bringing racks, wheels, and pincers upon the stage to excite pathos. No doubt but a very pathetic tragedy might be written upon "the Chamber of the Amputation," cutting for the stone, or the Cæsarean operation; but actual and tangible horrors do not belong to poetry. We do not exhibit George Barnwell upon the ladder to affect the gallery now, as was originally done; and the best picture of Apollo flaying Marsyas, or of the Martyrdom of St. Bartholomew, would be regarded as more disgusting than one of a slaughter-house or of a dissecting-room.

"What news to-morrow may bring of Monday's riots, God knows—the loss of some lives, I expect; and this I am sure of, that if government refrain much longer from exerting those means which are intrusted to it for the preservation of public security, the alternative will be, ere long, between revolution and a military system.

"Dec. 8, 1816.

"I am more sorry than surprised to see so many sailors in the mob. It has always been

importance, that he exhorted him, with all possible earnestness, to hold out the six days of the examination. Strong medicines were given him to enable him to support it, and he was pronounced the first man of his year. But life was the price which he was to pay for such honors as this; and Henry is not the first young man to whom such honors have proved fatal. He said to his most intimate friend, almost the last time he saw him, that were he to paint a picture of Fame crowning a distinguished under-graduate after the Senate-house examination, he would represent her as concealing a death's head under a mask of beauty."—*Remains of H. K. White*, vol. i., p. 46

* This allusion is to Wilson's "City of the Plague."

the custom to disband as many men as possible at the conclusion of a war, but there has been often a great cruelty in this, and in the present instance a great and glaring impolicy. The immediate cause of that distress which was felt in the beginning of the year, was an enormous diminution of the national expenditure; the war, a customer of fifty millions, being taken out of the market, and consequently, a great number of hands put out of employ. Now surely to spend less, and turn off more hands, is only an Irish way of remedying this.

"You, who know how much my thoughts have been led toward the subject, will not be surprised to hear that I am writing Observations upon the Moral and Political State of England. What I have at different times written in the Quarterly has sometimes been mutilated, and was always written under a certain degree of restraint to prevent mutilation. But I have heard of these things from many quarters, and seen that where the author was not suspected they have produced an impression. And I am disposed to think it not unlikely that I may do some present good, and almost certain that if the hope be disappointed for the present, it must sooner or later take effect. There is plenty of zeal in the country, and abundance of good intentions, which, if they were well directed, might be of infinite service. There are great and sore evils which may certainly be alleviated, if not removed; and there are dangers which we ought to look fairly in the face. I have nothing to hope or fear for myself, and the sole personal consideration that can influence me is the desire of acquitting myself at least of the sin of omission. Better that a candle should be blown out than that it should be placed under a bushel. Whether I am ripe in judgment must be for others to determine; this I know, that I am grown old at heart. I bore up under the freshness of my loss with surprising strength, and still carry a serene front; but it has changed me more than years of bodily disease could have done; and time enough has now elapsed to show how very little it will ever effect in restoring my former nature. It is a relief and a comfort to employ myself usefully, or at least in endeavoring to be useful. God bless you, my dear Wynn!

"Yours most affectionately, R. S."

To John May, Esq.

"Keswick, Jan. 1, 1817.

"My dear Friend,

"Your last letter gave me great and most unexpected concern. I had indeed believed that you were sailing on a quiet sea, in no danger of shoals or tempests. By what principle, or what strange want of principle, is it that mercantile men so often, for the sake of the shortest reprieve from bankruptcy, involve their nearest friends and connections with them? I write to you in a frame of mind which you will easily conceive, looking back upon the year which has just closed, and reflecting on the trials with which we have both been visited during its course. Your loss, I would fain hope, may not prove altogether so great as you apprehend; and I would hope also that some prize in the lottery of life, full of change as it is, may one day or other replace it. Even at the worst it leaves you heart-whole. It will be long before I shall find myself so; and if life had no duties, I should be very far from desiring its continuance for the sake of any enjoyments which it can possibly have in store. I have the same sort of feeling that a man who is fondly attached to his family has when absent from them—as if I were on a journey. I yearn, perhaps more than I ought to do, to be at home and at rest. Yet what abundant cause have I for thankfulness, possessing as I do so many blessings, that I should think no man could possibly be happier, if I had not been so much happier myself. Do not think that I give way to such feelings—far less that I encourage them, or am weak enough to repine. What is lost in possession is given me in hope. I am now in my forty-third year: both my parents died in their fiftieth. Should my lease be continued to that term, there is a fair prospect of leaving my family well provided for; and let it fall when it may, a decent provision is secured. Before this object was attained, great natural cheerfulness saved me from any anxiety on this score, and there happily exists no cause for anxiety when I have no longer the same preservative. My house is in order, and whenever the summons may come I am ready to depart. Dearly as I love these children, my presence is by no means so necessary as it was to him who is gone. He drew in his intellectual life from me, and a large portion of mine is departed with him. It is best as it is, for he is gone in the perfection of his nature, and mine will not be the worse for the chastening which it has undergone. Hitherto the lapse of time only makes me feel the depth of the wound. It will not be always thus. A few years (if they are in store for me) will alter the nature of my regret. I shall then be sensible how different a being Herbert, were he living, would be from the Herbert whom I have lost, and the voices and circumstances which now so forcibly recall him will have lost their power. Too much of this. But holidays are mournful days to persons in our situation, and the strong forefeeling which I have always experienced of such possibilities, has always made me dislike the observance of particular days. Your god-daughter is the only child whose birth-day I have not contrived to forget, and hers has been remembered from the accident of its being May-day. * * * *

"God bless you, my dear friend!

"Yours most affectionately,

"Robert Southey."

To Grosvenor C. Bedford, Esq.

"Keswick, Jan. 4, 1817.

"My dear Grosvenor,

"The Courier of to-night tells me I am elected member of the Royal Institute of Amsterdam. Now I put it to your feelings, Mr. Bedford, whether it be fitting that a man upon whom honor is thus thrust, should be without a decent pair of pantaloons to receive it in. Such, however, is my condition; and unless you can prevail upon the Grand Hyde to send me some new clothes without delay, I shall very shortly become a *sans culottes*, however unwilling Minerva may be. Moreover, I have promised to pay a visit at Netherhall* toward the end of this month, and I must therefore supplicate for the said clothes *in formâ pauperis*.

"The packet wherein this will be inclosed carries up the conclusion of a rousing paper for Gifford, which, with some omissions and some insertions, will be shaped into the two first chapters of my book. It will not surprise me if in some parts it should startle Gifford. Are the government besotted in security? or are they rendered absolutely helpless by fear, like a fascinated bird, that they suffer things to go on. Are they so stupid as not to know that their throats as well as their places are at stake? As for accelerating my movements for the sake of holding a conversation which would end in nothing, though I have little prudence to ballast my sails, I have enough to prevent me from that. All that I possibly can do I am doing, under a secret apprehension that it is more likely to bring personal danger upon myself than to rouse them to exertion; but for that, no matter: it is proper that the attempt should be made; the country will stand by them if they will stand by the country.

"Were I to see one of these personages, and he were to propose any thing specific, it would probably be some scheme of conducting a journal *à la mode* the Anti-Jacobin. This is no work for me. They may find men who will like it, and are fitter for it.

"I think of being in town in April, *si possum*. My book, peradventure, may be ready by that time; but there is a large field before me, and many weighty subjects. Meantime, though I want nothing for myself, and certainly would not at this time accept of any thing, I should nevertheless be very glad if they would remember that I have a brother in the navy. God bless you! R. S."

CHAPTER XXII.

SURREPTITIOUS PUBLICATION OF WAT TYLER—CONSEQUENT PROCEEDINGS—IS ATTACKED IN THE HOUSE OF COMMONS BY WILLIAM SMITH—OFFER OF A LUCRATIVE APPOINTMENT CONNECTED WITH THE TIMES NEWSPAPER—TOUR IN SWITZERLAND—LETTERS FROM THENCE—ACCOUNT OF PESTALOZZI—OF FELLENBERG—IMPRESSIONS OF THE ENGLISH LAKES ON HIS RETURN—HIGH OPINION OF NEVILLE WHITE—NORFOLK SCENERY—SPECULATIONS ON ANOTHER LIFE—LIFE OF WESLEY IN PROGRESS—CURIOUS NEWS FROM THE NORTH POLE—LINES ON THE DEATH OF THE PRINCESS CHARLOTTE—CURE FOR THE BITE OF SNAKES.—1817.

My father's acceptance of the office of poet laureate, together with his writings in the Quarterly Review, had drawn down upon him no small measure of hostility from that party whose opinions assimilated to those he had formerly held. Acknowledged by friends and foes to be a powerful writer, and by his own admission apt to express himself bitterly upon subjects of moral and political importance, they could not endure that he who in early youth had advocated Republican principles, should have outgrown and outlived them, and now, in the maturity of his judgment, bring his active mind and busy pen to the strenuous support of existing institutions.

It seems, indeed, that high as party spirit often runs now, it boiled up in those days with a far fiercer current. The preceding quarter of a century had been one of continued excitement—commenced by the French Revolution, kept up by the long war, and more recently renewed by its glorious termination. A large party in the country seemed imbued with what, to speak tenderly, must be called an un-English spirit: they would have been glad if their prognostications of Bonaparte's invincibility had been realized. "The wish was father to the thought;" and it can hardly be supposed they would have grieved if the imperial eagle had been planted a second time upon the shores of Britain.

Such was Hazlitt, whom even Mr. Justice Talfourd's kindly pen describes as "staggering under the blow of Waterloo;"* and as "hardly able to forgive the valor of the conquerors." Such my father's friend, William Taylor of Norwich, who calls it "a victory justly admired, but not in its tendency and consequences satisfactory to a cosmopolite philosophy;" and says that "Liberty, toleration, and art have rather reason to bewail than to rejoice" at the presence "of trophies oppressive to the interests of mankind."†

Neither is it difficult to imagine with what views such persons must have regarded all those questions upon which my father's pen was most frequently employed; and to many of them his writings were peculiarly obnoxious, both as reminding them unpleasantly that "they had spoken a lying divination," and also as boldly enunciating those principles which they were endeavoring with heart and soul to undermine and destroy.

Moved, doubtless, by some feelings of the kind, an attempt was now made by certain persons (and eagerly taken up by others) to annoy and injure him, which need only to be related to characterize itself, without requiring the use of strong language on my part—an attempt, the chief effect of which was to increase his notoriety more than any other event in his whole life.

It appears that in the summer of 1794, when in his twenty-first year, he had thrown off, in a moment of fiery democracy, a dramatic sketch, entitled Wat Tyler, in which, as might be expected from the subject, the most leveling sentiments were put into the mouths of the *dramatis personæ*.

* The seat of his friend Humphrey Senhouse, Esq.

* Final Memorials of Charles Lamb, vol. ii., p. 130.

† Memoirs of William Taylor of Norwich, vol. ii., p 461.

The MS. of this production was taken up to town by his brother-in-law, Mr. Lovel, and placed in a bookseller's hands, Ridgeway by name; and my father happening to go up to town shortly afterward, called upon this person, then in Newgate, and he and a Mr. Symonds agreed to publish it anonymously. There was also present in Ridgeway's apartment a Dissenting minister, by name Winterbottom.

It seems, however, that this intention was quickly laid aside, for no proofs were ever sent to my father; and "acquiescing readily in their cooler opinion," he made no inquiries concerning the poem, and took so little thought about it as not even to reclaim the MS.; indeed, the whole circumstance, even at the time, occupied so little of his thoughts, that I have not been able to find the slightest allusion to it in his early letters,* numerous and wholly unreserved in expression as have been those which have passed through my hands.

In the spring of this year (1817), to my father's utter astonishment, was advertised as just published, Wat Tyler, by Robert Southey; the time having been seized for doing so, when the opinions it contained could be most strongly contrasted with those the writer then held and advocated, and when the popular feeling† was exactly in that state in which such opinions were likely to be productive of the greatest mischief.

The first step taken in the matter, with the advice of his friends, was to reclaim his property, and to apply for an injunction against the publisher. The circumstances connected with this, and the manner in which the application was defeated, will be found in the following letters.

To Grosvenor C. Bedford, Esq.

"Keswick, Feb. 15, 1817.

"MY DEAR G.,

"Do you remember that twenty years ago a letter, directed for me at your house, was carried to a paper-hanger of my name in Bedford Street, and the man found me out, and put his card into my hand? Upon the strength of this acquaintance, I have now a letter from this poor namesake, soliciting charity, and describing himself and his family as in the very depths of human misery. This is not the only proof I have had of a strange opinion that I am overflowing with riches. Poor wretched man, what can I do for him! However, I do not like to shut my ears and my heart to a tale of this kind. Send him, I pray you, a two-pound note in my name, to No. 10 Hercules Buildings, Lambeth; your servant had better take it, for fear he should have been sent to the work-house before this time. When I come to town, I will seek about if any thing can be done for him.

"I wrote to Wynn last night to consult him about Wat Tyler, telling him all the circumstances, and desiring him, if it be best to procure an injunction, to send the letter to Turner, and desire him to act for me. Three-and-twenty years ago the MS. was put into Ridgeway's hands, who promised to publish it then (anonymously, unless I am very much mistaken), and from that time to this I never heard of it. There was no other copy in existence except the original scrawl, which is now lying up stairs in an old trunk full of papers. I wish the attorney-general would prosecute the publisher for sedition; this I really should enjoy. Happy are they who have no worse sins of their youth to rise in judgment against them.

"Government are acting like themselves. Could I say any thing more severe? They should have begun with vigor and rigor; and then, when they had the victory, have made their sacrifices *ex proprio motu*, with a good grace. But they ought not, on any account, to have touched the official salaries—a thing unjust and unwise, which, instead of currying favor for them with the rabble, will make them despised for their pusillanimity. I have neither pity nor patience for them. Was ever paper used like this last article has been to please them! They have absolutely cut it down to their own exact measure; every thing useful is gone, and every thing original; whatever had most force in it was sure to be struck out. Of all the practical measures upon which I touched, one only has escaped, and that because it comes in as if by accident—the hint about transportation for sedition. If we come out of this confusion without an utter overthrow, it will be as we escaped the gunpowder plot—not by any aid of human wisdom, and God knows we have no right to calculate upon miracles. The prospect is very dismal; and it is provoking to think that nothing is wanting to secure us but foresight and courage; but of what use is railing, or advising, or taking thought for such things? I am only a passenger; the officers must look to the ship; if she is lost, the fault rests with them. I have nothing to answer for, and must take my share in the wreck with patience.

"Murray offers me a thousand guineas for my intended poem in blank verse, and begs it may not be a line longer than Thomson's Seasons!! I rather think the poem will be a post-obit, and in that case twice that sum, at least, may be demanded for it. What his real feelings toward

* In of the reviews of the first volume of this work, it is remarked (naturally enough) as strange that Wat Tyler is not mentioned in the account of his Oxford life, when it was written. My reason for the omission was, that there being no mention of it in the papers or letters relating to that period, its history seemed properly to belong to the time of its surreptitious publication; especially as, had it not been so published, its very existence would never have been known.

† As a proof how well the movers in this business had calculated both the mischief the publication, at such a time, was likely to do, and the annoyance it would probably give my father, I may quote the following letter, in which a play-bill of Wat Tyler was inclosed:

To Robert Southey, Esq., Poet Laureate and Pensioner of Great Britain.

"Whittington, July 11, 1817.

"SIR,

"Your truly patriotic and enlightened poem of *Wat Tyler* was last night presented to a most respectable and crowded audience here, with cordial applause; nor was there a soul in the theater but as cordially lamented the sudden deterioration of your principles, intellectual and moral, whatever might have been the cause thereof.

"Yours, JACK STRAW."

me may be, I can not tell; but he is a happy fellow, living in the light of his own glory. The Review is the greatest of all works, and it is all his own creation; he prints 10,000, and fifty times ten thousand read its contents, in the East and in the West. Joy be with him and his journal.

"It is really amusing to see how the rascals attack me about the court, as if I were a regular courtier, punctual in attendance, perfect in flattery, and enjoying all that favor, for the slightest portion of which these very rascals would sell their souls, if they had any. Malice never aimed at a less vulnerable mark.

"God bless you! R. S."

"Longman has just sent me the Resurrection of Sedition. The verses are better than I expected to find them, which I think you will allow to be a cool philosophical remark."

To Messrs. Longman and Co.

"Keswick, Feb. 15, 1817.

"Dear Sirs,

"There is, unluckily, a very sufficient reason for not disclaiming Wat Tyler—which is, that I wrote it three-and-twenty years ago.

"It was the work, or rather the sport, of a week in the summer of 1794: poor Lovel took it to London, and put it into Ridgeway's hands, who was then in Newgate. Some weeks afterward I went to London and saw Ridgeway about it; Symonds was with him, and they agreed to publish it (I believe, or rather I am *sure*, the publication was to have been anonymous), and what remuneration I was to have was left to themselves, as dependent upon the sale. This was the substance of our conversation, for nothing but words passed between us. From that time till the present, I never heard of the work: they, of course, upon better judgment, thought it better left alone; and I, with the carelessness of a man who has never thought of consequences, made no inquiry for the manuscript. How it has got to the press, or by whose means, I know not.

"The motive for publication is sufficiently plain. But the editor, whoever he may be, has very much mistaken his man. In those times and at that age, and in the circumstances wherein I was placed, it was just as natural that I should be a Republican, and as proper, as that now, with the same feelings, the same principles, and the same integrity, when three-and-twenty years have added so much to the experience of mankind, as well as matured my own individual intellect, I should think revolution the greatest of all calamities, and believe that the best way of ameliorating the condition of the people is through the established institutions of the country.

"The booksellers must be disreputable men, or they would not have published a work under such circumstances. I just feel sufficient anger to wish that they may be prosecuted for sedition.

"I would write to Turner, if my table were not at this time covered with letters; perhaps, if you see him, you will ask his opinion upon the matter—whether it be better to interfere, or let it take its course.

"Yours very truly, R. Southey."

To C. H. Townshend, Esq.

"Keswick, Feb. 16, 1817.

"My dear Chauncey,

"If there be any evil connected with poetry, it is that it tends to make us too little masters of ourselves, and counteracts that stoicism, or necessary habit of self-control, of which all of us must sometimes stand in need. I do not mean as to our actions, for there is no danger that a man of good principles should ever feel his inclination and his duty altogether at variance. But as to our feelings. You talk of mourning the loss of your trees, and not enduring to walk where you were wont to see them. I can understand this, and I remember when I was little more than your age saying that

"'He who does not sometimes wake
And weep at midnight, is an instrument
Of Nature's common work;'

but the less of this the better. We stand in need of all that fortitude can do for us in this changeful world, and the tears are running down my cheeks when I tell you so.

"Thomas Clarkson I know well: his book upon Quakerism keeps out of sight all the darker parts of the picture; their littleness of mind, their incorrigible bigotry, and their more than popish interference with the freedom of private actions. Have you read his history of the Abolition of the Slave Trade? I have *heard* it from his own lips, and never was a more interesting story than that of his personal feelings and exertions. I have happened in the course of my life to know three men, each wholly possessed with a single object of paramount importance—Clarkson, Dr. Bell, and Owen of Lanark, whom I have only lately known. Such men are not only eminently useful, but eminently happy also; they live in an atmosphere of their own, which must be more like that of the third heaven than of this every-day earth upon which we toil and moil.

"I am very ill pleased with public proceedings. The present ministry are deficient in every thing except good intentions; and their opponents are deficient in that also. These resignations ought to have been made during the pressure of war, uncalled for, when they would have purchased popularity. They come now like miserable concessions forced from cowardice, and reap nothing but contempt and insult for their reward. Nor ought they at any time to have resigned part of their *official* appointments, because the appointments of office are in every instance inadequate to its expenses, in the higher departments of state. They should take money from the sinking fund, and employ it upon public works, or *lend* it for private ones, stimulating individual industry by assisting it with capital, and thus finding work for idle hands, and food for necessitous families. From the same funds they should purchase waste lands, and enable speculators and industrious poor to *colonize* them; the property of the lands remaining in the nation, as a source of certain revenue, improving in proportion to the prosperity of the country.

"God bless you!

"Your affectionate friend, R. S."

To Grosvenor C. Bedford, Esq.

"Feb. 19, 1817.

"MY DEAR GROSVENOR,

"This poor wretched paper-hanger* has sent me another letter, because I did not reply to his first. Men are too prone to take offense at importunity, finding anger a less uncomfortable emotion than pity; this indeed it is; and for that reason I scold my wife and my children when they hurt themselves. As to this unhappy man, I hope you have sent him the two pounds; it will do him very little good, but it is really as much as I can afford to give him for the sake of the name, and a great deal more than I ever got by it.

"The tide seems to be turning, and if government will but check the press they would soon right themselves. In this part of the country I hear that travelers (the bagmen) collect their money more easily than on their last rounds, and receive more orders. A fellow was selling Cobbett's twopenny Register and other such things at Rydal the other day; he was, or appeared to be, a sailor, and his story was that he was going to Whitehaven, and a gentleman had given him these to support himself on the road by selling them.

"In grief and in uneasiness I have often caught myself examining my own sensations, as if the intellectual part could separate itself from that in which the affections predominate, and stand aloof and contemplate it as a surgeon does the sufferings of a patient during an operation. This I have observed in the severest sorrows that have ever befallen me, but it in no degree lessens the suffering; and whenever I may have any serious malady, this habit, do what I may to subdue it, will tend materially to impede or prevent recovery. But in petty vexations it has its use. I was more vexed than I ought to have been about this publication of Wat Tyler; for, though I shook off the first thoughts, or, rather, immediately began to consider it in the right point of view as a thing utterly unimportant, still there was an uneasiness working like yeast in my abdomen, and my sleep was disturbed by it for two nights; by that time it had spent itself, and I should now think nothing more about it if it were not necessary to determine how to act. Wynn will find the thing more full of fire and brimstone, perhaps, than he imagines; and yet, perhaps, the wiser way will be not to notice it, but let it pass as a squib. Indeed, I could laugh about it with any person who was disposed to laugh with me. I shall hear from him again to-morrow, and probably shall receive a letter from Turner by the same post. Turner has a cool, clear head; I have very little doubt that they will coincide in their opinion, and, be it what it may, I shall act accordingly. God bless you!

"R. S."

To Sharon Turner, Esq.

"Keswick, Feb. 24, 1817.

"MY DEAR TURNER,

"My brother has written to dissuade me strongly from proceeding in this business. My own opinion is, that if I do not act now, the men who have published the work will compel me to do so at last, by inserting my name in such a manner as to render the measure unavoidable. Indeed it was inserted as a paragraph in the Chronicle, which I suppose they paid for as an advertisement. Therefore I think it best to take the short and open course, believing that in most cases such courses are the best. However, I have sent Harry's letter to Wynn, and, if his arguments convince him, have desired him to let you know. This was done yesterday, and if you have not heard from him before this reaches you, it may be concluded that he thinks it best to proceed. I suppose there can be no doubt of obtaining the injunction. The statement is perfectly accurate; I know not whether it be of any use to let you know that at the time the transaction took place I was under age. I was just twenty when the poem was written, and saw these booksellers about four months afterward.

"I fully assent to what you say concerning political discussions, and intermeddle with them no further than as they are connected not only with the future good, but, as appears to me, with the immediate safety of society. It is not for any men, or set of men, that I am interested, nor for any particular measures. But with regard to the fearful aspect of these times, you may perhaps have traced the ground of my apprehensions in Espriella, in the Edinburgh Register, and in the Quarterly, more especially in a paper upon the Poor about four years ago. It is now come to this question, Can we educate the people in moral and religious habits, and better the condition of the poor, so as to secure ourselves from a mob-revolution; or has this duty been neglected so long, that the punishment will overtake us before this only remediable means can take effect? The papers which I shall write upon the real evils of society will, I hope, work for posterity, and not be wholly forgotten by it; they proceed from a sense of duty, and, that duty discharged, I shall gladly retire into other ages, and give all my studies to the past and all my hopes to the future.

"My spirits, rather than my disposition, have undergone a great change. They used to be exuberant beyond those of almost every other person; my heart seemed to possess a perpetual fountain of hilarity; no circumstances of study, or atmosphere, or solitude affected it; and the ordinary vexations and cares of life, even when they showered upon me, fell off like hail from a pent-house. That spring is dried up; I can not now preserve an appearance of serenity at all times without an effort. and no prospect in this

* See *antè*, p. 347.

world delights me except that of the next. My heart and my hopes are there.

"I have a scheme to throw out somewhere for taking the Methodists into the Church, or borrowing from Methodism so much of it as is good, and thereby regenerating the Establishment. There is little hope in such schemes, except that in process of time they may produce some effect. But were it effected now, and would the Church accept the volunteer services of lay coadjutors, I should feel strongly inclined to volunteer mine. This is a dream, and I fear the whole fabric will fall to pieces even in our days.

"Believe me,

"Yours with affection and esteem,

"ROBERT SOUTHEY."

To the Rev. Herbert Hill.

"Keswick, Feb. 28, 1817.

"MY DEAR UNCLE,

"Your copies of Brazil are, I hope, by this time delivered at the doctor's, and in a day or two I shall send the third volume to the press; for if I should only get through a single chapter before my journey, it will be so much gained. My movements will be upon a wide scale. I purpose to start for London the second week in April, and, if you are then in Hampshire, to run down to you for a week, as soon as I have rested myself, and shaken hands with Bedford and Rickman; and on May-day, or as soon after as my companions can be ready, I start with Senhouse to Netherhall, and my former *compagnon de voyage*, Nash, for the Continent. From six weeks to two months is to be the length of our furlough, during which we mean to get as far as Lago Maggiore and Milan, back over the Alps a second time, and, seeing as much as we can of Switzerland, to return by way of the Rhine, and reach home as early as possible in July.

"I learn from to-day's Courier that Brougham attacked me in the House of Commons. I hope this affair will give no friend of mine any more vexation than it does me. Immediately upon seeing the book advertised, I wrote to Wynn and to Turner, giving them the whole facts, and proposing to obtain an injunction in Chancery. How they will determine I do not know. Perhaps, as Brougham has thus given full publicity to the thing, they may not think it advisable to proceed, but let it rest, considering it, as it really is, of no importance. Men of this stamp, who live in the perpetual fever of faction, are as little capable of disturbing my tranquillity as they are of understanding it.

"I have just finished the notes and preface to the Morte d'Arthur, a thing well paid for. For the next Quarterly, I have to review Mariner's Tonga Islands (including a good word for our friend the captain*), and to write upon the Report of the Secret Committees; but I shall fly from the text, and, saying as little as may be upon the present, examine what are the causes which make men discontented in this country, and what the means which may tend to heal this foul gangrene in the body politic. Never was any paper so emasculated as my last; and yet it was impossible to resent it, for it was done in compassion to the weakness, the embarrassment, and the fears of the ministry. They express themselves much indebted to me. In reply to their intimations of a desire to show their sense of this, I have pressed a wish that Tom be remembered when there is a promotion in the navy. For myself, I want nothing, nor would I, indeed, accept any thing. They give me credit for a reasonable share of foresight, and perhaps wish that my advice had been taken four years ago.

"God bless you! R. S."

* Captain, afterward Admiral, Burney, who published a collection of voyages in the South Seas.

It was now decided, upon the advice of his legal friends, that application should be made to the Court of Chancery* for an injunction to restrain the publication of Wat Tyler. This was done, but without success, upon the singular ground that as the work was calculated to do an injury to society, the author could not reclaim his property in it. This, which would seem a just decision in the case of the *piracy* of an immoral, blasphemous, or seditious work, applies very differently in the case of a publication, set forth without the consent or knowledge of the author, and apparently gives liberty to any scoundrel to plunder a man's writing-desk, and send forth to the public any chance squibs he may have thrown off in an idle hour for the amusement of his friends.

These fellows must have reaped a rich harvest by their roguery, 60,000 copies being said to have been sold at the time.

To the Editor of the Courier.

"In Courier, March 17, 1817.

"SIR,

"Allow me a place in your columns for my 'last words' concerning Wat Tyler.

"In the year 1794, this manuscript was placed by a friend of mine (long since deceased) in Mr. Ridgeway's hands. Being shortly afterward in London myself for a few days, I called on Mr.

* The following was Lord Eldon's judgment upon this case: "I have looked into all the affidavits and have read the book itself. The bill goes the length of stating that the work was composed by Mr. Southey in the year 1794; that it is his own production, and that it has been published by the defendants without his sanction or authority; and, therefore, seeking an account of the profits which have arisen from, and an injunction to restrain, the publication. I have examined the cases that I have been able to meet with containing precedents for injunctions of this nature, and I find that they all proceed upon the ground of a title to the property in the plaintiff. On this head a distinction has been taken to which a considerable weight of authority attaches, supported as it is by the opinion of Lord Chief-justice Eyre, who has expressly laid it down, that a person can not recover in damages for a work which is in its nature calculated to do an injury to the public. Upon the same principle, this court refused an injunction in the case of Walcot (Peter Pinder) v. Walker, inasmuch as he could not have recovered damages in an action. After the fullest consideration, I remain of the same opinion as that which I entertained in deciding the cases referred to. Taking all the circumstances into my consideration, it appears to me that I can not grant this injunction until after Mr. Southey shall have established his right to the property by action." Injunction refused.

Ridgeway, in Newgate, and he and Mr. Symonds agreed to publish it. I understood that they had changed their intention, because no proof-sheet was sent to me, and, acquiescing readily in their cooler opinion, made no inquiry concerning it. More than two years elapsed before I revisited London; and then, if I had thought of the manuscript, it would have appeared a thing of too little consequence to take the trouble of claiming it for the mere purpose of throwing it behind the fire. That it might be published surreptitiously at any future time, was a wickedness of which I never dreamed.

"To these facts I have made oath. Mr. Winterbottom, a Dissenting minister, has sworn, on the contrary, that Messrs. Ridgeway and Symonds having declined the publication, it was undertaken by himself and Daniel Isaac Eaton; that I *gave* them the copy as their own property, and gave them, moreover, a fraternal embrace, in gratitude for their gracious acceptance of it; and that he, the said Winterbottom, verily believed he had a right *now*, after an interval of three-and-twenty years, to publish it as his own.

"My recollection is perfectly distinct, notwithstanding the lapse of time; and it was likely to be so, as I was never, on any other occasion, within the walls of Newgate. The work had been delivered to Mr. Ridgeway; it was for him that I inquired, and into his apartments I was shown. There I saw Mr. Symonds, and there I saw Mr. Winterbottom also, whom I knew to be a Dissenting minister. *I never saw Daniel Isaac Eaton in my life;* and as for the story of the embrace, every person who knows my disposition and manners will at once perceive it to be an impudent falsehood. Two other persons came into the room while I was there; the name of the one was Lloyd—I believe he had been an officer in the army; that of the other was Barrow. I remembered him a bishop's boy at Westminster. I left the room with an assurance that Messrs. Ridgeway and Symonds were to be the publishers; in what way Winterbottom might be connected with them, I neither knew nor cared, and *Eaton I never saw.* There is no earthly balance in which oaths can be weighed against each other; but character is something in the scale; and it is perfectly in character that the man who has published Wat Tyler under the present circumstances, should swear—as Mr. Winterbottom has sworn.

"Thus much concerning the facts. As to the work itself, I am desirous that my feelings should neither be misrepresented nor misunderstood. It contains the statement of opinions which I have long outgrown, and which are stated more broadly because of this dramatic form. Were there a sentiment or an expression which bordered upon irreligion or impurity, I should look upon it with shame and contrition; but I can feel neither for opinions of universal equality, taken up as they were conscientiously in early youth, acted upon in disregard of all worldly considerations, and left behind me in the same straightforward course as I advanced in years. The piece was written when such opinions, or rather such hopes and fears, were confined to a very small number of the educated classes; when those who were deemed Republicans were exposed to personal danger from the populace; and when a spirit of anti-Jacobinism prevailed, which I can not characterize better than by saying that it was as blind and as intolerant as the Jacobinism of the present day. The times have changed. Had it been published surreptitiously under any other political circumstances, I should have suffered it to take its course, in full confidence that it would do no harm, and would be speedily forgotten as it deserved. The present state of things, which is such as to make it doubtful whether the publisher be not as much actuated by public mischief as by private malignity, rendered it my duty to appeal for justice, and stop the circulation of what no man had a right to publish. And this I did, not as one ashamed and penitent for having expressed crude opinions and warm feelings in his youth (feelings right in themselves, and wrong only in their direction), but as a man whose life has been such that it may set slander at defiance, and who is unremittingly endeavoring to deserve well of his country and of mankind. ROBERT SOUTHEY."

A letter addressed by Mr. Foster to Mr. Cottle, and published by him in his Reminiscences of Coleridge and Southey,* rather involves the matter in more difficulty than explains it.

"I wonder if Mr. Southey ever did get at the secret history of that affair. The story, as I heard it, was, that Southey visited Winterbottom in prison, and, just as a token of kindness, gave him the MS. of Wat Tyler. It was no fault of Winterbottom that it was published. On a visit to some friends at Worcester, he had the piece with him, meaning, I suppose, to afford them a little amusement at Southey's expense, he being held in great reproach and even contempt as a turn-coat. At the house where Winterbottom was visiting, two persons, keeping the piece in their reach at bedtime, sat up all night transcribing it, of course giving him no hint of the maneuver. This information I had from one of the two operators."

My father distinctly states he did not *give* the MS. to any body, and that he did not put it into Winterbottom's hands *at all.* But even if it had been so, how came Winterbottom to appear in court, and justify the publication upon oath, if the circumstances were as Mr. Foster relates?

It might have been supposed, that, with the proceedings before the lord chancellor, the matter would have ended; that the surreptitious publication of the crude and hasty production of a youth of twenty, long since forgotten by the writer, would hardly have been deemed worthy the attention of the public, especially as he had never concealed or suppressed his former opinions, which stood plainly on record in his early published works.

* P. 235.

But the opportunity was too tempting to be lost, and the subject was twice brought forward in Parliament—once by Mr. Brougham, the second time by William Smith, the member for Norwich, who, arming himself for the occasion with Wat Tyler in one pocket and the Quarterly Review in the other, stood forth in the House of Commons to contrast their contents.

In reply to this attack,* which was answered at the time by Mr. Wynn, my father published a letter to William Smith, defending himself against the charges brought against him, and stating his past and present opinions, and his views as to the condition of the country and the measures most likely to promote the welfare of the community. This letter, with the remarks that called it forth, will be found at the end of this volume, where I think it right to place it, as, from my father's reprinting it in his Essays, it appears plainly that he intended it should be preserved, and as the history of Wat Tyler is incomplete without it.

To Humphrey Senhouse, Esq.

"Keswick, March 22, 1817.

"My dear Senhouse,

"You see I am flourishing in the newspapers as much as Joanna Southcote did before her expected accouchement; and I have not flourished in Chancery,† because a Presbyterian parson has made oath that I gave the MSS. to him and to another person whom I never saw in my life. There is no standing against perjury, and therefore it is useless to pursue the affair into a court of law. I have addressed two brief letters to William Smith in the Courier, and there the matter will end on my part, unless he replies to them. In the second of those letters you will see the history of Wat Tyler, as far as it was needful to state it. There was no occasion for stating that about a year after it was written I thought of making a serious historical drama upon the same subject, which would have been on the side of the mob in its main feelings, but in a very different way; and, indeed, under the same circumstances, I should have brained a tax-gatherer just as he did. The *refaccimento* proceeded only some fifty or threescore lines, of which I only remember this short passage, part of it having been transplanted into Madoc. Some one has been saying, *a plague on time!* in reference to Tyler's gloomy state of mind, to which he replies,

"'Gently on man doth gentle Nature lay
The weight of years; and even when over-laden
He little likes to lay the burden down.
A plague on care, I say, that makes the heart
Grow old before its time.'

"Had it been continued, it might have stood beside Joan of Arc, and perhaps I should have become a dramatic writer. But Joan of Arc left me no time for it then, and it was dismissed, as I supposed, forever from my thoughts. I hear that in consequence of this affair, and of the effect which that paper in the Quarterly produced, Murray has printed two thousand additional copies of the number; and yet the paper has been dismally mutilated of its best passages and of some essential parts. I shall have a second part in the next number to follow up the blow.

"My fear is that when commerce recovers, as it presently will, government should suppose that the danger is over, and think that the disease is removed because the fit is past. There are some excellent remarks in Coleridge's second lay sermon upon the overbalance of the commercial spirit, that greediness of gain among all ranks to which I have more than once alluded in the Quarterly. If Coleridge could but learn how to deliver his opinions in a way to make them read, and to separate that which would be profitable for all from that which scarcely half a dozen men in England can understand (I certainly am not one of the number), he would be the most useful man of the age, as I verily believe him in acquirements and in powers of mind to be very far the greatest.

"Yours very truly, Robert Southey."

In the minds of many men who were not disposed to slander my father, nor to entertain hostile feelings toward him, there yet remained an impression that he attacked with intemperate language the same class of opinions which he himself had once held. The next letter shows us how he defended himself against this imputation, when represented to him by Mr. Wynn.

To C. W. W. Wynn, Esq., M.P.

"Keswick, April 13, 1817.

"My dear Wynn,

"Do you not see that the charge of my speaking acrimoniously against persons for thinking as I once thought is ridiculously false? Against whom are the strong expressions used, to which you refer in the Quarterly Review and the Registers? Against the rank Bonapartists, with whom I had never any more resemblance than I have with the worshipers of the devil in Africa; and against those who, without actually favoring him as Whitbread did, nevertheless thought it hopeless to make our stand against him on the ground where we had every possible advantage. And as for the Jacobin writers of the day—in what have I ever resembled them? Did I ever address myself to the base and malignant feelings of the rabble, and season falsehood and sedition with slander and impiety? It is perfectly true that I thought the party who uniformly predicted our failure in Spain to be ignorant,* and pusillanimous, and presumptuous—surely, surely, their own words, which are given in the Register, prove them to have been so. Can you have forgotten in 1809–10, how those persons who thought with me that there was reasonable

* Mr. Wilberforce wrote to my father at this time, saying he could not feel satisfied until he had informed him that he was not in the House of Commons when William Smith brought the subject forward, or his voice would also have been heard in his defense.

† My father seems to have mistaken the grounds of the chancellor's decision. Probably he had only been informed of the result, and had not seen the judgment.

* "The paper in the Quarterly Review is directed against the Edinburgh Reviewer, whose words are quoted to justify the epithets."—*R. S.*

ground for hope and perseverance were insulted as idiots, and laughed to scorn? For my own part, I never doubted of success; and proud I am that the reasons upon which my confidence was founded were recorded at the time. Had you been in power, you would have thought otherwise than as you did, because you would have known more of the state of Europe. Arms were sent from this country to Prussia as early as the autumn of 1811. Believe me, the terms in which I have spoken of the peace party are milk and water compared to what I have seen among the papers with which I have been intrusted. But enough of this.

"If you saw me now, you would not think otherwise of my temper under affliction than you did in the summer. I have never in the slightest degree yielded to grief, but my spirits have not recovered, nor do I think they ever will recover, their elasticity. The world is no longer the same to me. You can not conceive the change in my occupations and enjoyments: no person who had not seen what my ways of life were *can* conceive how they were linked with his life. But be assured that I look habitually for comfort where it is to be found.

"God bless you! I shall be in town on the 24th, at my brother's, and leave it on the 1st of May.

"Yours affectionately, R. S."

An incident that occurred in the midst of the Wat Tyler controversy must now be noticed, as one which, had my father thought fit to take advantage of it, would have changed the whole current of his life, and which offered him the most favorable prospects of pecuniary advantage of any which presented themselves either in earlier or later life.

This was a proposal made privately, through the medium of his friend, Mr. Henry Crabbe Robinson; and, in the first instance, the simple question was asked whether, "if an offer were made him to superintend a lucrative literary establishment, in which he would have—if he desired it—a property, of which the emolument would be very considerable, and which would give him extensive influence over the whole kingdom, he were in a condition to accept it;" or, rather, whether he was willing to listen to the details of such a proposal. "But," it was added, "if he was so attached to his delightful residence, and to that kind of literary employment which alone gives fame, and must, in its exercise, be the most delightful, an immediate answer to that effect was requested."

My father had no doubt from whom the proposal came and to what it referred, being aware of his friend's intimacy with Mr. Walter, the proprietor of the Times; but so completely was he wedded to his present mode of life, so foreign to his habits would this sort of occupation have been, combined with a residence in London, and so much more strongly was his mind set upon future and lasting fame than upon present profit, that he did not even request to be informed of the particulars of the offer, but at once declined it, upon the plea that no emolument, however great, would induce him to give up a country life, and those pursuits in literature to which the studies of so many years had been directed. "Indeed," he adds, "I should consider that portion of my time which is given up to temporary politics grievously misspent, if the interests at stake were less important.' *

The situation alluded to was that of writing the chief leading article in the Times, together, I suppose, with some general authority over the whole paper; and the remuneration which it was intended to offer was £2000 a year, with such a share in the profits as would have enabled him to realize an independence in a comparatively short time.

In a former letter my father speaks of an intention of making a tour of the Continent in the course of the spring. His habits of laborious study rendered some perfect relaxation absolutely necessary, and traveling abroad was the only way in which he could obtain it. At home he *could not* be unemployed; he had no tastes or pursuits of any kind to lead him from his books, and any journey he might take in his own country was only a series of hurried movements from one friend to another. Of London, the reader need not be told, he had not merely a dislike, but absolutely a "horror;" and thus his mind was hardly ever completely unbent except on the few occasions when he could afford himself a foreign excursion.

From such a change (which at this time was particularly needful to him) no one ever derived more benefit or more pleasure. With his traveling garments he put on totally new habits, and set out with the determination to make the most of all pleasures and the least of all inconveniences, being thus as good-humored and as accommodating a "compagnon de voyage" as it was possible to conceive. His journal on this occasion (like all his other journals) is elaborately minute, and shows how perseveringly he must have labored at it in spite of fatigue. Every circumstance is detailed; in every place he seems to find objects of interest which would altogether escape the eye of an ordinary traveler. Indeed, the industry of his pen, the activity of his mind, and the quickness of his perceptive faculties, are nowhere so plainly shown as in these records of his foreign journeys.

Every spare moment of his time being thus occupied, his letters during this journey contain little more than the outlines of his route; a few of them, however, will not be thought out of place here.

To Mrs. Southey.

"Neufchatel, Wednesday, May 28, 1817.

"MY DEAR EDITH,

"Yesterday we entered Switzerland, and reached this place after a week's journey from Paris, without let, hinderance, accident, or inconvenience of any kind.

* R. S. to H. C. R., March 13, 1817.

"It is with the greatest difficulty that I find time to keep a journal. We rise at five, and have traveled from ten to twelve hours every day, going about twenty miles before breakfast. Hunger would hardly permit us to do any thing in the way of writing before dinner, if there were not always something to see while dinner is preparing; and after dinner it requires an effort of heroic virtue to resist the pleasures of wine and conversation, and it becomes almost impossible, upon taking the pen in hand, to resist sleep. This morning we lay in bed till seven, that we might have the full enjoyment of a whole holiday. I remember at Westminster the chief gratification which a whole holiday on a Sunday afforded was that of lying abed till breakfast was ready at nine o'clock.

"Our windows are within a stone's throw of the lake, and we see the Alps across it. The lake is like a sea in its color, its waves, and its voice, of which we are, of course, within hearing. The Alps, of which we have the whole extent in view, can not be less than fifty miles distant in the nearest point, directly across the lake, and Mont Blanc, which is at the extremity on the right, about fourscore. If our horizon at Keswick were wide enough, I could sometimes show you the Alps in the clouds. They have precisely the appearance of white cumulated clouds, at the verge of the sky, resting upon the earth, and silvered with sunshine; and from such clouds they are only to be distinguished by their definite outline and permanent forms. It is idle to compare this country with our own; or, rather, it would be worse than idle to form any comparison for the purpose of depreciating either. Part of our yesterday's journey* was so like Cumberland, that I could fancy myself within an hour's walk of home; and this forced upon me such a sense of time and distance, and separation, that the tears were more than once ready to break loose. The mountains through which we passed from Pontarlier to this place rise behind the town, and in that direction the view as to its natural objects might be English. A huge harbor, or, still better, an arm of the sea, with such a sky as I have described, will give you a full idea of the rest.

"We hear dismal stories of famine and distress; but the scene continually recedes as we approach it, nor have we seen any indication of it whatever. From all that I can collect, the bad harvest of last year has acted here as it does in England, and must every where; it presses severely upon that class of persons who stood in need of economy before, and who, with economy, had a little to spare for others. There are plenty of beggars throughout France, and much squalid misery; but the children of the peasantry are as hale, and apparently as well fed, as far as all appearances of flesh and blood may be trusted, as those in our own country. What I have seen of France, about five hundred miles, from Calais to Pontarlier, is, on the whole, less interesting than an equal distance in Great Britain would appear to a foreign traveler; I mean that he would meet with a country more generally beautiful, finer parts, and better towns. But there have been very fine parts upon this journey, with a character and beauty of their own. In Switzerland every step must be interesting, and, go in what direction you will, it is impossible to go wrong.

"Nothing surprised me more in France than that there should be no middle-aged women among the peasantry; they appear to pass at once from youth to hagged old age, and it is no exaggeration to say that they look like so many living and moving mummies. Fond as they are of finery in youth (for they are then tricked out in all the colors of the rainbow), in old age their dress is as wretched and squalid as their appearance. I see nothing among them of the gayety of which we have heard so much in former times. Not a single party have we seen dancing throughout the whole journey. The weather, indeed, has been unusually cold, but certainly not such as would check the propensities of a light-heeled generation, if they ever were as fond of a dance as their light-hearted progenitors. I must say, to their credit, that we have uniformly met with civility; not the slightest insult or incivility of any kind has been offered to us; and if some extortion has been practiced generally at the hotels, it is no more than what is done every where, and perhaps more in England than any where else.

"God bless you! Give my love to all.

"Your affectionate husband, R. S."

To Mrs. Southey.

"Turin, Wednesday, June 11, 1817.

"MY DEAR EDITH,

"I wrote to you on this day fortnight from Neufchatel, since which time all has gone well with us, and we have traveled over very interesting ground. Half a day brought us to Yverdun, where the other half was passed for the sake of seeing Pestalozzi.* The next day to Lausanne,

* Across the Jura.

* "The castle is a huge, plain, square building, with few windows, and a round tower at each corner with an extinguisher top. This has been assigned to Pestalozzi; and having taken up our quarters at the Maison Rouge, forth we sallied to pay our respects to this celebrated personage.

"We ascended the steps and got into the court; the first person whom we accosted was a boy, who proved to be a young Philistine, and replied with a petition for petite charité; just then we got sight of one of the scholars, and at his summons Pestalozzi himself came out to us. I have seen many strange figures in my time, but never a stranger than was now presented to our view: a man whose face and stray tusk-like teeth would mark him for fourscore, if his hair, more black than gray, did not belie the wrinkles of his countenance; this hair a perfect glib in full undress, no hat or covering for the head, no neckcloth, the shirt collar open and a pair of coarse dark trowsers, and a coat, if coat it may be called, of the same material, which Hyde would as little allow to be cloth as he would the habiliment to be 'a coat at all.' He speaks French nearly as ill as I do, and much less intelligibly, because his speech is rapid and impassioned, and, moreover, much affected by the loss of his teeth. I introduced myself as a friend of Dr. Bell, who had read M. Julien's book, and the American work upon his system, but was desirous of obtaining a clearer insight into it. In his gesticulations to welcome us he slipped into a deep hole, and might very easily have met with a serious hurt. He led me into a small schoolroom, hung round with vile portraits of some favorite pupils, apparently works of the school; his own bust was

where, for the mere beauty of the place, we stayed a day. Tuesday to Geneva, seeing Fernay on the way. Wednesday we halted to see this famous, most ugly, most odd, and most striking city, compared to which Lisbon is a city of sweet savors. Friday to Aix—*that* Aix where the adventure of King Charlemagne and the archbishop happened: Pasquier (in whom I found the story) mistakes it for Aix-la-Chapelle. There is a lake here, and a magnificent one it is. N. and S. both made sketches of it before breakfast on Friday. We reached Les Echelles that night, and Saturday visited the Chartreuse: this was a horse expedition, and a whole day's work; but we were most amply rewarded for the heat and fatigue which we endured. I am fully disposed to believe, with Wordsworth, that there is nothing finer in Switzerland than this. The place took us two stages out of our way, which we had to retrace on Sunday; they happened to be remarkably interesting ones, having the mountain pass of the Echelles in one, with a tunnel through the mountain, and by the road in the other the most glorious waterfall I ever beheld. That evening we entered the Savoy Alps at Aiguebelle, and slept at La Grande Maison, a sort of large Estalagem in the midst of Borrowdale scenery upon a large scale. Nash made a view from the window. I do not stop to describe things, because my journal will do all this. Monday we continued our way up the valley, following the course, or, rather, ascending the River Arco: such a river! the color of my coat precisely, which, though Mr. Hyde admits it to be a very genteel mixture as well calculated to hide the dust, is a very bad color for a river; but for force and fury it exceeds any thing that I had ever before seen or imagined: we followed it as far as Lans le Bourg, a little town at the foot of Mount Cenis, and itself as high above the sea as the top of Skiddaw. Yesterday (Tuesday) we crossed Mount Cenis, descended into the plain of Piedmont, and, after the longest of all our days' journeys in point of time, reached Turin just as it grew dark.

"From Besançon to this place it has been one succession of fine scenery, yet with such variety that every day has surprised us. Fine weather began on the 1st of June, and here in Italy we have found a great difference of climate. On the other side the Alps, the cherries are not larger than green pease; here they are ripe. Currants, oranges, and Alpine strawberries are in the markets, and apricots, which are perfectly worthless.

"Our journey has been in all respects pleasant, and I shall find the full advantage of it in the knowledge which it has given me, and the new images with which it has stored my memory. Of the Alps, I will only say here that they make me love Skiddaw better than ever, and that Skiddaw will outlast them; at least, will outlast all that we have yet seen, for they are falling to pieces. The wreck and ruin which they display in many places are hardly to be described.

"We are burned like gipsies, especially Senhouse. 'All friends round Skiddaw' has been our daily toast; and we drank it in all kinds and qualities of wine. As for news, we know not how the world goes on, and have ceased to think about it. The only thing for which we are anxious is to get letters from home, and this we shall do when we get to Mr. Awdry's. If I could but know that all was well!

"God bless you! Good night, my own dear Edith. R. S."

To John May, Esq.

"Brussels, Aug. 1, 1817.

"MY DEAR FRIEND,

"I wrote you a long letter* from Geneva on our way to Italy, and since that time I have

there, strikingly like him, but large enough for Goliath, he himself being rather below the middle size. There happened to be a display of fencing, where the *beau monde* of Yverdun were at this time assembled, and the military band giving them tunes between the acts. Here his tutors were gone, and many of his boys, but in the evening, he said, he hoped to show us practically the system which he now explained: the sum of his explanation was, that true education consists in properly developing the talents and faculties of the individual. It was not likely that so metaphysical a head should think more of Dr. Bell, than Dr. Bell, in his practical wisdom, thinks of such metaphysics. I mentioned Owen of Lanark, and the Essay upon the Formation of Character, and presently perceived that I had touched the right string. We parted till the evening. A large party were dining at the hotel, as if it were a club or public meeting, which, however, the waiter said was not the case; but there was unusual business in the house; perhaps many persons had come from the country round to see the fencing. We walked about the town, and saw the view which it commands.

"We met Pestalozzi in a walk without the town. He had dressed himself, and was in a black coat, but still without a hat, and he was arm-in-arm with a figure more extraordinary than his own: a man some twenty-five or thirty years of age, dressed in a short and neat slate-colored jacket and trowsers trimmed with black, his bonnet of the same materials and color, and his countenance so full, so fixed, so strongly and dismally charactered, that a painter might select him for one of the first disciples of St. Francis or of Loyola. In the course of our walk we went behind the castle into a large open garden, and there we saw some of the pupils employed in developing their bodily powers: a pole, about eighteen feet high, was securely fixed in an inclined position against a ladder; the boys ascended the ladder and slid down the pole; others were swinging in such attitudes as they liked from a gallows. About six, P. called upon us to show us the practice of his system; it was exhibited by two very intelligent teachers as applied to drawing and arithmetic. In drawing, they were made to draw the simplest forms, and were not instructed in the laws of perspective till the eye and hand had acquired correctness; just as we learn to speak by habit before we know the rules of grammar. In arithmetic, it appeared to me that the questions served only to quicken the intellect, but were of no utility in themselves, and acted upon boys just as the disputes of the schoolmen formerly acted upon men. A son of Akerman's, in the Strand, was one of the boys, and said he was much happier than at an English school. His cousin of the same name, a German by birth, is one of the teachers; he had been in England, where he knew Wordsworth, and he studied under Mr. Johnson at the Central School, and he had traveled in Switzerland with Dr. Bell. He also was very curious concerning Owen; with him I had much conversation, and was much pleased with him. M. Julien also was introduced to us; author of those books which I bought at Aix-la-Chapelle. We wrote our names at parting, and although Mr. P. knew no more of mine than he did of Tom Long the carrier's, he was evidently gratified by our visit, and we parted good friends, with all good wishes."—*From his Journal.*

* This seems to have been a letter of elaborate description. It never reached its destination, having been destroyed by the person to whom it was given to put into the post, for the sake of appropriating the postage money!

written twice to London, so that I conclude you would hear by roundabout means that I had reached Milan, and afterward that we had safely returned into Switzerland. From Geneva we made for Mont Cenis, and turned aside from Chambery to visit the Grande Chartreuse, which, after all that we have since seen, remains impressed upon our minds as one of the finest imaginable scenes. * * * * At Milan I purchased some books. Thence to Como, where I found Landor, and we remained three days. Bellaggio, twenty miles from Como, upon the fork of the lake, is the finest single spot I have ever seen, commanding three distant lake views, each of the grandest character. Lugano was our next stage; and somewhere here it is, that, if climate and scenery alone were to be consulted, I should like to pitch my tent; perhaps at Laveno, upon the Lago Maggiore. The Isola Bella, upon that lake, is of all extravagant follies the most absurd. Having crossed the lake, we entered upon the Simplon road, which, on the whole, I do not think so fine as the passage of Mont Cenis; but it is foolish to compare things which are in so many respects essentially different. In the Maurienne, and, indeed, when you begin to descend into Piedmont, the world seems tumbling to pieces about your ears, of such perishable materials are the mountains made. In the Simplon you have generally rocks of granite. A glorious Alpine descent brought us into the Valais, which, even more than the Maurienne, is the land of goîtres and cretins, both more numerous and more shocking to behold than I could have believed possible. At Martigny we halted and crossed to Chamouny by the Tête Noir. In the album at the Montanvert I found John Coleridge's adventures in going to the Garden, as it is called: unluckily, the ink with which he wrote has made them in part illegible.

"We returned by the Tête Noir as we came, the Col de Balme being still covered in great part with snow; and proceeding by Vevay and Lausanne, returned to Mr. Awdry's, at Echichens, where we rested three days. Just four weeks had elapsed since we left that place, and it was a high enjoyment to find ourselves again among friends. * * * * * Proceeding to Berne,* we sent our carriage to Zurich, and struck into the Oberland, where we traveled ten days by land and water, on horseback or on foot, sometimes in cars and sometimes in carts. The snow rendered it impossible to cross the Grimsel without more risk than it would have been justifiable to incur. We slept on the Righi. At Zurich a day's halt was necessary for the love of the washerwoman. We then set off homeward in good earnest, through the Black Forest. * * * We then made for Frankfort and Mentz, and down the left bank of the Rhine to Cologne, where we saw the three kings, and a very considerable number of the eleven thousand virgins—certainly some thousands of them—a sight more curious than

* The following account of Fellenberg's Institution at Hofwyl, near Berne, may interest the reader: "Immediately after breakfast we drove to the noted spot. Fellenberg was not within when I delivered Sir T. Acland's letter and the book with which he had intrusted me; a messenger was dispatched to seek him, and a young man meanwhile carried us over the institution, and to a warehouse full of agricultural machines and instruments made upon the new principles, many of them so exceedingly complicated that it seemed as if the object had been how to attain the end desired by the most complex means; to the smiths, the blacksmiths, &c., &c.; we also visited the dairy, which was really a fine one, being so contrived that in hot weather half the floor is covered with cold water, and in time of severe frost with hot; the granaries, &c., and the place of gymnastics, where the boys are taught to climb ropes, and walk upon round poles. About an hour had been passed in this manner when F. returned. His countenance is highly intelligent; his light eyes uncommonly clear and keen; his manners those of a man of the world, not of an enthusiast. He entered into a long detail, rather of his own history than of his system. He had been the only member of the Council, he said, who, at the first invasion, proposed vigorous resistance, so as to make all Switzerland à la Vendée: they talked of shooting him, &c. Afterward, some of the Swiss directory who knew him, and whom he knew to be desirous of doing the best they could for their country under such calamitous circumstances, induced him, as he was at Paris on private business, to remain there as secretary to the embassy, and serve Switzerland as well as he could against her own embassador and the French government. This, I think, was intended as an apology for his political life. His object, he said, was, in the first place, to fulfill his duty as father of a family and as a citizen. He wished to restore the moral character of Switzerland; to raise her again to her former respectable state; and to make her the means of rendering services to Europe which other powers might receive from her without jealousy. This part of his plan turned out to be a wild scheme of instituting a seminary for those who were destined by birth to hold offices—princes, peers, and statesmen: they were to be educated so as to know and love each other: the purest Christianity was to be practically taught; and his institution was then to co-operate with the Christian Alliance, which was the favorite scheme of the Emperor Alexander and the Emperor of Austria. This part of his institution, though very high prices were paid by the individuals, did not support itself, the expense of masters being so great. The agronomic part afforded funds, from the farm (which appeared in beautiful order) and the manufacture of agricultural implements upon his improvements, the demand for them being great. All that we had seen were about to be sent off to those who had bespoken them. About 200 workmen are employed; a third part assisted in the education of poor destitute children—there were only about thirty; these amply supported themselves by the employments in which they were trained. The aristocracy of Berne discouraged him; treated him as a visionary, and even forbade the circulation of those books which expounded his views; I should not be able to get them any where in Switzerland, only at Geneva: so he gave me the collection. As for the seminary for statesmen, I can not but suspect there is more of humbug than of enthusiasm in it. F. neither looks nor talks like a man who can suppose himself destined to found a school like the philosophers of old. If he has any enthusiasm, it is respecting agriculture, which he spoke of as the means of developing moral virtues; and he was proud of his inventions, and evidently hurt that the Board of Agriculture had not acknowledged the receipt of some which he had presented to them, and not published the result of experiments made with them. He had also made experiments of great importance upon the nature of different soils, as to their property of retaining heat and moisture. Of Dr. Bell he was disposed to speak slightingly, saying he was an enthusiast and an excellent schoolmaster, but unfit for a director. Upon this point I told him of Madras: he thought that the doctor pushed the principle of emulation too far, and used means for encouraging a spirit which is in itself but too prevalent. On this point he spoke in a manner which in some measure accorded with my own judgment.

"Kosciuzko's name was in the book of visitors. He requested me, at my leisure, to give him some account of the best works which had been published in England during the French Revolution, that he might send for them for his library; for, though he did not speak our language, he understood it, and was desirous that our literature should be cultivated on the Continent. He had about 250 acres in cultivation, and inspected his laborers from a tower with a telescope; because, as one of his people said, he can not be in all places at the same time.'"

any of its kind in Portugal or Spain. Here we arrived last night. * * * * * I have made large purchases, which, with the Acta Sanctorum, now at last completed, will fill three chests. Verbiest has promised to dispatch them immediately. You may well imagine how anxious I am to hear from home, and how desirous to get there. As for news, we have lived so long without it that the appetite seems almost extinguished. By mere chance, I got at Zurich a German account of Massena's campaign in Portugal, written by a physician of his army. My knowledge of the subject assisted me greatly in making out the meaning, and I have found in it some curious matter. As far as I can learn, this is the only original document concerning the war which has yet been published in Germany.

"I have been perfectly well during the journey, and the knowledge it has given me amply repays the expense both of money and of time. It has been with great difficulty that I could keep up my Journal, so fully has every day and every hour been occupied, from five and frequently four in the morning. I have, however, kept it. My spirits have been equal to any demand which outward circumstances might make upon them; but to live always out of one's self is not possible, and in those circumstances which frequently occur amid the excitement and exhilaration of such a journey, my lonely feelings have perhaps been more poignant than they would have been amid the even tenor of domestic life; but I have learned to give them their proper direction, and when I am once more at home, I shall feel the benefit of having traveled.

"God bless you, my dear friend! And believe me most truly and affectionately yours,

"ROBERT SOUTHEY."

To C. W. W. Wynn, Esq., M.P.

"Keswick, Aug. 23, 1817.

"MY DEAR WYNN,

" * * * * * * *

They tell me, both here and in town, that traveling has fattened me. Certainly it agreed with my bodily health most admirably, whether it be attributable to early rising, continual change of air, or copious libations of good wine, or to all these. The early rising is unluckily the only practice which it would be possible to continue here. As for the wine,* when I think of the red wines of Savoy (the Montmelian in particular), and the white wines of the Rhine and the Moselle, I feel something as the children of Israel did when they remembered the flesh-pots of Egypt. Were I to settle any where on the Continent, Switzerland should be the country, and probably Lausanne the place. There are lovelier places in the Oberland of Berne, and the adjacent small cantons; but Lausanne has all those comforts which are desirable, and there is as good society in the canton of Vaud as need be desired. We could not gain admittance into Gibbon's garden, though his house belongs to a banker on whom we had bills. The assigned reason for refusing was, that the way lay through a chamber which was occupied by an invalid. I confess that I doubted this, and could not believe that the only way into the garden should be through a bed-chamber. This was a mortifying disappointment. As some compensation, however, our own apartments were not more than one hundred yards off, and opened upon a terrace which commanded exactly the same view of the lake and mountains, with no other difference of foreground than a hundred yards will make in looking over gardens and groves of fruit-trees. *

"Does this country, you will ask, appear flat and unprofitable after Alpine scenery? Certainly not. It has lost very little by the comparison, and that little will soon be regained. Skiddaw is by much the most imposing mountain, for its height, that I have yet seen. Many mountains, which are actually as high again from their base, do not appear to more advantage. I find here, as Wordsworth and Sir G. Beaumont had told me I should, the charm of proportion, and would not exchange Derwentwater for the Lake of Geneva, though I would gladly enrich it with the fruit-trees and the luxuriant beauties of a Swiss summer. Their waterfalls, indeed, reduce ours to insignificance. On the other hand, all their streams and rivers are hideously discolored, so that that which should be one of the greatest charms of the landscape is in reality a disgusting part of it. The best color which you see is that of clean soap-suds; the more common one that of the same mixture when dirty. But the rivers have a power, might and majesty which it is scarcely possible to describe.

"God bless you, my dear Wynn!

"Yours most affectionately, R. S."

To John May, Esq.

"Keswick, Oct. 13, 1817

"MY DEAR FRIEND,

"The notion of writing again that letter which the rascal Louis destroyed at Geneva has, I verily believe, prevented me from beginning one in the natural order of things. I can place myself at Thebes or at Athens on every occasion, dive into Padalon, or scale Mount Calasay;* but to remember what I then wrote, further than the journal you have seen might remind me of the facts, is beyond my power. Let us see, however, what can be done, with as little repetition as possible, of what you have taken the trouble to decipher. In speaking of Paris, I probably might have remarked what an out-of-door life is led by the inhabitants, and how prodigiously busy those people are who have nothing to do. There is more stir and bustle than in London, and of a very dif-

* Let not the reader suppose from this and other commendations of the juice of the grape, that my father was inclined to over-indulgence therein, for no man was ever more strictly temperate. Indeed, his constitution required more generous living than he ordinarily gave it; and part of the benefit he always derived from continental traveling was, as he here intimates, from his partaking more freely of wine when abroad than in the regularity of his domestic life.

* See the Curse of Kehama.

ferent character. In London they bear the stamp of business. You see that the crowds who pass by you in Cheapside have something to do, and something to think of; and in Paris you see as clearly that restlessness and dissipation bring people into the street because they have nothing to do at home. I should think France decidedly inferior to England in beauty of country; yet I did not find the scenery altogether so uninteresting as I had been taught to expect. Picardy has much historical interest to an Englishman, and perhaps the recollection of great events makes me enjoy scenes which might else have been insipid; for I thought of the struggle between Burgundy and France; and in tracts where there was little more than earth and sky to be seen, I remembered that that same earth had been trodden by our countrymen before the battles of Cressy and Agincourt, and that that same sky had seen their victory. The towns, also, have many interesting antiquities, where an antiquarian or artist would find enough to employ him. The rivers have a magnitude and majesty to be found in few English streams. On the other hand, there is a want of wood or of variety of wood. Poplars give a sameness to the scene, and a sort of sickly coloring, very different from the deep foliage of our oaks and elms. The very general custom of housing the cattle is unfavorable to the appearance of the country; there is a want of life, and motion, and sound. I believe, also, that there are fewer birds than in England. I scarcely remember to have seen a crow or a bird of prey. The most beautiful part of France which we saw (except the Jura country, which has a Swiss character) was French Flanders, which is, indeed, exceedingly beautiful. The country from Lisle to St. Omer's may vie with the richest parts of England. John Awdry was much disappointed with the South of France; perhaps this was because he entered it from Switzerland and Savoy; but the features, as he described them, were naturally unfavorable. The country upon the Loire has been much extolled. Landor told me it had the same fault which I had observed in other parts—a pale and monotonous coloring from the poplars, which was not relieved by vineyards, and in summer by sands which the river then left bare. We came upon a fine country as we approached Besançon. The air of the Jura Mountains seemed congenial to me; and if I did not look upon the people with some partiality because they were mountaineers, they were a better race in many respects than the natives of Burgundy and Champagne. Were I to visit Switzerland again, I should wish to see more of the Jura. I do not think that a traveler can enter Switzerland in any better direction than by way of Pontarlier and Neufchatel. If the wine of this latter territory could reach England, I should think it would have a great sale, for it has the flavor of Burgundy and the body of Port. If the duties are lowered (as I understand they are likely to be), it will find its way by the Rhine. *

"If the general use of tea could be introduced, it might prove a general benefit. A French breakfast has neither the comfort nor the domestic character of an English one; it is had better at a restaurateur's or an hotel than at home. But domestic habits are what are wanting in France; and if it were the fashion to drink tea, they would be very much promoted by it. In Morocco, tea is gradually superseding the use of coffee. I do not know why it is so little liked upon the Continent of Europe, when among us it has become one of the first necessaries of life. We tried it sometimes, but scarcely ever with success; and it is curious enough that we never on any occasion met with cream, except at Chalets in Switzerland, which is famous for it. Neither in France, Switzerland, Italy, Germany, nor the Netherlands, rich in dairies as all these countries are, do the inhabitants ever appear to use it. Perhaps I described the lakes of Neufchatel and Geneva in my last letter, and the abominable odor of the great city of Calvinism.

"Since my return we have had much company, and, in consequence, I have been led into much idleness.* Winter is now setting in: although the weather continues fine, the days are shortening fast; long evenings will confine me to my desk, and the retirement which this place affords during the dark season is such that I am in no danger of being disturbed. At present, I am finishing a paper upon Lope de Vega for the next Quarterly, and preparing the first chapter of the Peninsular War for the press.

"Believe me, yours most affectionately,

"ROBERT SOUTHEY."

To Chauncey Hare Townshend, Esq.

"Oct. 31, 1817.

"MY DEAR CHAUNCEY,

"During this fine autumn (the finest which we can remember in this country) I have frequently regretted that you were not with us upon our mountain excursions, and thought sometimes how busily your hammer would have been at work among the stones, over which I was treading as ignorantly as the cart-horse in our company.

"You have not estimated Neville White more favorably than he deserves. There does not breathe a better or a nobler heart. Men are sometimes strangely out of their place in this world: there, for instance, is a man living in Milk Street, and busied about Nottingham goods, who, if he were master of a palace and a princely fortune, would do honor to the one, and make the best possible use of the other. I felt toward him just as you have done, at first sight; and recognizing instantly the character, scarcely perceived that the individual was a stranger. There is more in these sympathies than the crockery class of mankind can conceive, or than our wise men have dreamed of in their philosophy.

"Your picture of the Norfolk scenery is very lively and very just. I have been twice in my life at Norwich, and once at Yarmouth, many

* His friend Mr. Bedford had been passing some weeks at Keswick, to their mutual enjoyment; and Mr. Rickman had also been there for a short time.

years ago, long enough to have drawn from that open and level country some images, which were introduced in Thalaba. I remember writing an epistle in blank verse from thence in 1798,* which had some descriptive lines that might be worth transcribing, if they were at hand. It was the unbroken horizon which impressed me, appearing so much wider than at sea; and the sky-scapes which it afforded. I had the same impression in passing through Picardy; and if I lived in such a country, should perhaps find as many beauties in the sky as I do here upon the earth. Any where I could find food for the heart and the imagination, at those times when we are open to outward influences, except in great cities. If I were confined in them, I should wither away like a flower in a parlor window. Did you notice the cry of the bittern in that country? I heard it between Yarmouth and Norwich. Its spiral flight, when it takes wing, is as remarkable and as peculiar as its cry. This bird has been extirpated here; only one has been seen since I have resided at Keswick, and that was shot by a young Cantab, who ate it for his dinner, and had no more brains in his head than the bittern.

"Having nothing to hope in this world, and nothing to desire in it for myself, except as quiet a passage through it as it may please God to grant, my mind, when it takes its course, recurs to the world which is to come, and lays as naturally now the scenes of its day-dreams in Heaven as it used to do upon earth. I think of the many intimacies I have made among the dead, and with what delight I shall see and converse with those persons whose lives and writings have interested me, to whom I have endeavored to render justice, or from whom I have derived so much pleasure and benefit of the highest kind. Something, perhaps, we shall have to communicate, and oh! how much to learn! The Roman Catholics, when they write concerning Heaven, arrange the different classes there with as much precision as a master of the ceremonies could do. Their martyrs, their doctors, their confessors, their monks, and their virgins, have each their separate society. As for us poets, they have not condescended to think of us; but we shall find one another out, and a great many questions I shall have to ask of Spenser and of Chaucer. Indeed, I half hope to get the whole story of Cambuscan bold; and to hear the lost books of the Faëry Queen. Lope de Vega and I shall not meet with equal interest, and yet it will be a pleasant meeting.

"What are you now about? If I had seen you here, where we could have conversed at leisure and without reserve, I would have told you of my own projects, formed in youth and now never to be resumed, talked over your own, and have endeavored to show you where you might gather the freshest laurels.

"God bless you!

"R. S."

* See *ante*, p. 103.

*To the Reverend John Jebb.**

"Keswick, Dec. 6, 1817.

"SIR,—A volume like yours needs no other introduction than its own merits. I received it last night, and rejoice to see such topics treated in a manner so judicious, so forcible, and so impressive. You are treading in the steps of the great and admirable men by whom our Church has been reformed and supported; and those who are to come after us will tread in yours. Unless I deceive myself, the state of religion in these kingdoms is better at this time than it has been at any other since the first fervor of the Reformation. Knowledge is reviving as well as zeal, and zeal is taking the best direction. We stand in need of both when evil principles are so actively at work.

"I am writing the Life of Wesley in such a manner as to comprise our religious history for the last hundred years. It is a subject which I have long meditated, and may God bless the labor. Perhaps you can give me some light into the reasons why Methodism should have made so little progress in Ireland, where the seed seems to have fallen upon a most ungenial soil, though it was scattered with abundant care. In Scotland its failure may be explained by the general respectability of the Scotch clergy, the effect of education, the scattered population, and the cold and cautious character of the people. Is the jealousy with which the Romish priests watch over their deluded flocks sufficient to account for its failure in Ireland? If so, why was not Quakerism equally unsuccessful?

"I will not apologize for asking your opinion upon this subject. Even if we were not both fortunate enough to possess the same valuable friends, we are now known sufficiently to each other; and men of letters, who hold the same faith, and labor, though in different ways, for the same cause, are bound together by no common ties.

"Believe me, sir, with sincere respect,

"Your obedient servant,

"ROBERT SOUTHEY."

To Walter Savage Landor, Esq.

"Keswick, Dec. 17, 1817.

"Perhaps the Lugano Gazette may not have given you the great news from the North, which excites much more interest in me than any thing which is going on at present in the political world. The Greenlandmen, last season, got as far as 84°, and saw no ice in any direction; they were of opinion, that if they could have ventured to make the experiment, they might have reached the pole without any obstruction of this kind. The coast of East Greenland, which had been blocked up for four or five centuries, was open. It is believed that some great convulsion of nature has broken up the continent of ice which has during those centuries been accumulating; and it is certain that the unnatural cold winds which were experienced throughout the whole

* Afterward Bishop of Limerick. The book referred to is his first publication; a volume of sermons, with notes.

of May last, from the S. and S.W., were occasioned by this ice floating into warmer latitudes. This effect is more likely to have been produced by volcanic eruption than by earthquakes alone, because for the last two years the fish have forsaken the Kamtschatka coast, so that the bears (ἰχθυόφαγοι) have been carrying on a civil war among themselves, and a war *plus quam civile* with the Russians. Earthquakes would not discompose the fish much, but they have a great objection to marine volcanoes. We are fitting out four ships for a voyage to the pole and the northwest passage. We shall have some curious facts about the needle; possibly even our climate may be improved, and trees will grow large enough for walking sticks in Iceland.

"The amusements of Como may very probably become the amusements of England ere long.* This I think a likely consequence, from the death of the Princess Charlotte. In the lamentations upon this subject there has been a great deal of fulsome canting, and not a little faction; still, among the better part and the better classes of society, there was a much deeper and a more general grief than could have been expected or would easily be believed. Two or three persons have told me that in most houses which they entered in London the women were in tears.

"'Tis not the public loss which hath impress'd
This general grief upon the multitude;
And made its way at once to every breast,
The old, the young, the gentle, and the rude.
'Tis not that in the hour which might have crowned
The prayers preferred by every honest tongue,
The very hour which should have sent around
Tidings wherewith all churches would have rung,
And all our echoing streets have pealed with gladness,
And all our cities blazed with festal fire,
That then we saw the high-raised hope expire,
And England's expectation quenched in sadness.
This surely might have forced a sudden tear.
Yet had we then thought only of the state,
To-morrow's sun, which would have risen as fair,
Had seen upon our brow no cloud of care.
It is to think of what thou wert so late;
Oh, thou who liest clay-cold upon thy bier,
So young and so beloved, so richly bless'd
Beyond the common lot of royalty;
The object of thy worthy choice possess'd,
The many thousand souls that pray'd for thee,
Hoping in thine a nation's happiness;
And in thy youth, and in thy wedded bliss,
And in the genial bed—the cradle dress'd—
Hope standing by, and joy a bidden guest.
'Tis this that from the heart of private life
Makes unsophisticated sorrows flow:
We mourn thee as a daughter and a wife,
And in our human natures feel the blow.†

"Have you succeeded in getting sight of the aspide? In Cyprus they stand in such dread of this serpent, that the reapers have bells fixed to their sides and their sickles: κοῦφ they call it there. One traveler names it the asp, and another asks *veterum aspis?* so I suppose it to be your neighbor. I do not know if the venom of your serpent produces death (as some others do), by paralyzing the heart, but it may be worth knowing, that in that case the remedy is to take spirit of hartshorn* in large doses, repeating them as long as the narcotic effect is perceived. A surgeon in India saved himself in this manner, by taking much larger doses than he could have prescribed to any other person, because he understood his own sensations, and proportioned the remedy accordingly. He took a tea-spoonful of the spiritus ammoniæ compositus in a Madeira glassful of water every five minutes for half an hour, and seven other such doses at longer intervals (according to the symptoms) before he considered himself out of danger; in the whole, a wine-glassful of the medicine. This is a very valuable fact, the medicine having lost its repute in such cases, because it was always administered in insufficient doses.

"God bless you! R. S."

CHAPTER XXIII.

RETROSPECT OF LIFE—REVIEWING—LIFE OF WESLEY—USES OF AFFLICTION—EDINBURGH ANNUAL REGISTER—WESTMORELAND ELECTION—HUMBOLDT—PAPER ON THE POOR LAWS—COBBETT—NUTRITIVE QUALITIES OF COFFEE—MILMAN'S POEM OF SAMOR—OFFER OF LIBRARIANSHIP OF THE ADVOCATES' LIBRARY, EDINBURGH—SCARCITY OF LITERARY MEN IN AMERICA—RITCHIE—MUNGO PARK—RECOLLECTIONS OF HIS TOUR ON THE CONTINENT—HE IS ATTACKED FROM THE HUSTINGS AT A WESTMORELAND ELECTION—WISHES TO PRINT HIS POEMS IN A CHEAPER FORM—MOB MEETINGS—CONGRATULATIONS TO MR. JUSTICE COLERIDGE ON HIS MARRIAGE—LITERARY ADVICE—HABITS OF ASCETICISM NOT UNFAVORABLE TO LONG LIFE—MR. WILBERFORCE VISITS KESWICK—SCHOOL REBELLION—REMARKABLE SEASON—COMPARATIVE HAPPINESS OF CHILDHOOD AND RIPER YEARS—CHANGES IN THE CRIMINAL LAW WANTED.—1818.

AFFAIRS in the political world had now somewhat settled down, and the immediate fear of an insurrectionary movement had passed away.

The original intention of the government in wishing my father to come up to town for the purpose of conferring with him was, as he had supposed, to endeavor to induce him to conduct a political journal which should aim at counteracting the influence of the seditious and anarchical portion of the daily and weekly press. This, however, was a scheme which no inducement they could have offered would have persuaded him to enter into; and, indeed, we have seen that he had declined an offer of the same nature, which would have combined far greater independence of action with large pecuniary advantages. It appears, however, that they were by no means so anxious that he should write "*ex proprio motu*," as under their own especial influence; and he was urged to employ the Quarterly Review as a vehicle for his opinions and

* This refers to the Princess of Wales, then living at Como.

† This has never been published. The Funeral Song for the Princess Charlotte is a much more elaborate and beautiful composition.

* Spirit of hartshorn, immediately applied, is the best remedy for the sting of a wasp: there may be some affinity in the two cases, only the application is inward in the one, and outward in the other.—*Ed.*

arguments, in preference to a separate and independent publication.

This, in the first instance, he consented to do; and the result was that article "On the Rise and Progress of popular Disaffection"* which excited the "ponderous displeasure" of Mr. William Smith; but for some time he still adhered to his intention of embodying his views of the dangers and evils of the existing state of society in England, and the remedies, in a small volume fitted in size and price for general circulation.

Other avocations, however, intervened, and, together with the improved aspect of public affairs, caused him to lay aside this idea for the present. "As to politics," he writes, at the close of the year, "I have nothing to do with them now. The battle has been won; but that, indeed, was a cause in which I would have spent something more precious than ink." * * "When I touch upon politics," he continues, "it will be with a wider range and a larger view than belongs to any temporary topics." It seems probable, indeed, that the Colloquies on the Progress and Prospects of Society took their rise from the ideas thus aroused.

The first letter with which the new year opens shows pleasingly how abiding were his feelings of gratitude to his early friend Mr. Wynn, and also speaks of his present literary employments.

To C. W. W. Wynn, Esq., M.P.

"Keswick, Jan. 1, 1818.

"MY DEAR WYNN,

"Many happy returns of the new year to you and yours. It is now thirty years since you and I first met in Dean's Yard, and in the course of these years half the human race who were then living have gone under ground. How long either of us may keep above it, God knows; but while we do, there is little likelihood that any circumstances can break or loosen an attachment which has continued so long. Your path has been just what might have been predicted—straight, honorable, and in full view, only that one might have expected to have found you on the other side the house and in office; and one day or other (the sooner the better) I trust to see you there. What mine might have been without your helping hand, when I was among the bogs and briers, I know not. With that help it has been a very pleasant uphill road, with so many incidents by the way that the history of them would make no bad Pilgrim's Progress, especially as I am now at rest among the Delectable Mountains, and have little more to do than to cross the river whenever my turn comes.

"We are enjoying a beautiful winter here. No snow has yet fallen in the valley, and it lies on the fells not raggedly, but in an even line, so that Skiddaw and Grisdale bear no distant resemblance to the Swiss mountains, and imbibe tints at morning and evening which may vie with any thing that ever was seen upon Mont Blanc or Jungfrau.

"I am writing for the Quarterly Review upon the Poor Laws, or, rather, upon the means of improving the lower classes—a practical paper, containing, I think, some hints which any clergyman or other influential person in a parish may usefully improve. It is not unlikely that I may gradually withdraw from the Review—that is to say, as soon as I can live without it. It takes up far too great a portion of my time; for, although no man can take to task-work with less reluctance, still, from the very circumstance of its being task-work—something which must be done, and not what I desire at the time to do—it costs me twice or thrice the time of any other composition, as much in the course of the year as it took to write Thalaba or Kehama. This last poem is going to press for a fourth edition; they sell slowly and steadily.

"The life of Wesley is my favorite employment just now, and a very curious book it will be, looking at Methodism abroad as well as at home, and comprehending our religious history for the last hundred years. I am sure I shall treat this subject with moderation. I hope I come to it with a sober judgment, a mature mind, and perfect freedom from all unjust prepossessions of any kind. There is no party which I am desirous of pleasing, none which I am fearful of offending; nor am I aware of any possible circumstance which might tend to bias me one way or other from the straight line of impartial truth. For the bigot I shall be far too philosophical; for the libertine, far too pious. The Ultra-churchman will think me little better than a Methodist, and the Methodists will wonder what I am. Ἅγια ἁγίοις will be my motto.

"My books from Milan have reached London—something more than 100 volumes. Ramusio is among them, and the Gesta Dei. I have not yet heard of my Acta Sanctorum, the arrival of which will form a grand day in my life. Little leisure as I find for poetry, and seldom, indeed, as I think of it, there is yet a sort of reluctance in me wholly to give up any scheme of a poem on which I have ever thought with any degree of fondness; and because I had meditated a Jewish poem many years ago, I bought at Milan the great Bibliotheca Rabinica of Barlotacci as a repository of materials. Could I have afforded to have written verses during those years when nobody bought them, I verily believe I should have written more than any of my predecessors. God bless you! R. S."

To Walter Scott, Esq.

"Keswick, March 10, 1818.

"MY DEAR SCOTT,

"I am glad that the first tidings which informed me of your illness told of your recovery also. There is an enjoyment of our absent friends, even of those from whom we are far distant, in talking and thinking of them, which makes a large part of the happiness of life. It is a great thing to be in the same place with a friend, it is something to be in the same planet; and whenever you are removed to a better, there are few

* This article was reprinted in his Essays.

men whose loss will be more widely felt in this, for I know no one who has administered so much delight to so extensive a part of the public. I hope your illness has left no weakness behind it. We stand in need, sometimes, of visitations which may lead us to look toward eternity, and in such cases the stroke is merciful when it falls on the body. There is a joyousness, too, in the sense of returning health — a freshness of sensation, such as one might expect from a draught of the fountain of youth.

"About four months ago, John Ballantyne wrote to ask me if he should dispose of my property in the Ed. An. Register to Constable, upon the same terms as those of the other persons who had the same share in it. As I had given it up for a lost concern, I was very glad to hear that I was to have about the same sum which the shares had cost, in a bill from Constable at twelve months' date; four months, however, have elapsed, and I have heard nothing further. Perhaps, if you have an opportunity, you will do me the kindness to ask how the matter stands.

"The neighboring county is in an uproar already with the expected election. —— has succeeded in producing as much turbulence there as he could desire; and if we may judge of what the play will be by what the rehearsal has been, it may prove a very serious tragedy before it is over. I am out of the sphere of this mischief. We shall have mobs, I think, upon the Poor-Law question, which is as perilous in its nature as a corn bill, and yet must be taken in hand. I know not whether the next Quarterly Review will look the danger in the face, and say honestly that we must be prepared to meet it. Preventive measures are very easy, and would be found effectual. How grievously do we want some man of commanding spirit in the House of Commons to do constantly what Canning only rouses himself to do now and then. There is, however, good promise in the solicitor general; to him, I think, we may look with hope, and to Peel.

"I saw Humboldt at Paris; never did any man portray himself more perfectly in his writings than he has done. His excessive volubility, his fullness of information, and the rapidity with which he fled from every fact into some wide generalization, made you more acquainted with his intellectual character in half an hour than you would be with any other person in half a year. Withal, he appeared exceedingly good-natured and obliging. It was at Mackenzie's that I met him.

"Remember us to Mrs. Scott and your daughter, who is now, I suppose, the flower of the Tweed.

"Believe me, my dear Scott,
"Ever affectionately yours,
"ROBERT SOUTHEY."

In a preceding letter my father refers to an article on the Poor Laws which he was then preparing for the Quartely Review. This was a subject he would hardly have taken up of himself, being well aware of his inability to handle topics requiring a clear head for statistical calculation and political economy. He had, however, been urged to it by Mr. Rickman, who furnished him with information and argument on all those points he felt himself unequal to—"as a history of the poor rates, a *catalogue raisonné* of the abominable effects of the Poor Laws, an *exposé* of the injudicious quackeries which from generation to generation had made bad worse."

It appears that although "the Poor-Law question and its remedies, if to be remedied," would have seemed, of all subjects, one of the least objectionable for discussion, Gifford at first had some fears lest it might be rather above the temperature of the Review, and to his hesitation about inserting it (before he had seen it) the following letter refers, while the next shows that a perusal of the paper removed his objections.

To John Rickman, Esq.

"April 5, 1818.

"MY DEAR R.,

"I apprehend, as you know, some such demurrer on the part of the feeble. They are, I believe, the only persons who, when engaged in mortal combat, were ever afraid of provoking their enemies, or striking them too hard. *

"Murray wrote me a brief note the other day, wherein, without any mention of this paper, he said he never desired to see another article upon either politics or religion in the Review, because they are 'certain of offending a great mass of people.' I replied to this at some length in a way which for a little while would impress the magnus homo; but because Mackintosh and a few other Ops. praise a number which does them no harm, he fancies because they are pleased the rest of his readers must be pleased too. This is the mere impression for the moment; but that the Review will ever proceed in a bold, upright, and straightforward course is not to be expected.

"I have a chance letter from Stuart: he says Cobbett has fallen one third in sale, and all such publications are declining, but the anarchists are as active as ever, and new opportunities will occur for bringing their venom into life. 'These wretches,' he continues, 'are effecting their purposes by libeling; they are driving off the ground every man that can oppose them; they are conquering by scandal, and ministers wish as much as others to keep out of the way. Unless this spirit of scandal is put down, unless the licentiousness of the press be restrained, certainly it will effect a revolution—restrained, I mean, by new laws and new regulations. It is altogether, as at present practiced, a *new thing*, not older than the French Revolution. I can perceive every one shrinking from it—you, me, Wordsworth, Coleridge, &c. Every one about the press dreads Cobbett's scandal; and thus, when a man throws off all consideration of character, he has all others in his power. Even the ministry, too, and their friends, I think, shrink from those who fight their battles, when covered with filth in the fray.'

"Stuart is wrong in two points. This sort of scandal is certainly as old as Junius and Wilkes, perhaps much older; and he mistakes my feelings upon the subject and Wordsworth's.

"God bless you! R. S."

To John Rickman, Esq.

"April 11, 1818.

"MY DEAR R.,

"I am not a little pleased that the paper has passed through the hands of Gifford with so little mutilation. * * My letter to Murraymagne in reply to his intended act of exclusion has had its proper effect; but behold, the said Murraymagne does not regard the Poor-Law paper as political: 'Such papers as these,' he says, 'are exceedingly desirable for the Review, because they are of essential service to the country, and they must obtain for us the esteem of all well-thinking men.' He only meant that we should avoid all *party* politics. I wish he did mean this. However, for the present, we have got a most important paper—most important in two points—for strengthening authority, as much as for its remedy for the evil of the Poor Laws. * * * *

"The second Police Report is not of the character which you supposed. There is much valuable matter in it; and, indeed, both Reports furnish stronger positions for me than for the enemy to occupy. The Bow Street men appear to great advantage in both. It really appears as if the coffee shops would almost supersede dram-drinking, so comfortable do the working classes find *warmth* and *distention* (your philosophy). Do you know that of all known substances coffee produces the most of that excitement which is required in fatigue? The hunters in the Isle of France and Bourbon take no other provision into the woods; and Bruce tells us that the viaticum of the Galla, in their expeditions, consists of balls of ground coffee and butter, one per diem (I believe), the size of a walnut, sufficing to prevent the sense of hunger. I have just made a curious note upon the same subject for the History of Brazil: a people in the very heart of South America, living beside a lake of unwholesome water, instead of making maize beer, like all their neighbors, carbonized their maize—as good a substitute for coffee as any which was used under Bonaparte's commercial system; and this was their sole beverage, and it was found very conducive to health.

"Edith May has found a brazen or copper spear-head upon Swinside, in a craggy part of the mountain, where it may have lain unseen for centuries. It is perfectly green, but not corroded; exceedingly brittle, quite plain, but of very neat workmanship, as if it had been cast—one of my spans in length.

"God bless you! R. S."

To Chauncey Hare Townshend, Esq.

"Keswick, April 12, 1818.

"MY DEAR CHAUNCEY,

'I have just finished Henry Milman's poem, a work of great power. But the story is ill constructed, and the style has a vice analogous to that which prevailed in prose about one hundred and seventy years ago, when every composition was overlaid with strained thoughts and far-fetched allusions. The faults here are a perpetual stretch and strain of feeling; and the too frequent presence of the narrator, bringing his own fancies and meditations in the foreground, and thereby—as in French landscape engraving—calling off attention from the main subject, and destroying the effect. With less poetry Samor would have been a better poem. Milman has been endeavoring to adapt the moody and thoughtful character of Wordsworth's philosophical poetry to heroic narration: they are altogether incompatible; and Wordsworth himself, when he comes to narrate in his higher strains, throws it aside like a wrestler's garment, and is as severe a writer as Dante, who is the great master in this style. If Milman can perceive or be persuaded of his fault, he has powers enough for any thing; but it is a seductive manner, and I think that as our poetry in Cowley's days was overrun with conceits of thought, it is likely in the next generation to be overflown with this exuberance of feeling.

"This is a great error. That poetry (I am speaking of heroic narrative) which would reach the heart, must go straight to the mark like an arrow. Away with all trickery and ornaments when pure beauty is to be represented in picture or in marble; away with drapery when you would display muscular strength. Call artifices of this kind to your aid in those feebler parts which must occur in every narrative, and which ought to be there to give the other parts their proper relief.

"Henry Milman was here, with an elder brother, about four years ago, who lodged at Keswick for some twelve months. He is a fine young man, and his powers are very great. They are, however, better fitted for the drama than for narration; the drama admits his favorite strain of composition, and is easier in its structure. Indeed, it is as much easier to plan a play than a poem of such magnitude as Samor, as it is to build a gentleman's house than a Cathedral.

"Do you know any thing of Sir George Dallas? He has sent me some marvelous verses by a son of his not yet thirteen—as great a prodigy as I have ever read of. Verse appears as easy to him as speech; Latin verse is at his fingers' end like English; and he has acted a part in a play of his own composition like another young Roscius.

* * * * * * *

"I am busy with history myself, and have written no poetry for many months; why this disuse, there is here hardly room to explain, if it were worth explanation The account of Lope de Vega in the last Quarterly is mine, as you would probably guess. I have read widely in Spanish poetry; and might in historical and literary recollections call myself half a Spaniard, if, being half a Portuguese also, this would leave any room for the English part of my intellectual being. I anticipate much pleasure in showing you the treasures with which I am surrounded here upon these shelves.

"God bless you! R. S."

In the course of the spring of this year, an offer was made to my father of an appointment, which it might have been imagined would have been more suited to his habits and likings than any other that had been proposed to his acceptance, and which, indeed, had it been made to him in earlier life, it is more than probable he would have gladly taken advantage of. This was the situation of librarian to the Advocates' Library at Edinburgh; the salary £400 a year, with the prospect of an increase, and the labor of making a catalogue attached to it. "Few persons," he says, speaking of this offer, "would dislike such labor less, but I am better employed. I do not love great cities. I will not remove further from my friends (being already too far from them); and having, God be thanked, no pecuniary anxieties, I am contented where I am and as I am, wanting nothing and wishing nothing."

In thus expressing his freedom from pecuniary anxiety (of which, in reality, he had so large a share), it seems probable that he alluded chiefly to the small provision the laureateship had enabled him to secure for his family by means of a life insurance. In other respects, however he might feel in moments of high hope and active exertion, when he perceived his reputation steadily rising, and his work becoming more remunerative, there were many times when the consciousness came over him that his subsistence depended upon his ability to follow day by day "his work and his labor until the evening;" and when the feeling that sickness might at any time, and that old age certainly would "dim the eye, and deaden the memory, and palsy the hand," came across him like a cloud over the face of the sun.

This the reader will see strikingly exemplified in a letter to Mr. Bedford, written at the close of the year, which forms a singular contrast to the expressions my father uses respecting this offer. It would seem, indeed, that he had taken root so firmly among the mountains of Cumberland, and was so unwilling to encounter the difficulties of a removal, and to take upon him new habits of life, that he exercised unconsciously a kind of self-deception whenever an offer was made to him, and conjured up for the time feelings of security from anxiety which had no solid foundation, but which served for the time to excuse him to himself for declining them.

To John Kenyon, Esq.

"Keswick, June 13, 1818.

"My dear Sir,

"Your letter to Mr. Coleridge, which has this day arrived, enables me to thank you for Dobrizhoffer, and for the good old Huguenot Jean de Leny. The American by whom the letter was sent to my brother's has not yet made his appearance at the Lakes. When he comes I will provide him with an introduction to Wordsworth, if he should not bring one from London; and if he is particularly desirous of seeing live poets, he shall have credentials for Walter Scott. I suppose an American inquires for them as you or I should do in America for a skunk or an opossum. They are become marvelously abundant in England, so that publications which twenty years ago would have attracted considerable attention, are now coming from the press in shoals unnoticed. This makes it the more remarkable that America should be so utterly barren: since the Revolution they have not produced a single poet who has been heard of on this side of the Atlantic. Dwight and Barlow both belong to the Revolution; and well was it for the Americans, taking them into the account, that we could not say of them, *tam Marte, quam Mercurio*

"I am very sorry that your friend Ritchie should have gone upon an expedition which has proved fatal to every one who has yet undertaken it, and which I think the amateur geographizing 'gentlemen of England who sit at home at ease' are altogether unjustifiable in pursuing at such a cost of valuable lives. The object is not tantamount, as it is in a voyage of discovery. In such voyages men are only exposed to some additional risk in the way of their profession, and the reward, if they return safe, is certain and proportionate; but here, Mungo Park went upon his second expedition literally because he could not support his family after the first. If, however, Ritchie should live to accomplish his object, I am no ways apprehensive that his reputation will be eclipsed by his intended rival Ali Bey, that solemn professor of humbug having always made less use of his opportunities than any other traveler. * * * * * *

"If you go through Cologne (as I suppose you will), do not fail to visit St. Ursula and the Eleven Thousand Virgins, whose relics form the most extraordinary sight that the Catholic superstition has to display. You will also find the Three Kings in the same city well worthy a visit to their magnificent shrine. From thence to Mentz and Frankfort you will see every where the havoc which the Revolution has made; further I can not accompany your journey. We came to Frankfort from Heidelburg and the Black Forest.

"Your most truly, Robert Southey."

To C. W. W. Wynn, Esq., M.P. (Boulogne).

"Keswick, Aug. 4, 1818.

"My dear Wynn,

"I envy you your French wines, and in a less degree your French cookery also, both indispensable in the alderman's heaven, where the stomach is infinite, the appetite endless, and the dinner eternal. I should envy, also, your bathing upon that noble beach, if Derwentwater were not within reach, and, still better, the rock baths in Newlands, which are the perfection of bathing. What you say of the country about Boulogne is just what I should have supposed it to be from what we saw upon the road, and the place itself is a very interesting one. I slept there, and did not leave it till noon the next day, happening to have an acquaintance there. * I had been told that the road to Paris was uninteresting, but to me it appeared far otherwise; for even if it had not possessed an historical interest of the highest kind to an Englishman, the scenery itself is in many parts very striking.

"You will be better pleased to hear that, if the carriers do not disappoint me, I may expect to-morrow to receive my three cases of books, with the Acta Sanctorum, and some fourscore volumes besides, the gatherings of my last year's journey from Como to Brussels. Far better, and far more agreeably, would my time and thoughts be employed with the saints of old than with the sinners of the present day, with past events and in other countries than with the current politics of our own. Heaven knows I have no predilection for a train of thought which brings with it nothing elevating and nothing cheerful. But I can not shut my eyes either to the direct tendency of the principles which are now at work, or to their probable success; inevitable indeed, and at no very distant time, unless some means be taken for checking the progress of the evil.

"The state of religious feeling appears to differ much in different part of France. In most places we found that the churches were very ill attended, but at Auxerre they were so full that we literally could not decently walk in to examine them as we wished to have done. In Switzerland the Protestant cantons have suffered more than the Catholic ones. I had good opportunities of inquiring into this in the Pays de Vaud, and the state of religion in Geneva is now notorious. Upon the banks of the Rhine, all the inhabitants who were not actually employed in the fields seemed to be busy in performing a pilgrimage. It was a most striking sight to see them—men, women, and children, toiling along bareheaded, under a July sun, singing German hymns. I suspect that the progress of irreligion has kept pace with the extent of French books in the Catholic part of Europe, and that where they have not found their way the people remain in the same state as before. But if things remain quiet for one generation, the Catholic Church will recover its ascendency; its clergy are wise as serpents, and, with all their errors, one can not, considering all things, but heartily wish them success.

"You should go to St. Omer's, if it were only to groan over the ruin of its magnificent Cathedral. The country between that place and Lisle is the perfection of cultivated scenery, and the view from Cassel the finest I have ever seen over a flat country.

"God bless you, my dear Wynn! I half hope Parliament may be sitting in December, that I may meet you in town!

"Yours most affectionately, R. S."

The commencement of the next letter refers to some remarks of Mr. Bedford upon a pamphlet (in the form of that addressed to William Smith), which my father had drawn up in reply to an attack which was made upon him during a contested election in Westmoreland. He had been accused from the hustings of having busied himself greatly on the Tory side, and he was denounced to an excited multitude as one rolling in riches unworthily obtained. To the former charge he could have given a direct denial, not having taken any part whatever in the matter; the latter one need not be further alluded to than as proving some little forbearance on his part in not carrying out his intention of publishing a reply. It is right to add that a counter-statement was made from the same place, on a subsequent occasion, by the same person.

To Grosvenor C. Bedford, Esq.

"Keswick, Sep. 6, 1818.

"MY DEAR GROSVENOR,

"If you had written to me in extenuation, as you term it, I should have been as nearly angry with you as any thing could make me, for how could I possibly attribute any thing you had said to any motive but the right one, or wherefore should I be more displeased with you for not liking my extended epistle more than you were with me for not liking your Dalmatian wine? The roughness of the one did not suit my palate, nor the asperity of the other your taste. And what of that? I dare say you think quite as favorably of your wine as before, and I am not a whit the less satisfied with my style objurgatory. But let that pass. * * * * *

"I have just purchased Gifford's Ben Jonson. He supposes that the laureate continues to receive his tierce of Spanish Canary, and recommends him yearly to drink to old Ben in the first glass. Tell him, if he will get me reinstated in my proper rights, I will drink to Ben Jonson not once a year, but once a day, and to him also. By the manner in which he speaks of Sidney's Arcadia, I conclude that either he has never read the book, or has totally forgotten it.

"So you are to have a Palace-yard meeting to-morrow. How few weeks have elapsed since Hunt was beaten and blackguarded in the face of the mob till his own miscreants hooted at him, and yet, you see, he is in full feather again. The fellow ought to be tried for sedition; he would certainly be found guilty, for the jury, as yet, would be nothing worse than Burdettites, and, therefore, disposed to give him his deserts; and, during his confinement, he should be restricted to prison diet, kept from all intercourse with visitors, and left to amuse himself with the Bible, the Prayer-book, and Drelincourt upon death, or the Whole Duty of Man, for his whole library. At the end of two years he would come out cured. *

"God bless you! R. S."

To John Taylor Coleridge, Esq.

"Keswick, Sept. 8, 1818.

"MY DEAR SIR,

"I am glad to hear that you have taken your chance for happiness in that state in which alone there is a chance of finding it. Men in your station too frequently let the proper season go by, waiting till they can afford to start with a showy establishment. Among those who have not more than an ordinary share of good principles, this is a very common cause of libertine habits; and they who escape this evil incur another, which is sometimes not less fatal. They look out for a wife when they think themselves rich enough, and this is like going to market for one: the choice on their part is not made from those feelings upon which the foundation of happiness must be laid; and, on the other part, they are accepted, not for their own sakes, but for the sake of the establishment which they offer. Similarity of disposition is not consulted, and there is generally in such cases a disparity of years, which is not very likely to produce it. You have chosen a better course, and may God bless you in it.

"The most profitable line of composition is reviewing. You have good footing in the Quarterly, and I am glad of it, for heretofore there has been vile criticism in that journal upon poetry, and upon fine literature in general. This connection need not preclude you from writing for the British Review. Translation is of all literary labor the worst paid—that is, of all such labor as is paid at all; and yet there are so many poor hungry brethren and sisters of the gray goose-quill upon the alert, that new books are sent out from France and Germany by the sheet as they pass through the press, lest the translation should be forestalled.

"Any thing which is not bargained for with the booksellers is, of course, matter of speculation, and success is so much a matter of accident (that is to say, temporary success) in literature, that the most knowing of them are often as grievously deceived as a young author upon his first essay. Biography, however, is likely to succeed; and, with the London libraries at hand, the research for it would be rather pleasurable than toilsome. History, which is the most delightful of all employments (*experto crede*), is much less likely to be remunerated. I have not yet received so much for the History of Brazil as for a single article in the Quarterly Review. But there are many fine subjects which, if well handled, might prove prizes in the lottery. A history of Charles I. and the Interregnum, or of all the Stuart kings, upon a scale of sufficient extent, and written upon such principles as you would bring to it, would be a valuable addition to the literature of our country—useful to others, as well as honorable to yourself. Venice offers a rich story, and one which, unhappily, is now complete. Sweden, also, is a country fruitful in splendid and memorable events. For this, indeed, it would be necessary to acquire the Norse languages. Sharon Turner acquired them, and the Welsh to boot, for a similar purpose, without neglecting the duties of his practice. It may almost be asserted that men will find leisure for whatever they seriously desire to do. * *

"Believe me, yours faithfully,

"ROBERT SOUTHEY."

To Sharon Turner, Esq.

"Keswick, Sept. 21, 1818.

"MY DEAR TURNER,

"You have taken, I see, Cornano for your physician. Had I made the same experiment, I should have been disposed to prefer a diet of roots, fruits, and esculent plants to bread, which is so likely to be adulterated. There is as much difference in the stomachs of men as in their tempers and faces; severe abstinence is necessary for some, and others feed high and drink hard, and yet attain to a robust old age; but, unquestionably, the sparing system has most facts in its favor, and I have often remarked with wonder the great length of life to which some of the hardest students and most inveterate self-tormentors among the monastic orders have attained. Truly glad shall I be if you derive from your system the permanent benefit which there seems such good reason to expect. Both you and I must wish to remain as long as we can in this 'tough world' for the sake of others. Thank Heaven, it is no rack to us, though we have both reached that stage in our progress in which the highest pleasure that this life can afford is the anticipation of that which is to follow it.

"You have made a wise determination for your son William, for I believe that medical studies are of all others the most unfavorable to the moral sense. Anatomical studies are so revolting, that men who carry any feeling to the pursuit are glad to have it seared as soon as possible. I do not remember ever in the course of my life to have been so shocked as by hearing Carlisle relate some bravados of young men in this state when he was a student himself.

"I wonder you should have any qualms at going to the press, knowing, as you do, how capriciously at best, and, in general, with what injustice and impudent partiality praise or blame is awarded by cotemporary critics, and how absolutely worthless their decrees are in the court of posterity, by which the merits of the case must be finally determined. I am so certain that any subject which has amused your wakeful hours must be worthy to employ the thoughts of other men, and to give them a profitable direction, that, without knowing what the subject is, I exhort you to cast away your fears.

"Remember me most kindly to your household.

"Yours affectionately, R. SOUTHEY."

To C. W. W. Wynn, Esq., M.P.

"Keswick, Nov. 4, 1818.

"MY DEAR WYNN,

"Since I wrote to you at Boulogne, the greater part of my time has been consumed by interruptions of which I ought not to complain, seeing they must needs be beneficial to my health, however they may be felt in the sum total of the year's work. I have had for a guest C——. There is something remarkable in the history of this family. His grandmother was a she-philosopher, a sort of animal much worse than a she-bear. Her housekeeper having broken her leg, she was exceedingly indignant at not being able to convince her that there was no such thing as pain; and when the poor woman complained that the children disturbed her by playing in a room over her head, she insisted upon it that that was impossible, because it was the nature of sound to ascend; and, therefore, she could not be disturbed unless they played in the room under her. This good lady bred up her children as nearly as she could upon Rousseau's maxims, and was especially careful that they should receive no religious instruction whatever. Her daughter had nearly grown up before she ever entered a church, and then she earnestly entreated a friend to take her there from motives of curiosity. This daughter has become a truly religious woman. The son has not departed from the way in which he was trained up; but as he is not a hater of religion, only an unbeliever in it, and has a good living in his gift, he chooses that his only son should take orders, this living being the most convenient means of providing an immediate establishment for him!

"C—— introduced himself to me about three years ago by sending me some poems, which for a youth of seventeen were almost better than should be wished. * * When he first proposed to visit me, his father was thrown into a paroxysm of anger, notwithstanding the *mollia tempora fandi* had been chosen for venturing to make the request; but he suffered him to see me in London last year. He had formed a notion that I was a Methodist, and drank nothing but water; and I believe it raised me considerably in his estimation when C—— assured him that I seemed to enjoy wine as much as any man.

* * * * * * *

"Wilberforce, also, has been here with all his household, and such a household! The principle of the family seems to be that, provided the servants have faith, good works are not to be expected from them, and the utter disorder which prevails in consequence is truly farcical. The old coachman would figure upon the stage. Upon making some complaint about the horses, he told his master and mistress that since they had been in this country they had been so lake-and-river-and-mountain-and-valley-mad, that they had thought of nothing which they ought to think of. I have seen nothing in such pell-mell, topsy-turvy, and chaotic confusion as Wilberforce's apartments since I used to see a certain breakfast-table in Skeleton Corner.* His wife sits in the midst of it like Patience on a monument, and he frisks about as if every vein in his body were filled with quicksilver; but, withal, there is such a constant hilarity in every look and motion, such a sweetness in all his tones, such a benignity in all his thoughts, words, and actions, that all sense of his grotesque appearance is presently overcome, and you can feel nothing but love and admiration for a creature of so happy and blessed a nature.

"A few words now concerning myself. It was my intention to have spent the Christmas in London; a very unexpected cause induced me to delay my journey. More than six years have elapsed since the birth of my youngest child: all thoughts of having another had naturally ceased. In February or March, however, such an event may be looked for. My spirits are more depressed by this than they ought to be; but you may well imagine what reflections must arise. I am now in my forty-fifth year, and if my life should be prolonged, it is but too certain that I should never have heart again to undertake the duty which I once performed with such diligence and such delightful hope. It is well for us that we are not permitted to choose for ourselves. One happy choice, however, I made when I betook myself to literature as my business in life. When I have a heart at ease, there can be no greater delight than it affords me; and when I put away sad thoughts and melancholy forebodings, there is no resource so certain.

"I begin to be solicitous about making such a provision as should leave me at ease in my ways and means, if loss of health or any other calamity should render me incapable of that constant labor, from which, while health and ability may last, I shall have no desire to shrink. When my next poem is finished, I shall be able to do what has never before been in my power—to demand a sum for it.

"God bless you, my dear Wynn!

"Yours most affectionately, R. S."

To John May, Esq.

"Keswick, Nov. 16, 1818.

"MY DEAR FRIEND,

" * * * * * * *

I know something of rebellions, and generally suspect that there has been some fault in the master as well as in the boys, just as a mutiny in a man-of-war affords a strong presumption of tyranny against the captain. Without understanding the merits of this case, it is easy to perceive that the boys believed their privileges were invaded, and fancied that the Magna Charta of Eton was in danger (the Habeas Corpus in schools is in favor of the governors—a writ issued against the subject and affecting him *in tail*), —— took the patriotic side, acting upon Whig principles. They are very good principles in their time and place, and youth is a good time and school a good place for them. When he grows older, he will see the necessity of subordination, and learn that it is only by means of order that liberty can be secured. * * I have a fellow-feeling for ——, because I was myself expelled from Westminster, not for a rebellion (though in that, too, I had my share), but for an act of authorship. Wynn, and Bedford, and Strachey (who is now chief secretary at Madras), and myself, planned a periodical paper in emulation of the Microcosm. It was not begun before the two former had left school, and Bedford and I were the only persons actually engaged in it. I well remember my feelings when the first number appeared on Saturday,

* A part of Christ Church, so called, where Mr. Wynn's rooms were situated.

March 1, 1792. It was Bedford's writing, but that circumstance did not prevent me from feeling that I was that day born into the world as an author; and if ever my head touched the stars while I walked upon the earth, it was then. It seemed as if I had overleaped a barrier, which till then had kept me from the fields of immortality, wherein my career was to be run. In all London there was not so vain, so happy, so elated a creature as I was that day; and, in truth, it was an important day in my life; far more so than I or than any one else could have anticipated, for I was expelled for the fifth number. The subject of that number was *flogging*, and Heaven knows I thought as little of giving offense by it as of causing an eclipse or an earthquake. I treated it in a strange, whimsical, and ironical sort of manner, because it had formed a part of the religious ceremonies of the heathens, and the fathers had held that the gods of the heathens were our devils, and so I proved it to be an invention of the Devil, and therefore unfit to be practiced in schools; and though this was done with very little respect for the Devil, or the fathers, or the heathen gods, or the schoolmasters, yet I as little expected to offend one as the other. I was full of Gibbon at the time, and had caught something of Voltaire's manner. And for this I was privately expelled from Westminster, and for this I was refused admission at Christ Church, where Randolph, from the friendship which he professed for my uncle, could not else have decently refused to provide for me by a studentship; and so I went to Baliol instead, in a blessed hour, for there I found a man of sterling virtue (Edmund Seward), who led me right when it might have been easy to have led me wrong. I used to call him *Talus* for his unbending morals and iron rectitude, and his strength of body also justified the name. His death in the year 1795 was the first severe affliction that I ever experienced; and sometimes even now I dream of him, and wake myself by weeping, because even in my dreams I remember that he is dead. I loved him with my whole heart, and shall remember him with gratitude and affection as one who was my moral father, to the last moment of my life; and to meet him again will at that moment be one of the joys to which I shall look forward in eternity. My dear John May, I have got into a strain which I neither intended nor foresaw. Misfortunes, as the story says, are good for something. The stream of my life would certainly have taken a different direction if I had not been expelled, and I am satisfied that it could never have held a better course. * * * * * *

"God bless you, my dear friend!

"Believe me, most truly and affectionately yours, ROBERT SOUTHEY."

To Grosvenor C. Bedford, Esq.

"Keswick, Nov. 28, 1818.

"MY DEAR GROSVENOR,

"This is a most remarkable season with us. On the 20th of November we had French beans at dinner, and now (on the 28th) there has not been the slightest snown on the mountains, nor the slightest appearance of frost in the valley. The late flowers continue to blossom still, and the early ones are pushing forward as if it were spring. The great scarlet poppy has two large buds ready to burst, and your favorite blue thistle has brought forth a flower. But, what is more extraordinary, the annual poppies, whose stalks, to all appearance dead and dry, were left in the ground merely till Mrs. Lovel should give directions for clearing them away, have in many instances shot out fresh leaves of diminutive size, and produced blossoms correspondently small, not bigger than a daisy. This is in our own garden, which, as you know, has no advantages of shelter or situation; in happier spots the gardens have more the appearance of September than of winter.

"Gifford will tell you that I have been speaking a good word in behalf of the historical painters. (By-the-by, get Nash to take you to see Haydon's great picture, which is prodigiously fine.) I am now upon the Copyright question, which I shall make as short a possible; a few days will finish it, and a few days more finish a paper upon the Catacombs, in which I have brought together a great collection of facts from out-of-the-way sources, some of them very curious. The Copyright must have a place in the present number, and no doubt it will, being much more for Murray's interest than mine. The Catacombs will eke out my ways and means for the next quarter, and I shall have done with the Quarterly Review for the next six months.

"I shall not move southward till both the Brazil and the Wesley are finished. Three winter months will do wonders, as I hope to be entirely free from interruptions. Other circumstances would not allow me to leave home before March, nor will I move then unless these works are off my hands. I shall then start fairly, without impediment, and in full force for the Peninsular War; and thus my life passes, looking to the completion of one work for the sake of beginning another, and having to start afresh for a new career as often as I reach the goal; and so I suppose it will be, till I break down and founder upon the course. But if I live a few years longer in possession of my faculties, I will do great things.

"God bless you! R. S."

To C. W. W. Wynn, Esq., M.P.

"Keswick, Nov. 30, 1818.

"MY DEAR WYNN,

"I was truly glad to hear of your daughter's recovery. I have been in a storm at sea, in a Spanish vessel, and the feeling, when the weather had so sensibly abated that the danger was over, is the only one I can compare with that which is felt in a case like yours upon the first assurance that the disease is giving way. Those writers who speak of childhood or even youth as the happiest season of life, seem to me to speak with little reason. There is, indeed, an exemption from the cares of the world, and from those anxieties which shake us to the very center. But, as far as my own experience goes, when we are exempt from trials of this nature, our happiness, as we grow older, is more in quantity, and higher in degree as well as in kind. What hopes we have are no longer accompanied with uneasiness or restless desires. The way before us is no longer uncertain; we see to the end of our journey; the acquisition of knowledge becomes more and more delightful, and the appetite for it may truly be said to grow with what it feeds on; and as we set our thoughts and hearts in order for another world, the prospect of that world becomes a source of deeper delight than any thing which this could administer to an immortal spirit. On the other hand, we are vulnerable out of ourselves, and you and I are reaching that time of life in which the losses which we have to endure will be so many amputations. The wound may heal, but the mutilation will always be felt. Not to speak of more vital affections, the loss of a familiar friend casts a shade over the remembrance of every thing in which he was associated. You and I, my dear Wynn, are less to each other than we were in old times. Years pass away without our meeting; nor is it at all likely that we shall ever again see as much of each other in this world as we used to do in the course of one short term at Oxford; and yet he who is to be the survivor will one day feel how much we are to each other, even now—when all those recollections which he now loves to invite and dwell upon will come to him like specters.

"However, I hope that both you and I may be permitted to do something more before we are removed; and I can not but hope that you will take upon yourself a conspicuous part in that reformation of the criminal laws, which can not much longer be delayed; nor do I know any one (setting all personal feelings aside) by whom it could so fitly be taken up. That speech of Frankland's was perfectly conclusive to my mind; but that alterations are necessary is certain, and the late trials for forgery show that they must be made, even now, with a bad grace, but with a worse the longer they are delayed. To me it has long appeared a safe proposition that the punishment of death is misapplied whenever the general feeling that it creates is that of compassion for the criminal. A man and woman were executed for coining at the same time with Patch. Now what an offense was this to the common sense of justice! There is undoubtedly, at this time, a settled purpose among the Revolutionists to bring the laws into contempt and hatred, and to a very great degree it has succeeded. The more reason, therefore, that where they are plainly objectionable they should be revised. But for the principle of making the sentence in all cases proportionate to the crime, and the execution certain, nothing in my judgment can be more impracticable, and I am sure nothing could lead to greater injustice than an attempt to effect it. The sentence must be sufficient for the highest degree of the crime, and a discretionary power allowed for tempering it to the level of the lowest. You would take up the matter with a due sense of its difficulty, and with every possible advantage of character, both in the House and in the country; and, moreover, the disposition of the ministers ought to be, and I really should suppose would be, in your favor. * *

"God bless you, my dear Wynn! R. S."

CHAPTER XXIV.

NERVOUS FEELINGS — ANXIETIES FOR THE FUTURE—RECOLLECTIONS OF EARLY JOURNEYS —PRUDENCE OF ANTICIPATING POPULAR OPINION—ODE ON THE QUEEN'S DEATH—HAYDON —WORDSWORTH—LIFE OF WESLEY—HOME POLITICS — SWITZERLAND — CRITICISMS ON A VOLUME OF POEMS BY MR. E. ELLIOTT—BIRTH OF A SON—HISTORY OF BRAZIL—RISING POETS—WAVERLEY NOVELS—REASONS FOR DECLINING TO ATTEND THE WESTMINSTER MEETING — COLLEGE RECOLLECTIONS — RELIGION NECESSARY TO HAPPINESS—NOTICES OF THE LAKE COUNTRY—MR. WORDSWORTH'S "WAGONER"—ADVISES ALLAN CUNNINGHAM ON LITERARY PURSUITS—LORD BYRON'S HOSTILITY—PROBABLE RECEPTION OF THE HISTORY OF BRAZIL—CRABBE'S POEMS—PETER ROBERTS —LITERARY EMPLOYMENTS — COLONIZATION NECESSARY—TOUR IN SCOTLAND—DESIRABLENESS OF MEN OF MATURE YEARS TAKING HOLY ORDERS — JOHN MORGAN IN DIFFICULTIES — PROJECTED JOURNEY.—1818–1819.

THE following is the letter before alluded to, as showing so strong a contrast to that freedom from anxiety and confidence in himself which seemed to possess him at the time he refused the offer of librarian to the Advocates' Library at Edinburgh. It is, indeed, no matter of wonder that, sensitively constituted as he was by nature, and compelled to such incessant mental occupation, such feelings should at times come over him; and we may see in them the sad forewarnings of that calamity by which his latest years were darkened.

But if he was not altogether what he so well describes the stern American leader to have been,

"Lord of his own resolves, of his own heart absolute master,"*

he certainly possessed no common power over himself; and he here well describes how needful was its exercise.

To Grosvenor C Bedford, Esq.

"Keswick, Dec. 5, 1818.

"MY DEAR GROSVENOR,

"It is, between ourselves, a matter of surprise to me that this bodily machine of mine should have continued its operations with so few derangements, knowing, as I well do, its excessive susceptibility to many deranging causes. The nitrous oxyd approaches nearer to the notion of

* Vision of Judgment.

a *neurometer* than any thing which perhaps could be devised; and I was acted upon by a far smaller dose than any person upon whom it had ever been tried, when I was in the habit of taking it. If I did not vary my pursuits, and carry on many works of a totally different kind at once, I should soon be incapable of proceeding with any, so surely does it disturb my sleep and affect my dreams if I dwell upon one with any continuous attention. The truth is, that though some persons, whose knowledge of me is scarcely skin deep, suppose I have no nerves, because I have great self-control as far as regards the surface; if it were not for great self-management, and what may be called a strict intellectual regimen, I should very soon be in a deplorable state of what is called nervous disease, and this would have been the case any time during the last twenty years.

"Thank God, I am well at present, and well employed: Brazil and Wesley both at the press; a paper for the Quarterly Review in hand, and Oliver Newman now seriously resumed; while for light reading I am going through South's Sermons and the whole British and Irish part of the Acta Sanctorum.

"In the MSS. of Wesley, which passed through Gifford's hands while you were absent, there was a chapter which I wished you to have seen, because both in matter and manner it is among the best things I have written. It contained a view of our religious history down to the accession of the present family—not the facts, but the spirit of the history. You will be pleased to see how I have relieved and diversified this book, which will be as elaborate as a Dutchman's work, and as entertaining as a Frenchman's.

"I want now to provide against that inability which may any day or any moment overtake me. You are not mistaken in thinking that the last three years have considerably changed me; the outside remains pretty much the same, but it is far otherwise within. If hitherto the day has been sufficient for the labor, as well as the labor for the day, I now feel that it can not always, and possibly may not long be so. Were I dead there would be a provision for my family, which, though not such as I yet hope to make it, would yet be a respectable one. But if I were unable to work, half my ways and means would instantly be cut off, and the whole of them are needed. Such thoughts did not use to visit me. My spirits retain their strength, but they have lost their buoyancy, and that forever. I should be the better for traveling, but that is not in my power. At present the press fetters me, and if it did not, I could not afford to be spending money when I ought to be earning it. But I shall work the harder to enable me so to do.

"God bless you! R. S."

To Chauncey H. Townshend, Esq.

"Keswick, Dec. 10, 1818.

"MY DEAR CHAUNCEY,

"You made the best use of your misfortune at Kendal. The most completely comfortless hours in a man's life (abstracted from all real calamity) are those which he spends alone at an inn, waiting for a chance in a stage-coach. Time thus spent is so thoroughly disagreeable that the act of getting into the coach, and resigning yourself to be jumbled for four-and-twenty or eight-and-forty hours, like a mass of inert matter, becomes a positive pleasure. I always prepare myself for such occasions with some closely-printed pocket volume, of pregnant matter, for which I should not be likely to afford leisure at other times. Erasmus's Colloquies stood me in good stead for more than one journey; Sir Thomas More's Utopia for another. When I was a schoolboy I loved traveling, and enjoyed it, indeed, as long as I could say *omnia mea mecum;* that is, as long as I could carry with me an undivided heart and mind, and had nothing to make me wish myself in any other place than where I was. The journey from London to Bristol at the holidays was one of the pleasures which I looked for at breaking up; and I used generally to travel by day rather than by night, that I might lose none of the expected enjoyment. I wish I had kept a journal of all those journeys; for some of the company into which I have fallen might have furnished matter worthy of preservation. Once I traveled with the keeper of a crimping-house at Charing Cross, who, meeting with an old acquaintance in the coach, told him his profession while I was supposed to be asleep in the corner. Once I formed an acquaintance with a young deaf and dumb man, and learned to converse with him. Once I fell in with a man of a race now nearly extinct—a village mathematician; a self-taught, iron-headed man, who, if he had been lucky enough to have been well educated and entered at Trinity Hall, might have been first wrangler, and perhaps have gone as near toward doubling the cube as any of the votaries of Mathesis. (Pray write a sonnet to that said personage.) This man was pleased with me, and (perhaps because I was flattered by perceiving it) I have a distinct recollection of his remarkable countenance after an interval of nearly thirty years. He labored very hard to give me a love of his own favorite pursuit; and it is my own fault that I can not now take the altitude of a church tower by the help of a cocked hat, as he taught me, or would have taught, if I could have retained such lessons.

"It is an act, not absolutely of heroic virtue, but of something like it, my writing to you this evening. Four successive evenings I have been prevented from carrying into effect the fixed purpose of so doing; first by the general's dropping in to pass the last evening with me before his departure, then by letters which required reply without delay; and this afternoon, just before the bell rang for tea, a huge parcel was brought up stairs, containing twenty volumes of the Gospel Magazine, in which dunghill I am now about to rake for wheat, or for wild oats, if you like the metaphor better.

"Yours affectionately, R. SOUTHEY."

To John Rickman, Esq.

"Dec. 11, 1818.

"MY DEAR R.,

" * * * * * * *

I sometimes try to persuade myself that mine is a Turkish sort of constitution, and that exercise and out-of-door air are not needful for its well-being; but the body begins to require better management than it did; it will not take care of itself so well as it did twenty years ago, and I need not look in the glass for a memento that I have begun the down-hill part of my journey. So be it. There is so much for my heart, and hope, and curiosity at the end of the stage, that if I thought only of myself in this world, I should wish that I was there.

"It is a strange folly, a fatality, that men in power will not see the prudence of anticipating public feeling sometimes, and doing things with a grace for the sake of popularity, which must be done with ignominy upon compulsion. For instance, in Lord Cochrane's affair, it was wrong to condemn him to the pillory; but if that part of the sentence had been annulled before popular opinion was expressed, the prince would have gained credit instead of being supposed to yield to the newspapers. There is another case in the suicide laws. * * And again in the matter of forgery; the law must be altered, and this not from the will of the Legislature, but by the will of the London juries! The juries, however, if they go on in their present course, will do more than this—they will prove that the very institution of juries, on which we have prided ourselves so long, is inconsistent not only with common sense, but with the safety of society and the security of government. I wish, when the question of forgery comes before the House (as it surely must do), that something may be said and done also for restoring that part of the system which makes the jurymen punishable for a false verdict.

"I have written shortly about the Copyright question for the Q. R., and put in a word, without any hope of a change in my time, upon the absurd injustice of the existing laws. My own case hereafter will plead more strongly against them than it is in my power to do now, as, according to all appearances, my copyrights will be much more valuable property after my death than they have ever yet proved.

"God bless you!

"Always and affectionately yours, R. S."

To John Rickman, Esq.

"Jan. 1, 1818.

"MY DEAR R.,

"Many happy new years to you and yours, and may you go on well however the world goes. Go as it may, it is some satisfaction to think that it will not be the worse for any thing that you and I have done in it. And it is to be hoped that our work is not done yet. I have a strong hope that something may be effected in our old scheme about the reformed convents, and that would be as great a step toward amending the condition of educated women as the establishment of savings' banks has been for bettering the state of the lower classes.

"I am reading Coxe's Memoirs of Marlborough, by far the best of his books. Marlborough appears to more advantage in all respects the more he is known. The reading is not gratuitous, for I am to review the work.

"Longman sent me Müller's Universal History, a surprising work, though I find him deficient in knowledge and in views in the points where I am competent to be his judge. Have you seen Fearon's Sketches of America? It is very amusing to see a man who hates all the institutions of his own country compelled to own that every thing is worse in America, and groan while he makes the confession; too honest to conceal the truth, and yet bringing it up as if it were got at by means of emetic tartar, sorely against his stomach. I wish I were not too busy to write a careful review of this book.

"Did I tell you concerning Morris Birbeck, that he sunk £8000 by a speculation in soap, and was Lord Onslow's tenant, which said Lord Onslow indited upon him this epigram:

"'Had you ta'en less delight in
Political writing,
Nor to vain speculations given scope,
You'd have paid me your rent,
Your time better spent,
And besides—washed your hands of the soap.'

"God bless you! R. S."

To Mr. Ebenezer Elliott, Jun.

"Keswick, Jan. 30, 1819.

"MY DEAR SIR,

"I received your little volume yesterday.* You may rest assured that you ascribed the condemnation in the Monthly Magazine to the true cause.

"There are abundant evidences of power in it; its merits are of the most striking kind; and its defects are not less striking, both in plan and execution. The stories had better each have been separate, than linked together without any natural or necessary connection. The first consists of such grossly improbable circumstances, that it is altogether as incredible as if it were a supernatural tale; it is also a hateful story, presenting nothing but what is painful. In the second, the machinery is preposterously disproportionate to the occasion. And in all the poems there is too much ornament, too much effort, too much labor. You think you can never embroider your drapery too much; and that the more gold and jewels you can fasten on it, the richer the effect must be. The consequence is, that there is a total want of what painters call breadth and keeping, and, therefore, the effect is lost.

"You will say that this opinion proceeds from the erroneous system which I have pursued in my own writings, and which has prevented my poems from obtaining the same popularity as those of Lord Byron and Walter Scott. But look at those poets whose rank is established beyond

* This volume of poems was entitled "Night."

all controversy. Look at the Homeric poems—at Virgil, Dante, Ariosto, Milton. Do not ask yourself what are the causes of the failure or success of your cotemporaries; their failure or success is not determined yet—a generation, an age, a century will not suffice to determine it. But see what it is by which those poets have rendered themselves immortal; who, after the lapse of centuries, are living and acting upon us still.

"I should not speak to you thus plainly of your fault—the sin by which the angels fell—if it were not for the great powers which are thus injured by misdirection; and it is for the sake of bearing testimony to those powers, and thereby endeavoring to lessen the effect which a rascally criticism may have produced upon your feelings, that I am now writing. That criticism may give you pain, because it may effect the minds of persons not very capable of forming an opinion for themselves, who may either be glad to be encouraged in despising your production, or grieved at seeing it condemned. But in any other point of view it is unworthy of a moment's thought.

"You may do great things if you will cease to attempt so much—if you will learn to proportion your figures to your canvas. Cease to overlay your foregrounds with florid ornaments, and be persuaded that, in a poem as well as in a picture, there must be lights and shades; that the general effect can never be good unless the subordinate parts are kept down, and that the brilliancy of one part is brought out and heightened by the repose of the other. One word more.

"With your powers of thought and language, you need not seek to produce effect by monstrous incidents or exaggerated characters. These drams have been administered so often that they are beginning to lose their effect; and it is to truth and nature that we must come at last. Trust to them, and they will bear you through. You are now squandering wealth with which, if it be properly disposed, you may purchase golden reputation.

"But you must reverence your elders more, and be less eager for immediate applause.

"You will judge of the sincerity of my praise by the frankness of my censure.

"Farewell! And believe me, yours faithfully, R. SOUTHEY."

To Walter Scott, Esq.

"March 11, 1819.

"MY DEAR SCOTT,

"My conscience will not let me direct a letter to your care without directing one to yourself by the same post.

"A great event has happened to me within this fortnight—the birth of a child, after an interval of nearly seven years, and that child a son. This was a chance to which I looked rather with dread than with hope, after having seen the flower of my earthly hopes and happiness cut down. But it is well that these things are not in our own disposal; and without building upon so frail a tenure as an infant's life, or indulging in any vain dreams of what may be, I am thankful for him now that he is come.

"You would have heard from me ere long, even if Mr. Ticknor* had not given a spur to my tardy intentions. I should soon have written to say that you will shortly receive the concluding volume of my History of Brazil, for I am now drawing fast toward the close of that long labor. This volume has less of the kite and crow warfare than its predecessors, and is rich in information of various kinds, which has never till now come before the public in any shape. Indeed, when I think of the materials from which it has been composed, and how completely, during great part of my course, I have been without either chart or pilot to direct me, I look back with wonder upon what I have accomplished. I go to London in about seven weeks from this time, and as soon as I return the Peninsular War will be sent to press.

"Our successors (for you and I are now old enough in authorship to use this term) are falling into the same faults as the Roman poets after the Augustan age, and the Italians after the golden season of their poetry. They are overlaboring their productions, and overloading them with ornament, so that all parts are equally prominent, every where glare and glitter, and no keeping and no repose. Henry Milman has spoiled his Samor in this way. It is full of power and of beauty, but too full of them. There is another striking example in a little volume called Night, where some of the most uncouth stories imaginable are told in a strain of continued tiptoe effort; and you are vexed to see such uncommon talents so oddly applied, and such Herculean strength wasted in preposterous exertions. The author's name is Elliott, a self-taught man, in business (the iron trade, I believe) at Rotherham. He sends play after play to the London theaters, and has always that sort of refusal which gives him encouragement to try another. Sheridan said of one of them that it was "a comical tragedy, but he did not know any man who could have written such a one." I have given him good advice, which he takes as it is meant, and something may come of him yet.

"It was reported that you were about to bring forth a play, and I was greatly in hopes it might be true; for I am verily persuaded that in this course you would run as brilliant a career as you have already done in narrative, both in prose and rhyme, for as for believing that you have a double in the field—not I! Those same powers would be equally certain of success in the drama; and were you to give them a dramatic direction, and reign for a third seven years upon the stage, you would stand alone in literary history. Indeed, already I believe that no man ever afforded so much delight to so great a number of his cotemporaries in this or any other country.

"God bless you, my dear Scott! Remem-

* The accomplished author of "The History of Spanish Literature." Harper & Brothers, 1850.

ber me to Mrs. S. and your daughter, and believe me,

"Ever yours affectionately,
"ROBERT SOUTHEY."

To Grosvenor C. Bedford, Esq.

"Keswick, April, 9, 1819.

"MY DEAR G.,

" * * * * * * * *

Even if I were in town, I certainly should not go to the Westminster meeting. The chance of seeing some half dozen men with whom I might exchange a few words of recognition and shake hands, would not make amends for the melancholy recollection of those whom I loved better and used to see at the same time. Moreover, I have an absolute hatred of all public meetings, and would rather go without a dinner than eat it in such an assembly. I went to the Academy's dinner for the sake of facing William Smith; but I go to no more such.

"My wish will be to see as much of my friends as I can, and as little of my acquaintance; and, therefore, I mean to refuse all such invitations as would throw me among strangers or indifferent persons, except in cases where I owe something for civilities received; for I do not want to see lions, and still less do I desire to be exhibited as one, and go where I should be expected to open my mouth and roar.

"There is another reason* why I would not attend the Westminster meeting. As I never went during Vincent's life, it might seem as if I felt myself at liberty to go there now, and had not done so before. Whereas, so far was I from harboring any resentment toward Vincent, or any unpleasant feeling of any kind, that I have long and with good reason looked upon my expulsion from Westminster as having been in its consequences the luckiest event of my life; and for many years I should have been glad to have met the old man, in full persuasion that he would have not been sorry to have met with me.

"I had a beautiful letter† yesterday from poor Walter Scott, who has been on the very brink of the grave, and feels how likely it is that any day or hour may send him there. If he is sufficiently recovered, I shall meet him in London; but his health is broken beyond all prospect or hope of complete recovery. He entreats me to take warning, and beware of overworking myself. I am afraid no person ever took that advice who stood in need of it, and still more afraid that the surest way of bringing on the anticipated evil would be to apprehend it. But I believe that I manage myself well by frequent change of employment, frequent idling, and keeping my mind as free as I can from any strong excitement.

"God bless you, my dear Grosvenor!

"R. S."

* Of your reasons for declining to be present at the Westminster meeting, one class I do not approve, and the other I do not admit. How it will look that you go to it after Vincent's death, never having gone to it during his life, is no question, for it will have no look at all, for nobody will look at it. This is just one of the feelings that a man has when *he knows* that he has a hole in his stocking, and fancies, of course, that the attention of all the company is attracted to it. The last time I ever saw the old dean, he spoke of you with kindness and approbation, and, I thought, with pride. * * If I were to have you here on that day, I should tie a string round your leg and pull you in an opposite direction to that in which I meant to drive you. Swallow that and digest it."—*G. C. B. to R. S., April* 12, 1819.

† See Life of Sir Walter Scott, 2d edit., vol. vi., p. 41.

To the Rev. Nicholas Lightfoot.

"Keswick, May 29, 1819.

"MY DEAR LIGHTFOOT,

"So long a time had elapsed without my hearing from you, or by any accident of you, that I began to fear what might have been the cause of this long silence, and was almost afraid to inquire. I am very sorry that Mr. Bush did not make use of your name when he was at Keswick last summer; he could have brought with him no better introduction, and I have always time to perform offices of attention and hospitality to those who are entitled to them. He left a good impression here as an excellent preacher; indeed, I have seldom or never heard a more judicious one. The account which he gave you of my way of life is not altogether correct. I have no allotted quantum of exercise, but, as at Oxford, sometimes go a long while without any, and sometimes take walks that would try the mettle of a younger man. And a great deal more of my time is employed in reading than in writing; if it were not, what I write would be of very little value. But that I am a close student is very true, and such I shall continue to be as long as my eyes and other faculties last.

"You must apply in time if you design to place your son at Oriel; it is now no easy matter to obtain admission there, nor, indeed, at any college which is in good reputation. I almost wonder that you do not give the preference to old Baliol for the sake of old times, now that the college has fairly obtained a new character, and is no longer the seat of drunkenness, raffery, and indiscipline, as it was in our days. It is even doubtful whether if I were an under-graduate now I should be permitted to try my skill in throwing stones for the pleasure of hearing them knock against your door. Seriously, however, altered as the college is, there would be an advantage in sending your son there, where you have left a good name and a good example. Poor Thomas Howe,* I believe, led but a melancholy life after he left college; without neighbors, without a family, without a pursuit, he must have felt dismally the want of his old routine, and sorely have missed his pupils, the chapel bells, and the common room. A monk is much happier than an old fellow of a college who retires to reside upon a country living. And how much happier are you at this day, with all the tedium which your daily occupation must bring with it, than if you had obtained a fellowship, and then waited twenty years for preferment.

"Believe me, my dear Lightfoot, yours affectionately as in old times, R. SOUTHEY."

* His college tutor. See *antè*, p. 73.

The following letter I found copied among my father's papers, but without name or date; it evidently, however, belongs to this period, and is, I think, worthy of insertion here, as showing his aptness to suggest religious thoughts whenever an occasion presented itself, and the judicious manner in which he does so.

"Keswick, 1819.

"I have behaved very ill in having so long delayed replying to a lady's letter, and that letter, too, one which deserved a ready and a thankful acknowledgment. Forgive me. I am not wont to be thus discourteous; and in the present instance there is some excuse for it, for your letter arrived at a time of much anxiety. My wife had a three months' illness after the birth of a son; and during that time it was as much as I could do to force my attention to business which could not be left undone. My heart was not enough at ease to be addressing you.

"The number of unknown correspondents whom I have had in my time does not lessen my desire of seeing you, nor abate that curiosity which men feel as strongly as women, except that they have not the same leisure for thinking of it.

* * * * * * *

"You tell me that the whole of your happiness is dependent upon literary pursuits and recreations. It is well that you have these resources; but, were we near each other, and were I to like you half as well upon a nearer acquaintance as it appears to me at this distance that I should do, I think that when I had won your confidence I should venture to tell you that something better than literature is necessary for happiness.

"To confess the truth, one of the causes which have prevented me from writing to you earlier has been the wish and half intention of touching upon this theme checked by that sort of hesitation which sometimes (and that too often) prevents us from doing what we ought for fear of singularity. That you are a woman of talents I know; and I think you would not have given me the preference over more fashionable poets, if there had not been something in the general character of my writings which accorded with your feelings, and which you did not find in theirs. But you have lived in high life; you move in circles of gayety and fashion; and though you sympathize with me when I express myself in verse, it is more than probable that the direct mention of religion may startle you, as something unwarranted as well as unexpected.

"I am no Methodist, no sectarian, no bigot, no formalist. My natural spirits are buoyant beyond those of any person, man, woman, or child, whom I ever saw or heard of. They have had enough to try them and to sink them, and it is by religion alone that I shall be enabled to pass the remainder of my days in cheerfulness and in hope. Without hope there can be no happiness, and without religion, no hope but such as deceives us. Your heart seems to want an object, and this would satisfy it; and if it has been wounded, this, and this only, is the cure.

"Are you displeased with this freedom? Or do you receive it as a proof that I am disposed to become something more than a mere literary acquaintance, and that you have made me feel an interest concerning you which an ordinary person could not have excited?

* * * * * *

"Scott is very ill. He suffers dreadfully, but bears his sufferings with admirable equanimity, and looks on to the probable termination of them with calmness and a well-founded hope. God grant that he may recover! He is a noble and generous-hearted creature, whose like we shall not look upon again."

To Wade Browne, Esq.

"Keswick, June 15, 1819.

"My dear Sir,

"When you hear that my journey to the south must be postponed till the fall of the leaf, I fear you will think me infirm of purpose, and as little to be depended on as the wind and weather in this our mutable climate. Its cause, however, lies rather in a good, obstinate principle of perseverance than in any fickleness of temper. This history, of which the hundredth sheet is now upon my desk, will confine me here so far into the summer (beyond all previous or possible calculation), that if I went into the south as soon as it is completed, I should be under the necessity of shortening my stay there, and leaving part of my business undone, in order to return in time for a long-standing engagement, which in the autumn will take me into the Highlands. All things duly considered, it seems best to put off my journey to London till November, by which time all my running accounts with the press will be settled.

* * * * * *

"Cuthbert, who is now four months old, is beginning to serve me as well as his sisters for a plaything. The country is in its full beauty at this time—perhaps in greater than I may ever again see it, for it is reported that the woods on Castelet are condemned to come down next year: this, if it be true, is the greatest loss that Keswick could possibly sustain, and in no place will the loss be more conspicuous than from the room wherein I am now writing. But this neighborhood has suffered much from the ax since you were here.* The woods about Lodore are gone; so are those under Castle-Crag; so is the little knot of fir-trees on the way to church, which were so placed as to make one of the features of the vale; and, worst of all, so is that beautiful birch grove on the side of the lake between Barrow aud Lodore. Not a single sucker is springing up in its place; and, indeed, it would require a full century before another grove could be reared which would equal it in beauty. It is lucky that they can not level the mountains nor drain the lake; bnt they are doing what they

* See the beginning of Colloquy X., On the Progress and Prospects of Society.

The following letter I found copied among my father's papers, but without name or date; it evidently, however, belongs to this period, and is, I think, worthy of insertion here, as showing his aptness to suggest religious thoughts whenever an occasion presented itself, and the judicious manner in which he does so.

"Keswick, 1819.

"I have behaved very ill in having so long delayed replying to a lady's letter, and that letter, too, one which deserved a ready and a thankful acknowledgment. Forgive me. I am not wont to be thus discourteous; and in the present instance there is some excuse for it, for your letter arrived at a time of much anxiety. My wife had a three months' illness after the birth of a son; and during that time it was as much as I could do to force my attention to business which could not be left undone. My heart was not enough at ease to be addressing you.

"The number of unknown correspondents whom I have had in my time does not lessen my desire of seeing you, nor abate that curiosity which men feel as strongly as women, except that they have not the same leisure for thinking of it.

* * * * * * *

"You tell me that the whole of your happiness is dependent upon literary pursuits and recreations. It is well that you have these resources; but, were we near each other, and were I to like you half as well upon a nearer acquaintance as it appears to me at this distance that I should do, I think that when I had won your confidence I should venture to tell you that something better than literature is necessary for happiness.

"To confess the truth, one of the causes which have prevented me from writing to you earlier has been the wish and half intention of touching upon this theme checked by that sort of hesitation which sometimes (and that too often) prevents us from doing what we ought for fear of singularity. That you are a woman of talents I know; and I think you would not have given me the preference over more fashionable poets, if there had not been something in the general character of my writings which accorded with your feelings, and which you did not find in theirs. But you have lived in high life; you move in circles of gayety and fashion; and though you sympathize with me when I express myself in verse, it is more than probable that the direct mention of religion may startle you, as something unwarranted as well as unexpected.

"I am no Methodist, no sectarian, no bigot, no formalist. My natural spirits are buoyant beyond those of any person, man, woman, or child, whom I ever saw or heard of. They have had enough to try them and to sink them, and it is by religion alone that I shall be enabled to pass the remainder of my days in cheerfulness and in hope. Without hope there can be no happiness, and without religion, no hope but such as deceives us. Your heart seems to want an object, and this would satisfy it; and if it has been wounded, this, and this only, is the cure.

"Are you displeased with this freedom? Or do you receive it as a proof that I am disposed to become something more than a mere literary acquaintance, and that you have made me feel an interest concerning you which an ordinary person could not have excited?

* * * * * *

"Scott is very ill. He suffers dreadfully, but bears his sufferings with admirable equanimity, and looks on to the probable termination of them with calmness and a well-founded hope. God grant that he may recover! He is a noble and generous-hearted creature, whose like we shall not look upon again."

To Wade Browne, Esq.

"Keswick, June 15, 1819.

"My dear Sir,

"When you hear that my journey to the south must be postponed till the fall of the leaf, I fear you will think me infirm of purpose, and as little to be depended on as the wind and weather in this our mutable climate. Its cause, however, lies rather in a good, obstinate principle of perseverance than in any fickleness of temper. This history, of which the hundredth sheet is now upon my desk, will confine me here so far into the summer (beyond all previous or possible calculation), that if I went into the south as soon as it is completed, I should be under the necessity of shortening my stay there, and leaving part of my business undone, in order to return in time for a long-standing engagement, which in the autumn will take me into the Highlands. All things duly considered, it seems best to put off my journey to London till November, by which time all my running accounts with the press will be settled.

* * * * * *

"Cuthbert, who is now four months old, is beginning to serve me as well as his sisters for a plaything. The country is in its full beauty at this time—perhaps in greater than I may ever again see it, for it is reported that the woods on Castelet are condemned to come down next year: this, if it be true, is the greatest loss that Keswick could possibly sustain, and in no place will the loss be more conspicuous than from the room wherein I am now writing. But this neighborhood has suffered much from the ax since you were here.* The woods about Lodore are gone; so are those under Castle-Crag; so is the little knot of fir-trees on the way to church, which were so placed as to make one of the features of the vale; and, worst of all, so is that beautiful birch grove on the side of the lake between Barrow aud Lodore. Not a single sucker is springing up in its place; and, indeed, it would require a full century before another grove could be reared which would equal it in beauty. It is lucky that they can not level the mountains nor drain the lake; bnt they are doing what they

* See the beginning of Colloquy X., On the Progress and Prospects of Society.

me freely; I would gladly be of use to you, if I could.

"Farewell, and believe me,

"Your sincere well-wisher,

"ROBERT SOUTHEY."

To C. H. Townshend, Esq.

"Keswick, July 20, 1819.

"MY DEAR CHAUNCEY,

" * * * * * * *

I have not seen more of Don Juan than some extracts in a country paper, wherein my own name is coupled with a rhyme which I thought would never be used by any person but myself when kissing one of my own children in infancy, and talking nonsense to it, which, whatever you may think of it at present as an exercise for the intellect, I hope you will one day have occasion to practice, and you will then find out its many and various excellences. I do not yet know whether the printed poem is introduced by a dedication* to me, in a most hostile strain, which came over with it, or whether the person who has done Lord Byron the irreparable injury of sending into the world what his own publisher and his friends endeavored, for his sake, to keep out of it, has suppressed it. This is to me a matter of perfect unconcern. Lord Byron attacked me when he ran amuck as a satirist; he found it convenient to express himself sorry for that satire, and to have such of the persons told so whom he had assailed in it as he was likely to fall in with in society—myself among the number. I met him three or four times on courteous terms, and saw enough of him to feel that he was rather to be shunned than sought. Attack me as he will, I shall not go out of my course to break a spear with him; but if it comes in my way to give him a passing touch, it will be one that will leave a scar.

"The third and last volume of my Opus Majus will be published in two or three weeks; they are printing the index. What effect will it produce? It may tend to sober the anticipations of a young author to hear the faithful anticipations of an experienced one. None that will be heard of. It will move quietly from the publishers to a certain number of reading societies, and a certain number of private libraries; enough between them to pay the expenses of the publication. Some twenty persons in England, and some half dozen in Portugal and Brazil, will peruse it with avidity and delight. Some fifty, perhaps, will buy the book because of the subject, and ask one another if they have had time to look into it. A few of those who know me will wish that I had employed the time which it has cost in writing poems; and some of those who do not know me will marvel that in the ripe season of my mind, in the summer of reputation, I should have bestowed so large a portion of life upon a work which could not possibly become either popular or profitable. And is this all? No, Chauncey Townshend, it is not all; and I should deal insincerely with you if I did not add, that ages hence it will be found among those works which are not destined to perish, and secure for me a remembrance in other countries as well as in my own; that it will be read in the heart of S. America, and communicate to the Brazilians, when they shall have become a powerful nation, much of their own history which would otherwise have perished, and be to them what the work of Herodotus is to Europe. You will agree with me on one point at least—that I am in no danger of feeling disappointment. But you will agree, also, that no man can deserve or obtain the applause of after ages, if he is too solicitous about that of his own.

"God bless you! R. S."

To C. W. W. Wynn, Esq., M.P.

"Keswick, July 22, 1829.

"MY DEAR WYNN,

"I give you joy of your escape from late hours in the House of Commons and a summer in London. I congratulate you upon exchanging gas-lights for the moon and stars, and the pavement of Whitehall for your noble terraces, which I never can think of without pleasure, because they are beautiful in themselves, and carry one back to old times — any thing which does this does one good. Were I to build a mansion with the means of Lord Lonsdale or Lord Grosvenor, I would certainly make hanging gardens if the ground permitted it. They have a character of grandeur and of permanence, without which nothing can be truly grand, and they are fine even in decay.

"I will come to you for a day or two, on my way to town, about the beginning of December. This will be a flying visit; but one of these summers or autumns, I should like dearly to finish the projected circuit with you which Mr. Curry cut short in the year 1801, when he sent for the most unfit man in the world to be his secretary, having nothing whatever for him to do; and many years must not be suffered to go by. My next birth-day will be the forty-fifth, and every year will take something from the inclination to move, and perhaps, also, from the power of enjoyment.

"I was not disappointed with Crabbe's Tales. He is a decided mannerist, but so are all original writers in all ages; nor is it possible for a poet to avoid it, if he writes much in the same key and upon the same class of subjects. Crabbe's poems will have a great and lasting value as

---

* This dedication, which is sufficiently scurrilous, is prefixed to the poem in the Collected Edition of Lord Byron's Life and Works, with the following note by the Editor:

"This dedication was suppressed in 1815 with Lord Byron's reluctant consent; but shortly after his death its existence became notorious, in consequence of an article in the Westminster Review, generally ascribed to Sir John Hobhouse; and for several years the verses have been selling in the streets as a broadside. It could, therefore, serve no purpose to exclude them on this occasion."—*Byron's Life and Works*, vol. xv., 101.

The editor seems by this to have felt some slight compunction at publishing this dedication; but he publishes for the first time another attack upon my father a hundred-fold worse than this, contained in some "Observations upon an Article in Blackwood's Magazine," without any apology. This subject, however, will more properly fall to be noticed hereafter.

pictures of domestic life, elucidating the moral history of these times—times which must hold a most conspicuous place in history. He knows his own powers, and never aims above his reach. In this age, when the public are greedy for novelties, and abundantly supplied with them, an author may easily commit the error of giving them too much of the same kind of thing. But this will not be thought a fault hereafter, when the kind is good, or the thing good of its kind.

"Peter Roberts is a great loss. I begin almost to despair of ever seeing more of the Mabinogion; and yet, if some competent Welshman could be found to edit it carefully, with as literal a version as possible, I am sure it might be made worth his while by a subscription, printing a small edition at a high price, perhaps 200, at £5 5*s*. I myself would gladly subscribe at that price per volume for such an edition of the whole of your genuine remains in prose and verse. Till some such collection is made, the 'gentlemen of Wales' ought to be prohibited from wearing a leek; ay, and interdicted from toasted cheese also. Your bards would have met with better usage if they had been Scotchmen.

"Shall we see some legislatorial attorneys sent to Newgate next session? or will the likely conviction of —— damp the appetite for rebellion which is at present so sharp set? I heard the other day of a rider explaining at one of the inns in this town how well the starving manufacturers at Manchester might be settled by parceling out the Chatsworth estate among them. The savings' banks will certainly prove a strong bulwark for property in general. And a great deal may be expected from a good system of colonization; but it must necessarily be a long while before a good system can be formed (having no experience to guide us, for we have no knowledge how these things were managed by the ancients), and a long while, also, before the people can enter into it. But that a regular and regulated emigration must become a part of our political system, is as certain as that nature shows us the necessity in every bee-hive. God bless you! R. S."

A large portion of the autumn of this year was occupied in a Scottish tour, to which the following letter refers. Of this, as of all his journeys, he kept a minute and interesting journal, and the time and attention required for this purpose prevented him from writing any but short and hurried letters.

To Mr. Neville White.

"Keswick, Oct. 14, 1819.

"MY DEAR NEVILLE,

"You need not be warned to remember that all other considerations ought to give way to that of health. A man had better break a bone, or even lose a limb, than shake his nervous system. I, who never talk about my nerves (and am supposed to have none by persons who see as far into me as they do into a stone wall), know this. Take care of yourself; and if you find your spirits fail, put off your ordination and shorten your hours of study; Lord Coke requires only eight hours for a student of the law, and Sir Matthew Hale thought six hours a day as much as any one could well bear; eight, he said, was too much.

"I was about seven weeks absent from home. My route was from Edinburgh, Loch Katrine, and thence to Dunkeld and Dundee, up the east coast to Aberdeen, then to Banff and Inverness, and up the coast as far as Fleet Mound, which is within sight of the Ord of Caithness. We crossed from Dingwall to the Western Sea, returned to Inverness, took the line of the Caledonian Canal, crossed Ballachulish Ferry, and so to Inverary, Loch Lomond, Glasgow, and home. This took in the greatest and best part of Scotland; and I saw it under the most favorable circumstances of weather and season, in the midst of a joyous harvest, and with the best opportunities for seeing every thing, and obtaining information. I traveled with my old friend Mr. Rickman, and Mr. Telford, the former secretary, and the latter engineer to the two committees for the Caledonian Canal and the Highland Roads and Bridges. They also are the persons upon whom the appropriation of the money from the forfeited estates, for improving and creating harbors, has devolved. It was truly delightful to see how much government has done and is doing for the improvement of that part of the kingdom, and how much, in consequence of that encouragement, the people are doing for themselves, which they would not have been able to do without it.

"So long an absence involves me, of course, in heavy arrears of business. I have to write half a volume of Wesley, and to prepare a long paper for the Q. R. (a Life of Marlborough) before I can set my face toward London, so I shall probably pass the months of February and March in and about town. * * * A great many Cantabs have been summering here, where they go by the odd name of *Cathedrals*.* Several of them brought introductions to me, and were good specimens of the rising generation. * * God bless you, my dear Neville!

"Yours affectionately, R. SOUTHEY."

To Mr. Neville White.

"Keswick, Nov. 20, 1819.

"MY DEAR NEVILLE,

"I wish, for your sake, that the next few months were over—that you had passed your examination, and were quietly engaged in the regular course of parochial duty. *In labore quies*, you know, is the motto which I borrowed from my old predecessor Garibay. It is only in the discharge of duty that that deep and entire contentment which alone deserves to be called happiness is to be found, and you will go the way to find it. Were I a bishop, it would give me great satisfaction to lay hands upon a man like you, fitted as you are for the service of the altar by principle and disposition, almost beyond

* This was a Cumberland corruption of "Collegian."

any man whom I have ever known. I have long regarded it as a great misfortune to the Church of England that men so seldom enter it at a mature age, when their characters are settled, when the glare of youth and hope has passed away; the things of the world are seen in their true colors, and a calm and sober piety has taken possession of the heart. The Romanists have a great advantage over us in this.

"You asked me some time ago what I thought about the Manchester business. I look upon it as an unfortunate business, because it has enabled factious and foolish men to raise an outcry, and divert public attention from the great course of events to a mere accidental occurrence. That the meeting was unlawful, and in *terrorem populi*, is to me perfectly clear. The magistrates committed an error in employing the yeomanry instead of the regulars to support the civil power; for the yeomanry, after bearing a great deal, lost their temper, which disciplined troops would not have done. The cause of this error is obviously that the magistrates thought it less obnoxious to employ that species of force than the troops—a natural and pardonable mistake.

"It is no longer a question between Ins and Outs, nor between Whigs and Tories. It is between those who have something to lose, and those who have every thing to gain by a dissolution of society. There may be bloodshed, and I am inclined to think there will, before the Radicals are suppressed, but suppressed they will be for the time. What may be in store for us afterward, who can tell? According to all human appearances, I should expect the worst, were it not for an abiding trust in Providence, by whose wise will even our follies are overruled.

"God bless you, my dear Neville!

"Yours affectionately,

"ROBERT SOUTHEY."

To Grosvenor C. Bedford, Esq.

"Keswick, Dec. 3, 1819.

MY DEAR GROSVENOR,

" * * * I must trespass on you further, and request that you will seal up ten pounds, and leave it with Rickman, directed for Charles Lamb, Esq., from R. S. It is for poor John Morgan, whom you may remember some twenty years ago. This poor fellow, whom I knew at school, and whose mother has sometimes asked me to her table when I should otherwise have gone without a dinner, was left with a fair fortune, from £10,000 to £15,000, and without any vice or extravagance of his own he has lost the whole of it. A stroke of the palsy has utterly disabled him from doing any thing to maintain himself; his wife, a good-natured, kind-hearted woman, whom I knew in her bloom, beauty, and prosperity, has accepted a situation as mistress of a charity-school, with a miserable salary of £40 a year, and this is all they have. In this pitiable case, Lamb and I have promised him ten pounds a year each as long as he lives. I have got five pounds a year for him from an excellent fellow, whom you do not know, and who chooses on this occasion to be called A. B., and I have written to his Bristol friends, who are able to do more for him than we are, and on whom he has stronger personal claims, so that I hope we shall secure him the decencies of life. You will understand that this is an *explanation* to you, not an *application*. In a case of this kind, contributions become a matter of feeling and duty among those who know the party, but strangers are not to be looked to.

"God bless you! R. S."

To Grosvenor C. Bedford, Esq.

"Keswick, Dec. 20, 1819

MY DEAR G.,

" * * * * * * * *

I have been obliged to complain to Gifford of the mutilations which he has made in this paper. Pray recover the manuscript if you can, or, what would be better, the set of proof-sheets. It is very provoking to have an historical paper of that kind, which, perhaps, no person in England but myself could have written, treated like a schoolboy's theme. Vexed, however, as I am, I have too much liking for Gifford to be angry with him, and have written to him in a manner which will prove this. * * * *

"Your godson, thank God! is going on well, and his father has nothing to complain of, except, indeed, that he gets more praise than pudding. I had a letter last night which would amuse you. A certain H. Fisher, 'printer in ordinary to his majesty,' of Caxton Printing-office, Liverpool, writes to bespeak of me a memoir of his present majesty in one or two volumes octavo, pica type, long primer notes, terms five guineas per sheet; and 'as the work will be sold principally among the middle class of society, mechanics and trades people, the language, observations, *facts*, &c., &c., to suit them.' This is a fellow who employs hawkers to vend his books about the country. You see, Grosvenor, 'some have honor thrust upon them.'

"A Yankee also, who keeps an exhibition at Philadelphia, modestly asks me to send him my painted portrait, which, he says, is very worthy of a place in his collection. I am to have the pleasure of sitting for the picture and paying for it, and he is to show it in Yankee land, admittance so much!

"God bless you! R. S."

To Grosvenor C. Bedford, Esq.

"Keswick, Dec. 22, 1819.

"MY DEAR G.,

"Shields's note is a curiosity in its kind. It is so choicely phrased. But he is very civil, and I would willingly task myself rather than decline doing what he wishes me to do. If, however, by a general chorus he means one which is to recur at the end of every stanza, an ode must be framed with reference to such a burden, or else it would be a burden indeed; and, indeed, it would be impossible to fit one to stanzas of such different import as these. If, on the other hand, a concluding stanza is meant, more adapted for a 'flourish of trumpets,' &c., I am afraid I can not find one, but I will try.* The poem, as it now stands, is not a discreditable one; so far from it, indeed, that if I execute the scheme of my visionary dialogue (upon which my mind runs), I should introduce it—that upon the princess's death, and a few pieces more to be written for the occasion, which would come in like the poems in Boëthius.

"I thought I had explained to you my intentions about my journey. Being sufficiently master of my time, whether I set out a month sooner or later may be regulated solely by my own convenience, so that I return with the summer. I have to finish Wesley, which will be done in five weeks, taking it coolly and quietly. I have to finish the review of Marlborough, which will require three weeks. One of them is my mornings', the other my evenings' work. And if I am satisfied about the payment for my last paper, I shall recast the article upon the New Churches, and perhaps prepare one other also, in order to be beforehand with my ways and means for the spring and summer. But if there be any unhandsome treatment, I will not submit to it, but strike work as bravely as a radical weaver. In that case, the time which would have been sold to the maximus homo of Albemarle Street will be far more worthily employed in finishing the Tale of Paraguay, which has proceeded more slowly than tortoise, sloth, or snail, but which, as far as it has gone, is good. Indeed, I must finish it for publication in the ensuing year, or I shall not be able to keep my head above water. The sum of all this is, that I intend to work closely at home till the end of February, to pass a few days at Ludlow on my way to town, arrive in London about the second week of March, pass five or six weeks, partly at Streatham, partly in town; go to Sir H. Bunbury's for a few days, and perhaps stretch on into Norfolk for another week or ten days, and find my way back to Keswick by the end of May.

"A merry Christmas to you! God bless you!

"R. S."

CHAPTER XXV.

OPINIONS ON POLITICAL AND SOCIAL SUBJECTS—CURIOUS BEQUEST FROM A LUNATIC—LETTER TO HIM—DISLIKE OF THE QUAKERS TO POETRY—LIFE OF WESLEY—COLLOQUIES WITH SIR THOMAS MORE—SIR HOWARD DOUGLAS—THE KING'S DEATH—PROSPECTS OF SOCIETY—REV. PETER ELMSLEY—NEW FASHION OF POETRY OF ITALIAN GROWTH—DON JUAN—POLITICAL FOREBODINGS—PARALLEL ROADS IN SCOTLAND—DEATH OF THE DUKE DE BERRI—BEGUINAGE SCHEME—ENGLISH SISTERHOODS—HIS BROTHER EDWARD—JOHN MORGAN—LAUREATE ODES—THE LIFE OF WESLEY—LETTER IN RHYME FROM WALES—ACCOUNT OF HIS RECEIVING THE HONORARY DEGREE OF D.C.L. AT OXFORD—RETURN HOME—CONGRATULATIONS TO NEVILLE WHITE ON HIS MARRIAGE—OPINIONS ON THE LIFE OF WESLEY—EXCUSES FOR IDLENESS—OCCUPATIONS—LETTER FROM SHELLEY—PROJECTED LIFE OF GEORGE FOX—MR. WESTALL AND MR. NASH—THE VISION OF JUDGMENT—CLASSICAL STUDIES—RODERIC TRANSLATED INTO FRENCH—BIOGRAPHICAL ANECDOTE—DEATH OF MISS TYLER—BIRTHDAY ODE—PORTUGUESE AFFAIRS.—1820, 1821.

In the preceding pages the reader has had several specimens of the obloquy which my father's political writings had entailed upon him. It may yet be allowed me once more to say a few words upon this subject before we enter upon this last period of his intellectual life, in which all his opinions and currents of thought were fixed and defined.

It has been the fashion with many of those persons whose opinions were most opposed to those my father held in later life, taking up their cue from the abuse which was for a long period showered upon him in the *Liberal* journals, to assume, as an undoubted truth, that at some particular period his views had changed totally and suddenly, under the influence of unworthy motives; that he had veered round (like a weathercock upon a gusty day) from the leveling opinions set forth in Wat Tyler to high Toryism; that he was a "renegade," an "apostate," a "hireling," and I know not what; and they attributed this change, on the one hand, to the mortification he felt at the squibs of the Anti-Jacobin, and at the various satirical attacks which he experienced; and, on the other, to the hope of basking in court smiles, and comfortably "feathering his nest" under ministerial favor. His pension (which, the reader need not be reminded, left him a poorer man than it found him) was by some considered as the pivot upon which he had turned round; and the laureateship, paid by the magnificent income of £90, and taken at a time when the office was considered as all but ridiculous, was by such persons regarded as the second instalment of a series of payments for this tergiversation. Others, again, unable to find that these had been the agents in effecting the changes in his views, and determined to discover some unworthy causes for the alteration rather than frankly attribute it to time, experience, increased knowledge, and calm and deliberate conviction, have declared that it was his connection with the Quarterly Review which chiefly influenced the course of his life and opinions; not choosing to suppose, with greater charity, that the Quarterly Review exhibited those opinions, but did not make them, or to confess that they were the spontaneous growth of his own mind.

I think it needless now to attempt to rebut charges like these, because the candid reader of

* "If I give the composer more trouble than poor Pye did, I am sorry for it, but I can no more write like Mr. Pye than Mr. Pye could write like me. His pie-crust and mine were not made of the same materials."—*R. S. to G. C. B.*

the preceding pages, having seen the ardor and frankness with which my father expressed the same opinions in his unguarded correspondence which he advocated in his public writings, will hardly be disposed to acquiesce in them, especially as his reasons for refusing to join the Edinburgh Review, at a period antecedent to the existence of the Quarterly, are on record.

But as my father's views upon politics have been so often misrepresented and misunderstood, a brief sketch of the chief of these can hardly be misplaced here; and I am the more impelled to make such a sketch, because I have lately seen it asserted that "the only opinions England has cause to dread are those held and advocated by Robert Southey during middle life." A notable sentence, showing how little his political opponents either know or consider how many of the improvements and changes which he advocated have been, or are now being, carried into effect, with the approbation of the best and most distinguished men of all parties.

Now, as in politics there are two great and opposite evils to be dreaded—tyrannical government on the one hand, and anarchy on the other—my father believed that the time for dreading the former was gone by, and that the latter danger was imminent; and on this account, as we have seen, he directed his energies to supporting the supreme authority, by urging the adoption of strong measures toward the seditious writers and speakers of the time, by opposing such proposals as seemed to have a tendency to strengthen the democratic element, and by himself proposing and urging the adoption of measures for improving the condition of the poorer classes.

Under these three heads are comprised, I believe, most of my father's political acts. Of the two first I need not speak: they are sufficiently understood; but on the third I would wish to dilate a little further. Let me, however, first guard against being supposed to claim infallibility for my father in his political opinions. Doubtless he sometimes erred in his estimate both of the good and the evil likely to result from certain measures. Who, indeed, has not so erred? What politician or what party does not occasionally anticipate exaggerated effects, alike from what they support or what they deprecate? But I would submit that, with respect to the *ultimate* effects of those great measures he most strongly opposed, time has not yet fully set his seal upon them; that we have not yet seen the whole results either of Catholic Emancipation or of the Reform Bill; and with respect to Free Trade, when its effects have already so far outrun the calculations of its first movers, surely he must be a bold man, however much he may wish it to succeed, who will say it is not still an experiment.

But while the correctness or the fallacy of my father's opinions, and of those who thought with him upon these points, in great measure has yet to be decided, I would lay much more stress upon his views on social subjects — upon his earnest advocacy of those measures he thought most calculated to ameliorate the condition of the lower orders, and to cement the bonds of union between all classes of society, and this as proving that both in early and in later life the objects he aimed at were the same, although he had learned to think that political power was not the panacea for all the poor man's evils.

Among the various measures and changes he advocated may be named the following, many of which were topics he handled at greater or less length in the Quarterly Review, while his opinions upon the others may be found scattered throughout his letters: National education to be assisted by government grants. The diffusion of cheap literature of a wholesome and harmless kind. The necessity of an extensive and well-organized system of colonization, and especially of encouraging female emigration. The importance of a wholesome training for the immense number of children in London and other large towns, who, without it, are abandoned to vice and misery. The establishment of Protestant sisters of charity, and of a better order of hospital nurses. The establishment of savings' banks in all the small towns throughout the country. The abolishment of flogging in the army and navy, except in cases flagrantly atrocious. Alterations in the poor laws. Alterations in the game laws.* Alterations in the criminal laws, as inflicting the punishment of death in far too many cases. Alterations in the factory system, for the benefit of the operative, and especially as related to the employment of children. The desirableness of undertaking national works, reproductive ones if possible, in times of peculiar distress.† The necessity of doing away with interments in crowded cities. The system of giving allotments of ground to laborers; the employment of paupers in cultivating waste lands. The commutation of tithes; and, lastly, the necessity for more clergymen, more colleges, more courts of law.

A man whose mind was full of projects of this kind ought, I think, to be safe from sentences of indiscriminate condemnation, and, indeed, when we remember how few of them had occupied the attention of politicians when he wrote of them, it must be allowed that he was one of the chief pioneers of most of the great and real improvements which have taken and are taking place in society in our own times; and though some may still think his fears of a revolution were exaggerated, yet who can say how far the tranquillity we enjoy has not been owing to the preventive and curative measures which he and others who thought with him so perseveringly labored to bring about?

The various literary employments upon which he was engaged in 1819–20 have been frequently referred to in his letters. The Life of Wesley was in the press. The Peninsular War he was busily employed upon; he had also in prog-

* The changes he advocated in the game laws have long since taken place, but, alas! without the good effects anticipated from them.

† Such as of later years has occurred in Ireland and Scotland.

ress the Book of the Church, and the Colloquies with Sir T. More; and to the Quarterly Review he was, as we know, a constant contributor, not so much from choice as from necessity.

But, in addition to all his other manifold employments, the laureateship was an inconvenient tax upon his time, and a considerable one upon his ingenuity. The regular task-work was still required, and he was, at the same time, too desirous of rendering the laurel more honorable than it had been, to be content with merely those common-place compositions, which no one could hold more cheaply than he did himself, often designating them as "simply good for nothing," and declaring "that next to getting rid of the task which the laureateship imposed upon him, of writing stated verses at stated times, the best thing he could do was to avoid publishing them except on his own choice and his own time."

The death of the king, which occurred in January, 1820, now seemed to call for some more particular effort on his part; and as this event had been for some time expected, he had been turning over in his mind in what way he could best pay his official tribute, and at the same time produce something of real merit. We have seen that from his youth he had been desirous of making the experiment of writing a poem in hexameter verse, and it has been noticed that in the year 1799 he commenced one in that measure. He now, therefore, determined upon the plan and structure of the Vision of Judgment, which it may be supposed was a work of no small time and labor, and with this addition to his other employments he might well say that his "head and his hands were as full as they could hold, and that if he had as many heads and as many hands as a Hindoo god, there would be employment enough for them all."

One other subject may also be mentioned as occupying his thoughts at this time, though probably in a less degree than it would have occupied the thoughts of most persons. He has mentioned in his autobiography that his great uncle, John Canon Southey, had left certain estates of considerable value in trust for his great nephew, John Southey Somerville, afterward Lord Somerville, and his issue, with the intent that if he, who was then a child, should die without issue, the estates should descend to the Southeys. Lord Somerville was lately dead without issue, and my father was under the impression that he had a legal claim to the property, and was at this time taking advice upon the subject. It turned out, however, that Canon Southey had not taken proper care that his intention should be carried into effect, for the opinions upon his claim were not sufficiently favorable to encourage him to take legal proceedings in the matter.

This disappointment he bore as quietly as he had done others of the same kind, and while by no man would a competence have been more thankfully welcomed and regarded as a greater blessing, and I believe I may add, better employed, he was far too wise to disturb himself with unavailing regrets, and never allowed these untoward circumstances to give him one moment's disquiet. In the present instance he most philosophically looked on the bright side of the matter. "Twice in my life," he says, "has the caprice of a testator cut me off from what the law would have given me had it taken its course, and now the law interferes and cuts me off from what would have been given me by a testator. It is, however, a clear gain to escape a suit in Chancery."

To C. W. W. Wynn, Esq., M.P.

'Keswick, Jan. 18, 1820.

"MY DEAR WYNN,

"I have two things to tell you, both sufficiently remarkable. Lord Bathurst, supposing that I had a son growing up, called on Croker lately to offer me a writership for him. I never saw Lord B., nor have I any indirect acquaintance with him. The intended kindness, therefore, is the greater.

"A curious charge has been bequeathed me —the papers of a man who destroyed himself on the first day of this year, wholly, I believe, from the misery occasioned by a state of utter unbelief. I never saw him but once. Last year he wrote me two anonymous letters, soliciting me to accept this charge. I supposed him, from what he said, to be in the last stage of some mortal disease, and wrote to him under that persuasion. And I rather imagined that the religious character of my second reply had offended him, for I heard nothing more till last week, when there came a letter from an acquaintance of mine telling me his name, his fate, and that the papers were deposited by the suicide himself the day before he executed his fatal purpose, to await my directions. I have reason to believe that, with all proper respect to the dead as well as to the living, a most melancholy but instructive lesson may be deduced from them. His letters are beautiful compositions, and he was a man of the strictest and most conscientious virtue!

"The jury pronounced him insane, which perhaps they would not have done had they seen the paper which he addressed to them. That cruel law should be repealed, and I wish you would take the credit of repealing it. It is in every point of view barbarous. A particular prayer for cases of this kind should be added to our Burial Service, to be used in place of those parts that express a sure and certain hope for the dead. God bless you! R. S."

Upon a careful examination of the papers here alluded to, my father found that it would be quite impossible to make any use of them, as they contained the strongest internal evidences of the perfect insanity of the writer. The reader will probably be interested by the insertion here of the letter* which my father conceived had offended the person to whom it was addressed. This, however, it had not done; on the contrary, it had affected him considerably, but he reasoned in-

* My father's first letter to —— has not been preserved.

sanely upon it, and it seems not improbable that it had caused him to postpone for a while his wretched intention of suicide, which it appears he had determined upon for six years.

To ———.

"Keswick, March 2, 1819.

"Your letter, my dear sir, affects me greatly. It represents a state of mind into which I also should have fallen, had it not been for that support which you are not disposed to think necessary for the soul of man.

"I, too, identified my own hopes with hopes for mankind, and at the price of any self-sacrifice would have promoted the good of my fellow-creatures. I, too, have been disappointed in being undeceived; but having learned to temper hope with patience, and when I lift up my spirit to its Creator and Redeemer, to say, not with the lips alone, but with the heart also, 'Thy will be done,' I feel that whatever afflictions I have endured have been dispensed to me in mercy, and am deeply and devoutly thankful for what I am, and what I hope to be when I shall burst my shell.

"O, sir, religion is the one thing needful. Without it, no one can be truly happy (do you not feel this?); with it, no one can be entirely miserable. Without it, this world would be a mystery too dreadful to be borne—our best affections and our noblest desires a mere juggle and a curse, and it were better, indeed, to be nothing than the things we are. I am no bigot. I believe that men will be judged by their actions and intentions, not their creed. I am a Christian; and so will Turk, Jew, and Gentile be in Heaven, if they have lived well according to the light which was vouchsafed them. I do not fear that there will be a great gulf between you and me in the world which we must both enter; but if I could persuade you to look on toward that world with the eyes of faith, a change would be operated in all your views and feelings, and hope, and joy, and love would be with you to your latest breath—universal love—love for mankind, and for the Universal Father, into whose hands you are about to render up your spirit.

"That the natural world, by its perfect order, displays evident marks of design, I think you would admit, for it is so palpable that it can only be disputed from perverseness or affectation. Is it not reasonable to suppose that the moral order of things should in like manner be coherent and harmonious? It is so if there be a state of retribution after death. If that be proved, every thing becomes intelligible, just, beautiful, good. Would you not, from the sense of fitness and of justice, wish that it should be so? And is there not enough of wisdom and power apparent in creation to authorize us in inferring that whatever upon the grand scale would be the best, therefore must be?

"Pursue this feeling, and it will lead you to the cross of Christ.

"I never fear to avow my belief that warnings from the other world are sometimes communicated to us in this; and that, absurd as the stories of apparitions generally are, they are not always false, but that the spirits of the dead have sometimes been permitted to appear. I believe this, because I can not refuse my assent to the evidence which exists of such things, and to the universal consent of all men who have not *learned* to think otherwise. Perhaps you will not despise this as a mere superstition when I say that Kant, the profoundest thinker of modern ages, came, by the severest reasoning, to the same conclusion.

"But if these things are, then there is a state after death; and if there be a state after death, it is reasonable to presume that such things should be.

"You will receive this as it is meant. It is hastily and earnestly written, in perfect sincerity, in the fullness of my heart. Would to God that it might find its way to yours. In case of your recovery, it would reconcile you to life, and open to you sources of happiness to which you are a stranger.

"But whether your lot be for life or death, dear sir, God bless you! R. S."

To Bernard Barton, Esq.

"Keswick, Jan. 21, 1820.

"Dear Sir,

"You propose a question* to me which I can no more answer with any grounds for an opinion, than if you were to ask me whether a lottery ticket should be drawn blank or prize, or if a ship should make a prosperous voyage to the East Indies. If I recollect rightly, poor Scott, of Amwell, was disturbed in his last illness by some hard-hearted and sour-blooded bigots, who wanted him to repent of his poetry as of a sin. The Quakers are much altered since that time. I know one, a man deservedly respected by all who know him (Charles Lloyd the elder, of Birmingham), who has amused his old age by translating Horace and Homer. He is looked up to in the society, and would not have printed these translations if he had thought it likely to give offense.

"Judging, however, from the spirit of the age, as affecting your society, like every thing else, I should think they would be gratified by the appearance of a poet among them who confines himself within the limits of their general principles. They have been reproached with being the most illiterate sect that has ever arisen in the Christian world, and they ought to be thankful to any of their members who should assist in vindicating them from that opprobrium. There is nothing in their principles which should prevent them from giving you their sanction; and I will even hope that there are not many persons who will impute it to you as a sin if you should call some of the months by their heathen names.†

* The question was, whether the Society of Friends were likely to be offended at his publishing a volume of poems.

† "One in the British Friend did impute this as a sin,

I know of no other offense that you are in danger of committing. They will not like virtuous feelings and religious principles the worse for being conveyed in good verse. If poetry in itself were unlawful, the Bible must be a prohibited book.

"I shall be glad to receive your volume, and you have my best good wishes for its success. The means of promoting it are not within my power; for though I bear a part in the Quarterly Review (and endure a large portion of the grossest abuse and calumny for opinions which I do not hold, and articles which I have not written), I have long since found it necessary, for reasons which you may easily apprehend, to form a resolution of reviewing no poems whatever. My principles of criticism, indeed, are altogether opposite to those of the age. I would treat every thing with indulgence except what is mischievous; and most heartily do I disapprove of the prevailing fashion of criticism, the direct tendency of which is to call bad passions into full play.

"Heartily hoping that you may succeed to your utmost wishes in this meritorious undertaking, I remain, dear sir, yours faithfully,

"ROBERT SOUTHEY."

To John Rickman, Esq.

"Jan. 28, 1820.

"MY DEAR R.,

" * * * My knowledge is never so ready as yours. The less you trust your memory, the worse it serves you; and for the last five-and-twenty years I have hardly trusted mine at all; the consequence has been, that I must go to my notes for every thing, except the general impressions and conclusions that much reading leaves behind.

"Upon the deficiency of our Ecclesiastical Establishment and its causes, you will find an historical chapter in my Life of Wesley, agreeing entirely with your notes in all the points on which we have both touched. Since that chapter was written, I have got at sundry books on the subject—Kennet's Case of Impropriations, Henry Wharton's Defense of Pluralities, Staveley's History of Churches—each very good and full of sound knowledge; Eachard's Contempt of the Clergy, and Stackhouse's Miseries of the Inferior Clergy—books of a very different character, but of great notoriety in their day; and two recent publications by a Mr. Yates, which contain a great deal of information. I was led to them by the mention made of them in Vansittart's speech upon the New Churches. * *

"I must borrow from some of the black letter men Sir Thomas More's works, which are tolerably numerous; and when I am in London, I must ask you to turn me loose for two or three mornings among the statutes at large, for I must examine those of Henry the Seventh in particular. There is something about the process of sheep-farming in those days which I am not sure that I understand. The double grievance complained of is, that it appropriated commons and turned arable land into pasture. Now, could this latter commutation answer in a country where the demand must have been as great for meal and malt as for wool and mutton? What I perceive is this, that down to the union of the two Roses, men were the best stock that a lord could have upon his estates; but when the age of rebellions, disputed succession, and chivalrous wars was over, money became of more use than men, and the question was not, who could bring most vassals into the field, but who could support the largest expenditure; and in Sir Thos. More's days the expenditure of the fashionables was infinitely beyond any thing that is heard of in ours. So I take it they did as —— is now doing: got rid of hereditary tenants who paid little or nothing, in favor of speculators and large breeders who could afford to pay, and might be rack-rented without remorse. I shall put together a good deal of historical matter in these interlocutions, taking society in two of its critical periods—the age of the Reformation, and this in which we live.

"God bless you! R. S."

To Grosvenor C. Bedford, Esq.

"Keswick, Feb. 11, 1820.

"MY DEAR GROSVENOR,

"When you see Gifford (and when you go near his door I wish you would make it a reason for calling), will you tell him that among the many applications to which, like himself, I am exposed on account of the Quarterly Review, there is one from Sir —— ——, concerning whose book I wrote to him some three or four months ago. I very much wish he would get Pasley to review that book. It would hardly require more than half a dozen pages; and I believe the book deserves to be brought forward, as being of great practical importance. If, as I apprehend, it shows that we are so much superior to the French in the most important branch of war in theory, as we have proved ourselves to be in the field, the work which demonstrates this ought to be brought prominently into notice, more especially as the notoriety which the Quarterly Review may give to Sir ——'s refutation of Carnot's theories may tend to prevent our allies from committing errors, the consequence of which must be severely felt whenever France is able to resume her scheme of aggrandizement. * * * * . . .

"Do you know that one of those London publishers who are rogues by profession is now publishing in sixpenny numbers a life of the king, by Robert Southy, Esq., printed for the author. 'Observe to order Southy's Life of the King, to avoid imposition.' J. Jones, Warwick Square, is the ostensible rogue, but the anonymous person who sent me the first number says '*alias Oddy*.' I have sent a paragraph to the Westmoreland Gazette, which may save some of my neighbors from being taken in by this infamous trick, and have written to Longman to ask

twenty-five years after this was written."—*Selections from the Poems and Letters of Bernard Barton*, p. 111.

whether it be advisable that I should take any further steps. He must be the best judge of this, and if he thinks I ought to apply for an injunction, he will hand over my letter to Turner, by whose opinion I shall be guided. The scoundrel seems to suppose that he may evade the law by misspelling my name.

"The death of the king will delay my departure two or three weeks beyond the time which I had intended for it; for if I do not finish the poem, which I must of course write before I leave home, my funeral verses would not appear before the coronation. In my next letter I shall probably horrorize you about these said verses, in which I have made some progress.

"I have about a fortnight's work with Wesley, not more; and not so much if this sort of holiday's task had not come to interrupt me. I versify very slowly, unless very much in the humor for it, and when the passion of the part carries me forward. This can never be the case with task verses. However, as I hope not to go beyond two or three hundred lines, I imagine that, at any rate, a fourth part is done. I shall not be very long about it. If I manage the end as well as I have done the beginning, I shall be very well satisfied with the composition.

"All well, thank God, at present.

"God bless you! R. S."

To Walter Savage Landor, Esq.

"Keswick, Feb. 20, 1820.

"Your poem has not found its way to me. It is either delayed or mislaid at Longman's. Oh that you would write in English! I can never think of your predilection for Latin verse but as a great loss to English literature.

"The times make less impression upon me than upon men who live more in the political world. The *present*, perhaps, appears to you, at a distance, worse than it is. The future will be what we may choose to make it. There is an infernal spirit abroad, and crushed it must be. Crushed it will be, beyond all doubt; but the question is, whether it will be cut short in its course, or suffered to spend itself like a fever. In the latter case, we shall go on through a bloodier revolution than that of France, to an iron military government — the only possible termination of Jacobinism. It is a misery to see in what manner the press is employed to poison the minds of the people, and eradicate every thing that is virtuous, every thing that is honorable, every thing upon which the order, peace, and happiness of society are founded. The recent laws have stopped the two-penny supply of blasphemy and treason, and a few of the lowest and vilest offenders are laid hold of. But the mischief goes on in all the stages above them.

"Do you remember Elmsley at Oxford—the fattest under-graduate in your time and mine? He is at Naples, superintending the unrolling the Herculaneum manuscripts, by Davy's process, at the expense of the prince regent — I should say, of George IV. The intention is, that Elmsley shall ascertain, as soon as a beginning is made of one of the rolls, whether it shall be proceeded with or laid aside, in hope of finding something better, till the whole have been inspected.

"A fashion of poetry has been imported which has had a great run, and is in a fair way of being worn out. It is of Italian growth—an adaptation of the manner of Pulci, Berni, and Ariosto in his sportive mood. Frere began it. What he produced was too good in itself and too inoffensive to become popular; for it attacked nothing and nobody; and it had the fault of his Italian models, that the transition from what is serious to what is burlesque was capricious. Lord Byron immediately followed, first with his Beppo, which implied the profligacy of the writer, and lastly with his Don Juan, which is a foul blot on the literature of his country, an act of high treason on English poetry. The manner has had a host of imitators. The use of Hudibrastic rhymes (the only thing in which it differs from the Italian) makes it very easy.

"My poems hang on hand. I want no monitor to tell me it is time to leave off. I shall force myself to finish what I have begun, and then—good night. Had circumstances favored, I might have done more in this way, and better. But I have done enough to be remembered among poets, though my proper place will be among the historians, if I live to complete the works upon yonder shelves.

"God bless you! ROBT. SOUTHEY."

To John May, Esq.

"Keswick, Feb. 22, 1820.

"MY DEAR FRIEND,

" * * * * * * *

You know what a rose-colored politician I was during the worst years of the war. My nature inclines me to hope and to exertion; and in spite of the evil aspects on every side, and the indications which are blackening wherever we look, I think that if we do not avert the impending dangers we shall get through them victoriously, let them come thick and threatening as they may. But it will not be without a heavy cost. The murder of the Duc de Berri surprised me more than a like tragedy would have done at home, where such crimes have perseveringly been recommended in those infamous journals, most of which have been suppressed by the late wholesome acts. The effect of such things (as it is the end also of all revolutions) must be to strengthen the executive power. As no man can abuse his fortune without injuring it, so no people can abuse their liberty without being punished by the loss of it, in whole or in part. * *

"Is it within the bounds of a reasonable hope that an improved state of public opinion, and an extended influence of religion, may prevent the degradation which, in the common course of things, would ensue, after one or two halcyon generations? How justly did the Romans congratulate themselves upon the security which they enjoyed under Augustus; but how sure was the tyranny, and corruption, and ruin which ensued? Our chance of escaping the same process of decay depends upon the question whether religion or infidelity is gaining ground; and if I am asked this question, I must comfort myself by the wise and good old saying, 'Well, masters, God's above.'

"You have heard, no doubt, of the discovery of Cicero de Republica? This was brought to my mind at this moment by a thought whether we might not be verging toward a state of things in which a general wreck of literature and destruction of libraries would make part of the plans of reform. The proposal of a new alphabet has been made by a German reformer, and approved by an English one, *because one of its effects would be to render all existing books useless!* It was said of old that there was nothing so foolish but some philosopher had said it. Alas! there is nothing so mischievous or so atrocious but that men are found in these days mad enough and malignant enough to recommend and to defend it.

"Yours most affectionately,

"ROBERT SOUTHEY."

To John Rickman, Esq.

"March 1, 1820.

"MY DEAR RICKMAN,

"Your guess about the Parallel Roads* has this in its favor, that if Glen Roy mean the king's glen, the word Roy would not have been used before there was an intercourse between the Scotch and the French; they were never such friends with our Normans as to have taken it from them. In point of time, therefore, this would suit well. On the other hand, in that age chroniclers delighted as much in a good show as in a good battle, and Froissart would hardly have failed to describe a hunting party upon so grand a scale as that for which these roads were made. It appears to be impossible that they should have been made for any other purpose; and when our friends at Corpach procure a list of the names of places, and some Gael is found learned enough to translate them, this main fact, I have no doubt, will be established. There is some possibility that by this means, also, we may come near the age; not by the language (for I believe the Gaelic is not like the Welsh, in which the date of a composition may be inferred with some certainty by its language), but by the names of some of the party, and perhaps of some of the implements used.

"You are quite right in thinking funded property better than landed property for charitable institutions, as being rather more than less secure, safe from fraudulent management, and requiring no trouble. There remains an objection from the uncertainty of the value of money; but it appears to me impossible that money should ever fall in value as it has done since the Middle Ages; perhaps even such an advance in prices as has taken place within our own recollection will never again occur—I mean, as affecting every thing. In the view which I take of the improvement of society, stability is one of the good things to be expected.

"I like your Beguinage scheme in all its parts. Endowments (analogous to college fellowships) would grow out of it in due course of time; and great part of the business of female education would be transferred to these institutions, to the advantage of all parties.

"The Duc de Berri will do more good by his death than he would ever have done by his life. I had been saying that such a tragedy in France surprised me much more than it would have done in England. The will, I knew, was not wanting, and intelligence soon came that the purpose had been formed. Your Oppositionists will call this discovery* a most unfortunate business, and such, I trust, it will prove for them. The jury who acquitted Thistlewood and Watson, the Oppositionists in Parliament and out of it who ridiculed the green bag plot, and the subscribers to Hone & Co., are much more deeply implicated in the guilt of this business than they would like to be told. They have given every encouragement to traitors, and thereby have made themselves morally art and part in the treason. What a fortunate thing that the Habeas Corpus was not suspended! in that case these miscreants would most of them have been in confinement, and the Whigs lamenting over them, and promoting subscriptions for them as the victims of oppression. The gallows will now have its due. * * * *

"God bless you! R. S."

The following was the "Beguinage scheme" alluded to in the foregoing letter:

"A local habitation is all I wish for where a secular nunnery is to be established; acres enough to preserve the integrity of aspect from encroachment and to prevent intrusion. * * * * My notion of a female establishment is, that any benefactor erecting a set of chambers shall thereby acquire a right (alienable by will, gift, or sale, like other property) to place inmates there on certain conditions, such as that security shall be given that each enjoy a competent income, not less than £——, while she resides there; that she shall be bound to the necessary rules of female decorum, on pain of instant expulsion, and to such other rules as are indispensable to the well-being of the community, but that nothing like common meals shall be proposed. The ladies to choose their own mutual society—of which there would be enough—and to make all minor arrangements among themselves. I believe, for external appearance, to

* "I read in Froissart (chap. lxi.) that the King of Scotland (Robert II.) was at that time absent from Edinburgh, being in the Highlands on a hunting party. The Parallel Roads in Glen Roy might be freshly made at that time, the Scottish kings having had recent opportunity of enlarging their ideas as prisoners or auxiliaries in England and France; and the listed field of a tournament might give the hint for a grand apparatus—a hunting spectacle. Game might be preserved in the neighborhood for royal diversion."—*J. R. to R. S., Feb.* 20, 1820.

* Of the Cato Street conspiracy.

prevent expense and vanity, and to restrain the number of idle applications, a uniform dress would be proper; and for many purposes, as for prayers, bad weather, and peripatetic exercise, a large room would be a respectable adjunct to the edifice, and for which the fundatores might be taxed a per centage upon their several chambers. Under such easy laws as these, and considering how fashionable and how laudable is the appetite for virtuous patronage, I do not see how it could fail that among the female nobility and other opulent females many would be ready so to invest part of their money. None of it could be spent more for their own reputation and respectability; and, considering that the individuals admitted would not of necessity (nor usually) be *maintained* by the foundress of the chamber, but recommended to her by those who might have interest or gratification in giving security for the maintenance of the inmate, I can not but think that the foundress, the immediate patron of the admitted female—who might thus exonerate himself from care and anxiety, were better motive wanting—and the admitted female, whose maintenance for life, or, at least, for a specified term of years, must be secured before her admission, would all find motive enough for falling into a plan, simple and unambiguous in its arrangement, and (if not wofully mismanaged) of the highest respectability.

"I do not know whether you are prepared to agree with me as to the necessity of a secured income to each female, but I have inquired enough in and about such female societies (such there are for clergymen's widows at Bromley, at Winchester, at Froxfield, at Lichfield, and, I dare say, elsewhere) as to be fully convinced that respectability can not be otherwise maintained. * * * In short, there must be a classification of relief, and I treat of the upper classes, observing only that many would be exalted into that upper class were the means of so exalting them easy, and obvious to the wealthy. Few wills would be without bequests of the competent annuity to some humble friend; various societies would be at various rates—I should say from £50 to £100 per annum, or some such minimum—and if a wealthy foundress resided herself, she would have larger facility for beneficence than display. The love of the community, so conspicuous among monks in former times, would found libraries, plantations, walks, cloisters, gaudy days, whether obit or birth-day, medical attendance, a chaplain, perhaps. For government, the foundresses must legislate."*

The reader will remember an interesting account of a Beguinage at Ghent,† and the recurrence to the subject at various intervals throughout my father's life shows how much interest he felt in it.

How far this plan of Mr. Rickman's, without considerable modification, might answer, seems doubtful, and something more of the nature of an asylum for persons of very limited means, or for those left altogether desolate, appears greatly wanted.

Institutions of this kind, however, so long as their object is limited to the benefit of their own inmates, have not in them a sufficient largeness of purpose and general utility to command the interest and admiration of mankind to any wide extent.

But when regarded in another light, as an influential machinery for the moral and religious cultivation of the people, they become highly important. My father has unfolded his own ideas upon this subject in the latter part of the Colloquies with Sir Thomas More, using frequently the same phrases, and making the same suggestions which occur in these letters, whether his own or his friend's; and he there indicates certain principles which seem essential to the well-being of such communities. There must be a center of union sufficient to overpower, or at least to keep in harmonious subjection individual characters; this can only be supplied by religion and the habit of obedience. "Human beings," he remarks, "can not live happily in constrained community of habits without the aid of religious feeling, and without implicit obedience to a superior;" but he did not expect that these requirements would be easily met with in this age, and he attributes the little success of some institutions to the want of them.

It seems also an absolute essential that they should have their definite work; an object which may fill their thoughts and occupy their energies; and this my father suggests, arguing that they ought to be devoted to purposes of Christian charity, and showing how wide a field is open to the members of such societies in attendance upon the sick, in affording Christian consolation, and in the relief and the education of the poor; and with reference to such offices as these, he concludes with the hopeful prognostic that "thirty years hence the reproach may be effaced, and England may have its Sisters of Charity."

We have happily seen that in this respect, as in some others, the tide has turned, and some institutions have sprung up whose existence is based upon these two principles. While, however, I sincerely rejoice that such a beginning has been made, I may be allowed to express a fear that as yet, with the enthusiasm of persons following a new and exciting idea, they have adopted too much of the minutiæ and austerities of convent discipline to be widely acceptable to the English mind, and consequently to be extensively beneficial; for the rigid strictness of the rules (in some houses at least) is likely to deter any one from entering them who respects and values the cheerfulness and rational liberty of domestic life, such as it appears in most religious families, and the quantity and fatigue of the duties required is such as can only be endured by persons in robust health; and thus the very class who most need such a residence as an asylum, and who, under a more moderate system,

* J. R. to R. S., Feb. 20, 1820.

† See *ante*, p. 319.

might be both contented and useful, are altogether excluded. It would seem, indeed, to be desirable that the inmates of such sisterhoods should aim at making as small a distinction as possible, consistently with their great objects and principles, between themselves and other sensible, industrious, and devout English ladies. Some differences there must be; but such as, without being necessary, are only likely to offend, should surely be studiously avoided.

In the following letter my father alludes to his youngest brother Edward, who has not been mentioned in these pages since his boyhood. The subject is a painful one, and I may be excused from entering into it further than to say that every effort had been made, both by his uncle, Mr. Hill, and his brothers, to place him in a respectable line of life, and induce him to continue in it. He possessed excellent abilities, and had received a good education; and if he would have chosen any profession, they would have prepared him for it. He was placed first in the navy, and afterward in the army, but in vain; and he finally took to the wretched life of an actor in provincial theaters. My father here sufficiently indicates the course ultimately pursued toward him by his brothers, who, in fact, did every thing it was possible to do for him. He died in 1845.

To Grosvenor C. Bedford, Esq.

"March 1, 1820.

"MY DEAR G.,

"Though I never examined an account in my life (holding it a less evil to be cheated than to cast up long sums, and fret myself about *l. s. d.*), yet I think there is an error in yours, for you have not debited me for the Westminster subscription, which must surely have been paid within the last three months.

"I thank you for your solicitude concerning my readiness to give. But you do not know when I turn a deaf ear. The case of poor Page's family is the only one in which I had not a cogent motive; there, perhaps, there was no better one than a regard to appearances—a tax to which I have paid less in the course of my life than most other persons. My unhappy brother Edward has at least the virtue of being very considerate in his demands upon me. They come seldom, and are always trifling. At present he is ill, perhaps seriously so. All that can be done for him is to take care that he may not want for necessaries while in health, nor for comforts (as far as they can be procured) when health fails him.

"In John Morgan's case I acted from the double motive of good will toward him and his wife, and of setting others an example—which has had its effect. There was an old acquaintance there; and for the sake of his mother, at whose table I have been a frequent guest, I would have done more for him than this, had it been in my power.

"People imagine that I am very rich, that I have great interest with government, and that my patronage in literature is sufficient to make an author's fortune, and to introduce a poet at once into full celebrity.

"Turner is about to take an opinion concerning my claims, both in law and in equity, to the Somersetshire estates. Where I to recover them, I should have great satisfaction in resigning my pension. The laureateship I would keep as a feather, and wear it as Fluellen did his leek.

"Last night I finished the Life of Wesley; but I have outrun the printer as well as the constable, and it may be four or five weeks before he comes up to me. Now I go *dens et unguis* to my Carmen, which, if I do not like when it is done, why I will even skip the task, and prepare for the coronation. Alas! the birth-days will now be kept; learn for me on what days, that I may be ready in time. I do not know why you are so anxious for rhyme. The rhythm of my Congratulatory Odes is well suited for lyrical composition; and the last poem which I sent you was neither amiss in execution, nor inappropriate in subject. God bless you! R. S."

To Grosvenor C. Bedford, Esq.

"March 26, 1820.

"MY DEAR GROSVENOR,

"Before I see you, you will receive the Life of Wesley,* whereof only about two sheets remain to be printed. Some persons have expressed their expectations that the book will have a huge sale. I am much more inclined to think that it will obtain a moderate sale and a durable reputation. Its merit will hardly be appreciated by any person, unless it be compared with what his former biographers have done; then, indeed, it would be seen what they have overlooked, how completely the composition is my own, and what pains it must have required to collect together the pieces for this great tesselated tablet. The book contains many fine things—pearls which I have raked out of the dunghill. My only merit is that of finding and setting them. It contains, also, many odd ones—some that may provoke a smile, and some that will touch the feelings. In parts I think some of my own best writing will be found. It is written with too fair a spirit to satisfy any particular set of men.

* "There are at this day half a million of persons in the world (adult persons) calling themselves Methodists, and following the institutions of John Wesley; they are pretty equally divided between the British dominions and the United States of America; and they go on increasing year after year. They have also their missionaries in all parts of the world. The rise and progress of such a community is, therefore, neither an incurious nor an unimportant part of the history of the last century. I have brought it no further than the death of the founder. You will find in it some odd things, some odd characters, some fine anecdotes, and many valuable facts, which the psychologist will know how to appreciate and apply. My humor (as it would have been called in the days of Ben Jonson) inclines me to hunt out such subjects; and whether the information be contained in goodly and stately folios of old times, like my noble Acta Sanctorum (which I shall like to show you whenever you will find your way again to your old chamber which looks to Borodale), or in modern pamphlets of whity-brown paper, I am neither too indolent to search for it in the one, nor so fastidious as to despise it in the other. In proof of this unabated appetite, I have just begun an account of our old acquaintance the Sinner Saved, in the shape of a paper for the Q. R."—*To Richard Duppa, Esq., March 25, 1820.*

For the 'religious public' it will be too tolerant and too philosophical; for the Liberals it will be too devotional; the Methodists will not endure any censure of their founder and their institutions; the High-Churchman will as little be able to allow any praise of them. Some will complain of it as being heavy and dull; others will not think it serious enough. I shall be abused on all sides, and you well know how little I shall care for it. But there are persons who will find this work deeply interesting, for the subjects upon which it touches, and the many curious psychological cases which it contains, and the new world to which it will introduce them. I dare say that of the twelve thousand purchasers of Murray le Magne's Review, nine hundred and ninety-nine persons out of a thousand know as little about the Methodists as they do about the Cherokees or the Chiriguanas. I expect that Henry will like it, and also that he will believe in Jeffrey,* as I do.

"God bless you! R. S."

In April, May, and June my father was absent from home, during which time he visited his friend Mr. Wynn, in Wales, spent some wearisome weeks in society in and about London, and finally received the honorary degree of D.C.L. at the Oxford commemoration.

The following letters are selected, because they give some slight idea of that affectionate playfulness which, in a character like his, ought not to be wholly passed over in silence.

To Edith May Southey.

"Shrewsbury, April 25, 1820.

"Having nothing else to do for a dismal hour or two, I sit down to write to you, in such rhymes as may ensue, be they many, be they few, according to the cue which I happen to pursue. I was obliged to stay at Llangedwin till to-day; though I wished to come away, Wynn would make me delay my departure yesterday, in order that he and I might go to see a place whereof he once sent a drawing to me.

"And now I'll tell you why it was proper that I should go thither to espy the place with mine own eye. 'Tis a church in a vale, whereby hangs a tale, how a hare being pressed by the dogs and much distressed, the hunters coming nigh and the dogs in full cry, looked about for some one to defend her, and saw just in time, as it now comes pat in rhyme, a saint of the feminine gender.

"The saint was buried there, and a figure carved with care, in the church-yard is shown, as being her own; but 'tis used for a whetstone (like the stone at our back door), till the pity is the more (I should say the more's the pity, if it suited with my ditty), it is whetted half away—lack-a-day, lack-a-day!

"They show a mammoth's rib (was there ever such a fib?), as belonging to the saint Melangel. It was no use to wrangle, and tell the simple people, that if this had been her bone, she must certainly have grown to be three times as tall as the steeple.

"Moreover, there is shown a monumental stone, as being the tomb of Yorwerth Drwndwn (*w*, you must know, serves in Welsh for long *o*). In the portfolio there are drawings of their tombs, and of the church also. This Yorwerth was killed six hundred years ago. Nevertheless, as perhaps you may guess, he happened to be an acquaintance of mine, and therefore I always have had a design to pay him a visit whenever I could, and now the intention is at last made good. *

"God bless you! R. S."

A very different record of the same scenes is preserved in my father's poems. One of the guests at Llangedwin during his stay there was Bishop Heber, and the meeting was remembered on both sides, for in Heber's journal there is an allusion to Oliver Newman, which must have been read to him at this time; and ten years later my father embodied, in his lines On the Portrait of Bishop Heber, a graceful memorial of his friends, and the spots which he visited in their company.

"Ten years have held their course
Since last I look'd upon
That living countenance,
When on Llangedwin's terraces we paced
Together, to and fro.
Partaking there its hospitality,
We with its honor'd master spent,
Well-pleased, the social hours;
His friend and mine—my earliest friend, whom I
Have ever, through all changes, found the same,
From boyhood to gray hairs,
In goodness, and in worth, and warmth of heart.
Together then we traced
The grass-grown site, where armed feet once trod
The threshold of Glendower's embattled hall;
Together sought Melangel's lonely Church,
Saw the dark yews, majestic in decay,
Which in their flourishing strength
Cyveilioc might have seen;
Letter by letter traced the lines
On Yorwerth's fabled tomb;
And curiously observed what vestiges,
Moldering and mutilate,
Of Monacella's legend there are left,
A tale humane, itself
Well-nigh forgotten now."*

To Bertha, Kate, and Isabel Southey.

"June 26, 1820.

"Bertha, Kate, and Isabel, you have been very good girls, and have written me very nice letters, with which I was much pleased. This is the last letter which I can write in return; and as I happen to have a quiet hour to myself, here at Streatham, on Monday noon, I will employ that hour in relating to you the whole history and manner of my being ell-ell-deed at Oxford by the vice-chancellor.

"You must know, then, that because I had written a great many good books, and more especially the Life of Wesley, it was made known to me by the vice-chancellor, through Mr. Heber, that the University of Oxford were desirous of showing me the only mark of honor in their

* Jeffrey was the name given to the invisible cause of certain strange noises which annoyed the Wesley family. —See *Life of Wesley*, vol. i., p. 445.

* In both the ten volume and one volume edition of my father's poems, this poem "On the Portrait of Bishop Heber" bears the wrong date of 1820. It was written in 1830.

power to bestow, which was that of making me an LL.D.—that is to say, a doctor of laws.

"Now you are to know that some persons are ell-ell-deed every year at Oxford, at the great annual meeting which is called the Commemoration. There are two reasons for this: first, that the University may do itself honor by bringing persons of distinction to receive the degree publicly as a mark of honor; and, secondly, that certain persons in inferior offices may share in the fees paid by those upon whom the ceremony of ell-ell-deeing is performed. For the first of these reasons, the Emperor Alexander was made a Doctor of Laws at Oxford, the King of Prussia, and old Blucher, and Platoff; and for the second, the same degree is conferred upon noblemen, and persons of fortune and consideration who are any ways connected with the University, or city, or county of Oxford.

"The ceremony of ell-ell-deeing is performed in a large circular building called the theater, of which I will show you a print when I return, and this theater is filled with people. The under-graduates (that is, the young men who are called Cathedrals at Keswick) entirely fill the gallery. Under the gallery there are seats, which are filled with ladies in full dress, separated from the gentlemen. Between these two divisions of the ladies are seats for the heads of houses, and the doctors of law, physic, and divinity. In the middle of these seats is the vice-chancellor, opposite the entrance, which is under the orchestra. On the right and left are two kind of pulpits, from which the prize essays and poems are recited. The area, or middle of the theater, is filled with bachelors and masters of arts, and with as many strangers as can obtain admission. Before the steps which lead up to the seats of the doctors, and directly in front of the vice-chancellor, a wooden bar is let down, covered with red cloth, and on each side of this the beadles stand in their robes.

"When the theater is full, the vice-chancellor, and the heads of houses, and the doctors enter: those persons who are to be ell-ell-deed remain without in the divinity schools, in their robes, till the convocation have signified their assent to the ell-ell-deeing, and then they are led into the theater, one after another, in a line, into the middle of the area, the people just making a lane for them. The professor of civil law, Dr. Phillimore, went before, and made a long speech in Latin, telling the vice-chancellor and the dignissimi doctores what excellent persons we were who were now to be ell-ell-deed. Then he took us one by one by the hand, and presented each in his turn, pronouncing his name aloud, saying who and what he was, and calling him many laudatory names ending in issimus. The audience then cheered loudly to show their approbation of the person; the vice-chancellor stood up, and repeating the first words in issime, ell-ell-deed him; the beadles lifted up the bar of separation, and the new-made doctor went up the steps and took his seat among the dignissimi doctores.

"Oh Bertha, Kate, and Isabel, if you had seen me that day! I was like other issimis, dressed in a great robe of the finest scarlet cloth, with sleeves of rose-colored silk, and I had in my hand a black velvet cap like a beef-eater, for the use of which dress I paid one guinea for that day. Dr. Phillimore, who was an old schoolfellow of mine, and a very good man, took me by the hand in my turn, and presented me; upon which there was a great clapping of hands and huzzaing at my name. When that was over, the vice-chancellor stood up, and said these words, whereby I was ell-ell-deed: 'Doctissime et ornatissime vir, ego, pro auctoritate meâ et totius universitatis hujus, admitto te ad gradum doctoris in jure civili, honoris causâ.' These were the words which ell-ell-deed me; and then the bar was lifted up, and I seated myself among the doctors.

"Little girls, you know it might be proper for me, now, to wear a large wig, and to be called Doctor Southey, and to become very severe, and leave off being a comical papa. And if you should find that ell-ell-deeing has made this difference in me, you will not be surprised. However, I shall not come down in a wig, neither shall I wear my robes at home.

"God bless you all!

"Your affectionate father,

"R. SOUTHEY."

To the Rev. Neville White.

"Keswick, July 6, 1820.

"MY DEAR NEVILLE,

"There is no better proof that two fellow-travelers are upon a proper understanding with each other than when they travel together for a good length of time in silence, each thinking his own thoughts, and neither of them feeling it necessary to open his lips for the sake of politeness. So it is with real friends: I have not written to congratulate you on your change of state till now, because I could not do it at leisure, I would not do it hastily, and *I knew* that *you knew* how completely every day, hour, and minute of my time must be occupied in London. Never, indeed, was I involved in a more incessant succession of wearying and worrying engagements from morning till night, day after day, without intermission; here, there, and every where, with perpetual changes of every kind, except the change of tranquillity and rest. During an absence of nearly eleven weeks, I seldom slept more than three nights successively in the same bed. At length, God be thanked, I am once more seated by my own fireside—perhaps it is the only fire in Keswick at this time; but, like a cat and a cricket, my habits or my nature have taught me to love a warm hearth; so I sit with the windows open, and enjoy at the same time the breath of the mountains and the heat of a sea-coal fire.

"And now, my dear Neville, I heartily wish you all that serious, sacred, and enduring happiness in marriage which you have proposed to yourself, and which, as far as depends upon yourself, you have every human probability of finding, and I make no doubt as far as depends upon your consort also. Such drawbacks as are inseparable from our present imperfect state, and such griefs as this poor flesh is heir to, you must sometimes expect, and will know how to bear. But the highest temporal blessings as certainly attend upon a well-regulated and virtuous course of conduct now as they did during the Mosaic dispensation; for what other blessings are comparable to tranquillity of mind, resignation under the afflictive dispensations of Providence, faith, hope, and that peace which passeth all understanding? However bitter upon the palate the good man's cup may be, this is the savor which it leaves; whatever his future may be, his happiness depends upon himself, and must be his own work. In this sense, I am sure you will be a happy man; may you be a fortunate one also.

"I had the comfort of finding all my family well, the children thoroughly recovered from the measles, though some of them somewhat thinner, and the mother a good deal so, from the anxiety and the fatigue which she had undergone during their illness. You hardly yet know how great a blessing it is for a family to have got through that disease—one of the passes perilous upon the pilgrimage of life. Cuthbert had not forgotten me; five minutes seemed to bring me to his recollection; he is just beginning to walk alone—a fine, stout, good-humored creature, with curling hair, and eyes full of intelligence. How difficult it is not to build one's hopes upon a child like this.

"I am returned to a world of business; enough to intimidate any one of less habitual industry, less resolution, or less hopefulness of spirit. My time will be sadly interrupted by visitors, who, with more or less claims, find their way to me during the season from all parts. However, little by little, I shall get on with many things, of which the first in point of time will be the long-intended Book of the Church. I told you, if I recollect rightly, what the Bishop of London had said to me concerning the Life of Wesley. You will be glad to hear that Lord Liverpool expressed to me the same opinion when I met him at Mr. Canning's, and said that it was a book which could not fail of doing a great deal of good. Had that book been written by a clergyman, it would have made his fortune beyond all doubt. But it will do its work better as having come from one who could have had no view to preferment, nor any undue bias upon his mind. If I live, I shall yet do good service both to the Church and State.

"My visit to Oxford brought with it feelings of the most opposite kind. After the exhibition in the theater, and the collation in Brazen-nose Hall given by the vice-chancellor, I went alone into Christ Church walks, where I had not been for six-and-twenty years. Of the friends with whom I used to walk there, many (and among them some of the dearest) were in their graves. I was then inexperienced, headstrong, and as full of errors as of youth, and hope, and ardor. Through the mercy of God, I have retained the whole better part of my nature; and as for the lapse of years, that can never be a mournful consideration to one who hopes to be ready for a better world whenever his hour may come. God bless you! R. S."

To Grosvenor C. Bedford, Esq.

"Keswick, July 29, 1820.

"My Dear Grosvenor,

"It is very seldom that a whole month elapses without some interchange of letters between you and me; and, for my part, in the present instance, I can not plead any unusual press of business, or any remarkable humor of industry. But, then, I can plead a great deal of enjoyment. I have been staying in the house all day—a great happiness after the hard service upon which my ten trotters were continually kept in London. I have been reading—a great luxury for one who during eleven weeks had not half an hour for looking through a book. I have been playing with Cuthbert, giving him the Cries of London to the life, as the accompaniment to a series of prints thereof, and enacting lion, tiger, bull, bear, horse, ass, elephant, rhinoceros, the laughing hyena, owl, cuckoo, peacock, turkey, rook, raven, magpie, cock, duck, and goose, &c., greatly to his delight and somewhat to his edification, for never was there a more apt or more willing pupil. Whenever he comes near the study door, he sets up a shout, which seldom fails of producing an answer; in he comes, tottering along, with a smile upon his face, and *pica pica* in his mouth; and if the picture-book is not forthwith forthcoming, he knows its place upon the shelf, and uses most ambitious and persevering efforts to drag out a folio. And if this is not a proper excuse for idleness, Grosvenor, what is?

"But I have not been absolutely idle, only comparatively so. I have made ready about five sheets of the Peninsular War for the press (the main part, indeed, was transcription), and William Nicol will have it as soon as the chapter is finished. I have written an account of Derwent Water for Westall's Views of the Lakes. I have begun the Book of the Church, written half a dialogue between myself and Sir Thomas More, composed seventy lines for Oliver Newman, opened a Book of Collections for the Moral and Literary History of England, and sent to Longman for materials for the Life of George Fox and the Origin and Progress of Quakerism, a work which will be quite as curious as the Wesley, and about half the length. Make allowances for letter writing (which consumes far too great a portion of my time), and for the interruptions of the season, and this account of the month will not be so bad as to subject me to any very severe censure of my stewardship.

"The other day there came a curious letter from Shelley, written from Pisa. Some of his friends persisted in assuring him that I was the author of a criticism* concerning him in the Quarterly Review. From internal evidence, and

* My father was not the writer of this article.

from what he knew of me, he did not and would not believe it; nevertheless, they persisted; and he writes that I may enable him to confirm his opinion. The letter then, still couched in very courteous terms, talks of the principles and slanderous practices of the pretended friends of order, as contrasted with those which he professes, hints at challenging the writer of the Review, if he should be a person with whom it would not be beneath him to contend, tells me he shall certainly hear from me, because he must interpret my silence into an acknowledgment of the offense, and concludes with Dear-Sir-Ship and civility. If I had an amanuensis, I would send you copies of this notable epistle, and of my reply to it.

"God bless you, Grosvenor!

"Yours as ever, R. S."

To Bernard Barton, Esq.

"Keswick, Nov. 24, 1820.

"My dear Sir,

"In reply to your questions concerning the Life of George Fox, the plan of the work resembles that of the Life of Wesley as nearly as possible. Very little progress has been made in the composition, but a good deal in collecting materials, and digesting the order of their arrangement. The first chapter will contain a summary history of the religious or irreligious dissensions in England, and their consequences, from the rise of the Lollards to the time when George Fox went forth. This will be such an historical sketch as that view of our ecclesiastical history in the life of Wesley, which is the most elaborate portion of the work. The last chapter will probably contain a view of the state of the society at this time, and the modification and improvement which it has gradually, and almost insensibly received. This part, whenever it is written, and all those parts wherein I may be in danger of forming erroneous inferences from an imperfect knowledge of the subject, I shall take care to show to some member of the society before it is printed. The general spirit and tendency of the book will, I doubt not, be thought favorable *by* the Quakers as well as *to* them; and the more so by the judicious, because commendation comes with tenfold weight from one who does not dissemble his own difference of opinion upon certain main points. Perhaps in the course of the work I may avail myself of your friendly offer, ask you some questions as they occur, and transmit certain parts for your inspection.

"Farewell, my dear sir, and believe me,

"Yours, with much esteem,

"Robert Southey."

It would seem that a rumor had got abroad at this time that the Society of Friends were somewhat alarmed at the prospect of my father's becoming the biographer of their founder; for, a few weeks later, Bernard Barton writes to him, telling him that he had seen it stated in one of the magazines that "Mr. Southey could not procure the needful materials, owing to a reluctance on the part of the Quakers to intrust them to him." And he goes on to say: "But although I have stated that I see no objection to intrusting thee with any materials which thou mayest consider at all essential to thy undertaking, I think I can see, and I doubt not thou dost, why some little hesitation should exist in certain quarters. Thy name is, of course, more likely to be known as that of a poet; and though poets as well as poetry are, I should hope, of rather increasing good repute among us, yet some distrust of their salutary tendency, which too much of our modern poetry may perhaps justify, still, perhaps, operates to their disadvantage. Then, again, many of us are very plain matter-of-fact sort of people, making little allowance for poetical license, and little capable of appreciating the pure charm and hidden moral of superstition and legendary lore. Now supposing thy Old Woman of Berkeley—St. Romuald—the Pope, the Devil, and St. Antidius—or the Love Elegies of Abel Shufflebottom, to have fallen in the way of such personages, and then for them to be abruptly informed that the author of them was about compiling a Life of George Fox, &c., thou wilt, I think, at once see a natural and obvious cause for hesitation in really very respectable and good sort of people, but with little of poetry in them."

In this there is some reason as well as some humor; the report, however, was without foundation; and it was not from want of the offer of sufficient materials that the Life of George Fox was never written. Other labors crowded closely one upon the other, and this was only one more to be added to the heap of unfulfilled intentions and half-digested plans which form the melancholy reliquiæ of my father's literary life, leaving us, however, to wonder, not at what he left undone, but at what he did.

To W. Westall, Esq.

"Keswick, Dec. 8, 1820.

"My dear Westall,

"Your letter arrived yesterday, by which post, you know (being Thursday), it could not be answered. By this night's I shall write to Murray, saying that you will deliver the drawings to him, and informing him of the price. That they have in them that which is common to poetry and painting I do not doubt, and I only wish it were possible for you to engrave them yourself. The first edition of the book would then bear a high value hereafter. In describing that scene on the side of Walla Crag, I have introduced your name in a manner gratifying to my own feelings, and which I hope will not be otherwise to yours.

"I am glad to hear you are employed upon your views of Winandermere. My topographical knowledge in that quarter is but imperfect; but, when you want your letter-press, if you can not persuade Wordsworth to write it (who would be in all respects the best person), I will do for you the best I can.

"Allow me to say one thing before I conclude. When you were last at Keswick there was an uncomfortable feeling in your mind toward Nash: I hope it has passed away. There is not a kinder-hearted creature in the world than he is; and I *know* that he has the truest regard for you, and the highest possible respect for your genius. Any offense that he may have given was entirely unintentional. Forget it, I entreat you: call upon him again as you were wont to do; it will rejoice him, and you will not feel the worse for having overcome the feeling of resentment. I need not apologize for saying this; for, indeed, I could not longer forbear saying it, consistent with my regard both for him and for you.

"All here desire their kind remembrances. We can not send them to Mrs. Westall, because you did not give us an opportunity of becoming known to her; but, I pray you, present our best wishes, and believe me,

"Yours affectionately,

"ROBERT SOUTHEY."

The prints referred to in the commencement of the foregoing letter were for the Colloquies with Sir Thomas More. The concluding paragraph of it had a special interest in Mr. Westall's eyes, as, with a rare willingness to receive such advice, he had immediately acted upon it, and renewed his friendly intercourse with Mr. Nash. And he reflected upon it with the more satisfaction, as a few weeks only elapsed before Nash was suddenly cut off.

Nash was a mild, unassuming, and most amiable person, bearing meekly and patiently a severe bodily infirmity, which, in its consequences, caused his death. My father first became acquainted with him in Belgium in 1815: he spent several summers at Greta Hall, a guest dear both to young and old; and to his and to Mr. W. Westall's pencil the walls of our home owed many of their most beloved ornaments.

Since the commencement of the publication of this volume, Mr. Westall has also "departed to his rest;" and I will take this opportunity of noticing the sincere regard my father entertained for him as a friend, and the estimation in which he held him as an artist, considering him as by far the most faithful delineator of the scenery of the Lakes.

His death has taken away one more from the small surviving number of those who were familiar "household guests" at Greta Hall, and to whom every minute particular of the friend they so truly loved and honored had its own especial interest.

To the Rev. Neville White.

"Keswick, Dec. 14, 1820.

"MY DEAR NEVILLE,

" * * * * * * * *

I shall have a poem to send you in the course of a few weeks, planned upon occasion of the king's death (which you may think no very promising subject), laid aside eight months ago, when half written, as not suited for publication while the event was recent, and now taken up again, and almost brought to a conclusion. The title is, 'A Vision of Judgment.' It is likely to attract some notice, because I have made—and, in my own opinion, with success—the bold experiment of constructing a meter upon the principle of the ancient hexameter. It will provoke some abuse for what is said of the factious spirit by which the country has been disturbed during the last fifty years; and it will have some interest for you, not merely because it comes from me, but because you will find Henry's name not improperly introduced in it. My laureateship has not been a sinecure: without reckoning the annual odes, which have regularly been supplied, though I have hitherto succeeded in withholding them from publication, I have written, as laureate, more upon public occasions (on none of which I should otherwise have ever composed a line) than has been written by any person who ever held the office before, with the single exception of Ben Jonson, if his Masques are taken into the account.

The prevailing madness has reached Keswick,* as well as other places; and the people here, who believe, half of them, that the king concealed his father's death ten years for the sake of receiving his allowance, and that he poisoned the Princess Charlotte (of which, they say, there can be no doubt; for did not the doctor kill himself? and why should he have done that if it had not been for remorse of conscience?), believe, with the same monstrous credulity, that the queen is a second Susannah. The Queenomania will probably die away ere long, but it will be succeeded by some new excitement; and so we shall go on as long as our government suffers itself to be insulted and menaced with impunity, and as long as our ministers are either unwilling or afraid to exert the laws in defense of the institutions of the country.

"I have a book in progress upon the state of the country, its existing evils, and its prospects. It is in a series of dialogues, and I hope it will not be read without leading some persons both to think and to feel as they ought. In more than one instance I have had the satisfaction of being told that my papers in the Quarterly Review have confirmed some who were wavering in their opinions, and reclaimed others who were wrong. *

"God bless you, my dear Neville! R. S."

To Grosvenor C. Bedford, Esq.

"Keswick, Jan. 5, 1821.

"MY DEAR G.,

"As for altering the movement of the six stanzas,† you may as well ask me for both my ears,

* Some riots had been expected on the occasion of the queen's trial. My father writes at the time, "King Mob, contrary to his majesty's custom, has borne his faculties meekly in this place, and my windows were not assailed on the night of the illumination. I was prepared to suffer like a Quaker; and my wife was much more 'game' than I expected. Perhaps we owed our security to the half dozen persons in town who also chose to light no candles. They had declared their intention of making a fight for it if they were attacked, and they happened to be persons of consideration and influence. So all went off peaceably. The *tallow chandler* told our servant that it was expected there would be *great disturbances;* this was a hint to me, but I was too much a Trojan to be taken in by the man of *grease*."—*To G. C. B., Nov.* 17, 1820.

† Of the Ode for St. George's Day, published with the Vision of Judgment.

or advise me to boil the next haunch of venison I may have, which, next to poaching a Simorg's* egg, would, I conceive, be the most inexpiable of offenses. I cast them purposely in that movement, and with forethought.

"Why should the rest of the world think meanly of me for offering a deserved compliment to Haydon?† or for what possible reason consider it as a piece of flattery to a man who might fancy it his interest to flatter me, but whom I can have no imaginable motive for flattering? That point, however, you will press no further when I tell you that the very day after the passage was written Haydon himself unexpectedly appeared—that I read him the poem as far as it had then proceeded—and that he, who, from the nature of his profession, desires cotemporary praise more than any thing in the world except abiding fame, values it quite as much as it is worth. You have shown me that I was mistaken about Handel, yet I think the lines may stand, because the king's patronage of his music is an honorable fact.

"I have to insert Sir P. Sidney among the elder worthies, and Hogarth among the later; perhaps Johnson also, if I can so do it as to satisfy myself with the expression, and not seem to give him a higher praise than he deserves. Offense I know will be taken that the name of Pitt does not appear there. The king would find him among the eminent men of his reign, but not among those whose rank will be confirmed by posterity. The Whigs, too, will observe that none of their idols are brought forward: neither Hampden, nor their Sidney, nor Russell. I think of the first as ill as Lord Clarendon did; and concerning Algernon Sidney, it is certain that he suffered wrongfully, but that does not make him a great man. If I had brought forward any man of that breed, it should have been old Oliver himself; and I had half a mind to do it.

"I have finished the explanatory part of the preface, touching the meter—briefly, fully, clearly, and fairly. It has led me (which you will think odd till you see the connection) to pay off a part of my obligations to Lord Byron and ——, by some observations upon the tendency of their poems (especially Don Juan), which they will appropriate to themselves in what proportion they please. If —— knew how much his character has suffered by that transaction about Don Juan, I think he would hang himself. And if Gifford knew what is said and thought of the Q. R. for its silence concerning that infamous poem, I verily believe it would make him ill. Upon that subject I say nothing. God bless you! R. S."

To the Rev. Neville White.

"Keswick, Jan. 12, 1821.

"MY DEAR NEVILLE,

"It appears to me that whatever time you bestow upon the classics is little better than time lost. Classical attainments are not necessary for you, and even if you were ten years younger than you are, they would not be within your reach. This you yourself feel; you had better, therefore, make up your mind to be contented without them, and desist from a study which it is quite impossible for you to pursue with any advantage to yourself.

"My dear Neville, it is a common infirmity with us to overvalue what we do not happen to possess. In your education you have learned much which is not acquired in schools and colleges, but which is of great practical utility—more, probably, than you would now find it if you had taken a wrangler's degree or ranked as a medallist. You have mingled among men of buiness. You know their good and their evil, the characters which are formed by trade, and the temptations which are incident to it. You have acquired a knowledge of the existing constitution of society, and situated as you will be, in or near a great city, and in a trading country, this will be of much more use to you professionally than any university accomplishments. Knowing the probable failings of your flock, you will know what warnings will be most applicable, and what exhortations will be most likely to do them good.

"The time which classical studies would take may be much more profitably employed upon history and books of travels. The better you are read in both, the more you will prize the peculiar blessings which this country enjoys in its constitution of Church and State, and more especially in the former branch. I could write largely upon this theme. The greater part of the evil in the world—that is, all the evil in it which is remediable (and which I take to be at least nine tenths of the whole)—arises either from the want of institutions, as among savages; from imperfect ones, as among barbarians; or from bad ones, as in point of government among the Oriental nations; and in point of religion among them also, and in the intolerant Catholic countries. In your own language you will find all you need—scriptural illustrations, and stores of knowledge of every kind.

"What you say concerning my correspondence, and the latitude which you allow me, is both kind and considerate, as is always to be expected from Neville White. I do not, however, so easily forgive myself when a long interval of silence has been suffered to elapse. A letter is like a fresh billet of wood upon the fire, which, if it be not needed for immediate warmth, is always agreeable for its exhilarating effects. I, who spend so many hours alone, love to pass a portion of them in conversing thus with those whom I love.

"You will be grieved to hear that I have lost my poor friend Nash, whom you saw with us in the autumn. He left us at the beginning of November, and is now in his grave! This has been a severe shock to me. I had a most sincere regard for him, and very many pleasant recollections are now so changed by his death, that they will never recur without pain He was so thor-

* See Thalaba, book xi., verse 10.

† This refers to an allusion to Haydon in the Vision of Judgment.

oughly amiable, so sensible of any little kindness that was shown him, so kind in all his thoughts, words, and deeds, and, withal, bore his cross so patiently and meekly, that every body who knew him respected him and loved him. Very few circumstances could have affected me more deeply than his loss.

"Remember me most kindly to your excellent mother and to your sisters. You are happy in having had your parents spared to you so long. The moral influences of a good old age upon the hearts of youth and manhood can not be appreciated too highly. We are all well at present, thank God. God bless you, my dear Neville!

"Yours affectionately,

"ROBERT SOUTHEY."

To Grosvenor C. Bedford, Esq.

"Keswick, Jan. 26, 1821.

"MY DEAR GROSVENOR,

"Yesterday evening I received 'Roderic, Dernier Roi des Goths, Poëme tradui de l'Anglais de Robert Southey, Esq., Poëte Laureat, par M. le Chevalier * * *.' Printed at Versailles, and published at Paris by Galignani. It was accompanied by a modest and handsome letter from the translator, M. Chevalier de Sagrie, and by another from Madame St. Anne Holmes, the lady to whom it is dedicated. This lady has formerly favored me with some letters and with a tragedy of hers, printed at Angers. She is a very clever woman, and writes almost as beautiful a hand as Miss Ponsonby of Llangollen. She is rich, and has lived in high life, and writes a great deal about Sheridan, as having been very intimate with him in his latter years. Me, Mr. Bedford, unworthy as I am, this lady has chosen for her *poëte favori*, and by her persuasions the chevalier has translated Roderic into French. This is not all: there is a part of the business which is so truly booksellerish in general, and French in particular, that it would be a sin to withhold it from you, and you shall have it in the very words of my correspondent St. Anne.

"'There is one part of the business I can not pass over in silence: it has shocked me much, and calls for an apology; which is—The Life of Robert Southey, Esq., P.L. It never could have entered my mind to be guilty of, or even to sanction, such an impertinence. But the fact is this: the printer and publisher, Mr. Le Bel, of the Royal Printing-office Press in Versailles (printers, by-the-by, are men of much greater importance here than they are in England), insisted upon having the life. He said the French know nothing of M. Southey, and in order to make the work sell, it must be managed to interest them for the author. To get rid of his importunities, we said we were not acquainted with the life of Mr. Southey. Would you believe it? this was verbatim his answer: "N'importe! écrivez toujours, brodez! brodez-la un peu, que ce soit vrai ou non ce ne fait rien; qui prendra la peine de s'informer?" Terrified lest this ridiculous man should succeed in his point, I at last yielded, and sent to London to procure *all the lives;* and from them, and what I had heard from my dear departed friend, Richard Brinsley Sheridan, we drew up the memoir.'

"Grosvenor, whoever writes my life when the subject has an end as well as a beginning, and does not insert this biographical anecdote in it, may certainly expect that I will pull his ears in a true dream, and call him a jackass.

"The Notice sur M. Southey, which has been thus compounded, has scarcely one single point accurately stated, as you may suppose, and not a few which are ridiculously false. *N'importe*, as M. Le Bel says, I have laughed heartily at the whole translation, and bear the translation with a magnanimity which would excite the astonishment and envy of Wordsworth, if he were here to witness it. I have even gone beyond the Quaker principle of bearing injuries meekly: I have written to thank the inflicter. Happily it is in prose, and the chevalier has intended to be faithful, and has, I believe, actually abstained from any interpolations. But did you ever hear me mention a fact worthy of notice, which I observed myself—that wherever a breed of peacocks is spoiled by mixture with a white one, birds that escape the degeneracy in every other part of their plumage show it in the *eye* of the feather? The fact is very curious; where the perfection of nature's work is required, there it fails. This affords an excellent illustration for the version now before me; every where the eye of the feather is defective. It would be impossible more fully to exemplify how completely a man may understand the general meaning of a passage, and totally miss its peculiar force and character. The name of M. Bedford appears in the *Notice*, with the error that he was one of my *College* friends, and the fact that Joan of Arc was written at his house. The dedication to him is omitted.

"God bless you! R. S.

"What a grand bespattering of abuse I shall have when the Vision appears! Your walk at the Proclamation was but a type of it—only that I am booted and coated, and of more convenient stature for the service. Pelt away, my boys, pelt away! if you were not busy at that work, you would be about something more mischievous. Abusing me is like flogging a whipping-post. Harry says I have had so much of it that he really thinks I begin to like it. This is certain, that nothing vexes me except injudicious and exaggerated praise, *e. g.*, when my French friends affirm that Roderic is acknowledged to be a better poem than the Paradise Lost!!"

To John May, Esq.

"Keswick, March 4, 1821.

"MY DEAR FRIEND,

"Yesterday I received a letter from my uncle with the news of Miss Tyler's death, an event which you will probably have learned before this reaches you. My uncle is thus relieved from a considerable charge, and from the apprehension which he must have felt of her surviving him.

She was in the eighty-second year of her age. She will be interred (to-morrow, I suppose) in the burial-place of the Hills, where her mother and two of the Tylers are laid, and my father with five of my brothers and sisters.

"Her death was, even for herself, to be desired as well as expected. My affection for her had been long and justly canceled. I feel no grief, therefore; but such an event of necessity presses for a while like a weight upon the mind. Had it not been for the whim which took her to Lisbon in the year of my birth, you and I should never have known each other; my uncle would never have seen Portugal, and in how different a course would his life and mine, in consequence, have run! I have known many strange characters in my time, but never so extraordinary a one as hers, which, of course, I know intimately. I shall come to it in due course, and sooner than you may expect, from the long intervals between my letters.

"Yesterday's post brought me also an intimation from my musical colleague, Mr. Shield, that 'our most gracious and royal master intends to command the performance of an Ode at St. James's on the day fixed for the celebration of his birth-day.' Of course, therefore, my immediate business is to get into harness and work in the mill. Two or three precious days will be spent in producing what will be good for nothing; for as for making any thing good of a birth-day ode, I might as well attempt to manufacture silk purses from sows' ears. Like Warton, I shall give the poem an historical character; but I shall not do this as well as Warton, who has done it very well. He was a happy, easy-minded, idle man, to whom literature in its turn was as much an amusement as rat-hunting, and who never aimed at any thing above such odes.

"*March* 20.—I now send you the fourth letter of the promised series, dated at the beginning nearly four months before it was brought to an end. Were I to proceed always at this rate with it, I should die of old age before I got breeched in the narrative; but with all my undertakings, I proceed faster in proportion as I advance in them. Just now I am in the humor for going on; and you will hear from me again sooner than you expect, for I shall begin the next letter as soon as this packet is dispatched. It is a long while since I have heard from you, and I am somewhat anxious to hear how your affair goes on in Brazil. If O Grande Marquez could have been raised from the dead, he would have had courage and capacity to have modeled both countries according to the circumstances of the age. But I am more anxious about the manner in which these events may affect you, than concerning their general course; that is in the will of Providence; and with regard to the state of the Peninsula and of Italy, I really see so much evil on both sides, and so much good intent acting erroneously on both, that if I could turn the scale with a wish, I should not dare to do it.

"God bless you, my dear friend!

"Yours affectionately, R. S."

To Grosvenor C. Bedford, Esq.

"Keswick, April 15, 1821.

"MR. BEDFORD—SIR,

" * * * * * * * *

I have received invitations to dine with the Literary Fund * * * and with the Artists' Benevolent Institution. These compliments were never before paid me. Cobbett, also, has paid me a compliment equally well-deserved and of undoubted sincerity. He marks me by name as one of those persons who, when the Radicals shall have effected a reformation, are, as one of the first measures of the new government, to be executed. As a curious contrast to this, the committee of journeymen who propose to adopt what is practicable and useful in Owen's plan, quote in their Report the eleventh stanza of my ode,* written in Dec., 1814, as deserving 'to be written in diamonds.' This is the first indication of a sort of popularity which, in process of time, I shall obtain and keep, for the constant tendency of whatever I have written. * * * Wordsworth was with me last week. Oddly enough, while I have been employed upon the Book of the Church, he has been writing a series of historical sonnets upon the same subjects, of the very highest species of excellence. My book will serve as a running commentary to his series, and the one will very materially help the other; and thus, without any concerted purpose, we shall go down to posterity in company. * * * * * *

"God bless you! R. S."

CHAPTER XXVI.

THE VISION OF JUDGMENT—LORD BYRON—MR. JEFFREY'S OPINION OF HIS WRITINGS—WORDSWORTH'S ECCLESIASTICAL SONNETS — STATE OF SPAIN—SCARCITY OF GREAT STATESMEN —THE εικων βασιλικη—HOBBES'S BEHEMOTH —FAILURE OF AN ATTEMPT TO RECOVER SOME FAMILY ESTATES—LONELY FEELINGS AT OXFORD—THE VISION OF JUDGMENT APPROVED BY THE KING—AMERICAN VISITORS—DISAPPROVAL OF THE LANGUAGE OF THE QUARTERLY REVIEW TOWARD AMERICA — AMERICAN DIVINITY—ACCOUNT OF NETHERHALL—BOHEMIAN LOTTERY — HAMPDEN — A NEW CANDIDATE FOR THE PROTECTION OF THE GAME LAWS—STATE OF IRELAND—SIR EDWARD DE-

* The following is the stanza here referred to:

"Train up thy children, England, in the ways
Of righteousness, and feed them with the bread
Of wholesome doctrine. Where hast thou thy mines
But in their industry?
Thy bulwarks where, but in their breasts?
Thy might, but in their arms?
Shall not their numbers, therefore, be thy wealth,
Thy strength, thy power, thy safety, and thy pride?
Oh grief, then, grief and shame,
If in this flourishing land
There should be dwellings where the new-born babe
Doth bring unto its parent's soul no joy;
Where squalid poverty
Receives it at its birth,
And on her withered knees
Gives it the scanty food of discontent."

RING—DECREE OF THE LONG PARLIAMENT—SPANISH AMERICA—HUMBOLDT'S TRAVELS—STATE OF ITALY, OF SPAIN, AND OF ENGLAND. —1821.

THE Vision of Judgment was now, at last, published, and my father had not overrated the measure of opposition and abuse with which its appearance would be hailed. Nor was this at all to be wondered at; for, besides the unfriendly criticisms of his avowed enemies and opponents, the poem, both in its plan and execution, could not fail to give offense to many of those persons most disposed to receive favorably the productions of his pen. The editor hopes he will not be thought chargeable with any want of filial respect if he thinks it right here to express his own regret that such a subject should have been chosen, as, however solemnly treated, it can hardly be said to be clear from the charge of being an injudicious attempt to fathom mysteries too deep for human comprehension; and it must be allowed, that to speculate upon the condition of the departed, especially when under the influence of strong political feelings, is a bold, if not a presumptuous undertaking.

My father adopted, as we have seen, his leading thoughts from Dante's great poem, not reflecting that Dante himself, if it were not for the halo thrown around him by his antiquity and the established fame of his transcendant genius combined, would in these days be very offensive to many sincerely religious minds.

But while undoubtedly the Vision of Judgment had the effect of shocking the feelings of many excellent persons, the storm of abuse which greeted its author did not come from them, nor did it arise from any regret that spiritual matters should be thus handled. It was the preface and not the poem which called them forth.

Now, whatever may be the opinion which any person may form of my father's writings, one thing has always been conceded—that in none of them did he appeal to the darker passions of human nature, or seek to administer pernicious stimulants to a depraved taste; that in none did he paint vice in alluring colors, calling evil good and good evil; and that in all of them there is a constant recognition of the duties, the privileges, and the hopes derived from revealed religion.

There was, therefore, a perfect contrast between his writings and those of some of the most popular authors of that day; and in the Quarterly Review he often used unsparing language concerning those writers who were in the habit of spreading among the people Free-thinking opinions in religion, and base doctrines in morals.

These things would naturally create a bitter enmity against him in the minds of all who, either by their own acts or by sympathy, were implicated in such proceedings; and the more definite and pointed remarks which he took occasion to make in his preface to the Vision of Judgment upon the principles and tendencies of these writers, wound up his offenses to a climax in their estimation, and set in motion the array of opposition and invective to which I have just alluded. Before, however, noticing more particularly the remarks themselves, and the rejoinder and counter-rejoinder they called forth, we will look a little at the relative position of the parties with respect to their writings.

Lord Byron, as is well known, in his English Bards and Scotch Reviewers, had satirized my father in common with many others, but not in any peculiarly objectionable manner; and when, as has been noticed, they met once or twice in London society in the year 1813, it was with all outward courtesy. From that time Lord Byron became year after year more notorious, and his writings more objectionable in their tendency. But while my father could not but greatly disapprove of many portions of them, he had been far too busily employed to trouble himself much about Lord Byron. He rarely alludes to him in his letters; for every allusion that I have found, I have printed. For some years he had made it a rule never to review poetry; and while he regarded him as a man of the highest talents, using them in a manner greatly to be lamented, and notoriously profligate as to his private life, he had never said this in print, and rarely seems to have spoken of him at all.

Lord Byron, on the other hand, appears to have regarded my father with the most intense dislike, which he veiled under an affectation of scorn and contempt which it is impossible to believe he could really feel. He had pronounced* his talents to be "of the first order," his prose to be "perfect," his Roderic "the first poem of the time," and therefore he could not think meanly of his abilities; and widely as he differed from him on political subjects, that could be no reason for the bitter personal animosity he displayed toward him. This is sufficiently shown in many passages of his published letters, and more particularly in his Don Juan; which, in addition to the allusions in the poem itself, came over for publication with a Dedication to him prefixed to it, couched in coarse and insulting terms. This was suppressed at the time (the editor states with Lord Byron's reluctant consent); but its existence was well known, and it is now prefixed to the poem in the collected edition of his works.

But the feelings with which Lord Byron regarded my father were still more plainly shown in some observations upon an article in Blackwood's Magazine, published for the first time in his Life and Works, but written, be it observed, *before* the remarks on the Satanic School in the preface to the Vision of Judgment.

The writer in Blackwood, it appears, had alluded to Lord Byron having "vented his spleen" against certain "lofty-minded and virtuous men," which he interprets to mean "the notorious triumvirate known by the name of the Lake Poets;" and he then goes on to make various charges against my father, which it is impossible to characterize by any other epithet than false and

* See Byron's Life and Works, vol. ii., p. 268, and vol. vii., p. 239.

calumnious. These were based upon the assumed fact that, on his return from the Continent in 1817, my father had circulated slanderous reports respecting Lord Byron's mode of life;* and upon this supposition, which was *wholly without foundation*, he proceeds in a strain of abuse which I will not sully these pages by quoting; suffice it to say, that when, at a later period, Lord Byron, in a letter to Sir Walter Scott, declares his intention of "working the laureate as soon as he could muster *Billingsgate* enough,"† he had a plentiful supply of it in those then unpublished pages. It is painful to have to recur to these deeds of the dead; but it is necessary, because these facts prove that Lord Byron's attacks upon my father preceded my father's comments upon him, and were altogether unprovoked; and also because his authority is still occasionally employed by others for the purpose of bringing my father's name and character into contempt.

Now I have made these observations solely to show upon which of the two (if upon either) the blame of a malicious or contentious temper must rest, not because I assume these calumnies to have been the reason why my father censured Lord Byron's writings.‡ The worst of these insults he certainly never saw; the other he was acquainted with; but while the effect of it must undoubtedly have been to remove any delicacy with regard to hurting Lord Byron's feelings, I am perfectly justified in asserting that, if there had not existed a great public cause—a question of the most vital principles—my father would never, upon that provocation, have gone out of his way to lift his hand against him.§ He conceived it to be his duty, as one who had some influence over the opinions of others, to condemn, as strongly as possible, works, the perusal of which he conscientiously believed was calculated to weaken the principles, corrupt the morals, and harden the heart.

With respect to the remarks in the preface to the Vision of Judgment, while it must be admitted they are stern and severe, they are surely not more so than the occasion justified. They are no personal invective, but simply a moral condemnation of a class of publications, and to be judged by a consideration of the whole question whether they were deserved or not. The question itself as to the spirit and tendency of many of Lord Byron's writings has never, by the public, been considered *apart* from his rank, his genius, and his redeeming qualities: admiration and adulation operated on the one hand, fear on the other; for while he himself and his advocates attributed the condemnation of his writings to "cowardice," with far greater truth might that be alleged as a reason for the praise of many and the silence of more.*

It was natural, then, that my father should meet with a large share both of abuse and blame for daring thus to attack the enemy in his stronghold; and while some marveled at his imprudence, there was one great writer who said more than that with strange inconsistency. Mr. Jeffrey, in the Edinburgh Review, suppressing the remarks themselves, attributed them wholly to envy; and it is not a little curious to observe, coupled with this, his own estimate of Lord Byron's writings, some portions of which I can not resist quoting here.

After various remarks, leveled apparently at my father, concerning "the base and the bigoted venting their puny malice in silly nicknames," he goes on to say,

"He has no priest-like cant or priest-like reviling to apprehend from us; we do not charge him with being either a disciple or an apostle of Satan, nor do we describe his poetry to be a mere compound of blasphemy and obscenity. On the contrary, we believe he wishes well to the happiness of mankind."

After speaking of the immoral passages and profligate representations in his writings, which, he says, are not worse than Dryden, or Prior, or Fielding, justly adding, however, that "it is a wretched apology for the indecencies of a man of genius that equal indecencies have been forgiven to his predecessors," he proceeds:

"It might not have been so easy to get over his dogmatic skepticism, his hard-hearted maxims of misanthropy, his cold-blooded and eager expositions of the non-existence of virtue and honor. Even this, however, might have been comparatively harmless, if it had not been accompanied with that which may look at first sight like a palliation—the frequent presentment of the most touching pictures of tenderness, generosity, and faith.

"The charge we bring against Lord Byron, in short, is, that his writings have a tendency to destroy all belief in the reality of virtue, and to make all enthusiasm and constancy of affection ridiculous; and this is effected, not merely by direct maxims and examples of an imposing or seducing kind, but by the constant exhibition of the most profligate heartlessness in the persons

* With reference to this accusation, which was made through some other medium during Lord Byron's life, my father says, in a letter to the editor of the Courier, "I reply to it *with a direct and positive denial*;" and he continues, "If I had been told in that country that Lord Byron had turned Turk or monk of La Trappe—that he had furnished a harem or endowed a hospital, I might have thought the account, whichever it had been, possible, and repeated it accordingly, passing it, as it had been taken, in the small change of conversation, for no more than it was worth. But making no inquiry concerning him when I was abroad, because I felt no curiosity, I heard nothing, and had nothing to repeat."—See Appendix. I may add that there is no allusion to Lord Byron either in my father's letters written during that tour or in his journal.

† See Life and Works of Byron, vol. v., p. 300.

‡ See Appendix.

§ Had he seen the other attack, he *could* not have remained silent under it.

* Mr. Jeffrey, in the Edinburgh Review, says, "Lord Byron complains bitterly of the detraction by which he has been assailed, and intimates that his works have been received by the public with far less cordiality and favor than he was entitled to expect. We are constrained to say that this appears to us a very extraordinary mistake. In the whole course of our experience we can not recollect a single author who has so little reason to complain of his reception; to whose genius the public has been so early and constantly just; to whose faults they have been so long and so signally indulgent."—*Edinburgh Review*, No 72.

of those who have been transiently represented as actuated by the purest and most exalted emotions, and the lessons of that very teacher who had been but a moment before so beautifully pathetic in the expression of the loftiest conceptions.

"*This* is the charge which *we* bring against Lord Byron. We say that, under some strange misapprehension of the truth and the duty of proclaiming it, he has exerted all the powers of his powerful mind to convince his readers, directly and indirectly, that all ennobling pursuits and disinterested virtues are mere deceits and illusions, hollow and despicable mockeries for the most part, and at best but laborious follies. Love, patriotism, valor, devotion, constancy, ambition —all are to be laughed at, disbelieved in, and despised! and nothing is really good, as far as we can gather, but a succession of dangers to stir the blood, and of banquets and intrigues to soothe it again. If the doctrine stood alone, with its examples, we believe it would revolt more than it would seduce; but the author has the unlucky gift of personating all those sweet and lofty illusions, and that with such grace, and power, and truth to nature, that it is impossible not to suppose for the time that he is among the most devoted of their votaries, till he casts off the character with a jerk; and the moment after he has moved and exalted us to the very height of our conceptions, resumes his mockery of all things sacred and sublime, and lets us down at once on some coarse joke, hard-hearted sarcasm, or relentless personality, as if to show

'Whoe'er was edified, himself was not.'"*

It is difficult to imagine how any thing more severe, and at the same time more just, than these remarks could have been penned; but I may fairly ask, with what consistency could the writer of them reckon my father as among the base and the bigoted for his remarks on the "Satanic School?" He does not, he says, charge Lord Byron with being either a disciple or an apostle of Satan; but had he striven to picture forth the office of such a character, could he have done it better? What method more subtle or more certain could the Enemy of Mankind use to enlarge the limits of his empire than "*to destroy all belief in the reality of virtue*"—to convince men that all that is good, noble, virtuous, or sacred is "*to be laughed at, disbelieved in, and despised?*" Consciously or unconsciously, the reviewer in these passages has embodied the very system which those whose philosophy is based upon Holy Scripture believe that the Evil Spirit is continually pursuing against the souls of men. He has said, virtually, only at greater length and more persuasively, exactly the same thing my father had said in those very passages he sneers at and condemns.

These remarks, including the quotation, have extended further than I could have wished; but the clergyman who finds cheap editions of Don Juan and Shelley's Queen Mab lying in the cottages of his rural flock, who knows that they are sold by every hawker of books throughout the country, and that they are handed about from one to the other by school-boys and artisans to supply shafts for the quiver of ribald wit and scoffing blasphemy, can hardly be thought out of season if, when this subject is forced upon him, he allows his own feeling concerning such works to appear; and it is not unimportant, while doing so, to have pointed out the strong coincidence, upon this question in real opinion, which existed between two writers, in general so opposed to each other as my father and the editor of the Edinburgh Review.

* Edinburgh Review, No. 72.

As may well be imagined, the passage alluded to concerning the Satanic School roused Lord Byron's anger to the uttermost, and he replied to it in a strain which compelled a rejoinder from my father, in a letter addressed to the Editor of the Courier, the effect of which was to make his lordship immediately sit down and indite a cartel, challenging my father to mortal combat, for which purpose both parties were to repair to the Continent. This challenge, however, never reached its destination, Lord Byron's "friend," Mr. Douglas Kinnaird, wisely suppressing it.

The passage itself, Lord Byron's reply, and the rejoinder, together with a letter written in 1824 on the appearance of Captain Medwin's work, the reader will find in the Appendix to this volume.

To the Rev. Neville White.

"Keswick, April 25, 1821.

"MY DEAR NEVILLE,

"I heartily give you joy of your dear wife's safe deliverance, and of the birth of your first child—an event which, of all others in the course of human life, produces the deepest and most permanent impression.

"Who hath not proved it, ill can estimate
The feeling of that stirring hour—the weight
Of that new sense; the thoughtful, pensive bliss.
In all the changes of our changeful state,
Even from the cradle to the grave, I wis
The heart doth undergo no change so great as this.

"So I have written in that poem which will be the next that I hope to send you; but I transcribe the lines here because you will feel their truth at this time. Parental love, however, is of slower growth in a father's than in a mother's heart: the child, at its birth, continues, as it were, to be a part of its mother's life; but upon the father's heart it is a *graft*, and some little time elapses before he feels that it has united and is become inseparable. God bless the babe and its parents, and spare it and them, each for the other's sake, amen!

"Tilbrook wrote to tell me his disapprobation of my hexameters. His reasons were founded upon some musical theory, which I did not understand further than to perceive that it was not applicable. His opinion is the only unfavorable one that has reached me; that of my friend Wynn, from whom I expected the most decided displeasure, was, that he 'disliked them less than he expected.' Women, as far as I can learn, feel and like the meter universally, without attempting to understand its construction. My brethren of the art approve it, and those whom I acknowledge for my peers are decidedly in its favor. Many persons have thanked me for that part of the preface in which Lord Byron and his infamous works are alluded to. * *

"I am going on steadily with many things, the foremost of which is the History of the War. The first volume will be printed in the course of September next. Whether it will be published before the other two, depends upon the booksellers, and is a matter in which I have no concern. I am proceeding also with my Dialogues, and with the Book of the Church—two works by which I shall deserve well of posterity, whatever treatment they may provoke now from the bigoted, the irreligious, and the factious. But you know how perfectly regardless I am of obloquy and insult. Your brother Henry gave me that kind of praise which is thoroughly gratifying, because I know that I deserve it, when he described me as fearlessly pursuing that course which my own sense of propriety points out, without reference to the humor of the public.

"In the last Quarterly Review you would recognize me in the account of Huntington. I am preparing a life of Oliver Cromwell for the next.

* * * * *

"Believe me, my dear Neville,
"Yours most affectionately,
"ROBERT SOUTHEY."

To C. H. Townshend, Esq.

"Keswick, May 6, 1821.

"MY DEAR CHAUNCEY,

"I received your little parcel this afternoon, and thank you for the book, for the dedication, and for the sonnet. As yet I have only had time to recognize several pieces which pleased me formerly, and to read a few others which please me now.

"The stages of your life have passed regularly and happily, so that you have had leisure to mark them with precision, and to feel them, and reflect upon them. With me these transitions were of a very different character; they came abruptly, and, when I left the University, it was to cast myself upon the world with a heart full of romance and a head full of enthusiasm. No young man could have gone more widely astray, according to all human judgment, and yet the soundest judgment could not have led me into any other way of life in which I should have had such full cause to be contented and thankful.

"The world is now before you; but you have neither difficulties to struggle with, nor dangers to apprehend. All that the heart of a wise man can desire is within your reach. And you are blessed with a disposition which will keep you out of public life, in which my advice to those whom I loved would be—never to engage.

"Your Cambridge wit is excellent of its kind. I am not acquainted with Coleridge of King's, but somewhat intimately so with one of his brothers,* now at the bar, and likely to rise very high in his profession. I know no man of whose judgment and principles I have a higher opinion. They are a remarkably gifted family, and may be expected to distinguish themselves in many ways.

"The Wordsworths spoke of you with great pleasure upon their return from Cambridge. *He* was with me lately. His thoughts and mine have for some time been unconsciously traveling in the same direction; for while I have been sketching a brief history of the English Church, and the systems which it has subdued or struggled with, he has been pursuing precisely the same subject in a series of sonnets, to which my volume will serve for a commentary, as completely as if it had been written with that intent. I have reason to hope that this work will be permanently useful; and I have the same hope of the series of Dialogues with which I am proceeding. Two of the scenes in which these are laid are noticed in your sonnets—the Tarn of Blencathra and the Ruined Village. Wm. Westall has made a very fine drawing of the former, which will be engraved for the volume, together with five others, most of which you will recognize. One of them represents this house, with the river and the lake, and Newlands in the distance.

"Are you going abroad? or do you wait till the political atmosphere seems to promise settled weather? God knows when that will be! For myself, I know not what to wish for, when, on the one side, the old governments will not attempt to amend any thing, and, on the other, the Revolutionists are for destroying every thing. Spain is in a deplorable state, which must lead to utter anarchy. If other powers do not interfere (which I rather hope than think they will not), the natural course of such a revolution will serve as an example *in terrorem* to other nations. True statesmen are wanted there, and not there alone, but every where else; why it is that there has not been a single man in Europe worthy of the name for the last century, is a question which it might be of some use to consider. Burke would have been one, had he not been always led away by passion and party, and an Irish imagination. It is something in the very constitution of our politics which dwarfs the breed, for we have had statesmen in India.

* * * * * * * *

"God bless you!
"Yours affectionately, R. SOUTHEY."

To John Rickman, Esq.

"Keswick, May 13, 1821.

"MY DEAR RICKMAN

"The present Oliver Cromwell, whose book serves me for a heading in the Quarterly Review, has led me into an interesting course of reading, and I am surrounded with memoirs of that age. Among other books, I have been reading the Εικων Βασιλικη, which never fell in my

* Now Mr. Justice Coleridge.

way before. The evidence concerning its authenticity is more curiously balanced than in any other case, except, perhaps, that of the two Alexander Cunninghams; but the internal evidence is strongly in its favor, and I very much doubt whether any man could have written it in a fictitious character—the character is so perfectly observed. If it be genuine (which I believe it to be as much as a man can believe the authenticity of any thing which has been boldly impugned), it is one of the most interesting books connected with English history. I have been reading, also, Hobbes's Behemoth; it is worth reading, but has less of his characteristic strength and felicity of thought and expression than the Leviathan. There is one great point on which he dwells with unanswerable wisdom—the necessity that public opinion should be directed by government, by means of education and public instruction.

"The course of the revolution in Portugal and Brazil will be to separate the two countries, and then, I fear, to break up Brazil into as many separate states as there are great captaincies; these, again, to be subdivided among as many chieftains as can raise ruffians enough to be called an army. There is, however, some check to these in the fear of the negroes, which may reasonably exist in great part of the country. This mischief has been brought about by Portuguese journals printed in London since the year 1808, and directed always to this end.

"God bless you! R. S."

To the Rev. Nicholas Lightfoot.

"Keswick, June 2, 1821.

"My dear Lightfoot,

"Your letter brings to my mind how it happened that the last which I received from you remained unanswered. I began a reply immediately, but having expressed a hope that business might probably soon lead me into the west country, and intimated a little too confidently the likelihood of my succeeding to some good family estates there in consequence of Lord Somerville's death, the letter was laid aside till I could be more certain. Shortly afterward I went to London, and the result of my legal inquiries there was, that, owing to the clumsy manner in which a will was drawn up, estates to the value of a thousand a year in Somersetshire, which, according to the clear intention of the testator, ought now to have devolved upon me, had been adjudged to Lord Somerville, to be at his full disposal, and were by him either sold or bequeathed to his half-brothers, so that the whole is gone to a different family. You know me well enough to believe that this never deprived me of an hour's sleep nor a moment's peace of mind. The only ill effect was, that I fancied your letter had been answered, and wondered I did not hear from you again, which wonder nothing but never-ending business has prevented me from expressing to you long ere this.

"God knows how truly it would have rejoiced me to have seen you at Oxford. My heart was never heavier than during the only whole day which I passed in that city. There was not a single cotemporary whom I knew; the only person with whom I spoke, whose face was familiar to me, was Dr. Tatham! except poor Adams and his wife, now both old and infirm. I went in the morning to look at Baliol, and as I was coming out he knew me, and then I recognized him, which otherwise I could not have done. I *dined* there in the hall at ten o'clock at night, and the poor old woman would sit up till midnight that she might speak to me when I went out. After the business of the theater was over I walked for some hours alone about the walks and gardens, where you and I have so often walked together, thinking of the days that are gone, the friends that are departed (Seward, and C. Collins, and Allen, and poor Burnet), time, and change, and mortality. Very few things would have gratified me so much as to have met you there. I had applause enough in the theater to be somewhat overpowering, and my feelings would have been very different if you had been there, for then there would have been one person present who *knew* me and loved me.

"My lodging was at Oriel, in the rooms of an under-graduate, whose aunt is married to my uncle. Coplestone introduced himself to me and asked me to dinner the next day, but I was engaged to return to London and dine with Bedford. There is no one of our remembrance left at Baliol except Powell, and him I did not see. The master and the fellows there showed me every possible attention; I had not been two hours in Oxford before their invitation found me out.

"The king sent me word that he had read the Vision of Judgment twice, and was well pleased with it; and he afterward told my brother (Dr. S.) at the drawing-room that I had sent him a very beautiful poem, which he had read with great pleasure.

"You will be pleased to hear that the Bishop of London, the Bishop of Durham, and Lord Liverpool told me, when I was in town last year, that the Life of Wesley was a book which in their judgment could not fail of doing a great deal of good.

"Always and affectionately yours,

"Robert Southey."

Among the great variety of strangers who found their way to Greta Hall with letters of introduction, there were a considerable proportion from America—travelers from thence, as my father humorously observes in one of his previous letters, inquiring as naturally for a real live poet in England as he would do for any of the wild animals of their country. Since that time, however, America has made rapid strides in literature, and native authors are not such rarities now as they were then. In this way he had made many agreeable and valuable acquaintances, and with several of them the intercourse thus begun was continued across the Atlantic: and he was the more rejoiced at the opportunity of showing them any attention in his power, because he had been most unjustly accused of holding and expressing opinions very unfavorable to America. Several papers had appeared in the Quarterly Review manifesting an unfriendly feeling toward that country, and these were ascribed to him,* while he was protesting against them privately, and strongly condemning the spirit in which they were written. This, however, was only one out of many instances in which the offenses of the Quarterly Review were laid to his charge.

The gentleman (Mr. Ticknor, of Boston) to whom the two following letters are addressed was one of the most literary of his American visitors, and a feeling of mutual respect and good will quickly sprang up between them, kept up by an occasional correspondence.

In the course of one of the evenings he passed at Greta Hall, my father had read to him the commencement of his poem of Oliver Newman, to which reference has occasionally been made, with which Mr. Ticknor had been much pleased; and, in consequence of the scene being laid in his native country, the MS. of the poem, when finished, was promised to him: to this the commencement of the following letter refers. Alas for the uncertainty of our intentions! No further progress of any moment was ever made in it; constant occupations of a different kind imperatively called for all his time and thoughts; many cares and more sorrows thickened upon him in these later years of his life; and the effort to resume the subject, though often contemplated, was never made.

To George Ticknor, Esq.

"Keswick, Aug. 19, 1821.

"MY DEAR SIR,

"That I intended to thank you for the books you sent me from London in 1819, the unfinished letter which I have now fished up from the bottom of my desk will show; and it is better to say *peccavi* than to apologize for the old and besetting sin of procrastination. That I had received them, you would probably infer from the mention of Fisher Ames in the Quarterly Review. This omission has been attended with frequent self-reproaches, for I am sure you will not suppose that you were forgotten; but I looked forward to an honorable amends in sending you the manuscript of my New England poem as soon as it should be completed. When that will be I dare not promise; but the desire of sending you that first fair copy, part of which was put into your hands when you were here, is not one of the least inducements for taking it up speedily as a serious and regular occupation.

"I found your parcel last night, on my return home, after a fortnight's absence. Its contents will be of the greatest use to me. I have already looked through Callender and the Archæology, and find in the former applicable information not in my other authorities, and in the latter many curious facts. Our old divine, Dr. Hammond, used to say, that whatever his course of study might be in the first part of the week, something always occurred in it which was convertible to use in his next sermon. My experience is of the same kind, and you will perceive that these books will assist me in many ways.

"My little girls have not forgotten you. The infant whom you saw sleeping in a basket here in this library, where he was born three weeks before, is now, God be thanked, a thriving and hopeful child. Kenyon will be here in the course of the week, and we shall talk of you, and drink to our friends in New England. This is less picturesque than the votive sacrifices of ancient times, but there is as much feeling connected with it.

"Mr. Everett sent me the two first numbers of his quarterly journal, telling me that I should not need an apology for the sentiments which it expresses toward England. I am sorry that those opinions appear to have his sanction, esteeming him highly as I do, and desirous as I am that the only two nations in the world who really are free, and have grown up in freedom, should be united by mutual respect and kindly feelings, as well as by kindred, common faith, and the indissoluble bond of language. Remember me most kindly to him, and to Mr. Cogswell also.

"I am collecting materials for a Life of George Fox, and the Rise and Progress of Quakerism. Perhaps some documents of American growth may fall in your way. We are never likely to meet again in this world; let us keep up this kind of intercourse till we meet in a better.

"God bless you!

"Yours affectionately,

"ROBERT SOUTHEY."

The following is the letter referred to as inclosed in the preceding one. I place it here as containing some interesting remarks upon American literature.

To George Ticknor, Esq.

"Keswick, Aug. 13, 1819.

"MY DEAR SIR,

"I did not receive your friendly letter, and the books which you sent to Murray's, till the last week in May, at which time I supposed you would be on your voyage homeward. Long ere this I trust you will have reached your native shores, and enjoyed the delight of returning to your friends after a long absence. Life has few greater pleasures.

"You have sent me a good specimen of American divinity. I very much doubt whether we have any cotemporary sermons so good; for, though our pulpits are better filled than they were in the last generation, we do not hear from

* "I returned to the post-office the other day three half crowns worth of abuse sent from New Orleans in the shape of extracts from Yankee newspapers. Every disrespectful thing said of America in the Q. R. is imputed to me in that country, while I heartily disapprove of the temper in which America is treated. Such things, however, are not worth notice; and lies of this kind for many years past have been far too numerous to be noticed, unless I gave up half my time to the task."—*To G. C. B., Jan.* 5, 1820.

them such sound reasoning, such clear logic, and such manly and vigorous composition as in the days of South and Barrow. What is said in the memoir of Mr. Buckminster of the unimpassioned character of our printed sermons is certainly true; the cause of it is to be found in the general character of the congregations for which they were composed, always regular church-going people, persons of wealth and rank, the really good part of the community, and the Formalists and the Pharisees, none of whom would like to be addressed by their parish priest as miserable sinners standing in need of repentance. Sermons of country growth seldom find their way to the press; in towns the ruder classes seldom attend the Church service, in large towns because there is no room for them; and indeed, in country as well as town, the subjects who are in the worst state of mind and morals never enter the church doors. Wesley and Whitefield got at them by preaching in the open air, and they administered drastics with prodigious effect. Since their days a more impassioned style has been used in the pulpit, and with considerable success. But the pith and the sound philosophy of the elder divines are wanting. Your Buckminster was taking the right course. The early death of such a man would have been a great loss to any country.

"You have sent me, also, a good specimen of American politics in the works of Fisher Ames. I perused them with great pleasure, and have seldom met with a more sagacious writer. A great proportion of the words in the American vocabulary are as common in England as in America. But, provided a word be good, it is no matter from what mint it comes. Neologisms must always be arising in every living language; and the business of criticism should be, not to reprobate them because they are new, but to censure such as are not formed according to analogy, or which are merely superfluous. The authority of an English reviewer passes on your side of the Atlantic for more than it is worth; with us the Review of the last month or the last quarter is as little thought of as the last week's newspaper. You must have learned enough of the constitution of such works to know that upon questions of philology they are quite unworthy of being noticed. The manner in which they are referred to in the vocabulary led me to this, and this leads me to the criticisms upon Bristed and Fearon's books in the Quarterly Review. I know not from whom they came, but they are not in a good spirit. R. S."

To John May, Esq.

"Keswick, Aug. 26, 1821.

"My dear Friend,

"How little are our lots in life to be foreseen! It might reasonably have been thought that, if any man could have been secured against ill fortune in his mercantile concerns by prudence, punctuality, method, and the virtues and habits which the mercantile profession requires, you, above all men, would have been uniformly and steadily prosperous; and yet to what a series of anxieties and losses have you been exposed, without any fault, or even any thing which can justly be called incautious on your part! This, however, is both consolatory and certain, that no good man is ever the worse for the trials with which Providence may visit him, and the way in which you regard these afflictions exemplifies this.

"Since I received your letter I made my proposed visit to the sea-coast with the two Ediths and Cuthbert. We were at Netherhall, the *solar* of my friend and fellow-traveler Senhouse, where his ancestors have uninterruptedly resided since the days of Edward II. (when part of the present building is known to have been standing), and how long before that no one knows. Some of his deeds are of Edward I.'s reign, some of Henry III.'s, and one is as far back as King John. We slept in the tower, the walls of which are nine feet thick. In the time of the great Rebellion the second of the two sons of this house went to serve the king, the elder brother (whom illness had probably detained at home) died, and the parents then wished their only surviving child to return, lest their ancient line should be extinct. A man who held an estate under the family was sent to persuade him to this, his unwillingness to leave the service in such disastrous times being anticipated; but the result of this endeavor was, that Senhouse, instead of returning, persuaded the messenger to remain and follow the king's fortunes. They were at Marston Moor together, and at Naseby. In the last of those unhappy fields Senhouse was dreadfully wounded, his skull was fractured, and he was left for dead. After the battle his faithful friend searched for the body, and found him still breathing. By this providential aid he was saved; his skull was pieced with a plate of metal, and he lived to continue the race. His preserver was rewarded by having his estate enfranchised; and both properties continue at this day in their respective descendants. This is an interesting story, and the more so when related as it was to me, on the spot. The sword which did good service in those wars is still preserved. It was made for a two-fold use, the back being cut so as to form a double-toothed saw.

"Netherhall stands upon the little river Ellen, about half a mile from the sea, but completely sheltered from the sea wind by a long high hill, under cover of which some fine old trees have grown up. The Ellen rises on Skiddaw, forms the little and unpicturesque lake or rather pool which is called Overwater, near the foot of that mountain, and, though a very small stream, makes a port, where a town containing 4000 inhabitants has grown up within the memory of man on the Senhouse estate. It was called Maryport, after Senhouse's grandmother, a very beautiful woman, whose portrait is in his dining-room. His father remembered when a single summer-house standing in a garden was the only building upon the whole of that ground, which is now covered with streets. The first sash windows in Cumberland were placed in the tower in which we slept by the founder of this town; and when his son (who died about six years ago, at the age of eighty-four or five) first went to Cambridge, there was no stage-coach north of York.

"Old as Netherhall is, the stones of which it is built were hewn from the quarry more than a thousand years before it was begun. They were taken from a Roman station on the hill between it and the sea, where a great number of Roman altars, &c., have been found. Some of them are described by Camden, who praises the Mr. Senhouse of his time for the hospitality with which he received him, and the care with which he preserved these remains of antiquity. * * It was a bishop of this family who preached Charles I.'s coronation sermon, and the text which he took was afterward noted as ominous: 'I will give him a crown of glory.' The gold signet which he wore as a ring is now at Netherhall. God bless you!

"Yours most affectionately,

"ROBERT SOUTHEY."

To Grosvenor C. Bedford, Esq.

"Keswick, Sept. 9, 1821.

"MY DEAR GROSVENOR,

"I wish to possess a castle in Bohemia. My good aunt Mary has the like desire; and as there are two castles to be had there, together with twelve villages (enough to qualify me, in all conscience, for a baron of the holy Roman empire), I beseech you, with as little loss of time as may be, to transmit, in such manner as Herries may best direct, the sum of two pounds to W. H. Reinganum, Banquier, No. 13 Rue Zeil, Frankfort sur Maine, to purchase one ticket in my name, and one in my aunt Mary's, in the lottery for the seven estates in Bohemia which are to be *played for* at Vienna on the 1st of next month; and I invite you, Grosvenor, to purchase a ticket also, and let us go shares in the adventure; and if we get the prize, we will make a merry and memorable journey to Prague, and you shall take your choice of seven titles for your baronship, to wit, Zieken, Wolschow, Koyschitz, Shunkau, Libietitz, Prytanitz, and Oberstankau.

"Just suppose, Grosvenor, that Fortune, in one of her freaks, was to give us this prize, and we were to set out for the purpose of taking possession of twelve villages, two chateaux, seven farms, and several mills and manufactures, and valued judicially at 894,755 florins of Vienna. I suppose the inhabitants are included. The notion, I think, will amuse you as much as it does us. So buy the tickets, Grosvenor. The castles in question are certainly two of the King of Bohemia's castles, because they make the great prize in an imperial lottery; but whether they are two of the seven castles the history of which Corporal Trim began to Uncle Toby, I pretend not to determine. By all means, however, let us have a chance for them. I should like a good fortune well, and much the better if it were a queer one, and came in a comical way.

"So God bless you, Grosvenor! and make us both barons, and my aunt a Bohemian baroness. R. S."

To the Rev. Neville White.

"Keswick, Oct. 20, 1821.

"MY DEAR NEVILLE,

" * * * * * * * *

You form a just opinion of the character and tendency of William Taylor's conversation. A most unfortunate perversion of mind has made him always desirous of supporting strange and paradoxical opinions by ingenious arguments, and showing what may be said on the wrong side of a question. He likes to be in a state of doubt upon all subjects where doubt is possible, and has often said, 'I begin to be too sure of that, and must see what reasons I can find against it.' But when this is applied to great and momentous truths, the consequences are of the most fatal kind. I believe no man ever carried Pyrrhonism further. But it has never led him into immoralities of any kind, nor prevented him from discharging the duties of private life in the most exemplary manner. There never lived a more dutiful son. I have seen his blind mother weep when she spoke of his goodness; and his kindness and generosity have only been limited by his means.

"What is more remarkable is, that this habitual and excessive skepticism has weakened none of the sectarian prejudices in which he was brought up. He sympathizes as cordially with the Unitarians in their animosity to the Church and State as if he agreed with them in belief, and finds as strong a bond of union in party spirit as he could do in principle.

"With regard to his talents, they are very great. No man can exceed him in ingenuity, nor in the readiness with which he adorns a subject by apt and lively illustrations. His knowledge is extensive, but not deep. When first I saw him, three-and-twenty years ago, I thought him the best-informed man with whom I had ever conversed. When I visited him last, after a lapse of eight years, I discovered the limits of his information, and that upon all subjects it was very incomplete.

"Of his heart and disposition I can not speak more highly than I think. It is my belief that no man ever brought a kindlier nature into this world. His great talents have been sadly wasted; and, what is worse, they have sometimes been sadly misemployed. He has unsettled the faith of many, and he has prepared for his own old age a pillow of thorns. To all reasoning, the pride of reason has made him inaccessible; and when I think of him, as I often do, with affection and sorrowful forebodings, the only foundation of hope is, that God is merciful beyond our expectations, as well as beyond our deserts.

"Thank you for the copy of Cromwell's Letters. The transcriber has tasked his own eyes, and mine also, by copying them in the very form of the writing. I can not attempt to read them by candle-light. You will by this time have seen my sketch of Cromwell's Life. It is the only article of mine which was ever printed in the Quarterly Review without mutilation. Gifford has made only one alteration; that, however, is a very improper one. I had said that Hampden might have left behind him a *name scarcely inferior to Washington's;* and he has chosen to alter this to a *memorable name*, not calling to mind that his name *is* memorable. The sentence is thus made nonsensical. Pray restore the proper reading in your copy of the Review. Murray wishes me to fill up the sketch for separate publication. I am fond of biography, and shall probably one day publish a series of English lives. I spent a week lately at Lowther Castle, and employed all my mornings in reading and extracting from a most extensive collection of pamphlets of Cromwell's age.

* * * * * * *

"God bless you, my dear friend!

"Yours very affectionately,

"ROBERT SOUTHEY."

To Grosvenor C. Bedford, Esq.

"Keswick, Nov. 11, 1821.

"MY DEAR GROSVENOR,

"Lakers and visitors have now disappeared for the season, like the swallows and other birds who are lucky enough to have better winter quarters allotted to them than this island affords them. The woodcocks and snipes have arrived, by this token, that my bookbinder here sent me a brace of the latter last week; and this reminds me to tell you, that if you ever have an owl dressed for dinner, you had better have it boiled, and smothered with onions, for it is not good roasted. *Experto crede Roberto.*

"Two or three weeks ago, calling at Calvert's, I learned that Raisley C. had committed the great sin of shooting an owl. The criminality of the act was qualified by an ingenuous confession, that he did not know what it was when he fired at it; the bird was brought in to show us, and then given me that I might show it to your godson, owls and monkeys being of all created things those for which he has acquired the greatest liking from his graphic studies. Home I came with the owl in my hand, and in the morning you would have been well pleased had you seen Cuthbert's joy at recognizing, for the first time, the reality of what he sees daily in Bewick or in some other of his books. Wordsworth and his wife were here, and as there was no sin in eating the owl, I ordered it to be dressed and brought in, in the place of game, that day at dinner. It was served up without the head, and a squat-looking fellow it was, about the size of a large wild pigeon, but broader in proportion to its length. The meat was more like bad mutton than any thing else. Wordsworth was not valiant enough to taste it. Mrs. W. did, and we agreed that there could be no pretext for making owls game and killing them as delicacies. But if ever you eat one, by all means try it boiled, with onion sauce.

"I asked your opinion, a good while since, concerning a dedication for the Peninsular War, and hitherto you have not opined upon the subject in reply. It has this moment, while I am writing, occurred to me, that I could, with sincere satisfaction in so doing, inscribe it to Lord Sidmouth. I have always felt thankful to him for the peace of Amiens, and should like to tell him so in public, as I once did *vivâ voce*. And I should do it the more willingly if he is going out of office, which I rather think he is.

"Gifford will have a paper upon Dobrizhoffer from me for this next number. Will you tell him that in a volume of tracts at Lowther, of Charles I.'s time, I found a Life of Sejanus by P. M., by which initials some hand, apparently as old as the book, had written Philip Massinger. I did not read the tract, being too keenly in pursuit of other game; but I believe it had a covert aim at Buckingham. I have not his Massinger, and therefore do not know whether he is aware that this was ever ascribed to that author; if he is not, he will be interested in the circumstance, and may think it worthy of further inquiry.

"My History is in good progress. I am finishing the longest chapter in the volume, and one of the most interesting. It contains the events in Portugal from the commencement of the insurrection in Spain till the arrival of our expedition.

"God bless you! R. S."

To the Rev. Neville White.

"Keswick, Nov. 29, 1821.

"MY DEAR NEVILLE,

* * * * * * *

"What you relate of William Taylor is quite characteristic of the manner in which he abuses his own powers, playing the mere sophist, and disregarding the opinions and feelings of others; careless how he offends and hurts them, though as incapable as man can be of giving intentional pain, or doing intentional wrong. He was not serious, for he knows very well that to call for proof of a negative is an absurdity, and that reason *and discourse of reason* are very different things. If he misleads some, his example operates as a warning upon others. They see how he has squandered his abilities, and that the hereditary blindness which he has some cause to apprehend, and of which he lives in fear, is not the darkest evil in his prospect. There is no rest but in religious faith, and none know this more feelingly than they who are without it.

"It would not surprise me if an expert Roman Catholic priest (where he to come in his way) should ensnare him in a spider's web of sophistry, more skillfully constructed than his own, and of a stronger thread. The pleasure of defending transubstantiation would go a long way toward making him believe in it.

"What a state is Ireland in at this time! The horrors of the Irish massacres may be credited in their whole extent, because we see that the same temper is exhibited at this time, and the same atrocities perpetrated in retail, opportunity being all that is wanted for committing them upon the great scale. The state of things in that country is a reproach to human nature, and our government has much to answer for. They must know that such a people ought to be kept under military law till they are fit for any thing better; that they stand in need of Roman civilization, and that no weaker remedy can possibly suffice. Cromwell's government, if it had lasted twenty years longer, would have civilized that island. His tyranny was as useful there and in Scotland as it was injurious in England, because they were barbarous countries, and he introduced order and despotic justice into both. But in England we had order and justice before his time. The rebellion dislocated both, and it was not possible for him to repair the evil in which he had been so great an agent. * *

"God bless you, my dear Neville!

"Yours affectionately,

"ROBERT SOUTHEY."

The reader will have observed in his later letters to Mr. May frequent allusion to Brazilian affairs as affecting his fortunes, and in the following one my father speaks of his having transferred to him for his present use what little money he had at command, and expressing a regret at not being able more effectually to assist him in his difficulties. These passages, though relating to matters of a private nature, I am glad to have the opportunity of publishing, with Mr. May's approval, as illustrative of the kindness of my father's heart, the warmth and stability of his friendships, and his grateful remembrance of many similar services rendered to him by his friend in past years.

To John May, Esq.

"Keswick, Dec. 10, 1821.

"MY DEAR FRIEND,

"It is not often that I allow myself to wish the accidents of fortune had been more in my favor, and that I were in possession of that property which, in the just ordinary course of things, ought to have devolved upon me; but I can not help feeling that wish now.

"By this post I write to Bedford, desiring that he will transfer to you £625 in the three per cents. I wish it was more, and that I had more at command in any way. I shall in the spring, if I am paid for the first volume of my history as soon as it is finished. One hundred I should, at all events, have sent you then. It shall be as much more as I may receive.

"One word more. I entreat you break away from business, if it be possible, as early in the spring as you can, and put yourself in the mail for this place. Though you can not leave your anxieties behind you, yet you may, by means of change of air and scene, be assisted in bearing them, and lay in here a store of pleasant recollections, which in all moods of mind are wholesome.

"I can not write to you about indifferent things, troubled as you needs must be, and sympathizing as I must do with you. Yet I trust that you now know the extent of the evil, and that, when this storm is weathered, there may be prosperity and comfort in store for one who so eminently deserves them.

"God bless you, my dear friend!

"Yours most affectionately,

"ROBERT SOUTHEY."

To the Rev. Neville White.

"Keswick, Dec. 11, 1821.

"MY DEAR NEVILLE,

"When the Life is reprinted, I can modify the passage which expresses an essential difference of opinion upon religious subjects with Henry. That difference is certainly not now what it was then, but it is still a wide one; though, had Henry lived till this time, I believe there would scarcely have been a shade of difference between us. I am perfectly sure that, with a heart and intellect like his, he would have outgrown all tendency toward Calvinism, and have approached nearer in opinion to Jeremy Taylor than to the Synod of Dort.

"You wrong the government with regard to Ireland. They neither now have, nor ever have had, a wish to keep the savages in that country in their state of ignorance and barbarity; and it would surprise you to know what funds have been established for their education. I know Dr. Bell was surprised at finding how large the endowments were, and felt that on that score it was not means that were wanting, but the just direction of them. How to set about enlightening such a people as the wild Irish is one of the most difficult duties any government was ever called upon to perform, obstructed as it is by such a body of priests, who can effectually prevent any better instruction than they themselves bestow. I want more information concerning certain parts of Irish history than I possess at present; but in one or more of the works which I have in hand I shall trace the evils of Ireland to their source. Meantime, this I may safely assert, as a general deduction from all that I have learned in the course of history, that the more we know of preceding and coexisting circumstances and difficulties, the more excuse we shall find for those men and measures which, with little knowledge of those circumstances, we should condemn absolutely. This feeling leads not to any thing like indifference concerning right and wrong, nor to any lukewarmness or indecision in opinion, but certainly to a more indulgent and charitable tone of mind than commonly prevails.

"God bless you, my dear Neville!

"And believe me yours affectionately,

"ROBERT SOUTHEY."

To Walter Savage Landor, Esq.

"Keswick, Dec. 19, 1821.

"At last I have received the books*—a rich cargo, in which I shall find much to amuse, and not a little to profit by. As yet, I have only had

* A present of various foreign books from Mr. Landor.

time to catalogue them, and look into them as this was done. In so doing, I saw that you had given a Jesuit the lie for what he said of the cause of the first rebellion. A lying Jesuit he is; but in this instance the falsehood is merely chronological. The Long Parliament passed a decree forbidding all persons to bow at the name of Jesus; Sir Edward Dering made a very eloquent speech upon the occasion, which I shall send you ere long in the little sketch of our Church history which I am preparing. This decree was subsequent to the Irish massacre. The fact which the Jesuit might have dwelt upon with advantage is, that the intolerance of the Parliament seeking to enforce the penalty of death against recusant priests, when Charles, like his father, was inclined to toleration, gave a pretext for the rebellion, and furnished those who instigated it with means for alarming and enraging the populace.

"I shall send your letter to Wordsworth, who will, I am sure, be much gratified at seeing what you say of him. His merits are every day more widely acknowledged, in spite of the duncery, in spite of the personal malignity with which he is assailed, and in spite of his injudicious imitators, who are the worst of all enemies.

"Nothing can be more mournful than the course of events abroad. All that the Spanish-Americans wanted they would have obtained now, in the course of events, without a struggle, if they had waited quietly. A free trade could not, from the first, have been refused them, nor any internal regulations which they thought good; and now the separation would have taken place unavoidably. As it is, it has cost twelve years of crime and misery. It is a most interesting part of the world for its natural features, for what we know of its history, and for what we do not—how some parts should have attained to so high and curious a state of civilization, and how the greater part of its inhabitants should have sunk so completely into savages. I will send you, in the next package, Humboldt's Travels, as far as they are published. He is among travelers what Wordsworth is among poets. Of Italian nobility I would take your opinion without hesitation, knowing nothing of them myself; but in Spain and Portugal I would have had a house of peers, were it only in respect to great names, and those heroic remembrances which are the strength and glory of a nation. The nobles were, for the most part, deplorably degenerate; but as a bad spirit had degraded, a better one would improve the next generation, and I would demolish nothing but what is injurious. My fear is, that they will demolish every thing, and this fear I have felt from the beginning. Deeply, therefore, as I detested the old misrule, I did not rejoice in the Spanish and Portuguese revolutions. In Portugal I wished for a great minister, such as Pombal would have been in these times; in Spain, for a court revolution, which should have sent Ferdinand to a monastery, and established a vigorous ministry under his brother's name, by whom the reforms which the country needed might have been steadily but gradually effected. I entirely agree with you that old monarchical states can not be made republican, nor new colonial ones be made monarchical.

"Since the disappearance of the queen's fever this country has been unusually calm: little is heard of distress, and less of disaffection. Of the latter we shall hear plentifully when the bills of restriction are expired, and of the former also when it shall be found (as it will be) that the renewed activity of our manufacturers will have again glutted the South American markets.

"God bless you! R. S."

CHAPTER XXVII.

RELIGIOUS FEELINGS—THE BOOK OF THE CHURCH—HISTORY OF THE PENINSULAR WAR—LORD BYRON—SPANISH AFFAIRS—MR. LANDOR'S NEW WORK—IMPROVEMENTS IN LONDON—EFFECTS OF GENERAL EDUCATION—VISIT FROM MR. LIGHTFOOT—DR. CHANNING AND THE REV. CHRISTOPHER BENSON—GENERAL PEACHEY—DWIGHT'S TRAVELS—EDITORSHIP OF THE QUARTERLY REVIEW—THE LAUREATESHIP—WAYS AND MEANS—THE PENINSULAR WAR—COURSE OF HIS READING—CATHOLIC EMANCIPATION—ILLUSTRATIONS OF RODERIC—POSTHUMOUS FAME—THE QUARTERLY REVIEW—AMERICAN VISITORS—WORDSWORTH'S POETRY—MR. MORRISON—OWEN OF LANARK—DANGER OF THE COUNTRY—BLANCO WHITE—THE FRENCH IN SPAIN—JOURNEY TO LONDON—ROWLAND HILL—THE DAILY STUDY OF THE SCRIPTURES RECOMMENDED.—1822–1823.

THE careful reader can hardly have failed to observe the gradual progress of my father's mind upon religious subjects, and to have marked how his feelings on those points had deepened and strengthened from the frequent references he makes to them as the only sure foundation for rational happiness. Few men, indeed, had ever the thoughts of the life to come more constantly present to them; and his anticipations of a happy futurity are so frequent as to have met with the charge of an overweening confidence approaching to irreverence. But, although his manner of speaking may have been such as to seem irreverent to other minds constituted differently from his own, his nature was not really so; and the truth would seem to be, that from a fervid imagination combined with strong positive faith, and a habit of mind the opposite to the Pyrrhonism he lamented in his friend William Taylor, he realized the idea of another life so vividly as to make him express himself on that subject with an unusual familiarity. The point which he most frequently alludes to, and which he appears to dwell upon with the greatest pleasure, is that of the meeting of "the spirits of just men made perfect;" and the natural buoyancy of his temperament, united with the wide charitableness of his creed, saved him from the misgivings which would have checked more timid religionists, both in contemplating the future state itself, and in peopling the blessed mansions with those whom he honored and loved.

The very course of his studies and the habits of his life forced upon him such continual thoughts of the "mighty dead" that they seem to have been almost like living and breathing companions, and his wishes to meet and commune with them face to face became like the intense desire we sometimes feel to meet a living person known intimately yet not personally.

I can not resist quoting here his own lines on the subject, written a few years before this period of his life:

I.

"My days among the dead are past;
Around me I behold,
Where'er these casual eyes are cast,
The mighty minds of old;
My never-failing friends are they,
With whom I converse day by day.

II.

"With them I take delight in weal,
And seek relief in woe;
And while I understand and feel
How much to them I owe,
My cheeks have often been bedewed
With tears of thoughtful gratitude.

III.

"My thoughts are with the dead, with them
I live in long past years;
Their virtues love, their faults condemn,
Partake their hopes and fears;
And from their lessons seek and find
Instruction with an humble mind.

IV.

"My hopes are with the dead! Anon
My place with them will be,
And I with them shall travel on
Through all futurity;
Yet leaving here a name, I trust,
That will not perish in the dust."*

I have before spoken of the prevalence of skeptical opinions (p. 200) among young men of the higher classes at the commencement of this century, and I have mentioned that many of my father's acquaintances and some of his friends were at one period or another troubled with doubts upon religion. Accordingly, as opportunity occurred, he often endeavored, when he had any reasonable hopes of doing good, to impress upon such persons the perfect adaptation of Christianity to the wants and nature of man, and especially the deep and never-failing sources of comfort it affords in all times of sorrow and trouble.

To one of these friends who had passed through the stages of doubt and settled into a firm conviction of the truth of Christianity, and whom he had the happiness of knowing he had been partly instrumental, through Providence, in leading to this better mind, the following letter was addressed.

To ——

"Keswick, Feb. 8, 1822.

"My dear ——,

"I heard with sorrow of your ill health. Perhaps you are at this time a happier man than if you were in the enjoyment of vigorous health, and had never known sickness or sorrow. Any price is cheap for religious hope. The evidence for Christianity is as demonstrative as the subject admits: the more it is investigated, the stronger it appears. But the root of belief is in the heart rather than in the understanding; and when it is rooted there, it derives from the understanding nutriment and support. Against Atheism, Materialism, and the mortality of the soul, there is the *reductio ad absurdum* in full force; and for revealed religion there is the historical evidence, strong beyond the conception of those who have not examined it; and there is that perfect adaptation to the nature and wants of man, which, if such a revelation had not already been made, would induce a wise and pious man to expect it, as fully as a Jew expects the Messiah. For many years my belief has not been clouded with the shadow of a doubt.

"When we observe what things men will believe who will not believe Christianity, it is impossible not to acknowledge how much belief depends upon the will.

"I shall have a large share of abuse in the course of this year. In the first place, my Book of the Church, which I am writing *con amore* and with great diligence, will strike both the Catholics and the Puritans harder blows than they have been of late years accustomed to receive. The Emancipationists, therefore, and the Dissenters will not be pleased; and you know the temper of the latter. My History of the War smites the Whigs, and will draw upon me, *sans* doubt, as much hatred from the Bonapartists in France as I have the satisfaction of enjoying from their friends in England. This volume is in great forwardness; more than five hundred pages are printed. As for Lord Byron and his coadjutors in the Times, Chronicle, &c., &c., I shall, of course, not notice the latter, and deal with his lordship as he may deserve and as I may feel inclined. I have the better cause and the stronger hand.

"God bless you!

"Yours affectionately,

"R. Southey."

---

* I have an additional pleasure in quoting these lines here, because Mr. Wordsworth (now, alas! himself numbered among those "mighty dead") once remarked that they possessed a peculiar interest as a most true and touching representation of my father's character. He also wished three alterations to be made in them, in order to reduce the language to correctness and simplicity. In the third line, because the phrase "casual eyes" is too unusual, he proposed

"Where'er I chance these eyes to cast."

In the sixth line, instead of "converse," "commune;" because as it stands, the accent is wrong.

In the second stanza, he thought

"While I understand and feel,
My cheeks have often been bedewed,"

was a vicious construction grammatically, and proposed instead,

"My pensive cheeks are oft bedewed."

These suggestions were made too late for my father to profit by them.

To the Rev. Herbert Hill.

"Keswick, Feb. 24, 1822.

"My dear Uncle,

" * * * * * * *

With regard to Lord Byron, I have suffered him to attack me with impunity for several years. My remarks upon the Satanic School were general remarks upon a set of public offenders; and it was only in reply to the foulest personalities that I attacked him personally in return. The sort of insane and rabid hatred which he has long entertained toward me can not be increased; and it is sometimes necessary to show that forbearance proceeds neither from weakness nor from fear.

"Your copy of Landor's book was franked up through the Admiralty to Gifford. His Latin, I believe, is of the best kind; but it is, like his English, remarkably difficult: the prose, however, much less so than the verse. The cause of this obscurity it is very difficult to discover.

"My correspondence with Frere has been very brisk. Something, also, I have had from Whittingham, and am every day expecting answers to further questions which I have sent; but the most valuable papers which I have yet had are from Sir Hew Dalrymple, relating to his first communications with the Spaniards, and the whole proceedings in the south of Spain, while the junta of Seville ruled the roast. They will cause me to cancel a few pages, and replace them with fuller details. Luckily, the greater part comes in time to be introduced in its place without any inconvenience of this kind. These papers have given me a clear insight into many points with which I was imperfectly acquainted before. They contain also proof of scandalous neglect on the part of ministers, or something worse than neglect—a practice of leaving their agents without instructions for the sake of shifting the responsibility from themselves. At the commencement of the troubles in Spain, out of thirty-four dispatches—certainly the most important that any governor of Gibraltar ever had occasion to send home—Lord Castlereagh never acknowledged more than two. I have heard our government complained of for this sort of conduct, which, in fact, is practiced in every department of state; but this is the most glaring proof of it that has ever fallen in my way.

"God bless you! R. S."

To Walter Savage Landor, Esq.

"Feb. 29, 1822.

"In looking over your volumes,* you will, I think, wherever you perceive that a passage has been struck out, perceive at the same time for what reason it was omitted. The reason for every omission was such that, I am persuaded, you would, without hesitation, have assented to it, had you been upon the spot. A most powerful and original book it is, in any one page of which—almost in any single sentence—I should have discovered the author, if it had come into my hands as an anonymous publication. Notice it must needs attract; but I suspect that it will be praised the most by those with whom you have the least sympathy, and that the English and Scottish Liberals may perhaps forgive you even for being my friend.

"I have not been from home since the summer of 1820. Even since that time, London has been so altered as to have almost the appearance of a new city. Nothing that I have seen elsewhere can bear comparison with the line of houses from Regent's Park to Carleton House. A stranger might imagine that our shop-keepers were like the merchants of Tyre, and lived in palaces. I wish the buildings were as substantial as they are splendid; but every thing is done in the spirit of trade. Durability never enters into the builder's speculations, and the unsubstantial brick walls are covered with a composition which seems to have the bad property of attracting moisture in a remarkable degree. In Regent's Park, before the houses are finished, the cornices are perfectly green with slimy vegetation. The most impressive sight to me was St. Paul's by gas-light. I do not think any thing could be more sublime than the effect of that strong light upon the marble statues; and the darkness of the dome, which the illumination from below served only to render visible. They have attempted to warm this enormous building by introducing heated air; but, after expending £800 in stoves and flues, the effect was to render the quire unendurably cold, for the whole body of cold air from the dome came rushing down, so that the attempt has been given up as hopeless.

"In London I scarcely went out of the circle of my own immediate friends. But as I went east and west upon a round of flying visits to old friends and familiar acquaintances, some of whom I had not seen for more than twenty years, I had opportunity enough of perceiving a more general disposition to be satisfied with things as they are, than ever existed within my memory at any former time. There happened to be no question afloat with which any party feeling could be connected, and the people were sensible of their general prosperity. Few, indeed, are they who apprehend the momentous consequences of the changes which are taking place. One effect of general education (such as that education is) is beginning to manifest itself. The two-penny journals of sedition and blasphemy lost their attraction when they no longer found hunger and discontent to work upon. But they had produced an appetite for reading. Some journeymen printers who were out of work tried what a weekly two-penny-worth of miscellaneous extracts would do; it answered so well, that there were presently between twenty and thirty of these weekly publications, the sale of which is from 1000 to 15,000 each. How I should like to talk with you concerning the prospects of the Old World and of the New.

"God bless you! R. S."

* The proof-sheets of a work of Mr. Landor's, on the Writings of Charles Fox, had passed through my father's hands.

To Grosvenor C. Bedford, Esq.

"Keswick, July 12, 1822.

"MY DEAR GROSVENOR,

"My old friend Lightfoot is with me, whom you remember at Oxford, and whom I had not seen since we parted upon leaving Oxford eight-and-twenty years ago. The communication between us had never been broken. I had a great regard for him, and talked of him often, and oftener thought of him; and, as you may suppose, the more I became known and talked of in the world, the larger part I occupied in his thoughts. So at length he mustered up resolution to make a journey hither from Crediton during his Midsummer holidays, being master of the grammar school there.

"He declares me to be less altered in appearance and manners than any man whom he ever saw. I should not have known him; and yet he has worn better than I have; but he is thinner, and altogether less than when he was a young man, and his face has lengthened, partly because he has lost some of his hair. His life has been laborious, uniform, successful, and singularly happy.

"He trembled like an aspen leaf at meeting me.* A journey to Cumberland is to him as formidable a thing as it would be for me to set off for Jerusalem, so little has he been used to locomotion. And he has shocked Edith May by wishing that the mountains would descend to fill up the lakes and vales, because then I should return to the south and be within reach of him.

"The only thing short of this which would be likely to remove me from this country, would be, if upon Gifford's giving up the management of the Quarterly Review, it were to be offered me and made worth my acceptance. In that case I should probably, from prudential reasons, think it proper to accept the offer, and fix myself within ten or twelve miles of town. But this is not likely, and I am not sure that it would be desirable.

"What a pleasure it is in declining life to see the friends of our youth such as we should wish them to be; and how infinitely greater will be the pleasure of meeting them in another world, where progression in beatitude will be the only change!

"God bless you! my dear Grosvenor.

"R. S."

In the course of the summer Dr. Channing made a brief visit to Keswick, bearing a letter of introduction to my father, from whom it seems he had requested one to the Rev. Christopher Benson, the late master of the Temple. This is interesting as relating to two distinguished individuals. I may add that my father used to speak of Mr. Benson as the most impressive and pleasing preacher he had ever heard, "so as to admit of no comparison with any other."

* In another letter he says, "I shall never forget the manner in which he met me, nor the tone in which he said, 'that, having now seen me, he should return home and die in peace.'"—*Sept.* 1, 1822.

To the Rev. Christopher Benson.

"Keswick, July 17, 1822.

"DEAR SIR,

"Dr. Channing, of Boston, in New England, is equally distinguished in his own country by the fervor and eloquence of his preaching, and the primitive virtues of his life. I take the liberty of introducing him to you, because you will feel yourself in accord with him upon many of the most important points and because I am very desirous that he should see and converse with one who holds as high a rank in Old England as he does in America. I have learned from him with some surprise that, under the name of Unitarianism, Arianism is the prevailing doctrine in the Massachusetts' states, and that he himself is of that persuasion. But I have told him that he will find himself much more in sympathy with our clergy than with the Dissenters, and this he already apprehends. He is in opulent circumstances, and has devoted, and almost spent, himself in the ministerial duties.

"I need say no more of him; his conversation and the truly Christian temper of his mind, notwithstanding the doctrinal errors which he holds, will sufficiently recommend him. But I feel the necessity of apologizing for the liberty which I am taking with you. You will, I trust, impute it to the true cause, and not be offended if, in excuse for it, I say to you that, having had the good fortune once to hear you in the pulpit, and having since perused with the greatest satisfaction the series of your discourses, I earnestly wish that this excellent American should receive the most favorable impressions of the English Church. When I spoke of you to him last night, and put your volume into his hands, I did not know whether you were in this or in a better world. To-day, by mere accident, I learn that you have happily resumed your labors, and, yielding to the first impulse, I offered this introduction to Dr. Channing with as much pleasure as he manifested at receiving it.

"When you visit this your native county, you would gratify me greatly by giving me an opportunity of personally repeating an apology for this intrusion, and offering you such hospitality as my means afford.

"Believe me, dear sir, yours, with the highest esteem and respect,

"ROBERT SOUTHEY."

The following letter refers to an amusing adventure which had just happened to General Peachey, whose name has before occurred, and who was one of my father's most friendly and hospitable neighbors. His seat was on one of the islands in Derwentwater, and a more lovely spot fancy could not picture. It was not, however, a convenient residence, especially for a dinner-party in unfavorable weather; for, although the passage was short, still silks and satins suffered woefully when the waves rose high, and occasionally covered the fair wearers with their spray, and great was the reluctance to leave blazing fires and lighted rooms for pitchy darkness, and a voyage not only unpleasant, but sometimes formidable.

Many adventures, generally, however, of a more ludicrous than perilous kind, occurred in consequence of this watery barrier. Large parties have been compelled to remain all night, the gentlemen bivouacking round the drawing-room fire; sometimes a dense fog came on, so that the rowers lost their way, and either wandered up and down the lake for several hours, or landed their hapless boat loads on some distant fenny or stony shore, to act, unwillingly, to the life "the Children of the Mist." On one occasion the general himself, returning home unexpectedly, found it impossible to cross, and after waiting upon the inhospitable shore till he was wet and weary, made his way up to Greta Hall in sad plight.

The general was a great lover of aquatics, and his favorite amusement was a sailing boat, which, in spite of all warnings (for the sudden gusts which rush down the mountain gorges render the smaller lakes extremely unsafe for sailing on), he persevered in navigating with more boldness than skill. More than once his only place of refuge was the keel of his vessel, on which he hung till help arrived, and sometimes he was driven hopelessly aground on the mid-shallows of the lake. All these accidents, however, served as good stories to circulate around his cheerful board, and many was the hearty laugh he raised and joined in at his own misadventures. The reader will find scattered up and down this volume occasional allusions to pleasant days passed in his company, nor did any one entertain a truer respect and a more friendly regard for my father. With him departed the open hand and kind heart of a true English gentleman.

To the Rev. Nicholas Lightfoot.

"Keswick, Sept. 16, 1822.

"My dear Lightfoot,

"The general has lately had a narrow, though ludicrous escape. He upset himself with an umbrella in a little skiff which Sir Frederic Moreshead had given him. It was within hearing of his own island. The skiff was corked so that it could not sink, but being half full of water after he had righted it, it was not possible for him to get in, and he being well buttoned up against a stormy day in a thick great-coat, was in no plight for swimming; so he held on, and hallooed stoutly for assistance. His two men hastened off in his little boat, the large one happening to be on the opposite shore. The general had presence of mind enough to consider that if he attempted to get into the little boat he should in all likelihood pull her under water, and that neither of the men could swim; he therefore very coolly directed them to take the rope of the skiff and tow it to the island with him at the end, and in this way he came in like a Triton, waving his hat round his head, and huzzaing as he approached his own shores. I ought to have told you that there came an invitation from him for you to dinner the day after your departure.

"John May left me this day fortnight, and Dr. Bell departed some days after him. The exercise which I took with him completed the good work which was begun with you, and has left me in a better state than I had been in for the two last years. By way of keeping it up while the season permits (nothing being so salutary to me as vigorous exercise), I went up Skiddaw Dod this morning—one of the expeditions which is reserved for your next visit; on my return I found a letter from my brother Henry, saying he shall be here on Wednesday. This will give me ten days more of laking and mountaineering, if the weather permit.

"The temptation which the country holds out to that exercise which is peculiarly necessary for me must be weighed among the many reasons for remaining in it; for, with my sedentary habits and inactive inclinations, I require every inducement to draw me out. But whether I remain or remove I shall see you, my dear Lightfoot, often again (God willing) both in Devonshire and wherever I may be. I shall certainly come down to you when next I visit London, which will probably be in February or March.

"During the little time I had for business I have written about half a paper for the Quarterly, upon a history of the Religious Sects of the last century, by the ex-Bishop Gregoire. The book is curious for its strange mixture of revolutionary feelings with Catholic bigotry, and for the account which it gives of irreligion in France. It gives me matter for an interesting paper, to be wound up with some seasonable observations upon the progress of infidelity at home. God bless you, my dear Lightfoot!

"Yours affectionately,

"Robert Southey."

To Dr. Southey.

"Keswick, Oct. 30, 1822

"My dear Harry,

"As soon as you departed I settled regularly to my habitual course of life, which has been so much to my benefit broken up through the summer. At the same time I very dutifully began to observe your directions, and have walked every day with the exception of one stormy one. This is against the grain, but I feel the benefit of it, and therefore do not grumble.

"The American books have arrived, and I am reading with much interest Dwight's Travels in his own country—a posthumous work. The author (whose unhappy name is Timothy) wrote in his youth, some forty years ago, an heroic poem upon the Conquest of Canaan, which was puffed and reprinted in London. Its stilted versification was admired in those days, but it had little or no real merit. Dwight, however, though a bad poet—because of a bad school—was a sensible man, and he kept a journal of his travels, and prepared it for publication, from a conviction that a faithful description of New England in all its parts, such as it then was, would in a few generations become exceedingly interesting, however unimportant it might appear if published as soon as it was written. A great deal, of course, is only interesting locally; but, on the whole, the picture of what the country is, his fair views of the state of society then, with its advantages and disadvantages, and the number of curious facts which are brought together, make it very well worth reading. I would give a good deal to see as trustworthy and minute an account of the Southern States. This is just the sort of book which ought to be digested into a review.

"The Quarterly Review will not do itself any good by the mealy-mouthed manner in which it has dealt with Lord Byron. The excuse for its previous silence is wretched; and to preach a sermon in refutation of so silly a piece of sophistry as Cain is pitiful indeed. To crown all, while they are treating his lordship with so much respect, and congratulating themselves on the improved morality of his productions—out comes 'the Liberal.' I have only seen some newspaper extracts from this journal, among them the description of myself. He may go on with such satire till his heart aches, before he can excite in me one uncomfortable emotion. In warring with him, I have as much advantage in my temper as Orlando had in his invulnerable hide. But there is no necessity for striking a blow at one who has so completely condemned himself. I wish the Liberals joy of their journal.*

"Love from all. God bless you!

"ROBERT SOUTHEY."

To the Rev. Nicholas Lightfoot.

"Keswick, Nov. 8, 1822.

"MY DEAR LIGHTFOOT,

"By my brother Henry's means, I have found how the impediment between me and your cider may be removed. If you will direct it for me to the care of George Sealy, Esq., Liverpool, and ship it for that place, letting me know by what vessel it is sent, he will look after it there and forward it to Keswick, and then we will all drink your health in the juice of the apple. It will need a case to protect it from the gimlet.

"There is little chance of any circumstance drawing me from this country to reside in the vicinity of London—at least I can foresee none. The question whether or not the Quarterly Review should do so has been fairly considered and decided, in consequence of Gifford's dangerous illness. He had written to me soon after you left us, saying he could not long continue to conduct the Review, and he knew not where to look for a successor. He was not ill at the time, and therefore my consideration of the matter was not hastily, but deliberately made. If I had chosen to propose myself, the office must have been mine, of course. The objections to it were, that the increased expenditure which I must incur near London would fully consume any increase of income which I should have obtained, and therefore the time consumed in the mere management of the journal would have been a dead loss. This time would be unpleasantly as well as unprofitably spent in corresponding upon the mere business of the Review, examining communications, and either correcting them myself where there was any thing erroneous, imprudent, or inconsistent with those coherent opinions which the journal should have maintained under my care, or in persuading the respective writers to amend and alter according to that standard. Lastly, it seemed that there was nothing which could recompense me for the sacrifice which it needs would be to quit a country in which I take so much delight, and of which all my family are as fond as myself; and there was this weightier consideration—that if I gave up the quantity of time which the management of such a journal requires, it would take away all reasonable hope of my completing the various great works for which I have been so long making preparations.

"I talked this matter over with John May, who entered entirely into my feelings. The next point, having fully made up my mind concerning myself, was to secure the succession (as far as my influence extended) for some person with whom I could freely and heartily co-operate. John Coleridge is just such a person; and having ascertained that he would like the situation, I mentioned him to Gifford and to Murray. Gifford's illness has occurred since. He is better at present, and I have good reason to believe it is all but settled that John Coleridge is to become the editor of the Quarterly Review. Without taking him from his profession, it will render him independent of it, and place him at once in a high and important situation.

" * * * * This is a long explanation, and yet I think you will like to know the *how* and the *why* of my proceedings. In consequence, I may possibly take more part in the Review, and certainly more interest in it; because, knowing the tenor of his opinions, and his way of thinking, I am sure he will admit nothing that either in matter or manner could offend a well-regulated mind. He will hold a manly and straightforward course, and censure will always come with weight and effect, because it will never be unduly or insolently applied. * * * * * * *

"Believe me, my dear Lightfoot,

"Yours affectionately,

"R. SOUTHEY."

To Grosvenor C. Bedford, Esq.

"Keswick, Dec. 20, 1822.

"MY DEAR G.,

"I have no written form of admission to the office of laureate, and very well remember being surprised at the thoroughly unceremonious manner of my induction. At the day and hour appointed (a very memorable one, the Prince Regent going to Parliament just after the news of the battle of Leipsic had been made public), I went to a little low, dark room in the purlieus of

* "Lord Byron has rendered it quite unnecessary for me to resent his attacks any further. This last publication is so thoroughly infamous that it needs no exposure. It may reach a second number if it escape prosecution, but hardly a third. He and Leigh Hunt, no doubt, will quarrel, and their separation break up the concern."—*To the Rev. Neville White, Nov.* 16, 1822.

St. James's, where a fat old gentleman usher, in full buckle, administered an oath to me, in presence of a solitary clerk; and that was all, payment of fees excepted, which was not made at the time. Walter Scott, I recollect, was amused at the description which I sent him of this ceremony, and said it was a judgment upon me for inserting among the Notes to the Cid a reflection of Sir John Finett's upon the 'superstition of a gentleman usher.' Whether any entry was made, and whether I signed my name, I can not call to mind, it being nine years ago. Gazetted, however, I was, and P. L. I have been from that time. But how can this concern you?

"You know the proverb, that he who is not handsome at twenty, wise at forty, and rich at fifty, will never be rich, wise, or handsome. *Quoad* my handsomeness—handsome is as handsome does, and whatever I may have been, they have made a pretty figure of me in magazines. There is a portrait in a German edition of my smaller poems, which it will be a treat for you to see. You will never again complain of your ugly likeness below stairs. Concerning the second part of the adage, certain it is that about the age of forty, my views upon all important subjects were matured and settled, so that I am not conscious of their having undergone any change since, except in slight modifications upon inferior points. But for the last part of the story—rich at fifty—I certainly shall not be, nor in the way to be so.

"When I deliberated, if deliberating it can be called, about the Quarterly Review, the single motive on one side was the desire of having an adequate and sure income, which I have never had since I discontinued the Edinburgh Annual Register, because it ceased to pay me for my work. My establishment requires £600 a year, exclusive of other calls. The average produce of my account with Longman is about £200; what I derive from the Exchequer you know; the rest must come from the gray goose quill; and the proceeds of a new book have hitherto pretty generally been anticipated. They may float me for a second year, perhaps. Roderic did for three years, with the help of the Pilgrimage; then the tide ebbs, and so I go on. At present it is neap tide in the Row. My tale of Paraguay, when I can finish it, will about make it high water.

"This is all very well while I am well; but if any of the countless ills which flesh is heir to should affect my health, eyesight, or faculties, I should instantly be thrown into a state in which my income would only amount to about half my expenditure. Concerning death I have no anxieties. * * On that score I am easy, and not uneasy upon any other. But I have said all this to explain why it was that I could even ask myself the question whether it would become me to take the Quarterly Review into my own hands. I am quite satisfied that it would not; but that it behooves me to go on, as I have always hitherto done, hopefully, contentedly, and thankfully, taking no further care for the morrow than that of endeavoring always to be able to say, sufficient for the day has been the work thereof.

"I have made a valiant resolution that the produce of this History shall not be touched for current expenses, looking to it always as the work wherewith I was to begin to make myself independent. The Book of the Church I must eat, but I will not eat these Peninsular quartos. The Whigs may nibble at them if they please.

"I have just received an official communication from Sir William Knighton, which, though it be marked *private*, there can be no unfitness in my communicating to you. It is in these words: 'I am commanded by the king to convey to you the estimation in which his majesty holds your distinguished talents, and the usefulness and importance of your literary labors. I am further commanded to add, that his majesty receives with great satisfaction the first volume of your valuable work on the late Peninsular War.' This is the letter, and at the head of it is written, 'Entirely approved. G. R.' Is not this very gracious? and how many persons there are whom such a communication would make quite happy. For myself, I am sorry there are so few persons connected with me who can be gratified by it, and wish my good Aunt Mary had been here to have enjoyed it. I may deposit it with my letters affiliatory from the Cymmrodorion, &c., and I might write upon the packet that contains them *vanitas vanitatum, omnia vanitas*. Not that I would be understood as affecting, in the slightest degree, to undervalue what I am continually laboring to deserve.

"God bless you! R. S."

To Grosvenor C. Bedford, Esq.

"Keswick, Jan. 27, 1823.

"MY DEAR GROSVENOR,

"I am very glad to see Herries's appointment. By all that I have heard for many years past, a more unfit person than —— could not possibly have been in that situation; to get him out, and to have so efficient a man in his stead, is indeed a great point. It is the very place in which I have wished to see Herries. I hope and trust, now, that such means as the existing laws afford will be steadily employed for checking the license of the press. The radical country papers continually lay themselves open to prosecution; and I am certain that repeated prosecutions would go far toward stopping the mischief which they are doing at present, and have so long been doing with impunity. A strict watch over these, and over Cobbett, would soon suppress them.

"I know nothing of the sale of my book; Murray has not written to me since it appeared. Only two opinions of it have reached me, except those of my friends—one in a complimentary letter from Mr. Littleton, the member for Staffordshire; the other in a letter of the *ci-devant* Grand Parleur, which Rickman sent me; and certainly nothing could be more flattering than what he said of it—that it was 'a Thucydidean history, which would last as long as our country and our language.' I must confess, however, that I am not aware of any other resemblance than what the title suggests; though I have always flattered myself that my other historical work might, in more points than one, be compared with Herodotus, and will hereafter stand in the same relation to the history of that large portion of the new world, as his work does to that of the old.

"We had an adventure this morning, which, if poor Snivel* had been living, would have set up her bristles in great style. A foumart was caught in the back kitchen: you may, perhaps, know it better by the name of polecat. It is the first I ever saw or smelled, and certainly it was in high odor. Poor Snivel! I still have the hairs cut from her tail thirty years ago; and if it were the fashion for men to wear lockets, in a locket they should be worn, for I never had a greater respect for any creature upon four legs than for poor Sni. See how naturally men fall into relic worship, when I have preserved the memorials of that momentary whim so many years, and through so many removals!

"To give you some notion of my heterogeneous reading, I am at this time regularly going through Shakspeare, Mosheim's Ecc. Hist., Rabelais, Barrow, and Aitzema, a Dutch historian of the seventeenth century, in eleven huge full folios. The Dutchman I take after supper, with my punch. You are not to suppose that I read his work verbatim: I look at every page, and peruse those parts which relate to my own subjects, or which excite curiosity; and a great deal I have found there.

"We have not seen the face of the earth here for fifteen days—a longer time than it has ever been covered with snow since I came into the country. I growl at it every day. It seems a long while since I have heard from you. God bless you! R. S."

To Humphrey Senhouse, Esq.

"Keswick, July 11, 1822.

"My dear Senhouse,

"I am sorry to say that the prospect before me is not such as to allow much hope of my seeing Holland† this year. Time, the printers, and the constable are leagued together to oppose my wishes: I shall overcome the alliance, but not till the season will be too far advanced. Perhaps I could be ready by the vintage, which would be no unpleasant sight; but then the days are shortening, and daylight is the thing which travelers can least spare.

"My winter has not been idly spent, but it has not carried me so far forward as I had anticipated, chiefly because writing a book is like building a house—a work of more time and cost than the estimate has been taken at. This is the chief reason. But something, I confess, must be set down to my besetting sin—a sort of miser-like love of accumulation. Like those persons who frequent sales, and fill their own houses with useless purchases, because they may want them some time or other; so am I forever making collections, and storing up materials which may not come into use till the Greek Calends. And this I have been doing for five-and-twenty years! It is true that I draw daily upon my hoards, and should be poor without them; but in prudence I ought now to be working up these materials rather than adding to so much dead stock.

"This volume, when it appears, will provoke a great branch of the Satanic confederacy—the Bonapartists. It is the most damning record of their wickedness that has yet appeared in this country, and in a form to command both attention and belief. Only yesterday I learned from General Whittingham, who was in the battle of Medellin, that the French had orders to give no quarter. A wounded Spanish officer was brought into the room where Victor was at supper, and Victor said to him, 'If my orders had been obeyed, sir, you would not have been here.' Those orders were obeyed so well, that the French dragoons that night rubbed their right arms with soap and spirits, to recover the muscles from the fatigue they had undergone in cutting the fugitives down. God bless you!

"Yours affectionately,

"Robert Southey."

To Grosvenor C. Bedford, Esq.

"Keswick, Feb. 23, 1823.

"My dear Grosvenor,

"Your letter comes in aid of a purpose which I had entertained, of putting together what I have said upon the Catholic question in the Edinburgh Annual Register, recasting it, and publishing it, with some needful additions, in the form of a pamphlet. About a week ago I put down in my note-book the first sketch of an arrangement, and actually began to compose what I have to say as a letter to some M.P.; not that it was meant to be addressed to any individual one; but having argued with Wilberforce and Sir Thomas Acland upon the subject, I knew in what light they considered it. The course which affairs have taken in Ireland will probably have the good effect of quashing the question for this year, and in that hope I am willing to postpone my own purpose till a season which may be more convenient to myself, and when aid of this kind may be more needed.

"The arguments lie in a nut-shell. The restraints which exclude the Catholics from political power are not the cause of the perpetual disorder in Ireland; their removal, therefore, can not be the cure. Suppose the question carried, two others grow from it, like two heads from the hydra's neck when one is amputated: a Catholic establishment for Ireland, at which Irish Catholics *must* aim, and which those who desire rebellion and separation will promote—a rebellion must be the sure consequence of agi-

* A dog belonging to Mr. Bedford in early days.

† My father had for some time wished to visit the Low Countries, and had planned a tour there with Mr. Senhouse, who had been his companion in a former journey. This was not accomplished until 1825, when Mr. S. was not able to accompany him.

tating this. The people of Ireland care nothing for emancipation—why should they? but make it a question for restoring the Catholic Church, and they will enter into it as zealously as ever our ancestors did into a crusade.

"The other question arises at home, and brings with it worse consequences than any thing which can happen among the potatoes. The repeal of the Test Act will be demanded, and must be granted. Immediately the Dissenters will get into the corporations every where. *Their* members will be returned; men as hostile to the Church and to the monarchy as ever were the Puritans of Charles's age. The Church property will be attacked in Parliament, as it is now at mob meetings and in radical newspapers; reform in Parliament will be carried; and then farewell, a long farewell, to all our greatness.

"Our Constitution consists of Church and State, and it is an absurdity in politics to give those persons power in the *State* whose duty it is to subvert the *Church*. This argument is unanswerable. I am in good hopes that my Book of the Church will do yeoman's service upon the question. God bless you! R. S."

To Grosvenor C. Bedford, Esq.

"Keswick, May 25, 1823.

"My dear Grosvenor,

"Westall has sent me four of the six prints for Roderic; the others are not yet finished. I am very much pleased with these. If I were persuaded, according to the custom of these times, that it is absolutely necessary to find some fault with every thing, I might perhaps say that the engraver has aimed at throwing too much expression into the eyes in some of the plates. Those which are come are Roderic at the Foot of the Cross, Adosinda showing him the Dead Bodies, Florinda at her Confession, and the Death of Count Julian. The first strikes me as the best, and for this reason, that the subject is altogether picturesque—it explains itself sufficiently; whereas, to know what the others mean, the poetical situation must be understood. I am much more desirous that this speculation should succeed on Westall's account than on my own. He had set his heart upon it, in the belief that it would be of service to me to have my poems thus illustrated (as the phrase is), and in the feeling that the publishers were acting unhandsomely in having such things done for every writer of any note except myself. The success would have been certain had it been done some years ago. At present it is very doubtful.

"How is Chantrey? Something like a message from him has been brought me by Mr. Gee, expressing a wish that I would sit to him when I come to London. When will that be, you ask? And many, I dare say, ask the same question, who know not what pains, as well as thought, I must take for the morrow before I can afford two months of traveling and expenditure. To-night I shall finish with Queen Mary's reign; Elizabeth's will require not a long chapter; James's a short one. The next is one of the most important in the book, but easily and soon written, because the materials are ready. Another chapter comes down to the Revolution, and one more will conclude. Then I shall set out for town, and eat ice there instead of oysters. * *

"God bless you! R. S."

To Grosvenor C. Bedford, Esq.

"Keswick, June 15, 1823.

"My dear G.,

"The worst symptom of advancing age which I am sensible of in myself is a certain anxiety concerning ways and means; to that cause I impute it, for I am sure it does not belong to my disposition.

"You tell me it is not politic to work entirely for posthumous fame. Alas! Grosvenor, had you forgotten when you wrote that sentence that by far the greater portion of my life has been consumed in providing for my household expenses? As for reputation, of that, God knows, I have as much as either I deserve or desire. If I have not profited by it, as some of my cotemporaries have by theirs, the fault is not owing to my living out of sight. What advantage could it possibly be to me to meet great men at dinner twice or thrice in the season, and present myself as often at court? There is, I dare say, good will enough among some of the men in power to serve me, if they knew how; but if they asked me how, I should not be able to point out a way.

* * * * * * *

"Is it impossible for you to break away from London, and lay in a stock of fresh health and spirits by help of fresh air and exhilarating exercise? I wish you would come here and stay with me till I could return to town with you. You would do me good as well as yourself. God bless you! R. S."

To George Ticknor, Esq.

"Keswick, July 16, 1823.

"My dear Sir,

"If, as I trust, you have received my first volume of the Peninsular War, and the lithographic views which my friend, William Westall, has engraved to accompany it, you will perceive that, negligent as I have been in delaying so long to thank you for the books, and to reply to your welcome letter, I had not been wholly unmindful of you. Without attempting to excuse a delay for which I have long reproached myself, I may say that it has been chiefly, if not wholly occasioned by an expectation that I might have communicated to you Gifford's retirement from the management of the Quarterly Review, and the assumption of that management by a friend of mine, who would have given it a consistent tone upon all subjects. Poor Gifford was for several months in such a state that his death was continually looked for. His illness has thrown the journal two numbers in arrear; he feels and acknowledges his inability to conduct it, and yet his unwillingness to part with a power which he can not exercise has hitherto stood in the way of any other arrangement.

"I have more than once remonstrated both with him and Murray upon the folly and mischief of their articles respecting America; and should the journal pass into the hands of any person whom I can influence, its temper will most assuredly be changed. Such papers, the silence of the journal upon certain topics on which it ought manfully to have spoken out, and the abominable style of its criticism upon some notorious subjects, have made me more than once think seriously of withdrawing from it; and I have only been withheld by the hope of its amendment, and the certainty that through this channel I could act with more immediate effect than through any other. Inclosed you have a list of all my papers in it. I mean shortly to see whether Murray is willing to reprint such of them as are worth preserving, restoring where I can the passages which Gifford (to the sore mutilation of the part always, and sometimes to the destruction of the sense and argument) chose to omit, and beginning with the Moral and Political Essays.

"Your friends and countrymen who come to Keswick make a far shorter tarriance than I could wish. They 'come like shadows, so depart.' Dr. Channing could give me only part of a short evening. Randolph of Roanoake no more: he left me with a promise that if he returned from Scotland by the western side of the island, he would become my guest: if he could have been persuaded to this, it would have done him good, for he stood in need of society, and of those comforts which are not to be obtained at an inn. Mr. Eliot passed through about five weeks ago, and on Monday last we had a younger traveler here—Mr. Gardner. No country can send out better specimens of its sons.

"Coleridge talks of bringing out his work upon Logic, of collecting his poems, and of adapting his translation of Wallenstein for the stage, Kean having taken a fancy to exhibit himself in it. Wordsworth is just returned from a trip to the Netherlands: he loves rambling, and has no pursuits which require him to be stationary. I shall probably see him in a few days. Every year shows more and more how strongly his poetry has leavened the rising generation. Your mocking-bird is said to improve the strain which he imitates; this is not the case with ours.

"Nov. 2, 1823.

"I conclude this too-long-delayed letter on the eve of my departure for London. From thence, in the course of the next month, I shall send you the Book of the Church. Gifford is so far recovered that he hopes to conduct the Review to the 60th number. I have sent him the commencement of a paper upon Dwight's book, which I shall finish in town. The first part is a review of its miscellaneous information; the second will examine the points of difference between an old country and a new one, the advantages and disadvantages which each has to hope and to fear, and the folly of supposing that the institutions which suit the one must necessarily be equally suitable to the other.

"Farewell, my dear sir. Remember me to Alston and my other New England friends; and be assured that to them and to their country I shall always do justice in thought, word, and deed.

"God bless you!

"Yours with sincere esteem,

"ROBERT SOUTHEY."

To the Rev. Nicholas Lightfoot.

"Keswick, Sept. 23, 1823.

"MY DEAR LIGHTFOOT,

"The summer, or what might have been the summer, has slipped away, and the autumn, or what ought to be the autumn, is passing after it, and I have not yet been further from my fireside than a morning's walk could carry me.

"I can tell you, however, now, that I shall start from home with my daughter Edith as early as possible in November, or, if possible, before the beginning of that month; and that after halting a week or ten days in London, I shall pursue my course to Crediton.

"The summer has brought with it its usual flock of strangers, some of them sufficiently amusing. My civilities to them are regulated something by the recommendations with which they present themselves, and a little more, perhaps, by their likeability, which depends something upon the *cut of their jib*. You know how impossible it is not to read faces, and be in some degree influenced by what we see in them. We have had two travelers from New England—young men both, and well qualified to keep up the good impression which their countrymen have left here. Last week we had an Englishman, who, having traveled in the Levant, and been made prisoner by the Bedouins, near Mount Sinai, chooses to relate his adventures instead of publishing them, and tells Arabian stories after the manner of the professed story-tellers in the East. I wish you had seen him the other evening gravely delivering a tale of a magic ring (it was a full hour long) to a circle of some sixteen persons in this room, the vicar being one of the number. But the most interesting stranger who has found his way here is a Somersetshire man—Morrison by name, who, at the age of two or three and thirty, and beginning with little or nothing, has realized some £150,000 in trade, and was then bound to New Lanark, with the intention of vesting £5000 in Owen's experiment, if he should find his expectations confirmed by what he sees there. This person is well acquainted with the principal men among the free-thinking Christians; he likes the men, but sees reason to doubt their doctrine. He seems to be searching for truth in such a temper of mind that there is good reason for thinking he will find it.

"My household are in tolerable order. It has been increased this year by the acquisition of a most worthy Tom-cat who, when the tenants of the next house departed, was invited to this, where he received the name of Rumpelstilzchen, and has become a great favorite. I can not say of him as Bedford does of a similar animal, that he is the *best-for-nothing cat* in the world, because he has done good service upon the rats, and been successively promoted to the rank of baron, viscount, and earl. In most other things we are as you left us, except that just now the waters are not in their place, having overflowed their banks.

"God bless you, my dear Lightfoot!

"Yours affectionately, R. SOUTHEY."

To the Lord Bishop of Limerick.

"Keswick, Oct. 22, 1823.

"MY LORD,

"I ought to have thanked you for your Visitation Sermon and for your Charge, both worthy of the hand from which they come. I have thought, also, more than once, of expressing to yourself, as I have done to others, the sincere pleasure which your promotion gave me, from a public not less than a personal feeling, in these times, when it is of such especial importance that such stations should be so filled.

* * * * * * *

"My anticipations would be of the darkest kind if it were not for a calm, unhesitating reliance upon Providence. Our institutions had need be strong when they are so feebly defended, and so formidably and incessantly assailed. Uncompromising courage was almost the only quality of a statesman which Mr. Pitt possessed, and that quality has not been inherited by his successors. At present they seem to think that all is well because the manufacturers are in employ, and there is no seditious movement going on; and they would hardly look upon that writer as their friend who should tell them that this quiet is only upon the surface; that the leaven is at work; and that there is less danger from the negroes in Demerara or Jamaica than from a manufacturing population such as ours, with such a party of determined radicals and besotted reformers in Parliament to excite them. Would that I could perceive the remedy as clearly as I do the evil! I have, however, for some time been deliberately putting together my thoughts upon this subject in a series of Colloquies upon the Progress and Prospects of Society, taking for my motto three pregnant words from St. Bernard, *Respice, aspice, prospice.* I am neither so vain nor so inexperienced as to imagine that any thing which I may offer will change any man's opinions; but I may fix them when they are unconfirmed, make the scale turn when it is wavering, and give a right bias to those who are beginning their career.

"There is hope for us at home, because our institutions are so good that it is quite certain, if they were subverted, the miserable people would soon desire nothing so much as their reestablishment; and moreover, with the commonest prudence, they are strong enough to resist a revolutionary attack. But if we look abroad, the contending parties are both in such extremes of evil, that I know not from which the worst consequences are to be apprehended, the establishment of old governments or the triumph of new ones. You would be pleased, I am sure, with the paper concerning Spain in the last Quarterly. It is by my friend Blanco White (Leucadio Doblado), a Spanish priest, who came over to this country in 1810, a thorough Jacobin and a thorough unbeliever, and is at this time as sincere a Protestant and as devout a minister as any whom the Church of England has in her service. There are few men whom I respect so highly.

"Before this letter reaches your lordship I shall be on the way to London, and as I shall not finally leave it before the beginning of February, it is possible that I may have the pleasure of meeting you there. It will indeed gratify me to accept of your obliging invitation, if I can one day find opportunity and leisure: there is much in your country which I should like to see, and many points upon which I should gladly seek for information. My Annual Ode two years ago was upon the king's visit to Ireland, and the condition of that country. It would naturally have concluded with some complimentary and hopeful mention of Marquis Wellesley, but my spirit failed. I felt that the difficulties of his situation were more than he could overcome, and the poem remained in this respect imperfect.

"That poem of Langhorn's has certainly a Hebrew cast; but it must be rather a proof that this form of composition is the natural figure of passion than of imitation. The principle, as a principle, he could not have understood; nor was he, being a lawyer, likely to have had any learning of that kind; nor, indeed, being a Catholic, even to have been conversant with the scriptural style. The part given in the Quarterly Review is about a third of the poem, but the whole is in the same high and sustained strain of feeling.

"I am putting the last hand to my long-promised Book of the Church. It will give great offense to the Catholics, and to all those Dissenters who inherit the opinions of the Puritans. But I hope and trust that it will confirm in many, and excite in more, a deep, well-founded reverence for the Establishment.

"Believe me, my lord, with great respect and regard, your lordship's obliged and obedient servant, ROBERT SOUTHEY."

The reader may possibly have remarked it as an omission, that among the many persons addressed and alluded to in my father's letters, the name of Charles Lamb should have so rarely occurred, especially as they were well known to entertain mutual feelings of close friendship, and admiration of each other's talents. The cause of this has been, on the one hand, that Lamb never preserved the letters he received, and, on the other, that such of those written by him to my father as were of peculiar interest are well known in Mr. Justice Talfourd's interesting sketch of his life.

The correspondence, indeed, between them,

though not frequent, was yet of a most familiar and interesting character; and to visit his early friend,* for they had been intimate for nearly twenty years, was one of the choicest pleasures my father always looked forward to in going to London.

At the time of his present visit to the metropolis, a momentary interruption to their friendship occurred, which requires to be noticed here.

In a recent number of the Quarterly (for July, 1823), in a paper upon the Progress of Infidelity, my father had taken occasion to remark upon the Essays of Elia, that it was a book which wanted only a sounder religious feeling to be as delightful as it was original. At this expression, with which my father himself had not been satisfied, but had intended to alter in the proof-sheet, which, unfortunately, was not sent him, Lamb was greatly annoyed; and having previously taken umbrage at some incidental reference to him in former articles, which in his hasty anger he attributed erroneously to my father's pen, he now addressed a very long letter of remonstrance to him by name, in the London Magazine for October (1823). In this, which was republished after his death in his collected works, he dwells particularly upon a point which I have before touched upon, as much, I think, as is necessary at my hands, that some person might affix a charge of a want of a sufficiently reverential habit of speaking on religious topics upon my father himself, and also upon the circumstance of his having taken so large a license in jesting upon subjects of Diablerie, and in facetious commentaries upon the Legends of Rome; acquitting him, at the same time, of all intentional irreverence, and affirming that he himself had learned from him something of the habit.

This letter, which contained, besides, much more that was written in a resentful spirit, was put into my father's hands soon after his arrival in London, and he was greatly astonished at its contents. He says, speaking of it in a letter to Mr. Moxon (July 15, 1837), "When he published that letter to me in the London Magazine, so little was I conscious of having done any thing to offend him, that upon seeing it announced in the contents of that number, I expected a letter of friendly pleasantry. My reply was to this effect, that if he had intimated to me that he was hurt by any thing which had been said by me in the Quarterly Review,† I would in the next number have explained or qualified it to his entire satisfaction; this, of course, it was impossible for me to do after his letter; but I would never make sport for the Philistines by entering into a controversy with him. The rest was an expression of unchanged affection, and a proposal to call upon him." And in another letter he says, "On my part there was not even a momentary feeling of anger. I was very much surprised and grieved, because I knew how much he would condemn himself. And yet no resentful letter was ever written less offensively; his gentle nature may be seen in it throughout."

Lamb's answer to my father's letter, fully confirming this expectation, may fitly be placed here.

C. Lamb, Esq., to R. Southey, Esq.

"E. I. H., Nov. 21, 1823.

"DEAR SOUTHEY,

"The kindness of your note has melted away the mist that was upon me. I have been fighting against a shadow. That accursed Quarterly Review had vexed me by a gratuitous speaking of its own knowledge* that the Confessions of a Drunkard was a genuine description of the state of the writer. Little things that are not ill meant may produce much ill. That might have injured me alive and dead. I am in a public office, and my life is insured. I was prepared for anger, and I thought I saw, in a few obnoxious words, a hard case of repetition directed against me. I wish both magazine and review

* In referring back to the account of my father's short residence at Burton in the year 1797, I find I have omitted to notice a visit which Charles Lamb there paid him, and which must have been the commencement of their intimacy. Mr. Justice Talfourd states that their first introduction to each other took place through Mr. Coleridge in 1799, but of this I did not find any traces in my father's letters, doubtless because his mind was then fully occupied with his own difficulties and distresses. Their most frequent intercourse was in 1802, when Lamb was living at the Temple, and London for the last time was my father's place of abode.

† Charles Lamb's bitter feelings against the Quarterly and its editor originated in an allusion to him in one of the earlier numbers, where, in speaking of a criticism of his on the great scene in Ford's play of The Broken Heart, where "Calantha dances on after hearing at every pause of some terrible calamity, the writer had affected to excuse Lamb as a maniac."[1] On seeing the passage, which the circumstances of Lamb's life rendered so peculiarly obnoxious, my father had written to Murray to express his sorrow at its having been permitted to appear, and received from Gifford, who, it seems, was himself the writer of it, an explanation so honorable to him, that I am extremely glad to be able to insert it here, especially as my father greatly regretted that he had not sent it to Mr. Justice Talfourd.

"James Street, Buckingham Gate, Feb. 13, 1812.

"MY DEAR SIR, * * * * * * *

"I break off here to say that I have this moment received your last letter to Murray. It has grieved and shocked me beyond expression; but, my dear friend, I am innocent as far as the intent goes. I call God to witness that in the whole course of my life I never heard one syllable of Mr. Lamb or his family. I knew not that he ever had a sister, or that he had parents living, or that he or any person connected with him had ever manifested the slightest tendency to insanity. In a word, I declare to you, *in the most solemn manner*, that all I ever knew or ever heard of Mr. Lamb was merely his name. Had I been aware of one of the circumstances which you mention, I would have lost my right arm sooner than have written what I have. The plain truth is, that I was shocked at seeing him compare the sufferings and death of a person who just continues to dance after the death of her lover is announced (for this is all her merit) to the pangs of Mount Calvary; and not choosing to attribute it to *folly*, because I reserved that charge for Weber, I unhappily, in the present case, ascribed it to madness, for which I pray God to forgive me, since the blow has fallen heavily where I really thought it would not be felt. I considered Lamb as a thoughtless scribbler, who, in circumstances of ease, amused himself by writing upon any subject. Why I thought so I can not tell, but it was the opinion I formed to myself, for I now regret to say I never made any inquiry upon the subject, nor by any accident in the whole course of my life did I hear him mentioned beyond the name. * * * *

"I remain, my dear sir, yours most sincerely,

"W. GIFFORD."

* This was one of the passages before referred to, as wrongfully ascribed to my father.

[1] See Final Memorials of C. Lamb, vol. i., p. 215.

were at the bottom of the sea. I shall be ashamed to see you, and my sister (though innocent) will be still more so, for this folly was done without her knowledge, and has made her uneasy ever since. My guardian angel was absent at that time.

"I will make up courage to see you, however, any day next week (Wednesday excepted). We shall hope that you will bring Edith with you. That will be a second mortification; she will hate to see us; but come and heap embers; we deserve it, I for what I have done, and she for being my sister.

"Do come early in the day, by sunlight, that you may see my Milton. I am at Colebrook Cottage, Colebrook Row, Islington. A detached whitish house, close to the New River, end of Colebrook Terrace, left hand from Sadler's Wells.

"Will you let us know the day before?

"Your penitent, C. LAMB."

In a letter to Bernard Barton of the same day, he thus alludes to the expected meeting: "I have a very kind letter from the laureate, with a self-invitation to come and shake hands with me. This is truly handsome and noble. 'Tis worthy my old ideas of Southey. Shall I not, think you, be covered with a red suffusion?"

The proposed visit was paid, and "the affectionate intimacy, which had lasted for almost twenty years, was renewed only to be interrupted by death."

To Mrs. Southey.

"London, Dec. 30, 1823.

"MY DEAR EDITH,

"We have been this morning to hear Rowland Hill. Mrs. Hughes called at his house last week to know when he would preach, and was answered by a demure-looking woman that (the Lord willing) her master would preach on Sunday morning at half past ten, and in the evening at six. So this morning I set off with E. May, Mrs. and Anne Rickman. We were in good time, and got into the free seats, where there were a few poor people, one of whom told us to go round to another door, and we should be admitted. Another door we found, with orders that the door-keepers should take no money for admittance, and a request that no person would enter in pattens. Door-keeper there was none, and we therefore ventured in and took our seats upon a bench beside some decent old women. One of these, with the help of another and busier old piece of feminity, desired us to remove to a bench behind us, close to the wall; the seats we had taken, they said, belonged to particular persons; but if we would sit where she directed till the service was over, we should then be invited into the pews, if there was room. I did not immediately understand this, nor what we were to do in the pews when the service was at an end, till I recollected that in most schism shops the sermon is looked upon as the main thing for which the congregation assemble. This was so much the case here, that people were continually coming in during all the previous part of the service, to which very little attention was paid, the people sitting or standing as they pleased, and coughing almost incessantly.

"I suppose what is properly called the morning service had been performed at an early hour, for we had only the communion service. Rowland Hill's pulpit is raised very high, and before it, at about half the height, is the reader's desk on his right, and the clerk's on his left, the clerk being a very grand personage with a sonorous voice. The singing was so general and so good that I joined in it, and, doubtless, made it better by the addition of my voice. During the singing, after Rowland had made his prayer before the sermon, we, as respectable strangers, were beckoned from our humble places by a gentleman in one of the pews. Mrs. R—— and her daughter were stationed in one pew between two gentlemen of Rowland's flock, and E. May and I in another, between a lady and a person corresponding very much in countenance to the character of a tight boy in the old Methodistical magazines. He was very civil, and by finding out the hymns for me, and presenting me with the book, enabled me to sing, which I did to admiration.

"Rowland, a fine, tall old man, with strong features, very like his portrait, began by reading three verses for his text, stooping to the book in a very peculiar manner. Having done this, he stood up erect and said, 'Why the text is a sermon, and a very weighty one too.' I could not always follow his delivery, the loss of his teeth rendering his words sometimes indistinct, and the more so because his pronunciation is peculiar, generally giving *e* the sound of *ai*, like the French. His manner was animated and striking, sometimes impressive and dignified, always remarkable; and so powerful a voice I have rarely or never heard. Sometimes he took off his spectacles, frequently stooped down to read a text, and on these occasions he seemed to double his body, so high did he stand. He told one or two familiar stories, and used some odd expressions, such as 'A murrain on those who preach that when we are sanctified we do not grow in grace!' and again, 'I had almost said I had rather see the Devil in the pulpit than an Antinomian!' The purport of his sermon was good; nothing fanatical, nothing enthusiastic; and the Calvinism which it expressed was so qualified as to be harmless. The manner that of a performer, as great in his line as Kean or Kemble, and the manner it is which has attracted so large a congregation about him, all of the better order of persons in business. E. May was very much amused, and I am very glad I have heard him at last. It is very well that there should be such preachers for those who have no appetite for better-dressed food. But when the whole service of such a place is compared with the genuine devotion and sober dignity of the Church service, properly performed, I almost wonder at the taste which prevails for garbage.

"One remark I must not omit. I never before understood the unfitness of our language for music. Whenever there was an *s* in the word, the sound produced by so many voices made as loud a hissing as could have been produced by a drove of geese in concert, or by some hundred snakes in full chorus.

* * * * * * *

"Lane is making a picture which promises to be as good as Phillips's print is bad, base, vile, vulgar, odious, hateful, detestable, abominable, execrable, and infamous. The rascally mezzotinto scraper has made my face fat, fleshy, silly, and sensual, and given the eyes an expression which I conceive to be more like two oysters in love than any thing else. But Lane goes on to the satisfaction of every body, and will neither make me look like an assassin, a Methodist preacher, a sensualist, nor a prig.

"God bless you! R. S."

To Edith May Southey.

"London, Tuesday, Dec. 30, 1823.

"My dear Daughter,

"I have sent you a Bible for a New Year's gift, in the hope that with the New Year you will begin the custom of reading, morning and night, the Psalms and Lessons for the day. It is far from my wish that this should be imposed as a necessary and burdensome observance, or that you should feel dissatisfied and uneasy at omitting it, when late hours or other accidental circumstances render it inconvenient. Only let it be your ordinary custom. You will one day understand feelingly how beneficially the time has been employed.

"The way which I recommend is, I verily believe, the surest way of profiting by the Scriptures. In the course of this easy and regular perusal, the system of religion appears more and more clear and coherent, its truths are felt more intimately, and its precepts and doctrines reach the heart as slow showers penetrate the ground. In passages which have repeatedly been heard and read, some new force, some peculiar meaning, some home application which had before been overlooked, will frequently come out, and you will find, in thus recurring daily to the Bible, as you have done among the lakes and mountains which you love so well, in the Word of God, as in his works, beauties and effects, and influences as fresh as they are inexhaustible. I say this from experience. May God bless the book to the purpose for which it is intended! and take you with it, my dear, dear child, the blessing of

"Your affectionate father,

"Robert Southey."

After pursuing his intended course into the West of England, and visiting his aged aunt at Taunton, and his friend Mr. Lightfoot at Crediton, my father reached home early in the next year, for the incidents and correspondence of which we must open a new chapter.

CHAPTER XXVIII.

PLAN FOR UNITING THE WESLEYAN METHODISTS WITH THE CHURCH—AMUSING DOMESTIC SCENE—OPINIONS OF THE BOOK OF THE CHURCH—RODERIC TRANSLATED INTO DUTCH VERSE—EFFECTS OF THE NITROUS OXYD—ENMITY MORE ACTIVE THAN FRIENDSHIP—ODD BOOKS IN READING—LORD BYRON'S DEATH—CAUSE OF THE DELAY IN THE PUBLICATION OF THE PENINSULAR WAR—ESTIMATE OF HUMAN NATURE—THE BOOK OF THE STATE—WISHES TO PROCURE THE PUBLICATIONS OF THE RECORD COMMITTEE—REASONS FOR DECLINING TO BE NAMED ONE OF THE ROYAL LITERARY ASSOCIATES—PREVALENCE OF ATHEISM—HISTORY OF THE MONASTIC ORDERS—THE DOCTOR, ETC.—LOVE OF PLANNING NEW WORKS—HABIT OF READING WHILE WALKING—WESLEYAN METHODISTS—LONG LIFE NOT DESIRABLE—MR. TELFORD—LORD BYRON—THE QUARTERLY REVIEW—PLAN OF OLIVER NEWMAN—STATE OF IRELAND—HE IS ATTACKED IN THE MORNING CHRONICLE—BIBLE AND MISSIONARY SOCIETIES—EVILS OF SEVERE REVIEWALS—SMEDLEY'S POEMS—MR. BUTLER'S REPLY TO THE BOOK OF THE CHURCH—REASONS FOR NOT VISITING IRELAND—LITERARY OBLIGATIONS—VINDICIÆ ECC. ANGLICANÆ IN PROGRESS—WISHES TO MAKE A TOUR IN HOLLAND—WANT OF READINESS IN SPEECH—HAYLEY.—1824–1825.

At the conclusion of the "Life of Wesley," after a brief summary of his character, my father expresses a hope that the Society of Methodists might cast off the extravagances which accompanied its growth, and that it would gradually purify itself from whatever was objectionable in its institution; and he adds that "it is not beyond the bounds of reasonable hope that, conforming itself to the original intention of its founders, it may again draw toward the Establishment from which it has receded, and deserve to be recognized as an auxiliary institution, its ministers being analogous to the regulars, and its members to the tertiaries and various confraternities of the Romish Church."

These remarks, it appears, and the work in general, had met with the approbation of some of the Wesleyans, notwithstanding the dislike* with which, as a body, they regarded this Life of their Founder; and, as might have been expected, certain internal commotions and divisions began to arise among them, which at one time seemed likely to lead to the results he here desiderates.

The first intimation he received of this was in the following curious communication from Mark Robinson, of Beverley, which awaited his return

* "The *mystery of the faith* kept in *a pure conscience* is indeed a mystery to Mr. Southey. * * * The day will come when the friend and pupil of Hume, and the bold historian of 'The Decline and Fall of the Roman Empire,' and the compiler of the 'Life of Wesley,' may be considered as having been engaged in the same work as '*kicking against the pricks.*'"—*Preface to the Rev. Henry Moore's Life of Wesley.*

home, which may not unfitly be inserted here, as giving an interesting view of the feelings, wishes, and movements of a considerable portion of the Methodists at that time.

From Mark Robinson to Robert Southey, Esq.

"Beverley, Jan. 13, 1824.

"SIR,

"I am encouraged by the representations I have received of your affability and willingness to afford information to those who apply to you, to lay before you a matter which has given me no little concern; and in the hope that you will favor me with your views upon the subject, I will proceed without further introduction.

"It has for several years appeared to me, and several respectable friends of mine, who, as well as myself, are all members of the Wesleyan Methodist Society, in which we have for many years filled official situations, that the rapid dissent which we believe the traveling preachers have been chiefly instrumental in effecting in the society from the Established Church is much to be lamented, and that in the same proportion in which the society have departed from the original plan of Methodism, in the same proportion they have missed their way. We think that a secession from the Church has engendered a sectarian spirit, and given to the preachers a kind of influence over the people which, we fear, in many of its consequences, will be injurious both to their piety and liberty, leading them to exchange the former for party zeal, and the latter for a too ready acquiescence in all the measures of the preachers. We lately opened a correspondence with the Church Methodists in Ireland, from which we learn—what you, sir, are probably already acquainted with—that, in 1817, the Methodist Conference in Ireland, after exciting the societies throughout the country to petition them for the sacraments, determined upon giving them to all who should desire it. In consequence, 7000 among them, among whom were many of the most respectable members in Dublin and other principal places, withdrew from the Conference connection and established a separate itineracy, and that they have now about 14,000 in close connection with them. We learn, also, that the Bishop of Waterford called together the clergy of his diocese, and sent for one of the itinerant preachers of the connection, who so fully satisfied his lordship and the clergy that they all, without one dissenting voice, promised to give the Church Methodists countenance and support. What particularly satisfied this meeting was the declaration of the preachers that the society had settled their chapels on trustees *conditionally*, that if they should ever leave the Church, these chapels should go to the crown. They hold no meetings in canonical hours, and receive the sacrament at the hands of the clergy. The bishop and many of his clergy have contributed to the erection of the Waterford Chapel, and not only numbers of the Church people attend the chapel on the Sunday evenings, but also the clergy themselves.

"This correspondence we have named to several, both of the evangelical and orthodox clergy, none of whom raise any objection to it, and most of whom are its warm advocates. I lately received an invitation from the evangelical clergy in Hull to meet them in this business; and, in company with M. T. Sadler, Esq., of Leeds, who is one of our most able coadjutors, I attended the meeting. The clergy were unanimously of opinion that Church Methodism would meet with general support throughout the country, and that the pious clergy would give it their support. It has also been named in a private way to many of our magistrates and other respectable gentlemen, who profess to think well of it. We feel confident that there is an intention in the minds of some of the leading Conference preachers to get up, not so much a plan of regular dissent as a *rival Church*. This we think strongly indicated by the introduction of baptism, of the Lord's Supper, burial of the dead, the reading the Church service, vergers with their uniform and wands, and especially the preachers having in the two last Conferences attempted to introduce *episcopal ordination:* the leading preachers to be bishops, and the remainder regular clergymen. We are also of opinion that the preachers holding a regular Conference or Convocation, from which they exclude *all* the people, may in the end not only endanger the liberties of their own people, but of the country at large. Pray, sir, is there any good precedent for such a meeting? Did not the proctors make part of the Conference or Convocation of the English clergy, and are not all the ecclesiastical laws subject to the control of his majesty in Chancery, and of the civil courts? We have it in contemplation to petition the next Conference to admit a fair representation of the people, and to beg that they will deliberate measures for the gradual return of the societies to Church Methodism.

"Mr. Sadler is perhaps known to you as the author of an excellent pamphlet addressed to Walter Fawkes, Esq., late member for the county of York, in which he has refuted that gentleman's arguments in favor of a reform in Parliament. I had forgotten to say that if the Conference will not listen to our request at all, we purpose applying to our Irish friends to send over some efficient preachers, which we believe they will do.

"I may add, that your excellent conclusion of the Life of Wesley has also contributed to induce me to take the liberty of troubling you on this subject, conceiving that our plan is not very dissimilar to what you refer to. * * * We shall highly value your opinion and advice, and shall feel much obliged by as early a reply as you can conveniently favor us with.

"I am, for myself and friends, sir,

"Your most obedient servant,

"MARK ROBINSON."

My father immediately transmitted a copy of this letter to Dr. Howley, at that time Bishop of London, who in his reply gives a valuable testimony to the importance and utility of the "Book of the Church."

The Bishop of London to R. Southey, Esq.

"London, Feb. 25, 1824.

"MY DEAR SIR,

"At the time of receiving your communication of Feb. 20, it had been my intention for some days to trouble you with a line to express the high satisfaction which I have derived from your Book of the Church.

"It contains a most interesting sketch of a subject which, to the generality of readers, is almost unknown; and as it can not fail to be popular from the beauty of its execution, will, I trust, have the effect of turning the attention of many persons, who have hitherto been indifferent to such matters, through ignorance, to the nature of the dangers which this country has escaped, and the blessings of various kinds which have been secured to it through the National Church Establishment. I could have wished for references to the original writers, more especially as Lingard has made such a display of his authorities. But perhaps you had reasons for withholding them at present. A wish has been expressed by many judicious persons that the work might be published in a reduced form for the benefit of the lower classes, whose minds would be elevated by the zeal and virtue of the first Reformers.

"Your communication is very interesting and important; great difficulties, I fear, lie in the way of an open and formal reunion with the body of the Church, and I am apprehensive the movement, if it has any effect, will terminate in swelling the numbers, and perhaps the reputation of a party, which count among its members many exemplary clergymen, not sufficiently alive either to the benefits of order, or to the prejudice resulting to religion from the aspersions thrown on the character of their brethren who differ with them in opinion on particular points. I am, however, not without hopes that in certain situations, more especially in parts of the colonies, a union of purpose and action at least may silently take place, which, under discreet management, would be productive of much advantage to the one great cause; but this must be effected by prudent use of opportunities, and not, I think, by formal treaty.

"With repeated thanks for your valuable communication, and with sincere respect, I remain,

"My dear sir, your faithful servant,

"W. LONDON."

Here, for the present, the matter rested. Mark Robinson continued, however, to correspond at intervals with my father, who took considerable interest in the subject, and brought it forward in his "Colloquies with Sir T. More," expressing a strong opinion as to the practicability and desirableness of "embodying as Church Methodists those who would otherwise be drawn in to join one or other of the numerous squadrons of dissent." This gave, again, some little impetus to the exertions of Robinson and his friends; but no results of any consequence followed. The subject will be found again alluded to at a later period.

I have placed these two letters together, as leading the one to the other. We next find my father communicating the news of his return to Mr. Bedford, and amusing him with a promised account of a scene which the two friends in some "Butlerish" mood had planned beforehand.

The horn here referred to was a long straight tin instrument, such as, in the olden times, mail-coach guards were wont to rouse slumbering turnpike keepers and drowsy ostlers with, before the march of music introduced them to key bugles and cornopeans, and long before rail-roads went steeple-chasing it across the country, and shrill steam whistles superseded these more dulcet sounds. It had been procured chiefly for the sake of the amusement the unpacking it would afford (though there might also be some latent intention of awakening the mountain echoes with it). Mrs. Coleridge professed an exaggerated horror of all uncouth noises, and "half in earnest, half in jest," played, not unwillingly, her good-humored part in these pantomimic scenes, which my father enjoyed with true boyish delight.

To Grosvenor C. Bedford, Esq.

"Keswick, Feb. 23, 1824.

"MY DEAR GROSVENOR,

"Here then I am, nothing the worse for having been wheeled over fifteen hundred miles in the course of fifteen weeks. I no longer feel the effect of motion in my head, nor of jolting in my tail. I have taken again to my old coat and old shoes; dine at the reasonable hour of four, enjoy as I used to do the wholesome indulgence of a nap after dinner, drink tea at six, sup at half past nine, spend an hour over a sober folio and a glass of black currant rum with warm water and sugar, and then to bed. Days seemed like weeks while I was away, so many and so various were my engagements; and now that I am settling to my wonted round of occupations, the week passes like a day. If my life is not like that of the *prisca gens mortalium*, it is quite as happy; and when you hear *Qui fit Mecænas* quoted, you may reply that you know one man, at least, who is perfectly contented with his lot.

"I was charged by Edith particularly to describe to her how Mrs. Coleridge looked when the fatal horn should first be exhibited to her astonished eyes. The task which my daughter imposed upon me my powers of language are not sufficient to discharge. The horn, I must tell you, was made useful as a case for Westall's lithographic print of Warwick Castle. The doctor packed it carefully up with my umbrella in brown paper, so that no person could possibly discover what the mysterious package contained; and great curiosity was excited when it was first observed at home. Mrs. C. stood by (I sent for her) while the unpacking was deliberately performed. The string was untied, not cut; I unbound it round after round, and then methodically took off the paper. The first emotion was an expression of contemptuous disappointment at sight of the umbrella, which I was careful should be first discovered. But when the horn appeared, the fatal horn, then, oh, then—

"Grosvenor, it was an expression of dolorous dismay which Richter or Wilkie could hardly represent unless they had witnessed it—it was at once so piteous and so comical. Up went the brows, down went the chin, and yet the face appeared to widen as much as it was elongated by an indefinable drawing of the lips which seemed to flatten all the features. I know not whether sorrow or resentment predominated in the eyes; sorrow as in the Dutch manner, she pitied herself; or anger when she thought of me, and of your brother from whom I received the precious gift, and whose benevolence I loudly lauded. She wished him at Mo-ko (where that is, I know not), and me she wished to a worse place, if any worse there be. In the midst of her emotion, I called upon Sarah to observe her well, saying that I was strictly charged by my daughter to make a faithful and full report. The comical wrath which this excited added in no slight degree to the rich effect. Here I blew a blast, which, though not worthy of King Ramiro, was nevertheless a good blast. Out she ran; and yet finally, which I hold to be the greatest triumph of my art, I reconciled her to the horn; yes, reconciled her to it, by reminding her that rats might be driven away by it, according as it is written in the story of Jeffry.*

"God bless you, Grosvenor! I should probably have prattled through the remainder of the sheet, but a parcel from the Row has arrived, and that always occasions an evening of dissipation. Yours affectionately, R. S."

To John May, Esq.

"Keswick, March 7, 1824.

"My dear Friend,

"What success this proposal† of my brother's may meet with remains to be seen. If he can obtain 200 subscribers, Longman will take the risk of printing 750 copies. The book will be respectable and useful, comprising a regular view of all that has occurred in those islands from their discovery to the present time. Take it for all in all, it is perhaps as disgraceful a portion of history as the whole course of time can afford; for I know not that there is any thing generous, any thing ennobling, any thing honorable or consolatory to human nature to relieve it, except what may relate to the missionaries. Still it is a useful task to show what those islands have been and what they are; and the book will do this much more fully, clearly, and satisfactorily than has ever yet been done.

"Three weeks have now nearly elapsed since my return, and they seem like so many days, so swiftly and imperceptibly the days pass by when they are passed in regular employment and uniform contentment. My old course of life has become as habitual as if it had never been interrupted. The clock is not more punctual than I am in the division of the day. Little by little I get on with many things. The Peninsular War is my employment in the forenoon. The Tale of Paraguay after tea. Before breakfast, and at chance times, as inclination leads, I turn to other subjects, and so make progress in all. The only thing at present wanting to my enjoyment is to have something in the press, that I might have proof-sheets to look for—and I shall not be long without this.

"*Sunday 7th.*—To-day I have received a letter from Locker, who delivers me a message from the Bishop of Durham, thanking me for what I have done in the Book of the Church. The Bishop of London wrote to express his 'high satisfaction.' Both regret that I have not referred to my authorities*—an omission which appears to be generally thought injudicious. The truth is, that when I began the book it was with an expectation that it would not exceed a single duodecimo volume; and that even when enlarged it is still a mere epitome for the most part, to which I should feel that a display of authorities was out of place. After the proofs of research and accuracy which I have given, I have a right to expect credit; and, in fact, the more my credit is examined, the higher it will stand. Whoever may examine my collections for this and for my other historical works (and doubtless they will one day be inspected), will find that I have always prepared many more materials than I have used. * * * * *

"Believe me, my dear friend,

"Yours most affectionately,

"Robert Southey."

To Grosvenor C. Bedford, Esq.

"March 27, 1824.

"My dear Grosvenor,

* * * * * * * *

"To-day I received the first volume of Roderic in Dutch verse, translated by the wife of Bilderdijk, who is one of the most distinguished men of letters in that country. The translation appears to be very well done, as far as I am able to judge; that is, I can see in the trying passages she has fully understood the original; and her command of her own language is warranted by her husband's approbation, who is a severe critic as well as a skillful poet himself. He must be near eighty years of age, for he tells me he has been now threescore years known as an author. His letter to me is in Latin. The book comes in a red morocco livery; it is dedicated to me in an ode, and a very beautiful one, describing the delight she had taken in the poem, and the consolation she had derived from it, when parts of it came home to her own feelings in a time of severe affliction.

"She calls me the *Crown Poet.* I mean to

* See Life of Wesley, vol. i., p. 445.

† For the publication of a Chronological History of the West Indies, by Capt. T. Southey.

* This omission was supplied in a later edition.

send her a set of the Illustrations as soon as I know how to transmit them. The packet came to me through a merchant at Amsterdam, who inclosed it in a Dutch-English letter of his own, and an essay upon the character of my Cid, which he had read in some literary society, and printed afterward. They give me praise enough in Holland: I would gladly commute some of it for herrings and Rhenish wine.

* * * * * * *

"Do let me hear from you.

"God bless you! R. S."

To Grosvenor C. Bedford, Esq.

"Keswick, April 27, 1824.

"MY DEAR GROSVENOR,

"Your letter was as welcome as this day's rain, when the thirsty ground was gaping for it. Indeed, I should have been uneasy at your silence, and apprehended that some untoward cause must have occasioned it, if I had not heard from Edith that you had supplied her exchequer.

"I should, indeed, have enjoyed the sight of Duppa in the condition which you describe, and the subsequent process of transformation.* How well I can call to mind his appearance on his return from the theater one-and-twenty years ago! Little did I think that day that the next time I was to enter that theater would be in a red gown to be bedoctored, and called every thing that ends in *issimus*. And yet of the two days, the former was one of the most cheerful in my life, and the latter, if not the most melancholy, I think the very loneliest.

"Murray writes to me that he has put the Book of the Church to press for a second edition. I make no alterations, except to correct two slips of the pen and the press: where the Emperor Charles V. is called Queen Catharine's brother instead of her nephew, and Henry IV. printed for III., and to omit an anecdote about Gardiner's death, which Wynn tells me has been disproved by Lingard. I do not know what number Murray printed. But if there should appear a probability of its obtaining a regular sale, in that case I shall be disposed to think seriously of composing a similar view of our civil history, and calling it the Book of the State, with the view of showing how the course of political events has influenced the condition of society, and tracing the growth and effect of our institutions; the gradual disappearance of some evils, and the rise of others. Meantime, however, I have enough upon my hands, and still more in my head.

"Hudson Gurney said to me he wished the king would lay his commands on me to write the history of his father's reign. I wish he would, provided he would make my pension a clear £500 a year, to support me while I was writing it, and then I think I could treat the subject with some credit to myself.

"God bless you! R. S."

To Grosvenor C. Bedford, Esq.

"Keswick, May 6, 1824.

"MY DEAR GROSVENOR,

"In the evil habit of answering familiar letters without having them before me, I forgot to notice your question* respecting the nitrous oxyd, which, however, I should not have done, had the thing been as hopeful as you supposed it to be. What I said was simply this, that the excitement produced by the inhalation was not followed by any consequent debility or exhaustion; on the contrary, that it appeared to quicken all the senses during the remainder of the day. One case occurred in which the gas seemed to produce a good effect upon a palsied patient. A fellow who had lost the use of his hands (a tailor by trade) was so far cured that he was turned out of the house for picking pockets.

"The difficulty in finding two hundred subscribers† arises from this, my dear Grosvenor, that our friends are never so ready to bestir themselves in our affairs as our enemies. There are half a score persons in the world who would take some pains to serve me, and there are half a hundred who would take a great deal more to injure me. The former would gladly do any thing for me which lay *in* their way; the latter would go *out* of theirs to do any thing against me. I do not say this complainingly, for no man was ever less disposed to be querulous; and, perhaps, no one ever had more friends upon whose friendship he might justly pride himself.

* Mr. Bedford's humorously exaggerated description may amuse the reader: "A circumstance occurred here a little while ago which I wish you could have witnessed. Henry had set off to dine at Mrs. Wall's at the next door. Miss Page and I had finished our meal, when there sounded a hard knock; when the door opened, a figure presented itself in the dim after-dinner light of the season, whose features were not easily discernible, when 'Look at me! what shall I do?' broke out in accents of despair, and betrayed poor Duppa. On one of the dirtiest days of this dirty and yet unexhausted winter, he had left Lincoln's Inn on foot to meet the gay party at Mrs. Wall's. A villain of a coachman had driven by him through a lake of mud in the Strand, and Duppa was overwhelmed with alluvial soil. A finer fossil specimen of an odd fish was never seen. He looked like one of the statues of Prometheus in process toward animation—one half life, the other clay. I sent immediately for Henry to a consultation in a case of such emergency. The hour then seven, the invitation for half past six; the guests growing cross and silent; the fish spoiling before the fire; the hostess fidgety! What could be done? Shirts and cravats it was easy to find; and soap and water few regular families in a decent station of life are without. But where were waistcoats of longitude enough? or coats of the latitude of his shoulders? But, impranso nihil difficile est: we stuffed him into a special selection from our joint wardrobes. Henry rolled round his neck a cravat, in size and stiffness like a Holland sheet starched, and raised a wall of collar about his ears that projected like the blinkers of a coach-horse, and kept his vision in an angle of nothing at all with his nose; would he look to the right or the left, he must have turned upon the perpetual pivot of his own derriere. * * * * Thus rigged, we launched him, and fairly he sped, keeping his arms prudently crossed over the hiatus between waistcoat and breeches, and continually avoiding too erect a posture, lest he should increase the interstitial space; he was a fair parallel to what he was upon another awful occasion, when we both saw him revolving himself into a dew after the crowd of the Oxford Theater."—*G. C. B. to R. S., April 16, 1824.*

* Mr. Bedford was a sufferer from almost complete deafness, and he had imagined that my father, in some former letter, had spoken of the nitrous oxyd as efficacious in that infirmity.

† To his brother Thomas's History of the West Indies.

But it is the way of the world; and the simple reason is, that enmity is a stronger feeling than good will.

* * * * * * *

"I am reviewing Hayley's Life for the desire of lucre; a motive which, according to a writer in the Lady's Magazine, induced me to compile the Book of the Church, and is, indeed, according to this well-informed person, the leading principle of my literary life. How thoroughly should I be revenged upon such miserable wretches as this, if it were possible for them to know with what infinite contempt I regard them!

"Shall I tell you what books I have in reading at this time, that you may see how many ingredients are required for garnishing a calf's head? A batch of volumes from Murray relating to the events of the last ten years in Spain; Bishop Parker, De Rebus sui Temporis; Cardinal D'Ossat's Letters; the Memoir of the Third Duke de Bourbon; Whitaker's Pierce Plowman; the Mirror for Magistrates; the Collection of State Poems; Tiraboschi, and the Nibelungen in its original old German, and its modern German version, the one helping me to understand the other. Some of them I read after supper, some while taking my daily walk; the rest in odds and ends of time; laying down the pen when it does not flow freely, and taking up a book for five or ten minutes by way of breathing myself.

* * * * * * *

"God bless you! R. S."

To Henry Taylor, Esq.

"Keswick, May 26, 1824.

"MY DEAR SIR,

"I thank you for your note. Its information is of a kind to make one thoughtful; but the sorrow which I felt was not such as you were disposed to give me credit for.*

"I am sorry Lord Byron is dead, because some harm will arise from his death, and none was to be apprehended while he was living; for all the mischief which he was capable of doing he had done. Had he lived some years longer, he would either have continued in the same course, pandering to the basest passions and proclaiming the most flagitious principles, or he would have seen his errors and sung his palinodia—perhaps have passed from the extreme of profligacy to some extreme of superstition. In the one case, he would have been smothered in his own evil deeds; in the other, he might have made some atonement for his offenses.

"We shall now hear his praises from all quarters. I dare say he will be held up as a martyr to the cause of liberty, as having sacrificed his life by his exertions in behalf of the Greeks. Upon this score the Liberals will beatify him; and even the better part of the public will for some time think it becoming in them to write those evil deeds of his in water, which he himself has written in something more durable than brass. I am sorry for his death, therefore, because it comes in aid of a pernicious reputation which was stinking in the snuff.

"With regard to the thought that he has been cut off in his sins, mine is a charitable creed, and the more charitable it is the likelier it is to be true. God is merciful. Where there are the seeds of repentance in the heart, I doubt not but that they quicken in time for the individual, though it be too late for the world to perceive their growth. And if they be not there, length of days can produce no reformation.

"In return for your news, I have nothing to communicate except what relates to the operations of the desk. I am going to press with the second volume of the Peninsular War, after waiting till now in hope of obtaining some Spanish accounts of the war in Catalonia, which it is now pretty well ascertained are not to be found in Spain, though how they should have disappeared is altogether inexplicable, unless the whole account of the books and their author, Francesco di Olivares, given by a certain John Mitford some four or five years ago, in Colburn's Magazine, is fictitious. I am reviewing Hayley's Memoirs. Hayley has been worried as school-boys worry a cat. I am treating him as a man deserves to be treated who was in his time, by popular election, king of the English poets; who was, moreover, a gentleman and a scholar, and a most kind-hearted and generous man, in whose life there is something to blame, more to admire, and most of all to commiserate. My first introduction to Spanish literature I owe to his notes; I owe him, therefore, some gratitude. I have written some verses too, and am going on with the Tale of Paraguay resolutely to its conclusion.

"Farewell, my dear sir; and believe me, yours with sincere regard,

"ROBERT SOUTHEY."

To Grosvenor C. Bedford, Esq.

"Keswick, June 1, 1824.

"MY DEAR GROSVENOR,

"You deserve to be rated for saying that nothing is so cold as friendship, in saying which you belie yourself, and in inferring it as my opinion from what I said,* you belie me. A friend will not take half the trouble to do you a trifling service, or afford you a slight gratification, that an enemy would to do you a petty mischief, annoy your comfort, or injure your reputation. But this same enemy would not endanger himself for the pleasure of doing you a serious injury, whereas the friend would go through fire and water to render you an essential benefit, and, if need were, risk his own life to save yours. Now and then, indeed, there appears a devil-incarnate who seems to find his only gratification in the exercise of malignity; but these are monsters, and

* "You will, I do not doubt, consider his death as useful to the world; but do you not feel personal commiseration?"—*H. T. to R. S., May* 14, 1824.

* "I could not but smile at the mode in which you speak of the difficulties of getting 200 subscribers to your brother's book. Had I said any thing half as censoriously true, how you would have rated me! But true it is there is nothing so cold as friendship, nothing so animated as enmity."—*G. C. B. to R. S., May* 13, 1824.

are noted as such. If I formed an estimate of human nature from what I observed at school, I should conclude that there was a great deal more evil in it than good; if from what I have observed in after life, I should draw the contrary inference. Follies disappear, weaknesses are outgrown, and the discipline of society corrects more evils than it breeds. You and I, and Wynn, and Elmsley, and Strachey are very much at this time what each must always have expected the others to be. But who would have expected so much abilities from the two A.'s (mischievously as those abilities are directed)? Who would have thought that B——, boorish and hoggish as he was, would have become a man of the kindest manners and gentlest disposition; and that C—— would have figured as a hero at Waterloo? It is true that opposite examples might be called to mind; but the balance would be found on the right side.

"I am much gratified by what you tell me from Mr. Roberts.* Such opinions tend greatly to strengthen my inclination for setting about a Book of the State, which, though not capable of so deep and passionate an interest, might be made not less useful in its direct tendency. The want of books would be an obstacle, for I am poorly provided with English history, and have very little help within reach. I should want (and do want for other objects also) the publications of the Record Committee. They were originally to be purchased, but they were beyond my means. The sale of them is given up, I think (at least there was a report recommending that it should be discontinued, as producing little), and the remaining copies must be lying in lumber; and yet, though there is a pleasant opinion abroad that I can have any thing from government which I please to ask for, I might as well whistle for a south wind against this blast from the east, as ask for a set of these books, well assured as I am that there is no man living to whom they would be of more use, or who would make more use of them. My end is not answered by borrowing books of this description, and I will explain to you why; when a book is my own, I read or look through it, and mark it as I proceed, and then by very brief references am enabled to refer to and compose from it at any future time. But if it is a borrowed book, the time which it costs to provide myself with extracts for future use may be worth more than the cost of the work, a lesson which I have learned of late years at no little price.

"God bless you! R. S."

To the Rev. Nicholas Lightfoot.

"Keswick, June 16, 1824.

"MY DEAR LIGHTFOOT,

"I told you my reasons for declining the proposal of being named one of the Royal Literary Associates. Had it been a mere honor, I should have accepted it as a matter of course and of courtesy. In my situation, any individual who pleases may throw dirt at me, and any associated body which pleases may stick a feather in my cap: the dirt does not stick, the feathers are no encumbrance if they are of no use, and I regard the one as little as the other. But in this case the feather was clogged with a condition that I was to receive a £100 a year, for which it was to be my duty every year to write an essay, to be printed, if the committee approved it, in their transactions. What should I gain by doing that once a year for this committee which I may do once a quarter for the Quarterly Review? and which I could not do without leaving a paper in that Review undone. With this difference, that what I write in the Review is read every where, is received with deference, and carries with it weight; whereas their transactions can not by possibility have a fiftieth part of the circulation, and will either excite ridicule, or drop still-born from the press. I would have accepted a mere honor in mere courtesy, and I would thankfully have accepted profit; but when they contrived so to mix up both as to leave neither the one nor the other, all I had to do was civilly to decline the offer.

"God bless you, my dear Lightfoot!

"Yours affectionately, R. S."

To ——, Esq.

"Keswick, Aug. 7, 1824.

"MY DEAR SIR,

"Your letter is not of a kind to remain unacknowledged, and my time is often less worthily employed than it will be in making a few remarks upon some parts of it.

"You tell me of the prevalence of Atheism and Deism* among those persons with whose opinions you are acquainted. Are those persons, think you, fair representatives of the higher orders, whom you suppose to be infected with such opinions in the same proportion? Or are they not mostly young men, smatterers in literature, or literati by profession?

"Where the principles of reasonable religion have not been well inculcated in childhood, and enforced by example at home, I believe that infidelity is generally and perhaps necessarily one step in the progress of an active mind. Very many undoubtedly stop there; but they whose hearts escape the corruption which, most certainly, irreligion has a direct tendency to produce, are led into the right path, sooner or later, by reflection, inquiry, and the instinct of an immortal spirit, which can find no other resting-place in its weal, no other consolations in its afflictions. This has been the case in the circle of my experience, which has not been a contracted one. I have mixed with men of all descrip-

* "Mr. Roberts is delighted with the Book of the Church, and desires me to say that he never read any thing that afforded him so much at once of entertainment, and information, and general instruction upon any subject."—*G. C. B. to R. S., May* 13, 1824.

* "In numbering those with whose opinions I am acquainted, I find one half of them to be Atheists and two thirds of the remainder Deists: I should not be surprised if this were found to be about the general proportion in the higher orders of society, and infidelity has been brought among the lower orders by political disaffection." —— *to R. S., Aug.* 1, 1824.

tions—Atheists, Roman Catholics, and Dissenters of every kind, from the Unitarians, whose faith stands below zero, to the disciples of Richard Brothers and Joanna Southcote, whose trash would raise the thermometer to the point of fever heat. I have seen them pass from one extreme to another, and had occasion to observe how nearly those extremes meet. And now, when I call to mind those persons who were unbelievers some thirty years ago, I find that of the survivors the greater and all the better part are settled in conformity with the belief of the national Church, and this conformity in those with whom I am in habits of peculiar and unreserved friendship I know to be sincere. A very few remain skeptical and are unhappy; and these, with the best feelings and kindest intentions, have fallen into degrading and fatal habits, which gather strength as they grow older and older, and find themselves more and more unable to endure the prospect of a blank futurity. Some others, who were profligates at the beginning, continue to be so.

"According to my estimate of public opinion, there is much more infidelity in the lower ranks than there ever was before, and less in the higher classes than at any time since the Restoration. The indifferentists—those who used to conform without a thought or feeling upon the subject—are the persons who have diminished in numbers. Considering the connection of infidelity with disaffection in all its grades, and the alliance for political purposes between Catholics, Dissenters, and unbelievers, I think with you that a tremendous convulsion is very likely to be brought about; but I am not without hope that it may be averted; and even should it take place, I have no fear for the result, fatal as it must needs be to the generations who should witness the shock.

"The progress of my own religious opinions has been slow, but steady. You may probably live to read it; and, what is of more consequence, may, without reading it, follow unconsciously the same course, and by God's blessing rest at last in the same full and entire belief.

"Yours very truly,

"Robert Southey."

To Grosvenor C. Bedford, Esq.

"Keswick, Oct. 4, 1824.

"My dear Grosvenor,

"Murray states that, having conversed with Heber and some other literary friends upon my proposed History of the Monastic Orders, 'he now comprehends its probable interest and popularity,' and shall be happy to come to 'closer quarters upon the subject.' He says something of future papers for the Quarterly Review, asking me to undertake the Pepys' Memoirs and Sir Thomas Brown's Works, and writes requesting a brief sketch of my monastic plan. I have told him little more than that it may be included in six octavo volumes, and comprises matter hardly less varied and extensive than Gibbon's Decline and Fall of the Roman Empire. If he offers me £500 per volume, I will, ere long, make it my chief employment, but he shall not have it for less, and I am in no haste to proceed with the negotiation, being at present sufficiently employed, and to my heart's content.

"The '*medical practitioner*' would not have puzzled you if Fortune had permitted us to have been somewhat more together during the last ten years. Yet you have heard from me the name of Doctor Daniel Dove, and something, I think, of the Tristramish, Butlerish plan of his history, which, if the secret be but kept, must, I think, inevitably excite curiosity as well as notice. I have lately taken a pleasant spell at it, and have something more than a volume ready; that is to say, something more than half of what I propose to publish, following it or not with as much more according to its sale and my own inclination. One reason why I wished for you here at this time was to have shown it to you, and to have had your help, for you could have excellently helped me, and I think would have been moved in spirit so to do. If I finish it during the winter, of which there is good hope, I will devise some pretext for going to town, where I must be while it is printed, to avoid the transmission of proofs, by which it would be easy, from calculation of time, to ascertain how far they had traveled, and so, of course, to discover the author, to whom the printers are to have no clew.

"God bless you! R. S."

To John Rickman, Esq.

"Keswick, Oct. 10, 1824.

"My dear Rickman,

"My literary employments have never, in the slightest degree, injured my health; for, in truth, I neither am, nor ever have been, a close student. If I do not take sufficient exercise, it is not from any love of the desk, but for the want of a companion or an object to draw me out when the season is uninviting; and yet I overcome the dislike of solitary walking, and every day, unless it be a settled rain, walk long enough, and far, and fast enough, to require the wholesome process of rubbing down on my return. At no time of my life have I applied half so closely to my employment as you always do to yours. They impose upon me no restrictions. There is nothing irksome in them; no anxiety connected with them; they leave me master of my time and of myself; nor do I doubt but they would prove conducive to longevity, if my constitution were disposed for it.

"With regard to the prudence of working up ready materials rather than laying in more, upon whatever I employ myself, I must of necessity be doing both. The work which I am most desirous of completing is the History of Portugal, as being that for which most preparation has been made, and most time bestowed on it; and when the Peninsular War shall be completed, by God's blessing, a week shall not elapse before it goes to the press, for it has been long in much greater forwardness than any work which I ever before began to print.

"I am, however, conscious now of a disposition the reverse of Montaigne's, who loved, he said, rather to forge his mind than to furnish it. Avarice, you know, is the passion of declining years, and avaricious I confess myself to be of the only treasure I have ever coveted or ever shall possess. My temper or turn of mind inclines also to form new projects. But it is one thing to perceive what might be done, and another to dream of doing it. No doubt, wherever Mr. Telford is traveling, he can not help seeing where a line of road ought to be carried, a harbor improved, or a pier carried out. In like manner, I see possibilities, and capabilities, and desirabilities, and I think no more of them. God bless you! R. S."

To Grosvenor C. Bedford, Esq.

"Keswick, Oct. 12, 1824.

"MY DEAR GROSVENOR,

"With regard to my labors in English history, the plan which I not long ago communicated to you, of sketching it in a Book of the State down to the accession of the reigning family, and following that by the Age of George the Third, is all that I *dream* of accomplishing. The works on which I ought to employ myself, Grosvenor, are those for which I have laid in stores, on which a large portion of my previous studies may be brought to bear, and for which no other person is at present, or is likely to be hereafter, so well qualified. Such a work was the History of Brazil, and such will be, if I live to accomplish it, that of the Monastic Orders.

"I can not but smile at your grave admonitions* concerning the Doctor, and would give something to have the satisfaction of reading to you the chapters which were written last week. Such a variety of ingredients I think never before entered into any book which had a thread of continuity running through it. I promise you there is as much sense as nonsense there. It is very much like a trifle, where you have whipped cream at the top, sweetmeats below, and a good solid foundation of cake well steeped in ratafia. You will find a liberal expenditure of long-hoarded stores, such as the reading of few men could supply; satire and speculation; truths, some of which might beseem the bench or the pulpit, and others that require the sanction of the cap and bells for their introduction; and, withal, a narrative interspersed with interludes of every kind, yet still continuous upon a plan of its own, varying from grave to gay, and taking as wild and yet as natural a course as one of our mountain streams.

"I am reading Scaliger's Epistles at this time, treading in my uncle's steps, who gave me the book when I was in town. Not long ago I finished Isaac Casaubon's. Oh, what men were these! and, thank God! men will never be wanting like them in one respect at least—that they will pursue the acquisition of knowledge with as much zeal as others follow the pursuit of wealth, and derive a thousand-fold more pleasure in the acquirement. God bless you! R. S."

To Grosvenor C Bedford, Esq.

"Keswick, Oct. 30, 1824.

"MY DEAR GROSVENOR,

"Your ill news had reached me some days ago.*

"There are many things worse than death. Indeed, I should think any reasonable person would prefer it to old age, if he did not feel that the prolongation of his life was desirable for the sake of others, whatever it might be for himself. If the event be dreaded, the sooner it is over the better; if it desired, the sooner it comes; and desired or dreaded it must be. If there were a balloon-diligence to the other world, I think it would always be filled with passengers. You will not suppose from this that I am weary of life, blessed with enjoyments as I am, and full of employment. But if it were possible for me (which it is not) to regard myself alone, I would rather begin my travels in eternity than abide longer in a world in which I have much to do and little to hope.

"Something upon this topic you will see in my Colloquies. They will go to press as soon as I hear from Westall in what forwardness the engravings are. Murray has announced the second volume of the War for November; it would require the aid of some other devils than those of the printing-office to finish it before the spring, and this he knows very well, both the MS. and the proof-sheets passing through his hands. Just one quarter is printed, and I am about a hundred pages ahead of the printers. Of late I have made good progress in forwarding various works, in the hope of clearing my hands and bettering my finances. I can not get on fast with the Tale of Paraguay because of the stanza, but on with it I am getting, and am half through the third canto; a fourth brings it to its close. A good deal has been done to the Colloquies, which will gain me much abuse now, and some credit hereafter; and a good deal to the Doctor, which I should very much like to show you. You shall see me insult the public, Mr. Bedford, and you will see that the public wonders who it is that insults them, for I think that I shall not be suspected.

* * * * * * *

"God bless you! R. S."

To John Rickman, Esq.

"Keswick, Nov. 9, 1824.

"MY DEAR R.,

"I see by the papers that Mr. Telford recommends paving roads where there is much heavy

* Mr. Bedford seemed to be under the apprehension that the "Cap and Bells" would be in too great requisition during the composition of the Doctor. "I am too ignorant," he says, "of Dr. D. D.'s concerns to be able to speak about him, but there is one thing which ought not to be lost sight of, that a joke may be very well received across a table which would be considered the dullest in the world in print. The success of Tristram Shandy affords no argument in favor of a second attempt to induce the public to join in making fools of themselves."—*Oct. 7, 1824.*

* Of the dangerous illness of their mutual friend, the Rev. Peter Elmsley.

carriage. In some of the Italian cities the streets are paved in stripes. The wheels run upon two lines of smooth pavement, as over a bowling green, with little sound and no jolting, and the space between, on which the horses go, is common pitching. This is the case at Milan and Como, and probably in most other places. Macadamizing the streets of London is likely, I think, to prove Quackadamizing. But the failure will lead to something better.

"Lord Byron is gibbeted by his friends and admirers. Dr. Stoddart sent me those papers in which he had commented upon these precious conversations. The extracts there and in the Morning Herald are all that I have seen, and they are quite enough. I see, too, that Murray has been obliged to come forward. * * I am vindictive enough to wish that he had known how completely he failed of annoying me by any of his attacks. —— should be called Lord B.'s blunderbuss. There is something viler in regrating slander, as he has done, than in originally uttering it.

"If this finds you in town, and you can lay your hand on the Report on the Salmon Fishery, I should like to have it, as a subject of some local interest. I am working away steadily, and with good will, making good progress with my second volume and with the Colloquies. We are all well, and Cuthbert in the very honey-moon of puerile happiness, being just breeched. God bless you! R. S."

To George Ticknor, Esq.

"Keswick, Dec. 30, 1824.

"My dear Sir,

"I have delayed thus long to acknowledge and thank you for your last consignment of books in the hope of telling you, what I am now at last enabled to do, that Gifford has finally given up the Quarterly Review, and that, after the forthcoming number, it will be under John Coleridge's management. This is a matter which I have had very much at heart, that there might be an end of that mischievous language concerning your country. I opposed it always with all my might, and forced in that paper upon Dwight's Travels; yet in the very next number the old system was renewed. You may be assured that they have occasioned almost as much disgust here as in America. So far is it from being the language or the wish of the government, that one of the cabinet ministers complained of it to me as most mischievous, and most opposite to the course which they were desirous of pursuing. There is an end of it now, and henceforth that journal will do all in its power toward establishing that feeling which ought to exist between the two nations. Let me be peace-maker; and use what influence you have that the right hand of good will may be accepted as frankly as it is offered.

"I know not what the forthcoming number may contain, but I can answer for the Review afterward. A friend of mine (Hughes, who wrote a pleasant book about the South of France) is preparing a paper upon your literature; and Buckminster's sermons are reprinting at my suggestion.

"Now, then, let me thank you for Philip's War, so long desired; for G. Fox, digged out of his burrows, and their companions. These Quaker books are very curious; it is out of such rubbish that I have to pick out the whole materials for my intended edifice, and good materials they are when they are found. Before this reaches you I shall have finished the Tale of Paraguay, which has hung like a millstone about my neck, owing to the difficulty which the stanza occasioned. As soon as I am rid of it I shall take up the New England poem as a regular employment, and work on with it steadily to the end. A third part is done; I am not making a hero of Philip, as it now seems the fashion to represent him. In my story the question between the settlers and the natives is very fairly represented, without any disposition either to favor the cause of savage life against civilization, or to dissemble the injuries which trading colonists (as well as military ones) have always committed upon people in an inferior grade of society to themselves. Better characters than the history affords me, or, to speak more accurately, characters more capable of serving the purposes of poetry, I need not desire. The facts are not quite so manageable. I may say, as a friend of mine *heard* Bertrand de Moleville say when, after relating a story, he was told that the facts were not as he had stated them, *Ah, monsieur! tant pis pour les faits*. So I must deal with them in fiction as a Frenchman deals with facts in history; that is, take as little truth, and mingle it with as much invention as suits my object. To what an extent the French do this I should hardly have thought credible, if I had not daily evidence in their memoirs upon the Peninsular War, comparing them with the undeniable documents in my hands.

"My niece desires me to thank you for the sweet story of Undine, which is surely the most graceful fiction of modern times. Some other pieces of the same author have been translated here, all bearing marks of the same originality and genius.

"I had made a half promise of going to Ireland, to visit one of the best and ablest persons there, the Bishop of Limerick; but it is not likely that the intention can be fulfilled. An Irishman, well informed of the state of things there, writes to me in these words: 'Pray don't think of going to Ireland. I would not insure any man's life for three months in that unhappy country. The populace are ready for a rebellion; and if their leaders should for their own purpose choose to have one, they may have to-morrow a second edition of the Irish massacre.'

"Wordsworth was with me lately, in good health, and talked of you. His brother, the Master of Trinity, has just published a volume concerning the Εικων Βασιλικη, a question of no trifling importance both to our political and literary history. As far as minute and accumulative evidence can amount to proof, he has proved it to be genuine. For myself, I have never, since I read the book, thought that any unprejudiced person could entertain a doubt concerning it. I am the more gratified that this full and satisfactory investigation has been made, because it grew out of a conversation between the two Wordsworths and myself at Rydal a year or two ago.

"Remember me to all my Boston friends; it is a pleasure to think I have so many there. The only American whom I have seen this year is Bishop Hobart, of New York. God bless you!

"Yours affectionately,

"ROBERT SOUTHEY."

A most atrocious attack having appeared about this time upon my father in the Morning Chronicle, he took counsel with some legal friends as to the expediency of prosecuting that paper for a libel. "You will see Turner," he writes at the time to Mr. John Coleridge, "though he recommends a course which I shall not follow—that of proceeding by information, and involving myself in expense and trouble, for the purpose of giving a solemn denial to charges which most certainly are not believed by the miscreant himself who made them. He wishes to avoid any appearance of an attack on my part upon the press and the Morning Chronicle; whereas it appears to me, that if I have an opportunity of punishing that newspaper for its abuse of the press, I ought just as much to do it in this case as I would bring a fellow to justice for assaulting me on the highway. Allowing them as large a latitude as they desire for political abuse, I would rest solely upon the charge of 'impious and blasphemous obscenities.'* * *

"Should it appear as clear in law as it is in equity that it is a foul and infamous libel, which any judge and any jury must pronounce such, then certainly I would bring an action for damages against the Morning Chronicle, without caring who the author may be, that paper having not only inserted it, but called attention to it in its leading paragraph. The rest may be thrown overboard. Let them revile me as an author and a politician till their hearts ache. Their obloquy serves only to show that my opinions have an influence in society which they know and feel; and if it gives me any feeling, it is that of satisfaction at seeing to what base and unmanly practices they are obliged to descend. But this goes beyond all bounds of political and even personal animosity; there can be no villainy of which a man would not be capable who is capable of bringing forward such charges upon such grounds. True it is that my character needs no vindication, and I would not lift a finger to vindicate it; but if I have a villain by the throat, I would deliver him over to justice. Nevertheless, if you and Turner agree in opinion that I had better let the matter alone, I shall, without hesitation, follow the advice; and it is well to bear in mind that there has more than once been manifested a most reprehensible disposition on the part of the judges to favor the wrong side, lest they should be suspected of leaning toward the right."

The advice of these friends being that he should not adopt legal proceedings, he patiently acquiesced. A private remonstrance was, however, carried to the editor by Allan Cunningham, who was well acquainted with him, and who showed him an anonymous letter my father had received from the writer of the published attack, which was couched in terms of the most horrible and disgusting kind. The editor affected to recognize "the hand of a young nobleman;" to which Allan Cunningham replied, "that he would sooner have cut his hand off than have written such a letter;" and to the excuse that Mr. Southey had "insulted the Scotch and the Dissenters," he rejoined, "that, had this been the case, he, who was a Scotchman and a Presbyterian, would never have been his friend." The attack was also promptly replied to by his friend Mr. Henry Taylor, whom he thanks in the following letter for his friendly interposition.

To Henry Taylor, Esq.

'Keswick, Jan. 10, 1825.

"MY DEAR SIR,

"I thank you for both your letters—the one in writing, and the one in print. As laws, judges, and juries in these days always favor the wrong party, partly from principle, partly from fashion, and a little in the middle, if not the latter case, from fear, I am advised not to prosecute the Morning Chronicle, and as I have no desire ever to put myself in the way of anxiety, the advice is deferred to without hesitation or reluctance. A more atrocious libel was never admitted into a newspaper, bad as the newspapers have long been. You suspect something more than the malignity of party spirit in it; so did I; and that suspicion has been verified by an anonymous letter from the author, which reached me this day. The letter is as blackguard as words can make it, and comes from a red-hot Irish Roman Catholic, who shows himself in every sentence to be ripe for rebellion and massacre. It is well they have no Prince Hohenlohe among them, who can kill at a distance as well as cure; for if they had, I should certainly be murdered by miracle.

"But I thank you heartily for what you have done. The letter is what it should be—manly, scornful, and sincere. I am very glad to have such a friend, and not sorry to have such enemies. They can only stab at my character, which they may do till they are tired without inflicting a scratch. The only mournful thing is to think that the newspapers should be in the hands of men who not only admit such infamous slanders, but lend their active aid to support them.

"The last Review not having reached me, I have not seen your father's paper upon Banks.

* He conceived this to have been founded "*literally* upon an extract from a Roman Catholic Book of Devotions to the Virgin Mary, in the first volume of the Omniana."

In that upon Landor, I liked every thing that had no reference to him, and nothing that had. The general tenor I should, no doubt, have liked better if Gifford had not struck out the better parts; but nothing could have reconciled me to any thing like an assumption of superiority toward such a man. Porson and I should not have conversed as he has exhibited us, but we could neither of us have conversed better.

"My letter to the Courier* was in all its parts fully justified by the occasion which called it forth. I am never in the habit of diluting my ink. The sort of outcry against it is in the spirit of these *liberal times*. These gentlemen of the press assert and exercise the most unlimited license in their attacks, and allow no liberty of defense.

"I shall publish a vindication of the Book of the Church, in reply to Mr. Butler, with proofs and illustrations. In this I shall treat him with the respect and courtesy which he so well deserves, but I will open a battery upon the walls of Babylon. Think of the Acta Sanctorum—more than fifty ten-pounders brought to bear in breach. God bless you!

"Yours affectionately,

"ROBERT SOUTHEY."

To John Taylor Coleridge, Esq.

"Keswick, Jan. 30, 1825.

"MY DEAR SIR,

"There is certainly a most pernicious set of opinions mixed up both with the Bible and Missionary Societies—so there is with the Abolitionists—and yet we can not have the good without the evil, and it is no little advantage when the men who hold these opinions direct some of their restless zeal into a useful channel. In that point of view the Missionary Societies are so many safety-valves. Even the best men whom they send abroad would be very likely to be mischievous at home.

"Bishop Law (the present bishop's father) advances an opinion that the true nature of revealed religion is gradually disclosed as men become capable of receiving it, generations as they advance in knowledge and civilization outgrowing the errors of their forefathers, so that in fullness of time there will remain neither doubt nor difficulties. He was a great speculator; whether, like one of his sons, he speculated too far, I do not know, but in this opinion I think he is borne out by history. Providence condescends to the slowness of Christian understandings, as it did to the hardness of Jewish hearts. All these societies proceed upon a full belief in the damnation of the heathen: what their future state may be is known as little as we do concerning our own, but this we know in both cases, that it must be consistent with the goodness of our Father who is in heaven. * * * Yet you could get no missionaries to go abroad unless they held this tenet. The Socinians, you see, send none, neither do the Quakers.

"The Quarterly Review has been overlaid with statistics, as it was once with Greek criticism. It is the disease of the age—the way in which verbose dullness spends itself. The journal wants more of the *literæ humaniores*, and in a humaner tone than it has been wont to observe. I think a great deal of good may be done by conciliating young writers who are going wrong, by leading them with a friendly hand into the right path, giving them all the praise they deserve, and advising or insinuating rather than reprehending. Keats might have been won in that manner, and perhaps have been saved. So I have been assured. Severity will have ten times more effect when it is employed only where it is well deserved.

"Do not over-work yourself, nor sit up too late, and *never continue at any one mental employment after you are tired of it*. Take this advice from one who has attained to great self-management in this respect.

"God bless you! R. SOUTHEY.

"Smedley's poems are very clever, but he seems quite insensible to the good which is connected with and resulting from this mixture of weakness, enthusiasm, and sectarian zeal. It does nothing but good abroad, and that good would not be done without it. The Bible Society has quadrupled the subscribers to the Bartlett's Buildings' one, and given it a new impulse. I hate cant and hypocrisy, and am apt to suspect them wherever there is much profession of godliness; but, on the other hand, I do not like men to be callous to the best interests of their fellow-creatures."

To John May, Esq.

"Keswick, March 16, 1825.

"MY DEAR FRIEND,

"It is a very old remark that one sin draws on another; and, as an illustration of it, I believe one reason why you have not had a letter from me for so long a time is that my Autobiography has been standing still. This is the first symptom of amendment, and, in pursuance of it, when this letter is dispatched, I propose to begin the 17th of the Series.

"Thus much has been left undone, and now for what I have been doing. You may have learned from John Coleridge that I sat to work for him as soon as he was installed into his new office,* and sent him a paper upon the Church Missionary Society, and a few pages upon Mrs. Baillie's Letters from Lisbon.

"You must have heard of Mr. Butler's attack upon the Book of the Church. My uncle says of it—his contradicting you and saying that you had misstated facts may have the same answer as Warburton gave to one of his antagonists: 'it may be so for all he knows of the matter.' The Bishop of London wrote to ask if I intended to answer it, for if I did not they must look about for some person who would, 'as it had imposed upon some persons who ought to have

* Concerning Lord Byron.

* As successor to Gifford in the editorship of the Quarterly Review.

known better, and he hoped I should demolish what he called his flimsy structure of misstatements and sophistry.' Upon my replying that it was my intention so to do, he communicated to me an offer of any books that might be useful from Lambeth. But it does not do to have bulky volumes sent 300 miles, when the object is to consult them perhaps only for half an hour. However, I shall avail myself of this permission when next I may be at Streatham. My reply will bear this title, 'Vindiciæ Ecclesiæ Anglicanæ'—the Book of the Church Vindicated and Amplified. The first portion of the manuscript would reach London this morning on its way to the press.

"Last week I spent at Rydal with Wordsworth, going thither partly in the hope that change of air might rid me of a cough, which, though apparently slight, has continued upon me long enough to show that it is deep seated. It was left behind some two months ago by an endemic cold that attacked the throat in a peculiar manner. I am better for the change. But it will be necessary for me to take a journey as soon as the summer begins, in the hope of escaping that annual attack which now regularly settles in the chest. I meant to have visited Ireland, but this I must give up on Edith's account, for I was strongly advised not to go by a man in power, who knew the country well, and said he would not insure any man's life there for three months: and this, with a sort of cut-throat anonymous letter from an Irishman (the same that made that infamous attack upon me in the Chronicle), abusing me as an Orange Boy in the foulest and most ferocious terms, has made her believe that I should be in danger there; and, of course, I should not think it right to leave her with that impression upon her mind. My intention, therefore, is to make a hasty visit to Streatham, and run down again to the west, unless I should meet with a suitable companion who would go over with me to Holland for three or four weeks.

"God bless you, my dear friend!

"Yours most affectionately,

"ROBERT SOUTHEY."

To the Rev. William Lisle Bowles.

"Keswick, March 19, 1825.

"MY DEAR SIR,

"I am induced to write to you by a letter which I have this day received from G. Peachey. In answer to the request which he communicates, though I am little behind you in the vale of years, and likely, perhaps, to reach the end of our mortal journey by a shorter road, yet, should I prove the survivor, any wish which you may please to signify I will faithfully, and to the best of my power, discharge. There are three cotemporaries, the influence of whose poetry on my own I can distinctly trace. Sayers, yourself, and Walter Landor. I owe you something, therefore, on the score of gratitude.

"But to a pleasanter subject. Peachey tells me that you had begun to print some observations upon Mr. Butler's book, but that you have suppressed them upon hearing that I was engaged in answering it. I am sorry for this, because the more answers that are called forth the better. False and shallow as the book is (the Bishop of London calls it, very justly, 'a flimsy structure of misstatements and sophistry'), it imposes upon shallow readers, and is gladly appealed to as an authority by the Liberals, who are at this time leagued against the Church. Every answer that may appear would have a certain circle, within which no other can act with equal effect; and I am so persuaded of this, that I desired Murray not to announce my intended work, lest it should have the effect of preventing others from coming forward in the same good cause. I hope, therefore, that you will resume the pen. The Church ought not to be without defenders at this time. If the Catholic writers had been put down whenever they appeared during the last five-and-twenty years, as they might and ought to have been, by an exposure of their gross and impudent misrepresentations, that party would not have been so daring as it now is.

"Dr. Phillpotts* is answering the theological part of Butler's.† My business, of course, must be, to attack him along the whole of his line, which I am doing most effectually. For the sake of relieving the tone of controversy, I take the opportunity of introducing biographical and historical matter, and call my work, therefore, Vindiciæ Ecclesiæ Anglicanæ—The Book of the Church Vindicated and Amplified. My temper is not controversial. I had much rather be industriously and thankfully reading old books, than detecting the defects and vices of new ones; but when I am provoked to it, I can wield a sledgehammer to as good purpose as my old friend Wat Tyler himself. God bless you, my dear sir!

"Yours very truly,

"ROBERT SOUTHEY."

To Henry Taylor, Esq.

"Keswick, March 28, 1825.

"MY DEAR SIR,

"Now then for my summer movements. Do not think me actuated by mere fickleness if I

* Now Bishop of Exeter.

† Dr. Phillpotts had thus courteously communicated his intention to my father:

"Stanhope, Durham, Feb. 28, 1825.

"MY DEAR SIR,

"I know not whether it may interest you to be informed that (feeling as I do the absolute necessity of some detailed confutation of Mr. Butler's statement of the doctrines of his Church, contained in the Letter X. of his book, especially when so many various misstatements of those doctrines are continually made by other writers and speakers) I have resolved speedily to undertake that work; indeed, I am at present as busy with it as infirm health will permit. Mr. Butler's book did not fall in my way until these three or four weeks.

"You will do me the justice of believing that I do not presume to interfere in any way with your work. That you are preparing a proper punishment for his offense against you I can not doubt, nor would I weaken the effect of that punishment from the most powerful of modern writers by any interference of mine. I strictly confine myself to the mere theological matters.

"Allow me to offer you my heartiest thanks for your very *admirable book*.

"Yours my dear sir, most sincerely,

"H. PHILLPOTTS."

propose crossing the Channel instead of the Severn, and drinking Rhenish wine instead of Welsh ale. I want to see Holland, which is a place of man's making, country as well as towns. I want monastic books, which it is hopeless to look for in England, and which there is every probability of finding at Brussels, Antwerp, or Leyden. In the course of three or four weeks, going sometimes by trekschuits and sometimes upon wheels, we might see the principal places in the Dutch Netherlands, visit the spot where Sir Philip Sidney fell, talk of the Dousas and Scaliger at Leyden, and obtain such a general notion of the land as would enable us better to understand the history of the Low Country wars. Neville White would perhaps join us; and always, in traveling, three persons are better than two, especially as neither you nor I (I suspect) are such good men of business as not to be glad if a better could be found to officiate as paymaster. Tell me if you like this scheme. If you do, I will write to Neville without delay, and be ready to start from London by the 1st of June.

"I had heard of * * * as an American by birth, a man of great talents and unhappy opinions, which, from him, had spread widely among his cotemporaries at Cambridge. Jeremy Bentham is now to such young men what Godwin was two or three-and-thirty years ago; for those who pride themselves most upon thinking for themselves, are just as prone as others *jurare in verba magistri*, only it must be a *magister* of their own choosing.

"I never made a speech since I was a school-boy, and am very certain that I never had any talent for speaking. Had I gone to the bar, my intent was to have spoken always as briefly and perspicuously as possible, and have endeavored to win a jury rather by appealing to their good sense than by mystifying their understanding. Burke's speeches, which will always be read, were never listened to; many members used to walk out of the House when he stood up. I believe that I derived great advantage from the practice sometimes of translating, sometimes of abridging, the historical books which are read in certain forms at Westminster; and, in like manner, I am inclined to think a habit of speaking upon business might be acquired by giving orally the substance of what one has just read. I have none of that readiness which is required for public life, or even which is looked for among *diners out*. When I am reading I have it; few things then escape me in any of their bearings. My mind is never so prompt as it is then. In writing it is sometimes too fast, sometimes too slow.

"So you do not like Hayley. I was born during his reign, and owe him something for having first made me acquainted by name with those Spanish writers of whom I afterward knew much more than he did. Compare him with ordinary country gentlemen, and see what he gains by his love of literary pursuits. Compare him with the general run of literary men, and see to what advantage his unenvious and liberal spirit appears.

"My Vindication is in the press. It contains a fuller account of Bede than can be found elsewhere; and I shall introduce in it lives of St. Francis and of good John Fox, whom the Papists hate worse than they do the Devil, and belie as virulently and as impudently as they do your friend, ROBERT SOUTHEY."

To Henry Taylor, Esq.

"Keswick, May 2, 1825.

"MY DEAR H. T.,

"You do not expect enough from Holland. It is a marvelous country in itself, in its history, and in the men and works which it has produced. The very existence of the country is at once a natural and a moral phenomenon. Mountaineer as I am, I expect to *feel* more in Holland than in Switzerland. Instead of climbing mountains, we shall have to ascend church towers. The panorama from that at Harlaem is said to be one of the most impressive in the world. Evening is the time for seeing it to most advantage.

"I have not yet forgotten the interest which Watson's Histories of Philip II. and III. excited in me when a school-boy. They are books which I have never looked into since; but I have read largely concerning the Dutch war against the Spaniards, on both sides, and there is no part of Europe which could be so interesting to me as historical ground. Perhaps my pursuits may have made me more alive than most men to associations of this kind; but I would go far to see the scene of any event which has made my heart throb with a generous emotion, or the grave of any one whom I desire to meet in another state of existence.

"My translatress, Katharina Wilhelmina Bilderdijk, is old enough to be your mother. She dedicates her translation to me in a very affecting poem, touching upon the death of her son, whom she lost at sea, and in what manner, before she knew his death, she had applied certain passages in Roderic to herself. * * * *

"God bless you! R. S."

CHAPTER XXIX.

TOUR IN HOLLAND—HE IS LAID UP AT LEYDEN AT MR. BILDERDIJK'S—REV. R. PHILLIPS—MR. BUTLER—MR. CANNING—MOTIVES FOR CHOOSING FRIENDS—VISITORS TO KESWICK—TENDENCY OF HIS ECCLESIASTICAL WRITINGS—SISTERS OF CHARITY—THE QUARTERLY REVIEW—METAPHYSICS—RULES FOR COMPOSITION—KNOWLEDGE OF HISTORY THE FIRST REQUISITE FOR A STATESMAN—THE BULLION QUESTION—JACOB CATS—WISHES TO WRITE A CONTINUATION TO WARTON'S HISTORY OF POETRY—MR. BILDERDIJK—DANGERS OF THE MANUFACTURING SYSTEM—EFFECTS OF TIME UPON THE MIND—HIS OWN RELIGIOUS FEELINGS—SHORT TOUR IN HOLLAND—DEATH OF HIS YOUNGEST DAUGHTER—WISHES AS TO POSTHUMOUS PUBLICATIONS—LETTER TO HIS DAUGH-

TERS ON THE DEATH OF THEIR SISTER.—1825–1826.

The reader has seen that my father had been for some time contemplating a tour in Holland; and his arrangements being now completed, he left home the end of May, and after passing a week in London, and joining there the other members of the party, consisting of Mr. H. Taylor, Mr. Neville White, and Mr. Arthur Malet, a young officer, they crossed the Channel from Dover to Boulogne, and made their way from thence first of all to Brussels.

The revisiting this place and the field of Waterloo recalled, naturally, many sad thoughts to my father's mind. He says in his Journal, "I hope I shall never see this place again. On my first and second visit Henry Koster and Nash were with me; and I pleased myself with bringing away little memorials for Herbert. Nash was with me again two years later—'where are they gone, the old familiar faces!'"

A visit to Verbeyst, however, the great bookseller of Brussels, from whom, in 1817, he had purchased the Acta Sanctorum (fifty-two vols. folio), and many other valuable works, brought back pleasanter remembrances. "Right glad," he says, "I was to find him in a larger house, flourishing to his heart's content, and provided with books to mine. He has more than 300,000 volumes, among which I passed the whole morning, till it was time to go to the bankers' before the hours of business had elapsed. On our return (for Neville was with me) Verbeyst had provided claret, Burgundy, and a loaf of bread, on which I regaled; and with the help of his wife, the handsome, good-natured woman whom I saw eight years ago, we made out some cheerful conversation. Verbeyst tells me he is building a house on the Boulevards; the *salle* is as large as the whole house which he now occupies, the whole edifice big as the dwelling of an English lord, and the garden as large as the Grand Place. I am glad that the world goes so well with them."

This journey, however, was doomed to be an unfortunate one, from an apparently trifling cause. Before leaving England, my father had received a slight injury on the foot, owing to a tight shoe, and traveling in hot weather had much inflamed it; then at Bouchain the diseased spot was chosen by one of those little gentry, whose name and presence are alike disagreeable, for his attacks, and the wound soon assumed a somewhat alarming appearance. At Antwerp, he says, "here I am a prisoner, with my foot poulticed, heartily wishing myself at home." After a few days, however, the surgeon permitted him to proceed on his journey, which he did in great pain, suffering more from this trifling cause in one week than he ever remembered to have endured in his whole life; and when the party reached Leyden, he was again obliged to put himself under a surgeon's hands.

Here, however, he quickly and most fortunately met with kind friends and a temporary home. He has before mentioned (see letter to Mr. Bedford, March 27, 1824) receiving a copy of Roderic translated into Dutch by Mrs. Bilderdijk, and a letter from her husband, a man who was highly distinguished in the literature of his country; it was, in a great measure, for the purpose of seeing them that he had come to Leyden, and no sooner were they aware of his situation than they insisted upon his being removed to their residence, to which he at first reluctantly consented.* This, of course, broke up the party. Mr. Neville White and Mr. A. Malet pursued their own course, while Mr. Taylor "stayed by the wreck." There my father remained more than three weeks, most hospitably treated and most kindly nursed. "My time," he says, "has passed most profitably and happily; and I have formed a friendship in this family which time will not weaken nor death divide."

His letters from thence will supply all other needful particulars.

To Mrs. Southey.

"Leyden, Thursday, June 30, 1825.

"MY DEAR EDITH,

"My foot is going on as well as possible, and will, according to all appearances, be completely healed in the course of three or four days. Having begun with this statement, *pour votre tranquillité*, as the aubergists at Besançon said at every word, I have next to tell you that I am quartered at Mr. Bilderdijk's, where every imaginable care is taken of me, and every possible kindness shown, and where I have all the comforts which Leyden can afford.

"How I came here you are now to learn. Upon applying to Mr. B. to procure a lodging for Henry Taylor and myself, he told me there was a difficulty in doing it, gave a bad account of Leyden lodgings, and proposed that we should both go to his house. Such an offer was not lightly to be accepted. Henry Taylor made inquiries himself, and looked at lodgings which would have contented us; but when he was asked for how long they might be wanted, and said a week or perhaps ten days, the people said that for so short a time he might be lodged at a hotel. The matter ended in my yielding to solicitations which were so earnest that I could not doubt their sincerity, and in his remaining at the hotel. So on Tuesday morning Neville and Arthur Malet departed for the Hague; they may fall in with us at Ghent or they may not, as it may happen. And in the evening I and my lame leg, and my trunk and bag, were deposited at Mr. Bilderdijk's.

* This reluctance quickly vanished before the kind friendliness of the Bilderdijks. "I shall not easily forget," Mr. H. Taylor writes to him after their return, "the easy confidence of good will and true welcome with which you threw yourself upon the sofa the first time you entered the house, and the satisfaction to yourself with which you rejoiced your host and hostess for three weeks, by listening to all that the mind of the 'Heer' could unfold in his singular intertexture of tongues, and by accepting, and eating, and drinking all that the heart of the 'Vraue,' in her profusion of Dutch delicacies, could invent. Such confidence as yours was certainly never better bestowed."—*H. T. to R. S., Oct.* 20, 1825.

"You may imagine how curious I was to see the lady of the house,* and yet I did not see her when we first met, owing to the shade of the trees and the imperfectness of my sight. She was kind and cordial, speaking English remarkably well, and with very little hesitation, without any foreign accent. The first night was not well managed: a supper had been prepared, which came so late, and lasted so long by the slowness which seems to characterize all operations in this country, that I did not get to bed till one o'clock. My bedroom is on the ground floor, adjoining the sitting-room in which we eat, and which is given up to me. Every thing was perfectly comfortable and nice. I asked for my milk at breakfast,† and when Mr. Droesa, the surgeon, came in the morning, I had the satisfaction of hearing that he should not dress the wound again in the evening, but leave it four-and-twenty hours, because there was now a disposition to heal. Mr. Bilderdijk brought me some curious manuscripts of the eldest Dutch poets; the morning passed pleasantly. Henry Taylor dined with us at half past two; dinner lasted, I hardly know how, till six or seven o'clock. I petitioned for such a supper as I am accustomed to at home, got some cold meat accordingly, and was in bed before eleven. I slept well, and the foot is proceeding regularly toward recovery. Mr. Droesa just left me before I begun to write. By Sunday I hope to be able to walk about the house, and then my imprisonment will soon be over. I am in no pain, and suffer no other inconvenience than that of keeping the leg always on a chair or settee.

"You will now expect to hear something of the establishment into which I have been thus, unluckily shall I say, or luckily, introduced. The house is a good one, in a cheerful street, with a row of trees and a canal in front; large, and with every thing good and comfortable about it. The only child, Lodowijk Willem, is at home, M. Bilderdijk being as little fond of schools as I am. The boy has a peculiar, and, to me, an interesting countenance. He is evidently of a weak constitution; his dress neat, but formal, and his behavior toward me amusing from his extreme politeness, and the evident pleasure with which he receives any attempt on my part to address him, or any notice that I take of him at table. A young vrouw waits at table. I wish you could see her, for she is a much odder figure than Maria Rosa‡ appeared on her first introduction, only not so cheerful a one. Her dress is black and white, perfectly neat, and not more graceful than a Beguine's. The cap, which is very little, and has a small front not projecting further than the green shade which I wear sometimes for my eyes, comes down to the roots of the hair, which is all combed back on the forehead; and she is as white and wan in complexion as her cap; slender, and not ill made; and, were it not for this utter paleness, she would be rather handsome. Another vrouw, who appears more rarely, is not in such plain dress, but quite as odd in her way. Nothing can be more amusing than Mr. Bilderdijk's conversation. Dr. Bell is not more full of life, spirits, and enthusiasm; I am reminded of him every minute, though the English is much more uncouth than Dr. Bell's.* He seems delighted to have a guest who can understand, and will listen to him; and is not a little pleased at discerning how many points of resemblance there are between us; for he is as laborious as I have been; has written upon as many subjects; is just as much abused by the Liberals in his country as I am in mine, and does 'contempt' them as heartily and as merrily as I do. I am growing intimate with Mrs. Bilderdijk, about whom her husband, in the overflowing of his spirits, tells me every thing. He is very fond of her and very proud of her, as well he may; and, on her part, she is as proud of him. Her life seems almost a miracle after what she has gone through.

* * * * * * *

"*Friday morning.*—My foot continues to mend, and proceeds as well as possible toward recovery. I can now, with the help of a stick, walk from room to room. My time passes very pleasantly. A more remarkable or interesting a person, indeed, than my host it was never my fortune to meet with; and Mrs. Bilderdijk is not less so. I shall have a great deal to talk about on my return. Early next week I hope to be at liberty; and I may travel the better, because we move here by trekschuits, so that the leg may be kept up. Now do not you vex yourself for an evil which is passed, and which has led to very pleasant consequences. Once more God bless you! R. S."

I well remember my pleasure at receiving the following letter, being at that time seven years of age. It is, I think, so good a specimen of a letter to a child, that the reader will not regret its insertion.

To C. C. Southey.

"Leyden, July 2, 1825.

"My dear Cuthbert,

"I have a present for you from Lodowijk Willem Bilderdijk, a very nice, good boy, who is of the age of your sister Isabel. It is a book of Dutch verses, which you and I will read together when I come home. When he was a little boy and was learning to write, his father, who is very much such a father as I am, made little verses for him to write in his copy-book; and these verses pleased some good people so much, that leave was asked to print them. They were printed from Lodowijk's writing, and have been thought so fit for the purpose, that a great many of them have been sold. Lodowijk will write his name and yours in the book. He is a

* She was not less curious to see him, and, on Mr. Bilderdijk's return from the hotel, eagerly inquired "how he looked;" to which the reply was given that "he looked as Mr. Southey *ought* to look:" a description which delighted my father exceedingly.

† A basin of hot milk was for many years my father's substitute for tea or coffee at breakfast.

‡ A Portuguese servant.

* Dr. Bell spoke with a strong Scotch accent.

very gentle, good boy, and I hope that one of these days somewhere or other he and you may meet.

"I must tell you about his stork. You should know that there are a great many storks in this country, and that it is thought a very wicked thing to hurt them. They make their nests, which are as large as a great clothes basket, upon the houses and churches, and frequently when a house or church is built, a wooden frame is made on the top for the storks to build in. Out of one of these nests a young stork had fallen, and somebody, wishing to keep him in a garden, cut one of his wings. The stork tried to fly, but fell in Mr. Bilderdijk's garden, and was found there one morning almost dead; his legs and his bill had lost their color, and were grown pale, and he would soon have died if Mrs. Bilderdijk, who is kind to every body and every thing, had not taken care of him, as we do of the dumbeldores when they have been in the house all night. She gave him food, and he recovered. The first night they put him into a sort of summer-house in the garden, which I can not describe to you, because I have not yet been there; the second night he walked to the door himself that it might be opened for him. He was very fond of Lodowijk, and Lodowijk was as fond of his *oyevaar*, which is the name for stork in Dutch, though I am not sure that I have spelled it rightly, and they used to play together in such a manner that his father says it was a pleasure to see them; for a stork is a large bird, tall and upright, almost as tall as you are, or quite. The oyevaar was a bad gardener; he ate snails, but with his great broad foot he did a great deal of mischief, and destroyed all the strawberries and many of the smaller vegetables. But Mr. and Mrs. Bilderdijk did not mind this, because the oyevaar loved Lodowijk, and therefore they loved the oyevaar, and sometimes they used to send a mile out of town to buy eels for him, when none could be had in Leyden.

"The very day I came to their house the stork flew away. His wings were grown, and most likely he thought it time to get a wife and settle in life. Lodowijk saw him rise up in the air and fly away. Lodowijk was very sorry, not only because he loved the oyevaar, but because he was afraid the oyevaar would not be able to get his own living, and therefore would be starved. On the second evening, however, the stork came again and pitched upon a wall near. It was in the twilight, and storks can not see at all when it is dusk; but whenever Lodowijk called *Oye! oye!* (which was the way he used to call him), the oyevaar turned his head toward the sound. He did not come into the garden. Some fish was placed there for him, but in the morning he was gone, and had not eaten it; so we suppose that he is married, and living very happily with his mate, and that now and then he will come and visit the old friends who were so good to him.

"It is very happy for me that I am in so comfortable a house, and with such excellently kind and good people * * where I learn more of the literature, present and past state, and domestic manners of the country, than it would have been possible for me to do in any other manner.

"Yesterday Mr. Bilderdijk received a letter from Algernon Thelwall, who is at Amsterdam, saying he had heard that I was here, and expressing a great desire to see me. Both Mr. and Mrs. Bilderdijk speak very highly of him. This news is for your mamma. I shall have a great deal to tell her on my return.

"I hope you have been a good boy, and done every thing that you ought to do, while I am away. When I come home you shall begin to read Jacob Cats with me. My love to your sisters and to every body else. I hope Rumpelstilzchen has recovered his health, and that Miss Cat is well, and I should like to know whether Miss Fitzrumpel has been given away, and if there is another kitten. The Dutch cats do not speak exactly the same language as the English ones. I will tell you how they talk when I come home.

"God bless you, my dear Cuthbert!

"Your dutiful father,

"ROBERT SOUTHEY."

To Mrs. Southey.

"Leyden, Thursday, July 7, 1825

"MY DEAR EDITH

" * * * This is our manner of life. At eight in the morning Lodowijk knocks at my door. My movements in dressing are as regular as clock-work, and when I enter the adjoining room, breakfast is ready on a sofa-table, which is placed for my convenience close to the sofa. There I take my place, seated on one cushion, and with my leg raised on another. The sofa is covered with black plush. The family take coffee, but I have a jug of boiled milk. Two sorts of cheese are on the table, one of which is very strong, and highly flavored with cummin and cloves: this is called Leyden cheese, and is eaten at breakfast laid in thin slices on bread and butter. The bread is soft, in rolls, which have rather skin than crust; the butter very rich, but so soft that it is brought in a pot to table, like potted meat. Before we begin Mr. B. takes off a little gray cap, and a silent grace is said, not longer than it ought to be; when it is over he generally takes his wife's hand. They sit side by side opposite me; Lodowijk at the end of the table. About ten o'clock Mr. Droesa comes and dresses my foot, which is swathed in one of my silk handkerchiefs. I bind a second round the bottom of the pantaloon, and if the weather be cold I put on a third, so that the leg has not merely a decent, but rather a splendid appearance. After breakfast and tea Mrs. B. washes up the china herself at the table. Part of the morning Mr. B. sits with me. During the rest I read Dutch, or, as at present, retire into my bed-room and write. Henry Taylor calls in the morning, and is always pressed to dine, which he does twice or thrice in the week.

We dine at half past two or three, and the dinners, to my great pleasure, are altogether Dutch. You know I am a valiant eater, and having retained my appetite as well as my spirits during this confinement, I eat every thing which is put before me. Mutton and pork never appear, being considered unfit for any person who has a wound, and pepper, for the same reason, is but sparingly allowed. Spice enters largely into their cookery; the sauce for fish resembles custard rather than melted butter, and is spiced. Perch, when small (in which state they are considered best), are brought up swimming in a tureen. They look well, and are really very good. With the roast meat (which is in small pieces), dripping is presented in a butter-boat. The variety of vegetables is great. Peas, peas of that kind in which the pod also is eaten, purslain, cauliflowers, *abominations*,* kidney beans, carrots, turnips, potatoes. But, besides these, many very odd things are eaten with meat. I had stewed apples, exceedingly sweet and highly spiced, with roast fowl yesterday; and another day, having been helped to some stewed quinces, to my utter surprise, some ragout of beef was to be eaten with them. I never know, when I begin a dish, whether it is sugared or will require salt; yet every thing is very good, and the puddings excellent. The dinner lasts very long. Strawberries and cherries always follow. Twice we had cream with the strawberries, very thick, and just in the first stage of sourness. We have had melons also, and currants—the first which have been produced. After coffee they leave me to an hour's nap. Tea follows. Supper at half past nine, when Mr. B. takes milk, and I a little cold meat with pickles, or the gravy of the meat preserved in a form like jelly; olives are used as pickles, and at half past ten I go to bed. Mr. B. sits up till three or four, living almost without sleep.

"Twice we had a Frisian here, whom we may probably see at Keswick, as he talks of going to England on literary business. Halbertsma† is his name, and he is a Mennonite pastor at Deventer.* Twice we have had the young Count Hoogmandorp, a fine young man, one of the eight who for six weeks watched day and night by Mr. B. in his illness; and once a Dr. Burgman, a young man of singular appearance and much learning, drank tea here. My host's conversation is amusing beyond any thing I ever heard. I can not hope to describe it so as to make you conceive it. The matter is always so interesting, that it would alone suffice to keep one's attention on the alert; his manner is beyond expression animated, and his language the most extraordinary that can be imagined. Even my French can not be half so odd. It is English pronounced like Dutch, and with such a mixture of other language, that it is an even chance whether the next word that comes be French, Latin, or Dutch, or one of either tongues shaped into an English form. Sometimes the oddest imaginable expressions occur. When he would say 'I was pleased,' he says 'I was very pleasant;' and instead of saying that a poor woman was wounded, with whom he was overturned in a stage-coach in England, he said she was severely *blessed*. Withal, whatever he says is so full of information, vivacity, and character, and there is such a thorough good nature, kindness, and frankness about him, that I never felt myself more interested in any man's company. Every moment he reminds me more and more of Dr. Bell.

* Broad beans, which he always so denominated.

† "Mr. Halbertsma is a very good and learned man, who has particularly directed his attention to the early languages of these countries, and is now planning a journey to England for the purpose of transcribing some MSS. of Junius's which are at Oxford. He speaks English, and made his first essay at conversing with an Englishman with me. His pronunciation was surprisingly good, considering that till that moment he had never heard English spoken by an Englishman. But the Frisians have nothing in their own language which it is necessary for them to forget: he read me some verses in their tongue that I might hear the pronunciation. To my ear they were much less harsh than the Dutch, being wholly free from gutturals. The language, however, is regarded as a barbarous dialect." I subjoin a few other extracts from his Journal:

"Very few of the Mennonites retain the orthodox faith of their fathers. In this generation they have generally lapsed into Socinianism, which, with other kindred *isms*, prevails extensively in Holland, Pantheism being the stage to which the speculative Atheists in this country proceed. Another people, like the unbelievers in England, all act in favor of Romanism and in league with it. Their principle is, that superstition is necessary for the vulgar; so they would have a papal establishment, with infidel priests and an indifferent government. The Romanists are palpably favored, and visibly increase in numbers. At the Fête de Dieu, the king committed the gross offense to his own religion of having his palace decorated in honor of the procession. This could not gratify his Romish subjects so much as it has disgusted all those who know how to appreciate the blessings of the Reformation; for the great body of the Dutch people are attached to that religion, the enjoyment of which their ancestors purchased so dearly.

"The government has followed that base policy which all restored kings seem to follow, as if to show, if persons alone were to be considered, how little they have deserved their restoration. The old enemies of the house of Orange are favored and preferred; the old friends, true servants and sufferers in their cause, are left with their sufferings for their reward. The system of Liberalism prevails; the press is made an engine of mischief here as in England; and every thing that presumptuous ignorance and philosophism can do, is doing to undermine the religion and morals of the people.

"During the triumph of the anti-stadtholder faction, popular feeling manifested itself in some odd ways. The body of the people have always been gratefully attached to the house of Orange, as it became them to be. To prevent all manifestation of that feeling, the ruling faction forbade the market-women to expose carrots for sale. They were enjoined, on pain of fine, to keep them covered under other greens. Carroty cats were hunted down to be extirpated, and marigolds rooted up by men sent for the purpose. Of course, such measures provoked the spirit which they were desired to suppress. The fishwomen cried orange-salmon through the streets, marigold seeds were scattered every where, and particularly in the gardens of the factious, and pigeons were dyed orange color and let fly. The two latter tricks excited some superstitious feeling.

"The University here has sadly declined. There are not thirty professors, and not more than 300 students. The want of able men and the appointment of unfit ones has occasioned the decline. Freshmen are called *greens*, and a ceremony was (and perhaps is) used in ungreening them, and admitting them to their full academical privileges. Bread, according to its degree of fineness, was called in military and academic towns, from the rank of those who might be supposed to eat it, cadet's, captain's, or colonel's bread; and here, from greens' up to professor's bread; the sort above which was called prophet's. If a fisherman offered for sale a remarkably fine and large fish, a haddock, for example, he will say it is a professor among haddocks."—*From his Journal.*

* The Mennonites were Dutch Baptists.

"I gather by one word which dropped from him that Mrs. B. is his second wife. They are proud of each other, as well they may. She has written a great many poems, some of which are published jointly with some of his, and others by themselves. Many of them are devotional, and many relate to her own feelings under the various trials and sufferings which she has undergone. In some of them I have been reminded sometimes of some of my own verses, in others of Miss Bowles's. One would think it almost impossible that a person so meek, so quiet, so retiring, so altogether without display, should be a successful authoress, or hold the first place in her country as a poetess. The profits of literature here are miserably small. In that respect, I am, in relation to them, what Sir Walter Scott is in relation to me. Lodowijk (thus the name is spelled) is a nice, good boy, the only survivor of seven children. He is full of sensibility, and I look at him with some apprehension, for he is not strong, and I fear this climate, which suits his father better than any other, is injurious to him. Tell Cuthbert that the oyevaar has paid him another visit, and that Lodowijk's other playmate is a magnificent tabby cat, as old as himself, who, however, is known by no other name than puss, which is good Dutch as well as English.

"English books are so scarce here that they have never seen any work of mine except Roderic. Of course I have ordered over a complete set of my poems and the History of Brazil, and as E. May is in London, I have desired her to add, as a present from herself to Mrs. B., a copy of Kirke White's Remains. I can never sufficiently show my sense of the kindness which I am experiencing here. Think what a difference it is to be confined in a hotel, with all the discomforts, or to be in such a family as this, who show by every word and every action that they are truly pleased in having me under their roof.

"I manage worst about my bed. I know not how many pillows there are, but there is one little one which I used for my head till I found that it was intended for the small of my back. Every thing else I can find instruction for, but here is nobody to teach one how to get into a Dutch bed, or how to lie in one. A little bottle of brandy is placed on the dressing-table, to be used in cleansing the teeth. Saffron is used in some of the soups and sauces. The first dish yesterday was marrow in a tureen, which was eaten upon toast. I eat every thing, but live in daily fear of something like suety pudding or tripe. About an hour before dinner a handsome mahogany case containing spirits is produced; a glass waiter is taken out of it, and little tumblers with gilt edges, and we have then a glass of liqueur with a slice of cake. Deventer cake it is called; and an odd history belongs to it. The composition is usually intrusted only to the burgomaster of that city, and when the baker has made all the other ingredients ready, the chief magistrate is called upon, as part of his duty, to add that portion of the materials which constitute the excellence and peculiarity of the Deventer cake. I shall have much to tell you, for I know not where I have heard so much to amuse, so much to affect, so much to interest and inform me as since I have been a prisoner here. * * * * * *

"Love to the children. God bless you, my dear Edith!

"Your affectionate husband, R. S."

To Miss Katherine Southey.

"Amsterdam, Saturday, July 16, 1825.

"MY DEAR KATE,

" * * * Tuesday we had a pleasant day on the water, and saw at the sluices of the Rhine enough to undeceive us concerning the common statements about this country. That the sea is higher than the towers of Leyden is altogether false: the truth is, that the general level of Holland is above the low-water mark, and a little below that of high-water; and though the lands are much below the rivers and canals, it is because the beds of the rivers have been raised by what they bring down, or because the lands were formerly large meres or deep morasses, which have been drained. Wednesday I went with Henry Taylor to the Hague, saw the museum of pictures, called on one of my Dutch curmudgeons, Mr. De Clerc, who is an improvisatore poet, and returned in the evening. Thursday I settled my business as to booksellers. Oh, joy when that chest of glorious folios shall arrive at Keswick! the pleasure of unpacking, of arranging them on the new shelves that must be provided, and the whole year's repast after supper which they will afford! After dinner we took what Mr. Bilderdijk calls a walk in a carriage, and drank tea in a village, where we had a very entertaining scene with the hostess—a woman shaped very much like a jumping Joan, supposing the said Joan to be tall, and lean in the upper half. Her birth-day had occurred a few days before, and on that occasion a poem had been addressed to her by the surgeon's man: this poem she brought to Mr. Bilderdijk to read, and he read it just as Mr. Wordsworth would have read a piece of doggerel, if under like circumstances it had been brought to him in some such public house as John Stanley's. The woman stood by in silent delight at hearing her own praises entoned by his powerful voice, and set off by his gestures and emphatic manner: Mrs. Bilderdijk kept her countenance to admiration. I sat by, not knowing whether the verses were good or bad, but infinitely amused by the scene, and the girl of the public house coming out at the unusual sound, stood among the shrubs of the garden listening—like Eve in the Paradise Lost.

"Yesterday our kind friends accompanied us a little way in the trekschuit on our departure, and we parted with much regret on both sides. If Mr. Bilderdijk can muster spirits for the undertaking, they will come and pass a summer with me, which of all things in the world would give me most pleasure, for never did I meet with more true kindness than they have shown me, or with two persons who have in so many essential respects so entirely pleased me. Lodowijk, too, is a very engaging boy, and attached himself greatly to me; he is the only survivor of eight children whom Mr. Bilderdijk has had by his present wife, and of seven by the first! I can truly say, that, unpleasant as the circumstance was which brought me under their roof, no part of my life ever seemed to pass away more rapidly or more pleasantly. We got to Harlaem by dinner-time, and to Amsterdam afterward.

"God bless you, my dear child!

"Your affectionate father, R. S."

To the Rev. Robert Philip.

"Keswick, Aug. 15, 1825.

"My dear Sir,

"On returning home after an absence of several weeks, I found, and was pleased to find, your friendly letter and the books which accompanied it. For the one relating to South America, I must beg you to express my thanks where they are due. Having inquired so diligently into the history and condition of that wide country during many years, I am glad to possess any documents which may enable me to correct or otherwise improve the result of my researches. But it will not be my fortune to revise the work. Excepting Mrs. Baillie's little book concerning Lisbon, I have not reviewed a book of travels for many years.

"I thank you for your own volume. You have undertaken a labor of love where it was greatly needed, and you will have your reward. I can not doubt but that some of the seed which you have sown will take root and bring forth fruit.

"No person can look with more eagerness than I do for your Life and Times of Whitefield, nor will any one who peruses it be better disposed to be pleased with the perusal. The points on which I may expect you to differ from me are not unimportant ones, but they are less important than those on which I am sure that we agree; and my temper will always lead me to consider a fair and generous opponent almost as a friend.

"I am busied at present in demolishing the flimsy sophistries of Mr. Butler, treating him, however, with the courtesy which is due to a kind-hearted man and an old acquaintance. Milner will receive a different treatment. What think you of his saying Whitefield *believed* that the Angel Gabriel attended on his congregation, and quoted a story which I have told to prove it? He says also that I have avowed the Moravian doctrine of instantaneous conversion, and refers to a passage (vol. iv., p. 159) which exposes the fallacy of the reasoning by which Wesley was led to believe it. And of such direct and impudent falsehoods his strictures are full. I have, however, rather to enlarge my statements than to vindicate them, and the greater part of my book will be historical and biographical.

"Mrs. Southey joins with me in remembrance to Mrs. Philips, and desires me to say she has not forgotten the few but pleasant hours in which we enjoyed your conversation seven summers ago.

"Yours with sincere esteem and regard,

"Robert Southey."

To Henry Taylor, Esq.

"Keswick, Oct. 22, 1825.

"My dear H. T.,

" * * * * * * *

Canning came here from Lowther, and sat about half an hour with me. My acquaintance with him is of some five years standing, and of course slight, as it is very rarely that circumstances bring me in his way. Had we been thrown together in early life—that is, if I had been three years older, and had been sent to Eton instead of Westminster—we might probably have become friends. 'Very ordinary intelligence' has never sufficed for me in the choice of my associates, unless there was extraordinary kindness of disposition, or strength of moral character to compensate for what was wanting. When these are found, I can do very well without great talents; but without them, the greatest talents have no attractions for me. If Canning were my neighbor, we might easily become familiar, for we should find topics enough of common interest, and familiarity grows naturally out of an easy intercourse where that is the case. But I am very sure that his good opinion of me would not be increased by any thing that he would see of me in general society.

"With regard to my writings, I am well aware that some of them are addressed to a comparatively small part of the public, out of which they will not be read. Probably not half a dozen even of those persons who are most attached to me ever read all that I have published. But if immediate reputation were my object, I know not how it could more surely be attained than by writing to such different classes as those among whom my different books find readers for the sake of the subject matter. The truth, however, is, that this never enters into my consideration. I take up a subject because it interests me. I treat it in the manner which seemeth best in my own eyes, and when it has been sent forth to take its chance, the only care which I have concerning it is to correct and improve it in case it should be reprinted.

"The Bishop of Chester has been here, and Mackintosh breakfasted with me and spent an evening also. He has been in Holland, but knows Bilderdijk only by name and by reputation.

"My books arrived about a month ago, and I have been in a high state of enjoyment ever since. But I have had another pleasure since their arrival, which is to learn that the second edition of Wadding's Annales Minorum, for want of which I was fain to purchase the first of Verbeyst, has been bought for me at Rome by Senhouse, this being seventeen volumes, the first only eight. To me, who desire always the fullest materials for whatever I undertake, this is a great acquisition. My after-supper book at present is Erasmus's Letters, from which I know not whether I derive most pleasure or profit.

"The tendency of my ecclesiastical writings, whether controversial or historical, is not to disturb established delusions, but to defend established truths. It is not to any difference of religion that the better character of the lower orders in France must be ascribed—the persons who are under forty years of age and above twenty having grown up without any—but to the difference of national manners, amusements, &c., the way in which our manufactures are carried on, and the effect which, within the last thirty years, the poor-laws have produced. So far, however, as religion comes into the account, it is in favor of the French for these reasons, that the lowest class have a religion there, which here very generally they have not (I speak of large towns and manufacturing districts where the neglected population have outgrown the churches); that a bad religion is better than none; and that the effects of the Roman Catholic system (as of Methodism) become more and more injurious as you trace them up from the lowest to the higher ranks. This I shall this minute note as a subject to be pursued in my Colloquies. * * * * * *

"God bless you! R. S."

To Dr. Gooch.

"Keswick, Dec. 18, 1825.

"MY DEAR GOOCH,

"I can not refer you to any other account of the Sisters of Charity than is to be found in Helyot's Histoire des Ordres Monastiques, a very meager but useful book; compared to what a history ought to be, it is somewhat like what a skeleton is to the body. When I was first in the Low Countries, I endeavored to collect what information I could concerning the Beguines, and got into their principal establishment at Ghent. Their history is curiously uncertain, which I found not only from themselves, but from pursuing the subject in books; and as I have those books at hand, I can at any time tell you what is not known about them, for to that the information which they contain amounts. The Beguines are as much esteemed in the Low Countries as the Sœurs de la Charité in France; but I have incidentally learned from books that scandal used to be busy with them. A profession of religion naturally affords cover for hypocrisy, and it is therefore to be expected that scandal should sometimes arise, and more frequently be imputed; but the general utility of the institution is unquestionable; and I do not know that there is any thing to be set against it, for they are bound by no vows, nor to any of those observances which are at once absurd and onerous. I will have the notes which I made concerning them at Ghent transcribed for you. As your adventures were in Flanders, not in France, have you not mistaken the Beguines for the Sisters of Charity?

"It is not surprising that your letters in Blackwood should have produced so much impression. The subject comes home to every body, and that Yarmouth story is one of the most touching incidents I ever remember to have heard. As an example to prove how much a principle of humanity is wanting, look by all means for an account of the Foundling Hospital at Dublin, where the most damnable inhumanity of its kind upon record was practiced by the nurses for a course of years. The mortality was monstrous. I think it appeared that these wretches who dealt in infant suffering used sometimes to murder the children by sitting upon them in the carts wherein they conveyed them from the hospital to the country.

"The change of ministry in the Quarterly Review is the only change of such a kind which could have affected me for evil and for good.

"As for my importance to the Review, it is very little. Just at this juncture I might do harm by withdrawing from it; but at any other time I should be as little missed as I shall be, except in my own family and in some half a dozen hearts besides, whenever death shakes hands with me. The world closes over one as easily as the waters. Not, however, that I shall sink to be forgotten.

"But as for present effect, the reputation of the Review is made, and papers of less pith and moment than mine would serve the bookseller's purpose quite as well, and amuse the great body of readers, who read only for amusement or for fashion, more. God bless you!

"Yours affectionately,

"R. SOUTHEY."

To Henry Taylor, Esq.

"Keswick, Dec. 31, 1825.

"MY DEAR H. T.,

"I have pursued so little method in my own studies at any time of my life, that I am, in truth, very little qualified to direct others. Having been from youth, and even childhood, an omnivorous reader, I found myself, when I commenced man, with a larger stock of general information than young men usually possess, and the desultory reading in which I have always indulged (making it, indeed, my whole and sole recreation) has proved of the greatest use when I have been pursuing a particular subject through all its ramifications.

"With regard to metaphysics I know nothing, and therefore can say nothing. Coleridge, I am sure, knows all that can be known concerning them; and if your friend can get at the kernel of his 'Friend' and his 'Aids to Reflection,' he may crack peach-stones without any fear of breaking his teeth. For logic—that may be considered indispensable, but how far that natural logic which belongs to good sense is assisted or impeded by the technicalities of the schools, others are better able to determine than I am, for I learned very little, and nothing which I ever learned stuck by me unless I liked it.

"The rules for composition appear to me very simple; inasmuch as any style is peculiar, the peculiarity is a fault, and the proof of this is the easiness with which it is imitated, or, in other words, caught. You forgive it in the original for its originality, and because originality is usually connected with power. Sallust and Tacitus are examples among the Latins, Sir T. Brown, Gibbon, and Johnson among our own authors; but look at the imitations of Gibbon and Johnson! My advice to a young writer is, that he should weigh well what he says, and not be anxious concerning *how* he says it; that his first object should be to express his meaning as perspicuously, his second as briefly as he can, and in this every thing is included.

"One of our exercises at Westminster was to abridge the book which we were reading. I believe that this was singularly useful to me. The difficulties in narration are to select and to arrange. The first must depend upon your judgment. For the second, my way is, when the matter does not dispose itself to my liking, and I can not readily see how to connect one part with another naturally, or make an easy transition, to lay it aside. What I should bungle at now may be hit off to-morrow; so, when I come to a stop in one work, I lay it down and take up another.

"For a statesman, the first thing requisite is to be well read in history. Our politicians are continually striking upon rocks and shallows which are all laid down in the chart. As this is the most important and most interesting branch of knowledge, so also is it one to which there is no end. The more you read the more you desire to read, and the more you find there is to be read; and yet I would say this to encourage the student, not to dismay him, for there is no pleasure like this perpetual acquisition and perpetual pursuit. For an Englishman there is no single historical work with which it can be so necessary for him to be well and thoroughly acquainted as with Clarendon. I feel at this time perfectly assured, that if that book had been put into my hands in youth, it would have preserved me from all the political errors which I have outgrown. It may be taken for granted that —— knows this book well. The more he reads concerning the history of those times, the more highly he will appreciate the wisdom and the integrity of Clarendon. For general histories of England, Hume's is not ranked higher than it deserves for its manner, and the perpetual presence of a clear intellect. Henry may be classed with Rapin as laborious and heavy. I have never had an opportunity of reading Carte, in whom I believe there is much good matter. For matter and research, Turner's is very much the best, as far as it goes. But were your friend, as an exercise in composition, to undertake the history of a single reign, it would surprise him to find into how wide a field of reading he would be led, and how much he would discover that has been overlooked.

"The advice I would give any one who is disposed really to read for the sake of knowledge, is, that he should have two or three books in course of reading at the same time. He will read a great deal more in that time and with much greater profit. All travels are worth reading, as subsidiary to reading, and, in fact, essential parts of it: old or new, it matters not—something is to be learned from all. And the custom of making brief notes of reference to every thing of interest or importance would be exceeding useful.

"Enough of this. Do you know who wrote that paper in Blackwood which you sent me? for I should like to know. Whoever the author be, I very much agree with him. But when you say that conciliation and comprehension should be the policy of the Church, I agree only as to the latter. Comprehension is the principle upon which the Articles were framed, but for conciliating enemies, Heaven bless those who attempt it! There are two things which may endanger the Church. The Catholic Question is one, scandalous promotions are the other. Its safety just now consists in public opinion acting upon the government in both cases, and in some degree controlling it. The bigotry which is in the Church is hurtful enough, but not so hurtful as the promotion of unworthy men who take the bigoted party just as they would take the strongest side in case of danger.

* * * * * * *

"A humorous French criticism upon the Tale of Paraguay has found its way into the Westmoreland Gazette, that I have shown off my professional knowledge too much in dwelling upon vaccination and the cow-pox. This I get by my doctorship.

"God bless you! R. S."

To Grosvenor C. Bedford, Esq.

"Keswick, Feb. 18, 1826.

"My dear Grosvenor,

* * * * * * *

"You can not hold the Bullion Question in greater abhorrence than I do. It is the worst plague that ever came out of Pandora's Scotch mull. I can not but think that government is altogether wrong in abolishing small notes; they should allow of none which have not the stamp of national credit, but without small bills there will be a want of sufficient currency. And as for forgery, Heaven help the wits of those who do not perceive that for one who can forge there will be twenty who can coin. Peel has never recovered the credit with me which he lost by becoming a bullionist, and Ricardo's opinion I hold in so little respect that I am glad he has not an English name.

"Do you remember me buying a Dutch grammar in the 'cool May' of 1799, and how we were amused at Brixton with the Dutch grammarian who pitied himself, and loved his good and rich brother? That grammar is in use now; and Cuthbert and I have begun upon Jacob Cats, who, in spite of his name, and of the ill-looking and not-much-better-sounding language in which he wrote, I verily believe to have been the most useful poet that any country ever produced. In Bilderdijk's youth, Jacob Cats was to be found in every respectable house throughout Holland, lying beside the hall Bible. One of his longer poems, which describes the course of female life, and female duties from childhood to the grave, was in such estimation, that an ornamental edition of it was printed solely for bridal presents. He is, in the best sense of the word, a domestic poet; intelligible to the humblest of his readers, while the dexterity and felicity of his diction make him the admiration of those who are best able to appreciate the merits of his style. And for useful practical morals, maxims for every-day life, lessons that find their way through the understanding to the heart, and fix themselves there, I know of no poet who can be compared to him. Mi *Cats* inter omnes. Cedite Romani Scriptores, cedite Graii!

"I believe you know (which is not yet to be made known) that I have engaged to continue Warton's History of English Poetry, and bring it down to the close of the last century; that is, I mean to conclude with Hayley, Cowper, and Darwin, and stop just where my own time begins. It is to be in three or four octavo volumes, as the subject may require, for which I am to have £500 each, paid as each is finished. What leads me to speak of this is, that you may understand how I am led from history and polemics to the humaner study of Jacob Cats. My plan, like Warton's, includes and requires excursive views of the literature of other countries. How far these commercial storms may extend, there is no foreseeing; but as I am not to begin printing before the beginning of next year, it is likely that things will go on smoothly again by that time.

* * * * * * *

"God bless you! R. S."

To the Lord Bishop of Limerick (Dr. Jebb).

"Keswick, April 17, 1826.

"MY LORD,

"I will be at your door at ten o'clock on Saturday, the 20th of May, unless any mishap should prevent me.

"It was not without some degree of shame that I received your kind letter—the shame which arises from a consciousness of having omitted what ought to have been done; for I have often thought of writing to you, and intended to write, and as often some avocation has made me postpone it till that more convenient season, which never arrives for one who is always employed, and but too frequently interrupted.

"My last year's journey proved an eventful one, both for evil and good. I traveled in the hope of cutting short an annual catarrh, which is of such a nature that, unless the habit of its recurrence can be overcome, its work must, in a very few visits more, be completed. The experiment succeeded perfectly, and so far all was well. I sent home, also, a goodly consignment of folios and of smaller fry from Brussels and from Leyden; heavy artillery, to be mounted in ny batteries against Babylon. But my ill fortune began at Douay, whither I went on my outward journey, partly for the sake of taking a line which I had not traveled before; chiefly because I had an ancestor buried there, the first Sir Herbert Croft, who turned Romanist in the reign of James I., and died there among the Benedictines. Happily for me, his son returned to the faith in which he had been borne. I wished to see his grave; but when I came to the Benedictine church, I was in the same case as Yorick, when he looked for the tombs of Amandus and Amanda. The church had been gutted, the monuments destroyed, in the Revolution; and the crypt, wherein he was buried, was filled with rubbish. However, I saw the shell of the building; and I saw, also, the outside of that college where so many treasons had been plotted, and so much mischief for these kingdoms hatched. But at Douay or at Bouchain I was bitten on the foot by the vilest of all insects; an accidental hurt, which was but just healed, had disposed the part for inflammation. The weather was intensely hot; by the time I reached Antwerp, I was unable to put that foot to the ground; and having proceeded to Leyden, whither, happily, I had a strong motive for proceeding, I was told that, had the inflammation continued to proceed for another day, the limb would have been in danger. So there I lay nearly three weeks under a surgeon's hands. Such, however, was my good fortune, that I never passed three weeks more happily. Bilderdijk, whose wife translated Roderic into Dutch verse, and who is himself, take him for all in all, the most extraordinary and admirable person whom I have ever known, took me into his house. Here I was nursed as if I had been their brother; and thither, as they can not come and visit me, I am going to see them once more; were Leyden ten times as distant as it is, I would take the journey, for the pleasure which I shall give and receive. I knew him only by letter till I was cast upon their compassion. But Bilderdijk is one of those men whose openness of heart you perceive at first sight; and when I came to know them both, if I had sought the world over, it would not have been possible for me to have found two persons with whom I should have felt myself more entirely in unison, except, indeed, that my host stands up, like a true Hollander of the old stamp, for the Synod of Dort.

"He is above seventy years of age, and considering what he has gone through in mind and body, it is marvelous that he is alive. From infancy he has been an invalid; and in childhood was saved, after his case was pronounced hopeless, by a desperate experiment of his own father's—to change the whole mass of his blood by frequent bleeding. But, in consequence, his system acquired such a habit of making blood, that periodical bleeding has been necessary from that time; and now, in his old age, after every endeavor to prolong the intervals, he is bled every six weeks. His pulse is always that of a feverish man. He has never slept more than four hours in the four-and-twenty, and wakes always unrefreshed, and in a state of discomfort, as if sleep exhausted him more than the perpetual intellectual labor in which he is engaged. None of his countrymen have written so much, or so variously, or so well; this is admitted by his enemies; and he has for his enemies the whole body of Liberals and time-servers. His fortune was completely wrecked in the Revolution; and having been the most confidential and truest friend of the Stadtholder, he has received the usual reward of fidelity after a Restoration. The house of Orange, like other restored families, has thought it politic to show favor to their enemies and neglect their friends. A small pension of about £140 is all that he has; and a professorship, which the king had promised, is withheld, lest the Liberals should be offended.

"His life has been attempted in popular commotions; he has almost wanted bread for his family in exile, having had eight children by a first wife, seven by the present! one boy of twelve years old is the only one left, whose disposition is every thing that can be desired, but his constitution so feeble that it is impossible to look at him without fear. The mother is four-and-twenty years younger than her husband, and in every respect worthy of him; I have never seen a woman who was more to be admired and esteemed for every thing womanly; no strangers would suppose that so unassuming a person was in high repute as a poetess. Bilderdijk's intellectual rank is at once indicated by his countenance; but he is equally high-minded and humble, in the best sense of those epithets; and both are so suited to each other, so resigned to their fortunes, so deeply and quietly religious, and, therefore, so contented, so thankful, and so happy, that it must be my own fault if I am not the better for having known them.

"This theme has made me loquacious. You see that, if I suffered for visiting Holland instead of Ireland, the evil was amply overpaid. For your renewed invitation I can not thank you as I ought, nor say more at present than that in all likelihood I shall be most happy to accept it. We shall see what twelve months will bring forth.

"Farewell, my lord, till May 20. I beg my kind regards to Mr. Forster, and remain,

"With sincere respect and esteem, your lordship's obliged and faithful servant,

"ROBERT SOUTHEY."

To John Rickman, Esq.

"Keswick, April 26, 1826.

"MY DEAR R.,

" * * * * * I can have no opinion about the Corn Laws, having no concern in them, which might make me overcome an habitual or natural inaptitude for such complicated questions. But with regard to the general question of Free Trade, I incline to think that the old principle, upon which companies of the various trades were formed for the purpose of not allowing more craftsmen or traders of one calling in one place than the business would support, was founded in good common sense; and as a corollary, that if some more effectual step is not put to the erection of new cotton mills, &c., than individual prudence is ever likely to afford, at some time or other the steam-engine will blow up this whole fabric of society. Three years ago, I was assured that, at the rate of increase then going on in Manchester, that place would, in ten years, double its manufacturing population. When we hear of the prosperity of those districts, it means that they are manufacturing more goods than the world can afford a market for, and the ebb is then as certain as the flow; and in some neap tide, Radicalism, Rebellion, and Ruin will rush in through the breach which hunger has made.

"You have had more than your share of this world's business. I doubt whether any other man who has worked so hardly has worked so continuously and so long. Our occupations withdraw us all too much from nearer and more lasting concerns. Time and nature, especially when aided by any sorrows, prepare us for better influences; and when we feel what is wanting, we seek and find it. The clouds then disperse, and the evening is calm and clear, even till night closes.

"Long and intimate conversance with Romish and sectarian history, with all the varieties of hypocritical villainy and religious madness, has given me the fullest conviction of the certainty and importance of these truths, from the perversion and distortion of which these evils and abuses have grown. There is not a spark of fanaticism left in my composition: whatever there was of it in youth, spent itself harmlessly in political romance. I am more in danger, therefore, of having too little of theopathy than too much—of having my religious faith more in the understanding than in the heart. In the understanding I am sure it is; I hope it is in both. This good in myself my ecclesiastical pursuits have certainly effected. And if I live to finish the whole of my plans, I shall do better service to the Church of England than I could ever have done as one of its ministers, had I kept to the course which it was intended that I should pursue. There is some satisfaction in thinking thus. God bless you! R. S."

In the following month of June, my father, in company with Mr. H. Taylor and Mr. Rickman, made a short tour in Holland, and again visited the Bilderdijks in Leyden. This was a rapid journey, and his letters during the course of it do not possess sufficient novelty to interest the reader. His return home was a mournful one: he found his youngest daughter, Isabel, laid on a bed of sickness, from which she never rose.

Well do I, though but a child, remember that return, as we hastened to meet him, and changed, by our sorrowful tidings, his cheerful smile and glad welcome to tears and sadness. It was the first time I had seen sorrow enter that happy home: and those days of alternate hope and fear, and how he paced the garden in uncontrollable anguish, and gathered us around him to prayer when all was over, are vividly impressed on my mind.

This, too, was the "beginning of troubles;" and from this shock my mother's spirits, weakened by former trials, and always harassed by the necessary anxieties of an uncertain income, never wholly recovered.

To Grosvenor C. Bedford, Esq.

"Sunday night, July 16, 1826.

"MY DEAR GROSVENOR,

"I have lost my sweet Isabel. There was hope of her recovery till yesterday evening, when my misgivings were dreadfully confirmed by symptoms which I knew too well. This evening she departed in a swoon, without a struggle, as if falling asleep.

"Under this heavy affliction we have the support of religion—the sure and only source of comfort. I am perfectly tranquil and master of myself, suffering most for what my wife suffers, who yet exerts herself with Christian fortitude. But the body can not be controlled like the mind, and I fear I shall long feel the effects of an anxiety which has shaken every fiber. Were it not for the sake of my family, how gladly would I also depart and be at rest.

"God bless you, my dear Grosvenor.

"R. S."

To Grosvenor C. Bedford, Esq.

"July 19, 1826.

"MY DEAR GROSVENOR,

"Τετελεσται. I have seen the mortal remains of my sweet Isabel committed earth to earth. And what I must now do is, to find occupation in the business of this world, and comfort in the thought of the next. The loss which I suffered ten years ago was greater; the privation, perhaps, not so great; and there were not so many to partake and augment the sorrow.

"It would be acting a friend's part, Grosvenor, if you would come to me a few weeks hence. My mind will soon regain its wonted composure, and keep to itself all thoughts which would awaken the grief of others. But I should be truly glad to have you here, and the house would be the better for the presence of an old friend. My poor wife would recover the sooner if some such turn were given to her thoughts, and we might enjoy each other's company; for I should enjoy it at leisure, which it is impossible that we should ever do in London. Indeed, I know not when I shall have heart enough to leave home again for a long absence.

"I wish to show you some things, and to talk with you about others; one business in particular, which is the disposal of my papers whenever I shall be gathered to my fathers and to my children. That good office would naturally be yours, should you be the survivor, if the business of the Exchequer did not press upon you, like the world upon poor Atlas's shoulders. I know not now upon whom to turn my eyes for it, unless it be Henry Taylor. Two long journeys with me have made him well acquainted with my temper and every-day state of mind. He has shown himself very much attached to me, and would neither want will nor ability for what will not be a difficult task, inasmuch as that which is of most importance, and would require most care, will (if my life be spared but for a year or two) be executed by my own hand. You do not know, I believe, that I have made some progress in writing my own life and recollections upon a large scale. This will be of such certain value as a post obit, that I shall make it a part of my regular business (being, indeed, a main duty) to complete it. What is written is one of the things which I am desirous of showing you. If you ever look over my letters, I wish you would mark such passages as might not be improper for publication at the time which I am looking forward to. You, and you alone, have a regular series which has never been intermitted. From occasional correspondents, plenty of others, which, being less confidential, are less careless, will turn up. I will leave a list of those persons from whom such letters may be obtained, as may probably be of avail.

"I am not weary of the world, nor is the world weary of me; but it is fitting that I should prepare, in temporal matters, for the separation which must take place between us, in the course of years, at no very distant time, and which may occur at any hour.

"Our love to Miss Page. She will feel for us the more, because she knows what we have lost.

"God bless you, my dear Grosvenor!

"R. S."

I can not better conclude this chapter than with the following beautiful letter:

To Edith May, Bertha, and Katherine Southey.

"July 19, 1826.

"MY DEAR DAUGHTERS,

"I write rather than speak to you on this occasion, because I can better bear to do it, and because what is written will remain, and may serve hereafter for consolation and admonishment, of which the happiest and best of us stand but too often in need.

"If any thing could at this time increase my sorrow for the death of one who was the pride of my eyes and the joy of my heart, it would be that there are so many who have their full share in it. When your dear mother and I were last visited with a like affliction, you were too young to comprehend its nature. You feel and understand it now; but you are also capable of profiting by it, and laying to your hearts the parental exhortations which I address to you while they are wounded and open.

"This is but the first trial of many such which are in store for you. Who may be summoned next is known only to the All-wise Disposer of all things. Some of you must have to mourn for others; some one for all the rest. It may be the will of God that I should follow more of my children to the grave; or, in the ordinary course of nature and happiest issue, they may see their parents depart. Did we consider these things wisely, we should perceive how little it imports who may go first, who last; of how little consequence sooner or later is, in what must be. We must all depart when our time comes—all to be reunited in a better state of existence, where we shall part no more.

"Our business here is to fit ourselves for that state—not by depreciating or renouncing those pleasures which may innocently and properly be enjoyed, but by correcting the faults to which we are prone, cultivating our better dispositions, doing the will of God by doing all we can for the good of others, and fixing our dearest hopes on Heaven, which is our resting-place and our everlasting home.

"My children, you have all brought into the world good dispositions: I bless God for it, more than for all the other blessings which he has vouchsafed me. But the best dispositions require self-watchfulness, as there is no garden but what produces weeds. Blessed be God, I have never seen in either of you any one symptom of an evil nature. Against great sins there is no occasion to warn you; but it is by guarding against little ones that we acquire a holy habit of mind, which is the sure foundation of happiness here and hereafter.

"You know how I loved your dear sister, my sweet Isabel, who is now gathered to that part of my family and household (a large one now!) which is in Heaven. I can truly say that my desire has ever been to make your childhood happy, as I would fain make your youth, and pray that God would make the remainder of your days. And for the dear child who is departed, God knows that I never heard her name mentioned, nor spoke, nor thought of her, without affection and delight. Yet this day, when I am about to see her mortal remains committed earth to earth, it is a grief for me to think that I should ever, by a harsh or hasty word, have given her even a momentary sorrow which might have been spared.

"Check in yourselves, then, I beseech you, the first impulses of impatience, peevishness, ill-humor, anger, and resentment. I do not charge you with being prone to these sins; far from it; but there is proneness enough to them in human nature. They are easily subdued in their beginnings; if they are yielded to, they gather strength and virulence, and lead to certain unhappiness in all the relations of life. A meek, submissive, obliging disposition is worth all other qualities. I beseech you, therefore, to bear and forbear, carefully to guard against giving offense, and more carefully (for this is the more needful admonition) to guard against taking it. A soft answer turneth away wrath. There is no shield against wrongs so effectual as an unresisting temper. You will soon find the reward of any conquest which you shall thus obtain over yourselves: the satisfaction is immediate; and the habit of equanimity which is thus easily acquired, will heighten all your enjoyments here, as well as enable you the better to support those afflictions which are inseparable from humanity.

"Your sister is departed in her innocence: 'of such is the kingdom of Heaven.' For you, if your lives are prolonged, there will be duties and trials in store, for which you must prepare by self-government, and for which God will prepare you if you steadfastly trust in his promises, and pray for that grace which is never withheld from humble and assiduous prayer.

"My children, God alone knows how long I may be spared to you. I am more solicitous to provide for your peace of mind and for your everlasting interest than for your worldly fortunes. As I have acted for myself in that respect, so do I feel for you. The longer I may live, the more, in all likelihood, will be the provision which may be made for you; large it can never be, though, whenever the hour comes, there will be enough, with prudence and good conduct, for respectability and comfort. But were it less, my heart would be at rest concerning you while I felt and believed that you were imbued with those principles, and had carefully cultivated in yourselves those dispositions which will make you heritors of eternal life.

"I copy this letter for each of you with my own hand. It will be read with grief now. But there will come a time when you may think of it with a solemn rather than melancholy pleasure, and feel grateful for this proof of love. Take it, then, with the blessing of

"Your afflicted and affectionate father,

"ROBERT SOUTHEY."

CHAPTER XXX.

HE IS RETURNED TO PARLIAMENT FOR THE BOROUGH OF DOWNTON—DECLINES TO TAKE HIS SEAT—GROWTH OF HIS OPINIONS—HIS AUTOBIOGRAPHY—EMIGRATION—THE EDINBURGH ANNUAL REGISTER A USEFUL OCCUPATION TO HIM—SHARON TURNER'S HISTORY OF ENGLAND—AMBITION—FRUITLESS EFFORTS TO INDUCE HIM TO SIT IN PARLIAMENT—REASONS FOR DECLINING TO DO SO—FORTUNATE COURSE OF LIFE—DIFFERENT MODES OF PREACHING NECESSARY TO DIFFERENT CONGREGATIONS—HE IS WISHED TO UNDERTAKE THE EDITORSHIP OF THE GARRICK PAPERS—ILLNESS OF MR. BILDERDIJK—DEATH OF BARD WILLIAMS—A QUAKER ALBUM—DOMESTIC AFFLICTIONS—STATE OF HOLLAND—DEATH OF LORD LIVERPOOL—DISLIKE OF POLITICAL ECONOMY—FOREIGN QUARTERLY REVIEW—STATE OF THE SCOTCH KIRK—POLITICS, HOME AND FOREIGN—RELATIVE HAPPINESS OF NATIONS—DECREASING SALE OF HIS WORKS—NATIONAL EDUCATION.—1826–1827.

DURING my father's absence in Holland, one of the most curious of the many odd circumstances of his life occurred to him, and one which proved that, notwithstanding the amount of obloquy, misrepresentation, and enmity his writings had stirred up against him, there were not wanting striking instances of their producing the effect he so earnestly desired.

While passing through Brussels, to his great astonishment, a report reached him that he was elected a member of Parliament, no intimation of the likelihood of such an honor being thrust upon him having previously reached him.

On his arriving in London, he found the following letter awaiting his return :

"July 10, 1826.

"A zealous admirer of the British Constitution in Church and State, being generally pleased with Mr. Southey's 'Book of the Church,' and professing himself quite delighted with the summary* on the last page of that work, and entertaining no doubt that the writer of that page really felt what he wrote, and, consequently, would be ready, if he had an opportunity, to support the sentiments there set forth, has therefore been anxious that Mr. Southey should have a seat in the ensuing Parliament; and having a little interest, has so managed that he is at this moment in possession of that seat under this single injunction :

"Ut sustineat firmiter, strenue et continuo, quæ ipse bene docuit esse sustinenda."

This was without signature, but the handwriting was recognized as that of Lord Radnor, to whom my father was personally an entire stranger.

His answer, addressed to a mutual friend, was in the following terms :

To Richard White, Esq.

1 Harley Street, July 1, 1826.

"MY DEAR SIR,

"I heard accidentally at Brussels that I had been returned for the borough of Downton, and on my arrival here on Wednesday last, I found a letter, announcing, in the most gratifying and honorable manner, that this distinction had been conferred upon me through the influence of the writer, whose name had not been affixed; had that, however, been doubtful, the writing was recognized by my old and intimate friend Mr. John May.

"Our first impulses in matters which involve any question of moral importance are, I believe, usually right. Three days allowed for mature consideration have confirmed me in mine. A seat in Parliament is neither consistent with my circumstances, inclinations, habits, nor pursuits in life. The return is null, because I hold a pension of £200 a year during pleasure. And if there were not this obstacle, there would be the want of a qualification. That pension is my only certain income; and the words of the oath (which I have looked at) are too unequivocal for me to take them upon such grounds as are sometimes supplied for such occasions.

"For these reasons, which are and must be conclusive, the course is plain. When Parliament meets, a new writ must be moved for, the election as relating to myself being null. I must otherwise have applied for the Chiltern Hundreds.

"It is, however, no inconsiderable honor to have been so distinguished. This I shall always feel; and if I do not express immediately to your friend my sense of the obligation he has conferred upon me, it is not from any want of thankfulness, but from a doubt how far it might be proper to reply to an unsigned communication. May I therefore request that you will express this thankfulness for me, and say at the same time that I trust, in my own station, and in the quiet pursuance of my own scheme of life, by God's blessing, to render better service to those institutions, the welfare of which I have at my heart, than it would be possible for me to do in a public assembly.

"I remain, dear sir,

"Yours with sincere regard,

"ROBERT SOUTHEY."

To Dr. Southey.

"Keswick, July 20, 1826.

"MY DEAR HARRY,

"I am now endeavoring to turn to my employment, as the rest of my sad household must do. The girls, as well as their mother, are sorely shaken, and sometimes I think ominously of the old proverb, which says, welcome evil if thou comest alone!

"With regard to the mode of getting out of Parliament, I am very willing that others should decide for me, in the total indifference with which I regard the question. Being aware of the nullity of the return, I abstain from franking,* and this is all that it concerns me to do. As for the impediment arising from the pension, nothing could have been easier than to have removed it, by having the pension made for life instead of during pleasure, or transferred to my wife. Herries could have done this, or you could have had it done, for it was, in fact, asking nothing but the alteration of a few words; with regard to the qualification, no one could have censured me if I had gone into Parliament, and as so many others do, with one prepared for the nonce. I am so sure that my life will be seen in its proper light when it is at an end, that misrepresenta-

* The following is the concluding passage in the Book of the Church here referred to : "From the time of the Revolution the Church of England has partaken of the stability and security of the State. Here, therefore, I terminate this compendious, but faithful view of its rise, progress, and political struggles. It has rescued us, first, from heathenism, then from papal idolatry and superstition; it has saved us from temporal as well as spiritual despotism. We owe to it our moral and intellectual character as a nation; much of our private happiness, much of our public strength. Whatever should weaken it, would, in the same degree, injure the common weal; whatever should overthrow it, would, in sure and immediate consequence, bring down the goodly fabric of that Constitution, whereof it is a constituent and necessary part. If the friends of the Constitution understand this as clearly as its enemies, and act upon it as consistently and as actively, then will the Church and State be safe, and with them the liberty and prosperity of our country."

* This resolution he steadily persevered in, notwithstanding the entreaties of his family for "one frank" in memory of his temporary M.P.-ship, and the persecution of autograph collectors.

tions, however malicious, serve only to make me smile; and I am amused at thinking that many persons will be as much surprised at discovering what manner of man Southey really was, as all the world was when Madame d'Eon was found to be of the masculine gender.

"This odd affair, however, will be of some use; it keeps my name fresh before the public, and in a way, too, which raises it in vulgar estimation. Had I arrived here in a chaise instead of coming in the mail, the people would have drawn me home in triumph; and there was a consultation about chairing me, which ended in the true conclusion that perhaps I should not like it. The General* had these honors (except the chairing) yesterday afternoon. They drew him from the turnpike to his own landing-place, and he made a speech from the boat. How he must have enjoyed this, and how we should have enjoyed it, if that very hour had not been one of the bitterest of our lives. God bless you!

"Your affectionate brother,

"R. SOUTHEY."

To Henry Taylor, Esq.

"Keswick, Aug. 31, 1826.

"MY DEAR HENRY TAYLOR,

"I have read your long letter with much interest. The question of political economy may stand over till I find a proper place for touching upon it. Concerning the Irish question you quote the Edinburgh Register; the question is pursued in the fourth volume of that work. There is just now a much more urgent question relating to Ireland. I know not how man and beast are to be saved from perishing there by famine without parliamentary assistance, promptly and efficiently administered. The pasturage is wholly destroyed by drought, the potatoes nearly so. As late as last week they had had no rain.

"Political questions will never excite any difference of feeling between us in the slightest degree. I have lived all my life in the nearest and dearest intimacy with persons who were most opposed to me in such things: whether you or I be right is of no consequence to our happiness, present or future, and of very little as to our usefulness in society. The other point whereon you touch is of more importance.

"The growth and progress of my own opinions I can distinctly trace, for I have been watchfully a self-observer. What was hastily taken up in youth was gradually and slowly modified, and I have a clear remembrance of the how, and why, and when of any material change. This you will find (I trust) in the Autobiography which I shall leave, and in which some considerable progress is made, though it has not reached this point. It will be left, whether complete or not (for there is the chance of mortality for this) in a state for the press, so that you will have no trouble with it. There will be some in collecting my stray letters, and selecting such, in whole or in part, as may not unfitly be published, less for the sake of gratifying public curiosity than of bringing money to my family.

"One thing more will remain, which is to edit my poems from the corrected copies which are in my possession. Some pieces there will be to add, and some fragments, if I do not finish what is begun. The rise and growth of all my long poems may be shown (if it be thought worth while) from the memoranda made during their progress. To those who take an interest in such things, these will be curious, as showing how the stories developed themselves, what incidents were conceived and rejected, and how the plans were altered as the composition advanced. But for this how much, or how little, or if any, will be matter of discretion, to be decided as time and circumstances may serve.

"I spoke to Lockhart about the Georgics, and he was very glad to hear of your father for the subject, and of the subject for your father. God bless you!

"Yours affectionately, R. S."

To Henry Taylor, Esq.

"Keswick, Oct. 11, 1826.

"MY DEAR H. T.,

"Thank you for the New Zealander's portrait. It may lead one to speculate whether a well tattooed face remains capable of any other individual expression than what the eye gives. In a portrait it appears that eyes, nose, and mouth go for nothing.

"You seem right in thinking that Upper Canada is the country to which government should direct such emigrants as may be at its disposal. But when the full necessity of widely colonizing shall be generally perceived and felt, I hope something like a spirit of enterprise may be excited in adventurers of the middle and higher ranks, and that men may be found who will be ambitious of founding a settlement and a family in a new world. New Holland is the country for them. I doubt whether all history can supply such another instance of stupid misgovernment as has been exhibited in stocking that country with *male* convicts, without any reference to the proportion of the sexes. You ought with all speed to ship off 'in good condition' as many female volunteers as the Magdalen, the hospitals, and the streets can supply.

"But I want to hear of colonists of a better stamp than those who are sent abroad by law or driven thither by necessity; and such, I think, may be found. It is a matter of necessity to provide an outlet for our overgrown population, who will otherwise soon become the wild beasts of society; but it is a matter of perspective policy, not less important in its consequences, to provide also for the overflow of the educated classes.

"I was at Lowther for three days last week, and met Lord Beresford there. The priests in Ireland, he says, are loaded and primed, and have their fingers upon the trigger.

"God bless you! R. S."

* General Peachey, then newly elected M.P. for Taunton.

To Henry Taylor, Esq.

"Keswick, Nov. 13, 1826.

"MY DEAR H. T.,

"You are right in supposing that I should have made a bad statesman,* and you may add to it that for no one line of life should I have been well qualified except for the clerical profession. But had I been placed in political life, I might very probably have erred more from want of decision than from deciding too rapidly.

"The Benedictine Order was established long before the twelfth century—early in the sixth—and swallows up all other rules in the Western world. It was in the twelfth that the two great Mendicant orders (the Franciscan and Dominican) were established. By help of those orders, and of that said Wadding whereon you pun, I shall make a *ramp* among the Roman Catholics. Do but imagine how Butler and Bishop Bramston (who is an old acquaintance of mine) will look when I set Sister Providence upon her head before them!

"The Register was perhaps the most successful occupation for myself in which I was ever engaged. It led me to look into the grounds of my own opinions—to modify some, to change others, and to confirm other some. If you remember it, when you are reading the Peninsular War, you will perceive that imperfect information had led me sometimes wrong, and that sometimes I had erred in forming my own opinion. But, on the whole, it is very satisfactory to find how much more frequently I was right in combining facts and forming conclusions. Do you know that the Whigs held a Council of War, and resolved to have me brought as a culprit before the House of Commons for certain remarks in that Register upon some of their worshipful body; but their decision was reversed upon an appeal, I suppose, from Whig drunk to Whig sober. It was a great pity, for I should have had good advisers and good friends, have made my own cause good, and have punished them to my heart's content. God bless you! R. S."

To Sharon Turner, Esq.

"Keswick, Nov. 12, 1826.

"MY DEAR TURNER,

"Thank you for your new History, which I have read with great attention, great pleasure, and great advantage. It places Wolsey in a worse light than that in which Cavendish had led me to view him; but Cavendish saw only the better parts of his character, and was necessarily ignorant of the crooked policy which you have exposed. I am pleased to see how nearly your estimate of Harry's character accords with mine; and not less pleased to think that my inquiries should have in some degree stimulated you to undertake and accomplish so great an undertaking as this volume. I could wish that the style had in some places been less ambitious.

"On Wednesday next I shall write to the speaker, and lay down my M.P.-ship. No temptation that could have been offered would have induced me to sacrifice the leisure and tranquillity of a studious and private life. Free from ambition I can not pretend to be, but what ambition I have is not of an ordinary kind: rank, and power, and office I would decline without a moment's hesitation, were they proffered for my acceptance; and for riches, if I ever perceive the shadow of a wish for them, it is not for their own sake, but as they would facilitate my pursuits, and render locomotion less inconvenient. The world, thank God! has little hold on me. I would fain persuade myself that even the desire of posthumous fame is now only the hope of instilling sound opinions into others, and scattering the seeds of good. All else I have outlived. I have suffered severely since we parted. Little, indeed, when I breakfasted with you last, did I apprehend the affliction which was impending over me, and which had even then begun its course. But the will of God be done! My bodily health has not recovered the shock, nor will it speedily, I fear. I am, however, now in full activity of mind, and feel the perfect leisure which winter brings with it in this place as a relief and comfort.

* * * * * * *

"I hope and trust you will find courage and health to go on till the end of Elizabeth's reign—in which I am sure you will make great discoveries. Remember me most kindly to your family, and believe me always,

"Yours affectionately,

"ROBERT SOUTHEY."

The two following letters contain the sequel of my father's strange adventure respecting the representation of the borough of Downton: the second was apparently not written till some time after the circumstances to which it relates, but it will most appropriately be inserted here.

To Grosvenor C. Bedford, Esq.

"Keswick, Friday, Dec. 8, 1826.

"MY DEAR GROSVENOR,

"Hear the second part of the history of my parliamentary affairs:

"On Wednesday I received a note from Harry, saying that a plan had been formed for purchasing a qualification for me; that Sir Robert In-

* "I have thought, as I read the Edinburgh Annual Register, how apt you were to state a strong reason as a conclusive one. To every extensive measure weighty objections exist, whatever reasons there may be to overrule them. Had you been a statesman instead of an author, the habits of your mind would have been more scrutinizing as to the merits, more inquisitive as to the defects of what, upon the whole, you should see cause to approve. If not, you would have been very far from what is called, in official phrase, 'a safe man.'"—*H. T. to R. S., Nov.* 10, 1826.

I may quote here, as applicable to these remarks, a passage from a letter of my father's written some years later: "What —— —— complains of in Sadler's speeches and in his book, is exactly what you have complained of in certain of my compositions; that confidence which a man feels whose opinions are established upon his religious belief, and who looks to the moral consequences in every thing, and will no more admit of any measures which oppose that belief, or lead to consequences injurious to it, than a mathematician will listen to any thing that contradicts an axiom, or a logician to a train of reasoning which starts from a false postulate."—*R. S. to H. T., April* 8, 1829.

glis had just communicated this to him, and was then gone to Lord R. to ask him to keep the borough open: that he (Harry) doubted whether a sufficient subscription could be raised, but supposed that under these circumstances I should not refuse the seat, and desired my answer by return of post, that he might be authorized to say I would sit in Parliament if they gave me an estate of £300 a year!

"I rubbed my eyes to ascertain that I was awake, and that this was no dream. I heard Cuthbert his Greek lesson, and read his Dutch one with him. I corrected a proof-sheet. And then, the matter having had time to digest, I wrote in reply as follows:

"'My dear H.,

"'An estate of £300 a year would be a very agreeable thing for me, Robert Lackland, and I would willingly change that name for it: the convenience, however, of having an estate is not the question which I am called upon to determine. It is (supposing the arrangement possible—which I greatly doubt), whether I will enter into public life at an age when a wise man would begin to think of retiring from it; whether I will place myself in a situation for which neither my habits, nor talents, nor disposition are suited, and in which I feel and know it to be impossible that I should fulfill the expectations of those who would raise the subscription. Others ought to believe me, and you will, when I declare that in any public assembly I should have no confidence in myself, no promptitude, none of that presence of mind, without which no man can produce any effect there. This ought to be believed, because I have them all when acting in my proper station and in my own way, and therefore can not be supposed to speak from timidity, nor with any affectation of humility. Sir Robert Inglis and his friends have the Protestant cause at heart, and imagine that I could serve it in Parliament. I have it at heart also—deeply at heart—and will serve it to the utmost of my power, "so help me God!" But it is not by speaking in public that I can serve it. It is by bringing forth the knowledge which so large a part of my life has been passed in acquiring; by exposing the real character and history of the Romish Church, systematically and irrefragably (which I can and will do) in books which will be read now and hereafter; which must make a part, hereafter, of every historical library; and which will live and act when I am gone. If I felt that I could make an impression in Parliament, even then I would not give up future utility for present effect. I have too little ambition of one kind, and too much of another, to make the sacrifice. But I could make no impression there. I should only disappoint those who had contributed to place me there; and in this point of view it is a matter of prudence, as well as in all others, of duty, to hold my first resolution, and remain contentedly in that station of life to which it has pleased God to call me. If a seat in Parliament were made compatible with my circumstances, it would not be so with my inclinations, habits, and pursuits, and therefore I must remain Robert Lackland.

"'You will not suppose that I despise £300 a year, or should lightly refuse it. But I think you will feel, upon reflection, that I have decided properly in refusing to sit in Parliament under any circumstances. R. S.'

"To-day (Friday) Harry has received this letter from me, and I have received the following one from him:

"'My dear Robert,

"'Lord R.'s answer to Sir Robert Inglis is nearly in the following words: "Mr. —— was returned upon public grounds solely, without previous communication, or even acquaintance. It has since been seen under his handwriting that the situation was not to his taste, and did not accord with his habits of life."

"'I believe these are the very words of Lord R.'s answer to an excellent letter from Inglis. Thus ends your very singular adventure. If you could have got an estate by it, the story would have told better. As it is, the estimation in which you are held by many great and good men has been proved in the most satisfactory manner. Sir Robert did not tell me the names of those who had expressed their willingness to subscribe, nor with whom the scheme had originated (not with himself), but he seemed sanguine of success. H. H. S.'

"God bless you! R. S."

To Sir R. H. Inglis, Bart.

(Without date.)

"My dear Sir Robert,

"For some time I have been intending to thank you for your very kind intentions and exertions in my behalf, and to explain, more clearly than could be done in a hasty reply to my brother's letter, the motives upon which my decision in that matter was formed. The event has proved that it was fortunate, but I wish you to be satisfied that it was *rightly made*—I might say *deliberately* also; for, though little expecting to be invited in such a manner, I have often said, and always felt, that no prospects of ambition or advantage should induce me to enter into public life.

"In replying to my brother, I spoke only of unfitness for Parliament, and disinclination for it, which were in themselves sufficient reasons. I did not speak of the separation from my family for four or five months in the year, which would have been necessary, nor of the probable effect upon my health, nor of the interruption of pursuits which, from other causes, have been and are already too much interrupted.

"If I had taken a seat in Parliament when it was at my option, the express condition was that of doing my duty there; and of this a pretty regular attendance must have been an indispensable part. But early and regular hours are necessary for my constitution, which is not strong, has always been accustomed to this, and has been shaken; and though I have neither the habits nor the feelings of a valetudinarian, some management is required to keep me as well as I am, and the loss of sleep is what I could not bear. Separate from my family I must have been during the session: this would have interfered with the education of my little boy, would have been some loss to my daughters, and would have still more depressed the spirits of my wife, which are constitutionally low, and have received shocks from which I fear there is little hope of their recovering. The motives, therefore, must be very strong which could overpower these considerations: in these times I know of no public duties which could be strong enough; nor is there any thing on the score of private advantage which should lead me to change the whole system of my life. It is very possible that, being in Parliament, I might have made my way into some minor office, which would have given me a good income: this is even likely, because I have friends who would have helped me when they saw me in a situation where I could help myself, and because my capability and fitness for such business might have been acknowledged. But in that case no leisure would have been left for my own pursuits, and all hope must have been given up of completing those projects, upon which and in preparing for which the greater part of my life has been employed. Thus I should have done worse than buried my talent; I should have thrown it away.

"That my way of life has been directed by a merciful Providence, I feel and verily believe. I have been saved from all ill consequences of error and temerity, and by a perilous course have been led into paths of pleasantness and peace—a sufficient indication that I ought to remain in them. Throughout this whole business I have never felt any temptation to depart from this conviction. I may be wrong in many things, but not in the quiet confidence with which I know that I am in my proper place. *Inveni portum; spes et fortuna valete;* the only change to which I look forward is a possible migration to the south when my lease expires, if I should live so long. But there are so many obstacles in the way of this, that I may probably be spared from what to me would be a very painful and unwilling removal.

"This is an egotistic letter. I felt, however, that some such exposition was due to you, lest I should seem either to have acted unreasonably or to feel unthankfully. But be assured, in this whole odd episode of my life, there is nothing which I shall remember with more pleasure than the very kind and friendly part which you have taken in it.

"Believe me, dear Sir Robert,

"Yours very truly, R. S.

"I must not forget that I have a favor to ask. An old friend, for whom I have a very high and well-founded regard, is to be balloted for at the Athenæum on the 9th of February. Kenyon is his name. Upon the list of members I see the names of Mr. Dealtry and Mr. H. S. Thornton. Will you say to them that I should be greatly obliged by their votes on this occasion, and that they could not be bestowed upon a man better qualified in all respects for the admission which he is seeking?"

To the Rev. James White.

"Keswick, Dec. 14, 1826.

"MY DEAR JAMES,

"You need not be assured that I am very glad accident should have enabled me to put you in the way of being usefully, though arduously employed,* and in a station where I hope you may make your own way to something better. To be sure nothing can be less agreeable than the description which you give both of your fold and your flock; the only set-off against this is the reflection that, the worse the people are, the more good you may do them. When once it is known that you perform the service impressively, like a man whose heart is in his work, you will not preach to empty benches.

"If I preached to a wealthy congregation, my general aim would be to awaken them from that state of religious torpor which prosperity induces. I should, therefore, dwell upon the responsibility which is attached to the good things of this world; upon sins of omission, and the straitness of the gate. But to a congregation like yours, my general strain would be consolatory; forgiveness and mercy would be my favorite theme. In the former case it is necessary to rouse, if not to alarm; in the latter, to encourage and invite. In the former, to dwell upon the difficulty of attaining to salvation; in the latter, upon its easy terms, and the relief which it offers to those who are heavy laden.

"Concerning schools, no person can be more unfitted for advising you on that business (or, indeed, on any other) than I am. But of this I am sure, that, in such a parish as yours, an *infant* school is the most useful and necessary establishment that could be formed. The people of this country are not yet aware of the consequence of youthful depravity; how widely it extends, and how early it begins. In any attempts of this kind, you will have the mothers with you; and, indeed, at all attempts at moral reformation, the women are so immediately interested, that their good will is sure to attend upon any endeavors at bettering the condition of their children, or preserving their sons, brothers, husbands, and fathers from vice. Do not, however, aim at too much, and thereby exhaust yourself, even if you do not otherwise defeat your own purpose. Fill your church, and establish, as soon as you can, an infant school; and as you feel what more is wanted, you will discover by what means to bring it about.

"In your case, I would never touch upon controversial subjects, especially those which relate to Popery. The character of being a charita-

* Mr. James White had been appointed to the incumbency of St. George's, Manchester, through my father's recommendation.

ble, earnest, and pious preacher will make its way among some of the Irish Romanists, and lead them further than they are aware of toward a perception of the difference between the religion of the Gospel and the superstitions by which they are enthralled. But were you to touch upon the points of difference, it would serve only to put their priests upon the alert, and make them watch over their flock more strictly. I would pursue a different course at Dublin, because the two parties are in hostile array there, and the weapons of controversy must be used.

"But your task seems to me, in this respect, a pleasanter one. If I judge rightly of the circumstances in which you are placed, your call is to proclaim good tidings, and preach the promises of the Gospel. Those who are in misery—I had almost said, in the vices to which misery too often leads—have little need of its threats.

"But enough of this. I have no acquaintance in Manchester to whom I can introduce you; but, going there in what may be called a public character, you will soon find acquaintance, and I have no doubt friends. There is this advantage in large cities (and a great one it is), that you are sure of finding some persons there with whom it is both pleasant and profitable to associate.

"Believe me, my dear James,

"Always yours, with sincere regard,

"Robert Southey."

To Grosvenor C. Bedford, Esq.

"Keswick, Dec. 24, 1826.

"My dear Grosvenor,

"I will undertake the arrangement of the Garrick Papers very willingly for the lucre of gain, and not for the love of the subject; for the sake of being well paid, and not for the sake of being well talked of. But I will do it for lucre, for goodly remuneration, and 'most sweet guerdon,' which you know is better.

"It will take me more time to do this than it would any other person, for this simple reason—that I should take more pains about it; not in the composition, but in making myself thoroughly acquainted with all the literary points on which it would be necessary to touch. On the other hand, my general acquaintance with English literature is such, that there is no point upon which I have not some stock of knowledge at command. Less than a thousand guineas the booksellers ought not to think of offering, nor I of taking; and if there be a chance of getting more, let it be intimated that I rate my name and services as they ought to be rated. There's a magnanimous sentence! And with that sentence I leave the subject to work in the proper quarter, and to sleep with me till I hear of it again. Observe that I suppose the Life to be included in the two volumes, not to form one by itself.

* * * * * * *

"Tuesday, 26th.

"If Colburne could see my table at this time, he would think my studies were not the most appropriate for the task which he wishes me to undertake. Here is a volume of Jackson's Works (folio)—in my judgment the most valuable of all our English divines; there is a Portuguese poem, in twenty books, upon the Virgin Mary. Here is the English translation of Father Paul's History of the Council of Trent. Here is a Latin folio upon the Divi Tutelares of Popish Christendom, by the Jesuit Macedo, who had so much to do with Queen Christina's conversion. Here is a volume of Venema's Hist. Eccl. Institutiones. Here is the Report upon Emigration, and there is a thick, dumpy, and almost cubical small quarto, containing some 1400 closely-printed pages in Latin—De Miraculis Mortuorum, by an old German physician, who was moriturus himself when he composed the work. Miracula here are to be understood in the sense of phenomena. The book is exceedingly curious, and would furnish the Master of the Rolls with much matter both of amusement and cogitation, if it should ever fall in his way. I will therefore add that the author's name is Garmannus, and the date of the book 1709. Here is a volume of the Acta Sanctorum on another table, and one of Baronius on the floor.

"From this apparatus you will conclude that I have a second volume of Vindiciæ in hand.

"God bless you! R. S."

To Henry Taylor, Esq.

"Keswick, Jan. 24, 1827.

"My dear H. T.,

" * * * You do not tell me that you are better, which is what I most wish to hear. If a wish could bring you and your father here, you should see these mountains as they are now, in the full glory of snow, and clouds, and sunshine.

"I have a melancholy letter from Leyden. Mrs. Bilderdijk has been for fifteen weeks confined to her chamber, and mostly to her bed, and it is not intimated that she is recovering. B. himself speaks of his own health and faculties as sensibly impairing day by day. The only hopeful sign is the warmth and animation with which he writes. I wish I could go to see him this year; but that is not possible, and therefore I can hardly hope to meet him again in this world. I am now reading his fragment of the Deluge, and shall go through the rest of his works, in full intention of making them known, sooner or later, and, with your help, to the English readers.

"My old acquaintance (those, I mean, who were elders when I was a young man) are dropping on all sides. One very remarkable one is just gone to his rest after a pilgrimage of fourscore years. Edward Williams, the Welsh bard, whom, under his Welsh name of Iolo,* some lines in Madoc were intended to describe and

* "There went with me
Iolo, old Iolo, he who knows
The virtues of all herbs of mount or vale,
Or greenwood shade, or quiet brooklet's bed;
Whatever lore of science or of song
Sages and bards of old have handed down."
Madoc in Wales, VIII.

gratify. He was the most eccentric man I ever knew, in whose eccentricity there was no affectation, and in whose conduct there was nothing morally wrong. Poor fellow! with a wild head and a warm heart, he had the simplicity of a child and the tenderness of a woman, and more knowledge of the traditions and antiquities of his own country than it is to be feared will ever be possessed by any one after him. I could tell you some odd anecdotes of him which ought not to be lost.

"God bless you! R. S."

To Henry Taylor, Esq.

"Keswick, Jan. 31, 1827.

"My dear H. T.,

"I inclose to you a letter of thanks, which you will have the goodness to let your man leave at the United Service Club. Captain Mangles was thrown in my way here by mere chance last summer as the stage-coach companion of ——, a Quaker of a new description from Philadelphia, who brought letters to me. The Quaker was ambitious of being what Shakspeare tells us the Prince of Darkness is; so he wore black, and drank healths, and was superfine in his manners, and had with him the greatest curiosity of its kind that I have ever seen—a Quaker album, in which the spirit had moved all his Quaker acquaintance to bestow the highest eulogiums upon the happy owner, and to pray for his spiritual welfare. But the gem of the book was a composition by his royal highness the Duke of Sussex.

"The Quaker did not know the name of his traveling companion, but from his account I knew who he must be, and accordingly made the Quaker introduce him here. And the end of this is, that Captain Mangles has sent me a copy of his travels, which were printed for private distribution, and of which he could not lay his hands on a copy till now. * * * *

"I am now going to the Emigration paper, and I have taken up Oliver Newman, where I shall be *in medias res;* a little way further, and then it will become an object to complete it.

"God bless you! R. S."

To Walter Savage Landor, Esq.

"Keswick, Feb. 21, 1827.

"I know not how I have lost sight of you so long, nor whether this may find you at Florence, nor what may have befallen you in the interval since we have communicated. No such affliction, I hope, as has befallen me, in the loss of my youngest daughter. Seven months have elapsed since we suffered this bereavement. She was the flower of my family—and a lovelier flower this earth never produced. It was long before I could recover heart for any thing, and sometimes I fear that my spirits will never again be what they have been. My wife's, I have but too much cause to apprehend, have received a shock from which they will not recover. Yet we have much left for which to be thankful; and, above all, I am thankful for that settled and quiet faith which makes me look on to the end of my journey as a point of hope.

"My friend Kenyon talks of going to Italy this year, and if he goes, I shall get him to carry my last book.

"Last summer, like the one preceding, I traveled for my health. On the first occasion I came back with erysipelas (the effect of an accident), which undid the good that had been done; and the shock which awaited my return the second time in like manner counteracted the benefit I had found.

"Holland is to me a very interesting country. Except Amsterdam, which outstinks Lisbon, I like every thing in it. There is a greater appearance of domestic comfort and decent wealth, and less appearance of vice, poverty, and wretchedness, than in any other part of Europe that I have seen, and I verily believe than in any other part of the world. In prospect there is enough to sadden one, for the bright days of Holland are gone by, and there seems no likelihood—scarcely, indeed, a possibility—that they ever should return. Decay is felt there, but it is not apparent, and you must inquire and look for it before you perceive that it is going on. But the Dutch merchants are not like the English, who so generally live up to the full measure of their prosperity. In their best times they have been frugal; and they are very generally, at this time, living upon the interest of old capital, great part of which is vested in the English funds.

"You will not wonder when you call to mind in how many things the two nations resemble each other, that Dutch poetry should in its character of thought and feeling resemble English, much more than the English resembles that of any other nation, ancient or modern. Their poets have been as numerous, in proportion to the country, as their painters, and not a few of them as skillful in their art. One has two things to get over in the language, its ugliness and its difficulty: I wish I could overcome the latter as well as I have got over the first.

"While I am writing the post has brought news that Lord Liverpool has had an apoplectic stroke, which is likely to be fatal, but which certainly incapacitates him from ever taking any further part in public affairs. How often do I wish that you were in England. The curious state of things in this country can hardly be understood, even by an Englishman, at a distance; the strange complexity and contrariety of interests, the strange coalitions, the ferment of opinions, and the causes which are at work to bring about greater changes in the constitution of society than even the last half century has produced. No guess can as yet be formed as to the effect that this accident will produce upon the administration. Canning's health is broken, and, in my judgment, it would be fortunate for his reputation if this cause should prevent him from taking possession of the premiership. Every one had confidence in Lord Liverpool; there are none who will have confidence in him; with all his brilliancy of talent, with all his personal good qualities (and they are such that he is liked wherever he is known), he must ever be distrusted as a statesman. New scenes are opening upon us, new men will come forward, and some of the old ones be seen in new characters; but for statesmen, such as they are and long have been in England, there will always be an abundant supply. What can be expected as long as St. Pitt and St. Fox have their red letter days in the political calendar?

"I would give a great deal to enjoy three such days as those which I passed at Como now ten years ago.

"God bless you! R. S."

To Henry Taylor, Esq.

"Keswick, April 12, 1827.

"MY DEAR H. T.,

"If the Utilitarians would reason and write like you, they would no longer deserve to be called Futilitarians. But the metapoliticians have dealt with their branch of policy as the metaphysicians have with their branch of philosophy—they have muddied and mystified it.

"It is not the habit of my mind to despise nor to undervalue the sort of knowledge which I do not possess, but I know enough of political economy to have perceived in the father of the British school (Adam Smith) that the wealth of nations is every thing in that school, and the morality and happiness of nations nothing; and in the other writers which have fallen in my way, I have found their knowledge so little, and their presumption so great, as to excite in me a greater degree of contempt than I usually feel for any thing in the shape of a book.

"To all that you say in its general import I agree; but when you tell me that a tax of £1000 per week laid upon capitalists would have the sure effect of throwing 1000 weekly laborers out of employ, it appears to me that you suppose a connection between cause and effect, as certain as those in chemical and mechanical combinations, and overlook the infinite number of modifying and disturbing circumstances which often in chemical, and more often in political experiments, occasion some wholly unexpected result.

"I shall very soon methodize some of my views, tending to this proposition, that the prime object of our policy should be to provide for the well-being and employment of the people. Whatever lessens wages and throws men out of employ is so far an evil. There may be evil that leads to good, and good that leads to evil, and both may be instanced in the effects of machinery. If you like to see my speculations as they go through the press, let Murray direct the proofs of my Colloquies to you, and I will perpend any comments that you may make upon their contents. * * * * *

"I have been asked to write for the Foreign Quarterly, and replied, as willingly as for John Murray, *at the same price*. An attempt was then made to wheedle me into giving them an article for their first number at ten guineas a sheet; or, if that failed, then they would screw up their price to £50 for the article. I answered, not in the style of Jupiter Tonans, but *more meo*, that I wrote such things for lucre, and for nothing else, and that, if they had screwed their price to the sticking point, I certainly should not lower mine to meet it. * * This brought an apology for tradesman-like dealing, and a hope that I would be pleased to accept the £100. To which I condescended, saying that the manner of dealing belonging to the race was to be looked upon in the individuals as a sort of original sin.

"The Royal Society of Literature have voted me a gold medal, and asked me to come and receive it. I thank them for the medal, but decline the journey. * * * * *

"God bless you! R. S."

To Henry Taylor, Esq.

"Keswick, April 23, 1827.

"MY DEAR H. T.,

" * * * * * * *

No inference concerning Ireland can be drawn from the state of Canada, where we have continued the system which we found there, and where I am inclined to think there is a better condition of society than is likely to be found in the Upper Province. Look at the evidence concerning Maynooth College, and you will see that it has produced and could produce nothing but evil.

"In Scotland the *general* condition of the clergy is above the standard in England. In villages and remote places, indeed, the manse is generally the best house, perhaps the only good one, and appears like a mansion in comparison with the dwellings about it. Still the Kirk has been injured by spoliation, and the manner in which Episcopacy was betrayed there at the Revolution is one of the stains upon that portion of our history. It would have been better for the Scotch if a proportion of their clergy had been drawn from the higher ranks. There would have been less bigotry in the Kirk, and more learning, of which there has been a lack. I doubt whether the Kirk has produced half a dozen works worthy of preservation. Sure I am that I could name a score of English divines, any one of whose writings would weigh down in sterling worth all that has ever come from the Kirk of Scotland since Episcopacy was abolished, for Leighton was of their Episcopal Church.

"The prizes of our Church draw into it unfit men; yet it is a small part of the prizes which falls to their share; and I think that, in proportion, more unworthy clergy will be found in the middle and lower than in the higher ranks of the Church. The evil (an evil certainly there is) is corrigible by public opinion. You will see that I have touched upon it.

"God bless you! R. S."

To John Rickman, Esq.

"Keswick, April 23, 1827.

"MY DEAR R.,

"Among all the ups and downs which you

have witnessed in this country in the course of five-and-twenty years, you have never, I think, seen things more in what lawyers call hotch-potch than they are at present. Who is right and who wrong I have little means of knowing, and as little curiosity to know. But I think Canning an unsafe minister, and doubt whether any administration which he can form can stand, with such strong interests and strong feelings as will be arrayed against it.

"The prospect is discouraging enough both at home and abroad. I can not but apprehend that we have got ourselves into a situation in Portugal from which it will not be easy to withdraw without some loss of reputation. Every one who knows the Portuguese must know that they are neither in a humor nor in a state to receive a new Constitution; and if Don Miguel likes a journey to Madrid better than a voyage to Brazil, we shall find ourselves fooled by France, laughed at by Spain, and on no desirable terms with Portugal.

"Then at home we have to contend with the effects of the liberal system in trade, with the march of intellect, and the consequences of the manufacturing system. The new ministry will not sleep upon roses. Canning, I think, will not last long, whether he maintains his ascendency or not. At the time of Lord Londonderry's death, his friends, I know, thought that his health would not stand the wear and tear of public business, if it should be of a harassing kind; and, therefore, they rather wished he had gone to India at that time.

"I mean to take my family to Harrogate about the latter end of next month for three or four weeks. The place is ugly; but there are interesting objects to be seen, and if my womankind are the better for the waters and the excursion, I shall be content to drink stinking water instead of the ordinary wine on the other side of the Channel. * * * * * *

"God bless you! R. S."

To Henry Taylor, Esq.

"Keswick, May 5, 1827.

"MY DEAR FRIEND,

" * * * * Machiavelli has shown you why Mitford (had there been no French Revolution) would have sided with the tyrants instead of the democracies of Greece in his history. Read the history of any despotism, and your feelings become republican; read that of any republic, and you become monarchical. The happiest age of the world, as far as its happiness depends upon earthly governments, was that of the Antonines, and the reign of Augustus before it; and we all know to what these reigns led, not accidentally, but by the sure effects of such a system. As far as relates to government and religion, this country is the most favored under heaven; not only above all others at this time, but above all others of any time. But our prosperity was hardly won, and is not two centuries old. The Venetian was the most durable of European governments, and an infernal one it was, though it was the object of admiration to the Liberals of the Great Rebellion.

"The great works of the Egyptians, Greeks, Romans, and Spanish Moors were *not* erected in barbarous ages, but in times of very high civilization. Taxation, probably, was not far short of its present amount; the Moors had a tenth of all produce and rents, and wars cost the government nothing, so that there was revenue to spare. God bless you!

"Yours affectionately, R. S."

To the Rev. Neville White.

"Keswick, May 5, 1827.

"MY DEAR NEVILLE,

* * * * * * *

"I do not see how these ministerial changes can affect my brother Tom's future prospects. * * * My means have always been precarious. My books are less productive than they were ten years ago; very materially so, as Longman could tell you. Their novelty is gone by, and, with all the reputation which I have fairly won, I have never been a fashionable, still less a popular author. At the end of the first twelve month's sale my profits upon the Tale of Paraguay fell short of eighty pounds. I have, God be thanked, been able to make a moderate provision for my family, but not by any thing that I have laid by; solely by my life insurance, my books, copy-rights, and papers. In other respects I am in a worse situation than I was ten or fifteen years ago. My poems had then a much greater sale, and I stood upon better ground in the Quarterly Review. * * * * * * I am writing a paper at present for the first number of a Foreign Quarterly; possibly it is the last that I may ever write for a review. There was an engagement which might have enabled me at once to have come to this resolution, but the last year's failure compelled the publisher to recede from it. I do not, however, expect any difficulty in renewing it elsewhere, and have no fear that that Providence which has hitherto made the labor of the day sufficient for its support, will withdraw from me its continued blessing. * * * I have always done for my brother Tom all I could, and not seldom to my own embarrassment in so doing. * * *

"The question about National Education you will see discussed in my Colloquies, when they are completed. Here is the gist of the question. The human mind is like the earth, which never lies idle. You have a piece of garden ground. Neglect it, and it will be covered with weeds, useless to yourself and noxious to your neighbors. To lay it out in flowers and shrubbery is what you do not want. Cultivate it, then, for common fruits and culinary plants. So with poor children Why should they be made worse servants, worse laborers, worse mechanics, for being taught their Bible, their Christian duties, and the elements of useful knowledge? I am no friend of the London University, nor to Mechanics' Institutes. There is a purpose in all these things of excluding religion, and preparing the way for the overthrow of the Church. But God will confound their devices; and my principle is, that where a religious foundation is laid, the more education the better. Will you have the lower class *Christians* or *brutes?* * *

"God bless you, my dear friend!

"Yours affectionately, R. S."

The great question concerning National Education has made rapid strides since these letters were written; and it is more than ever necessary that all who value the Christian character of the nation should strenuously exert themselves, both in promoting religious education and in preventing an irreligious one. There are several highly interesting letters in the second volume of Dr. Arnold's Life, showing that he laid down principles almost identically the same as that stated here, and resigned his fellowship of the London University because its constitution "did not satisfy the great principle that Christianity should be the base of all public education in the country."

Dr. Arnold's mode of working out this theory would have been different to that which my father would have advocated; but it is very worthy of remark, that even he, whose views of "Church principles" were so very peculiar, and so far removed from those commonly held by "Churchmen," acknowledged and insisted upon it.

CHAPTER XXXI.

VISIT TO HARROGATE—ALBUM VERSES—LORD COLCHESTER—CONSTITUTIONAL BASHFULNESS—THE PROSPECT OF ANOTHER LIFE THE ONLY SOLID FOUNDATION FOR HAPPINESS—PROPOSES TO COLLECT HIS POLITICAL ESSAYS—MR. CANNING—HOME POLITICS—PROJECTED LIFE OF WOLFE—GROUND OF HIS OPINIONS—MR. MAY—MR. COTTLE—MR. KING—INTERCOURSE WITH MR. WORDSWORTH'S FAMILY—THE QUARTERLY REVIEW—DESIRABLENESS OF PUTTING AN END TO IMPRISONMENT FOR SMALL DEBTS—DISAGREEABLE DUTIES REQUIRED FROM PUBLIC OFFICERS—ANCIENT STATUTES—UNDERTAKES TO EDIT THE VERSES OF AN OLD SERVANT—BISHOP HEBER—DIFFICULTIES OF A REMOVAL—THE PENINSULAR WAR—ENGAGES TO CONTRIBUTE TO THE KEEPSAKE—URGES MR. BEDFORD TO VISIT KESWICK—GOES TO LONDON—SITS TO SIR THOMAS LAWRENCE AND SIR F. CHANTREY—TRANSLATION OF DAVILA NOT LIKELY TO SUCCEED—HIS UNCLE'S DEATH—CHOICE OF A FEW STANDARD ENGLISH WORKS—HIS SON'S STUDIES—JACKSON'S SERMONS—LIFE OF NELSON—DECLINING SALE OF HIS WORKS—VISIT FROM LIEUT. MAWE—INTEREST IN MR. MAY'S AFFAIRS—REMARKS ON THE ANNUALS—NEW THEORY OF THE WEATHER—LITERARY EMPLOYMENTS—INTENDED VISIT TO THE ISLE OF MAN.—1827–1828.

MY father had now for some years found that a summer journey was absolutely necessary for his health, especially for the purpose of warding off, or at least breaking the violence of, the "hay asthma;" a complaint which, by its regular periodical visitations, seemed to have rooted itself in his system, and threatened to undermine his constitution.

His greatest delight and most complete relaxation was, as we have seen, a foreign excursion; but, finding that several of his household required some change of air, he determined to take them to Harrogate, where he had the additional inducement of being joined by Mr. Wordsworth and some of his family.

From thence he writes in somewhat low spirits respecting a distressing infirmity which had now afflicted him for many years, and latterly had rendered all walking exercise extremely painful, and from which he had not at that time any hopes of being relieved.

To Grosvenor C. Bedford, Esq.

"Harrogate, June 10, 1827.

"MY DEAR GROSVENOR,

" * * * * * * *

At my age there can be no expectation that time will remove any bodily infirmity. The probability is, that I shall, ere long, be totally unable to walk; and to look for any chance of good fortune that would set me upon wheels, would be something like looking for a miracle. I am thankful, therefore, that my disposition and sedentary habits will render the confinement which appears to await me a less evil than it would be to most other persons. The latter years of our earthly existence can be but few at the most, and evil at the best; but he who is grateful for the past, and has his hopes in futurity, may very well be patient under any present privations, and any afflictions of which the end is in view.

"There is enough in this neighborhood to repay me for a short tarriance here, even with the discomforts which, especially in my case, are felt always in an absence from home. As yet I have only seen William Herbert's garden, where there is a splendid display of exotics; the grounds at Plumpton, where the rocks very much resemble the scenery of Fontainebleau; the cave where Eugene Aram buried the body of Daniel Clarke; the hermitage carved in the rock at Knaresborough; and the dropping well, which, in my childhood, I longed to see, as one of the wonders of England. Knaresborough is very finely situated, and I should spend some of my mornings in exploring all the points of view about it if I were able to move about with ease. I wish you were here; the place itself is pleasanter than I had expected to find it. We are on a common, with a fine, dry, elastic air; so different from that of Keswick, that the difference is perceptible in breathing it, and a wide horizon, which in its evening skies affords something to compensate for the scenery we have left. The air would, I verily believe, give you new life, and among the variety of springs there is choice of all kinds for you. * * * * * *

"So much for Harrogate. Now for a word or two concerning my own pursuits. You will or may, if you please, see a paper of mine upon the Moorish History of Spain in the first number of the Foreign Quarterly, when it is published. The Foreign Quarterly pays me £100 for my paper, but I do not calculate upon doing any thing more for it. There are hardly readers enough who care for foreign literature to support a journal exclusively devoted to it, certainly not enough to make it a very lucrative speculation; and unless it were so, it could not afford to pay me as I am accustomed to be paid.

"A lady here, whom we never saw, nor ever before heard of, sent her album for Wordsworth and myself to write in, with no other preliminaries than desiring the physician here, Dr. Jaques, to ask leave for her! When the book came, it proved to be full of pious effusions from all the most noted Calvinist preachers and missionaries. As some of these worthies had written in it texts in Hebrew, Chinese, and Arabic, I wrote in Greek, 'If we say that we have no sin,' &c., and I did *not* write in it these lines, which the tempting occasion suggested:

"What? will-we, nill-we, are we thrust
Among the Calvinistics—
The covenanted sons of schism,
Rebellion's pugilistics.
Needs must we then ourselves array
Against these state tormentors;
Hurrah for Church and King, we say,
And down with the Dissenters.

"Think how it would have astonished the fair owner to have opened her album, and found these verses in it, signed by R. S. and W. W.

"It will be charity to write to me while I am here, where, for want of books, I spell the newspaper. God bless you! R. S."

To John Rickman, Esq.

"Keswick, July 30, 1827.

"MY DEAR RICKMAN,

"I am out of humor with myself respecting Lord Colchester,* as if from shyness on my part there had been a want of due attention to him. He called on his arrival to thank me for having made all arrangements for his movement in this neighborhood, and came just as I had a party assembling for dinner; and having that party, I did not, of course, ask him for the evening, which otherwise I should have done. The next day I went to his inn a little after seven in the evening, meaning, if he had not been wearied with the round which he had taken, to have asked him to drink tea in a pleasanter room than the inn affords. But he proved to be at dinner, for which reason I merely left my card; and then, because his rank stood in the way, and made me fearful of appearing to press myself upon him, I did not write a note to invite him up, which I should have done had he been Mr. Abbott. The next day brought me a very obliging note from him, after his departure. He has had from us good directions and commissariat services, but not that personal attention which I wished to have paid him.

"In this way, through a constitutional bashfulness, which the publicity of authorship has not overcome, and through the sort of left-handed management (I do not mean *sinister*) which that bashfulness occasions, I have repeatedly appeared neglectful of others', and have really been so of my own interests. Upon the score of such neglect, no man living has more cause for reproach than I have; but it passes off with only a transitory sense of inward shame, occurring more or less painfully when occasion calls to mind some particular sin of omission.

* * * * * * *

"I believe, my dear R., that most men, by the time they have reached our age, are ready, whatever their pursuits may have been, to agree with Solomon, that they end in vanity. If they are not mere clods, muck-worms, they come to this conclusion—wealth, reputation, power, are alike unsatisfactory when they are attained, alike insufficient to content the heart of man, which is ever discontented till it has found its rest. This it finds in the prospect of immortality, in the anticipation of a state where there shall be no change, except such as is implied in perpetual progression. When we have learned to look forward with that hope, then we look back upon the past without regret, and are able to bear the present, however heavy and painful sometimes may be its pressure. There is no other support for a broken spirit—no other balm for a wounded heart.

"You have overworked yourself, which I have ever been afraid of doing. The wonder is that you have not suffered more severely and irremediably; and that, while so working, you should have yet been able to lay in that knowledge of other kinds which renders you (as I have found you during well-nigh thirty years) the most instructive of all companions. Ant-like, you have toiled during the summer, and have stored your nest: my summer work leaves me as little prepared for winter as the grasshopper; but this is rather my fortune than my fault, and therefore no matter of self-reproach.

"What you have to do is to extricate yourself from all unnecessary and ungrateful business, and give the time which you may thus gain to more healthful and genial pursuits—books, to which inclination would lead you, and, above all, traveling. I wish you could have gone with Henry Taylor and his father—a man whom you would especially like; still more do I wish you would come here and take a course of mountaineering—upon which I should very gladly enter, and which would be to my bodily benefit. And then we might talk at leisure and at will over the things of this world and the next.

"God bless you, my dear friend! R. S."

To John Rickman, Esq.

"Keswick, August 15, 1827.

"MY DEAR RICKMAN,

"I am about to reprint in a separate form

* Mr. Rickman had written to tell him that Lord Colchester was going to the Lakes, and intended calling upon him, and requesting him to give him some information as to the best mode of seeing the country.

such of my stray papers as are worth collecting from the Quarterly Review, &c., beginning with two volumes of Essays, Moral and Political. For this I have the double motive of hoping to gain something by the publication,* and wishing to leave them in a corrected state. Shall I print with them your remarks upon the economical reformers in the Edinburgh Annual Register of 1810, and your paper upon the Poor Laws? Certainly not if you have any intention of collecting your own papers, which I wish you would do. But if you have no such intention, or contemplate it at an indefinite distance, then it would be well that so much good matter should be placed where it would be in the way of being read; and there I should like it to be as some testimony and memorial of an intimacy which has now for thirty years contributed much to my happiness, and, in no slight degree, to my intellectual progress. In this case I will take care to notice that the credit of these papers is not due to me, either specifying whose they are, or leaving that unexplained, as you may like best.

* * * * * * *

"Your foresight concerning poor Mr. Canning has been sadly realized. Sorry I am for him, as every one must be who had any knowledge of the better part of his character. But I know that his death is not to be regretted, either for his own sake or that of the country, for he had filled his pillow with thorns, and could never again have laid down his head in peace. I do not disturb mine with speculating what changes may or may not follow; nor, in truth, with any anxieties about them. Perhaps it may be desirable that the Whigs should be allowed rope enough, and left to plunge deeper and deeper in the slough of their Irish difficulties. They can never satisfy the Macs and the great O's without conceding every thing which those gentlemen please to demand, and that can not be done without bringing on a civil war.

"I am about to write a Life of General Wolfe,† which will be prefixed to his letters. The letters will disappoint every one. Can you tell me or direct me to any thing that may assist me in it? There is the taking of Loisbourg, and the campaign in which he fell. The rest must be made up by showing the miserable state of the army; his merits as a disciplinarian, being in those days very great; my memorabilia concerning Canada, abundance of which are marked in books which I read long since, and by whatever other garnish I can recollect. My pay for the task-work is to be 300 guineas.

"God bless you! R. S."

To Henry Taylor, Esq.

"Keswick, Sept. 13, 1827.

"My dear H. T.,

"I am sorry to hear that cares have been knocking at your door; they must have gone out of their way, methinks, to call there. I thought that you had no thorns either in your sides or your pillow. Tidings after an absence of a few weeks afford, indeed, at all times, matter for uneasy apprehension; and if you and I had this to learn, the two journeys which we have taken together would have taught it us.

"I found a great want of you (as they say in this country) during your absence. One likes to have one's friends in a local habitation, where at any time they may be found; to be out of reach is too like being out of the world. It often came into my thoughts that, if H. T. were in London, I should have written to him upon such and such occasions, and quite as often that I should have had some brief notices of the strange turns of the wheel.

"You distrust opinions, you tell me, when you perceive a strong tenor of feeling in the writer who maintains them. The distrust is reasonable, and is especially to be borne in mind in reading history. My opinions are (thank God!) connected with strong feelings concerning them, but not such as can either disturb my temper or cloud my discernment, much less pervert what I will venture to call the natural equity of my mind. I proceed upon these postulates: 1. That revealed religion is true; 2. That the connection between Church and State is necessary; 3. That the Church of England is the best ecclesiastical establishment which exists at present, or has yet existed; 4. That both Church and State require great amendments; 5. That both are in great danger; and, 6. That a revolution would destroy the happiness of one generation, and leave things at last worse than it found them.

"If our institutions are worth preserving, we can not be attached to them too strongly, remembering always that the only way to preserve them is by keeping them in good repair. The two duties upon which I insist are those of conservation and improvement. We must improve our institutions if we would preserve them; but if any go to work upon the foundations, down must come the building.

"How is it possible to reflect upon the history of former times without inquiring what have been the good and evil consequences of the course which things have taken at the age which you are considering? It is, surely, no useless speculation to inquire whether good results which have been dearly purchased might not have been obtained at less cost. If I were to build a house, I should consult my neighbor, who might tell me how I might go to work more advantageously than he had done. *What might have been* is a profitable subject for speculation, because it may be found useful for what yet *may be*.

"God bless you! R. S."

To John May, Esq.

"Keswick, Sept. 15, 1827.

"My dear Friend,

" * * * I can very well enter

* This hope was not realized; they never paid their expenses!

† This intention was never carried into effect, it being found impossible to procure sufficient materials.

into the melancholy part of your feelings upon this transplantation to a strange city, though that city is to me the place in the world, as far as mere place can go, where I should feel myself most at home. *Where* is your bank, and where your dwelling-house? Tell me, that I may see them in my mind's eye when I think of you. I never thought to have seen Bristol again; but, now that you are there, I may find in my heart to revisit it, and show you the houses where my childhood and youth were passed.

"You ought to become acquainted with my old friend Joseph Cottle, the best-hearted of men, with whom my biographical letters will one day have much to do. It would give him great pleasure to see any one with whom he could talk about me. Make an hour's leisure some day and call upon him, and announce yourself to him and his sisters as my friend. You will see a notable portrait of me before my name was shorn, and become acquainted with one who has a larger portion of original *goodness* than falls to the lot of most men.

"I would have you know King, the surgeon, also, with whom I lived in great intimacy, and for whom I have a great and sincere regard. His wife is sister to Miss Edgeworth. A more remarkable man is rarely to be found, and his professional skill is very great.

"These are the only friends in Bristol who are left to me, and perhaps I can say nothing that will recommend them more to you than when I add that they are both warmly attached to me.

"Now for my household and personal concerns. The Harrogate expedition answered its purpose in some degree for us all. * * Your god-daughter has been living a most active life between this place and Rydal Mount, with which a constant interchange of visits has been going on since our return, not to speak of occasional meetings half way; and for a mountain excursion with the Bishop of Chester, who went up Saddleback with us last week. My hay asthma was not prevented by the journey, but it was shortened. I escaped with a visit of one month instead of a visitation of three, and am willing to think that the last two years, by cutting the disease short, have weakened its habit and shaken its hold. The Harrogate waters have also materially benefited my digestion, so that, on the whole, though far from a sound man, I am in better condition than for some time past.

"The Quarterly Review and I have made up our differences, and my paper, which had been unceremoniously postponed since January last, leads the van in the new number. I learn from John Coleridge that his mind is made up in favor of what is called Catholic Emancipation, and therefore I am very glad the Review is in other hands; for, if it had taken that side, I should certainly have withdrawn from it, and have done every thing in my power to support a journal upon my own principles, which as certainly would have been started; and which, in fact, has been prevented from starting by my refusal to conduct it, on the ground that the Quarterly Review will keep its course. I am reviewing Hallam's Constitutional History for the Christmas number, and have engaged to review Barantes's History of the Dukes of Burgundy for the Foreign Quarterly. Gillies, a nephew of the historian, is the projector of this, and edits it conjointly with a Mr. Frazer, whom I know only by letter. Scott writes in it. * * *

"God bless you!

"Yours most affectionately, R. S."

To John Rickman, Esq.

"Keswick, Sept. 18, 1827.

"MY DEAR RICKMAN,

" * * * Your scheme for putting an end to previous imprisonment for all minor offenses has always seemed to me one of the most practicable and useful suggestions that has ever been offered for preventing much evil and saving much expense. And I can not but hope it will be carried into effect, in the way of which good it will at least be put by bringing it again forward.

"Wordsworth, in his capacity of Stamp Distributor, received a circular lately requiring him to employ persons to purchase soda powders when sold without a stamp, and then lay an information against the venders. It seems as if they were resolved so to reduce the emolument in the public services, and connect such services with them, that no one with the habits and feelings of a gentleman shall enter or continue in it.

"Mr. N. breakfasted with me, and we talked of you and Mr. Telford. He maintained what seemed to me a most untenable assertion, that pauperism has decreased since the Restoration, and says the returns prove this. Now it is certain that the poor-laws were not so misapplied as to breed paupers till within our own times; nor did the manufacturers in those days increase and multiply in whole districts.

"In looking through the statutes of Henry VII., I have found that an abatement or allowance, as it is called, of '£6000 in every fifteenth and tenth (*i. e.*, upon the two), was made in relief, comfort, and discharge of the poor towns, cities, and burghs in the realm, wasted, desolate, and destroyed, or over greatly impoverished, or else to such fifteenth or tenth over greatly charged.' This allowance to be divided according to former example. I will hunt this subject back, and endeavor to ascertain whether a deduction was made from the impost on the money distributed in relief.

"The statutes, I clearly see, have not yet been read as you have taught me to read. Though I have only examined this reign, several curious inferences have appeared which I believe others have neglected to make. I find a disposition in the older laws to keep the lower classes in castes, making the child follow his father's calling, and a law allowing no one to be apprenticed in any town, unless the parents had lands or rent to the amount of £20 a year. The laws opposed the strong desire of bettering their condition, which the laboring people manifested, and the only liberty allowed was of breeding their children to learning. Henry VII. repealed the restrictions upon apprenticeship, upon the petition of the Norwich people, but for that city only, going to work experimentally in his laws.

"I learn, too, that the cross-bow would have superseded the bow and arrow, even if fire-arms had not been introduced, and that there was a great anxiety to keep that weapon from the people. The higher orders had an obvious interest in continuing the use of those weapons which were least effective against armor; and the cross-bow, like the musket, was a leveler a weak hand could discharge; it required as little practice as a gun, and generally went with surer aim than the arrow, perhaps with greater force.

"H. T. tells me that Huskisson's health can never stand the fatigue of his Parliamentary business. Do not you overwork yourself, however much it may be the taste of ministers and post-horses to be so sacrificed.

"God bless you! R. S."

During the few weeks my father passed at Harrogate in the early part of the summer, he received an application from a poet in humble life, John Jones by name, to peruse and give his opinion of some poems. He was struck with the simple-hearted frankness of the writer, and with the feeling and natural piety displayed in his verses, and he replied to him in such a manner as to give encouragement to a further communication of his productions; and finally he undertook to edit a small volume of poems, prefacing it by a biographical sketch of the lives of uneducated poets.

As in many other cases, his good nature in this one drew on him much more expenditure of time and trouble than he at first anticipated; but he thought himself well repaid by the perfect happiness he had been the means of affording Jones, and by his warm gratitude, and also by having been enabled to put him in possession of a sum of money which might assist in procuring comforts for his latter years. Some further particulars concerning him will be found in the following letters.

To Grosvenor C. Bedford, Esq.

"Keswick, Oct. 31, 1827.

"My dear Grosvenor,

" * * * Thank you for the interest you take in my scheme for serving honest John Jones. There is no one point, Grosvenor, in which you and I accord more entirely than in our feelings concerning servants, and our behavior toward them. The savings' bank may do for this class all, or almost all, that you desire, if there be but religious education to give them an early sense of duty, which I think it will be more easy to give than to bring about the desired amendment in the behavior of their superiors. To amend that, there must be a thorough reform in our schools, public and private, which should cut up the tyranny of the boys over their juniors by the roots.

"You have seen exactly in the true light what my views and motives are with regard to Jones. I want to read a wholesome lecture in this age of Mechanics' Institutes and of University College. I want to show how much moral and intellectual improvement is within the reach of those who are made more our inferiors than there is any necessity that they should be, to show that they have minds to be enlarged, and feelings to be gratified, as well as souls to be saved, which is the only admission that some persons are willing to make, and that grudgingly enough; and if I can, by so doing, put a hundred pounds into Jones's pocket (which, if a few persons will bestir themselves for me, there is every likelihood of doing,) I shall have the satisfaction of giving him a great deal of happiness for a time, and of rendering him some substantial benefit also. * * * * *

"Did you see my paper upon the Spanish Moors in the Foreign Quarterly? I have another to write for one of the journals into which it has split, upon M. de Barantes's History of the Ducs de Bourgogne. This and a paper upon the Emigration Report for the Quarterly Review will be taken in hand immediately on my return. Lope de Vega will arrive about the 15th, and I look for a noble importation from Brussels before Christmas, consisting of the books which I purchased there last year, and others of which a list was left with Verbeyst, the best of booksellers, who gives me, when I deal with him, as good Rhenish as my 'dear heart' could desire, and better strong beer than ever hero drank in Valhalla out of the skull of his enemy.
* * * * *

"We are fitting up an additional room for books, and if you do not next year come to see me in my glory among them, why you will commit a sin of omission for which you will not forgive yourself when it is no longer to be repaired.

"God bless you! R. S."

To Mrs. Hodson.

"Keswick, Nov. 16, 1827

"My dear Madam,

"Mr. Charles Hodson may, perhaps, have told you that I was likely to bring forward the rhymes of an old servant for publication by subscription, and that, in that case, it was my intention to solicit your assistance in procuring names for my list.

"The man's name is John Jones—it could not be a more unpoetical one, but he could not help it—the Muses have forgiven him for it, and so I hope will you. He lives with Mr. Bruere of Kirkby Hall, near Catterick, and has served the family faithfully for twenty years. Mr. Otter (the biographer of Dr. Clark) assures me of this. Jones is just of my age, in his fifty-fourth year. If I can get a tolerably good list of subscribers, I will offer the list and the book to Murray, and get what I can for it. The price may be from 7*s.* 6*d.* to 10*s.* If we have any good success, something may be obtained which would assist him in the decline of life.

"Do not suppose that I present him to notice as a heaven-born genius, and that I have found another Bloomfield. There is enough to show that Nature had given him the eye, and the ear, and the heart of a poet; and this is sufficient for my purpose; quite so to render any reader satisfied that he has bestowed his bounty well in subscribing to the volume. The good sense and good feeling of the man are worth more than his genius; and my intention is to take the opportunity for showing how much intellectual enjoyment, and moral improvement in consequence, is within the reach of persons in the very humblest ways of life; and this moral cultivation, instead of unfitting them for their station, tends to make them perform their duties more diligently and more cheerfully; and this I mean to oppose to the modern march of intellect, directed as that is with the worst intentions and to the worst ends. This will be the subject of my introduction, with some remarks upon the poetry of uneducated men. Jones tells his own story, and I am sure you will be pleased with it and his manner of telling it, and with the simplicity and good sense of his letters.

"Reginald Heber's Journal (his East Indian one) will very soon be published. There was a man whom the world could very ill spare; but his works and his example will live after him. Alas! the works of the wicked survive them also; but the example of their lives too often is forgotten. My household desire their kindest remembrances to you and Mr. Hodson, to whom I beg mine also. We were some of us much the better for the Harrogate waters, and, indeed, I myself continue to feel the benefit which I derived from them.

"Believe me, my dear madam,

"Yours, with sincere regard,

"ROBERT SOUTHEY."

My father's residence at Keswick placed him so much out of the world, that his friends naturally often endeavored to persuade him to move nearer London, not only because they wished to have more frequent opportunities of seeing him, but also because they thought a less remote part of the country would be better in many respects, both for himself and his family.

But the time was now past when such a change was practicable. He was, as it were, fast anchored by his large library; and this, with other causes, combined to keep him to the end in his mountain home.

In the following letter he refers to a possible motive for removal. What this was does not appear, but from other letters I conjecture it to have been the chance of one of his daughters settling in the south.

To Henry Taylor, Esq.

"Keswick, Nov. 22, 1827.

MY DEAR H. T.,

"My lease expires in the spring of 1831. So long, if I should live so long, I shall certainly remain where I am, and indeed, at this time the house is undergoing some alterations to render it more habitable in its worst parts, and to afford more accommodation for my books, the last cargo from Verbeyst's being on the way. The obstacles to a removal afterward are so great on the score of inclination, inconvenience, and expense, that, among all possible chances, I see but one which will overcome them. * * Supposing the motives to exist, and the obstacles to be surmountable, Bath is the place on which I should fix. I should like my old age to be passed in the scenes of my childhood, and if I am not to sleep the ιερον υπνον with my children here, I should wish to be gathered to my fathers.

"I hardly think you would be sorry if I produced another such volume of controversy as the Vindiciæ, of which historical and philosophical disquisition would be the meat, and controversy only the seasoning; for the form of a second volume is what I should choose, having, in fact, begun one sixteen months ago, and made abundant notes for it.

"It is very certain that, when two sets of cutthroats played their favorite game against each other during the Peninsular War, my wishes were always with the Spanish party, though they might have been just as great ruffians as the other. But, surely, I have neither dissembled nor extenuated the cruelties of the Spaniards; and it is upon the leaders of the French army that my reproach falls, who had their full share in Bonaparte's guilt. I have *not* relied rashly upon Spanish and Portuguese authorities, but the scale on which I have related events in which the British army had no share is not what —— likes. * * * * I take my side, and that warmly, but my desire is to be just, and so far strictly impartial. Now when I add that in proceeding with my third volume I shall bear your observations in mind, you will not do me the injustice to suppose that they needed, or could need, any thing like an apology.

"It would have been well for me if I had always had friends as able and as willing to stand forward in my defense as you are. But I have had back-friends instead, as well as enemies. They have done me some injury, as far as regards the sale of my books; other harm it has been out of their power to do. My character is not mistaken by those who know me; and for the world at large (the world! that little portion of it, I mean, which concerns itself with such things), it may safely be left to the sure decision of time. Under more favorable circumstances I might have accomplished more and better things. But when the grave-digger has put me to bed, and covered me up, it will not be long before it will be perceived and acknowledged that there are few who have done so much. * * *

"God bless you!

"Yours affectionately,

"R. S."

To Allan Cunningham, Esq.

"Keswick, Feb. 24, 1828.

"My dear Allan Cunningham,

"I will do any thing for you;* but I wish you had been fifteen days earlier in your application; for just so long ago young Reynolds (son of the dramatist) called here, and, introducing himself by a letter, then introduced Charles Heath. Charles Heath proceeded expeditiously to business, presented me with a 'Keepsake' from his pocket, said that he had been into Scotland for the express purpose of securing Sir Walter's aid, that he had succeeded, that he now came to ask for mine, and should be happy to give me fifty guineas for any thing with which I would supply him. Money—money, you know, makes the mare go—and what, after all, is Pegasus but a piece of horse-flesh? I sold him, at that price, a pig in a poke; a roaster would have contented him: 'perhaps it might prove a porker,' I said; improvident fellow as I was not to foresee that it would grow to the size of a bacon pig before it came into his hands! I sold him a ballad-poem entitled 'All for Love, or a Sinner well Saved,' of which one-and-twenty stanzas were then written. I have added fifty since, and am only half way through the story. It is a very striking one, and he means to have an engraving made from it. First come, first served, is a necessary rule in life; but if I could have foreseen that you would come afterward, the rule should have been set aside; he might have had something else, and the bacon pig should have been yours.

"Heath said that Sharpe was about to start a similar work of the same size and upon the same scale of expense: this, I take it for granted, is yours; and he seemed to expect that these larger Annuals would destroy the dwarf plants. The Amulet will probably survive, because it has chosen a walk of its own, and a safe one. The Bijou is likely to fall, as Lord Goderich's administration did, for want of cordiality among the members concerned in it. Alaric will hold out like a Goth. Ackerman understands the art of selling his wares, and has, in that respect, an advantage over most of his rivals. Friendship's Offering is perhaps in the worst way. But these matters concern not the present business, which is—what can I do for you? One of two things.

"I can finish for you an Ode upon a Gridiron,† which is an imitation of Pindar, treating the subject as he treats his, heroically and mythologically, and representing both the manner and character of his poetry more closely than could be done in a composition of which the subject was serious. I should tell you that though I think very well of this myself, it is more likely to please a few persons very much than to be generally relished.

"Or, I can write for you a life of John Fox the Martyrologist, which may, I think, be comprised in five or six-and-twenty of your pages. This, however, you can not have in less than three months from this time.

"Now, take your choice; and, remember, that when you go into your own country, you are to make Keswick in your way, and halt with me.

"Yours with sincere regard,

"Robert Southey.

"Heath has sold 15,000 of the Keepsake, and has bespoken 4000 yards of silk for binding the next volume!!!"

To Grosvenor C. Bedford, Esq.

"Keswick, March 30, 1828.

"My dear Grosvenor,

"There used to be a quicker interchange of letters between you and me when we were younger, and each, with less to think of, had a great deal more to say.

"I think you will see me, God willing, about the third week in May; but my way is not as yet quite clear, nor am I sure what stoppages it may be expedient to make upon the road. The only sure thing is, that I shall remain as short a time as possible in and about town, having to make a wide western circuit on the way home. I should take this circuit with much greater satisfaction if you would make a good, honest, hearty engagement to meet me at Keswick on my arrival there. The man Grosvenor ought to bear in mind that neither he, nor the man Southey, have any right to put off things from year to year, in reliance upon the continuance of life and ability; that they are both on the high road to threescore, both in that stage of existence in which all flesh may fitlier be called hay than grass, because the blossom is over, and the freshness, and the verdure, and the strength are past. But let us meet while we can. Nothing would do more good both to Miss Page and you than to pass your autumn here, and nothing would do me more good than to have you here.

"The paper upon Emigration in this last Quarterly Review is mine, or, rather, upon the causes which render a regulated emigration necessary. Our fabric of society, Grosvenor, is somewhat in the condition that the Brunswick Theater was before the crash—too much weight suspended from the roof; and, to make things worse, we allow all sort of undermining, and are willing to let every thing be removed that was erected for securing the building. They talk, I see, of abolishing the Exchequer. I will forgive them if they do it in time to emancipate you; yet I wish you to have the next step first, and then, Grosvenor, peradventure you may be the last auditor, and I the last laureate. Well, it will matter little to us when we are in the Ghost: you will not haunt Palace Yard, and I shall not haunt the levee.

"God bless you! * * * *

"R. S."

In the last letter my father speaks of an in-

* Mr. Cunningham at this time had accepted the editorship of Sharpe's forthcoming annual, called The Anniversary.

† This fragment, which has not been published before, will be found in the Appendix.

tended visit to London. His object in this was two-fold, and neither of them of a cheerful kind: the first, to see his uncle, Mr. Hill, for the last time, who, at the age of seventy-nine, was rapidly approaching his latter end; the second, to place himself under the surgeon's hands for the removal, if possible, of the infirmity I have before alluded to.

With respect to this latter intention, his careful consideration for the feelings of others was strongly shown. Knowing the weak state of my mother's spirits, and the natural anxiety which all his family would feel if they knew he was about to undergo a painful operation, and one not unattended with danger, he concealed altogether his purpose; nor did they receive the slightest intimation of it until, with a trembling hand, from his bed he penned a few lines communicating the safe and successful result. "God be thanked," he says, "I shall no longer bear about with me the sense of a wearying and harassing infirmity * * * and, though you will not give me credit for being a good bearer of pain, because I neither like to have my fingers scorched by a hot plate, nor scarified by that abominable instrument called a pin, Mr. Copeland will. * * Henry Taylor and Bedford have been the most constant of my visitors, but I have had inquiries out of number, and none among them more frequent than the Bishop of Limerick."

Among his other London engagements after his recovery, he had to sit to Sir T. Lawrence, for Sir Robert Peel, and also to Sir Francis Chantrey, who was very desirous of executing a bust of him. The former of these was, on the whole, the most successful likeness of my father taken in later life; at least it is generally considered so. He used to speak of the process of sitting to Sir T. Lawrence as a very agreeable one; as, the more easy and unembarrassed the conversation, the better for the painter, who also sometimes requested my father to read to him some of his poems, as affording opportunities of catching the various expressions of his countenance in the most natural manner, the blending of which into one harmonious whole is, I suppose, the greatest triumph of art.

With Sir Francis Chantrey he was more intimate, and thither their mutual friend, Mr. Bedford, always accompanied him: and there, too, was Allan Cunningham; so the molding went on merrily, for Chantrey loved a good story, and the reader need not be told that Mr. Bedford would both give and take a joke.

The sculptor, however, was not so successful as the painter; and, though he made several attempts to improve the likeness by after-touches, he never regarded his task as satisfactorily accomplished, though many persons were well satisfied with it; indeed, although he promised my father a marble copy of it, he would never fulfill his promise, always purposing to amend his work.

After his death, I believe it was purchased by Sir R. Peel.

To Mrs. Hodson.

"Keswick, Aug. 14, 1828.

"MY DEAR MADAM,

"I wish there were but one ten thousand of those persons in England who talk about new books and buy them, whether they read, mark, and inwardly digest them or not, that felt half as much interest in any forthcoming or expected work of mine as you are pleased to express, and as I should be unjust, as well as ungrateful, if I did not give you credit for. Alas! my third volume of the Peninsular War is far from complete—very far. It must be a close and hard winter's work that will make it ready for publication in the spring.

"My way to London toward the latter end of May was, I confess, through Ripon, but it was in the mail-coach, for I performed the whole journey without resting on the way. It was any thing but a pleasant one. I went to see an uncle (my best friend) for the last time in this world; his continuance, at the age of fourscore, in pain, infirmity, and earthly hopelessness, not being to be desired,* even though his deliverance must be, in a mere worldly view, a great misfortune to his family. He married in his sixtieth year, and has six children. I went, also, in the secret determination of undergoing a surgical operation, if it should be deemed expedient, for an infirmity which had long afflicted me. Thank God! it has succeeded, and I am once more a sound man, which I had not been for some twelve years.

"If I am now not quite as able to skip over the mountains as I was when first my tent was pitched here, it will be owing only to the gradual effect of time, not to any disablement from a painful and dangerous cause.

"No publisher, I am afraid, in this age, would venture to bring out a translation of Davila. The sale of books is grievously diminished within the last six or eight years (I speak feelingly). To have any success, a book must be new—a single season antiquates it; it must come from a fashionable name (nobility is now turned to a marketable account in this way); or it must be personal, if not slanderous; but, if slanderous, then best of all. It is the general diminution of income consequent on the depreciation of agricultural produce, and the experiments in free trade which has affected the booksellers, new books being the first things which persons who feel it necessary they should retrench find they can do without.

"And who, in this most ignorant age, reads Davila? Most ignorant I call it relative to historical reading; for, if our statesmen, so called

* "I would not, as I saw thee last,
For a king's ransom have detain'd thee here,
Bent, like the antique sculptor's limbless trunk,
By chronic pain, yet with thine eye unquench'd,
The ear undimm'd, the mind retentive still,
The heart unchanged, the intellectual lamp
Burning in its corporeal sepulcher.
No: not if human wishes had had power
To have suspended Nature's constant work,
Would they who loved thee have detain'd thee thus,
Waiting for death."
Dedication to Colloquies with Sir T. More.

by the courtesy of England, read Davila, and such historians as Davila, they could not commit such blunders as they have committed, are committing, and will commit; nor should we at this time have had cause to apprehend changes, and consequent convulsions, from which we must look alone to Providence to preserve us. Were there more of sound knowledge, there would be more of sound principle and of sound feeling. If Davila were published, some two or three of the worthies who dug up and mutilated the remains of Hampden might, perhaps, if they were to know that it was the book which Hampden studied when he was preparing himself and the nation for a rebellion and subversion of the lawful government, have thought it worth while to peruse it with the same sort of patriotic foresight.

"I am writing some verses describing the whole gallery of my portraits for Allan Cunningham's annual volume. Such volumes are among the plagues of my life; but Allan Cunningham is a right worthy man, and I owe him something for having carried a remonstrance from me to the editor of the Morning Chronicle, on occasion of some atrocious attacks upon me in that paper.

"I have made an arrangement with Murray concerning John Jones's rhymes. He will publish them, and give Jones the whole of his subscription copies; they amount to little more than 200 at present, but the list may be increased as much as we can. The verses will go to press as soon as Murray enables me to prepare the introduction by procuring for me the works of certain low and untaught rhymers of whom I wish to speak—Taylor the Water Poet, Stephen Duck, &c. Believe me, yours very truly,

"ROBERT SOUTHEY."

To John May, Esq.

"Keswick, Sept. 22, 1828.

"MY DEAR FRIEND,

"Before this reaches you, you will have heard that my dear uncle is relieved from the burden of age and infirmity which pressed upon him so heavily in his latter days. This day brought me the news of his deliverance, and it was the first that I had of his illness; but I was prepared for it, knowing that the first breath of wind must shake the dry leaf from the tree.

"It is somewhat remarkable, that either on the night before or after his decease (I am not certain which, but think it was the former) I was very much disturbed throughout the night in dreams concerning him. I seldom remember to have suffered so much in sleep, or to have wept more than I did then, thinking that I saw him, as I had last seen him, bent and suffering, helplessly and hopelessly, and that he reproved, or rather reasoned with me for allowing myself to be so affected. This is perfectly explicable; but it impressed me strongly at the time; and if, in some of his latter hours, his thoughts were directed toward me (as they may have been), I could find a solution which would accord with my philosophy, though it may not be dreamed of in that of other men.

"I have long looked for this event, and however important in one point of view the prolongation of his life might appear, I could not, if wishes or prayers could have done it, have stretched him upon the rack of this world longer.

"There is some comfort in thinking that he now knows, if he never knew it before, how truly I loved and honored him. I often indulge the belief that toward our dead friends our hearts are open and our desires known.

* * * * * * *

"God bless you, my dear friend!

"Yours most affectionately,

"R. SOUTHEY."

To Grosvenor C. Bedford, Esq.

"Keswick, Nov. 28, 1828.

"MY DEAR GROSVENOR,

"You may get the whole of Sir Thomas Brown's works more easily, perhaps, than the Hydrotaphia in a single form. The folio is neither scarce nor dear, and you will find it throughout a book to your heart's content. If I were confined to a score of English books, this, I think, would be one of them; nay, probably it would be one if the selection were cut down to twelve. My library, if reduced to those bounds, would consist of Shakspeare, Chaucer, Spenser, and Milton; Lord Clarendon; Jackson, Jeremy Taylor, and South; Isaac Walton, Sidney's Arcadia, Fuller's Church History, and Sir Thos. Brown; and what a wealthy and well-stored mind would that man have, what an inexhaustible reservoir, what a Bank of England to draw upon for profitable thoughts and delightful associations, who should have fed upon them!

" * * * I am glad you have passed six weeks pleasurably and profitably, though grudging a little that they were not spent at Keswick, where, among other things, I should like you to see the additional book-room that we have fitted up, and in which I am now writing, dividing my time between the two book-rooms by spells, so that both may be kept well aired. It would please you to see such a display of literary wealth, which is at once the pride of my eye, and the joy of my heart, and the food of my mind; indeed, more than metaphorically, meat, drink, and clothing for me and mine. I verily believe that no one in my station was ever so rich before, and I am very sure that no one in any station had ever a more thorough enjoyment of riches of any kind or in any way. It is more delightful for me to live with books than with men, even with all the relish that I have for such society as is worth having.

"I broke off this morning (not being a post day) for the sake of walking to Lodore, to see the cataract in its glory, after heavy rain in a wet season. A grand sight it was, and a grand sound. The walk, however, has just induced enough of agreeable lassitude to disincline me for my usual evening's pen-work.

"Your godson comes on well with his books, and, if you are disposed to make him a godfather's gift, you may send him a Septuagint, that being a book in which Michaelis advises that all who are intended for the theological profession should be grounded at school. Intentions, or even wishes, I hardly dare form concerning him; but this, I am sure, is the best and happiest profession which a wise man could choose for himself, or desire for those who are dear to him.

* * * * *

"God bless you! R. S."

To Grosvenor C. Bedford, Esq.

"Keswick, Dec. 8, 1828.

"MY DEAR GROSVENOR,

"I do not wonder that neither you nor your friend are acquainted with the name of Jackson as a divine, and I believe the sight of his works would somewhat appal you, for they are in three thick folios. He was Master of Corpus (Oxford) and vicar of Newcastle-upon-Tyne in the early part of Charles the First's reign, but his works were not published in a collective form till after the Restoration, when they were edited by Barnabas Oley, who was also the editor of George Herbert's remains. In our old divines there is generally something that you might wish were not there: less of this in Jackson, I think, than in any other, except South; and more of what may truly be called divine philosophy than in any or all others. Possibly you might not have the same relish for Jackson that I have, and yet I think you would find three or four pages per day a wholesome and pleasant diet.

"If you have not got the sermons of my almost-namesake, Robert South (who was, moreover, of Westminster), buy thou them forthwith, O Grosvenor Charles Bedford! for they will delight the very cockles of thy heart. * *

"I can not give full credit to your story* about the Life of Nelson. It is not likely that the American government, which is as parsimonious as Mr. Hume would wish ours to be, should incur the expense; and if they had, it is very unlikely that I should not have heard of it from the Americans who find their way to me, or those American acquaintance who give them letters of introduction. If the fact were so, it should be put in the newspapers. But I dare say that, if Henry will cross-question his informant, he will find that it has been asserted upon very insufficient grounds. As for our government doing any thing of this kind, they must first be taught to believe that it is part of their duty to provide wholesome instruction for the people. This they will learn when they have had sufficient cause to repent of their ignorance, and not *till* then. For myself, I am very far from complaining of government, to which, indeed, I owe much more than to the public. You know what his majesty is pleased to allow me through your hands. Now from the said public my last year's proceeds were—for the Book of the Church and the Vindiciæ, per John Murray, *nil;* and for all the rest of my works in Longman's hands, about £26. In this account, you know, the Peninsular War and the Life of Nelson are not included, being Murray's property. But the whole proceeds of my former labors were what I have stated them for the year ending at midsummer last, so that, if it were not for reviewing, it would be impossible for me to pay my current expenses. As some explanation, I should tell you that Roderic, and Thalaba, and Madoc are in new editions, which have not yet cleared themselves. They are doing this very slowly, except Roderic, from which, if it had been clear, I should have received £35.

"There are many causes for this. The Annuals are now the only books bought for presents to young ladies, in which way poems formerly had their chief vent. People ask for what is new; and to these may be added, that of all the opponents of the great and growing party of Revolutionists, I am the one whom they hate the most, and of all the supporters of established things, the one whom the anti-Revolutionists like the least; so that I fight for others against many, but stand alone myself

"God bless you! R. S."

To John May, Esq.

"Keswick, Dec. 11, 1828.

"MY DEAR FRIEND,

"If my long summer absence, and the continual interruptions which followed it to the middle of October, had not brought most heavy arrears of business upon my hands, you would have heard from me ere this. It seems my fate, like yours, to have more business as I advance in life, and less leisure for what I should take more delight in; however, God be praised who gives me strength and ability to go on, and enables me to support what, even with the best and most careful economy, is necessarily an expensive household.

"Dec. 15.

"I have been prevented from finishing this letter by the unexpected appearance of Lieut. Mawe, who has come from Peru down the Orellana, being the first Englishman who has ever descended that river. He has brought his manuscript to me before it goes to the press. I had seen him at Chantrey's just on his arrival, and he is wishing now that my History of Brazil had fallen in his way before he began his expedition. You may suppose how interesting I find his conversation and his journal. The account which he gives of Para is not favorable; trade is de-

* "I met a Mr. Brandreth at my brother's a few days ago, who has lately returned from the West Indies. He says the American government has printed an edition of your Life of Nelson, sufficiently numerous for a distribution on fine paper to every officer, and on coarse paper to every man in their fleet. This is what should have been done here long ago, and would have been done if our statesmen had been any thing better than politicians, or considered the people of the country as any thing but mere machines, unendowed with feelings or motives of action. It ought to be in the chest of every seaman, from the admiral to the cabin-boy. But our rulers have long been in the habit of calculating the people only by arithmetical figures, and look upon them only in the mass, without taking human character into the account. 'We politicians, you know,' said the late Lord Londonderry once to a friend of mine, 'have no feelings.' No, indeed, should have been the answer, nor do you reckon upon any in others."—*G. C. B. to R. S., Dec.,* 1828.

clining for want of specie; the English and American merchants are obliged to take produce in payment, and on that account price their goods, it is said, 30 per cent. above what they otherwise would do, and this makes them too dear for the market. Steam-boats, whenever they are introduced, will alter the condition of that country, and produce apparently a most beneficial effect.

"God bless you, my dear friend! and bring you through all those difficulties which you had so little reason to expect, and had done nothing to bring upon yourself. The inflictions of injustice are, I suppose, the most difficult of all evils to bear with equanimity: evils which arise from our own faults we receive as their chastisement and our own deserts; those which Heaven is pleased to inflict are borne as being its will. I hope and trust that there are better days in store for you. Alas! how ill do times and seasons sometimes suit with our views and wishes. Had you been removed to Bristol four-and-twenty years sooner, I should never have been removed from it.

"Once more, with kind remembrances from all here,

"Yours most affectionately, R. S."

To Allan Cunningham, Esq.

"Keswick, Dec. 21, 1828.

"MY DEAR ALLAN,

"Having no less than seven females in family, you will not wonder that as yet I have seen little more than the prints in your book* and its table of contents. It is, I do not doubt, quite as good in typographical contents as any of its rivals. The truth is, that in this respect there can be little to choose between; they are one and all of the same kind; the same contributors are mostly to be found in all of them, and this must of necessity bring the merits of all pretty much to an average. I am not sure that it would be for your interest to monopolize three or four writers, whose names happen to be high on the wheel of Fortune, if by so doing you should exclude some of those that are at present on the lower spokes. To me it seems the best policy that you should have many contributors, because every one would, from self-love, wish to promote the sale of the volume; and, moreover, every writer is the center of some little circle, within which what he may write is read and admired. But the literary department, make what exertions you will, must be as inferior in its effect upon the sale to the pictorial one as it is in its cost. At the best, Allan, these Annuals are picture-books for grown children. They are good things for the artists and engravers, and, therefore, I am glad of their success. I shall be more glad if one of them can be made a good thing for you; and I am very sure that you will make it as good as a thing of its kind can be made; but, at the best, this is what it must be.

"I have not seen the Keepsake yet, neither have I heard from its editor. He has 'o'erstepped the modesty of puffing' in his advertisements, and may very likely discover that he has paid young men of rank and fashion somewhat dearly for the sake of their names. You know upon what terms I stand with that concern.

"You wish for prose from me. I write prose more willingly than verse from habit, and because the hand of Time is on me; but, then, I can not move without elbow room. Grave subjects which could be treated within your limits do not occur to me; light ones I am sure will not; playfulness comes from me more naturally in verse. I have one or two stories which may be versified for you, either as ballads or in some other form, and which will not be too long. Want of room, I am afraid, would apply equally to a life of John Fox, which would better suit the Quarterly Review, if Dibdin should bring out his projected edition. Sometimes I think the bust may afford me a subject; but whether it would turn out song or sermon, I hardly know, perhaps both in one.

"Your book is very beautiful. The vignettes are especially clever. Of the prints Sir Walter interests me most for its subject, Pic-a-Back perhaps for its execution. It is the best design I ever saw of Richard Westall's. To make your book complete as exhibiting the art of the age, I should like something from Martin and something from Cruikshank, otherwise I do not see how it could be improved.

"God bless you!

"Yours very truly,

"ROBERT SOUTHEY."

To Grosvenor C. Bedford, Esq.

"Keswick, Dec. 29, 1828.

"MY DEAR GROSVENOR,

"I have two things to tell you, each good in its kind—the first relating to the moon, the second to myself.

"It is not likely that you should recollect a poor, harmless, honest old man, who used to deliver the letters when you were at Keswick; Joseph Littledale is his name, and, if you remember him, it will be by a chronic, husky cough, which generally announced his approach. Poor Littledale has this day explained the cause of our late rains, which have prevailed for the last five weeks, by a theory which will probably be as new to you as it is to me. 'I have observed,' he says, 'that when the moon is turned upward, we have fine weather after it; but if it is turned down, then we have a wet season; and the reason I think is, that when it is turned down, it holds no water, like a basin, you know, and then down it all comes.' There, Grosvenor, it will be a long while before the march of intellect shall produce a theory as original as this, which I find, upon inquiry, to be the popular opinion here.

"Next concerning myself. A relation of my friend Miss Bowles heard at a dinner-party lately that Mr. Southey had become a decided Methodist, and was about to make a full avowal of

* The Anniversary

his sentiments in a poem called the Sinner well Saved.* 'The title,' said the speaker, 'shows plainly what it is. But I have seen it; I have had a peep at it at the publisher's, and such a rant!!' * * * *

"I am about to begin a paper upon Surtees's History of the County of Durham for the next Quarterly Review, a subject which requires no more labor than that of looking through the three folios, and arranging what matter of general interest they contain in an amusing form; and this is comparatively easy work. Moreover, I am about a Life of Ignatius Loyola for the Foreign Review. My books having nearly come to a dead stand-still in their sale, it becomes necessary for me to raise my supplies by present labor, which, thank God! I am at present very well able to do. I shall work hard to make provision for a six weeks' holiday, commencing early in May, when I mean (if we all live and do well, and alas! Grosvenor, how little is this to be depended upon!) to remove my women-kind to the Isle of Man for sea air and bathing if they like it. The island is worth seeing, and there is no place where we could get at so little expense, or live so cheaply when there. We are but two stages from Whitehaven, and from thence there is a steam-packet. There I shall go over the whole island, and write verses when it rains.

"*Wednesday*, 31.— * * * I did not know that there was a folio edition of South. Six octavo volumes of his sermons were published during his life, five more after his death, from his manuscripts which had not been corrected for the press. The Oxford edition comprises the whole in seven octavos. One sermon among the posthumous ones is remarkable, because it was evidently written (probably in his younger days) as a trial of skill, in imitation of Sir Thomas Brown. * * *

"God bless you, my dear Grosvenor!

"R. S."

CHAPTER XXXII.

PERSONAL APPEARANCE—HABITS OF DAILY LIFE—EXCURSIONS—HIS HOUSE AND LIBRARY—ELEEMON—GROWTH OF HIS OPINIONS—THE CATHOLIC QUESTION—CONTROVERSY WITH MR. SHANNON—BALLADS FROM ROMISH LEGENDS—RENEWED HEALTH AND POWERS—MR. WORDSWORTH—VERBEYST, THE BRUSSELS BOOKSELLER—POLITICS—HIS HEALTH—VISIT TO NETHERHALL—LITERARY EMPLOYMENTS—THE CO-OPERATIVE ASSOCIATION—DR. PHILLPOTTS—SOME RESULTS OF HIS COLLOQUIES—ALLAN CUNNINGHAM'S LIVES OF THE PAINTERS—ARTICLE IN THE QUARTERLY REVIEW UPON PORTUGAL—PROSPECTS OF SOCIETY AT HOME—MICHAEL T. SADLER—IGNATIUS LOYOLA—CARLISLE—HERAUD—DESIRABLENESS OF MEN IN LATER LIFE TAKING HOLY ORDERS—THE COLLOQUIES—CHURCH METHODISM—MRS. OPIE—MR. HORNBY—INSTITUTION FOR TRAINING NURSES OPENED—CAUSES OF ITS FAILURE—MARRIAGE OF MISS COLERIDGE—LITERARY EMPLOYMENTS—MR. LANDOR—MR. WORDSWORTH—RECOMMENDATION OF BERKELEY'S MINUTE PHILOSOPHER—VISIT TO MRS. HODSON AND COL. HOWARD.—1829.

HAVING now arrived at that portion of my father's life which comes within the immediate sphere of my own recollections, I may be permitted to speak somewhat more familiarly than I have yet been enabled to do, both of himself personally and of the habits of his daily life. Being the youngest of all his children, I had not the privilege of knowing him in his best and most joyous years, nor of remembering Greta Hall when the happiness of its circle was unbroken. Much labor and anxiety, and many sorrows, had passed over him; and although his natural buoyancy of spirit had not departed, it was greatly subdued, and I chiefly remember its gradual diminution from year to year.

In appearance he was certainly a very striking looking person, and in early days he had by many been considered as almost the *beau idéal* of a poet. Mr. Cottle describes him at the age of twenty-two as "tall, dignified, possessing great suavity of manners, an eye piercing, a countenance full of genius, kindliness, and intelligence;" and he continues, "I had read so much of poetry, and sympathized so much with poets in all their eccentricities and vicissitudes, that to see before me the realization of a character which in the abstract so much absorbed my regards, gave me a degree of satisfaction which it would be difficult to express." Eighteen years later Lord Byron calls him a prepossessing looking person, and, with his usual admixture of satire, says, "To have his head and shoulders I would almost have written his Sapphics;" and elsewhere he speaks of his appearance as "Epic," an expression which may be either a sneer or a compliment.

His forehead was very broad; his height was five feet eleven inches; his complexion rather dark, the eyebrows large and arched, the eye well shaped and dark brown, the mouth somewhat prominent, muscular, and very variously expressive, the chin small in proportion to the upper features of his face. He always, while in Keswick, wore a cap in his walks, and partly from habit, partly from the make of his head and shoulders, we never thought he looked well or like himself in a hat. He was of a very spare frame, but of great activity, and not showing any appearance of a weak constitution.

My father's countenance, like his character, seems to have softened down from a certain wildness of expression to a more sober and thoughtful cast; and many thought him a handsomer man in age than in youth; his eye retaining always its brilliancy, and his countenance its play of expression.

* A Roman Catholic legend, taken from the "Acta Sanctorum," versified, and published in the collected edition of his poems, under the title of "All for Love, or a Sinner well Saved."

The reader will remember his Republican independency when an under-graduate at Oxford, in rebelling against the supremacy of the college barber. Though he did not continue to let his hair hang down on his shoulders according to the whim of his youthful days, yet he always wore a greater quantity than is usual; and once, on his arrival in town, Chantrey's first greetings to him were accompanied with an injunction to go and get his hair cut. When I first remember it, it was turning from a rich brown to the steel shade, whence it rapidly became almost snowy white, losing none of its remarkable thickness, and clustering in abundant curls over his massive brow.

For the following remarks on his general bearing and habits of conversation I am indebted to a friend:

"The characteristics of his manner, as of his appearance, were lightness and strength, an easy and happy composure as the accustomed mood, with much mobility at the same time, so that he could be readily excited into any degree of animation in discourse, speaking, if the subject moved him much, with extraordinary fire and force, though always in light, laconic sentences. When so moved, the fingers of his right hand often rested against his mouth and quivered through nervous susceptibility. But, excitable as he was in conversation, he was never angry or irritable; nor can there be any greater mistake concerning him than that into which some persons have fallen when they have inferred, from the fiery vehemence with which he could give utterance to moral anger in verse or prose, that he was personally ill-tempered or irascible. He was, in truth, a man whom it was hardly possible to quarrel with or offend personally and face to face; and in his writings, even on public subjects in which his feelings were strongly engaged, he will be observed to have always dealt tenderly with those whom he had once seen and spoken to, unless, indeed, personally and grossly assailed by them. He said of himself that he was tolerant of persons, though intolerant of opinions. But in oral intercourse the toleration of persons was so much the stronger, that the intolerance of opinions was not to be perceived; and, indeed, it was only in regard to opinions of a pernicious moral tendency that it was ever felt.

"He was averse from argumentation, and would commonly quit a subject when it was passing into that shape, with a quiet and good-humored indication of the view in which he rested. He talked most and with most interest about books and about public affairs; less, indeed hardly at all, about the characters and qualities of men in private life. In the society of strangers or of acquaintances, he seemed to take more interest in the subjects spoken of than in the persons present, his manner being that of natural courtesy and general benevolence without distinction of individuals. Had there been some tincture of social vanity in him, perhaps he would have been brought into closer relations with those whom he met in society; but, though invariably kind and careful of their feelings, he was indifferent to the manner in which they regarded him, or (as the phrase is) to his *effect* in society; and they might, perhaps, be conscious that the kindness they received was what flowed naturally and inevitably to all, that they had nothing to give in return which was of value to him, and that no individual relations were established.

"In conversation with intimate friends he would sometimes express, half humorously, a cordial commendation of some production of his own, knowing that with them he could afford it, and that to those who knew him well it was well known that there was no vanity in him. But such commendations, though light and humorous, were perfectly sincere; for he both possessed and cherished the power of finding enjoyment and satisfaction wherever it was to be found—in his own books, in the books of his friends, and in all books whatsoever that were not morally tainted or absolutely barren."

His course of life was the most regular and simple possible, and, indeed, in his routine he varied but little from the sketch he gave of it in 1806 (see *antè*, p. 199). When it is said that breakfast was at nine, after a little reading,* dinner at four, tea at six, supper at half past nine, and the intervals filled up with reading or writing, except that he regularly walked between two and four, and took a short sleep before tea, the outline of his day during those long seasons when he was in full work will have been given. After supper, when the business of the day seemed to be over, though he generally took a book, he remained with his family, and was open to enter into conversation, to amuse and to be amused. It was on such times that the most pleasant fireside chattings and the most interesting stories came forth; and, indeed, it was at such a time (though long before my day) that The Doctor was originated, as may be seen by the beginning of that work and the Preface to the new edition. Notwithstanding that the very mention of "my glass of punch," the one, temperate, never exceeded glass of punch, may be a stumbling-block to some of my readers, I am constrained, by the very love of the perfect picture which the first lines of The Doctor convey of the conclusion of his evening, to transcribe them in this place. It was written but for a few, otherwise The Doctor would have been no secret at all; but those few who knew him in his home will see his very look while they reperuse it, and will recall the well-known sound:

"I was in the fourth night of the story of the Doctor and his horse, and had broken it off, not,

* During the several years that he was partially employed upon the Life of Dr. Bell, he devoted two hours before breakfast to it in the summer, and as much time as there was daylight for during the winter months, that it might not interfere with the usual occupations of the day. In all this time, however, he made but little progress in it, partly from the nature of the materials, partly from the want of sufficient interest in the subject.

like Scheherazade, because it was time to get up, but because it was time to go to bed. It was at thirty-five minutes after ten o'clock on the 20th of July, in the year of our Lord 1813. I finished my glass of punch, tinkled the spoon against its side, as if making music to my own meditations, and having fixed my eyes upon the Bhow Begum, who was sitting opposite to me at the head of her own table, I said, 'It ought to be written in a book.'"

This scene took place at the table of the Bhow Begum,* but it may easily be transferred to his ordinary room, where he sat after supper in one corner, with the fire on his left hand and a small table on his right, looking on at his family circle in front of him.

I have said before, as indeed his own letters have abundantly shown, that he was a most thoroughly domestic man, in that his whole pleasure and happiness was centered in his home; but yet, from the course of his pursuits, his family necessarily saw but little of him. He could not, however he might wish it, join the summer evening walk, or make one of the circle round the winter hearth, or even spare time for conversation after the family meals (except during the brief space I have just been speaking of). Every day, every hour had its allotted employment; always were there engagements to publishers imperatively requiring punctual fulfillment; always the current expenses of a large household to take anxious thoughts for: he had no crops growing while he was idle. "My ways," he used to say, "are as broad as the king's high road, and my means lie in an ink-stand."

Yet, notwithstanding the value which every moment of his time thus necessarily bore, unlike most literary men, he was never ruffled in the slightest degree by the interruptions of his family, even on the most trivial occasions; the book or the pen was ever laid down with a smile, and he was ready to answer any question, or to enter with youthful readiness into any temporary topic of amusement or interest.

In earlier years he spoke of himself as ill calculated for general society, from a habit of uttering single significant sentences, which, from being delivered without any qualifying clauses, bore more meaning upon their surface than he intended, and through which his real opinions and feelings were often misunderstood. This habit, as far as my own observation went, though it was sometimes apparent, he had materially checked in later life, and in large parties he was usually inclined to be silent, rarely joining in general conversation. But he was very different when with only one or two companions; and to those strangers who came to him with letters of introduction, he was both extremely courteous in manner, and frank and pleasant in conversation, and to his intimates no one could have been more wholly unreserved, more disposed to give and receive pleasure, or more ready to pour forth his vast stores of information upon almost every subject.

I might go on here, and enter more at length into details of his personal character, but the task is too difficult a one, and is perhaps, after all, better left unattempted. A most intimate and highly-valued friend of my father's, whom I wished to have supplied me with some passages on these points, remarks very justly, that "any portraiture of him, by the pen as by the pencil, will fall so far short both of the truth and the ideal which the readers of his poetry and his letters will have formed for themselves, that they would be worse than superfluous." And, indeed, perhaps I have already said too much. I can not, however, resist quoting here some lines by the friend above alluded to, which describe admirably in brief my father's whole character:

"Two friends
Lent me a further light, whose equal hate
On all unwholesome sentiment attends,
Nor whom may genius charm where heart infirm attends.

"In all things else contrarious were these two:
The one a man upon whose laureled brow
Gray hairs were growing! glory ever new
Shall circle him in after years as now;
For spent detraction may not disavow
The world of knowledge with the wit combined,
The elastic force no burden e'er could bow,
The various talents and the single mind,
Which give him moral power and mastery o'er mankind.

"His sixty summers—what are they in truth?
By Providence peculiarly blest,
With him the strong hilarity of youth
Abides, despite gray hairs, a constant guest,
His sun has veered a point toward the west,
But light as dawn his heart is glowing yet—
That heart the simplest, gentlest, kindliest, bless'd,
Where truth and manly tenderness are met
With faith and heavenward hope, the suns that never set."*

What further I will venture to say relates chiefly to the external circumstances of his life at Keswick.

His greatest relaxation was in a mountain excursion or a pic-nic by the side of one of the lakes, tarns, or streams; and these parties, of which he was the life and soul, will long live in the recollections of those who shared them. An excellent pedestrian (thinking little of a walk of twenty-five miles when upward of sixty), he usually headed the "infantry" on these occasions, looking on those gentlemen as idle mortals who indulged in the luxury of a mountain pony; feeling very differently in the bracing air of Cumberland to what he did in Spain in 1800, when he delighted in being "gloriously lazy," in "sitting sideways upon an ass," and having even a boy to "propel" the burro. (See *antè*, p. 135.)

Upon first coming down to the Lakes he rather undervalued the pleasures of an al-fresco repast, preferring chairs and tables to the greensward of the mountains, or the moss-grown masses of rock by the lake shore; but these were probably the impressions of a cold, wet summer, and having soon learned thoroughly to appreciate these pleasures he had his various

* Miss Barker, the Senhora of earlier days, who was living at that time in a house close to Greta Hall. (See *antè*, p. 318.)

* Notes to Philip van Artevelde, by Henry Taylor.

chosen places, which he thought it a sort of duty annually to revisit. Of these I will name a few, as giving them, perhaps, an added interest to some future tourists. The summit of Skiddaw he regularly visited, often three or four times in a summer, but the view thence was not one he greatly admired. Sca-Fell and Helvellyn he ranked much higher, but on account of their distance did not often reach. Saddleback and Causey Pike, two mountains rarely ascended by tourists, were great favorites with him, and were the summits most frequently chosen for a grand expedition; and the two tarns upon Saddleback, Threlkeld and Bowscale tarns, were among the spots he thought most remarkable for grand and lonely beauty. This, too, was ground rendered more than commonly interesting, by having been the scenes of the childhood and early life of Clifford the Shepherd Lord. The rocky streams of Borrowdale, high up beyond Stonethwaite and Seathwaite, were also places often visited, especially one beautiful spot, where the river makes a sharp bend at the foot of Eagle Crag. The pass of Honistar Crag, leading from Buttermere to Borrowdale, furnished a longer excursion, which was occasionally taken with a sort of rustic pomp in the rough market carts of the country, before the cars which are now so generally used had become common, or been permitted by their owners to travel that worst of all roads. Occasionally there were grand meetings with Mr. Wordsworth, and his family and friends, at Leatheswater (or Thirlmere), a point about half way between Keswick and Rydal; and here as many as fifty persons have sometimes met together from both sides of the country. These were days of great enjoyment, not to be forgotten.

There was also an infinite variety of long walks, of which he could take advantage when opportunity served, without the preparation and trouble of a preconcerted expedition: several of these are alluded to in his Colloquies. The circuit formed by passing behind Barrow and Lodore to the vale of Watenlath, placed up high among the hills, with its own little lake and village, and the rugged path leading thence down to Borrowdale, was one of the walks he most admired. The beautiful vale of St. John's, with its "Castle Rock" and picturesquely placed little church, was another favorite walk; and there were a number of springs of unusual copiousness situated near what had been apparently a deserted, and now ruined village, where he used to take luncheon. The rocky bed of the little stream at the foot of Causey Pike was a spot he loved to rest at; and the deep pools of the stream that flows down the adjoining valley of New Lands,

> "Whose pure and chrysolite waters
> Flow o'er a schistose bed,"

formed one of his favorite resorts for bathing.

Yet these excursions, although for a few years he still continued to enjoy them, began in later life to wear to him something of a melancholy aspect. So many friends were dead who had formerly shared them, and his own domestic losses were but too vividly called to mind with the remembrance of former days of enjoyment, the very grandeur of the scenery around many of the chosen places, and the unchanging features of the "everlasting hills," brought back forcibly sad memories, and these parties became in time so painful that it was with difficulty he could be prevailed upon to join in them.

He concealed, indeed, as the reader has seen, beneath a reserved manner, a most acutely sensitive mind, and a warmth and kindliness of feeling which was only understood by few, indeed, perhaps, not thoroughly by any. He said, speaking of the death of his uncle, Mr. Hill, that one of the sources of consolation to him was the thought that perhaps the departed might then be conscious how truly he had loved and honored him; and I believe the depth of his affection and the warmth of his friendship was known to none but himself. On one particular point I remember his often regretting his constitutional bashfulness and reserve; and that was, because, added to his retired life and the nature of his pursuits, it prevented him from knowing any thing of the persons among whom he lived. Long as he had resided at Keswick, I do not think there were twenty persons in the lower class whom he knew by sight; and though this was in some measure owing to a slight degree of short-sightedness, which, contrary to what is usual, came on in later life, yet I have heard him often lament it as not being what he thought right; and after slightly returning the salutation of some passer-by, he would again mechanically lift his cap as he heard some well-known name in reply to his inquiries, and look back with regret that the greeting had not been more cordial. With those persons who were occasionally employed about the house he was most familiarly friendly, and these regarded him with a degree of affectionate reverence that could not be surpassed.

It may perhaps be expected by some readers that a more accurate account of my father's income should be given than has yet appeared; but this is not an easy matter, from its extreme variableness, and this it was that constituted a continual source of uneasiness both to others and to himself, rarely as he acknowledged it. A common error has been to speak of him as one to whom literature has been a mine of wealth. That his political opponents should do this is not so strange; but even Charles Lamb, who, if he had thought a little, would hardly have written so rashly, says, in a letter to Bernard Barton, recently published, that "Southey has made a fortune by book drudgery." What sort of a "fortune" that was which never once permitted him to have one year's income beforehand, and compelled him almost always to forestall the profit of his new works, the reader may imagine.

His only certain source of income* was his

* I speak of a period prior to his receiving his last pension, which was granted in 1835.

pension, from which he received £145, and the laureateship, which was £90: the larger portion of these two sums, however, went to the payment of his life insurance, so that not more than £100 could be calculated upon as available, and the Quarterly Review was therefore for many years his chief means of support. He received latterly £100 for an article, and commonly furnished one for each number. What more was needful had to be made up by his other works, which, as they were always published upon the terms of the publisher taking the risk and sharing the profits, produced him but little, considering the length of time they were often in preparation, and as he was constantly adding new purchases to his library, but little was to be reckoned upon this account. For the Peninsular War he received £1000, but the copy-right remained the property of the publisher.

With regard to his mode of life, although it was as simple and inexpensive as possible, his expenditure was with difficulty kept within his income, though he had indeed a most faithful helpmate, who combined with a wise and careful economy a liberality equal to his own in any case of distress. One reason for this difficulty was, that considerable sums were, not now and then, but regularly, drawn from him by his less successful relatives.

The house which for so many years was his residence at Keswick, though well situated both for convenience and for beauty of prospect, was unattractive in external appearance, and to most families would have been an undesirable residence. Having originally been two houses, afterward thrown together, it consisted of a good many small rooms, connected by long passages, all of which, with great ingenuity, he made available for holding books, with which, indeed, the house was lined from top to bottom. His own sitting-room, which was the largest in the house, was filled with the handsomest of them, arranged with much taste, according to his own fashion, with due regard to size, color, and condition; and he used to contemplate these, his carefully-accumulated and much-prized treasures, with even more pleasure and pride than the greatest connoisseur his finest specimens of the old masters; and justly, for they were both the necessaries and the luxuries of life to him; both the very instruments whereby he won, hardly enough, his daily bread, and the source of all his pleasures and recreations—the pride of his eyes and the joy of his heart.

His Spanish and Portuguese collection, which at one time was one of the best, if not itself the best to be found in the possession of any private individual, was the most highly-prized portion of his library. It had been commenced by his uncle, Mr. Hill, long prior to my father's first visit to Lisbon; and having originated in the love Mr. Hill himself had for the literature of those countries, it was carried forward with more ardor when he found that his nephew's taste and abilities were likely to turn it to good account. It comprised a considerable number of manuscripts, some of them copied by Mr. Hill from rare MSS. in private and convent libraries.

Many of these old books being in vellum or parchment bindings, he had taken much pains to render them ornamental portions of the furniture of his shelves. His brother Thomas was skillful in calligraphy; and by his assistance their backs were painted with some bright color, and upon it the title placed lengthwise in large gold letters of the old English type. Any one who had visited his library will remember the tastefully-arranged pyramids of these curious-looking books.

Another fancy of his was to have all those books of lesser value, which had become ragged and dirty, covered, or rather bound, in colored cotton prints, for the sake of making them clean and respectable in their appearance, it being impossible to afford the cost of having so many put into better bindings.

Of this task his daughters, aided by any female friends who might be staying with them, were the performers; and not fewer than from 1200 to 1400 volumes were so bound by them at different times, filling completely one room, which he designated as the Cottonian library. With this work he was much interested and amused, as the ladies would often suit the pattern to the contents, clothing a Quaker work or a book of sermons in sober drab, poetry in some flowery design, and sometimes contriving a sly piece of satire at the contents of some well-known author by their choice of its covering. One considerable convenience attended this eccentric mode of binding—the book became as well known by its dress as by its contents, and much more easily found.

With respect to his mode of acquiring and arranging the contents of a book, it was somewhat peculiar. He was as rapid a reader as could be conceived, having the power of perceiving by a glance down the page whether it contained any thing which he was likely to make use of—a slip of paper lay on his desk, and was used as a marker, and with a slight penciled S he would note the passage, put a reference on the paper, with some brief note of the subject, which he could transfer to his note-book, and in the course of a few hours he had classified and arranged every thing in the work which it was likely he would ever want. It was thus, with a remarkable memory (not so much for the facts or passages themselves, but for their existence and the authors that contained them), and with this kind of index both to it and them, that he had at hand a command of materials for whatever subject he was employed upon, which has been truly said to be "unequaled."

Many of the choicest passages he would transcribe himself at odds and ends of times, or employ one of his family to transcribe for him; and these are the extracts which form his "Common-place Book," recently published; but those of less importance he had thus within reach in case he wished to avail himself of them. The quickness with which this was done was very remarkable. I have often known him receive a parcel of books one afternoon, and the next have found his mark throughout perhaps two or three different volumes; yet, if a work took his attention particularly, he was not rapid in its perusal; and on some authors, such as the old divines, he "fed," as he expressed it, slowly and carefully, dwelling on the page, and taking in its contents deeply and deliberately, like an epicure with his "wine searching the subtle flavor."

His library at his death consisted of about 14,000 volumes; probably the largest number of books ever collected by a person of such limited means. Among these he found most of the materials for all he did, and almost all he wished to do; and though sometimes he lamented that his collection was not a larger one, it is probable that it was more to his advantage that it was in some degree limited. As it was, he collected an infinitely greater quantity of materials for every subject he was employed upon than ever he made use of, and his published Notes give some idea, though an inadequate one, of the vast stores he thus accumulated.

On this subject he writes to his cousin, Herbert Hill, at that time one of the librarians of the "Bodleian:" "When I was at the British Museum the other day, walking through the rooms with Carey, I felt that to have lived in that library, or in such a one, would have rendered me perfectly useless, even if it had not made me mad. The sight of such countless volumes made me feel how impossible it would be to pursue any subject through all the investigations into which it would lead me, and that therefore I should either lose myself in the vain pursuit, or give up in despair, and read for the future with no other object than that of immediate gratification. This was an additional reason for being thankful for my own lot, aware as I am that I am always tempted to pursue a train of inquiry too far."

To Henry Taylor, Esq.

"Keswick, Jan. 19, 1829.

"My dear H. T.,

"You are right in your opinion of the last scene in Eleemon,* but it can not be altered now, and I am not sure that it ever can, for the bond is there. When you read the original story, you will see how much it owes to the management of it; what was offensive I could remove, but there remained an essential part which I could neither dignify nor get rid of. All I could do was to prepare for treating it in part satirically, by concluding the interest in the penultimate canto, and making the reader aware that what remained was to be between the bishop and the arch lord chancellor. And after all, the poem is only a sportive exercise of art, an *extravaganza* or capriccio to amuse myself and others.

"Dear H. T., however fast my thoughts may germinate and flower, my opinions have been of slow growth since I came to years of discretion, and since the age of forty they have undergone very little change; but increase of knowledge has tended to confirm them. My friends—those whom I call so—have never been the persons who have flattered me; if they had, they would not have held that place which they possess in my esteem.

"The experiment of pauper colonies has been long enough in progress to satisfy such a man as Jacob of its success. Remember what a matter-of-fact man he is: all the travels which have fallen in my way agree with him.

"I require a first outlay, from the money expended in work-house and poor-rates. Feed the pauper while he builds his cottage, fences his allotment, and digs his garden, as you feed him while he breaks stones or lives in idleness. You think of the plow, I of the spade; you of fields, I of gardens; you of corn land, I of grass land; and I treat these measures, not as substitutes for emigration, but as co-operatives with it; I want to increase potatoes and pigs as well as peasantry, who will increase whether pigs and potatoes do or do not. The land on which this is going on in Germany and Holland is worse than the worst of our wastes. The spade works wonders. God bless you! R. Southey."

To the Rev. Neville White.

"Keswick, Jan. 20, 1829.

"My dear Neville,

"Among the other causes which have from day to days, and from days to weeks, and from weeks to months, put off the intention of writing to you, one has been the hope and expectation of hearing from you. *Of* you I heard an ugly story—that my head had fallen on yours;* in which accident I, as well as you, had a merciful escape, for if that bust had been your death, it would have left a life-long impression upon my spirits.

* * * * * * *

"I am very much taken up with reviewing, without which, indeed, I should be in no comfortable situation; for the sale of my books in Longman's hands, where the old standers used to bring in about £200 a year, has fallen almost to nothing: at their present movement, indeed, they would not set my account with him even before seven years' end. The Book of the Church, too, is at a dead stand-still; and for the Vindiciæ, that book never produced me so much as a single paper in the Quarterly Review. The Foreign Review enables me to keep pace with my expenditure; but the necessity of so doing allows far too little time for works on which I might more worthily be employed.

"Though I am not sanguine, like my brother Tom, and have no dreams of good fortune coming to me on one of the four winds, I have,

* This poem is entitled "All for Love, or a Sinner well Saved."

* A bust of my father, which Mr. Neville White possessed, had fallen upon him, but, fortunately, without doing serious injury.

reach in case he wished to avail himself of them. The quickness with which this was done was very remarkable. I have often known him receive a parcel of books one afternoon, and the next have found his mark throughout perhaps two or three different volumes; yet, if a work took his attention particularly, he was not rapid in its perusal; and on some authors, such as the old divines, he "fed," as he expressed it, slowly and carefully, dwelling on the page, and taking in its contents deeply and deliberately, like an epicure with his "wine searching the subtle flavor."

His library at his death consisted of about 14,000 volumes; probably the largest number of books ever collected by a person of such limited means. Among these he found most of the materials for all he did, and almost all he wished to do; and though sometimes he lamented that his collection was not a larger one, it is probable that it was more to his advantage that it was in some degree limited. As it was, he collected an infinitely greater quantity of materials for every subject he was employed upon than ever he made use of, and his published Notes give some idea, though an inadequate one, of the vast stores he thus accumulated.

On this subject he writes to his cousin, Herbert Hill, at that time one of the librarians of the "Bodleian:" "When I was at the British Museum the other day, walking through the rooms with Carey, I felt that to have lived in that library, or in such a one, would have rendered me perfectly useless, even if it had not made me mad. The sight of such countless volumes made me feel how impossible it would be to pursue any subject through all the investigations into which it would lead me, and that therefore I should either lose myself in the vain pursuit, or give up in despair, and read for the future with no other object than that of immediate gratification. This was an additional reason for being thankful for my own lot, aware as I am that I am always tempted to pursue a train of inquiry too far."

To Henry Taylor, Esq.

"Keswick, Jan. 19, 1829.

"My dear H. T.,

"You are right in your opinion of the last scene in Eleemon,* but it can not be altered now, and I am not sure that it ever can, for the bond is there. When you read the original story, you will see how much it owes to the management of it; what was offensive I could remove, but there remained an essential part which I could neither dignify nor get rid of. All I could do was to prepare for treating it in part satirically, by concluding the interest in the penultimate canto, and making the reader aware that what remained was to be between the bishop and the arch lord chancellor. And after all, the poem is only a sportive exercise of art, an *extravaganza* or capriccio to amuse myself and others.

"Dear H. T., however fast my thoughts may germinate and flower, my opinions have been of slow growth since I came to years of discretion, and since the age of forty they have undergone very little change; but increase of knowledge has tended to confirm them. My friends—those whom I call so—have never been the persons who have flattered me; if they had, they would not have held that place which they possess in my esteem.

"The experiment of pauper colonies has been long enough in progress to satisfy such a man as Jacob of its success. Remember what a matter-of-fact man he is: all the travels which have fallen in my way agree with him.

"I require a first outlay, from the money expended in work-house and poor-rates. Feed the pauper while he builds his cottage, fences his allotment, and digs his garden, as you feed him while he breaks stones or lives in idleness. You think of the plow, I of the spade; you of fields, I of gardens; you of corn land, I of grass land; and I treat these measures, not as substitutes for emigration, but as co-operatives with it; I want to increase potatoes and pigs as well as peasantry, who will increase whether pigs and potatoes do or do not. The land on which this is going on in Germany and Holland is worse than the worst of our wastes. The spade works wonders. God bless you! R. Southey."

To the Rev. Neville White.

"Keswick, Jan. 20, 1829.

"My dear Neville,

"Among the other causes which have from day to days, and from days to weeks, and from weeks to months, put off the intention of writing to you, one has been the hope and expectation of hearing from you. Of you I heard an ugly story—that my head had fallen on yours;* in which accident I, as well as you, had a merciful escape, for if that bust had been your death, it would have left a life-long impression upon my spirits.

* * * * * * *

"I am very much taken up with reviewing, without which, indeed, I should be in no comfortable situation; for the sale of my books in Longman's hands, where the old standers used to bring in about £200 a year, has fallen almost to nothing: at their present movement, indeed, they would not set my account with him even before seven years' end. The Book of the Church, too, is at a dead stand-still; and for the Vindiciæ, that book never produced me so much as a single paper in the Quarterly Review. The Foreign Review enables me to keep pace with my expenditure; but the necessity of so doing allows far too little time for works on which I might more worthily be employed.

"Though I am not sanguine, like my brother Tom, and have no dreams of good fortune coming to me on one of the four winds, I have,

* This poem is entitled "All for Love, or a Sinner well Saved."

* A bust of my father, which Mr. Neville White possessed, had fallen upon him, but, fortunately, without doing serious injury.

and this it is that constitutes the *gravamen* of the charge against ministers. They took none of those measures which might have prevented this alternative; they suffered the danger to grow up, knowingly, willfully, and I can not but add, *treacherously*; and now they make the extent of that danger their excuse for yielding to it. They have deceived their friends, and betrayed the Constitution.

"Now any war is so dreadful a thing, that even when it becomes (as it may) a duty to choose it as the least of two evils, a good man, in making such a choice, must bid farewell forever to all lightness of heart. There will be hours of misgiving for him, let his mind be ever so strong; and sleepless nights and miserable dreams, when the thorns in his pillow prevent him not from sleeping. This we shall be spared from. It is not our resistance to this pusillanimous surrender that will bring on the last appeal. It must be made at length, but under circumstances in which our consciousness will be that the course which we should have pursued from the beginning would have prevented it.

"This is our position. Let us now look at that in which Mr. Peel and his colleagues have placed themselves. They have pledged themselves to impose securities; the more violent Catholics have declared that they will submit to none: and the Bishop of London (who said he should be satisfied with the *minimum* of security) has said in Parliament that he can devise none. And here Phillpotts, who, I dare say, was honestly upon the quest, is at fault. The difficulties here may again break off the treaty, and in such a manner that those Emancipators who think securities necessary must come round, in which case as much may be gained by an accession of strength as has been lost by this pitiful confession of weakness. I am inclined to think that these preliminary difficulties will not be got over.

"But if the measure be passed, and the Protestant flag should be struck, and the enemy march in with flying colors, there may possibly be a sort of honey-moon session after the surrender. Then comes the second demand for despoiling the Irish Church, and the Catholic Association is renewed in greater strength, and upon much more formidable grounds. Meantime the Irish Protestants will lose heart, and great numbers will emigrate, flying while they can from the wrath to come. Grief enough, and cause enough of fear, there will be for us in all this; but as to peace of mind, we should be in a Goshen of our own. And there is hope in the prospect; for all pretext of civil rights is then at an end. It becomes a religious claim leading at once to a religious war. The infidel party may still adhere to the papists; their other partisans can no longer do so. And I think, also, that France is not so likely to take part in a war upon papal grounds, as in one which would be represented as a liberal cause.

"I know but one danger in the present state of things which might have shaken a constant mind; that arising from the great proportion of Irish Catholics in the army. The Protestant strength of Ireland was enough to counterpoise it. But if the duke was affected by this danger, he will take means for lessening it before the crisis comes on.

"These are my speculations, partaking perhaps of the sunshine of a hopeful and cheerful disposition. Had I been intrusted with political power at this time, I would, upon the principle that we are to trust in Providence, but act according to the clear perception of duty, have resisted this concession even to blood. In this I differ from Blanco White. I am sorry to see the part which he is taking; but I am quite sure he has a single eye, and casts no sinister looks with it.

"God speed you, my dear friend, not in this contest alone, but in every thing. I wish you success the more, because it will be creditable to the University—to the national character. The mass of mankind, while we are what our institutions make us, *must* be time-servers. (The old Adam in our nature is less active than the old Serpent in our system of society.) When they shift with the wind, they only change *professions*, not principles, upon questions which they understand imperfectly. But if I see a good majority of persons who have preferment to look for, either in the Church or the Law, voting according to their former convictions, when tergiversation is the order of the day, it will be a hopeful symptom, and serve in a small degree as a set-off against the mortification which individual cases of defection can not but occasion at this time.

"Yours affectionately,

"ROBERT SOUTHEY."

My father's paper on the Catholic Question in the Quarterly Review appears to have met with royal approbation, for the king expressed a wish that it should be printed in a separate form for more general circulation. This, however, Mr. Murray, apparently having more regard to profit than loyalty, would not consent to, saying that those who wished to read the article might purchase the number which contained it. But as it found favor with many persons, as might be expected, it was extremely unpalatable to those who held views of an opposite nature; and in a pamphlet upon the Roman Catholic claims by the Rev. Mr. Shannon, it was alluded to in very strong terms, and the writer further expressed his confident hopes that my father was not the author, because there was a spirit in it so "utterly inhuman" toward Ireland and its Catholic population, and because, when in his company several times more than twenty years previously, he "remembered well the enthusiasm of his feelings in speaking of the wrongs and sufferings of Ireland, and the energy of language in which he expressed his ardent wishes for the restoration of Catholic rights;"* and he went on to say,

* This passage was extracted in the Times newspaper with this remark: "The article against the Irish Roman Catholics and their claims, which appeared in the last number of the *Quarterly Review*, has generally been ascribed to the pen of Dr. Southey; we are not in the secret on such matters, nor do we think it of any consequence to settle the authorship of such a piece of acrimonious declamation; but we allude to it for the purpose of introducing

that "the generous warmth of indignant feeling may easily be supposed to abate in the cooler temperament of an advancing age; but it is impossible that the moral sense should undergo so complete a transformation, except from causes which are liable to suspicion."

This misrepresentation of a private conversation which had taken place so long ago, naturally surprised and annoyed exceedingly my father, and he wrote to Mr Shannon on the first instant very courteously, saying that he had no doubt he had persuaded himself that the statement was correct, but that it was altogether inaccurate in every thing which would appear to him material; and he concluded by saying that Mr. Shannon owed him a public acknowledgment for a public wrong.

This, however, Mr. Shannon was not inclined to make; and as he persisted in maintaining that his impression of what my father's opinions had been was correct, and that he had not committed any offense against the established usages of society in thus bringing forward his recollections of a private conversation, the correspondence assumed a somewhat angry tone. The following letter, which concluded it, I insert here, as giving pretty clearly a summary both of these circumstances and of my father's opinions respecting Ireland.

To the Rev. Richard Shannon.

"Keswick, March 2, 1829.

"SIR,—I thank you for your pamphlet; but I find that the extract from it in The Times is faithfully given, and I repeat that you have offered me a personal wrong, as unprovoked as it is unwarrantable. You have egregiously mistaken what my opinions were when we met. You have uncharitably misrepresented what they are now; and you have imputed to me suspicious motives for a change which has no other exist-

a note relative to the doctor from a convincing and able *Address to the Clergy on behalf of the Roman Catholic Claims*, just published by the Rev. Mr. Shannon, of Edinburgh. As we take it for granted that the reverend gentleman is stating a fact, we must conclude, that if Dr. Southey be the author of the article in question, he has to add another inconsistency to that long list of tergiversations and conflicting professions which have occurred in his transition from the Jacobin leveler of altars and thrones to the loyal and high-church poet laureate, of which he ought to be reminded every year by receiving a copy of *Wat Tyler* along with the annual butt of sack."

In consequence of this, a long letter was addressed to the editor of the Times by Mr. Henry Taylor, some portions of which I subjoin here, as answering well both Mr. Shannon's charges and those of the Times' editor.

"Mr. Shannon has found in the article 'an inhuman spirit toward the Irish.' I have searched the article through, and I know not where in it Mr. Shannon could find a trace of such a spirit, or a pretext for his charge. At page 573, the writer speaks of the readiness with which the Irish would rebel for the sake of their religion. 'In that faith,' he says, 'they would be ready to inflict or to endure any thing, to deserve the heaviest punishment that outraged humanity might demand and offended justice exact, and to undergo it with a fortitude which, arising from deluded conscience, excites compassion even more than it commands respect.' If these are the feelings with which the writer would regard the Irish in rebellion, what are the measures by which he would keep them out of it? 'The Emperor Acbar bore upon his signet this saying: "I never saw any one lost upon a straight road." This is a straight road—to restrain treason, to punish sedition, to disregard clamor, and by every possible means to better the condition of the Irish peasantry, who are not more miserably ignorant than they are miserably oppressed. Give them employment in public works, bring the bogs into cultivation, facilitate for those who desire it the means of emigration. Extend the poor laws to Ireland; experience may teach us to guard against their abuse—they are benevolent, they are necessary, they are just. * * * Better their condition thus—educate the people, execute justice, and maintain peace. * * * Let every thing be done that can relieve the poor—every thing that can improve their condition, physically, morally, intellectually, and religiously.'

"As far as human feelings and not political opinions are in question, I know not by what spirit Mr. Shannon would desire this writer to have been actuated, nor do I know by what spirit any writer could have been actuated who could find 'an inhuman spirit' in this.

"Surely Mr. Shannon might find it in his power to differ from Mr. Southey (as I do) on the Catholic Question, without imputing to him malevolent feelings, corrupt motives, and an advocacy of gross oppressions. The difference is on a controvertible political question, to the advocates of which, on either side, injurious language is obviously misapplied; and at the same time that I am willing to give due credit to Mr. Shannon for his exertions in a cause to which I wish all success, I regret that he has been betrayed, in this instance, into a mode of proceeding which is no evidence of the abilities attributed to him, and which is, moreover, in more than one respect, rather inconsistent with the feelings of propriety which belong to his profession, and, I have no doubt (political zeal apart), to himself also.

"Mr. Southey has been, at all times, an enemy to oppression of all sorts. Mr. Shannon found him so in his conversations twenty-five years ago, and whether in his writings or in his discourse, to those who understand his views, he will never appear otherwise. True it is that at the present time Mr. Southey considers the nearest dangers of society to arise from a too rapid accession of power to the ill instructed. A man acting under this conviction will naturally apply himself with more solicitude to exhibit to the people the benefits which they derive from existing institutions, than to detect for them their grievances. But, as in this article (if it be his), so in all his other writings, he never stints the language of reprobation when there is real oppression to be written of. Men may differ from him as to the measures which may be applicable to our system of society; but if they see him aright, they will see him, in spirit and in purpose, as sincere a lover of liberty, and as indignantly opposed to injustice, as ever he was in his boyhood, when he thought that he saw a short way out of the evils of society.

"You, or the writer of your paragraph, have spoken of 'the long list of his tergiversations.' In so speaking you have joined the common cry of those enemies of Mr. Southey whom his political writings have raised up against him. The only fact which can be assumed as a foundation for such charges is, that Mr. Southey held republican opinions in his very early youth, and that he changed them soon after he had arrived at man's estate. That he profited by the change is wholly false. And to suppose that any worldly considerations could have affected his opinions, or touched for a moment the sincerity of his mind, would seem to any one who knew him as absurd as to suppose that Nelson wanted courage or that Sheridan wanted wit. When, with the growth of his knowledge and understanding, his Utopian systems gave way, he attached himself to the Constitution of his country—and here 'the long list of his tergiversations' comes to an end.

"Mr. Southey is a public man, and you have a right to animadvert on the opinions of his which are or have been before the public, whether they come out in a way which is usual, or by the means of gentlemen who shall conceive themselves to have mastered them in two or three private conversations at Mr. Southey's table, and to be enabled to expound them now. You must allow me, however, to express regret that an editor, whose paper owes, I think, a part of its weight to the use of some little discrimination in the language of invective, should have suffered himself to join in a vulgar cry of inferior party writers, and to cast a reflection for what he can scarcely think to be matter of reproach. For the distinguished individual in question, men of ability ought to have at least one sort of respect, and all who know him must have every possible respect. I can not help thinking, therefore, that you would have better prefaced your extract from Mr. Shannon's publication if you had admonished him (with all due acknowledgment of his merits and exertions) that he would do well, in making toward a just end, to be just on the way, and to pursue liberality with a liberal feeling.

"I am, sir, your obedient servant, H. T."

ence than in your own erroneous recollections and intemperate judgment.

"If what you called the Catholic rights were touched upon in our table-talk, it is likely that a subject which was not at that time prominent would be lightly dismissed, willing as we both were to dwell rather upon points of agreement than of difference. I remember distinctly our difference concerning the union with England, and no other. Nor do I suppose that we differ now upon any thing else relating to Ireland, except upon the question whether concession to the Romanists is likely to remedy the evils of that poor country or to aggravate them. On that question it is well known to all my friends that my views have never undergone any alteration; and they were formed and declared as early as the year 1801, when the question first came before me. For what possible motive could I have dissembled them to you? I have never expressed an opinion which I did not hold, nor held one which I feared to express—to maintain when I was persuaded that it was right, or to abandon if convinced that it was wrong.

"With regard to the Quarterly Review, I never will allow that any one has a right to call upon me individually respecting any composition (not of a personal character) which has not my name affixed to it. But I maintain every argument which is urged in that paper; I assent to every assertion which it contains; I hold every opinion which is advanced there. Elsewhere I have published arguments, assertions, and opinions of the same kind, bearing upon the same conclusion. And whosoever charges me with inhumanity for this, or affirms that it is designed to render the Irish objects of horror and execration, calumniates me. I have been used to misrepresentation and calumny, but I did not expect them, sir, from you.

"It is a fair course of argument to assert that the miseries of Ireland were not caused by the laws which exclude the Roman Catholics from legislative power, and to infer that they can not be remedied by the repeal of those laws; and the question is, whether those premises can be proved by historical facts, and that inference established by just reasoning. You can not condemn the British government more severely than I do for having suffered the great body of the Irish people to remain to this day in as barbarous a state as the Scotch and the Welsh were till they were civilized, the first by their Kirk, the second by the laws. That the Irish have been thus barbarous from the earliest times may be learned by their own annals; that they are so still is proved at every assizes in that unhappy country, and almost in every newspaper. That they should be in this condition is the fault of their aristocracy, their landlords, and their priests, and the reproach of their rulers. But in what state of mind must that person be who accuses another of inhumanity, and holds him up as the enemy of the Irish nation, because he has asserted these truths!

"I could say more, sir, were it not vain to address one whose sense of the usages of society is so perverse that he deems it no breach of honor and hospitality to bring old table-talk before the public for the purpose of depreciating me; whose prepossessions are so obstinate that rather than think it possible his own recollections, after more than twenty years, may have deceived him, he will believe me guilty of deliberate falsehood; whose Christian charity is so little, that because I think the Protestant Church establishments in England and Ireland will be endangered by admitting Roman Catholics into the Legislature, he imputes suspicious motives to me, and accuses me of seeking to render the Irish people objects of horror and execration; and, finally, whose notions of moral feeling are so curiously compounded, that because these heinous charges are accompanied with some complimentary phrases to the injured person on the score of his talents, he is actually surprised that an indignant remonstrance should be expressed in a tone which he calls uncourteous! Finding it, therefore, in vain to expect from you a reparation of the wrong which you have offered, I shall take a near and fitting opportunity for publicly contradicting* your statement, and repelling your injurious charges and calumniatory insinuations.

"ROBERT SOUTHEY."

My father's convictions upon the subject of the admission of Roman Catholics into the Legislature were most strongly rooted in his mind: he had, indeed, always held that all rights should be conceded to them, and all restrictions removed in matters which had not a close relation to political power; but to invest them with that power he considered as the most perilous experiment that could by possibility be tried in a Protestant country. Deeply read in Roman Catholic history, and probably more fully acquainted with the principles and practices of that Church, as set forth by her own writers, than most of his cotemporaries, he could not divest himself of the idea that her sincere members must necessarily be actuated by the same spirit as of old. He felt that if he were of that faith his whole heart and soul would be bent upon the overthrow of the Protestant Church—that he would have striven to be a second Loyola; and believing one of the moving principles of the Roman Catholic religion to be that the end justified the means, he did not see how any securities that might be taken from members of that persuasion could be strong enough to overcome what he considered *ought* to be a paramount duty on their part.

Some of his friends, indeed, endeavored to persuade him that Romanism would accommodate itself to the times if it were permitted to do so; but he could not be convinced of this, and he consequently viewed the passing of the Roman Catholic Bill with very dark forebodings.

* This was done by a few brief remarks in the Preface to the Colloquies with Sir Thomas More.

To George Ticknor, Esq.

"Keswick, March 17, 1829.

"MY DEAR SIR,

"Mere shame has for some time withheld me from writing, till I could tell you that my Colloquies, which have so long been in the press, were on the way to you. They will be so by the time this letter is half seas over. I am expecting by every post the concluding proofs; and you will receive with them a little volume consisting of two poems,* from the subjects of which (both are Romish legends), and perhaps a little from the manner also, you might suppose the writer was rejuvenescent. Both were, indeed, intended for some of our Annuals, which are now the mushrooms of literature; but the first in its progress far outgrew all reasonable limits for such a collection, and the latter was objected to because it might prevent the annual from selling in Roman Catholic circles—an anecdote, this, which is but too characteristic of the times.

"Rejuvenescent, however, in a more important sense of the word, thank God, I am. When your consignment arrived at Keswick last summer, I was in London, under Copeland the surgeon's hands. By an operation which some years ago was one of the most serious in surgery, but which he (more than any other person) has rendered as safe as any operation can be, I have been effectually relieved from an infirmity which had afflicted me about twelve years, and which often rendered me incapable of walking half a mile. Now I am able to climb the mountains; and as then I was never without a sense of infirmity when I moved, I never walk now without a consciousness of the blessing that it is to have been thus rendered sound. This sort of second spring prevents me from feeling the approach of age as I otherwise might do. Indeed, Time lays his hand on me gently: I require a glass only for distant objects; for work, my eyes serve me as well as ever they did; and this is no slight blessing when most of my cotemporaries have taken to spectacles.

"Nevertheless, I have mementoes enough in myself and in those around me. The infant whom you saw in his basket has now entered upon his eleventh year, and is making progress in Dutch and German as well as Greek and Latin. The youngest of my remaining daughters has ceased to be a girl. She who was the flower of them (and never was there a fairer flower)—you will remember her—is in heaven; and were it not for the sure hope we have in looking forward, I could not bear to look back.

"This year, I trust, will see good progress made in Oliver Newman, the poem being so far advanced that it becomes an object to take it earnestly in hand and complete it. With us no poetry now obtains circulation except what is in the Annuals; these are the only books which are purchased for presents, and the chief sale which poetry used to have was of this kind. Here, however, we are overrun with imitative talent in all the fine arts, especially in fine literature; and if it is not already the case with you, it will very soon be so. I can see some good in this: in one or two generations, imitative talent will become so common that it will not be mistaken, when it first manifests itself, for genius; and it will then be cultivated rather as an embellishment for private life than with aspiring views of ambition. Much of that leveling is going on with us which no one can more heartily desire to promote than I do—that which is produced by raising the lower classes. Booksellers and printsellers find it worth while now to publish for a grade of customers which they deemed ten years ago beneath their consideration. Good must result from this in many ways; and could we but hope or dream of any thing like long peace, we might dream of seeing England in a state of intellectual culture and internal prosperity such as no country has ever before attained. But all the elements of discord are at work; and though I am one of the last men to despair, yet I have no hope of living to see the end of the troubles which must ere long break out—the fruits of this accursed Catholic Question, let it now take what course it may.

"Wordsworth has had a most dangerous fall, headlong, from his own mount, but providentially received no serious injury. He is looking old, but vigorous as ever both in mind and body. Remember me to all my Boston friends, and present my thanks to Mr. Norton for his edition of Mrs. Hemans's poems, which reached me safely. I was very sorry that he found me here in a crowd, in consequence of which I saw much less of him and his very agreeable companions than we all wished to have done.

"God bless you, my dear sir!

"Yours, with sincere regard,

"ROBERT SOUTHEY."

* The titles of these were, "All for Love, or a Sinner well Saved," and "The Pilgrim to Compostella."

My father had given commission for a considerable number of books to the great "bibliopole" of Brussels, which were so long in making their appearance that Mr. Taylor had expressed some opinions derogatory to his qualities as a good and punctual bookseller, which called forth the following amusing letter in his defense.

To Henry Taylor, Esq.

"April 13, 1829.

"MY DEAR H. T.,

"I must not let you think ill of Verbeyst. He had sundry books to provide for me, some of which are not easily found; for example, the continuators of Baronius, a set of Surius, and Colgar's very rare Lives of the Irish Saints, without which I could not review O'Connor's collection of the Res Hibernicarum Script. Last year, when he had collected these, his wife fell ill and died. *Bien des malheurs*, he says, he has had since he saw me, and that they had left him in a lethargic state, from which he is only beginning to recover. * * *

"You must not think ill of Verbeyst: he has

the best stock of books I ever met with, and at the lowest prices. * * No, H. T., if you had bought as many books of Verbeyst as I have, and had them in your eye (as they are now in mine), and had talked with him as much as I have done (and in as good French), and had drunk his Rhenish wine and his beer, which is not the best in the world, because there is, or was, as good at West Kennet, but than which there is not, never was, and never can be better —no, H. T., if you remembered the beer, the wine, and the man himself, as I do, you would not and could not entertain even the shadow of an ill or an angry thought toward Verbeyst. Think ill of our fathers which are in the Row, think ill of John Murray, think ill of Colburn, think ill of the whole race of bibliopoles except Verbeyst, who is always to be thought of with liking and respect.

"A joyful day it will be when the books come, and he promises them by the first ship—perhaps it may be the second. But come they will at last, if wind and waters permit; and, if all be well, when they arrive I shall not envy any man's happiness (were I given to envy) on that day.

"I have told you of the Spaniard who always put on his spectacles when he was about to eat cherries, that they might look the bigger and more tempting. In like manner, I make the most of my enjoyments, and, though I do not cast my cares away, I pack them in as little compass as I can, carry them as conveniently as I can for myself, and never let them annoy others. God bless you! R. S."

The next letter is out of place as to date, but, I think, so peculiarly in it as to subject, that I may be excused the anachronism.

To Henry Taylor, Esq.

"Oct. 8, 1829.

"MY DEAR H. T.,

"I have been jumping for joy: Verbeyst has kept his word; the bill of lading is in Longman's hands, and by the time this reaches you I hope the vessel, with the books on board, may be in the river, and by this day month they will probably be here. Then shall I be happier than if his majesty King George the Fourth were to give orders that I should be clothed in purple, and sleep upon gold, and have a chain about my neck, and sit next him because of my wisdom, and be called his cousin.

"Long live Verbeyst! the best, though not the most expeditious of booksellers; and may I, who am the most patient of customers, live long to deal with him. And may you and I live to go to the Low Countries again, that I may make Brussels in the way, and buy more of his books, and drink again of his Rhenish wine and of his strong beer, better than which Jacob von Artevelde never had at his own table, of his own brewing—not even when he entertained King Edward and Queen Philippa at the christening. Would he have had such a son as Philip if he had been a water-drinker, or ever put swipes to his lips? God bless you! R. S."

To Walter Savage Landor, Esq.

"April 14, 1829.

"The bookseller sent me the first volume of your unpublished series. Some things in it I wished away; with very many more you know how truly I must be delighted. Lucullus and Cæsar especially pleased me, as one of the most delightful of these conversations throughout.

"You will not suppose that I am one of the sudden converts to Catholic Emancipation. Those conversions have the ill effect of shaking all confidence in public men, and making more converts to parliamentary reform than ever could have been made by any other means. For myself, I look on almost as quietly at these things from Keswick as you do from Florence, having done my duty in opposing what I believe to be a most dangerous measure, and comforting myself with the belief that things will end better than if it had been in my power to have directed their course. I suppose the next movement of the Irish Catholics, when the next movement of the drama begins, will be put down by the Duke of Wellington with a high hand; but the ghost of the Catholic Question will be far more difficult to lay than the Question itself would have been: there will be a great emigration of Protestants from Ireland; the struggle will be for Catholic domination there, and we shall have the war upon a religious ground, not upon a civil pretext.

"We are likely to have Historians of the American War on both sides of the water. Jared Sparks, who is to publish Washington's Correspondence, came over to examine our state papers. In his search, and in that which took place in consequence of it, so much matter has been ferreted out that the government wishes to tell its own story, and my pulse was felt; but I declined, upon the ground that others could perform the task as well, and that I have other objects which it was not likely that any other person would take up with the same good will, and equal stock in hand to begin with.

"My health, thank God, is good, and the operation I underwent last June has restored me to the free use of my strength in walking, a matter of no trifling importance for one who was born to go afoot all the days of his life. I can now once more climb the mountains, and have a pleasant companion in my little boy, now in his eleventh year. Whatever may be his after fortunes, he will have had a happy childhood, and, thus far, a happy boyhood. The change which my death would make in his happiness, and in that of others, is the only thing which casts a cloud over my prospect toward eternity. I wish I could see you and your children; and I have a hope that this may yet be, though I know not when.

"God bless you! R. S."

On page 465 my father speaks of an intended

visit to the Isle of Man in the following May, and all preparations were now made for this excursion, which was, however, destined to be cut short by what seemed an untoward circumstance, though it did not prove so in its results. On arriving at Whitehaven, we found some accident had occurred to the machinery of the steam-vessel in which we were to have crossed, and, in consequence, it was determined that we should fix ourselves for a time at some watering-place on the coast. Chancing, however, on our road to call at Netherhall, the seat of my father's old friend and fellow-traveler, Mr. Senhouse, he found him just recovering from an illness, and glad of the cheerful change my father's company afforded him; and our morning call was prolonged, by his hospitable pressure, to a five weeks' visit.

This led further to Mr. Senhouse being induced to remove with his family to Keswick for the latter part of the summer and the autumn, which he did for several successive years, and a great addition was thus made to the pleasant summer society there. Many were the morning excursions and evening dances held in consequence; and although my father was at no time a partaker of the latter, and occasionally looked grave at late hours, yet no one rejoiced more to see others enjoy themselves.

These were the best days of Keswick in my recollection: there were always parties of Oxford and Cambridge students passing the long vacation there, and with the resident society and the frequent presence of visitors, for some years our season was a very gay and joyous one. My father's occupations, however, though suffering some necessary interruptions, slackened little because of the idleness around him.

To Henry Taylor, Esq.

"June 20, 1829.

"MY DEAR H. T.,

"Here is a tit-bit of information to you respecting publishers and public taste. One of ——'s best novelists writes to me thus: 'You are not aware, perhaps, that my publisher employs supervisors, who strike out any thing like dissertation, crying out ever for bustle and incident, the more thickly clustered the better. Novel readers, say these gentry, are impatient of any thing else; and they who have created this depraved appetite must continue to minister to it.'

"I have been amused by reading in the Atlas that I resemble Leigh Hunt very much both in my handwriting and character, both being 'elegant *pragmatics*.' A most queer fish, whose book and epistle will make you laugh when you come here next, calls me, in verse, 'a man of Helicon.' 'Elegant Pragmatic' I think pleases me better.

"I am now working at the Peninsular War. Canga Arguelles has published a volume of remarks upon the English histories of that war: it is, in the main, a jealous but just vindication of his countrymen against Napier. In my case he has denied one or two unimportant statements, for which my authorities are as good as his, and pointed out scarcely any mistake except that of paper money, for stamps, in a case where the people burned those of the intrusive government. I am not a little pleased to see that he has not discovered a single error of the slightest importance; but I am justly displeased that, professedly writing to vindicate his countrymen against the injurious and calumniating representation of the English writers, he has not specially excepted me from such an imputation, as he ought in honesty to have done.

"I am also in the last part of a queer poem for Allan Cunningham. The hay-asthma keeps off and on with me, sometimes better, sometimes worse, sometimes wholly suspended, and never much to be complained of. As soon as my dispatches are made up, I shall set off with it, in the intention of bathing in the Greta, unless a shower should prevent me.

"God bless you! R. S."

To Henry Taylor, Esq.

"July 8, 1829.

"MY DEAR H. T.,

"* * * * * * *

I have no wish to see the Examiner.* What there is there proceeds either from the Elegant Pragmatic himself, or from Hazlitt, both of whom hate me, but have a sort of intellectual conscience which makes them respect me in spite of themselves. But it is evident that the constant hostility of newspapers and journals must act upon an author's reputation like continued rain upon grass which is intended to be cut for hay; it beats it to the ground and ruins the harvest, though the root may remain unhurt. Booksellers, if they understood their own interest, ought to counteract this.

* * * * * * *

"As for my readiness to admit any exculpation of the Spaniards, I shall not acknowledge any such bias till I see that any writer has more distinctly perceived their manifold errors, or more plainly stated them.

"Lockhart has sent me Doddridge's Correspondence to review: a pleasant and easy subject, though the first half volume, which is all I have read, is a most curious specimen of elaborate insipidity. From his youth Doddridge kept short-hand copies of all the letters which he wrote! and the series begins in his nineteenth year, and any thing so vapid, so totally devoid of easy and natural playfulness, I could hardly have conceived. Withal, he was an excellently good man, and when I have read his works (to which I am an entire stranger at present, but I have sent to Lockhart for them), I may then perceive that he has deserved his reputation as a writer. At any rate, insipid materials may be made into a good dish by the help of suitable seasoning and sauces, and I like to deal with no subjects so well as those which I can play with.

* A review of the Colloquies had appeared in that paper, and Mr. Taylor had offered to send him the number that contained it.

"Blackwood I have not seen.

"I have the raw materials of more ballads ready to be worked out, and am about a prelude, which I think you will like, to the next. Allan offers £35 per sheet, which is good pay for light and pleasant work, and I retain the right of reprinting hereafter.

"God bless you! R. S."

To John Rickman, Esq.

"Keswick, July 9, 1829.

"My dear R.,

"Do you know any thing of an association which began at Brighton about two years ago, and which Gooch writes me word from thence 'is prospering splendidly considering the paucity of its means.' It is a slip of Owenism grafted upon a sound common sense stock. 'The whole principle is (Gooch *loquitur*) for a number to join to form a common property by small weekly subscriptions, which, instead of being vested in savings' banks or benefit societies, is vested in business. They have already got a shop, a mackerel boat, and a garden of twenty-eight acres, all of which are prospering; so that the common property in capital accumulates in two ways, by the weekly subscriptions and by the profits of trade. In conducting these trades they employ their own members, and as they increase their trade they will employ more, till the whole number will be employed in the service: then the community will be complete, although scattered; but they hope, ultimately, to live together on their own land in a kind of village, like the Beguines of Ghent. The practice is spreading among the working classes in various parts of the island, and seventy similar institutions have already been formed. The knowledge of it has been diffused by a weekly paper called the Co-operator, consisting of four pages, price one penny: it sells upward of 12,000. I have drawn up (Gooch *loquitur*) an account of it for the Quarterly; but will the editor put it in?' Brighton is near enough to one of your haunts for you to inquire further into this, if it strikes you as it does me at this distance and Gooch upon the spot.

* * * * * * *

"God bless you! R. S."

To the Rev. Nicholas Lightfoot.

"Keswick, July 12, 1829.

"My dear Lightfoot,

"The very wish which you have expressed to me, that your sons should become acquainted with my kinsmen (who, though my first cousins, are of their generation, not of yours or mine), I had formed, and was thinking of expressing to you. I dearly love inherited attachments, and am never better pleased than when I see a likelihood of their striking root.

"Your bishop (Dr. Phillpotts) was at the head of the school when I entered it in its midway form, so there should be four or five years' difference in our age. Of course I well remember him, because of his station; but had he been in any other part of the school among the οι πολλοι, I should call him to mind as distinctly by his profile as he does me by my name, though I do not suppose that a single word was ever exchanged between us.

"Whether the seed which I have scattered in my Colloquies will produce fruit in due season, I perhaps may not live to see; but some of it appears to have taken root. Among the letters, pertinent and impertinent, which have reached me relating to it, there are two from strangers which show this. The one is from Sir Oswald Mosely, about the Church Methodists, entering into the views which I have expressed, and proposing to form an association for furthering their progress. Upon this subject I have declined giving him any opinion till I shall have seen Sadler, the member for Newark, whom I have engaged to see at Lowther in the autumn, and who, I know, takes much interest in this attempt. The other relates to the scheme for directing the personal charity of females to hospitals rather than prisons; to the sick rather than to the profligate. This is from Mr. Hornby, the Rector of Winwick, who had before hinted at such a thing in a sermon preached upon the opening of the Liverpool Infirmary, and who now offers his purse and his personal exertions to promote it. You will readily suppose that I am gratified by this. But I have neither time, nor inclination, nor talents to take upon myself any part in forming such societies. If the voice of one crying in the mountains is heard, all that I am capable of doing is done.

* * * * * * *

"One way in which I feel the effect of time is that I neither walk so fast as formerly nor willingly so far, and that I have sometimes a sense of weakness, which is, no doubt, as a memento that I shall presently be an old man. And yet I hope to have some pleasant days with you upon the lakes and the mountains yet. God bless you, my dear old friend!

"Yours most affectionately,

"R. Southey."

To Allan Cunningham.

"Keswick, July 23, 1829.

"My dear Allan,

"I have read your first volume, and with very great pleasure. You need not ask any one how biography ought to be written. A man with a clear head, a good heart, and an honest understanding will always write well; it is owing either to a muddy head, an evil heart, or a sophisticated intellect that men write badly, and sin either against reason, or goodness, or sincerity.

"There may be secrets in painting, but there are none in style. When I have been asked the foolish question what a young man should do who wishes to acquire a good style, my answer has been that he should never think about it, but say what he has to say as perspicuously as he can, and as briefly as he can, and then the style will take care of itself.

"Were you to leave nothing but these Lives,

you need not doubt of obtaining the remembrance which you court and desire.

"I wish I could tell you any thing which might be found useful in your succeeding volumes. I knew Barry, and have been admitted into his den in his worst (that is to say, his maddest) days, when he was employed upon his Pandora. He wore at that time an old coat of green baize, but from which time had taken all the green that incrustations of paint and dirt had not covered. His wig was one which you might suppose he had borrowed from a scare-crow; all round it there projected a fringe of his own gray hair. He lived alone, in a house which was never cleaned; and he slept on a bedstead with no other furniture than a blanket nailed on the one side. I wanted him to visit me. 'No,' he said, 'he would not go out by day, because he could not spare time from his great picture; and if he went out in the evening, the Academicians would waylay him and murder him.' In this solitary, sullen life he continued till he fell ill, very probably for want of food sufficiently nourishing; and after lying two or three days under his blanket, he had just strength enough left to crawl to his own door, open it, and lay himself down with a paper in his hand, on which he had written his wish to be carried to the house of Mr. Carlisle (Sir Anthony) in Soho Square. There he was taken care of; and the danger from which he had thus escaped seems to have cured his mental hallucinations. He cast his slough afterward; appeared decently dressed and in his own gray hair, and mixed in such society as he liked.

"I should have told you that, a little before his illness, he had with much persuasion been induced to pass a night at some person's house in the country. When he came down to breakfast the next morning, and was asked how he had rested, he said remarkably well; he had not slept in sheets for many years, and really he thought it was a very comfortable thing.

"He interlarded his conversation with oaths as expletives, but it was pleasant to converse with him; there was a frankness and animation about him which won good will as much as his vigorous intellect commanded respect.

"There is a story of his having refused to paint portraits, and saying, in answer to applications, that there was a man in Leicester Square who did. But this he said was false, for that he would at any time have painted portraits, and have been glad to paint them. God bless you!

"Yours very truly, R. S."

To Henry Taylor, Esq.

"Keswick, Aug. 6, 1829.

"MY DEAR H. T.,

"I have declined a proposal from Fraser to write a popular history of English literature, *à-la-mode* Murray's Family Library, in four volumes, because, in the first place, it can not be prudent to engage in schemes where, besides author and bookseller, there is a certain middle man, or undertaker, to have his portion of the profits; secondly, because I hope to execute such a work upon a fitting scale, and in a manner correspondent to the subject; and, lastly, because I will clean my hands of all existing engagements and projects before I admit even a thought of any thing new, except in the way of mere recreation.

"Lockhart tells me my paper upon Portugal has had the rare fortune of pleasing all parties: I looked at it, therefore, to find out what there was wrong in it, but I could not discover. He asks for a similar paper upon Spain, but can not have it, because much that is true of the one country is true of the other, and because I am not so thoroughly acquainted with the subject. Concerning Portugal no other foreigner can know so much; concerning Spain, many may know more.

"It is well for me that I like reviewing well enough to feel nothing irksome in the employment; but as life shortens on me, I can not help sometimes regretting that so large a share of the little which is left must continue so to be employed till the last.

"When are you coming? we talk of you and wish for you every day.

* * * * * * *

"You think me easily pleased with people. Perhaps no one tolerates them more easily; but I am not often contented, in the full sense of that term, any more with men than with books. In both I am thankful for the good that is mixed with ill; but there are few of either which I like well enough to take my heart, and incorporate them, as it were, with it.

"But I must go on with the Life of Loyola, so God bless you! R. S."

To Dr. Gooch.

"Keswick, Aug. 8, 1829.

"MY DEAR GOOCH,

"If your letter had contained a pleasanter account of your own convalescence, it would have been one of the most agreeable that I ever received. There is zeal enough in the world and good will enough to do all the work which is wanted, if they can but be rightly directed. It is neither a natural nor a fit state of things that there should be more zeal and activity on the wrong side than the right.

"I believe, as you do, that great and permanent good may be effected by colonization, by cultivating waste lands, and by co-operative societies. There will be difficulties in these latter, when the question arises where the limits of private property are to be fixed. In every Utopian romance which has fallen in my way, a despotism of laws, as strict as any military discipline, is always part of the scheme.

"Such a man as is wanted in Parliament I think we shall find in Sadler, whom I am to meet in the course of next month at Lowther. I have to talk about Church Methodism with him; the first time I ever heard his name was in connection with that subject, as being the person on whose countenance and support the prime mover (Mark Robinson, of Beverley) most counted. Sir

Oswald Mosely has been moved by my Colloquies to consult me about the fitness of forming a lay association for promoting this scheme; in my reply I deferred answering that question till I should have conversed with Sadler. I will talk to him also about the co-operation and the poor. We have ground on which to fix our levers, and strong arms with which to work them.

"As for the political economists, no words can express the thorough contempt which I feel for them. They discard all moral considerations from their philosophy, and in their practice they have no compassion for flesh and blood.

"I am writing a life of Ignatius Loyola for the Christmas number of the Foreign Review. The last number has not reached me, and of its contributors I only know that an Edinburgh person, by name Carlisle, has written the most striking ones upon German literature, and that the paper upon Klopstock is by a young man whom I introduced to it, whose name is Heraud—a man of extraordinary powers, and not less extraordinary industry and ardor; he seems capable of learning any thing, except how to check his own exuberance in verse.

"God bless you, my dear Gooch! With hands fuller than I could wish them, and with a head fuller than my hands, and perhaps a heart fuller than my head, I must leave books and papers to go pic-nic-ing upon the hills, where I wish you could be with us.

"Yours affectionately, R. S."

To the Rev. Neville White.

"Keswick, Aug. 21, 1829.

"My dear Neville,

* * * * * * *

"I am very glad that you have got through your degrees, and in a way to satisfy yourself as well as others, which in your case (contrary to most other cases) was the more difficult thing. Set your heart now at rest with the certain knowledge that you have taken more pains to qualify yourself for your profession than most members of it who have entered it in the ordinary course of education for that purpose. One great evil of our Church is, that men are ordained at too early an age. How it could be otherwise I do not know in our state of society, but of this I am very sure, that at such an age it must be by rare circumstances that either the heart or understanding are ripe for such a charge.

"You will have perceived that in those Colloquies I have been careful not to offend those whom I endeavored to impress, and that I have sometimes rather pointed at a wound than probed it. Prudence required this. Some effect the book is producing, for it has drawn on some correspondence respecting Sisters of Charity and Church Methodists, and will, in all likelihood, cost me in this way more time than I can well afford.

"As for the sale of the book I know nothing, which no knowledge is proof sufficient that it has not as yet been great. Nor, indeed, is it likely to be. But I am satisfied with myself for having written it, and believe that in due time it will bring forth fruit after its kind; setting many persons to think, some, I should expect, to feel, and some few, I should hope, to act.

"This has been hastily written amid much interruption; and I must now conclude, with our best remembrances to your fireside (for I conclude you have a fire), and my more especial ones to your good mother, who, if we looked at things as we ought, should be considered now as one of the happiest of human beings, sure as she is of her reward, and near it. I thank God for many things, and for nothing more than that he has enabled me to look onward to death with desire rather than with dread.

"God bless you, my dear Neville!

"Yours most affectionately, R. S."

In consequence of the subject of Female Hospital Nurses and Church Methodism having been touched upon in the "Colloquies," my father had been led into a correspondence with the Rev. J. Hornby of Winwick, who took a lively and active interest in both these subjects. The following is the only letter of my father to Mr. Hornby which has been preserved.

To the Rev. J. J. Hornby.

"Keswick, Aug. 27, 1829.

"Dear Sir,

"It is long since any thing has given me so much pleasure as your letter. You have looked at the subject in all its hopeful bearings with the true spirit of Christian philosophy.

"When I received the first communication concerning Church Methodism from Mark Robinson (in February, 1824), I thought it of sufficient importance to send a copy to the present primate, with whom I had personal acquaintance enough to authorize me in so doing. I did not let Robinson know this, because it would have been giving myself a false appearance of consequence in his eyes—would have been taking upon myself more than I had any right or reason to do; and might also have raised vain expectations in him. In my letters to him, then and afterward, I could do nothing more than express hearty wishes for the success of what appeared to me a most desirable attempt.

"The answer which I received from Fulham was in these words. [See letter from the Bishop of London, *antè*, p. 421.]

"It seemed to me at the time that the Bishop of London supposed these seceding Methodists to ask for more than they actually did; that they required nothing like a formal treaty, but merely to have their offered services accepted and countenanced. I thought, also, that there could be little danger in this case, from the description of clergy to which he alluded; because, such among them as hold Calvinistic doctrines (and these are the only dangerous ones) would not be likely to co-operate with Wesleyan Methodists.

"Robinson told me that Archdeacon Wrangham favored his views; and he counted also, through his means, upon the good wishes of the

Archbishop of York. He tried to effect a union with the Irish Church Methodists, and some of their preachers came over in consequence; but this attempt failed. And I know nothing more of the connection which he was endeavoring to form. I read, indeed, sundry pamphlets, which related mainly to personal disputes, the sort of matter into which such things easily degenerate; and I made inquiries concerning Robinson's character, which were satisfactorily answered. When I see Mr. Sadler I shall no doubt be able to obtain full information.

"You and I are perfectly agreed in this, that without some such assistance from without, as well as strenuous exertions within, the Church Establishment of this kingdom can not hold its place. The Dissenting minister has his subordinate helpers every where, the clergyman acts alone. Would I could persuade myself that even with such assistance the overthrow of the Establishment might be averted! But no better means of strengthening it can now be devised, and no likelier ones of preparing the way for its eventual restoration, if, as I too surely fear, this generation should not pass away without seeing it as prostrate as it was in the Great Rebellion.

"You say that you would not ministerially co-operate in any plan of this kind which was disapproved by those to whom ministerial deference and subordination are due. This, of course, I should have expected from you; and, indeed, if the scheme were pursued upon any other principle, it could end only as Methodism has ended, in producing another schism. In the movers and promoters of such a scheme there is too much probability of meeting either with much zeal or too little—with fervent sincerity untempered by discretion, or with mere worldly wisdom—with wild enthusiasts, or with men who look to it only as a politic expedient for supporting a Church which it is their interest to uphold, which they plainly perceive to be in danger, and which they suppose to be even weaker than it is, because they are conscious that they themselves have none of the spirit whereby alone it can be preserved. I know not whether there is more danger from the hot head or the cold heart, but I know which is to be regarded with most dislike. No good work, however, upon any great scale, has ever been undertaken in which fanatics and formalists have not thrust themselves forward to make and to mar. Both must be counted on; and if the work go forward with a blessing upon its purpose, both will be made useful.

"You would not concur in any plan the object of which was to create schism in the body of the Methodists, neither would I bestow a thought upon any such object. But Methodism is already torn by schisms; the specific schism which a mere politic churchman would have wished to bring about, has been made, and in that schism the only organized Methodists are to be found with whom we could co-operate, or who would co-operate with us; for the Revivalists and Ranters are out of the question; and the Conference have something to lose by such co-operation, and nothing to gain by it. The Conference would not give up its system of confession, even if it were to concede matters less demonstrably mischievous. It would not allow you to be rector in your own parish, nor the bishop to be bishop in his own diocese. Its ministers would stand upon their privileges, preach during the hours of Church service, and administer the sacrament. Instead of assisting you to feed your flock, their aim would be to collect as many of your sheep as they could into their own fold.

"But the Church Methodists, if they are true to their own professions, would be just such auxiliaries as are wanted. The scheme, as relating to any single parish, should seem not to be difficult with their help; they would bring whatever is good in the Wesleyan discipline, rejecting its watch-nights and its confessions; they would act as catechists when parents are unable to perform that duty in their own families; and by their meetings and their local preachers, they would introduce and keep up devotional habits. Much may be done in this way But for the work of startling the sinner and making the deaf hear, I think that in most places the aid of itinerant preachers will be wanted; and when we come to itinerancy, we come upon the difficulties and some of the dangers of organizing, supporting, and governing such a class of men. Yet these are the men who can 'create a soul under the ribs of Death;' these are the firemen who seem to be in their proper element when they are breathing amid flames and smoke; whom practice has rendered, as it were, fire proof, and who are thus enabled to snatch brands from the burning. I know not whether any such men have as yet appeared among the Church Methodists; but when work of this kind is to be done, the supply of laborers seldom fails of being equal to the demand.

"In any parish where a society were once methodized, it might be possible to ingraft upon their discipline a plan of looking after the sick for the purpose of administering to their bodily necessities. Women might be found to take upon themselves, if not, like the Beguines, the charge of nursing, yet of assisting in, and in some degree superintending it, avoiding, however, any perilous exposure of themselves, and thereby their own families, to infection; for by such exposure the probable evil that may be incurred exceeds the good that can possibly be done.

"There is some hope also (though fainter) that Methodism, thus regulated and kept in subordination, may be rendered useful in another way. The Co-operative societies are spreading and must spread. I believe that their principle will act upon the whole foundation of society with a force like that of crystallization; and every society which is formed into a little community of its own will surely be withdrawn from the national Church, unless by some such aid as that of Methodism it can be kept or brought within the pale. But this is a wide as well as most momentous subject. And it is time that I should conclude. Believe me, dear sir, yours, with sincere respect, ROBERT SOUTHEY."

Mrs. Opie to R. Southey, Esq.

"Tottenham, 6th mo. 8th, 1829.

"MY DEAR FRIEND,

"I did not know till our yearly meeting was begun the obligation which thou hadst conferred on me, so little worthy of such an enviable distinction as that of being noticed by thee. I will own to thee that my first emotion on reading thy animated and eloquent words* was one of uncontrollable anguish, because the bitter recollection instantly came over my mind that *he* whom they would *most* have pleased would never see them; but happier feelings succeeded, attended by a strong sense of gratitude to thee.

"On the important subject which thou hast thus brought before my consideration, I have not time even to give an opinion, as I am preparing to set off for Paris next fourth day (Wednesday). * * * * I was in hopes of being able to read thy valuable and interesting book through before I wrote to thee, but I have scarcely had an hour of uninterrupted leisure since our yearly meeting closed, and have not read more than a third of the first volume. The introduction is exquisite, I think, and amusing enough to allure even *common* readers to their benefit.

"I intend to turn my visit to Paris to the best account *possible*, and shall see their hospitals, prisons, &c.; and I hope to spend a month pleasantly and profitably, though in that city of *abominations*—past, present, and to come.

"It is twenty-seven years since I was there last; what changes in nations, men, and things have taken place since that time! And how many individuals whom we admired and respected have gone to their long homes since 1802!

"But there is One above '*who changeth not;*' and from this conviction I always derive consolation, when the sense of what I have lost presses heavily upon me.

"Farewell! with the best wishes for thy happiness, and that of thy interesting group, which I picture to myself in thy library, welcoming the wet and wandering guest,

"I am thy affectionate and obliged,

"A. OPIE."

To Mrs. Opie.

"Keswick, Aug. 30, 1829.

"MY DEAR MRS. OPIE,

"I should have replied to your letter immediately upon receiving it, if the answer could have reached you before your departure for Paris, because I suspect from one part of that letter that the copy of my Colloquies which I requested Murray to send you as soon as they were published had not found its way to you. Should this be the case, I pray you cause inquiry to be made for it of his people. You might well wonder that having been moved to call upon you as I have there done, I should leave you to hear of it by chance.

"Though far from any approach to Quakerism myself, I have always justified your transition to it, thinking that under your circumstances the change was both a natural and a happy one. I should have been better pleased if you had not consented to corrupt the king's English, against which debasement, I think, your example, when you conformed in other things, might perhaps have produced some effect, proud of such a proselyte as, however it may *seem*, the society must be; not that this is a matter of any moment, except that I do not like to see you conform to any thing which is not reasonable and worthy of yourself. But the mere change to a state of religious feeling and a strict sect would not have induced me to address you so publicly and pointedly upon a subject which I have very much at heart, from a deep sense of its utility, if I had not heard an expression of yours relating to 'prison duties,' which I think (though highly meritorious in itself) is not the best direction which heroic charity can take. But the words proved that *that* charity had taken possession of you, and that you were ready to follow wherever it might lead.

"You and I have lived in an age of revolutions, and the greatest, as affecting this country, and ultimately the whole of Europe and of the Christian world, is yet to come. The evils of the manufacturing system and the misery of the poor are approaching a crisis, and unless some effectual remedies are speedily applied, the foundations of society will be overthrown. You will agree with me that moral and religious discipline must be one of those remedies, though we might differ concerning its form. But forms will not stand in the way between us here. Quakers and Moravians will co-operate in any great and good work with a single mind, where other sectarians have always a secondary motive lurking in all of them, and uppermost in many or in most.

* * * * * * *

"I see so distinctly the dangers which beset us, and the only means by which they are to be resisted, that if the objects which I have at heart could be promoted by my preaching in the fields and market-places, I would go forth and do so. But my power is in the ink-stand, and my place is here, where I will take every opportunity of enforcing upon such of the public as have ears to hear, truths necessary for their political salvation, did they look no further.

"When I designated you so plainly in that Colloquy, I wrote under the influence of strong feeling; but I have ever since been calmly convinced that I neither spoke too strongly nor said too much. Amelia Opie, I know no person so qualified, and, let me say, so *prepared*, as you to take the lead in a great work of goodness; and if you are of one mind with me in this, I verily believe it will be done.

"God bless you!

"Yours with sincere regard, R. S."

* In the Colloquies, vol. ii., p. 230, my father had mentioned, only not by name, Mrs. Fry and Mrs. Opie, as women prepared by charitable enthusiasm to take the lead in establishing societies for improving hospitals, &c.

I place the next letter a little out of order in respect to date, as being a reply to the preceding one.

Mrs. Opie to R. Southey, Esq.

"Norwich, 11th mo. 24th, 1829.

"MY DEAR FRIEND,

"Illness and other circumstances over which I have seemed to have no power, have, ever since my return to Norwich, prevented my writing to thee, though I can say with truth that I have thought of thee every day, and pondered often over thy letter with grateful and increasing interest.

"It reached me at Paris. I did not for a moment think of answering it then, because I was wholly unacquainted with the societies to which it alludes, and could not obtain the necessary information. But on my return to England I found Elizabeth Fry deep in thy book, and *believing* that she had *already* made a few steps at least in the career to which thou hast pointed in thy eloquent address to me.

"I did not agree with her as to the expediency of the delay, but consented to accompany her on a visit to Dr. Gooch, the result of which he has probably communicated to thee. He gave us ample information relative to the co-operative societies, and last night the friend with whom I am staying read aloud an excellent article on that subject in the Quarterly, and I greatly admire many of the plans on which the society act. I wish it was indispensable for every member to be a religious as well as a moral character. *

"*En attendant*, let me know more of thy views in relation to Elizabeth Fry and myself. Thy letter was truly gratifying to me, but humbling also, as it led me to look into myself, and feel how little worthy I am of such an appeal, and how little able to answer it as it ought to be answered.

"I left Paris (where I stayed four months and a fortnight at the house of a near and dear relation) with a heart full of love and gratitude toward every person there, but also filled with pity, strong disapprobation, and alarm. Still, when I consider the efforts making by many pious and good persons to spread the knowledge of the truth as it is in Christ Jesus among them, I can answer the question, '*Can these bones live?*' not only 'Thou knowest,' but that I think *they will*. Farewell!

"I am thy grateful and affectionate friend,

"A. OPIE."

I do not find traces of any further correspondence with Mrs. Opie upon this subject; several other letters, however, passed between my father and Mr. Hornby, chiefly upon the plan of educating a better order of persons as nurses for the poor; and, through the exertions of the latter, a beginning was made, which unfortunately was prevented by untoward circumstances from producing any permanent results.

It appears that Mr. Hornby, in concert with Adam Hodgson, Esq., of Liverpool, undertook to set on foot an institution for this purpose as an experiment, and to maintain it for two years. They hired a house, engaged a matron, received a number of inmates, and had educated and sent out some few as nurses. Other individuals now became anxious to join them in the responsibility and superintendence; and there not being a sufficient unity of purpose among all the managers, the scheme, which was prospering admirably, fell to the ground. As soon as it appeared that they were educating a valuable class of persons, it was sought to make them available to the upper classes as monthly nurses; and this being an entire perversion of the original plan, Mr. Hornby and Mr. Hodgson withdrew at the end of the two years, and the whole scheme quickly fell to the ground.

The autumn of the year was marked by a great change in the household at Greta Hall. From the time of my father's first settling at Keswick, where it will be remembered he found Mr. and Mrs. Coleridge residing, she and her only daughter had formed part of the family circle, and now the latter was to change, not her name (for she was about to marry her cousin, the late Henry Nelson Coleridge), but her state and residence; and Mrs. Coleridge was about to take up her permanent residence with them. This, of course, was like the parting with a sister.

To John May, Esq.

"Keswick, Sept. 19, 1829.

"MY DEAR FRIEND,

" * * * * * * *

I will tell you Murray's opinion of the Colloquies. The sale, he says, would have been ten-fold greater if religion and politics had been excluded from them! The profits, I dare say, will be very little.

* * * * * * * *

"My third volume of the War is in the press, and my hand has been only taken from it for a short interval, that I might do the needful work of reviewing, by which alone does it seem practicable for me to keep clear with the world. I have written for the London Review a short but very interesting account of Lucretia Davidson, an American poetess, killed, like Kirke White, by over-excitement, in her seventeenth year. It is a most affecting story. There have been three papers of mine in that work—in the first, second, and fifth numbers; and, as they promise that there shall be no further delay in payment, I should not like to withdraw from it. * *

"I might be paid at the same rate for Sharpe's London Magazine; but, when that was converted into a magazine, it passed from the hands of Allan Cunningham into those of Theodore Hook and Dr. M'Ginn, with neither of whom did I wish to associate myself.

* * * * * * *

"But I am looking forward with much satisfaction to next year, as setting me free from the Peninsular War, and thereby leaving me at liberty to commence printing the History of Portugal. I shall be able to live by reviewing, and yet win time enough from that employment to compose this history from the materials which have been so long in preparation, and to carry it through the press. And I shall get by it something better than money: the profits, indeed, can not be so small as to disappoint me, or to make me in the slightest degree indisposed to the task.

"The best news I can send you of myself must be something like an echo of your own letter—that I go on working steadily, with little to hope, but cheerfully, and in full belief that the situation in which I am placed is that which is best for me. Had I kept the path wherein I was placed, I might have been a bishop at this day—probably should have been; and therefore I bless God even for having gone astray, since my aberrations have ended in leading me to a happier, a safer, and (all things considered) a more useful station.

"If there be a later history of Bristol than Barrett's, it must be a better one; there is no earlier. I do not know the spot which you call the Fairies' Parlor by that name; but I could show you some haunts of mine upon those Downs, and in that neighborhood, which I know not whether I should have most pain or pleasure in revisiting. Henry Coleridge and his bride are now lodging in Keswick: her mother departs next week, and then we part, after six-and-twenty years' residence under the same roof. All change is mournful, and if I thought of myself only, I should wish to be in a world where there will be none.

* * * * * * *

"I want to finish the biographical letter in my desk; but you would pity me if you knew what I have in head, and in hand, and at heart, and saw the continual interruptions which cut up my time in large slices, or fritter it away. Withal, I have the blessing of being sound in body once more, and can ascend the mountains with something like the strength, and all the spirits of youth. I had more to say of projects, and of approaching evils and dangers, of which we are likely to see the beginning, but not the end. I was born during the American Revolution, the French Revolution broke out just as I grew up, and my latter days will, in all likelihood, be disturbed by a third revolution, more terrible than either. God bless you, my dear friend!

"Yours most affectionately, R. S."

To ——— ———.

"Oct., 1829.

"My dear Sir,

"I have not seen Landor's second edition, though Colburn was desired to send it me. Your judgment of the book is quite in conformity with mine, if (as I suppose) you except a few dialogues from the general censure, one or two being (to my feeling) nearly perfect. What you have heard me say of his temper is the best and only explanation of his faults. Never did man represent himself in his writings so much less generous, less just, less compassionate, less noble in all respects than he really is. I certainly never knew any one of brighter genius or of kinder heart.

"I am pleased, also, to find you expressing an opinion respecting Milton and Wordsworth which I have never hesitated to deliver as my own when I was not likely to do harm. A greater poet than Wordsworth there never has been nor ever will be. I could point out some of his pieces which seem to me good for nothing, and not a few faulty passages, but I know of no poet in any language who has written so much that is good.

"Now, ——, I want you, and *pray you* to read Berkeley's Minute Philosopher;* I want you to learn that the religious belief which Wordsworth and I hold, and which—I am sure you know in my case, and will not doubt in his—no earthly considerations would make us profess if we did not hold it, is as reasonable as it is desirable; is in its historical grounds as demonstrable as any thing can be which rests upon human evidence; and is, in its life and spirit, the only divine philosophy, the perfection of wisdom; in which, and in which alone, the understanding and the heart can rest.

* * * * * * *

"God bless you! R. S."

To Herbert Hill, Esq.

"Keswick, Nov. 29, 1829.

"My dear Herbert,

"Last year we were at this time looking for your arrival, and well pleased should we all be could we look for it now. I have been somewhat of a rambler of late. Having paid a short, though long-deferred visit at Lowther toward the latter end of last month, I joined Henry Coleridge and Sarah at Penrith, on their way to London, at noon one day, and on the evening of the next they dropped me at Ripon. We saw Rokeby in the morning (a singularly beautiful place), where I called on Mr. Morritt, whom I had not seen for seventeen years; and, on the way to Ripon, we saw Richmond.

"My visit near Ripon was to Mrs. Hodson, known as a poetess by her maiden name of Margaret Holford. One day I dined at Studley, but it was so wet a day that it was impossible to go to the Abbey, or see the grounds there. Another day Mr. Hodson took me to Aldborough, where are many Roman antiquities, and to the place where Paulinus is said to have baptized some thousand Saxons in the River Swale. Another

* To the same friend he writes at another time: "It is because your range of reading has lain little in that course that you suppose religious subjects have rarely been treated in a philosophical spirit. I believe you have cast an eye of wonder upon the three folios of Thomas Jackson's works, and that it would be hopeless to ask you to look into them for the philosophy and the strength of faith, and the warmth of sincere religious belief with which they abound. I do not recommend you to Dr. Clark as a philosophical writer, because I have never yet had an opportunity of reading him myself; but I believe you will find head-work to your heart's content there. But I again recommend you to Berkeley's Minute Philosopher and to Philip Skelton's work.

"But he did not arrive at his belief by philosophical reasoning; this was not the foundation, but the buttress. Belief should be first inculcated as an early prejudice—that is, as a duty; then confirmed by historical evidence and philosophical views. Whether the seed thus sown and thus cultivated shall bring forth in due season its proper fruit, depends upon God's mercy. Butler, I believe, was a very pious man, though the bent of his mind was toward philosophical inquiry; but you may find among our divines men of every imaginable variety of disposition and genius coming to the same center of truth. The older I grow the more contentment I find in their writings."

day I was at Newby (Lord Grantham's), where there is a fine collection of statues. Lady —— had contrived to introduce herself to me in the morning by a move which it required a good deal of the effrontery of high life to effect. The most interesting person whom I saw during this expedition was Mr. Danby, of Swinton Park, a man of very large fortune, and now very old. He gave me a book of his with the not very apt title of 'Ideas and Realities;' detached thoughts on various subjects. It is a book in which his neighbors could find nothing to amuse them, or which they thought it behooved them to admire; but I have seldom seen a more amiable or a happier disposition portrayed than is there delineated.

* * * * * * *

"This was a ten days' absence. I have since made a three days' visit to Colonel Howard at Levens, between Kendal and Milnthorpe, whom I knew by the name of Greville Upton when he was in college at Westminster, and had not seen since. He married an heiress, and took her name, taking with it four large estates, with a mansion upon each, in Westmoreland, Staffordshire, Surrey, and Norfolk. Such fortune has not often been so bestowed upon one who has made so good use of it. Levens is an old house of Elizabeth's age, and fitted up as in that age, with carved chimney-pieces, oak wainscots, and one room is hung with gilt leather. The gardens are in the old fashion, and, perhaps, the best specimen now remaining of their kind. They are full of yew trees cut into all imaginable and unimaginable shapes. One of them is called Dr. Parr, from its likeness to his wig. A guest who dines there for the first time is initiated by a potent glass (called the Levens' constable) of a liquor named Morocco, the composition of which is a family secret. It is like good strong beer, with a mixture of currant wine.

* * * * * * *

"God bless you, my dear Herbert! R. S."

CHAPTER XXXIII.

THE CO-OPERATIVE SOCIETIES—LITERARY EMPLOYMENTS—DEATH OF HIS BROTHER HENRY'S WIFE—EVILS OF OUR COMMERCIAL SYSTEM—CURE FOR LUMBAGO—GALIGNANI'S EDITION OF HIS POEMS—MILLER'S SERMONS—BISHOP HACKET—THE REFORM BILL—DR. GOOCH'S DEATH—THE EVANGELICAL CLERGY—LITERATURE OF DENMARK—RENEWS THE LEASE OF HIS HOUSE—ART OF COMPOSITION—HONE'S EVERY-DAY BOOK, ETC.—POLITICS—JOHN JONES—MR. SADLER—LITERARY EMPLOYMENTS—PAUPER COLONIES—THE MARCH OF INTELLECT—DENMARK—LIFE OF BISHOP HEBER—STATE OF FRANCE—MR. FLETCHER—ELLIS THE MISSIONARY—DR. BELL—POLITICS. —1830.

THE co-operative societies, which have been already alluded to in several letters, seem to have taken great hold of my father's mind, doubtless from their main principle assimilating to that upon which the Pantisocratic Utopia of his early youth was to have been founded, and he had persuaded his unromantic friend Mr. Rickman to take a considerable interest in them, and to make the co-operative papers his companions in a journey he was about to make in Scotland in the previous autumn. From thence he writes, "I have a large and undefined notion of investigating society with this view. How many actually independent incomes, or how much income is requisite as a nucleus wherein to sustain a population dependent upon the expenditure of that income, and on the expenditure of each other? I suspect that this involution is much more powerful and extensive than is usually supposed, insomuch that a common payment for the creation of independent gentry (idlers, if you please), pensioners and creditors of the public, is good instead of evil. The co-operative plan naturally prompts one to think of the circles, the repetition of patterns in paper hangings or carpets, whereof the whole papered room or carpet is made; and by means of the little orbits of Descartes, I think I could depict society usefully by condescending (you know I am in Scotland) on particulars, and by a camera-obscura view of the bustle of mankind."

This set my father's imagination working wonderfully, and after quoting this passage in a letter to Mr. Henry Taylor, he says, "Here I think we have something like a foundation for political economy to rest upon, your existing systems being built either upon sand or bottomless mud. My head is full of thought upon this subject and of seminal notions, which in due time will work out a channel for themselves. They are so busy there that I could almost fancy my work is but to begin, and that all I have hitherto done has only been in the school of preparation. Take notice, H. T., that the clock has just struck eight, that I dined at four, and drank only four glasses of green gooseberry wine; that after dinner I read some pages in Cudworth and the history of some half score Images of our Lady; that I then took half an hour's nap, and afterward drank tea; from which fact you are to conclude that I write now in perfect sobriety, and with a healthy pulse that keeps time at its usual sober moderate rate."

My father never had leisure to bring these notions into any thing like a definite form, and it is probable that, had he attempted to do so, one difficulty after another would have occurred, until he would have given up the matter in despair; and it may be doubted whether any but an odd superstructure could be built upon such a foundation as Mr. Rickman's.

The co-operative scheme itself was destined to disappoint its supporters; for, as soon appeared from the language of these very persons who had commenced so moderately, the most dangerous and socialistic opinions quickly began to gain ground among them, as appears from the following letter.

To John Rickman, Esq.

"Jan. 5, 1830.

"My dear R.,

"* * * * There was a meeting of co-operatives in London in November, I think, the proceedings of which were printed in the News newspaper, and afterward in a separate form. The rankest leveling language was held and applauded there, and the effect was to frighten one gentleman in this county, who, from Gooch's paper in the Quarterly Review, was disposed to encourage such a scheme in his own neighborhood. The best heads among them are very likely to take this wrong turn, and the worst mischief they will do by it, and the first also, will be to cut themselves off from the encouragement which, if they keep within bounds, it is clearly the interest of the land-owners to afford them. The Brighton writer must not preach about the growing omnipotence of such societies, if he would have them succeed. But this was to be expected, and is the greatest obstacle in the way of a very obvious and great good.

"I should like to see the inquiry which you suggested pursued as to the quantity of expenditure needful for keeping a community of some given number in well being, say five hundred persons. To know the rate of circulation and the quantity of the circulating medium would seem something like knowing that rate, &c., in the human body—a means, in some degree, of ascertaining when and how the system is disordered. But, in the social system, there is no danger of disease from overfulness. The circulation can neither be too free nor too fast.

"I do not know who wrote the article on Home Colonies. They appear to me very desirable; but I conceive a regular and also regulated system of emigration to be necessary, to do for us in peace more than can be done in war, by taking off the greater part of those who are restless at home, or who have no prospect of prosperity. I apprehend that in the Dutch poor colonies a great deal has been done by the best management of manures. The Dutch may have learned this from the Japanese.

"God preserve us from a population such as is devouring Ireland and threatening to devour us! Emigration must at last be resorted to, as the only preventive which can save us from this. Meantime we may improve one generation by setting them to cultivate bad land, and train their children for good colonists. I believe there is a great deal of cultivable waste land in the north of England, and that at Bagshot is of the very worst kind in the island.

"The absolute necessity of discipline, and the outcry which would be raised against any exercise of it, are doubtless most serious difficulties in the way, yet I think superable ones, supposing the experiment to be wisely conducted, so that it might bear close, and full, and even hostile inspection.

"I am to review Ellis's book. Pomare was probably a state convert, like Clovis and some of our first Saxon kings; yet not wholly so, for they were converted by politic missionaries, who, for the sake of such converts, made the new religion perfectly accommodating to all the practices which were tolerated by the old.

"God bless you and yours with a new year which may be prosperous in all things!

"R. S."

To Mrs. Hodson.

"Keswick, Jan. 20, 1830.

"My dear Mrs. Hodson,

"My poor brother Henry is left with seven young children, happily so young that five of them will not feel their loss, another soon cease to feel it, and only the eldest feel it long and lastingly; for he (poor boy) has some malformation about the heart which must keep him always at home, and his understanding and affections have acquired strength and intensity as if in compensation for the incurable malady of his frame. I had known my sister-in-law from her infancy, and loved her dearly, both for her own sake and her mother's, who, take her for all in all, was the sweetest woman I have ever been acquainted with. Louisa herself was one of the violets of the world; nothing could be gentler or kinder. She seemed never to think of herself, and was wholly devoted to her family.

* * * * * * *

"Norwich, Mrs. Opie tells me, is in a state of civil war; and infidelity is said to prevail there extensively among the weavers. I believe very few people who are not serving under its banners are aware how widely it has spread among all ranks, and of the imminent danger that threatens us from that cause. I am busy upon the Peninsular War, and in finishing a life of John Bunyan for a handsome edition of the Pilgrim's Progress, a task not of lucre, but of love. The moment it is done I must no longer delay the introduction of John Jones's verses. The Quarterly Review has only a short paper of mine upon Captain Head's book. The after number will have one on Mawe's Journal, and I must forthwith begin for it an account of the mission to Tahiti, which, however, you may read to more advantage in my text-book, Ellis's Polynesian Researches. I have engaged to compose a volume of Naval History, in biographical form, for the Cabinet Cyclopædia, not for love, but for lucre, though it will be done lovingly when in hand. And thus my life passes; little employments elbowing worthier and greater undertakings and shouldering them aside, and the necessity for providing ways and means preventing me from executing half of what I could and would have done for other generations. And yet, how much better is this than pleading causes, feeling pulses, working in a public office, or being a bishop with all the secular cares which a bishopric brings with it, not to speak of its heavier responsibilities.

"Believe me, my dear Mrs. Hodson,

"Yours very truly,

"Robert Southey."

To John Rickman, Esq.

"Feb. 16, 1830.

"MY DEAR R.,

"The co-operatives* ought to be very much obliged to you, and would be so if it were not the most difficult thing in the world to make men understand their own true interest.

"I suspect that in many things our forefathers were wiser than we are. Their guilds prevented trades from being overstocked, and would have by that means prevented over-production, if there had been any danger of it. The greedy, grasping spirit of commercial and manufacturing ambition or avarice is the root of our evils. You are very right in saying that in all handicraft trades wages are enough to allow of a very mischievous application of what, if laid by, would form a fund for old age; and I quite agree with you that tea and sugar must be at least as nutritious as beer, and in other respects greatly preferable to it. But there is a real and wide-spreading distress, and the mischief lies in the manufactories; they must sell at the lowest possible price; the necessity of a great sale at a rate of small profit makes low wages a consequence; when they have overstocked the market (which, during their season of prosperity, they use all efforts for doing), hands must be turned off; and every return of this cold fit is more violent than the former.

"There is no distress among those handicrafts who produce what there is a constant home demand for. But if we will work up more wool and cotton than foreigners will or can purchase from us, the evils of the country must go on at a rate like compound interest. Other nations will manufacture for themselves (a certain quantity of manufacturing industry being necessary for the prosperity of a nation), and this, with the aid of *tariffs*, may bring us to our senses in time.

"One tells me that there is likely to be a slight degree of consolidating pressure brought to bear upon the ministry; another, that they may very likely find themselves in a minority. I do not wish for a change of men, because I do not see what better men could do in their places. Eighteen months ago circumstances might have been directed to a wise statesman's will; now they must take their course: but, come what will, I shall never lose heart or hope.

* * * * * * *

"God bless you! Our best remembrances to your fireside. R. S."

To Allan Cunningham.

"Keswick, March 4, 1830.

"MY DEAR ALLAN,

"Thank you for your second volume,† which, if I had not been more than usually pressed for time, I should have read throughout at a sitting immediately on its arrival, but of which I have read enough to know that it is *very good.* Indeed, I do not see how that part which I have read could have been better.

"If your lumbago be severe, I can tell you that at Yarmouth cod-liver oil taken internally used to be considered as a specific for that complaint, but in what quantity taken I can not tell. It is a villainous complaint, as I know by some slight touches of it only; but complaints that threaten no serious consequences sit lightly on us even when they are heaviest. The flesh feels them, but not the spirit; and there it is we feel when those who are near and dear to us are suffering. Spring, I hope, will bring with it recovery to your household.

"I am put to the daily expense of two hours' walking to keep in order a liver which has a great inclination—as if the spirit of Reform had reached it—to try some new mode of action altogether inconsistent with the safety of the constitution. The remedy seems to answer well; and when the weather will allow me to take a book in my hand, it is not altogether lost time. I can read small print at the pace of three miles an hour; and when I have read enough to chew the cud upon, then in goes the pocket volume, and I add a mile an hour to my speed.

"Galignani has sent me his edition of all my poems, with his compliments. He has put Lawrence's name to the portrait, which is a worsened copy of 'Fitzbust the Evangelical.' He has got a most circumstantial memoir, in which every circumstance that is not totally false is more or less inaccurate; all Hazlitt's abuse of me is interwoven and mixed up with a hodge-podge of panegyric, which in its particulars is just as false. Some rubbish which I had thrown overboard is raked up; one poem given to me which is Crowe's, another which is Cottle's, and a third which is I forget by whom; and one or two pieces are printed twice over. Withal, it is a goodly volume; and will make my poems known on the Continent to the cost of their sale at home. I shall favor M. Galignani with a few lines, to be inserted in my epistle to you, whenever that is printed. Farewell, and believe me always

"Yours with hearty regard,

"ROBERT SOUTHEY."

To Henry Taylor, Esq.

"Keswick, March 8, 1830.

"MY DEAR H. T.,

"Lord John's budget is as much a masterpiece in its way as Lord Althorpe's. It really seems as if the aristocracy of this country were to be destroyed, so marvelously are they demented.

"While London is intent upon these debates, I have been reading Miller's* Sermons, 'intend-

* Mr. Rickman had written a paper on the subject for insertion in the Brighton Co-operator, and which he had sent to my father for his suggestions and remarks.

† Of The Lives of British Painters, &c., in Murray's Family Library.

* The Rev. John Miller, of Worcester College, Oxford. Of these discourses, my father says to another correspondent, "Would to God that such sermons were oftener delivered from our pulpits. Bad sermons are among the many causes which have combined to weaken the Church of England; they keep many from church, they send many to the meeting-house; hurtful they can hardly fail to be if they are not profitable: and one of the ways by which incompetent ministers disparage and injure the Establishment in which they have been ordained, is by de-

ed to show a sober application of scriptural principles to the realities of life.' Recommend them to your mother and Miss Fenwick, and to any of your friends who are not indisposed to read such books. I think you saw Miller here one evening, with a brother and sister. His sermons are unlike any others which I have ever read; they are thoroughly Christian in their spirit, and philosophical; comprehensible by the plainest understanding, and as satisfactory to the judgment as they are to the feelings.

"If I had leisure I could write a very curious essay, historical and critical, upon sermons.

* * * * * * *

"I have been reading, too, for the first time, Lord Chesterfield's Letters, with a melancholy feeling that the one and only *grace* which he despised might have made him a wise and good man.

"Bishop Hacket and I go on well after supper. His are comical sermons: half Roman Catholic in their conceits, full of learning which would be utterly unprofitable if it did not sometimes call forth a shrewd remark, seasoned with piety, and having good strong sense mixed up with other ingredients, like plums in a pudding which has not too many of them.

"I think you will have another change at the Colonial Office ere long. This ministry can not stand, if the aristocracy and monarchy are to be preserved. I believe they felt their weakness (how, indeed, could they fail to feel it after such a budget?), and therefore they went over to the Radicals at the eleventh hour, thinking so to find strength. Peel's is said to have been the best speech he ever made. I am curious to see how far 'the evil heart of fear' will carry —— upon this occasion. God bless you! R. S."

To Henry Taylor, Esq.

"March 14. [illegible]

"MY DEAR H. T.,

"Your views are darker than mine, though I see the danger clearly and look it fairly in the face. The bill will be thrown out, unless many members who are opposed to it absent themselves from the division in cowardice; and to some extent this no doubt will happen, as even public opinion inflicts no punishment upon moral cowardice, though when the poor *body* offends, it is punished with disgrace or with death.

"What astonishes me is, that the Greys, Russells, &c., do not look at the known character and certain motives of the men whose support they are actually courting at this time.

* * * * * * *

"I should like a law excluding from Parliament all persons against whom a verdict has been given for libels, public or private, adultery, or fraud of any kind, and all who, having been bankrupts, had not afterward paid their creditors in full.

"I am reading the Doctrine de Saint Simon, preparatory to a paper upon that subject. The subject is very curious, and the book written with great ability. God bless you! R. S."

To Mrs. Hodson.

"Keswick, March 16, 1830.

"MY DEAR MRS. HODSON,

" * * * * * * *

I have lost in Dr. Gooch one of the men in the world for whom I had the greatest regard. He saved this country from having the plague imported by a paper some years ago upon the subject in the Quarterly Review. That paper upon Anatomy in the last number is his, and the forthcoming one I believe will contain one upon Madhouses, the last subject that occupied him. Never was man more desirous of doing all in his power toward diminishing the sum of human misery.

"The article on the Internal Situation of the Country is not mine, nor do I know whose it is. You may be sure that I shall not be found complimenting the present ministry, nor even excusing them, further than by saying that they know not what they do. If I wish that they may keep their station, it is because I do not wish any other set of men so ill as to wish them in their place, and because I do not see any good which could be hoped for from such a change. Even the Swiss are looking with exultation for the downfall of British prosperity and power, which they believe to be fast approaching. But in this the enemies of England will be woefully deceived, whatever may happen to us at home.

"I am inclined to think that the Church is in more danger from the so-called Evangelical party among its own clergy than it would be from lay-assistance. These clergy are now about to form a sort of union—in other words, a convocation of their own, that they may act as a body. They have had a Clerical breakfast in London. The two Noels, Stewart, who is brother-in-law to Owen of Lanark, and was here with him some years ago, and Daniel Wilson, were the chief movers. There have been two reports of the speeches in the Record newspaper, and a Mr. M'Neil, who very sensibly objected to the whole scheme, had the whole meeting against him.

"Like you, I both dislike and distrust those who call themselves professors. They are just what the Pharisees were before them; but I want to embody in the service of the Church some of that honest enthusiasm which will otherwise be employed against it. I want field preachers while we have an ignorant and brutal population: there can be no other means of reclaiming them. They will not go to church—the preacher must go to them.

"Have you seen the Last Days of Sir Humphrey Davy? I knew him intimately in his

livering crude and worthless discourses, which chill devotion even where they do not offend and shock the understanding.

"These are, in the true sense of a word, which has been most lamentably misapplied—Evangelical. I do not know any discourses in which revealed truths and divine philosophy are brought home with such practical effect to all men. They have the rare merit of being at the same time thoroughly intelligible, thoroughly religious, and thoroughly discreet."

best days: he would have been a happier and a greater man than he was if he had been less successful in his fortunes. No man was ever yet the better for living in what is called the world. God bless you!

"Yours truly, ROBERT SOUTHEY."

To J. W. Warter, Esq.

"Keswick, March 18, 1830.

"MY DEAR WARTER,

* * * * * * *

"You are going to a country* which has more in its history and its literature to recommend it than in its objects of art or nature. But to an Englishman it is a very interesting land, and the language of all others most akin to our own, and consequently easier than any other foreign one whatever. You will readily acquire it, and find the value of the acquisition, as an aid toward other Northern tongues, and an indispensable step toward a lexicographical knowledge of our own.

"One subject will be very well worthy your inquiry there—the history of the Reformation, and the present state of the Church in Denmark and Sweden; for in those countries the work was more effectually done than any where else, and therefore, it should seem, more wisely. The Romanists have never recovered strength there, nor have any sects acquired head enough to be troublesome. I have long (for my own satisfaction) been desirous of obtaining more information on this subject than I know where to find.

"There is much sound learning in Denmark, though it may not be of that kind which is rated so much above its real worth in our English Universities. Their two most distinguished poets are Œhlenschlagen and Ingemann. If you will take over the Tale of Paraguay, and All for Love to them, these books may serve as an introduction, some civilities of this kind having heretofore passed between us: tell me, if you can make room for four such little volumes, where they may be sent for you.

"For the climate's sake I shall be glad if you migrate to Naples. Such a migration is likely, because nothing can be more according to the wisdom of English diplomacy than that a minister who has made himself acquainted with Northern interests should be sent to a Southern court, where he has every thing to learn. But I hope you will lay your Danish and German foundations first. The Goths, who overthrew the Roman empire, were not superior in a greater degree to the Romans whom they subdued, than the Northerns are now in literature to any thing that the South produces, or can produce as long as Italy is blasted by the Papal Upas.

* * * * * * *

"God bless you! R. S."

To Henry Taylor, Esq.

"April 15, 1830.

"MY DEAR H. T.,

"Our political evils I impute mainly to the progress of every thing in the country, except good morals and sound policy.

"The specific evil which I ascribe to the Catholic Relief Bill is, that it has destroyed the principle of the Constitution: the Revolution made it (and at a heavy price) essentially Protestant; it may be any thing now. Parties are in consequence broken up, the process of dislocation is going on, *every thing* is out of joint, and by-and-by all will fall to pieces.

"I am not well, but I am able to work, and shall walk, in old English phrase, 'for dear life;' though life is not so dear to me but that I could very willingly lay it down, if its continuance were not more desirable for others than myself. One pleasant thing, however, is, that I yesterday made arrangements for renewing my lease of this house; it expires in November next, six months earlier than I had thought; which is so much the better for me, for, getting rid now of the little furniture which belongs to the landlord, I take it from that time at a reduced rent for five years, extensible at my option to five more. This it was prudent to secure, though, in all likelihood, a smaller tenement will suffice for me before that time.

"So I look upon myself as settled for life. Lack of employment I shall have none, for scarcely a week passes without some application to me.

"Sir —— told my brother that I was a *fortunate* man: I have been, and am so, God be thanked, in almost every sense of the word, except that in which Sir G. is likely to understand it.

"God bless you! R. S."

To J. W. Warter, Esq.

"Keswick, April 23, 1830.

"MY DEAR WARTER,

" * * * * * * *

I went abroad for the first time at an early age, under circumstances not very dissimilar; for a shorter absence, but with much worse prospects. My disposition, however, was always hopeful; relying upon Providence, I could rely upon myself; and I can truly say that no anxiety concerning my worldly fortunes ever cost me a sleepless night or an uncomfortable hour. When I had little I lived upon little, never spending when it was necessary to spare; and hitherto, by God's blessing, my means have grown with my expenses.

"My voyage was to Portugal, and you know how much it has influenced the direction of my studies. My uncle advised me at that time to turn my thoughts toward the history of that country, when he saw how eagerly I was inquiring into its literature, and more especially its poetry. Then my mind was not ripe enough for historical pursuits; but the advice was not without effect; and when I went again to Portugal, after an absence of four years, I began to look for materials, and set to work.

"I am glad that Burton recommended the ecclesiastical history of Denmark and Sweden to

* Mr. Warter was about to be ordained as chaplain to the British Embassy at Copenhagen.

your attention. It is an interesting subject, and if you only sketched it in a paper for the Quarterly or the British Critic, it might be of use to you hereafter; still more if you found pleasure enough in the pursuit to follow it into its details and make a volume. And this might lead you at length to meditate a history of the three Scandinavian kingdoms—Norway, Sweden, and Denmark—a singularly rich subject, having in its early periods an English interest; a romantic one in its middle, and even later ages; and a moral and political one, in a high degree, at last.

"As for composition, it has no difficulties for one who will 'read, learn, mark, and inwardly digest' the materials upon which he is to work. I do not mean to say that it is easy to write well; but of this I am sure, that most men would write much better if they did not take half the pains they do. For myself, I consider it no compliment when any one praises the simplicity of my prose writings; they are written, indeed, without any other immediate object than that of expressing what is to be said in the readiest and most perspicuous manner. But in the transcript (if I make one), and always in the proof-sheet, every sentence is then weighed upon the ear, euphony becomes a second object, and ambiguities are removed. But of what is called *style*, not a thought enters my head at any time. Look to the matter, and the manner takes care of itself.

* * * * * * *

"Yours affectionately,

"ROBERT SOUTHEY."

To Henry Taylor, Esq.

"May 3, 1830.

"MY DEAR H. T.,

"Hone* might have thriven if he had gone on as badly as he begun. But he was meant for better things, and published, at a cost which could only be covered by a large popular sale, more curious things than these penny purchasers were prepared for; so, in outmarching the march of intellect itself, he outran the constable at the same time. His old sins averted from him one set of customers, and his better mind indisposed others, who would have dealt with him for garbage and such offal as goes to the swine-trough of vulgar taste.

"Add to this that he has ten children, and his embarrassments are accounted for. It is too likely that they will at last break, not his spirit, but his constitution and his heart.

"I hold with Wilmot Horton about emigration, and think Sadler erroneous in his opinions upon the law of primogeniture; but, in the main, his book is a most important one. He has trampled upon Malthus's theory, proving its absurdity and falsehood, and his own views of the law of population deduce from facts that it is what from feeling you would wish it to be. God bless you! R. S."

* "By-the-by, I have bought Hone's Every-day Book and his Table Book, and am sorry I had not seen them before my Colloquies were printed, that I might have given him a hearty good word there. I have not seen any miscellaneous books that are so well worth having; brimful of curious matter, and with an abundance of the very best wood-cuts. Poor fellow, he outwent the march of intellect; and I believe his unwearied and almost unparalleled industry has ended in bankruptcy. I shall take the first opportunity of noticing these books; perhaps it will be in Allan Cunningham's periodical."—*To H. Taylor, Esq.*

To the Rev. Robert Montgomery.

"Keswick, May 11, 1830.

"DEAR SIR,

"I had yesterday the pleasure of receiving your poems. As the note which accompanied them bears date in January, you may have wondered that they were not acknowledged sooner. Any single page of these volumes contains sufficient proof of ardor and power with which any thing may be done when they are disciplined. You are in the right path, with right principles to guide you, and good fortune, I trust, full in view. You have only to store your mind well (as you are storing it), and it will ripen of itself. You mention an introductory letter from one of the very best of men;* I shall be glad if this implies that you have an intention of coming into these parts, when I should have great pleasure in becoming personally acquainted with you.

"Believe me, dear sir, yours with sincere good will, ROBERT SOUTHEY."

To Mrs. Hodson.

"Keswick, May 15, 1830.

"MY DEAR MRS. HODSON,

"The poor king, it is to be hoped, will be released from his sufferings before this reaches you, if, indeed, he be not already at rest; it was thought on Monday that he could not live four-and-twenty hours. God be merciful to him and to us! He failed most woefully in his solemn and sworn duty on one great occasion, and we are feeling the effects of that moral cowardice on his part. The duke expected to remove all parliamentary difficulties by that base measure, instead of which he disgusted by it all those adherents on whom he might have relied as long as he had continued to act upon the principles which they sincerely held; rendered all those despicable who veered to the left-about with him, and found himself as a minister weaker than either the Whigs whom he sought to propitiate, or the Brunswickers (as they are called), whom he has mortally offended.

"William IV., it is believed, will continue the present ministers, but act toward them in such a way that they will soon find it necessary to resign. Then in come Lord Holland and the Whigs, in alliance with the flying squadron of political economists under Huskisson. Beyond this nothing can be foreseen, except change after change; every successive change weakening the government, and, consequently, strengthening that power of public opinion which will lay all our institutions in the dust. Yet I neither despair nor despond, and you may be assured I will not be idle.

"The Peninsular War is my main employment

* The late Sharon Turner.

now. It is yet a long way from its completion, but in good steady progress. I have at this time a head and both hands full. John Jones's attempts in verse will make their appearance shortly; there is a long introduction—in fact, a chapter, of the history of English poetry, which ought to content those subscribers who will not feel the touches of nature which are in this poor man's verses, but *will* feel the rudeness and the faults. I have taken public leave of all such tasks, and declined all inspection of manuscripts, &c., in a way which will amuse you; but I am very far from repenting of what I have done in this way and in this case: in *this* case, because I have rendered some little service, and afforded great delight, to a very worthy poor man.

"In the next Quarterly Review I have papers upon Mawe's passage over the Andes, and the conversion of Tahiti, where, with all my admiration for the spirit in which the missionaries begin and prosecute their work, you will see that I am not blind to the consequences of Calvinistic Christianity. This reminds me of Reginald Heber, upon whose portrait I have written a poem, which will appear in the forthcoming volume of his Letters.

"With our united remembrances to Mr. Hodson, always very truly yours,

"ROBERT SOUTHEY."

To John Rickman, Esq.

"June 8, 1830.

"MY DEAR R.,

"In increase of population, would not the increased proportion of infants augment the per centage of mortality quite as much as the increase of youth would lessen it?

"And will not insufficient diet among the poor balance the effect of improved diet upon the general scale? The lower classes were worse fed formerly, but, except in seasons of extreme dearth, I do not think there were any who died of slow starvation, which is now no uncommon death. This we know in this place, where poor rates, formerly low, have prodigiously increased.

"Did I tell you that a semi-official offer of ground in the New Forest has been made, for the purpose of trying a pauper colony, if government could have found an amateur philanthropist to undertake the management of it. The person fixed upon was a clergyman, an old schoolfellow of mine; not wanting in good will for doing his duty at any time, but not so far wanting in common prudence as to take upon himself such a charge.

"A great deal depends upon the issue of the present struggle in France. The people will not be satisfied with a limited monarchy; they must either be under a tyrannical democracy or an absolute king. If the crown should succeed, I should think it bad policy in this country to oppose any schemes of French conquest on the Barbary shore; there is room enough for ambition there, but at such a cost that France, with such an issue open, would feel little inclination or strength for troubling the repose of Europe.

"The march of intellect has had an odd effect upon Sharon Turner. He thinks past history is likely to attract so little attention in future, and carry with it so little interest, that he advised me to begin my series of British Biography with Sir William Temple! A few steps more in the march, and we shall have to begin the history of philosophy with Jeremy Bentham, and the history of England with Joseph Hume, and the history of literature with the foundation of the London University.

"God bless you! R. S.

"I am working very steadily, and improving a most wet and wintery season by the fireside."

To J. W. Warter, Esq.

"Keswick, June 9, 1830.

"MY DEAR WARTER,

* * * * * * *

"Are there any remains at Shrewsbury of the Amphitheater which in Elizabeth's reign had been made there in an old quarry between the city walls and the Severn? Churchyard the poet (a Shrewsbury man) describes it as holding ten thousand spectators the area served for bear-baiting, wrestling, &c., and on better occasions your school predecessors acted plays there; certainly in a more classical theater than the Dormitory at Westminster. Sir Philip Sidney, and his friend and biographer Lord Brooke, entered that school on the same day; and it was then in as high estimation as any public school in England.

"Danish is so easy and straightforward a language that you may make yourself acquainted with it without study, while you are studying German, and enlarge your vocabulary thereby, without confounding your grammar. Danish seems to me the easiest language into which I have ever looked, not excepting Spanish and Portuguese; but German is as difficult as Greek, and the difficulty is very much of the same kind. I am glad you are under the necessity of acquiring the one; the other you can not help acquiring. Lamentable experience makes me know how much is lost by a *monoglot* traveler: that epithet, perhaps, is not exactly what should be applied to myself, who get on with a mingle-mangle of many languages, put together without regard to mood, tense, gender, number, or person; but my ear is the very worst in the world at catching sounds, and I have therefore more difficulty in understanding others than in making them understand me.

* * * * * * *

"Do not think any thing which relates to the manners or appearance—the in- or out-of-door nature—of a foreign country unworthy of noticing in your journal or note-book. At your age I was satisfied with two or three lines of memoranda, when the same objects would now give me good matter for perhaps as many pages. I should like to know a great deal more of Denmark than I can gather from books; there is no later book than Lord Moleworth's that gives me any satisfaction, and in that there is very much wanting. Coxe is, as he always was, dry and dull, giving only the *caput mortuum* of what information he had gathered, which was generally from the most accessible authorities, when it did not consist of statistic details. Later travelers tell us a great deal more of Sweden. I want to know why Denmark is a poor country, the people being industrious, and the government neither oppressive nor wasteful. Two years ago, having occasion to make some inquiry concerning foreign funds, I thought Danish the safest, looking upon the government as safe, and the nation as honorable and honest, and not likely to be involved in wars or revolutions. But I was informed that it paid the interest of its debt with borrowed money, and, therefore, that it was not a safe stock in which to invest money. This came from a person more than ordinarily versed in such things; but the stock has gradually risen ten per cent. since that time, and will be more likely to keep up than that of any other country, if there should be a convulsion in France, which God in his mercy avert.

"We are in no slight danger here, unless the Whigs are alarmed in time at the progress of their own opinions. In this country there are symptoms of their being so. But it must be a strong sense of their own danger in the men of property that can save us from a popular parliamentary reform in the course of the next Parliament, the direct consequence of which will be a new disposal of Church property, and an equitable adjustment with the fund-holders, terms which in both cases will be soon found to mean spoliation.

* * * * * * *

"Meantime it is a comfort to know that though man *pro*poses, the *dis*posal is ordered by a higher power. God bless you! R. S."

To Henry Taylor, Esq.

"Keswick, July 10, 1830.

"My dear Henry Taylor,

"I dare say it will generally be felt that Mrs. Heber's book does not support the pretensions which its title, and still more its appearance, seems to hold forth. The materials would have appeared to more advantage in a different arrangement.

"There is certainly an air of book-making about the publication, which is not lessened by the funebrial verses that it contains. Mine might have accompanied the portrait, in which case they would have seemed to be appropriately introduced; in fact, they were composed with that design. But this book ought not to detract from his reputation, the estimate of which must be taken from those things which he prepared for the press, and from his exertions in India. He was a man of great reading, and in his Bampton Lectures has treated a most important part of the Christian faith with great learning and ability. His other published sermons are such that I am not surprised my brother Henry should think him the most impressive preacher he ever heard.

"As a poet he could not have supported the reputation which his Palestine obtained, for it was greatly above its deserts, and the character of the poem, moreover, was not hopeful; it was too nicely fitted to the taste of the age. Poetry should have its lights and shades, like painting; like music, its sink and swell, its relief and its repose. So far as the piece was intended for success in a competition for a prize, and for effect in public recitation, it was certainly judiciously done to make every line tell upon the ear. But to all such poetry the motto under one of Quarle's Emblems may be applied, '*tinnit, inane est*.'

"He had a hurried, nervous manner in private society, which covered much more ardor and feeling than you would have supposed him to possess. This I believe entirely disappeared when he was performing his functions; at which time, I have been assured, he seemed totally regardless of every thing but the duty wherein he was engaged.

"Few persons took so much interest in my writings, which may partly have arisen from the almost entire coincidence in our opinions and ways of thinking upon all momentous subjects, the Catholic Question alone excepted. Mrs. Heber told me that I had no little influence in directing his thoughts and desires toward India; and I have no doubt that some lines in Joan of Arc set him upon the scheme of his poem on the death of King Arthur. My personal acquaintance with him was but little, but we knew a great deal of each other through Charles Wynn.

* * * * * * *

"I *am* fond of irregular rhymeless lyrics, a measure wherein I have had few to approve and still fewer to imitate me. The proof of the poetry, however, is not like that of the pudding, in the taste of those who partake it. Thalaba might very probably have been popular had it been in rhyme. None of my lyrical pieces could have been so; and methinks it makes little difference whether there be three or four to admire them, or five or six.

"There are friendships of *chance* and friendships of *choice*, and it was of the former which I meant to speak; they are the more numerous, and probably the more lasting, because, generally beginning earlier, they have time to strike root in us, and partake of the nature of a habit, as the latter may be said to do, in some degree, of a passion. For the same reason, you are not so likely to be deceived in them. One whom you have known from early boyhood may disappoint your hopes and expectations; but you will seldom be deceived in your moral estimate of him; if he was ingenuous and kind-hearted, he will continue so through life. A good apple-tree may be blighted or cankered in its growth, but it will never produce crabs.

"Ministers will delay the meeting of Parliament as long as they can, just as schoolboys would prolong their holidays if they could. But they may be flattered or frightened into any thing, good, bad, or indifferent: no persons who ever filled that station before have been politically so weak, and most pitiably conscious they are of their weakness. A promise to convoke it without delay may probably be extorted from them. 'Gentlemen' have other business than that of the nation to attend to in the month of September, and I do not expect them to meet till they have had a campaign against the pheasants as well as the partridges; so I look to be in town somewhere in October.

* * * * * * *

"God bless you! R. S."

To J. W. Warter, Esq.

"Keswick, Aug. 25, 1830.

"MY DEAR WARTER,

"The late events in France have placed both that country and this, in some respects, in the same sort of relation to each other that they were in forty years ago, after the fall of the Bastile, where my distinct and full recollections of history begin. *There* they are in the honeymoon of their new revolution, and here they are applauded and admired by persons as rash as those who fraternized with the old French Revolutionists, and as ignorant. Their language now is more open and more violent, because they are much more numerous, and perfectly aware of their own power. Yet, on the whole, I am inclined to think that the course of events is rather likely to retard our progress toward revolution than to accelerate it; a *formal* revolution I mean, the *moral* one having already been brought about.

"The aristocracy are likely to be awakened to a sense of danger: in this country, indeed, I know that they are so, though they want either the courage or the honesty to make their public conduct agree with their private declarations. But this course of double dealing can not long be continued if Europe should be involved again in revolutionary wars, from which I hardly see how it can escape, for I can not think that the new King of the French will possess that throne in peace.

"As to military means, we have never been so well prepared for war, and the excitement which it would bring with it, and the impulse which it would give to every branch of industry, would put an end at once to all the present distress, whatever might be the eventual consequences of a war expenditure.

"But enough of this subject, which occupies more of my thoughts than I could wish.

"I have written a biographical paper for the Quarterly Review which will interest you much, if you have not already read the book from which it is composed. It is the Life of Oberlin, a pastor of the Ban de la Roche in the Vosges Mountains. I am upon the latter part of a reviewal of Dymond's Moral and Political Philosophy; and I have sent off a short paper upon the Negro-English New Testament, for printing which the Bible Society has been greatly inveighed against. The Testament is a great curiosity, and I think myself very fortunate in having obtained one. But I do not join in the outcry against the Bible Society; in my judgment they are completely justified in having printed it, but every means for superseding it ought to be used, by teaching either Dutch or English in all the English schools.

* * * * * * *

"God bless you! R. S."

To the Rev. Neville White.

"Keswick, Aug. 27, 1830.

"MY DEAR NEVILLE,

"James Stanger gave me your message yesterday evening, and thereby made me perceive that I must have been mistaken in supposing I had written to you immediately after Mr. Fletcher's visit. I received from him the Religio Medici, which I was very glad to see; and I now say to you, what I then said to him, that when the book is ready I will do the best in my power to serve it in the Quarterly Review. It will be a very beautiful edition of an author whom I value most highly. I was much pleased with Mr. Fletcher himself, and wish there were more booksellers so well-principled and so well-disposed.

"Since his appearance we have had much anxiety concerning Cuthbert; first from a slight but decided attack of scarlet fever, and, before he had recovered his strength, from a much more serious bilious one, which alarmed us greatly, and left him exceedingly reduced. By God's mercy he has been spared to us, and is, I think, gaining strength now day by day. I endeavor to be thankful for this and for other mercies, and, without an endeavor, am always mindful of the uncertainty of human life; without endeavor I say, because that feeling has become habitual.

* * * * * *

"Ellis, the missionary, whose book I reviewed in the last Quarterly Review, has been here, and we were very much pleased with him. I was gratified by hearing from Sir Robert Inglis, in a letter which I received yesterday, that he thought that reviewal of mine was likely to be of much use; the circles in which he moves afford him opportunities of observing how the observations which I made upon the errors of the Missionaries, and the dangers consequent upon those errors, are received among persons who have some influence in directing their proceedings.

"This letter would have been finished and dispatched yesterday if Dr. Bell had not unexpectedly arrived on a flying visit, or, rather, on his way to Scotland. He is a marvelous person for his years, and yet I see a difference since he was here in 1828.

"Edward, the eldest of my uncle's sons, is passing the long vacation with me, and has been joined here by the third brother, Erroll. I hope to have much comfort in these young relations, and have now more satisfaction than I can express in manifesting toward them my love for their father. God bless you, my dear Neville!

"Yours most affectionately, R. S."

To Mrs. Hodson.

"Keswick, Sept. 10, 1830.

"MY DEAR MRS. HODSON,

"You might have had another reason for dis

believing the statement of my appearing as a witness in behalf of Mr. St. John Long, to wit, that I am not likely to put myself into the hands of a quack. Probably he has had a patient of the same name, and the news' reporters supposed it to be me. It was contradicted in the Times by my brother (I suppose), who perhaps thought it some derogation to his own doctorship as well as mine.

"I am troubled at the course of events, yet I can find some considerations, which, if they do not allay my disquietude, have in them a growing comfort. Had it been in my power to turn the balance between the contending principles of France—which were Liberalism and Jesuitism—I should have laid my hand with great misgiving on either scale; and if I had decided on that which was, for the time, the cause of order, and brought with it the least immediate evil, it would have been with no clear conviction or good will. The complete triumph of the old Bourbon system would be the re-establishment of such a religion and such a court as those of Louis XIV. and Louis XV. Charles X. did not desire such a court, neither did the dauphin his son, but they both deemed it their duty to do all that could be done by sovereign power for the holy Roman Catholic Church.

"The royal family fully understood that a scheme for expelling them and putting the son of Philippe Egalitè in their place had been carrying on ever since the battle of Waterloo, but they were strangely mistaken with regard to their strength, and did not calculate on the means of resistance which had been *prepared*. Otherwise, they had troops on whom they could have perfectly relied, who could have been brought up, for they were within two days' march.

"It is better as it is, for they had put themselves glaringly in the wrong by the Ordinances, having been wholly in the right before. You might have been with them for mere political considerations (and those only temporary ones) if they had succeeded, but you could not have been with them in principle and in heart. But all three are now united in the Duke de Bordeaux's cause. Oh, how blind of intellect and dead of heart must the Duke of Orleans be to have thrown away such an opportunity of securing himself a good and glorious name! Had he insisted upon that child's right, and the plain policy of maintaining it—had he acted for him as a faithful regent—he would have had, not the mere recognition of unwilling courts, nor the 'hey, fellow!' recognition of Cobbet and Co., but the sure support of all the European powers, and the grateful attachment of all the old Royalists, and of all Frenchmen who desire tranquillity; and his name would have become as illustrious as that of Washington.

"Did you ever read the Abbé Terasson's Sethos? There this duke might have found a better model for himself than Fénélon exhibited for his pupil in Telemachus. It is so fine a romance in part of its story, and in its conception of moral greatness, that I have always wondered how a Frenchman could have written it. But Louis Philippe is already tasting the bitter relish of that ambition which was sweet at the first draught. Take away from his party the adventitious supporters (who make use, or hope to make use of him as an instrument, one faction against another), and his party is the weakest in France: the Napoleonists are stronger; so are the Republicans; so are the Loyalists. These last would be the most numerous if quiet voices were ever counted in clamorous times. The Republicans are the most active and the most daring, and therefore they are most likely to have their day of triumph. War then becomes inevitable, and the new king's best policy, as against both Republicans and Napoleonists, may be to keep a mischievous nation quiet at home by engaging in hostilities with his neighbors, and taking up the old scheme of fraternization and conquest. This is what I expect, and then huzza for another battle of Waterloo!

"Believe me, always yours very truly,

"ROBERT SOUTHEY."

To John Rickman, Esq.

"Sept. 11, 1830.

"MY DEAR R.,

"Parliamentary reform is no longer a doubtful matter; in some shape or other it must come; and, in fact, the present state of things gives us some of its worst effects, as seen in Yorkshire and Middlesex. The old ground of defense, therefore, that the system works well, is no longer tenable; indeed, I have long seen that what wise men ought to look to is to devise in what manner they may best construct a raft from the wreck of the old ship. I would have fought her to the water's edge rather than have run among the breakers in the vain hope of escaping the enemy's fire.

"It has been said that the king meant by his own prerogative to issue writs for Birmingham, Manchester, and perhaps Leeds and Sheffield. I wish he would, because it is better this should be done as an act of grace than of yielding; and it would be wholesome to exert the prerogatives in a way that would be popular. The qualification might be fixed at a reasonable standard, and then let the cry for universal suffrage take its course.

"A curious circumstance has come to my knowledge, showing that the Liberals were ready to strike a blow before the Ordinances gave a good color to their cause. A Frenchman employed in Child's banking-house in their foreign correspondence, at £170 a year, asked leave (before the Ordinances were fixed) to go to Paris, and was refused; he said he *must* go; they said, if so, they must fill up his place. He then told them that he was one of the National Guard; that he was bound, as such, by a secret oath, to repair to Paris whenever he might be summoned, and wherever he might be, disregarding all other objects: the summons had reached him, and go he must. He went accordingly, and would arrive just in time for the struggle.

"Has any thought been given at the Admiralty to the effect which steam navigation must produce upon naval war? I fear we shall have to make our experiments in actual war, and learn that as we did engineering in Spain.

"By good fortune, our enemies are as ignorant in it as ourselves. God bless you!

"R. S."

CHAPTER XXXIV.

JOURNEY TO LONDON—UNEASY LIFE THERE—NATIONAL EDUCATION—GOES INTO HAMPSHIRE AND TO THE WEST OF ENGLAND—CORRESPONDENCE WITH LORD BROUGHAM RESPECTING THE ENCOURAGEMENT OF LITERATURE AND SCIENCE—ADVICE AS TO THE CHOICE OF A PROFESSION—MISS BOWLES—JOANNA BAILLIE—POLITICS—NECESSITY OF NATIONAL EDUCATION—THE OBSERVANCE OF THE SABBATH—THE REFORM BILL—PROSPECTS OF THE COUNTRY—IVAN VEGEEGHAN—JOURNEY TO CHELTENHAM ON DR. BELL'S AFFAIRS—SIR WALTER SCOTT—MR. WORDSWORTH—STRANGE NOTION OF ANASTASIUS HOPE—MR. KENYON—MR. POOLE—GENERAL PEACHEY—HIS PROSPECTS NOT SO GOOD AS FORMERLY—THE CHOLERA—LITERARY EMPLOYMENTS—STATE OF FEELING IN THE COUNTRY—JOURNEY TO LIVERPOOL, MANCHESTER, ETC.—IS INVITED TO STAND FOR A PROFESSORSHIP AT GLASGOW—REGRETS MR. MAY'S REMOVAL FROM BRISTOL—RIOTS IN THAT CITY—THE CHOLERA—THE EXCHEQUER LIKELY TO BE ABOLISHED—PUBLICATION OF HIS POLITICAL ESSAYS.—1830–1831.

TOWARD the end of the following month (October) my father was on the move for London, whither he traveled slowly, having Mr. Henry Taylor for a companion, who had been passing a short time at Keswick. Their route lay by the great North Road, through York and Doncaster, at which latter place they amused themselves with fixing upon the identical house in which Dr. Daniel Dove had lived. While they were walking round the town, an incident occurred, which is related in The Doctor, &c., and may not unfitly be mentioned here: "The group inside a shaving shop (Saturday evening) led us to stop for a minute, and a portrait over the fire induced us to walk in and look at it. It was an unfinished picture, and would probably have been a good one had it been completed. Upon inquiring whose it was, the barber said it had been in his possession many years before he knew; some friend had given it him because he said his shop was the proper place for it, the gentleman looking, by his dress, as if he was just ready to be shaved, with an apron under his chin. One day, however, the portrait had attracted a passing stranger's notice, as it had done ours, and he recognized it (as I did upon hearing this) for a portrait of Garrick."*

* To Mrs. Southey, Oct., 1830.

This visit to London was partly on business—as he found it desirable occasionally to confer personally with his publishers—and partly for the sake of being nearer to the scene of action in those stirring times. This was as well for the purpose of writing upon the state of the times in the Quarterly Review, as also because he was then planning a new series of Colloquies, on moral and political subjects, in which Mr. Rickman was to be the interlocutor. A considerable portion of the work was written in the course of the following year by these two parties, and even part of it set up in type; but the plan of a joint composition did not answer, being, as might be supposed, very unfavorable to any thing like close reasoning and logical deduction, and from this and other causes it was never completed.

The following letter to Dr. Bell shows how restless a life he was compelled to lead in London.

To the Rev. A. Bell, D. D.

"London, Nov. 25, 1830.

"MY DEAR SIR,

"I came home at twelve this morning,* that I might write to you fully by this post, and found on my table a hand-bill of such a nature that I deemed it my duty to lose no time in sending it to the Home Office: it invites a subscription for arming the people against the police. Before this could be done, in came a caller, then another; and it is now three o'clock. Would that it were possible for me to convince you of what it is so desirable for you to be convinced of—not merely that your system must make its way universally (for you have never doubted that), nor that your own just claims will one day be universally acknowledged (for this also you can not doubt), but that such efforts as you now weary and vex yourself with making, and as you wish me to assist in, can not possibly promote the extension of the system. * * *

"The best thing that I can do, after touching upon the necessity of national education in the Christmas number (of the Quarterly Review), will be to prepare a paper upon the subject as early as possible; a task the more necessary, because many persons, I perceive, are beginning to apprehend that the progress of education among the lower classes has done more harm than good. It is, you know, not a matter of opinion with me, but of feeling and religious belief, that the greater the diffusion of knowledge, the better will it be for mankind, provided that the foundation be built upon the rock, and that, above all things, the rising generation be instructed in their duties. I shall be well employed, therefore, in showing that where any harm has been done by education, it is because that education has been imperfect, or because its proper object has been perverted by untoward circumstances, and the present state of the nation is such that I shall be enabled to do this with better hope.

"I am entering far more into general society than in any of my former visits to London, for

* From breakfasting out.

the purpose of seeing and hearing all within my reach. The Duchess of Kent sent for me to dinner on Wednesday last; there was a large party, not one of whom I had ever seen before. With the duchess, who seems a very amiable person, I had a very little conversation, though quite as much as she could possibly bestow upon me; but with Prince Leopold, the only person to whom I was introduced, I had a great deal. I see men who are going into office, and men who are going out, and I am familiar enough with some of them to congratulate the latter, and condole with and commiserate the former. I meet with men of all persuasions and all grades of opinion, and hear their hopes and their fears, and have opportunities (which I do not let slip) of seeing the mechanism of government, and observing how the machine works. I was to have dined with the archbishop on Wednesday, when the duchess made me put off my engagement. * * * * * *

"My table is now covered with notes, pamphlets, and piles of seditious papers. You may imagine how I long to be at home and at rest. To-day I dine with Mr. Croker, who is likely to be prominent in opposition. The duke will not; neither, by what I hear, will Sir R. Peel. But I do not think it possible that the present administration can hold together long; and Peel, who is now without an equal in the Commons, has only to wait patiently till he is made minister by common consent of the nation.

"Farewell, my dear sir; and believe me always sincerely and affectionately yours,

"Robert Southey."

My father was much gratified, on the occasion of this visit to the Duchess of Kent, by her bringing the Princess Victoria, then eleven years of age, to tell him she had lately read with pleasure his Life of Nelson. "With the archbishop," he says in another letter, "I dined afterward, Wordsworth, Dr. Wordsworth, and Joshua Watson being of the party. The Duke of Wellington sent me a card, but I could not accept the invitation. But the oddest thing which befell me was, that as I rose from my knee at the levee, my hand was unexpectedly caught hold of and shaken by Lord Brougham."*

He continued in London until the end of December, when he went down into Sussex with Mr. Rickman, and, after a few days, proceeded to his friend Miss Bowles, at Buckland, near Lymington, where he found perfect quiet and leisure to finish a paper for the ensuing number of the Quarterly Review. A few brief extracts from his account of his journey thither will show how observant a traveler he was, even over ground which most persons would find little to interest them in: "* * * Our road lay through Kingston, where Huntingdon the Sinner Saved commenced his manner of living by faith; Esher, where Prince Leopold lives; Cobham, where some whimsical nobleman used to keep a hermit (he had three in succession in the course of one year); Guildford, where we had time to go into the prettiest alms-houses in the kingdom, a foundation of Archbishop Abbot, into its chapel, where there are some rich painted windows and a good portrait of the founder; and Godalming, where I saw the church in passing. * * At Chichester, one of the canons, Mr. Holland (who married Murray's sister), expected us. The Cathedral is a very interesting pile on many accounts, and much finer than books or common report had led me to expect. A bookseller showed me a letter of Cowper's and some MS. notes of his written in Johnson's Life of Milton. Chillingworth's grave is in the cloisters, near Mr. Holland's door. Dr. Chandler, the dean, came to us in the Cathedral library, where, among other rarities, is the oldest volume of English sermons by Bishop Fisher. Bernard Barton's brother also joined us there, to be introduced to me. After luncheon, Mr. Holland took me to see his Chichester poet, Charles Crocker, a shoe-mender, a very industrious, happy, and meritorious man, who is perhaps the best example of the good that may be done by education to persons in his rank of life. His poems are of very considerable merit. Then we went on the city walls, and lastly into the bishop's palace, so that I saw all that could be shown me in Chichester, a cheerful, pleasant city."* The next letter gives some account of his further movements.

To the Rev. J. W. Warter.

"Crediton, Jan. 12, 1831.

"My dear Warter,

"Here I arrived last night on my way home, and at the furthest point from it to which my circuit has extended; and here, at last, I have some hours upon which no demand will be made. This is the first use of my first interval of leisure. How I have been distracted in London no one can fully understand, unless they have been living with me there; and how I have been busied tooth and nail during eleven days after I left it and got to Miss Bowles's, near Lymington, you may judge when you know that in that time I wrote the concluding article of the Quarterly Review all but the first seven pages.

* * * * * * *

"As to the state of the country, I am more hopeful than most persons. The change of ministry was the best thing that could have occurred, because the Whigs *must* do what they would never have allowed the Tories to do; they must unsay much of what they have said; they must undo (as far as that is possible) much of what they have done. They are augmenting the army, which they compelled their predecessors to reduce. They have called for a yeomanry force, which they made their predecessors disband. They are endeavoring to curb the license of the press. I think they must suspend the Habeas Corpus Act. I believe they must restore the one pound bills; I expect that they will find it

* At that time lord chancellor.

* To Mrs. Southey, Dec. 30, 1830.

impossible not to go to war; and I am sure that if the question of Parliamentary Reform should not be thrust aside by other events, it could not be brought forward so well by any other persons as by the *Whigs in power*. They have great stakes in the country, and they are now heartily afraid of the democracy which they have so long been flattering. They have raised the devil, and it is proper that they should have the task of laying him. But in this, all who think and feel as I do will lend them a cordial support; not for their sakes, but for the sake of ourselves and of the nation. While the government is what it is, we must support it in whatever hands it may be.

"We shall get through our difficulties, and the better if there be war to help us. The property of the country is yet strong enough to restore order. And if we have a change in the form of representation grounding it on property, and nowhere on numbers, we may gain by such a change more than we should lose by it. Soon we shall have a stronger government, and something like police in the country as well as in London.

* * * * * * *

"I leave this place (whither I came only to spend three days with my old fellow-collegian Lightfoot) on Saturday morning for Taunton, there to see my Aunt Mary, the last of my father's generation; a dear excellent old lady, in whom I see what I am indebted for to the Southey part of my blood. Monday I go to Bristol, where I have not been for twenty years. I mean once more to look at the scenes of my birth and childhood, and have so much love for the place that I have the serious intention of writing a poem, descriptive, historical, and desultory, in honor of my native city.

"You may suppose how impatient I am to reach home, and resume once more the even tenor of my usual life. I bought a good many books in London, three or four consignments of which have arrived, and others are on the way. Some skill in packing will be required for arranging them. Neither my head nor hands were ever so full as at this time, and I hope, with God's blessing, to get through a world of work.

"And now, my dear Warter, God bless you!

"Yours affectionately,

"ROBERT SOUTHEY."

It would seem that my father felt considerable surprise at Lord Brougham's friendly greeting at the levee, partly because they had little or no personal acquaintance, having, I believe, only met once at Edinburgh in 1805 (see *antè*, p. 195), and partly because they had been so strongly opposed in politics, neither having spared the other when occasion served. Time, however, had somewhat softened the political asperities of both, and the greeting was only the prelude to a friendly letter from his lordship, which reached my father while on his journey, but to which he had not leisure to reply until his return. I subjoin it here, with the answer, having Lord Brougham's kind permission to do so.

The Lord Chancellor Brougham and Vaux to R. Southey, Esq.

"Althorp, Jan., 1831.

"DEAR SIR,

"I was prevented by various interruptions from writing to you while I was at Brougham upon a subject which greatly interests me, and I therefore take the earliest opportunity of bringing it before you.

"The government of this country have long been exposed, I fear justly, to the charge of neglecting science and letters. I feel it an impossible thing for me, whose life has been passed more or less in these pursuits, to allow this stain to rest upon any administration with which I am connected, and therefore that it is my duty, as far as in me lies, to turn the attention of the present government to the best means of encouraging scientific and literary pursuits. With this view I have applied to the two men at the head of the physical and mathematical sciences, in my opinion, and I can not look into the department of literature without being met by your name. I may probably apply in like manner to one or two more men distinguished in the same field, but I have not as yet selected any such. My wish is to have the benefit of your unreserved opinion upon the questions:

"1st. Whether or not Letters will gain by the more avowed and active encouragement of the government?

"2d. In what way that encouragement can the most safely and beneficially be given them?

"Under the first head is to be considered, no doubt, the chances of doing harm as well as the prospect of doing good. Thus it seems obvious that there is one danger to be guarded against—the undue influence of government—capable of being perverted to political and party purposes. This includes the risk of jobs for unworthy persons, and the exclusion of men of merit. The applause of the public, it may be said, is a safe test and unbiased reward of merit; not to be easily, at least not permanently, perverted to wrong ends. I throw out this as one consideration, showing that the case is not so clear of doubt as it at first may seem to be.

"Under the second head several things present themselves for consideration. If the risk of abuse were not great, it is plain that pecuniary assistance would be the most desirable means of helping genius, because many a man of genius is forced out of the path of original inquiry and of refined taste by the necessities of his situation, and is obliged to spend his talents on labor little better than mechanical. But the difficulties of arranging such aid systematically are so great, and the risk of abuse so imminent, that I question if more can be done in this way than by lending occasional assistance.

"The encouragement of societies has been already tried, not perhaps in the best way, but still a good deal has been thus attempted. These are susceptible of considerable improvement. A judicious foundation of prizes is another mode deserving consideration.

"The distribution of honors has been very partially tried, and many have proposed a more regular admission of men of science and letters to rank, confined to their own lives in cases where hereditary honors might be burdensome to their families. An order of merit has been proposed by some. But as all novelties in such a matter (of opinion and public feeling) are to be shunned, one of the existing orders of knighthood, as the Guelphic, has been by others suggested as free from the objection.

"I throw out these things more for the purpose of bringing your mind to the details of the matter than with the view of exhausting the subject.

"It will afford me great satisfaction to be favored with your opinion upon the question as fully as your leisure may permit. I shall, of course, keep it entirely to myself.

"It may very possibly turn out that, after all, nothing material can be accomplished; but, at any rate, I can not allow this opportunity to pass without trying all means of accomplishing an object so desirable; and my anxiety on this score must plead my excuse for troubling you with so long a letter.

"I am, dear sir, your faithful servant,

"BROUGHAM."

To the Lord Chancellor Brougham and Vaux.

"Keswick, Feb. 1, 1831.

"MY LORD,

"The letter which your lordship did me the honor of addressing to me at this place found me at Crediton, in the middle of last month, on a circuitous course homeward. It was not likely that deliberation would lead me to alter the notions which I have long entertained upon the subject that has, in this most unexpected manner, been brought before me; but I should have deemed it disrespectful to have answered such a communication without allowing some days to intervene. The distance between Devonshire and Cumberland, a visit upon the way to my native city, which I had not seen for twenty years, and the engagements arising upon my return home after an absence of unusual length, will explain, and I trust excuse, the subsequent delay.

"Your first question is, whether Letters would gain by the more avowed and active encouragement of the government?

"There are literary works of national importance which can only be performed by co-operative labor, and will never be undertaken by that spirit of trade which at present preponderates in literature. The formation of an English Etymological Dictionary is one of those works; others might be mentioned; and in this way literature might gain much by receiving national encouragement; but government would gain a great deal more by bestowing it. Revolutionary governments understand this; I should be glad if I could believe that our legitimate one would learn it before it is too late. I am addressing one who is a statesman as well as a man of letters, and who is well aware that the time is come in which governments can no more stand without pens to support them than without bayonets. They must soon know, if they do not already know it, that the volunteers as well as the mercenaries of both professions, who are not already enlisted in this service, will enlist themselves against it; and I am afraid they have a better hold upon the soldier than upon the penman, because the former has, in the spirit of his profession and in the sense of military honor, something which not unfrequently supplies the want of any higher principle, and I know not that any substitute is to be found among the gentlemen of the press.

"But neediness, my lord, makes men dangerous members of society, quite as often as affluence makes them worthless ones. I am of opinion that many persons who become bad subjects because they are necessitous, because 'the world is not their friend, nor the world's law,' might be kept virtuous (or, at least, withheld from mischief) by being made happy, by early encouragement, by holding out to them a reasonable hope of obtaining, in good time, an honorable station and a competent income, as the reward of literary pursuits, when followed with ability and diligence, and recommended by good conduct.

"My lord, you are now on the Conservative side. Minor differences of opinion are infinitely insignificant at this time, when, in truth, there are but two parties in this kingdom—the Revolutionists and the Loyalists; those who would destroy the Constitution, and those who would defend it. I can have no predilections for the present administration; they have raised the devil, who is now raging through the land; but, in their present position, it is their business to lay him if they can; and so far as their measures may be directed to that end, I heartily say, God speed them! If schemes like yours, for the encouragement of letters, have never entered into their wishes, there can be no place for them at present in their intentions. Government can have no leisure now for attending to any thing but its own and our preservation; and the time seems not far distant when the cares of war and expenditure will come upon it once more with their all-engrossing importance. But when better times shall arrive (whoever may live to see them), it will be worthy the consideration of any government whether the institution of an Academy, with salaries for its members (in the nature of literary or lay benefices), might not be the means of retaining in *its* interests, as connected with their own, a certain number of influential men of letters, who should hold those benefices, and a much greater number of aspirants who would look to them in their turn. A yearly grant of £10,000 would endow ten such appointments of £500 each for the elder class, and twenty-five of £200 each for younger men; these latter eligible of course, and preferably, but not necessarily, to be elected to the higher benefices as those fell vacant, and as they should have approved themselves.

"The good proposed by this, as a political measure, is not that of retaining such persons to act as pamphleteers and journalists, but that of preventing them from becoming such, in hostility to the established order of things; and of giving men of letters, as a class, something to look for beyond the precarious gains of literature, thereby inducing in them a desire to support the existing institutions of their country, on the stability of which their own welfare would depend.

"Your lordship's second question—in what way the encouragement of government could most safely and beneficially be given—is, in the main, answered by what has been said upon the first. I do not enter into any details of the proposed institution, for that would be to think of fitting up a castle in the air. Nor is it worth while to examine how far such an institution might be perverted. Abuses there would be, as in the disposal of all preferments, civil, military, or ecclesiastical; but there would be a more obvious check upon them; and where they occurred, they would be less injurious in their consequences than they are in the state, the army, and navy, or the Church.

"With regard to prizes, methinks they are better left to schools and colleges. Honors are worth something to scientific men, because they are conferred upon such men in other countries; at home there are precedents for them in Newton and Davy, and the physicians and surgeons have them. In my judgment, men of letters are better without them, unless they are rich enough to bequeath to their family a good estate with the bloody hand, and sufficiently men of the world to think such distinctions appropriate. For myself, if we had a Guelphic order, I should choose to remain a Ghibelline.

"I have written thus fully and frankly, not dreaming that your proposal is likely to be matured and carried into effect, but in the spirit of good will, and as addressing one by whom there is no danger that I can be misunderstood. One thing alone I ask from the Legislature, and in the name of justice—that the injurious law of copyright should be repealed, and that the family of an author should not be deprived of their just and natural rights in his works when his permanent reputation is established. This I ask with the earnestness of a man who is conscious that he has labored for posterity.

"I remain, my lord, yours, with due respect,
"ROBERT SOUTHEY."

To Herbert Hill, Esq.

"Keswick, Feb. 5, 1831.

"MY DEAR HERBERT,

"You may be perfectly at ease as to my anticipations of the changes which I might find at Crediton; they had no relation to any thing but the knowledge that we must all of us either improve or worsen as we grow older, and that at no time is this more apparent than when we pass to man-hood or woman-hood. Those whom I had left girls were now become young women; the change is not so great as from kitten-hood to cat-hood; but if ever you have children of your own, you will then know how the joyousness which they impart diminishes, and the anxieties increase as they grow up. A little of this one feels for those friends to whom we are most attached; and you know that I have as hearty a regard for —— as he has for me. I never knew a better man, and have never known a happier one. A blessing seems to have attended him through life.

* * * * * * *

"Now for your own speculations as to the choice of a profession. And let me begin by admonishing you that this is a choice between risks, uncertainties, and difficulties (discomforts might be added to the list), not between two ways, each pleasant alike, and each leading surely to the resting-place which is the object of the journey.

"You hesitate between the professions of theology and medicine. Morally and intellectually, both are wholesome studies for one who enters upon them with a sound heart and a proper sense of duty. I should not say the same of the law, for that must, in my judgment, be always more or less injurious to the practitioner. The comparative advantages and disadvantages seem to be these: the medical profession will require you to live in a town, most likely in London, or certainly in one of the larger cities; this may be a recommendation or otherwise, according to your inclinations. It requires means for supporting you till you get into practice, and this is slow and up-hill work, as well as being in a great degree uncertain; you may make a great fortune by it, but not till late in life, and your labors increase with your success.

"As a clergyman, then, you have your fellowship till you choose to vacate it; a less busy, but a less anxious life is before you. Talents and industry may do more for you as a clergyman; good manners and good nature may tell to better account as a physician. But the prudential balance is so nearly equipoised, that the determination may fairly be a matter of free choice. With regard to the studies in which they would engage you, I think you would like that of physic best at first, but that the older you grew the better you would like and feel the value of those to which theology would lead you.

"Opinions must always be inherited, and happy are we who can refer to the title-deeds upon which ours are founded. As you read more and observe more, what are now prejudices will become principles, and strike root as such, and as such bring forth fruit in due season. *Nullius addictus, &c.*, is the boast of vanity and sciolism. There are very few who do not put faith in their apothecary and their lawyer, and we are less likely to be deceived when we confide in the opinions which have been held by men of whose learning, and ability, and integrity no doubt can be entertained. If the writers from whom I now derive most pleasure and most profit had been put into my hands when I was at your age, I should have found little in them that was attractive. Our higher intellectual faculties (perhaps it were better to say our spiritual ones) ripen slowly, but then they continue to improve till the bodily organ fails. Take this maxim with you, that in divinity, in ethics, and in politics there can be no new truths. Even the latter is no longer an experimental science, and woe be to those who treat it as such!

* * * * * * * *

"God bless you! R. S."

To Mrs. Hodson.

"Keswick, Feb. 7, 1831.

"My dear Mrs. Hodson,

"You may infer how incessantly I was engaged during my abode in town from the 1st of November to the 27th of December, when you are told that I could not possibly find time for writing more than the first six pages of that paper in the Quarterly Review, though the number was waiting for it. The remainder was written at Caroline Bowles's, where I shut myself up for eleven days, refusing all invitations, seeing no visitors, and never going out, except when she mounted her Shetland pony, and I walked by her side for an hour or two before dinner. That paper, however, is but the first fruits of my journey. I have a great deal more to say, and am busily employed in saying it.

"When I met Joanna Baillie at Rogers's, her sister and my daughter Bertha constituted the whole party; for, as to literary parties, they are my abomination. She is a person whom I admired as soon as I read her first volume of Plays, and liked when I saw her as much as I had admired her before. I never talk much in company, and never carry abroad with me the cheerful spirits which never forsake me at home. But I was not *sad* that morning, though perhaps my thoughts might sometimes be more engaged than they ought to have been by the engagements of various kinds which were pressing upon me. Bertha said of me in one of her letters from town that I used to look as if I had more to think of than I liked. This was only because it was so much, not that I looked at the course of events with any thing like despondency. Very far from it; I found few persons so hopeful, so confident as myself; but those few were exactly the persons on whose judgment I have most reliance. The Whigs have already increased the army, called for the yeomanry force which they had disbanded, and begun to prosecute for sedition. I expect to see them suspend the Habeas Corpus, reissue one pound notes, and go to war. We have at least a government now, and we have only had the shadow of one before since the great defection; and the men in power must, of necessity, do what their opposition would have prevented or deterred their predecessors from doing. This advantage is worth purchasing at the cost of that minimum of reform which is to be looked for at their hands.

"Yours very truly, R. Southey."

To Captain Southey.

"Keswick, Feb. 13, 1831.

"My dear Tom,

" * * * * * * * *

Heartily glad I am to be at my own desk by my own fireside, and once more at rest. In London I could not find any time for writing any thing; it was less interruption to let in all callers than to receive and answer notes if they were excluded. I was at the most important debates which I could attend conveniently, because my quarters were with Rickman. I walked into the city on the Lord-mayor's Day and the day before, and saw the sort of multitude which had been brought together for mischief, and from various quarters I heard what the mischief was—a Cato-street scheme, with this difference only, that instead of attacking the ministers at a dinner-party, the king and the Duke of Wellington were to have been killed in their carriages, and the new police massacred.

"The Quarterly Review was kept waiting for my paper. But yet I have a great deal to say upon the state of public affairs, both through the medium of the Quarterly and in other ways. As soon as possible I mean to address a series of letters to the people.

"Murray is now reprinting my Moral and Political Papers, in a small cheap form, like his Family Library. About half a volume is printed, and in revising them for the press it is mournful to see that they are in the main as applicable now as when they were written, and that much of the present evil might have been averted if the warning which was then given had been taken in time. The evil has now, I think, become so great that it must draw on a remedy. And it is like a special judgment upon the Whigs, who have raised the devil, that they should be in a position which makes it their business to lay him if they can. They must do every thing which they used to declaim against; and, happily, they can do it, because there will be no factious opposition to them.

"The Duchess of Kent sent for me one day to dine with her; the reason, as I learned from Sir John Conroy, being that she thinks of making a Northern tour with the little princess, and intended to ask me what tour she should take, and what time it would require. No such questions, however, could the duchess ask, for there were more than twenty persons at dinner, of whom I only got at the names of those nearest me, and of course she could have very little conversation with me. I took it quietly, felt as I should have done at a *table d'hôte* where all were strangers, made a good dinner, and withdrew as soon as my brother's carriage came for me at a quarter before ten.

* * * * * * *

"God bless you! R. S."

To the Rev. Neville White.

"Keswick, March 21, 1831.

"My dear Neville,

" * * * * * * * *

You know, my dear Neville, that I have endeavored always to impress upon the public the necessity of educating the people. If that education is either so conducted, or left so imperfect as in many cases to do harm rather than good, the fault is not in the principle, but in the mismanagement of it. The great evil which at present it produces is that of making young persons discontented with the stations which they were intended to fill, and thus producing more claimants for the stations one degree higher than can be provided for in that class. Whenever the education which such persons receive shall become universal, this mischief must necessarily cease. It produced nothing but good in Scotland, because it was universal there.

"A more difficult question is how to render the religious instruction which children receive at school of more effect. And where parents neglect, as they so very generally do in that station of life, this duty, I do not see how this is to be done by schools and teachers. We want a reformation of manners to effect that without which manners, alas! can not be reformed. This is evident, that boys and girls are taken from school precisely at that age when they become capable of, in some degree, understanding and feeling what till then they have only learned by rote. Then it is that the aid of catechists is wanting. In a small parish the clergyman can do much; in large ones I do not wonder that they are deterred from attempting what with their utmost exertions they could not possibly accomplish.

"I am perfectly satisfied that no children ought to be left without education, so much as to enable them to read, write, cipher, and understand their moral and religious duties. But about infant schools I do not see my way so clearly, and am not sure whether some harm is not done, both to parent and child, by taking so much off the parent's hands. No doubt it is a choice between evils. Of this I am sure, that half the crimes which disgrace this nation are brought on by *street education*, which goes on in villages as well as in towns. So far as infant schools tend to prevent this, they are greatly beneficial.

"You ask me about Magdalen institutions. There is scarcely any form of misery that can have so strong a claim upon compassion as that which these are intended to alleviate. Often as the intention may be disappointed, one case in which it succeeds may compensate for fifty disappointments. And these poor creatures are not so generally, I might say uniformly, to be distrusted as prison converts. In prisons, I believe, the common effect is, that the cleverest criminals add hypocrisy to their other sins.

"Look again at what I have said concerning the observance of Sunday, and you will perceive that I have argued against Dymond's liberal notions about the day, and also against, not a religious, but a puritanical observance of it; for that, I am sure, tends to promote irreligion. Of the two extremes I would choose rather the popish than the puritanical Sabbath. Let us keep the mean.

"James Stanger is expected here next week, but for a short time only. He is a very valuable man, and I have a sincere respect for him, though very far from being as good a neighbor as he might like to find me, and, were he less considerate than he is, might expect me to be. But I have no time for neighborly intercourse.

"No room is left for politics. My hope is that the ministers will not think it expedient to resign till war begins, for something would seem wanting in political justice if it were not to be begun under their administration. God forgive them for the mischief they are doing by their portentous budget of reform, and for calling in, as they have done and are doing, the aid of the villainous press, in order to carry it by intimidation. Passages in the ——, which even the editor would not dare to write, are said to have been supplied to him for this purpose.

"Our kind remembrances to your fireside.

"God bless you, my dear Neville!

"Yours affectionately, R. SOUTHEY."

To Grosvenor C. Bedford, Esq.

"Keswick, May 3, 1831.

"MY DEAR GROSVENOR,

"Would that I were more at leisure to converse with those who are at a distance; but leisure and I seem to have parted company forever in this world, and occupation does not bring with it that quiet now which it used to do in less uneasy times.* Not that I have lost either heart or hope; for, though nothing can be worse than all the manifestations of public feeling from all sides, I expect that the delusion will in a great degree be removed when the present excitement has spent itself; and though I have no reliance whatever upon the good sense of the people, there is yet goodness enough in the nation to make me trust in full faith that Providence will not deliver us over to our own evil devices, or rather to those of our rulers. Those who gave Earl Grey credit for sagacity, believed, upon his own representations, that time had moderated his opinions, and that he would always support the interests of his order. Provoked at the exposure of his whole cabinet's incapacity, which their budget brought forth, he has thrown himself upon the Radicals for support, bargained with O'Connell, and stirred up all the elements of revolution in this kingdom, which has never been in so perilous a state since the Restoration.

"The poor people here say they shall all be 'made quality' when this 'grand reform' is brought about. 'O it is a grand thing!' The word deceives them; for you know, Grosvenor, it 'stands to feasible' that *reform* must be a good thing, and they are not deceived in supposing

* "If I were in the seventeenth year of my age instead of the fifty-seventh, I might, perhaps, like the prospect of a general revolution in society, looking only at the evils which it was to sweep away, and the good with which it was to replace them. But I am old enough to know something of the course on which we have entered. Anarchy is the first stage—and there the road divides, one way leading by a circuitous route, and so difficult a one as to be scarcely practicable, back to the place from whence we start; the other by a broad and beaten way to military despotism. The tendency is to a despotism of institutions, which, when once established, stamps a whole people in its iron mold and stereotypes them."—*To H. Taylor, Esq., March* 13, 1831.

that its tendency is to pull down the rich, whatever may be its consequences to themselves.

"May 14.

"This letter has lain more than a week unfinished in my desk. To-day's paper tells me that his Right Honor* has gained his election; and this I am very glad of, hoping, however, that the head of the family, or one of those uncles who can so well afford it, will bear the costs. There is no statesman to whom I ascribe more of the evils which are gathering round us than Lord Grenville. The Catholic Question was an egg laid and hatched in that family, and Leda's egg was not prolific of more evils to Troy than that question has proved, is proving, and will prove to these kingdoms.

* * * * * * *

"I saw Lord —— this morning: he said 'we are going to wreck;' and I was shocked to see how ill he looked—twenty years older than when I dined with him at Croker's in December last. It is not bodily fatigue, but anxiety, that has produced this change; the clear foresight of evils which are coming in upon us with the force of a spring-tide before a high wind. Every one whom I see or hear from is in worse spirits than myself, for I have an invincible and instinctive hope that the danger will be averted by God's mercy. In the present state of the world nothing seems to proceed according to what would have been thought likely. Who, for example, could have expected that France would not have been at war before this time, or that Louis Philippe would have been still on his uneasy throne? Who would have supposed that Russia would have been defeated in its attempt to suppress the Poles? or that Austria could have put down the insurrection in Italy? I say nothing of the madness which king, cabinet, and people have manifested at home, because they really seem to be acting under a judicial visitation of insanity. But I am almost ready to conclude that we shall weather this storm, because all probabilities and all appearances are against it. Some unexpected event may occur; the war for which France has been preparing upon so formidable a scale may break out in time, and in a way which will render it impossible for our ministers to remain at peace; or such a revolution may be effected in that country as will frighten the king and ministry here into their senses. Some death may take place which may derange the administration; some schism may make it fall to pieces; the agricultural insurrections and the burnings may begin again, and act in prevention of a revolution which they would otherwise inevitably follow; or, perhaps, the cholera morbus may be sent us as a lighter plague than that which we have chosen for ourselves.

"Be the end of these things what it may, Grosvenor, '*we's never live to see't*,' as an old man of Grasmere, whom Betty knew, said upon some great changes which were taking place in his time; '*but we's, may be, hear tell*,' he added, and so say I.

"Further, I say, come to Keswick this year; and remember, Grosvenor, that you and I have not many 'next years' to talk of, even if life were less precious than it is.

"I have a great deal to say to you, and a great deal to show you, if I had you by the fireside, and in the boat, and on the ascent of Skiddaw, and two or three other mountains, where I would walk beside your horse, if your own feet were too sensitive to perform their own duty.

* * * * * * *

"God bless you! R. S."

* Mr. Wynn.

To Dr. Southey.

"Keswick, June 27, 1831.

"My dear H.,

"I returned home* on Friday, and Bertha arrived the same night, safe, and if not sound, yet much better than she had of late been, and I hope on the convalescent list. My journey ended as I expected, in my declining the proposed executorship, and giving good counsel to no purpose. The poor old doctor† may live long, or soon be taken off. He is completely speechless, but in full possession of all his other faculties, and his mind is as quick and vigorous as ever. Nevertheless, I have reason to believe that the will will be contested, on a most untenable plea of insanity in the testator. If so, I must appear as a witness.

"The proofs which awaited my return I have got through; not so the letters, which are, as usual, *de omnibus et quibusdam aliis*. There were the proofs of an article upon the New Christianity and New System of Society, started by the St. Simonites in France; proofs of my Essays, of which half the first volume is printed, and which I dedicate to Inglis; and proofs of the Peninsular War. This will be ready for publication in November. You have got my Brazilian small stock out of the fire in good time: I should have thought myself lucky to get out at 50; and wonder that they have not fallen so low as to prove that there are no purchasers. No other revolution could be so injurious to the commerce of this country, nor produce such interminable evils in its own.

"Recommend Ivan Vejeeghan, a *Russian* Gil Blas, to those who wish to see a lively description of society in Poland and Russia. It contains a better account than can any where else be met with. Were the rest of the world undisturbed and unaffected by what may happen in and around Poland, the war there might be regarded with much indifference, as a process which can not worsen the moral condition of either people, and might possibly improve it, though that possibility is a very poor one. But how any thing better than a barbarous government, whether it be an oligarchy or a despotism, can be constructed in a country where there is no middle class, nor any persons in a condition to be raised into

* The next letter explains the object of this journey fully.

† Dr. Bell.

such a class, I do not perceive. The peasants are serfs, and trade is in the hands of Jews, the vilest, filthiest, and most superstitious of their race.

"If I had Aladdin's lamp, the genius should transport me, and my household and my books, to Cintra; though, just now, perhaps, one might be safer under the paternal protection of Ferdinand than of Miguel. But I verily believe that Spain and Portugal are the safest countries in Europe, and that Spain will be a most peaceable and flourishing one for some years to come. God bless you! R..S."

To the Rev. Neville White.

"Keswick, July 15, 1831.

"MY DEAR NEVILLE,

"When your letter arrived I was absent from home on a melancholy business, obeying, indeed, a call from my poor old friend Dr. Bell, who told me that he was speechless and in a perilous state, and that he greatly desired to see me. I found him totally deprived of speech, by a gradual paralysis of the organs, but no otherwise in danger of death than that death is daily probable at his advanced age, and that this paralysis may extend to the neighboring parts and prevent his swallowing, or descend and stop the digestive functions.

"He had deposited £120,000 3 per cents. in the hands of certain trustees belonging to the University of St. Andrews, and when I arrived this sum had been divided into twelve parts, six of which went to the University and town, and four for founding Madras schools at Edinburgh, Glasgow, Aberdeen, and Inverness. I was consulted about the disposal of the remaining two, and my advice was that he should dispose of one for the augmentation of small livings (which might have been so managed by vesting it in trustees as to call forth an equal sum from Queen Anne's bounty, and thus augment forty livings), and apply the other to founding his own schools in the parishes so augmented: to which suggestion I trusted for making the other acceptable. He was delighted at first with the thought, and readily agreed to it. But the next day he returned to the one thought which has always possessed him, and education was to have it all. I urged in vain that the Church of England had some claim for a part of the large sum which had almost wholly been derived from it.

"There will be a residue of his property, and I suspect of considerable amount, by his anxiety as to the disposal of it. About this, too, I was consulted, but to no purpose, for all will go in some shape or other to schools. I pleaded for his relations earnestly, but in vain. He considers it his duty to devote his whole property to the object which has occupied his whole life.

"He wished me to be one of his executors; but this was impossible, without neglecting my own business for an indefinite time. As his will then stood, he had bequeathed a thousand pounds each to me and Wordsworth, with the charge of editing his works. The will was to be re-made, and I think it not unlikely that his bequest may be omitted at last; for though I believe there is no person for whom he has a higher regard, and though I am sure that the advice which I gave him can not have lowered me in his esteem, whatever it may in his liking, yet if he weighs me in the balance against a Madras school to be established in any part of Scotland, my scale will kick the beam.

"He has been a most devoted friend to children: he has loved them with all his heart, so indeed as to have left little room in it for any other affections. I passed four mournful days with him, and was absent twelve days from home, which is to me a serious loss of time.

* * * * * * *

"About the Liturgy I have left mysel little room to write. It wants few alterations, and those very easy and unobjectionable. I would divide the Morning from the Communion Service; the two together, with the addition of a sermon, being far too long both for the priest and the people. Some of the first lessons might better be changed, and a few of the Psalms passed over, as not being for edification. When Church reformation begins, if revolution does not render it unnecessary, I fear we shall find many Judases in the Establishment. It was more by her own treacherous children that she was overthrown in the Great Rebellion than by the Puritans. But this must ever be the case.

* * * * * * *

"God preserve us from the cholera morbus, from which nothing but his mercy can preserve us! It is a fearful thought that perhaps *in his mercy* he may bring it upon us as the least of the evils which we deserve! Yet I have that comfortable reliance upon Providence, that even in these times I am not cast down.

"God bless you, my dear Neville! And believe me always

"Yours most affectionately,

"ROBERT SOUTHEY."

To Henry Taylor, Esq.

"Keswick, July 15, 1831.

"MY DEAR H. T.,

"This day being Friday, when no letters go for London, I intended to have sent you a note of introduction to Sir Walter; but this day's newspaper brings account that he has had another attack, and is in extreme danger. I fear this is true, because I wrote to him last week,* and should most likely have heard from him in reply if he had been well. His *make* is apoplectic, and I dare say he has overworked himself, with much wear and tear of anxiety to boot, which is even more injurious. Latterly his spirits have failed him, a good deal owing to the prospect of public affairs: that, indeed, can exhilarate such persons only as ——, and those who hope to fish in troubled waters.

"The sort of statesman that we want is a man who yields nothing that he ought not to yield,

* The later letters to Sir W. Scott have not come into my hands.—ED.

who would dispute all the way from London to Witton-le-Weir, taking Oxford on the road; who will summon cab-men when it is proper so to do, and engage with a whole quarterly meeting of Quakers in argument.

* * * * * * *

"Wordsworth, in all likelihood, will be at home at the time you wish. I saw him last week; he is more desponding than I am, and I perhaps despond less than I should do if I saw more clearly before me. After seeing the reign (I can not call it the government) of Louis Philippe's last twelve months, Poland resisting Russia, and Italy not resisting Austria, William IV dissolving Parliament in order to effect parliamentary reform, and Prince Leopold willing to become king of the Belgians, who can tell what to expect, or who would be surprised at any thing that was most unexpected, most insane, or most absurd! Certainly what seems least to be expected is that we should escape a revolution, and yet I go to sleep at night as if there were no danger of one.

* * * * * * *

"Have you seen the strange book which Anastasius Hope left for publication, and which his representatives, in spite of all dissuasion, have published? His notion of immortality and heaven is, that at the consummation of all things, he, and you, and I, and John Murray, and Nebuchadnezzar, and Lambert the fat man, and the living skeleton, and Queen Elizabeth, and the Hottentot Venus, and Thurtell, and Probert, and the twelve apostles, and the noble army of martyrs, and Genghis Khan and all his armies, and Noah with all his ancestors and all his posterity—yea, all men and all women, and all children that have ever been or ever shall be, saints and sinners alike, are all to be put together, and made into one great celestial eternal human being. He does not seem to have known how nearly this approaches to Swedenborg's fancy. I do not like the scheme. I don't like the notion of being mixed up with Hume, and Hunt, and Whittle Harvey, and Phillpotts, and Lord Althorpe, and the Huns, and the Hottentots, and the Jews, and the Philistines, and the Scotch, and the Irish. God forbid! I hope to be I myself; I, in an English heaven, with you yourself—you, and some others, without whom heaven would be no heaven to me.

"God bless you! R. S."

To John Kenyon, Esq.

"Keswick, Sept. 11, 1831.

"My dear Kenyon,

"I am always glad to receive a letter from you. It reminds me of many pleasant meetings, and of years upon which, though they have long gone by, it is not yet become painful to look back.

"Something we must all have to regret; I have done much since you first became acquainted with me, but much less than I hoped to have done, than I should have done under more favorable circumstances, and than I might have done under those in which I have been placed. You have chosen rather to enjoy your fortune than to advance it; and with your power of enjoyment, I am far from thinking that you have chosen ill. You would be neither a wiser, happier, or better man if you were sitting on the bench all be-robed and be-wigged as Mr. Justice Kenyon, nor if you were in the House of Commons, flitting, like the bat in the fable, between two contending parties, and not knowing to which you properly belonged. Men make a great mistake when they fancy themselves useful members of society because they are busy or bustling ones. You have seen a great deal of the world, and your recollections and observations, were you to employ yourself in preserving them, might produce something which posterity would not willingly let perish.

"Poole will be here on a flying visit next week: he says it will be his last visit to the North. I know not why it should be so, if he continue, as he tells me he now is, in good health. I have lately lost in Duppa one who, though somewhat less than a friend, was much more than an acquaintance. In him the link is broken which connected me with some who are gone before me to their rest, and with places which I shall never again see. Some pages of Espriella are his writing; and not a few of my cheerful recollections have ceased to be cheerful now, because he forms a part of them. I have very few friends younger than myself, and this is a misfortune.

"The general* is here, in good health and spirits. It is very pleasant to see the perfect boyishness with which he enters into all youthful sports. He spells Sir Nicholas's name, plays forfeits, dances, and wears a false nose, as gravely and with as much serious enjoyment as he used to play the cymbals five or six-and-twenty years ago. Senhouse also is here with his family. Both desire to be remembered to you.

"I am writing some Colloquies, but not with the same interlocutor; and I am collecting my political papers, lest my claims to unpopularity should be forgotten: some of my friends may say the publication in this respect being ill-timed to a nicety. This year will clear my hands of the Peninsular War, and then the History of Portugal will go to press, the work which I have most at heart. Whether any thing will come of the collections which I have made for other undertakings not less extensive in their kind, God knows. I sometimes fear that I shall have the reflection at last of having heaped up much treasure of this kind in vain.

"God bless you!

"Yours very sincerely,

"Robert Southey."

To John May, Esq.

"Keswick, Oct. 1, 1831.

"My dear Friend,

"* * * * * * *

The prospect before me is not so clear as it was.

---

* General Peachey.

The state of politics has affected every branch of business, and none more than that upon which I have to depend. It can not be long before it be determined whether the Quarterly Review will continue to pay me at its former rate, or whether I must withdraw from it, and look about for other means of support. Other employment, equally profitable and certain in its profit as this has hitherto been, it may not be easy to find; but I have no fear of getting on well at last, and my disposition saves me from all disquietude which is produced by needless anxiety.

"Your own cares at this time can have left you little leisure for those fears which the moral, political, and physical state of Europe awaken in every one who has leisure to look before him and around him. The spirit of insubordination, connected with every thing that is most false and perilous in politics, morals, and religion, has extended so widely, so all but generally, throughout the working classes, that the white inhabitants in Jamaica are not in more danger from the negroes than we are from our servile population. This spirit has been greatly aided by the agitation which the Reform Bill has excited; and whatever plan of reform may be at length agreed on, and to whatever extent it may be carried, the consequences of such a ferment must long be felt. One issue leads to certain revolution, the other gives only a chance of averting it. With these prospects at home, and the cholera rapidly advancing to the opposite coast of the Continent (it is daily expected at Hamburg), I do not think that England, since it was England, has ever been threatened by such serious dangers; for any pestilence must be more dreadful than in former times, in proportion to the increased density of our population and the rapidity of communication throughout the country, and any revolution, instead of throwing down (as in former convulsions) a few high towers and old houses like a storm of wind, would rend and overthrow the foundations of society like an earthquake. These reflections occur to me so frequently and with so much force, that the deprecations in the Litany which apply to these specific dangers have for some time made part of my prayers at night and morning.

"My occupations of late have been the Peninsular War, of which I hope to see the end in a few weeks after my return; the Colloquies on the vulgar Errors of the Age, for which Westall has made some most beautiful drawings; and a review of Moore's Life and Death of Lord Edward Fitzgerald, which I must take with me to finish in Shropshire. The reprint of my Essays might have been completed long since, if Murray had pleased. But he is the most incommunicable of men; and the book hitches upon some notion of his that the papers upon the Catholic Question, which were intended to conclude the volumes, would injure their sale. I tell him that those who hate my opinions will not buy my books, whether those papers are included or not; and that those who agree with me will like to have what the collection professes to be, the whole of my Political Essays. But here the matter rests, and the press stands still.

"One thing I had nearly forgotten to tell you. A selection from Wordsworth's poems for young persons has answered so well, that a similar volume from mine is now in the press; and if this succeeds, as it may *almost* be expected to do, there will be a companion to it of prose selections. In this way I may derive some little profit, now that the sale of the works themselves is at a dead stop; and in this way some good will be done, as far as the selections circulate. Two mottoes have fallen in my way for them, which I think you will deem applicable:

> 'Nullo imbuta veneno
> Carmina,'

is the one; both are from Janus Douza: the other,

> 'Quales filiolis suis parentes,
> Quales discipulis suis magistri,
> Tuto prælegere et docere possint.'

"Believe me always, my dear and excellent friend,

"Yours most affectionately,

'ROBERT SOUTHEY."

To John Rickman, Esq.

"Keswick, Oct. 14, 1831.

"MY DEAR RICKMAN,

"Since you last heard from me I have taken a round of about 300 miles—by way of Liverpool to Shrewsbury, and by way of Manchester home; and, among all the persons with whom I fell in, in stage-coaches and at inns, there was but one reformer, and he a Londoner. The others generally wanted a little encouragement to draw them out, but, when I had spoken boldly, were glad to declare themselves.

"Manchester* was perfectly quiet when The Times described it as being in a state of dreadful excitement. There was alarm enough on the day of the meeting, but the Radicals, having routed the Whigs to their heart's content, spent the evening in jollity instead of mischief. The Whigs called the meeting, the Radicals had their own way at it, and both have done what the Conservative party would have wished them to do.

"Among the means which have occurred to me for lessening the power of the newspapers, one is, that the debates should be officially published, and sold at a low price, so that their comparative cheapness might carry them into circulation. I would have also, whether connected with the debates or not, a paper as official as the Moniteur, and as authentic as the Gazette, in which government should relate as much news as can possibly be related, never deceiving the people. This, if ably conducted, might prevent much delusion and consequent mischief. * *

"God bless you! R. S."

* "The borough-reeve of Manchester tells James White that if that town were rid of about thirty fellows, who are the notorious movers of all political mischief there, it would be as quiet and as well-disposed as any place in England. Does that government deserve the name of government which has no power to keep such fellows in order?"—*To J. Rickman, Esq., Oct.* 25, 1831.

On my father's return from this short journey, he found an invitation awaiting him to offer himself as a candidate for the Professorship of Humanity at Glasgow, and it was represented to him that the chances of success were not doubtful. "Under the present circumstances of the publishing trade," he says, "it would have become a question of prudence in which inclination must not have been suffered to interfere, if it had not so happened that the invitation found its way to me too late to admit of my making inquiries concerning particulars which it did not communicate. If, as I suspect, the professors are required to subscribe the Kirk's Articles of Faith, there could have been no choice."

To a suggestion from another friend of the practicability of obtaining some permanent position of this kind, he says, "Headships are out of the question both as to the requisite knowledge and the way of attaining them. No, H. T., I have nothing to look for but what comes out of this ink-stand. There may be some temporary inconvenience, but, unless all things are subverted about me, that ink-stand will supply my wants till death or infirmity overtake me. For the first I am sufficiently prepared as to worldly affairs; for the latter, I trust that Providence will save me from it, or support me under it."*

To Herbert Hill, Esq.

"Keswick, Oct. 30, 1831.

"My dear Herbert,

" * * * * * * *

The study of the Fathers opens so wide a field, that I, who have long cast a longing eye thitherward, have been afraid to enter it, because it was too late in the day for me; and yet few men can be prepared in mind and inclination for such pursuits early enough to go through with them. Routh, I suppose, has published most of what your friend recommends to you. It is in the early Fathers that you will find least admixture of other than theological matter; their successors offer a mine which has been very imperfectly worked as yet of historical materials; that is, for the history of manners and opinions. Let nothing of this kind escape you. I not unfrequently find notes useful which were made five-and-thirty years ago, when I could little foresee to what use they would be applied.

"In a note of Isaac Reed's to Dodsley's Old Plays, he quotes a MS. from 'a chest of papers formerly belonging to Mr. Powell (Milton's father-in-law), and then existing at Forest Hill, about four miles from Oxford, where, he says, in all probability, some curiosities of the same kind may remain, the contents of these chests (for I think there are more than one) having never yet been properly examined.' This note was written fifty years ago, and most likely the papers have now disappeared; but it may be worth while to inquire about them, for the bare possibility of discovering some treasures.

"I am, I hope, settled to my winter's work, heartily glad to be so, though with darker prospects than at any former time. But I am in good hopes, and trust that, though we are under the worst ministry that ever misconducted the affairs of a great nation, Providence will preserve us. Even if they succeed in bringing upon themselves the destruction which they deserve, you will live to see a restoration of the monarchy and the Episcopal Church.

"God bless you!

"Yours affectionately, R. S."

* To Henry Taylor, Esq., Oct. 23, 1831.

To the Rev. J. W. Warter.

"Keswick, Dec. 27, 1831.

"My dear Warter,

"The merry Christmas that we wish you will be over before our wishes can reach Copenhagen, and the new year will be far on its way to February—may it, however, be a happy one in its course! None within my memory has ever opened with such threatening aspects; but this consideration, which enters night and morning into my prayers, affects me very little at other times, partly because I am too busy to entertain it, partly because my constitutional hilarity overcomes it, and still more, perhaps, because I have a strong persuasion, such as might almost be called an abiding trust, that Providence will visit this country, sinful as it is, rather in mercy than in vengeance.

"The misconduct of those people who let the cholera *into* Sunderland has been, if possible, exceeded by that of the government which has let it *out!* instead of shutting it up and extinguishing it in the first house where it appeared. But even in the king's speech the question of contagion is spoken of as doubtful, and the government have dealt with this pestilence just as they did with the Catholic Question—allowed the evil to increase till they could plead its extent as an excuse for yielding to it: they kept up the farce of a quarantine upon the ships, and allowed free intercourse by land. The cholera is now as fairly denizened as the small-pox.

"I have always thought Copenhagen one of the safest places from this disease, because your government there is an efficient one in such cases, and is perfectly aware of the danger, and yet has few points to guard, which being guarded it can not be brought to you. In England it will have as free a course as sedition, treason, and blasphemy. This house is as favorably situated as any one can be that is not at a distance from an inhabited place; and with this assurance we shall commit ourselves to God's mercy, if it should be imported into Keswick.

* * * * * * *

"You ask me about the insurrection at Bristol. Government are well informed that it was part only of a wider scheme, in which Birmingham, Nottingham, and other places were to have taken part. The bishop behaved manfully; the mob were masters of the city, and one of the minor canons waited upon him before the hour of service, and represented to him the propriety of postponing it. 'My young friend,' said the bishop, with great good nature, laying his hand upon his shoulder as he spake, 'these are times in which it is necessary not to shrink from danger. Our duty is to be at our post.' The service accordingly was performed as usual, and he himself preached. Before evening closed, his palace was burned to the ground, and the loss which he sustained (besides that of his papers) is estimated at £10,000. Except the books and papers which were consumed there, nothing has been destroyed but what may be replaced; for, though the fire has done no good (that is, though it has burned none of those filthy dens of wretchedness with which all our cities are disgraced), it has touched none of the antiquities of the place. A letter from Bristol gives this description, by an eye-witness, of what was going on all night in Queen's Square, the main scene of action: 'The mob gave notice of the houses they meant to attack by knocking at the doors, and they allowed the family a quarter of an hour to escape. This interval they spent in dancing: they cleared a circle in the middle of the square, and went round hand in hand, prisoners in their prison dresses (drunk with the delight of having been set free) and women of the worst description. The light from the blazing houses made them all appear black; and the dance was to many of them the dance of death, for they were so improvident for their own escape, that they set many rooms and different stories on fire at the same time, and when the roofs fell in many of them were seen to drop into the burning ruins.' It is not known how many perished there, but the number killed and wounded by the soldiers was not short of 500.

"This event has made the decent part of the people understand what the populace are, and has made the populace fear the soldiers. Latterly, indeed, the mob were so drunk that a handful of resolute men might have knocked them on the head, as sailors kill seals upon an unfrequented island.

"The truth is, that the West Indian planters are not in more danger from their negroes than we are from our servile population. The old habit of obedience is destroyed, and what is even worse, there is no longer the bond of mutual interest between the workmen, whether in manufactures or agriculture, and their employers. The poor are poorer than they ought to be; they know this, and they know their own numbers and their strength. Where this is the case, no system that depends upon cheap labor for its prosperity can continue. Great changes in the constitution of our society are therefore inevitable; but the changes which our ministers are moving earth and hell to effect, can not even alleviate any one existing evil: their direct tendency is to give more power to that part of the people who have already far too much, and who, in truth, can not possibly have too little, in any well-ordered state.

"How much matters of this kind have been in my thoughts during the last three-and-twenty years, you will see whenever my Essays reach you. I expect daily to see them advertised.

* * * * * * *

"I am glad to hear that you have been buying books. I have subscribed to the Bibliotheca Anglo-Saxonica; and to Jonathan Boucher's Glossary, which is at last about to be completed and published as a Supplement to Johnson. If the continuation be as good as Boucher's own part, it will be the best work of its kind, I believe, in any language. Cuthbert and I are reading the Merchant of Venice in the Friesland dialect, Halbertsma having sent me, from Deventer, a translation by Posthumous of that play and of Julius Cæsar.

"God bless you! R. S."

To Grosvenor C. Bedford, Esq.

"Keswick, Dec. 28, 1831.

"My dear Grosvenor,

"You have taken a wise man's view of the prospect before you; only in one point I think you anticipate something worse than is at all likely to happen, for it is by no means likely that your retiring allowance will be so niggardly as to impose upon you the necessity of any retrenchment. I shall be sorry when this vile measure is carried into effect, believing, upon your judgment, that it is a bad measure in itself; but I should be sorry for it as a mere change, unless there were some great and certain good to arise from it; and even then I should be sorry, for the sake of the poor old Exchequer itself, and my more than forty years' acquaintance with it. But for your sake, certainly, if your future allotment depended upon my will, your harness should be taken off, and to grass you should go for the rest of your life, but with a comfortable shed for winter and bad weather, and plenty of good winter food there, and warm litter. Whatever becomes of the Exchequer, this would be my wish for you. The latter years of life ought to be our own; by the time we reach the threshold of old age, the cares of the world have had from us all that ought to be exacted for them.

* * * * * * *

"You ought, by this time, to have received my Essays, reprinted from the Quarterly Review, and the Edinburgh Annual Register; and with the passages restored which poor Gifford cut out, that is, where I was lucky enough to recover either the MSS. or the proofs. Except the dedication to Sir Robert Inglis, they contain nothing that will be new to you; but you will like to have them thus collected; and when you are cutting the leaves open, you will see many proofs of melancholy foresight. My intention was, if these volumes should obtain a tolerable sale, to follow them with similar volumes ecclesiastical, historical, literary, and miscellaneous, about eight or ten of which my stores would supply. But in the present state of things an encouraging sale is not to be expected, especially for a book containing the most unpopular opinions expressed in the strongest language in which I could convey them.

"At present, thank God, we are all in tolerable health, and in good spirits: these, you know, never fail me. Your godson is a tall fellow, nearly as tall, and only some months younger than I was when you first saw me across the school, little thinking at the time what you and I should be to each other in after years.

"God bless you, my dear G. My love to Miss Page and your brother, and as many new years to you all as may be happy ones. The Smoker* is desired to accept the assurances of their high consideration from the Cattery of Cats' Eden.

"R. S."

CHAPTER XXXV.

FEARS OF A REVOLUTION—THE CHOLERA MORBUS—MARY COLLING—CHARLES SWAIN—DR. BELL'S DEATH—POLITICAL APPREHENSIONS—OFFER OF PROFESSORSHIP AT DURHAM—FEW MEN KNOWN THOROUGHLY—COMPARISON BETWEEN PUBLIC AND PRIVATE EDUCATION—OPINION OF MR. SWAIN'S POETRY—KNOWLEDGE NOT THE FIRST THING NEEDFUL—HISTORY OF PORTUGAL—REVIEW OF BOWLES'S ST. JOHN IN PATMOS—MARY COLLING—VISIT TO LOWTHER—LORD MAHON—PRINCE POLIGNAC—POLITICAL PROSPECTS—LORD NUGENT—LORD BROUGHAM—THE CORN-LAW RHYMER—DANGERS OF THE COUNTRY—THE FACTORY SYSTEM—LORD ASHLEY—AMERICAN DIVINITY—THE CHURCH OF ENGLAND—ALISON'S HISTORY OF EUROPE—DEATH OF A FAVORITE CAT—HISTORY OF BRAZIL—DR. BELL—ALLAN CUNNINGHAM'S LIVES OF THE PAINTERS—FRENCH POLITICS—EBENEZER ELLIOTT—PROSPECTS OF THE COUNTRY—THE DOCTOR—MARRIAGE OF HIS ELDEST DAUGHTER—THE CORN LAWS—HABITS OF DAILY LIFE—HENRY TAYLOR'S PLAYS—ZOPHIEL—REMONSTRANCE IN A CASE OF CRUELTY.—1832–1834.

MY father's apprehensions concerning the state and prospects of the country at this time may, perhaps, to persons reading them now, appear exaggerated and unfounded; and, indeed, we are often apt to think lightly both of our own fears and those of others when the danger has passed by. But these feelings were not confined to himself, for many others shared them fully. Every reader of Sir Walter Scott's life will remember with what fears he had viewed the approach of the present crisis. Mr. Rickman, with a cool, clear head, and with peculiar opportunities of knowing the feelings and wishes of the various parties in the House of Commons, saw the danger clearly, at the same time that he believed it would be averted. Mr. Wordsworth, too, looked at the prospects of the country and the signs of the times with the darkest apprehension, and, not being endowed with such elastic spirits as my father, was occasionally much depressed by his fears.

It must, however, be remembered that, notwithstanding the opinion my father held of the pernicious tendency of the measures the Whig party were then advocating—opinions confirmed and strengthened by the means adopted to carry those measures, and by the feelings with which so many of the poorer classes regarded them—yet he had never lost his heart, hope, or a confidence that there was that stability in the country which, under Providence, would withstand the shock.

But he had other causes for looking gloomily at the course of events—private reasons as well as political ones. "The Great Trade," as it has been called, shared in the general stagnation. Men's minds were too full of the stirring politics of the time to read any thing except newspapers and pamphlets, the sale of his own works was altogether at a stand, and publishers naturally were unwilling to enter into new engagements. The Quarterly Review was suffering from its being on the unpopular side, and he was beginning to fear lest his main support should fail him; yet his spirits did not fail him, and in a little time the prospect began to look brighter.

To the Rev. Neville White.

"Keswick, June 3, 1832.

"MY DEAR NEVILLE,

"Though the old-fashioned wish of a Merry Christmas and a Happy New Year would now be after date, it is not too late to express a wish that God's blessing may be with you and yours in this year and in all the years that shall follow it, and that His special mercy may protect you, whatever evils this nation may be afflicted with.

"Lord Althorpe thinks the arrival of the cholera is the greatest national calamity that could befall us; this he says, because, being Chancellor of the Exchequer, he dreads the effect which an extended quarantine must produce upon the revenue; and truly, after the experiments in free trade, and the repeal of taxes, which has cut down the national income without affording the slightest perceptible relief to any portion of the people, he may apprehend this consequence.

"It is many years ago, long before the Colloquies were begun, that the likelihood of a visitation of pestilence occurred to me, when thinking of the condition of this country and the ways of Providence. Considering the condition of the poor, the miserable population which the manufacturing system had collected in great bodies, and the zeal with which the most mischievous opinions were propagated, I thought, with David, that pestilence was the lightest evil that could be expected, and therefore that, perhaps, it was the likeliest.

"The possibility of such a political crisis as the present was never in my thoughts. Who, indeed, could have dreamed that we should ever have a ministry who would call in the mob for the purpose of subverting the Constitution? The fearful question which a few months must resolve is, whether pestilence will arrest the progress of revolution, or accelerate it, by making the populace desperate. Nothing can more dangerously tend to make them so than the opinion which is

* A favorite cat of Mr. Bedford's.

given in all the newspapers that it is a disease from which the more fortunate classes seem to be exempt; and that unclean habits, crowded habitations, and poor diet render men peculiarly liable to it.

"10th. On the morning after I had written the above, the Ballot for January 1 was sent me, where, in the leading article, ——, by whom it is edited, endeavors to excite the populace by means of the cholera, telling them that they, and they alone, are the marked victims of this pestilence, and that it is oppression which has made them so! and that the rich are safe, because they are rich, and have all the comforts of life!

"The king, I am told, will make as many peers as his ministers choose; and nothing then remains for us but to await the course of revolution. I shall not live to see what sort of edifice will be constructed out of the ruins, but I shall go to rest in the sure confidence that God will provide as is best for His church and His people.

"My tenderest regards to your dear mother, and those of my fireside to you and yours.

"God bless you, my dear friend!

"Yours most affectionately, R. S."

To the Rev. James White.

"Keswick, Feb. 8, 1832.

"MY DEAR JAMES,

"The endless round of occupation in which my days are passed has prevented me from thanking you, as long ago I ought and intended to have done, for the trouble and the care which you took for and of my daughter. This delay lies on my conscience for another reason, though happily what I have to say is not yet too late; it is to give you my most serious and earnest opinion, that when the cholera reaches Manchester, your duty is *not* to look after the sick. Upon the Roman Catholic system it would be; it is not upon the principle of the Reformed Church. The progress of the disease is too rapid, and when it proves fatal, its effects are also too violent, to admit of any good being done by religious instruction: this matter I have talked over with Mr. Whiteside here, and he entirely agrees with me. Preach rousing sermons to your people, tell them death is at their doors, and exhort them to hold themselves in readiness for his summons. Do as you are doing to prepare against the evil by other means, but do not expose yourself unnecessarily to infection when it comes. No man is less likely to take it than you are, your very ardor being the best prophylactic; *but you are not to presume upon that.*

"I think it would be prudent if those who have authority were to enjoin that the funeral service should not be performed where the disease is raging in individual cases, nor even over many at one time, but that, when the disease has ceased, there should be a general service in every place for those who have died of it; this would much lessen the spread of the contagion, and have a solemn effect at last.

"One good I confidently hope for from this visitation. The preparatory measures of precaution have made the squalid misery of the lower orders matter of public notoriety. What you and I have so long known, and what was always known to those whose business or duty leads them among the poor, is now brought publicly to the knowledge of those who, if not ignorant of it, might at least excuse their gross inattention to this great and crying evil by affecting to be so. They who are insensible to the moral evils of such poverty, and even to its political dangers, may be roused by the physical consequences, when they see it acting as a recipient and conductor not only for sedition and rebellion, but for pestilence also. * *

"There will be only a short paper of mine in the next Quarterly Review upon Mary Colling's Fables. You will be interested with her story, and amused, perhaps, with the introduction of the Poet Laureate of Trowbridge.

"Pray remember me to Mr. Swain when you see him. I had been much pleased with his poems, and was not less pleased with him, for, indeed, he seemed to be in all things such as I could have wished to find him.

"To-night I begin the last chapter of the Peninsular War, and you may well suppose that I shall proceed rapidly, seeing the end so near.

"Take care of yourself; that is, do not attempt more than flesh and blood can perform. You can do no greater good to others than by sparing yourself, and keeping yourself in health for the service of some more manageable flock in a different sort of pasture.

"God bless you, my dear James!

"Yours affectionately, R. S."

To John May, Esq.

"Keswick, Feb. 18, 1832.

"MY DEAR FRIEND,

" * * * * * * *

I know no one who has been pursued by such a series of unmerited afflictions: one may use such language in speaking of calamities that are brought on by the actions of our fellow-creatures.

" * * * * * * *

If I had been called to Cheltenham, I should certainly have gone on to Bristol; but as yet I have received no further intelligence from thence than a few lines from the poor old doctor's secretary, informing me of his death, and saying that when the trustees arrived, official information would be sent to me.* I persuade myself that it is not likely I shall be called from home, disagreeable as it would be, and especially inconvenient at this time.

"No man can care much about public affairs

* "I have just received news of Dr. Bell's death from his faithful secretary Davies, who says that 'official information will be dispatched to me when the trustees arrive.' When it comes, I fear it may call me to Cheltenham; but certainly I shall not go if the business can be done by proxy. Poor old man, he is now at rest from his discovery, which was a perpetual torment to him, whatever good it may ultimately produce to others. But I had a great liking for the better parts of his strongly-marked character; and his death, though expected, and for his own sake long to have been desired, takes full possession of my mind just now, and troubles it."—*To H. Taylor, Esq., Jan.* 31.

when his own troubles are pressing heavily upon his heart and mind. But I greatly fear that the time is hastening on when public concerns will affect the vital interests of every individual. Wordsworth is made positively unhappy by this thought. I should be so if my mind were not constantly occupied, for I see most surely that nothing but the special mercy of Providence can save us from a revolution; and I feel, also, that we have much more reason to fear the Almighty's justice than to rely upon his mercy in this case; yet I rely upon it, and keep my heart firm in that reliance.

"Feb. 20.

"Yesterday brought me the expected letter from Dr. Bell's trustees. He has left me £1000. He had left me also his furniture, &c., but this he revoked in a codicil a few days before his death, giving some unintelligible reason for so doing, and adding at the same time a bequest of £100 to my dear Isabel* as his godchild; his memory, therefore, had completely failed him at that time. The legacy to me is the largest he has left; and most welcome it is, as something on which I may rely (as far as any thing dependent upon the fearful insecurity of human life, and of all our social institutions in these days, may be relied on) for Cuthbert's support at Oxford: it relieves me from any difficulty respecting means, if he and I should live so long, and this frame of things should be kept together.

"I collect from the trustees' letter that Dr. Bell changed his intention concerning the publication of his works, which he had desired Wordsworth and myself to superintend, but it seems he still wished and expected that I should draw up an account of his life. Upon this I shall have further information, no doubt, in due time. Poor man! the last letter I received from him told me that he had bequeathed to me his furniture, and that therefore I must be prepared to set off for Cheltenham as soon as I should be informed of 'an event which could not be far distant.' If I had done so, how uncomfortably should I have felt on my arrival there! * * * * God bless and support you, my dear friend, and bring you through all difficulties into a peaceful port.

"Yours most affectionately, R. S."

To Henry Taylor, Esq.

"Keswick, March 2, 1832.

"My dear H. T.,

" * * * * * * *

In how different a situation should we now be if ministers had looked to the real evils of the country, and left the imaginary ones alone! The great remedy for pauperism can be nothing but constant emigration, to which I would have all pauper children destined who are orphans, or whose parents have deserted them: they are easily transported, easily settled, and in this manner best provided for. Always bearing in mind that the country can not be healthy unless the great drain of emigration is kept open, the means of more immediate relief which I should look to would be, from bringing wastes into cultivation, thinking it profit enough if those who must otherwise be supported by the public can raise their own food there.

"I wish government would employ —— upon a digest of the agricultural surveys—a work of national importance, for which he is peculiarly qualified, and in the course of which much would suggest itself upon this very subject of the poor.

"I like your simile of the pyramid,* and am content with it—content that the work should be a lasting one, and, though seen by few, heard of by many. The commonwealth of Readingdom is divided into many independent circles. Novel and trash readers make by much the largest of the communities; I think the religious public rank next in numbers; then perhaps come those who affect poetry: history is read by those only who are desirous of information, and of these very few like to have it at length, or, indeed, can afford time for it. But in every generation there are some. My story belongs to a brilliant part of our own history, and to a most important one in that of two other countries; it is sure, therefore, of a place in the *Bibliotheca Historica* of all three.

"The History of Portugal, if I live to execute it, will be my best historical work. There, as in the Brazil, industry in collecting materials, and skill in connecting them, may be manifested, and a great deal brought to light which will be deemed of no little interest in the history of European society and of the human mind. A good deal of the Peninsular story required, as you observe, little more than the mere patience of detailing it on my part; but the whole has an entireness of subject which can belong to the history of very few wars, and an interest from the importance of the cause and the peculiarity of the circumstances which is quite as uncommon. I believe none of my works have been read with more eagerness by those into whose hands it has come, and you know I never look for a wide public. It is more profitable to have your reputation spread itself in *breadth;* I am satisfied with looking to the probable *length* of mine. God bless you! R. S."

The next letter was in reply to one containing some overtures from some of the authorities at Durham as to whether my father would be disposed to accept a Professorship of History in that University. The fact of his being willing to listen to and consider the details of an offer†

* Isabel Southey died in 1826.

* "I shall be very glad to see the third volume of the Peninsular War appear. It will be a great work, I suppose the greatest of its kind, and yet I should almost regret to see you engage again in any narrative of so much detail; a great portion of the labor bestowed upon such a work must be not of a kind to bring into play the faculties of your mind in all their extent and variety, and I doubt whether now or henceforward the growth of literature will admit of works being constructed on such a scale. This sort of Great Pyramid will be allowed to be a wonderful structure, but it will not be commonly resorted to"—*H. T. to R. S., Feb. 28, 1832.*

† With reference to the offer, he says, in a letter to Mr. Bedford, after stating that it is solely from prudential mo-

of this kind, at his age and with his habits, shows that a change had come over him, and that a settled income had become a matter of far greater importance in his eyes than formerly.

This scheme, however, as he anticipated, soon fell to the ground, the remuneration it was intended to offer not being such as he could prudently have accepted.

To George Taylor, Esq.

"Keswick, March 3, 1832.

"MY DEAR SIR,

"Your letter which I have this day received proposes for my consideration a question of prudence, which can be answered only when the particulars are made known. At present I can say no more than that it is a matter in which my inclinations shall not be allowed to have more than their due weight, but that it must be no inconsiderable advantage which could induce me to alter my habits of life, and divide the remainder of it between two places of abode; for, though not so rooted here as to be absolutely irremovable, I am *leased* to the spot, and my library also binds me to it. Perhaps no consideration could induce me wholly to leave it; but Durham is an easy distance, and periodical migrations, though attended with some discomfort, would probably be wholesome for my family, and not hurtful to myself.

"But I will dismiss from my mind at present all thoughts of this kind, and of the difficulties and objections on one side, and on the other the plans which would readily present themselves to be sketched and shaped. It would be losing time to think of these things now; only I may say that my estimate of what would be to be done goes far beyond Mr. ——'s. My consideration would be, not with how little labor I might go through the functions of the professorship, but how I might best discharge them for the benefit of those whom I should have to address, and for my own credit hereafter.

"Farewell, my dear sir. Present our kind remembrances to Mrs. Taylor, and believe me always

"Yours, with great and sincere regard,

"ROBERT SOUTHEY."

To H. Taylor, Esq.

"Keswick, March 7, 1832.

"MY DEAR H. T.,

" * * * * * * *

Most men play the fool in some way or other, and no man takes more delight in playing it than I do, in my own way. I do it well with children, and not at all with women, toward whom, like John Bunyan, 'I can not carry myself pleasantly,' unless I have a great liking for them. Most men, I suspect, have different characters even among their friends, appearing in different circles in different lights, or rather showing only parts of themselves. One's character, being *teres atque rotundus*, is not to be seen all at once. You must know a man *all round*—in all moods and all weathers—to know him well; but in the common intercourse of the world, men see each other in only one mood—see only their manners in society, and hear nothing that comes from any part lying deeper than the larynx. Many people think they are well acquainted with me who know little more of me than the cut of my jib and the sound of my voice.

"The probabilities, I think, are much against the Durham scheme. It will not appear to them worth *their while* to make it worth *mine;* they will consider what, according to common prudence, they might be expected to afford; as I must what, upon the same ground, I ought to accept. The two prudentials are not likely to agree, and they will never know what they lose in failing to engage me, for, were I to live and do well, my work would be worth far more to them than my name. God bless you! R. S."

To Grosvenor C. Bedford, Esq.

"Keswick, April 1, 1832.

"MY DEAR GROSVENOR,

"If you had been within reach of me a week ago, when I wrote *Laus Deo* at the end of the Peninsular War, I should have taken my hat and my walking-stick, and set out for the satisfaction of singing 'O be joyful' in your presence and with your aid. The volume, since I wrote to you in December, has outgrown my expectations by more than a hundred pages, so much more detail have I been led into by my materials than at first sight had been anticipated.

* * * * * * *

"From this you will conclude that I am in good health and in good spirits, notwithstanding the dismal prospect of public affairs. On private scores, however, I have uneasiness enough, of which it were useless to speak where no good can be obtained.

* * * * * * *

"As for the likings or dislikings, Grosvenor, which are formed at first sight or upon casual acquaintance, no one who has lived long in the world will attach more importance to them than they deserve. Complicated as every human character must be, we like or dislike just that part of it which happens to present itself to our observation; and perhaps the same person, in another point of view, makes a very different impression. It is so with countenances, and it is so even with natural scenery. Upon a second journey I have sometimes looked in vain for the beauties which delighted me on the first; and, on the other hand, I have discovered pleasing objects where I had formerly failed to perceive them. I know very well in what very different lights I myself must appear to different people, who see me but once, or whose acquaintance with me is very slight: not a few go away with the notion that they have seen a stiff, cold, reserved, disobliging sort of person; and they judge rightly as far as they see, except that no one

tives, he "deemed it right to listen to the overture. It is not in the natural or fitting course of things that I should be put in harness at an age when I ought rather to be turned out to grass for the remainder of my days."

should be deemed disobliging merely for taking no pains to make himself agreeable where he feels no inclination to do so.

"This I think is the greatest disadvantage that notorious authorship brings with it. It places one in an unfair position among strangers: they watch for what you say, and set upon you to draw you out, and whenever that is the case, in I go like a tortoise or hodmandod into my shell.

* * * * * * *

"God bless you, my dear G.! R. S."

To Grosvenor C. Bedford, Esq.

"Keswick, April 15, 1832.

"My dear G.,

"There are Greek and English Lexicons now; but if your nephew is intended for a public school, the better way, as he would be a day-boy (which I look upon to be the greatest of all advantages), would be to send him to Westminster as soon as he was fit for the second form: I do not say for the petty, because the work of the first two years may probably be as well got at home in six months. Had I lived in London, Cuthbert should certainly have gone to Westminster as a day-boy. There is in schemes of education, as in every thing else, a choice of evils: no *safe* process—*that is impossible.* My settled opinion is, that the best plan is a public school, where the boy can board at home: upon this I have no doubt. When he can not, the question between public and private education is so questionable, that in most cases a feather might turn the scale. With me it was turned by the heavy weights of distance and expense, and the consideration that life is uncertain; and by educating my son at home, I was at least sure of this, that his years of boyhood would be happy.

"Your godson whom you are not likely to see unless you come to Keswick, is nearly, if not quite, as tall as his godfather, though he completed his thirteenth year only in February last. His knowledge of Greek is about as much as I carried with me into the fifth form; his Latin rather less than I brought to Westminster, the truth being that I am not qualified to teach him either critically; but what he lacks can be superadded easily in due time. We went through the Pentateuch (omitting the Levitical parts), Joshua, and Judges, in your present of the Septuagint, and read the same portion of the Bible on the same day in German and Dutch. Having got so far, I substituted Herodotus for the Septuagint, and added the Swedish to our biblical readings. We now read Herodotus and Homer on alternate days. God alone knows what may be appointed for him or for me. * * *

"I am reviewing Lord Nugent's Life of Hampden, with the intention of winding up with some remarks on the present state of affairs. One of the amiable correspondents of the Times asks, in to-day's paper, whether *I* am one of the Duke of Wellington's advisers! a question which shows how much this fellow knows either about the duke or me.

"God bless you! R. S.

"The Cattery of Cats' Eden congratulate the Cat without a name upon his succession in Stafford Row."

To Charles Swain, Esq.

"Keswick, May 1, 1832.

"My dear Sir,

"Do not look upon my invitation to you as a matter of politeness, a motive from which I never act further than the common law of society requires.

"Respect for you and your talents, and the use you have made of them, was my motive. Your poetry is made of the right materials. If ever man was born to be a poet, you are: and if Manchester is not proud of you yet, the time will certainly come when it will be so.

"Come when you will, and stay as long as you can, I shall be sincerely happy to receive you here. I wish you were with us now; the sun shines, the birds are busy, the buds beginning to open. There is a vernal spirit abroad which carries joy to young hearts, and brings the best substitute for it to those whose season for joy is past, not to return again.

"God bless you!

"Yours affectionately,

"Robert Southey."

To the Rev J. W. Warter.

"Keswick, June 20, 1832.

"My dear Warter,

" * * * * * * *

Oxford or Cambridge are good places of residence for men who, having stored their minds well, want well-stored libraries which may enable them to pursue their researches and bring forth the fruits of them. But the plant which roots itself there will never attain any vigorous growth. The mind must be a very strong and a very active one which does not stand still while it is engaged in *tutoring*, and both universities now are little more than manufactories in which men are brought up to a certain point in a certain branch of knowledge, and when they have reached that point they are kept there.

"But, after all, knowledge is not the first thing needful. Provided we can get contentedly through the world, and (be the ways rough or smooth) to heaven at last, the sum of knowledge that we may collect on the way is more infinitely insignificant than I like to acknowledge in my own heart. Indeed, it is not easy for me always to bear sufficiently in mind that the pursuits in which I find constant interest and increasing enjoyment must appear of no interest whatever to the greater part not merely of mankind, but of the educated part even of our own countrymen. I forget this sometimes when I am wishing for others, opportunities by which perhaps they would not be disposed to profit.

* * * * * * *

"I wish I could answer Sarmento's question to my own satisfaction. If I could follow my inclinations, a week would not elapse before the History of Portugal would be in the press. But this work can only have that time allotted to it which can be won from works of necessity, and that not yet. I hope my affairs are in such a train that next year it will become my chief object in those *subsecive* hours, for which I can find no English word. Once in the press, it would go on steadily, for the subject has been two-and-thirty years in my mind. So long is it since I began not merely to collect materials, but to digest them, and for at least two thirds of the history I have only to recompose in the process of transcribing what has long been written. I believe no history has ever yet been composed that presents such a continuous interest of one kind or another, as this would do, if I should live to complete it. The chivalrous portion is of the very highest beauty; much of what succeeds has a deep tragic interest; and then comes the gradual destruction of a noble national character brought on by the cancer of Romish superstition.

"But I have other letters to write by this post, and therefore must conclude. God bless you!

R. S."

To the Rev. W. Lisle Bowles.

"Keswick, July 30, 1832.

"MY DEAR SIR,

"This morning I received your St. John in Patmos, two months after the date of the note which accompanied it: this is mentioned, that you may not think I have been slow in acknowledging and thanking you for it. I have just read the poem through, and with much pleasure. Yours I should have known it to have been by the sweet and unsophisticated style upon which I endeavored, now almost forty years ago, to form my own. You have so blended the episodical parts that they do not in any degree disturb the solemn and mysterious character of the whole.

"You will not, I am sure, suppose that I could for even a moment feel hurt by your remarks in the preface. After having reviewed in the Quarterly Review Grahame's Georgics, Montgomery's Poems, and his World before the Flood, and Landor's Count Julian, I found it necessary to resolve that I would not review the work of any living poet. Applications to me from strangers, and from others in all degrees of acquaintanceship, were so frequent, that it became expedient to be provided with a general reason for refusing, which could offend no one; there was no other means of avoiding offense. Many would otherwise have resented the refusal, and more would have been more deeply displeased if they had not been extolled according to their own estimate of their own merits. From this resolution I did not consider myself as departing when I drew up the account of Mary Colling; her story and her character interested me greatly, and would, I thought, interest most readers. I wished to render her some service, and have the satisfaction of knowing that this has been in some measure effected. It was a case wherein a little praise, through that channel, might be the means of producing some permanent benefit to one who has gentle blood in her veins, and whose sweet countenance, if you look at her portrait, will say more in her favor than any words of mine could do.

"I have no wish to encourage the growth of humble authors, still less of adventurers in literature, God knows. But I earnestly wish, especially in an age when all persons can read, to encourage in all who have any love of reading that sort of disposition which would lead them to take pleasure in your poems and in mine, and in any which are addressed, as ours always have been, to the better feelings of our nature. The tendency of our social system has long been to brutalize the lower classes, and this it is that renders the prospect before us so fearful. I wish to see their moral and intellectual condition as much as possible improved; it seems to me that great improvement is possible, and that in bettering their condition the general good is promoted.

"Would that there were a hope of seeing you here, that I might show you this lake and these mountains, and these books, and talk with you upon subjects which might make us forget that we are living in the days of William IV., Earl Grey, the Times newspaper, and the cholera morbus. God save the first, and deliver us from the rest!

"Believe me, my dear sir, yours, with sincere respect and regard,

"ROBERT SOUTHEY."

To the Rev. Neville White.

"Keswick, August 19, 1832.

"MY DEAR NEVILLE,

"It rarely happens in these times that the post brings me any matter for rejoicing; but it never at any time brought me a communication which gave me more thorough delight than your letter which arrived this morning. You have now the reward of your deserts, and it is no slight comfort to see that desert has been thus rewarded. All circumstances, too, are as you could have wished them to be; for, though your lot has not fallen in a beautiful country, it is near Norwich, and therefore a desirable location for you. Walpole is a name which from childhood I have regarded with good will, and henceforth I shall regard it with still better.

"I shall certainly look in upon you on my next journey to London. When that may be I know not, but certainly not before the spring, and perhaps not so soon. Engagements will keep me to the desk, and, happily, inclination would never take me from it.

"I shall like dearly to see you in your Rectory: to a certain degree you will once more have to form new habits, but in this instance the change is likely to be salutary.

"I dare say that the duties of your parish will be much less fatiguing than those in which you engaged as a volunteer in Norwich, and they will be more agreeable, because, in a little while, as soon as your parishioners know you, you will perceive the fruits of them. Any clergyman who does his duty as you will do it must soon be loved by his flock, and then no other station in life can be so happy.

"I wish James were emancipated from his bondage, and settled as his bishop ought to settle him, where he might enjoy the well-deserved reward of his labors, and some rest from them.

"Much against my will, I am going to Lowther Castle on Friday next, to remain till Monday. Lord Lonsdale asks me in so kind a manner, saying that he is always unwilling to take me from my employments, that I can not refuse to go; and his object is to introduce me to Lord Mahon, whom I know only by letter, but whose way of thinking and pursuits make him desire to become acquainted with me. It is gratifying to perceive that there are persons growing up whose minds have been influenced by my writings, and that here and there the seed which during so many years I have been casting on the waters, has taken root, and is beginning to bring forth fruit after its kind.

"God bless you, my dear Neville! With the kindest congratulations and remembrances of my household, and my own especially to your dear mother and your wife, believe me always,

"Yours most affectionately,

"ROBERT SOUTHEY."

To John Rickman, Esq.

"Keswick, Oct. 15, 1832.

"MY DEAR R.,

"I have been working hard upon a paper on French affairs, which I shall finish to-morrow. A pamphlet by Prince Polignac furnishes the text and much of the matter for it. This was sent me by Sir Robert Adair, who is his particular friend, and I have since, through the same channel, had a letter from the poor prisoner himself.* Adair has also sent me a curious pamphlet, written to vindicate the Belgian revolution from the *disgrace* of having any thing in common with the last French one.

"It is very difficult to foresee any thing in the present state of Europe. Nothing could have seemed more improbable than the preservation of peace thus long. If it be still preserved, the struggle between the government and the Chamber will go on till the nation distinctly see that it is, in fact, a question whether there is to be any government or none, and then the least unlikely termination would be that Soult would enact the part of Monk, and Louis Philippe make a merit of having acted as king, in order to preserve the monarchy till he could safely transfer it to the legitimate prince. To this or to another military despotism it must come.

"Last night we had the M. of Hastings here, who voted with the ministry, and now apprehends the consequences. Wynn thinks there is a reaction in the country; C——, on the contrary, believes revolution to be imminent and inevitable. I will not say that every thing depends upon the new elections, but much certainly does; and I suspect that the Radicals, when the time comes, will be found much more alert and active than their opponents are prepared to expect, or, perhaps, to withstand. We are only *sure* of one Conservative member from this county, Matthias Attwood's success being doubtful.

"Oddly enough, while American notions of government are obtaining ground in Europe, the United States themselves seem likely to be disunited, and give practical proof of the instability of any such system. No doubt our West Indian planters would call upon America to receive them into the Union, and be received accordingly, if the Slave Question were not likely to be the cause of quarrel between the Southern States and the Congress. Most likely I shall write a paper upon this question for the Christmas number. From the way in which the emancipators on the one hand, and the colonial assemblies on the other, are proceeding, we shall soon have those islands in the condition of St. Domingo.

* * * * * * *

"Murray has published a letter to himself by Lord Nugent, which letter abuses me by name, à-la-William Smith. It has been published more than a fortnight, and he has never sent it me, nor do I know any thing of it, except at second hand from a newspaper. If I should think it worth while to take any notice of this attack, it will be very briefly, and through the newspapers; but I must make myself angry before I can bestow even the little time upon such a business which it would require.

"God bless you! R. S."

To John May, Esq.

"Keswick, March 1, 1833.

"MY DEAR FRIEND,

" * * * * If any one had told me that I should ever feel an anxious interest in any promise of the Lord Chancellor Brougham's, it would have seemed a most improbable supposition, and yet I am now solicitous about two of his promises—that to which you are looking, and that which he made to Henry about the Lunacy Commission. I have known men who make promises without the slightest intention of keeping them, rather with the full intention of never performing them. This is not Brougham's case: in such things he does not look so far forward; and he is a good-natured man, much too good-natured ever to raise hopes, meaning to disappoint them. * * * *

"This year will not pass away without greater changes than the last. It is already apparent that the reformed Parliament will not work. Government by authority has long been defunct. Government by influence was put to death by the Reform Bill, and nothing is left but government by public opinion.

"I have gone through the whole evidence concerning the treatment of children in the factories, and nothing so bad was ever brought to light before. The slave trade is mercy to it. We know how the slave trade began and imperceptibly increased, nothing in the beginning being committed that shocked the feelings and

* See Appendix.

was contrary to the spirit of the age. Having thus grown up, it went on by succession, and of later years has rather been mitigated than made worse. But this white slavery has risen in our own days, and is carried on in the midst of this civilized and Christian nation. Herein it is that our danger consists. The great body of the manufacturing populace, and also of the agricultural, are *miserably* poor; their condition is worse than it *ought* to be. One after another, we are destroying all the outworks by which order, and, with it, property and life, are defended, and this brutalized populace is ready to break in upon us. The prelude which you witnessed at Bristol was a manifestation of the spirit that exists among them. But in the manufacturing districts, where the wages of the adults are at a starvation rate, and their children are literally worked to death —murdered by inches—the competition of the masters being the radical cause of these evils, there is a dreadful reality of oppression, a dreadful sense of injustice, of intolerable misery, of intolerable wrongs, more formidable than any causes which have ever moved a people to insurrection. Once more I will cry aloud and spare not. These are not times to be silent. Lord Ashley has taken up this Factory Question with all his heart, under a deep religious sense of duty. I hear from him frequently. If we are to be saved, it will be, I will not say *by* such men, but for the sake of such men as he is—men who have the fear of God before their eyes, and the love of their fellow-creatures in their hearts.

"God bless you, my dear friend! Remember me most kindly to your two daughters; and believe me always yours most affectionately,

"R. SOUTHEY."

To the Lord Bishop of Limerick.

"Keswick, March 6, 1833.

"MY LORD,

"I am greatly obliged to you for your edition of Burnet's Lives, made still more valuable by the Introduction, the Prefaces, and the Notes with which they are enriched. No books are read with more interest than such as this, and none are likely to do so much good.

"The Americans seem more awake to the uses of exemplary biography than we are. They lose no opportunity of pronouncing funeral orations; and in what may be called the ordination charge of a Unitarian minister, the old pastor recommends that biographical discourses should be delivered from the pulpit occasionally instead of sermons, instancing as fit subjects such men as Watts, Lindsey, and Howard. This will remind you of the Roman Catholic practice, to which we are indebted for such books as the Flos Sanctorum.

"But the American Unitarians come nearer to the Romanists on more dangerous ground. Two volumes have lately been sent me from New England of sermons by James Freeman, a very old and very amiable man, exceedingly beloved and reverenced by his friends and his flock. Had they come to me as a collection of essays, in which any thing religious or devotional might or might not incidentally be introduced, I should have been pleased with the happy disposition that they indicate, the benevolent spirit that pervades them, and their occasional felicity of expression, and, I may add, with what might then have deserved to be called their unobtrusive piety; but as discourses from a gray-haired pastor to his people, I could not peruse them without sorrow, nor, indeed, sometimes without astonishment. He tells his congregation, 'Alms, when they are bestowed from pious and benevolent principles, will carry you to Heaven: they will deliver you from death, and never suffer you to descend into a place of darkness. This is rendering it may be said, the path to everlasting happiness very plain and easy. True; but I do not render it easier and plainer than the Scriptures have made it.'

"No wonder that the Roman Catholics increase at Boston, as they do in Holland and elsewhere, wherever such Christianity is preached. 'The Almighty,' he says, 'sent down from His throne such men as Copernicus, Kepler, and Newton to enlighten the world.'

"In an Ordination Charge he says, 'In this age of the Church it is unnecessary that you should read the Fathers, except for improvement in morals and devotion, because others have read them for you, and have extracted from them almost all the facts that they contain.'

"These are some of the fruits which Puritanism has brought forth in America. It seems as if in our own country the experiment was about to be repeated of improving the vineyard by breaking down the fences, and letting the cattle and the wild beasts in. The crisis is probably very near at hand: I see my way much more distinctly into it than out of it. For the last two years it has been evident that O'Connell has formed an alliance offensive and defensive with the political unions. He relies upon them either to frighten the ministers out of their coercive measures by a demonstration of physical force, embodied, mustered, and ready to take the field, or, if they fail in this, he expects them to hoist the tricolor flag, and march upon London whenever he gives the signal for rebellion in Ireland. Brandreth's insurrection in 1817, the projected expedition of the Blanketeers a little later, and the Bristol riots, were all parts of a widely-concerted scheme, which has only been from time to time postponed till a more convenient season, and is now thoroughly matured, and likely to be attempted upon a great scale whenever the leaders of the movement think proper. I am not without strong apprehensions that before this year passes away, London may have its Three Days.

"But earnestly as such a crisis is to be deprecated, I do not fear the result. It may even come in time to save us from the otherwise inevitable overthrow of all our institutions by the treachery and cowardice of those who ought to uphold them. The Whigs will never give over the work of destruction which they have so prosperously begun till the honester Destructives are armed against them, and threaten them with their due reward. The sooner, therefore, that it comes to this, the better.

"Meantime there is a comfort in seeing by the London election that a great change has taken place in public opinion there: there is a comfort in knowing that the Church of England and of Ireland could never at any time have been better able to bear hostile inquiry, and to defend themselves than now; above all, there is a never-failing comfort in a constant reliance upon Providence, and this, God be thanked, I am enabled to feel.

"I beg my kindest remembrances to Mr. Forster; and remain, with the greatest respect, my lord, your lordship's obliged and obedient servant,

"ROBERT SOUTHEY."

To the Rev. Neville White.

"Keswick, April 10, 1833.

"MY DEAR NEVILLE,

"Your letter, which I have this morning received, came when I was just about to reply to that of March 11th. You may judge how my other correspondents fare by the length of time that your letters remain unanswered, there being none which I receive more gladly or to which I reply with more interest; and yet more than half my mornings are consumed in letter-writing; though, as far as possible, I have, from necessity, cut off all useless correspondence, and curtailed the rest.

"Now, my dear Neville, to the other part of your letter—the uses and the danger of the Church Establishment. I will touch upon one of its uses which happened to be noticed in conversation yesterday with Wordsworth by the wayside. He mentioned of what advantage the Church of England had been to that great body of Dissenters among whom the Unitarian heresy has spread, and your country was particularly instanced. A great part of the Presbyterian congregations lapsed with their preachers, as sheep follow the bell-wether; but of those who remained orthodox, the majority found their way into the right fold. They held the doctrines of the Church before in the main, differing from them only in points where our Articles most wisely have left room for difference; and they now found by experience the insufficiency of their own discipline, and the want of such a standard as the Establishment preserves.

"Public property the Church indeed is—most truly and most sacredly so—and in a manner the very reverse of that in which the despoilers consider it to be so. It is the only property which is public—which is set apart and consecrated as a public inheritance, in which any one may claim his share who is properly qualified. You have your share of it, I might have had mine. There is no respectable family in England, some of whose members have not, in the course of two or three generations, enjoyed their part in it; and many thousands are at this time qualifying themselves to claim their portion. Upon what principle can any government be justified in robbing them of their rights?

"Church property neither is nor ever has been public property in any other sense than this. The whole was originally private property, so disposed of by individuals in the way which they deemed most beneficial to others, and most for the good of their own souls. How much of superstition may have been mingled with this, matters not. Much of this property was wickedly shared among themselves by those persons who forwarded the Reformation as a scheme of spoliation, and in other ways materially impeded its progress. Yet they did nothing so bad as the Whig ministry are preparing to do, for they, no doubt, mean to give to the Romish clergy what they take from the Irish Protestant Church.

"You should read Townsend's pamphlet upon Lord Henley's absurd and mischievous schemes. It is a most able and manly composition, and the name and character of the writer carry weight with them. God bless you!

"Yours most affectionately, R. S."

To A. Alison, Esq.

"Keswick, April 17, 1833.

"MY DEAR SIR,

"I am much obliged to you for your History. It reached me on Monday evening last, so that I have only had time to run through the whole, and peruse those parts which arrested me.

"A better book could not possibly have been made upon that subject within the same limits, nor could the subject be treated in a manner more likely to be in the highest degree useful, if any thing in these times could be addressed with effect to the understanding of an infatuated nation.

"The events which you have so vividly described are fresh in my memory, for I was just old enough to take the liveliest interest in them as they occurred, and young enough for that interest to have all the eagerness of hope. I thought as highly of the Girondists as you have spoken of them, but was too young and too ignorant to see their errors as you have done. I entered, therefore, warmly into their views, and no public event ever caused me so much pain as the fate of Brissot and his associates—till I lived to see our own Constitution destroyed. Few of that party hold the same place in my estimation now—perhaps only Isnard and Vergniaud, for their speeches (which is all that we know of them), and Madame Roland, whose great qualities can not be estimated too highly. But of the rest, too many were as profligate as they were superficial and irreligious. Brissot, who was in some respects the best of them, has been greatly lowered in my mind since I read two volumes of his Memoirs, and a collection of nine volumes of his works. He was an amiable man in his private relations, but as a man of letters not above the third or fourth rank; and that enthusiasm which sometimes supplied to him the place of sound principle, could not supply his want of judgment.

"I do not see the name of Helen Maria Williams among your references; if you have not seen her letters, you would find in them more particulars concerning this party than in any other work that has fallen in my way. With all the cotemporary works I am well acquainted; later ones I have not happened to meet with, and have not sought. The best that I have met with relating to the early period is Puisaye's—the two or three first volumes—his latter volumes relate chiefly to the miserable intrigues among the emigrants; but there is some very interesting matter respecting his own life among the Chouans. I have been twice in company with Puisaye, and never saw a finer countenance, nor one that I could more readily have confided in.

"Are you accurate as to Barrère's death?* I very well remember that in 1805 or 1806 the newspapers said he was attached to the French embassy at Lisbon; and though this was not the case, the impression upon my mind is, that he was employed under Bonaparte's government.

"You have a good word for General Biron at his death. If this were the *ci-devant* duc, he was altogether unworthy of it, having been one of the most profligate and thoroughly worthless of the French nobility.

"Danton and Robespierre quarreled at one of the political clubs before the 10th of August: high words ended in a challenge: they met, and the duel was prevented by the interference of an Englishman, who went out as a second to the one, and represented to them how injurious it would be to the cause of liberty if either of them should fall. That Englishman was the present James Watt of Soho, and from him I heard this remarkable fact.

"But I must conclude, once more thanking you for the book, which is every thing that such a book ought to be in all respects, except that for my own gratification I wish this part of your subject had been extended to four volumes instead of being compressed into two; the booksellers and the public would no doubt be of a different opinion, but it is because men are too busy or too idle to read what ought to be read, that they who engage in state affairs are ignorant of what they ought to know, and hence the consequences that we have seen, and those which we may foresee.

"I very well remember when you and Mr. Hope came in upon our cheerful party. Our friend Mr. Telford, whom I saw here last, was depressed in spirits by his growing deafness; this was more than two years ago, and I fear that the cause is not likely to be removed at his age.

"Should any circumstance lead you into this country, I hope you will give me an opportunity of shaking you once more by the hand, and own me a fellow-laborer in the field of history.

"Believe me, my dear sir,

"Yours very truly,

"ROBERT SOUTHEY."

* This observation was quite just, and was corrected in the next edition.—*A. A.*

My father's fondness for cats has been occasionally shown by allusion in his letters, and in The Doctor is inserted an amusing memorial of the various cats which at different times were inmates of Greta Hall. He rejoiced in bestowing upon them the strangest appellations; and it was not a little amusing to see a kitten answer to the name of some Italian singer or Indian chief, or hero of a German fairy tale, and often names and titles were heaped one upon another, till the possessor, unconscious of the honor conveyed, used to "set up his eyes and look" in wonderment. Mr. Bedford had an equal liking for the feline race, and occasional notices of their favorites therefore passed between them, of which the following records the death of one of the greatest.

To Grosvenor C. Bedford, Esq.

"Keswick, May 18, 1833.

"MY DEAR G.,

"* * * * * * *

Alas! Grosvenor, this day poor old Rumpel was found dead, after as long and happy a life as cat could wish for, if cats form wishes on that subject.

"His full titles were:

"The Most Noble the Archduke Rumpelstiltzchen, Marquis Macbum, Earl Tomlemagne, Baron Raticide, Waowhler, and Skaratch.

"There should be a court mourning in Catland, and if the Dragon* wear a black ribbon round his neck, or a band of crape à la militaire round one of the fore paws, it will be but a becoming mark of respect.

"As we have no catacombs here, he is to be decently interred in the orchard, and cat-mint planted on his grave. Poor creature, it is well that he has thus come to his end after he had become an object of pity. I believe we are each and all, servants included, more sorry for his loss, or rather more affected by it, than any one of us would like to confess.

"I should not have written to you at present had it not been to notify this event.

* * * * * * *

"God bless you! R. S."

"Did I tell you that my History of Brazil has led the English merchants who trade with Monte Video to claim an exemption from certain duties: the attorney general pronounces that they have established a *primâ facie* claim to that exemption; the officers of the customs are instructed to act upon that opinion; and one house alone saves £1200 by this, by their own statement to me, for I have had several letters upon the subject, soliciting information during the inquiry.

* * * * * * *"

To John May, Esq.

"Keswick, May 20, 1833.

"MY DEAR FRIEND,

"Dr. Bell's amanuensis (Davies) has arrived at Keswick with the poor doctor's papers: he is established in lodgings at the bottom of the garden, and I go to him every morning at seven,

* A cat of Mr. Bedford's.

and remain with him till nine, inspecting a mass of correspondence which it will take several months to go through. Dr. Bell, from the time he went to India in 1787, seems to have preserved every paper—first, for the interest which he took in them, and latterly, no doubt, with a persuasion that whatever related to him would be deemed of importance by posterity, and with a sure conviction that the more fully he was known the higher would be the opinion formed of his character; and this is certainly the case till the latter part of his life, when his own system obtained such complete possession of his heart and soul as to leave room for nothing else.

"My acquaintance with him began in 1809, but it was not till two or three years afterward that I began to know him intimately, and then I believe there was no person among the connections of his latter life for whom he entertained a more sincere regard. From that time it was his wish that I should undertake the office which has now been committed to me, and I have great pleasure in thinking that his life and correspondence will not disappoint the expectations which he had formed.

"Having been several weeks at this task, I have now become as well acquainted with the first half of his life as the most unreserved letters could make me, and this has made me understand how little we know of men with whom we become acquainted after a certain age, and upon what different foundation the friendships of boyhood, of youth, and of maturity rest; but, withal, the older they are (like good Rhenish wine), the finer is the relish. If you and I had first met in London ten years later than we did in Lisbon, our intimacy could never have been what it is.

"This session of Parliament is not likely to pass over without some fearful struggle. The mob in London stand in fear of the soldiers, and still more of the police. The want of such a police has given them the upper hand at Manchester, Birmingham, and Sheffield, and elsewhere; and, in the confidence of their union and their numbers, it seems to me more than probable that they will attempt a simultaneous march upon London, such as the Blanketeers intended about fourteen years ago. In that case there will be an insurrection in London, unless they are stopped on the way and defeated; and well will it be if the metropolis suffers nothing worse than it did in 1780. This is certain, that if any resistance to the revolutionary spirit is intended by the government, it must be made soon, and made effectually, otherwise there will be no security for life or property in England. Meantime, I am not distressed with anticipations of evil: near as it may be, it does not yet disturb me when I lie down at night, nor enters into my dreams. We are in the hands of Providence; and though I do not see by what human agency it is to be brought about, I know that the Almighty can deliver us, and feel as if he would. God bless you, my dear old friend! Yours most affectionately,

"Robert Southey."

To Allan Cunningham, Esq.

"Keswick, June 3, 1833.

My dear Allan,

"Thank you in my own name, and in my daughter Bertha's, for the completing volumes of your Painters. The work is very far the best that has been written for the Family Library, and will continue to be reprinted long after all the others with which it is now associated. I do not except the Life of Nelson from this; the world cares more about artists than admirals after the lapse of centuries; and as long as the works of those artists endure, or so long as their conceptions are perpetuated by engravings, so long will a lively interest be excited by their lives, when written as you have written them.

"Give your history of the rustic poetry of Scotland the form of biography, and no bookseller will shake his head at it unless he is a booby. People who care nothing about such a *history* would yet be willing to read the lives of such poets, and you may very well introduce all that you wish to bring forward under cover of the more attractive title. The biography of men who deserve to be remembered always retains its interest.

"Are you right as to Lawrence's birth-place? The White Hart, which his father kept at Bristol, is in the parish of Christ Church, not St. Philip's, which is a distant part of the city.

"Sir George Beaumont's marriage was in 1774, the year of my birth; he spent that summer here, and Faringdon was with him part of the time, taking up their quarters in the little inn by Lowdore. Hearne, also, was with him here, either that year or soon afterward, and made for him a sketch of the whole circle of this vale from a field called Crow Park. Sir George intended to build a circular banqueting-room, and have this painted round the walls. If the execution had not always been procrastinated, here would have been the first panorama. I have seen the sketch, now preserved on a roll more than twenty feet in length.

"Sir George's death was not from any decay. His mother lived some years beyond ninety, and his health had greatly improved during the latter years of his life. He was never better than when last in this country, a very few months before his death. The seizure was sudden: after breakfast, as he was at work upon a picture, he fainted; erysipelas presently showed itself upon the head, and soon proved fatal.

"I know that he painted with much more ardor in his old age than at other times of his life, and I believe that his last pictures were his best. In one point I thought him too much of an artist: none of his pictures represented the scene from which he took them; he took the features, and disposed them in the way which pleased him best. Whenever you enter these doors of mine, you shall see a little piece of his (the only one I have) which perfectly illustrates this: the subject is this very house, and scarcely any one object in the picture resembles the reality. His wish was to give the character—the spirit of the scene. But whoever may look upon this picture hereafter with any thought of me, will wish it had been a faithful portrait of the place.

"He was one of the happiest men I ever knew, for he enjoyed all the advantages of his station, and entered into none of the follies to which men are so easily tempted by wealth and the want of occupation. His disposition kept him equally from all unworthy and all vexatious pursuits; he had as little liking for country sports as for public business of any kind, but had a thorough love for art and nature; and if one real affliction or one anxiety ever crossed his path in any part of his life, I never heard of it. I verily believe that no man ever enjoyed the world more, and few were more humbly, more wisely, more religiously prepared for entering upon another state of existence.

"He became acquainted with Coleridge here before I came into this country; this led to his friendship with Wordsworth, and to his acquaintance with me (for more than acquaintance it can hardly be called). He has lodged more than once in this house, when it was in an unfinished state: this very room he occupied before the walls were plastered.

"Next to painting and natural scenery, he delighted in theatricals more than in any thing else. Few men read so well, and I have heard those who knew him intimately say that he would have made an excellent actor.

"Thank you for your good word in the Athenæum. I had not heard of it before: little of the good or evil which is said of me reaches this place; and as I believe the balance is generally largely on the wrong side (enmity being always more on the alert than friendship), my state is the more gracious. The new edition of Byron's works is, I think, one of the very worst symptoms of these bad times.

"I am glad to hear of your sons' welfare; they will all find your good name useful to them through life.

"Since this letter was begun, the influenza laid hold on me and all my children; all except Cuthbert had it very severely. I was completely prostrated by it for a full week, and it has left me emaciated and weak; nor, indeed, is my chest yet completely rid of it. However, I begin to walk about, and have resumed my usual habits.

"God bless you, my dear Allan! My daughter joins in kind remembrances to Mrs. Cunningham. Believe me always

"Yours affectionately,

"ROBERT SOUTHEY."

To Lord Mahon.

"Keswick, Oct. 22, 1833.

"MY DEAR LORD MAHON,

"Long ago I ought to have thanked you for your paper, which had been so unbecomingly interpolated in the Quarterly Review. And now, having just completed that portion of our naval history which has never been brought together, I was about to have done this with my first leisure, when you give me a second occasion for thanks, both on my own part and on Cuthbert's, whose eyes were lit up upon finding himself thus unexpectedly remembered.

"The French play is French indeed, and in its own way far exceeds Calderon's Cisma de Inglaterra. I shall place it among my curiosities. The Loi sur l'Instruction Primaire I am glad to possess, because the subject must, ere long, take up much of my thoughts when preparing for the press the Life and Correspondence of Dr. Bell. This task will lead me to inquire into the history of scholastic education, its present state, primary schools, Sunday schools—the good and the evil—the too much and the too little. There are no other means by which the character of society might so beneficially and so surely be changed; but even in this the practical difficulties are so many, that the man must have either great warmth of enthusiasm or great strength of principle who is not rendered almost hopeless when he contemplates them.

"Your account of the state of affairs in France is almost what I should have wished it to be. Louis Philippe, in his own country at least, is a Conservative; and if the Duc de Bordeaux ever succeeds to the throne (which, if he lives, I think, as well as hope, he will), it were better both for him and for France that some years should have their course before this restoration takes place; better for him, because he must acquire more knowledge in his present condition than he possibly could as a reigning prince, and better for France, because in a few years death will have removed those persons whom it might be alike injurious to punish or to pardon. When vengeance has been long delayed, its just infliction seldom fails to call forth compassion, even for great criminals; and a still worse effect has followed in all restorations when old adherents are neglected, and old enemies not only forgiven, but received into favor, and trusted and rewarded. For these reasons, and because the citizen king will govern with a stronger hand than the legitimate king, I incline to wish that Louis Philippe may reign long to curb his subjects, and break in the people to habits of obedience by the vigorous exercise of his power.

"This reminds me of the spirit which is breathed in the Corn-Law Rhymes. I have taken those poems as the subject of a paper for the Christmas Review, not without some little hope of making the author reflect upon the tendency of his writing. He is a person who introduced himself to me by letter many years ago, and sent me various specimens of his productions, epic and dramatic. Such of his faults in composition as were corrigible, he corrected in pursuance of my advice, and learned, in consequence, to write as he now does, admirably well, when the subject will let him do so. I never saw him but once, and that in an inn in Sheffield, when I was passing through that town. The portrait prefixed to his book seems intentionally to have radicalized, or rather ruffianized, a countenance which had no cut-throat expression at that time. It was a remarkable face, with pale gray eyes, full of fire and meaning, and well suited to a frankness of manner and an apparent simplicity of character such as is rarely found in middle age, and more especially rare in persons engaged in what may be called the warfare of the world. After that meeting I procured a sizarship for one of his sons; and the letter which he wrote to me upon my offering to do so is a most curious and characteristic production, containing an account of his family. I never suspected him of giving his mind to any other object than poetry till Wordsworth put the Corn-Law Rhymes into my hands, and then, coupling the date of the pamphlet with the power which it manifested, and recognizing also scenery there which he had dwelt upon in other poems, I at once discovered the hand of my pupil. He will discover mine in the advice which I shall give him. It was amusing enough that he should have been recommended to my notice as an uneducated poet in the New Monthly Magazine.

"In such times as these, whatever latent evil there is in a nation is brought out. This man appeared always a peaceable and well-disposed subject till Lord Grey's ministry, for their own purposes, called upon the mob for support, and then, at the age of fifty, he let loose opinions which had never before been allowed to manifest themselves, and the fierce Puritanism in which he had been bred up burst into a flame. * *

"And believe me always yours with sincere regard, ROBERT SOUTHEY."

To the Rev. J. Miller.

"Keswick, Nov. 16, 1833.

"MY DEAR SIR,

"The 'Suggestions,'* which I have to thank for your welcome letter, came to me about three weeks ago, from Mr. Charnock of Ripon, through Mrs. Hodson—the Margaret Holford of former days. With whom they have originated I have not heard, nor do I sufficiently understand what is hoped for from the proposed association, or how it can act. But that any association formed on such principles will have my cordial good wishes, and all the support that I can give it in my own way, you need not be assured.

"Among the many ominous parallelisms between the present times and those of Charles the First, none has struck me more forcibly than those which are to be found in the state of the Church; and of those, this circumstance especially—that the Church of England at that time was better provided with able and faithful ministers than it had ever been before, and is in like manner better provided now than it has ever been since. I have been strongly impressed by this consideration; it has made me more aprehensive that no human means are likely to avert the threatened overthrow of the Establishment; but it affords also more hope (looking to human causes) of its restoration.

"The Church will be assailed by popular clamor and seditious combinations; it will be attacked in Parliament by unbelievers, half-believers, and misbelievers, and feebly defended by such of the ministers as are not secretly or openly hostile to it. On our side we have God and the right. Οἰστέον καὶ ἐλπίστεον must be our motto, as it was Lauderdale's in his prison. We, however, are not condemned to inaction, and our hope rests upon a surer foundation than his.

"He, no doubt, built his hopes upon the strange changes which take place in revolutionary times. Some of those changes are likely to act in our favor. The time can not be far distant when the United States of America, instead of being held up to us for an example, will be looked to as a warning. Portugal and Spain will show the egregious incapacity and misconduct of the present administration; and Louis Philippe, becoming a Conservative for his own sake, must also 'seek peace and ensue it,' because the liberal principles to which France would appeal in case of a Continental war would overthrow his throne. It can not be his policy to excite revolutionary movements in other countries, while all his efforts are required for repressing them at home. Our revolutionary ministers, therefore, will not find so ready an ally in him as he might find in them, if it were his object to bring on a general war; and if we get on without any financial embarrassments (which we may do, as long as peace is maintained), there will be no violent revolution here. We may have an easy descent; and when the state machine has got to the bottom, and is there fast in the quagmire, the very people who have made the inclined plane for it, and huzzaed as it went down with accelerated speed, when they see what the end of that way is, will yoke themselves to it to drag it up again, if they can, with labor and with pain.

"I am constitutionally cheerful, and, therefore, hopeful. God has blessed me with good health and buoyant spirits, and my boyish hilarity has not forsaken me, though I am now in my sixtieth year.

"Of late I have been employed, profitably for myself, and therefore necessarily, in Messrs. Longman's great Cabinet manufactory. I am now preparing a friendly lecture to the Corn-Law Rhymer in the Quarterly. I taught him, as he says, the art of poetry, and I shall now endeavor to teach him something better, and bring him to a sense of his evil ways. I shall endeavor also to prepare for the same number, as a sort of companion or counterpart to the lives of Oberlin and Neff, a life of the Methodist blacksmith, Samuel Hick, who was born without the sense of shame, and, nevertheless, was useful in his generation.

"But I am preparing for an undertaking of some importance—the Lives of the English Divines, upon a scale like that of Johnson's Lives of the Poets—to accompany a selection *from*

* "The 'Suggestions' here spoken of were entitled, 'Suggestions for the Promotion of an Association of the Friends of the Church;' but the association never was formed. The practical result was 'The Oxford Tracts;' but the whole theory and management fell into other (and exclusive) hands, so that any direct influence and work of the 'Suggestions' must ever remain unknown and undefined. Perceval's and Palmer's Narratives of the Theological Movement tell all that is to be told on the subject." —*J. M.*

manner and an apparent simplicity of character such as is rarely found in middle age, and more especially rare in persons engaged in what may be called the warfare of the world. After that meeting I procured a sizarship for one of his sons; and the letter which he wrote to me upon my offering to do so is a most curious and characteristic production, containing an account of his family. I never suspected him of giving his mind to any other object than poetry till Wordsworth put the Corn-Law Rhymes into my hands, and then, coupling the date of the pamphlet with the power which it manifested, and recognizing also scenery there which he had dwelt upon in other poems, I at once discovered the hand of my pupil. He will discover mine in the advice which I shall give him. It was amusing enough that he should have been recommended to my notice as an uneducated poet in the New Monthly Magazine.

"In such times as these, whatever latent evil there is in a nation is brought out. This man appeared always a peaceable and well-disposed subject till Lord Grey's ministry, for their own purposes, called upon the mob for support, and then, at the age of fifty, he let loose opinions which had never before been allowed to manifest themselves, and the fierce Puritanism in which he had been bred up burst into a flame. * *

"And believe me always yours with sincere regard, ROBERT SOUTHEY."

To the Rev. J. Miller.

"Keswick, Nov. 16, 1833.

"MY DEAR SIR,

"The 'Suggestions,'* which I have to thank for your welcome letter, came to me about three weeks ago, from Mr. Charnock of Ripon, through Mrs. Hodson—the Margaret Holford of former days. With whom they have originated I have not heard, nor do I sufficiently understand what is hoped for from the proposed association, or how it can act. But that any association formed on such principles will have my cordial good wishes, and all the support that I can give it in my own way, you need not be assured.

"Among the many ominous parallelisms between the present times and those of Charles the First, none has struck me more forcibly than those which are to be found in the state of the Church; and of those, this circumstance especially—that the Church of England at that time was better provided with able and faithful ministers than it had ever been before, and is in like manner better provided now than it has ever been since. I have been strongly impressed by this consideration; it has made me more aprehensive that no human means are likely to avert the threatened overthrow of the Establishment; but it affords also more hope (looking to human causes) of its restoration.

"The Church will be assailed by popular clamor and seditious combinations; it will be attacked in Parliament by unbelievers, half-believers, and misbelievers, and feebly defended by such of the ministers as are not secretly or openly hostile to it. On our side we have God and the right. Οἰστέον καὶ ἐλπιστεον must be our motto, as it was Lauderdale's in his prison. We, however, are not condemned to inaction, and our hope rests upon a surer foundation than his.

"He, no doubt, built his hopes upon the strange changes which take place in revolutionary times. Some of those changes are likely to act in our favor. The time can not be far distant when the United States of America, instead of being held up to us for an example, will be looked to as a warning. Portugal and Spain will show the egregious incapacity and misconduct of the present administration; and Louis Philippe, becoming a Conservative for his own sake, must also 'seek peace and ensue it' because the liberal principles to which France would appeal in case of a Continental war would overthrow his throne. It can not be his policy to excite revolutionary movements in other countries, while all his efforts are required for repressing them at home. Our revolutionary ministers, therefore, will not find so ready an ally in him as he might find in them, if it were his object to bring on a general war; and if we get on without any financial embarrassments (which we may do, as long as peace is maintained), there will be no violent revolution here. We may have an easy descent; and when the state machine has got to the bottom, and is there fast in the quagmire, the very people who have made the inclined plane for it, and huzzaed as it went down with accelerated speed, when they see what the end of that way is, will yoke themselves to it to drag it up again, if they can, with labor and with pain.

"I am constitutionally cheerful, and, therefore, hopeful. God has blessed me with good health and buoyant spirits, and my boyish hilarity has not forsaken me, though I am now in my sixtieth year.

"Of late I have been employed, profitably for myself, and therefore necessarily, in Messrs. Longman's great Cabinet manufactory. I am now preparing a friendly lecture to the Corn-Law Rhymer in the Quarterly. I taught him, as he says, the art of poetry, and I shall now endeavor to teach him something better, and bring him to a sense of his evil ways. I shall endeavor also to prepare for the same number, as a sort of companion or counterpart to the lives of Oberlin and Neff, a life of the Methodist blacksmith, Samuel Hick, who was born without the sense of shame, and, nevertheless, was useful in his generation.

"But I am preparing for an undertaking of some importance—the Lives of the English Divines, upon a scale like that of Johnson's Lives of the Poets—to accompany a selection from

* "The 'Suggestions' here spoken of were entitled, 'Suggestions for the Promotion of an Association of the Friends of the Church;' but the association never was formed. The practical result was 'The Oxford Tracts;' but the whole theory and management fell into other (and exclusive) hands, so that any direct influence and work of the 'Suggestions' must ever remain unknown and undefined. Perceval's and Palmer's Narratives of the Theological Movement tell all that is to be told on the subject." —*J. M.*

rance we anticipated much entertainment, and have not been disappointed. When I went down to dinner, he told me with great glee that the book which had come that morning was one of the queerest he had ever seen. He had only looked into it, but he had seen that there was one chapter without a beginning, and another about Aballiboozonorribang (for so he had got the word), which, whether it was something to eat, or whether it was the thing in the title-page, he could not tell, for in one place it was called the sign of the book, and in another you were told to eat beans if you liked, but to abstain from Aballiboozo.

"At tea he was full of the chapter about the warts and the moonshine, and all the philosophers in the dictionary. At supper he was open-mouthed about the sirloin of a king, and the schoolmaster's rump; he would read to me about the lost tribes of Israel; and concluded by wishing he had not seen the book, for he should be troubled by dreaming about it all night.

"To-day he says that there is more sense in the second volume, but he does not like it so well as the first. That there is not much in the book about the doctor; and, indeed, he does not know what it is about, except that it is about every thing else; that it was very proper to put &c. in the title-page; that the author, whoever he is, must be a clever man, and he should not wonder if it proved to be Charles Lamb. You may imagine how heartily we have enjoyed all this.

"A letter from Wordsworth tells us that the book has just arrived there, and that one of W.'s nephews (a Fellow of Trinity College, Cambridge, and a very clever and promising person) had got hold of it, was laughing while he looked over the contents, and had just declared that the man who wrote the book must be mad.

"God bless you, my dear Grosvenor!

"R. S."

To Henry Taylor, Esq.

"Keswick, Jan. 16, 1834.

"My dear H. T.,

"Edith departed yesterday from the house in which she was born. God grant that she may find her new home as happy as this has been to her, though the cheerfullest days of this have long been past. Her prospects are fair; and, what is of most consequence, she is intrusted to safe hands.

"As my household diminishes, there will be room for more books. These I shall probably continue to collect as long as I can, living in the past, and conversing with the dead—and The Doctor.

"God bless you! R. S."

To John May, Esq.

"Keswick, May 2, 1834.

"My dear Friend,

"* * * * * * *

The days pass so rapidly with me because of their uniformity, that I am made sensible of their lapse only by looking back, and feeling with surprise, and sometimes with some sorrow, and some shame also, the arrears which they have brought upon me in their unheeded course.

"See how the day is disposed of! I get out of bed as the clock strikes six, and shut the house-door after me as it strikes seven. After two hours with Davies,* home to breakfast, after which Cuthbert engages me till about half past ten, and when the post brings no letters that either interest or trouble me (for of the latter I have many), by eleven I have done with the newspaper, and can then set about what is properly the business of the day. But letters are often to be written, and I am liable to frequent interruptions, so that there are not many mornings in which I can command from two to three unbroken hours at the desk. At two I take my daily walk, be the weather what it may, and when the weather permits, with a book in my hand; dinner at four, read about half an hour; then take to the sofa with a different book, and after a few pages get my soundest sleep, till summoned to tea at six. My best time during the winter is by candle-light: twilight interferes with it a little; and in the season of company I can never count upon an evening's work. Supper at half past nine, after which I read an hour, and then to bed. The greatest part of my miscellaneous work is done in the odds and ends of time.

* * * * * * *

"To make any amendment of the Poor Laws what it ought to be, one leading principle should be, that while relief is withheld from the worthless pauper, or administered only in such measure as to keep him from famishing, it should be afforded to the deserving poor (as it could then be afforded) more liberally, and that none should be condemned to a work-house but those who deserve it as a punishment. It should be made apparent that all industrious laborers, all of good character, would gain by the proposed alteration; for every possible artifice and exertion will be used to make the people believe that this is a law passed by the rich against the poor, and there never was a time when it was more easy to stir up a servile war, nor when such a war would have been so greatly to be dreaded. May God preserve us!

* * * * * * *

"It is needless to say how gladly I would use any endeavors in my power toward effecting your wishes with regard to the Poor Commission, or in other ways. They are worth little, I well know, but, however little, they shall be zealously made when we know in what channel they must be directed. We may see great changes, and, perhaps, great troubles, before the appointments are made; for, though Louis Philippe has won one great battle for us, we may yet have another to fight at home.

* * * * * * *

"God bless you, my dear old friend!

"Yours most affectionately, R. S."

---

* Mr. Davies, the late Dr. Bell's secretary, was then lodging in Keswick, within five minutes' walk of Greta Hall.

To Lord Mahon.

"Keswick, May 12, 1834.

"MY DEAR LORD MAHON,

"Thank you for Sir Robert Peel's speech. I do not wonder at the effect which it produced. But could it be believed of any ministers, except the present, that in the course of a week after the close of the debate in which that speech was delivered, they should have returned to their old base policy of complimenting and truckling to O'Connell?

"In reading that entertaining paper upon the modern French drama in the last Quarterly Review, I fancied that we were obliged to you for it. It is, indeed, curiously characteristic of the people and the times.

"You will, I think, be pleased with the forthcoming play upon the history of Philip van Artevelde. The subject was of my suggesting, as eminently dramatic, and the first part (which is all that I have seen) is written with true dramatic power. But so was the author's former tragedy, Isaac Comnenus, which met with few readers, and was hardly heard of. To obtain immediate popularity, an author must address himself to the majority of the public—and the vulgar will always be the majority—and upon them the finer delineations of character and of human feeling are lost.

"If you have not seen Zophiel,* it is well worth your reading, as by far the most original poem that this generation has produced. If —— or —— had treated the same subject, they would have made it most mischievously popular; but, exceptionable as it is, the story is told with an imaginative power to which the one has no pretensions, and with a depth of feeling of which both were by nature incapable. The poem has attracted no notice; the chief cause of the present failure I suppose to be that it is not always perspicuously told. The diction is surprisingly good; indeed, America has never before produced any poem to be compared with it.

"The authoress (Mrs. Brooks) is a New Englander, of Welsh parentage. Many years ago she introduced herself to me by letter. When she came to this place, and sent up a note to say she had taken lodgings here, I never was more surprised, and went to call upon her with no favorable expectations. She proved, however, a most interesting person, of the mildest and gentlest manners, and my family were exceedingly taken with her. Coming fresh from Paris, she was full of enthusiasm for the Poles, for whom the profits of this poem were intended, if there should be any; and she had a burning thirst for fame, which seems now to have become the absorbing passion of her most ardent mind. I endeavored to prepare her for disappointment by moderating her confident hopes. She left her manuscript in my hands at her departure. When I had failed to obtain a publisher for it, some of her American connections engaged with a bookseller in Great Queen Street, and I corrected the proof-sheets.

"Believe me, my dear lord,

"Yours with sincere regard,

"ROBERT SOUTHEY."

To Grosvenor C. Bedford, Esq.

"Keswick, July 3, 1834.

"MY DEAR G.,

"I have been prevented from writing before, first, by being too busy with proof-sheets and letters, and secondly by being too idle, company and the season having idled me.

* * * * * * *

"The day before yesterday I commanded a cart party to Honister Crag, and walked the whole way myself, twenty-one and a half miles by Edward Hill's pedometer, without difficulty or fatigue; so you see that, notwithstanding a touch of the hay-asthma, I am in good condition, and have a pair of serviceable legs.

"Henry Taylor's Tragedies are of the very best kind. I am exceedingly glad that you have taken to one another so well. He is the only one now living, of a generation younger than yours and mine, whom I have taken into my heart of hearts.

"I certainly hope that you may be set free from all official business with such a pension as your long services and your station entitle you to; for I have no fears of your feeling any difficulty in the disposal of your time, or any other regret for the cessation of your long-accustomed business than what always belongs to the past, and what in this case may arise from the dissolution of an old establishment, which, for the very sake of its antiquity, ought to have been preserved. You will get more into the country than you otherwise could have done, and you will come here and take a lease of health and good spirits from the mountains. I shall pass through London with Cuthbert on our way to the West in the autumn. Our stay will hardly exceed a week.

* * * * * * *

"Just now I am very busy, finishing a third volume of Naval History. This is my sheet anchor. In the way of sale The Doctor has clearly failed; yet it may be worth while to send out another volume, and so, from time to time, at longish intervals, till the design is completed. This may be worth while, because the notice that each will excite will keep the name alive, and act advantageously when it comes to be included in the posthumous edition of my works. Meantime, the pleasure that I and my household, and a very few others who are behind the curtain, will receive, will be so much gain. It will not be amiss to throw out hints that Henry Taylor may be the author, having shown in his plays both the serious and the comic disposition and power.

"My cousin, Georgiana Hill, is here for the first time, and as happy as you may suppose a girl of eighteen is likely to be on such an occasion. Did I tell you that I have a pony, the best

* Zophiel, or the Bride of Seven, by Maria del Occidente.

of ponies (given me by Sir T. Acland)? and I have bought a light chair, in which Cuthbert or Bertha drive out their mother. If I could give you a good account of *her*, all would be well. But her spirits are so wretchedly nervous, and I begin to fear so hopelessly so, that I have need of all mine.

"God bless you, my dear G.! My love to Miss Page. R. S."

The following letter was addressed to a party from one of the universities who were at that time *reading* at Keswick, and it is inserted for the sake of showing how strong was his abhorrence of all cruelty. I have seen his cheek glow, and his eye darken and almost flash fire, when he chanced to witness any thing of the kind, and heard him administer a rebuke which made the recipient tremble. Like some other gentle natures, when his indignation was roused—and it was only such cases that did fairly rouse it—he was stern indeed.

In reading or speaking of any cases of cruelty or oppression, his countenance and voice would change in a most striking manner.

This letter was sent without a signature, and transcribed by another hand.

"Keswick, July 12, 1834.

"Young Gentlemen,

"It has come to the knowledge of the writer that one of your amusements here is to worry cats—that you buy them from those owners who can be tempted to the sin of selling them for such a purpose, and that you employ boys to steal them for you.

"A woman who was asked by her neighbor how she could do so wicked a thing as to sell her cat to you, made answer that she never would have done it if she could have saved the poor creature, but that, if she had not sold it, it would have been stolen by your agents, and therefore she might as well have the half crown herself.

"Neither her poverty nor her will consented, yet she was made to partake in your wickedness because she could not prevent it. She gave up to your barbarity a domestic animal—a fireside companion, with which her children had played, and which she herself had fondled on her lap. You tempted her, and she took the price of its blood.

"Are you incapable, young gentlemen, of understanding the injury you have done to this woman in her own conscience and in the estimation of her neighbors?

"Be this as it may, you can not have been so ill taught as not to know that you are setting an evil example in a place to which you have come for the ostensible object of pursuing your studies in a beautiful country; that your sport is as blackguard as it is brutal; that cruelty is a crime by the laws of God, and theft by the laws also of man; that in employing boys to steal for you, and thus training them up in the way they should not go, you are doing the devil's work; that they commit a punishable offense when serving you in this way, and that you commit one in so employing them.

"You are hereby warned to give up these practices. If you persist in them, this letter will be sent to all the provincial newspapers."

One other trifling circumstance I may briefly notice here as occurring at this time—a request from the Messrs. Galignani that he would write a brief sketch of Lord Byron's life and literary character, to be prefixed to their edition of his works, leaving "the remuneration entirely to himself." It is hardly needful to add that the proposal was not entertained.

CHAPTER XXXVI.

PERSONAL RECOLLECTIONS—MODE OF TUITION—MY MOTHER'S ILLNESS AND REMOVAL TO YORK—FEELINGS UNDER AFFLICTION—EVIL EFFECTS OF ANXIETY UPON HIS HEALTH—CORRESPONDENCE WITH SIR R. PEEL CONCERNING THE OFFER OF A BARONETCY—JOURNEY TO SUSSEX—RETURN TO KESWICK—GRANT OF AN ADDITIONAL PENSION—LITERARY EMPLOYMENTS—THE DOCTOR—DEATH OF MISS HUTCHINSON—MR. WYON'S MEDALLIONS—PRESENT FEELINGS AND EMPLOYMENTS—SPANISH LITERATURE—WESTMINSTER SCHOOL—CAUSES OF ITS DECLINE—STATE OF HIS SPIRITS—JACKSON'S WORKS—FEELINGS OF THANKFULNESS FOR HIS NEW PENSION—NOVEL MODE OF BOOK-BINDING—LITERARY EMPLOYMENTS—RECOLLECTIONS OF C. LAMB—SINGULAR EFFECTS OF SOUND AND LIGHT—STATE OF THE CHURCH—LIFE OF COWPER—DIFFICULTY OF LEAVING HOME—IS SUBPŒNAED TO A TRIAL AT LANCASTER.—1834–1836.

As my task draws nearer to its conclusion it becomes naturally more painful, and the more so because, in chronicling the events which darkened my father's later years, they rise up so vividly before my own sight.

"It is my youth, that where I stand
Surrounds me like a dream.
The sounds that round about me rise
Are what none other hears;
I see what meets no other eyes,
Though mine are dim with tears."*

A happier home or a happier boyhood than mine had been it would not be easy to conceive. My father had so strongly imprinted on his memory the sad changes through which his own "gentle spirit" had to pass in childhood and boyhood—

"The first grief he felt,
And the first painful smile that clothed his front
With feelings not his own;"

and how, on first quitting home,

"Sadly at night
He sat himself down beside a stranger's hearth;
And when the lingering hour of rest was come
First wet with tears his pillow"—

* Henry Taylor.

that he resolved that the early years of his own children should be as happy as he could make them. He had again become the "father, teacher, playmate," all in one, though probably with far less heart and hope than in earlier years; and he had given up as much time as he could possibly spare to my education. This, however, was somewhat of a desultory and irregular kind, more amusing and attractive, perhaps, than very profitable, at least as regarded the attainment of a good foundation for correct scholarship. He was himself far from being an accurate classic; indeed, he had spoiled his Latinity by continually reading bad Latin—"feeding upon monkish historians;" and although he did his best to put me in the right way, I found I had much up-hill work to undergo at too late a period, having learned the practice from him of catching at the general meaning of a passage without much knowledge or examination of its construction—"making a shy at it," as school-boys say—an evil habit as regards ordinary purposes, though doubtless profitable for him whose glance was so keen and so sure.

He had also an odd plan (conducing to this same end), which he practiced a good deal with me in modern tongues, of reading the original aloud, and making me render it into English by the ear; and this he would do with the Dutch, German, Danish, and Swedish, being particularly partial to the Northern tongues, and wishing to become more versed in them himself. French he disliked exceedingly; and he did not teach me Spanish and Portuguese, which he knew thoroughly, probably for that very reason.

Another odd practice I may mention. After reading a portion of Homer in our daily studies, he would make me read aloud the same portion in every translation he possessed—Pope, Cowper, Chapman, and Hobbes—a process more amusing than profitable; and he would do the same thing with Virgil, out of Sotheby's magnificent Polyglott.

In other matters I was left very much to myself, allowed to run riot amid the multitude of books, and permitted, if not encouraged, to indulge a desultory appetite for odd reading; and here again some objects were sacrificed which might have been attained had I been encouraged to read less and more carefully.

But while this sort of bringing up had, as all *home* education must have, some disadvantages, I must always feel grateful for it, as enabling me to have that appreciation of my father's character—that companionship with him and freedom from reserve, that "perfect love that casteth out fear," which I could never have felt had I been earlier sent out into the world. The most certain evil of the many years of school-boy life is the want of friendship between father and son. To all of us, indeed, Greta Hall was a most delightful home. The daily walks; the frequent excursions "by flood and fell;" the extreme beauty of the surrounding country, his own keen appreciation of and deep delight in which had extended to his children; the pleasant summer society, full of change and excitement; the quieter enjoyments of winter, all tended to attach us more to it, perhaps, than was desirable. We "loved it, not wisely, but too well."

But its best days were over: he had said so with a too true foreboding, when, in the first month of the year, his eldest daughter had changed her name, and departed to another home on the distant coast of Sussex; and it being now thought necessary that I should be placed under her husband—Mr. Warter's tuition—to be prepared for Oxford, my father prepared to take me thither. But the pain of quitting a peculiarly happy home is not much, if at all, diminished by postponement.

"Then, in truth, we learn
That never music like a mother's voice,
And never sweetness like a father's smile,
And never pleasures like that home-born throng,
Circling calm boyhood, has the world supplied."*

And like to this were my father's own anticipations. "This," he says, "will never again be Cuthbert's home, in the whole full meaning of that word. He will come to it at vacation times, but never more will he have that sense of home comfort and home happiness here, the want of which is very ill compensated by all the hopes, and emulations, and excitement of the world on which he must now enter. I shall miss him sadly, and begin to perceive that books, which have always been the chief pleasure of my life, will soon be the only ones with which there are no regrets to mingle."†

But these plans were destined to be sadly and suddenly disconcerted for the time. I have before alluded to the weak and nervous state of my mother's spirits; and of late, total loss of appetite and sleep had caused serious apprehensions, which were, alas! too well founded; for, just as we were on the point of departing, the melancholy truth became apparent that she was no longer herself. It is, perhaps, rash to endeavor to search into the causes of these mysterious visitations of Providence; but it may, I think, fairly be alleged, that an almost life-long anxiety about the uncertain and highly precarious nature of my father's income, added to a naturally nervous constitution, had laid the foundation for this mental disease; and my father himself also now felt and acknowledged that Keswick had proved, especially of later years, far too unquiet a residence for her weakened spirits and that much company and frequent visitors had produced exactly the opposite effect to what he had hoped. Her immediate removal seemed to offer the best hope of restoration, and this step was at once taken.

To Grosvenor C. Bedford, Esq.

"York, Thursday night, Oct. 2, 1834.

"MY DEAR GROSVENOR,

"After what Henry Taylor has imparted to you, you will not be surprised at learning that I have been parted from my wife by something worse than death. Forty years has she been the

* Robert Montgomery.

† To H. Taylor, Esq., Aug. 21, 1834.

life of my life, and I have left her this day in a lunatic asylum.

"God, who has visited me with this affliction, has given me strength to bear it, and will, *I know*, support me to the end, whatever that may be.

"Our faithful Betty is left with her. All that can be done by the kindest treatment and the greatest skill we are sure of at the Retreat. I do not expect more than that she may be brought into a state which will render her perfectly manageable at home. More is certainly possible, but not to be expected, and scarcely to be hoped.

"To-morrow I return to my poor children. There is this great comfort, that the disease is not hereditary, her family having within all memory been entirely free from it.

"I have much to be thankful for under this visitation. For the first time in my life, I am so far beforehand with the world that my means are provided for the whole of next year, and that I can meet this additional expenditure, considerable in itself, without any difficulty. As I can do this, it is not worth a thought; but it must have cost me much anxiety had my affairs been in their former state.

"Another thing for which I am thankful is, that the stroke did not fall upon me when the printers were expecting the close of my naval volume, or the Memoir of Dr. Watts. To interrupt a periodical publication is a grievous loss to the publishers, or, at least, a very serious inconvenience.

* * * * * * *

"Some old author says, 'Remember, under any affliction, that Time is short; and that, though your Cross may be heavy, you have not far to bear it.'

"I have often thought of those striking words.

"God bless you, my dear Grosvenor! My love to Miss Page; she, I know, will feel for us, and will pray for us. R. S."

To Henry Taylor, Esq.

"York, Oct. 2, 1834.

"My dear H. T.,

"Yesterday I deposited my dear wife in the Retreat for Lunatics, near this city, and to-day I visited her there. To-morrow I return home, to enter upon a new course of life.

* * * * * * *

"Recovery is possible, but I do not attempt to deceive myself by thinking that it is likely. It is very probable that she may be brought into a state which will no longer require restraint. In that case, I shall engage a proper attendant from this place, bring her home, appropriate two rooms to her use, and watch over her to give her all the comforts of which she may be capable, till death do us part.

* * * * * * *

"The call upon me for exertion has been such, that, by God's help, I have hitherto felt no weakness.

"That this is a far greater calamity than death would have been, I well know. But I perceive that it can be better borne at first, because there is a possibility of restoration, and, however feeble, a hope; therefore that collapse is not to be apprehended which always ensues when the effort which the circumstances of a mortal sickness, and death, and burial, call forth in the survivor, is at an end.

"Mine is a strong heart. I will not say that the last week has been the most trying of my life, but I will say that the heart which could bear it can bear any thing.

"It is remarkable that the very last thing I wrote before this affliction burst upon me in its full force was upon Resignation, little foreseeing, God knows, how soon and how severely my own principles were to be put to the proof. The occasion was this: Mrs. Hughes thought it would gratify me to peruse a letter which she had just received from one of her friends—a clergyman who had recently suffered some severe domestic affliction. He said that his greatest consolation had been derived from a letter of mine, which she had allowed him to transcribe some years ago, and which he verily believed had at that time saved his heart from breaking. The letter must have been written upon my dear Isabel's death. I have no recollection of it; but that must have been the subject, because Mrs. Hughes and her husband had both been exceedingly struck with her, and declared—when such a declaration could without unfitness be made—that she was the most radiant creature they had ever beheld.

"This made me reflect upon the difference between religious resignation and that which is generally mistaken for it, and, for immediate purpose, in no slight degree supplies its place. You will see what I was thus led to write in its proper place.

"Davies came with me here, and has been of great use. God bless you, my dear H. T.!

"R. S."

To H. Taylor, Esq.

"Keswick, Oct. 6, 1834.

"My dear H. T.,

"Your letter did not surprise me, though it would from almost any one else. Thank you most heartily for your offer. But at present it is better that I should be alone, and that the girls should be left to themselves with Miss Hutchinson. For me this is best, because nothing is so painful as the reaction of your own thoughts after you have been for a while drawn away from them, if this be attempted too soon. When I can enjoy your company, I shall be most thankful for it; and as you know I shall not give myself to melancholy, you need not apprehend any ill consequences from my being alone.

"The worst of my business has been got through. I had Cuthbert at his lessons this morning; to-day will clear off the remaining and less important letters, and to-morrow I hope to resume my work; not, however, forcing myself to it, but following the course which my own instinct will point out.

"Miss Fenwick will like to see the last passage which I wrote before this calamity burst upon me, and certainly with no *pro*spective feelings. It will be safe with her if you tell her from whence it is extracted. God bless you!

"R. S."

"'He had looked for consolation where, when sincerely sought, it is always to be found, and he had experienced that religion effects in a true believer all that philosophy professes, and more than all that mere philosophy can perform. The wounds which stoicism cauterizes, Christianity heals.

"'There is a resignation with which, it may be feared, most of us deceive ourselves. To bear what must be borne, and submit to what can not be resisted, is no more than what the unregenerate heart is taught by the instinct of animal nature. But to acquiesce in the afflictive dispensations of Providence—to make one's own will conform in all things to that of our heavenly Father—to say to Him, in the sincerity of faith, when we drink of the bitter cup, "Thy will be done"—to bless the name of the Lord as much from the heart when He takes away as when He gives, and with a depth of feeling of which, perhaps, none but the afflicted heart is capable: this is the resignation which religion teaches, this the sacrifice which it requires. This sacrifice L. had made, and he felt that it was accepted.'"

This was, indeed, a sad return—this an awful separation between those who had been so long, so truly united; to this death had been a light evil, for when are we so near as then—

"'Tis but the falling of a leaf,
The breaking of a shell,
The rending of a veil."

But what a gulf is there "fixed" between the reasoning and the unreasoning mind?

Yet even now, when sorrow had indeed "reached him in his heart of hearts," he sought for all sources of comfort, for all motives for resignation and thankfulness. Writing to Mr. Warter from York, he says, "I can not but regard it as a special mercy that this affliction should have fallen upon me at a time when there were no extraneous circumstances to aggravate it, the grievous thought excepted of the grief it would cause at Tarring. How easily might it have happened when I was pressed for time to bring out a volume for periodical publication, the delay of which would have been a most serious loss to the publishers—nor could it have occurred when I was so perfectly able to support the expense. My dear Edith had laid by money for a time of need which will fully cover the mournful demand upon me. Moreover, Mr. Telford* has left me £200; and, independent of this, I am, for the first time in my life, so far beforehand with the world, that I have means at command for a whole year's expenditure, were my hand to be idle or palsied during that time. There is, therefore, no reason for anxiety concerning the means of meeting this additional expenditure.

"Thank God, my strength has not failed nor my health suffered."

This, as may well be imagined, is a period not to be remembered without pain: the anxiety attendant upon absence, and the constantly varying accounts while the issue was yet doubtful and there was room for hope, though but slenderly grounded, had the most injurious effect upon my father's naturally sensitive mind. He kept up, indeed, wonderfully, and a common observer would have remarked but little change in him, except that he was unusually silent; but to his family the change was great indeed. Yet he bore the trial patiently and nobly; and when, in the following spring, it was found that the poor sufferer was likely in all respects to be better under his own roof, and the period of suspense, and doubt, and alternate hope and fear had passed away, it was marvelous how much of the old elasticity remained, and how, though no longer happy, he could be contented and cheerful, and take pleasure in the pleasures of others. A few extracts from his letters will show his state of mind and feeling at this time. About three weeks after his return home, he says, "This morning's letter is decidedly favorable, and I feel its effects. Hitherto I have not recovered my natural sleep at night: plenty of exercise and quiet employment fail of their wonted effect in producing it, because in darkness and solitude uncomfortable thoughts prevent sleep for a while, and then trouble it. I should not be the better for society nor for leaving home. There is nothing to be done but to pursue the same course of self-management, live in as much hope as it may be reasonable to encourage, and, above all, to bear always in mind that we have both entered on the last of our seven stages. In a very few years, what may have befallen us in the course of these years may be of some interest to any one who may write my life, but it will be of no consequence to us, whose lot, doubtful as it is for the short remaining portion of our time, is, I trust, fixed for eternity."*

A little later he says to another friend, "I am beginning to sleep better the last few days, and I do every thing that is likely to keep myself in bodily and mental health, walking daily in all weathers, never overtasking myself, or forcing

* "That kind old man, Mr. Telford, has (most unexpectedly) left me £200. His will, like his life, is full of kindness; bequests to all whom he loved, and all who had served under him so as to deserve his good opinion; and to the widows of such as had gone before them, a larger portion than would have been allotted to their husbands. Mr. Rickman is one of the executors, and put a copy of the will into my hands, doubling it at the place which concerned me. After the surprise and the first emotion, it was some time before I smiled at recollecting the whimsical manner in which I was designated thus:

To Thomas Campbell, poet, £200.
" Robert Southey, do. £200.

He had completed and put to press a history of all his works. It will be a splendid book, with about seventy engravings. He was far the greatest man that has ever appeared in his profession, and has left behind him the greatest works; and as no man in that profession has left a greater name, so, I verily believe, no one in any line has ever left a better; for he was thoroughly disinterested, and as kind-hearted and considerate as man could be."—*To Mrs. J. W. Warter, Sept.* 11, 1834.

* To H. Taylor, Esq., Oct. 23, 1834.

myself to a distasteful employment, yet never remaining idle. But my spirits would assuredly give way were it not for a constant reference to another world, and a patient hope of God's mercy in this."*

With one more extract I will conclude this year—the saddest of all I have had yet to chronicle: "I find it a grievous thing that I must now, for the first time, think about *ways* as well as *means*. For the last eight-and-thirty years I had nothing to do but to provide the means in my own quiet way, and deliver them over to one of the best stewards that ever man was blessed with. The ways were her concern, and her prudence and foresight exempted me from all trouble as well as from all care. My daughters can not yet stand here in their poor mother's place, and I must be more accustomed to my new situation before I introduce them to it. Nothing can possibly exceed the good sense and good feeling which they have manifested under our present affliction; but their attentions to me give me a very painful sense of how much importance I am to their happiness. Cuthbert, also, is a great comfort to me. Whatever course I may find it necessary to take, his removal to Sussex will not be delayed beyond the commencement of the spring."†

The new year brought nothing cheerful with it to our now diminished and saddened circle. The regular report from York was the only object of interest, and that, while it varied a little, and sometimes raised temporary hopes, yet, on the whole, gradually prepared us for the conviction that no permanent restoration was to be expected, and that the most that could be looked for was such an improvement as would permit the sufferer to be taken care of under her own roof.

The days thus passed by in an almost unbroken routine of regular employment—my father himself working, if possible, more closely than ever—when an event occurred which broke the current of his thoughts for a time, and which, in its sequel, proved a most fortunate occurrence for the comfort of his remaining years, and one which helped very materially to lighten the still darker days which were yet in store.

One morning, shortly after the letters had arrived, he called me into his study. "You will be surprised," he said, "to hear that Sir Robert Peel has recommended me to the king for the distinction of a baronetcy, and you will probably feel some disappointment when I tell you that I shall not accept it, and this more on your account than on my own. I think, however, that you will be satisfied I do so for good and wise reasons;" and he then read to me the following letters, and his reply to them.

Sir Robert Peel to R. Southey, Esq.

"Whitehall Gardens, Feb. 1, 1835.

"My dear Sir,

"I have offered a recommendation to the king (the first of the kind which I have offered), which, although it concerns you personally, concerns also high public interests, so important as to dispense with the necessity on my part of that previous reference to individual feelings and wishes which, in an ordinary case, I should have been bound to make. I have advised the king to adorn the distinction of baronetage with a name the most eminent in literature, and which has claims to respect and honor which literature alone can never confer.

"The king has most cordially approved of my proposal to his majesty; and I do hope that, however indifferent you may be personally to a compliment of this kind, however trifling it is when compared with the real titles to fame which you have established, I do hope that you will permit a mark of royal favor to be conferred in your person upon the illustrious community of which you are the head.

"Believe me, my dear sir, with the sincerest esteem,

"Most faithfully yours,

"Robert Peel."

This was accompanied with another letter marked *private*.

Sir Robert Peel to R. Southey, Esq.

"Whitehall, Feb. 1, 1835.

"My dear Sir,

"I am sure, when there can be no doubt as to the purity of the motive and intention, there can be no reason for seeking indirect channels of communication in preference to direct ones. Will you tell me, without reserve, whether the possession of power puts within my reach the means of doing any thing which can be serviceable or acceptable to you, and whether you will allow me to find some compensation for the many heavy sacrifices which office imposes upon me in the opportunity of marking my gratitude as a public man, for the eminent services you have rendered, not only to literature, but to the higher interests of virtue and religion?

"I write hastily, and perhaps abruptly, but I write to one to whom I feel it would be almost unbecoming to address elaborate and ceremonious expressions, and who will prefer to receive the declaration of friendly intentions in the simplest language.

"Believe me, my dear sir, with true respect,

"Most faithfully yours,

"Robert Peel.

'P.S. I believe your daughter is married to a clergyman of great worth, and perhaps I can not more effectually promote the object of this letter than by attempting to improve his professional situation. You can not gratify me more than by writing to me with the same unreserve with which I have written to you."

Robert Southey, Esq., to Sir Robert Peel.

"Keswick, Feb. 3, 1835.

"Dear Sir,

"No communications have ever surprised me

* To John May, Esq., Nov. 12, 1834.

† To G. C. Bedford, Esq., Dec. 18, 1834.

so much as those which I have this day the honor of receiving from you. I may truly say, also, that none have ever gratified me more, though they make me feel how difficult it is to serve any one who is out of the way of fortune. An unreserved statement of my condition will be the fittest and most respectful reply.

"I have a pension of £200 conferred upon me through the good offices of my old friend and benefactor, Charles W. Wynn, when Lord Grenville went out of office; and I have the laureateship. The salary of the latter was immediately appropriated, as far as it went, to a life insurance for £3000. This, with an earlier insurance for £1000, is the whole provision that I have made for my family; and what remains of the pension after the annual payments are made, is the whole of my certain income. All beyond must be derived from my own industry. Writing for a livelihood, a livelihood is all that I have gained; for, having always something better in view, and therefore never having courted popularity, nor written for the mere sake of gain, it has not been possible for me to lay by any thing. Last year, for the first time in my life, I was provided with a year's expenditure beforehand. This exposition might suffice to show how utterly unbecoming and unwise it would be to accept the rank which, so greatly to my honor, you have solicited for me, and which his majesty would so graciously have conferred. But the tone of your letter encourages me to say more.

"My life insurances have increased in value. With these, the produce of my library, my papers, and a posthumous edition of my works, there will probably be £12,000 for my family at my decease. Good fortune, with great exertions on the part of my surviving friends, might possibly extend this to £15,000, beyond which I do not dream of any further possibility. I had bequeathed the whole to my wife, to be divided ultimately between our four children; and having thus provided for them, no man could have been more contented with his lot, nor more thankful to that Providence on whose especial blessing he knew that he was constantly, and, as it were, immediately dependent for his daily bread.

"But the confidence which I used to feel in myself is now failing. I was young, in health and heart, on my last birth-day, when I completed my sixtieth year. Since then I have been shaken at the root. It has pleased God to visit me with the severest of all domestic afflictions, those alone excepted into which guilt enters. My wife, a true helpmate as ever man was blessed with, lost her senses a few months ago. She is now in a lunatic asylum; and broken sleep and anxious thoughts, from which there is no escape in the night season, have made me feel how more than possible it is that a sudden stroke may deprive me of those faculties, by the exercise of which this poor family has hitherto been supported. Even in the event of my death, their condition would, by our recent calamity, be materially altered for the worse; but if I were rendered helpless, all our available means would procure only a respite from actual distress.

"Under these circumstances, your letter, sir, would in other times have encouraged me to ask for such an increase of pension as might relieve me from anxiety on this score. Now that lay sinecures are in fact abolished, there is no other way by which a man can be served, who has no profession wherein to be promoted, and whom any official situation would take from the only employment for which the studies and the habits of forty years have qualified him. This way, I am aware, is not now to be thought of, unless it were practicable as part of a plan for the encouragement of literature; but to such a plan perhaps these times might not be unfavorable.

"The length of this communication would require an apology, if its substance could have been compressed; but on such an occasion it seemed a duty to say what I have said; nor, indeed, should I deserve the kindness which you have expressed, if I did not explicitly declare how thankful I should be to profit by it.

"I have the honor to remain,

"With the sincerest respect,

"Your most faithful and obliged servant,

"ROBERT SOUTHEY."

Young as I then was, I could not, without tears, hear him read, with his deep and faltering voice, his wise refusal and touching expression of those feelings and fears he had never before given utterance to to any of his own family. And if any feelings of regret occasionally come over my mind that he did not accept the proffered honor, which, so acquired and so conferred, any man might justly be proud to have inherited, the remembrance at what a time and under what circumstances it was offered, and the feeling what a mockery honors of that kind would have been to a family so afflicted, and, I may add, how unsuitable they would be to my own position and very straitened means, make me quickly feel how justly he judged and how prudently he acted.

The next letter shows how thankfully he anticipated the possibility of such a result as soon afterward followed, from his communication in reply to Sir Robert Peel.

To the Rev. Neville White.

"Keswick, Feb. 16, 1835.

"MY DEAR NEVILLE,

" * * * * * * *

You will see by the papers that a baronetcy has been offered to me. The offer came in a letter from Sir Robert Peel, and nothing could be more handsome than the way in which it was made. I may tell you (what must be known only to those from whom I have no secrets) he accompanied it with another letter, inquiring, in the kindest manner, if there was any way wherein he could serve me. I replied by an unreserved statement of my circumstances, showing how utterly unbecoming and unwise it would be to accept of such, when I had absolutely nothing to bequeath with it. From the manner in which my answer was received (which I know not from himself, but from two other authentic sources), I have reason to believe that, as soon as in his power, I may receive some substantial benefit.

"It was signally providential that I should have been enabled to meet the expenses which my domestic affliction has occasioned, and which, at any former time, would most seriously have embarrassed me; and what a blessing it will be if Providence should now, by this means, relieve me from all the anxieties attendant upon a precarious income—anxieties which, as you know, I have not felt before, because I was confident in my own powers of exertion; but how precarious these powers are, this recent visitation has made me feel too sensibly.

"God bless you, my dear Neville! I am in the midst of packing, and the arrangements which are necessary upon leaving home. It will be the first time that I ever left it without looking forward joyfully to the time of my return. But, by God's blessing, I shall soon become accustomed to a small family. If my hopes of a permanent income are realized, I shall be able, after another year, to devote myself wholly to my own great works, regardless of booksellers, and without imprudence I shall be able to travel for health's sake whenever it may be expedient. In short, I shall be thankful for the past, make the best I can of the present, and look on to the future in humble, and yet, I trust, sure and certain hope.

"Yours most affectionately,

"ROBERT SOUTHEY."

In the preceding letter my father speaks of being on the point of leaving home. This was for the purpose, first, of conveying me into Sussex, and then, if it should be found practicable, of removing my mother to Keswick. This proved to be the case. A brief extract from a letter written to me from Scarborough, where he remained for a short time after leaving York with his sad charge, will show the unvaried tone of his feelings under affliction. "The monotony of this week is a curious contrast to the excitement and movements of the preceding month. The first great change in your life has taken place during this interval, and I am about to enter upon not the least in mine—so different will my household be from what it has formerly been, and so much will it be reduced. Your sisters will find themselves supported in the performance of their duties; and after the emotion which our return must produce is over, their spirits, I doubt not, will rally. We shall always have enough to do, they as well as myself; and this is certain, that they who are resigned to God's all-wise will, and endeavor to do their duty in whatever circumstances they are placed, never can be thoroughly unhappy—never, under any affliction, can find themselves without consolation and support."* And again, after a few days, he writes to Mr. May: "The far greater number of incurable patients in the asylum are kept there that they may be out of the way of their respective families, though they are perfectly harmless. This may be necessary in some cases, but where it is not necessary it seems to me that we are no more justified in thus ridding ourselves of a painful duty than we should be in sending a wife or a mother to die in an infirmary, that we might escape the pain and trouble of attending upon a death-bed."*

* March 27, 1835.

Immediately after his return, when his hopes had been raised by a temporary improvement, he writes: "I had never any thought of leaving the girls with their mother, and transferring to them a duty which I am better able to bear. * * * If any thing should be done for me (which it would be equally unwise to build upon, and unjust to doubt, though, to be sure, it is not easy to sit between the two stools)—if, I say, my circumstances should be rendered easy, I believe it would have a happy effect upon her who, for some twenty years, has been anxious over much upon that score; though, in the morning of life, when all my exertions and all her economy were required, and if either had failed in their respective duties we must have sunk, her spirits failed as little as mine."†

Two days later the suspense was ended.

Sir Robert Peel to R. Southey, Esq.

"Whitehall, April 4, 1835.

"MY DEAR SIR,

"I have resolved to apply the miserable pittance at the disposal of the crown, on the Civil List Pension Fund, altogether to the reward and encouragement of literary exertions. I do this on public grounds; and much more with the view of establishing a principle, than in the hope, with such limited means, of being enabled to confer any benefit upon those whom I shall name to the crown—worthy of the crown, or commensurate with their claims.

"I have just had the satisfaction of attaching my name to a warrant which will add £300 annually to the amount of your existing pension. You will see in the position of public affairs a sufficient reason for my having done this without delay, and without previous communication with you.

"I trust you can have no difficulty in sanctioning what I have done with your consent, as I have acted on your own suggestion, and granted the pensions on a public principle—the recognition of literary and scientific eminence as a public claim. The other persons to whom I have addressed myself on this subject are Professor Airey, of Cambridge, the first of living mathematicians and astronomers—the first of this country, at least—Mrs. Somerville, Sharon Turner, and James Montgomery, of Sheffield.

"Believe me, my dear sir,

"Most faithfully yours,

"ROBERT PEEL."

* March 30, 1835.

† To H. Taylor, Esq., April 2, 1835.

received (which I know not from himself, but from two other authentic sources), I have reason to believe that, as soon as in his power, I may receive some substantial benefit.

"It was signally providential that I should have been enabled to meet the expenses which my domestic affliction has occasioned, and which, at any former time, would most seriously have embarrassed me; and what a blessing it will be if Providence should now, by this means, relieve me from all the anxieties attendant upon a precarious income—anxieties which, as you know, I have not felt before, because I was confident in my own powers of exertion; but how precarious these powers are, this recent visitation has made me feel too sensibly.

"God bless you, my dear Neville! I am in the midst of packing, and the arrangements which are necessary upon leaving home. It will be the first time that I ever left it without looking forward joyfully to the time of my return. But, by God's blessing, I shall soon become accustomed to a small family. If my hopes of a permanent income are realized, I shall be able, after another year, to devote myself wholly to my own great works, regardless of booksellers, and without imprudence I shall be able to travel for health's sake whenever it may be expedient. In short, I shall be thankful for the past, make the best I can of the present, and look on to the future in humble, and yet, I trust, sure and certain hope.

"Yours most affectionately,
"ROBERT SOUTHEY."

In the preceding letter my father speaks of being on the point of leaving home. This was for the purpose, first, of conveying me into Sussex, and then, if it should be found practicable, of removing my mother to Keswick. This proved to be the case. A brief extract from a letter written to me from Scarborough, where he remained for a short time after leaving York with his sad charge, will show the unvaried tone of his feelings under affliction. "The monotony of this week is a curious contrast to the excitement and movements of the preceding month. The first great change in your life has taken place during this interval, and I am about to enter upon not the least in mine—so different will my household be from what it has formerly been, and so much will it be reduced. Your sisters will find themselves supported in the performance of their duties; and after the emotion which our return must produce is over, their spirits, I doubt not, will rally. We shall always have enough to do, they as well as myself; and this is certain, that they who are resigned to God's all-wise will, and endeavor to do their duty in whatever circumstances they are placed, never can be thoroughly unhappy—never, under any affliction, can find themselves without consolation and support."* And again, after a few days, he writes to Mr. May: "The far greater number of incurable patients in the asylum are kept there that they may be out of the way of their respective families, though they are perfectly harmless. This may be necessary in some cases, but where it is not necessary it seems to me that we are no more justified in thus ridding ourselves of a painful duty than we should be in sending a wife or a mother to die in an infirmary, that we might escape the pain and trouble of attending upon a death-bed."*

* March 27, 1835.

Immediately after his return, when his hopes had been raised by a temporary improvement, he writes: "I had never any thought of leaving the girls with their mother, and transferring to them a duty which I am better able to bear. * * * If any thing should be done for me (which it would be equally unwise to build upon, and unjust to doubt, though, to be sure, it is not easy to sit between the two stools)—if, I say, my circumstances should be rendered easy, I believe it would have a happy effect upon her who, for some twenty years, has been anxious over much upon that score; though, in the morning of life, when all my exertions and all her economy were required, and if either had failed in their respective duties we must have sunk, her spirits failed as little as mine."†

Two days later the suspense was ended.

Sir Robert Peel to R. Southey, Esq.

"Whitehall, April 4, 1835.

"MY DEAR SIR,

"I have resolved to apply the miserable pittance at the disposal of the crown, on the Civil List Pension Fund, altogether to the reward and encouragement of literary exertions. I do this on public grounds; and much more with the view of establishing a principle, than in the hope, with such limited means, of being enabled to confer any benefit upon those whom I shall name to the crown—worthy of the crown, or commensurate with their claims.

"I have just had the satisfaction of attaching my name to a warrant which will add £300 annually to the amount of your existing pension. You will see in the position of public affairs a sufficient reason for my having done this without delay, and without previous communication with you.

"I trust you can have no difficulty in sanctioning what I have done with your consent, as I have acted on your own suggestion, and granted the pensions on a public principle—the recognition of literary and scientific eminence as a public claim. The other persons to whom I have addressed myself on this subject are Professor Airey, of Cambridge, the first of living mathematicians and astronomers—the first of this country, at least—Mrs. Somerville, Sharon Turner, and James Montgomery, of Sheffield.

"Believe me, my dear sir,
"Most faithfully yours,
"ROBERT PEEL."

* March 30, 1835.
† To H. Taylor, Esq., April 2, 1835.

to be sent to the Rev. John Miller, and the following letter was written in reply to one from him concerning it. In common with many others, it seems from the first he had believed my father to be the author.

To the Rev. John Miller.

"Keswick, July 20, 1835.

"My dear Sir,

"A copy of the 'unique Opus' came to me upon its first appearance, with my name printed in red letters on the back of the title-page, and 'from the author' on the fly leaf, in a disguised hand; in which hand, through the disguise, I thought I could recognize that of my very intimate friend, the author of Philip van Artevelde. He, however, if my theory of the book be well founded, is too young a man to be the author. I take the preparatory postscript to have been written in sincerity and sadness; and if so, Henry Taylor was a boy at the time when (according to the statement there) the book was begun.

"It may, I think, be inferred from every thing about the book and in it, that the author began it in his blithest years, with the intention of saying, under certain restrictions, *quidlibet de quolibet*, and making it a receptacle for his shreds and patches; that, beginning in jest, he grew more and more in earnest as he proceeded; that he dreamed over it and brooded over it—laid it aside for months and years, resumed it after long intervals, and more often latterly in thoughtfulness than in mirth; fancied, perhaps, at last, that he could put into it more of his mind than could conveniently be produced in any other form; and having supposed (as he tells us), when he began, that the whole of his yarn might be woven up in two volumes, got to the end of a third without appearing to have diminished the balls that were already spun and wound when the work was commenced in the loom, to say nothing of his bags of wool.

"To the reasons which he has assigned for not choosing to make himself publicly known, this no doubt may be added, that the mask would not conceal him from those who knew him intimately, nor from the few by whom he might wish to be known; but it would protect his face from dirt, or any thing worse that might be thrown at it.

"I see in the work a little of Rabelais, but not much; more of Tristram Shandy, somewhat of Burton, and perhaps more of Montaigne; but methinks the *quintum quid* predominates.

"I should be as much at a loss to know who is meant by REVERNE as you have been, if I had not accidentally heard that the only person to whom the authorship is ascribed, upon any thing like authority, is the Rev. Erskine Neale. Mrs. Hodson (formerly Margaret Holford) being in the neighborhood of Doncaster, and desirous to hunt out, if she could, the history of the Opus, inquired about it there, and was assured by a bookseller that it was written by this gentleman, who had once resided in that place, but was then living at Hull. A clergyman whom she met there confirmed this, and there seemed to be no doubt about it in Doncaster. It is plain, therefore, that REVERNE designates this Great-every-where-else-unknown; but I would not swear the book to him upon such evidence.

"I can resolve another of your doubts. The concluding signature is not in the Garamna tongue, but in cryptography, or what might more properly be called, in Dovean language, comicography. If you look at it, and observe that k, e, w spell Q, you will find that when the nut is cracked it contains no kernel.

"So much concerning a book which is a great favorite with my family, and has helped them sometimes to beguile what otherwise must have been hours of sorrow. Ten months have elapsed since our great affliction came upon us. * * * * * * This is the fortieth year of our marriage, and I know not whether the past or the present seems now to me most like a dream.

"Amid these griefs, you will be glad to know that some substantial good has befallen us. One of the last acts of Sir Robert Peel's administration was to give me a pension of £300, in addition to that of £200 which I before possessed, the new one being (I am told) free from deductions, and this will emancipate me from all booksellers' work when my present engagements are completed. If my life be prolonged, I shall then apply myself to the histories of Portugal, of the Monastic Orders, and of English Literature, from the point where Warton breaks off. Do not conclude that, in entertaining such designs at my age, I am *immemor sepulchri;* for of the first at least three fourths of the labor has been performed, and I have been very many years preparing for all three, hoping the time might come when I could afford to make them my chief employment.

"Farewell, my dear sir. Present my best wishes to your brother and sister, and believe me always yours with the sincerest respect and regard,

Robert Southey."

To John May, Esq.

"Keswick, Aug. 1, 1835.

"My dear Friend,

" * * * * * * *

Since my last letter we have had a severe shock in the death of Miss Hutchinson, Mrs. Wordsworth's sister, who was one of the dearest friends these poor girls had, and who was indeed to me like a sister. She had been with us in all our greatest afflictions. Her strength had been so much exhausted in nursing Miss Wordsworth the elder, and with anxiety for Dora, that after a rheumatic fever, from which she seemed to be recovered, she sunk at once, owing to mere weakness: an effusion on the brain was the immediate cause. Miss Wordsworth, whose death has been looked upon as likely any day for the last two years, still lives on. Her mind, at times, fails now. Dora, who is in the most precarious state herself, can not possibly amend while this anxiety continues, so that at this time Wordsworth's is a more afflicted house than my own.

They used to be two of the happiest in the country. But there is a time for all things, and we are supported by God's mercy.

"Our health, thank God, continues good. * * * * If I could leave home with satisfaction, I should go either to Harrowgate or Shap (if Shap, which I hope, would do) for the sake of the waters. But my poor Edith likes none of us to leave her, and requests us not to do so. This, of course, would induce me to bear with any thing that can be borne without danger. Nor, indeed, should I willingly leave my daughters, who stand in need of all that can be done to cheer them in the performance of their duty, and who are the better because they exert themselves to keep up their own spirits for my sake.

"You will see how unprofitable it would be for me, under these circumstances, to look beyond the present any where—except to another world. In the common course of nature, it can not be long before all the events of this life will be of no further importance to me than as they shall have prepared me for a better. To look back over the nine-and-thirty years which have elapsed since you and I first met at Lisbon, seems but as yesterday. Wednesday, the 12th, completes my sixty-first year; and the likelihood is, that before a fourth part of the like interval has passed, you and I shall meet—where there will be no more sorrow nor parting.

"God bless you, my dear old friend, and bring us thither in His own good time. My love to your dear daughters.

"Yours most affectionately,

"ROBERT SOUTHEY."

To Grosvenor C. Bedford, Esq.

"Keswick, Sept. 29, 1835.

"MY DEAR G.,

"Mr. Wyon has killed two birds with one shot. Seeing how perfectly satisfied every body here was with his medallion of me, he asked for an introduction to Wordsworth, which I was about to have offered him. Off he set in good spirits to Rydal, and, not finding Wordsworth there, was advised to follow him to Lowther. To Lowther he went, and came back from thence delighted with his own success, and with the civilities of Lord and Lady Lonsdale, who desired that they might have both medallions. Nothing, I think, can be better than Wordsworth's, and he is equally pleased with mine.

"He tells me of some unpublished poems of Cowper, which he is in hopes of obtaining for me.

* * * * * * * *

"To-morrow will be just twelve months since we set out on our miserable journey to York! One whole year! At our time of life there can not be many more to look on to at *most*. If her illusions are like dreams to her, the reality is like a dream to me, but one from which there is no awaking.

"Yet, Grosvenor, I need not say that in doing all which can be done, there is a satisfaction which, if it be not worth all it costs, is worth more than any thing else. My spirits are as you might expect them to be—somewhat the better, because it is necessary that they should make the best appearances, and always equal to the demand upon them, for which I can never be sufficiently thankful. And what a blessing it is to be relieved from all anxiety concerning my ways and means, just at the time when it must otherwise have made itself felt in a way which it had never done before.

"I very much regret that you could not come here this summer. That 'more convenient season,' for which you have so long waited, may now be put off till the Greek Kalends; and, for aught I can see, any movement of mine to the South may be as distant. Here I shall remain, as long as it is best for these members of my family that I should remain here, and that is likely to be as long as our present circumstances continue.

"Happily, while my faculties last, I shall never be in want of employment. At present I have rather more than is agreeable; but when the pressure is over, it will never be renewed. Just now two presses are calling upon me, a third longing for me, and a fourth at which I cast a longing eye myself. The two which, like the daughter of the horse-leech, cry Give, give, are employed upon Cowper and the Admirals. The third is asking for the new edition of Wesley; and the quantity of a good Quarterly Article must be written before that can be satisfied. Two, or, at the most, three chapters would give me my heart's desire with the other. But the Admirals will cover all my extraordinaries for two years to come largely; and when the edition of Cowper is finished I shall receive sweet remuneration to the amount of 1000 guineas, which, however, will be well earned.

"By-the-by, you are likely to possess Henderson's life; and if so, I wish you would write me a letter about him, for he gave such a lift to Cowper by reciting John Gilpin, that a page or two to his honor might, with great propriety, be introduced.

"I shall finish my first volume in the course of a few days; the life will go far into the second. As much as possible, I have woven the materials into the narration, and made Cowper tell his own story; but still the work is a web.

"Will you believe that I had forgotten your direction, and that it took me five minutes to recollect it! *Saville* Row was running in my head; I danced for joy when I shouted Εὐρήκα.

"R. S.

"Sharpe recommended John Gilpin to Henderson. The last communication I ever had with him was a note confirmatory of this."

To the Rev. John Warter.

"Keswick, Oct. 1, 1835.

"MY DEAR W.,

"Poor Karl* is to start on Monday, the 12th, if no mishap intervene. * * * His sisters will miss him woefully. As for me, the

* The German abbreviation of my name, which he commonly used.

blossoms of my life are shed, and I stand like a tree in winter—well rooted, and, as yet, whole at the heart, and with its head unscathed. There is this difference, that the tree will put forth its foliage again.

"Time, however, passes rapidly with us; every day brings its employments, and my interest in them is unabated. Last week I received a parcel sent by Quillinan from Porto, containing Gil Vincente's works, a present from one of the editors. My uncle would have rejoiced with me over it, but in losing him I lost the only person who could fully enter into that branch of my pursuits. The book is printed at Hamburg, from a copy of the first edition in the Gottenburg Library: I believe there is no other copy of that edition in Europe, and none of the only other one are in England, that other, moreover, having been expurgated by the Inquisition. More than any other writer Gil V. may be called the father of the Spanish drama. He was a man of most extraordinary genius, his satire so undaunted, that it accounts for the almost utter annihilation of his work. As connected with the history of Portuguese manners and literature, this republication is the most important work that could have been undertaken. I sup upon him every night.

"Grimshaw and his publishers, by taking the evangelical line, have removed the only uncomfortable circumstance in my way, which was the care I must otherwise have taken (in consideration to the publishers) not to say any thing that would have been unpalatable to that party.
* * * * *

"The first fine day in next week, Bertha, Kate, Karl, and I are to accompany the Lord High Snab* to his estate, and there each of us is to plant a yew-tree, which planting I am to celebrate in a poem that is to live as long as the yew-trees themselves, live they ever so long. I need not tell you how happy the Lord High Snab is at the prospect of both the fête and the poem. It does one's heart good to see a man so thoroughly happy who so thoroughly deserves to be so. * * * * * *

"God bless you! R. S."

The following letter was written in reply to a communication from the Rev. T. G. Andrews, dean of Westminster, on the subject of Westminster School, which at that time had greatly declined in numbers. Mr. Andrews, who took great interest in the matter, from "his family having been there for more than 200 years," had written, urging my father, as an Old Westminster, to write some verses in commendation of the school, and with some allusion to the eminent men who had been educated there, which might be read on the anniversary dinner, and printed afterward for circulation.

To the Rev. Gerrard Thomas Andrews.

"Keswick, Nov. 12, 1835.

"Dear Sir,

"I can not but be much gratified by a letter like yours, and should be still more so did I think it likely, or even possible, that I could comply with a request that does me so much honor.

"I know what poems ought to be which are designed for a public meeting—terse, pointed, and, above all, short. But I know, also, that I am given to prolixity, and that, if I could find leisure, or muster resolution to begin upon such a subject, it would lead me astray from the desired object. The musings of an old man might draw some quiet tears from a solitary reader, but at such an assembly they would be as much out of place as their author himself.

"My time is more fully occupied than can be well conceived by any one who is not acquainted with my habits of mind and the number of my pursuits. Moreover, I have outlived the inclination for writing poetry. To be asked for an epitaph, or to contribute something to a lady's album, gives me much more annoyance than I ever felt at hearing Dr. Vincent say to me, 'Twenty lines of Homer, and not go to breakfast.'

"Some causes of the decline at Westminster are of a permanent nature. Preparatory schools, which were not heard of fifty years ago, have annihilated the under school. King's College and the London University take away a large proportion of the day boys, who were very numerous in my time. Proprietary schools (another recent invention) are preferred by anxious parents; and too many patrician ones, though the father were at Westminster himself, forsake a falling house, and send their boys to Harrow or to Eton. A school declines faster as soon as it is known to be declining. The *religio loci*, which with you is an hereditary feeling, and with me a strong one, can do little, I fear, to counteract so many co-operating causes.

"Your father was before my time. I should love and venerate his name, even did I know nothing more of him than his kindness to Herbert Knowles.*

"I was placed at Westminster in the under fourth, a few weeks before Dr. Smith left it, in 1788. Botch Hayes was then usher of the fifth, and left it in disgust because he was not appointed under-master. Most of my cotemporaries have disappeared; but in Charles W. W. Wynn and Grosvenor Bedford I have still two of my dearest friends; and if I were beholden to the old school for nothing more than their friendship, I should have reason enough to bless the day on which I entered it.

"Believe me, dear sir,

"Yours with sincere respect,

"Robert Southey."

To C. C. Southey.

"Keswick, Dec. 16, 1835.

"My dear Cuthbert,

"Twice I wished for you yesterday; first at

* A playful appellation given to Dr. Bell's late amanuensis, Mr. Davies, who had lately purchased a small mountain farm near Keswick, called High Snab, whither for some years we made annual visits. The yew-trees died, and of the poem, which was to have been in the form of an epistle addressed to his eldest daughter, only a few lines were ever written.

* See *antè*, p. 343.

breakfast, because it was a beautiful morning, and my feet itched for a ten miles' walk. But you are in Sussex, Davies is in Shropshire, and I have not even a dog for a companion.

"Secondly, you were wished for two hours afterward, when I had settled to my work, for then came the box of books from Ulverston. You would have enjoyed the unpacking. It is the best batch they ever sent home: thirty-six volumes, besides three for Bertha and five of Kate's.

"I should like, if it were possible, always to communicate my pleasures, and keep my troubles to myself. Here was no one to admire the books with us.

"You remember* when the miller invited me, to whom he had never spoken before, to rejoice with him over the pig that he had killed, the finest that he had ever fattened, and how he led me to the place where that which had ceased to be pig, and was not yet bacon, was hung up—scalded, exenterate, and hardly yet cold—by the hind feet.

"Mr. Campbell's† man Willy, in like manner, yesterday called on his acquaintance to admire a salmon which he had kippered the preceding night; the kitchen floor had been cleaned and swept, and the salmon was displayed on it, while Willy, half-seas over in the forenoon, pointed out to his master the beauty of the fish: he had never killed one in such condition before—it was worth seven shillings.

"About six weeks hence I hope to rejoice both over Cowper and the Admirals, though not to take my leave of them then. But I hope to have a volume of each completed, and am now keeping on *pari passu* with both. The Evangelical Magazine has outdone its usual outdoings in abusing the first volume. They say I shall be known to posterity as embalmed in Lord Byron's verse for an incarnate lie. The whole article is in this strain, and it has roused Cradock's indignation as much as it has amused me; for it is written just as I should wish an enemy to write. God bless you, my dear boy!

"R. S."

To Grosvenor C. Bedford, Esq.

"Keswick, Jan. 7, 1836.

"MY DEAR GROSVENOR,

"The best thing I can wish for myself, on the commencement of a new year (among those things which 'stand to feasible'), is, that it may not pass away without your making a visit to Keswick. Other *hope* for the year I have none, and not much (to confess the truth) of this. Time, however, passes rapidly enough; and good part of it, by help of employment, in a sort of world of my own, wherein I seem abstracted from every thing except what occupies my immediate attention. The most painful seasons are when I lie down at night and when I awake in the morning. But my health continues good, and my spirits better than I could possibly have expected, had our present circumstances been foreseen. * * It is remarkable that, of all employments at this time, the *Life of Cowper* should be that on which I am engaged. Enough of this. God bless you!

"R. S."

To John May, Esq.

"Keswick, Jan. 30, 1836.

"MY DEAR FRIEND,

"Your letter arrived this morning. I sent off by this day's post the last portion of manuscript for my second volume; and having so done, I lay aside all thoughts of Cowper till Monday morning, giving myself thus what may be called a quarter's holiday this evening. Methinks time has taken from me nothing which is so much to be regretted as leisure, or rather nothing of which I should so certainly, as well as allowably, wish to be possessed again. However, I live in hope of working my way to it. When Cowper and the Admirals are off my hands, I will engage in nothing that does not leave me master of my own time. It will be still too little for what I once hoped to perform.

"Cradock has advertised for the 13th; so on Monday, the 15th, your copy ought to be in Harley Street. The Life will extend to half a volume more, and with it my hurry ends, but not my work.

"I am very glad to hear that you are reading Dr. Thomas Jackson, an author with whom, more almost than any other, one might be contented in a prison. There is hardly any thing in his works which I wished away, except one shocking passage about the Jews. For knowledge, and sagacity, and right-mindedness, I think he has never been surpassed. You will be much pleased, also, with Knox's Remains, and his correspondence with Bishop Jebb.

"There is no change for the better in our domestic circumstances. All hope is extinguished, while anxiety remains unabated, so sudden are the transitions of this awful malady. I can never be sufficiently thankful that my means of support are no longer precarious, as they were twelve months ago. The fear of being disabled, which I never felt before, might too probably have brought on the evil which it apprehended, when my life seemed to be of more consequence to my family than at any former time, and my exertions more called for. Thank God, Sir Robert Peel set me at ease on that score. Would to God that you were relieved from your cares in like manner! We have both cause to return thanks for the happiness that we have enjoyed, and for the consolations that are left us. If the last stage of our journey should prove the most uneasy, it will be the shortest. It is just forty years since we met in another country; most probably, before a fourth part of the time has elapsed, we shall meet in another state of existence.

"We have both great comfort in our children. Perhaps one reason why women bear affliction (as I think they generally do) better than men

* I remember it very well, and how my father rejoiced the man's heart by admiring the goodly sight.

† A gentleman resident at Keswick, with whom he was very intimate.

is, because they make no attempt to fly from the sense of it, but betake themselves patiently to the duties, however painful, which they are called upon to perform. It is the old emblem of the reed and the oak—they bend, and therefore they are not broken; and then comes peace of mind, which is the fruit of resignation.

"Secluded as we now are from society, my daughters find sufficient variety of employment. They transcribe a good deal for me: indeed, whatever I want extracted of any length from books—most of my notes. One room is almost fitted up with books of their binding: I call it the *Cottonian* library; no patch-work quilt was ever more diversified. They have just now attired two hundred volumes in this fashion. Their pleasure, indeed, in seeing the books in order, is not less than my own; and, indeed, the greater part of them are now in such order, that they are the pride of my eye as well as the joy of my heart.

"On Monday I begin to give my mornings again to the Admirals, that is, as many mornings as my ever-growing business of letter-writing may leave leisure for—letters in half of which I have no concern, and in the other half no pleasure. The fourth volume will contain the lives of Essex, Raleigh, Sir William Monson, Blake, and Monk. Then, not to extend unreasonably a work which was not intended by the publisher at first for more than two volumes, I shall drop the biography, and wind up in one volume more, with the Naval History from the Revolution, in continuous narrative. A good pretext for this is, that the age of naval enterprise and adventure, and, consequently, of personal interest, was past, and the interest thenceforth becomes political; events are regarded, not with reference to the principal actors, as in Drake's time, but to their bearings upon the national affairs. I shall be glad when this work is completed, because, though of all my books I have been best paid for it, it is that which I have taken the least interest in composing, and which any one who would have bestowed equal diligence upon it might have executed quite as well.

* * * * * * *

"The snow has confined me three days to the house. It is now rapidly thawing, to my comfort, for I feel as if the machine wanted that sort of winding up which is given to it by daily exercise. God bless you, my dear old friend! May I live to write a great many more books; and may you and your daughters live, and read, and like them all. No small part of the pleasure which I take in writing arises from thinking how often the work in which I am engaged will make me present, in a certain sense, with friends who are far away.

"Yours most affectionately,

"Robert Southey."

To Edward Moxon, Esq.

"Keswick, Feb. 2, 1836.

"My dear Sir,

"I have been too closely engaged in clearing off the second volume of Cowper to reply to your inquiries concerning poor Lamb sooner. His acquaintance with Coleridge began at Christ's Hospital; Lamb was some two years, I think, his junior. Whether he was ever one of the *Grecians* there, might be ascertained, I suppose, by inquiring. My own impression is, that he was not. Coleridge introduced me to him in the winter of 1794–5, and to George Dyer also, from whom, if his memory has not failed, you might probably learn more of Lamb's early history than from any other person. Lloyd, Wordsworth, and Hazlitt became known to him through their connection with Coleridge.

"When I saw the family (one evening only, and at that time), they were lodging somewhere near Lincoln's Inn, on the western side (I forget the street), and were evidently in uncomfortable circumstances. The father and mother were both living; and I have some dim recollection of the latter's invalid appearance. The father's senses had failed him before that time. He published some poems in quarto. Lamb showed me once an imperfect copy: the Sparrow's Wedding was the title of the longest piece, and this was the author's favorite; he liked, in his dotage, to hear Charles read it.

"His most familiar friend, when I first saw him, was White, who held some office at Christ's Hospital, and continued intimate with him as long as he lived. You know what Elia says of him. He and Lamb were joint authors of the Original Letters of Falstaff. Lamb, I believe, first appeared as an author in the second edition of Coleridge's Poems (Bristol, 1797), and, secondly, in the little volume of blank verse with Lloyd (1798). Lamb, Lloyd, and White were inseparable in 1798; the two latter at one time lodged together, though no two men could be imagined more unlike each other. Lloyd had no drollery in his nature; White seemed to have nothing else. You will easily understand how Lamb could sympathize with both.

"Lloyd, who used to form sudden friendships, was all but a stranger to me, when unexpectedly he brought Lamb down to visit me at a little village (Burton) near Christ Church, in Hampshire, where I was lodging in a very humble cottage. This was in the summer of 1797, and then, or in the following year, my correspondence with Lamb began. I saw more of him in 1802 than at any other time, for I was then six months resident in London. His visit to this county was before I came to it; it must have been either in that or the following year: it was to Lloyd and to Coleridge.

"I had forgotten one of his school-fellows, who is still living—C. V. Le Grice, a clergyman at or near Penzance. From him you might learn something of his boyhood.

"Cottle has a good likeness of Lamb, in chalk, taken by an artist named Robert Hancock, about the year 1798. It looks older than Lamb was at that time; but he was old-looking.

"Coleridge introduced him to Godwin, shortly after the first number of the Anti-Jacobin Magazine and Review was published, with a caricature of Gillray's, in which Coleridge and I were introduced with asses' heads, and Lloyd and Lamb as toad and frog. Lamb got warmed with whatever was on the table, became disputatious, and said things to Godwin which made him quietly say, 'Pray, Mr. Lamb, are you toad or frog?' Mrs. Coleridge will remember the scene, which was to her sufficiently uncomfortable. But the next morning S. T. C. called on Lamb, and found Godwin breakfasting with him, from which time their intimacy began.

"His angry letter to me in the Magazine arose out of a notion that an expression of mine in the Quarterly Review would hurt the sale of Elia: some one, no doubt, had said that it would. I meant to serve the book, and very well remember how the offense happened. I had written that it wanted nothing to render it altogether delightful but a *saner* religious feeling. *This* would have been the proper word if any other person had written the book. Feeling its extreme unfitness as soon as it was written, I altered it immediately for the first word which came into my head, intending to remodel the sentence when it should come to me in the proof; and that proof never came. There can be no objection to your printing all that passed upon the occasion, beginning with the passage in the Quarterly Review, and giving his letter.

"I have heard Coleridge say that, in a fit of derangement, Lamb fancied himself to be young Norval. He told me this in relation to one of his poems.

"If you print my lines to him upon his Album Verses, I will send you a corrected copy. You received his letters, I trust, which Cuthbert took with him to town in October. I wish they had been more, and wish, also, that I had more to tell you concerning him, and what I have told were of more value. But it is from such fragments of recollection, and such imperfect notices, that the materials for biography must, for the most part, be collected.

"Yours very truly,
"ROBERT SOUTHEY."

To Henry Taylor, Esq.

"Keswick, March 12, 1836.

"MY DEAR H. T.,

"When I went to Lisbon the second time (in 1800), it was for my health. An illness (the only one I ever had) had weakened me, and I was liable to sudden pulsations of the heart, which seemed to indicate some organic derangement. It was inferred, or rather ascertained, that they arose from nervous excitability, because the moment I apprehended them they returned; and this conclusion was confirmed by a circumstance which has led me to this relation. Going out of our sitting-room one morning, I happened to hear the maid draw the bed-curtains, preparatory to making the bed in the chamber opposite. From that time, while I remained in those lodgings, I never went out of the room in the early part of the day without hearing the same sound distinctly, though it came from within instead of without.

"Now let me tell you a more curious circumstance, of which I made a memorandum as soon as I returned. About two months ago I was going to the lake, and reading as I went. It was a bright, frosty day, and my Scotch bonnet (in which I appear like a Gaberlunzie man) afforded no shelter to the eyes, but, having been used to wear it, I was not inconvenienced by the light. Just on the rising ground, where the view of the lake opens, I suppose the sun came more directly upon my eyelids, but the page which I was reading appeared to be printed in red letters. It happened to be a page in which one book of a Latin poem ended and another began: the heading of this latter was, of course, in considerably larger types these changed their color first, and became red as blood; the whole page presently became so, and the opposite page presented a confused intermixture of red and black types when I glanced on it, but, fixing my eyes, the whole became rubric also, though there was nothing then so vivid as the large letters of the heading. The appearance passed away as my position to the sun was altered.

"This phenomenon never occurred to me before, but I observed it particularly, because, if my memory does not deceive me, I have more than once read of the same thing, and always as of something supernatural in the history of a Romish saint, or a fanatic of some other denomination. According to the mood of mind in which it occurred, it would be taken for a manifestation of grace or of wrath.

* * * * * * *

"God bless you! R. S."

To Herbert Hill, Esq.

"Keswick, April 2, 1836.

"MY DEAR HERBERT,

" * * * * * * *

James II.'s conduct in obtruding a Romish president upon Magdalen was not worse than that of the present ministry in appointing Dr. Hampden to the professorship of divinity. If they had given him any other preferment, even a bishopric, it would have been only one proof among many that it is part of their policy to promote men of loose opinions; but to place him in the office which he now holds was an intentional insult to the University. In no way could the Whigs expect so materially to injure the Church as by planting Germanized professors in our schools of divinity. Thank God, there is too much sound learning in the land for them to succeed in this. Not the least remarkable of the many parallels between these times and those of Charles I. is to be found in the state of the clergy: from the time of the Reformation they had never been in so good a state as when the Church was for a while overthrown; and since the Restoration they have never been in so good a state as at present. I mean, that there has never been so great a proportion of learned and diligent able men: men whose lives are conformable to their profession, who are able to defend the truth, and who would not shrink from any thing which they may be called upon to suffer for its sake.

"Have you read 'Subscription no Bondage?' Some one (I forget who) sent it me last year. Maurice* is said to be the author's name; an abler treatise I have never read.

"I am glad that you are studying German, and that you sometimes write verses, not only as a wholesome exercise for thoughts and feelings which hardly find utterance in any other form, but also because if you ever become a prose writer, you will find the great advantage of having written poetry. No poet ever becomes a mannerist in prose, nor falls into those tricks of style which show that the writer is always laboring to produce effect.

"The third volume of Cowper will be published next week. The remaining part of the Life extends far into it. The dealers in weekly and monthly criticism appear to think it as much a matter of course that I am now to be beplastered with praise as they once did that I was to be bespattered with abuse. On both occasions I have often remembered what the Moravian said to Wesley: *Mi frater, non adhæret vestibus.* To make amends, however, the Evangelical party have declared war against me, and I am told that in some places as much zeal is manifested in recommending Grimshawe's edition as in canvassing for a vacant lectureship. My main labor is over, but a good deal yet remains to be done in biographical notices, some of which will probably form a supplementary volume. As for materials, I have been fed by the ravens. The information which I have come upon unexpectedly, or which has been supplied to me from various quarters to which no application was made, because I did not know that such documents existed, has been surprisingly great.

"It would have amused me much if you and Edward had exhibited your skill in special pleading upon the delectable book 'The Doctor,' as you intended. To convince a man against his will, you know, is no easy matter; and if you substitute knowledge for will, what must it be then? That the writer has at first or second hand picked up some things from me, is plain enough; if it be at first hand, there is but one man upon whom my suspicion could rest, and he is very capable of having written it, which is no light praise. He possesses all the talents that the book displays, but not the multifarious sort of knowledge, nor are the opinions altogether such as he would be likely to express. So if it be his, he must have had assistance, and must also have hung out false lights. However, some friends of Henry Taylor's tell him that Dr. Bowring is the author; not the Dr. Bowring who is now M.P., who has had a finger in every revolutionary pie for the last fifteen years (and ought, indeed, to be denoted as dealer in revolutions and Greek scrip), but a retired practitioner of that name at Doncaster. H. Taylor's informants know every thing about him. The tedious chapters about Doncaster give some probability to this statement. You have it, however, as it came to me, for what it is worth; and the next volume, perhaps, if next there should be, may throw more light upon the authorship.

"God bless you, my dear Herbert!

"R. S."

To John May, Esq.

"Keswick, June 13, 1836.

"My dear Friend,

"Time passes on so rapidly with me in the regular course of constant occupation, that it seems only a few days since that letter arrived which yours of this morning reminds me is two months old. * * *

"There is no change in my poor Edith, nor is there likely to be any. Thank God, there is no suffering, not even so much as in a dream (of this I am fully convinced), and her bodily health is better than it had been for very many years. * * * * *

"Only one of my daughters is with me at present. Kate has been prevailed on to go to Rydal, and if it be possible to remove poor Dora Wordsworth to the coast (which is her only chance of recovery), she will go with her. The loss of Miss Hutchinson, which was the greatest we could have sustained out of our own nearest kin, has drawn the bonds of affection closer between dear Dora and my daughters, who were almost equally dear to the dead.

* * * * * * *

"You will not wonder that the Life of Cowper was a subject better suited to my own state of mind at this time than almost any other could have been. It was something like relief to have thoughts, from which it is not possible that I could escape, diverted as it were from home. There are passages which I dare say you will have perceived would not have been written unless I had had something more than a theoretical knowledge of this most awful of all maladies. * *

"I shall be very glad to see John Coleridge. The bishop sent me his kind remembrances from Demerara the other day. You ask if there be any likelihood of seeing me in town? Not at present; nor is it possible for me to say when it may be fitting for me to leave home. My presence, though it may be little comfort to my poor wife, is a very great one to my daughters; my spirits help to keep up theirs, and with what they have to do for me in the way of transcribing, and the arrival of letters and packets which would cease during my absence, they would feel a great blank were they left to themselves. In her quieter moods, too, my poor Edith shows a feeling toward me, the last, perhaps, which will be utterly extirpated. How often am I reminded of my own lines, and made to feel what a woeful thing it is

'When the poor flesh surviving, doth entomb
The reasonable soul.'

"You and I, my dear friend, have been afflicted in different ways, and both heavily. But the

* Rev. F. Maurice, Professor at King's College, London.

time is not far distant when we shall have all losses restored, and understand that the ways of Providence are always merciful to those who put their trust in it. * * * *

"Bedford and his cousin, Miss Page, are coming to lodge at the foot of the garden in the course of a fortnight. I have known him from the year 1788; we became familiar in 1790, intimate in 1791, and have kept up a constant and most intimate intercourse ever since. So you may suppose how much I shall enjoy his society. Mary Page, too, is the oldest of my female friends.

"God bless you, my dear old friend! and believe me always

"Yours most affectionately,

"ROBERT SOUTHEY."

In consequence of the presence of these friends, whose coming my father anticipates at the close of the last letter, this summer passed more cheerfully than those which for some time had preceded it; nor, indeed, could any persons have more thoroughly enjoyed each other's society. Mr. Bedford, though afflicted with almost complete deafness, as well as other infirmities, had lost none of his natural cheerfulness and relish for odd humor and boyish jokes; and my father was never weary of talking into his trumpet. They had, indeed, both preserved up to so late a period of life more natural vivacity and elasticity of mind than falls to the lot of most persons even in youth, and both regarded it as a signal blessing that they had done so.

The cheerfulness of the summer was further increased by the circumstance of another old "Westminster" (the Rev. Edward Levett, late of Hampstead) passing some months at Keswick; and although they had rarely met since their boyish days, this tie quickly brought them into intimacy.

Soon after their departure, my father was surprised by a subpœna to appear as a witness at the assizes at Lancaster, in what was commonly called "The great Will Case," involving a property called the Hornby Castle Estate. The late possessor, whose name was Marsden, was presumed to have been a person of weak intellect, under the control of his steward, to whose son he had bequeathed the estate, worth from £6000 to £7000 a year. Admiral Tatham, the heir-at-law, challenged Marsden's competency to make a will; and one of the points upon which his counsel (Mr., now Sir Cresswell Cresswell) relied was the internal evidence contained in a series of letters purporting to be the production of the testator.

For the purpose of giving opinion upon these letters, several literary men had been subpœnaed —Dr. Lingard, the historian (who had been a witness on a former trial, as knowing the testator personally), Mr. Wordsworth, my father, Dr. Shelton Mackenzie, and others. The following letter shows it was decided not to examine these witnesses, and Mr. Wordsworth was the only one sworn.

To H. Taylor, Esq.

"Keswick, Sept. 10, 1836.

"MY DEAR H. T.,

"The papers may have told you that Wordsworth's evidence was not received. The point at issue was, whether certain letters produced in the testator's hand-writing could all be composed by the same person, or whether they did not imply such a difference of intellect, and contain such different peculiarities of spelling and style, as to be proofs of a long-laid scheme for defrauding the heir-at-law.

"The argument whether this course of inquiry should be gone into was raised as soon as W. had been sworn in the box, and was yielded by the plaintiff's counsel (Cresswell)—less, I think, in deference to the advice of the judge, than because he saw that, in the event of a favorable verdict, Pollock was preparing to make it the plea for another trial.

"I wish you could have seen us at a board of law the preceding evening; and how Pollock was taken aback when he heard Wordsworth called into the box; and how well he recovered, and skillfully took his ground, though every step of his argument was sophistical. Wordsworth is now a 'Sworn Critic, and Appraiser of Composition;' and he has the whole honor to himself—an honor, I believe, of which there is no other example in literary history.

"We went on Tuesday, Quillinan accompanying us. On Wednesday we returned to Rydal, where I slept that night and the next morning I walked home without the slightest fatigue. But when Wordsworth marvels that I can do this, and says that I must be very strong to undertake such a march, it shows that he is an old man, and makes me conscious that I am on the list of the elders.

"The journey has been useful as an experiment; and my plans are now laid for a long circuit. About the middle of October, as soon as the volume of Admirals can be finished—upon which I go doggedly to work from this day—I hope to start with Cuthbert for the West of England. We shall halt in Shropshire, and perhaps in Warwickshire, on the way to Bristol, thence to Taunton, Devonshire, and the Land's End. I shall show him all the scenes of my childhood and youth, and the few old friends who are left; convey him to Tarring, and then come to London for two or three weeks, taking up my abode there with Rickman. God bless you!

"R. S."

Dr. Shelton Mackenzie has kindly favored me with his recollections of this meeting with my father, of great part of which I avail myself here.

"At our meeting on the preceding evening, Mr. Wordsworth gave his opinion of the letters to this effect, judging from external as well as internal evidence, that though they came from one hand, they did not emanate from one and the same mind; that a man commencing to write letters might do so very badly, but as he advanced in life, particularly if, like Marsden, he wrote many letters, he would probably improve in style; such improvement being constant, and not capricious. That is, if he gradually learned to spell and write properly, he would not fall back at intervals into his original errors of composition and spelling—that if once he had got out of his ignorance, he could not fall back into it, except by design—that the human mind advances, but can not recede, unless warped by insanity or weakened by disease. The conclusion arrived at, which facts afterward proved, was, that the inequality in the letters arose from their being composed by different persons, some ignorant and some well informed, while another person always copied them fairly for the post.

"This is the sum of what Mr. Wordsworth at great length and very elaborately declared as the result he had arrived at. It was thought piled on thought, clear investigation, careful analysis, and accumulative reasoning.

"While Wordsworth was speaking, I noticed that Southey listened with great attention. Once or twice Wordsworth referred to him for his coincidence in an argument, and Southey very laconically assented. Dr. Lingard's opinion was already on record, and my friend and myself very briefly stated ours to be precisely the same as Wordsworth's. The next day Wordsworth was put into the witness-box, was sworn, and his examination had commenced, in fulfillment of Mr. Cresswell's promise to the jury that they should hear the opinion of eminent literary characters as to the compound authorship of Marsden's letters. But Sir F. Pollock, the leader on the other side, objected to such evidence, alleging that they might as well examine a batch of Edinburgh reviewers; and that it was substituting speculative opinion for actual fact, besides taking from the jury the power of judgment founded upon opinion. After a long argument, it was decided that this evidence was inadmissible; but, as the verdict eventually showed, the jury evidently thought that there was good reason why such evidence was set aside.

"While a friend went for a magistrate's order for us to see the Castle (which is used as the prison), Southey, Wordsworth, and myself had a brisk conversation.

"From the spot on which we stood (a sort of terrace) there was a fine view of the Irish sea, the country around Lancaster, and to the north the mountains of Cumberland and Westmoreland, which last were eagerly pointed out by Wordsworth. I hazarded the remark that an American had compared these mountains with some in the vicinity of his own Hudson River, and this led to a conversation about America. 'I always lamented,' said Southey, 'that Gifford's anti-American feeling should be so prominent in the Quarterly; but he was obstinate, and the more I remonstrated the more he persevered.' We spoke of American reprints of English works, and Wordsworth said it was wonderful what an interest they took in our literature—'it was the yearning of the child for the parent;' while Southey remarked, with a smile, 'Rather the yearning of the robber for his booty: they reprint English works, because it pays them better than to buy native copyrights; and until men are paid, and paid well for writing, depend on it that writing well must be an exception rather than the rule.'

"We now went to visit Lancaster Castle, which need not here be described. After enjoying the fine view from the Keep, we went to see the Penitentiary, within the castle. Dr. Lingard had left us before this, and the ball of conversation was kept up between Wordsworth, Southey, and myself. The principal subject was American literature, with which, at that time, I was pretty well acquainted. Wordsworth could scarcely believe that of a three volume work, published here at a guinea and a half, the reprint was usually sold in New York for two shillings—in later days the price has been as low as sixpence, the great sale making a fraction of profit worth looking for. Wordsworth expressed a strong desire to obtain an American reprint of any of Southey's works; but Mr. Southey appeared quite indifferent. 'I should be glad to see them,' said he, 'if the rogues would only give me a tithe of what the work of my brains may yield to them.'

"Returning to the terrace leading to the courts, Wordsworth and Mr. Quillinan went into the town, while Southey and myself walked up and down for about half an hour. 'I am glad,' said he, 'that they would not take our evidence. It was nothing but matter of opinion, and if twenty men of letters swore one way on one day, twenty more would swear the reverse on the next day, and with equal conscientiousness.' I said that I suspected the *offering* such evidence was enough, as its rejection made the jury suspect there was a cause for not hearing it. 'Like enough,' said he, laughing heartily, 'that would be a true lawyer's trick!'

"Southey then inquired whether some lines on the death of a child, which had gone the round of the newspapers shortly before, were not my composition. Learning that they were, he said, 'The solace of song certainly does mitigate the sufferings of the wounded spirit. *I* have suffered deeply, and I found a comfort in easing my mind through poetry, even though much of what I wrote at such times I have not let the world see. It is a bitter cup,' added he, 'but we can not expect the ties of kindred to remain forever. One by one, as we live on, our friends and our relations drop through the broken arches of the bridge of life.'

"He spoke freely of his cotemporaries. Lingard he praised for true earnestness, and a desire to state the facts. Another living historian he praised as 'one of the most learned men in Europe.' He regretted that Robert Montgomery should have been as much overpraised at first as he was latterly abused. He eulogized the genius of Mary Ann Browne, then living at Liverpool, and said that he thought she had as much ability as Mrs. Hemans, with less mannerism. He said that the Corn-Law Rhymer was a sort of pupil of his own: 'he sent me his verses when he was a youth; I pointed out their defects, and he was not above trying to amend and remove them. There are parts of Elliott's poems,' added he, 'not surpassed in the language.'

"We spoke of Wordsworth, and he said, 'A clear half of what he has written will remain. Who can say how much of the rest of us will survive? Scott, for example; no one thinks of his poetry now.' I ventured to say that in Scott's case, as in his own, the excellence of their prose had thrown their poetry into the shade. 'That is a flattering apology,' said he; 'but our prose may, from its very quantity, if from no other cause, have crowded down our poetry. One thing I do know; to write poetry is the best preparation for writing prose. The verse-maker gets the habit of weighing the meanings and qualities of words, until he comes to know, as if by intuition, what particular word will best fit into the sentence. People talk of my style! I have only endeavored to write plain English, and to put my thoughts into language which every one can understand.' He mentioned Cobbett as one of the best writers of English we had yet possessed. 'He has a Saxon basis, derived from his education in the heart of an English county, where the Saxon roots occur once or twice in every sentence uttered by the peasantry. Cobbett,' he added, 'has done and said many foolish things; but he writes English such as every one, from Chaucer to Sir Thomas More, and from More to Cowper, can not fail to comprehend. He is very much in earnest, and writes without stopping to pick out pretty words, or round off polished sentences.'

"I mentioned his Life of Nelson. 'That,' said he, 'was a *Quarterly* article, and I expanded it into a book. I was afraid of the sea phrases; but I had no fear of making the book liked by the public, for I had material for ten times the extent I was bound to, and the man I wrote of lived in the nation's heart.'

'The question of memory was touched upon, from my mentioning the dates of some events we spoke of. 'Now,' said he, 'I could as soon fly as recollect these dates. I have trusted so little to memory, that memory will do little for me when I press her. I have a habit of making notes of what I should treasure in my mind, and the act of writing seems to discharge it from the mind to the paper. This is as to particulars; the main points of a subject I recollect very well.'

"To my surprise, when I inadvertently named Byron, he rather encouraged the subject. 'You think,' said he, 'that if we had been personally acquainted there would probably have been few unkind feelings between us. We did meet, more than once, in London society. I saw that he was a man of quick impulses, strong passions, and great powers. I saw him abuse these powers; and, looking at the effect of his writings on the public mind, it was my duty to denounce such of them as aimed at the injury of morals and religion. This was all; and I have said so in print before now. It has been said that I, who avowed very strong opinions in my youth, should not have condemned others; but, from my youth until now, my desire has been to improve the condition, moral, religious, and physical, of the great body of mankind. The means which I once thought best suited to effect this are not the means which, after forty years' constant thought, I would now employ. My purpose remains the same as it was in youth—I would use different machinery.'

"After this conversation we parted. Southey went to his friends at their inn, while I went to mine for some American reprints of English and Scotch magazines which I had with me. When I rejoined them they were at luncheon. Mr. Wordsworth again expressed a desire to obtain any reprints of Southey's poems; and Southey said, 'I wish they would reprint my History of Brazil.' I said, alluding to the size of the work, that this would be a heavy affair. 'Yes,' said he, 'it is in three thick quartos, and therefore quite out of the reach of common purchasers. It is a very curious fact that this very work has added some £1200 a year to the income of a commercial house in London. They claimed some exemption (of duties, I think he said) from information given them by a passage in that work, and thus they gain more by it in one year than the author can expect for the labor and research of many.'

"Shortly after they departed, both poets kindly inviting me to correspond with them, and pressing me to visit them, if ever I went within 'a day's march' of either. I never again saw these poets, but enjoyed the correspondence of each.

"The personal appearance and demeanor of Southey at this time (he was then aged 62) was striking and peculiar. The only thing in art which brings him exactly before me is the monument by Lough, the sculptor. Like many other young men of the time, who had read Byron with great admiration, I had imbibed rather a prejudice against the laureate. This was weakened by his appearance, and wholly removed by his frank conversation. He was calm, mild, and gentlemanly; full of quiet, subdued humor; the reverse of ascetic in his manner, speech, or actions. His bearing was rather that of a scholar than of a man much accustomed to mingle in general society. Indeed, he told me that, next to romping with his children when they were children, he 'enjoyed a tête-à-tête conversation with an *old* friend or a *new*. With one,' added he, 'I can talk of familiar subjects which we have discussed in former years, and with the other, if he have any brains, I open what to me is a new mine of thought. The educated Americans whom I have conversed with always leave me something to think of.'

"In any place Southey would have been pointed at as 'a noticeable man.' He was tall, slight, and well made. His features were striking, and Byron truly described him as 'with a hook nose and a hawk's eye.' Certainly his eyes were peculiar—at once keen and mild. The brow was rather high than square, and the lines well defined. His hair was tinged with gray, but his head was as well covered with it — wavy and flowing—as it could have been in youth. He by no means looked his age: simple habits, pure thoughts, the quietude of a happy hearth, the friendship of the wise and good, the self-consciousness of acting for the best purposes, a separation from the personal irritations which men of letters so often are subjected to in the world, and health, which up to that time had been so generally unbroken, had kept Southey from many of the cares of life, and their usually harrowing effect on mind and body. It is one of my most pleasant recollections that I enjoyed his friendship and regard."

CHAPTER XXXVII.

JOURNEY IN THE WEST OF ENGLAND—THE LIFE OF COWPER—LITERARY ADVICE TO A LADY—HIS SON'S PROSPECTS — NEW EDITION OF HIS POEMS—PROSPECTS OF THE COUNTRY—LAMB'S LETTERS — THE DOCTOR — FAILURE OF THE PUBLISHERS OF THE LIFE OF COWPER—THANKS TO DR. S. MACKENZIE FOR REVIEWING THE NEW EDITION OF HIS POEMS—CERTAINTY OF A FUTURE STATE—DEATH OF HIS WIFE. — 1836–1837.

Since the commencement of this last and bitterest sorrow which had befallen my father, he had devoted himself wholly to the office of lightening, as far as possible, the affliction both to the poor sufferer herself and to all his household. He had never quitted home, and, with the rare exception of a single friend, had seen no society whatever.

This sort of life, however, although his health did not appear yet to suffer, was naturally deemed so likely to prove permanently injurious to him, that his friends had often and strongly urged him to leave home for a time, and recruit himself by change of air and scene.

But, while assenting to the desirableness of such a change, he had considerable difficulty in making up his mind to attempt it. My mother had become a constant object of solicitude; his presence was often useful, always a source of as much pleasure as she was capable of receiving; and he knew, moreover, that in absence there would always be a certain amount of anxiety, which would materially diminish the good to be gained. He felt, also, the comfort his presence was to his daughters, and the blank which the absence of his continual cheerfulness would make to them.

It happened, however, that the brief, enforced absence at Lancaster, which has just been noticed, came opportunely to decide him. He found that, after the momentary discomfort had passed away, his absence did not make any very material difference; and he determined to seize the time present, although the year was already so far advanced, for a journey of considerable length, in which I was to be his companion. Our progress was an extremely circuitous one; and as almost every halting-place was at the house of some hospitable friend, it was all pure pleasure to me; and, indeed, he himself enjoyed it as much as any one could do whose thoughts and heart were elsewhere: he appreciated every minute beauty of the country we passed through with all his natural quickness of perception, the frequent meetings with old friends were a source of evident pleasure, and with the remembrance of old times his spirits seemed occasionally to recover their old buoyancy; neither, indeed, could he help being gratified with the reception he every where met with.

Our first halting-place was at Lord Kenyon's beautiful seat, near Oswestry, whence the following letter was written, in which the reader will find an outline of our route.

To Charles Swain, Esq.

"Gredington, Oct. 27, 1836.

"My dear Sir,

"No compliment has ever been addressed to me which gratified me more than your Dedicatory Sonnet, and one only which gratified me so much (that of Henry Taylor's Philip van Artevelde); both for the same reason, because both are in themselves singularly beautiful, and I know that both were written with sincerity.

"This letter is written from my first halting-place on a very wide circuit. Cuthbert and I left home on Monday, bound for the Land's End, from whence I shall turn back with him to Sussex, and, having deposited him there, proceed to London. There my purpose is to remain a fortnight, after which I shall perform my promise of visiting Neville White whenever I went again to town, and then make the best of my way home. It is an unfavorable season for making such a journey, but my brother, Dr. Southey, advised and urged me to break from home, and not rely too confidently upon a stock of health and spirits on which there were large demands.

"Being able to do this (which I hardly expected till a fortunate *subpœna* to Lancaster put it to the proof), I had the additional motive of going to examine the only collections of Cowper's letters which have not been intrusted to me—those of Mr. Bagot, which I am to peruse with his son, near Birmingham, and those of Joseph Hill, which were bequeathed as an heirloom, with a good estate, to Jekyll. I go to Mr. Bagot's on Monday next, and shall have access to Mr. Jekyll's MSS. in London. There can be little doubt of my finding in these collections (especially in the latter) materials for my supplementary volume.

"There was a third inducement for this journey. I wished to show Cuthbert the scenes of my childhood and youth, which no one but myself could show him, and to introduce him to a few old friends, all that are left to me in that part of England. Probably it may be my last journey to those parts. We hope to reach Bristol on Thursday, Nov. 3, and intend to remain a week there.

"Direct to me at Mr. Cottle's, Bedminster,

Bristol. Cottle published my Joan of Arc in 1796, and there are very few who entertain a warmer regard for me than he has done from that time.

"The lines which I have written in Miss ——'s album are on the opposite page to that upon which O'Connell and Joseph Bonaparte have inscribed their effusions. You will see that mine did not require any premeditation:

"'Birds of a feather flock together;
But *vide* the opposite page!
And thence you may gather I'm not of a feather
With some of the birds in this cage.'

"As soon as Cowper is completed, Longman means to commence a monthly publication of my poems in ten volumes. The volumes shall be sent you duly as they are published. Very few of my successors in this generation would be so well entitled to them as an acknowledgment of their merit, fewer still as a mark of personal regard.

"Cuthbert desires his kind remembrances; and believe me always, my dear sir, yours with sincere regard, ROBERT SOUTHEY."

From Gredington we proceeded, after paying some visits on the way, to Bristol, where the publisher of Joan of Arc in 1796, Mr. Cottle, hospitably entertained us. From his hands my father had received, when struggling with his early difficulties, many most substantial acts of kindness which he was always prompt to mention and acknowledge, and under his roof, and with his sisters, my mother had been left after their romantic marriage. Here, therefore, were many mournful thoughts awakened, though no one could yield to them less, or dwell more wisely than he did upon every alleviation. We visited together all his old haunts—his grandmother's house at Bedminster, so vividly described in his Autobiography—the College Green where Miss Tyler had lived—the house where he was born—the schools he had been sent to. He had forgotten nothing—no short cut—no by-way; and he would surprise me often by darting down some alley, or thridding some narrow lane, the same which in his school-boy days he traversed. We went to Westbury to look for Martin Hall,* the house where he had passed one of the happiest portions of his life; but no trace of it could be found; and we were then told, I believe erroneously, that the walls of a nunnery inclosed the place where it stood; at all events, the general features of the place were so changed, that my father did not recognize the house again, if indeed it was then standing.

This was a pleasant visit, and my father's enjoyment was greatly enhanced by the company of Mr. Savage Landor, who was then residing at Clifton, and in whose society we spent several delightful days. He was one of the few men with whom my father used to enter freely into conversation, and on such occasions it was no mean privilege to be a listener. We also visited Corston—his first boarding-school, and found all there exactly as he has described it in his Autobiography and in the "Retrospect."

I was much struck with his strong attachment to his native city, and his appreciation of all the beauties of the neighborhood; and I have often wondered he did not take up his abode there or in the neighborhood in earlier life.

Our next visit is described in the following letter:

To Grosvenor C. Bedford, Esq.

"Bedminster, Nov. 10, 1836.

"MY DEAR G.,

"Right glad should I be to feel myself sufficiently at rest and at leisure for writing at full length to you; but little rest shall I have, and as little leisure, till we meet in London some six weeks hence.

"We left home on Monday the 24th, crossed the Mersey, and got to Chester the next evening, and the next day reached Lord Kenyon's to dinner. Gredington (his house) is in Flintshire, not far from old Bangor, where the monks were massacred, and one of the small meres which are not uncommon in Cheshire touches upon his grounds. The view is very splendid: Welsh mountains in the distance, stretching far and wide, and the fore and middle ground undulated and richly wooded. There we remained till Friday morning, and then posted to Sweeny Hall, near Oswestry, where Mr. Parker had a party to meet me at dinner. I called there on Davies's mother and his two sisters, who are just such women as the mother and sisters of so thoroughly worthy a man ought to be. The former lives in a comfortable cottage which he purchased for his father some years ago, the two others are married; and the pleasure of seeing these good people, and of seeing with what delight they heard me talk of Davies, would have overpaid me for my journey.

"Saturday we reached Mr. Warter's (near Shrewsbury) to dinner, stayed there Sunday, and on Monday proceeded to Birmingham, from whence we took chaise for Mr. Egerton Bagot's at Pipe Hayes.

* * * * * * *

"Two mornings were fully occupied in reading Cowper's letters with him, and transcribing such as had hitherto been withheld.

"At four on Wednesday the chaise which I had ordered at Birmingham arrived, and took us to the Hen and Chickens. We then *flew* (that is to say, went in a fly) about a mile out of that town, to drink tea with Mr. Riland, a clergyman, who married a sister of Robert Wolsely (your cotemporary at Westminster), and who has now and then communicated with me by letter. We had a pleasant evening; after which we returned, like dutiful chickens, to rest under the Hen's wings.

"Thursday we came to Bristol, and took up our quarters here at Bedminster with Cottle. Here I have been to the church which I used to attend with my mother and grandmother more than half a hundred years ago; and I have shown

* See *antè*, p. 104.

Cuthbert my grandmother's house—what was once my garden of Eden. At church I was placed in a seat exactly opposite the spot on which our pew had stood; but the whole interior of the church had been altered. A few monuments only remained as they had been. November 8. Tuesday, we walked with Landor about the finest parts of the neighborhood; but the house which I inhabited for one year at Westbury, and in which I wrote more verses than in any other year of my life, has been pulled down. Yesterday I took the North Pole* to Corston, and went into the house in which I had been at school fifty-five years ago.

"We go on Saturday to visit Bowles at Bremhill, and shall stay there till Wednesday.

"To-day I have a letter from home with accounts not on the whole unfavorable, but upon which I must not allow myself to dwell. Right glad shall I be, or rather right thankful (for gladness and I have little to do with each other now) to find myself at home again. I am well, thank God, and my spirits seldom fail; but I do not sleep better than at home, and lose that after-dinner nap, which has for some time been my soundest and most refreshing sleep. On the whole, however, I expect to find myself the better for this journey, when I return to remain by the wreck. You will not wonder that I am anxious to be there again, and that I have a satisfaction in being there—miserable as it is—which it is impossible to feel any where else.

"God bless you, my dear Grosvenor!

"R. S.

"Our love to Miss Page."

To Miss Katharine Southey.

"Wells, Wednesday evening,
"Nov. 16, 1836.

"My dear Kate,

* * * * * * *

"Look at the history of Bremhill, and you will see Bowles's parsonage; it is near the fine old church, and as there are not many better livings, there are few more pleasantly situated. The garden is ornamented in his way, with a jet-fountain, something like a hermitage, an obelisk, a cross, and some inscriptions. Two swans, who answer to the names of Snowdrop and Lily, have a pond to themselves, and if they are not duly fed there at the usual time, up they march to the breakfast-room window. Mrs. Bowles has also a pet hawk called Peter, a name which has been borne by two of his predecessors. The view from the back of the house extends over a rich country, to the distant downs, and the white horse may be seen distinctly by better eyes than mine, without the aid of a glass. * * *

"Much as I had heard of Bowles's peculiarities, I should very imperfectly have understood his character if I had not passed some little time under his roof. He has indulged his natural timidity to a degree little short of insanity, yet he sees how ridiculous it makes him, and laughs himself at follies which nevertheless he is continually repeating. He is literally afraid of every thing. His oddity, his untidyness, his simplicity, his benevolence, his fears, and his good-nature, make him one of the most entertaining and extraordinary characters I ever met with. He is in his seventy-third year, and for that age is certainly a fine old man, in full possession of all his faculties, though so afraid of being deaf, when a slight cold affects his hearing, that he puts a watch to his ear twenty times in the course of the day. Our reception was as hospitable as possible, Mrs. Bowles was as kind as himself, and every thing was done to make us comfortable. * * * * * *

"The bishop, unluckily, is at Weymouth; he wrote to Bowles to say how glad he should be to see us; but he will not be in Wells till this day week. Whether the dean (Goodenough) is here, the people of the inn can not tell. *

"Tell your dear mother that I earnestly wish to be at home again, and shall spend no time on the way that can be spared.

"Love to all. So good night; and God bless you! R. S."

* An appellation given to the editor by Mr. Bedford.

The next letter gives in brief an account of great part of the journey; and I think is not uninteresting, as showing his capabilities of bearing fatigue, and of deriving some pleasure from such a routine of visits as might reasonably have been expected to be wearisome to him.

To John Rickman, Esq.

"Linton, Dec. 7, 1836.

"My dear R.,

"After a course as erratic as that of a comet which has been driven out of its way (if comets are liable to such accidents), here we are, in certainly the most beautiful spot in the West of England. I was here in 1799, alone, and on foot. At that time the country between Porlock and Ilfracombe was not practicable for wheel carriages, and the inn at Linton received all travelers in the kitchen. Instead of that single public house, there are now several hotels, and in its accommodation, and in the number of good houses which have been erected by settlers, Linton vies with any watering-place in Devonshire.

"We were within a few miles of this place a fortnight ago, when Poole parted with us at Holnicot, Sir T. Acland's, Somersetshire House; but Sir T. persuaded us to accompany him to Killerton, that we might see the road that he has opened along the side of the Exe, and then return to the south coast by way of Barnstaple. At Killerton we met Scoresby the *Ceticide*, now the Reverend, and the Earl of Devon. We paid our visit to Mrs. Hodson at Dawlish, and there met Colonel Napier, brother to the Peninsular historian, and Mrs. Crawford, widow of the general, who was killed at Ciudad Rodrigo. Thursday last we breakfasted with Charles Hoare, the banker, who is uncle to both Sir Thomas and Lady Acland. He has a beautiful house, which he built himself, near Dawlish. From thence

Sir Thomas drove us to Mamhead, where Sir Robert Newman has built, and is now busily decorating, the most gorgeous mansion I have ever seen. Here Lord Devon met us, and took us to Powderham Castle. The Poor-Law Bill is working well here, they tell me; and it has had the good effect of bringing the better kind of country gentlemen in contact with the farmers, who used to think that gentlemen knew nothing, and are now convinced that they are better informed than themselves.

"We stayed one night at Powderham, and went next day to my old friend Lightfoot's, near Crediton; there we spent three comfortable days in a parsonage, having every thing about us that the heart of man could desire. To-morrow we return to Barnstaple, and go to Mr. Buck's, the chief of the North Devon Conservatives, near Bëdeford, who has offered us hospitality, and to show us Clovelly and Hartland. Sir Thomas talks of meeting us again at Bude. * * * At Poole's we met Mr. Cross, whose discoveries astonished the Wittenagemot at Bristol. You would like his frank, unassuming manner. * * We saw the storm of Tuesday, Nov. 29, from a house on the beach at Dawlish, which was considered to be in danger, if the wind had not changed when it did. The effect of the change more resembled what I suppose may be that of a hurricane than any thing I ever witnessed before: it whirled the waves about, and the whole surface of the sea was covered with spray flying in all directions. On Saturday week we were called out to a fire which consumed a large farm-house, not far from Lightfoot's. It will be well if the ensuing week passes without our seeing a shipwreck; for when the winter commences with storms, they seem generally to prevail through it, as far as my observation extends, or rather as far as my recollection can be trusted.

"This wandering life is as little suited to my inclination as to my habits; but it has its use in shaking up the system and in refreshing old recollections. Much of what I see and hear will at some time or other turn to account, I hope; and, moreover, it will be a good thing for Cuthbert to have seen my old friends and so much of his own country!

"God bless you! R. SOUTHEY."

From Linton, after visiting Mr. Buck at Hartland Abbey, and meeting Sir Thomas Acland at Bude Haven, who had ridden fast and far that he might welcome my father in three counties,* we pursued our way down the iron-bound north coast of Cornwall, visiting the most remarkable places. Tintagel,† the reputed birth-place of King Arthur (see some of the first chapters of Morte d'Arthur), interested him greatly; and the rugged scene lacked no accompaniments of storm and tempest which could increase its grandeur, for we could hardly keep our footing while we viewed it; and to have scaled the rocks which lead up to it would have been impossible in such weather, and dangerous enough at any time.

Further down the coast we visited that singular tract of sand which has been rendered well known by the discovery of the ancient British Church of Peranzabuloe (or St. Peran in the Sands), which, when we saw it, was again half buried. The structure itself was of the rudest and humblest kind; and what struck us most forcibly was, that the sand all around was filled with small fragments of human bones, indicating a burial-place at some distant period of far greater extent than the size of the building or the population of the country would have led any one to think necessary. I suppose, however, it had been an oratory, and not a parish church. We were told that, a few days before our visit, the sand shifting during a storm had exposed to view a row of stone coffins without covers, with the skeletons in them nearly perfect; but they had been again buried by the last turn of the wind, which, indeed, was already driving the sand, which is exceedingly deep and loose, over the remains of the little church itself.

Helston was our furthest resting-place, where the Rev. Derwent Coleridge was then residing; from whence we visited the Land's End, with the wild grandeur of which my father was particularly struck. St. Michael's Mount, in Penzance Bay, also pleased him greatly; and he was delighted at seeing the identical chair from which Rebecca Penlake was thrown, as narrated in his well-known ballad. It is situated on the outside of the church tower, and is evidently part of an old lantern or place to light a beacon fire on.

One other scene also which he had described in verse he was much pleased at now being able to visit for the first time, viz., the Well of St. Keyne, near Liskeard, which we saw during a brief visit to the Rev. W Farwell; and during this excursion, which was impracticable on foot, I saw my father for the first and last time in my life mount on horseback. That he had ever been a good rider I should think very doubtful; but on this occasion he surpassed my expectations. Our Christmas was passed at Tavistock, at the Rev. E. Bray's, whose wife is the well-known novelist and the kind editress of Mary Colling's simple verses. My father had known her for some time as a not unfrequent correspondent, but not until now personally. A second visit to Mr. Lightfoot ended our western sojourn.

* At Holnicot, in Somersetshire; Killerton, in Devonshire; and Bude, in Cornwall.

† I find this place well described in a topographical account of Cornwall:

"Reft from the parent land by some dire shock,
Majestically stands an island rock,
On whose rough brow Tintagel's donjon keep
Sternly uprears and bristles o'er the deep:
Her arches, portal tower, and pillars gray
Lie scattered, all in ruinous decay.
And wild the scene; from far is heard the roar
Of billows breaking on the shingly shore;
And at long intervals the startling shriek
Of the white tenants of the lofty peak;
Beneath in caverns raves the maddening surge,
Around with ruins capp'd grim rocks emerge,
And Desolation fills his gloomy throne,
Raised on the fragments of an age unknown."

To Miss Katharine Southey.

"Stockleigh Pomeroy, Jan. 1, 1837.

"MY DEAR DAUGHTER,

"Whichever it be to whom this letter is due (for I keep ill account of such things), I begin with such wishes to both, and to all others at home, and all friends round Skiddaw or elsewhere, as the first day of the year calls forth.

* * * * * * *

"It was some comfort to hear that your dearest mother listened to my letters, and asked some questions; and it is some comfort to know that my presence is not wanted, while it is in vain to wish that it were wished for. I shall be home by the middle of February; glad to be there, and glad that I have taken a journey which has warmed some old attachments, and been in many respects of use. As for Cuthbert, he declares that it would have been worth while to make the whole journey for the sake of seeing Mary Colling. Verily I never saw any person in and about whom every thing was more entirely what you could wish, and what it ought to be. She is the pattern of neatness and propriety, simplicity and good sense. Her old master, Mr. Hughes, is as proud of her as if she was his daughter. They live in a small house, the garden of which extends to the River Tavy, a beautiful stream; and her kitchen is such a kitchen for neatness and comfort, that you would say at once no person who could not be happy there deserved to be happy any where else. Strangers (and there are many whom Mrs. Bray's book draws to Tavistock and Dartmoor) generally inquire for her, and find means to see her, and she has already a little library of books which have been presented to her by such persons.

* * * * * * *

"Mr. Bray's is the only house in which I have eaten upon pewter since I was a child; he has a complete service of it, with his crest engraved upon it, and bright as silver. The house (built for him by the Duck, as the Duke of Bedford is called in Tavistock) is a very good one, the garden large and pleasantly laid out; it includes some of the ruins, and a door from it opens upon a delightful walk on the Tavy. In spite of the weather we had two pleasant walks, one of about ten miles, the other about six; but of Dartmoor we could see nothing. Our time passed pleasantly, Mary paying us a visit every day; some more Fables in her own hand-writing will be among the most interesting autographs that I have to dispose of.

"So much for Tavistock. I see it to great disadvantage. The Tavy is like our Greta in its better parts, the water was quite as clear; but snow has the effect of making water look dirty, and Mr. Bray compared the foam of the river to soap-suds; a simile not less apt than that of Sir Walter, who likens the foam of a dark stream to the mane of a chestnut horse. The small patches of snow on the banks looked like linen laid there to dry or to bleach. The beauty of brook and torrent scenery was thus totally destroyed; yet I could well imagine what the country is at a better season, and in all such scenery it resembles Cumberland.

"I may fill up what remains of this paper with some epitaphs, which I wrote down from the tombs in Bremhill church-yard. The first two were as follows, on a Dissenter and his wife; and because they were Dissenters, Bowles, in reference to the latter, wrote the third, on one of his own flock.

"'E. W. 1800.

"'A loving wife, a friend sincere,
A tender mother, sleepeth here.'

"'W. W. 1834.

"'Here in the silent dust lies one
Beloved of God.
Redeemed he was by Christ,
Wash'd in his precious blood,
And faithful was his name.
From tribulation great he came,
In love he lived, in Christ he died;
His life desired, but God denied.'

"Bowles, who loves not the Dissenters more than I do, wrote, in contrast to this, the following inscription, on a neighboring tomb-stone:

"'Reader, this heap of earth, this grave-stone mark!
Here lie the last remains of poor John Dark.
Five years beyond man's age he lived, and trod
This path each Sabbath to the house of God;
From youth to age, nor ever from his heart
Did that *best prayer our Savior taught* depart.
At his last hour with lifted hands he cried,
Thy kingdom come, Thy will be done! and died.'

"This was a hit at those who went to meeting instead of church, and never used the Lord's Prayer; moreover, it alluded to the Dissenter wishing to live longer if he could.

"And now God bless you all! Heartily indeed do I wish myself at home; but I am far from repenting of my journey.

"Your dutiful father, R. S."

To Henry Taylor, Esq.

"Buckland, Jan. 8, 1837.

"MY DEAR H. T.,

" * * * * * * *

If I have learned to look with indifference upon those whom I meet in casual society, it is because in early life circumstances (and disposition also) made me retire into myself, like a snail into his shell; and in later years, because so many new faces have come to me like shadows, and so departed. Yet I was not slow in my likings when young, nor has time rendered me so: it has only withheld me from making any advances toward intimacy with persons, however likeable, whom it is certain that I can have very few opportunities of seeing again, and no leisure for conversing with by letter.

"It is, indeed, most desirable to knit our friends in a circle; and one of those hopes which, thank God, have in me the strength of certainties, is that this will be done in the next stage of our existence, when all the golden links of the chain will be refined and rendered lasting. I have been traveling for the last ten weeks through places where recollections met me at every stage, and this certainly alone could render such recollections endurable. My faith in that future which can not be far off never fails.

"God bless you! R. S."

To Miss Katharine Southey.

"Tarring, Feb. 8, 1837.

"MY DEAR KATE,

" * * * * * * *
Yesterday I and Karl had a walk of some fourteen or fifteen miles, to the Roman encampments of Sisbury and Chankbury. The latter commands a noble prospect over the Weald. We had also a remarkable view of Worthing, which appeared like a ruined city (Balbec or Palmyra) in the distance, on the edge of what we knew to be the sea, but what might as well have been a desert; for it was so variegated with streaks of sunshine and of shade, that no one ignorant of the place could have determined whether it were sea or sky that lay before us.

* * * * * * *

"I shall come home hungry for work, for sleeping after dinner, and for walking with a book in my hand. The first thing I have to do is to write a preface for Cowper's Homer—little more than an evening's employment. Then I set about reviewing Mrs. Bray's book, and carefully reading through Joan of Arc, that it may be sent immediately to the press; for the first volume of my Poetical Works is to appear on July 11 (a month after Cowper is finished), and we wish to have two or three more through the press, so as to prevent all danger of delay in the publication. Then there are two volumes of Cowperiana to prepare (for which I am to have, as is fitting, separate pay), and two volumes more of Admirals, besides other things—enough to do, but not too much; for I see my way through all, and was never in better trim for work.

* * * * * * *

"And now, God bless you all! Rejoice, Baron Chinchilla, for I am coming again to ask of you whether you have every thing that a cat's heart can desire! Rejoice, Tommy Cockbairn, for I must have a new black coat! and I have chosen that it should be the work of thy hands, not of a London tailor. Rejoice, Echo, for the voice which thou lovest will soon awaken thee again in thy mountains! Rejoice, Ben Wilson, for sample clogs are to be sent into the West country, for the good of the Devonshire men! R. S."

To —— ——.

"Keswick, March, 1837.

"MADAM,*

"You will probably, ere this, have given up all expectation of receiving an answer to your letter of December 29. I was on the borders of Cornwall when that letter was written; it found me a fortnight afterward in Hampshire. During my subsequent movements in different parts of the country, and a tarriance of three busy weeks in London, I had no leisure for replying to it; and now that I am once more at home, and am clearing off the arrears of business which had accumulated during a long absence, it has lain unanswered till the last of a numerous file, not from disrespect or indifference to its contents, but because, in truth, it is not an easy task to answer it, nor a pleasant one to cast a damp over the high spirits and the generous desires of youth.

"What you are I can only infer from your letter, which appears to be written in sincerity, though I may suspect that you have used a fictitious signature. Be that as it may, the letter and the verses bear the same stamp, and I can well understand the state of mind which they indicate. What I am you might have learned by such of my publications as have come into your hands; and had you happened to be acquainted with me, a little personal knowledge would have tempered your enthusiasm. You might have had your ardor in some degree abated by seeing a poet in the decline of life, and witnessing the effect which age produces upon our hopes and aspirations; yet I am neither a disappointed man nor a discontented one, and you would never have heard from me any chilling sermons upon the text, 'All is vanity.'

"It is not my advice that you have asked as to the direction of your talents, but my opinion of them; and yet the opinion may be worth little, and the advice much. You evidently possess, and in no inconsiderable degree, what Wordsworth calls 'the faculty of verse.' I am not depreciating it when I say that in these times it is not rare. Many volumes of poems are now published every year without attracting public attention, any one of which, if it had appeared half a century ago, would have obtained a high reputation for its author. Whoever, therefore, is ambitious of distinction in this way, ought to be prepared for disappointment.

"But it is not with a view to distinction that you should cultivate this talent, if you consult your own happiness. I, who have made literature my profession, and devoted my life to it, and have never for a moment repented of the deliberate choice, think myself nevertheless bound in duty to caution every young man who applies as an aspirant to me for encouragement and advice, against taking so perilous a course. You will say that a woman has no need of such a caution—there can be no peril in it for her. In a certain sense this is true; but there is a danger of which I would, with all kindness and all earnestness, warn you. The day-dreams in which you habitually indulge are likely to induce a distempered state of mind; and in proportion as all the ordinary uses of the world seem to you flat and unprofitable, you will be unfitted for them without becoming fitted for any thing else. Literature can not be the business of a woman's life, and it ought not to be. The more she is engaged in her proper duties, the less leisure will she have for it even as an accomplishment and a recreation. To those duties you have not yet been called, and when you are you will be less eager for celebrity. You will not seek in imagination for excitement, of which the vicissitudes of this life, and the anxieties from which you must not hope to be exempted, be your state what it may, will bring with them but too much.

* The lady to whom this and the next letter are addressed is now well known as a prose writer of no common powers.

"But do not suppose that I disparage the gift which you possess, nor that I would discourage you from exercising it. I only exhort you so to think of it and so to use it as to render it conducive to your own permanent good. Write poetry for its own sake—not in a spirit of emulation, and not with a view to celebrity: the less you aim at that, the more likely you will be to deserve, and, finally, to obtain it. So written, it is wholesome both for the heart and soul; it may be made the surest means, next to religion, of soothing the mind, and elevating it. You may embody it in your best thoughts and your wisest feelings, and in so doing discipline and strengthen them.

"Farewell, madam. It is not because I have forgotten that I was once young myself that I write to you in this strain, but because I remember it. You will neither doubt my sincerity nor my good will; and, however ill what has here been said may accord with your present views and temper, the longer you live the more reasonable it will appear to you. Though I may be but an ungracious adviser, you will allow me, therefore, to subscribe myself, with the best wishes for your happiness here and hereafter,

"Your true friend,

"ROBERT SOUTHEY."

To the same.

"Keswick, March 22, 1837.

"DEAR MADAM,

"Your letter has given me great pleasure, and I should not forgive myself if I did not tell you so. You have received admonition as considerately and as kindly as it was given. Let me now request that, if you ever should come to these lakes while I am living here, you will let me see you. You would then think of me afterward with the more good will, because you would perceive that there is neither severity nor moroseness in the state of mind to which years and observation have brought me.

"It is, by God's mercy, in our power to attain a degree of self-government, which is essential to our own happiness, and contributes greatly to that of those around us. Take care of over-excitement, and endeavor to keep a quiet mind (even for your health it is the best advice that can be given you): your moral and spiritual improvement will then keep pace with the culture of your intellectual powers.

"And now, madam, God bless you!

"Farewell, and believe me to be your sincere friend, ROBERT SOUTHEY."

To H. Taylor, Esq.

"Keswick, March 30, 1837.

"MY DEAR H. T.,

"I too, as you may suppose, speculate (and sometimes more largely than is wise) upon Cuthbert's past, present, and future. The past is past, and could not, I believe, all things considered, have been changed for the better; for the good and evil of public education and of private, as compared with each other, are so nearly balanced, that it would be difficult to say on which side the advantages preponderate. But life is uncertain, and it was a great object with me, feeling that uncertainty, to make his boyhood happy. Moreover, the expense of a public school would have cost me no little anxiety, and must have put me to my shifts.

* * * * * * *

"For the future, he knows my predilection, and knows also that he is just as free to choose his own profession as if I had none. I indulge in no dreams respecting my life or his, or into which their prolongation enters. But if he lives, I think he would be happier in a country parsonage than at the bar, or as a physician, or in a public office. He is free to choose. I may live to see his choice, but not to know the result of it. God bless you! R. S."

"If you have never read Roger North's Lives of the Lord-keeper Guildford and his other two brothers, let me recommend them to you. Bating the law matters, you will be amused by every thing else. There is an edition in three octavos, published a few years ago. His Examen is also well worth reading by any one who wishes to understand our history from the Restoration to the Revolution.

"The influenza is leaving me slowly, and I wait for milder weather to get out of doors."

To the Rev. W. L. Bowles.

"Keswick, April 25, 1837.

"MY DEAR MR. BOWLES,

"I have to thank you for the honor which you intend me in your forthcoming edition—a very great honor I can not but consider it, especially remembering (what I shall never forget) the improvement, as well as the delight, which I derived from your poems more than forty years ago, and have acknowledged in a general preface (just drawn out) to my own. The Conscript Fathers of the Row have set me upon a collected edition of them.

"The booksellers in one respect have rendered me a service by accelerating what I looked forward to as a posthumous publication, for I might otherwise have deferred the necessary preparations, waiting for a more convenient season, till it would have been too late. Indeed, it requires some resolution to set about a task which brings in review before me the greater part of my life—old scenes, old feelings, and departed friends. No doubt the reason why so many persons who have begun to write their own lives have stopped short when they got through the chapter of their youth is, that the recollections of childhood and adolescence, though they call up tender thoughts, excite none of that deeper feeling with which we look back upon the time of life when wounds heal slowly and losses are irreparable.

"The mood in which I have set about this revision is like that a man feels when he is setting his house in order. I waste no time in attempting to mend pieces which are not worth mending; but upon Joan of Arc, which leads the way, as having first brought me into notice, a good deal of patient labor has been bestowed. The faults of language have been weeded out, and as many others as it was possible to extirpate. This would have been a preposterous attempt if the poem had been of a piece before; but it was written in 1793, rewritten in 1795, and materially altered in 1797, and what has been done now makes the diction of the same character throughout. Faults enough of every other kind remain to mark it for a juvenile production.

"The men who are now in power are doing the greatest injury they can to the Church by strengthening the only strong argument that can be brought up against the alliance between Church and State. They certainly overlook all considerations of character, station, acquirements, and deserts in the disposal of their preferment, and regard nothing but the interests of their own party. It will tend to confirm the American Episcopalians in the only point upon which they differ from their English brethren, and I am more sorry for this than for the handle which it gives to the Dissenters at home; for in these dark times, the brightest prospect is that of the Episcopal Church in America, and yet without an alliance with the State, and endowments for learned and laborious leisure, it never can be all that a church ought to be.

"I am a good hoper, even when I look danger full in the face. We are now in great danger of a severer dearth than any within our memory. Here in Cumberland, at this time, there is scarcely the slightest appearance of spring. Last year the hay failed, and the sheep are now dying for want of food. The gardens have suffered greatly by frosts, which continued till last week, and most of the grain which was sown in the early spring is lost. The manufacturers are out of employ, and the cold fit of our commercial disease is likely to be the most formidable that we have ever experienced. Mischief of course is at work in the manufacturing countries, and it will be tremendously aided by the New Poor-Laws, which are not more useful in some of their enactments than they are inhuman in others. I fear, however, nothing so much as a premature change of ministry. Let the present men remain to reap what they have sown. You and I can not live to see the issue of all these changes that are in progress, but, as an old man in this neighborhood said, 'mayhap we may hear tell.'

"God bless you, my dear sir! Present my kind regards to Mrs. Bowles, and believe me,

"Yours affectionately,

"ROBERT SOUTHEY."

To Edward Moxon, Esq.

"Keswick, July 19, 1837.

"MY DEAR SIR,

"I received Lamb's Letters yesterday evening, and not very wisely looked through both volumes before I went to bed, for, as you may suppose, they kept possession of me during the night. Of late I have seen much of myself in a way that thus painfully brings back the past; Sir Walter's Memoirs first, then Joseph Cottle's Recollections of so many things which had better have been forgotten, and now these Memorials of poor Charles Lamb. What with these, and the preparation of my own poems for an edition which I have set about in the same mood of mind as if it were designed for posthumous publication, my thoughts and feelings have been drawn to the years that are past far more than is agreeable or wholesome.

* * * * * * *

"I wish that I had looked out for Mr. Talfourd the letter* which Gifford wrote in reply to one in which I remonstrated with him upon his designating Lamb as a poor maniac. The words were used in complete ignorance of their peculiar bearings, and I believe nothing in the course of Gifford's life ever occasioned him so much self-reproach. He was a man with whom I had no literary sympathies; perhaps there was nothing upon which we agreed except great political questions; but I liked him the better ever after for his conduct on this occasion. He had a heart full of kindness for all living creatures except authors; *them* he regarded as a fishmonger regards eels, or as Isaac Walton did slugs, frogs, and worms. I always protested against the indulgence of that temper in his Review, and I am sorry to see in this last number that the same spirit still continues there.

"A few remarks I will make upon these volumes as they occur to me. There was nothing emulous intended in Coleridge's Maid of Orleans. When Joan of Arc was first in the press (1795), he wrote a considerable portion of the second book, which portion was omitted in the second edition (1798), because his style was not in keeping with mine, and because the matter was inconsistent with the plan upon which the poem had been in great part recast. All that Coleridge meant was to make his fragment into a whole.

"I saw most of Lamb in 1802, when he lived in the Temple, and London was my place of abode—for the last time, God be thanked!

"It was not at Cambridge that Lloyd was attracted to Coleridge. He introduced himself to him at Bristol in 1796, resided with him afterward at Stowey, and did not go to Cambridge till three or four years later, after his own marriage.

* * * * * * *

"Remember me to Mrs. Moxon, and believe me always yours very truly,

"ROBERT SOUTHEY.

"Remember me most kindly to Mr. Rogers when you see him. I am sorry that Cary has been so ill treated. It may be hoped that the archbishop may think it fitting to mark his sense of the transaction by giving him some preferment

"Mr. Talfourd has performed his task as wel as it could be done, under all circumstances. The book must be purely delightful to every one, the very few excepted to whom it must needs recall melancholy recollections."

The reader will have observed, from various passages in my father's letters, the extreme pains

* See *antè*, p 417.

and trouble he had taken to conceal the true authorship of The Doctor; the publication of this book, and the mystification about it, in which he contrived to involve so many people, being one of his chief sources of amusement—indeed, his only recreation during his later years.

The two first volumes had been published at hap-hazard, the work being so unlike any other that had ever appeared that he could form no anticipation of what its reception would be. With that reception (although the sale was never a large one) he was fully satisfied, and encouraged to continue it at much greater length than he at first intended; indeed, had his faculties and life been spared, there is no knowing where it would have ended.

When first he determined upon anonymous publication, it is certain he did not expect that the authorship would be so uniformly and confidently ascribed to him as proved to be the case, otherwise he might have hesitated at a step which ultimately involved him in so many statements, which, if not amounting to an absolute denial of the fact, yet sounded like it to the persons to whom they were written; and in some cases his friends felt hurt at what he had said in pure playfulness, and at being led on by his own expressions to assert positively that they knew he was not the author. He was himself from the first determined that this should not be like the authorship of the Waverley Novels—a secret and no secret. The vast extent of odd and out-of-the-way reading manifested, the peculiar vein of humor, the admixture (distasteful to some minds, delightful to others) of light topics with grave ones, and the strong opinions so plainly expressed on political and social subjects, all combined to stamp him so positively as the author, to those who knew him personally or his writings well, that it required something more than a mere playful shifting off of the charge to convince them to the contrary. To some of these persons he admitted it, in a way which did not commit them to keeping it a secret, and yet enabled them to escape acknowledging that they knew him to be the writer; to others, whom he was more anxious to mystify, he said more than they thought he ought to have said. But, after all, it must be said he never denied the authorship in direct terms, nor indeed said more on the subject than is asserted in hundreds of cases when any secret is intended to be kept; and if the matter seemed to occupy more of his attention and call forth more ingenuity than it was worth, it must be remembered it was the amusement of what would otherwise have been sad hours, and a relief from painful recollections and melancholy thoughts.

Among other expedients to put the critics and literary public on a wrong scent, one was to send all the original letters of acknowledgment for the first two volumes (among them an ingenious one from himself) to the late Theodore Hook, as a person who might fairly be suspected of having been the writer; and it was hoped he would have spoken of this hoax being passed upon him, and thus have given a fair pretext for fixing the authorship upon him. It does not appear, however, that he took up the joke with any zest, or that the matter was heard of until the letters were found among his papers after his death.

To H. Taylor, Esq.

"Keswick, Aug. 12, 1837.
My 63d Birth-day.

"My dear H. T.,

"* * * * * * *

I am amused to hear that before the fourth volume could be permitted to circulate in the Book Club at Harrow, the chapter relating to the Loves of Nobs's Sire and Dam was cut out, as being too loose and licentious for this virtuous age. O soul of Sir John Falstaff!

"I think of a special Inter-chapter upon the occasion, proposing a reform of our vocabulary; for example, that as no one ventures to pronounce the name of a she-dog before female ears, the principle of decency should be *carried through* (as reformers phrase it), and we should speak of a she-horse, a she-cow; he-goat and she-goat are in use, so ought he-sheep and she-sheep to be; or Tom-sheep, as no one has objected to Tom-cat: then touch upon the Family Shakspeare, and hint at a Family Bible upon a plan different from all others.

* * * * * * *

"People say they *know* me to be the author. As how? There are two ways: one is, by being in the secret. Now it must be presumed that none who are would commit so gross a breach of confidence as to proclaim it. The other way is, they know it by particular circumstances and by internal evidences; their knowledge, therefore, is worth just what their opinion may be—no more.

"This is certain, that some of my nearest relations and oldest friends have not been intrusted with the secret: in this way we have a good right to discredit the assertions of persons who show so little sense of what they ought to have considered a moral obligation.

"God bless you! R. S.

"We dined yesterday in the bed of one of the Borrowdale streams. Karl, and Erroll Hill, Kate, Miss Muckle, Davies, and I. Just when we had finished our dinner came on a noble thunder-storm. The subject would have been good for a picture: rocks and umbrellas sheltered some of us well. I was among the fortunate. Erroll and Davies got well soaked. We sat it out like so many Patiences, except that Patience, though she may have been in as heavy a storm, was never in so merry a mood. The force of the storm was at Armboth, about two miles from us, where some sheep were killed and other mischief done. Lowdore was nearly dry in the morning, and on our return it was in great force. I did not think an hour's rain could possibly have swollen the streams so much. God bless you!

"R. Southey."

The following letter refers to some apprehension my father had been, and indeed was then under, respecting the payment for his Life of

Cowper, and labor in editing his works, in consequence of the insolvency of the firm of Baldwin and Cradock, who were the publishers, and who had engaged him to prepare the edition. With his usual equanimity, however, in such matters, although the sum at stake was for him a large one, he had not suffered himself to be at all discomposed, and patiently awaited the result, which was not so favorable as he had anticipated; for, in addition to much trouble, and of necessity some anxiety, he received £250 less than the stipulated payment.

To Mrs. Hodson.

"Keswick, Oct. 27, 1837.

"MY DEAR MRS. HODSON,

"Happily, pecuniary assistance is not needed. There is reason to think I shall suffer no eventual loss. The price to have been paid me was 1000 guineas. That sum not having been paid upon the completion of the work, the copyright rests with me, and the property of the edition can not be sold without my assignment. The sum was intended to cover Cuthbert's expenses through his University course. Even if it should be materially diminished, or lost, it will not distress me. Dr. Bell left me £1000: that sum is vested in the French funds, and, if need be, may be drawn out for this purpose. But my own opinion is, that the copyright is good security for payment in full. I had written good part of a letter in reply to yours, saying that I have no other concern with the publishers of my poems than to receive from them half the eventual profits, which half is not the lion's half. I was writing also playfully about The Doctor; but it was an effort, and I had no heart to go on, for our long tragedy is drawing to its close. The change has been very rapid. Thank God, there is no suffering either of body or mind. How long this may last it is impossible to say. To all appearance she is in the very last stage of emaciation and weakness. There is no strength for suffering left; she will probably fall asleep like an infant, and you may imagine what a comfort it is for me to believe, as I verily do, after two-and-forty years of marriage, that no infant was ever more void of offense toward God and man. I never knew her to do an unkind act nor say an unkind word.

"We are as well as we can be in this state. The event has long been to be desired—the worst has long been past—and when one sharp grief is over, we shall be thankful for her deliverance from the body of this death.

"God bless you, my dear Mrs. Hodson!

"ROBERT SOUTHEY."

To Dr. Shelton Mackenzie.

"Keswick, Nov. 3, 1837.

"MY DEAR SIR,

"I am greatly obliged to you for the efficient and timely assistance* which you have given to a publication that needs all the aid it can muster. Longman proposed it, not because there was any call for such an edition, but because he did not like that Galignani should have the market to himself. My own intention was to prepare for a posthumous collection, which I was confident would prove a good post-obit for my children. The Conscript Fathers of the Row thought that the present ought not to be neglected for prospective views, and I gave up my own opinion, thinking that they were better qualified to form a judgment upon such points. They then proposed giving only a vignette title-page. Upon that point I represented that any such parsimony would be fatal to the project; for if they made the book inferior in its appearance to the other works which had been published in the same manner and at the same price, it was neither more nor less than a confession that they had no reliance upon their own speculation, and did not think the work in sufficient repute for them to venture the same outlay upon it, which was readily advanced upon the credit of more fashionable names. They yielded to this argument, and have performed their part well.

"What I aimed at in my Prefaces was to say neither too little nor too much, and to introduce no more of my own history than was naturally connected with the rise and progress of the respective poems. But of this there will be a great deal. Many years ago I began to write my own Life and Recollections in letters to an old and dear friend. About half a volume was produced in this way, till it became inconvenient to afford time for proceeding; and, to confess the truth, my heart began to fail. This, no doubt, is the reason why so many autobiographies proceed little beyond the stage of boyhood. So far all our recollections are delightful as well as vivid, and we remember every thing; but when the cares and the griefs of life are to be raised up, it becomes too painful to live over the past again.

"Doubtful, or more than doubtful as it is whether I shall ever have heart to proceed with these letters, your advice shall have the effect of making me say more than I had thought of saying in these prefaces.

"Wat Tyler is printed in the second volume, and in the third there will be the Devil's Walk at much greater length than it has ever appeared.

"You will have your reward for refusing to conduct a journal that aims at a mischievous end. The time is fast coming when it will be seen that measures of true reform are to be expected from those only one of whose chief endeavors it is to preserve what is good.

"Farewell, my dear sir; and believe me always very truly and thankfully yours,

"ROBERT SOUTHEY."

To —— ——

"Keswick, Nov. 3, 1837.

"MY DEAR SIR,

"I have never seen the book to which you

* Dr. S. Mackenzie had reviewed the new edition of my father's poems in the Liverpool paper which he conducted, and had strongly urged him, by letter, not to be too brief in his autobiographical prefaces.

allude, but I suppose it to be that which bears the fictitious name of Search. The end which I should propose and expect from any theological investigation would be simply a conviction that Christianity is neither a fable cunningly devised, nor a superstition which has sprung from a combination of favoring causes, but that it is a scheme of Providence indicated by prophecies and proved by miracles. With this consent of the understanding, I should be satisfied in Y——'s case. The rest would assuredly follow in due time and in natural course.

"I could agree with you that 'personal identity unbroken by death' were little to be desired, if it were all—if we were to begin a new life in the nakedness of that identity. But when we carry with us in that second birth all that makes existence valuable, our hopes and aspirations, our affections, our eupathies, our capacities of happiness and of improvement—when we are to be welcomed into another sphere by those dear ones who have gone before us, and are in our turn to welcome there those whom we left on earth, surely, of all God's blessings, the revelation which renders this certain is the greatest. There have been times in my life when my heart would have been broken if this belief had not supported me. At this moment it is worth more than all the world could give.

* * * * * * *

"Nov. 4.

"The end can not be far off, and all is going on most mercifully. For several days, when I have supported her down stairs, I have thought it was for the last time; and every night, when she has been borne up, it has seemed to me that she would never be borne down alive. Thank God, there is no pain, no suffering of any kind, and only such consciousness as is consolation.

"God bless you! R. S."

To Joseph Cottle, Esq.

"Keswick, Nov. 16, 1837.

"My dear Cottle,

"It pleased God to release my poor dear Edith this morning from a pitiable state of existence, though we have always had the consolation of thinking it was more painful to witness than to endure. She had long been wasting away, and for the last month rapidly. For ten days she was unable to leave her bed. There seemed to be no suffering till excess of weakness became pain, and at no time any distress of mind; for being sensible where she was and with whom, and of the dutiful affection with which she was attended, she was sensible of nothing more.

"My poor daughters have been mercifully supported through their long trial. Now that the necessity for exertion is over, they feel that prostration which in such cases always ensues. But they have discharged their duties to the utmost, and they will have their reward. It is a blessed deliverance! the change from life to death, and from death to life! inexpressibly so for her.

"My dear old friend, yours affectionately, in weal or in woe, Robert Southey."*

CHAPTER XXXVIII.

MELANCHOLY THOUGHTS—INTENDED MOVEMENTS—REFLECTIONS ON HIS WIFE'S DEATH—LETTER FROM MR. BEDFORD—THE COPYRIGHT BILL—REVIEW IN THE EXAMINER—HIS WIFE CONTINUALLY BROUGHT TO MIND—WEAK STATE OF HIS HEALTH AND SPIRITS—MISS EDGEWORTH—INVITATION TO C. SWAIN—LETTER TO HIS SON ON COMMENCING A COLLEGE LIFE—STATE OF HIS HEALTH AND SPIRITS—LITERARY OCCUPATIONS—FROUDE'S REMAINS—THE DOCTOR—TOUR IN FRANCE—RETURN HOME—GREAT STORM—SAVONAROLA—CHATTERTON—MARRIAGE WITH MISS BOWLES—FAILURE OF MIND—HIS DEATH.—1837–1843.

I have just closed a melancholy chapter, and I must open another—the last—in which there is nothing cheerful to record. During the three years that my mother's afflicted state continued, my father had borne up wonderfully, and after the first shock had passed away, his spirits, though of course not what they had been, were uniformly cheerful, and he had found in the performance of a sacred duty that peace and comfort which in such paths is ever to be found. But when the necessity for exertion ceased, his spirits fell, and he became an altered man. Probably the long-continued effort began now to tell upon him, and the loss of her who for forty years, in sickness and health, had been the constant object of his thoughts, now caused a blank that nothing could fill. "I feel," he says, in one of his letters, "as one of the Siamese twins would do if the other had died, and he had survived the separation." He seemed, indeed, less able to accommodate himself to his altered circumstances than might have been expected from the turn of his mind and the nature of his pursuits.

To Henry Taylor, Esq.

"Keswick, Nov. 20, 1837.

"My dear H. T.,

"An ever-present sense of the uncertainty of all human projects does not, and indeed ought not, to prevent me from forecasting what course it may be best to pursue under any probable circumstances. For this I have had but too much opportunity for some time past, and temptation to it as well, for it was some kind of relief from the present and the past.

"About the middle of January Karl must begin his residence at Oxford. I think of giving him charge of Kate to London, from whence she will proceed to Tarring.

"Bertha and I must winter where we are. The house can not be left without a mistress.

"We shall find salutary occupations enough till Cuthbert returns about the end of March for

* This is endorsed, "The last letter which Joseph Cottle received from his old friend Robert Southey."

a month's recreation. That brings me to the month of May. By that time my extraordinaries will be provided for by the Admirals (whatever becomes of Cowper) or by the Q. R., for which I have two papers in hand (Sir T. Browne, and Lord Howe). Then, too, Miss Fricker will come from the Isle of Man to keep Mrs. Lovel company, and, in fact, look after the house during the summer months, thus placing Bertha and myself at liberty.

"In May, then (I do not look so far forward without misgivings)—but if all go on well, by God's blessing in May—I hope to leave home with Bertha and our invaluable Betty, whose services to us for five-and-twenty years, through weal and woe, have been beyond all price, who loves my children as dearly as if they were her own, and loved their poor mother with that sort of attachment which is now so rarely found in that relation, and served her with the most affectionate and dutiful fidelity to the last. The house might safely be left in her charge; but she needs recruiting as much as we do. So I shall go first with Bertha and her into Norfolk, and pass a week or ten days with Neville White, discharging thus a visit which was miserably prevented three years ago. Then we go to London, making little tarriance there, and that chiefly for Betty's sake, on whom the sight of London will not be thrown away. By that time Kate will have got through both her stay at Tarring and her visit to Miss Fenwick; and depositing Bertha at Tarring, I think of taking Kate with me to the West. One friend there I have lost since my last journey: it must have been about this very day twelve months that I shook hands with him, little thinking that it was for the last time. But there are still some persons there who will rejoice to see us. Old as my good aunt is, she may very probably be living; there is Elizabeth Charter there, and there is Lightfoot, with either of whom we should feel at home; on our way back there would be Miss Bowles; and very possibly Mrs. Brown may be in Devonshire.

"God bless you! R. S.

"It has been snowing this morning for the first time in the valley, but the snow having turned to rain, I shall presently prepare for my daily walk, from which nothing but snow deters me."

To Grosvenor C. Bedford, Esq

"Keswick, Nov. 24, 1837.

"MY DEAR G.,

"This event could not have been regarded otherwise than as a deliverance at any time, since there ceased to be a hope of mental restoration; and for several weeks it was devoutly to be desired. Yet it has left a sense of bereavement which I had not expected to feel, lost as she had been to me for the last three years, and worse than lost. During more than two thirds of my life, she had been the chief object of my thoughts, and I of hers. No man ever had a truer helpmate, no children a more careful mother. No family was ever more wisely ordered, no housekeeping ever conducted with greater prudence or greater comfort. Every thing was left to her management, and managed so quietly and so well, that, except in times of sickness and sorrow, I had literally no cares.

"I always looked upon it as conducing much to our happiness that we were of the same age, for in proportion to any perceptible disparity on that point, the marriage union is less complete; and so completely was she part of myself, that the separation makes me feel like a different creature. While she was herself, I had no sense of growing old, or, at most, only such as the mere lapse of time brought with it: there was no weight of years upon me; my heart continued young, and my spirits retained their youthful buoyancy. Now, the difference of five-and-thirty years between me and Bertha continually makes me conscious of being an old man. There is no one to partake with me the recollections of the best and happiest portion of my life; and for that reason, were there no other, such recollections must henceforth be purely painful, except when I connect them with the prospect of futurity.

"You will not suppose that I encourage this mood of mind. But it is well sometimes to look sorrow in the face, and always well to understand one's own condition.

* * * * * * *

"Meantime you may be assured that I shall not be wanting in self-management, as far as that can avail; that I shall think as little as I can of the past, and pursue as far as possible my wonted course of life.*

---

* I transcribe here the chief part of Mr. Bedford's admirable reply to this letter:

"MY DEAR SOUTHEY,

"Your letter, as you may suppose, is one of the highest interest to me, as affording a perfect picture of your present state of mind and feelings; and it is also satisfactory.

"However much the separation may have been anticipated, or, for her sake, even desirable, I am not at all surprised that you feel the sense of bereavement as you do at this moment, or that your recollection rather reverts to her in her happier days than in the last few years of sickness and helplessness. It is quite natural, and the period for such recollections will run its course, to be succeeded by a tender, a cherished, and in its effects a most consolatory feeling.

"If you and I had not resembled each other in some material points, we could not have maintained an unbroken intimacy for five-and-forty years, and when I speak from observation and experience of myself, I speak for you also. I may therefore, on these grounds, say that I believe few men have preserved the youth of their minds as long as we have. For my own part I am truly grateful for this, for I consider such a possession as one of Heaven's best blessings, inasmuch as it affords a protection against the evils of life, and, like youth of body, contains an elastic power of resistance to every blow, and encourages the spring and growth of hope in the very depth of misfortune. My dear Southey, I have no hesitation in believing that in due time you will again be such as you have been. You have great and happy means within your own reach for attaining this desirable state, in the society of your own excellent children, with whom you have ever lived so much like a brother, that I can not believe the difference in your mutual years can create any strong line of demarkation between you. You will now consider them with (if possible) increased love, and they will look to you with more reverent affection. Surely these must operate to break down the bar which difference of years might else interpose between you, to prevent that perfect intercourse and fellow-feeling which will constitute so much of your happiness and theirs. Recollection will operate to strengthen the tie on both sides. I have often called to mind the last act of my dear father's life that dis-

"Remember me most kindly to Miss Page. God bless you, my dear Grosvenor! R. S."

To H. Taylor, Esq.

"Keswick, Dec. 2, 1837.

"My dear H. T.,

"I have received Spring Rice's circular about the pensions, and take for granted that it comes as a mere circular, and therefore requires no answer.

"Moore and I being coupled upon this occasion, it is not likely that our pensions will be objected to, on either side of the House, upon the ground that literature, like any other profession, brings with it its own emoluments. But if that argument should be used against an enlargement of the copyright, which is not unlikely, it will be fitting that some one should state how the case stands in my instance: that, followed as a profession, with no common diligence and no ordinary success, it has enabled me to live respectably (which, without the aid of my first pension, it would not have done), and that all the provision I have been able to make for my family consists in a life insurance, of which about three fourths are covered by the salary of the laureateship. Were I to die before Talfourd's Bill passes, the greater part of my poems and no little of my prose would be seized immediately by some rascally booksellers, as property which the law allowed them to scramble for. It is true that, as the law now stands, I secure a new term of copyright by the corrected edition now in course of publication; but these fellows would publish from the former copies, and thereby take in all those purchasers who know nothing about the difference between one edition and another.

"It is well that Windham is not living, and that there is no one in either house on whom his mantle has fallen, for he would surely have taken the opposite side to Talfourd, and argued upon the folly of altering an established law for the sake of benefiting one or two individuals in the course of a century. He would ask what the copyrights are which would at this time be most beneficial to the family of the author: the Cookery Book would stand first; within my recollection, the most valuable would have been Blair's Lectures, the said Blair's Sermons, Taplin's Farriery, Burn's Justice, and Lindley Murray's English Grammar.

* * * * * * *

"Monday, 4.

"Thank you for the Examiners; they shall be duly returned. I would never desire better praise, and must not complain because there is more of it than is good. In the piece which they praise as resembling Cowper, there is nothing Cowperish; and, on the other hand, in the substitution of the general crimes of the Terrorists in France for the instances of Brissot and Madame Roland, there is nothing but what is in perfect accord with the pervading sentiment of the poem. Madame Roland's praise is left where it was appropriate, in the second volume. As for Brissot, I knew him only by newspapers, when his death, and that of the great body of the Girondists with him, kept me (as I well remember) a whole night sleepless. But I know him now by two volumes of his Memoirs, which, though *made up*, are from family materials; and I know him by nine volumes of his own works, and thereby know that he was a poor creature. And I know by Garat's book that the difference between the Brissotines and the Jacobines was that, playing for heads, the Brissotines lost the game.

"God bless you! R. S."

To Henry Taylor, Esq.

"Keswick, Dec. 14, 1837.

"My dear H. T.,

" * * * * * * *

It can not often have happened that any one should have a lost wife brought to his mind in the way that I am continually reminded of my poor Edith. Before any of my children were old enough to make extracts for me, it was one of her pleasures to assist me in that way. Many hundred notes in her writing (after so many have been made use of) are arranged among the materials to which every day of my life I have occasion to refer, and thus she will continue to be my helpmate as long as I live and retain my senses. But all these notes bring with them the vivid recollection of the when, and the where, and the why they were made; and whether the sight of her hand-writing will ever be regarded without emotion, is more than I can promise myself.

"God bless you! R. S."

To Grosvenor C. Bedford, Esq.

"Keswick, Dec. 29, 1837.

"My dear G.,

"I was not aware that it was so long since you had heard *from* me; *of* me you could only have heard from H. T., with whom I have a pretty constant communication, owing to the transmission of proofs. These come thick; there has been little tinkering in the third volume, but the sixth, on which I am at work, requires a good deal, in repairing some old wefts and strays, and preparing prolegomena. Moreover, I am reviewing Barrow's Life of Lord Howe; so you see I am not idle.

"In other respects I can give no good report of myself. There is every possible reason to be thankful for my poor Edith's release, and God knows I am truly thankful for it. But my spirits, which bore up through three trying years, and continued to do so while there was immediate necessity for exertion, show as yet no tendency

played consciousness, and always with such pleasure as I look for for you. Henry and I were standing on each side of the bed, with one of his hands in each of ours. He had long lain quite still, and only breathed, when, to our joint surprise, he lifted one, the disabled arm, and brought our two hands in union across his breast. After that he never moved for several hours, but passed imperceptibly to a state, I hope and trust, of happiness. Excuse me for this, but I always dwell upon the recollection of that act with delight, and though it be of the tenderest character, it is unmingled with pain. * * * * * * *

"Ever yours, my dear Southey,

"G. C. Bedford."

to recover that elasticity which they lost when the necessity ceased. Time will set all to rights. As the days lengthen, I shall be able to rise earlier, which will be a great benefit, the worst hours being those in which I lie awake, and they are many. The best are those when I am employed, and you know I am not given to idleness; but it behooves me to manage myself in this respect. Except in the main point of sleep, the bodily functions go on well. I walk duly and dutifully. But I am as much disposed to be silent in my own family now, as I ever was in company for which I felt little or no liking; and if it were not plainly a matter of duty to resist this propensity, I should never hear the sound of my own voice.

* * * * * * *

"Nothing more has been heard of Baldwin and Cradock's affairs. But I must tell you what it will give you pleasure to hear. As soon as Lightfoot learned that the sum which I had (as I thought) provided for carrying Cuthbert through the University was supposed to be in danger of being lost, he offered to relieve me from all anxiety upon that score. Knowing the sincerity of that offer, I am just as much obliged to him as if there were any necessity for accepting it. But Dr. Bell's legacy is available for that purpose. And as for my Cowperage, if it be recovered, as I think it will, so much the better; if it be lost, it will never enter into the thoughts that keep me wakeful at night, or in the slightest degree trouble me by day.

* * * * * * *

"To-day (30th) the sun shines, and it is some satisfaction to see that there still is a sun, for he has been so long among the *non apparentibus*, that if I jumped to my conclusions as eagerly as some of our modern philosophers, I might have pronounced him to be not in existence.

"Your brother ought to reflect that though it is many a poor fellow's duty to expose his life upon deck, and to lose it there, it is no man's duty to die at the desk; and, as I once heard a medical student say, when he expressed his satisfaction at having escaped being taken upon a resurrectionary party, 'there is no glory in it.' The first duty of any man, upon whose life the happiness or the well-being of others is in great degree dependent, is to take care of it. God bless you! Our love to Miss Page. R. S."

To Dr. Shelton Mackenzie.

"Keswick, Jan. 25, 1838.

"MY DEAR SIR,

"I am much obliged to you for your good services in one paper, and the Canadian news in another. It has never been my fortune to be engaged with any bookseller who made good use of the periodical press to promote the sale of any of my works. They lay out lavishly in advertisements, when a tenth part of the money so expended would, if laid out in extracts, produce ten times the effect.

"I recollect hearing of Miss Edgeworth* at Dr. Holland's, but have no recollection of seeing her there; but I very well remember seeing her more than once at Clifton in 1800, at which time her father said to me, 'Take my word for it, sir, your genius is for comedy.' He formed this opinion, I believe, from some of the Nondescripts, and one or two Ballads which had just then appeared in the Annual Anthology. This, I think, will be worth mentioning in the Preface to the Ballads. When you write to Miss Edgeworth, present my thanks for her obliging message, and say that I am pleased at being remembered by her.

"It is mortifying to think how few situations there are in this country for men of letters—fewer, I believe, than in any other part of civilized Europe—and what there are, leave the occupant very little leisure to profit by the stores of learning with which he is surrounded. The editorship of the ——, or of any literary journal, would be a more agreeable office than that of a public librarian, in this respect that your own mind would have more scope; and private librarians there are very few. Lord Spencer, I suppose, must have one as a matter of necessity. The only instance within my knowledge in which a man of letters was invited to such an appointment not because the library was extensive enough to need his attendance, but because it was thought desirable for him, is that of Jeremiah Wiffen, and no doubt he owed it to his being a native of Woburn. The Duke of Bedford might otherwise never have heard of him, nor cared for him if he had. Farewell, my dear sir.

"Yours very truly,

"ROBERT SOUTHEY."

To Charles Swain, Esq.

"Keswick, March 9, 1838.

"MY DEAR SIR,

"Since you heard from me last I have been so much shaken that there is little likelihood of my ever being myself again. But it would be ungrateful indeed in me to complain, who have had a greater share of happiness than falls to the lot of one in ten thousand, and that happiness of a higher degree and of much longer continuance, with health that had scarcely ever been interrupted, and with a flow of spirits that never ebbed. I can not be too thankful for these manifold blessings, let the future be what it may.

"Cuthbert comes home the first week in April for about a month's vacation. Can you give yourself a holiday, and pass with us as much of that month as you can spare? I can not now climb the mountains with you—not for want of strength,

* Dr. Mackenzie had mentioned to Miss Edgeworth that my father was employed in working up materials for his own life, and had communicated the substance of her reply, which was as follows:

"I thank you for telling me that Southey is engaged in literary biography. His Life of Nelson is one of the finest pieces of biography I know. I have seen its effects on many young minds. I had the honor of meeting Mr. Southey some years since, at our mutual friend's, Dr. Holland's, in London. But such is the nature of that sort of town intercourse, that I had not opportunity of hearing much of his conversation, and he none of mine; therefore I can hardly presume that he remembers me. But I would wish to convey to him, through you, the true expression of my respect for his character, and admiration of his talents, and of the use he has made of them."

still less of inclination, but because of an infirmity (I know not how or when occasioned) but recently discovered, which condemns me to caution, at least, for the rest of my life. But I shall be heartily glad to see you, and to make your visit as pleasant as I can. You were the last guest whom my dear Edith received with pleasure.

"Most persons, I believe, are displeased with any alterations that they find in a favorite poem; the change, whether for the better or the worse, balks them, as it were, and it is always unpleasant to be balked. In tinkering one's old verses, there is a great chance of making two flaws where you are mending one. However, to my great joy, I have now done with tinkering; the last pieces which required correction on the score of language are in that volume of Ballads (beginning with The Maid of the Inn), which come next in order of publication. I know not yet how the adventure is likely to turn out. The number struck off at first was 1500, which the publishers say will just about cover the expenses, leaving the profit to arise from any further use of the stereotype and the engravings. Something may be expected from the occasional sale of separate portions, for which merely a new title-page will be required; in that way the long poems may tempt purchasers by their cheapness. But, apart from all other considerations, I am very thankful that I was persuaded, against my inclination, and in some degree, also, against my judgment, to undertake such a revision of my poetical works. The sort of testamentary feeling with which it was undertaken may prove to have been *an ominous one:* certain it is, that if the task had been deferred but a few months, I should never have had heart to perform it, though it was a duty which I owe to myself and to the interests of my family.

"And now, my dear sir, God bless you!

"Yours with sincere regard,

"ROBERT SOUTHEY."

To C. C. Southey, Esq.

"Keswick, Feb. 7, 1838.

"MY DEAR CUTHBERT,

"It is right that you should clearly understand what you have to reckon on for your ways and means. Two hundred a year will be a liberal allowance, probably above the average at Queen's, which has not the disadvantage of being an expensive college. Whether I live or die, this is provided for you. If I live and do well, my current occupations will supply it. In any other event, there is Dr. Bell's legacy in the French Funds, even if the Cowperage should not be forthcoming.

"It is an uncomfortable thing to be straitened in your situation; but, for most under-graduates, it is far more injurious to have too much. If you can save from your income, I shall be glad; and I have confidence enough in you to believe that you would have much more satisfaction in saving from it than you could derive from any needless expenditure. I do no not mean that you should receive less from me, if you find that you can do with less, but that you should lay by the surplus for your own use. Next to moral and religious habits, habits of frugality are the most important; they belong, indeed, to our duties. In this virtue your dear mother never was surpassed. Had it not been for her admirable management, this house could not have been kept up, nor this family brought up as they were. God never blessed any man with a truer helpmate than she was to me in this and in every other respect, till she ceased to be herself.

"I dwell upon this, not as supposing you need any exhortation upon the subject, for I have the most perfect confidence in you; no father ever had less apprehension for a son in sending him to the University. But frugality is a virtue which will contribute continually and most essentially to your comfort; without it, it is impossible that you should do well, and you know not how much nor how soon it may be needed. It is far from my intention, if I should live till you take your degree, to hurry you into the world, and bid you shift for yourself as soon as you can. On the contrary, there is nothing on which I could look forward with so much hope as to directing your studies after you have finished your collegiate course, and training you to build upon my foundations. That object is one which it would be worth wishing to live for. But when you take your degree, I, if I should then be living, shall be hard upon threescore and ten. My whole income dies with me. In its stead there would be (at this time) about £8000 immediately from the insurance, and this is all that there will be (except £200 or £300 for current expenses) till my papers and copyrights can be made available. At first, therefore, great frugality will be required, though eventually there may be a fair provision for all. I make no estimate of my library, because, if it please God that you should make use of the books in pursuing my course, they would be of more value to you than any sum that could be raised by dispersing them.

"It is fitting that you should bear all this in mind, but not for discouragement. Your prospects, God be thanked, are better than if you were heir to a large estate—far better for your moral and intellectual nature, your real welfare, your happiness here and hereafter.

"God bless you, my dear Cuthbert!

"Your affectionate father,

"ROBERT SOUTHEY."

To the Rev. Neville White.

"Keswick, Feb. 14, 1838.

"MY DEAR NEVILLE,

"Long ago I ought to have written to you, but to you and my other friends I have as little excuse to offer as an insolvent debtor can make to his creditors. Of late, indeed, I have waited not so much for a more convenient season as for better spirits and for better health. I have been very much out of order in many ways—old infirmities reappeared and brought others in their train, and I could both see and feel such changes in myself as induced a not unreasonable apprehension that my constitution was breaking up. I have had recourse, under my brother's direction, to tonics and opiates: they have quieted the most distressing symptoms, and abated others, and I hope that milder weather, when it comes, will rid me of what I suppose to be rheumatic affection in the right hip. So much for my maladies. No one can have enjoyed better health than I have been favored with during what has now not been a short life, nor has any one been blessed with a greater portion of happiness—happiness not to be surpassed in this world in its kind and degree, and continued through a long course of years. I never can be too thankful to the Giver of all good.

"I have recovered sufficiently to be in trim for work, though it is hardly to be expected that I should do any thing with the same heart and hope as in former days. However, I shall do my best, and endeavor, by God's mercy, to take the remaining stage of my journey as cheerily as I can.

"Remember me most kindly to your fireside; and believe me always, my dear Neville, yours with true and affectionate regard,

"ROBERT SOUTHEY."

At this time he was laboring under apprehension of an infirmity which, though not dangerous, would have prevented him taking active exercise, and caused him great inconvenience and discomfort, and this naturally preyed somewhat on his spirits; fortunately, however, he determined at once to seek London advice, and went up to town to consult Sir B. Brodie, who quickly relieved his apprehension, pronouncing that there was no real cause for alarm.

He consequently returned home, reassured on this point.

To Miss Charter.

"Keswick, April 11, 1838.

"DEAR MISS CHARTER,

"I am much obliged to you for all the trouble you have taken; trouble being, I am sorry to say, the only privilege accruing at present from the title of friend, which you have possessed with me for so many years, and will continue to hold while we retain any remembrance of the past.

* * * * * * *

"I have now been returned a week, in which time I have been fully employed in writing letters and correcting proof-sheets, except yesterday, when great part of the day was passed upon the sofa, for the sake of putting to sleep a cold in the head. The weather has been wet and stormy; and it is better that I should keep within doors, than continue to brave all weathers, as I was wont to do, till I get into good condition again, if it please God. Shaken as I have been, there is still a reasonable hope of this.

" * * Kate is at Mr. Rickman's now. Bertha was very busily employed during my absence in painting and papering—making alterations which are not the less melancholy because it was necessary that they should be made. She has made a good choice in her cousin Herbert; and happy man is his dole, I may say with equal truth. They may have long to wait before he gets a living; but meantime there is hope, without which life is but a living death. He loves literature, and his situation as second librarian at the Bodleian is favorable for literary pursuits. My papers may be intrusted to his care, if I should die before Cuthbert is old enough to superintend their publication.

* * * * * * *

"Cuthbert's vacation is only for a month. He must be at chapel on Sunday the 29th. I shall proceed the more earnestly with my work, that I may have the shorter time to pass in solitude and silence. What I have to do is to get through a volume of the Admirals, in which little progress has been made, and a reviewal of Sir Thomas Browne's works. My Poems require no further tinkering; I have only to correct the proofs of the remaining three volumes, and to write the prefaces to them. Arranged and dated as the Poems now are, they communicate to those who have known me well much of my history and character; and a great deal has been reserved which there would have been no propriety in telling the public while I am in the land of the living. There is nothing, thank God, which I could wish to be concealed after my death; but the less that a living author says of himself (except in verse), the better. God bless you, dear Miss Charter!

"Yours with sincere regard, R. S."

To ——— ———.

"Easter Monday (April 16), 1838.

"MY DEAR SIR,

" * * * * * * *

God forgive those who bring upon others any unhappiness which could be prevented by a wiser and kinder course of conduct. If we could be spared the misery which others make for us, little would there be but what might be borne with wholesome resignation as the appointment of Providence, or as the proper consequence of our own errors and misdeeds.

"Time will do all for you, and will probably not be long in doing it. With an old subject like me there is more to do, and of that kind that there is little hope it can be done before the curtain falls. I could always, when I went from home, leave all my habits behind me. It is a far different thing to feel that I have lost them—that my way of life is changed, the few points which are unchangeable serving only to make the change in all other respects more sensible.

"I thank God I am well in health, having easily got rid of a cold; and now that all the proofs in your packet have been got through, and directions given to the printer concerning the eighth volume, I shall make up my dispatches, set my clogs by the fire, and emerge from solitude; not to look for society which is not to be found, nor to be wished for, out of a very small circle which every year contracts, but to take a dutiful walk. God bless you! R. S."

To Henry Taylor, Esq.

"Keswick, June 10, 1838.

"My dear H. T.,

'Whether Hope and I shall ever become intimate again in this world, except on the pilgrimage to the next, is very doubtful; nor ought it to be of much importance to a man in his sixty-fourth year. I have had a large portion of happiness, and of the highest kind: five-and-thirty years of such happiness few men are blessed with. I have drunk, too, of the very gall of bitterness; yet not more than was wholesome: the cup has been often administered, no doubt because it was needed. The moral discipline through which I have passed has been more complete than the intellectual. Both began early; and, all things considered, I do not think any circumstances could have been more beneficial to me than those in which I have been placed. If not hopeful, therefore, I am more than contented, and disposed to welcome and entertain any good that may yet be in store for me, without any danger of being disappointed if there should be none.

"I am very glad that Kate is to join Miss Fenwick; but I must warn both Kate and Dora against converting dormitories into loquitories, and talking each other to death before they get to the end of their journey. God bless you!

"R. S."

To the Rev. John Miller.

"Keswick, July 21, 1838.

"My dear Sir,

"I was very much pleased with Bishop Jebb's first opinion of your Bampton Lectures, and not less pleased with the greater part of his more elaborate critique. I did not agree with him in any of his objections, nor has a fresh perusal of that critique, after reading your Preface, altered or even modified my first impression in the slightest degree. It appears to me that you were right in noticing his remarks as fully as you have done, and that it could not have been done in a better spirit nor in a more conclusive manner.

"The publication of Froude's Remains is likely to do more harm than —— is capable of doing. 'The Oxford School' has acted most unwisely in giving its sanction to such a deplorable example of mistaken zeal. Of the two extremes —the too little and the too much—the too little is that which is likely to produce the worst consequence to the individual, but the too much is more hurtful to the community; for it spreads, and rages too, like a contagion.

* * * * * * *

"I hear, though I have not seen, that another volume of The Doctor is announced. You and I, therefore, may shortly expect it, if the masked author keeps his good custom of sending it to us. Some letters, published in the Sheffield Mercury, have been collected into two small volumes, entitled 'The Tour of the Don.' They contain a chapter which is headed 'Doncaster and the Doctor.' The writer reminds the Doncasterians of the visit, 'not a clandestine one,' of the worthy laureate to their good town, some ten years agone, accompanied, as some may recollect, by his lovely daughter, 'the dark-eyed Bertha;' and this he mentions as one of the facts which 'appear indubitably to identify the author of The Doctor with the author of Thalaba.' The conclusion would not have followed, even if the premises had been true. But the truth upon which he has built a fallacious argument is, that about ten years ago I passed a night at *Sheffield* on the way to London. My daughter *Edith* was one of our traveling party; and certainly there was nothing clandestine in the visit, for I wrote notes to Montgomery and to Ebenezer Elliott to come to me at the inn—the only time I ever saw either of those remarkable men. James Everett, a Methodist preacher, and also a remarkable man, heard from one of them where I was, and volunteered a visit. So it was soon known that I was in Sheffield. It is not often that a mistake of this kind can so plainly be explained. 'Well,' Latimer used to say, 'there is nothing hid but it shall be opened.'

"Farewell, my dear sir; and believe me always yours with sincere regard and respect,

"Robert Southey."

For some time my father had been meditating a short journey on the Continent, to which his friends also urged him, in the hopes it might aid in re-establishing his health and spirits, which, though both were somewhat amended, seemed greatly to need some change. A party of six was accordingly soon formed for the purpose, and a tour arranged, through Normandy, Brittany, and a part of Touraine, to terminate at Paris.

The party consisted of Mr. Senhouse, of Netherhall, who had been with my father in Switzerland in 1817; Mr. Kenyon, also a friend of long standing; Mr. Henry Crabbe Robinson, and Captain Jones, R.N.; my father and myself made up the number. At the end of August we all met in London, and, crossing to Calais, commenced our excursion, the course of which is indicated in the next letter, and which proved as agreeable as favorable weather, an interesting line of country, and a party disposed to be pleased with every thing could make it.

In all we saw my father took much interest, and while we were actually traveling, the change and excitement seemed to keep his mind up to its usual pitch. He bore all inconveniences with his wonted good humor, and his vast stores of historical knowledge furnished abundant topics of conversation.

Still, however, I could not fail to perceive a considerable change in him from the time we had last traveled together: all his movements were slower, he was subject to frequent fits of absence, and there was an indecision in his manner, and an unsteadiness in his step, which was wholly unusual with him.

The point in which he seemed to me to fail most was, that he continually lost his way, even in the hotels we stopped at; and, perceiving this, I watched him constantly, as, although he himself affected to make light of it, and laughed at his own mistakes, he was evidently sometimes painfully conscious of his failing memory in this respect.

His journal also, for he still kept up his old habit of recording minutely all he saw, is very different from that of former journeys—breaks off abruptly when about two thirds of our tour was completed, and shows, especially toward the close, a change in his hand-writing, which, as his malady crept on, became more and more marked, until, in some of the last notes he ever wrote, the letters are formed like the early efforts of a child.

To John May, Esq.

"Dieppe, Sept. 2, 1838.

"MY DEAR JOHN MAY,

"Thus far our journey has been in all respects favorable. You saw us proceeding with weather which was only too fine, inasmuch as it soon became hot and dusty, such weather bringing with it a plague of flies, who insisted upon being inside passengers, and whenever I was inclined to doze, and, indeed, could not keep awake, some one of the Egyptian enemies presently awakened me by alighting upon the most prominent feature of my face. We had a short and pleasant passage the next morning, and remained one day at Calais for the purpose of engaging carriages for the journey, Kenyon having recommended that we should travel post, as the only means by which we could command our own time, choose our own route, stop where we would, and remain as long as seemed good to us at any place. This I had found the most advisable mode when traveling with poor Nash and Senhouse in 1817.

"I am now writing at Blois, on Friday, Sept. 28. Our faces were turned homeward when we left Nantes on Sunday last, Sept. 23. We had then accomplished the two chief objects of our journey—that is, we had been to Mount St. Michael's and to Carnac, the only two days concerning which there could be any solicitude concerning the state of the weather. In both instances we were most fortunate. We came to the mount during the neap tides and in a clear day, escaping thus all dangers and inconveniences that, at ordinary tides, the state of the weather might have occasioned, and fogs at any time. Cuthbert and I had seen our own St. Michael's Mount in 1836. The French is the more remarkable, because of its position, which is always a waste either of water or of sand. The mount itself is not much higher, if at all, I think, than the Cornish Mount, but the superstructure of building is much greater, including a small fishing town, a large prison, a garison, houses for the governor and other officers, and, on the summit, a church. Our own mount, on the contrary, is far the more beautiful object, and, except a few mean houses at the landing-places, there is nothing to excite any uncomfortable reflections. The rock itself reminded me of Cintra in this respect, that it consisted in great part of rocks piled on rocks, and on the summit the governor's house and the church very much resembled in their situation the Penha Convent. The mount stands also in a small bay, and is itself a beautiful object, in a part of the country which is itself regarded as the most genial part of the West of England.

"Another place which we were desirous of seeing was the great Druidical monuments, known by the name of Carnac, from the nearest village. They are the most extensive Druidical remains that have yet been discovered, the stones at the lowest computation not being fewer than four thousand, and extending in parallel lines over a great extent of country; none of these are so large as those of Stonehenge, and they are all single stones. But there are many of considerable magnitude, and many have been destroyed before a stop was put by authority to such destruction, and many are built up in walls; but there remains enough to astonish the beholder.

"To-day we have seen the Castle of Amboise, which Louis Philippe began to repair when he was Duke of Orleans, but which, though it is a beautiful place, commanding fine views, and in itself a comfortable palace, there being nothing too large to be inconsistent with comfort, he has never set foot in himself. I can account for this only by supposing that as the very beautiful chapel which they are repairing contains the intended mausoleum for himself and his royal family, that consideration may dispose him to regard it with a melancholy feeling, which he is not willing to induce.

"To-morrow we shall see what is most worth seeing at Blois, and proceed after breakfast to Orleans, where we shall remain on Sunday. I should tell you that I have seen Joan of Arc's monument at Rouen, and the Castle of Chinon, and the apartment in the ruins there in which she had her first interview with the king; so, when I shall have seen Orleans, I shall have sufficient knowledge of the localities to correct any mistakes into which I may, indeed must, have fallen.

"The other places of most interest which we have seen are Havre, by which port I propose returning, Honfleur, Caen, Bayeux, Granville, St. Malo, Nantes, Angers, Saumur, Tours. Normandy and Bretagne we have seen satisfactorily, and were as much delighted with Normandy as we were surprised by the miserable condition and more miserable appearance of our Breton cousins: they seem not to partake in the slightest degree of that prosperity which is every where else apparent in France. Louis Philippe is both Pontifex and Viafex maximus, if there be such a word. The roads are undergoing, at the expense of government, a most thorough repair, greatly to our annoyance in traveling over them in the course of remaking. I know not how many suspension bridges we have seen, finished or in progress, and every large place bears evident marks of improvement upon a great scale.

"I hope to be at Paris on the 4th or 5th of October. There our party separates: Kenyon and Captain Jones proceed to the Low Countries; Robinson remains a while at Paris; Cuthbert, I, and Mr. Senhouse make our way by one steamer down the Seine to Havre, and by another from Havre to Southampton. From thence Cuthbert proceeds to London and Oxford, Senhouse to Cumberland, and I to Lymington, where I shall remain a few weeks with Miss Bowles, and get through some work, where I shall be free from all interruption.

"I have had no opportunity of purchasing any books, there being no old book shops in any of the great towns through which we have passed; but at Paris my only business will be to look for those which I want.

"And now, my dear old friend, God bless you! Remember me to your daughters, and believe me always yours most affectionately,

"Robert Southey."

To John Rickman, Esq.

"Buckland, Lymington, Oct., 1838.

"My dear R.,

"I heard good accounts of you on my journey, and having since seen that you were present at the prorogation, venture to infer that you are no longer under the oculist's care.

"Nothing could be more fortunate than my expedition was in every thing. The weather was as fine as it could be. During six weeks there was not one wet day; what rain fell was generally by night, and never more than sufficed for laying the dust and cooling the air. We got to Carnac. Chantrey had desired me to look for some small red stones,* which Buckland, or some of his disciples, had been much puzzled about, because they are not pebbles of the soil, and have all evidently been rubbed down to different angles. Just such stones so rubbed are used by Chantrey's own people in polishing the finer parts of their statuary; and he fancied this was proof that the people who erected the stones at Carnac must have used them for some similar purpose. I came to the conclusion that the *Celts*, which are so hard and so highly polished, were brought to that high polish by these instruments.

"The Bretons are the most miserable people I have ever seen, except those inhabitants of the Alps who suffer with goîtres, and among whom the Cretons are found. They look, indeed, as if they lived in an unhealthy country, and as if they were only half fed. Yet I know not that there are any causes to render it insalubrious: it is not ill cultivated, and there is no want of industry in the inhabitants. The only cause that I can imagine for their squalid appearance and their evidently stunted stature (if that cause be sufficient) is their extreme uncleanness. The human animal can not thrive in its own filth, like the pig; and the pig, no doubt, is a very inferior creature in its tame state to what it is when wild in the forest.

"I never saw so many dwarfs any where as in Brittany—more, indeed, when traveling through that province than in the whole course of my life.

* We found a number of these stones, all in one place, as if they had been poured out in a heap, nearly overgrown with grass and weeds. I brought some home, and took them to Sir F. Chantrey, who recognized them as of the same description as those he had seen before.—Ed.

"There is one work which Mr. Telford would have regarded with great interest if he ever happened to see it—the Levée, as it is called, which protects a large tract of country from the inundations of the Loire. This work is of such antiquity that it is not known when it was commenced, but it seems first to have been taken up as a public work by our Henry II. Perhaps there is no other embankment which protects so great an extent of country.

"I am finishing here the reviewal of Telford's book, which I hope to complete in about a week's time, taking care not to make it too long, and therefore passing rapidly over his latter works, and winding up in the way of a eulogium, which no man ever was more worthy of.

"I derived all the benefit that I hoped for from my journey, and am in good condition in all respects. God bless you! R. S."

To Mrs. Hodson.

"Keswick, Feb. 18, 1839.

"My dear Mrs. Hodson,

"My movements last year did not extend beyond Normandy and Bretagne, and when I turned my face toward England, it was in a steam packet from Havre to Southampton, by good fortune just before that stormy weather set in, which, with few intervals, and those but short, has continued ever since. Normandy pleased me as much as I had expected, and my expectations were pitched high. We were six in company, and no journey could have been more prosperous in all respects. The weather never prevented us from seeing any thing that we wished, and we met no mishap of any kind.

"Cuthbert and I parted when we left the steam packet. He made the best of his way to Oxford; I remained some weeks in Hampshire, and on returning to Keswick found my youngest daughter suffering under a serious attack of the influenza;* an insidious disease, from which, though we were assured that she was well recovered, she has not yet regained strength. You may possibly have heard from the newspapers that I have resolved upon a second marriage. I need not say that such a marriage must be either the wisest or the weakest action of a man's life; but I may say that in the important points of age, long and intimate acquaintance, and conformity of opinions, principles, and likings, no persons could be better suited to each other. The newspapers, indeed, have stated that Miss Bowles is thirty years younger than me, which, if it were true, would prove me to be something worse than an old fool.

"You will be glad to hear that I am likely to recover something from Baldwin and Cradock. The trustees of their affairs had the modesty to expect that I should receive a dividend of one shilling in the pound, to be followed by a second and final dividend of the same amount. But upon finding that I was prepared to file a bill in Chan-

* Upon this a sharp attack of pleurisy had supervened, and we were for some little time in alarm as to the result. —Ed.

cery against them, they have proposed to pay me eight hundred pounds—a composition which I am advised to accept, and shall think myself fortunate when it is fairly paid.

"This place and the surrounding country suffered greatly in the late hurricane: it was quite as violent as that which I witnessed at Dawlish, and of much longer duration. I never felt the house so shaken. Indeed, there were persons who came as soon as it was daybreak to see what had become of us, and whether we were buried in the ruins of the house. Happily, we suffered no serious injury, having chiefly to regret that the whole front of the house, which was covered with ivy, has been completely stripped of it. The havoc among the trees* has been such as the oldest persons do not remember to have seen or heard of. Few days have passed without a storm since the great one. The winds are piping at this time, and so continued is the sound that my head is almost as much confused by it as if I were at sea. The weather concerns me much more than the affairs of state, and I know as little of current literature as if there were neither magazines nor reviews. My state is the more gracious. And if there were no newspapers in the world, and no rail-roads, I should begin to think that we might hope to live once more in peace and quietness.

"I heard of Landor during my last transit through London, and saw one of the very best portraits of him by a young artist that I ever remember to have seen. The picture, too, was as good as the likeness. The artist did not succeed so well with Kenyon, whose head upon the canvas might very well have passed for the Duke of York's.

"You will think that I am bent upon continuing in the old ways when I tell you that it is my intention never again to travel by a rail-way, if there be any means of proceeding by any other mode of conveyance. It is very certain that the rapidity of rail-way traveling, if long continued, has a tendency to bring on a determination of blood to the head: this is one of the unforeseen and unforeseeable results of a mode of traveling so unlike any thing that was ever before in use. Mail-coach traveling will be fast enough for me, if I should ever travel again after the journey to which I am now looking forward of four hundred miles, which I mean to take with no other rest than what is to be had in the mail. But I expect to doze away the time. When I was a schoolboy there was nothing I should have liked better than such a journey.

"Present my kind remembrances to Mr. and Mrs. Blencowe, &c.

"Believe me, my dear Mrs. Hodson,

"Yours with sincere regard,

"ROBERT SOUTHEY."

* "A poplar, mentioned in the proem to the Tale of Paraguay, was torn up by the roots. It had become for some years a mournful memorial, and though I should never have had heart to fell it, I am not sorry that it has been thus removed. But do not suppose that I ever give willing admission to thoughts of unprofitable sadness."—*To H. Taylor, Esq., Jan.* 8, 1839.

To Walter Savage Landor, Esq.

"Buckland, March 31, 1839.

"MY DEAR LANDOR,

"The portrait of Savonarola is safely lodged at Keswick; I should have thanked you for it sooner, if I had known whither to direct to you. I have seldom seen a finer picture or a finer face; the countenance seems to bespeak credit for one whose character may perhaps be still considered doubtful.

"Mr. C. Bowles Fripp wrote to me some time last year, asking me to supply an epitaph for the proposed monument to Chatterton. I said to him, in reply, that I was too much engaged to undertake it; that, as far as related to Chatterton, I had done my duty more than thirty years ago; that of all men, men of genius were those who stood least in need of monuments to perpetuate their memory. Moreover, as to an epitaph, I never would attempt to compose any thing of the kind, unless I imagined that I could do it satisfactorily to myself, which in this case appeared to me impossible. How, indeed, could the circumstances of Chatterton's history be comprised in a monumental inscription? It is to the credit of Bristol that my fellow-townsmen should show how different a spirit prevails among them now from that which was to be found there fifty years ago; but how this might best be effected I know not.

"The portrait of Chatterton, which Mr. Dix discovered, identifies itself if ever portrait did. It brought his sister, Mrs. Newton, strongly to my recollection. No family likeness could be more distinctly marked, considering the disparity of years.

"My daughter Bertha's marriage to her cousin, Herbert Hill, is especially fortunate in this respect, that for a few years it will remove her no further from Keswick than Rydal. Very different has been her elder sister's lot; for being, to all likelihood, fixed upon the coast of Sussex (and the very worst part of it), she has been lost to us ever since. I have now only one daughter left, and my son divides the year between college and home. Oxford has done him no harm; indeed, I never apprehended any. Reduced in number as my family has been within the last few years, my spirits would hardly recover their habitual and healthful cheerfulness if I had not prevailed upon Miss Bowles to share my lot for the remainder of our lives. There is just such a disparity of age as is fitting; we have been well acquainted with each other more than twenty years, and a more perfect conformity of disposition could not exist; so that, in resolving upon what must be either the weakest or the wisest act of a sexagenarian's life, I am well assured that, according to human foresight, I have judged well and acted wisely, both for myself and my remaining daughter. God bless you!

"ROBERT SOUTHEY."

On the 5th of June my father was united to Miss Bowles, at Boldre Church, and returned to Keswick with her the latter end of the following August.

I have now almost arrived at the conclusion of my task, yet what remains to be said calls up more painful recollections than all the rest.

The reader need not be told that the sorrows and anxieties of the last few years of my father's life had produced, as might be expected, a very injurious effect upon his constitution, both as to body and mind. Acutely sensitive by nature, deep and strong in his affections, and highly predisposed to nervous disease, he had felt the sad affliction which had darkened his latter years far more keenly than any ordinary observer would have supposed, or than even appears in his letters. He had, indeed, then, as he expressed himself in his letter declining the baronetcy, been "shaken at the root;" and while we must not forget the more than forty years of incessant mental application which he had passed through, it was this stroke of calamity which most probably greatly hastened the coming of the evil day, if it was not altogether the cause of it, and which rapidly brought on that overclouding of the intellect which soon unequivocally manifested itself.

This, indeed, in its first approaches, had been so gradual as to have almost escaped notice; and it was not until after the sad truth was fully ascertained that indications of failure (some of which I have already alluded to) which had appeared some time previously were called to mind. A loss of memory on certain points; a lessening acuteness of the perceptive faculties; an occasional irritability (wholly unknown in him before); a confusion of time, place, and person; the losing his way in well-known places—all were remembered as having taken place when the melancholy fact had become too evident that the powers of his mind were irreparably weakened.

On his way home in the year 1839, he passed a few days in London, and then his friends plainly saw, what, from the altered manner of the very few and brief letters he had latterly written, they had already feared, that he had so failed as to have lost much of the vigor and activity of his faculties. The impressions of one of his most intimate friends, as conveyed at the time by letter, may fitly be quoted here. "I have just come home from a visit which affected me deeply. * * It was to Southey, who arrived in town to-day from Hampshire with his wife. * * He is (I fear) much altered. The animation and peculiar clearness of his mind quite gone, except a gleam or two now and then. What he said was much in the spirit of his former mind as far as the matter and meaning went, but the tone of strength and elasticity was wanting. The appearance was that of a placid languor, sometimes approaching to torpor, but not otherwise than cheerful. He is thin and shrunk in person, and that extraordinary face of his has no longer the fire and strength it used to have, though the singular cast of the features and the habitual expressions make it still a most remarkable phenomenon. Upon the whole, I came away with a troubled heart." * * After a brief account of the great trials of my father's late years, the writer continues: "He has been living since his marriage in Hampshire, where he has not had the aid of his old habits and accustomed books to methodize his mind. All this considered, I think we may hope that a year or two of quiet living at his own home may restore him. His easy, cheerful temperament will be greatly in his favor. You must help me to hope this, for I could not bear to think of the decay of that great mind and noble nature—at least not of its premature decay. Pray that this may be averted, as I have this night."*

On the following day the same friend writes, "I think I am a little relieved about Southey to-day. I have seen him three times in the course of the day, and on each occasion he was so easy and cheerful that I should have said his manner and conversation did not differ, in the most part, from what it would have been in former days, if he had happened to be very tired. I say for the most part only though, for there was once an obvious confusion of ideas. He lost himself for a moment; he was conscious of it, and an expression passed over his countenance which was exceedingly touching—an expression of pain and also of resignation. I am glad to learn from his brother that he is aware of his altered condition, and speaks of it openly. This gives a better aspect to the case than if he could believe that nothing was the matter with him. Another favorable circumstance is, that he will deal with himself wisely and patiently. The charm of his manner is perhaps even enhanced at present (at least when one knows the circumstances) by the gentleness and patience which pervade it. His mind is beautiful even in its debility."

Much of my father's failure in its early stages was at first ascribed by those anxiously watching him to repeated attacks of the influenza—at that time a prevailing epidemic—from which he had suffered greatly, and to which he attributed his own feelings of weakness; but alas! the weakness he felt was as much mental as bodily (though he had certainly declined much in bodily strength), and after his return home it gradually increased upon him. The uncertain step—the confused manner—the eye once so keen and so intelligent, now either wandering restlessly, or fixed, as it were, in blank contemplation, all showed that the overwrought mind was worn out.

One of the plainest signs of this was the cessation of his accustomed labors; but, while doing nothing (with him how plain a proof that nothing could be done), he would frequently anticipate a coming period of his usual industry. His mind, while any spark of its reasoning powers remained, was busy with its old day-dreams—the History of Portugal—the History of the Monastic Orders—the Doctor—all were soon to be taken in hand in earnest—all completed, and new works added to these.

For a considerable time after he had ceased to compose, he took pleasure in reading, and the

* August 24, 1839.

habit continued after the power of comprehension was gone. His dearly-prized books, indeed, were a pleasure to him almost to the end, and he would walk slowly round his library looking at them, and taking them down mechanically.

In the earlier stages of his disorder (if the term may be fitly applied to a case which was not a perversion of the faculties, but their decay) he could still converse at times with much of his old liveliness and energy. When the mind was, as it were, set going upon some familiar subject, for a little time you could not perceive much failure; but if the thread was broken, if it was a conversation in which new topics were started, or if any argument was commenced, his powers failed him at once, and a painful sense of this seemed to come over him for the moment. His recollection first failed as to recent events, and his thoughts appeared chiefly to dwell upon those long past, and as his mind grew weaker, these recollections seemed to recede still further back. Names he could rarely remember, and more than once, when trying to recall one which he felt he ought to know, I have seen him press his hand upon his brow and sadly exclaim, "Memory! memory! where art thou gone?"

But this failure altogether was so gradual, and at the same time so complete, that I am inclined to hope and believe there was not, on the whole, much painful consciousness of it; and certainly for more than a year preceding his death he passed his time as in a dream, with little, if any, knowledge of what went on around him.

One circumstance connected with the latter years of his life deserves to be noticed as very singular. His hair, which previously was almost snowy white, grew perceptibly darker, and I think, if any thing, increased in thickness and a disposition to curl.

But it is time I drew a veil over these latter scenes. They are too painful to dwell on.

"A noble mind in sad decay,
When baffled hope has died away.
And life becomes one long distress
In pitiable helplessness.
Methinks 'tis like a ship on shore,
That once defied the Atlantic's roar.
And gallantly through gale and storm
Hath ventured her majestic form;
But now in stranded ruin laid,
By winds and dashing seas decayed,
Forgetful of her ocean reign,
Must crumble into earth again."*

In some cases of this kind, toward the end some glimmering of reason reappears, but this must be when the mind is obscured or upset, not, as in this case, apparently worn out. The body gradually grew weaker, and disorders appeared which the state of the patient rendered it almost impossible to treat properly; and, after a short attack of fever, the scene closed on the 21st of March, 1843, and a second time had we cause to feel deeply thankful when the change from life to death, or more truly from death to life, took place.

It was a dark and stormy morning when he was borne to his last resting-place, at the western end of the beautiful church-yard of Crosthwaite. There lies his dear son Herbert—there his daughters Emma and Isabel—there Edith, his faithful helpmate of forty years. But few besides his own family and immediate neighbors followed his remains. His only intimate friend within reach, Mr. Wordsworth, crossed the hills that wild morning to be present.

Soon after my father's death, various steps were taken with a view to erecting monuments to his memory, and considerable sums were quickly subscribed for that purpose, the list including the names of many persons, not only strangers to him personally, but also strongly opposed to him in political opinion. The result was that three memorials were erected. The first and principal one, a full length recumbent figure, was executed by Lough, and placed in Crosthwaite church, and is certainly an excellent likeness, as well as a most beautiful work of art. The original intention and agreement was that it should be in Caen stone, but the sculptor, with characteristic liberality, executed it in white marble at a considerable sacrifice.

The following lines, by Mr. Wordsworth, are inscribed upon the base:

"Ye vales and hills, whose beauty hither drew
The poet's steps, and fixed him here; on you
His eyes have closed; and ye loved books, no more
Shall Southey feed upon your precious lore,
To works that ne'er shall forfeit their renown
Adding immortal labors of his own—
Whether he traced historic truth with zeal
For the state's guidance or the Church's weal,
Or fancy disciplined by curious art
Informed his pen, or wisdom of the heart,
Or judgments sanctioned in the patriot's mind
By reverence for the rights of all mankind.
Wide were his aims, yet in no human breast
Could private feelings meet in holier rest.
His joys—his griefs—have vanished like a cloud
From Skiddaw's top; but he to Heaven was vowed
Through a life long and pure, and steadfast faith
Calm'd in his soul the fear of change and death."

But this was not the only tribute to my father's memory paid in connection with the church where he had so long worshiped. The structure itself, though not unecclesiastical in its style and plan, had little architectural beauty; and the interior, at the time I am referring to, was much in the same state as ordinary country churches—a flat ceiling, the stone pillars and arches covered with whitewash, and a multitude of pews of all shapes, and sizes, and colors. A small gallery at the west end had been added a few years before, and a very handsome organ presented by James Stanger, Esq., of Lairthwaite, Keswick. This gentleman had taken a most active part in furthering the erection of the monument; and rightly deeming that the introduction of a beautiful work of art would only show in a strong light the deficiencies of the structure, as well as moved by the pious wish to dedicate largely of his substance to the Church, he determined upon a total renovation of the building, of the heavy expense of which he bore by far the largest part.

* Robert Montgomery. The fourth line is altered from the original.

The exterior stone-work was renewed, the pillars and arches restored to their original state, an open roof with ornamented rafters was substituted for the flat ceiling, the pews were taken away, the chancel was fitted with oak stalls beautifully carved, and the nave and aisles with uniform open seats. He also presented a very handsome painted east window. This good example was not lost, for three other painted windows and a beautiful communion service were presented by residents in the immediate neighborhood; and a fourth was added by the parishioners generally, as a testimonial to Mr. Stanger.

When all was completed, the monument was removed to its appointed place, immediately facing the east door, and, together with the changes and embellishments of the church itself, forms a most lasting and gratifying testimonial to the estimation in which my father was held in the place where so large a portion of his life had been spent.

Committees were also formed in London and in Bristol for the same purpose, and busts and tablets erected in Westminster Abbey, and in the Cathedral church of his native city.

I must now make a few observations upon the materials which have passed through my hands in the preparation of this volume. I stated at the commencement my intention of making my father his own biographer, and I have endeavored to render this work consistent with itself throughout in its autobiographical character.

In selecting from the masses of correspondence which have passed through my hands, there has necessarily been considerable labor and difficulty, the amount and nature of which can only be understood by those who have been similarly employed. One of my chief difficulties has been to avoid repetition, for the same circumstance is commonly to be found related, and the same opinions expressed to most of his frequent and familiar correspondents; so that what a Reviewer calls "significant blanks and injudicious erasures" are very often nothing more than what is caused by the cutting out of passages, the substance of which has already appeared in some other letter, and, according to my judgment, more fully and better expressed. It may probably be observed that my selections from the correspondence of the later years of his life are fewer in proportion than of the former ones; but for this several reasons may be given. A correspondence is often carried on briskly for a time, and then dropped almost entirely, as was the case between Sir Walter Scott and my father, although the friendly feelings of the parties were undiminished; in other cases the interchange of letters continued, though they contained nothing sufficiently interesting for publication. With others, again, as with Mr. Rickman, Mr. H. Taylor, and Mr. Bedford, the correspondence increased in frequency, and necessarily the interest of single letters diminished, as it was carried on by a multitude of brief notes; and this, which in these two cases resulted from facilities in franking, it seems likely will be so general a result of the New Postage System, that in another generation there will be no correspondences to publish. With respect to the correspondence with Mr. Wynn, much to my regret, I was unable to procure any letters of later date than 1820, owing to their having been mislaid; since his decease they have been found and kindly transmitted to me by his son; but, unfortunately, it was too late for me to make any present use of them.

In addition to these causes, it may also be mentioned, that his correspondence with comparative strangers and mere acquaintances occupied a continually increasing portion of his time. The number of letters he received from such persons was very great, and almost all had to be answered, so that but little time was left for those letters he had real pleasure in writing. Every new work he engaged in entailed more or less correspondence, and some a vast accession for a time, and these letters generally would not be of interest to the public. The Life of Cowper involved him in a correspondence of considerable extent with many different persons: many of these letters I could have procured, and some were sent to me; but they were not available, from the limits of this work, neither would their contents be of general interest. I may, however, take this opportunity of expressing my thanks to those gentlemen who have sent me letters of which I have not made any use, but for whose kindness I am not the less obliged.

While, however, I have necessarily been compelled to leave out many interesting letters, I feel satisfied that I have published a selection abundantly sufficient to indicate all the points in my father's character—to give all the chief incidents in his life, and to show his opinions in all their stages. I am not conscious of having kept back any thing which ought to have been brought forward—any thing excepting some free and unguarded expressions which, whether relating to things or persons, having been penned in the confidence of friendship and at the impulse of the moment, it would be as unreasonable in a reader to require as it would be injudicious and improper in an editor to publish. And if in any case I may have let some such expression pass by uncanceled, which may have given a moment's pain to any individual, I sincerely regret the inadvertency.

APPENDIX.

Extract from Mr. William Smith's Speech in the House of Commons, March 14, 1817.

"THE honorable member then adverted to that tergiversation of principle which the career of political individuals so often presented. He was far from supposing that a man who set out in life with the profession of certain sentiments, was bound to conclude life with them. He thought there might be many occasions in which a change of opinion, when that change was unattended by any personal advantages, when it appeared entirely disinterested, might be the result of sincere conviction. But what he most detested, what most filled him with disgust, was the settled, determined malignity of a renegado. He had read in a publication (the Quarterly Review), certainly entitled to much respect from its general literary excellences, though he differed from it in its principles, a passage alluding to the recent disturbances, which passage was as follows: 'When the man of free opinions commences professor of moral and political philosophy for the benefit of the public, the fables of old credulity are then verified; his very breath becomes venomous, and every page which he sends abroad carries with it poison to the unsuspicious reader. We have shown, on a former occasion, how men of this description are acting upon the public, and have explained in what manner a large part of the people have been prepared for the virus with which they inoculate them. The dangers arising from such a state of things are now fully apparent, and the designs of the incendiaries, which have for some years been proclaimed so plainly, that they ought, long ere this, to have been prevented, are now manifested by overt acts.'

"With the permission of the House, he would read an extract from a poem recently published, to which, he supposed, the above writer alluded (or, at least, to productions of a similar kind), as constituting a part of the virus with which the public mind had been infected:

"'My brethren, these are truths, and weighty ones:
Ye are all equal; Nature made ye so.
Equality is your birth-right; when I gaze
On the proud palace, and behold one man
In the blood-purpled robes of royalty,
Feasting at ease, and lording over millions;
Then turn me to the hut of poverty,
And see the wretched laborer, worn with toil,
Divide his scanty morsel with his infants,
I sicken, and, indignant at the sight,
Blush for the patience of humanity.'

"He could read many other passages from these works equally strong on both sides; but, if they were written by the same person, he should like to know from the honorable and learned gentleman opposite why no proceedings had been instituted against the author. The poem *Wat Tyler* appeared to him to be the most seditious book that ever was written; its author did not stop short of exhorting to general anarchy; he vilified kings, priests, and nobles, and was for universal suffrage and perfect equality. The Spencean plan could not be compared with it: that miserable and ridiculous performance did not attempt to employ any arguments; but the author of Wat Tyler constantly appealed to the passions, and in a style which the author, at that time, he supposed, conceived to be eloquence. Why, then, had not those who thought it necessary to suspend the Habeas Corpus Act taken notice of this poem? why had they not discovered the author of that seditious publication, and visited him with the penalties of the law? The work was not published secretly, it was not handed about in the darkness of night, but openly and publicly sold in the face of day. It was at this time to be purchased at almost every bookseller's shop in London: it was now exposed for sale in a bookseller's shop in Pall Mall, who styled himself bookseller to one or two of the royal family. He borrowed the copy from which he had just read the extract from an honorable friend of his, who bought it in the usual way; and, therefore, he supposed there could be no difficulty in finding out the party that wrote it. He had heard, that when a man of the name of Winterbottom was, some years ago, confined in Newgate, the manuscript had been sent to him, with liberty to print it for his own advantage, if he thought proper; but that man, it appeared, did not like to risk the publication, and therefore it was now first issued into the world. It must remain with the government and their legal advisers to take what step they might deem most advisable to repress this seditious work and punish its author. In bringing it under the notice of the House, he had merely spoken in defense of his constituents, who had been most grossly calumniated, and he thought that what he had said would go very far to exculpate them. But he wished to take this bull by the horns."—See *Hansard's Parl. Debates*, vol. xxxvii., p. 1088.

A Letter to William Smith, Esq., M.P., from Robert Southey, Esq.

"1817.

"SIR,—You are represented in the newspapers as having entered, during an important discussion in Parliament, into a comparison between certain passages in the Quarterly Review, and the opinions which were held by the author of Wat Tyler three-and-twenty years ago. It appears further, according to the same authority, that the introduction of so strange a criticism, in so unfit a place, did not arise from the debate, but was a premeditated thing, that you had prepared yourself for it by stowing the Quarterly Review in one pocket, and Wat Tyler in the other; and that you deliberately stood up for the purpose of reviling an individual who was not present to vindicate himself, and in a place which afforded you protection.

"My name, indeed, was not mentioned; but that I was the person whom you intended, was notorious to all who heard you. For the impropriety of introducing such topics in such an assembly, it is further stated that you received a well-merited rebuke from Mr. Wynn, who spoke on that occasion as much from his feelings toward one with whom he has lived in uninterrupted friendship for nearly thirty years, as from a sense of the respect which is due to Parliament. It is, however, proper that I should speak explicitly for myself. This was not necessary in regard to Mr. Brougham: he only carried the quarrels as well as the practices of the Edinburgh Review into the House of Commons. But as calumny, sir, has not been your vocation, it may be useful, even to yourself, if I comment upon your first attempt.

"First, as to the Quarterly Review. You can have no other authority for ascribing any particular paper in that journal to one person or to another, than common report; in following which, you may happen to be as much mistaken as I was when upon the same grounds I supposed Mr. William Smith to be a man of candor, incapable of grossly and wantonly insulting an individual.

"The Quarterly Review stands upon its own merits. It is not answerable for any thing more than it contains. What I may have said or thought in any part of my life no more concerns that journal than it does you or the House of Commons; and I am as little answerable for the journal as the journal for me. What I may have written in it is a question which you, sir, have no right to ask, and which certainly I will not answer. As little right have you to take that for granted which you can not possibly know. The question, as respects the Quarterly Review, is not who wrote the paper which happens to have excited Mr. William Smith's displeasure, but whether the facts which are there stated are true, the quotations accurate, and the inferences just. The reviewer, whoever he may be, may defy you to disprove them.

"Secondly, as to Wat Tyler. Now, sir, though you are not acquainted with the full history of this notable production, yet you could not have been ignorant that the author whom you attacked at such unfair advantage was the aggrieved, and not the offending person. You knew that this poem had been written very many years ago, in his early youth. You knew that a copy of it had been surreptitiously obtained and made public by some skulking scoundrel, who had found booksellers not more honorable than himself to undertake the publication. You knew that it was published without the writer's knowledge, for the avowed purpose of insulting him, and with the hope of injuring him, if possible. You knew that the transaction bore upon its face every character of baseness and malignity. You knew that it must have been effected either by robbery or by breach of trust. These things, Mr. William Smith, you knew! and, knowing them as you did, I verily believe, that if it were possible to revoke what is irrevocable, you would at this moment be far more desirous of blotting from remembrance the disgraceful speech which stands upon record in your name, than I should be of canceling the boyish composition which gave occasion to it. Wat Tyler is full of errors, but they are the errors of youth and ignorance; they bear no indication of an ungenerous spirit or of a malevolent heart.

"For the book itself, I deny that it is a seditious performance; for it places in the mouths of the personages who are introduced nothing more than a correct statement of their real principles. That it is a mischievous publication, I know, the errors which it contains being especially dangerous at this time. Therefore I came forward to avow it, to claim it as my own property, which had never been alienated, and to suppress it. And I am desirous that my motives in thus acting should not be misunderstood. The piece was written under the influence of opinions which I have long since outgrown, and repeatedly disclaimed, but for which I have never affected to feel either shame or contrition; they were taken up conscientiously in early youth, they were acted upon in disregard of all worldly considerations, and they were left behind in the same straightforward course, as I advanced in years. It was written when Republicanism was confined to a very small number of the educated classes; when those who were known to entertain such opinions were exposed to personal danger from the populace; and when a spirit of anti-Jacobinism was predominant, which I can not characterize more truly than by saying that it was as unjust and intolerant, though not quite as ferocious, as the Jacobinism of the present day. Had the poem been published during any quiet state of the public mind, the act of dishonesty in the publisher would have been the same; but I should have left it unnoticed, in full confidence that it would have been forgotten as speedily as it deserved. But in these times it was incumbent upon me to come forward as I have done. It became me to disclaim whatever had been erroneous and intemperate in my former opinions, as frankly and as fearlessly as I once maintained them. And this I did, not as one who felt himself in any degree disgraced by the exposure of the crude and misdirected feelings of his youth (feelings right in themselves, and wrong only in their direction), but as one whom no considerations have ever deterred from doing what he believed to be his duty.

"When, therefore, Mr. William Smith informed the House of Commons that the author of Wat Tyler thinks no longer upon certain points as he did in his youth, he informed that legislative assembly of nothing more than what the author has shown during very many years in the course of his writings—that while events have been moving on upon the great theater of human affairs, his intellect has not been stationary. But when the member for Norwich asserts (as he is said to have asserted) that I impute evil motives to men merely for holding now the same doctrines which I myself formerly professed, and when he charges me (as he is said to have charged me) with the malignity and baseness of a renegade, the assertion and the charge are as *false* as the language in which they are conveyed is coarse and insulting.

"Upon this subject I must be heard further. The Edinburgh Review has spoken somewhere of those vindictive and jealous writings in which Mr. Southey has brought forward his claims to the approbation of the public. This is one of those passages for which the editor of that review has merited an abatement in heraldry, no such writings ever having been written; and, indeed, by other like assertions of equal veracity, the gentleman has richly entitled himself to bear a *gore sinister tenné* in his escutcheon. Few authors have obtruded themselves upon the public in their individual character less than I have done. My books have been sent into the world with no other introduction than an explanatory Preface as brief as possible, arrogating nothing, vindicating nothing; and then they have been left to their fate. None of the innumerable attacks which have been made upon them has ever called forth, on my part, a single word of reply, triumphantly as I might have exposed my assailants, not only for their ignorance and inconsistency, but frequently for that moral turpitude which is implied in willful and deliberate misstatement. The unprovoked insults which have been leveled at me, both in prose and rhyme, never induced me to retaliate. It will not be supposed that the ability for satire was wanting, but, happily, I had long since subdued the disposition. I knew that men might be appreciated from the character of their enemies as well as of their friends, and I accepted the hatred of sciolists, coxcombs, and profligates, as one sure proof that I was deserving well of the wise and of the good.

"It will not, therefore, be imputed to any habit of egotism, or any vain desire of interesting the public in my individual concerns, if I now come forward from that privacy in which, both from judgment and disposition, it would have been my choice to have remained. While among the mountains of Cumberland I have been employed upon the Mines of Brazil, the War in the Peninsula, and such other varieties of pursuit as serve to keep the intellect in health by alternately exercising and refreshing it; my name has served in London for the very shuttlecock of discussion. My celebrity for a time has eclipsed that of Mr. Hunt the orator, and may perhaps have impeded the rising reputation of Toby the sapient pig. I have reigned in the newspapers as paramount as Joanna Southcote during the last month of her tympany. Nay, columns have been devoted to Mr. Southey and Wat Tyler which would otherwise have been employed in bewailing the forlorn condition of the Emperor Napoleon, and reprobating the inhumanity of the British cabinet for having designedly exposed him, like Bishop Hatto, to be devoured by the rats.

"That I should ever be honored by such a delicate investigation of my political opinions was what I never could have anticipated, even in the wildest dreams of unfledged vanity. Honor, however, has been thrust upon me, as upon Malvolio. The verses of a boy, of which he thought no more than of his school exercises, and which, had they been published when they were written, would have passed without notice to the family vault, have not only been perused by the lord chancellor in his judicial office, but have been twice produced in Parliament for the edification of the Legislature. The appetite for slander must be sharp-set when it can prey upon such small gear! As, however, the opinions of Mr. Southey have not been thought unworthy to occupy so considerable a share of attention, he need not apprehend the censure of the judicious if he takes part in the discussion himself, so far as briefly to inform the world what they really have been, and what they are.

"In my youth, when my stock of knowledge consisted of such an acquaintance with Greek and Roman history as is acquired in the course of a regular scholastic education—when my heart was full of poetry and romance, and Lucan and Akenside were at my tongue's end, I fell into the political opinions which the French Revolution was then scattering throughout Europe; and following these opinions with ardor wherever they led, I soon perceived the inequalities of rank were a light evil compared to the inequalities of property, and those more fearful distinctions which the want of moral and intellectual culture occasions between man and man. At that time and with those opinions, or rather feelings (for their root was in the heart and not in the understanding), I wrote Wat Tyler, as one who was impatient of 'all the oppressions that are done under the sun.' The subject was injudiciously chosen, and it was treated as might be expected by a youth of twenty, in such times, who regarded only one side of the question. There is no other misrepresentation. The sentiments of the historical characters are correctly stated. Were I now to dramatize the same story, there would be much to add, but little to alter. I should not express these sentiments less strongly, but I should oppose to them more enlarged views of the nature of man and the progress of society. I should set forth with equal force the oppressions of the feudal system, the excesses of the insurgents, and the treachery of the government; and hold up the errors and crimes which were then committed as a warning for this and for future ages. I should write as a man, not as a stripling; with the same heart and the same desires, but with a ripened understanding and competent stores of knowledge.

"It is a fair and legitimate inference, that no person would have selected this subject, and treated it in such a manner at such a time, unless he had, in a certain degree, partaken of the sentiments which are expressed in it; in *what* degree he partook them is a question which it requires more temper as well as more discretion to resolve than you, sir, have given any proof of possessing. This can only be ascertained by comparing the piece with other works of the same author, written about the same time or shortly afterward, and under the influence of the same political opinions; by such a comparison it might be discerned what arose from his own feelings, and what from the nature of dramatic composition. But to select passages from a dramatic poem, and ascribe the whole force of the sentiments to the writer as if he himself held them, without the slightest qualification, is a mode of criticism manifestly absurd and unjust. Whether it proceeded in this instance from excess of malice, or deficiency of judgment, is a point which they who are best acquainted with Mr. William Smith may be able to determine.

"It so happens that sufficient specimens of Mr. Southey's way of thinking in his youth are before the world, without breaking open escritoires, or stealing any more of his juvenile papers which he may have neglected to burn. The poem to which, with all its faults, he is indebted for his first favorable notice from the public, may possibly have been honored with a place in Mr. William Smith's library, as it received the approbation of all the dissenting journals of the day. It is possible that their recommendation may have induced him to favor Joan of Arc with a perusal, and not improbably in a mood which would indulge its manifold demerits in style and structure for the sake of its liberal opinions. Perhaps, too, he may have condescended to notice the minor poems of the same author, sanctioned as some of these also were at their first appearance by the same critical authorities In these productions he may have seen expressed an enthusiastic love of liberty, a detestation of tyranny wherever it exists and in whatever form, an ardent abhorrence of all wicked ambition, and a sympathy not less ardent with those who were engaged in war for the defense of their country and in a righteous cause—feelings just as well as generous in themselves. He might have perceived, also, frequent indications that, in the opinion of the youthful writer, a far happier system of society was possible than any under which mankind are at present existing, or ever have existed since the patriarchal ages—and no equivocal aspirations after such a state. In all this he might have seen something that was erroneous and more that was visionary, but nothing that savored of intemperance or violence. I insist, therefore, that inasmuch as Wat Tyler may differ in character from these works, the difference arises necessarily from the nature of dramatic composition. I maintain that this is the inference which must be drawn by every honest and judicious mind; and I affirm that such an influence would be strictly conformable to the fact.

"Do not, however, sir, suppose that I shall seek to shrink from a full avowal of what my opinions have been: neither before God nor man am I ashamed of them. I have as little cause for humiliation in recalling them, as Gibbon had when he related how he had knelt at the feet of a confessor; for while I imbibed the Republican opinions of the day, I escaped the Atheism, and the leprous immorality which generally accompanied them. I can not, therefore, join with Beattie in blessing

> 'The hour when I escaped the wrangling crew,
> From Pyrrho's maze and Epicurus' sty,'

for I was never lost in the one, nor defiled in the other. My progress was of a different kind. From building castles in the air to framing commonwealths was an easy transition; the next step was to realize the vision; and in the hope of accomplishing this, I forsook the course of life for which I had been designed, and the prospects of advancement, which I may say, without presumption, were within my reach. My purpose was to retire with a few friends into the wilds of America, and there lay the foundations of a community upon what we believed to be the political system of Christianity. It matters not in what manner the vision was dissolved. I am not writing my own memoirs, and it is sufficient simply to state the fact. We were connected with no clubs, no societies, no party. The course which we would have pursued might have proved destructive to ourselves, but as it related to all other persons, never did the aberrations of youth take a more innocent direction.

"I know, sir, that you were not ignorant of this circumstance: the project, while it was in view, was much talked of among that sect of Christians to which you belong: and some of your friends are well acquainted with the events of my life. What, then, I may ask, did you *learn* concerning me from this late surreptitious publication? Nay, sir, the personal knowledge which you possessed was not needful for a full understanding of the political opinions which I entertained in youth. They are expressed in poems which have been frequently reprinted, and are continually on sale; no alterations have ever been made for the purpose of withdrawing, concealing, or extenuating them. I have merely affixed to every piece the date of the year in which it was written—and the progress of years is sufficient to explain the change.

"You, Mr. William Smith, may possibly be acquainted with other persons who were Republicans in the first years of the French Revolution, and who have long since ceased to be so, with as little impeachment of their integrity as of their judgment; yet you bring it as a heinous charge against me, that, having entertained enthusiastic notions in my youth, three-and-twenty years should have produced a change in the opinions of one whose life has been devoted to the acquirement of knowledge.

"You are pleased, in your candor, to admit that I might have been sincere when I was erroneous, and you, who are a professor of modern liberality, are not pleased to admit that the course of time and events may have corrected me in what was wrong, and confirmed me in what was right. True it is that the events of the last five-and-twenty years have been lost upon you; perhaps you judge me by yourself, and you may think that this is a fair criterion; but I must protest against being measured by any such standard. Between you and me, sir, there can be no sympathy, even though we should sometimes happen to think alike. We are as unlike in all things as men of the same time, country, and rank in society can be imagined to be; and the difference is in our mind and mold, as we came from the Potter's hand.

"And what, sir, is the change in the opinions of Mr. Southey, which has drawn upon him the ponderous displeasure of William Smith? This was a point upon which it behooved you to be especially well informed before you applied to him the false and insolent appellation which you are said to have used, and which I am authorized in believing that you have used. He has ceased to believe that old monarchical countries are capable of Republican forms of government. He has ceased to think that he understood the principles of government, and the nature of man and society, before he was one-and-twenty years of age. He has ceased to suppose that men who neither cultivate their intellectual nor their moral faculties can understand them at any age. He has ceased to wish for revolutions even in countries where great alteration is to be desired, because he has seen that the end of anarchy is military despotism. But he has not ceased to love liberty with all his heart, and with all his soul, and with all his strength; he has not ceased to detest tyranny wherever it exists, and in whatever form. He has not ceased to abhor the wickedness of ambition, and to sympathize with those who are engaged in the defense of their country and in a righteous cause; if, indeed, he had, he might have been sure of the approbation, not only of Mr. William Smith, and of those persons who were, during the war, the sober opponents of their country's cause, but of the whole crew of ultra Whigs and anarchists, from Messrs. Brougham and Clodius down to Cobbett, Cethegus, and Co.

"Many were the English who wished well to the French at the commencement of their revolution; but if any of those Englishmen have attached the same interest to the cause of France through all the changes of the Revolution—if they have hoped that Bonaparte might succeed in the usurpation of Portugal and Spain, and the subjugation of the Continent —the change is in them, in their feelings and their principles, not in me and in mine. At no time of my life have I held any opinions like those of the Bonapartists and Revolutionists of the present day; never could I have held any communion with such men in thought, word, or deed; my nature, God be thanked! would always have kept me from them instinctively, as it would from toad or asp. Look through the whole writings of my youth, including, if you please, Wat Tyler—there can be no danger that its errors should infect a gentleman who has called upon the attorney-general to prosecute the author; and he would not be the worse were he to catch from it a little of the youthful generosity which it breathes. I ask you, sir, in which of those writings I have appealed to the base or the malignant feelings of mankind; and I ask you whether the present race of revolutionary writers appeal to any other? What man's private character did I stab? Whom did I libel? Whom did I slander? Whom did I traduce? These miscreants live by calumny and sedition; they are libelers and liars by trade.

"The one object to which I have ever been desirous of contributing according to my power, is the removal of those obstacles by which the improvement of mankind is impeded; and to this the whole tenor of my writings, whether in prose or verse, bears witness. This has been the pole-star of my course; the needle has shifted according to the movements of the state vessel wherein I am embarked, but the direction to which it points has always been the same. I did not fall into the error of those who, having been the friends of France when they imagined that the cause of liberty was implicated in her success, transferred their attachment from the Republic to the military tyranny in which it ended, and regarded with complacency the progress of oppression because France was the oppressor. 'They had turned their faces toward the east in the morning to worship the rising sun, and in the evening they were looking eastward still, obstinately affirming that still the sun was there.'* I, on the contrary, altered my position as the world went round. For so doing, Mr. William Smith is said to have insulted me with the appellation of renegade; and if it be indeed true that the foul aspersion passed his lips, I brand him for it on the forehead with the name of SLANDERER. Salve the mark as you will, sir, it is ineffaceable! You must bear it with you to your grave, and the remembrance will outlast your epitaph.

"And now, sir, learn what are the opinions of the man to whom you have offered this public and notorious wrong; opinions not derived from any contagion of the times, nor entertained with the unreflecting eagerness of youth, nor adopted in connection with any party in the state, but gathered patiently, during many years of leisure and retirement, from books, observation, meditation, and intercourse with living minds who will be the light of other ages.

"Greater changes in the condition of the country have been wrought during the last half century than an equal course of years had ever before produced. Without entering into the proofs of this proposition, suffice it to indicate, as among the most efficient causes, the steam and the spinning engines, the mail-coach, and the free publication of the debates in Parliament: hence follow, in natural and necessary consequence, increased activity, enterprise, wealth, and power; but, on the other hand, greediness of gain, looseness of principle, half knowledge (more perilous than ignorance), vice, poverty, wretchedness, disaffection, and political insecurity. The changes which have taken place render other changes inevitable; forward we must go, for it is not possible to retrace our steps; the hand of the political horologe can not go back, like the shadow upon Hezekiah's dial; when the hour comes, it must strike.

"Slavery has long ceased to be tolerable in Europe; the remains of feudal oppression are disappearing even in those countries which have improved the least; nor can it be much longer endured that the extremes of ignorance, wretchedness, and brutality should exist in the very center of civilized society. There can be no safety with a populace half Luddite, half Lazzaroni. Let us not deceive ourselves. We are far from that state in which any thing resembling equality would be possible; but we are arrived at that state in which the extremes of inequality are become intolerable. They are too dangerous, as well as too monstrous, to be borne much longer. Plans which would have led to the utmost horrors of insurrection have been prevented by the government, and by the enactment of strong but necessary laws. Let it not, however, be supposed that the disease is healed because the

* I quote my own words, written in 1809.

ulcer may skin over. The remedies by which the body politic can be restored to health must be slow in their operation. The condition of the populace, physical, moral, and intellectual, must be improved, or a *Jacquerie*, a *Bellum Servile*, sooner or later, will be the result. It is the people at this time who stand in need of reformation, not the government.

"The government must better the condition of the populace; and the first thing necessary is to prevent it from being worsened. It must no longer suffer itself to be menaced, its chief magistrate insulted, and its most sacred institutions vilified with impunity. It must curb the seditious press, and keep it curbed. For this purpose, if the laws are not at present effectual, they should be made so; nor will they then avail, unless they are vigilantly executed. I say this, well knowing to what obloquy it will expose me, and how grossly and impudently my meaning will be misrepresented; but I say it, because, if the licentiousness of the press be not curbed, its abuse will most assuredly one day occasion the loss of its freedom.

"This is the first and most indispensable measure, for without this all others will be fruitless. Next in urgency is the immediate relief of the poor. I differ *toto cœlo* from Mr. Owen, of Lanark, in one main point. To build upon any other foundation than religion is building upon sand. But I admire his practical benevolence; I love his enthusiasm; and I go far with him in his earthly views. What he has actually done entitles him to the greatest attention and respect. I sincerely wish that his plan for the extirpation of pauperism should be fairly tried. To employ the poor in manufactures is only shifting the evil, and throwing others out of employ by bringing more labor and more produce of labor into a market which is already overstocked.

"Wise and extensive plans of foreign colonization contribute essentially to keep a state like England in health; but we must not overlook the greater facility of colonizing at home. Would it not be desirable that tracts of waste land should be purchased with public money, to be held as national domains, and colonized with our disbanded soldiers and sailors, and people who are in want of employment, dividing them into estates of different sizes, according to the capability of the speculators, and allotting to every cottage that should be erected there a certain proportion of ground? Thus should we make immediate provision for those brave men whose services are no longer required for the defense of their country; thus should we administer immediate relief to the poor, lighten the poor-rates, give occupation to various branches of manufacture, and provide a permanent source of revenue, accruing from the increased prosperity of the country. There never was a time when every rood of ground maintained its man; but surely it is allowable to hope that whole districts will not always be suffered to lie waste while multitudes are in want of employment and of bread.

"A duty scarcely less urgent than that of diminishing the burden of the poor-rates, is that of providing for the education of the lower classes. Government must no longer, in neglect of its first and paramount duty, allow them to grow up in worse than heathen ignorance. They must be trained in the way they should go; they must be taught to 'fear God and keep his commandments, for this is the whole duty of man.' Mere reading and writing will not do this: they must be instructed according to the established religion; they must be fed with the milk of sound doctrine, for states are secure in proportion as the great body of the people are attached to the institutions of their country. A moral and religious education will induce habits of industry; the people will know their duty, and find their interest and their happiness in following it. Give us the great boon of parochial education, so connected with the Church as to form part of the establishment, and we shall find it a bulwark to the state as well as to the Church. Let this be done; let savings' banks be generally introduced; let new channels for industry be opened (as soon as the necessities of the state will permit) by a liberal expenditure in public works, by colonizing our waste lands at home, and regularly sending off our swarms abroad, and the strength, wealth, and security of the nation will be in proportion to its numbers.

"Never, indeed, was there a more senseless cry than that which is at this time raised for retrenchment in the public expenditure, as a means of alleviating the present distress. That distress arises from a great and sudden diminution of employment, occasioned by many coinciding causes, the chief of which is, that the war-expenditure of from forty to fifty millions yearly has ceased. Men are out of employ: the evil is, that too little is spent, and, as a remedy, we are exhorted to spend less. Every where there are mouths crying out for food, because the hands want work; and at this time, and for this reason, the state-quack requires further reduction. Because so many hands are unemployed, he calls upon government to throw more upon the public by reducing its establishments and suspending its works. *O lepidum caput!* and it is by such heads as this that we are to be reformed!

"'Statesmen,' says Mr. Burke, 'before they value themselves on the relief given to the people by the destruction (or diminution) of their revenue, ought first to have carefully attended to the solution of this problem: Whether it be more advantageous to the people to pay considerably and to gain in proportion, or to gain little or nothing and to be disburdened of all contribution.' And in another place this great statesman says, 'The prosperity and improvement of nations have generally increased with the increase of their revenues; and they will both continue to grow and flourish as long as the balance between what is left to strengthen the efforts of individuals, and what is collected for the common efforts of the state, bear to each other a due reciprocal proportion, and are kept in a close correspondence and communication.' This opinion is strikingly corroborated by the unexampled prosperity which the country enjoyed during the war—a war of unexampled expenditure; and the stupendous works of antiquity, the ruins of which at this day so mournfully attest the opulence and splendor of states which have long ceased to exist, were in no slight degree the causes of that prosperity of which they are the proofs. Instead, therefore, of this senseless cry for retrenchment, which is like prescribing depletion for a patient whose complaints proceed from inanition, a liberal expenditure should be advised in works of public utility and magnificence; for if experience has shown us that increased expenditure during war, and a proportionately increasing prosperity, have been naturally connected as cause and consequence, it is neither rash nor illogical to infer that a liberal expenditure in peace upon national works would produce the same beneficial effect without any of the accompanying evil. Money thus expended will flow like chyle into the veins of the state, and nourish and invigorate it. Build, therefore, our monuments for Trafalgar and Waterloo, and let no paltry considerations prevent them from being made worthy of the occasion and of the country—of the men who have fought, conquered, and died for us—of Nelson, of Wellington, and of Great Britain! Let them be such as may correspond in splendor with the actions to which they are consecrated, and vie, if possible, in duration with the memory of those immortal events. They are for after ages: the more magnificent they may be, the better will they manifest the national sense of great public services, and the more will they excite and foster that feeling in which great actions have their root. In proportion to their magnificence, also, will be the present benefit, as well as of future good; for they are not like the Egyptian pyramids, to be raised by bondsmen under rigorous task-masters; the wealth which is taken from the people returns to them again, like vapors which are drawn imperceptibly from the earth, but distributed to it in refreshing dews and fertilizing showers. What bounds could imagination set to the welfare and glory of this island, if a tenth part, or even a twentieth, of what the war expenditure has been, were annually applied in improving and creating harbors, in bringing our roads to the best possible state, in colonizing upon our waste lands, in reclaiming fens and conquering tracts from the sea, in encouraging the liberal arts, in erecting churches, in building and endowing schools and colleges, and war upon physical and moral evil with the whole artillery of wisdom and righteousness, with all the resources of science, and all the ardor of enlightened and enlarged benevolence?

"It is likewise incumbent upon government to take heed lest, in its solicitude for raising the necessary revenue, there should be too little regard for the means by which it is raised. It should beware of imposing such duties as create a strong temptation to evade them. It should be careful that all its measures tend as much as possible to the improvement of the people, and especially careful nothing be done which can tend in any way to corrupt them. It should reform its prisons, and apply some remedy to the worst grievance which exists—the enormous expenses, the chicanery, and the ruinous delays of the law.

"Machiavelli says that legislators ought to suppose all men to be naturally bad; in no point has that sagacious statesman been more erroneous. Fitter it is that governments should think well of mankind; for the better they think of them, the better they will find them, and the better they will make them. Government must reform the populace, the people must reform themselves. This is the true reform, and compared with this all else is *flocci, nauci, nihili, pili.*

"Such, sir, are, in part, the views of the man whom you have traduced. Had you perused his writings, you could not have mistaken them; and I am willing to believe that if you had done this, and formed an opinion for yourself, instead of retailing that of wretches who are at once the panders of malice and the pioneers of rebellion, you would neither have been so far forgetful of your parliamentary character, nor of the decencies between man and man, as so wantonly, so unjustly, and in such a place, to have attacked one who had given you no provocation.

"Did you imagine that I should sit down quietly under the wrong, and treat your attack with the same silent contempt as I have done all the abuse and calumny with which, from one party or the other, anti-Jacobins or Jacobins, I have been assailed in daily, weekly, monthly, and quarterly publications, since the year 1796, when I first became known to the public? The place where you made the attack, and the manner of the attack, prevent this.

"How far the writings of Mr. Southey may be found to deserve a favorable acceptance from after ages, time will decide; but a name which, whether worthily or not, has been conspicuous in the literary history of its age, will certainly not perish. Some account of his life will always be prefixed to his works, and transferred to literary histories and to the biographical dictionaries, not only of this, but of other countries. There it will be related that he lived in the bosom of his family, in absolute retirement; that in all his writings there breathed the same abhorrence of oppression and immorality, the same spirit of devotion, and the same ardent wishes for the amelioration of mankind; and that the only charge which malice could bring against him was, that as he grew older his opinions altered concerning the means by which that amelioration was to be effected; and that, as he learned to understand the institutions of his country, he learned to appreciate them rightly, to love, and to revere, and to defend them. It will be said of him, that in an age of personality he abstained from satire, and that during the course of his literary life, often as he was assailed, the only occasion on which he ever condescended to reply was when a certain Mr. William Smith insulted him in Parliament with the appellation of renegade. On that occasion it will be said that he vindicated himself as it became him to do, and treated his calumniator with just and memorable severity. Whether it shall be added that Mr. William Smith redeemed his own character by coming forward with honest manliness and acknowledging that he had spoken rashly and unjustly, concerns himself, but is not of the slightest importance to me.

"ROBERT SOUTHEY."

Two Letters concerning Lord Byron, published in Southey's Essays, 2 vols., Murray, 1832.

"HAVING, in the preface of my 'Vision of Judgment,' explained the principle upon which the meter of that poem is constructed, I took the opportunity of introducing the following remarks:

"'I am well aware that the public are peculiarly intolerant of such innovations, not less so than the populace are of any foreign fashion, whether of foppery or convenience. Would that this literary intolerance were under the influence of a saner judgment, and regarded the morals more than the manner of a composition—the spirit rather than the form! Would that it were directed against those monstrous combinations of horrors and mockery, lewdness and impiety, with which English poetry has, in our days, first been polluted! For more than half a century English literature had been distinguished by its moral purity—the effect, and, in its turn, the cause of an improvement in national manners. A father might, without apprehension of evil, have put into the hands of his children any book which issued from the press, if it did not bear, either in its title-page or frontispiece, manifest signs that it was intended as furniture for the brothel. There was no danger in any work which bore the name of a respectable publisher, or was to be procured at any respectable bookseller's. This was particularly the case with regard to our poetry. It is now no longer so; and woe to those by whom the offense cometh! The greater the talents of the offender, the greater is his guilt, and the more enduring will be his shame. Whether it be that the laws themselves are unable to abate an evil of this magnitude, or whether it be that they are remissly administered, and with such injustice that the celebrity of an offender serves as a privilege whereby he obtains impunity, individuals are bound to consider that such pernicious works would neither be published nor written, if they were discouraged, as they might and ought to be, by public feeling. Every person, therefore, who purchases such books, or admits them into his house, promotes the mischief, and thereby, as far as in him lies, becomes an aider and abettor of the crime.

"'The publication of a lascivious book is one of the worst offenses which can be committed against the well-being of society. It is a sin, to the consequences of which no limits can be assigned, and those consequences no after repentance in the writer can counteract. Whatever remorse of conscience he may feel when his hour comes (and come it must!) will be of no avail. The poignancy of a death-bed repentance can not cancel one copy of the thousands which are sent abroad; and as long as it continues to be read, so long is he the pander of posterity, and so long is he heaping up guilt upon his soul in perpetual accumulation.

"'These remarks are not more severe than the offense deserves, even when applied to those immoral writers who have not been conscious of any evil intention in their writings, who would acknowledge a little levity, a little warmth of coloring, and so forth, in that sort of language with which men gloss over their favorite vices, and deceive themselves. What, then, should be said of those for whom the thoughtlessness and inebriety of wanton youth can no longer be pleaded, but who have written in sober manhood and with deliberate purpose? Men of diseased* hearts and depraved imaginations,

* "*Summi poetæ in omni poetarum sæculo viri fuerunt*

who, forming a system of opinions to suit their own unhappy course of conduct, have rebelled against the holiest ordinances of human society, and hating that revealed religion which, with all their efforts and bravadoes, they are unable entirely to disbelieve, labor to make others as miserable as themselves, by infecting them with a moral virus that eats into the soul! The school which they have set up may properly be called the Satanic School; for, though their productions breathe the spirit of Belial in their lascivious parts, and the spirit of Moloch in those loathsome images of atrocities and horrors which they delight to represent, they are more especially characterized by a Satanic spirit of pride and audacious impiety, which still betrays the wretched feeling of hopelessness wherewith it is allied.

"'This evil is political as well as moral; for, indeed, moral and political evils are inseparably connected. Truly has it been affirmed by one of our ablest and clearest reasoners,† that "the destruction of governments may be proved, and deduced from the general corruption of the subjects' manners, as a direct and natural cause thereof, by a demonstration as certain as any in the mathematics." There is no maxim more frequently enforced by Machiavelli than that, where the manners of a people are generally corrupted, there the government can not long subsist: a truth which all history exemplified; and there is no means whereby that corruption can be so surely and rapidly diffused as by poisoning the waters of literature.

"'Let rulers of the state look to this in time! But, to use the words of South, if "our physicians think the best way of *curing* a disease is to *pamper* it, the Lord in mercy prepare the kingdom to suffer what He by miracle only can prevent!"

"'No apology is offered for these remarks. The subject led to them; and the occasion of introducing them was willingly taken, because it is the duty of every one, whose opinion may have any influence, to expose the drift and aim of those writers who are laboring to subvert the foundations of human virtue and of human happiness.'

"Lord Byron, in his next publication, was pleased to comment upon this passage in the ensuing words:

"'Mr. Southey, too, in his pious preface to a poem, whose blasphemy is as harmless as the sedition of Wat Tyler, because it is equally absurd with that sincere production, calls upon the "Legislature to look to it," as the toleration of such writings led to the French Revolution—*not* such writings as Wat Tyler, but as those of the "Satanic School." This is not true, and Mr. Southey knows it to be not true. Every French writer of any freedom was persecuted: Voltaire and Rousseau were exiles, Marmontel and Diderot were sent to the Bastile, and a perpetual war was waged with the whole class by the existing despotism. In the next place, the French Revolution was *not* occasioned by any writings.

"'It is the fashion to attribute every thing to the French Revolution, and the French Revolution to every thing but its real cause. That cause is obvious. The government exacted too much, and the people could neither *give* nor *bear more*. Without this, the encyclopedists might have written their fingers off without the occurrence of a single alteration.

"'And the *English* Revolution (the first, I mean), what was it occasioned by? The *Puritans* were surely as pious and moral as Wesley or his biographer. Acts—acts on the part of government, and *not* writings against them, have caused the past convulsions, and are leading to the future.

"'I look upon such as inevitable, though no revolutionist. I wish to see the English Constitution restored, and not destroyed. Born an aristocrat, and naturally one by temper, with the greater part of my present property in the funds, what have *I* to gain by a revolution? Perhaps I have more to lose in every way than Mr. Southey, with all his places and presents for panegyrics and abuse into the bargain. But that a revolution is inevitable, I repeat. The government may exult over the repression of petty tumults; these are but the receding waves, repulsed and broken for a moment on the shore, while the great tide is still rolling on, and gaining ground with every breaker. Mr. Southey accuses us of attacking the religion of the country; and he is abetting it by writing lives of *Wesley!* One mode of worship is merely destroyed by another. There never was, nor ever will be, a country without a religion. We shall be told of *France* again; but it was only Paris and a frantic party which for a moment upheld their dogmatic nonsense of theophilanthropy. The Church of England, if overthrown, will be swept away by the reclaimers, and not by the skeptics. People are too wise, too well-informed, too certain of their own immense importance in the realms of space ever to submit to the impiety of doubt. There may be a few such diffident speculators, like water in the pale sunbeam of human reason, but they are very few; and their opinions, without enthusiasm or appeal to the passions, can never gain proselytes, unless, indeed, they are persecuted: *that*, to be sure, will increase any thing.

"'Mr. S., with a cowardly ferocity, exults over the anticipated "death-bed repentance" of the objects of his dislike, and indulges himself in a pleasant "Vision of Judgment," in prose as well as verse, full of impious impudence. What Mr. S.'s sensations or ours may be in the awful moment of leaving this state of existence, neither he nor we can pretend to decide. In common, I presume, with most men of any reflection, *I* have not waited for a "death-bed" to repent of many of my actions, notwithstanding the "diabolical pride" which this pitiful renegado, in his rancor, would impute to those who scorn *him*.

"'Whether, upon the whole, the good or evil of my deeds may preponderate, is not for me to ascertain; but as my means and opportunities have been greater, I shall limit my present defense to an assertion (easily proved, if necessary), that I, "in my degree," have done more real good in any one given year, since I was twenty, than Mr. Southey in the whole course of his shifting and turn-coat existence. There are several actions to which I can look back with an honest pride, not to be damped by the calumnies of a hireling. There are others to which I recur with sorrow and repentance; but the only *act* of *my* life, of which Mr. Southey can have any real knowledge, as it was one which brought me in contact with a near connection of his own, did no dishonor to that connection nor to me.

"'I am not ignorant of Mr. Southey's calumnies on a different occasion, knowing them to be such, which he scattered abroad on his return from Switzerland, against me and others. They have done him no good in this world; and if his creed be the right one, they will do him less in the next. What *his* "death-bed" may be, it is not my province to predicate; let him settle it with his Maker, as I must do

probi; in nostris id vidimus et videmus; neque alius est error a veritate longiùs quàm magna ingenia magnis necessario corrumpi viti is. Secundo plerique posthabent primum, hi malignitate, illi ignorantia; et quum aliquem inveniunt styli morumque vitiis notatum, nec inficetum tamen nec in libris edendis parcum, eum stipant, prædicant occupant, amplectuntur. Si mores aliquantulum vellet corrigere, si stylum curare paululum, si fervido ingenio temperare, si moræ tantillum interponere, tum ingens nescio quid et vere epicum, quadraginta annos natus, procuderet. Ignorant verò febriculis non indicari vires, impatientiam ab imbecillitate non differre; ignorant a levi homine et inconstante multa fortasse scribi posse plusquam mediocria, nihil compositum, arduum, æternum."—Savagius Landor, De Cultu atque Usu Latini Sermonis. This essay, which is full of fine critical remarks and striking thoughts felicitously expressed, reached me from Pisa, while the proof of the present sheet was before me. Of its author (the author of Gebir and Count Julian) I will only say in this place, that to have obtained his approbation as a poet, and possessed his friendship as a man, will be remembered among the honors of my life, when the petty enmities of this generation will be forgotten, and its ephemeral reputations shall have passed away.

† South.

with mine. There is something at once ludicrous and blasphemous in this arrogant scribbler of all works, sitting down to deal damnation and destruction upon his fellow-creatures, with Wat Tyler, the Apotheosis of George the Third, and the Elegy on Martin the Regicide all shuffled together in his writing-desk. One of his consolations appears to be a Latin note from a work of Mr. Landor, the author of "Gebir," whose friendship for Robert Southey will, it seems, "be an honor to him when the ephemeral disputes and ephemeral reputations of the day are forgotten."

"'I, for one, neither envy him "the friendship" nor the glory in reversion which is to accrue from it, like Mr. Thelusson's fortune, in the third and fourth generation. This friendship will probably be as memorable as his own epics, which (as I quoted to him ten or twelve years ago in "English Bards") Porson said "would be remembered when Homer and Virgil are forgotten, and not till then." For the present I leave him.'"

The foregoing passage, which has here been given at length, called forth the first of the ensuing letters.

LETTER I.

To the Editor of the Courier.

"Keswick, Jan. 5, 1822.

"SIR,—Having seen in the newspapers a note relating to myself, extracted from a recent publication of Lord Byron's, I request permission to reply through the medium of your journal.

"I come at once to his lordship's charge against me, blowing away the abuse with which it is frothed, and evaporating a strong acid in which it is suspended. The residuum, then, appears to be, that 'Mr. Southey, on his return from Switzerland (in 1817), scattered abroad calumnies, knowing them to be such, against Lord Byron and others.' To this I reply with *a direct and positive denial.*

"If I had been told in that country that Lord Byron had turned Turk or monk of La Trappe—that he had furnished a *harem* or endowed a hospital, I might have thought the report, whichever it had been, possible, and repeated it accordingly, passing it, as it had been taken, in the small change of conversation, for no more than it was worth. In this manner I might have spoken of him as of Baron Gerambe, the Green Man, the Indian Jugglers, or any other *figurante* of the time being. There was no reason for any particular delicacy on my part in speaking of his lordship; and, indeed, I should have thought any thing which might be reported of him would have injured his character as little as the story which so greatly annoyed Lord Keeper Guilford—that he had ridden a rhinoceros. He may ride a rhinoceros, and though every one would stare, no one would wonder. But making no inquiry concerning him when I was abroad, because I felt no curiosity, I heard nothing, and had nothing to repeat. When I spoke of wonders to my friends and acquaintances on my return, it was of the flying-tree at Alpnach, and the eleven thousand virgins at Cologne —not of Lord Byron. I sought for no staler subject than St. Ursula.

"Once, and only once, in connection with Switzerland, I have alluded to his lordship; and as the passage was curtailed in the press, I take this opportunity of restoring it. In the Quarterly Review, speaking incidentally of the 'Jungfrau,' I said 'it was the scene where Lord Byron's *Manfred* met the Devil and bullied him, though the Devil must have won his cause before any tribunal, in this world or the next, if he had not pleaded more feebly for himself than his advocate, in a cause of canonization, ever pleaded for him.'

"With regard to the others, whom his lordship accuses me of calumniating, I suppose he alludes to a party of his friends, whose names I found written in the album at Mont Anvert, with an avowal of atheism annexed, in Greek, and an indignant comment in the same language, underneath it. Those names, with that avowal and the comment, I transcribed in my note-book, and spoke of the circumstance on my return. If I had published it, the gentleman in question would not have thought himself slandered by having that recorded of him which he has so often recorded of himself.

"The many opprobrious appellations which Lord Byron has bestowed upon me, I leave as I find them, with the praises which he has bestowed upon himself.

"'How easily is a noble spirit discern'd
From harsh and sulphurous matter that flies out
In contumelies, makes a noise, and stinks.'

Ben Jonson.

But I am accustomed to such things; and so far from irritating me are the enemies who use such weapons, that when I hear of their attacks, it is some satisfaction to think they have thus employed the malignity which must have been employed somewhere, and could not have been directed against any person whom it could possibly molest or injure less. The viper, however venomous in purpose, is harmless in effect while it is biting at the file. It is seldom, indeed, that I waste a word or a thought upon those who are perpetually assailing me. But abhorring as I do the personalities which disgrace our current literature, and averse from controversy as I am, both by principle and inclination, I make no profession of non-resistance. When the offense and the offender are such as to call for the whip and the branding-iron, it has been both seen and felt that I can inflict them.

"Lord Byron's present exacerbation is evidently produced by an infliction of this kind, not by hearsay reports of my conversation four years ago, transmitted him from England.

"The cause may be found in certain remarks upon the Satanic School of Poetry, contained in my preface to the Vision of Judgment. Well would it be for Lord Byron if he could look back upon any of his writings with as much satisfaction as I shall always do upon what is there said of that flagitious school. Many persons, and parents especially, have expressed their gratitude to me for having applied the branding-iron where it was so richly deserved. The Edinburgh Reviewer, indeed, with that honorable feeling by which his criticisms are so peculiarly distinguished, suppressing the remarks themselves, has imputed them wholly to envy on my part. I give him, in this instance, full credit for sincerity: I believe he was equally incapable of comprehending a worthier motive, or inventing a worse; and, as I have never condescended to expose, in any instance, his pitiful malevolence, I thank him for having in this stripped it bare himself, and exhibited it in its bald, naked, and undisguised deformity.

"Lord Byron, like his encomiast, has not ventured to bring the matter of those animadversions into view. He conceals the fact that they are directed against authors of blasphemous and lascivious books; against men who, not content with indulging their own vices, labor to make others the slaves of sensuality like themselves; against public panders, who, mingling impiety with lewdness, seek at once to destroy the cement of social order, and to carry profanation and pollution into private families and into the hearts of individuals.

"His lordship has thought it not unbecoming in him to call me a scribbler of all work. Let the word *scribbler* pass; it is an appellation which will not stick like that of *the Satanic School.* But, if a scribbler, how am I one of *all work?* I will tell Lord Byron what I have *not* scribbled, what kind of work I have *not* done:

"I have never published libels upon my friends and acquaintances, expressed my sorrow for those libels, and called them in during a mood of better mind, and then reissued them when the evil spirit, which for a time had been cast out, had returned and taken possession, with seven others more wicked than himself. I have never abused the power, of which every author is in some degree possessed, to wound the character of a man or the heart of a woman. I have never sent into the world a book to which I did not dare affix my name, or which I feared to claim in a court of justice, if it were pirated by a knavish bookseller. I have never manufactured furniture for the brothel. None of *these things* have I done; none of the foul work by which literature is perverted to the injury of mankind. My hands are clean! There is no damned spot upon them! no taint, which all the perfumes of Arabia will not sweeten!

"Of the work which I *have* done it becomes me not here to speak, save only as relates to the Satanic School, and its Coryphæus, the author of Don Juan. I have held up that school to public detestation as enemies to the religion, the institutions, and the domestic morals of the country. I have given them a designation *to which their founder and leader answers*. I have sent a stone from my sling which has smitten their Goliath in the forehead. I have fastened his name upon the gibbet for reproach and ignominy, as long as it shall endure. Take it down who can!

"One word of advice to Lord Byron before I conclude. When he attacks me again, let it be in rhyme. For one who has so little command of himself, it will be a great advantage that his temper should be obliged to *keep tune*. And while he may still indulge in the same rankness and violence of insult, the meter will, in some degree, seem to lessen its vulgarity. ROBERT SOUTHEY."

LETTER II.

To the Editor of the Courier.

"Keswick, Dec. 8, 1824.

"SIR,—On a former occasion you have allowed me, through the channel of your journal, to contradict a calumnious accusation as publicly as it had been preferred; and though, in these days of slander, such things hardly deserve refutation, there are reasons which induce me once more to request a similar favor.

"Some extracts from Captain Medwin's recent publication of Lord Byron's Conversations have been transmitted to me by a friend, who, happening to know what the facts are which are there falsified, is of opinion that it would not misbecome me to state them at this time. I wish it, however, to be distinctly understood, that in so doing I am not influenced by any desire of vindicating myself; that would be wholly unnecessary, considering from what quarter the charges come. I notice them for the sake of laying before the public one sample more of the practices of the Satanic School, and showing what credit is due to Lord Byron's assertions. For that his lordship spoke to this effect, and in this temper, I have no doubt, Captain Medwin having, I dare say, to the best of his recollection, faithfully performed the worshipful office of retailing all the effusions of spleen, slander, and malignity which were vented in his presence. Lord Byron is the person who suffers most by this; and, indeed, what man is there whose character would remain uninjured, if every peevish or angry expression, every sportive or extravagant sally, thrown off in the unsuspicious and imagined safety of private life, were to be secretly noted down and published, with no notice of circumstances to show how they had arisen, and when no explanation was possible? One of the offices which has been attributed to the Devil is that of registering every idle word. There is an end of all confidence or comfort in social intercourse if such a practice is to be tolerated by public opinion. When I take these Conversations to be authentic, it is because, as far as I am concerned, they accord, both in matter and spirit, with what his lordship himself had written and published; and it is on this account only that I deem them worthy of notice—the last notice that I shall ever bestow upon the subject. Let there be as many 'More last Words of Mr. Baxter' as the 'reading public' may choose to pay for, they will draw no further reply from me.

"Now, then, to the point. The following speech is reported by Captain Medwin as Lord Byron's: 'I am glad Mr. Southey owns that article* "Foliage," which excited my choler so much. But who else could have been the author? Who but Southey would have had the baseness, under pretext of reviewing the work of one man, insidiously to make it a nest-egg for hatching malicious calumnies against others? I say nothing of the critique itself on "Foliage;" but what was the object of that article? I repeat, to vilify and scatter his dark and devilish insinuations against me and others. Shame on the man who could wound an already bleeding heart—be barbarous enough to revive the memory of an event that Shelley was perfectly ignorant of, and found scandal on falsehood! Shelley taxed him with writing that article some years ago; and he had the audacity to admit that he had treasured up some opinions of Shelley ten years before, when he was on a visit to Keswick, and had made a note of them at the time.'

"*The reviewal in question I did not write.* Lord Byron might have known this if he had inquired of Mr. Murray, who would readily have assured him that I was not the author; and he might have known it from the reviewal itself, wherein the writer declares in plain words that he was a cotemporary of Shelley's at Eton. I had no concern in it, directly or indirectly; but let it not be inferred that in thus disclaiming that paper, any disapproval of it is intended. Papers in the Quarterly Review have been ascribed to me (those on Keats's Poems, for example), which I have heartily condemned both for their spirit and manner. But for the one in question, its composition would be creditable to the most distinguished writer; nor is there any thing either in the opinions expressed, or in the manner of expressing them, which a man of just and honorable principles would have hesitated to advance. I would not have written that part of it which alludes to Mr. Shelley, because, having met him on familiar terms, and parted with him in kindness (a feeling of which Lord Byron had no conception), would have withheld me from animadverting in that manner upon his conduct In other respects, the paper contains nothing that I would not have avowed if I had written, or subscribed, as entirely assenting to, and approving it.

"It is not true that Shelley ever inquired of me whether I was the author of that paper, which purporting, as it did, to be written by an Etonian of his own standing, he very well knew I was not. But in this part of Lord Byron's statement there may be some mistake, mingled with a great deal of malignant falsehood. Mr. Shelley addressed a letter to me from Pisa, asking if I were the author of a criticism in the Quarterly Review upon his Revolt of Islam, not exactly, in Lord Byron's phrase, *taxing* me with it, for he declared his own belief that I was not, but adding that he was induced to ask the question by the positive declaration of some friends in England that the article was mine. Denying, in my reply, that either he or any other person was entitled to propose such a question upon such grounds, I nevertheless assured him that I had not written the paper, and that I had never, in any of my writings, alluded to him in any way.

"Now for the assertion that I had the audacity to admit having treasured up some of Shelley's opinions when he had resided at Keswick, and having made notes of them at the time. What truth is mixed up with the slander of this statement I shall immediately explain, premising only, that as the opinion there implied concerning the practice of noting down familiar conversation is not applicable to me, I transfer it to Captain Medwin for his own especial use.

"Mr. Shelley having, in the letter alluded to, thought proper to make some remarks upon my opinions, I took occasion, in reply to comment upon his, and to ask him (as the tree is known by its fruits) whether he had found them conducive to his own

* A volume of poems by Mr. Leigh Hunt. The reader who may be desirous of referring to the article will find it in vol. [illegible] of the Quarterly Review, p. [illegible].—R. S.

happiness, and the happiness of those with whom he had been most nearly connected. This produced a second letter from him, written in a tone partly of justification, partly of attack. I replied to this also, not by any such absurd admission as Lord Byron has stated, but by recapitulating to him, as a practical illustration of his principles, the leading circumstances of his own life, from the commencement of his career at University College. The earliest facts I stated upon his own authority, as I had heard them from his own lips; the latter were of public notoriety. Here the correspondence ended. On his part it had been conducted with the courtesy natural to him; on mine, in the spirit of one who was earnestly admonishing a fellow-creature.

"This is the correspondence upon which Lord Byron's misrepresentation has been constructed. It is all that ever passed between us, except a note from Shelley, some years before, accompanying a copy of his *Alastor*, and one of mine in acknowledgment of it. I have preserved his letters, together with copies of my own; and if I had as little consideration for the feelings of the living as Captain Medwin has displayed, it is not any tenderness toward the dead* that would withhold me now from publishing them.

"It is not likely that Shelley should have communicated my part of this correspondence to Lord Byron, even if he did his own. Bearing testimony, as his heart did, to the truth of my statements in every point, and impossible as it was to escape from the conclusion which was then brought home, I do not think he would have dared produce it. How much or how little of the truth was known to his lordship, or with which of the party at Pisa the insolent and calumnious misrepresentations conveyed in his lordship's words originated, is of little consequence.

"The charge of scattering dark and devilish insinuations is one which, if Lord Byron were living, I would throw back in his teeth. Me he had assailed without the slightest provocation, and with that unmanliness, too, which was peculiar to him; and in this course he might have gone on without giving me the slightest uneasiness, or calling forth one animadversion in reply. When I came forward to attack his lordship, it was upon public, not upon private grounds. He is pleased to suppose that he had mortally offended Mr. Wordsworth and myself many years ago, by a letter which he had written to the Ettrick Shepherd. 'Certain it is,' he says, 'that I did not spare the Lakists in it, and he told me that he could not resist the temptation, and had shown it to the fraternity. It was too tempting; and as I could never keep a secret of my own (as you know), much less that of other people, I could not blame him. I remember saying, among other things, that the Lake poets were such fools as not to fish in their own waters. But this was the least offensive part of the epistle.' No such epistle was ever shown to Mr. Wordsworth or to me; but I remember (and this passage brings it to my recollection) to have heard that Lord Byron had spoken of us in a letter to Hogg, with some contempt, as fellows who could neither vie with him for skill in angling nor for prowess in swimming. Nothing more than this came to my hearing; and I must have been more sensitive than his lordship himself could I have been offended by it. But if the contempt which he then expressed had equaled the rancor which he afterward displayed, Lord Byron must have known that I had the *flocci* of his eulogium to balance the *nauci* of his scorn, and that the one would have *nihili-pilified* the other, even if I had not well understood the worthlessness of both.

"It was because Lord Byron had brought a stigma upon English literature that I accused him; because he had perverted great talents to the worst purposes; because he had set up for pander-general to the youth of Great Britain as long as his writings should endure; because he had committed a high crime and misdemeanor against society, by sending forth a work in which mockery was mingled with horrors, filth with impiety, profligacy with sedition and slander. For these offenses I came forward to arraign him. The accusation was not made darkly, it was not insinuated, nor was it advanced under the cover of a review. I attacked him openly in my own name, and only not by his, because he had not then publicly avowed the flagitious production by which he will be remembered for lasting infamy. He replied in manner altogether worthy of himself and his cause. Contention with a generous, honorable opponent leads naturally to esteem, and probably to friendship; but, next to such an antagonist, an enemy like Lord Byron is to be desired—one who, by his conduct in the contest, divests himself of every claim to respect; one whose baseness is such as to sanctify the vindictive feeling that it provokes, and upon whom the act of taking vengeance is that of administering justice. I answered him as he deserved to be answered, and the effect which that answer produced upon his lordship has been described by his faithful chronicler, Captain Medwin. This is the real history of what the purveyors of scandal for the public are pleased sometimes to announce in their advertisements as 'Byron's Controversy with Southey!' What there was 'dark and devilish' in it belongs to his lordship; and had I been compelled to resume it during his life, he who played the monster in literature, and aimed his blows at women, should have been treated accordingly. 'The Republican Trio,' says Lord Byron, 'when they began to publish in common, were to have had a community of all things, like the Ancient Britons—to have lived in a state of nature, like savages, and peopled some island of the blessed with children in common, like ——. A very pretty Arcadian notion!' I may be excused for wishing that Lord Byron had published this himself; but, though he is responsible for the atrocious falsehood, he is not for its posthumous publication. I shall only observe, therefore, that the slander is as worthy of his lordship as the scheme itself would have been. Nor would I have condescended to have noticed it even thus, were it not to show how little this calumniator knew concerning the objects of his uneasy and restless hatred. Mr. Wordsworth and I were strangers to each other, even by name, at the time when he represents us as engaged in a satanic confederacy, and we never published any thing in common.

"Here I dismiss the subject. It might have been thought that Lord Byron had attained the last degree of disgrace when his head was set up for a sign at one of those preparatory schools for the brothel and the gallows, where obscenity, sedition, and blasphemy are retailed in drams for the vulgar. There remained one further shame—there remained this exposure of his private conversations, which has compelled his lordship's friends, in their own defense, to compare his oral declarations with his written words, and thereby to demonstrate that he was as regardless of truth as he was incapable of sustaining those feelings suited to his birth, station, and high endowments, which sometimes came across his better mind. ROBERT SOUTHEY."

* In the preface to his Monody on Keats, Shelley, as I have been informed, asserts that I was the author of the criticism in the Quarterly Review upon that young man's poems, and that his death was occasioned by it. There was a degree of meanness in this (especially considering the temper and tenor of our correspondence) which I was not then prepared to expect from Shelley, for that he *believed* me to be the author of that paper I certainly do not believe. He was once, for a short time, my neighbor. I met him upon terms, not of friendship indeed, but certainly of mutual good will. I admired his talents; thought that he would outgrow his errors (perilous as they were); and trusted that, meantime, a kind and generous heart would resist the effect of fatal opinions which he had taken up in ignorance and boyhood. Herein I was mistaken. But when I ceased to regard him with hope, he became to me a subject for sorrow and awful commiseration, not of any injurious or unkind feeling; and when I expressed myself with just severity concerning him, it was in direct communication to himself.—*R. S.*

THE GRIDIRON.

A PINDARIC ODE.

1.

Broiling is best; bear witness, gods and men!
Awake, my pen;
Promoted from some goose or gander's pinion
To be the scepter wherewithal I sway
The Muses' wide dominion!
And thou, my spirit, for a loftier flight
Than ere the Theban eagle gain'd, prepare;
Win with strong impulse thine ethereal way,
Till from the upper air,
Subjected to thy sight,
Regions remote and distant ages lie,
And thine unbounded eye
All things that are on earth or were in time descry.

2.

Broiling is best; from Jove begin the strain,
High-thundering Jupiter, to whom belong
The Gridiron and the song.
Whence came the glorious Gridiron upon earth?
O daughter of Mnemosyne, relate
When, where, and how the idea uncreate,
That from all ages in the all-teeming mind
Had slept confined,
Received in happy hour its formal birth.
Say, Muse, for thou canst tell
Whate'er to gods or men in earliest days befell:
Nor hath Oblivion in her secret cell,
Wherein with miserly delight
For aye by stealth
She heaps her still accumulating wealth,
Aught that is hidden from thy searching sight.

3.

'Twas while the Olympian gods
Were wont among yet uncorrupted nations
To make from time to time their visitations,
Disdaining not to leave their high abodes
And feast with mortal men:
To Britain were the heavenly guests convened;
Its nymphs and sylvan gods assembled then,
From forest and from mountain,
From river, mere, and fountain;
Thither Saturnian Jove descended;
With all his household deities attended;
And Neptune with the oceanic train,
To meet them in his own beloved isle,
Came in his sea-car sailing o'er the main.
In joy that day the heav'ns appear'd to smile,
The dimpled sea to smile in joy was seen,
In joy the billows leap'd to kiss the land;
Yea, joy like sunshine fill'd the blue serene,
Joy smooth'd the waves, and sparkled on the sand;
Winds, woods, and waters sung with one consent;
The cloud-compelling Jove made jovial weather,
And earth, and sea, and sky rejoiced together.

4.

The sons of Britain then, his hearty hosts,
Brought forth the noble beef that Britain boasts,
To please, if please they might, their mighty guest.
And Jove was pleased, for he had visited
Men who on fish were fed,
And those who made of milk their only food,
A feeble race, with children's meat content,
Whey-blooded, curd complexion'd. But this sight
Awaken'd a terrestrial appetite
That gladden'd his dear heart. The chief
Of gods and men approving view'd
The Britons and their beef;
His head ambrosial in benignant mood
He bent, and with a jocund aspect bless'd
The brave Boöphagi, and told them broil'd was best.

5.

He touch'd his forehead then,
Pregnant this happy hour with thought alone,
Not riving with parturient throbs, as when
Panoplied Pallas, struggling to come forth,
Made her astonish'd Mater-pater groan,
And call on Vulcan to release the birth.
He call'd on Vulcan now, but 'twas to say
That in the fire and flame-eructant hill
The sweltering Cyclops might keep holiday,
For his own will divine,
Annihilant of delay,
Should with creative energy fulfill
The auspicious moment's great intent benign.
So spake the All-maker, and before the sound
Of that annunciant voice had pass'd away,
Behold upon the ground,
Self-form'd, for so it seem'd, a Gridiron lay.

6.

It was not forged by unseen hands,
Anticipant of Jove's commands,
Work worthy of applause,
And then through air invisibly convey'd,
Before him upon Earth's green carpet laid.
Jove in his mind conceived it, and it was;
But though his plastic thought
Shaped it with handle, feet, and bars, and frame,
Deem not that he created it of naught.
Nothing can come of nothing: from the air
The ferrean atoms came;
The air, which, poising our terraqueous ball,
Feeds, fosters, and consumes, and reproduces all.

7.

Now the perfect Steak prepare!
Now the appointed rites begin!
Cut it from the pinguid rump,
Not too thick and not too thin;
Somewhat to the thick inclining,
Yet the thick and thin between,
That the gods, when they are dining,
May commend the golden mean.
Ne'er till now have they been bless'd
With a beef-steak duly dress'd;
Ne'er till this auspicious morn
When the Gridiron was born.

8.

Gods and demigods alertly
Vie in voluntary zeal:
All are active, all are merry,
Aiding, as they may, expertly,
Yet in part the while experi-
mentally the expected meal.
Then it was that call'd to birth,
From the bosom of the earth,
By Apollo's moving lyre,
Stones, bituminous and black,
Ranged themselves upon the hearth
Ready for Hephæstus' fire:
While subjacent fagots crack,
Folds of fog-like smoke aspire,
Till the flames with growing strength
All impediment subdue,
And the jetty gloss at length
Is exchanged for Vulcan's hue.
Now with salt the embers strew,
In faint explosion burning blue.
All offending fumes are gone,
Set, oh set the Gridiron on!

9.

But who is she that there
From Jove's own brain hath started into life?
Red are her arms, and from the elbow bare;
Clean her close cap, white and light,
From underneath it not a hair
Straggles to offend the sight.
A fork bidented, and a trenchant knife,
She wields. I know thee! yes, I know thee now,
Heiress of culinary fame;
Clothed with pre-existence thou!
Dolly of the deathless name!
Thy praise in after days shall London speak,
O kitchen queen,
Of pearly forehead thou and ruby cheek!
And many a watery mouth thy chops will bless,
Unconscious they and thou alike, I ween,

That thou hadst thus been ante-born to dress
For Jupiter himself the first beef-steak.

10.

O Muse divine, of Jove's own line, expound
That wonderful and ever-only birth
Like which the womb of Possibility
(Aye-and-all-teeming though it be)
Hath brought no second forth.
What hand but thine, O Muse divine, can sound
The depth of mysteries profound
Sunk in arcanal ages and in night?
What but thy potential sight,
Piercing high above all height,
Reach them in the abyss of light?

11.

It were ignorance or folly
To compare this first-born Dolly
With Athenè ever young;
Gray-eyed, grave, and melancholy,
In her strength and in her state,
When from her cranial egg the goddess sprung
Full-fledged, in adamantine arms connate.
Verily produced was she
In her immortality;
This of Dolly was a fan-
tastic birth, or, rather, man-
ifestation soon to be
Revoked into non-entity.

* * * *

Thus far, apparently, is completed; that which follows is transcribed from loose slips of paper.

Anticipating all her wishes,
Spirits come with plates and dishes.
Can more be needed? Yes, and more is here.
Swifter than a shooting-star,
One to distant Malabar
Speeds his way, and, in a trice,
Brings the pungent Indian spice.
Whither hath Erin's guardian genius fled?
To the Tupinamban shore
This tutelary power hath sped;
Earth's good apples thence he bore,
One day destined to abound
On his own Hibernian ground,
Praties to be entitled then,
Gift of gods to Irishmen.

* * * *

And strike with thunder from my starry seat
Those who divorce the murphies from the meat.

* * * *

Bring me no nectar, Hebe, now,
Nor thou, boy Ganymede!
He said, and shook his smiling brow,
And bade the rock with porter flow—
The rock with porter flow'd.
Not such as porter long hath been
In these degenerate days, I ween;
But such as oft, in days of yore,
Dean of St. Peter's, in thy yard,
Though doors were double lock'd and barr'd,
I quaff'd as I shall quaff no more;
Such as loyal Whitbread old,
Father of the brewers bold,
From his ample casks preferr'd
When he regaled the king, the good King George
the Third.

* * * *

Far more than silver or than gold
The honest pewter pot he prized,
And drank his porter galvanized.

* * * *

Teetotallers, avaunt, and ye who feed,
Like grubs and snails, on root, or stem, or weed;
Nor think
That by such diet and such drink
Britain should rule the main.

LIST OF THE PUBLICATIONS OF ROBERT SOUTHEY, ESQ.

1. Poems by R. Southey and R. Lovell. 1 vol. Cottle, 1794.
2. Joan of Arc. 1 vol. 4to. Cottle, 1795.
3. Letters from Spain and Portugal. 1 vol. Cottle, 1797.
4. Minor Poems. 2 vols. Cottle, 1797–1799.
5. Annual Anthology. 2 vols. Biggs and Cottle, 1799–1800.
6. Thalaba. 2 vols. Longman, 1801.
7. Chatterton's Works, edited by R. Southey and J. Cottle. 3 vols. 1802.
8. Amadis of Gaul. 4 vols. Longman, 1803.
9. Metrical Tales and other Poems. 1 vol. 1805.
10. Madoc. 1 vol. 4to. Longman, 1805.
11. Palmerin of England. 4 vols. Longman, 1807.
12. Specimens of English Poets. 3 vols. Longman, 1807.
13. Letters from England, by Don Manuel Espriella. 3 vols. Longman, 1807.
14. Remains of Henry Kirke White, edited by R. Southey. 2 vols. Longman and others, 1807.
15. Chronicle of the Cid. 1 vol. 4to. Longman, 1808.
16. Curse of Kehama. 1 vol. 4to. Longman, 1810.
17. Omniana. 2 vols. Longman, 1812.
18. Life of Nelson. 2 vols. Murray, 1813.
19. Roderic, the Last of the Goths. 1 vol. 4to. Longman, 1814.
20. Carmen Triumphale and Carmina Aulica. 1 vol. Longman, 1814.
21. Minor Poems (re-arranged, &c.). 3 vols. Longman, 1815.
22. Lay of the Laureate. 1 vol. Longman, 1816.
23. Specimens of later British Poets.
24. Pilgrimage to Waterloo. 1 vol. Longman, 1816.
25. Morte d'Arthur. 2 vols. 4to. Longman, 1817.
26. Letter to William Smith. A Pamphlet. Murray, 1817.
27. History of Brazil. 3 vols. 4to. Longman, 1810–1817–1819.
28. Life of Wesley. 2 vols. Longman, 1820.
29. Expedition of Orsua. 1 vol. Longman, 1821.
30. A Vision of Judgment. 1 vol. 4to. Longman, 1821.
31. Book of the Church. 2 vols. Murray, 1824.
32. Tale of Paraguay. 1 vol. Longman, 1825.
33. Vindiciæ Ecclesiæ Anglicanæ. 1 vol. Murray, 1826.
34. History of the Peninsular War. 3 vols. 4to. Murray, 1822–1824–1832.
35. Lives of Uneducated Poets—Prefixed to Verses by John Jones. 1 vol. Murray, 1829.
36. All for Love and the Legend of a Cock and a Hen. 1 vol. Longman, 1829.
37. Colloquies on the Progress and Prospects of Society. 2 vols. Murray, 1829.
38. Life of John Bunyan, for an Edition of the Pilgrim's Progress. Murray and Major, 1830.
39. Select Works of British Poets, from Chaucer to Jonson, edited with Biographical Notices. 1 vol. Longman, 1831.
40. Naval History of England. 4 vols. and part of the 5th, in Lardner's Cabinet Cyclopædia. Longman, 1833–1840.
41. The Doctor, &c. 7 vols. Longman. Vols. 6 and 7, edited by the Rev. J. Wood Warter, 1834–1847.
42. The Life and Works of Cowper. Edited. 15 vols. Baldwin and Cradock, 1835–1837.
43. Collected Edition of his Poems. 10 vols. Longman, 1837, 1838. Also complete in 1 volume. 1847.
44. Common-place Book, 1st, 2d, and 3d Series. A fourth is announced. Edited by the Rev. J. Wood Warter. Longman.
45. Oliver Newman, and other Fragments. Edited by the Rev. H. Hill. 1 vol. Longman, 1845.

Contributions to Periodical Literature.

Articles communicated by Robert Southey to the first four volumes of the Annual Review.

VOL. I. (1802).

Sauer's Account of Commodore Billing's Expedition to the Northern part of Russia.
Mackenzie's Voyages from Montreal, &c.
Fischer's Travels in Spain.
Acerbi's Travels in Sweden.
Mrs. Guthrie's Travels in the Crimea.
Pallas's Travels in the S. Provinces of Russia.
Olivier's Travels in Turkey.
Wrangham's Poems.
Poetry by the Author of Gebir.*

VOL. II. (1803).

Burney's History of Discoveries in the South Sea.
Clarke's Progress of Maritime Discovery.
Curtis's Travels in Bombay.
Grandpré's Voyage to Bengal.
Davies's Travels in America.
Muirhead's Travels in the Low Countries.
New Military Journal.
Wittman's Travels in Turkey.
Malthus on the Principles of Population.
Transactions of the Missionary Society.
Myle's History of the Methodists.
Godwin's Life of Chaucer.
Ritson's Ancient English Romances.
Mant's Life of J. Warter.
Hayley's Poems.
Kirke White's Clifton Grove.
Lord Strangford's Camoëns.
Owen Cambridge's Works.

VOL. III. (1804).

Barrow's Travels.
Barrow's China.
Froissart's Chronicles.
Address from the Society for the Suppression of Vice.
Seward's Life of Darwin.
Scott's Sir Tristram.
Cupid turned Volunteer.
Falconer's Shipwreck.
Churchill's Poems.
Crowe's Lewesdon Hill.
Transactions of the Missionary Society.

VOL. IV. (1805).

Bruce's Travels to the Source of the Nile.
Clarke's Naufragia.
Present State of Peru.
Griffith's Travels.
Roscoe's Life of Leo X.
Cayley's Life of Sir Walter Raleigh.
Tisbault's Anecdotes of Frederic the Great.
Greswell's Memoirs of Angelus Politianus.
Ellis's Specimens of Early Metrical Romances.
Todd's Spenser.
Bowles's Spirit of Discovery.
Hayley's Ballads.
Boyd's Penance of Hugo.
Report on the Poems of Ossian.

The Historical part of the Edinburgh Annual Register for 1808, 1809, and 1810.

Articles contributed to the Quarterly Review from 1808 to 1838; viz.:

No. 1. Baptist Mission in India.
2. Portuguese Literature.
3. South Sea Missionaries.
— Lord Valencia's Travels.
4. Holmes's American Annuals.
5. Life of Nelson. Enlarged afterward, and published separately.
6. Veeson's Residence at Tongataboo.
— Graham's Georgics.
7. Observador Portuguez. On the French Occupation of Portugal.
No. 8. Faroë Islands.
— On the Evangelical Sects.
11. Bell and Lancaster. Enlarged afterward, and published separately.
12. The Inquisition.
— Montgomery's Poems.
13. Sir G. Mackenzie's Iceland.
14. French Revolutionists.
15. Landor's Count Julian.
— D'Israeli's Calamities of Authors.
16. On the Manufacturing System and the Poor.
19. Bogue and Bennet's History of the Dissenters.
21. Nicobar Islands.
— Montgomery's World before the Flood.
22–23. Chalmers's British Poets.
23. Forbes's Oriental Memoirs.
24. Lewis and Clarke's Travels in North America.
— Remains of Barré Roberts.
25. Miot's French Expedition to Egypt.
26–27. Life of Wellington.
28. Alfieri.
29. Madame La Roche Jacquelin's Memoirs.
— On the Poor.
30. Ali Bey's Travels in Morocco.
— Foreign Travelers in England.
31. Parliamentary Reform.
32. Koster's Travels in Brazil.
— Rise and Progress of Disaffection.
33. Mariner's Tonga Islands.
35. Lope de Vega.
39. Evelyn's Memoirs.
— On the Means of improving the People.
41. Copy-right Act.
42. Cemeteries and Catacombs of Paris.
43. Monastic Institutions.
45. Coxe's Life of Marlborough.
46. New Churches.
48. Life of W. Huntington, S. S.
50. Life of Cromwell.
52. Dobrizhoffer.
53. Camoëns.
55. Gregoire's History of Religious Sects.
56. Gregoire's History of Theophilanthropists.
57. Burnet's Own Times.
58. Dwight's Travels in New England.
61. New Churches.
62. Life of Hayley.
— Mrs. Baillie's Lisbon.
63. Church Missionary Society.
64. Life of Bayard.
65. Roman Catholic Church and Waldenses.
66. Sœur Nativité.
67. Sumatra.
68. Britton's Cathedral Antiquities.
69. Dr. Sayers's Poems.
— Head's Journey across the Pampas.
72. Butler's Reply concerning Sœur Nativité.
73. Hallam's Constitutional History of England.
74. Emigration Report
75. Ledyard's Travels.
— Chronological History of the West Indies.
76. Roman Catholic Question and Ireland.
77. Elementary Education, and the new Colleges in London.
78. Surtees's History of Durham.
81. State of Portugal.
82. Poems by Lucretia Davidson.
— Smyth's Life of Captain Beaver.
83. Head's Forest Scenes in Canada.
85. Ellis's Polynesian Researches.
86. Negro New Testament.
87. Dymond's Essays on Morality.
— Moral and Political State of the Nation.
88. Life of Oberlin.
89. Babœuf's Conspiracy.
90. Doctrine de St. Simon.
91. Life and Death of Lord E. Fitzgerald.
93. Mary Colling.
94. Lord Nugent's Life of Hampden.
95. Prince Polignac and the Three Days.
97. Life of Felix Neff.

* My father reviewed Gebir in the Critical Review. I regret that I can not obtain a list of his contributions to that periodical.—ED.

No. 113. Mawe's Voyage down the Amazon, and Captain Smyth.
118. Mrs. Bray's Tamar and Tavy, and Sir Geo. Head's Home Tour.
123. Barrow's Life of Lord Howe.
126. Life of Telford.

In the Foreign Quarterly Review.

Barantes's History of the Dukes of Burgundy.
On the Spanish Moors.
Life of Ignatius Loyola.

PRINCE POLIGNAC TO R. SOUTHEY, ESQ.

"Ham, ce 14 7bre, 1832.

"MONSIEUR,—J'ai appris, par l'intermédiare d'un ami à qui je suis tendrement attaché, que vous vous occupiez en ce moment d'un travail relatif aux circonstances qui ont accompagné la lutte que le trône des Bourbons a eu à soutenir dans les derniers jours de Juillet, 1830, vous proposant pour but, dans ce travail, de rectifier les erreurs qu'une calomnie victorieuse a cherché à propager dans le public.

"Personne mieux que vous, monsieur, ne peut accomplir si noble tâche, et avec plus d'espoir de succès; votre talent bien connu, vos principes, vos sentiments généreux feront obtenir à la vérité ce triomphe que la force et les passions du moment ont pu seules lui arracher.

"Quant à moi, dont le nom se trouve nécessairement associé au drame révolutionnaire dont la malheureuse France a offert le spectacle à l'Europe, il me serait impossible de vous peindre tous les élans de ma reconnaissance; ceux-là seuls peuvent en mesurer l'étendue qui, habitués à étudier le cœur humain, comprendront ce que le mien a dû souffrir en me voyant, en face d'un peuple égaré et irrité, forcé de garder le silence. J'ai dû accepter—ainsi que je le mandais à un de mes amis, à une époque peu éloignée de celle où nous sommes—j'ai dû accepter tous les genres d'accusation qu'on a voulu entasser sur ma tête. Je me suis considéré comme le chef d'un vaisseau, au moment d'un grand naufrage; le vaisseau, c'était la Royauté exilée qu'on cherchait encore à atteindre en me frappant; j'ai gardé pour moi les coups qu'on lui reservait; l'équipage, c'était mes collégues: un devoir impérieux m'imposait l'obligation de ne pas compromettre leur sûreté; je me suis tû lorsque cette sûreté pourait être compromise. L'histoire, j'ose le dire, ne retrace pas une situation plus compliquée que celle dans laquelle je me suis trouvé; jamais plus de sentimens de diverse nature froissés et brisés, n'ont torturé le cœur d'un homme; jamais l'honneur ne désarma mieux sa victime.

"Ces moments cruels sont passés sans doute; le temps est venu calmer l'irritation des esprits; les évènements qui se sont succédés ont pu désiller bien des yeux, désabuser bien des esprits, et l'on pourrait se demander, si le moment ne serait pas enfin arrivé de révéler les mystères du passé et de présenter quelques explications devenues nécessaires pour ma justification.

"Je pourrais faire à cette question une réponse affirmative; mais j'ajouterai que je ne saurais être la personne chargée d'une semblable tâche; ma présence dans la lice réveillerait des amours propres, raviverait des ressentiments presque éteints; elle pourrait troubler ce repos momentaire que la lassitude du mal entraine souvent après lui. Il est des circonstances où le bon citoyen doit même savoir accepter les effets de la calomnie par amour pour la paix. La postérité, ou peut-être de mon temps encore, la plume de quelque main amie expliquera mon silence; il sera compris par l'homme de bien.

"D'ailleurs, le langage et les actes de ceux qui se sont faits mes accusateurs ont déjà commencé ma justification, et celle-là, au moins, n'a aucun des inconvénients que je viens de signaler.

"En effet, quelques-uns d'entr'eux reprochent aux ministres de Charles X. d'avoir violé la charte de 1814, en faisant une fausse application de l'article 14 renfermé dans cette même charte; mais eux, qu'ont-ils fait le 29 Juillet, 1830, après que les fameuses ordonnances furent retirés par Charles X.? ils brisèrent la charte toute entière; ils détrônèrent le souverain à qui ils avaient prêté serment de fidélité, qui, d'après cette charte, était irresponsable, et dont la personne devait être inviolable; ou bien, ils ne cherchaient alors qu'un prétexte pour détruire la charte qu'ils invoquaient et pour renverser le trône qu'ils entouraient de leurs serments; et, dans ce cas, il y avait hypocrisie de leur part, ou bien les reproches qu'ils dirigent aujourd'hui contre les ministres de Charles X. doivent retomber sur eux; car, en supposant que les ministres de ce monarque aient fait une fausse interprétation de l'article 14, leurs accusateurs ont fait plus, ils ont brisé une charte et une couronne.

"D'autres, par leurs aveux, justifient d'une manière plus éclatante encore les ordonnances de Charles X. Ils déclarent qu'il y a eu, sous la restauration, une conspiration permanente contre les Bourbons; ils en nomment les chefs, ils en indiquent et la marche et le but, lequel était, disent ils, de renverser à la fois et le trône et la charte; ils se vantent d'avoir, dans les derniers temps du règne des Bourbons, rendu tout gouvernement *impossible;* c'est ainsi, qu'en révélant leur anciens projets, qui, au reste, étaient bien connus du gouvernement en 1830, ils disculpent le souverain qu'ils ont détrôné, puisqu'ils prouvent qu'il n'a agi que dans un but de défense personnelle et pour repousser des attaques qui menaçoient le trône et la tranquillité publique.

"Il suffirait donc aujourd'hui, pour justifier Charles X. et ses conseillers, d'enrégistrer les aveux qui remplissent les colonnes des journaux Français. L'histoire impartiale se chargera sans doute de ce soin.

"Dans une brochure que j'ai publiée au commencement de cette année, et que je prie la personne qui a la bonté de vous transmettre cette lettre, de vouloir bien vous faire passer, j'ai prouvé la légalité des ordonnances du 27 Juillet, 1830; j'ai même prouvé que les adversaires de la couronne avaient, soit dans leurs discours à la tribune parlementaire, soit dans leurs écrits, interprété le sens de l'article 14 de l'ancienne charte de la même manière que l'avait interprêté la couronne en 1830. Or, que disait cet article? *que le roi pourrait faire des ordonnances pour la sûreté de l'état.* Qui oserait dire aujourd'hui que l'état n'était pas alors en danger? qui pourrait nier que le trône ne fut, à cette époque, miné de tous côtés, et qu'une révolution ne menaçât la France? mais les passions frappent et ne raisonnent pas.

"Vous excuserez, monsieur, la longueur des détails dans lesquels je suis entré; j'ai cru devoir vous les soumettre, sachant que votre judicieux discernement et votre impartialité vous portent à ne pas juger des causes seulement par leurs effets, ni à vous laisser séduire par des apparences trompeuses. Je terminerai cette lettre par quelques observations sur la note que vous avez entre les mains, intitulée *Note sur quelques circonstances relatives aux évènements de Juillet*, 1830.

"De graves erreurs, à ce qu'il me semble, se sont propagées concernant le nombre de troupes confiées au Maréchal Duc de Raguse, lors des troubles qui éclatèrent à Paris vers la fin de Juillet, 1830. Vous pouvez maintenant juger combien sont erronnées les bruits qu'on s'est plu à repandre à ce sujet. Une simple observation suffit pour en démontrer la fausseté. N'est-il pas évident, en effet, que, si le Duc de Raguse n'eût eu à sa disposition que cinq à six mille hommes, comme on la prétendu, il y eût eu, de sa part, une coupable impéritie à adopter le plan qu'il suivit le 28 Juillet, au moment où l'insurrection avait acquis son plus haut dégré d'intensité. Ce plan consistait, comme on le sait, à diviser ses troupes en trois colonnes, lesquelles devaient traverser Paris dans sa plus grande longueur, puis se répandre dans les rues nombreuses de la capitale. L'exécution de ce plan me parut même audacieux; les résultats n'en furent point heureux; la plus grande partie des troupes, ainsi divisées en petits corps épars dans des rues étroites, eurent beaucoup de peine à revenir sur leurs pas, et à surmonter les obstacles et les dangers qui s'opposaient à leur retour. Quoiqu'il en soit, on ne peut, sans faire injure aux talents militaires, ou aux sentiments de loyauté et de fidélité du Maréchal Duc de Raguse, supposer que, dans l'état de fermentation générale dans laquelle se trouvait alors la capitale, il eût osé tenter l'exécution d'un semblable plan avec cinq, huit, et même dix mille hommes; cependant il la tenta; donc, il crut que les forces qu'il commandait étaient suffisantes pour en assurer la réussite.

"Ce n'est point tout, après la journée du 28 la seule, on peut le dire, dans laquelle les rues de Paris furent le théâtre d'une lutte sanglante, puisque le lendemain matin la capitale fut évacuée, le Duc de Raguse, malgré la résistance opiniâtre qu'il avait rencontrée, dit hautement à mes collègues, à moi-même et à d'autres officiers présens, qu'il se maintiendrait un mois dans la position qu'il occupait alors; cette position était le Louvre, les Tuileries, les deux quais de la rivière et les Boulevards: il ajouta qu'elle *était inexpugnable*, et insista pour que j'en donnasse connaissance au roi, ce que je fis aussitôt. Il est donc hors de doute, qu'à cette époque, le Duc de Raguse avait encore la ferme conviction, que ses forces étaient suffisantes pour s'opposer aux efforts de l'insurrection, bien que toutes les troupes, qui des divers points de la division militaire placée sous son commandement se dirigeaient sur Paris, ne l'eussent point encore rejoint.

"Ainsi voilà deux faits avérés, incontestables, l'un desquels s'est passé avant l'action et l'autre après l'action, qui, sans autre commentaire, prouvent l'absurdité des bruits que des journaux Français et étrangers se sont plus à accréditer relativement à l'insuffisance des forces qui furent confiées au Duc de Raguse, au mois de Juillet, 1830.

"Le 29 Juillet, au matin, Paris fut tout-à-coup évacué, presque sans coup férir; je cessai d'être ministre, et de prendre par conséquent part aux évènements qui se sont succédés: qu'elles furent les causes de cette retraite précipitée, qui livra la capitale aux insurgés et la monarchie à ses ennemis, c'est à l'histoire qu'il appartient de les approfondir: quant à moi je les ignore encore.

"Il n'est peut-être pas inutile, monsieur, que je prévienne une objection qui pourrait être faite à deux assertions contenues dans la note qui vous a été transmise, et qui, au premier abord, semblent se contredire. Il y est dit, au commencement de la 2me page, que, dans le court délai de trois semaines qui s'écoula depuis le moment où le principe des ordonnances fut arrêté, et celui où elles furent signées, *tout mouvement considérable de troupes devenait impossible:* plus loin, à-peu-près à la septième page, il est dit, au contraire, que *dans l'espace de huit ou dix jours, une force d'environ cinquante-cinq à soixante mille hommes se serait trouvée sous les murs de Paris*. Ces deux assertions, quoique contradictoires en apparence, ne le sont cependant pas. Il suffit, pour s'en assurer, de réfléchir à quelle époque se rapportent les mouvements militaires auxquels l'une et l'autre de ces assertions fait allusion. La première époque se rapporte à un temps qui précédait les évènements de Juillet, auquel temps il était important de ne pas éveiller l'attention publique, ni celle des journaux, sur des déplacements de troupes que le gouvernement n'eût pu expliquer, et qui eût pu faire naître des soupçons sur la nature des mesures qu'on voulait adopter; la seconde époque se rapporte, au contraire, à un temps subséquent à l'insurrection de Paris. Toutes les précautions indiquées ci-dessus devenaient alors inutiles: à la première époque, les mouvements de troupes devaient se combiner avec la sûreté de quelques localités importantes qui exigeaient une surveillance spéciale, telles que Lyon, Rouen, Nantes, Bordeaux, &c., qu'on ne pouvait laisser dépourvues de forces militaires. On jugea même prudent d'augmenter, dans le courant de Juillet, le nombre de troupes qui étaient alors en garnison dans quelques-unes des villes que je viens de citer. À l'autre époque, au contraire, tout devait céder devant la nécessité de sauver la capitale. On pouvait, on devait même négliger la sûreté de quelques points moins importans. Enfin, à la première époque, les mouvements de troupes ne pouvoient s'opérer que régulièrement, étapes par étapes, ce qui les rendaient difficiles et lents, tandis qu'à l'autre époque, la rapidité de ces mouvements en faisait seule le mérite: l'ordre était donné aux troupes de s'avancer à *marches forcées;* les étapes étoient doublées; on eût pu même, au besoin, transporter les troupes en chariots.

"J'ai cru, monsieur, devoir vous donner ces explications, qui furent devenues inutiles si le rédacteur de la note que vous avez entre les mains eût mieux exprimé sa pensée; les détails qu'elle contient seront rapportés avec plus de développement dans un travail qui se prépare, mais dont la publication doit être encore ajournée; et c'est à vous, monsieur, que je serai redevable du premier essai qui aura été tenté d'éclairer le public sur des circonstances peu connues des uns et calomnieusement interprétées par les autres: une semblable tâche ne pouvait être entreprise par une plume plus éloquente, plus habile, ni qui fit mieux présager le succès.

"C'est avec regret, monsieur, que je me suis vu forcé d'emprunter une main étrangère pour tracer les lignes que j'ai l'honneur de vous addresser; mais la faiblesse de mes yeux et d'autres incommodités inhérentes à la position dans laquelle je me trouve en ce moment, m'en ont fait une nécessité. Je n'ai pas, cependant, voulu terminer ma lettre sans charger moi-même de vous réitérer l'expressions de ma vive réconnaisance, ni sans vous prier d'agréer ici l'assurance de mes sentimens d'estime et de haute considération. LE PRINCE DE POLIGNAC.

"To DR. SOUTHEY, &c., &c. &c."

THE END.

www.ingramcontent.com/pod-product-compliance
Lightning Source LLC
LaVergne TN
LVHW021231110826
845150LV00002B/308